D0890168

Rodale's Encyclopedia of Indoor Gardening

Rodale's Encyclopedia of Indoor Gardening

Edited by Anne M. Halpin

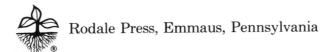 Rodale Press, Emmaus, Pennsylvania

Opposite, flower and buds of jasmine, Jasminum polyanthum.

Copyright © 1980 by Rodale Press, Inc.
All rights reserved. No part of this publication may be
reproduced or transmitted in any form or by any means,
electronic or mechanical, including photocopy, recording, or
any information storage and retrieval system without the
written permission of the publisher.

Printed in the United States of America

Library of Congress Cataloging in Publication Data
Main entry under title:

Rodale's encyclopedia of indoor gardening.

    Bibliography: p.
    Includes indexes.
    1. Indoor gardening. 2. House plants. 3. Organic
gardening. I. Halpin, Anne Moyer. II. Title: Encyclopedia
of indoor gardening.
SB419.R74   635.9'65   80-17019
ISBN 0-87857-319-4   hardcover

    2 4 6 8 10 9 7 5 3 1   hardcover

Editorial Staff
Associate Editor: Brenda Bortz
Assistant Editors: Nancy E. Lee, Suzanne L. Nelson
Proofreader: Jane Sherman

Art Director: K. A. Schell
Associate Art Director: Jerry O'Brien
Design Assistants: Ed Courrier, George Retseck , Carol Ann Sabik

Project Photographer: Margaret Smyser
Photography Assistants: Sara Bell (Chief Co-ordinator and Stylist), Christie Tito
Contributing Photographers: Dr. Gary F. Leatham, Charles Marden Fitch

Illustrators: Jacquelyn Diotte, Joan M. Frain, Brian Swisher

Botanical Consultant: Dr. Dudley J. Raynal, Associate Professor of Botany
    State University of New York, College of Environmental Science and Forestry,
    Syracuse, New York
Editorial Consultant: Dr. Michael J. Balick
Design Consultant: Bruce McIntosh
Photographic Consultant: Tom Roth, The Corner Greenery

Contents

Introduction

This book is a guide to growing many kinds of plants in all kinds of indoor environments. You will learn in these pages how using indoor space offers you the opportunity to live with foliage and flowering plants all year, and how it extends the range of your gardening activities by stretching the growing season for outdoor crops. If you're new to the world of indoor gardening, you will find plenty of basic information to get you started. If you're already a plant-lover, we hope you will be inspired to try some new plants you've never grown before.

We have worked with many expert writers and consultants in the fields of botany and horticulture to gather together the best, most reliable information available on growing plants indoors. But as you read, remember that horticultural practices vary widely among amateurs and experts alike. The cultural techniques that work for one gardener don't always produce the best results for everyone. Part of the joy of growing plants is in developing an awareness of what each one needs, and in finding the cultural techniques that work best for you. So don't be afraid to

Above, inflorescence of summer torch bromeliad, Billbergia pyramidalis *var.* concolor.

experiment. You will enjoy the greatest success if you adapt the guidelines given in these pages to fit the particular environment in which your plants are growing.

HOW TO USE THIS BOOK

In organizing this book, we have grouped the information into several major sections. Chapters 1 through 3 will introduce you to the world of plants. We hope these chapters will convey a sense of the wonder and pleasure of sharing your home with plants. They will also acquaint you with the basic environmental considerations involved in growing and caring for plants indoors, such as light, moisture, and humidity. Chapters 4 through 9 explain the fundamental cultural techniques for successful indoor gardening, such as making soil mixtures, repotting, propagating, and controlling pests and diseases by organic means.

Chapters 10 through 24 discuss special kinds of plants. You will find here background information to help you recognize and understand the most popular plant families and groups—gesneriads, cacti and other succulents, orchids, and many others—and the special growth requirements of each group indoors.

Chapters 25 through 29 are devoted to helping you make the best use of the varied indoor environments where you can grow plants—light gardens, terraria and dish gardens, special indoor garden spaces, windowsills, and solar and traditional greenhouses. Chapter 30 explains how you can use plants to decorate your home.

The House Plant Encyclopedia following chapter 30 provides specific cultural information on 252 plants, along with a color photo of each one for ready identification. This is the place to go for quick reference on a particular plant.

The Appendix section lists addresses of plant societies, botanic gardens, and departments of agriculture, for further information.

UNDERSTANDING PLANT NAMES

Plants have many common names, and they can be confusing. Botanists use a standardized system of Latin nomenclature to identify and classify plants, and we have employed this system extensively in this book for the sake of accuracy and clarity. Botanical nomenclature is recognized internationally, and knowing the Latin name for a plant will be of great help to you in dealing with commercial plant suppliers and in communicating with other gardeners. The system of plant nomenclature is explained in chapter 1, under How Plants Are Named, and we urge you to read that section.

The botanical nomenclature in this book was done in accordance with *Hortus Third,* a widely recognized taxonomical reference compiled by the staff of the Liberty Hyde Bailey Hortorium at Cornell University. Species names, however, are all written with lower-case letters, in accord with generally accepted practice. Occasionally we ran across a species that is not listed in *Hortus Third;* where this occurred, the nomenclature was taken from other reliable sources.

The general index to this book lists plants only by botanical name. If you want to find information on a particular plant but you know only its common name, turn to the Index of Common Plant Names preceding the general index to find the botanical name of the plant. Then look in the general index to locate the pertinent page numbers.

We have tried to make this book as useful and as accurate as possible. We hope you enjoy it.

CHAPTER 1

About Plants

Plants can live without people.
People cannot live without plants.

With this truism, we begin our appreciation of plants, with which the human race has shared a long and complex history since our first appearance upon this green planet.

Plants manufacture their own food. In the process known as photosynthesis, in which the plant manufactures carbohydrates in the presence of light, chlorophyll, and carbon dioxide, oxygen is released as a by-product. It is to every green plant, from the one-celled alga of the sea to the towering California redwood, that we owe the bulk of our life-giving oxygen supply.

In addition, green plants provide virtually all of our food. Whether we eat plants directly, in the form of fruits, vegetables, and grains, or indirectly as grain and grass converted to eggs, milk products, or animal meat, we owe our lives — again — to green plants.

Plants provide wood to build our houses, coal and petroleum products to heat them, fibers for clothing, and derivatives for medicine. Even if we could live without plants, the quality of our lives would be severely diminished in their absence.

Not least, plants offer a balm to the soul and an inspiration to the spirit. Only when we have lived for a time without green plants can we appreciate them properly. Who has not returned from a desert without marveling at the sight of green trees and pastures? Who has not lived through an icy northern winter without, at its end, feeling sentiments akin to those of poet George Meredith:

> Now the North wind ceases,
> The warm South-west awakes,
> The heavens are out in fleeces,
> And earth's green banner shakes.

OUR CHANGING RELATIONSHIP TO PLANTS

The popular discovery of the science of ecology, no more than a few decades old, has led to a new appreciation of plants, which in turn has begun to alter our relationship to them. No longer do we look at plants simply as low forms of life placed on earth for our convenience and pleasure. Now, some scientists are paying attention to the way plants seem to respond to *us*. Only long after we began to look and listen for signs of intelligent life from distant planets did we turn our attentions toward possible communications from living bodies of a quite different, and closer, source.

There is a growing body of evidence to support the view that, indeed, plants can and do sense our presence, and that they react in definite and often predictable ways to our actions. Although much of this research is very controversial, and many reputable scientists reject the validity of the findings, it is an area of investigation that will receive increasing attention in the decades ahead, as man continues the never-ending quest to understand the world and his place in it.

Two popular books of the 1970s — *The Secret Life of Plants,* by Peter Tompkins and Christopher Bird, and *The Psychic Power of Plants,* by John Whitman (see Bibliography) — detail much of the psychic research that has been conducted in the last several decades. Perhaps the most controversial and best-known experiments are those of Cleve Backster, an American polygraph (lie detector) expert, who in 1966 reported that he had accidentally discovered that a house plant responded vigorously to his thoughts of harming that plant. Initially, he attached the polygraph electrodes to the leaves of a *Dra-*

Opposite, close-up of a fig leaf, Ficus *species.*

1

Green Revelations:
Two Pioneers in Plant Communication

The theories regarding communication between plants and people are controversial to say the least. But more and more researchers are beginning to believe that such theories hold at least some measure of truth. Two men whose work with plants is based on a firm belief in the interrelatedness of plants and humans are Marcel Vogel and Alan Chadwick.

A crystallographer and IBM scientist, Marcel Vogel has been researching the relationship between plants and people, meditative states, positive thought-transference, and telepathy. He believes that plants and people share a life force or cosmic en-

ergy (called prana) which surrounds all living things. This shared life force, he is convinced, makes it possible for people and plants to intercommunicate, and allows such communications from the plant to be tracked on a recording chart.

Plants, Vogel says, not only conduct thought, but they also visibly respond to love. He demonstrated this for our interviewer by passing his hand slowly under the leaves of a large philodendron in his living room, not touching the plant itself at all. Within a short time, the plant was visibly trembling and undulating, seemingly in a kind of delight.

Vogel works with children and sometimes with adults, teaching them to explore this type of communication with plants. "The way it works is this," he explained. "I send out a loving thought to the plant, and at the same time I enter its energy field, not touching the plant itself, but activating its prana or life-energy visibly, with both the physical massage and the loving feeling."

Vogel sees his work with plants as mirrors of human thought as a way to help people learn to achieve spiritual, intellectual, and emotional growth. From plants, says Vogel, we can learn the art of loving and know truly that when we think a

caena fragrans 'Massangeana' as a whim, but so surprising were the results of his experiments that he eventually established a foundation for the furtherance of such research.

Some experimenters now believe they have shown that plants react to music (liking chamber music and abhorring loud rock), have memory, are capable of communicating not only with people but with each other, display emotions, go through periods of depression, and exhibit definite personality characteristics. Others flatly dismiss the results of such research. The solution to the debate is nowhere in sight. What is certain, though, is that we have much to learn about the still-mysterious forces that bind together all life forms.

HORTICULTURAL THERAPY

In the last few decades, plants have been used in various forms of physical and emotional therapy for human beings. Six major

American universities now offer degrees in this new field, while others offer courses but no degrees.

Alice Burlingame, noted plant therapist and the author of *Hoe for Health,* and, with Donald P. Watson, *Therapy through Horticulture* (see Bibliography), defines the goal of horticultural therapy as increasing the patient's level of motivation through working with plants and flowers. Whether the patient's problems are mental or physical, caring for plants will reward him or her with a feeling of accomplishment, renewed confidence, and an interest in the future.

Most of us have already made use of the principles of horticultural therapy, probably without thinking about it. When children grow up and leave home, many people turn more actively to growing plants. It is not coincidental that many middle-aged people refer to their plants as "my babies." Many people have, after a severe emotional crisis, found comfort in tending plants, indoors or thought we release a tremendous power of force into space. By knowing that we *are* our thoughts, we will know how to use thinking for growth.

Another modern horticultural development, one which is based on work with devic, or spiritual, forces in nature, is the system of gardening known as bio-dynamic. Created in the early 1900s by mystic educator Rudolph Steiner, bio-dynamic gardening presupposes that nature is naturally abundant if one approaches it with the correct attitude and knowledge. Bio-dynamic gardening, whose proponents claim to produce harvests four to six times larger than those yielded by other methods of gardening, is attentive to the special qualities of each plant, and to the terrestrial and cosmic influences which affect it.

Alan Chadwick, who was tutored as a child by Steiner, is today the leading exponent of bio-dynamic gardening in the United States. To Chadwick, the plant realm is magnificent in its array, simply spirit made manifest. "The world is governed by pulsation," he says. "It is breathing in and out, and there really is no time.

"Throughout nature there is a balance," he continues. "There are plants which like certain plants, not others. With birds and insects and people, of course, too, it is the same. There are relationships and dysrelationships. In some cases unaccountable, but in all cases completely real. So, behind this whole matter of the garden there is a definite spiritual approach. One might call it soul, but what does that matter? It is a certain goodness of intent. When you approach the garden this way, you will have so many vegetables, fruits, and flowers you won't have enough friends to give them away to because, treated with goodness, nature always gives more than is required."

To people such as Marcel Vogel and Alan Chadwick, plants are much more than a convenient source of food or decoration to be used as we see fit. Instead, they are co-dwellers with us on this planet, and as such they deserve our care and our respect.

out. The involvement with other living and growing things somehow trains our sights on the future, and renews our faith in life itself.

Plants are, with increasing frequency, seen as an antidote to the cold and impersonal life in the city. The harried executive or office clerk, after spending endless days on cement and asphalt, readily appreciates a greener world awaiting his or her return home. These benefits of plants also help to explain the extraordinary recent popularity of house plants in both home and office. Today's interior decorators try to soften the stark lines of modern architecture with plants, often using large, tubbed specimens as visual and aesthetic focal points.

House plants are highly recommended for children, to help them to understand the basic lessons of life and death, and to appreciate the very nature of the world around them. The child who successfully grows a plant is rewarded quickly, and in a way that he can readily understand. It does not take long for him to learn that the plant depends on him for water, light, and food.

House plants also serve as an outlet for creative energies. The training of plants to forms, the construction of terraria, dish gardens, and bonsai arrangements — all are forms of living art, and some of them have been practiced for thousands of years.

Finally, the nurturing of plants can act as a daily tranquilizer for all of us. As noted house plant expert Elvin McDonald says in his book, *Plants as Therapy* (see Bibliography), "If you live and work with plants around you, there is always something that needs to be done for them and that will simultaneously help you get through everyday anxieties. As you wait for an important telephone call or recover from a difficult personal or professional confrontation, picking off dead leaves and flowers, watering a plant, or cleaning its leaves with a damp tissue can reduce anxiety far better than chain smoking, a stiff drink, or a tranquilizer."

Plants in the Office: Trees or large bushy plants in tubs (as shown here), hanging baskets with cascading plants, or small, neat dish gardens set on desk or cabinet tops bring a welcome touch of greenery to the stark, sterile atmosphere of a working environment.

A SHORT HISTORY OF GARDENING

Gardening — the growing of plants for food or ornament — is evident in all cultures and civilizations of recorded history, and its vestiges are apparent in archaeological records of prehistoric times.

It is generally accepted that gardening and farming (it is difficult to separate the two at man's early stage of development) began during the Neolithic period, as long as 8,000 years ago. Mankind made great social strides during this age, which saw the first use of polished stone tools, the making of pottery, the invention of weaving, the settlement of the world's first villages, and the domestication of animals. Human beings turned from hunters and gatherers into new and radically different creatures — ones who could, for the first time, exercise some degree of control over the environment and provide security through growing food, creating shelter, making clothing, and planning for common defense. The growing of plants was one of the new-found talents that helped to place our ancestors in a position superior to that of the other animals around them.

The first evidence of food cultivation appears at the oases at Jericho, in Palestine, around 6000 B.C. The next earliest evidence, in western Asia, dates back no earlier than 4500 B.C. It is not surprising that the first gardens appeared in the oases of the Middle Eastern deserts, however, since the surrounding terrain offered little hope of gathering food and, necessity always having been the mother of invention, the early desert-dwellers were soon forced to make best use of the small green oases in order to survive at all.

The propagation of plants, since it is a necessary part of gardening, also doubtless began during Neolithic times. Many of our food crops — and some of our popular house plants, as well — are available to us today because they were encouraged and improved by our ancestors of thousands of years ago. The date palm growing in the living room in today's suburban ranch house may well be a direct descendant of one cultivated by men and women before the time of Christ. Some plants, finding particular favor among people, have been propagated by cuttings for hundreds of years, so that each new plant is, in fact, a part of the parent plant. In this way, for instance, the grapevine 'Pinot Meunier' has been propagated for more than a thousand years.

Although early gardens were grown for food rather than pleasure, the growing of ornamental plants followed soon after — usually in the homes of the very rich, or in public places. The ancient Egyptians built beautiful walled gardens. The Mesopotamians constructed elaborate terraced gardens. After the biblical Garden of Eden, perhaps the most famous early garden was a Mesopotamian product — the Hanging Gardens of Babylon.

Styles and techniques of gardening were brought to different areas of the world by traders, explorers, conquerors, and others who had cause to leave their native lands. Thus the Moors introduced advanced Arabic styles and techniques to Spain. The planting of naturalistic gardens, which emulate nature instead of forcing plants into artificial forms, was widely practiced throughout Asia by the Buddhists, who regarded such gardens as sacred places. The Japanese learned the style from the Buddhists, and refined it through the centuries to the precise and breathtaking art it is today. Even the ancient Japanese art of bonsai — the training of certain plants by judicious pruning in small containers — was taken up by the Europeans in the form of dish gardens.

This history of gardening, after ancient times, becomes more interesting and complex. In Europe, early gardening styles were developed under the Roman Empire and tended to be classical in nature, closely following the other arts. The Crusaders introduced Asian techniques upon returning from their quests. During the Renaissance, the classical styles of ancient Greece and Rome were revived in Europe, nowhere on a grander scale than in Italy, where very formal gardens and marvelous fountains were in vogue, closely following styles in painting, music, and architecture.

The Spanish and Portuguese, early conquerors of America, brought their Moorish gardening techniques to the New World, where they merged with Inca and Aztec styles. In return, the New World introduced corn and potatoes to Europe.

Early gardening in North America was dominated by the necessity of growing food plants. Ornamental plantings were a rare luxury in the beginning, and house plants were probably unknown by the vast majority of colonists. During the time of George Washington, however, the English revived the naturalistic style — again paralleling trends in other arts — and brought this new style to the colonies. Early American public gardens were thus designed in the English style, and have remained so to the present day.

PLANTS MOVE INDOORS

Our love for green plants led us to bring them indoors at a very early point in history. We can only surmise that some plant lover, at some distant time, hit upon the idea of planting a favorite specimen in a clay pot or bowl and placing it indoors by a sunny window. From that day until this, certainly more than 2,000 years, people have passed along that idea to others.

We know that the ancient Greeks and Romans grew plants in pots in both courtyards and buildings. History shows, also, that indoor gardening made few strides in Europe through the Middle Ages, up until about the time of the discovery of the Americas. It was, in fact, the contact with the New World that, in part, spurred renewed interest in house plants, since some noble and otherwise wealthy Europeans delighted in displaying exotic plants brought from the New World, often growing them indoors to protect them. At this time, too, European traders returning from the Orient brought back plants to satisfy the rising demand of the affluent classes.

The masses, however, did not take up the cultivation of indoor plants until relatively recently. By 1875, the Victorian middle class had begun to emulate the upper class in adopting house plants as a sign of elegance and good breeding. Cacti, palms, and ferns were very popular at various times during the nineteenth century in North America as well as in Great Britain. The wealthy constructed greenhouses, solaria, and other indoor spaces — lighted by skylights — for the cultivation of favorite plants. These indoor areas were usually as large and elaborately designed as the family's wealth would allow. The less fortunate Victorian, although he could not afford to match the grand scale of the gentry and nobility, nevertheless carried out his plant-growing schemes in the same fanciful Victorian design. The plant stands, containers, and glass cases of the time were — like the art and architecture of the period — full of overblown gingerbread. By today's measures of taste, the Victorian style was, at best, "busy." Nevertheless, we do owe our nineteenth-century forebears a significant debt for bringing plants into the indoor environment of the middle-class family.

Throughout the history of gardening in modern times, the plant collector has remained a key figure. Often braving the most challenging of conditions — storms, shipwrecks, steamy jungles, hostile natives, disease, famine, and hordes of insects — the plant collector nevertheless forged on, looking for seeds and specimens of rare and beautiful plants in any corner of the world. Most of the collectors were commissioned by noble families, horticultural societies, or commercial dealers, and they were paid for their fortitude. Some, however, were simply well-to-do travelers who took pleasure in the quest for beauty among plants. It is these hearty adventurers, whatever their motivation, that we must thank for most of the standard house plants we enjoy today. Each has a history filled with tales of valor, suspense, and glory.

The other key figure of house plant history is the nurseryman/breeder. As soon as a demand for house plants arose, there were nurserymen trying to improve species and varieties, to create the most attractive and productive plant specimens and, thus, to attract the larger share of business. Plant improvement has been going on for thousands of years, as farmers have always chosen the best of food crops from which to gather seeds for the next year's plantings. The Incas practiced selective breeding of potatoes before the birth of Christ. The Egyptians similarly improved strains of grapes 4,000 years ago. In this simple way, all of our modern food plants have been altered significantly, often to a point where their distant ancestors would be virtually unrecognizable. As farmers chose the best seeds, so did ornamental plant nurserymen, much later in history, choose the largest, the healthiest, or the most colorful plants of any group to propagate for sale.

The first intentional breeding of a hybrid plant (an offspring of two plants of different varieties, species, or genera) is believed to have been carried out by the English nurseryman Thomas Fairchild in 1717. He crossed a carnation and a sweet William. Since that time, hybridization has been the most successful and dramatic way of improving plants to suit our needs and tastes. The techniques did not gain widespread popularity for many years, because of the difficulty involved in selecting proper parent plants, but during the nineteenth century, as a flood of exotic plants was introduced into Europe from all over the world, hybridization became quite common.

The progress of the indoor plant in America has paralleled its fortunes in Europe. Indoor plants did not gain favor among the American middle class until the late nineteenth century, at which time some plants — notably ferns and palms — gained popularity in both tasteful homes and public places. It was not until after World War II, however, that indoor plants began to assume more importance throughout the wider American society. At this time, there began a trend to family homes with large windows, airy rooms, patios, and terraces. As American architecture softened the lines between indoors and out, plants naturally found a place in the modern scheme of things. Plant health was enhanced not only by the brighter rooms, but also by the increased use of room and furnace humidifiers. People discovered that what was good for plants was good for themselves, as well. The increased use of fluorescent lighting also made the indoors a better environment for plants, since a combination of warm and cool fluorescent tubes provides a better spectrum of light than does the tungsten bulb, and does so less expensively.

The 1950s foreshadowed the increasing trends of the sixties and seventies, when America fell in love with the outdoors. These decades saw the coming of the environmental movement, when a reverence for the natural world was nourished as never before. As threats to the environment from pollution and depletion of natural resources were made clear, millions sought to preserve it. As the dangers of synthetic pesticides became widely known, millions turned to organic gardening, joining those stalwarts who had held this banner for 30 years or more. As many aspects of our daily lives seemed to be growing increasingly impersonal, millions sought to soften the edges of their own lives by turning to natural things. In all of these interrelated movements and trends, gardening — including indoor gardening — has found a ready role.

PLANT EXPLORATION AND INTRODUCTION: THE QUEST FOR NEW PLANTS

The plants in our homes today are descendants of plants brought back by plant hunters from distant corners of the world. Nonnative plants introduced into cultivation have changed our lives; once rare and unusual fruits and flowers are now grown and appreciated by gardeners in many countries. Familiar favorites include *Calceolaria* from the Andes of South America, *Maranta* from the lowland American tropics, many orchids from the Far East, *Cyclamen* from Europe, and *Primula* from China. Plant hunting has been going on since the days of the Egyptian pharaohs. The many expeditions undertaken through the years were often fraught with

adventure, danger, and frequently death for those brave enough to journey through continents in search of seeds or cuttings for their sponsor's gardens.

The earliest recorded expedition to gather exotic plants for introduction was sent to Somalia by Queen Hatshepsut of Egypt in 1495 B.C., for the purpose of obtaining frankincense trees. Once located, these were carefully dug up, packed in wicker baskets, slung on poles carried by slaves, and brought back to Egypt. After their long journey, the trees were planted in a temple garden at Thebes.

In the United States, the earliest introductions were simply an exchange of plants with private individuals in Europe, beginning in the 1700s. The United States government has been concerned primarily with plants that have economic uses, and it has been the academic institutions that traditionally have supported explorations for ornamental species. For example, the Arnold Arboretum of Harvard University sponsored various expeditions to the Far East, led by such immortal figures as Charles S. Sargent, Ernest H. Wilson, and Joseph F. Rock.

One major problem facing eighteenth- and early nineteenth-century collectors was the great strain placed on transplanted seedlings or bulbs during the long trip back to their intended countries. In the case of overseas voyages, many collected plants subsequently died during the months needed for transport, or else were dumped at sea to lighten the load on fragile vessels during harsh storms. Perhaps the most well known case of such a plant loss involved the H.M.S. *Bounty,* an English warship dispatched to pick up a load of valuable tropical trees in the Pacific Islands. On a return trip from Tahiti, the precious breadfruit trees placed on the ship's deck seemingly were given better care and more water than the crew.

On April 28, 1789, during the famous mutiny, the trees were tossed into the Pacific Ocean, and the plant collector, David Nelson, cast adrift in a small boat along with Captain

Bligh. After an arduous voyage, sailing in tossing seas from island to island in search of rations and rescue, Nelson died of "inflammatory fever," on July 20. In this case, as in many others, the price was high for the individual plant explorer.

Today it is usually private institutions or individuals who sponsor and participate in the search for ornamental plants, sometimes in cooperation with government agencies.

Probably the largest combined effort between a private American institution and a government agency ever undertaken to search out and introduce ornamental plants was the United States Department of Agriculture-Longwood Gardens Ornamental Plants Exploration Program, begun in 1956. The team effort of these two powerful organizations allowed for the solution of problems that had plagued plant explorers for centuries. The difficulties of a private individual traveling freely in a foreign country were eased by the government affiliations of the USDA. Funds for the collection of strictly ornamental plants were supplied by Longwood Gardens at Kennett Square, Pennsylvania, as they would be difficult to justify from a government agency whose major efforts were with agronomic crops.

Trained collectors were provided by both agencies, along with extensive growing, testing, and breeding facilities. Shipments of plants had been hindered in the past by local customs restrictions and limited commercial airline rates and schedules. Seeds, cuttings, and plants from these expeditions, however, were often shipped by air directly to Washington, D.C., in diplomatic pouches and mail. In addition, the introduction and early uses of plastic films occurred during this period, so that well-wrapped plants and cuttings could thus remain extra fresh for the several days required for transcontinental shipment.

Plant material was inspected upon arrival at its United States destination, and the USDA took care of any processing and post-entry quarantine that was required. Each plant was given a plant introduction number and records of its performance and distribution were kept. Over 10,000 new plants were introduced into the United States during the 13 expeditions which took place from 1956 to 1970. The explorers journeyed to many parts of the world in search of plants: southern Japan (1956), western Europe (1957), southern Brazil and Argentina (1958), Australia (1958–59), northern Europe (1959), northern Japan (1961), Nepal (1962), the USSR (1963 and 1971), Sikkim (1965), South Korea (1966), Taiwan (1967–68), and New Guinea (1970).

The final results may not be known for several decades. It often takes years to select, evaluate, genetically manipulate, propagate, and test ornamental material. However, among the more immediate successes are the well-known New Guinea impatiens, collected by H. F. Winters and J. J. Higgins in 1970 during a trip to the subtropical highlands of Australian New Guinea. These new impatiens hardly resemble those familiar species that have been our common summer bedding plants for so long. Most striking are the large flowers 1 to 2 inches (2.5 to 5 cm) across, with one kind sometimes attaining a diameter of 3 inches (8 cm). The plants range in size from a bushy 12 inches (30 cm) to over 36 inches (91 cm) tall. The decorative leaves are often variegated with white, yellow, and pink.

Another successful introduction, a *Chrysanthemum* hybrid known as 'White Spider Tokyo', had, by 1972, already grossed over a million dollars in the florist trade, only 15 years after its introduction from Japan by John L. Creech. There are many other examples of ornamental plants introduced from this program, and certainly we will be hearing about others of its "graduates" for a long time to come.

One of the independent plant societies working to promote the cultivation of exotic species through their membership is the

Palm Society. Among the major activities of the society are the publication of a quarterly journal, *Principes,* containing both scientific and popular papers, and the maintenance of the Seed Bank, a clearinghouse where members exchange, contribute, and receive seeds of various palm species. This type of introduction depends almost entirely on the volunteer efforts of a nucleus of amateurs and volunteers, who keep the day-to-day aspects of the program viable. Financial contributions received by the central office are used to help pay for a small portion of the expenses of a tropical botanist or collector who will be traveling to a locality rich in palm flora. The seeds are sent back from the field to the Seed Bank and immediately distributed to the regular members or those supporting a specific expedition.

An active member of the Palm Society, and one of the coordinators of the Seed Bank, is DeArmand Hull. Hull is a prime example of one who has been bitten by the "palm bug." Nights and weekends are spent working for the Seed Bank, coordinating the correspondence, rushing to the airport to receive fresh seed shipments, and hand-packaging these seeds into hundreds of small labeled bags, each with its own succinct biological data, to be mailed to the members.

Those receiving an individual packet in turn contribute two dollars to help defray collecting costs and postage fees. With this voluntary financial support, the Seed Bank has been able to provide for the re-collection and shipment of many rare and endangered species, for ultimate distribution to worldwide botanical gardens and individual members. These people assiduously cultivate the plants, often keeping notes that are later published in *Principes.* Thus, in addition to rescuing palm species that would otherwise be lost, horticultural observations and research also become a product of the Palm Society Seed Bank. During his vacations, Hull often journeys to tropical palm habitats and attempts to obtain live plant material first-hand.

Hull's persistence and dedication have paid off. His collection includes about 1,000 of the estimated 3,000 palm species that are known to exist. The efforts of many individuals such as Hull make the Palm Society perhaps the most important key to collecting, introducing, and preserving one of the world's more ornamental and important tropical plant families, the palm.

NATURAL HABITATS OF HOUSE PLANTS

Where, specifically, have our present-day house plants come from? The answer is not a simple one; plants currently cultivated in North America have their "roots" in all corners of the globe. For example, the showy-flowered camellias are native to China and Japan; the present floriferousness of the species we cultivate is the product of many years of selection and research. *Lantana,* cultivated as an indoor pot plant, is a weedy, climbing shrub from tropical and subtropical parts of both the Old and New World. Our beloved African violets (*Saintpaulia* spp.) are in nature herbaceous perennials that grow wild along the coastal regions of East Africa. The red tulip may be considered Holland's national flower, but its true origins are found among the 150 or so species scattered along the Mediterranean region and across Asia to Japan. The magnificently perfumed Madagascar jasmine (*Stephanotis floribunda*) is a vine native to Madagascar and Malaya. Each of our ornamental plants thus has a different and distinct origin. Over the past few decades, more and more of these gems have been making their way into our gardens, encouraged by our desire for the rare or unusual.

In habitats such as the rain forest described in A Journey down the Amazon, stressed environments are often the best places to find suitable plant material for cultivation. The edge of the forest, exposed tops of trees, and sites with poor soil are all possible hunting grounds. It is more likely that a plant which can survive under the stress of a little less water or in poorer soil than its neighbor will be a better candidate for our often less than ideal indoor environments.

The needs of hundreds of house plants are detailed in these pages. You will be better able to understand those needs, however, if you gain some idea of the native environment of the plants you choose to grow. The mere picturing of a dieffenbachia on the floor of a dense jungle can give us a much surer sense of why we must provide the conditions commonly recommended for that plant. When we learn that some of our tropical plants originated in environments with annual wet and dry seasons, it will be easier to remember to give those plants a seasonal rest, holding back fertilizer and applying water sparingly. Picturing the dry season of a South American rain forest will give us a clearer understanding of the needs of plants from that part of the world — much more so than if we were simply to follow, in a mechanical way, the usual recommendations for light, temperature, soil moisture, and humidity. Just as a smattering of knowledge about chemistry is important to the development of a good cook, so a little geographical knowledge is important to the success of an indoor gardener.

Many of our house plants come from tropical areas near the equator. The first thing to remember, in a very general sense, is that the days near the equator are always about 12 hours long, as are the nights. Plants originating from the equatorial region have become adapted to that light schedule over countless centuries. Knowing that, you can understand that, for these plants, being thrust out into the backyard of a Minnesota home during the very long days of summer may not be the vacation you had intended for the plants, but a real hardship instead. You can understand, too, that during the short days of November and December, some plants require supplemental light during the early evening hours. And if you have ever wondered why you must provide at least 12 hours of total darkness for your poinsettia, in order to get it to bloom for Christmas, a look at its southern Mexican origins will provide the answer.

In many tropical areas, also, temperature variations are very slight. Since there is little, if any, changing of the seasons, the temperatures in January are remarkably similar to those in July. There is always a moderate dip — perhaps 7° to 10°F (4° to 6°C) — at night. In contrast, temperate zone plants are used to seasonal variations of as much as 120°F (67°C), and many northern plants must go through an annual freezing period in order to grow and reproduce. If such plants are to bloom and to grow well indoors, this cold period must be simulated in a refrigerator or cold frame.

Most indoor gardeners tend to see plant families such as the cacti (Cactaceae) as a monolithic group, not realizing that there are vast differences among them, again relating to their native habitats. Some cacti come from lowland deserts where nighttime temperatures never dip to the freezing point. Others, however, come from semiarid mountain areas where hard freezes are common, and where even daytime temperatures are quite cool. Cacti have developed common characteristics because of their common response to poor soil, and because they have been forced to go for long periods without water. But to subject all cacti to hot temperatures throughout the year, assuming that they are all desert plants, is to ignore the importance of their varying origins. Some cacti will do far better spending the winter on an unheated sun porch, while others prefer the constant warmth of an indoor windowsill.

Because most of us are not in the position to see firsthand the natural habitats of the plants we grow, botanical, horticultural, ecological, and natural history studies are the best sources of this kind of information.

RE-CREATING ORIGINAL ENVIRONMENTS

Generally speaking, the further you can go in re-creating the original environments for your plants, the greater success you will have with them. The tools and equipment available to today's indoor gardeners have made such re-creation not only possible, but almost simple. True, you still cannot reproduce a miniature tropical rain forest in your home, but you can come close enough to grow plants that you will be proud to display, while maintaining a home atmosphere fit for people, as well.

The four major plant requirements — light, temperature, soil moisture, and humidity — are all within control with today's resources. Artificial lighting, thermostatic heating, and judicious watering will meet the first three requirements with little difficulty. The fourth — humidity — is the most difficult. Most tropical plants, for truly maximum home growth, require a level of humidity which we cannot sensibly provide. It is best, then, to compromise, to offer the greatest amount of humidity — again through artificial means — that we can reasonably provide.

It is wise, also, to select plants of similar geographic origin to share a common location in the home. Even if you do not know the specific origins of all your plants, group together those that have similar requirements. Low-light specimens that like warm temperatures and moist, woodsy soil can be grouped together in a large planter, where they can receive similar care. Plants that prefer lots of light and a drier soil can share a plant stand and a few hanging baskets near a south-facing window. You can arrange a rain forest collection, a desert collection, or even a North American woodland collection in a terrarium, where all the plants receive the same lighting, temperature, watering, and humidity. To intermingle plants of sharply varying requirements is to make things hard on yourself, as well as the plants.

INTRODUCING THE PLANT: SOME BASIC BOTANY

The plant is a wonderful thing, indeed. Every part of it has been shaped for a specific purpose. No part is unnecessary, and every reaction within the plant works in perfect concert with all the others, for a single purpose: to perpetuate the species.

Over eons of struggle, each plant has adapted itself to the environmental conditions in its own part of the world. The cactus, a marvel of adaptation, has developed a thick cuticle to protect it from freezing nights and water loss, enormously swollen stems to hold water reserves in times of drought, and sharp spines to protect the plant from animals that would otherwise devour it. The common dandelion sends its seed-bearing puffballs, virtually weightless, to the wind at just the right time, insuring future generations of its species. Many plants bear their seeds in pulpy fruits and berries that are attractive to birds. The birds eat the fruit, but expel the seeds, which are unharmed because of their tough coating. Each seed, falling to the ground, is coated in manure, which, by the time the seed is ready to germinate, has composted to the perfect point to nourish the young seedling when its roots are established in the ground. (Before roots are established the embryonic plant is nourished by reserves in the seed and by the cotyledon, or seed-leaf.) Indeed, all plants are marvels of adaptation.

PARTS OF THE PLANT
Leaf

The major purpose of the leaf is to manufacture food for the plant's growth. Contrary to the belief of many gardeners, plants do not depend on the "plant food" we buy for them. They manufacture their own food in the process known as photosynthesis. It is, in fact, this process, known only to plants, that is the source of food for all the animals of the earth. Plant foods are no more than mixtures of cer-

A Journey down the Amazon

Let us wander, in these few paragraphs, to a tropical rain forest located in the Amazon Valley of South America, and explore the habitat in which several of our familiar house plants are found.

Drifting along the Amazon River, the most striking sight is the huge trees that solidly line the river bank and dominate the surrounding landscape. Drawing nearer, there appears a way into the forest, along a small creek which feeds into the great river. We step off the boat, onto the moistened soil lining the side of this small stream, and begin to wander through the forest, walking along an aboriginal hunting trail winding through the otherwise dense jungle. Moving along, the spongy soil gives under our feet, its first six inches (15 cm) rich in organic matter.

This warm, lush, loamy environment supports several species of plants which are easily distinguished. *Dieffenbachia maculata,* the dumb cane, is a 36-inch (91 cm) stalk growing alongside the base of a tree. The white flowers of *Spathiphyllum floribundum* arise from the tufts of glossy foliage thriving in an inundated area. A multicolored *Calathea* is taking advantage of a ray of sunlight streaming down along the trail. Here these plants find their ideal environment: a warm temperature, indirect sunlight filtering in from the leafy canopy of trees above, continual humidity, moisture from the torrential rains, and rich soils laden with freshly decomposed organic matter contributed by the wealth of animal

and plant life that is found in the tropical rain forest.

Perfectly shaped, and safe from insect predators due to their occurrence in isolated patches and low natural density, the plants display a range of foliage and flowers that would be impossible to re-create in our temperate homes and greenhouses. Appressed to the trees are vining plants, which use these natural "stakes" to reach up 100 feet (31 m) or more into the canopy to seek more light or additional support for their grasping roots. The showy spathes of white and pink are displayed at staggered intervals along the length of the stem. The flight of dozens of insects creates a noisy activity around each bloom, as they seek their sustenance of nectar or pollen.

To the left of us lies the fallen limb of a large tree, broken off because it could no longer support the great profusion of bromeliads, peperomias, orchids, and other epiphytic plants which grew upon it. As we wander farther and farther into the forest, the realization dawns that we are witness to an incredible creation, a complete orchestration of plants, using each available inch of space to its fullest advantage, and at the same time making way for the successional species that will later develop. Several living layers can be distinguished: herbaceous ground plants, vines, low shrubs, upright palms, and large canopy trees. Combined they represent the living skeleton and body of the forest, and irrevocable change ultimately follows the disturbance of any single level.

Dense Jungle Forest: Ramrod-straight trees tower above the thick tropical vegetation of this Amazon rain forest. Filtered sun, warmth, high humidity, and a wealth of organic matter are the reasons for the luxuriant growth. Many of the foliage plants found in our homes, such as philodendrons, prayer plant, and Chinese evergreen, originated in this type of environment, along with such flowering beauties as angel-lily and certain orchids.

River Scene: Although the heyday of plant expeditions is over, it's not hard to imagine boats gliding along this river bearing eighteenth-century European plant hunters, in search of exotic plants to bring back to their sponsors. The lush jungle undoubtedly appeared as a treasure trove to these explorers, offering up its wealth of bromeliads and orchids, as well as other flowering and foliage plants.

tain essential minerals (sometimes in an organic base) that the plant needs to carry on certain chemical processes. The application of fertilizer to a plant is comparable to our taking vitamin supplements. It is insurance against an inadequate diet.

The leaf has an enormous surface area when compared to its mass. It is, in other words, flat, and this flatness suits its purpose perfectly. Its thinness lets in a great amount of light, and light is essential to its food manufacturing process. It also enhances the efficient absorption and diffusion of gases and water vapor through its thousands of openings. Also, the loss of water vapor from leaves in the process of transpiration enables plants to maintain a proper heat balance.

A cross section of an ordinary leaf would bear a striking resemblance to that of human skin. The outer layer of cells (the epidermis) is waterproof — not to keep water out of the leaf, but to hold it in during the food manufacturing process. Leaf functions must be conducted in water at all times. Were the epidermis not waterproof, the leaf would dry out and die in a matter of hours in the absence of rain.

Below the epidermis is a layer of upright-standing cells known as the palisade layer.

Inside the palisade cells are minute bits of material, football or biscuit shaped, called chloroplasts, which contain chlorophyll and give leaves their distinctive green color. In the middle of the leaf cross section is a large spongy layer, which also contains chloroplasts, and below that is the lower epidermis. Both the upper and lower leaf surfaces are pierced with small openings called stomata, which allow the absorption and diffusion of gases and water vapor during the chemical operations of this food factory. The vascular tissue (veins) in leaves serves to transport water and "food" throughout the leaf and to the stem.

The major chemical function of the leaf is the manufacture of food in photosynthesis. This complex process is undoubtedly among the most important in the world, for it is not only the source of food for both plants and animals, but also it releases oxygen as a by-product.

Photosynthesis is the phenomenon by which plants trap light and produce their food-for-growth. The "traps" are molecules of chlorophyll, a green pigment contained in the chloroplasts that are scattered throughout the upper cells of the plant leaves. Chlorophyll absorbs red and blue waves of light and

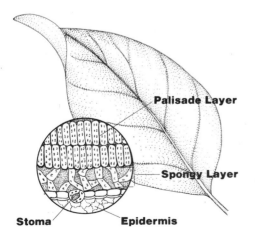

Palisade Layer

Spongy Layer

Stoma   **Epidermis**

Leaf Structure: A leaf, as it meets the eye, appears as a deceptively simple structure, a pleasant adornment for the plant. In reality, it is a sandwich of cellular layers which are responsible for assuring that adequate food will be manufactured to sustain the whole plant and fuel its growth. The epidermis, a waterproof outer layer of cells, has the all-important task of retaining water in the leaf so the chemical processes may continue. A layer of these cells forms both the upper and lower leaf surfaces. In both of these layers are found stoma, small openings which allow gases and water vapor to be taken in and released during chemical processes. Next to the lower epidermis is a spongy layer which houses chloroplasts, the chlorophyll-containing bodies which serve to trap the light necessary for photosynthesis. Next is the palisade layer composed of oblong cells lying beneath the upper epidermis; these, too, contain a full complement of chloroplasts.

reflects most of the green and yellow waves. Through a series of complex electrochemical processes, this light energy is used to combine atoms of hydrogen, carbon, and oxygen. The result is food energy — a sugar solution which is the "food" or photosynthate that plant cells need to survive. At night, when photosynthesis has stopped, the sugar is distributed to plant cells and consumed as the plant grows. If there is more sugar than the plant needs for immediate growth, the surplus is changed to starch or oils and stored in roots, tubers, bulbs, and seeds. The plant uses this stored food whenever it is unable to produce sufficient amounts of photosynthate.

Modern scientists, with all the resources at their disposal, have never been able to duplicate this process of photosynthesis. Scientists now understand some of the processes involved, but the large gaps in their understanding still bar the door to duplication.

Stem

The stem has two main functions. One is to support the plant. The other is to serve as a transportation system between the leaves and roots. For this second purpose, the stem contains two kinds of very specialized tissues. One, called xylem, comprises cells that carry water and dissolved minerals from the roots up to the leaves, where they are needed in the food manufacturing process. The other, called phloem, carries manufactured substances down to the roots and other parts of the plant.

The water in the leaves at the top of the tallest tree comes from the roots, a distance of literally hundreds of feet, through a series of tiny tubes made of xylem cells. The water is literally pulled up from the roots as water transpires from the leaf, much as water is pulled up from the glass through a straw when we drink it. The water-pulling action will be greatest during dry and windy days, least during calm and humid days. This is important to remember when you keep plants

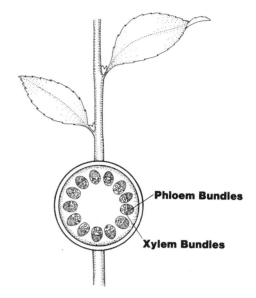

Specialized Transit System in a Stem: Food energy produced by the leaves must be distributed throughout the plant in order for growth to ensue. To make sure this happens, specialized tissues called phloem facilitate the transfer of manufactured food down to the roots and other parts of the plant. But in order for the manufacturing process to continue, water and dissolved minerals from the roots must in turn be brought up to the leaves. Another set of tissues called xylem carry out this function so that the cycle of food manufacture and distribution is complete.

outdoors for the summer. They will need watering more often, because of the more rapid water transpiration through the leaves.

In nonwoody, or herbaceous, plants (which includes most house plants) the xylem and phloem tissues are enclosed in long, tubular structures known as vascular bundles. When you break in half a rhubarb or celery stalk, the long strings you see are the vascular bundles. In woody plants (including trees, of course, but also some house plants, for example, poinsettias, avocados, and boxwood) the xylem is confined to the wood and the phloem to the bark. If just a tiny section of bark is cut from all around the trunk of a tree, the tree will die, since its roots will be deprived of food and soon will cease to gather minerals and water for the leaves.

Most house plants have soft or nonwoody stems. Canes are thick stems with pithy or hollow centers; among house plants, dieffenbachias and ti plants have canes. Some plants — notably the taller-growing ones — have a distinct main stem. But most of our popular house plants have no main stem, but send up many. A lateral or side shoot is a smaller stem growing from the primary one. A petiole is a leaf stalk, the stemlike structure supporting the leaf blade. An axil is the point at which a leaf stalk joins the stem, or where a smaller stem joins a larger one. A stolon, or runner, is a stem that grows along the surface of the ground. Often, a stolon produces roots at intervals along the stem, as is the case with strawberry geraniums.

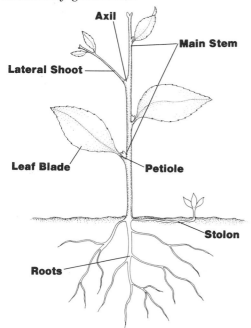

Basic Plant Structures: Jutting out to the left from the main stem is a lateral shoot bearing immature leaves. On the lower two leaves the petiole, the stemlike structure which supports the leaf blade, is apparent. The point where the petiole meets the stem is known as the axil. To the right of the plant, running slightly below the soil surface, is a stolon which eventually turns upward and emerges with a set of new leaves. The threadlike roots extend throughout the soil to serve as anchors, water and mineral absorbers, and storage units.

Certain plants have evolved modified stem structures to store the products of photosynthesis, depending on their environmental pressures. Cacti and succulents, as we have noted, have developed swollen stems (and leaves) for both water and food storage. Florists' gloxinias, caladiums, and a number of other plants are grown from tubers, which are nothing more than enlarged underground stems, again developed over time to store large amounts of sugar and water for future use. Bulbs, which are swollen underground stems with fleshy leaves, serve the same purpose. A corm is the enlarged base of a stem that usually grows erect; a rhizome, a horizontally growing stem, either wholly or partially underground. All are common parts of plants, adapted by some to serve as food and water storage areas under environmental pressure.

Roots

Roots serve to anchor the plant in the ground, to absorb water and the mineral salts dissolved in water, and to store manufactured food for future use. The xylem and phloem tissues begin in the roots and run up the stem and into the leaves, carrying raw materials upward to the leaf factory, and manufactured food down from the leaves into the roots as well as to the other parts of the plant.

It is important to understand the nature of roots if you are to develop an ability to care for plants. The water and minerals are not taken in by the older and tougher roots, but by the tiny root hairs that grow just behind the growing tip of the roots or rootlets. These root hairs work their way into spaces between soil particles where there is both air and water. They will force their way into any available space. In the last century, for instance, Charles Darwin discovered that roots will follow the burrows of earthworms, the burrows apparently providing a ready source of air, moisture, and mineral elements.

Actually, then, roots do not grow *in* soil,

but in the spaces between soil particles. You must be sure to provide indoor plants with a potting mixture that allows sufficient air spaces, yet contains no very large spaces where roots may dry out and die. In a proper soil or potting mixture, the moisture will cling to the soil particles, still leaving room for sufficient air. But if a potting mixture, no matter how well made, is kept saturated by overwatering, the root hairs will receive insufficient oxygen, will be unable to send water and food up to the stems and leaves, and the plant will eventually die. More house plants are killed by overwatering than by any other cause.

If the above is true, then why may some house plants be grown in water? The answer is that a plant grown in water will develop roots of a different nature, ones capable of deriving oxygen from the water itself. Not all plants can do this, however, and even among those that can be grown in water, many have difficulty in adjusting when later planted in soil.

It does no harm to most plants to cut back their roots somewhat when repotting, since — after a short period of shock — they will quickly develop new root hairs, usually in greater profusion than before. Often, plants whose roots are trimmed respond with new health and vigor, because of the stimulation provided by the thousands of new root hairs. Be sure, however, to prune the topgrowth of the plant proportionally; otherwise, the reduced root system will not be able to supply the stem and leaves adequately with water and minerals.

Flowers

We work so hard to encourage brightly colored and pleasantly scented flowers, in both our house and garden plants, that we sometimes believe that the plant is producing them just for our pleasure. Things fall into humbler perspective, however, when we stop to realize that plants produce bright and sweetly scented blossoms not for us, but to attract pollinating insects. After all, the flower — to the plant — is a sexual apparatus, a necessary part of its reproductive function, and the object is to get the insects to visit the plant, "sample" the pollen, and deposit it on the next flower, where pollination can occur. Not all plants depend on insects, of course; some rely on wind or water to transfer pollen from one plant to another.

Indoors, we encourage neither insects nor wind, and so we propagate plants by asexual methods, usually by cuttings or root division. Nevertheless, many indoor plants flower abundantly, producing beautiful and fragrant blossoms at nearly any time of year.

Briefly, the parts of the flower and the specific function of each:

Bracts are usually green, leaflike structures. (The bright red "flowers" on a Christmas poinsettia are not really flowers at all, but bracts which have changed color; the actual flowers surrounded by the bracts are quite small.)

Sepals are green or colorful floral organs which surround the inner parts (i.e., petals, stamens, and pistils) when the flower is in bud. In some flowers, such as orchids, the sepals are as colorful as the petals when the flowers are fully open.

Calyx is the collective term given to all of the sepals. The covering of a rose bud is its calyx.

Petals are the brightly colored tissues surrounding the inner apparatus. Different insects are known to be attracted to different colors, and to the intensity of color.

Corolla is the name botanists give to all the petals together.

Stamens are the male reproductive organs consisting of a stalk or filament and an anther at the top which bears the pollen.

Pistil is the name for the female sexual organ of the flower, containing the ovary. The pistil is contained inside the ring of stamens and inserted on the tip of the flower stem.

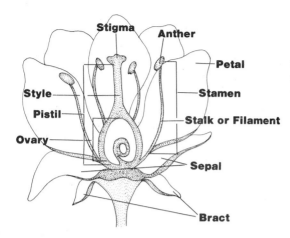

Structure of a Flower: Beautiful to behold, a flower is also an intricate assembly of parts which serve to aid pollination and surround the plant's reproductive organs. The leaflike structures lying just below the sepals are called bracts. Sepals are the variously colored or all-green parts which enclose the inner flower parts while the flower is still in bud; collectively these sepals are known as the calyx. The eye-catching, colorful tissues, usually the most distinctive aspect of the bloom, are known as petals; collectively they become the corolla. The four stalks shown here are the stamens or male reproductive organs, topped by the pollen-bearing anther. In the very heart of the flower is the pistil, the female sex organ, which houses the ovary. The elongated neck of the pistil is called the style, which terminates in the stigma. The sticky surface of the stigma helps hold the pollen grains to facilitate pollination and subsequent fertilization.

Stigma is the top part of the pistil which is supported by the style, a necklike portion of the pistil. The stigma is often covered by a sticky substance which facilitates pollen grains adhering to it. The pollen grains germinate here, then send tubes down into the ovary (the lower portion of the pistil that contains the ovule, which in turn contains the egg). When one of the tubes grows into one of the ovules, the sperm and egg cells are united and fertilization occurs. Each fertilized ovule may grow into a seed. (The process of fertilization is discussed in more detail in chapter 8.)

HOW PLANTS ARE NAMED

Do you have to know that Japanese boxwood is really *Buxus microphylla* var. *japonica*? Is it important to ask for *Plectranthus australis* when all you want is a Swedish ivy?

Sometimes it seems to gardeners that botanists attach Latin names to plants just to confuse outsiders. In truth, Latin or scientific names are necessary. Without them, it would often be impossible to keep plants in order, to tell one from the other, or even to order the plant you really want from a catalog. Many plants are known by different common names, not only in different countries, or different sections of our own country, but even among gardeners on the same block. If you asked for bluebells in New York, you would get one plant; in England or Scotland, perhaps two totally different plants; and in Japan, quite another plant. If you ordered a black pepper plant, you might get a nice house plant that grows edible peppercorns — or you might get a member of the deadly Nightshade family! An asparagus fern can be a trailer, a climber, or an upright-growing plant, because several different plants share this name.

It is not to confuse you, but to bring an end to confusion, that botanists name plants. They use Latin because it is the international language of biologists. Only by sharing this common language can a nurseryman in Belgium communicate accurately with a plant breeder in Poland or Brazil.

Usually the Latin names (often incorporating Greek) describe the plant. Take *Antirrhinum majus,* for instance. *Antirrhinum* is from the Greek words *anti* and *rhinos,* meaning "like a snout." *Majus* means "major" or "greater." Put them all together and you have a common species of a standard size snapdragon. Not all Latin plant names are descriptive, however. Some are used in honor of people. The Dahlia was named for noted Swedish botanist Andreas Dahl. The Poinset-

Plant Genealogy: What's in a Name?

Taxonomy, the identification and classification of plants, from the most primitive to the most advanced, is based on such characteristics as structural features, methods of reproduction, and the manner of producing food. Reproductive criteria are especially important because these are least likely to change over time.

Just as a country is divided into states, counties, and towns, so, too, is the plant kingdom divided. The basic and smallest unit in the classification system is the species. Members of a species are structurally similar, have a common heritage and (in nature) maintain their characteristic features through innumerable generations. Closely related species are grouped into genera (singular, genus). All philodendrons, for example, con-

stitute the genus *Philodendron,* but the way they deviate from their basic commonalities determines the species to which they belong.

Closely related genera are then grouped into families. Many genera make up the Arum family, among which are the genera *Aglaonema* (Chinese evergreen), *Dieffenbachia* (dumb cane), *Philodendron, Epipremnum* (pothos), and *Anthurium* — all of which have basic similarities in flower structure, but differ in other ways. The scientific names of most families end in "aceae." The Arum family is called Araceae. A group of related families composes an order; this scientific name ends either in "ae" or "ales." Spathiflorae, the Arum order, is comprised of the Arum family (Araceae), and the duckweed family (Lemnaceae). Plant orders are further grouped into

classes, which are in turn grouped into divisions.

Our current system of classifying plants went through a complex evolution. Ancient groupings of plants by Aristotle and others were quite simple: trees, shrubs, and herbs. Systematic botany began with the herbals of the sixteenth century. Men like Brunfels, Fuchs (after whom the fuchsia was named), and Bock studied local plants, carefully describing them and having woodcuts made in perfect likenesses — some of which still exist in museums around the world.

Herbalists went wrong, though, because they studied plants only in terms of their most obvious features, and for their economic and medicinal properties alone. Early attempts at plant grouping continued to be quite primitive. By 1623, however, genera and species

---

tia honors J. R. Poinsett, a Virginia statesman who introduced the plant into this country in the nineteenth century. Some are named after the place of origin of the plant — such as *californica, africanus,* or *japonica.*

Every plant has two scientific names, one specifying the genus (the generic name) and the other the species (the specific epithet). After a generic name is introduced, it is thereafter abbreviated. Thus *Antirrhinum majus,* if mentioned again soon after, becomes *A. majus.*

Both names are always written in italics. The generic name is always capitalized, but the specific name is always written in lowercase letters, even if it honors the name of a person.

Often there is a third part of the name,

which helps to distinguish among different varieties of the same genus and species. If a variety is found in nature, it is indicated by a third name which also appears in italics and is preceded by the abbreviation "var.," for "variety." If the variety was developed in cultivation, it is known as a cultivar, and is indicated in Roman type and preceded by the letters "cv." or surrounded by single quotes. Thus, Canary Islands ivy is *Hedera canariensis,* while the variegated form is *Hedera canariensis* 'Variegata'.

If a nonitalic name in quotes follows the genus name rather than the species name (e.g., *Begonia* 'President Carnot'), it is likely an interspecific hybrid. A hybrid may also be indicated by a multiplication sign, such as in *Caladium* × *hortulanum.*

were distinguished by names, and binomial nomenclature began to occur frequently. The arrangement of plants was still quite simplistic. They were grouped in categories of broad-leaved, bulbous, and rhizomatous monocotyledons (such as the Lily family and Orchid family); in dicotyledonous herbs; and into what was thought to be the most perfect group of plants: trees and shrubs. Flower and fruit characteristics were entirely neglected.

In the seventeenth century, John Ray's *Historia Plantarum* recognized the importance of the embryo. But it was in 1735 that Linnaeus, in his *Systema Naturae* (which described the basis for classifying all plants, animals, and minerals), placed plant gender and reproduction high on the list of classification priorities. Even so, from the point of view of the evolution of a natural system of classification, Linnaeus's system still fell short of the mark. He himself regarded the method as only temporary, and he died before he finished grouping his genera into orders. But he was on the way to arranging plants according to their simplest symmetry — not one of special features but the sum of their parts.

This natural system was further developed and gradually refined into the nomenclature we currently use. The first half of the nineteenth century saw an abundance of new systems, due in no small part to the improvement of the compound microscope.

Since earliest times, scientists have invented names for the plants they found on the basis of many factors. Often a genus or species will have a Greek or Latin derivation, as with colchicum, whose roots are a source of narcotic and poison. In the days of the pharaohs until the time of King James I, colchicums were used medicinally for the treatment of gout. Colchis, a city in ancient Greece where it grew profusely, was where Medea restored youth to the favored and poisoned her enemies with these potent roots.

The botanical name of the tulip tree, *Liriodendron,* is derived from two Greek words meaning tulip and tree — which refer to its tuliplike flowers.

At times, a plant's name will honor a public figure, as does the bird-of-paradise *(Strelitzia reginae),* a flower from the Cape of Good Hope named to honor Queen Charlotte, who came from Mecklenburg-Strelitz. Some plants take their names from mythological creatures, such as the iris, named for the rainbow goddess because of its wide range of color.

The binomial system (two names) was devised by the great Swedish botanist Carl von Linné. The trinomial system (three names) was developed later.

With the publication of his *Species Plantarum* in 1753, Linné created order out of chaos. This work described all the species of plants (by genus and species) that he had encountered at that time. He spent the greater part of his life classifying not only plants, but all living things. He considered it a great honor, and not at all unnatural, that his name was Latinized. To this day, he is known as Carolus Linnaeus.

The tremendous explosion of plant varieties has necessitated our keeping the binomial system of Linnaeus. Today, the awesome task of keeping track of all new plants, of recording their names, and of deciding on complex issues of nomenclature, falls to the International Commission for the Nomenclature of Cultivated Plants of the International Union of Botanical Sciences. Doubtless, ordinary gardeners would prefer to leave Latin nomenclature to the commission, remaining free to order Japanese boxwood, Swedish ivy, and snapdragons by their catalog names. Still the nomenclatural procedures are critical for classifying plants and every gardener will, at some time, rely on them to obtain the plants he really wants.

CHAPTER 2

Requirements for Plant Growth

TEMPERATURE

For each individual plant, there is a specific temperature range at which it will grow best, and there are maximum ranges beyond which it cannot live at all. If any plant is to succeed in your home, you must provide temperatures within its permissible range; for maximum health and growth, you must provide temperatures as close as possible to the ideal for that plant.

The plants we have chosen to cultivate for indoor growth are those that can enjoy, with us, common indoor temperatures. Most of them are tropical plants, whether they come from humid or dry regions. Most house plants can do well in a range of 60° to 80°F (16° to 27°C). Even so, there are those that prefer temperatures on the cooler side, and those that respond better to warmer conditions. It is important to check the requirements for every plant you wish to grow. And, if you are to avoid disappointment, do not attempt to grow a plant in temperatures outside its permissible range.

House plants are generally divided into three groups for this purpose: cool-temperature plants (preferring 40° to 60°F/4° to 16°C) such as *Cyclamen persicum, Fatsia japonica,* and *Araucaria heterophylla* (Norfolk Island pine); those thriving in intermediate temperatures (55° to 65°F/13° to 18°C) such as *Asparagus* species (asparagus fern), *Begonia, Coleus,* and *Pilea* species; and those which do best in warm conditions (65° to 75°F/18° to 27°C), which include *Monstera deliciosa* (Swiss cheese plant), *Ficus* species, and various species of *Aglaonema.* Few plants can take continuing temperatures over 80°F (27°C).

Some house plants can tolerate a far wider temperature range than others, and these are often our most popular plants for this very reason. The *Aspidistra,* for instance, although it is a temperate zone plant and does best under cool conditions, will survive (if not exactly thrive) even in overheated rooms. The same is true of heartleaf philodendron *(Philodendron scandens* subsp. *oxycardium),* palms, and grape ivy *(Cissus rhombifolia)* — all popular and tolerant house plants.

All plants, coded by their native environments, grow best when night temperatures drop 5° to 10°F (3° to 6°C) below daytime levels. At night, plants break down some of the food they had manufactured during the day in the presence of light. If the room temperature is too high at night, the rate of respiration will be too high and much of the stored food may be wasted. The result will be a slowing of growth because of insufficient food.

RELATIONSHIP OF TEMPERATURE TO HUMIDITY AND LIGHT

Although temperature affects all of a plant's metabolic reactions, it operates in concert with other environmental conditions, including light and humidity. Outdoors, in the tropics, our house plants can survive much higher temperatures than they can in our homes, because the outdoor environment also offers higher humidity and light intensity, enabling the plants to carry out metabolic processes at a fairly rapid rate. Inside, with insufficient light and low humidity, tropical temperatures can injure or kill these plants.

If any house plant is suffering because of high room temperatures, you can mitigate the ill effects by providing more humidity and light. In this way you will allow the plant

Opposite, plants thrive in the sunny, humid, warm environment of a greenhouse.

Temperature Needs of Some Common Plants

Plants for Cool Temperatures
(45° to 55°F/7° to 13°C at night; 50° to 60°F/10° to 16°C during the day)

Araucaria heterophylla (Norfolk Island pine)
Ardisia crenata (coral berry)
*Aspidistra elatior** (cast-iron plant)
Cacti and succulents*† (during winter rest period only)
Camellia japonica
Chrysanthemum spp.
Citrus spp.
Cyclamen persicum (Persian violet)
Euonymus japonica (spindle tree)
× *Fatshedera lizei* (tree ivy)
Fatsia japonica
Ficus pumila (creeping fig)
Freesia spp.
Grevillea robusta (silk oak)
Hedera helix cvs.* (English ivy)
Hyacinthus orientalis (hyacinth)
Hydrangea macrophylla
Jasminum spp. (jasmine)
Lilium longiflorum var. *eximium** (Easter lily)
Narcissus spp. (daffodil, narcissus)
Pittosporum tobira (mock orange)
Primula spp. (primrose)
Rhododendron spp. (azalea)
Rosa spp. (miniature rose)
Senecio × *hybridus* (cineraria)
Solanum pseudocapsicum (Jerusalem cherry)
Tradescantia spp. (wandering Jew)
Tulipa cvs. (tulip)
Zantedeschia aethiopica (white calla lily)
Zephyranthes grandiflora (Zephyr lily)

*Will also do well at medium temperatures.
†Will also do well at high temperatures.

Plants for Medium Temperatures
(55° to 60°F/13° to 16°C at night; 60° to 65°F/16° to 18°C during the day)

Abutilon spp. (flowering maple)
*Acorus calamus** (sweet flag)
Asparagus setaceus (asparagus fern)
*Aspidistra elatior** (cast-iron plant)
Asplenium nidus (bird's nest fern)
Aucuba spp. (gold-dust tree)
Begonia spp.
Brassaia actinophylla (schefflera)
Bromeliads†
Browallia spp. (bush violet)
Cacti and succulents*†
Calceolaria spp. (pocketbook plant)
Cissus antarctica† (kangaroo vine)
Citrus spp.*
Coleus × *hybridus*
Cryptanthus† (earth star)
Euphorbia milii var. *splendens*† (crown of thorns)

Plants for Medium Temperatures (continued)

Euphorbia pulcherrima (poinsettia)
Fuchsia spp.
Gardenia jasminoides
Gynura aurantiaca† (purple passion plant)
Hedera helix cvs.* (English ivy)
Hibiscus spp.
Hippeastrum spp. (amaryllis)
Hoya spp. (wax plant)
Justicia brandegeana (shrimp plant)
Kalanchoe spp. (panda plant)
Lilium longiflorum var. *eximium** (Easter lily)
Lithops spp.† (living stones)
Oxalis spp. (shamrock plant)
Palms
Peperomia spp.
Persea americana (avocado)
Pilea spp.
Piper nigrum (black pepper)
Platycerium bifurcatum† (staghorn fern)
Podocarpus spp.
Pteris spp. (brake fern)
Sansevieria spp.† (snake plant)
Saxifraga stolonifera (strawberry begonia)
Schlumbergera bridgesii (Christmas cactus)
Senecio mikanioides (German ivy)
Soleirolia soleirolii (baby's tears)
Tolmiea menziesii (piggyback plant)
Zantedeschia elliottiana (yellow calla lily)

*Will also do well at cool temperatures.
†Will also do well at high temperatures.

Plants for High Temperatures
(65° to 70°F/18° to 21°C at night; 70° to 80°F/21° to 27°C during the day)

Acalypha hispida (chenille plant)
Achimenes spp. (monkey-faced pansy)
Aechmea spp. (living vase plant)
Aglaonema spp. (Chinese evergreen)
Alternanthera spp. (copperleaf)
Aphelandra squarrosa (zebra plant)
Bromeliads*
Cacti and succulents*†
Caladium spp. (mother-in-law plant)
Calathea spp. (peacock plant)
*Cissus antarctica** (kangaroo vine)
Cissus rhombifolia (grape ivy)
Cocos nucifera (coconut palm)
Codiaeum variegatum var. *pictum* (croton)
Cordyline spp.
Cryptanthus spp.* (earth star)
Dizygotheca spp. (false aralia)
Dracaena spp.
Echeveria spp. (hen and chicks)
Epipremnum aureum (golden pothos, scindapsus)
Episcia spp. (flame violet)
Euphorbia milii var. *splendens** (crown of thorns)

Plants for High Temperatures (continued)

Ficus spp.
Geogenanthus undatus (seersucker plant)
*Gynura aurantiaca** (purple velvet plant)
Impatiens spp. (busy lizzie)
Lithops spp.* (living stones)
Malpighia coccigera (miniature holly)
Maranta spp. (prayer plant)
Mimosa pudica (sensitive plant)
Monstera deliciosa (Swiss cheese plant)
Pandanus veitchii (veitch screw pine)
Pelargonium spp. (geranium)
Philodendron spp.
*Platycerium bifurcatum** (staghorn fern)
Saintpaulia spp. and cvs. (African violets)
Sansevieria spp.* (snake plant)
Sinningia speciosa (florists' gloxinia)
Spathiphyllum spp. (peace lily)
Syngonium spp. (arrowhead)

*Will also do well at medium temperatures.
†Will also do well at cool temperatures.

to speed up its metabolic processes and to grow faster.

In dim light and high temperatures, plants tend to grow weak and spindly, with leaves spaced far apart on the stems. And in all cases, plants in warm locations need more frequent watering because of greater leaf transpiration.

The major problem in northern homes occurs during autumn and winter, when the days are short and the sun is low in the sky, yielding relatively little light, and central heating systems cut humidity drastically. In urban office buildings, summer is apt to present a different problem, in that daytime temperatures are often cooler than those at night, when the air conditioning is turned off. This day/night office temperature pattern is exactly the opposite of the plant's needs, and will interfere with its food manufacturing and growth processes.

Home temperatures vary greatly from room to room, and even in different spots within a room, especially in the winter. Bedrooms, usually kept cooler than other living areas, are often places for coolness-loving plants such as azaleas and gardenias. A kitchen or bathroom, offering higher than av-

Temperatures Vary within a Room: You can't assume that because the thermostat on the wall reads 65°F (18°C) an even temperature prevails throughout the room. For instance, plants on a windowsill can be baked by the heat of the sun, then chilled by night air while the rest of the room remains at a constant level. Cool drafts slip in wherever there's an opening, and even when a door is shut it can still allow cold air to enter underneath or through cracks in the frame—with the end result that temperature is lowered in the immediate area. A plant located above a radiator or heat vent will receive a daily blast of hot, dry air and will register its complaint with browning leaves that will eventually shrivel and fall off.

erage heat and humidity, may be a good location for ferns. An unheated sun porch may be perfect for some temperate zone plants, so long as the air does not freeze. Every plant should be placed in a spot that offers the closest to ideal conditions for that plant.

Within rooms, temperatures in winter can vary as widely as 30°F (17°C). A windowsill environment can be blazing hot during the day, when the full sun is streaming in, and can dip to as low as 45°F (7°C) during the night, while the room thermostat registers 65°F (18°C). The surface temperature of the window pane itself can be much colder, injuring the leaf of any plant touching it. In winter, no plant should be kept on a windowsill that is shut off from the rest of the room by a curtain.

Temperatures within a room are affected not only by windows, ill-fitting doors, and other sources of entrance for cold air, but also by heat vents and radiators. No plant should be placed directly above a heat source, nor should it be kept in a drafty location. Even a kitchen or bathroom exhaust fan will create air patterns that can affect plants.

Nearly as important as the actual temperature are the rates of change in temperature. Plants need time to adjust their chemical processes to rising or falling temperatures, and very sharp changes, even if they stay within the plant's permissible range, can produce shock and damage. In the tropical habitats to which so many house plants are native, temperature changes come gradually, with the setting and rising sun. It is not difficult, then, to see that a plant will not have time to react to quick changes produced artificially. If you return from a winter's weekend vacation, push up the thermostat gradually, hour by hour, if you value your plants' health. Do not keep plants near a heat vent or roaring fire at such times, either. If the house has been maintained at 62°F (17°C) for several days, the furnace will work furiously to raise the temperature only a few degrees, and heat vents will be releasing very hot air at the maximum rate. Temperature changes in the opposite direction are less likely to pose a problem, since the home will cool off at a slower rate.

Plants subjected to unsuitable temperatures show a variety of reactions, all of them bad. Excess heat will cause leaves to yellow, wilt, and eventually fall off. Growth will be weak and spindly, color will be light, and flower buds will drop prematurely. In addition, the high heat will make a plant more susceptible to insect and disease attack. On the other hand, if temperatures are too cold, leaves also will wilt. They will curl, and, if the situation is not corrected, turn brown and drop from the plant. The leaves of plants in cold drafts will often turn yellow and drop.

HANDLING TEMPERATURE PROBLEMS

Although we cannot adjust the temperatures in our homes to suit all house plants, it is undeniable that the best range for most plants — 60° to 80°F (16° to 27°C) — is a good one for human health, too. An automatic thermostat which lowers the temperature shortly before bedtime, and raises it again just before breakfast time, not only saves energy fuel and money but can lead to both plant and human health. The money spent for proper insulation will quickly be repaid in fuel savings, and warm clothing can enable us to lower the thermostat just a little more, both day and night. An ideal thermostat setting of 60° to 70°F (16° to 21°C), in fact, is becoming the standard in many energy-conscious homes today.

The preferred temperature range for individual plants is listed along with the discussion of each plant found in the Encyclopedia section of this book. In order to find the best location for a particular plant, you should invest in a maximum/minimum thermometer, the kind that not only tells the current temperature, but also the lowest and highest temperature it recorded since you last reset its controls. With this instrument, you can record the exact day/night range at any spot in the home, and you can fit a plant to that location (considering also other environmental factors such as light and humidity).

Plants that absolutely require cooler than average room temperatures, such as *Chrysanthemum, Cyclamen, Freesia, Primula,* and *Rhododendron* species — as well as spring bulbs you are forcing for winter bloom — can be kept on a sunny but unheated sun porch, or even in a cool part of the basement in good light, and can be brought into living areas for special occasions, perhaps just before company arrives until immediately after it has departed. To keep such flowering plants indoors permanently during winter is to shorten their useful lives.

If any plant must be kept in a location that is too warm, remember that you can mitigate the effects of heat by providing more light and humidity.

On very cold nights in the north, plants

close to a window can be placed on a plant stand equipped with wheels, so that the stand can be pulled back from the window in the evening. With this simple maneuver, you can save the plants from cold drafts that might otherwise inflict temporary or permanent injury. Draperies can be pulled on cold nights, also, to cut down on drafts. At the very least, a piece of cardboard or newspaper can be slipped in between plants and the window pane, to act as temporary insulation.

The same measures can be taken to protect plants from summer sun. During the hottest part of the day, a plant stand can be pulled back a foot or so (approximately 30 cm) from the window, to reduce light intensity. Light-filtering shades or sheer curtains also can help reduce temperatures and light intensity to a level healthful for plants.

LIGHT

Light is critically important to plants. As with temperature, each plant has its own preferences for light — not only the intensity of light, but the number of hours of light received each day. If you want your plants to flourish, you must check these requirements, then give each plant a location in your home that offers optimum light conditions.

PHOTOPERIODISM

Plants use light in the photosynthetic process to manufacture food. Light also is involved in many other processes, including seed germination, growth control, and root formation, and it is absolutely critical to flowering. Photoperiodism, or daylength, is the name given to the effects of duration of daily light and darkness. Since the discovery of this principle early in the twentieth century, all plants have been classified as short-day, long-day, or day-neutral types (all of which are discussed in more detail in chapter 25). Short-day plants are those which will not flower until sufficient daily hours of darkness are pro-

Thriving in Cool Temperatures: The lovely *Cyclamen persicum* graces the indoors with a multitude of lovely, fragile-looking blooms in fall and winter, but only if provided with cool temperatures. This plant is a logical choice for a home where the thermostat is kept low in the winter.

vided. Among house plants, poinsettias *(Euphorbia pulcherrima)* and Christmas cactus *(Schlumbergera bridgesii)* are commonly recognized short-day plants. Poinsettias need at least 12 hours of darkness daily, starting in October, to force blooming at Christmas. Florists and nurserymen have learned to provide the exact daily duration of darkness to be assured of holiday blooming.

Long-day plants are those that bloom during the long days of summer in our temperate zone, and include most of our popular garden annuals — petunias, black-eyed Susans, and marigolds, to name just a few. Among indoor plants, tuberous begonias and various *Fuchsia* species are long-day plants.

Day-neutral plants are those which will bloom freely in a variety of conditions. Among house plants, the prize representatives of this group are the African violets *(Saintpaulia* spp.). (See Artificial Lighting Requirements of Popular House Plants in chapter 25 for a listing of daylength requirements.)

PHOTOTROPISM

Some indoor gardeners give their plants a

quarter-turn every day, in order to get them to grow evenly. Others, less attentive, turn their plants only after they have grown lopsided in reaching toward the sun. No matter how attentive they are, however, gardeners have known for years that indoor plants seem to "stretch" toward the sun.

Although it would seem that plants reach toward the sun in order to soak up more of it, this is not actually the case. This phenomenon, called phototropism, has been discovered to be caused by the reaction of one of the plant's growth hormones, called auxins, to any source of light. The plant's hormones, much like our own, control many of its functions, including growth and flowering. Just as our hormones determine our eventual height, so do the plant's auxins determine its height.

Light tends to destroy auxins (although more are always being produced by the plant's growing tips). So, when light hits a plant stem, many of the auxins on the light side are destroyed. They concentrate, then, on the shaded side of the stem. And, since auxins promote growth, the shaded side grows more quickly than the sunny side, causing the bending of the stem toward the light. The plant appears to be turning toward the light, but actually it is growing away from the light. Intensity has nothing to do with the reaction and, indeed, some plants will react to lights no brighter than one-thousandth the luminosity of moonlight. If the growth functions are filmed with time-lapse photography, the resulting motion picture will show a plant "dancing" to the rhythms of its changing light.

The concentration of auxins in the shady parts of plants also explains why plants grow leggy and spindly in dim light. In this case, too many auxins are produced and the stem grows rapidly, but fewer leaves are produced. This phenomenon can easily be observed with an asparagus fern. Placed in a dim spot, the fern will form very rapidly growing shoots containing few leaves. Knowledge of how

Reaching for the Sun: A lazy indoor gardener who fails to turn a plant so that it receives an equal complement of light from all sides will one day find that nice, even growth has given way to a lopsided look. This neglected rubber tree is a prime example of phototropism, that "stretching" toward the light which is triggered by the plant's growth hormones.

auxins work is also important to the understanding of pruning, and this will be discussed in the next chapter.

THE LIGHT SPECTRUM

Each color of light, ranging from red to blue, has its own wavelength. Plants react most strongly to the light on the two ends of the spectrum — red and blue — both of which are offered by natural light, but not in good amounts by all artificial lighting. Red light is most important for stimulating the growth and blossoming of plants, while light at the blue end is instrumental in regulating the plant's respiratory system and for inducing bushy growth.

Modern fluorescent lights have enabled indoor gardeners to grow plants in places where it was previously impossible. Not only

Optimum Light Intensities for Various Groups of Decorative Plants

Low-Light Plants . . . need at least 25 footcandles, but prefer 75 to 200.

Examples:
Aglaonema spp., *Aspidistra elatior* (cast-iron plant), *Chamaedorea elegans* (neanthe bella palm), *C. erumpens* (bamboo palm), *Dracaena fragrans* 'Massangeana' (corn plant), *Howea forsterana* (kentia palm), *Peperomia caperata* (emerald ripple), *Philodendron scandens* subsp. *oxycardium* (common philodendron).

Medium-Light Plants . . . need at least 75 to 100 footcandles, but prefer 200 to 500.

Examples:
Aechmea fasciata (living vase plant), *Asparagus densiflorus* 'Sprengeri' (asparagus fern), *Brassaia actinophylla* (schefflera), Bromeliaceae (bromeliads–many spp.), *Cissus rhombifolia* (grape ivy), *Dieffenbachia amoena* and *D. exotica* (dumb cane), *Dracaena deremensis* (green dracaena), *D. deremensis* 'Warneckii' (white-striped dracaena), *D. marginata* (dragon tree), *Fatsia japonica* (Japanese aralia), *Ficus* spp., *Ligustrum lucidum* (wax leaf privet), *Maranta leuconeura* (prayer plant), *Nephrolepis exaltata* 'Bostoniensis' (Boston fern), *Philodendron* hybrids, *Phoenix roebelenii* (dwarf date palm), *Polyscias guilfoylei* (geranium-leaf aralia), *Rhapis excelsa* (lady palm), *Spathiphyllum* 'Mauna Loa' (white flag).

High-Light Plants . . . need at least 200 footcandles, but prefer 500 or more.

Examples:
Chamaerops humilis (European fan palm), *Cissus antarctica* (kangaroo vine), ✕ *Citrofortunella mitis* (calamondin), *Crassula* spp., *Eriobotrya japonica* (Japanese loquat), *Hoya* spp., *Pittosporum tobira* (mock orange), *Tradescantia* spp., (wandering Jew).

Very-High-Light Plants (including most flowering ornamentals and vegetables) . . . need at least 1,000 footcandles for slow growth, with up to 2,000 preferred.

Examples:
Allamanda spp. (golden trumpet), *Aloe variegata*, begonias (other than *B. metallica* and *B.* ✕ *rex-cultorum*), carnations, chrysanthemums, coleus, crotons, geraniums, lavender, marigolds, orchids (many spp.), passionflower, *Petunia hybrida* (cascading type), rosemary, roses, *Sedum morganianum* (burro's tail).

Germinating Seeds and Rooting Cuttings . . . need 600 to 2,000 footcandles.

Hardwood Cuttings . . . need up to 5,000 footcandles.

do fluorescent tubes offer a wider and more natural light spectrum, but they burn much more coolly than the older tungsten bulbs, thus allowing gardeners to concentrate more light on plants without burning them. The kinds and quality of light, and selection and use of artificial lighting systems, will be discussed more fully in chapter 25.

HANDLING LIGHT IN THE HOME

Few people realize what vast differences in light intensity exist within the home. Not only from room to room, but within the same room, the light can be many times brighter in one location than another. Although plants can handle changes in light, they do have their limits. Tropical plants, which once found homes on the jungle floor where the light was filtered through tall trees, often have a particularly difficult time in adjusting to long periods of direct sun. Too much sun, as well as too little, can injure a plant.

Aside from a greenhouse or glass-roofed solarium, the windowsill of a south-facing room is the brightest spot in the home. Some plants can find happiness there, including cacti and other succulents, geraniums (*Pelargonium* spp.), amaryllis (*Hippeastrum* spp.), and flowering plants from temperate zones. But many house plants can easily be injured in such a location, except during the short days of winter when the sun hangs low in the sky, offering indirect and weakened light.

Too Little Light Means Lost Variegation: The full display of variegation on the croton at left is a sure sign that the plant has received a bountiful supply of light. The croton at right has received too little light, with the very visible result that the variegation has faded, as the green, chlorophyll-laden areas have had to increase in order to manufacture enough food.

Generally, after a south-facing window, the next brightest is an east-facing one, followed by those facing west and north. Low-light plants often favor the steady, cool light of a north window. A southwest window in summer is often treacherous, particularly in the afternoon when the combination of heat and light intensity may be too much for tropical plants to handle.

Most house plants like some direct sun, usually no more than an hour or two a day. These plants will do well in either an east or west window, and can thrive in a south-facing room, if they receive some protection from the sun. As plants are moved back from the windowsill, the intensity of light falls off dramatically, so that in the middle of a room, the light intensity will have decreased 50 percent or more. Plants in the back corner of a south room, where no direct sun falls, may receive only 5 percent of the light that strikes plants on the windowsill.

These dramatic variations of light within a single room should be studied carefully, and plants placed accordingly, if you seek maximum plant growth and health. One way is to use a light meter. Focus the meter on a white piece of paper at different locations within the room and record the differences in the readings. In this way, you will gain a far better idea of the possibilities for plant location within that room. You may find a spot in an east room, near a window, receives about the same light intensity as a back corner of a south-facing room.

In making your light calculations, you also must take into account the changing light of the seasons, caused by the sun's changing position in the sky, and also other environmental factors such as humidity, temperature, and soil moisture. Plants can stand more light in the summer because rooms are usually more humid during that season, at least in northern homes. Soil will dry out more quickly when temperatures are high and room humidity is low.

LIGHT REFLECTION

The light in any room can be strongly intensified by reflective surfaces, both indoors and out. The white surface of a house next door, or the sun bouncing off a large bank of snow, can increase light inside a room by as much as 30 percent. Similarly, white walls in a room can provide 30 percent more light than dark walls can. A large mirror in the back of a room can flood an area with several times more light than it would otherwise receive. Consider these reflective factors when choosing locations for your plants.

Plants that receive too much light often react by curling their leaves downward and by losing their green color. Young leaves are affected first, turning pale and then yellow. Often, inexperienced indoor gardeners mistake such signs as evidence of lack of food and water.

The symptoms of too little light are perhaps more commonly recognized. Stems will become elongated and spindly, with few and stunted leaves. The plant will seem to be reaching desperately toward the strongest source of light available. In either situation, the obvious answer is to move the plant to a light position more to its liking. If plants have grown leggy, prune them to encourage bushy growth. Pale leaves of overexposed plants should return to greener color after they have been given a rest from direct sun for a week or two.

NATURAL VS. ARTIFICIAL LIGHT

Plants apparently do not care whether light comes directly from the sun or from artificial sources, so long as the light intensity, duration, and color is sufficient for its needs. Some plants, notably African violets, actually seem to thrive better under the constant and controlled light of fluorescent tubes, than the sharply varying intensities of natural sunlight. This is perhaps because the filtered light they received on the jungle floor was closer in character to fluorescent light than to the direct or indirect light of open sun.

HUMIDITY

The scenario is a common one, repeated in thousands of American homes every winter: the house plants begin to turn pale and sickly looking, their leaves curling downward. Some develop brown tips and edges. The Boston fern develops large brown patches, and they get larger by the day.

Someone tells the owner of these plants, quite correctly, that the room is too dry, that the plants are suffering from the lack of moisture. The plant owner, unable to think of any way to increase the room humidity, attempts to compensate for the lack by increasing soil moisture. He keeps the plants overwatered, and the situation only becomes worse. If help does not come, many plants may be lost.

What has happened is that the plants were, indeed, suffering from lack of humidity — water vapor in the air. In the plant's normal scheme of things, water is absorbed by the roots and distributed throughout the plant. It is used in the leaves to manufacture

food, then is transpired through the stomata and is replaced by more water drawn up from the roots. The drier the air becomes, however, the faster that water is transpired from the leaves — to a point where the roots cannot draw up enough to replace it. The leaves curl downward in an attempt to conserve water. The tips and edges of the plant, the last areas to receive water from the vascular system, are the first to become desiccated. Then the plant owner overwaters the plant, excluding oxygen from the roots. From that point, it is merely a question of whether the roots or topgrowth will be the first to die.

The problem of providing sufficient humidity is greatest in northern homes in the winter, where central heating provides no humidity without special equipment. The average home has a humidity level of approximately 20 percent during winter months or, as one humidifier salesman has said, "drier than the Sahara Desert." Basements tend to be much damper, with levels of 30 to 45 or 50 percent, but attics are notoriously low in humidity. Older homes and steam-heated apartments are the worst. But the problem occurs — usually to a lesser degree — also in air-conditioned homes and offices during the summer, when the humidity is kept low in order to increase human comfort during hot weather. (Incidentally, do not be fooled by those gigantic and healthy plants in modern office buildings. If you have wondered how they can thrive in dim corners and low humidity, the answer is that they often don't. Usually, the building employs a plant contractor who revolves plants periodically, carrying each plant back to the greenhouse for needed recuperation before returning it for another stint at the office.) Growing plants under lights can reduce humidity an additional 5 to 10 percent.

As with light, temperature, and soil moisture, each plant has its own preference for relative humidity, as well as permissible ranges beyond which it cannot survive for long. The cacti and succulents, along with a few other desert plants and some herbs, not only survive in low humidity (about 15 percent), but thrive in it. Some plants from highly humid tropical regions, including some orchids and jungle floor ferns, can get by only in very humid environments (70 to 80 percent relative humidity). Very high humidity is also desirable for germinating seeds and rooting cuttings. Most of our popular house plants, however, have requirements in between these two extremes. A relative humidity of 40 to 60 percent will keep most plants healthy and happy. This range, incidentally, is optimal for human health as well.

Air moisture is measured in terms of relative humidity, which is simply an expression of the percentage of water that the air can hold at a given temperature. When the television weather announcer tells you that the relative humidity is 100 percent, he means that the air can hold no more moisture at the current temperature. And when your home hygrometer (the instrument which measures relative humidity) shows a reading of 10 percent, you must take action if you want your prized plants to survive.

WAYS TO INCREASE HUMIDITY

Humidity can be increased by any of several methods, ranging from the installation of a humidifying device on your furnace system to the placing of containers of water in the rooms in which your plants live. Probably the best solution for small plants needing lots of humidity is to grow them in a terrarium. For larger plants, the answer will depend on your financial resources and, quite reasonably, on whether you own or rent your home.

Furnace Humidifiers

This solution, although expensive, is both effective and permanent, requires no further effort on your part (since it operates automatically), and is also a wise investment in your health.

Room Humidifiers

This is the second-best course to take, requiring a modest investment. A typical room model holds 4 to 7 gallons (15.1 to 26.5 l) of water and will evaporate from 3 to 3¾ pints (1.4 to 1.7 l) of water an hour, thus running for 9 to 16 hours before you must refill it. Most models are equipped with automatic shut-off devices and "time-to-refill" lights.

Misting

Plants that have smooth leaves often benefit from regular misting. By spraying foliage with fine water droplets, you are not only counteracting the effects of low humidity, but also are duplicating the nocturnal dew which is present outdoors.

In misting, however, it is important never to drench the plant with water or fill the leaf axils. This can encourage fungus diseases and insect attacks that would not otherwise be a problem. You can mist especially delicate plants as much as two or three times a day, but as with the plants in your outdoor garden, avoid wetting the foliage at night.

Grouping Plants

Since moisture transpires both from the leaves and from the sides of clay pots, you can help your plants to recapture some of this lost moisture if you group them together during the winter. In this way, the moisture lost by some plants will benefit others around them. Again, it is a help, but not the sole answer to a severe problem.

Pebble Trays

A pebble tray is any watertight shallow tray or other container that can hold an inch or two (2.5 or 5 cm) of pebbles. The potted plants are placed on top of the pebbles, and then the trays are filled with water just to the top of the pebbles, not blocking the drainage holes of the pots. The moisture evaporating and rising from the tray offers a continuing source of humidity for the plants and is a

Grouping to Minimize Moisture Loss: Dry air, the bane of many indoor gardeners, can be offset to some extent by grouping plants together. Moisture that is escaping from leaves and from the sides of pots will help boost the humidity level in the atmosphere immediately around the congregated plants.

truly effective way of combating insufficient moisture in a local area. It is the best low-cost answer in an apartment. Placing pots on a bed of damp sand will produce similar results.

Water Containers

Any water placed in a dry room will soon evaporate — and any evaporation will increase the humidity of that room. Radiators in old houses and apartments often were equipped with deep, narrow metal containers, hooked over the backs of the radiators. These, periodically filled with water, offered some room humidity at no cost and little effort. An aquarium will help in the same way. Keeping the sinks and bathtubs filled with a few inches (approximately 5 cm) of water also will help. Any container of water will aid both plants and humans in a dry home.

FIRST AID FOR WILTED PLANTS

If a plant is obviously suffering from low hu-

midity there are several ways in which you can offer rejuvenating moisture. You can carry the plant into the bathroom, run some hot water in the tub to create moderate steam, then turn off the water, turn on the light, close the door, and leave the plant there overnight. Or, you can mist the plant and erect a plastic tent over it, leaving an air space at the bottom. Individual plants which require still

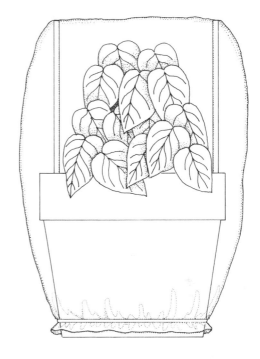

Rejuvenating a Wilted Plant: Don't despair when one of your plants is left drooping from lack of moisture. With a few common household items and close attention, you can create a humidity tent to revive the bedraggled specimen. First, find a large plastic bag that will comfortably cover both plant and pot. Exhale into the bag to inflate it, then slip it over the top of the plant and seal at the bottom with a snug-fitting rubber band. Never allow the bag to come in contact with the leaves; stick dowels or other suitable objects into the pot to extend above the top of the plant to act as a framework. Excessive heat and direct sun can harm the plant while it's in the bag, and for that reason should be avoided. Once the foliage has perked up, you can remove the bag and resume regular care.

higher humidity levels can be enclosed in plastic bags that are large enough to contain them without crowding. Blow up the bag like a balloon and attach it to the pot with a rubber band. Place a dowel on both sides of the plant, if necessary, to keep the bag from touching the leaves. Open the bag if room temperature rises above 75°F (24°C), or the plant may suffocate. If you use either of these enclosures, do not expose the plant to direct sun, because temperatures within the tent or bag might quickly rise to a point of danger.

WATERING

How often should I water my plants? How high is up? The answers to both questions are purely relative.

The water needs of plants not only vary from species to species and from one stage of plant growth to the next, but they also are influenced by the makeup of the growth medium, the composition and shape of the container, the plant's location in the home or greenhouse, and by seasonal and day-to-day changes in the growing climate.

There is a colorful array of ways to determine whether it's time to water. Some gardeners thrust a finger into the soil, figuring that if particles stick it is not yet time to water. Others insert a toothpick and water if it comes out clean. And others tap the sides of clay pots and water when they hear a clear, bell-like sound instead of a dull thud. With plants in plastic pots it is usually time to water when the soil surface is lighter in color, or when the plant seems lighter in weight.

Experienced indoor gardeners eventually learn to "know" when any plant needs water, especially if the plant has been a long-term guest in the home. Those with less gardening experience, or even experienced gardeners who are confronted with a new plant, will have to consider all the preceding factors before coming to an informed decision about watering policy.

Every plant has its own preferences for soil moisture. Some, like many ferns and gesneriads, like a soil that is constantly moist (but not soggy) while they are growing actively. Others, including most cacti and succulents, like the soil to become nearly dry throughout between waterings. Most common house plants like to be watered after the top layer of soil has become dry to the touch. Consult the Encyclopedia section later in this book for water requirements of plants.

Even if you know how much water each of your plants needs, however, you still have not answered the questions — how often should you water your plants? Here are some factors to consider in coming to that decision:

Plants in clay pots need watering more frequently than those in plastic or glazed ceramic pots, since water evaporates through the porous walls of the unglazed clay. Remember this when choosing containers for hanging plants or for others that are difficult to water. A plastic pot can reduce the number of waterings you must provide.

Plants in small pots need more frequent watering than those in large pots, since small pots offer more surface area relative to their mass. However, potbound plants need more water than those that have ample root space, since a potbound plant has relatively less water available for its hungry roots.

Recently pruned plants need less water than they did previous to pruning, since there are fewer leaves to feed while the root mass remains the same. Pruning your plants just before you leave for vacation is a good idea, since the plants' water needs will be somewhat diminished in your absence.

Plants with thin leaves need watering more often than those with fleshy leaves. Thin leaves are capable of retaining less water, thus requiring constant replenishment from the root and vascular systems.

Actively growing plants use more water than those in dormant or rest periods. Plants coming into bud need more water than they do at other times of year.

Plants potted in a heavy, peaty soil mixture need watering less often than those in light or sandy mixtures.

Plants in warm temperatures need watering more often than they do in cooler conditions.

Plants in a dry atmosphere need more water than those in high humidity, since leaf moisture will be lost more readily to the surrounding air when it is dry.

Plants need less water on cloudy, snowy, or dull, rainy days than they require when the weather is clear and bright.

Another important consideration is the time of day. In summer it is a good idea to water at noon, since the plants will lose more water through their leaves in the peak temperatures of afternoon. During the winter, though, watering in the early morning is best because it will leave a full day at rising temperatures for top-watered greenery to dry off before dark. Never water at night, for this will encourage soggy soil around plant roots and lingering moisture on leaves — both invitations to disease.

House plants kept outside during the summer need far more water than those remaining indoors. The major factor is the constant air movement outside, which carries away leaf moisture at a rapid rate.

TOO MUCH WATER

More house plants are killed by overwatering than by any other single factor. This killing with kindness is easy to understand, since it is normal for people to worry about plants drying out. In truth, the penalties of drying out from underwatering are far less severe than those caused by an excess of water.

A plant wilted from dryness can usually be revived by giving it water, misting it lightly, and placing it out of direct sun. The symptoms of overwatering, on the other hand, are more difficult to detect and far less reversible. An overwatered plant will soon display wilted and yellowed leaves, which will

eventually drop off (sometimes leading the owner to believe it needs still *more* water). In some cases, the lower leaves and the base of the stem will begin to rot, the leaf tips will become brittle, or scablike bubbles will appear on the undersides of leaves. When this happens, you can be sure that root damage — rot — also has occurred. It is best to repot the plant, trimming away all affected root and leaf portions, then put it in good light but out of direct sun. If the situation looks terminal, take some tip cuttings and start over.

WATER CHARACTERISTICS

The best water for plants is the pure, unpolluted, nontreated, warm rainwater that they once received in their natural habitats. Unfortunately, our drinking water, especially in urban areas, often does not meet this standard. Therefore, we must do the best we can with what we have.

Chlorine in water, in the amounts used in city systems, is not deadly to plants, although some gardeners believe that it may have some detrimental effects. Chlorine can easily be removed from water, however, by letting tapwater stand in a jug or pail for 24 hours. This procedure also will allow the water to warm up to room temperature.

Fluorine, on the other hand, has been shown to be definitely harmful to some plants, even in the amounts used in city water supplies. If your water is fluoridated, it may be best to capture rainwater for plant use. Do not use water washing down from the eaves of your house, however, for it is apt to be more polluted than tapwater. Instead, establish a rainbarrel in the backyard.

Home water softeners that use ion exchangers, such as Zeolite, replace natural calcium in the water with sodium, which can be harmful to plants because plants attempt to substitute it for calcium in the building of cell walls. Water used for plants should be tapped from the line before it enters the softening unit. In hard-water areas, the lime deposits in unsoftened water will not injure plants, although they will build up in the potting mixture, gradually increasing its alkalinity. An inexpensive pH testing kit, available in most house plant centers, will help you to keep an eye on the pH level of all your plants. Although each plant has its own narrow range of pH preference, the general range for most house plants is 5.5 to 7.5.

If you must water your plants with softened water, let the water sit overnight before using it. If your water is alkaline or hard, you can help neutralize its effect by watering plants once a month with a solution of 1 tablespoon (15 ml) of vinegar to 1 gallon (3.8 l) of water. You also can compensate for hard water by adding acidic organic supplements such as cottonseed meal to the potting mix of acid-loving plants like azaleas and gardenias.

Water for house plants should be at room temperature. Cold water from the tap comes as a shock to roots, and repeated applications can stunt growth and invite disease. A good idea is to keep two large jugs in service at all times, so that you can fill your watering cans and pebble trays with water of moderate temperature at any time.

WATERING METHODS

There are four common watering methods — top-watering, immersion, bottom-watering, and wick-watering. Of course, there are variations on all of these.

Top-Watering

Top-watering is the easiest and most commonly used technique, although not necessarily the most satisfactory. A watering can with a long, thin spout is ideal, since it allows the water to be placed in the middle of any pot without disturbing the plant or splashing water on the leaves. Water left standing on leaves can be injurious, especially to hairy-leaved plants such as African violets.

In top-watering, as in other methods,

enough water should be applied to soak the potting mixture thoroughly, then water should be withheld until the plant indicates the need for more. For most plants, this point will be when the top ½ inch (13 mm) of soil is dry to the touch. Never be a "daily dribbler," since frequent and light waterings will keep the top layer moist while desiccating roots in the lower half of the pot. Such shallow watering also will allow the buildup of harmful fertilizer salts, which are flushed from the pot with thorough watering.

With most plants, you can simply fill one pot nearly to the brim, then move on to each in succession until you have finished. Then,

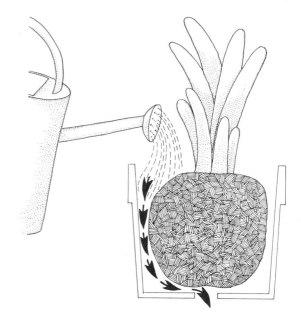

The Problem of a Shrinking Soil Ball: Water that flows out the pot bottom almost as soon as the plant has been watered should make you suspect soil ball shrinkage. A potting mix with a large proportion of peat moss which is allowed to dry out often shrinks away from the sides of the pot, leaving channels for the water to flow through without ever penetrating the soil where the roots are. If this happens, the only way to insure that water penetrates the entire soil ball is to use the immersion method. Measures to prevent shrinkage from occurring in the first place include switching to a mix lower in peat, or watering frequently enough so that the mix never dries out completely.

go back and examine each. If no water has run out of the drainage hole into the saucer, add a little more. In a half hour to an hour, go back and drain the water from all saucers. No plant should sit in a saucer of water for long; it is one sure way to deprive the plant of oxygen and encourage root rot.

If, in top-watering, the water runs out the drainage hole just seconds after you pour, you may be sure that the plant has water channels in its soil ball. What has happened, probably, is that the potting mixture has dried out and shrunk, leaving large air spaces between the soil ball and the pot wall. This often occurs when the potting mixture contains a large percentage of peat, which is prone to shrinkage. In such cases, the plant will never receive enough water through the top-watering method. It should be soaked thoroughly by the immersion method (described below), and then measures should be taken to see that channels do not develop in the future. Press the wet potting mixture down gently but firmly along the edges of the pot, then try to water often enough so that it does not dry out thoroughly in the future. You may want to change the potting mixture to one containing less peat.

Immersion

This method is by far the best for most house plants, but it also takes the most time. Many people top-water routinely, but treat plants to immersion once a month or as often as they have the time for it.

Immersion involves placing the potted plant in a larger container of water (bathtubs are often used) so that the water level comes up to the soil line but never over the rim of the pot. The plant absorbs water through the walls of the pot (plastic and glazed ceramic pots cannot be used) and through the drainage hole. The plant is left standing in the water until the soil surface is thoroughly moist, then is removed, left to drain fully, and replaced in its permanent location.

Bottom-Watering

This method, which some growers have long used with African violets, miniature citrus trees, and florists' gloxinias *(Sinningia speciosa)*, involves filling the saucer with water and letting the plant absorb it by capillary action. It is a rather inefficient method, since the potting medium often cannot draw up water at a satisfactory rate, and it encourages rot at the lower levels of the pot.

Wick-Watering

Only those plants which prefer a constantly moist soil — including gardenias, camellias, many ferns, and gesneriads — should be wick-watered. The process involves inserting an absorbent wick into the drainage hole and extending it to a water source to draw water slowly up into the soil by capillary action.

You can buy pots specially constructed for wick-watering, or suspend plants with wicks on grids over trays — methods that also boost humidity. A very inexpensive approach is to use standard plastic or clay pots and a length of a recycled nylon cord or 24-weight nylon clothesline. Half the cord should be inserted into the still-empty pot through a piece of fiberglass or aluminum screening (or nylon net) cut to fit the bottom of the container. The inside part of the wick should be held vertically and soil medium poured around it to a point halfway up the pot, where its end should be placed horizontally, to be covered by more potting mix and then the root ball of the plant. The other end of the wick should feed into a tray, bucket, or other reservoir of water below the plant. For best results, the reservoir should be no farther than eight inches (20 cm) below the surface of the soil.

If wick setups are not to your liking, you can set clay-potted plants atop a one-inch (2.5 cm) layer of sand or sphagnum moss in a plastic, aluminum, or galvanized tray. Those plants liking high moisture can be worked slightly down into the layer. If the sand or

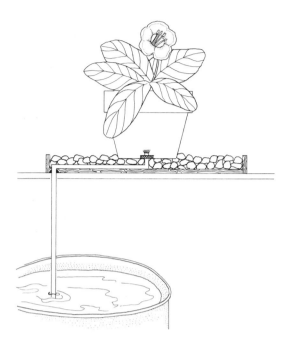

Wick-Watering: Moisture-loving plants such as gesneriads, camellias, gardenias, and many ferns can have their needs met by this watering method. It's not a magical force but rather capillary action that draws the water up from a reservoir into the pot. To facilitate this action, insert a length of absorbent wick into the drainage hole of a pot. The free end of the wick must then be suspended into a reservoir of water, in this case a bucket. In this particular set up, the humidity around the plant is boosted by setting it on a pebble-filled tray with an opening drilled to allow the wick to pass through.

moss is kept moist, the pot should take up enough water to keep the plant constantly moist.

Another wickless method of watering from below involves the use of a $\frac{3}{8}$ inch (10 mm) plastic "egg-crate" diffuser of the kind used in light fixtures. The plastic grid is cut to fit plant trays and placed inside them. Then enough water is added to cover the plastic slightly. Plants set on top of the plastic support absorb water through their drainage holes, and the water below the top of the grating helps raise the humidity.

Another effective method of bottom-wa-

tering involves the use of capillary matting, which can be purchased in various sizes. The mats can be cut to fit inside waterproof trays of whatever size you wish to use.

Place pots on the barely moistened mats and water the plants from above to establish capillary action. The soil mix must be in contact with the mat moisture, so do not use crocking in pots. Plastic pots with several holes are usually recommended because the thin bottoms allow easy contact between soil and mat moisture, but clay pots also may be used. A $\frac{1}{4}$-inch (6 mm) wick, or a "plug" of sphagnum moss in the drainage hole of a thicker clay or Styrofoam pot will act as a wick to the matting and also will prevent soil from dropping out to dirty the mat or to leave an air space large enough to break contact with mat moisture. The matting may be kept moist by a daily soaking with a watering can or a barely trickling hose. The mat may extend to a reservoir at one end of the bench (in a greenhouse), or you can spread the mat over a plastic crate set in the pan of water and allow one end to touch the water.

Wick-watering is easy and efficient — for those plants that are suited to the method. By using a deep tray, you can leave home for a month or more and never worry about your moisture-loving plants.

WATERING PLANTS FROM THE GREENHOUSE

Greenhouse plants are pampered and encouraged into optimum growth in the commercial greenhouse, where they receive ideal conditions for growth. Often, the home cannot match these conditions, and you will have to pay special attention to the new plants until they have become acclimated to their new location. Given high light conditions in the greenhouse, the plants were accustomed to moving water through their systems at relatively rapid rates. In your home, they will receive less light and will soon adjust to receiving less water. In the beginning, however, you should strive to provide ideal conditions for greenhouse plants, giving them prime space among your plants. Mist them often and watch their water needs carefully. In a matter of weeks, perhaps months, the plants should adjust to the environment you can reasonably be expected to provide.

AIR, VENTILATION, AND POLLUTION

In daylight, plants absorb carbon dioxide from the air and release oxygen. At night, they consume oxygen and release carbon dioxide. When this process became general knowledge, zealous nurses in hospitals began to remove plants from patients' rooms at night, fearing that the rooms' oxygen supply would become diminished. In truth, plants maintain a good balance of gases, and in no case will they rob oxygen from our air. So perfect is this balance, in fact, that many plants can live indefinitely in a sealed terrarium or bottle, reusing the gaseous elements in the air for steady growth and good health.

Generally, air that is good for our own health is good for that of plants. Slight air movement is beneficial to plants, as it allows the leaves to release moisture normally, and it is this transpiration that helps plants to remain cool in high temperatures. Good ventilation also may help to prevent fungus diseases from becoming established. Never crowd plants so that they are touching each other, because in doing so you will impede proper air movement and encourage disease. In winter, when windows are closed and air movement is likely to be reduced, a small room fan (not directed at the plants) will help to keep the air moving.

Cold or hot drafts are to be avoided at all times. Either can produce ill effects. Never place a plant in front of a cracked window in winter, or in the direct path of an air conditioner's airstream, or above a radiator or heat vent. When it comes to ventilation for plants, moderation and gentleness are the keys. Except for those cacti and other succulents that once grew in windswept deserts or mountain plateaus, and boxwood and other temperate zone specimens, the majority of house plants came from sheltered locations of mild climate, where dense tree and vine growth kept air movement constant but gentle. This is the atmosphere to strive for in the home.

Air pollution can be a serious threat to house plants, just as it is to us. Especially in industrial urban areas, the number of noxious chemicals in the air can be many and varied, including sulfur dioxide, hydrogen chloride, ammonia, chlorine, and ozone. All can cause damage or death to plants. Pollution symptoms include leaf drop or edge and tip burn on leaves. Plants may cease growth, become permanently stunted, or simply wilt and die. Flowering plants may never develop blossoms, or the blossoms may burst and drop before coming to flower.

Ferns and other plants of delicate leaf are often the first to show pollution's effects. If the problem is severe in your area, and you cannot protect plants by an air filtration system, it will be best to avoid the delicate plants and stay with succulents, *Aspidistra elatior,* and other thick-leaved and hardy specimens.

The effects of air pollution are commonly most severe during periods of high heat and humidity, when transpiration is retarded. On such days in industrial areas, use a fan to keep air moving around the plants.

The major pollutant in the home is manufactured gas, which contains ethylene and carbon monoxide, both deadly to plants. Natural gas does not contain these chemicals, and is not a serious threat. For both human and plant health, ranges using manufactured gas should be checked periodically and any sources of leaks corrected.

CHAPTER 3

Caring for Plants through the Year

The home that you give to house plants is necessarily an imperfect one for optimum growth of most plants. In order to give house plants the best chances for growth and health in this imperfect environment, you must provide each with the basic conditions of light, temperature, humidity, and soil moisture that it requires. Beyond those basic requirements, however, there are procedures of care that will bring rewards in better growth — pruning, training, and grooming, and special care during the changing seasons. These will be discussed in this chapter, along with tips on buying new plants and moving plants from one location to another.

PRUNING

Intelligent and regular pruning will produce healthy, bushy, compact, and attractive house plants. Further, it will reduce the chances of disease and encourage some plants to grow and flower more profusely. Unpruned plants tend to grow spindly, weak, and undisciplined in appearance. Pruning is a simple procedure that can be quickly carried out on most plants. If it is neglected, however, progressively more drastic and difficult pruning methods will be required. The watchword, then, is diligence. Regular pinching back of new growth may save much time and trouble later.

UNDERSTANDING PRUNING

In chapter 2, we discussed the role of certain plant hormones, called auxins, in phototropism — the tendency of plants to bend toward a light source. Auxins are important in causing plants to react favorably to pruning as well, since they are instrumental in regulating the plant's growth habits.

Prune for Better Blooms: The fuschia is a good example of a plant that will respond to pruning with a bumper crop of blooms. Soon after new growth appears, the stem tips can be pinched back, which also helps retain a compact, bushy shape.

Auxins are manufactured in the plant's young leaves and growth tips. From there, they flow down the shoot and into the plant's lower parts. By this process, the stems below grow longer as more young leaves are produced.

Auxins promote growth. That is one of the reasons why new leaves, which contain the highest concentrations of auxins, grow at a rate much faster than that of older leaves. When you pinch back a new shoot, the stem below it will grow less rapidly, since its supply of auxins is diminished, and the lateral buds below the growth tip are stimulated into new growth. The result is that, for every new growth shoot you pinch off, two or more will usually grow beneath it, while stems are retarded in elongation. The result will be a more bushy and compact plant.

Opposite, geraniums bloom cheerfully on a windowsill indoors while snow covers ground outside.

PRUNING METHODS

There are three general methods of pruning house plants. The least severe is called pinching back or stopping the growing tip. Some gardeners use a small, sharp scissors for the job, although most simply pinch off the shoot between the thumbnail and index finger.

Plants should be pinched back only during their active growing periods. Remember, though, that for every new shoot pinched, two or more are likely to take its place, meaning that you must do more and more pinching until the plant attains the desired compact and bushy form. Nearly all plants respond to pinching, and with those that are

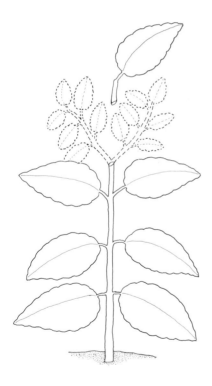

Pinching Back for Bushy Growth: You can often improve the appearance of a stalky but otherwise healthy plant by pinching off the growing tip during periods of active growth. At least two shoots will appear in place of the one you have removed, and a consistent program of pinching back will ultimately result in a fuller shape.

not bushy by nature, such as wandering Jew, *Coleus,* and some of the ivies, it is critical to the plant's attractive appearance.

The second pruning method, slightly more severe, is called softwood pruning. It involves removing young, leaf-bearing stems at a point just above a pair of leaves. A number of leaves may be removed in this manner, instead of just a growth tip, but the result is similar to stopping. Two or more new growth tips will soon emerge from the point of pruning, and the stem's growth will be temporarily retarded. Again, this encourages a more bushy and compact plant. Flowering plants which produce blossoms on new wood (such as *Fuchsia, Gardenia,* and *Pelargonium* species) will produce more blossoms if pruned back regularly. There are a few however, including *Bougainvillea* species, that produce blossoms on the previous year's wood. Pruning the new growth of a bougainvillea will mean that no flowers will be produced in the following year.

The third and most severe method is hardwood pruning, in which the plant is pruned clear back to hard wood, removing all leaves in that portion of the plant. Hardwood pruning is used only for old and badly neglected woody plants, and any plants so treated are going to be unattractive for as long as six months afterward, until after they have made substantial new growth.

In hardwood pruning, the cut should be made just above, and at a slight angle up and away from, a dormant bud. After the cut has been made, the wood should be given two or three days to heal and dry, then should be enclosed in a small plastic bag. The warmth and humidity provided by the bag will cause the wood to soften and will encourage the dormant bud to become active. Soon, new growth will appear and the bag can be removed safely.

Of course, all parts of a plant cannot be pruned down to hard wood at once, or there would be no leaves to manufacture food and the roots would soon die, unless new growth appeared immediately. Therefore, prune just a few branches at a time — never more than one-third of the plant. Even old and neglected plants can be given new life through hardwood pruning, although they will be unsightly for quite a while until their new beauty is created.

Plants Not to Prune

There are some plants that do not take particularly well to pruning, and others that cannot be pruned at all. Succulents (including cacti) are difficult to prune satisfactorily because of their swollen stems, which form permanent scars when cut. In any case, there is seldom a need to prune succulents.

Ferns and other plants that send up leaves directly from the soil line also do not need pruning. Another plant in this category is the peace lily (*Spathiphyllum* 'Clevelandii'). The Norfolk Island pine *(Araucaria heterophylla)* should not be pruned either, since removing the terminal leader of this plant causes it to lose its graceful symmetry.

Root Pruning

Just as the tops of plants respond well to pruning, so, sometimes, do the roots. A plant should be root pruned if it has become potbound and you do not want it to grow larger by repotting it in a larger container, or simply if the plant has grown too large and you want to make a smaller and more compact specimen of it.

Root pruning is best done in the spring, when growth is active. If pruning is done at this time, new roots will form quickly and the plant will avoid much shock. The procedure is a simple one, and may be quite invigorating to the plant. Remove the soil ball (which should be thoroughly moist, but not soggy) and, with a sharp and clean knife, cut away the outer inch (2.5 cm) of soil mass and roots (for a six-inch/15 cm pot; proportionally more or less for larger or smaller pots). Then repot the plant in the same container, adding fresh potting soil to fill in.

In root pruning, you remove many of the young rootlets and root hairs — the ones that absorb and transport water and minerals to the top parts of the plant. To prevent the plant from wilting because of the temporary inability of the roots to function efficiently, enclose it in a plastic bag supported by a wire or wood frame (do not let the plastic touch the foliage) and put it in a location out of direct sunlight. The increased humidity in the bag will lessen transpiration through the leaves, thus easing the burden on the roots.

After about a week, the plant will have sent out hundreds or thousands of new feeder roots enabling efficient uptake of water and nutrients. At that time, begin to remove the plastic bag gradually, first loosening it from the bottom, and day after day, easing it up the support frame, until after the fifth day, when it can be removed completely. When the plant has regained a normal appearance, prune back topgrowth in about the same proportion that the roots were pruned. In a very short time, the plant should take on new vitality, and the result in the end should be a more healthy and pleasing plant, of the right size for its location.

TRAINING

Many indoor plants, particularly those which are natural climbers or trailers, require some sort of supporting devices in order to show them off to best advantage. Among the climbers and trailers are arrowhead vine *(Syngonium podophyllum)*, black pepper *(Piper nigrum)*, Canary Islands ivy *(Hedera canariensis)*, creeping fig *(Ficus pumila)*, English ivy *(Hedera helix)*, grape ivy (*Cissus* spp.), kangaroo vine *(Cissus antarctica)*, *Pellionia* and *Philodendron* species, pothos *(Epipremnum aureum)*, velvet plant *(Gynura aurantiaca)*, and wax plant *(Hoya carnosa)*. These plants do not *have* to be trained on supports, of course. Training is just one alternative among several, others being the use of hanging baskets and, in a regular table pot, hard and periodic pruning.

There are many kinds of supporting devices, ranging from the single stake that will support a large arrowhead vine, to sphagnum moss cylinders for ivies, to elaborate and carefully designed topiary forms, shaped to make plants resemble animals or formal geometric patterns.

When securing any plant to a support, always tie it tightly around the support and loosely around the plant. In this way, you will get the firm support you desire, without

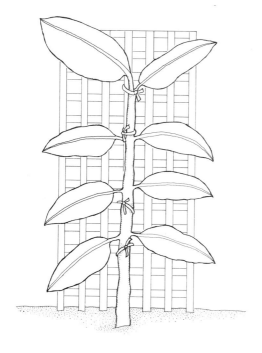

Using a Trellis: This lattice-work structure is a handy accessory for training climbing and trailing plants, or for use as a means of support (as shown here) until the plant is established. The simple, open-weave design provides plenty of vertical and horizontal surfaces to aid in attaching the plant. For small-diameter stems, paper-covered wire is suitable, but for larger plants, thick, soft yarn comes in handy. Loop it loosely around the plant and tightly around the trellis, and check from time to time on the positioning of the loops to see that they keep pace with the growth of the plant.

accidentally breaking the stems or impeding their growth. Paper-covered wire — the kind used to close plastic trash bags — is often recommended. Better, however, is the thick, soft yarn often used to decorate gift packages. Form a loose loop around the plant stem and a tight loop around the stake. As the plant grows, inspect the loops periodically and retie any that might be interfering with the plant's normal development.

For *Coleus* and other plants that tend to grow somewhat laterally from the base, when you would prefer more upward growth, you may use wire circles supported by stakes — resembling miniature tomato cages — to lift the stems at the base of the plant.

Trellises of many kinds are available at plant shops, or can be built in the home workshop. While the idea is to conceal most supports with lush foliage growth, many trellises are attractive in themselves and need not be hidden. All climbers will train themselves to trellises, although some might have to be tied loosely until they have established themselves on the form.

Ivies and other climbers that form aerial roots will grow especially vigorously on the moist environment of a sphagnum moss totem pole. This ingenious device is constructed of a stake, moss, and wire mesh.

Topiary, the training of plants to forms, is an activity better suited to outdoor than indoor gardening. Nevertheless, some indoor gardeners have achieved good results with boxwood (which is a slow-growing and woody plant), ivies, and baby's tears *(Soleirolia soleirolii).*

GROOMING PLANTS

The cleaning of foliage is important for two reasons. First, it helps to keep the stomata free of dust, thus allowing the leaves to carry out their normal rate of gas and water vapor exchange. Second, it allows the maximum amount of light to reach the leaves, helping the photosynthetic process.

A Totem Pole for Climbing Plants

Wrap a stake with a thick layer of moist sphagnum moss and secure it by wrapping green, plastic-covered wire mesh around it. A portion of the bare stake (pointed) should protrude from the bottom and will be inserted into the soil in the pot. Plant shoots of ivy all around the stake and, as they grow, tie them loosely to it. As soon as their aerial roots attach themselves to the moss, you may remove the supports. Very often, no tying is needed at all, since the vines seem to climb the stake quite readily on their own. Keep the sphagnum moss moist at all times, perhaps by inserting a very small clay pot into the top of the totem and watering through the pot's drainage hole.

Moss Totem Pole: This pole is easy to make and creates an effective display for the graceful growth of a climbing plant. Begin by wrapping a layer of moist sphagnum moss around a stake which has one pointed end. Secure the moss by encircling it with green, plastic-covered mesh which blends in with the overall green tone of the planting. When the moss-covered pole has been firmly positioned in the pot, shoots of climbing plants can be slipped into the soil around the pole base and encouraged to twine upward by being tied loosely to the mesh. When the plants have begun to climb, the ties can be removed.

The best time to clean plants is in the morning or early afternoon. If the plants are allowed to remain wet through the night, the chances of disease attack are increased. Wet plants also can suffer from cold drafts, which are more likely to occur in the evening hours.

Large leaves, such as those of rubber trees and the large philodendrons, can be dusted first with a very soft brush, then wiped gently with a moistened cloth. A small amount of a mild soap added to a pail of water will help to clean and will not injure the plant.

Plants with small leaves can be taken to the kitchen sink and sprinkled with tepid water from the sprinkler hose, or, in the absence of this sink attachment, with an ordinary plant mister. Use a fairly strong spray setting and be sure to reach the undersides of leaves, since most of the stomata are found there.

As a rule, do not clean foliage with anything other than the water and soap solution described above. Through the years, some harmful misinformation has been passed from gardener to gardener, recommending the use of beer, milk, household oil, or other cleaning agents — all of them potentially detrimental to plant health. Commercially available leaf-cleaning products also are not recommended, because many contain waxy substances that will block leaf pores.

Never wipe with water or polish cacti and succulents or plants with hairy leaves. Remove dust on these plants by brushing them gently with a soft camel's hair brush.

Once a flowering plant has bloomed and the flowers begin to fade, take the time to remove the spent blooms. Otherwise, the plant's energy goes into seed production, and unless the seeds are needed for propagation purposes, their development occurs at the expense of leaf and flower growth.

HOW TO BUY PLANTS

The least expensive way to obtain new plants is to beg or trade cuttings from friends. Root cuttings yourself and you will have all the low-cost plants you can possibly support.

Plants can be bought at neighborhood house plant sales, or sales sponsored by gar-

Judging Plants by Their Environment: The condition of the plant store is a good indication of the quality of the plants being sold. Dirty, poorly lit, cramped quarters foster the spread of pests and diseases, and you should think twice before purchasing a plant from the stock, no matter how nice it looks at the time. On the other hand, a neat, well-arranged display of plants in adequate light, like the one shown here, is your clue that care is taken to maintain the plants in the healthiest and best possible condition.

den clubs. Prices will be considerably lower than those at plant shops, but you should inspect each plant for signs of insects and disease, and isolate them from your other plants for at least three weeks until they have proven themselves trouble free.

Despite the sources of low-cost plants, every indoor gardener occasionally buys plants from shops, nurseries, or garden centers. The purchase of a small, inexpensive seedling of a familiar plant like *Peperomia* may safely be made on impulse at the supermarket or department store. You know the identity and basic needs of the plant and, if it should fail, your loss will not be great. But a substantial purchase, or one of a plant unknown to you, should be made somewhat more cautiously.

The appearance of the plant shop itself is usually a good indication of the quality of the plants you will find there. If the shop is dirty, littered with dead leaves, the plants jammed together in bad light or crowded up against a wall, you can guess that this is a store that thrives on high-volume sales, probably at bargain prices. No plant that dies turns out to be a bargain, however, and the possibility is good of that happening with plants purchased at an unkempt shop.

Another clue to the quality of plants found in a shop is the attitude and knowledge of the shop's owner and employees. Any reputable owner or clerk will take the time to answer your questions — and you should be prepared with questions. What is the common name of this plant? What is its Latin name? How large will it become? How much light should it have? How much water? Does it require high humidity? Ask these questions even if you know the answers to some of them. The owner or clerks in a reputable shop will know the answers and gladly share them with you. They care about their plants, and they want to see them succeed in your home. If a clerk avoids your questions or gives flippant answers, seek another source of plants.

There are bargains to be found in good stores if you choose plants carefully. A plant with an unusually large number of new growing tips will soon become as large as a more expensive plant. A large hanging basket cascading with grape ivy will cost far more than an empty planter and six or eight grape ivy seedlings. Yet, potted up in the planter, the seedlings will quickly grow to the size of those in the high-priced planted hanger. The same is true for Swedish ivy, pothos, and English ivy. A fast-growing schefflera *(Brassaia actinophylla)* will soon reach the height of a higher priced specimen. Three or four small Chinese evergreens *(Aglaonema* spp.) planted together will soon resemble plantings costing much more. Such bargains, alas, are seldom found among slow growers like the Norfolk Island pine.

PLANT INSPECTION

How can you be assured of buying healthy, full-rooted plants free of disease and insects? The best way is to know your shop owner, either from past dealings or on strong recommendation. Then, come prepared to make intelligent decisions. The following list of considerations might help you to prepare:

1. Never buy a plant the first day you see it, unless you are absolutely sure of satisfaction. Instead, think about the purchase for a day or two, as you check the requirements for its care; you might discover that your home conditions are unsuitable.

2. When buying any large plant, place a deposit and come back for the plant in two weeks. Should the plant be about to go into shock, having just arrived from the grower or wholesaler, it is better that it does so at the store rather than in your home. Any reputable store will hold a plant on deposit.

3. When buying any plant, inspect it carefully. Are the leaves turgid, richly green, and vibrant in appearance? Are there signs of new growth? If so, good. But — are there indications that the plant was recently pruned heavily, especially at the lower levels? If so, the shop owner might have been trying to conceal the effects of disease or shock. Have the leaves been trimmed on the tips or edges with a scissors? If so, the shop is trying to conceal browning, and the browning problem is likely to recur when you take the plant home. Inspect the roots as carefully as you can. Don't be afraid to dig down a little with your fingers to feel for indications of full-rootedness. Dark and scraggly roots are signs of an unhealthy plant (except with *Dracaena* species and cacti, in which dark and sparse roots are the rule). If the soil smells sour, you may legitimately suspect root rot.

4. Come with a hand lens and inspect for insects. Before buying plants, learn to recognize insects and the damage they create. (See chapter 9 for more information.)

5. Never buy a large and expensive plant that has been luxuriating in a greenhouse, especially during winter. The chances are good that it will not recover from the shock of being thrust into your dry and comparatively dim home. If you really love the plant, again make a deposit and ask the owner to take the plant out of the greenhouse for two weeks. If it still looks good after two weeks, complete the purchase.

6. Ask the owner whether he has subjected the plant to systemic treatment. Systemic insecticides are powerful, able to kill insects for more than two months with a single treatment. The insecticide is absorbed by the plant and the soil, and by porous clay pots, as well. It is dangerous to both humans and pets. That a plant has been so treated does not necessarily mean that you should not buy it (although a nontreated plant would obviously be preferable). It does mean, however, that you must exercise extreme caution in handling the plant for the first three months. Scrub the pot thoroughly, while wearing rubber gloves, and do it outdoors — not in the

(continued on page 48)

Buying House Plants by Mail

Nearly every newspaper, gardening magazine, and seed catalog has them — advertisements offering live house plants by mail, usually at bargain prices. Sometimes they're obviously too good to be true; sometimes they're bona fide opportunities to expand your plant collection cheaply. Telling the difference, and knowing what to do if your expectations aren't met, can save you frustration, time, and money. We asked some experts for advice:

"The first thing you should do," cautions Dr. Gilbert F. Daniels, president of the American Horticultural Society, "is know what the plant you're ordering really is. Advertisements or catalogs should list the scientific name and the common name; don't waste money on plants that aren't listed by name. And watch those Sunday supplement advertisements — not all of them are fraudulent, but some are; stay away from the so-called 'wonder plants'."

"If it seems too good to be true, then it probably isn't true," echoes Jane Foster, president of the Mailorder Association of Nurserymen (MAN), a trade association organized to protect the many legitimate plant shippers from the bad publicity earned by a few fly-by-night opportunists.

Obviously, shopping by mail can be a delight. Few greenhouses can afford to stock rarer species of house plants, and those that do often charge premium prices for them. If you have a taste for the exotic, mail ordering can be the best way to augment your indoor garden with unusual plants. But unfamiliarity can be a problem, too. An advertisement for "the horticultural breakthrough of the decade," with vivid hyperbole about a miracle plant's beauty, growth, flower or fruit production, or ability to survive under adverse conditions, may omit the fact that it performs those feats only in a greenhouse, or after being subjected to special treatment, or after a long period of dormancy. Unusual plants often have unusual needs. Reputable advertisers will tell you about those needs; rip-off artists won't. And miracles happen only in the movies, not in the greenhouse.

"If there were miracle plants, we'd surely have them in our catalog," says Klaus Neubner, senior vice-president in charge of horticultural activities for the George W. Park Seed Co., Inc., a major shipper of live house plants which does not deal in miracles.

Folks who get burned usually spend more time looking at the colorful pictures than reading the fine print — an unwise practice, according to Dr. Daniels.

"Believe it or not, some people still order what they think are mature plants because of a picture in an ad, and then are disappointed to find that they've bought tiny seedlings or — even worse — a packet of seeds." Dr. Daniels' advice is to read everything in the ad, especially the warranty. Most reputable plant shippers offer full replacement or refund warranties, and the ad should state that.

Foster advises prospective purchasers to look for the MAN seal, which shows that the advertiser subscribes to that organization's code of ethics. If you're buying from a new or unfamiliar source, place a small "test" order first, and keep a copy of your order and check. How well a shipper handles a small order is a good indication of his integrity.

Not getting what you thought you ordered is one problem, but getting what you ordered *in poor shape* is quite another. Low temperatures en route are probably responsible for most mail order house plant problems, with high temperatures and soil displacement running a close second. Companies like Park are continually refining and testing their packaging for protection against temperature extremes and shock (Neubner says that his company tumbles packaged plants in a clothes dryer — on low heat — to test their packaging!), but even so, the most well acclimated and well packaged plant can't survive much more than a ten-day journey in any weather. And, of course, the shipping service has a lot to do with that.

"Once a plant leaves our warehouse, we have no control over it," Neubner explains. "Accidents can happen; delays can occur. Ideally, a plant should be kept between 40° and 60°F (4° and 16°C) while en route, but we ship all year round and get an amazing number of plants through without freezing — more than 95 percent. Of course, it's not so good to let a plant sit in the mailbox for a couple of hours when the temperature's below freezing!"

High temperatures cause a buildup of ethylene gas within the carton, which causes leaves to yellow and fall. Heat can dry up the soil, too, and the combination can prove fatal to even the most carefully packaged plant. If you're ordering during the coldest or hottest months and have a choice of shippers, it's good practice to pick the fastest one, even if it means paying a little extra. And arrange to meet your plants so that they don't freeze or bake in your mailbox.

Some plants are easier to ship than others. Neubner says that Park has given up on shipping cape primrose *(Streptocarpus saxorum)* and removed it from their catalog; ferns tend to develop bruised tips, which are not serious impediments to subsequent growth, he adds; and baby's tears *(Soleirolia soleirolii)* tends to dry out rapidly en route, and should not be shipped long distances. Other than those, most plants can be shipped, whatever their size and sensitivities; it's a matter of preparation and packaging. Still, plants don't especially like to travel.

"Any plant that comes into the home will have suffered some trauma," says Dr. Daniels. "But if it's been mishandled or frozen, you'll know it right away — there are no delayed reactions." Emergency first aid may help save the traumatized plant.

"If the plant has been dried out, water it *lightly* and put it in well-filtered light for a few days," Neubner advises, adding that one criterion for a well-packaged plant is that it has been sent with enough soil to prevent drying out.

"If the soil has shaken loose — and that can happen no matter how carefully the plant was packaged — replace the soil and put the plant inside a 'tent' of plastic with a few air holes punched in it, to increase humidity. Make sure the plastic doesn't touch the leaves, though. Any yellow leaves will be lost, but often a marginal plant can be saved this way."

If it cannot, the disappointed purchaser should seek a refund or replacement rather than simply writing it off as a loss. If the package has been damaged, notify the carrier right away; both the postal service and private carriers have procedures for handling complaints. If the plant is dead or dying, or if it is not delivered as advertised, you should notify the company immediately by letter, describing the problem as accurately as possible, and asking specifically for a refund or replacement. MAN President Foster recommends sending a copy to her, c/o Jack-

son and Perkins, Medford, OR 97501.

If you get no reply, or an unsatisfactory reply, within 30 days, send a second letter to the shipper and enclose a copy of your first letter. In addition, send copies of the letter and the cancelled check, making sure you include the name and address of the company involved to MAN; the Federal Trade Commission (Washington, DC 20260, Attn: Consumer Protection Division); the Consumer Protection Division of the Attorney General's Office in the shipper's home state; the United States Postal Service (Washington, DC 20260, Attn: Thomas Chadwick); and the Mail Order Action Line service of the Direct Mail Marketing Association (6 E. 43rd St., New York, NY 10017). It helps to send the second letter by registered mail.

Garden Writers Association of America past President Corinne Willard addressed the problem at the 30th Anniversary Annual Meeting in late 1978. Her advice was to "write to the publication in which you read the ad. Complain to them. If more readers would do that, deceptive horticultural advertising could be eliminated because reliable publications would not accept (it)."

Buy by mail then, but do it with care. Ever since "Jack and the Beanstalk," folks have been trying to sell miracles; with a bit of healthy skepticism and a sharp pencil, you can drive the "miracle peddlers" out of business, and buy with confidence.

kitchen sink. Don't allow pets or children near the plant. (A plant treated with systemics might have a milky residue on the foliage, and it might have a peculiar, foul-sweet odor.)

After you have brought a plant home, inspect the potting mixture carefully. Sometimes, plants are potted in "shipping soil" by the grower. Typically, shipping soil is made from a large amount of peat with a little sand sprinkled over the surface. The purpose — for the grower — is to reduce the weight of the potted plant and thus save on shipping costs. The mixture looks good — dark and rich, with added sand for good soil texture. But in reality, no plant will survive for long in shipping soil; it should be repotted immediately. Anyone who has worked with peat can recognize it easily. If you are not sure, take a sample to a plant-loving friend, or remove some and let it dry out for a few days. If it is virtually weightless and caked hard when dry, it is probably peat. Some growers also use sea sand in the mixture. Often, the salt in this sand will kill a plant after the salt has been washed down into the potting mixture.

Even when you have exercised all cautions, it is still safest to isolate any new plant in your home for a few weeks. Inspect it every few days for signs of insect or disease activity. Only after you are sure it is not infested should you place it among your other plants.

MOVING PLANTS

The thought of moving plants, for anyone who has a large collection and has done the job before, is enough to throw the cheeriest of souls into a state of depression. It is a difficult and time-consuming job, often fraught with frustration and disappointment.

Moving across town presents little problem. Simply pack the plants in open cardboard cartons (separating the pots with wads of newspaper), load the boxes into the back

seat of the car, and proceed directly to your new home. In winter, be sure to protect the plants from freezing. Warm up the car before loading and, unless you have a garage that opens directly into the house, wrap each plant loosely with newspaper for the dash to the curb. Remember that even a few seconds of exposure to subfreezing temperatures can injure any tropical plant. In summer, again move the plants by car. Do not load them into the back of an open pickup truck; the strong wind will not only induce shock, but also is likely to break stems and branches. If the day is a hot one, do not stop along the way for any reason, leaving the plants to bake in the back of the car.

For short moves with large plants, pack sphagnum moss into the top of each pot, tie a plastic bag securely around the pot, fastening it around the crown or lower stem, and tip the plant on its side for the car ride. If the plant is too tall for the back seat of the car and must be placed in a van, load it last, in the very back. Be sure that the pot or tub is secured against sliding or tipping, and drive slowly.

Moving plants long distances across state lines is a different matter. Not only is it difficult, it is not even recommended. Nevertheless, if there are some plants to which you have grown hopelessly attached, there are precautions that you can take to increase their chances of safe arrival.

When moving across state lines, the first thing to do is to call your state department of agriculture and ask for the bureau of plant protection. Tell the bureau representative where you intend to move and when, and what kinds of plants you intend to move. You might learn that you will need a certificate of inspection before being allowed to bring plants into the new state. Usually, this requires your bringing all the plants to the state or county office shortly before moving, having them checked for insects and disease, and receiving the proper certification. Some states will send an inspector to your home if you have a large number of plants (although there may be an extra charge for this service). You might even learn that there are certain of your plants that you will not be able to bring into the new state. California, for instance, will not allow your Ponderosa lemon tree (or any other citrus) to be brought into the state.

Remembering that all plants have individual needs for light, soil moisture, humidity, and temperature, you must then plan to move them in the way that will provide for these needs as adequately as possible. No matter what method of transportation you choose, however, the plants will suffer shock and there will probably be some casualties.

Moving plants long distances in a moving van, along with your furniture and other belongings, is not a good idea. In winter, the plants would likely freeze. In summer, they would be injured or killed by excessive heat.

If you and your family will be moving personally by plane, it will be possible for you to take plants along as luggage or cargo, although if you have many plants, the cost will be high. Ask the airline representative about limitations on the size of boxes and for any other regulations that might apply. After you have satisfied these, prune the plants as severely as you can without harming them, and pack them upright into cartons supplied by the moving company. Cover the tops of the pots with aluminum foil or plastic, wrapping it tightly around the base of the plants to keep the soil from spilling out. Insulate the carton well by stapling 10 to 15 sheets of newspaper to all the inside walls, and put at least 40 sheets on the bottom. (Remember that luggage compartments of airplanes are likely to freeze at high altitudes, even in summer.) Support the pots or tubs as well as you can, perhaps cutting pieces of heavy Styrofoam to wedge among them, and stake the branches of large specimens so that they will not break if the carton is tipped. In cold weather, cover each plant with a plastic bag (trying not to let the plastic drape over any of

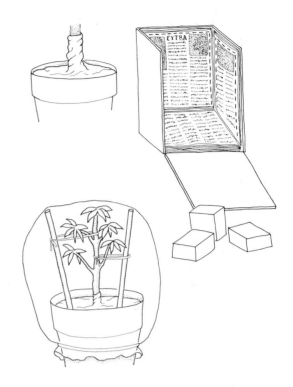

Getting Ready for Long Distance Travel: When preparing your plant for a journey of any length, make sure to provide warm, sheltered, and secure traveling accommodations. Begin the preparations with a thorough pruning, cutting back as far as you can without injuring the plant. To keep the potting mix in place, fasten a sheet of foil or plastic across the top of the pot, making sure the covering is firmly wrapped around the base of the plant. A large packing box should hold your plant comfortably, especially when a thick layer of newspaper is stapled in place to act as cushion and insulator. Large branches that might break easily should be staked for support. If your plant will be traveling during cold weather, protect it further by covering it with a plastic bag. Styrofoam blocks wedged between the base of the pot and the inside walls of the box can keep the plant from shifting around during transit.

the foliage). Then, cut some air holes in the top of the carton and write with a heavy marker on all sides and the top of the carton, "Fragile — Live Plants — This Side Up," drawing arrows pointing upward.

All of this should be done as closely as possible to flight time, to reduce plant shock to the minimum. Upon arriving at your destination, claim the plants as quickly as you can, open the tops of the cartons, and remove any plastic bags. Get the plants to their new home in short order and put them in a location of moderate light, out of direct sun. Withhold fertilizer completely and water lightly until they have recovered from any shock symptoms.

If you are taking a few plants with you for an auto trip of more than a day's duration, similar precautions are in order. Small plants can be packed conveniently into cardboard cartons from the grocery or liquor store, the kind with compartments. In summer, remember that many hours of wind blowing into the back of the car can increase leaf transpiration to a point where the plant is totally exhausted. If you park for lunch, try to find a spot out of the hot sun, and leave the windows cracked, as you would for the family dog. If you check into a motel in late afternoon, take the plants inside with you and check to see if they need water. If you stop during the cool of the evening, on the other hand, the plants will probably be fine in the car until morning.

When traveling by car in winter, remember the temperature requirements of your plants. A dinner stop can give interior car temperatures time to dip below the freezing mark. When you stop for the night at a motel, be sure to take the plants inside with you. It is safer, in any case, to insulate the plants as recommended for air travel.

It is also possible to ship plants by United Parcel Service or the United States Postal Service. The chances of damage in this case are certainly less than those presented by a moving company, but more than those of air freight. Check with representatives of either service before making your plans, and, should you choose either, pack the plants well, as you would for air freight shipment.

After considering all the perils and prob-lems of plant moving, you might come to the decision that most people choose. Select two or three of your favorite hardy varieties to take with you, then organize a plant sale. With the money you make, you can buy plants at your new location.

SEASONAL PLANT CARE

The Plant Institute of America estimates that one in four house plants dies during the first year of ownership, an annual loss of $300 million.

Despite the obvious boosts to the plant-growing industry, this is an enormous loss, and largely can be avoided if plants are given proper care throughout the year. In chapter 2, we discussed the basic requirements of plants for water, humidity, light, and temperature. Now, we will consider generally some of the special problems likely to be encountered with the changing of the seasons. If you heed the special seasonal needs of plants — keeping in mind that most of their basic needs do not change, whether the temperature outside is 90° or 0°F (32° or −18°C) — then your plants will not add to the fatality statistics.

The changing of the seasons in the northern temperate zone requires that indoor gardeners make special adjustments for tropical house plants, which thrive best under consistent conditions of light and temperature. A south windowsill might offer a perfect home for African violets during winter, when the sun remains low and its intensity is diminished, but they would certainly perish there during the intensely bright and hot days of summer. It is up to us to keep in mind the requirements of every plant, and to respond to them as conditions change with passing seasons.

Here, then, are some things to consider for each of the four seasons. We have not considered these month by month, since seasonal conditions change at different times in different places.

AUTUMN

Autumn marks the beginning of the indoor gardening season. Many house plants which have spent the summer outdoors are moved back inside at this time, and our desire to buy new plants is accelerated, in anticipation of winter.

Bringing Plants Indoors

Plants that have spent the summer outdoors may now be brought back inside. This is best done when the outside temperatures closely approximate those indoors, lessening the chances of temperature shock. September is the usual time in the northern half of the United States, October in the South. If you wait until outdoor temperatures at night hve dipped to 50° or 55°F (10° or 13°C), then you should keep the plants on a cool but protected sun porch for a week or so, letting them adjust to warmer indoor temperatures gradually. Be sure of the minimum temperature requirement of each individual plant, however, and don't let any be exposed to temperatures that could injure it.

Before bringing each plant inside, inspect it carefully for signs of disease and insects. If any are found, treat the plant promptly, using the methods recommended in chapter 9. Even if no signs of infestation are found, isolate all these plants in a separate room for several weeks, until you are absolutely sure that your other indoor plants will not become contaminated. Knock the soil ball out of each pot and inspect it for slugs or insect larvae. A few earthworms will not injure the roots (and they probably will not survive for long indoors, anyway), but the appearance of any insects or other pests signifies the need for immediate repotting in a fresh and pasteurized potting mix. You also might find that the summer outdoors has stimulated the plant's growth to a point where it is potbound. If so, either repot it (if you wish it to grow larger) or prune back both the top and roots (if you wish to keep the plant at its present size).

Light Conditions in Autumn

While the weather in October may remain perfectly mild and pleasant, the days at this season are quickly growing shorter, while the sun's intensity is steadily diminishing because of its lower position in the sky. The result is that your plants receive progressively less light each day, actually from the end of June until the end of December, at which time the days begin to lengthen again.

Autumn is the time to respond to the annual slowdown in growth as plants prepare for dormancy. Water plants less often, and apply fertilizer sparingly.

The Facts of Dormancy and Rest

Nearly all plants enter periods of dormancy at some time during the year, during which they will stop growing, stop blossoming, and may take on a faded and washed-out appearance. This is a perfectly natural and beneficial phase of their life cycle. After the dormant period, the plant will come back with renewed health and growth. It is important that indoor gardeners recognize the signs and times of dormancy for each plant, and that they cooperate by offering each reduced water and light and by withholding fertilizer completely. To do otherwise may injure the plant.

The time of year each plant enters its dormant period depends on its place of origin. The tuberous begonia *(Begonia × tuberhybrida),* for instance, which comes from Central America, north of the equator, rests in winter and renews itself in spring, just as our native plants do. The African violet, however, which is a native of the southern part of that continent, where the seasons mirror our own, blossoms freely all winter and then ceases flowering for a month or so in spring. Tropical foliage plants which originated close to the equator may show few or no signs of dormancy, since their native environment varies so slightly from winter to summer. Even these plants, however, have periods of

52

greater and lesser growth, requiring your appropriate response.

In general, the farther away from the equator the plant's point of origin, the more pronounced is its period of dormancy. Extreme examples are the deciduous trees of the north, which drop their leaves and rest for as long as six months of the year, and the common tropical grape ivy, which remains bright and green throughout the year, even though it grows more profusely at some times than at others. The prayer plant *(Maranta leuconeura)* generally loses some of its leaves each autumn, even when grown under artificial conditions of consistent light and temperature. Plants removed from their origins by many generations may still respond as they might under their native conditions.

The house plants with the most pronounced periods of dormancy include cacti and succulents, most flowering plants (fibrous-rooted begonias and gesneriads are exceptions), and bulbous and tuberous plants. Wax plants must be given a dormant period during winter if they are to bloom in spring. The poinsettia should be forced into dormancy after it has bloomed. Florists' gloxinias *(Sinningia speciosa)* should be rested completely over winter, their bare tubers stored in sand. The amaryllis *(Hippeastrum* spp.) can be forced into dormancy over the fall and early winter, then brought into spectacular bloom for the Christmas season. Every plant has its natural preferences for dormancy, although some may be manipulated without harm if we want to force them into bloom during certain times of the year. The critical dormancy needs of plants are discussed in the Encyclopedia section of this book.

You must respond to each plant's signals for dormancy as they appear. In general, reduce light and the number of waterings, give the plant a slightly lower temperature, and withhold fertilizer entirely, until active new growth begins.

The reduction of light is seldom a prob-

Not Dead but Dormant: You should by no means assume that this *Hippeastrum* has produced its last bloom and is now ready for the compost pile. To the contrary, if this dormant bulb is stored dry in a cool, dark place, it will burst forth at the end of dormancy with new growth, and can flower again.

lem in northern homes, since window light is naturally reduced at this time of year. More critical is the reduction of water, especially when considering that most indoor gardeners tend to overwater plants even during periods of their active growth. Plant experts stress that water should be given to a dormant plant only when that plant begins to wilt. Although this procedure might seem a severe one, it is highly beneficial. Look for the first signs of slight wilt, and water only then. But, as usual, be sure to water thoroughly. If you simply sprinkle the surface of the soil time after time, you will lose the entire lower root structure, harming the plant permanently. Water plants less often, but not less at each watering.

Fertilizer must be withheld completely when a plant has gone into a dormant period. For one thing, the plant's metabolic processes are operating at a seasonal low and the plant cannot absorb the fertilizer, thus creating a potentially dangerous accumulation of mineral salts that can cause root burn. For another, the soil will be kept dry, and fertilizer applied to dry soil also can cause root burn.

Humidity conditions are not critical during dormancy. Providing normal humidity, in fact, will aid the plant, since it will lessen the rate of transpiration from the leaves and thus aid in its tendency to slow down metabolic processes.

It is not difficult to tell when any plant breaks dormancy. New growth will appear, the plant will take on a bright and healthy appearance, and some which flower profusely will begin to flower again. Respond to this call by once again providing normal levels of light, fertilizer, water, and temperature.

WINTER

With the approach of winter, we seem to cling more than ever to our house plants — which is well, since they need our close attention during the cold months. Pruning, staking, watering, and fertilizing will be reduced, since many plants will have entered into dormancy, but both temperature and humidity must be watched carefully at this time.

House heat in winter is often surprisingly uneven, varying from room to room by as much as 15°F (8°C), and within a room by even more, since the mini-climate on a windowsill can be near freezing at night, and very hot during the day in the presence of full sun. The heat from a fireplace can trigger a nearby thermostat to cut off furnace heat, even though other rooms of the house may be quite cold. The answer is to keep several good thermometers at various strategic locations throughout the house. Include one maximum/minimum thermometer, the kind that will register the lowest and highest temperatures of any given period. You might find that some adjustments will have to be made, even though many plants are at rest and can stand lower temperatures at this time.

The humidity problem is most critical during winter, the result of central heating and a lack of outside air. Depend on a good hygrometer to check the relative humidity in different parts of the house, and follow the suggestions in chapter 2 to bring it up to an acceptable level.

Tropical plants that were sheltered from direct sun during the summer can now be brought into brighter locations, where they will respond well. This is especially true of African violets, which will continue to flower through the winter if given enough light.

Caring for Plants during Winter Vacations

Before going off for a skiing trip to Aspen or a two-week sojourn to a tropical isle, you must give some careful thought to your house plants.

The best solution, by far, is to ask a plant-loving friend to come in every few days and tend them for you. Often, reciprocal arrangements can be made among indoor gardeners.

You might decide, however, that you prefer to give the plants the opportunity to care for themselves in your absence. They can, for as long as three weeks.

The general idea, in preparing plants for their owner's absence for extended periods, is to water them normally, then slow down their respiration rates until you return. The usual method is to enclose large plants in clear plastic bags. Provide three or four stakes upon which to drape the plastic, being sure that the plastic does not touch the foliage. The effect will be a miniature greenhouse in which the plant will luxuriate for up to three weeks. Pull the plant back from the window so that it does not receive direct sunlight.

Smaller plants may be grouped and covered with an old leaky aquarium, or you may construct a plastic boxlike structure, using wooden lath strips. If the plants are placed on a pebble tray (see chapter 2) and covered with the plastic box, these plants, also, will not need attention for up to three weeks.

Some people simply group together as many plants as will fit into a shower stall, then keep ½ inch (13 mm) of water in the

Absentee Plant Tending: While you're gone your plants don't need to languish—just build them a plastic-enclosed compartment that will keep them alive for up to three weeks.

bottom of the stall, or as much as it will hold without coming up and over the plant's saucers. Close the shower curtain or door, keep the ceiling light on continuously during your absence, and the plants will be fine for a week or ten days.

A word of caution: Never overwater plants, then enclose them in plastic before going on vacation. The probable result will be root rot. Always drain pots in a normal manner before enclosing them.

Light duration should be given consideration during vacation periods, also. Never keep plants in a dark and windowless room for long periods. A room with windows may be kept unlit if the windows are open to light. In fact, you might find that some of your short-day plants will come into rare blossom when room lights are not turned on every night. Even so, most plants will thrive if given some additional light during the early evening hours, and this can be provided through the use of an inexpensive 24-hour timer. If you must keep a room light on con-

tinuously during your vacation, you need not fear for your plants. Ordinary room lights will not harm plants, even if kept on for several weeks at a time.

Plants that grow well in constantly moist soil may be handled easily with water wicks as described in chapter 2. In such cases, no plastic bags will be needed, since the plants can draw up as much moisture as they need until your return.

Upon returning from your vacation, inspect all plants carefully and water any that have become dry. Remove any plastic bags gradually over a period of several days, to help plants become accustomed once again to room conditions.

Other Activities

Between carrying out various house plant chores and projects and poring over new seed catalogs, gardeners pass away the winter with a minimum of discontent. The bulbs we stored for forcing in October will, during January, February, and March, be brought into bloom, bringing spring tantalizingly close. Residents of large cities are drawn to botanical gardens at this time of year. Then, about the end of February, it becomes clear that the days are growing longer. Although the temperature may remain frigid, the sun becomes brighter, rising higher in the sky with each passing day, and we begin to look for the first signs of spring in the lingering snow. At this time, survey all of your house plants once again. The African violets that bloomed profusely during winter on the south windowsill might now be placed in a position of slightly less light. Watch for signs of an end to plant dormancy, signified by new growth and intensified color of all foliage. When it happens, respond to plants' requirements by providing more water, good light, and the first application of fertilizer since that of last autumn. Ever so gradually, winter glides into spring, and it is with the company of house plants that the transition seems so graceful and painless.

Springtime Cuttings: The renewed burst of growth most plants experience in spring makes this the best time to take cuttings. The cuttings will root more readily and will mature aided by the season's warm temperatures and plentiful sunlight.

SPRING

The lengthening days of spring, leading to the longest day of the year at the time of the summer solstice in June, are beneficial to most house plants, which often show their greatest growth spurts at this time. The reason for the spurt of new growth lies in the increasing intensity and daily duration of light, which increases the photosynthetic process, enabling the plant to manufacture more food. Many plants also come out of dormancy in spring, and simply seem more eager to grow than at any other time.

Your treatment of plants in spring, as always, should be guided by their individual requirements. When new growth is rapid, respond by increasing waterings and giving all plants a dose of fertilizer.

Spring is also a good time to check the soil balls of all plants and to repot any that need it. A detailed discussion of potting and repotting can be found in chapter 6.

Propagation by Cuttings

Spring is the ideal time to take cuttings of leaves and stems for starting new plants. Since growth is particularly active now, the cuttings you take will root more easily, with a better than average chance for success. The ideal weather over spring and summer will give the new plants a good chance to become well established by autumn, when they can serve either as additions to your own collection or as gifts for friends. See chapter 8 to learn about propagation.

SUMMER

The summer months usually take us away from our indoor plants and into the outdoor garden, which certainly needs our close attention for at least four months. At this time, too, house plants are fairly well able to grow successfully with a minimum of care. Nevertheless, we must keep an eye on indoor plants during these warm months, if only to see that each is in the best summer location and is receiving adequate water.

Light and heat are the major considerations. Be sure that your tropical plants are not overexposed to strong sunlight. It is true that, with good light and air movement, plants can stand higher temperatures than they could otherwise. Nevertheless, nearly all plants should be protected from overexposure until September, when the sun's rays begin to lose their intensity. Pull plants back from south and west windows, or offer a light-filtering device such as bamboo or open-weave fabric curtains. Try to achieve the effect of a location under a tree, where the sun is filtered during the late morning and through the afternoon hours.

Remember, too, that the high light and

temperatures of summer will increase the rate of leaf transpiration, resulting in greater water requirements.

Plants' Vacation Outdoors

Many gardeners consider it an absolute necessity to summer their house plants outdoors, pointing to the lush growth that plants make when given this annual vacation. Other gardeners would never even consider it, pointing to the damage threatened by insects, disease, neighborhood dogs and cats, and the harsh effects of sun and wind. There is no clear winner in this debate. To decide what course you should follow, review the specific needs of each plant — temperature, humidity, light, and soil moisture — and then see whether you can provide these outdoors as well as indoors.

Summering Plants in a Lath House: Your plants can respond to a summertime outing with luxuriant growth. A lath house buffers them from intense summer rays and strong winds, allowing filtered sunlight and gentle air movement within the structure.

Probably only the cacti may be placed out in the hot summer sun and be expected to survive. Indeed, not all cactus species would benefit by the experience. Most house plants, since they are of tropical origin, enjoy about 12 hours a day of filtered sun, with good soil moisture and humidity and gentle air movement. Some — those that prefer some direct sun — will benefit from receiving 2 or 3 hours of sun in the cool of the morning. If you cannot provide proper conditions, then do not attempt to challenge your indoor plants with an outdoor environment unsuited to them.

There are many outdoor locations that are good for house plants. A sheltered terrace or patio, which receives only the morning sun, is often ideal. A brick wall under a large tree, or a lath house where only a little filtered sunlight slips through, is a good location for plants that grow well in bright light but not direct sun. A totally shaded spot will be fine for those plants that like locations of medium light.

Never remove plants from their pots when placing them outdoors. To do so is to invite disease and insects, and to encourage the plant's roots to spread too widely. Before bringing it back indoors in fall, you would have to trim off most of the new roots that had developed. Plants may be sunk into the ground in their pots, up to within an inch (2.5 cm) of the pot rims, and in this case you should either safeguard the drainage hole with a piece of plastic screening, to keep out soil-dwelling insects, or spread a two-inch (5 cm) layer of gravel at the bottom of a trench, placing the pots on the gravel and then filling in with soil.

If you do not sink pots into the ground, you should inspect the plants periodically to see whether they need water. The high temperatures, light, and air movement outdoors will cause any house plant to use more water than it does indoors.

Plants may be sunk into soil in large tubs and other containers and placed on a patio or terrace, where they will serve to make these outdoor living areas much more pleasant all summer long. Because of the shelter offered by patios and terraces, they are often the very best summer locations for plants. For extra color, complement house plants with bright, flowering garden annuals, also grown in containers.

Plants outdoors should be checked regularly for signs of disease, insect attack, and sunscald. If any is found to be affected, bring it indoors, isolate it, and begin treatment immediately. In the case of sunscald, the treatment will be simply to place the plant out of direct sun until it has recovered.

When to Move Plants Outdoors

The proper time to move any plant outdoors is when the temperature range outdoors falls within that plant's permissible range. Coolness-loving plants such as *Aloe variegata,* English ivy, *×Fatshedera lizei,* geraniums, wandering Jew, and wax plant, may go out when night temperatures will not dip below 50°F (10°C). Warmth-loving plants such as dieffenbachias, dracaenas, fiddleleaf fig *(Ficus lyrata),* palms, and others should not go out until night temperatures have risen to a minimum of 60°F (16°C).

Any plant should be introduced gradually to the outdoors. The combined shock of temperature and light changes, if introduced suddenly, can injure most plants. One way to "harden-off" plants to outdoor conditions is to carry them out for an hour the first day, two hours for the next few days, and for progressively longer periods over a week or ten days. A better (and far less time-consuming) way is to place the plants on an enclosed sun porch, opening the door for good air circulation during the warmer parts of the day. After a week on the sun porch, open the door fully for three days, then carry the plants to their outdoor locations on the morning of the next day.

Urban apartment dwellers find a variety of places to send their plants for the summer, including fire escapes, under skylights, on rooftops, and in window boxes. It is important to remember, however, that it is not necessary to summer plants outdoors. Do not feel that you will be mistreating them if you decide to, or must, keep them inside. You will be in the best of company, with those many gardeners who refuse to adopt the practice, either from principle or sorry experience.

Air Conditioning and Plants

Many gardeners of the southern and southwestern United States have learned to keep their plants indoors during the summer, exposing them to outdoor conditions only when temperatures have moderated in the autumn. Often, in these warmer areas, the question of the effects of air conditioning on plants arises, many gardeners fearing that the "unnatural" effects of air conditioning will harm plants. In truth, air conditioning will not harm plants, so long as the cold airstream is not directed upon any plant. House plants respond well at the same temperatures that bring comfort to us. Think of your comfort, therefore, and you will also be considering the plant's.

The major consideration when using air conditioning is to watch the humidity level in the room. Since all air conditioning units remove humidity from the air, some extra measures might have to be taken for moisture-lovers such as ferns.

Plant Care during Summer Vacations

The general principles of plant care during summer vacations are the same as those recommended earlier for winter vacations. Since room temperatures are likely to be higher during summer, however, it will be somewhat more difficult to slow down your plants' metabolic processes at this time. Light intensity also will present a problem, although this may be solved by moving plants away from bright windows or filtering light by the use of open-weave curtains or shades. Follow the procedures described under Caring for Plants during Winter Vacations.

CHAPTER 4

Containers

Containers for plants should be chosen with care if you wish to display house plants most effectively, and if you care about the health of your plants. The container must, in other words, be both aesthetically pleasing and highly functional.

The basic plant container is the classic clay flower pot, and it is well designed for its purpose. The clay (unglazed) is porous, allowing for both water and air to pass through its walls. It has a lip, making it easy to handle. Its sides are tapered, so that the soil ball may be removed easily. And, of course, it has a drainage hole. A better design would be hard to conceive, although some plastic pots are now close rivals.

Clay pots range from 2½ to 15 inches (6 to 38 cm) or more in diameter (measured at the rim). In addition to the standard clay flower pot, there are special variations of form for special purposes — orchid pots, bulb pans, half-pots, and seed pans. The last three are shorter and wider than the standard form, since their uses require less potting mixture.

Despite the popularity of clay pots, ones made of plastic now account for the vast majority of plant containers sold in stores and shops. They are less expensive, for one thing, and most are designed to a form that offers all the advantages of the classic clay model. The big difference between the two is that plastic is not porous, and the soil in these pots will retain water for longer periods. Plants growing in plastic pots must be watered less often, and it is especially important to provide for good soil drainage in plastic, in order to introduce sufficient amounts of air into the soil. Air cannot pass through the walls of a plastic pot, as it can through clay. Many people prefer the plastic pots because they are lightweight, easier to clean, will not

absorb odors and microscopic disease organisms, and are available in a wide variety of colors and textures. Among the most popular are those that have an attached saucer.

SAUCERS FOR POTS

Ordinary clay and plastic pots will require a saucer to catch draining water. Other than considering aesthetic values (the saucer ideally should match the pot), you should be aware that unglazed clay saucers are not

An Assortment of Clay Pots: Favorites with many indoor gardeners, unglazed clay pots come in a wide range of shapes and sizes to suit a multitude of gardening situations. In the foreground is a slotted pot for orchid growing. In the background can be seen two sizes of standard flower pots.

Opposite, some of the many sizes and shapes of clay pots available.

moisture proof. If you wish to use them on a prized wooden table, you can apply a coat of clear shellac to the upper surface of the saucer, thus making it watertight. Or, you may choose plastic saucers, the kind that are colored to resemble red clay.

CHOOSING THE RIGHT POT

After you have considered the functional qualities of a pot, you should assure yourself that it is aesthetically pleasing — that it suits the plant as well as your home decor or style. A glazed clay pot, painted with bright flowers, would certainly compete for attention with a modest *Peperomia* — and the pot would almost certainly win. A ceramic figure of a cartoon animal might be pleasing and humorous, but probably less so with a cactus growing out of its back. Some people cannot resist containers of this kind, and are perfectly happy with them. Others prefer to let the plant dominate the container. It is a matter of personal taste.

When you bring a plant home from the shop and wish to replant it, be sure to choose a pot of the right size. Ordinarily, a plant in a 2½-inch (6 cm) seedling pot may be transferred to a 3- or 3½-inch (8 or 9 cm) pot. Larger plants may need no repotting at all, unless they appear to be potbound. When repotting any plant, choose only the next larger size of pot. If you wish to use a special pot which happens to be too large, then double-pot the plant.

DOUBLE-POTTING

If you cannot find a decorative container you like that is suitable for plant growth, it is best to pot up the plant in a clay pot, then find a larger vessel in which to hide the clay pot. In this way, you can make use of containers that would otherwise be unsuitable for plants. Popular containers for double-potting include woven baskets, wooden tubs, antique crocks,

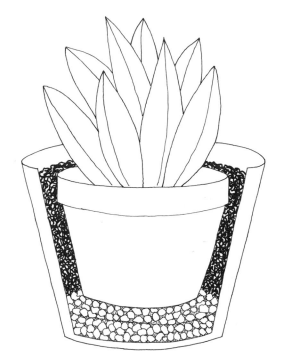

Double-Potting: This technique cuts down on the frequency of watering in addition to dressing up an ordinary clay pot. When the plant is watered, excess water will drain into the layer of charcoal and gravel at the bottom. Moistened sphagnum moss sandwiched between the pot walls helps conserve the water normally transpired through the clay pot.

brass buckets, and large soup tureens. Almost any container can be used for double-potting. The only caveat is that those which are not watertight should be made so. The easiest way is to line the container with several sheets of plastic, or plastic bags of a convenient size. The rims of the planter pots can be hidden just under a layer of sphagnum moss, along with all evidence of plastic.

In double-potting, the idea is to allow excess water from the clay pot to drain into the decorative container. Start, then, by putting a layer of gravel (mixed with one-tenth that amount of charcoal) in the bottom of the larger container. The layer should be at least one inch (2.5 cm) deep, but may be deeper. In very large containers, four inches (10 cm) is not unusual. Place the clay pot, which holds the plant, on top of the gravel, then pack

A Pot Proportioned to the Plant: A large, dramatic plant calls for an attractive container which can balance the height of the plant. This clay pot blends well with the wood paneling and the natural tones used in the decor. In addition, it is the correct size to hold the right amount of growing medium to sustain the plant.

sphagnum moss around the sides until it comes up to the rim of the clay pot. The top of the clay pot's rim should be just a shade lower than that of the larger container. If you wish, you may cover the clay rim very shallowly, so that it cannot be seen.

Double-potting has an advantage beyond that of aesthetics. The sphagnum moss, if kept moist (but not soggy), will lessen transpiration through the walls of the clay pot, and will reduce the number of times you must water. Excess water will drain through the hole of the clay pot into the gravel below. (Occasionally, remove the clay pot and see that not too much water is collecting in the gravel.) When you go out of town for a long weekend, water the plant normally and also moisten the sphagnum moss. The plant will do well in your absence.

INDOOR PLANTERS AND WINDOW BOXES

Another form of double-potting allows you to place several medium size or many smaller pots in a single large container. Sometimes, this takes the form of a window box, which can be attached to a windowsill indoors, just as it is outdoors. Plant stands are popular, and some of them are equipped with plant-growing lights. Any number of smaller plants may be displayed in these containers, so long as the rules of double-potting are followed. Keep each plant in the right size pot, and provide good drainage.

TUBS AND CROCKS FOR LARGE PLANTS

The selection of containers for treelike plants again depends on personal taste. Plants may be set into these containers directly, or may be double-potted. If double-potting is not employed, then be sure to offer proper drainage with a heavy layer of gravel and charcoal. Wooden containers may be built in the home shop or purchased at garden centers. Often, the kinds designed for outdoor container gardening are also suitable for large indoor plants. Some popular containers of larger size include old whiskey barrels (cut in half), copper kettles, antique stoneware crocks, large porcelain urns, and clay strawberry barrels. Again, all should be made watertight with plastic lining. Or, if you wish to go to the expense, copper lining is a permanent solution.

SMALL CONTAINERS FOR SEEDLINGS

Easiest of all for starting bedding plants or vegetables are the many kinds of peat pots, which you will transplant to the outdoor garden right along with the seedlings inside them. Some of these have fertilizer already in them (you can improvise this kind yourself by soaking standard peat pots and your peat moss filler in compost tea), while others come in attached blocks and even with a plastic tray. But there is no need to buy containers to get plants started; any two or three inch (5 or 8 cm) deep holders such as egg or milk cartons, margarine or cottage cheese containers, little juice cans and so on can be used to begin seedlings or transplant them or cuttings as long as you perforate the bottom to provide drainage.

HANGING CONTAINERS

There is a wide variety of hanging containers offered in plant shops. From airy wooden baskets and fancy ceramic pots to functional plastic pouches, hanging containers become more attractive as one's collection of plants grows and window space dwindles. Double-potting may be used with hanging containers, or drainage may be provided with gravel and charcoal in a watertight container. Saucers also may be used if the hanging device cradles the bottom of the container.

Naturally, we all hope that our hanging containers will soon be hidden with a profusion of green growth and colorful bloom. Since these hopes are not always realized, however, it is well to choose hanging containers that do not dominate the plant through bright color or overly bold design. Often, a hanging container takes on a different character when it is hung in the room above eye level, than it had when you examined it at the shop.

At one time, the only hanging container offered at stores was the traditional wire basket. It was meant for hanging outdoors, on porches, since it was impossible to control dripping water from this device. Generally, the bottom of the basket was lined with living sheet moss, green side out, then the potting mixture was added and the basket was planted. No gravel layer was required, since any excess water simply drained onto the porch. Indoors, of course, this is impractical. However, you can still use a wire basket indoors if you put a layer of plastic between the

Easy Conversion: A standard pot can be transformed into a hanging one with a little handiwork and a coat hanger. Mold the unhooked end around the pot, and use the hooked end to suspend your planter.

moss and a layer of drainage gravel, then add the potting mixture. You will have to mist the moss every day, in order to keep it bright green. Should it dry out and turn brown, it usually can be revived by remisting. Outdoors, the wire basket still performs admirably.

A standard three- or four-inch (8 or 10 cm) flower pot can be easily converted to a hanging container by straightening a coat hanger, then bending the unhooked end into a circle so it clasps the pot. On solid walls or upright supports you might attach wall brackets that hold single pots. Hangers for standard clay and plastic pots also can be made from rope, plastic cord, or wire. Attractive, inexpensive macrame hangers in a variety of materials and colors can be made at home or purchased.

Creative indoor gardeners have improvised plant hangers from a multitude of everyday materials. Towel racks, wagon wheels,

Build Your Own Hanging "Log" Basket

This decorative hanging basket accommodates one flower pot with a saucer. By using standard wood dowels, the container can be made in various sizes to fit the size pot you wish to place in it.

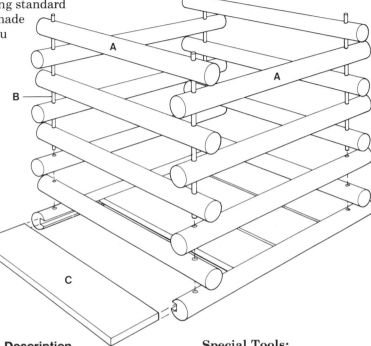

Materials:

Item	Quantity	Description
A. Sides	16	$3/4 \times 9$-inch hardwood dowel
B. Corner dowels	4	$1/4 \times 6$-inch hardwood dowel
C. Bottom	4	$1/4 \times 1\ 1/2 \times 7\ 1/8$-inch #2 pine
Hanger	1	8-foot leather thong
Glue	—	White vinyl glue
Finish	—	Boiled linseed oil and turpentine

Special Tools:

Hand drill or drill press

Procedure:

1. Cut 16 pieces of dowel for sides (A) according to the dimensions in the materials list.
2. Drill a $1/4$-inch hole $3/4$ inch in from each end of each dowel. Be sure to keep the holes parallel to one another.
3. Rout a $1/4$-inch groove 7 inches long in one side of two of the dowels to receive the bottom slats of the plant holder.
4. Cut corner dowels (B) according to the dimensions in the materials list.
5. Cut bottom slats (C) as described in the materials list.
6. Assemble the bottom, spacing the slats evenly across the bottom and gluing them in place.
7. Insert the corner dowels into the bottom dowels and stack the remaining 14 dowels alternately, like a log house, gluing each piece in place as it is installed.
8. Tie together the two ends of the 8-foot leather thong. Double the thong and hang the thong from each corner of the "log" planter.
9. Finish the unit with two coats of a mixture of equal parts boiled linseed oil and turpentine.

Build Your Own Hanging Planter for 3 Plants

This plant hanger is designed to hold three five-inch plant pots and their saucers. Be sure to buy the pots and their saucers first as assembly dimensions depend on these.

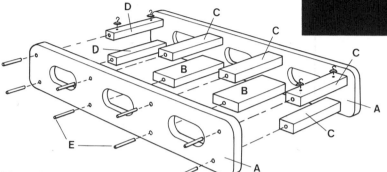

Special Tools:

Sabre or coping saw
Router
Hand drill or drill press

Materials:

Item	Quantity	Description
A. Sides	2	$\frac{3}{4} \times 4 \times 19$-inch #2 pine
B. Spacers	2	$\frac{3}{4} \times 2\frac{1}{4} \times 5\frac{3}{8}$-inch #2 pine
C. Spacers	4	$\frac{3}{4} \times 1\frac{1}{2} \times 5\frac{3}{8}$-inch #2 pine
D. Spacers	2	$\frac{3}{4} \times 1 \times 5\frac{3}{8}$-inch #2 pine
E. Dowels	20	$\frac{3}{16} \times 1\frac{1}{2}$-inch maple dowels
Glue	—	White vinyl glue
Finish	—	Boiled linseed oil and turpentine
Hooks	4	$\frac{1}{2}$-inch brass cup hooks
Chain	6 feet	Brass-plated chain
S hook	1	$\frac{3}{8}$-inch brass S hook

Procedure:

1. Cut all wooden sides and spacers to size according to the dimensions in the materials list.
2. Cut a 1-inch radius on each corner of the sides with a sabre or coping saw.
3. Lay out and cut out three holes in each side piece.
4. Rout a $\frac{1}{4}$-inch radius on all edges of the sides including the cutout holes and all the edges of the spacers, or break the edges with a sanding block.
5. Position the spacers so they are spaced evenly at a width that will provide a proper base for the saucer. The pot itself is not secured.
6. Glue the spacers.
7. Drill $\frac{3}{16}$-inch holes through the sides into the spacers for the dowels.
8. Connect the sides to the spacers, with glue and dowels.
9. Coat the plant hanger with two coats of a mixture of equal parts boiled linseed oil and turpentine.
10. Install four brass cup hooks on the top of the end spacers, and attach the hanging chain. Join the ends of the chains with an S hook.

ladders, drapery rods, basketball hoops, and lots of other household items can be suspended from the ceiling or mounted on the wall as decorative racks from which to hang plants. Sleek, sophisticated track-mounting systems also can be purchased and installed. Such systems can consist of a single track or a multi-level arrangement of hoops and bars.

Attractive plant hangers and hanging containers also can be constructed at home. Instructions for several different designs can be found in this chapter.

FEEDING AND WATERING HANGING CONTAINERS

Plants in containers that hang in the upper half of a room will be subject to more heat than those at windowsill level. They also will get more than their share of smoke and dust. They will require watering more often, and the extra water will carry away nutrients more quickly, meaning that they must be fertilized more often, as well. Make a special point of checking your hanging plants frequently, then, and double-pot them whenever you can, not only for the plants' health, but also for the time saving for you.

TRAYS

Shallow trays can be used to double-pot seedlings in 2½-inch (6 cm) containers, or they can be used as pebble trays for larger plants. The pebble tray (see chapter 2) is a device kept filled with pebbles and water. Potted plants are placed on top of the pebbles, and the evaporating water from the tray offers a continuing source of humidity for the plants. Often, unused trays can be found around the home to serve the purpose. If you can find none, then visit a hardware store and survey the plastic or rubber trays made for kitchen use. They come in a wide variety of sizes and colors, are inexpensive, and serve the purpose very well.

CLEANING CONTAINERS

All pots and other plant containers should be cleaned every other year, at least, or as soon as you notice a fairly serious accumulation of mineral salts along the edges of the pot. This accumulation is made by unused fertilizer and, in hard-water sections of the country, by limestone that accompanies tapwater. If the salts are not removed occasionally, they can build up to a point where plant health may be threatened.

Cleaning pots is a good chore for a Saturday morning when nothing else is going on. Remove the soil balls carefully from their pots, and put them on several layers of moist paper toweling. Scrub the pots, using a mild soap solution, then rinse them thoroughly and replace the plants immediately. If you wash only three pots at a time, the soil balls will not have a chance to dry out.

Any pot that has contained a diseased plant should be washed thoroughly, then soaked in boiling water for 20 minutes to destroy any traces of disease. Or the pot may be soaked in a solution of 1 part household bleach to 9 parts water, and rinsed thoroughly before reusing.

SPACE SAVERS

In an effort to conserve room space, manufacturers have come up with a dazzling array of plant stands, poles, lighted shelf units, and windowsill extenders to hold potted plants. Before buying any of them, consider carefully how your plants will be served by them. Many of the shelf arrangements will hold only very young or low-growing plants. Others are very versatile, capable of being worked in with bookshelf units and room dividers. There are some small planters equipped with a single plant-growing bulb — not the fluorescent kind — that would burn any fair size plant set beneath it.

To fill vertical space handsomely, you

Build Your Own Hanging 2-Tiered Planter

This plant hanger was designed to hold a standard 12-inch clay saucer in the lower level, and the top level is made from a 4-inch copper pot. The two wood pot supports are held together with brazing rod.

Special Tools:

Tools for bronze welding
Table saw
Drill press
Fly cutter
Router (optional)

Materials:

Item	Quantity	Description
A. Support frame	4	1 ⅛ × 1 ⅛ × 16-inch construction grade fir
B. Pot base	1	½ × 5 × 5-inch pine
C. Pot sides	1	2 × 4-inch copper drain pipe
Saucer	1	12-inch clay saucer
Brazing rod	8 feet	⅛-inch brazing rod
Brazing rod	4 feet	¹⁄₁₆-inch brazing rod
Sealer	—	Clear silicone caulk
Finish	—	Clear varnish

Procedure:

1. Cut four pieces of construction grade fir for the support frame (A), according to the dimensions in the materials list.
2. Cut a half-lap in the four pieces (A) so that the ends extend 1 ⅜ inches past the half-lap. Assemble frame.
3. Rout a ¼-inch radius on all edges of the frame (A), or break the edges with a sanding block.
4. Drill a ⅛-inch hole through the center of each half-lap joint.
5. Bend a ¾-inch circle on one end of four pieces of ⅛ × 23-inch brazing rod.
6. Insert the four pieces through the holes in the corners of the frame. Pull the brazing rod ends together at the top and weld them together. Weld a ring on the top and bottom of the juncture of the four rods.
7. Cut one piece of pine ½ × 5 × 5 inches for the base (B) of the top pot.
8. Using a drill press and fly cutter, cut a groove, a 4-inch circle, ¼ inch deep and ¼

inch wide, in the base (B) to receive the copper drain pipe (C).

9. Rout a ⅛-inch radius on all of the edges of the base (B), or break the edges with a sanding block.
10. Lay out and drill a ¹⁄₁₆-inch hole in each corner of the base (B).
11. Bend a ½-inch circle on one end of each of four pieces of ¹⁄₁₆ × 9 ½-inch brazing rod.
12. Insert the four pieces of brazing rod through the holes in the corners of the base (B), and pull them together at the top and weld the pieces. Weld a hook of ¹⁄₁₆-inch brazing rod on top of this juncture.
13. Place a piece of copper drain pipe (C) in the groove in base (B) to form the pot.
14. Coat the entire bottom of the pot with silicone caulk to waterproof the pot.
15. Finish all wood surfaces with two coats of waterproof varnish.

might stack some lightweight volcanic lava rocks over a steel pipe with a one-inch (2.5 cm) diameter, then dig out small pockets for cacti and other succulents. Or make a strawberry or flower tower by placing a circular column of chicken wire or one inch by two inch (2.5 cm by 5 cm) welded wire over a planter. Pour a layer of charcoal into the base of the column, then add a layer of potting mix. Moisten the mix and plant a small plant through the wire. A long-handled tweezers is helpful for this procedure. Lightly tamp the mix around the plant. Add another layer of mix, moisten it, and give the column a quarter-turn. Plant another small plant a little higher than the first one. Repeat the procedures until the column is planted. Fill in the container around the base of the column with charcoal or potting mix. When it's time to water, use a syringe or bulb-type baster to direct water to the base of each plant.

BUILT-IN PLANTERS

With some creative planning, planters can be built into new homes at little additional expense. In rooms at ground level, they can be sunk down to floor level beneath large windows, forming indoor gardens. Even in older homes, planters can be designed as room dividers and wall units. Artificial lighting can easily solve the problem in otherwise dim locations, so that nearly any location in the home is a potentially suitable one for large groupings of plants.

A Built-In Planter: A permanent planter serves to divide the living room from the dining room in this home. A plant track in the ceiling allows baskets of trailing plants to be hung from above to create an airy green curtain. The planter is filled with bark chips, and individually potted plants are then sunk into the chips, for an attractive finished look. Light fixtures over the planter may be turned on as needed, although these plants enjoy unimpeded light pouring in from a south-facing, floor-to-ceiling window.

CHAPTER 5

Tools for Indoor Gardening

Some indoor gardeners delight in buying every gadget that makes its way to the marketplace. Others prefer to buy no special tools at all, getting by with items recycled from the home. Most gardeners, however, take the middle ground, equipping themselves only with some basic plant tools. In this chapter, we will attempt to evaluate a number of basic and not-so-basic indoor gardening tools.

TOOLS FOR PLANTING AND CULTIVATING

Greenhouse gardeners, and those with built-in indoor garden beds, need to prepare larger amounts of soil than container gardeners. Screens for sifting soil and compost will be helpful in preparing a fine-textured planting medium. A simple screen can be made easily from four pieces of wood nailed to a frame to which you staple hardware cloth. Large amounts of potting medium can be mixed in an old dishpan if you don't have a potting bench.

For direct-planting in flats, borders, or benches, a dibble or spotting board will be helpful. To make a spotting board, fasten pieces of tapered wooden dowels to a board that will fit inside the flats or benches to be planted, and attach a handle to the opposite side. Or you can puncture the board with evenly spaced nails. Plain old sticks or dowels of various widths also make perfectly functional dibbles to dig holes for planting seeds or seedlings.

For a handy cultivating tool for benches or beds, snip off the hook of a wire coat hanger and fit the straight end inside a wood or bamboo handle — a more ambitious cultivator can be fashioned by twisting together several hanger ends.

SOIL TESTING KITS

It is a good idea to test your potting mixtures before using them, especially if you are experimenting with different formulas. The soil of plants in small pots does not have to be tested, since those plants will be repotted every few years, but those in large pots and tubs will benefit from testing every year or so, to check on nutrient and pH levels.

You may send soil samples to your county extension office, or you may buy your own testing kits. They are available in many

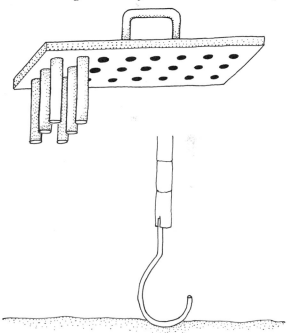

Tools for Planting and Cultivating: For evenly spaced holes of a uniform depth, try a homemade spotting board. It is easily constructed by attaching wooden dowels or nails to a piece of board. The hooked end of a coat hanger can be cut off and fitted inside a length of wood or bamboo for a handy cultivator.

Opposite, an assortment of helpful tools for indoor gardeners.

degrees of sophistication, the prices rising along with the sophistication. At the very least, your home testing kit will give some good indication of the levels of nitrogen, phosphorus, and potassium in the soil, as well as its pH level. County extension tests also will give the levels of some trace elements, and perhaps a reading of the organic matter content.

When you take a soil sample from a large tubbed specimen, be sure to get a fairly deep core sample for fair representation. If you top-dress the plant periodically, soil taken from the top of the pot will give misleading results.

BRUSHES AND SPONGES

A soft brush is needed to clean dust from hairy-leaved plants such as strawberry begonias *(Saxifraga stolonifera)* and African violets (*Saintpaulia* spp.), since misting can cause water spots on the foliage of such plants. Many brushes are offered in plant shops, but brushes of better quality may be found in art supply stores. Small sponges will be helpful in cleaning the foliage of large-leaved plants. A wire brush is useful for cleaning salt deposits from old containers.

WATERING DEVICES

A good watering can is essential to most indoor gardeners. It may be a decorative metal one or a lighter, less expensive plastic model. In either case, it should have a long spout that will allow you to distribute water into the center of a pot without getting too much on the foliage. The one-quart (946 ml) size is handy. Anything larger is tiring to lift as you water many plants, while a smaller can requires many trips between kitchen and plant rooms. It is a good idea to fill the can after you have finished watering, so that the water you use next time will be at room temperature and will have lost most of its chlorine. (Some gardeners maintain several jugs of water at all times, for the same reason.)

The 25- or 50-foot (7.5 or 15 m) plastic hoses made to be attached to the kitchen or bathroom faucet, featuring a release valve at the end, are handy if they are of good design and quality. With some models, however, the water is released at a very slow pace and the valve cannot be held down for long without tiring the hand, making this method more tiring and time consuming than the one using the old watering can. Be sure, also, that the faucet attachment will fit the faucet in your kitchen.

MISTERS AND SPRAYERS

Many indoor gardeners consider some type of mister/sprayer to be essential for optimum plant health, especially during the winter in northern areas, when humidity levels in centrally heated homes are low. Brass or porcelain misters, with thumb pumps, are often seen in department stores, gift shops, and mail order catalogs. They make attractive additions to the plant table or bookshelf. More practical, however, is the pint (473 ml) or quart (946 ml) plastic model, which holds more water and is operated by squeezing the pump. Thumb-pumping is a tiring business, if more than a half-dozen plants are involved. Regular misting, if done carefully, not only will help keep the foliage clean, but also can offer needed humidity to plants. Hairy-leaved plants do not respond well to misting.

MOISTURE METERS

A moisture meter is sometimes helpful if you are uncertain about how much water to give your plants. The beauty of the moisture meter is that it records moisture at the end of its probe, and you may insert the probe deeply into the pot. The soil on the surface might be dry, while lower levels are very wet. (If this is often the case, incidentally, you might have a drainage problem with that plant.)

Since most plants are likely to suffer from consistent overwatering, the greatest value of the moisture meter is in telling you when *not* to water plants. There are several kinds, one which indicates moisture by color, another with a dial that registers dry, moist, or wet. The models with the dial are generally more accurate. Moisture meters are rather tricky to use, so buy a good one and read the instruction booklet carefully, since the reading of one meter will often be different from that of another.

PRUNING TOOLS

A good, sharp knife is essential for pruning and taking cuttings. You can use an old kitchen knife, newly sharpened, or you may buy a special pruning knife. They are available in handy pocket models, featuring two blades. Whichever you choose, be sure that you keep the blade sharp and clean.

Some gardeners prefer to use the type of device that holds a single-edge razor blade, since the blade will be sharper than any knife, and it can be changed whenever it becomes dull. Should you choose this option, be sure to get the kind of holder designed for rug cutting, not the kind made for scraping paint from windows. The rug cutter is far handier to use in pruning.

Besides a knife, you will want a good pair of lightweight garden pruners, which may be found at any hardware store or garden center. Do not use the same pair for indoor and outdoor gardening, since there is always the danger of introducing outdoor diseases to your sheltered indoor plants.

Many indoor gardeners find that some more specialized tools such as floral scissors for trimming spent flowers, leaves, and stems, and nippers for pinching off delicate tips and small leaves also come in handy. Greenhouse gardeners may find a long-handled pruning tool indispensable for reaching across wide beds or benches.

THERMOMETERS

Every indoor gardener should have a few thermometers of good quality. Include one

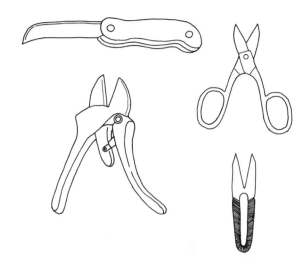

Tools for Pruning: There are a number of tools to choose from, all well suited for the task. Clockwise from upper left are a pruning knife, floral scissors, nippers, and garden pruners.

minimum/maximum thermometer, the kind that records the highest and lowest temperatures for any given period. By placing it among any group of plants for 24 hours, you can see at a glance whether those plants are staying within their preferred temperature range. Then you can reset the instrument and test another plant location. Thermometers are available which register on both the Centigrade and Fahrenheit scales.

HYGROMETERS

A hygrometer, the instrument that measures relative humidity in the air, is particularly valuable when you are growing tropical plants and other moisture lovers. The easiest kind to read is one which has a dial calibrated in percentages. Often, a hygrometer will be combined with a thermometer (and sometimes a barometer) in a common case, some of them very handsome for displaying. Again, however, do not let style be a substitute for quality.

Build Your Own Plant Carrier

Plant carriers are useful when you are required to move potted plants from one area to another, and they also come in handy for holding pots still when repotting.

This plant carrier was designed to hold eight flower pots. It provides holes to accept two pots each, of four different sizes.

Materials:

Item	Quantity	Description
A. Tray	1	$\frac{1}{2} \times 14\frac{1}{4} \times 28\frac{1}{4}$-inch exterior plywood
B. Ends	2	$\frac{3}{4} \times 5\frac{1}{2} \times 14\frac{1}{4}$-inch #2 pine
C. Tray support	1	$\frac{3}{4} \times 1\frac{1}{2} \times 27\frac{1}{2}$-inch #2 pine
Nails	—	4d finish nails
Glue	—	Waterproof glue
Paint	—	Exterior paint

Special Tools:

Saber saw
Router (optional)

1. Cut pieces A, B, and C to size according to the dimensions in the materials list.
2. Lay out and bore eight holes in tray (A) for the flower pots: two 3-inch; two 3 ½-inch; two 4-inch; and two 4 ½-inch.
3. Cut a dado ½ inch wide × ⅜ inch deep in the middle of the ends (B) to receive the plywood tray.
4. Lay out and drill two 1 ¼-inch holes in ends (B) and cut out the wood between the holes to form the handles of the plant carrier.
5. Lay out and cut a 1-inch radius on all four corners of the end pieces (B) with a saber saw.
6. Rout a ¼-inch radius on all edges of the end pieces (B), on the inside edges of the handle holes—and on the edges of the tray support (C)—or break these edges with a sanding block.
7. Assemble the carrier, using glue and 4d finish nails on all joints.
8. Finish by sanding all the surfaces.
9. Finish the carrier with two coats of paint.

PROPAGATION CASES

None but the most dedicated of indoor gardeners will want to invest in a sophisticated propagating case. For those who do wish to multiply their plants (as opposed to the majority who are trying to contain their numbers), the case is a valuable tool. There are a number of different models offered by various manufacturers, all of which have under-soil heating wires, controlled by a thermostat, and a clear plastic cover to hold in humidity and admit light. The larger ones have separate compartments for different groupings of plants, and some even have dual thermostats for the different compartments. They may be seen at some garden centers and department stores, and are often advertised in gardening magazines.

Less precise but less expensive propagating cases that will meet the needs of most gardeners can be constructed by following the directions for the plastic-enclosed flat in chapter 8, or the mist chamber in chapter 29.

MINIATURE TOOL SETS

These popular gift items, usually including a miniature rake, trowel, and perhaps one or two other tools, are certainly attractive, perched in their little wooden buckets, but their utility is limited. Most indoor gardeners simply use an old kitchen spoon to loosen the soil in large tubs, and a fork for smaller plants.

MISCELLANY

A 10-power magnifying glass is useful for spotting diseases and insects. When infestations do occur, you'll need to have on hand some cotton swabs for applying alcohol to pest colonies, and a bucket for mixing up a soapy solution to bathe affected plants.

Most gardeners will want to keep on hand some other odds and ends, such as soft yarn for tying up plants, green-colored bamboo stakes for supporting them, perhaps some attractive bark slabs for training a climbing philodendron or ivy, some trellises, driftwood for bromeliads, and labels for marking seedlings.

Both the ingenuity of gardeners in designing and building their own tools, and the plethora of gadgets that seem to appear in stores at each Christmas season, will provide indoor plant growers with all the equipment they can profitably use.

CHAPTER 6

Soils, Potting Mixtures, and Potting Techniques

The potting mixture you choose for each of your plants will be a key factor in that plant's future success. According to the mixture, plant roots will have room to grow and thrive, or they will be stunted and starved. Roots will receive the air they need, or will be suffocated by the lack of it; they will receive water in the proper amounts, or they will wither or rot from an insufficiency or excess of water. The nutrients in the potting mix will be made available to roots at a proper rate, or they will be withheld or delivered too quickly.

Thinking back once again to the wide disparity of our house plants' origins, we can appreciate that the potting needs of individual plants must differ, also. A begonia which thrived in the moist and humusy soil of a South American rain forest has potting needs quite different from those of the many cacti that are native to the semiarid regions of Mexico.

The subject of potting mixtures is one that divides plant experts sharply. Even for the same plant, there might be a dozen or more potting mixture recipes recommended by different experts. There are even some green thumbers who guard their potting mixture recipes jealously, much as a master chef guards his special sauce recipes. In this chapter, we will look at all the ingredients commonly used in potting mixtures, list some tested recipes for different mixtures, then consider various methods of potting and repotting.

It should be stressed that there is no single "right" mixture for any plant. Beginning with a mixture commonly recommended, however, most indoor gardeners, over years of experience, come upon their own favorite recipes. The one that seems to work best for one gardener might not be the best for another. It is an area for study and experimentation.

GARDEN SOIL

In their native environments, nearly all of our common indoor plants grew in soil, which provides the necessary water and mineral elements necessary to the life of the plant, as well as the living organisms necessary to the constant renewal of the soil itself.

In growing these plants indoors, then, it seems only logical to use soil as the potting medium. The matter is not quite so simple, however. The soil we obtain from our outdoor gardens is often dissimilar to that of the plants' native environments. In fact, most of our soils contain far less organic matter than those of tropical regions in which these plants once grew. In addition, pH levels might be different, and garden soils harbor some forms of life that can injure or kill plants. Because garden soils contain substances both beneficial and potentially harmful to house plants, indoor gardening experts are quite sharply divided regarding their use. Some use garden loam as a basic ingredient of the potting mixture, while others steer clear of it entirely, preferring soilless mixes. (Incidentally, throughout this book, the terms soil, soil mix, potting mixture, and potting medium are used interchangeably for the sake of convenience. All refer to any substance in which plants are potted.)

Since the subject of garden soil is a controversial and important one, it seems logical to consider it first in a list of potting mixture ingredients.

The soil in your garden is a living com-

Opposite, overgrown African violet badly in need of repotting.

munity, teeming with bacteria, fungi, and protozoa, many of which play important roles in breaking down raw organic matter into forms that plants can use as nutrients. There are insects and their larvae in soils, as well. Some are harmful to plants and others are highly beneficial. In the end, however, all leave their bodies to the soil, thus contributing to its store of organic matter.

A most important soil inhabitant is the earthworm, which acts as a highly efficient composting factory, consuming raw organic and mineral particles, mixing them together, and helping to break them down for plants to use. Soil that has passed through the bodies of earthworms registers levels of essential minerals several times higher than those of surrounding soil, the result of the earthworm's digestive process making these minerals available to plants. Some indoor gardeners put earthworms into the potting mixture, depending on them to perform the same services for house plants that they do for garden plants. Others say that earthworms disturb the roots of plants and should be excluded from pots. If you decide to experiment with earthworms in plant pots, be certain to choose one of the so-called "domesticated" species that can live in warm temperatures— either *Lumbricus rubellis* (the red worm or red wiggler) or *Eisenia foetida* (the brandling or banded worm). Nightcrawlers and common brown garden worms cannot live at room temperatures. Some food must occasionally be provided, as well, either a commercial earthworm mix or a sprinkling of cornmeal dug very shallowly into the soil surface. Last, earthworms must share with plants a common preference for a moist and humusy soil and a pH level near neutral. Earthworms cannot live in dry or highly acid soils.

Although life forms of all kinds are a critical component of soils, and their numbers are staggering (there may be more than a billion bacteria in a single gram of garden soil), together they account for a mere fraction of 1 percent of the total soil mass. The other ingredients, also important in nourishing plant life, include minerals, organic matter, water, air, and other gases. Water and air ordinarily fill the spaces between solid soil particles.

ORGANIC MATTER

Any once-living substance, plant or animal, constitutes organic matter. A good garden soil may contain as little as 1 or 2 percent organic matter. Virgin prairie soils or gardens that have been heavily composted may contain up to 10 percent. Peat or muck soils may contain 75 percent or more, although the nutrients in most of these soils are not in a form available to plants.

It is in the process of decay, made possible by the actions of earthworms and other invertebrates, and microorganisms, that mineral nutrients are released by organic matter and made available to plants. Organic matter, thus, acts as a storehouse for essential plant nutrients, releasing them slowly as plants are able to make use of them. The entire matter of plant nutrition and fertilizing will be taken up in chapter 7.

MINERALS

The mineral content of ordinary garden soil often accounts for about half of its total volume. Minerals come from the age-old crust of the earth itself, which through millions of years has been broken, crushed, and ground through the effects of underground disturbances and atmospheric weathering. The most important minerals to plant nutrition are phosphorus and potassium. Others, needed in lesser amounts, include aluminum, calcium, iron, magnesium, manganese, sulfur, boron, copper, zinc, and titanium; also cobalt, lithium, nickel, and molybdenum.

Despite the abundance of minerals in soil, many plants will starve if these elements are not made available to roots in soluble form. It is the function of earthworms and microorganisms to break down minerals, making them available to plants.

WATER

Water acts as the transportation system for soil minerals, carrying nutrients in solution from the soil to the plant's roots, where they are pulled up the stem and into every leaf, there to be used in the plant's food manufacturing process. The water is then transpired through the leaves' stomata into the air. Water is also necessary for the maintenance of earthworms and microorganisms. It accounts for perhaps 25 percent of soil volume, although the actual percentage varies greatly, depending on the amount of rainfall and the water-holding capacity of the particular soil. Water accumulates in the spaces between soil particles, and it adheres to the particles themselves. When water drains from a soil, it is replaced by air.

AIR

About 25 percent of the soil's volume is composed of air, although again the actual amount of air present at any given time depends on the amount of space available for it between soil particles, and the amount of water in the soil at that time. Large amounts of air will be forced from soil during a heavy rain. If you inspect a puddled area immediately after a heavy rain, you will see bubbles forming, just as you will when you water a dry plant. These bubbles indicate that air in the soil is being replaced by water, and it willl be reintroduced only as the water drains away or evaporates. Since air is just as important as water to soil and plant health, it is important that your treatment of plants allows for sufficient amounts of both, and an excess of neither.

A lack of air, either in overwatered soil or in those of poor texture, will impede the work of microorganisms, cause plant roots to suffocate and die, lead to a compact and dense soil, and prevent the oxidation of minerals, mak-ing them unavailable for plant use. You may insure an adequate supply of air for your house plants by giving them a good potting mixture and by watering properly.

SOIL TEXTURE AND STRUCTURE

Just as important as the chemical makeup of soil is its physical makeup, which is evaluated in terms of texture and structure. Soil texture refers to the proportional amounts of various size particles found in its composition. The largest particles are gravel, followed in descending order of size by sand, silt, and clay. Depending on the percentages of all these particles, a soil is often referred to (in ordinary gardening terms) as sand, loam, or clay. Soil scientists, of course, have hundreds of classification terms to describe soils of various textures.

Closely related to texture is soil structure, or crumb structure, which refers to its ability to form granules or aggregates. Granules or aggregates are small groups of sand, silt, and clay that adhere together. This grouping of particles is necessary to good garden soil, since it allows adequate spaces for air and water to enter. A sandy soil cannot form good aggregates because its particles are too coarse. Sandy soil cannot hold water for long, and is a poor storehouse for mineral elements because of its lack of organic matter and soil life. A heavy clay, on the other hand, cannot form good aggregates because it lacks larger particles. Heavy clays exclude both air and water, being too compact to allow either. The good middle ground is loam, which contains good proportions of sand, silt, and clay, together forming aggregates for air and water retention.

Plant roots grow in the spaces between soil aggregates, where the tiny root hairs can absorb both air and water to send up the vascular system to the stems and leaves. Realizing this, you can readily understand the importance of providing all indoor plants with a potting mixture of good structure.

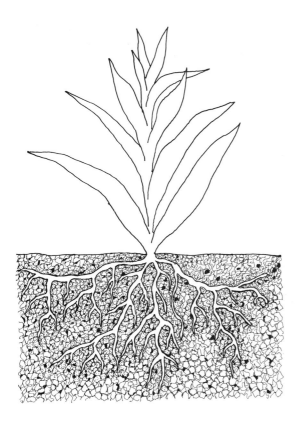

How Plant Roots Grow: The roots of your house plants don't actually grow in the soil; rather, they grow in the spaces between soil particles where their root hairs can reach out and find air and water.

Good garden loam may be used as a primary ingredient of all potting mixtures. Not only does it contain particles of different sizes to form good structure and texture, but it contains living substances (fungi and bacteria) capable of breaking down raw organic matter and thus providing a steady supply of nutrients for house plants. All commercial substitutes for garden soil—including sterilized potting soil, sterilized compost, peat moss, and sphagnum moss—are nonliving substances devoid of beneficial microorganisms. In a sterile potting environment, plants must receive fertilizer in soluble, available form. Further, the structure and texture

of such mixtures will never improve, but will steadily become worse, requiring more frequent repotting.

Select the best of garden loam for house plant use—the richest and most friable your garden has to offer. If you have no outdoor garden, do your best to beg or buy some from an organic gardening friend, or ask at garden centers or plant shops until you find good, unsterilized loam. Never gather soil from a farm field, unless you know it has been managed organically for at least several years. The herbicide residues in chemically treated soil can be detrimental to house plants.

Screen the soil roughly in order to remove stones and any plant debris. Never pulverize it finely, because in so doing you will destroy much of its structure. Return any earthworms you find to the outdoor garden.

Before you store the garden loam in plastic bags or other containers for future use, you should pasteurize it to kill nematodes, insects and their larvae, and other potentially harmful living organisms. Note that pasteurization is not the same as sterilization, which kills all living organisms.

PASTEURIZING SOIL

There are several convenient ways to pasteurize soil for indoor gardening. Soil can be spread several inches (approximately 5 cm) thick in flats or pans, covered tightly with foil or placed in a turkey roasting bag pierced in two places and tied at the end, and baked in the oven. You should be sure the soil is moist but not soggy, since water together with the heat helps to kill the organisms. A meat thermometer inserted through the foil or plastic into the middle of the soil (but not touching the container) will be very helpful. Set the oven at a very low temperature. Most ovens have a setting for 200°F (93°C) and some for low. Use low if you can and 200°F (93°C) if you must. Watch the thermometer and start timing when it reaches 150°F (65°C). Keep the temperature between 150° and 180°F

(65° and 82°C) for 30 minutes. If the temperature exceeds 180°F (82°C), turn the oven off.

This is the most reliable method, but you may be offended by the smell of the baking soil—it is not exactly pleasant, but you may grow to tolerate it. Other methods which may not smell as bad are less effective and certainly more messy. For example, you can pour boiling water over a flat of soil (or other container which has drainage) until the thermometer in the center reaches 180°F (82°C). Then cover the flat tightly with foil for at least 30 minutes. You might also try improvising methods such as steaming soil in a colander or pots. Just be sure to mind your thermometer and don't let the temperature get too high.

COMMERCIAL POTTING SOILS

Bagged preparations labeled as "potting soil" can be good for plants, or they can be fatal. Studies conducted by the Pennsylvania State University soil testing laboratory (reported in *Popular Gardening Indoors*, Dec. 1977–Jan. 1978, p. 33) revealed that, of 20 commercial brands of potting soil tested, 4 were capable of injuring or killing house plants.

How can this be so? The culprit seems to be the chemical fertilizer that some manufacturers add to potting soils. Apparently the company hopes that the fertilizer will give newly potted plants a burst of growth, thus impressing the buyer and causing him to become devoted to that particular brand. Often, however, the soluble salts in these mixes are far too strong for the young roots of newly potted plants—particularly those that have been rooted in water and have not yet developed root hairs to absorb minerals.

The situation is complicated when organic constituents in the mixture offer further nutrients. These organically derived nutrients are made available only at a rate consistent with the activity of microorganisms. In a plastic bag, exposed to high heat, microorganisms will multiply at a rapid rate and will release nutrients at a similar rate in doing so. If the mixture is sterile, microorganisms may be introduced into the potted mixture at a later date. The result in either case will be a double dose of mineral salts which many plants cannot handle. If eager plant owners decide to add a dose of fertilizer on their own, "to get the plant off to a good start," fatality is virtually assured. Roots will burn and die, and the plant will die.

Commercial potting soils can injure plants in still another way. In the mixing process, the manufacturer often strives for a product of fine and even texture, believing—usually correctly—that customers will be attracted to a soil with no bumps, no clots, no fragments of twigs or plant roots. In the process of such fine mixing, soil structure is destroyed completely. Were the packaged soil to be used alone (as many buyers are led to believe it should), it would offer a compact and dense environment in which roots could not find spaces to obtain air or water. Again, roots would suffocate and die, or rot from insufficient soil drainage.

Not all commercial potting soils are harmful, of course. But you must inspect any soil before using it. If it crumbles as you work it around in your hand, it probably has good structure. If it turns to powder when dry, the structure probably has been destroyed. It is probably not wise to use such soil, even if you add coarse sand, perlite, or vermiculite, which are the ingredients usually recommended to improve structure. Also read the label carefully, to see whether chemical fertilizers have been added, and to see the sources from which the soil was prepared. The label is not an infallible guide, since labeling laws vary from state to state, but it might prove helpful. After considering all the pros and cons, you might decide to use garden loam that you can trust. The little work which is involved in its preparation will be repaid in dollar savings and good plant health.

Potting Ingredients: The materials shown here contribute to the texture and nutrient value of potting mixes. Displayed from left to right, top row, are: charcoal, ground limestone, compost; middle row: sphagnum moss, leaf mold, vermiculite; bottom row: perlite, gravel, wood ashes.

OTHER POTTING INGREDIENTS

BONE MEAL

A good source of phosphorus and nitrogen, bone meal is a common ingredient of potting mixtures. Since it is a natural product, it offers a long-term source of nutrients with no danger of burning roots. Be sure to purchase sterilized or steamed bone meal, and not the raw form. Steamed bone meal is produced from green (fresh) bones, with all the fat content removed. The steaming process lowers the nitrogen content slightly, but increases the percentage of phosphorus. Steamed bone meal is also ground more finely than the raw form, making it more easily and quickly available to plants.

CHARCOAL

Every indoor gardener should maintain a small supply of charcoal, which is often used to help provide drainage, sweeten soils, and absorb impurities. It is added to pebble trays to prevent the standing water from becoming foul, and it is added to bottles in which plants are grown or rooted in water. It is also a good idea to add a little charcoal with the gravel you use to line pots. A layer of charcoal added to the terrarium, just above the gravel layer and below the potting mixture, can extend the life of the potting mixture.

Be sure to buy hardwood charcoal meant for plant use, and never barbeque briquettes, which often contain binders that can injure plants. You also may chip your own charcoal supply from partially burned hardwood in your fireplace.

COMPOST

Compost is a mixture of different organic materials, air, and water, with the possible addition of soil and minerals, which together have advanced so far in the process of decomposition as to be a valuable addition to soil for the growing of plants.

Nearly all organic gardeners use compost in potting mixtures, since it combines the advantages of water retention, structure-building characteristics, and a wide-ranging source of nutrients. Its versatility makes it preferable to both peat moss and leaf mold (although either might be recommended for special plant-growing purposes).

Although nearly all of us believe in the value of compost, few appreciate fully all the services it performs for our plants, both indoors and outdoors. Here are some of them:

—Compost builds soil structure, correcting both sandy and heavy clay soils by building aggregates and improving crumb structure.

—Compost absorbs water readily, even when dry (unlike peat moss). It can hold twice its weight in water, yet create air spaces for root health.

—Carefully blended compost is a good source of all the nutrients needed for plant health. Not only the big three—nitrogen, phosphorus, and potassium—are found in compost, but all the trace minerals, as well.

—Compost acts to neutralize soil toxins, particularly heavy metals that are harmful to plants (and humans) at certain levels of concentration. Actively decomposing organic materials produce acids which lock up iron, aluminum, and other metals in stable complexes, thus rendering them harmless to plants.

—Compost alters the pH level of the soil, making acid soils less acid and alkaline soils less alkaline. Compost is the great neutralizer, bringing all soils toward the center of the pH scale where most plants grow best.

—The humic acids in decaying compost stimulate the phenolase oxidative action and improve oxygen assimilation of plants. The result is faster growth of plants, particularly in their early stages. Thus, compost stimulates plant growth as no other form of fertilizer can.

There are many ways to make compost—in bins, boxes, plastic bags, and garbage cans; in strips, sheets, or trenches; in 14 months or 14 days. Directions for making compost for house plants can be found in chapter 7.

GRAVEL

The gravel used to line the bottom of pots should be clean, free from salt and chemical contaminants, from $\frac{1}{4}$ to $\frac{1}{2}$ inch (6 to 13 mm) in size, and irregular in shape so that it offers adequate spaces for water drainage. Broken clay pots are often substituted for gravel. If the broken pots formerly held diseased plants, be sure to boil the fragments to remove any traces of disease before using them. It is better to discard the pots which held diseased plants, and use other broken pots for crocking. The gravel found in packages at plant shops and garden centers is intended for decorative use and is expensive. For pot use, gather your own or pick up 50 pounds (22.5 kg) or so at a building supply center, when you buy your sand.

LEAF MOLD

Technically, leaf mold is another form of peat, since it is the partially decayed remains of plant material. In practice, it is referred to simply as leaf mold. It is also a form of compost, and the two are often used interchangeably in potting mixtures. Leaf mold has less water-retention capacity than peat moss has, but it is richer in nutrients, offering many trace elements that trees pull up from deep within the earth.

Leaf mold can seldom be purchased commercially, and so other sources must be found. Gardeners with outdoor space can make their own, very easily. In autumn, the fallen leaves are placed in any kind of a topless wire mesh or snow-fence enclosure, then tamped down and left to decompose. The process will take several years, although it can be hastened considerably if the leaves are first finely shredded, and material rich in nitrogen (such as chicken manure) is mixed into the pile. A mound of leaves left for several years to decompose will generate no heat—it is only with the addition of nitrogen that you will find your pile warming up.

If leaf mold is needed immediately, it can be gathered from the floor of any wooded area (after you have checked regulations and obtained the needed permission). In addition, most communities today do not incinerate the leaves they gather from curbs, but store them in huge piles where they break down slowly. Call your municipality's parks or street sanitation department to see whether you may gather up several bushels for home use. The good leaf mold will be at the bottom of the heap and toward the center, so some vigorous digging might be required. Any extra leaf mold that you don't use can be stored in a plastic bag until it is needed.

Leaf mold has many of the benefits of both peat moss and compost. It helps to build good structure in the potting mix and it retains water well. Leaf mold should be screened before using to remove pebbles, twigs, and other debris. You don't want to reduce it to very fine particles, though, because it is more effective as a soil conditioner when the particles are coarse.

All leaves are acid in nature, except for those of white ash, which are nearly neutral. The most highly acid leaves are those from conifers, oaks, and maples (all below 5.0 on the pH scale). Balsam fir, American beech, and hemlock range from 5.0 to 5.5. When leaf mold is used in a soil mix, some lime is usually added to neutralize the acidity.

LIME

Limestone (calcium carbonate) is a good source of calcium, a necessary element in plant nutrition. It is used in potting mixtures not for this nutrient, however, but as a neutralizer, bringing acid mixtures toward the neutral range on the pH scale. Lime helps to improve soil structure, since it causes clay soils to form aggregates, and it releases some of the phosphorus and potash from insoluble compounds, making them available for absorption by roots.

When buying lime for use in potting mixtures, be sure to get ground limestone or dolomitic limestone, and not quicklime, slaked lime, or hydrate of lime, all of which can kill soil life and cause root burn. Dolomitic limestone, made from the mineral rock dolomite, is preferred over other forms since it also contains the trace mineral magnesium.

The rate at which limestone can be used by plants depends on the size of its particles. Larger particles will require a longer time to be broken down for plant use, while very fine particles can be used immediately, as needed by plants. A mixture of particle sizes from very fine to somewhat coarse will provide for both immediate and long-range needs. For small and medium size indoor plants, however, it is better to use finely ground limestone. Since most indoor plants are repotted at least every few years, there is little need to provide for long-term usage. For large plants in tubs, which might never be repotted, some of the particles should be of the larger size.

PEAT MOSS

Peat is a broad and loosely applied term referring to the partially or entirely decomposed remains of plants. Peat moss is the peat obtained from peat bogs, usually containing the remains of plants of the genus *Sphagnum*. Thus, the term peat moss and sphagnum peat moss are interchangeable, technically, although the product you buy under the label "peat moss" is likely to be a fibrous reed or sedge peat. (Also, sphagnum peat is not the same as the live sphagnum moss that is used on top of the soil in terraria and dish gardens.) Confusing? Yes, because the various terms relating to peat have never been standardized in the plant world. Shredded sphagnum moss is far preferable to reed or sedge peat, which is dark brown and heavy. Sphagnum moss is sometimes labeled "Canadian peat moss" (it can also come from Germany or Ireland), while reed or sedge peat is often labeled "Michigan peat moss." But both kinds may come from bogs in New York or Wisconsin. Since labeling becomes more confusing as you delve more deeply into the subject, remember only that the best kinds for house plant use are shredded sphagnum moss and Canadian peat moss.

Peat bogs are ancient. It has been estimated that it takes nature 100 to 800 years to lay down a single foot (30 cm) of bog, and yet some bogs in the United States are 50 or more feet (15 m) deep. With the passing of each season, the sphagnum moss or the reeds and sedges die back to the ground, and their remains add to the store of peat below. As the bog grows older, the materials below become more and more compressed. At the very bottom of the bog, the oldest and most compressed materials are called sedimentary peat. It is worthless as an ingredient in potting soils.

The material in the middle portion of the bog is woody peat. It is formed from the remains of trees, shrubs, and undergrowth from the forest floor or swamp. Woody peat is not a good addition to house plant mixes.

The upper layer of bogs contains the sphagnum moss, or the reed and sedge peat, depending on the kind of plants grown there. Both are good additions to soil mixes, although, as noted, sphagnum moss is the better of the two. Sphagnum moss is light brown in color, while all other bog peats are dark brown to black.

Peat moss contains almost no plant nutrients. The little nitrogen it possesses is released so slowly to plants that it cannot be counted upon. In the culture of house plants, this lack of nutrients is often seen as an advantage, since it gives the grower more control over the nutrients which he or she introduces to the plants. More plants, after all, are injured by overfertilization than by underfertilization. The chief benefit of peat moss, rather, is as a soil conditioner. Since it can hold up to 15 times its dry weight in water, it is valued as an addition to lighter soils, to improve the nutrient retention capacity. It also can be combined with heavier soils to form aggregates for improved soil structure. Peat moss is often used in place of leaf mold or compost in potting mixtures, since all share certain characteristics.

The disadvantage of peat moss is that, once dry, it is very difficult to moisten again. For this reason, no potting mixture recipe calls for a very high percentage of it. Peat moss is also acidic in nature. Acid-loving plants, like azaleas, benefit from the addition of peat moss to the potting mix. However, a high percentage of peat moss in the mix may be too much of a good thing; depending on the pH level of other ingredients used, the resulting mixture may be too acid for plant health.

One caution to keep in mind when working with sphagnum peat is that it sometimes harbors a fungus, *Sporothrix schenckii*, which can cause inflammation or illness when its spores become embedded under the skin through a cut or scratch. The fungus can stay viable for several years, and begins to grow and produce spores in warm, moist conditions. To minimize any risk of exposure to the fungus, store sphagnum in a cool, dry place, always wear gloves when working with the peat, and be sure to keep work areas clean.

PERLITE

Perlite is volcanic rock that has been expanded by exposure to very high temperatures. It serves the same purpose as sand, and can be used as a substitute if builder's sand cannot be found. Perlite is slightly alkaline, which presents no problem when acid materials (leaf mold, peat moss, garden loam) are used in the potting mixture. It is also very light—so light, in fact, that over a period of time the perlite tends to work its way upward in the potting mixture, eventually concentrating at the top of the soil layer. When this happens, its structure-building benefits are lost to the lower levels. Like sand, perlite absorbs and holds little moisture. Unlike sand, perlite is expensive. It is available at garden centers and in plant shops.

SAND

Every indoor gardener should have on hand a large bucket of coarse, sharp, builder's sand. Do not use seashore residues. Do not use sand from river beds, which also will be rounded. When mixed with other potting ingredients, builder's sand will create good air and water spaces and help to build good structure, giving root hairs plenty of spaces to grow and feed. Builder's sand can be purchased inexpensively at building supply centers and at some garden centers and hardware stores.

VERMICULITE

This product, which is the mineral mica, expanded by heat, is similar in weight to per-

lite. Its particles are generally finer, however, and whereas perlite is white, vermiculite has a brown-gold color. Vermiculite can absorb and hold moisture, while perlite cannot. For this reason, the two are not interchangeable in the potting recipe, as is often supposed. Although vermiculite offers the dual advantages of holding moisture and adding to structure, it is really not very efficient at either. Peat moss is better for holding moisture, and sand is far better for building structure.

Because vermiculite is so light in weight, however, it is very desirable for soilless media and locations where weight is a problem (such as in large hanging pots).

WOOD ASHES

The ashes from your fireplace should never be thrown away. They are a valuable source of potash for both the indoor and outdoor gardens. Used in a mixture with compost and bone meal, they provide a balanced fertilizer for all house plants. The same cannot be said for coal ashes, which are likely to harm plants because of their potentially dangerous levels of sulfur and iron.

POTTING MIXTURE RECIPES

Recipes for potting mixtures may be as simple or complex as you wish. Many successful gardeners swear by this all-purpose mixture:

> 2 parts garden loam
>
> 1 part compost or leaf mold
>
> 1 part sharp sand or perlite
>
>> Add ½ cup (118 ml) of bone meal per peck (8.8 l) of above mix, or 1 tablespoon (15 ml) per quart (1.1 l).

Many others prefer this basic recipe:

> 1 part garden loam
>
> 1 part sand

1 part peat moss or leaf mold

    Add bone meal as for above.

Either mix will probably serve most of the plants you grow. There are certain groups of plants, however, that do better in special mixes. Desert cacti and succulents, for example, don't need as many nutrients in their soil, but do require a rapidly draining mix to forestall rotting. Epiphytic plants (tree crotch dwellers, which include various bromeliads, ferns, and orchids) need a light, porous mix that won't bind their roots and which retains water. Humus-loving plants such as caladiums, *Fittonia* species, prayer plants, and baby's tears require a heavy, nutrient-rich soil that absorbs and holds water well.

Either all-purpose mixture offers ample amounts of all the essential nutrients (assuming that your garden loam and compost are of a fairly good quality) and enough sand to assure good structure and drainage. A potting mix need be no more complicated than this, although some experts have developed and refined their recipes to contain a dozen or more ingredients. Others have developed special recipes for individual plants, including begonias, dieffenbachias, English ivy, *Ficus* species, palms, and philodendrons.

It is unnecessary to specialize to this degree. Here, however, are some special mixtures for special groups of plants that truly will do better in something other than an all-purpose mixture. More specific soil mixes for plant families such as orchids and gesneriads can be found in the appropriate chapters of this book. Soil requirements for individual plants are listed in the Encyclopedia section.

For humus-loving plants:

1 part garden loam

2 parts compost or leaf mold

1 part sharp sand or perlite

    Add ½ cup (118 ml) of bone meal per peck (8.8 l) of above mix, or

1 tablespoon (15 ml) per quart (1.1 l).

For desert-living cacti and other succulents (xerophytes):

1 part garden loam

1 part compost or leaf mold

1 part sharp sand or perlite

½ part crushed clay pot, brick, or small pebbles (approximately pea size)

    Add 1 cup (236 ml) bone meal and 1 cup (236 ml) ground limestone per bushel (35.2 l) of above mix, or 1 tablespoon (15 ml) of each to 2 quarts (2.2 l).

For epiphytes:

1 part garden loam

2 parts leaf mold, peat moss, osmunda fiber, or shredded fir bark

1 part sharp sand or perlite

½ part crushed clay pot, brick, or crushed gravel (approximately pea size)

    Add 1 cup (236 ml) bone meal per bushel (35.2 l) of above mix, or 1 tablespoon (15 ml) per 2 quarts (2.2 l).

Naturally, if your garden soil is sandy, the amount of sand added to the recipe should be reduced. Heavy soils will require somewhat more sand, although it is not wise to use heavy clay in the potting mixture, since it is difficult to mix with other materials.

SOILLESS MIXES

It was not until early in the 1950s that soilless mixes began to achieve popularity among house plant growers. Today, probably more than half of all indoor plants are grown without garden soil. Such mixes differ from soil-based blends in several ways.

For one thing, since these materials are mostly sterile at first use, they lack the many beneficial soil microorganisms that can convert organic nitrogen into the nitrate form readily taken up by plants. This means such mixes must first have immediately available nitrate provided in a starter solution. Another difference between soil and soilless blends is that the clay particles in soil hold nutrients in storage, releasing them gradually, while peat releases the nutrients it has absorbed all at once. The effect of this is that a wider range of plant foods must be added more often to soilless media. On the other hand, this very characteristic gives the indoor gardener greater and more immediate control over plant growth. Nearly all suppliers and plant shops prefer soilless mixes because of the consistent nature of their ingredients (garden soil, of course, is widely variable in character).

Today, there are special soilless mixes designed for special plants and plant groups, including African violets, orchids, azaleas and other acid-lovers, bromeliads, and even foliage plants. Some are intended for starting seedlings.

If you put together your own soilless mix instead of buying the prepackaged kind, you can save some money. Here is a recipe for one popular soilless blend:

> 3 parts peat
>
> 1 part coarse sand, perlite, or
>   vermiculite
>
>> Add 6 ounces (168 g) of ground
>> limestone per bushel (35.2 l) of
>> the above mix, to neutralize some
>> of the acidity of the peat.

PACKAGED POTTING MEDIA

Potting mixes (sometimes called "planter's mixes") are available in a wide variety of commercial brands, usually packaged in plastic bags containing from 1 to 40 pounds (0.45 to 18 kg). Sometimes the ingredients are listed on the label, sometimes not. Ironically, the character of commercial mixes—even when comparing different brands recommended for the same plant—is even more variable than that of garden soils. Dedicated and experienced organic gardeners know the nature of their garden soil, but will tend to mistrust a packaged mix, unless they've had success with it in the past.

Some packaged mixes are soilless, and contain nothing but peat and sand. This is, of course, a sterile mixture, offering no nutrients. Others contain a variety of ingredients, including leaf mold, charcoal, vermiculite, perlite, chemical fertilizers, and fine gravel. These mixes are sterilized to kill all soil organisms, meaning that, unless living soil or compost is added, the plants growing in the mix will have to be fed nutrients in soluble form. Plants growing in a sterile medium require more frequent fertilizing than those grown in a mixture containing topsoil and/or compost. Although the quick-acting chemical fertilizer in a prepackaged mix will give plants a "quick fix" and cause an initial growth spurt, the plants will be let down when the fertilizer has been depleted, and may receive root burn if the soil becomes dry or if they become dormant.

Organic gardeners who have a good source of both garden loam and compost usually prefer to mix up their own potting media. If garden loam is unavailable, a good packaged topsoil may be substituted. In the absence of compost, substitute packaged, composted sheep or cow manure. Both are available at garden centers, and sometimes at plant shops, at costs far below those of the packaged mixes.

A good potting mixture will offer an ample supply of all essential nutrients to support the plant for about six months. It should also be of an ideal texture, free of large stones and plant debris, but containing enough sand to provide good drainage and structure. Last, the pH of the mixture should be slightly acid for most plants, and moderately acid for azaleas and other plants requiring more than normal acidity.

ACIDITY/ALKALINITY

The pH scale, which runs from 0 to 14, reflects the level of acidity or alkalinity of any solution. Numbers at the lower end are in the acid range, while the higher numbers mean that the substance is alkaline in nature. Neutral solutions, neither acid nor alkaline, register 7 on the scale.

Each plant has its own pH preference, as well as maximum and minimum ranges beyond which it will not survive. Fortunately, nearly all house plants like a slightly acid soil, in the 6.5 to 6.9 range. No common house plants like an alkaline soil, while just a few— azaleas, chrysanthemums, citrus fruits, camellias, and gardenias—prefer a soil slightly more acidic, in the 6.2 to 6.6 range (except for *Gardenia jasminoides*, which prefers 4.5 to 5.0). Plants subjected to an overly alkaline soil will lose leaf color and produce stunted roots. Those exposed to an overly acid soil will respond by wilting and dropping leaves.

The gardener who mixes his own potting soils should consider pH, even though it is unlikely to cause a problem. Garden loams are naturally acid in most parts of the United States, but are alkaline in large areas of the Southwest. Unless gardeners in these areas have corrected their garden soils for the growing of outdoor flowers and vegetables, proper precautions should be taken.

Acid potting materials include humus, peat moss, and leaf mold, in addition to most topsoils. Alkaline materials include perlite, limestone, and eggshells (which some house plant growers crush and add to potting mixtures). The potting mixture recipes listed earlier in this chapter are well balanced, offering the proper pH level—slightly acid—for nearly all house plants. Should you have any

doubts about your own mixture, however, you should buy and use a pH-testing kit, available at most garden centers for a few dollars.

POTTING AND REPOTTING

There are two times when a plant should be repotted—when you have just brought it home from the plant shop and you suspect that it has been potted in shipping soil, and when it has outgrown its old pot, becoming potbound. In either case, repotting is a simple pleasant activity for a weekend in spring, when working with plants is a true pleasure.

Spring is, in fact, the ideal time to repot plants, since their roots are growing actively at this time and they will be able to overcome shock in a relatively short time. Each spring, all plants should be checked to see whether they have become potbound. Take each pot and gently turn it upside down, holding it in one hand with your middle and ring fingers straddling the main stem of the plant. Tap the pot rim against the edge of a table several times, and the entire soil ball should separate itself from the pot with ease. If it does not, it might be too wet; wait for few days and try again, or run a knitting needle around the edges of the soil line to loosen the soil ball.

After you have separated the two, examine the soil ball carefully. If the roots are twisting around the edges of the soil in a tangled mass, or if they are trailing out of the drainage hole, you may assume that they need more room to grow. If not repotted, the plant will eventually suffer because its root mass has grown too large to derive sufficient amounts of both water and nutrients from the surrounding soil. The plant will become stunted, and older leaves may lose their color and drop.

The question at this point is whether you wish to encourage the plant to grow larger, or prefer to hold it to its present size.

The Proper Way to Pot: This cross section reveals the layer of drainage material spread in the bottom of the pot, as well as the sequence of soil additions. Before the plant is set in the pot, a layer of potting mix is spread over the gravel. Once the soil ball is set on top of this layer, more potting mix is added around the sides and is gently tamped down. Keep in mind that the top of the soil ball should be at the same height in relation to the rim as it was in its former pot.

If you want to encourage growth, then find a pot which is one size larger. (Do not jump sizes, since most plants respond poorly when given a pot too large for immediate needs.) If you want to contain the plant's size, then prune both the roots and topgrowth, using the methods described in chapter 3.

POTTING ON

The process of repotting a plant in a larger container, called "potting on" by the British, should be planned in advance, since the plant should be watered three to four days prior to being repotted. Soak the new pot in water for 24 hours before using it, so that it will become saturated and not draw too much water from

the soil. If it has previously contained a diseased plant, scrub it thoroughly and boil it beforehand. (Do not boil plastic pots, of course.)

Use a potting mixture that is recommended for the particular plant. Unless the present mixture is diseased or otherwise deficient, it will not be replaced but simply augmented; the new potting mix is lightly packed around the old.

Line the bottom of the new pot with a shallow layer of gravel or broken crockery, along with a little charcoal, to provide for good drainage. Some plant experts now advise against doing this, since a piece of gravel could block the drainage hole, restricting drainage. If you are careful in the arrangement of the gravel, however, this will probably not cause problems. Placing a piece of broken pot—concave side down—over the hole will also do the trick. (If you do experience problems with poor drainage and waterlogged soil, try the procedure described in An Alternative Potting Method.)

Next, add a layer of potting mixture on top of the gravel, remove the soil ball from the old pot, and place it on top of this layer, centering it carefully. The top of the soil ball should be at the same height, in relation to the pot rim, that it was in an old pot. It may be placed very slightly lower, especially if there was too little room for top-watering in the old pot. If you see that the root ball is situated too low in the new pot, however, remove it and add more potting mixture until it rests at the proper height when pressed down gently.

Then, slowly work more potting mixture around the sides of the new pot, tamping it down lightly with your fingers (some people use a cork attached to a knitting needle) until its level matches that of the old soil ball.

Some people, after they have added the bottom layer of potting mix, set the old pot on top of it, being sure that both rims are equal in height, then work more potting mix between the two pots. The old pot is then

An Alternative Potting Method

Many root diseases are fostered by overwatering or poor drainage. Dr. Robert Raabe, a plant pathologist at the University of California at Berkeley, maintains that proper drainage is of the utmost importance for healthy roots. He warns all who will listen *not* to follow the frequently repeated advice to put a piece of crockery over the hole at the bottom of the pot. Worse yet, he says, is the practice of putting a layer of pebbles or crockery in the bottom of the pot.

In Dr. Raabe's experience, covering the drainage hole with a piece of crockery can impede drainage. Putting a layer of pebbles or crockery across the bottom creates large air pockets there which will entirely fill with water before any excess will drain from the pot. Thus, water is more likely to stand in the pot with such a crockery layer, and root rot may be promoted.

Dr. Raabe recommends the following procedures to promote good drainage:

1. Make sure the soil mix has enough sand (one-third of the mixture is a good proportion for many plants).

2. Press the soil mix down in the bottom of the pot, packing it firmly over the open hole so there are no extra spaces.

3. Water from the top, allowing any excess to drain completely out of the pot and then emptying the saucer.

gently twisted out and the soil ball takes its place. It should fit nicely, with just a little more tamping around the edges, and it should be centered well, too.

TOP-DRESSING

Plants growing in large tubs and containers cannot be repotted using the method described above, for obvious reasons. Although the job can be done with help from a friend or two, these plants are sometimes not repotted at all, but are top-dressed instead. The process involves no more than removing the top several inches of potting mixture (being careful not to injure roots) and replacing it with fresh mixture. The nutrients in the new soil will gradually wash down to the roots, providing a long-lasting source of minerals. Some gardeners top-dress large plants annually, while others do it no more than every two or three years.

After a plant has been repotted, or even top-dressed, it may exhibit some form of shock, although this should be minor and short lived. To aid the plant at this time, water it, drain it thoroughly, then keep it out of strong light for several days. After about a week, it may be returned to its original location. It will require watering less frequently than it did before, since there will be more soil to hold moisture, and it will probably not need fertilizer for six months, assuming that nutrient-rich soil and compost were used in the new potting mix.

CHAPTER 7

Plant Foods

In chapter 1, we saw how plant leaves manufacture food (sugar), combining carbon dioxide from the air and water from the roots, in the process known as photosynthesis. This is the major food-building process of the plant, but it is not the only one. The plant then uses these simple sugars to form starch, cellulose, or lignin—all carbohydrates.

Cellulose forms the cell walls of most plants, while lignin is the woody material of plants. Starch is a form of stored food that can be reconverted into sugar for the plant's energy needs. The tubers of plants, for example, are storage structures and are composed of nearly 100 percent starch.

Plants also build proteins, which are a constituent of protoplasm, the basic living substance of all cells, both plant and animal. Certain chemical elements are needed in the protein manufacturing process, including nitrogen, phosphorus, and potassium, which are needed in major amounts, and a series of other elements needed in lesser amounts—calcium, magnesium, sulfur, iron, zinc, molybdenum, boron, copper, and chlorine. Although these nutrients are generally needed only in small amounts, the lack of any one of them can impair the normal functioning of the plant.

All plants need all the essential nutrients, both major and minor. However, some need more of certain nutrients, and may call for extra amounts of certain nutrients during particular stages of their development. For instance, plants coming into flower need increased amounts of phosphorus. Foliage plants need high amounts of nitrogen for good growth. Geraniums will bloom more profusely if supplied with high amounts of potash and low amounts of nitrogen. Following is a discussion of the important nutrients for plant growth.

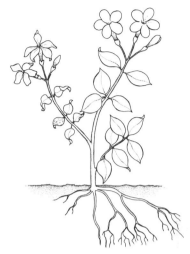

Proper vs. Improper Amounts of Nutrients:
To illustrate the effect which nitrogen, potassium, and phosphorus have on plant growth, the left side of this plant shows the result of nutrient deficiencies, while the right side shows good growth resulting from the proper amounts. Pale, poorly formed flowers are an indication the plant is not receiving enough potassium and phosphorus; full-colored flowers, properly formed, are signs that there is ample phosphorus. Leaves are barometers for nitrogen and potassium levels: too little nitrogen results in pale color and stunted growth, while a potassium deficiency causes leaf spots and curled edges that may even appear burned. A plant receiving the right amount of nitrogen will exhibit good green coloring and full development of leaves and stems. Too little potassium causes stunted root growth; the proper amount allows the roots to develop and supply the water and minerals needed for healthy growth aboveground.

NUTRIENT FUNCTIONS

Nitrogen is instrumental in the development of foliage and the healthy green color of plants. A lack of it will result in stunted growth and the loss of green color. An excess of nitrogen will cause unnaturally fast and succulent (weak) growth, subjecting plants to disease, and causing them to drop their buds. Too much nitrogen also can mask variegation of foliage. Flowering may be encouraged when nitrogen is withheld.

Opposite, different types of plants require different potting media and different fertilizers.

Phosphorus is an important constituent of the plant's genetic materials and plays an important role in seed development, thus being paramount in the continuation of any plant species. It is also important for good root and stem development, and for flower formation and color. A deficiency will cause stunted growth, poor flowering, and sterility of seeds. Too much phosphorus produces a weak, floppy appearance.

Potassium, often called potash, is essential for formation of carbohydrates and proteins. It is important to good root and stem development, production of flowers, and resistance against cold and disease. A potassium deficiency can cause stunted plants, the direct result of stunted roots. Leaves may be spotted, curled, or mottled, and show signs of "burn" around the edges.

Calcium is required for cell elongation and cell division, and is important in guarding against magnesium toxicity, in building healthy cells, and in neutralizing certain organic acids formed by the plant as by-products of metabolism. Pale leaf margins in the growing tip and young leaves might be a sign of calcium deficiency.

Magnesium, usually listed as a trace element, is actually needed in relatively large amounts. Without it, no chlorophyll could be manufactured, since each chlorophyll molecule must contain one atom of magnesium. This mineral is also necessary to the plant's utilization of nitrogen, phosphorus, and sulfur, and for protein formation. A magnesium deficiency will cause lower leaves to lose color, although the veins will remain green. If uncorrected, the problem will cause leaves to turn yellow and orange, then die.

Sulfur has a wide variety of roles in plant nutrition, combining with other chemicals to form sulfates and sulfur-containing vitamins. A deficiency will cause yellowing of expanding leaves.

Iron is important in the manufacture of chlorophyll and carbohydrates. A deficiency can cause chlorosis, again resulting in yellow leaves and stunted growth.

Zinc is known to be important to plant health, although scientists are just beginning to discover its exact roles. Zinc deficiency results in stunted growth, twisted, distorted leaves, and lowered resistance to disease.

Molybdenum is important for the fixation of gaseous nitrogen and nitrate assimilation. Its deficiency causes a drop in ascorbic acid levels in the plant, but this is rarely a problem, since molybdenum is widely distributed in soils and is needed in very small amounts by plants.

Boron is essential to many plant functions, including cell division, nitrogen and carbohydrate metabolism, flowering, and fruiting. Lack of boron kills shoot tips. It is seldom deficient in soils, however, so the garden loam you use in the potting mixture will supply plants with sufficient amounts.

Copper is an essential trace element, although its role is not fully understood. It is a component of some important enzymes, and thought to be involved in plant respiration and the utilization of iron. A deficiency will cause new growth tips to die.

Chlorine is another of the trace elements needed in minute amounts, but its role is not fully understood. It is deposited into soils with rainfall, and so its deficiency is rarely a problem.

SUPPLYING NUTRIENT NEEDS

All the major and minor nutrient elements can be supplied initially through compost and other naturally occurring materials—notably bone meal—in the potting mixture. By choosing a wide variety of materials in making compost, gardeners will not have to seek out special formulas or worry about the lack of any specific nutrient. The matter is put very well by William R. Van Dersal, in his book *Why Does Your Garden Grow?* (see Bibliography):

In the process of decay the complex materials that once formed living organisms are broken down into simpler compounds. In certain specific forms these simpler chemical substances can be taken up and used by the higher plants (trees, shrubs, grasses, and so on). You might think about this when you are considering the use of mulch in your garden. There is no fertilizer made that is as complete as decaying organic material. After all, organic material contains all the elements necessary to plant life. Frequently we do not know what all these elements are. Scientists are continually discovering new ones, and commercial fertilizer manufacturers may hasten to add them, but we apparently have much more yet to learn about such substances.

Synthetic fertilizers are available in a wide variety of commercial brands at garden centers, plant shops, department stores, and supermarkets. They are offered in powder, liquid, and tablet form. There are liquids designed to be sprayed directly on the plant's foliage, there to be absorbed directly, and there are tiny time-release pellets said to serve a plant's needs for three to four months.

The advantages of these products are that they offer ample amounts of the three major nutrients, and they are neat and easy to apply. The disadvantages are several. Chemical fertilizers supply only the nutrient elements guaranteed on the label. Trace elements have to be purchased separately, or as a component of a particular fertilizer formula. More important, these products contribute nothing to the structure or texture of the potting mixture, which is as important as the nutrients contained in it. Also, they can burn plant roots if misapplied.

Indoor gardeners can assure their plants of receiving all the essential nutrients—both major and minor—by using good compost and garden soil in the potting mixture, and then by supplementing this base with further additions of organic materials, which break down slowly and offer long-term benefits. Outdoors, the gardener may call upon a wide variety of materials for their nutritive contributions. For house plants, however, the list need not be large. Fish emulsion, found in stores wherever other house plant fertilizers are sold, has a 5-1-1 NPK (nitrogen-phosphorus-potassium) formula, a good one for foliage plants, and is—like chemical formulas—neat and easy to apply. Its nutrients are in a form readily available to plants, but, unlike synthetics, it will not burn roots.

Fish emulsion is usually applied in liquid form, when plants are watered. The one drawback to this fertilizer is its unpleasant smell. To avoid the problem, you can dilute fish emulsion further than the recommended strength, and use this weaker solution more often. Fish emulsion is also available in deodorized and capsule form. Capsules are buried in the soil and are said to give off no odor.

The nitrogen supply offered by fish emulsion is high, although it is rather low in both phosphorus and potassium. Therefore, it is a good idea to supplement this substance occasionally with another mixture of organic materials which contains higher percentages of these elements. A good one is:

2 parts wood ashes
(NPK 0.00–1.50–7.00)

1 part blood meal
(NPK 15.00–1.30–0.70)

1 part bone meal
(NPK 4.00–21.00 –0.20)

This mixture will result in an approximate 5-6-4 formula, one well balanced to supplement the 5-1-1 fish emulsion. But gardeners can mix their own formulas, based on the materials they have at hand. Gardeners in different parts of the United States have access to industrial wastes of various kinds—leather dust and fish scraps in New England, hoof meal and horn dust in large areas of the Midwest, Southwest, and the Plains states, cottonseed meal in the South, agricultural wastes on the West Coast. Rural gardeners can often obtain manure quickly and easily. Then, there are natural rock powders, including limestone, granite dust, and phosphate rock, that can often be purchased at garden centers. The one caution is that most organic materials must be thoroughly composted before they are used. Using the wood ash/blood meal/bone meal formula recommended above, no composting is necessary. But before using animal manures, fish scraps, seaweed, brewers' grains, and similar materials, be sure that they have been composted thoroughly, or damage can be inflicted on plants.

You can experiment with your own formulas, using the materials you have at hand. Many gardeners, for instance, already have coffee grounds in the kitchen, wood ashes in the fireplace or basement, and bone meal in the potting shed or garage. Using 4 parts coffee grounds, 1 part bone meal, and 1 part wood ashes, you may construct an approximate 2-4-1.65 formula.

To determine the NPK value of a homemade formula, refer to the chart listing NPK contents of various organic materials. Add the total percentage of nitrogen, phosphorus, and potassium in the materials used in your formula, then divide by the number of parts used in the formula. For example, to find the NPK rating of the coffee grounds/bone meal/wood ash formula mentioned above, proceed this way:

	N	P	K
4 parts coffee grounds	1.99	0.36	0.67
	1.99	0.36	0.67
	1.99	0.36	0.67
	1.99	0.36	0.67
1 part bone meal	4.00	21.00	0.20
1 part wood ashes	0.00	1.50	7.00
Total amounts	11.96	23.94	9.88
Divided by 6 (total parts)	1.99	3.99	1.65

The NPK rating of this formula, then, is approximately 2-4-1.65.

Here are some other formulas composed of commonly available ingredients:

NPK 2-8-3:	3 parts greensand 2 parts seaweed 1 part blood meal 2 parts phosphate rock
NPK 2-13-2.5:	1 part cottonseed meal 2 parts phosphate rock 2 parts seaweed
NPK 2.5-6-5:	1 part blood meal 1 part phosphate rock 4 parts wood ashes
NPK 0-5-4:	1 part phosphate rock 3 parts greensand 2 parts wood ashes
NPK 3-7-5:	1 part blood meal 1 part phosphate rock 3 parts wood ashes

Despite the wide variety of materials available for supplemental fertilization, the basis of organic gardening is still a good, all-purpose compost. If you choose your composting materials carefully, you need provide plants with nothing more. With the additions of materials rich in all the nutrients, your compost will provide all that is required for good plant health.

MAKING COMPOST FOR HOUSE PLANTS

Organic matter provides nutrients for plants only while it is decaying. Undecayed kitchen scraps hold no value as a fertilizer (although their potential value is significant), and neither does very old peat moss, which has decayed completely. It is only during the biochemical processes of decay that nutrients in organic matter are released to plants. That is, in fact, the purpose of composting—to return organic wastes to plant-growing environments in a state of partial decay.

NPK Content of Some Organic Materials Used in Composting and Fertilizing

For indoor gardeners who wish to mix their own compost formulas, here are the approximate NPK values of some commonly used materials:

	% Nitrogen	% Phosphorus	% Potassium
Alfalfa hay	2.45	0.50	2.10
Apple leaves	1.00	0.15	0.35
Blood meal	15.00	1.30	0.70
Bone meal	4.00	21.00	0.20
Brewers' grains (wet)	0.90	0.50	0.05
Cattail reed and water lily stems	2.02	0.81	3.43
Cattle manure (fresh)*	0.29	0.17	0.10
Coffee grounds	1.99	0.36	0.67
Cottonseed	3.15	1.25	1.15
Cottonseed meal	7.00	2.50	1.50
Eggshells	1.19	0.38	0.14
Fish scraps (fresh)	6.50	3.75	0.00
Granite dust	0.00	0.00	3.00–5.00
Greensand	0.00	1.50	5.00
Hen manure (fresh)*	1.63	1.54	0.85
Hoof meal and horn dust	12.50	1.75	0.00
Horse manure (fresh)*	0.44	0.17	0.35
Oak leaves	0.80	0.35	0.15
Orange culls	0.20	0.13	0.21
Peanut shells	0.80	0.15	0.50
Phosphate rock	0.00	30.00–50.00	0.00
Pine needles	0.46	0.12	0.03
Seaweed	1.68	0.75	4.93
Sheep manure (fresh)*	0.55	0.31	0.15
Swine manure (fresh)*	0.60	0.41	0.13
Tankage	6.00	5.00	0.00
Tea grounds	4.15	0.62	0.40
Tobacco leaves	4.00	0.50	6.00
Tomato leaves and stalks	0.35	0.10	0.45
Wheat (straw)	0.50	0.15	0.60
Wood ashes (unleached)	0.00	1.50	7.00

*Dried manures contain up to five times more NPK.

When a compost heap is only a few days old, it will begin to heat up quickly, the result of furious activity of microorganisms which break down the raw materials and multiply at a rapid rate. After a few weeks or months, the heap cools to a normal temperature and different species of microorganisms may replace earlier populations. It is at this stage—when the raw materials have been turned into a brown, crumbly, humuslike material, that compost is said to be "finished." It is finished, in one way, for it is then ready to be used in growing plants. But in another way, it is far from finished, since it will release its nutrients to plants, at a slow, safe, and effective pace, for many years to come. Chemical "time-release" fertilizers are but a poor imitation of nature's compost.

Long before man walked the earth, nature recycled all of its organic wastes. The dead leaves moldering on a forest floor, the brown pasture grass that yielded to winter's icy grip, the birds and animals that have lived out their natural spans, the creatures great and small, above and beneath the earth's surface—all are destined to return to the earth that spawned and nurtured them, in this amazing process known as decomposition. The gardener who composts his wastes is emulating nature's own sound methods. Of course, gardeners have learned how to make certain refinements, to help along and speed the process. In this way, the composter works in harmony with nature, while achieving his or her own gardening ends in a most scientific and efficient way.

COMPOSTING METHODS

Anyone with access to any outside space can build a compost heap. This includes urban homeowners with very small lots and even apartment dwellers with outside balconies. Gardeners who rent plots away from home can often construct a heap right alongside their gardens.

Successful composting demands three major ingredients: organic matter, heat, and microorganisms. Also important are sufficient quantities of nitrogen, water, and air.

We will begin by listing the steps in building a traditional heap, in the Indore method (named for the region in India where it was developed early in the century by the Englishman Sir Albert Howard, who was one of the earliest proponents of organic farming and gardening). Then we will discuss some variations used by gardeners with special problems (notably lack of space and the constituents of an urban setting).

The first step in the Indore method of composting is to select a level area 6 feet (1.8 m) wide and at least 6 feet (1.8 m) long (but as long as you wish). Dig out the topsoil from the area to a depth of 12 to 18 inches (30 to 46 cm), and heap the soil to one side for later use. Line the pit with rough brush to form a good drainage base.

Now, put down a six-inch (15 cm) layer of green matter—grass clippings, weeds, leaves, and so on. (Don't use leaves exclusively, for they will mat down and exclude air.)

On top of the green matter, put a two-inch (5 cm) layer of manure, followed by a sprinkling of topsoil mixed with powdered limestone or bone meal.

Repeat these layers—green matter, manure, topsoil with limestone—until the heap reaches about five feet (1.5 m) in height. Keep it watered—damp but not soggy—and after about six weeks turn the heap so that the materials on the outer edges go into the center of the heap where the greatest microorganism activity will be taking place. After two more months, the compost should be ready to use. A heap started in spring will be ready for use in the autumn.

A heap constructed in this way provides all the necessary ingredients for success. Organic matter is provided in the form of green matter and manure, both rich in nitrogen. The microorganisms are plentiful in both the topsoil and the manure, and it is the microorganisms that produce the necessary heat. The minimum six-foot by six-foot (1.8 m by 1.8 m) construction provides enough mass to assure proper heating; a very small heap cannot, since too much of its mass is in contact with the outside air. The turning of the heap and the green matter help to aerate the materials, providing proper oxygen for microorganisms. Some gardeners poke holes in the heap to provide air passages.

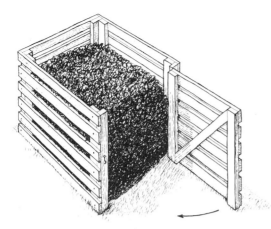

Lehigh Box for Composting: Making compost in your backyard becomes a neat, efficient operation with the use of this bin. Shown here is a single Lehigh box, but you will actually need two identical ones, placed side by side, once composting gets under way. They are easy to build and materials and size can be adapted to fit your particular situation.

Urban and suburban dwellers, of course, often cannot construct huge compost heaps in their backyards. More suitable here are various compost bins and other enclosures that both contain the heap and exclude dogs, rats, and other animals. A well-designed compost bin poses no public health or aesthetic problems.

Perhaps the most popular backyard bin is the so-called Lehigh box, which is really two boxes, each 4 to 5 feet (1.2 to 1.5 m) square, built side to side so that compost can be forked from one box to the other. While finished compost is ready on one side, new compost is working on the other. The bins are built in various ways, according to the gardener's available materials and ingenuity, but all have three stable sides and a front panel that is removable or hinged to fold down, so that the contents of the box are accessible. Many bins also have a hinged top, which is particularly advisable where animals might be a problem. Where slats are used, a ½-inch (13 mm) space should be left between them, to provide for aeration. If solid panels such as plywood are used, then ½-inch (13 mm) holes are drilled 6 to 12 inches (15 to

30 cm) apart. The bins can be painted dark green, or natural woods can be left in their rough state (some gardeners use split logs), so that the bins are actually quite attractive.

There are dozens of other compost structures, including some very attractive commercially built units. Some people simply dig post holes, fill them with organic matter, and level them off with six inches (15 cm) of topsoil. Compost also can be made in plastic leaf bags or trash barrels with tight-fitting lids; either produces compost anaerobically (without air) and causes no odor or pest problems at all. (Incidentally, if any compost heap produces unpleasant odors, it should be turned, to introduce more air, then covered lightly with soil.)

MATERIALS FOR COMPOSTING

Nearly any once-living material, plant or animal, is a candidate for the compost heap. Even unlikely materials such as hair clippings, vacuum cleaner dust, and the stuffing from old chairs can add to the organic store. Here is a list of some of the more popular composting materials, along with their approximate NPK percentages. Remember that the nutrient value of your compost, and its pH value, will depend on the materials you use to build it.

Alfalfa Hay (NPK 2.45—0.50—2.10)

Hay has many uses in the outdoor garden. For the compost heap, it offers good amounts of both nitrogen and potash. Hay is available at most larger garden centers, but you will be able to buy yours more cheaply from a farmer. Hay that has spoiled in the fields can often be purchased at nominal rates.

Blood Meal (NPK 15.00—1.30—0.70)

Powdered blood, an extremely good source of nitrogen, is available by the pound at garden centers, but the price is high. You might do better by going directly to a slaughterhouse. Since blood meal is used in animal feeds, also try feed mills or manufacturing plants.

Bone Meal (NPK 4.00—21.00—0.20)

Used principally as a source of phosphorus, bone meal can be purchased at plant shops and garden centers. Or, you may take your chances at a bone mill.

Brewers' Grains, Wet (NPK 0.90—0.50—0.05)

Brewers of beer and ale discard hops and other grains after they have been "spent." Most breweries will be happy to have you cart off all you can. Since the piles are wet and heavy, it is not an easy job, although a morning's work can provide many months' worth of free composting materials.

Cattle Manure, Fresh (NPK 0.29—0.17—0.10)

Manure is not only a good source of nutrients, but also contains bacterial activators (microorganisms) for the heap. If you are lucky, the manure you collect will contain some manure-type earthworms which will multiply in the heap. If you do not know a farmer who will give you a few bushels, try feedlots or slaughterhouses.

Horse Manure, Fresh (NPK 0.44—0.17—0.35)

An hour's worth of work at the local riding stables will bring rich rewards.

Kitchen Scraps

To discard kitchen scraps in landfills, dumps, incinerators, or sewage systems is a tragic waste of a great national resource. Compost yours daily, but bury them deeply in the center of the heap where they will not attract rodents, dogs, and cats.

Leaves

Most leaves are acid in nature, and should not form an overly high percentage of the compost heap. They should be shredded before going into the heap because, unshredded, they tend to mat and decompose very slowly. They also can be used alone to make leaf mold, which can be used in potting mixtures as described in chapter 6.

Sheep Manure, Wet (NPK 0.55—0.31—0.15)

Sheep manure is a better source of all three major nutrients than is cattle or horse manure, but lower in both nitrogen and phosphorus than poultry manure.

Tobacco Leaves (NPK 4.00—0.50—6.00)

In the late summer and early autumn, spoiled tobacco leaves can often be obtained from farmers who grow this crop. They are worth the hauling for their good amounts of nitrogen and potassium.

Wood Ashes (NPK 0.00—1.50—7.00)

Potash fertilizer costs money. Think of your fireplace ashes, therefore, as a form of cash rebate on your fireplace wood. Save all you can, for composting and for adding to both indoor and outdoor soils.

When compost is cool to the touch, is crumbly and dark brown, and has that characteristic earthy odor, you know that it is finished and ready to use. However, if the materials in the heap are still recognizable, or if the center of the heap is warm, you will know that the microorganisms are still working to break down materials.

If the heap does not heat up properly, the problem might be a lack of nitrogen or of microorganisms. Manure and topsoil will provide both. A musty odor, like that of rotting potatoes, is a sign of mold formation and is caused by a lack of sufficient air. Reconstruct the heap, using hay or shredded leaves to lighten it. If a strong ammonia odor is detected, it is a sign that the heap is losing nitrogen through the formation of free ammonia. An excess of either manure or lime can cause the problem. Again, reconstruct the heap, adding hay or plant debris to balance the materials properly and provide aeration. Extra soil will adsorb the ammonia and prevent its loss.

USING COMPOST WITH HOUSE PLANTS

Compost is used as an integral part of the potting mixture for all plants, as described in chapter 6. It also can be used to provide a continuing source of nutrients, either through top-dressing (in which it is sieved through a ¼-inch/6 mm screen and then scratched into the top inch or ½ inch/25 or 13 mm of potting soil) or by the application of compost tea.

COMPOST TEA

Compost tea is made in much the same way as ordinary tea. Generally, a burlap bag full of finished compost is inserted into a bucket or watertight barrel three-quarters full of water, then is stirred occasionally for two weeks or more, during which time the nutrients are leached into the water. The liquid should be brown in color; if it is black it may be too strong for house plants unless it is diluted before use. Another method of "brewing" compost tea requires no burlap bag, simply the mixing of the compost and water in the barrel. The liquid is then sieved into containers to be stored for future use.

Because of the bacterial activity and the resultant odors, it is a job best done outdoors. The barrel can remain outside until all signs of bubbling and belching are finished, at which time the liquid may be bottled and stored in the basement for year-round use with house plants. Because of the possibility of expansion of gases, it is best to cover the jars or bottles with a piece of aluminum foil, rather than tight-fitting lids or caps. The foil will seal in odors yet allow for the escape of gases, if necessary. A supply of compost tea made in August will be enough to feed your indoor plants all winter long.

If you do not have a compost pile but have access to well-rotted manure, you can use the methods described above to make a manure tea that is also useful as a plant food.

HOW OFTEN TO FERTILIZE

The question of how often to fertilize is, like that of how often to water, a relative one. It depends on the growth habits of the individual plant, its age, its location, and the time of year.

Plants need more fertilizer when they are growing rapidly, less when they are resting. Plants in a dormant state should not be fertilized at all; to do so would build up unused mineral salts in the soil to the point of overstimulating the plant. Generally speaking, you will want to fertilize about twice as often during the light-intensive period from April to September as you will from October to March. Plants that are being treated for serious insect or disease infestation should not be fertilized, since their metabolic systems will not be performing normally under such conditions. Do not fertilize young seedlings; when they are of sufficient size, they should be transplanted into a potting soil that offers plenty of nutrients for the first several months. Bear in mind that usually plants do better with frequent weak applications of nutrients than with infrequent strong doses, which can overstimulate growth and burn root tissues. Do not fertilize newly repotted plants for two months. Overfertilization kills more plants than underfertilization.

A good basic fertilization plan is to apply fish emulsion (or a similar NPK formula mixture) once every two weeks during the plant's active growing season, and to supplement this with a formula higher in phosphorus and potassium once a month. Occasionally, you may scratch some fresh compost into the top inch or ½ inch (25 or 13 mm) of soil, or apply compost tea instead of water. (Compost tea is described earlier in this chapter.) When plants are coming into flower, scratch in a few pinches of wood ashes, for needed potash. That's all there is to it. Instructions for fertilizing specific plants can be found in the Encyclopedia section of this book.

CHAPTER 8

Propagation

There is something eminently satisfying about watching a tiny green shoot emerge from a bed of rich brown soil, poking its way to light and life. That seemingly insignificant seed carries within it a patient, determined embryo which sometimes will remain dormant for decades before it finds the right moment to germinate into lush greenness. The excitement of observing the day-to-day drama of emerging new leaves and elongating, maturing stems awakens the gardener's instinct in us all. Although we are awed by the power of nature, we also feel somehow responsible for this creation as we nurture our tiny new charges. We are involved in a miracle every time we sow a seed.

This joy of fostering new life can be experienced by all indoor gardeners. Whether you have the total involvement of pollinating flowers, collecting and sowing the seeds, and sustaining the cycle to mature plant, or whether you simply remove and root cuttings from the ends of a plant's branches to produce new duplicate plants, you will feel the thrill of creation.

Plants really can become a part of your life, each evoking special memories and sentiments. You will be able to root a sprig of ivy from the wedding bouquet of a relative or friend, creating a living memory for her. Or you might clone a favorite *Episcia* for years by taking cuttings over and over again until you no longer know whether the original plant is the one hanging in your kitchen window, the one adorning your best friend's sun porch, or one carried off by a relative. The satisfaction of recounting how you started from seed the rubber plant *(Ficus elastica)* filling the corner of the living room can rekindle all the delight you felt when you first noticed it nudging its way through the soil.

Although the pleasure obtained from nurturing plants and watching them increase in size and number is reason enough to propagate them, the practicality of starting new plants from existing ones offers an additional bonus. As any plant lover knows, an incurable mania to acquire more and more plants often sets in soon after the first few house plants have been acquired. This is an expensive affliction if each new plant must be purchased. But once the techniques described in this chapter have been mastered, you will be able to increase your collection by propagating new plants from your old ones by rooting stem and leaf cuttings, dividing large plants, separating offsets, and germinating seeds.

You will be able to take a small cutting from your friend's rare and prized hybrid *Columnea* and grow one exactly like it. You also will be able to take cuttings from your own plants to give as very personal and inexpensive gifts to friends, or to sell at school benefits or garage sales.

Perhaps best of all, you will realize that propagating plants by sexual or asexual techniques does them no harm! Indeed, taking cuttings or divisions is actually a good way of pruning and shaping large plants, or rejuvenating old and overgrown plants. And if a plant is ailing and likely to die, you often can perpetuate it by propagating from some of its healthier parts. Displayed in an attractive vase, either alone or set off with a few cut flowers, such rooting cuttings can handsomely adorn a table or desk.

Whether they involve seeds or other plant parts, all of the methods described here, with the exception of grafting, are Nature's own ways of keeping the world alive and green. In learning and applying them, you will not be improving upon Nature, but only helping her along a little.

Opposite, close-up of Hibiscus *stigma with pollen.*

SEXUAL PROPAGATION

Nature created sex as a way of producing offspring which have a mixture of characteristics derived from the male and female parents. This variation in the offspring allows for successful evolution through survival of the fittest. The sex life of plants also makes it possible for plant breeders to selectively develop plants more desirable to man.

Sexual reproduction results in the production of seeds, and sexual propagation enables you to sow seeds in a container of soil. Normally, seeds resulting from any given cross are genetically different from one another and they produce plants that also look different. (You are genetically different from your brothers and sisters even though you have the same parents.) This principle holds true when you produce seeds from your own plants, even if you self-pollinate them. There always will be natural variations in the offspring (see Producing Your Own Seeds, later in this chapter). But if you purchase hybrid seeds from a seed company, these specially produced seeds will germinate into seedlings which appear to be identical.

Hybrid seeds are produced by a plant breeder who chooses particular male and female parents which when crossed produce seeds that will grow into plants appearing to be identical to each other. The key word here is "appearing," for plants of the first generation (F_1 hybrids) may look alike but not be genetically identical. Therefore, some members of the second generation of plants grown from hybrid seeds (F_2 hybrids) will probably look different from each other. In order to obtain hybrid plants yielding seeds that will grow into plants truly identical to their parents, at least six generations of self-pollination and careful selection are required — a pointless task where most house plants are concerned since hybrids can be easily cloned and quickly replicated genetically through some type of vegetative propagation.

In choosing parent plants that will produce a first generation of look-alike progeny, breeders also select and match those plants possessing desirable characteristics. By crossing a disease-resistant but not-too-attractive plant with a strain known for outstanding flowers or foliage, for example, a hybridizer might hope to obtain a plant that is both beautiful and hardy.

When hybridizers are breeding indoor plants, quality combined with strength is not as important as beauty blended with those characteristics that make a plant commercially viable. For example, a favorite gloxinia, *Sinningia* 'Sparkles', boasts superbly showy, upright rose-red blooms edged with white. But it also has brittle foliage that breaks readily in shipping and handling. Another gloxinia, *S. regina,* combines drooping flowers of a dull purple with wonderfully flexible leaves. Not surprisingly, at least one hybridizer has been cross-breeding these plants in the hope of getting their best traits to combine in just the right proportions. Such breeding requires a sound knowledge of the way in which inherited characteristics are transmitted in the specific plants involved.

Hybrid seeds are used extensively in modern horticulture and agriculture for growing grains, vegetables, and flowering annuals. Though seeds are available for foliage plants, they usually are not produced by hybridization, for until recently there has not been the interest or money available to produce hybrid seeds for such plants.

Where very exotic plants are involved, collectors are sent into tropical jungles, mountainous regions, and deserts all over the world to gather seeds from foliage or flowering plants. A host of variables in environmental conditions, such as variations in the weather, cause the seeds to be scarce some years and abundant other years. Sometimes the seeds that are gathered are difficult to germinate. The seed companies usually test such seeds and sell them only if they can be guaranteed to germinate at a prescribed level. If you purchase such nonhybrid seeds, you may get seedlings which differ in size, shape, or color, or perhaps in height, vigor, and resistance to disease — but of course that can be fun.

You may find that some of your flowering house plants will set seeds by themselves — some examples are firecracker flower *(Crossandra infundibuliformis),* cyclamen *(Cyclamen persicum),* and Jerusalem cherry *(Solanum pseudocapsicum).* If this does not happen naturally, you may experiment with hybridizing them yourself by hand pollination as described later under Producing Your Own Seeds. Pollinating your own plants can be a fun and rewarding hobby and you will end up with some very different and distinctive, if not always beautiful, plants.

Even if you have little or no interest in plant breeding, you can save money and experience special pleasure by growing house plants from seeds. Moreover, once you have mastered the art of germinating house plant seeds, you probably will want to get a head start on your vegetable garden by germinating seeds indoors in late winter or early spring. You will be able to grow disease-resistant tomatoes and other special varieties recommended in gardening books and magazines, but hard to find in flats at garden centers. You will be able to start long-season plants like watermelon, cantaloupe, and pumpkin early enough indoors to produce fruit even in northern climate zones.

Flowering annuals for outdoor borders likewise can be started indoors. Purchasing enough annuals to fill your flower beds can be very expensive, and if seeds are sown outdoors it may be August before many of them bloom. If you germinate marigolds, zinnias, snapdragons, and other bedding plants indoors, you will be able to enjoy pretty flowers all summer long. You can also grow from seeds a number of annuals, such as petunias, to bloom indoors during the winter, provided you can give them enough light. For information on brightening your home with annuals, see chapter 12.

TECHNIQUES FOR SUCCESS WITH SEEDS

TREATING SOILS, CONTAINERS, AND SEEDS TO PREVENT DISEASE

The tender tissues of a seedling are easy prey for disease organisms. Damping-off, a general term for rotting or molding of small seedlings, is a common disease caused by one or a combination of four fungi — namely, *Botrytis, Phytophthora, Pythium,* or *Rhizoctonia.*

The mycelium (body of the fungus) or spores (reproductive structures of the fungus) are universally present in the atmosphere, soil, well water, infected plants, or on the surface of seeds and plant parts. Spores of *Botrytis,* which also attack fallen leaves, flowers, wounded stems, and other dying plant parts, are carried on air currents. These ubiquitous organisms are always around, waiting to attack highly vulnerable seedlings. You should suspect damping-off if germinating seeds decay or rot before or during emergence, if the seedlings collapse and die because of stem rot at the soil level, or if they remain standing but die from being girdled by the fungus.

Since you are an organic gardener and do not want to spray with fungicides (which are not too effective against damping-off anyway), you will have to make sure that the disease is prevented. If you carefully follow the principles of sanitation outlined here but your seedlings die anyway, you can reasonably conclude that the problem is not damping-off, but rather excessive wetness or dryness of the growing medium, excessively high soil temperatures, or high soluble salt levels in the soil.

The major source of damping-off infection is the soil, so it is necessary to disinfect soil and to be sure that other components in the growing medium are sterile. Vermiculite and perlite are heated to high temperatures during their manufacture, and are guaranteed sterile until the bag is opened. Peat moss and sphagnum moss, though not heat processed, are generally considered to be pathogen free, too, because their high acid content inhibits development of most disease organisms. Sphagnum has some fungus-inhibiting property which directly discourages the growth of damping-off organisms, and is highly recommended for use without special treatment in propagating media. Soil and sand must be treated to eliminate any disease organisms.

The usual method is to heat-treat soil or a propagating mix containing soil or sand, to kill pathogens as well as weed seeds. The techniques for pasteurizing propagating and potting media are described in chapter 6.

For successful propagation, it also is important that containers, the work surface, and your hands are clean and free of disease organisms. Soak the pots, especially any that have contained diseased plants, in a solution of 1 part household bleach to 9 parts water for 20 minutes. It also is recommended that seeds be disinfected before sowing because the rough surface of the seed coat may harbor the spores of damping-off fungi which then will attack during germination. Sometimes seed companies will coat their seeds with fungicides before packaging them, but not always. It is wise to surface-sterilize all seeds not known to be pretreated just in case they are carrying disease pathogens.

One of the best ways to surface-sterilize seeds is to use the same 10 percent bleach solution recommended for sterilizing containers. Soak seeds in this liquid for five to ten minutes only. Bleach solution is deadly to fungal spores, and it also can be deadly to plant seeds if they are left in it for too long. Limiting the soaking to five to ten minutes will prevent injury to the sensitive inner tissues of the seeds. Seeds can be drained on several layers of cheesecloth lining a strainer (if they are tiny), or in the strainer alone if they are large enough not to fall through the holes.

If you prefer, you might try surface-sterilizing seeds with hot water. This treatment will kill many spores which may be on the inside of the seed coat as well as those on the surface. You must be very careful, however, since the water, if too hot, can kill the seeds, too. You will need a thermometer — a meat, dairy, or candy thermometer is best. Immerse the seeds in hot water at 120° to 135°F (49° to 58°C) for 15 to 30 minutes, using the thermometer to be sure the temperature of the water is within the correct range. It may be difficult to keep the water hot without returning it to the stove, thus risking overheating it and destroying the seeds. You can preheat the water to 135°F (58°C), and pour it over the seeds in a Thermos bottle, Styrofoam ice bucket, or other insulated container. Time the soaking carefully and when the treatment is over, pour off the water, retaining the seeds in cheesecloth or a strainer. Spread them out to cool and dry quickly, then store them in clean, dry envelopes, or plant them immediately.

SPECIAL PRETREATMENTS

Seeds perpetuate a plant species over time, and Nature has developed many techniques for keeping seeds alive without germinating for years, or for allowing them to germinate only when conditions for growth are ideal. This helps a plant compete in nature. But what's best in nature may not be best for your indoor gardening ventures, and you may need to treat certain seeds in specific ways to induce germination. This special handling may involve presoaking or otherwise scarifying (breaking through) the seed coat, and perhaps subjecting the seeds to cold temperatures.

All seeds need moisture to germinate. A hard seed coat provides protection against germination during dry, unfavorable weather. Often, the seeds will germinate only when the spring rains have thoroughly soaked the ground and softened the hard seed coats. Desert-dwelling plants, like cacti, have especially hard seed coats so they can even bypass a year if the spring is dry.

Other seeds — those of tomatoes, for instance — have germination inhibitors in the seed. Until a sufficient quantity of water is absorbed by the seed, resulting in leaching out these inhibitors, the seed will not germinate. Soaking seeds in water mimics heavy spring rains, softening the seed coats and leaching out inhibitors.

You should soak seeds for 24 hours before planting them, to insure even and rapid germination. Use water that has been boiled and cooled. You may shorten or lengthen the treatment time as you see fit; the crucial indicator is the splitting of the seed coat, which occurs after the inner parts of the seed swell from taking up water. This often requires 24 hours, but allow the seeds to soak longer if swelling has not occurred, and remove them sooner if they swell in less time.

An especially hard seed coat makes some seeds so waterproof that they may remain alive but dormant in the soil for years. Such seeds require scarification, which consists of scratching the seed coat with a file or sandpaper so that water can reach the inside of the seed. Commercial seed producers usually scarify seeds before packaging if this pretreatment is needed.

Other seeds need a cold period ranging from one hour to four months before they will germinate. Seeds needing cold pretreatment may have inhibitors which prevent them from germinating until springtime. Most of these are seeds of temperate zone plants that ripen their seeds in the fall. We don't know what really happens during chilling, but there are physiological changes in the seeds that require temperatures of 35° to 40°F (2° to 4°C), and must occur before germination can take place. Most house plants come from tropical climates, and so their seeds have not evolved with a chilling requirement.

However, if you are trying to germinate seeds from outdoor trees and shrubs such as boxwood or flowering dogwood, you may wish to stratify the seeds; that is, expose them to cold conditions to mimic winter weather. Stratification can be accomplished by soaking the seeds as previously described and then wrapping them in moist sphagnum moss and placing them in the refrigerator or anywhere the temperature is 35° to 40°F (2° to 4°C) for six weeks or longer. Bear in mind that soaking makes seeds more susceptible to injury, so they should be handled with care afterward. After cold treatment the seeds usually will germinate readily. Some seeds may have to be scarified before stratification.

TESTING FOR GERMINATION

Seeds from most tropical foliage plants are short lived. Since germination conditions are always optimum in their native environment, seeds germinate quickly after reaching the ground, the crevice of a tree trunk, or whatever their natural habitat might be. If you are taking seeds from your own plants, sow them immediately after collection. If you order seeds by mail, plant them immediately after they arrive for best results.

Seeds from other types of house plants usually keep better. Often seeds will be packaged in foil envelopes which are vacuum sealed to afford protection. Keep these pack-

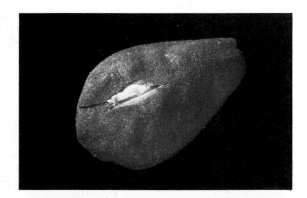

Scarified Seed: A hard, protective seed coat hinders germination by preventing water from entering a seed. Scratching the coat creates an opening that allows water to be absorbed by the seed and the process of germination to begin.

ages where they will be cool and dry — the refrigerator is a good place. Some seeds will keep for years this way. If you open a package and do not use all the contents, put the opened packet inside a small, tightly closed jar and store it in the refrigerator.

To be sure you have not overbleached or overheated your seeds, or to tell if seeds you have saved or gathered from year to year are viable, you can perform a simple germination test. Take five to ten seeds which you have surface-sterilized and soaked, and line them up in the center of a wet paper towel. Roll up the paper towel so that no two seeds touch, and wrap it tightly in plastic or Saran. After about a week, check every few days for germination. If 80 to 90 percent of the seeds germinate, you have achieved excellent results. Commercial seed suppliers test their seeds in a similar manner and do not sell any that do not have a high rate of germination. If none of your seeds have germinated after a week, wait another week. After that you might suspect that they were injured in surface-sterilizing or during scarification. Or the seeds could be too old, too dry, or too warm or cold. Try again, attempting to determine what the problem is. At least with a germination test you will save yourself all the trouble and frustration of sowing and tending the seeds fruitlessly. If the germination test is successful, you can be assured the seeds will germinate well when sown.

MEETING THE LIGHT OR DARKNESS REQUIREMENT FOR GERMINATION

You may read on the back of some seed packets that either light or darkness is required for germination. It is usually smaller seeds, such as those of coleus *(Coleus × hybridus),* begonias, and lettuce, that need light. This is because they do not contain enough stored food to sustain their growth to the light through very much soil. Their light requirement makes them wait until they are uncov-

ered or brought to the surface before germination can occur. These seeds must be placed near the surface of the soil, so that light falling on the seed coat after the seed has absorbed water can cause necessary chemical changes to take place, allowing the seed to germinate.

Larger seeds sometimes require darkness to germinate because they need to be planted deeply enough to do well. Seeds of the sensitive plant *(Mimosa pudica),* cyclamen, and parsley *(Petroselinum crispum)* all will germinate better and more uniformly if the seed flats are placed in a dark closet, or covered with newspaper for a few days.

Most seeds, however, have no special light or darkness requirements and can be germinated under natural light/dark cycles. If you want to speed germination, though, you can give these seeds 24 hours of light a day until the seedlings part the soil. According to the United States Department of Agriculture (USDA), best results come from placing the seeds six inches (15 cm) below a fluorescent fixture or reading lamp.

Directions on seed packets will tell you whether seeds have special light or darkness requirements, so read them carefully.

GERMINATION MEDIA

The same type of medium you use for vegetative propagation also can be used for germinating seeds. (See Propagation Media, under General Needs of Plants Being Propagated Vegetatively, later in this chapter, for detailed descriptions of various media and instructions on using them.) The same guidelines apply for seeds as well as cuttings and divisions — the medium should hold plenty of both water and air. Tiny seeds may need a finer textured medium than cuttings to keep them from drying out. If you are using vermiculite or perlite, purchase the finest texture; it is usually labeled propagating grade.

Vermiculite, perlite, peat, or sphagnum

can be used alone for germination media, but they contain no nutrients. Seedlings do grow while in the germination medium and often they do not carry enough stored food to sustain them during their entire stay in the seed flat. If you are using a soilless medium without nutrients, you should add organic fertilizers such as fish emulsion or seaweed extract in a solution at half the usual strength after the seeds have germinated. You are not running a risk of introducing damping-off with these two products since they are manufactured under sterilizing conditions. But do not use manure tea, as it may not be sterile and, if the manure is uncomposted, it can burn and damage tender seedlings.

Commercially prepared mixes are light and well draining, but they contain a small amount of chemical fertilizer to sustain seedlings for about three weeks. Jiffy-Mix, Pro-Gro, and Terra-Lite are such products commonly found in garden centers. These products are made of very fine vermiculite or perlite and very fine sphagnum moss with tiny crystals of fertilizer. Commercial growers almost universally use these mixes to start their seedlings.

To avoid the chemical fertilizer, you can easily make your own mix. Use ⅓ fine vermiculite, ⅓ finely shredded sphagnum moss, and ⅓ pasteurized soil. Mix these materials well and force them through a fine mesh screen to obtain the proper texture. The soil, which is not found in commercial mixes, will make this medium somewhat heavier, but also will provide the needed nutrients. Another good seed-starting blend containing nutrients in very low concentration consists of 2 parts potting soil, 1 part peat, and 1 part sand.

Media containing sphagnum will be difficult to wet at first because the sphagnum resists absorbing water. To be sure it is thoroughly moist, wet the medium the day before using it. Put it into a large plastic bag, a pot, or other container. Add water and stir the mix well. Do not overstir mixes containing vermiculite, as this material may compress and lose its moisture-and-air-holding capacity. The mix should be wet enough to stick together, but not so wet that it forms a ball when squeezed in your fist. If it makes a ball, allow it to dry for an extra day, or add a little more dry medium.

HOW TO SOW SEEDS

Some plants will seed themselves, and those equipped to eject seeds forcefully — for example, impatiens and life plant *(Biophytum zenkeri)* — will even propel their progeny into the pots of other plants. More often than not, though, the task of handling and germinating seeds will fall to you.

Instructions on the seed package usually will tell you how deep to plant the seeds. The rule of thumb is to cover seeds to a depth of two or three times their diameter. That is easy enough to do for large seeds such as cyclamen, or medium size seeds such as Jerusalem cherry *(Solanum pseudocapsicum)* or chives *(Allium schoenoprasum)*. But with tiny seeds such as those of begonias, gloxinias, or African violets, you're in trouble. It is rather difficult to plant something as small as a dust particle twice as deep as its size. The best you can do is to sprinkle these seeds on top of the soil, letting them plant themselves by falling between the soil particles when you mist-spray the soil surface.

Seeds should not be planted too close together. For seeds large enough to handle, spacing will not pose much of a problem. Drill holes of the proper depth about one inch (2.5 cm) apart using your finger, a pencil, or other dibble. Be sure to clean or sterilize the dibble first. Drop in the seeds and cover them. Or, make a small furrow of the correct depth, again using your finger or a tool. Place the seeds one to two inches (2.5 to 5 cm) apart, and cover with soil.

Smaller seeds require more skill to sow. A good method is to sow them directly from the packet. This way you do not touch the

(continued on page 110)

Build Your Own Basic Flat

For starting plants from seeds or propagating cuttings, nothing works better than a flat. Perfectly good flats can be easily made at home, often using scrap lumber. Flats can be made any size or shape; however, it is wise to make all your flats the same size, to give uniformity to your propagating efforts.

   The flat described here is used for the plastic-enclosed flat and the propagation bed projects explained later in this chapter. If you make your flats to these measurements, you will be able to follow those projects exactly.

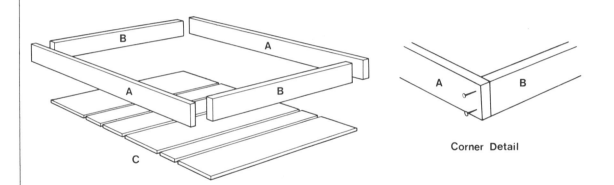

Corner Detail

Materials:

Item	Quantity	Description
A. Sides	2	$\frac{3}{4} \times 2\frac{1}{2} \times 24$-inch #2 pine
B. Ends	2	$\frac{3}{4} \times 2\frac{1}{2} \times 18\frac{1}{2}$-inch #2 pine
C. Bottom	1 or more	$\frac{5}{16} \times 20$-inch random width #2 pine
Nails	—	6d box nails
Nails	—	4d box nails

Procedure:

1. Cut sides (A) and ends (B) according to the dimensions in the materials list.
2. Nail sides (A) into ends (B), using 6d box nails, to form the sides of the flat.
3. Cut, from random width pine $\frac{5}{16} \times 20$ inches long, enough pieces (C) to cover the bottom of the flat.
4. Nail the slats to the bottom of the frame, using 4d box nails. Leave $\frac{1}{8}$ inch of space between the slats.

Build Your Own Propagation Bed

This unit was designed to cover two flats and convert them into a propagation bed. A simple wood frame covered with clear polyethylene plastic makes up the covering unit which helps to maintain high humidity levels in the bed. This propagation bed will give cuttings and heat-loving seedlings the warmth and humidity they need for good growth. If the humidity level inside the bed becomes too high, water droplets will form and run down the sides of the cover. When that happens, remove the cover and allow the medium to dry out a bit.

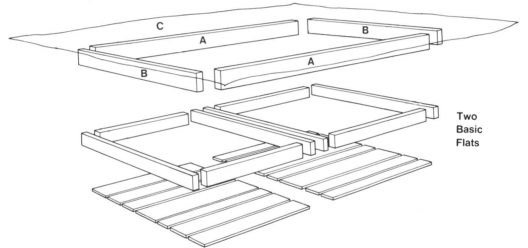

Two
Basic
Flats

Materials:

Item	Quantity	Description
A. Sides	2	¾ × 3 ½ × 42-inch #2 pine
B. Ends	2	¾ × 3 ½ × 24 ⅜-inch #2 pine
C. Plastic	1	3 × 5-foot polyethylene plastic
Nails	—	6d box nails
Staples	—	⁵⁄₁₆-inch staples
Basic flats	2	2 ½ × 20 × 24-inch wood flats

Procedure:

1. Cut sides (A) and ends (B) according to the dimensions in the materials list.
2. Nail sides (A) into ends (B) to form the frame.
3. Cover the frame with clear polyethylene plastic (C). Stretch the plastic over the top, down the sides, and around the bottom, and staple it to the inside of the frame.

seeds, thus avoiding the risk of contaminating them with dirty hands. If the seeds are not in a packet, you can take a small quantity in the palm of your (clean) hand, make a loose fist, and sprinkle the seeds over the soil gently and evenly.

Seeds can be either planted in rows or broadcast. When seeds are planted in rows, if you get damping-off in one area of the flat, it will spread down only the one row. If you broadcast seeds, damping-off in one small area may spread throughout the flat. However, broadcasting does allow more even coverage. To broadcast your seeds, first scatter them from side to side over the soil, then turn the flat 90 degrees and scatter the seeds from end to end. This will insure the most even coverage. Some experts even mix very fine seeds with an equal part of fine sand before spreading. The sand will thin the seeds advantageously, cover them adequately, and show you where you have sown them — a service that should keep you from ending up with a green mat of seedlings in one corner of the flat and nothing everywhere else. For the heavy-handed, mixing in a little sand can mean the difference between success and failure with tiny seeds.

You will find that a thin covering of very finely shredded sphagnum moss sprinkled over the seed bed is another aid against damping-off. After the seeds are planted, lightly dust the soil with a ¼ inch (6 mm) deep layer of sphagnum. If you cannot purchase a very fine grade, then force what you have through a fine mesh screen or through a flour sifter to obtain the proper texture. Sphagnum's fungistatic property will form a protective guard around the seedling at the soil surface — its most vulnerable spot. But you must be careful that the sphagnum is never allowed to dry out because it then can form a very hard, impenetrable sheet that water and seedlings will have a tough time getting through.

Cover the flat with glass or plastic to maintain high humidity until the seeds germinate, and keep the flat out of direct sun. (See Build Your Own Basic Flat and Build Your Own Propagation Bed for instructions on building simple, sturdy flats.) You should not have to water at all until germination is complete. But as soon as you see the first leaves emerging from the soil, remove the cover. Although seedlings still will need high humidity, they will be very susceptible to damping-off in an enclosed container. The air circulation and slight drying of the surface that occur with the cover removed will discourage disease, since fungi thrive on stagnant air and high moisture.

However you plant your seeds, avoid firming, tamping, or otherwise compressing the growing medium any time before or after sowing. Such compacted soil is poorly aerated and slow draining, and puddles on top when watered.

GERMINATION TEMPERATURES

Seeds are separated into several classes according to optimum temperature for germination. Most indoor tropical foliage plants or indoor flowering plants germinate best at warm temperatures of 70° to 75°F (21° to 24°C), and some tropical plants even prefer up to 85°F (29°C). You may have to provide bottom heat to get these temperatures. A good way to provide bottom heat is to build the flat described in Build Your Own Basic Flat and install heating cables before adding the soil mix. Bottom heat is discussed in more detail in Warmth, under General Needs of Plants Being Propagated Vegetatively, later in this chapter. A 5°F (about 2.5°C) drop in temperature is usually a good idea at night — this mimics the natural outdoor environment. Cool-season plants, including many vegetables and flowering annuals, will do best at daytime temperatures of 60° to 65°F (16° to 18°C), again with a slight drop at night. Many trees, shrubs, and perennials from the temperate zone need a daytime temperature of approximately

55°F (13°C) for best germination.

If you cannot provide these temperatures it does not mean the seeds will not germinate, but they may be slow, weak, or erratic in performance. Once the seeds have sprouted, reduce the heat, for while comparatively high temperatures are required for germination, root development proceeds best in the 63° to 77°F (17° to 25°C) range. Also, staying on the cool side will help reduce damping-off problems.

PROVIDING THE RIGHT LIGHT FOR SEEDLINGS

Once above ground, all seedlings need light to grow. Fluorescent lights usually give best results. The amount of light provided will be consistent, and the temperature will not fluctuate as much as in a sunny or shady window. Seedling tops should be 15 inches (38 cm) from a 40-watt cool white or warm white bulb with a reflector, or 10 to 13 inches (25 to 33 cm) from a Gro-Lite tube (the latter bulbs emit less radiant energy).

If you must keep your seedlings in the window, the bright light of an unshaded west or east window is best. Be sure to turn the flat each day so the seedlings will grow erect and not leaning toward the window. In a greenhouse you probably will have to shade the flat with cheesecloth or Saran shade screening, or place it under a bench, especially before seedlings emerge. Otherwise light and heat levels inside may become too intense and the seeds will burn. After you remove the solid cover, shade the seedlings as needed for attaining compact, dark green growth. If seedlings are pale and spindly, they need more light.

If your plants do not emerge quickly, do not be distraught. Have patience; germination can take time. With cacti, for example, some seedlings may be up the day after planting but others from the same sowing may not appear for two or three months. Sporadic germination can be expected from most of the tropical foliage plants, too, since they are not selected or bred for uniformity and reliable behavior. Other seeds (parsley, for example) will germinate evenly, but only after three weeks. You can gently dig up and examine a seed or two if you are getting really worried. The seeds may have rotted, damped-off before emerging from the soil, or you may have misjudged the hardness of the seed coat. If all looks well, keep waiting.

SOME ADVICE ON WATERING

Proper watering after germination is most important for healthy plants. Avoid the watering can if possible and water seedlings by subirrigation (from beneath). The stream of water from a watering can may dislodge small seedlings and wet their leaves and stems, creating an invitation for fungus attack. If you must water from above, use a watering can with a "rose" attachment that breaks the forceful jet of water into a shower of fine streams. Point the watering can away from the seedlings until the initial gush of big drops has given way to a steady, gentle rain of droplets. Then pass the can from side to side over the seedlings several times, being careful to move beyond the sides of the flat before you make each swing back over the plants. End the watering as you started — outside the flat. This method can help settle seeds into the planting medium and when carefully used, is almost as nondisruptive as bottom-watering.

To water from below, place the flat of seedlings in a few inches or centimeters of water in a sink or washtub. Observe carefully and when you see moisture beginning to reach the surface of the propagating medium, remove the flat from the water. Be sure the sink or tub is clean before you water in this way. In fact, it may be wise to scrub it out with a bleach solution.

Do not let seedlings dry out. Water-stress is hard on them at this delicate stage; they wilt easily, and may not recover. Even if watering does revive them, they may be more susceptible to damping-off and other injuries than if they always had been kept vigorous and turgid.

On the other hand, be careful to water seedlings only when the soil is somewhat dry. Overwatering will kill them just as surely as will underwatering.

HOW TO TRANSPLANT

The first leaves you will see on your seedlings are the cotyledons, or seed-leaves. These leaves were present inside the seed, and contain stored fat and carbohydrates to nourish the seedling. Many tropical foliage plants, bulbs, and grasses will have only one seed leaf since they belong to a large group of plants with one cotyledon (the monocots). Other plants are dicots and have two cotyledons. The cotyledons usually do not look characteristic of the plant you are trying to grow. The next set of leaves — called the first true leaves — will look more familiar. You will see the cotyledons begin to shrivel as the true leaves are forming.

After the first true leaves have appeared, it is time to thin the ranks. You can do this by pricking out the seedlings and transplanting them into another flat at a wider spacing, or by pulling out and discarding superfluous seedlings. To transplant, lift each seedling gently with a wooden plant label. You can make a notch in the end of the label by removing a splinter of wood, then use the label like a fork.

In thinning or transplanting, keep in mind that you do not want the seedlings too close together. The spacing depends somewhat upon the size of the leaves, which should never touch. For best results, the seedlings should be about three inches (8 cm) apart at this stage. You want them to be close enough to keep the humidity moderately high, but not so close as to invite damping-off by overcrowding. Spacing seedlings too close will cause them to shade one another, resulting in tall and spindly growth.

After transplanting, seedlings can spend several weeks in their new location. Fertilize with fish emulsion or seaweed extract if your medium contains no soil (see chapter 7 for information on using these fertilizers). When the leaves are touching again (there now should be three or four sets of leaves), it is time to pot up the new plants or to set them out in their permanent location. Separate the seedlings gently by lifting them with the large end of a plant label or gently digging them out with a spoon. Be sure to take along as much of each plant's root system as possible, and lift the plant so as to include intact much of the surrounding soil. Replant the young plants at the same level at which they formerly were growing. They may rot if you plant them too deep.

HARDENING-OFF

If you are germinating seeds for plants that will be planted outdoors in your vegetable or flower garden, you will need to harden-off the seedlings before they are planted outside. Hardening-off means slowly acclimating plants to a new, generally harsher environment. In the outdoor garden, plants will not experience the ideal growing conditions they are used to indoors.

The first step in the hardening-off process is to reduce the temperature around the seedlings and to discontinue any fertilizer applications. These measures will slow growth, and if lighting is good, food will accumulate in the plant. This stored food will make the seedlings better able to withstand transplant shock when moved outdoors. After about two weeks of these hardening conditions, the seedlings are ready to be planted in the outdoor garden.

You can create the necessary cool environment by placing the seedlings near a cool (50° to 60°F/10° to 16°C), nondrafty window. Some gardeners prefer to harden-off plants in a cold frame, keeping the sash closed at first, then opening it more and more until it is removed entirely for the last few days of the treatment. In the absence of a cold frame, plants in pots or boxes can be set outside in a partially shaded, sheltered place when the weather allows, and covered with canvas or brought back indoors overnight. Gradually, they can be moved into the open until they are capable of withstanding full sun and wind.

A WORD ABOUT PEAT POTS, PELLETS, AND CUBES

Instead of transplanting seedlings into a flat after germination, you can transplant into peat pots filled with your favorite medium, or into specially developed peat pellets or cubes. Made from compressed peat, these compact containers swell up when they absorb water. In addition to their convenience, peat pots, pellets, and cubes offer a major advantage. The root system of the seedling is not disturbed during transplanting, because you plant the container with the seedling in the soil. The roots keep growing through the sides of the container and into the soil.

However, containers made of peat can get quite soggy if overwatered, and also can dry out very rapidly in your home, where the atmosphere is not particularly humid. You will need to tend them very carefully.

You may even encounter disease problems with peat containers. Peat is sterile as it comes from the bog, but with the new manufacturing methods which use water to harvest the peat, many fungal spores, including even damping-off spores, get introduced into the peat. You may see molds or fungi (most of which should not themselves be disease causing) growing on the surface of peat containers after they have been wet for a few days. Since such white or green patches can spread and harbor damping-off, or render the peat waterproof, you should pretreat any peat containers that have been stored in the basement or garage. Soak them in water until slightly moist, and place them in a preheated oven at 180°F (83°C) for 30 minutes. (Note: Don't oven-sterilize containers covered with plastic netting, as the netting will melt and burn.)

When you plant the seedling in its peat container in its permanent location, be sure the container is buried at least $1/4$ inch (6 mm) below the soil surface, since if the peat is exposed to the air it can act as a wick and dry out the entire container. This will seriously damage delicate roots growing through the cube or pot. Because peat pots are notorious for being so tightly compressed that roots sometimes have difficulty growing through the walls, it is best to remove the bottom of the pot and also to tear the sides before planting; this will allow the roots to emerge and help the peat pot to disintegrate.

PRODUCING YOUR OWN SEEDS

If you do not remove the spent flowers from your plants, you might be rewarded with fruits from which you can gather seeds. This will often occur naturally on begonias, cyclamens, firecracker flowers, sinningias *(Sinningia concinna),* and spider plants *(Chlorophytum comosum),* to name a few. If you are lucky enough to have large and healthy old foliage plants such as Chinese evergreen *(Aglaonema modestum)* or corn plant *(Dracaena fragrans* 'Massangeana'), these too might flower and set seeds of their own accord. Of course, depending on luck, chance, and the plant's good will is a haphazard way of going about getting your own seeds.

If you want to take matters into your own hands, you may try hand pollination and play amateur plant breeder with any of your flower-forming plants. Knowing a little basic plant anatomy helps (see Parts of the Plant, in chapter 1). Most house plants have bisexual, or perfect, flowers. The pollen-containing anther sacs tip the stamens, which are the male organs. The anthers are often yellow, but may be pink, red, purple, or orange. The number of stamens in a bloom can vary greatly from genus to genus. A cactus flower has innumerable stamens in whorls inside the petals, while an African violet has only two.

The female structure of a flower is called the pistil. There is usually only one pistil in each flower, but the stigma — its tip — may be divided into three or five long or feathery parts. The stigma is sometimes brightly colored yellow, pink, orange, or purple. In the ovary are the ovules, or egg cells, which can develop into seeds if fertilized. Pollination occurs when a pollen grain containing two cells lands on a receptive stigma. The pollen then germinates, growing downward through the pistil with the tube cell, or tube nucleus, leading the way and the generative cell (which contains two sperm nuclei) following. When this pollen tube reaches the embryo sac in an ovule, the tube cell breaks down but one of the sperm nuclei from the generative cell fertilizes the egg and the other sperm nucleus fuses with two polar nuclei. This double fertilization must occur for seeds, or embryonic plants, to develop. But before this remarkable chain of events can take place, pollen must be transferred by insect, wind, or hand.

To hand pollinate a plant, you must try to get the pollen, by any means you can, onto

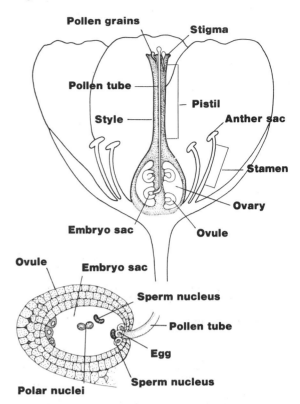

Pollination and Fertilization: A plant must be fertilized before it will produce seeds, and fertilization in turn is dependent on pollination. The large diagram shows a bisexual flower and depicts how pollination occurs. A pollen grain from the anther sac of the male stamen lands on or is carried to the stigma of the female pistil. The germinating grain then begins extending down the style, with the pollen tube reaching for the embryo sac, carrying along a generative cell. The detail shows an ovule at the moment when the pollen tube enters the embryo sac, and two sperm nuclei from the generative cell are released into the sac. One sperm nucleus fertilizes the egg at the base of the pollen tube, while the second sperm nucleus unites with two polar nuclei which have already joined together in the embryo sac. This dual fertilization is necessary for the development of seeds.

Begonia Seed Pod: A spent flower that was not plucked off yielded this pod laden with seeds.

the stigma. The tricky part comes in determining the appropriate time to perform the pollination. You will need a hand lens — the kind botanists, geologists, and entomologists have hanging around their necks when they are tramping around in the wilderness. With it you will be able to judge the proper time for pollination. When the flower opens, check the stigma with the hand lens once or twice a day. Usually it will be ready for pollination about two days after the flower opens. When the pistil is receptive, it will look full size and fuzzy. Often it also will be moist with a clear, sticky fluid. This period of readiness can last anywhere from a couple of hours to several days. Check the pollen, too. It will look loose and powdery when it is ready (except in African violets, where you will have to cut the anther sacs with nail scissors to release the pollen). If you are attempting to work with two plants, and the pollen you plan to use is ready before the stigma is prepared to accept it, you still can make the cross. Remove the pollen by cutting off the anthers, let them dry in open air for two days, then rub them between your fingers or through a sieve to release the pollen. Store pollen in a sterile glass vial and stopper the vial with absorbent cotton. Store the pollen in the freezer for later use. The viability of pollen varies tremendously from species to species. The pollen of some grasses (when not frozen) lives only a day or two, while that of the date palm can be saved by growers from year to year. Pansy and carnation pollen is reported viable for about three weeks and tomato and nasturtium pollen lasts for several months. Whatever the kind of pollen, you can prolong its life greatly by keeping it cold and dry.

Pollination is relatively simple. You can take a camel's hair paint brush, dab it into the loose pollen, and then brush it over the stigma. Or you may use your fingertip, a cotton swab, a twist of paper, or the eraser end of a pencil. You can even cut off the anther with a nail scissors and, holding it with tweezers, touch the anther sac to the stigma. Do be careful, though, to apply the pollen gently to avoid injuring the sensitive stigma. And remember, to maintain controlled pollinations it is necessary to replace your pollinator — or at least dip it in alcohol — each time you change your pollen source.

If you put the pollen back onto the

Ready for Pollination: This close-up of an amaryllis flower reveals the male and female structures during a period of readiness. The yellow anther sacs at ends of stamens are ready to liberate ripe pollen grains, which need to alight on the receptive stigma (seen here as the whitish, three-part tip of the pistil) in order for pollination and the subsequent fertilization to occur.

stigma of the same flower, another flower on the same plant, or onto a plant propagated asexually from the first plant, the process is called self-pollination. Placing the pollen on a flower from a genetically different plant of the same or another species is cross-pollination. Cross-pollination is most likely to result in seedlings which look different from the parents, having a mixture of their characteristics. Self-pollination is most apt to produce seedlings that look similar to the parent plant, but then again, it may not. Such unpredictable results make plant breeding more intriguing.

When making controlled crosses, you must insure that there is no self-pollination.

This is done by removing the stamens before the pollen is mature — a procedure appropriately called emasculation. Emasculation is best done just before the flower opens. Using a sharp razor blade, knife, or your fingernails, cut through the petals just below where they are attached and twist or cut off the stamens. Be sure not to injure or remove the column-like pistil, on which you will deposit pollen later. If there is any danger that pollen from other flowers on the same or a nearby plant might reach the exposed pistil, isolate the plant or cover the emasculated flower with a small bag until it is ready for hand pollination. After you have pollinated the flower(s), tie a tag to the flower stalk or wrap a label

Evaluating Coleus Hybrids: Plant breeder Jimmy Alston keeps careful records on those plants which exhibit the coloring and leaf shape he seeks to develop further through hybridization.

Alston studies the seedlings and selects plants that have the desirable traits. It isn't the most vigorous and fastest growing coleus seedlings that are most desirable. Although such plants would be selected for most species, in coleus they often have more undesirable green pigment in the leaves. The slow-growing, more brilliantly colored seedlings are the ones selected for further study.

Alston is trying to improve coleus by developing dramatically colored plants that branch naturally without pinching. His 'Tie-Dyed Gold' and 'Tie-Dyed Red' are colored in unusual speckled patterns rather than the typical marbling or zonation seen in other coleus. Plants with a distinctive leaf shape are another of Alston's goals, and his Lancer series sports unique swordlike foliage.

A Breeder's Search for a Better Coleus

Jimmy Alston has been a plant breeder at the Park Seed Company in Greenwood, South Carolina, for over eight years. Much of his efforts go toward overseeing the seed-testing program, a program in which Park evaluates all seeds before they are sold. Alston also hybridizes double gloxinias, begonias, sinningias, and amaryllis, but his favorite work is breeding coleus — no small task.

Individual coleus flowers are tiny and each flower on a raceme blooms at a different time, spanning a period of weeks. Alston artificially cross-pollinates each flower by hand, removing the anthers to prevent an unintentional self-pollination from sabotaging his experiments. It takes a month for the seeds to mature, and then he gets only four seeds from each laborious cross.

Should amateur breeders join the quest for the ultimate coleus? Alston suggests that beginners choose a plant that is simpler to work with than coleus. The amaryllis may be a sound choice, although this plant flowers only once a year. Begonias, he thinks, are good to start with, since their separate male and female flowers help eliminate much confusion.

around it. This should contain the date and the botanical names of both plants so you will have a record of what cross you made in case you want to repeat it. Now, sit back and wait.

But do not expect miracles. Some commercial African violet growers breed as many as 200,000 seedlings each year and among these they find only about 5 which are worthy of being propagated as improvements over previous plants. The rest are discarded. If you are working for a yellow African violet, do not expect instant success. Similarly, do not try to hybridize your amaryllis (*Hippeastrum* spp.) with your florists' gloxinia (*Sinningia speciosa*) and expect to get something really exciting. You will get nothing. Although you can pollinate anything with anything, to make that pollination work, fertilization has to occur. And fertilization occurs only when the parent plants have the same number of chromosomes. (Chromosomes are larger groups of the trait-determining factors containing genes and are found in two matching sets in just about every cell of every flowering plant.) Two plants of the same species always will have the same chromosome count. Plants in different genera, however, may not have the same number of chromosomes, so if you want to try such a cross, look up the chromosome numbers of both candidates in the bulletins of the appropriate plant society.

Matching chromosomes is just the first hurdle in successful cross-breeding. The genes must match in their functions as well as in their number and sometimes closely related plants coded by the same number of chromosomes cannot be crossed. One such cross thwarting hybridizers to date is between the genera *Streptocarpus* (cape primrose) and *Saintpaulia* (African violet). Wide crosses between distantly linked genera or even between families are sometimes possible in the laboratory, and the new asexual technique of cell fusion may one day make such apparently unlikely crosses commonplace. (See Un-

derstanding Plant Growth and Development, under Vegetative Propagation, for more on fusing cells.)

Taking into account the guidelines just given, go ahead and practice hand pollinations. You might self-pollinate a hybrid just to see what different traits find expression in its progeny. Or try crossing two fine hybrids with different backgrounds; you just might create a genetically superb plant. Another challenge is in mating a sophisticated cultivar with an unimproved species in the hope of upgrading the less developed plant's appeal or even of transferring a valuable trait from the humbler plant to the more extensively bred one. Or as parent plants you might choose different unimproved species with diverse traits — one such intriguing pair would be the many-flowered, early-blooming cactus *Lobivia arachnacantha* and the huge-flowered cactus *Echinopsis ancistrophora*.

In crossing bisexual plants, it often does not seem to matter which plant you select to donate the pollen and which to receive it. To cover every bet, many growers make the cross in both directions. Practically speaking, your chances of successful pollination should be greater if you use the plant with the longest flowers as the pollen source (in other words, pollinate the flowers with the shortest stigmas), since that way you can be surer that the pollen tube that develops will grow all the way from the stigma to the ovary — something that is obviously necessary for fertilization to occur. You would also do well to use the plant with fewer flowers as the pollen parent, for a single bloom produces thousands of pollen grains and you will want to apply pollen to as many flowers as feasible to increase the likelihood of fertilization. Remember, too, that it makes sense to give the more stressful job of seed production to the plant that is healthier and looks as if it has an ample supply of stored food.

After pollination is accomplished, you cannot do anything to help fertilization along. Just wait and be patient. If the flower petals fall off (assuming you left them intact) and the ovary begins to swell in a week or two, you can assume fertilization has occurred. If there are no signs that a seed-bearing fruit is beginning to develop, the pollen probably did not reach and fertilize the egg cells. If possible, try the cross at least two more times, using a different pair of flowers each time, before you assume that it cannot succeed.

The fertilized ovaries of some house plants, including cacti, grow into fleshy fruits, and the moist seeds inside must be washed and allowed to dry in the sun for a couple of days before they will germinate. Many of the flowering plants will form dry-looking seed capsules. Some examples are amaryllises, begonias, florists' gloxinias, *Streptocarpus* species, and African violets. You will know that the seeds of such plants are ready to harvest when the capsule changes color from dark green to dark brown, and begins to dry and split open. You do not want the pod to open and spill the seeds on the floor, so place a paper sandwich bag over it to catch the seeds.

When you collect the seeds, be sure they are thoroughly dry before you store them. Then keep them in an enclosed container in the refrigerator until you are ready to plant. African violet seeds, for instance, will keep for up to a year, but seeds of tropical foliage plants should be planted immediately.

When it comes to germinating the seeds, you are on your own. Packaged seeds usually come already scarified or stratified if needed, but you will have to do any necessary pregermination treatments yourself before sowing homegrown seeds. As a general rule, sterilize the seeds with bleach solution, soak them overnight in water, and then test for germination. If the germination percentage is high, then plant a few of the seeds. If none germinate, try scarifying or stratifying, as described earlier under Special Pretreatments. Seeds of tropical species should need no pretreatment, but you probably will need to experiment with the seeds of plants that

naturally live in environments where there are extreme seasonal changes. Seeds native to places with cold winters might need stratifying, whereas those from intermittently dry climates probably have a hard seed coat which will require scarifying. If you have patiently tried every possibility and all fail, you might search for further information in some of the books recommended in the Bibliography. As a last resort, get out a seed catalog and order seeds for the plants you want to enjoy.

If you should become skillful enough to bring plants to maturity from home-hybridized seeds and motivated enough to pursue plant breeding until you have created a unique and worthwhile new plant, you might want to register your prize specimen according to internationally agreed-upon rules. To proceed with registration, check with the appropriate plant society for the guidelines to nomenclature and try to make sure that you haven't unwittingly re-created a hybrid that already has been registered.

STARTING FERNS FROM SPORES

You can propagate your ferns sexually much as you would flowering plants. Spores are produced in spore cases which often are located on the undersides of the fronds. The spores inside look like dust. When spores are ejected naturally from the spore cases, they are blown about by the wind and land in a moist environment where each germinates into a tiny structure called a prothallus. The almost microscopic prothallus has both male structures (antheridia) and female structures (archegonia) on its underside.

Because the environment is so moist, there is a film of water over everything. The archegonia send out chemical substances into this water which attract the sperm from the antheridia. The sperm then swim into the archegonia and fertilize the eggs. Each fertilized egg develops into an embryo in the archegonium and keeps on growing into a mature fern. The new plant is nourished by the prothallus until it is large enough to make it on its own. See chapter 11 for more information on the life cycle of a fern.

You really do not have to understand the whole life cycle to get spores to grow into ferns. But it helps if you are aware of the conditions you must create to propagate successfully from spores.

You can buy fern spores, or you can collect them from your own plants. You will see the spore cases on the undersides of fertile fronds along the midrib or around the edges of leaflets. Many novice fern fanciers never notice them when they are green, and become alarmed when the spore cases turn brown.

The spore cases will slowly mature and change color until in most species they turn to shiny brown. At this point the spores are ready to collect. Cut off the frond and lay it on white paper with the spore cases facing down. Overnight the spore cases should pop open and the spores will drop onto the paper. When you lift the frond, they will form a tracery of it that looks like green or brown dust. Remove and discard any large pieces of spore case, then bend the paper and direct the spores into a paper envelope. Plan to use the spores within a few days and store them in the refrigerator in a tightly closed jar until then.

Green-colored spores are very short lived, so you should sow them as soon as possible. Depending on the species of fern, brown spores will keep for a year or many years if stored properly. It is a good idea to surface-sterilize fern spores before you sow them. Use a 5 percent solution of bleach (1 part bleach and 19 parts water). Sterilizing spores is a bit difficult since they may float on the surface of the solution and cling to the edges of the container. After the spores have been in the solution for five minutes, pour them off, catching them in a filter paper or in a tea strainer lined with a paper towel. Rinse with cooled, boiled water; let the paper dry in open air.

There are several different methods of germinating spores. Some favorites are to use finely screened soil (pasteurization is absolutely essential) or finely screened milled sphagnum. One part peat and 1 part sand also makes a good medium. You can use any container that you might use for germinating seeds, but two in particular are preferred by fern enthusiasts. One is a mason jar laid on its side. An inch (2.5 cm) of medium is placed on the lower side, and when the lid is screwed shut the environment stays quite humid.

Bricks sterilized in an oven by baking at 250°F (122°C) for 30 minutes are also popular. After the brick cools, cover the top with about an inch (2.5 cm) of milled sphagnum or soil, and set it in a shallow container kept constantly filled with water. The water will be drawn up to the surface of the brick by capillary action as needed, and the germinating spores will be consistently moist, but never soggy, and the surrounding air kept humid. This may be the most foolproof method of growing ferns from spores.

Keep whatever container you choose enclosed in glass or plastic to maintain very high relative humidity, with a film of moisture over everything. It is also very important that the soil and containers be scrupulously clean. Within this humid environment algae can invade and overrun all your baby ferns, and are as much to be feared as damping-off. Needless to say, pasteurize your medium and use bleach solution on your containers before you get under way.

Sprinkle the spores over the moist medium as you would fine seeds. Keep them moist, warm, and in indirect sunlight or under fluorescent tubes. Do not allow them to receive direct, burning sunlight. A north window is ideal.

In 4 to 14 days you should begin to see a haze of green on the medium, and eventually a mat of prothalli will appear. When you can distinguish individual prothalli from the haze, you should begin to aid in fertilization. Mist the green mat lightly once a week for three weeks to provide a water film for the sperm to swim in. After three weeks, fertilization should have occurred on many of the prothalli. Using tweezers, pull the mat apart into ¼-inch (6 mm) squares that include the medium, and set them about ½ inch (13 mm) apart in a new flat of medium. Keep them moist and covered with glass or plastic.

Tiny ferns will begin to appear, and they too can be separated when they become crowded. Plant them in 2½-inch (6 cm) pots of medium, keeping them moist at all times. Gradually reduce the humidity until they can survive without being enclosed.

This whole process may take seven months or more, so plan to be patient. However, you probably will find that you enjoy tending those baby maidenhair ferns (*Adiantum* spp.), Boston ferns *(Nephrolepis exaltata)* or holly ferns *(Cyrtomium falcatum).* In fact, if you get even a small percentage of the spores you collect to germinate into tiny ferns, you will have enough ferns to start a business or plant an old-fashioned fernery. (For more information on propagating ferns successfully, see chapter 11.)

VEGETATIVE PROPAGATION

Sexual propagation (seeds or spores) produces offspring with varying characteristics. But in asexual propagation the parent plant is duplicated exactly. Asexual or vegetative propagation occurs naturally and has been of immense importance in horticulture. Many plants in the wild reproduce asexually from vegetative parts. Roots growing and creeping underground on an aloe *(Aloe barbadensis)* produce buds (suckers) which grow into new plants. Branches of blackberry bend down to the ground in the autumn and grow roots where they touch the soil, forming separate plants. Boston ferns and airplane plants send out runners which establish new plants at their tips. *Cereus,* a cactus, will drop some of its branches to the ground, and these will root when the growing conditions are favorable.

The fallen leaves of the succulent jade plant *(Crassula argentea)* form tiny shoots and roots when they touch the ground. All of these new plants are separate individuals, but are genetically identical to the original plant.

The foregoing natural methods of vegetative propagation have been exploited by horticulturists as ways of circumventing the disadvantages of seed propagation. Seedlings may take too long to grow into mature plants, or the genetics of a plant may be too complicated to produce hybrid seeds. Seeds from some plants are slow to germinate or germinate over a long period of time, making the regular and uniform production of such plants very costly and difficult. Besides, it often requires as long as five to eight years to create a worthwhile hybrid line. So when uniformity of plant material is necessary and seed propagation is not practical, horticulturists turn to vegetative methods of propagation. Commercial growers often do likewise to produce large numbers of uniform plants to sell.

The word clone is used to describe a group of individual plants which are genetically identical, being propagated vegetatively from a particular selected plant and its vegetatively propagated offspring. Roses, florists' chrysanthemums, fruit trees, grapes, foliage plants, and many species of trees are often cloned and propagated exclusively by asexual means. Most of the plants you grow indoors probably have been propagated this way, and you can learn how to multiply your plants using many techniques of vegetative propagation.

UNDERSTANDING PLANT GROWTH AND DEVELOPMENT

In order to use asexual propagation techniques most effectively, it will be helpful to understand how plants grow. Plants increase in size in two ways, either by producing more cells (cell division) or by enlarging existing cells (cell elongation and enlargement). Most cell division occurs in meristematic cells. Groups of these — called meristems — are located in several places in the body of a plant.

Cells located at the tip of each stem and branch are constantly and rapidly dividing to form the new leaf and stem cells. These groups of specialized cells, called apical meristems, also produce auxin, a plant hormone. Auxin travels down the stem and influences how the rest of the plant grows. Lateral meristems are present in the dormant buds located in the axil of each leaf. These are identical to apical meristems except that they are dormant and will not become active and divide until they receive the proper hormonal signal. It is the auxin produced by the apical meristem which keeps the lateral meristems dormant, but when the apical meristem is removed (by pinching back the plant, for instance) the cessation of auxin flow allows the dormant lateral buds to "break" and grow into new branches and leaves.

Meristems also are present at the tips of each root, and divide and elongate to produce longer roots. The cambium is a group of meristematic cells located in the stem which divides to produce more cells which add to the girth of the stem.

Vegetative propagation of a plant usually is most successful if the piece of plant being used for propagation contains some meristematic cells. When you are rooting a cutting, the apical meristem gives rise to the new shoot and leaves. Less specialized cells (called parenchymal cells) from other parts of the plant undergo a change which causes them to become similar to meristem tissue, and these cells then begin dividing to form root tissue.

The cutting grows into an identical plant because it still has the same genes that the original plant had. The genes inside each cell function rather like blueprints, for they carry all the genetic information necessary to make a complete plant. Each cell retains that total information throughout the life of the plant,

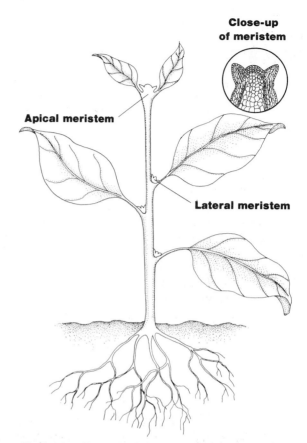

Close-up of meristem

Apical meristem

Lateral meristem

Meristems Responsible for Plant Growth: During the course of normal growth, the apical meristems at stem and branch tips are responsible for the formation of new leaves and the lengthening of stems. The lateral meristems, found in dormant buds nestled in leaf axils, have the same capability as apical meristems, but need a special hormonal signal to trigger their action. When you pinch the growing tip of a plant, this sets up the proper signal, causing the lateral buds to burst forth with new leaves and branches. Inset shows the grouping of cells in a meristem; the rapid cellular division, invisible to the naked eye, accounts for the readily visible signs of plant growth.

regardless of whether that cell is present in a leaf, a flower, or a root. In a leaf cell, for instance, every gene necessary to make a complete plant is present but only those needed to make that cell a leaf cell are active; other genes are turned off. When we propagate that leaf by removing it from the plant and placing it in moist sand, some genes previously

(continued on page 124)

Visit to a Brave New World

In a remote attic room, white-coated figures bend intently over large vats holding a special formula. Nearby, others under strange hoods perform exquisitely delicate operations on living tissue. The room is filled with the eerie sound of exhaled air being returned to the atmosphere through filters in the hoods. From time to time a rush of steam escapes from a huge pressure-cooker-like piece of equipment as one of the white-coated figures inserts or removes jars or test tubes containing The Formula. In an adjoining room, row upon row of test tubes squat silently beneath glaring fluorescent lights. Nourished by a super formula, the cells within each vial are regenerating rapidly into new individuals.

Though this breathy narrative reads like the set directions for a Hollywood thriller that could be dubbed "The Clone Zone," it is a fair description of business as usual in the tissue culture laboratory at Fetzer Greenhouses in Hartsville, Pennsylvania. Operating since November of 1975, the air-conditioned lab must maintain a hospitallike sterility, for fungal and bacterial contaminants from the air and the human body can grow on the nutrient medium, destroying the plant tissue being propagated. For this reason, the staff wears lab coats, most work is done while the technicians sit under hoods that filter all contaminants from the air, and the

Tissue Culture at Fetzer Greenhouses: Under sterile working conditions, an employee oversees the process of rapid regeneration which can yield up to 8,000 plants in the span of a week.

growth medium mixed in the vats is sterilized in an autoclave (a device that uses superheated steam under pressure).

The nutrient medium contains a standard formula of the 17 elements that plants are known to require for growth and that they normally obtain from the soil. Other ingredients that cells ordinarily receive from the growing plant are also added to the brew. These include sugar, vitamins, and hormones. (The manipulation of the plant tissue with hormones is the secret behind getting each individual plant species to grow in a test tube.) Once blended, the medium is solidified with agar, a gelatinous substance, and dispensed into test tubes or jars and sterilized.

Each prepared vial or jar then receives a minute amount of plant tissue called the explant. In the tissue culturing of most foliage plants, a technician aided by a microscope cuts off the shoot tip, which consists of the apical meristem, leaf primordia (cells that will become leaves), axillary buds, and other specialized cells. The tip, which can be as small as the head of a pin, is usually free of plant pathogens. When placed in a test tube and positioned under fluorescent light, the apical meristem grows quickly, and in a month the tube is filled with many tiny shoots.

The shoots then are separated, and each one is returned to a separate test tube to grow again into many shoots. Depending upon the rate of shoot production, thousands of plants can be generated from one shoot tip in several months. When plants are desired, the tiny shoots are transferred to a different medium where they grow roots. They then are planted in the greenhouse and treated like seedlings.

Compared with traditional sexual and asexual methods of propagation, tissue cultures makes possible great savings in labor, energy, and plant material costs. Fewer workers are needed in the lab than in a comparatively productive greenhouse, and although the technicians are paid more than less skilled greenhouse help, they also produce more — three employees in the Fetzer lab can propagate 7,000 to 8,000 plants each week. Less physical space relative to output is needed in the lab, which at Fetzers' covers 11,000 square feet, and heating and lighting such an enclosed area is much cheaper than warming a greenhouse in winter. The Fetzers also save money on plant materials, for they no longer need to buy seedlings or cuttings elsewhere for propagation purposes.

On the debit side, the start-up costs of a lab may be an obstacle for greenhouse owners who would like to have one. Constructing a facility comparable to Fetzers and stocking it with the rather specialized equipment required costs an estimated $50,000, with an additional $50,000 necessary to get the business well under way. (At Fetzers, costs were cut initially by converting an unused attic room into a lab, but this facility was quickly outgrown and is being replaced by a new structure.) Another possible problem in getting into tissue culture is finding the specially trained personnel needed to manage and work in such a lab.

There are, though, immediate horticultural as well as long-range economic benefits that help make up for the special challenges involved in this new method of propagation. Usually faster than traditional ways of multiplying plants, tissue culture allows the propagator to build up new and different plant material rapidly. For example, when the orchids grown at Fetzers for cut flowers are tissue cultured, they bloom in just $3\frac{1}{2}$ years — half the time required for orchids grown from seeds. Also, this kind of vegetative propagation is effective with some plants that do not respond well to older asexual methods. Plants grown from tissue culture are free of external bacterial and fungal diseases since they are generated in a sterile environment. More importantly, shoot-tip culture can be used to remove internal pathogens (bacteria, viruses, and mycoplasmas) from clones, following which clean plants may be built up in the sterile test tubes, where there is no chance of their becoming reinfected.

Because of the scientific precision and the special tools involved, tissue culture may never be widely popular with home gardeners (although home-tissue-culture kits are available). But it is a boon to large-scale growers and professional breeders, and increasing numbers of the plants sold commercially are being propagated by these techniques.

turned off will be reactivated to supply the information for cells to make new shoots and roots.

Since every cell in a plant has the blueprints for an entire plant, it is theoretically possible to propagate a plant from just a single cell. Scientists have actually done this with a few plant species using a method called tissue culture. Tissue culture requires a sterilized blend of the nutrients, hormones, and vitamins necessary for plant growth. A form of cloning, tissue culture has been a great benefit to scientists who study plant growth, but it is also an exciting way to propagate plants commercially. In recent years, many nurseries have set up tissue culture laboratories to propagate orchids, Boston ferns, African violets, gerberas, philodendrons, strawberry begonias, and other foliage plants. (See Visit to a Brave New World for a closer look at one such commercial operation.)

Recent breakthroughs in cell biology suggest that in the future tissue culture will be the basis for a revolution in plant breeding. Researchers have discovered that individual cells not only can regenerate whole plants, but with the help of certain biochemicals they can be fused first so the resulting plant is a genetically new one. Evolved through the pioneering work of Dr. Peter Carlson, who teaches at Michigan State University, the techniques of cell fusion are seen as the key to overcoming the natural incompatibility that has so far limited the varieties of plants obtainable through hybridization.

GENERAL NEEDS OF PLANTS BEING PROPAGATED VEGETATIVELY

House plants are most frequently propagated by cutting off and rooting small vegetative portions of the plant. Whether you are propagating a leaf cutting from a rex begonia (Begonia ×rex-cultorum), a softwood stem cutting from an English ivy (Hedera helix), or a sucker from a cast-iron plant (Aspidistra elatior), the severed part of the plant undergoes a shock because its supply of water and nutrients suddenly has been removed. You must nurse these cuttings through that shock by providing high humidity until complete plants are formed again. Many cuttings also benefit from or require light and extra warmth. Regardless of the plant part you are propagating, the methods you will be using to provide these essentials will be the same.

HUMIDITY

It may take some cuttings many weeks to regenerate new roots. Until that time, you must keep the atmosphere very humid to prevent dehydration of the plant until it can absorb water through its new root system. You can help by watering stock plants especially well about a day before taking cuttings. This will assure that cuttings are filled with water when severed from the parent plant. To keep cuttings from losing this water through transpiration (the natural loss of a plant's internal water through its stomates, or pores), raise the humidity around them immediately and maintain it at a high level. Commercial greenhouse growers usually propagate cuttings under conditions of 100 percent humidity by using intermittent misting systems. Cuttings are rooted in benches with water pipes running overhead or rising vertically in the form of towers several feet or meters high. This piping is fitted with fine spray nozzles, often controlled by automatic timers. The cuttings are sprayed for several seconds every few minutes (exact intervals are determined by solar radiation and ambient humidity) to keep a film of water on the surface of the leaves. This water film acts to slow transpiration, keeping the cutting turgid and fresh until roots are formed.

If you have a greenhouse, you may be able to design an automatic misting system similar to those used commercially by purchasing the specialized pipes and nozzles. Or you can build your own mist chamber, as described in chapter 29. But even without elaborate equipment, there are easy ways to supply ample humidity for cuttings.

The most common method is to enclose the propagating container. This assures 100 percent humidity inside, but can increase disease problems due to lack of fresh air. Plastic bags or sheets are excellent for enclosing propagating containers. (Polyethylene or polypropylene is best since either of these plastics is permeable to the respiration gases, oxygen and carbon dioxide.) One plastic sandwich bag will cover a single pot and a single cutting, while glass plates are more convenient for flats of small cuttings. See Build Your Own Propagation Bed, earlier in this chapter, for instructions on how to construct a plastic-covered bed.

PROPAGATION CONTAINERS

You will not need anything fancy or special in which to propagate your cuttings as long as the unit can be enclosed to keep in moisture. Individual cuttings may be rooted in small clay or plastic pots, or you may recycle yogurt or cottage cheese containers and Styrofoam cups, punching holes in the bottoms for drainage. Groups of cuttings may be placed in plastic shoe or bread boxes and you can punch drainage holes in these with a heated ice pick. Pyrex casserole dishes or fish tanks are also useful, but since these provide no drainage, you will need to take care with the watering can to avoid overwatering your young plants.

Place the individual pots inside plastic bags and tie each one shut. The plastic should not touch the leaves, for beads of water will form on the inside of the plastic and rot any plant parts that come in contact with them. You may find it useful to use one or more plant labels or pencils as supports to keep the plastic away from the plant.

The drops of water you see forming on the inside of the plastic cover indicate that there is enough water inside to keep the atmosphere at 100 percent humidity. But you do not want this moisture to be excessive, and a little fresh air is important, too. A few holes punched in the plastic will solve both problems. As long as there are small water beads forming on the plastic, the cuttings are moist enough. When the little droplets are no longer visible on the cover, add water to the growing medium. To help new plants under plastic make a gradual adjustment to less humid conditions, keep a pin nearby and perforate the bag once or twice several times a day when you are passing by. In a week or two the cover will be ragged and the plant beneath will have adjusted to the surrounding environment.

If you are using a hard plastic container as a propagating box, you can punch holes in the top with a heated ice pick to provide air. Or you can tilt the lid slightly to create a crack for air. Casserole dishes and glass-covered fish tanks should have their lids tipped a little, too, to allow some air movement. You can regulate the air exchange by the size of the opening you leave. Always try to keep a film of small water beads on the surface of the top, opening it a bit more if the beads look very large and closing it and watering if they fail to appear at all.

For another ready-made propagating case, consider using one of the glass or plastic domes made to keep baked goods or cheese moist and fresh. A cover large enough to fit over a three-layer cake can accommodate 30 cuttings housed in two-inch (5 cm) pots. Prop up the lid slightly for aeration as needed.

Be sure to provide a layer of gravel for drainage inside a fish tank or other container with no holes in the bottom. Since the sides of the glass containers are clear, you can prevent overwatering if you closely observe the propagating medium through the sides.

A wooden or plastic flat also makes a good propagating container, but trying to enclose it may pose an obstacle. You can always make the plastic-covered wooden frame described earlier, or a sheet of plastic alone may be used successfully as a cover if you construct supports for it (see Build Your Own Plastic-Enclosed Flat for directions).

PROPAGATION MEDIA

Even though the cut surface of the cutting can absorb only a small amount of water until roots form, a good propagating medium still should hold lots of water. It is the water evaporating from the propagating medium that keeps the humidity high around the cutting. A good propagating medium also should hold lots of air, since oxygen is needed for the conversion of the plant's sugar into the energy needed to grow new roots. It may seem impossible for a medium to hold large quantities of both water and air, but there are simple ways you can create such a medium for your cuttings.

Perlite is a very lightweight substance containing many pores that provide excellent water-holding capacity. Because it will not compact, the spaces between the particles have a good air-holding capacity. Vermiculite, another man-made mineral product, is also lightweight but tends to compact. Sand, which also provides adequate aeration, has fewer water-holding pores than either perlite or vermiculite. All three substances often are used alone for propagating plants. Because they provide no nutrients, a cutting should not be left in them after roots begin to form.

Peat or sphagnum moss occasionally are used alone for rooting cuttings. These materials have a tremendous capacity for holding water, but they also have a tendency to compact, depriving the plant of air. Peat and sphagnum are also notorious for being difficult to wet when dry. It takes about 24 hours for these products to thoroughly absorb water, so wet them the day before you plan to use them. Though peat and sphagnum are plant products, they are low in nutrients because they are only partly decomposed. Both

are highly acidic, which is a deterrent to damping-off, and sphagnum has a natural ability to inhibit the growth of bacteria and fungi. This fungistatic quality makes it especially useful in combating rot problems in the rooting medium. Rotting can occur in overwatered media at higher temperatures, and afflicted cuttings develop blackening of the stem.

Using soil alone for a propagating medium is a poor choice. Soil will compact and remain soggy after watering. There are few air spaces and the cuttings are very prone to rot. Although soil will supply nutrients, nutrients are not really necessary for rooting. However, cuttings should be transplanted out of a soilless propagating medium as quickly as possible after they root.

Often a mixture of various ingredients is made for propagating plants. A blend that contains one part each of peat, perlite or vermiculite, and soil will offer the positive qualities of each and minimize the negative ones. The soil is necessary only if cuttings will be left in the propagating mixture after they have rooted, as it will keep them from starving from lack of nutrients. If you plan to pot up cuttings as soon as they are rooted, you may use a half-and-half mixture of peat and perlite. Any combination you create with whatever ingredients are at hand will work if it drains quickly while still holding water. Be sure that you pasteurize any medium that includes soil or sand (see chapter 6 for instructions), and that you sterilize any containers that have held diseased or dead plants (directions are included under Sexual Propagation, earlier in this chapter). Use only healthy-looking cuttings, and cut them with tools sterilized in rubbing alcohol or in a solution of 9 parts water and 1 part household bleach.

ROOTING IN WATER

Sometimes the easiest way to root a cutting seems to be to drop it in a glass of water, ignore it, and be rewarded with roots in a few

Build Your Own Plastic-Enclosed Flat

For use as a propagation bed for rooting tall or very large cuttings, nothing will do a better job than a plastic-covered flat. Use either wire coat hangers or ⅛-inch wire to construct a simple framework over the flat. This framework is then used to support a layer of clear polyethylene plastic. The plastic can be pulled down and stapled to the flat for a more permanent unit, but be sure to leave one end loose to let you work inside the miniature greenhouse.

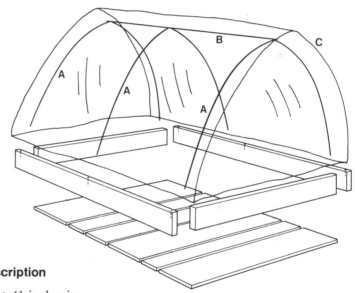

Special Tools:

Brazing torch or epoxy
Stapler
Hacksaw or wire cutters

Materials:

Item	Quantity	Description
A. Hoops	3	⅛ × 41-inch wire
B. Brace	1	⅛ × 22 ½-inch wire
C. Plastic	1	4 × 5-foot polyethylene plastic
Brazing rod	—	
Basic flat	1	2 ½ × 20 × 24-inch wood flat

Procedure:

1. Cut three pieces of ⅛-inch wire 41 inches long for the support hoops (A).
2. Drill six ⅛-inch holes in the top edge of the flat to receive the wire support hoops (A).
3. Form hoops and fit them into the holes.
4. Cut a piece of ⅛-inch wire 22 ½ inches long for the top brace (B), and braze it in place. Epoxy may be used in place of brazing. Soldering is not an option when working with steel.
5. Cover the frame with clear polyethylene plastic (C).

weeks or a month. Though this method often works, it is rarely advisable. Most plants, even if they root in the water, are under a hardship when propagated this way. There is very little air in the water, so the cutting may be slow to root. And the roots that are formed are different from those formed in soil. They are coarse and less branched, have fewer root hairs, and are more brittle. When you transplant that cutting to soil, it undergoes another shock because its roots are not adapted to absorb water from soil.

However, if you are tempted occasionally to propagate plants this way, there are a few tricks to make success more likely. Let any tapwater you plan to use for cuttings sit for 24 hours so it reaches room temperature and the chlorine in it evaporates. From time to time change the water in which cuttings are rooting to give them more oxygen and forestall the growth of algae. To keep cuttings in water vigorous and to speed early rooting, you might try adding a pinch each of rooting hormone and house plant fertilizer. After you transplant the rooted cutting into soil, pinch it back if you want the plant to branch thickly. You also should cover the pot with a plastic bag for a week or so to give the cutting high humidity while finer roots are being formed. If a cutting started in water has developed a welter of tangled roots, you can improve its chances of surviving the transition to soil by adding a potting medium around the roots while they are floating freely underwater. Just place the pot you are going to use under water up to its rim and hold the cutting so its roots are positioned properly in the pot. Then slowly drop soil into the pot and let it settle around the spread-out roots. When the roots are well covered, remove the newly potted plant from the water and allow it to drain.

It is also helpful to keep the newly potted plant for at least two weeks in the same place where it rooted in water. That way it will not have to adjust to different levels of light and warmth right away.

A few plants will not suffer from being propagated in water and may even prosper if grown indefinitely in water and never potted in soil. You might find this true of arrowhead vine *(Syngonium podophyllum)*, pothos *(Epipremnum aureum)*, Chinese evergreen, and the familiar heart-leaf philodendron *(Philodendron scandens* subsp. *oxycardium)* — all of which can live in water, though they should be fed occasionally to thrive.

LIGHT

Light is necessary to keep cuttings healthy and producing the energy needed to grow new roots. Very bright but indirect sunlight is best. Direct sunlight must be avoided since the heat from the rays will be trapped inside the plastic or glass cover and literally cook the unfortunate cuttings. Fluorescent lights do not give off much heat and are ideal for use in propagating plants. If you place the cuttings six to ten inches (15 to 25 cm) away from the tubes you need not worry that they will be overheated.

Cuttings are often propagated in full sun in greenhouses where intermittent mist is used. The evaporation of water film on the leaves cools them so the full sunlight does not burn or overheat the cuttings. Rooting is faster in bright light, so intermittent mist is a great aid to a commercial grower, who is usually in a greater hurry than you are. If you are using an enclosed chamber or polyethylene tent in the greenhouse, you will have to place it under the bench or shade it with cheesecloth or the cuttings will overheat.

WARMTH

New cuttings are in a state of shock. They need warmth to stay healthy and aid in regenerating new roots. This may be the most difficult requirement to meet, since the ideal temperature is 70° to 75°F (21° to 24°C) and many of us do not keep our homes this warm. If you place your cuttings in a window where they receive good light, they also may get cold drafts.

For rooting, the soil temperature is usually more important than the air temperature. Commercial plant propagators provide "bottom heat" for their cuttings by laying heating cables in the propagating medium, or by rooting the cuttings over steam heating pipes. Bottom heat which keeps the soil temperature at 70° to 75°F (21° to 24°C) can be provided at home by using heating cables with or without attached thermostats. These are sold at garden centers. If installed properly, a cable should maintain the promised temperature but a built-in thermostat can help. You also can buy specially heated mats, trays, and propagating boxes, but these often are not worth the money.

With a little electrical knowledge and mechanical skill, you can build your own wooden flat complete with bottom heat. Such a homemade unit is very practical and sturdy, and cheaper than those small plastic units sold by garden centers. You can build the flat described in Build Your Own Basic Flat, earlier in this chapter, and simply install a heating cable in the bottom of the flat before adding the propagation medium. If you do work with electrical heating cable, remember not to shorten it since the thickness and length of the wire were both precalculated to provide the proper heat. Be sure to purchase a cable that has a built-in, preset soil thermostat which maintains a uniform soil temperature.

Bottom heat provided by heating cables is reliable and accurate but expensive, since you will be drawing electricity 24 hours a day for several weeks. With a little imagination perhaps you can find free heat. For instance, you could locate your plastic-enclosed cuttings on a board on top of a radiator or near a hot air duct. Other warm spots are the top of the refrigerator or the top of the furnace or hot water heater. Some people place their cuttings on the top of a fluorescent lighting fixture, which transmits a suitably gentle

warmth. Use a thermometer to precheck all these places, remembering that roots grow best from 63° to 77°F (17° to 25°C). And be sure to provide enough light.

WHAT YOU NEED TO KNOW ABOUT ROOTING HORMONES

Although you may want to use rooting hormones just to speed up rooting, you will find that they are actually necessary for certain cuttings to root at all. Hormone powders are available at garden centers or through seed catalogs and should be used judiciously. They come in varying strengths, some of which are good for most house plants, others of which are recommended for woody material that is harder to root.

Rooting hormones contain talc as a carrying agent, and one or two kinds of synthetic auxins, usually NAA (naphthalene acetic acid) and/or IBA (indolebutyric acid). The natural hormone equivalent is the auxin called IAA (indoleacetic acid). Nature designed IAA to be unstable in the presence of light and high temperatures as a natural way of controlling its activity. However, because of this instability, IAA is rarely included in rooting preparations.

NAA and IBA are more stable than IAA but begin to lose effectiveness after six to eight months. Purchase only small quantities at a time and store the powder in a tightly closed container in a refrigerator or other cool place.

To use the powders, remove a small portion from the container onto a dish or piece of paper. Dip the cut end of the cutting into the powder to a depth of two inches (5 cm) and tap off the excess. Do not let frugality influence you here; throw away any leftover powder, since the cutting has contaminated the hormone with moisture and bacteria which will speed up the compound's deterioration.

You may wish to experiment with a method used by old-time English gardeners, who would embed a germinating grain seed in the base of a cutting as a rooting aid. A germinating seed contains a rich supply of auxins and will provide these to the cutting. Soak the grain seed and treat it just as you would if you were sprouting seeds for your salads or Chinese dishes. When it just begins to germinate, the proper time to use it has arrived. Push it gently into the bottom of a succulent cutting, or place it into a slit cut into the bottom of hard woody cuttings.

It is easy to tell when your cuttings are rooted and ready to be transplanted to their permanent homes. You will notice that new growth has begun on the top of the cutting. A slight tug on the cutting should meet with resistance at this time since roots will have formed before top growth resumed. Do not tug too vigorously, or you may injure delicate new roots.

Gently lift the cuttings from the propagating medium with a wooden plant label or spoon so as to avoid injuring roots. Choose a pot that is not too large for the small cutting or it may become waterlogged. Spread the roots apart gently and add soil appropriate for the plant. Give the pot a thump to settle the soil around the roots, and water. Watch the cutting carefully the first week or so for signs of stress such as wilting or yellowing. Provide extra humidity if wilting occurs.

Remember to label cuttings that can be easily confused, African violet leaf cuttings, for instance. Write the name of the plant on a square of masking tape and stick it around the stem of the cutting or on the pot.

PROPAGATING VARIOUS PLANT PARTS

HERBACEOUS AND SOFTWOOD STEM CUTTINGS

Sometimes the terms herbaceous cutting and softwood cutting are erroneously used interchangeably. These cuttings are handled the same way, but they come from two different types of plants. A softwood cutting is derived from a woody plant which has a seasonal growth cycle and produces new, succulent growth only during certain seasons, usually just in spring. Softwood cuttings are taken from this new growth. An herbaceous cutting is also from soft, succulent plant tissue, but the plant it comes from does not have a cycle of soft growth alternating with maturing woody growth; its tissues are always soft and succulent.

Begonias, coleus, impatiens, wandering Jews, and many gesneriads (such as African violets and gloxinias) that are commonly grown in the home or greenhouse can be propagated from herbaceous cuttings taken at any time of the year. Softwood cuttings of indoor plants might come from hydrangeas *(Hydrangea macrophylla),* for example, or miniature roses.

Herbaceous and softwood cuttings may be similar in that both may consist of soft, succulent, rapidly growing stem tissue. The shoots are not mature, and the growing shoot tip is producing lots of auxin, so the stems respond well when made into cuttings. Rooting is rapid and rooting powders often are not used, although some plants will respond to the lower concentrations. Some softwood cuttings, however, are thin, with little stored food, wilt easily, and tend to defoliate after a few weeks. These cuttings usually will respond well to auxin.

You usually will not need a knife to make these cuttings from well-grown plants. If your plants are turgid and fresh, the cutting will snap off under pressure from your fingers. The ideal cutting will bend slightly under light pressure and break in two when it is bent double. Cuttings from thinner, softer plants will need to be removed with a knife or razor blade. Since these more delicate cuttings also are more prone to fungus invasion, it is a good idea to wash your tools in a bleach solution before taking the cuttings. Break off the cutting, which should be about three to five inches (8 to 13 cm) long, just below the

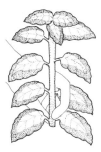

Herbaceous Cuttings: This healthy plant has been chosen as a likely prospect for yielding a cutting. A section is cut off below the fourth set of mature leaves, which are then removed before the cutting is set in water. From these stripped areas, as well as from other points along the stem, roots will emerge in about a month's time. The parent plant should not be forgotten; remove the bare stem from just above the next remaining pair of leaves, making a more attractive plant which in time will sprout new leaves.

third or fourth set of leaves. Strip the foliage off the lower one or two nodes (points where leaves emerge) before you insert the cutting into the rooting medium (which may be water in some cases). For best results, leave at least two stripped nodes underground or underwater, as nodes sometimes can produce roots more easily than internodes (spaces between nodes or leaves). It is also important to leave several healthy leaves above ground, especially on softwood cuttings. Also, be sure to break off the bare internode remaining on

your mother plant just above the next node. That unsightly stub will not grow new leaves and will die, inviting disease and decay.

Softwood and herbaceous cuttings root easily in less than a month if proper moisture, light, and humidity are provided. Since plants such as Persian violets, wax begonias, and coleus lose their succulence as they age, you might want to assure a supply of more tender, younger plants by systematically taking cuttings from one-year-olds, then discarding those donor plants that are losing their good looks.

SEMIHARDWOOD STEM CUTTINGS

Many of your indoor plants will be propagated from semihardwood cuttings. Gardenias *(Gardenia jasminoides),* calamondin *(×Citrofortunella mitis),* camellia *(Camellia japonica),* and holly *(Ilex* spp.) make magnificent indoor plants that are certainly worth propagating. When grown in the home or greenhouse, these plants experience periods of growth and periods when growth ceases, though they never lose all of their leaves and never become fully dormant in the sense that plants grown outdoors do. You will be most successful in propagating these plants if you take stem cuttings when the flush of growth has stopped, and the woody stem tissue is still young but has passed the soft stage. You will recognize this stage easily. It occurs when no more new leaves are being formed and when the youngest leaves have turned from that fresh green color to a deeper green.

Semihardwood cuttings root more easily if rooting hormone is applied, since they are slower to root than herbaceous cuttings. The hormone will reduce the time the cuttings spend in the stressful rootless condition and you will get more satisfactory results.

You will need a very sharp pruner, knife, or single-edged razor blade to remove the cutting because the stem will be a bit tough. These tools make clean, flat wounds that heal quickly and do not have rough edges in which harmful organisms might multiply. Scissors can be used, but they tend to bruise the tissue. If you feel more comfortable using scissors, make cuttings taken with them an extra ½ inch (13 mm) long, then place the cuttings on a board and remove the extra stem with a clean cut by a single-edged razor blade. Clean all tools in bleach solution before you take the cuttings.

A semihardwood cutting should be four to six inches (10 to 15 cm) long and cut at the node as described for softwood cuttings. Remove any stub from the mother plant. Leaves which would go below the surface of the medium should be removed. Be extra careful to supply high humidity for these cuttings, since it may take them up to two months to form roots. The length of time it takes for roots to develop really depends upon the kind of plant you are propagating, but for most, the addition of bottom heat will speed up rooting.

HARDWOOD STEM CUTTINGS

Hardwood cuttings are made from dormant woody stems of plants with seasonal growth cycles. This method is used primarily for outdoor deciduous trees and shrubs. Cuttings are made from fall to early spring after leaves have fallen and plants have become dormant. The cuttings are given high humidity and adequate moisture over winter until the long rooting process is completed. These cuttings do not require light but do respond to bottom heat and rooting powders. Air temperatures in the rooting area should be kept between 35° and 45°F (2° and 7°C) so that buds will receive their necessary chilling but will not grow out until roots are available to supply them with water. Since these cuttings are hard and woody, they are much easier to handle and much more resistant to disease than softwoods. Indoor plants do not experience a period of complete dormancy, so hardwood-cutting methods seldom are used by

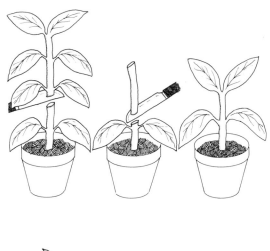

Semihardwood and Cane Cuttings: The top sequence shows how to take a semihardwood cutting. Choose a plant that is resting, and make a clean cut below the third or fourth pair of leaves. Before inserting into rooting medium, break off the lower leaves and apply rooting hormone. Care that includes plenty of humidity and bottom heat, plus a little patience, will be rewarded by the appearance of new roots. Trim the stem on the parent plant to just above the first set of remaining leaves. The bottom drawing shows how an unappealing, leafless stem can be put to good use through cane cuttings. Check the stem for scars where leaves used to be; cut 2-inch (5 cm) pieces, each including a scar. These pieces, placed horizontally at least 1 inch (2.5 cm) below the soil surface, will yield roots and shoots, as a whole new generation of plants is created.

the indoor gardener unless he or she wishes to propagate some outdoor trees and shrubs, such as azaleas.

CANE CUTTINGS

If your dragon tree *(Dracaena marginata)* is touching the ceiling and has an ugly bare stem, you may wish to rejuvenate it. You can cut off the top and root it as a semihardwood cutting, or you can air layer it (as described later). Either choice will leave you with a long leafless stem which can be made into many cane cuttings.

If you look closely at the cane or stem, you will see marks where the old leaves once grew (leaf scars). At the base of these scars is a dormant bud which can grow into a shoot if given the proper chance. That ugly cane is really a plethora of potential plants, since each bud will make a new plant. You can capitalize on this by cutting the cane into two-inch (5 cm) sections, each containing a node with a bud. A very sharp knife is needed for this operation — a Chinese cleaver can deliver a deft blow of the kind necessary to sever these very tough stems.

Place the stem sections so they are either upright, standing out of the propagating medium, or buried horizontally, about 1 to 1½ inches (2.5 to 4 cm) deep. Horizontal planting will give you a lusher plant, since early shoots grow from the center of a cane cutting, not from the end. Bottom heat greatly speeds up the regeneration process here; without it you still will be successful, but you will have to wait twice as long — maybe up to several months. Eventually, you will be rewarded with the sight of a shoot emerging from the hard stem surface and unfurling its tender leaves. The dormant bud will have broken and at the same time, roots will be forming from the cane.

Cane cuttings also may be rooted vertically in water, but submerging even part of the cutting for such a prolonged time is an invitation to rot or algae growth.

Plants often propagated by cane cuttings include Chinese evergreen, Hawaiian ti plant *(Cordyline terminalis),* and dumb cane *(Dieffenbachia picta).* Cane cuttings of ti plant often are mailed successfully from Hawaii to customers, since the tough stem is very durable. The cut ends often are sealed with wax to prevent the cane from drying out. Scrape off this wax before you plant the cane so it will be able to take up water.

LEAF CUTTINGS

A stem cutting already looks like a plant while rooting, so it does not seem to be hiding any secrets or promising any extraordinary miracles. But a leaf cutting is just a leaf or piece of a leaf. It hardly seems capable of regenerating several plants, and it is fascinating to watch it grow tiny plants from its edges or surface.

Only a few specific kinds of plants will perform this miracle of growing new plants from severed leaves. Generally they belong to species without branching stems. Leaf-propagated plants may be divided into two categories: those in which the plants form from the

New Plants through Vegetative Propagation:
A single streptocarpus leaf can produce a bumper crop of offspring from along the leaf blade once it has been removed from a mature plant, slit along a large vein, and set in the appropriate propagating medium.

leaf blade itself, and those in which the new plants grow from the petiole (leaf stem). Generally, leaf cuttings root more easily than they form new shoots.

Rex begonias, florists' gloxinias, snake plant *(Sansevieria trifasciata)* and *Streptocarpus* species are commonly propagated from pieces of leaves. Without doing any harm to the appearance of your plant, simply remove a leaf that is mature, but not old (usually one which is growing halfway between the outer edge and the center of the plant). New plants will grow from the leaf blade.

With gloxinias and rex begonias, you can use a whole leaf and regenerate one or several new plants, depending on the number of slits you make in the large leaf veins.

Make slits all the way through the veins on the undersides of the leaves. Next place the leaf on the surface of moist propagating mix. Pin it down with hairpins to assure good contact with the medium. Cover the container with plastic or glass and keep it in a warm place. Be patient; like all miracles, this one may be long in coming. If the mother leaf remains healthy, in one to two months tiny shoots and roots will form. The old leaf then will begin to shrivel and you can separate the youngsters from it and pot them individually when they are large enough to handle.

Where *Streptocarpus* or rhizomatous begonias, including rex begonias, are concerned, you might prefer to cut each leaf into two or three wedges. Using a single-edged razor blade or a sharp knife, cut each wedge in the shape of a triangle. Make sure a large vein goes through the center of each wedge and that the thicker end of the vein is at one point of the wedge. Root the wedges in the high humidity of a propagation case, preferably under artificial lights. Stand each one upright in a blend of vermiculite and perlite so the narrow tip of the triangle — the one where the broad end of the vein emerges — is buried in the soil. After this buried part of the vein sends out roots, the tiny leaves of a new

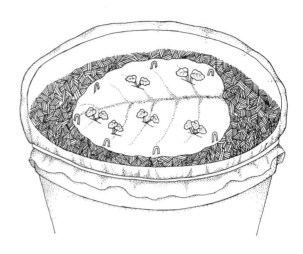

Propagating with Leaves: A single rex begonia leaf can produce a whole new crop of plants. At top, the entire leaf is used after the veins on the underside have been cut open. Hairpins are handy tools to hold the leaf against the moist propagating surface. A piece of plastic set on top of the pot and held on with string or a rubber band creates a miniature propagating case. When set in a warm spot, roots and shoots should appear. At bottom, a rex begonia leaf has been cut into triangular wedges. One side of each triangle should contain a large vein, with the thickest end of the vein at the point of the wedge. Insert this end into the moist propagating mix and cover with a piece of glass as shown here or with plastic as shown above. Roots will form from the pointed end, and tiny shoots will emerge alongside the wedge.

plant will break through the medium next to the wedge. When the leaves are half as tall as the wedge, lift the wedge-and-plant with a spoon, and transplant it to a small pot. Keep the new begonia in the propagation case until the leafy wedge withers.

Snake plant usually is propagated by cutting the long swordlike leaves into sections about two inches (5 cm) long and standing these upright in the propagating medium. You will see new shoots which formed underground emerging from the soil after about four weeks.

Many snake plants have striped, variegated edges of yellow or silver, but the new plants growing from the leaf cutting rarely will show this striped pattern, for they form from the genetically different cells in the center of the leaf. A plant like this is a genetic mosaic and is called a chimera (after the monster in Greek mythology who had the head of a lion, the body of a goat, and the tail of a dragon). The patterns exhibited by a chimera can be perpetuated only by vegetative propagation, and in the case of snake plant even the leaf cutting loses the striped character. Dividing the plant (as described later), however, will perpetuate the characteristic.

Leaves dropping naturally off the jade plant, hen-and-chickens (*Echeveria* spp.) and other succulents are so eager to reproduce that they will root and form tiny new plants without any special attention from you. Such leaf cuttings take a few weeks longer to root than stem cuttings from the same plant, and grow into an adult plant a little more slowly. Dig up the self-starting new plants when they are several inches or centimeters high and put them in two-inch (5 cm) pots. You can help along such cooperative plants yourself whenever you desire. Remove the succulent leaves at the point where they join the stem (there is no apparent petiole), and place them horizontally or vertically on top of barely moist sand or vermiculite. The cut surface of the leaf will callus over, and eventually roots and buds will emerge from the callus.

You will see the large leaf begin to shrivel and then you can separate the tiny plants and pot them up separately in small pots.

Other plants, such as peperomias and gesneriads such as African violets, grow new plants directly from the petiole. You should treat them rather like stem cuttings. Again, remove a leaf that is mature but not old — one from the middle ring of foliage — and stand it up in the propagating mix. New plants will arise from the petiole after it has formed roots. When plants are large enough to handle, you can sever them from the old leaf and plant them in individual pots. African violets can take up to nine months to go from leaf cutting to flowering plant.

LEAF-BUD CUTTINGS

Many plants will develop both shoots and roots from a leaf cutting; but other plants will grow only roots. To propagate shoots as well as roots from these plants, you have to include an axillary bud and a bit of stem tissue. The bud will grow into the stem of the new plant. When you take a leaf-bud cutting, you are actually taking a very small stem cutting along with the leaf cutting.

To make a leaf-bud cutting you usually cut off the leaf with about $1/4$ to $1/2$ inch (6 to 13 mm) of surrounding stem. This stem will contain the dormant axillary bud. You can handle a leaf-bud cutting like a stem cutting, placing it into the rooting medium so that the bud is under the surface of the moist medium. Roots are formed first, and then the bud will break and grow into a shoot which will poke its way through the soil. If you make the cutting improperly and do not include the bud, the leaf still may root, but it will never form any shoots, no matter how long you wait.

Croton *(Codiaeum variegatum* var. *pictum)* and polka dot plant *(Hypoestes phyllostachya)* are propagated this way by commercial plant propagators. Though these plants may be propagated easily from stem cuttings, many more new plants can be obtained by the leaf-bud cutting method. For this reason, commercial growers often take leaf-bud cuttings. But if you use a stem cutting, you will have a larger plant sooner. It is a trade-off between time and numbers, so decide whether you want lots of small plants or one larger plant before choosing your method.

LAYERING

When cuttings of stems or leaves are used for propagation, the cutting is under a great deal of stress since it has been severed from its natural supply of water and nutrients. This stress is too much, especially for hard-to-root species which take a long time to root; they die before roots form. Layering eliminates this stress, because rooting is done while the offspring is still attached to the mother plant.

You can bend or twist a stem so that it lies along the surface of the propagating medium, or it may even be buried, without being severed from the mother plant. This allows the continual flow of water and nutrients to the part being propagated until it has rooted and can be separated.

Layering is used most often to propagate outdoor trees and shrubs which are difficult to root, although it has many uses for indoor plants, too. You will find it fun and easy to root vines such as English ivy, pothos, and philodendron by layering. Sometimes every node can be tied down to make a new plant. Prayer plants (*Maranta* spp.), begonias, and any plants with long, flexible stems also can be propagated by layering.

To layer a given plant, take a lower stem that is at least 12 inches (30 cm) long and pin it with a hairpin to a flat, pot, or pan of propagating mix which you will set beside the mother pot. If you lay the stem on the medium, pinning it down at each node, the method is called serpentine layering. If you bend a shoot down to the medium, pinning it underground but allowing the shoot tip to

Two Types of Layering: A plant with long stems, such as a philodendron, can be encouraged to root by placing a section of stem firmly against or under the soil in an adjacent pot (top). The stem is shown buried, with a shoot tip reappearing on the surface to the right, a procedure known as simple layering. When new growth appears on the shoot tip, and gentle tugging reveals that roots have formed, the vining stem of the parent plant on the left may be cut above soil level, and the new plant potted up separately. A spider plant with hanging plantlets is a candidate for natural layering. Set a pot alongside the parent, and anchor the runner-borne plantlet in the soil to root. Once roots have formed, the runner can be snipped, and a new plant is born.

reemerge above the surface, you are practicing simple layering. With woodier plants such as azaleas or camellias, you can make a cut about halfway through the underside of the stem where it reaches the middle of the propagating pot, then twist the end of the stem upright and pin it so the cut is down into the medium. Auxin and sugars will accumulate at the cut and cause faster rooting. If you have a pothos, nephthytis, or philoden-dron with a particularly lanky and leafless stem tipped by a leaf, you can bury the base of the leaf and much of the bare stem just below the surface of a nearby pot of soil. In this indoor version of trench layering, you may have to weight down the buried stem with pebbles until it roots and can be sepa-rated from the mother plant.

The propagating medium should be kept moist, but the atmosphere does not have to be as humid as with cuttings. Be patient. Layering is a slow process, since the layers are being well supplied with water and nutri-ents while they are rooting.

NATURAL LAYERING WITH RUNNERS

When your strawberry begonia *(Saxifraga stolonifera)* develops its flock of tiny plantlets and your spider plant sends out its dangling babies, they are performing what can be called natural layering. Modified stems, called runners, are formed by these plants, and tiny new plantlets emerge at their tips or along their length even without the runners touching ground.

If you place a runner with its tiny plant onto a pot of soil, the new plant eventually will root. You then can cut the runner away from the parent plant and have a new plant. Rooting may go faster if you keep the pot enclosed in a plastic bag to keep the surface of the medium moist so delicate new roots do not dry out.

Any of the plants that are formed while still dangling in the air can be cut from the plant and propagated like stem cuttings if it is inconvenient to place propagating pots around the mother plant. But layering the runners is more satisfactory since it avoids the stress associated with severing the plants from their roots, and the new plants will nev-er suffer shock or setback.

Boston ferns form long, hairlike roots that will generate small forests of ferns if

they are pegged down, lightly covered with ⅓ inch (9 mm) of sphagnum moss, and kept moist for several months.

AIR LAYERING

Layering works only if the plant stems are flexible enough to be brought down to the level of the soil for propagation. Where stems cannot be bent down, the soil can be brought

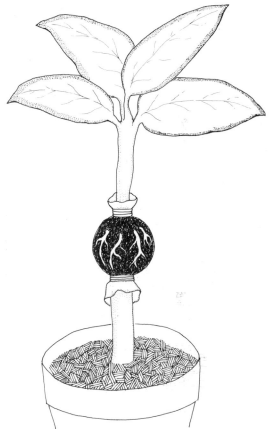

Air Layering: Tall, stiff stems that won't bend for simple layering can be accommodated by this method. First, scrape away a 1-inch (2.5 cm) ring of bark, then apply rooting hormone. Moisten some unmilled sphagnum moss and place it around the stem to cover the ring. A piece of plastic wrapped around the moss and tied or taped at top and bottom holds everything in place. When roots pop through the plastic, cut the stem below these new roots and move plant to its own pot.

up around the stem in a method called air layering. This method is used extensively for propagating foliage plants outdoors in Florida nurseries, and often is employed in northern climates for small trees and shrubs. You, too, will find it useful for propagating such plants as dieffenbachias, dracaenas, and the rubber plant. These plants tend to become tall and stalky with age, and a new, more compact plant can be obtained by air layering.

With a sterilized penknife or paring knife, scrape off a thin layer of bark in a strip about one inch (2.5 cm) wide that completely circles the stem where you want the roots to grow. Rub about ½ teaspoon (2.5 ml) of rooting hormone into the wound and then bandage it. First, wrap moist, unmilled sphagnum moss around the wound. Make sure the moss is not soggy, as too much moisture will slow rooting. Then wind plastic securely around the moss and tape the ends tightly with electrical tape. The moss should stay moist for months if it is wrapped carefully, but if you notice it drying out, then unwrap, moisten, and rewrap.

After several months, when you see roots through the plastic, cut off the top of the plant just below the roots and pot it up in a small pot. If the roots seem small for the size of the top, enclose the new plant in a plastic bag for about a month while a more sufficient root system is forming.

You may not know what to do with the bottom of the plant, and there are several choices you can make. You can throw it away if it is too large or unsightly. Or you can make cane cuttings from the bare stem and discard the rest of the plant. Or keep the pot of roots and tend it in the hope that new shoots will sprout from the roots.

DIVISION OF OFFSETS AND SUCKERS

You undoubtedly have had an African violet, a Boston fern, or an aloe that seemed to get fuller and fuller and change from a single plant into several plants. Sometimes this seems to happen overnight without your noticing. These plants are increasing naturally by forming offsets and suckers, and if they were growing free in the wild they would grow into a thicket of identical plants. You can take advantage of this mode of growth by separating the clumps into individual plants.

Offsets are new plants that grow from dormant buds located at the crown of the original plant. You might notice them on a strawberry begonia, Transvaal daisy *(Gerbera jamesonii)*, screw pine *(Pandanus veitchii)*, or African violet. *Cryptanthus* and other bromeliads also produce offsets. Suckers are plants that develop from shoot meristems that form spontaneously on roots of some plants, like agaves, aloes, anthuriums, and Chinese evergreens.

If you want to separate these offsets and suckers, first knock the mother plant out of its pot by turning the pot upside down and thumping it on the edge of a table or counter. Some newspapers spread around can help make the job less messy. Remove the root ball from the pot and look for natural places where the plants divide. In some cases, with aloe for instance, the small plants already will have roots. In such a situation, you can cut through the entire root ball with a large knife to divide it into sections or chunks. But to be sure you have enough roots to go with each plant, cut through only the large roots and then with your fingers pry apart and separate the rest of the roots so they do not get cut away from their own plant.

With other plants like African violets, some of the offsets may have roots and others will seem to be rootless and firmly attached to the larger plant. In this case use a sharp, clean knife to cut into the root ball between the crown of the individual rosettes of leaves, then pull and pry apart individual plants, trying to keep some roots with each plant.

Plants with roots may be potted up with little subsequent attention. Plants without roots must be treated as stem cuttings. Dust

Dividing a Rhizomatous Plant: A snake plant responds well to propagation by division. First, remove the plant carefully from the pot after running a knife along the inside surface. Check for weak points in the rhizome, or a point where it branches, as likely spots to make the separation. A quick tug or a clean slice with a knife divides the clumps, each including roots, several mature leaves, and some new growth. Let each division dry for a week to toughen the roots, increasing resistance to rot. Then, pot up in soil mix and provide several weeks of bright, filtered light and high humidity.

bases with hormones, stick into moist propagating medium, and keep enclosed for high humidity until roots form.

PROPAGATING UNDERGROUND STRUCTURES

Even if you call them all "bulbs," the underground storage and reproductive structures variously classified as bulbs, corms, rhizomes, tubers, and tuberous roots will grow into new plants for you just the same. These underground mysteries are described in chapter 1,

and you will find them on many herbaceous perennial plants which die back to the ground and remain dormant for several months of the year and then sprout new leaves.

Some plants, such as tuberous begonias *(Begonia ×tuberhybrida),* dahlias, and sweet potatoes, have enlarged roots, called tuberous roots. (Some botanists argue that the begonias actually have tubers.) On one end, tuberous roots have a bud (or buds) that is attached to the parent plant. This bud will form the stem growth of the new plant. The other end of the tuberous root forms adventitious roots when planted. To propagate new plants from tuberous roots, divide them from one another, making sure that each root has at least one bud at the top. The tubers can be potted up separately with the bud placed several inches or centimeters below the surface of the potting medium. If you place them in bright light, and water them only enough to keep the medium moist, you will be rewarded with new growth.

Tubers and rhizomes are other underground storage structures similar to tuberous roots, but while a tuberous root is a modified root, tubers and rhizomes are modified stems. These structures also have eyes or dormant buds.

In the tuber, such growth buds dot the surface at regular intervals, each eye consisting of one or more tiny buds which are partially surrounded by a scalelike leaf. Tubers usually can be cut in pieces, each piece having an eye, and planted. Each eye will produce a shoot. The Irish potato *(Solanum tuberosum)* is the most famous tuber of them all, but many ornamental plants grow from tubers, too. The elephant's ear *(Caladium ×hortulanum)* which may adorn your light garden with brilliantly colored leaves can be propagated by separating its tubers as you would tuberous roots. Cyclamens also have tubers.

Rhizomes usually are not as thick as tubers and often are creeping and branched.

Some of their dormant buds produce roots, while others found at the tip of each branch generate leaves and flower stalks. Rex begonias, snake plants, and some gesneriads grow from rhizomes which creep at or just below the soil surface. Like tubers, these rhizomes may be cut into pieces for propagation. Each piece should be several inches or centimeters long and must contain several buds, or nodes. Anchor the cutting in propagating medium, and keep evenly moist until roots and shoots appear. Then repot the young plant in a suitable growing medium.

Rhizomatous plants also can be divided, similar to the method described under Division of Offsets and Suckers. Wait a few days after watering to make sure the root ball will be dry enough to be manageable. Then slide it out of the pot, if necessary running a butter knife around the sides and pushing a pencil through the drainage hole to force it free. Sometimes rhizomes clamp onto the rim of a pot — break them if this occurs. In dividing rhizomes, make sure you trim away any that are discolored and soft, since they are likely to be diseased or dead. Divisions of the remaining healthy rhizomes will stand a better chance of surviving if each one includes one to two inches (2.5 to 5 cm) of roots, at least several mature leaves, and at least a sign of new growth. When possible, separate rhizomes at weak or branching points with a fast, firm tug. If they resist breaking cleanly, cut through them decisively with a very sharp knife or razor blade, as ragged, torn edges will invite rot.

Repot each division in an appropriate soil mix, preferably first dipping each wounded end in powdered sulfur as a further discouragement to rot. As an added safeguard, let the newly cut portion dry for at least a week before potting until it is callused enough to tolerate normal soil moisture. Water the new plants from below until growth starts. Keep them under plastic and in bright but indirect light for about two weeks, then remove the plastic and give the plants the

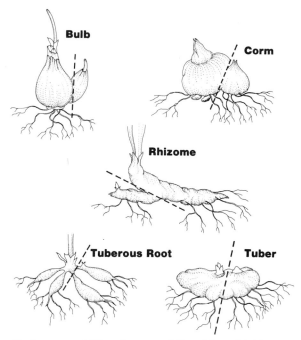

Underground Structures and How They Divide: The dotted lines indicate the points at which division can be done on each particular structure. Bulbs and corms produce offsets which can be removed immediately after foliage dies back, and then stored. Another method is to store the entire bulb or corm, then separate the offsets prior to planting. Rhizomes feature dormant buds along their surface; cut a piece of rhizome several inches or centimeters long, including at least several buds. With proper care these buds will be stimulated to produce roots, leaves, and flower stalks. Tubers should be cut into pieces, each piece containing tiny growth buds grouped together to form an eye. Tuberous roots can be separated, making sure that each piece has a bud on top from which a new plant will form.

kind of light they require to grow. Wait several months before you resume feeding as usual.

Bulbs and corms are swollen, modified underground storage stems. Corms consist mostly of solid stem tissue with nodes and internodes. Topped by a bud that sends forth leaves and a flower stalk, a corm develops new corms and small "cormels" around its base. A bulb, on the other hand, has vegetative and flower buds concealed inside it, surrounded protectively by fat, meaty leaves called scales, in which food is stored. Bulbs may form bulblets, or offsets, when they are mature, although some bulbs will reproduce only outdoors.

You can separate offsets from the main corm or bulb after the foliage has died back and the underground stem has become dormant. Offsets may be stored for several months if they are removed just after the plant dies back. Or you may store the whole plant and separate the new bulbs or corms just before planting. Keeping them in a cool, dry place, such as a garage or basement, will prevent the offsets from shriveling or using up their supply of stored food. With scaly bulbs, such as lilies, you can remove a few scales from the mother bulb without injuring it. Allow the cut surfaces to dry for a few days before planting the scales several inches or centimeters apart in a well-drained medium in furrows lined with sand, and cover them with up to two inches (5 cm) of sand or peat moss. Keep the pot or flat in indirect light and periodically check for the development of tiny bulblets along the edges of the scales. When these begin to crowd each other, remove the scales from the sand and separate and plant the bulblets. Another approach is to seal scales in a polyethylene bag with moist vermiculite, and keep them in a warm, dimly lit spot. When bulblets forming on the sides of the scales have roots ½ inch (13 mm) long you can detach the bulblets and plant them. They will need several cycles of growth and dormancy before they grow large enough to flower.

Some bulbs can be propagated by cutting them into sections. The trick is to make sharp cuts from top to bottom, between scales, and to include part of the basal plate in each piece. Treat such units like leaf cuttings, and plant them in a starting medium until they are sizable enough to transplant.

To encourage bulblet formation on hyacinths, which normally produce them only very slowly, scoop out the bottom of a mature bulb with a melon baller or steel teaspoon that has been dipped in alcohol. Do this after the leaves have died back in late summer. Cut through the center of the basal plate and destroy the main shoot. Another technique is to make three intersecting cuts across and through the basal plate in the shape of a single six-pointed star. Dust such cuts with sulfur and place the bulbs where the temperature is about 70°F (21°C) until the wounds are callused (about a week). Then keep them in a warm, dark place for three months. Next, plant each bulb with its bulblets 4 inches (10 cm) deep and winter it over at 40° to 45°F (4° to 7°C) to break dormancy of the bulblets. The next spring the bulblets will send up leaves and the mother bulb will start to disintegrate. That fall, dig up, separate, and replant the bulblets. You can get up to 24 of them from a scooped hyacinth bulb, and they should be big enough to flower in three or four years. At 5½ to 6 inches (14 to 15 cm) in diameter, they can be planted out, but let them grow an additional ½ inch (13 mm) in girth before forcing them indoors. This method also will work for amaryllis bulbs.

Tender bulbs such as amaryllis, Amazon lily *(Eucharis grandiflora),* and cape cowslip *(Lachenalia aloides)* are well suited to the home environment and often will increase in size and produce many offsets. When grown in plenty of light, an amaryllis may form several new bulblets each season which may be separated from the large bulb. These can be grown to flower in about two years.

If you do force spring-flowering bulbs (such as hyacinths, tulips, and narcissus) or corms (crocuses) indoors during the winter, you probably should discard the bulbs after they have finished flowering. They do not usually form offsets if grown in the home, where the temperatures are too high and the light not bright enough for them to reproduce. Enjoy such forced bulbs as they are, and do not trouble yourself with trying to perpetuate them as either indoor or outdoor plants.

CHAPTER 9

Keeping Plants Healthy

Sooner or later every house plant gardener encounters a plant that seems sick. Sometimes the probable cause is apparent. Most people can recognize aphids or mealybugs as insects and may attribute the decline of an ailing plant to their presence. But often the problem is less clear. Leaves which yellow, turn brown around the edges, or become spotted may all be due to a number of possible causes that are not as obvious. In fact, some symptoms are so unfamiliar that they are misleading; scale insects, for example, may be taken for normal growths of plant tissue.

There are at least three basic rules that you can follow to keep your plants healthy or to return them to that state.

First, admit only healthy plants to your collection. Isolate each new plant from the others for a week or two. Inspect it thoroughly for any insect pests or other problems it may be bringing into the house with it. A bath in mild soapy water followed by a clear rinse is a good idea for each newcomer.

Second, if all does not appear well with either a new or old acquisition, make efforts to identify the problem correctly. The information in this chapter should be helpful. Your local agriculture extension entomologist or plant pathologist can also help in identifying rare or difficult problems.

Third, individual attention to each plant is essential. Learn something about its native habitat and proper maintenance. House plants are more likely to become "sick" from improper care, such as overwatering or overfertilizing, than from invading insects or plant disease organisms. The encyclopedia section of this book lists the environmental needs of 250 individual plants, and chapter 2 contains a more complete discussion of how to fulfill those needs.

Of course, the key to success in indoor gardening is to recreate as faithfully as possible the natural environment from which each house plant (or its forebears) came. Plants of the forest floor, such as ferns, require a filtered light and high humidity. They may sunburn in bright light, showing yellow or brown spots on the leaves or drying of leaf tips. A combination of direct sun and dryness may make a plant more susceptible to mite infestations. It is important to select the proper light conditions suitable for each house plant in your care. You can provide the proper amount of humidity by such practices as massing plants together, misting the leaves, enclosing plants in terraria, or placing the pots on pebbles set in trays of water (as explained in chapter 2).

Even, moderate temperatures characterize the native environments of tropical and subtropical plants. Sudden chills, from cold water or drafts from a window, may cause leaf drop in these tender plants. Cold water

Cold Water Spots: Cold water will cause unattractive brown discolorations on the foliage of hairy-leaved plants such as this African violet. Water such plants carefully, even when the water you use is at room temperature, to avoid splashing water on the plants' leaves.

Opposite, close-up of mealybug on plant stem.

may spot certain hairy-leafed plants such as African violets. Tropical plants may safely spend the summer outdoors, in a sheltered spot, when the weather is evenly warm. Bring them back indoors well before the house heat is turned on, so they can adjust gradually to temperature and humidity changes.

Many of these plants come from environments where rainfall is high and soils are porous. The high temperature of these areas causes dead organic matter to decompose quickly. The remaining salts are promptly leached away by the rains, leaving the soil relatively low in nutrients. Plants from such areas, which are accustomed to quick-draining, nutrient-poor soils, are often susceptible to root rots or fertilizer burn when grown under indoor conditions. Overwatering, the other environmental danger to tropical plants, may yellow a plant's lower leaves or cause green algae to grow on the soggy soil surface.

Many cacti and other succulents come from semiarid areas where rains are intermittent and the soil dries out periodically. These plants have the ability to suck up water quickly through an extensive root system, often expanding visibly as they do so and holding the water for later use within the plant body. This gives them a competitive advantage over other forms of life in the environment, including soilborne pathogens, that are not able to store water in this way. Thus, letting the soil dry out between waterings is the best method of preventing root infections in these plants.

Cacti protect their succulent, watery interiors with a tough, waxy cuticle. Once this outer layer is breached, however, through either mechanical or insect injury, pathogenic fungi and bacteria quickly take hold. This can happen if the plant "sunburns." If a cactus is not rotated as it grows, the side constantly facing the sun will eventually toughen. If the plant is then moved, and the tender side is exposed to bright sunlight, it may turn yellow or pinkish, a sign that the

plant tissues have been damaged. To avoid sunburn, rotate your cacti regularly. If you have neglected to do so, mark the side of the pot facing the sun. That way you can orient the plant the same way again if the cactus should be moved.

THE INDOOR ENVIRONMENT AND PESTS

In the outdoor environment in which the house plant originally developed, there were insects and other organisms present that could feed upon it. There were microorganisms such as fungi, bacteria, and viruses present in the soil, air, and water that would invade the plant tissues and cause symptoms of disease. At the same time, however, there were many natural controls operating to hold in check the populations of potential pests. In the native habitat, insects have parasites, predators, and diseases that reduce their numbers. Microorganisms in soil and air live together in complex communities in which they compete with each other, providing checks and balances against the dominating proliferation of any one particular species.

By comparison, inside the house the number of species of organisms has been greatly reduced. Only a fraction of the outdoor ecosystem is represented. For example, potting soils may be pasteurized or sterilized. If a potentially pathogenic microorganism should enter that "clean" environment, it will find no competition from other organisms in a complex soil community. Aphids, mites, or other creatures that may colonize an indoor plant are not likely to be found by their natural enemies that are so abundant outdoors. The result is pest populations that may multiply unchecked when given a susceptible plant and suitable temperature, humidity, and light conditions. By eliminating the natural enemies of plant pests from the indoor environment, the indoor gardener is in the same predicament as the farmer or backyard gardener whose poison sprays have similarly disturbed the balance of nature. With the natural enemies gone, you must take over their work in controlling the pests.

There are two major advantages that the indoor environment offers, however. One is the opportunity to exclude potential pest organisms from the plants by using screens on windows and bringing only pest-free plants into the house. The other is the chance to manipulate the situation by washing your plants, moving them to a better environment (changing the light or humidity conditions, for example), letting the soil dry out or changing it altogether, and otherwise modifying the situation drastically in ways not possible with plants in the outdoor garden or field. Each plant can be treated individually without regard to the vagaries of outdoor weather or backyard soil conditions. Indoors, you have substantial control over the many factors that influence potential pests. With attention and ingenuity you can manage pest problems satisfactorily without resorting to the use of commercial synthetic pesticides.

PREVENTIVE MAINTENANCE

The most important component of any pest management program, indoors or out, is regular, careful inspection or monitoring. Watch your plants closely. By observing the reaction of each plant to the amount of light, water, fertilizer, and pruning it receives, or to the potting soil in which it is placed, you will learn to associate specific plant symptoms with reactions to various horticultural techniques. In other words, you will learn how your plant behaves. Thus, you will learn what is desirable practice and what is not, and you will know when your plant is exhibiting abnormal symptoms.

Careful monitoring will also permit you to discover pest populations when they are small. This is when they are easy to eliminate through simple, nontoxic methods.

One of the most effective ways to keep alert to the presence of any unwanted pests and to dispose of them before they get well established is to clean the plant regularly. Most urban environments are very dirty. Dust settles all over plants, clogging the pores (stomata) through which oxygen and carbon dioxide exchanges take place and reducing the amount of light that reaches the leaves.

Daily misting can help cut down on dust for those plants that need high humidity. Most small plants can be inverted and sloshed through a bucket of mild soapy water, then rinsed with clear water. Use paper or cloth wrapped around the stem and held in

To Clean Small Plants: Wrap a cloth or piece of paper around the stem and over the edges of the pot to hold the plant and soil in place. Then, invert the pot and dunk the plant in a bucket of mild, soapy water. Dip the plant in clear, room-temperature water to rinse.

place with your hands to prevent the soil from falling out. Use lukewarm water and a mild, fat-based soap, not a detergent, for this bath. Remember, before using any soap product, it should be tested on a leaf of the plant beforehand, particularly in the solution you will eventually use regularly on your plants. Plants too large for this operation can be sprinkled in the shower or hosed off (gently) outdoors. Plants still larger can be wiped clean with a sponge.

This periodic cleaning operation provides an opportunity to scrutinize all visible parts of the plant for signs of pest problems or disease. If anything suspicious is observed, control measures can be started during the process or immediately after.

Improving Drainage: Elevating pots on a tray of pebbles can help to eliminate salt buildup, because all excess water and fertilizer drain out of the pot with each watering.

As you inspect your plants, cut or pinch off discolored or dying leaves and stems. If the plant parts are not diseased, they can be added to a compost heap to nourish garden or house plants (as described in chapter 7). A white crust on the soil surface or sides of the pot is a sign of salt buildup. Flush these salts away with repeated watering in the sink or bathtub. Better yet, repot the plant in fresh soil in a clean pot. The encrusted pot should be soaked and scrubbed thoroughly to remove the salts. In fact, this is a good practice to follow when reusing any old pot. If the last plant to occupy the pot was diseased, sterilize the scrubbed, empty pot in the oven at 180°F (85°C) for 30 minutes before using it again.

Salt buildup can be a sign of improper watering techniques. To prevent a recurrence of the problem, elevate the pot on a pan or saucer filled with pebbles. The bottom of the pot should be high enough so that when you water, any excess will drain out and be unable to seep back again. Feeding your house plants with weak compost or manure tea also will help to eliminate salt buildup. These natural substances are less concentrated than commercial plant foods.

Many root diseases are fostered by overwatering or poor drainage. This is one of the most common problems seen by agriculture extension plant pathologists at plant clinics around the country. Proper drainage is of the utmost importance for healthy roots. See chapter 6 for advice on correct potting techniques to insure good drainage.

CONTROLLING PEST PROBLEMS

There are four approaches to controlling pest and disease problems in plants: physical, cultural, biological, and chemical. Washing your plants to remove pest infestations is an example of a physical control. Aphids, mealybugs, young scales, mites, and thrips all can be washed off by soap and water. The additional humidity also may cause disease outbreaks among the pests.

An old toothbrush, or a toothpick with a cotton swab, is useful for dislodging adult scales. You also can use a toothpick to lift up the scale to determine if it is alive, and what stage it is in. If the cotton is dipped in alcohol before being used to rub off colonies of mealybugs or aphids, you are actually combining a physical and a chemical control.

Cultural controls are those applied by modifying horticultural techniques such as watering, fertilizing, and pruning. They are particularly important in disease management, when their aim is to modify the plant's environment, but can prove useful in combating insects as well. Aphids, for example, are attracted by high nitrogen levels in the plant which are present in plant tips during the active growing season. Both feeding and reproduction of the aphids may therefore increase. When aphids attack a plant, cutting back on the amount of supplemental nitrogen being fed to the plant may help in controlling them.

Biological control refers to controlling pest insects, mites, or microorganisms through the use of parasites, predators, disease, or competitive organisms. Although the science is well developed for certain outdoor agricultural crops and ornamental plants, and for greenhouse situations, attempting to use biological control on house plants is a relatively new concept. Of course, every time you let a spider live within the house, you are practicing biological control of the insects which it kills for food. Potting plants in a soil mix that contains some garden humus and compost is also a form of biological control. With the inclusion of the organic matter, you are attempting to create a complex soil community that will prevent the development of high populations of undesirable soil microbes or fungi.

Nevertheless, the constraints of the house interior, where people usually fear insects, and the small amount of total space occupied by the plant and soil, make it

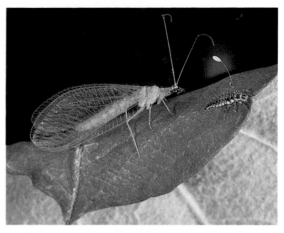

Lacewings: With their larvae, lacewings provide a means of biologically controlling aphid, mealybug, and whitefly infestations. Lacewing larvae can be placed on the infested plant, to consume the invading pests and their eggs. Placing the potted plant, along with its saucer, in a pan of water will insure that the lacewings will not leave the plant.

somewhat tricky to experiment with predators other than the two commonly commercially available species, green lacewings and predatory mites. Since there are numerous commercial sources of both and neither will fly away when placed on the plant, they are both well worth trying.

The larvae of green lacewings (*Chrysopa carnea*) eat a very wide variety of pest insects. Try them for aphid, mealybug, or whitefly infestations. Lacewings will arrive in the egg or young larval stage and should be distributed over the plant so that they don't eat each other. Predatory mites (usually *Phytoseiulus persimilis*) are shipped in a sealed straw or a similar container, and should also be spread around liberally. They will eat the common pest mites and mite eggs. Placing the plant, saucer and all, in a pan of water will prevent either lacewing or mite predators from leaving the plant. They will simply die off when they run out of insects to eat.

Exactly how many of either predator to release on each infested house plant has not yet been determined. However, most commercial suppliers offer a minimum order that is probably more than you will need, and purchasing the minimum will allow you plenty with which to experiment. For more detailed information on using biological controls indoors and in the home greenhouse, you can consult the book *Windowsill Ecology* by Dr. William H. Jordan, Jr. (see Bibliography).

The most drastic approach to disease and pest management is the use of chemical controls. There has been much confusion over the use of "organic" versus "chemical" insecticides. All organic materials are made up of chemicals, of course, so a better way of distinguishing between them is needed. "Plant-based" versus synthesized might be a more suitable way of expressing the difference. The plant-based insecticides are called botanicals.

While botanical insecticides can usually be relied upon to break down rapidly and lose their poisonous effects within a short time, they still may be very toxic at the time you are using them. The measure of toxicity of these substances is indicated by two numbers. The LD_{50} is the unit of measure. It means the lethal dose that kills 50 percent of a population of test animals (usually mice or rats). The higher the LD_{50} number, the *less* toxic the material, since it takes more of the compound to kill the test animals (measured in milligrams of toxin per kilogram of body weight of the test animals). On this scale pyrethrum has an LD_{50} of 200 (when given orally to rats), rotenone an LD_{50} of 132, and nicotine an LD_{50} of 50. These substances are all botanicals, and they all work as contact and stomach poisons against insects. But even though they are derived from plants, botanical insecticides can be extremely toxic. For example, nicotine, which is sometimes used in homemade solutions of soapy water and cigarette butts, is more toxic than malathion 50 (with an LD_{50} of 2,800), a popular commercially synthesized organophosphate recommended in many books on house plant care.

The point to keep in mind is that all chemical pesticides, botanical or not, are poisons and should be treated with respect. Some good rules to follow are:

1. Use insecticides *only* as a last resort when all other methods have failed and you feel you must save the plant.
2. Read the label carefully for instructions on which insects the poison can be used against successfully.
3. Do spraying outside the house or in a very well ventilated room. Any wind should be away from you.
4. Wear nonabsorbent, waterproof gloves and protective clothing.
5. Mix only as much insecticide as you will actually need, so you are not left with the problem of disposal.

The safest insecticides for house plants are water or soap and water. Most plants (except those with hairy leaves) can be dipped in or sponged with a solution of one to two tablespoons (15 to 30 ml) of a mild flaked soap like Ivory or Octagon dissolved in a gallon (4 l) of warm (not hot) water. Leave the solution on the plant for an hour or two, then rinse it off thoroughly.

A lightweight summer oil (or dormant oil) is also nontoxic to humans and effective in controlling young scales, spider mites, and mealybugs. There are several brands of oil sprays manufactured specifically for use on plants. These are available at plant nurseries, some hardware stores, and other places where plant care products are sold. Oil sprays can be used on most kinds of plants. However, they are not recommended for epiphytic plants, such as *Tillandsia* and *Angraecum* (comet orchid), because they can clog leaf pores and thus hinder nutrient absorption. Delicate ferns and hairy-leafed gesneriads also may not respond well to oil sprays.

Rubbing alcohol can be swabbed directly

on the insects or their egg masses. Do not let it touch the plant itself—alcohol can burn delicate foliage. Rinse off all of these materials after they have had a chance to act on the pests. Always remove plants from direct sunlight while they are being treated with any type of insecticide.

A number of the commercial insecticides may injure specific house plants. When using any toxic materials, always test them first on just a portion of the plant.

IDENTIFYING INSECTS AND MITES

In general, insects and mites can be divided into piercing and sucking, and chewing species, depending on the kind of mouthparts that they have. Both pests and the predators that control them may fall into either category. It so happens, however, that all the common house plant insect and mite pests have piercing and sucking mouthparts. This means that, unlike outdoor garden plants which show holes and missing sections as a result of insect feeding, house plants will usually display more subtle symptoms.

Where the mouthparts pierce the leaves, small spots may be visible. The cumulative effect of many feeding pests may be a stippling of the leaves. Or, the leaves may curl around a colony of aphids. Yellowing or other discolorations are also visible in plants under attack by insects. Small drops of glistening honeydew are produced by some pests (particularly aphids and mealybugs) and may attract ants. The first thing that you notice when mites are present may be the webs. The pictures accompanying this text will help you to identify the particular animal with which you are dealing. A low-power hand lens or magnifying glass is also very handy for this purpose.

When a plant becomes very badly infested, it is sometimes better to destroy the plant than to risk poisoning yourself or spreading the disease to other plants in your collection. If you can, take a cutting from a clean section of the plant, and start a new plant in fresh soil. Following are suggestions for controlling some common indoor plant pests.

APHIDS

Aphids are soft-bodied, sucking insects that usually cluster near the soft, growing parts of plants. They are generally green or black in color. Aphids produce a sugary excretion called honeydew, which is much liked by ants. If ants are found harvesting the honeydew, exclude them as described later. The aphids themselves can be removed by using a cotton swab dipped in alcohol. The whole plant may be washed in mild, soapy, lukewarm water, then rinsed with clear water. When the weather outdoors is warm, the infested plant may be placed in a partially shaded spot in the garden to attract natural enemies that may destroy the aphid infestation. Nicotine is also frequently used for

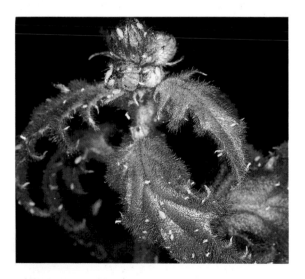

Aphids: These small insects attack both the indoor and outdoor garden. They are usually found near the young shoots and growing tips of the plant, such as the purple passion plant *(Gynura aurantiaca)* shown here.

aphid control. Be very careful not to come in contact with this highly toxic insecticide, either by skin contact or inhalation. Aphids are also very susceptible to biological control by lacewings.

Aphids are fascinating creatures. For much of every season the common species bear live young without mating. (And they multiply rapidly!) Aphid births can be observed with a hand lens. Take a good look before you wash them all away.

MEALYBUGS

Mealybugs are close relatives of aphids and, like them, are honeydew producers. They have soft, oval bodies, and frequently exude a white, waxy material, producing cottony fluffs over themselves where they are feeding. Like aphids, they suck plant juices, causing bud drop and foliage damage. Mealybugs tend to gather on the undersides of leaves, and in leaf axils. Recommended treatment is the same as for aphids: physical removal, water-washing, or washing with water and soap. They are also good candidates for biological control by lacewings.

When mealybugs colonize the roots of cacti or other succulents, sometimes the best solution is to repot the affected plants in fresh soil. After repotting succulents, except cacti, water them more frequently than you did previously. A badly infested cactus will respond well to having all the roots removed with a sharp, clean knife and the cut ends dusted with sulfur. The cactus body can then be set aside to dry on a windowsill that is sunny but not hot. Repot in fresh, dry soil when new, uninfested roots appear. This may take several months. Wait a month or so after repotting before watering the cactus again so that damage to the new roots will have time to heal.

MITES

These relatives of spiders (also called spider mites) are extremely tiny. In fact, they will

Mealybugs: Shown here clustered on a plant stem, mealybugs also tend to gather in leaf axils and on the undersides of leaves.

usually appear as no more than animated specks of dust. Their presence should be suspected when plant leaves show stippling or mottling, which is caused by the mites' piercing mouthparts. Depending on the species of mite, the leaves may fall when the infestation becomes severe, or they may become coated and tied together with very fine webs. Still another type of mite may attack flower beds and cause the flowers to be distorted, or stunt the entire plant.

Since mites can be spread easily on your hands and clothing (they are even blown on puffs of air), the first step in controlling them is to isolate plants that are suspected of being infested. Periodic washing, for those plants that can take it, can be a good means of control. Many pest mites are very susceptible to water sprays, the high humidity apparently affecting their reproduction. Wash your hands and arms after handling the infested plants so you don't spread mites to the rest of your collection.

A light summer oil is also often very effective on mites. So are commercially available mite predators. If you opt for biological controls, describe your problem to the insec-tary when you order mite predators so that they are sure to send you the best species for your situation. Because they multiply rapidly, it is sometimes difficult to keep mites from coming back, especially in winter. Introducing predators can help prevent recurring large infestations.

SCALE INSECTS

There are many scales of ornamental plants, some with hard shells over the body of the adult and some without. With many scales, only the males have wings and can fly. The

Spider Mites: These insects are so tiny they are often mistaken for specks of dust. Spider mites are visible here as light patches on some of the leaves of this *Impatiens*.

Scale Insects: Shown here on a palm leaf, scales are sometimes mistaken for normal growths of plant tissue.

young are called crawlers and can easily move away from the mother scale to find new feeding sites for themselves. This is when they are most vulnerable to washing off or predation by lacewings. Light summer oil will kill them also. Once scales settle at a permanent feeding site, a stiff brush usually will be required to dislodge them. Physical removal is the best method of control, though scales can also be killed with applications of soap or nicotine solutions.

Using a toothpick, lift off the hard outer shell of a common house plant scale. If the scale insect is alive, you will see the soft body of the mother insect inside. Sometimes she will be surrounded by her eggs. If the "eggs"

appear to move, the young are ready to emerge from under the scale and spread over the plant. Get ready to start control measures. If the scale is empty, the insect is dead. Inspect additional scales to determine whether some are alive and will therefore require control.

WHITEFLIES

These are most often a problem on tomatoes, cucumbers, and iris grown indoors. The adults can fly while the young are stationary. Adults are visible when a plant is disturbed— they look like bits of dust swirling about the plant. When cold the adults are often easy to wipe or vacuum up. The young (usually found on the leaf undersides) closely resemble small scale insects and often can be wiped off with a sponge. Soap and water, pyrethrum, or rotenone may offer some control, although it is very easy to develop resistant whitefly populations through overuse of insecticides. In many areas whiteflies already are resistant to most common garden insecticides.

Lacewing larvae will eat young whiteflies and there is a host-specific parasite (*Encarsia formosa*) that is available commercially. This parasite is useful in controlling whiteflies

Whiteflies: When a plant infested by whiteflies is disturbed, the insects fly about the plant in a small swarm, giving rise to the very apt nickname of "flying dandruff." Both young and adults are seen in this magnified view of the underside of a leaf.

when the days are at least 15 hours long (or supplemented with artificial lights), the temperature can be kept at 70°F (21°C) or more, and the light is fairly bright. In other words, you may have difficulty getting them to control an infestation in the house during midwinter in most of the United States. They are very valuable for artificially heated and lighted greenhouses at that time, however. Detailed directions for using these parasites are given in the book *Windowsill Ecology,* mentioned earlier.

ANTS

Occasionally ants will take up residence in a flower pot, or swarm over it to collect sweet honeydew from aphids, mealybugs, scales or whiteflies. If they are nesting in the pot, only repeated flooding will unseat them. One elegant method that has been used successfully is to provide them with an alternative and drier home. Place a bucket of compost next to the pot you wish to clear. Use a stick to form a bridge between the two containers. When the plant is soaked, the ants will emerge and carry their eggs and young across the bridge to safety. It may take repeated flooding, but finally all will leave. The bucket of compost can then be taken outside and dumped.

Where ants climb onto the plant from an adjacent area, the plant can be isolated by setting it up on an ant stand made with legs ringed with Stickem or Tanglefoot. This is a nontoxic material that ants will not cross. To prevent dust and lint being blown over the sticky material and thus dulling its effect, the legs of the stand can be threaded through upside-down cat food or tuna fish cans and the sticky barrier placed inside.

FUNGUS GNATS

These are tiny flies that live in, and eat, decaying organic matter. Organic gardeners are more likely to notice them, since there are

Ant Barrier: One way to keep ants away from plants is to construct a special stand on which to elevate pots. The legs of the stand are ringed with a sticky substance which ants will not cross. The sticky material can be shielded from dust and dirt by placing it inside small cans. The legs of the stand can also be set in cans of water to keep away ants. (Adapted from *The Integral Urban House: Self-Reliant Living in the City.* Farallones Institute. Sierra Club Books, 1979.)

bound to be some (as well as springtails, small jumping insects) in any unfinished compost you use to mulch the plants. The adult flies are harmless, but the immature gnat, or maggot, can damage plant roots. To avoid gnats, you can pasteurize your potting soil and compost in the oven (as described in chapter 6), or use a soil mix made up of commercial products exclusively, in order to have a low organic matter content in the soil mix. We know of one greenhouse where Stickem-covered papers are used to trap the adult flies if they become too plentiful.

Whiteflies Attracted to Yellow: When Dr. Webb shakes infested tomato plants, the whiteflies are immediately attracted to the yellow board.

A New Way to Control Whiteflies

Two USDA scientists have finally found a safe and sensible way to control whiteflies. Their control technique doesn't call for any chemicals, companion plants or the like. They paint small boards yellow and cover them with a sticky substance, and hang them in the greenhouse. The insects are attracted to the yellow, and become stuck to the boards.

Although it sounds simple, the results are nothing short of fantastic. During a visit to Dr. Ralph Webb in his laboratory at Beltsville, Maryland, he demonstrated the new techique in a greenhouse where the experimental whitefly population is reared. There, holding a piece of white paper about 18 inches (46 cm) from a tomato plant that was literally covered with whiteflies, he shook the plant. The flies immediately took to the wing and hovered around the top of the plant for a few seconds before settling back on the plant. Then substituting a yellow board for the piece of white paper, he shook the plant again. It was amazing to see about 70 percent of the flies go directly to the board. As Dr. Webb had promised, "they are attracted to the board like iron filings to a magnet."

Working with Dr. Floyd Smith, Dr. Webb has been experimenting with the whitefly control method since 1970. "Originally we needed a nonchemical way to control whiteflies while we experimented with other insects in the greenhouse," he recalled. Having read earlier work on color attractance of insects, he began to experiment with different colors and methods of use. Finally he decided on using an orange-yellow, as it had a far higher attractance rate than any other color.

The use of the sticky boards in other experiments was so successful that Dr. Smith convinced Dr. Webb they should do a controlled experiment to test just how effective the control method was. The results surprised even the two researchers.

In one experiment, the treated boards were placed between in-

PLANT DISEASES

The classical model for describing plant disease has been a triangular one of environment, susceptible plant, and causal agent. All three factors have to be present for disease to occur (Figure 1). With what is now known about competition and antagonism between the microorganisms, however, perhaps a fourth factor should be added—the absence of organisms antagonistic to the causal agent—and the model should be expanded to a rectangle (Figure 2). If you are interested in learning more about this fascinating subject, we recommend the book *Biological Control of Plant Pathogens* by Kenneth F. Baker and R. James Cook (see listing in Bibliography).

The reason for paying attention to this

fested tomato plants. The white-fly population was reduced by about 25 percent each day. In a second experiment on chrysan-themum plants, 12 treated boards completely eliminated a whitefly infestation within 24 hours.

In the most exciting experi-ment, the researchers combined the boards with a parasitic wasp (*Encarsia formosa*) and had what Dr. Webb calls virtually absolute control. The boards controlled the population of flying adults, and the parasites controlled the larvae.

Relying only on the boards, and what few natural parasites are available, Dr. Webb notes that the whitefly control will be "well beyond the economic threshold that commercial grow-ers aim for." He explained that the treated boards do not harm other natural predators or para-sites, and interfere only with the adult whitefly population.

Because of their mobility, once in a greenhouse, whiteflies quickly spread throughout an entire building. That, combined with a life cycle of about one month, gives the whitefly a reputation as one of the tough-est of all insects to control. Since whiteflies are highly mobile, the stationary boards are very effec-tive at attracting a high percent-age of the flies.

There are two ways to use this control method, Dr. Webb ex-plained. A treated board can be held and individual plants shaken to get rid of an intense population outbreak quickly, or you can hang the treated boards in the greenhouse, and they will control an existing population.

Dr. Webb has found that the boards work best when they measure about 12 inches (30 cm) square. He uses Rust-Oleum 659 yellow paint, but other similar shades would work as well. For the sticky substance, he has found that a product called Tack Trap gives the longest period of control, working for a year or more. However, the researchers also have had good results with other commercial trapping agents. They also have used SAE 90 motor oil and heavy mineral oil. For short-term use, the mineral oil has an effective-ness of from two to three weeks, and the motor oil about two weeks.

The only problem with the control method that Drs. Smith and Webb can find is that the sticky boards can be a nuisance hanging around the greenhouse. To solve this problem the two researchers tested different cages to keep the boards in. Af-ter experimenting they found that a green wire cage, with about a 2-inch (5 cm) square mesh opening worked best. Smaller mesh sizes reduced the effectiveness of the trap, but the 2-inch (5 cm) opening proved as effective as the uncaged boards, yet kept people, plants, and clothing from getting stuck.

To use the traps, Dr. Webb recommends a minimum of four treated boards for about every 150 square feet (13.5 sq m) of greenhouse space. The boards should be hung right in the mid-dle of the plant canopy, as whiteflies do not fly upward, they travel laterally. Once the boards are treated, they need no further care until they are either completely covered with trapped insects, or if mineral oil or motor oil is used, they lose their sticki-ness. Then all you have to do is clean off the boards, re-treat them, and forget about whitefly problems.

model is that it makes clear that by affecting any one of the four factors, we can prevent disease.

Breeding plants for resistance to disease is out of the hands of the average house plant gardener. It is up to the commercial growers who supply the plant marketplace. When you purchase garden vegetable seeds, resistance to specific pathogens is usually clearly an-nounced on the label of the packet. But in dealing with ornamentals, whether or not a particular variety is susceptible to the pathogens common to your area is less obvi-ous. Consequently, the house plant buyer is left with making as wise a choice as possible based on how healthy the plant looks in the

Figure 1:
The classical model for describing plant disease shows that three factors are necessary for disease to occur: a causal agent (the pathogen), a susceptible plant, and an environment that fosters the growth of the pathogen.

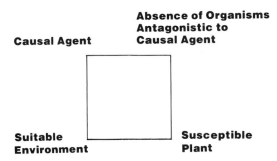

Figure 2:
Theories of the biological control of plant disease add a fourth factor to the classical model: the absence of organisms antagonistic to the causal agent.

store. Whatever information you can obtain from books or store clerks on how difficult the plant might be to raise also will be helpful.

As mentioned earlier, using compost in the soil mix or as a mulch on the soil surface is one method used by some organic growers to introduce competitive or antagonistic microorganisms into the soil environment. Until this science is more fully developed, we have no other strategies at our disposal for biological control of plant disease.

Most efforts to control house plant disease are thus focused on the two remaining factors, the causal agent and the suitable environment. In many cases the environment itself is the cause of the disease symptom: too much or not enough light, too much mois-

ture, too little humidity, too low or too high temperature, drafts, smog, overfertilizing, or too much salt in the water. The answer to each of these problems is apparent in the description of the problem itself, and simply modifying the environment is the desirable control measure.

However, in some cases changing the environment helps to control disease symptoms because something in the environment is especially suitable to a plant pathogen. Most often that something is water, either in the air or soil. Light also may be a factor in triggering a problem. And some soil mixes are more hospitable than others to soilborne plant pathogens.

The other efforts to control disease are usually directed at the causal agent itself. Pasteurizing the potting soil is an effort to eradicate potential problems. Removing diseased portions of the plant also may help, as may repotting in fresh soil. Isolating and, if necessary, destroying diseased plants so they will not spread their problem to others in the collection is an additional important tactic to which you may have to resort.

A final thought regarding diseased plants: when in doubt, throw it out. Take a cutting from a healthy piece of the plant and start over.

Following are some specific recommendations for controlling the most common house plant ailments.

ROOT, CROWN, AND STEM ROTS

A wide variety of fungi (*Phytophthora, Sclerotium, Pythium, Phoma* species and others) will cause the stems and roots of a plant to turn mushy. The whole top of the plant may eventually collapse and/or the leaves may look dark and waterlogged.

There is not much you can do with a plant that shows such symptoms. It has probably been overwatered. Crown rot can start if water is allowed to stand in the center

Crown Rot: Overwatering has caused crown rot on this *Phalaenopsis* orchid.

growing point in those plants such as African violets that grow from a basal rosette of leaves. Usually, seriously diseased plants should be destroyed.

Cacti, however, are exceptions to the rule. On these plants stem rot may start at punctures in the waxy cuticle. Infected stem sections should be cut out with a clean knife and the wounds dusted with sulfur powder. Then the entire cactus should be allowed to dry in a very bright place out of direct sun. If the diseased portion is very large, cut clear through the stem well below the rot where the tissue is firm and of normal color. This, in effect, will prune the plant back and encourage the growth of new shoots. Cut diagonally so any moisture will drain off, and dust the open wound with sulfur. Then allow the plant to dry thoroughly.

If the roots are rotted, the cactus should be removed from the soil, all roots cut off, and the cut points dusted with sulfur. Allow the plant to dry thoroughly on its side in a bright, dry place for several months until new roots appear. Then repot in dry soil.

LEAF SPOTS

Spots on the leaves can have a number of causes, such as cold drops of water falling on a warm plant, too much sunlight, or misting or spraying while the sun is shining on the plant. Where a fungus is the problem (species of *Stemphyllium*, *Alternaria*, *Fusarium* and other genera), it is best to remove the spotted leaves. Then reduce the humidity around the plants by separating them further from each other. Make sure that there is good air circulation around susceptible plants. Be careful not to get the foliage wet when you water.

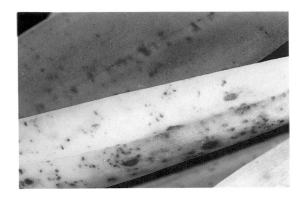

Leaf Spots: Spots on the foliage of this *Cattleytonia* orchid were caused by a fungus, *Gloeosporium affine*.

POWDERY MILDEWS

This is another fungus (*Sphaerotheca* sp.) that may be a reaction to humid conditions. It is evidenced by a grayish white, powdery growth that gradually spreads across plant leaves. Sometimes the leaves may dry up and die. This fungus sometimes may be controlled by dustings of powdered sulfur or a dip of wettable sulfur. Reduce the humidity and temperature around the plants, and make sure they are situated where light conditions are suitable.

Mildew: Pencil point indicates a fuzzy patch of mildew on a Rieger begonia.

BOTRYTIS BLIGHT

Botrytis appears as a gray, moldy growth causing rotting of leaves, stems, and flowers. Overwatering, overfeeding plants with nitrogen which may make them soft and succulent, or crowding them too close together are ways to invite problems with *Botrytis*. The best cure is to remove infected plant parts and try to correct the adverse conditions.

Botrytis Blight: Shown here on a *Cattleya*-type orchid; eventually turns plant parts brown and mushy.

DAMPING-OFF

This condition is seen most often in seedlings and is common indoors where the light may be poor and the seedbed kept too soggy. Water molds (*Pythium* spp.) will cause a marked thinning of the seedling stem where it enters the soil, and the plant will fall over. Not infrequently seedlings will fail to emerge from the soil at all. The percentage of mortality can be very high. Sterilizing the soil used for seedlings may be necessary if proper light and moisture conditions cannot be provided. In general, plant seeds closer to the soil surface than you would if you were planting them outdoors. Cover with sand, or a mixture of sand and powdered charcoal, to insure good drainage.

A House Plant Clinic

This chart has been put together for
quick reference, denoting the most common symptoms of
house plant troubles, along with causes and simple cures. Remember to
always test any dip or spray solution on a portion of the plant first.

SYMPTOM	CAUSE	TREATMENT
Yellow leaves	Lack of light	Move to brighter spot.
	Excess sunlight	Move to shadier spot.
	High temperature	Give 70°F (21°C) during day; 55° to 60°F (13G to 16°C) at night.
	Lack of nitrogen	Apply balanced plant food more often.
	Poor drainage	Repot, following methods recommended in chapter 6. Use good soil mix such as 1 part each sand, peat moss, vermiculite, and perlite.
	Too much water	Keep soil uniformly moist, never soggy. Some plants like to dry out between waterings. Water according to type and size of plant, porosity of container, and room temperature.
	Too little water (dry soil)	Water more frequently (see above).
	Soil not acid enough, as with azaleas and other acid lovers	Increase acidity with vinegar water or sulfur dust.
	Mite damage	Use magnifying glass on top and bottom sides of leaves to detect mites. Wash in plain water or soap and water. If mites remain, dip in or spray with a mixture of ½ cup (8 tablespoons or 118 ml) buttermilk, 4 cups (944 ml) wheat flour and 5 gallons (19 l) water.
	Nematodes (some species cause lumps on roots; others do not)	No control; discard pot and all by burning or regular refuse collection. (Do not use in compost pile.)
Browning of leaf tips (leaf tip burn)	Dry air	Increase humidity by double potting; place pots on pebbles in a tray with ½ inch (13 mm) of water; use room humidifier.
	Overfeeding	Excessive fertilizer salts burn roots, especially when plant is allowed to go dry. If overfed, knock plant from pot and flush soil ball under water faucet.
	Chemical ions in water or soil may supply excess fluoride, sodium, boron, or magnesium and injure sensitive plants. Chlorine may also cause salt damage.	Let tapwater stand overnight, or boil and cool to get rid of chlorine before watering plants. If tapwater is treated with fluoride, add 1 teaspoon (5 ml) of gypsum to 6-inch (15 cm) pot of soil to cancel fluoride; or 2 teaspoons (10 ml) limestone per 6-inch (15 cm) pot.
	Dry soil	Water more frequently.
	Commercial leaf-shining materials	Avoid using them; they can clog leaf pores.
	Leaves next to cold window in winter	Draw shades at night; move plants back.
	Pesticide burn	Test any pesticide on a small portion of the plant before using on entire plant. Do not hold spray cans too close; many aerosol sprays are not recommended for house plants. Better yet, don't use them at all.
	Diseases and insects	See individual listings and photos.

(chart continued on next page)

SYMPTOM	CAUSE	TREATMENT
Drooping foliage	Dry soil	Apply enough water to rejuvenate.
	Soil too wet (poor drainage); shuts off oxygen to roots, causing suffocation	Never let soil become soggy. See CAUSE: Poor drainage and Too much water, under SYMPTOM: Yellow leaves.
	Root rots due to various fungi (such as species of *Fusarium, Phytophthora, Pythium, Rhizoctonia, Sclerotium, Thielaviopsis,* and others) cause collapse at soil line	Use disinfected pots and pasteurized soil.
	Dormancy	If plant needs a dormant period, decrease water and light until active growth resumes.
Curling of leaves	Overwatering	Check plant's water preference. Never let soil become soggy.
	Dry soils	Keep soil moist, not soggy.
	Root rots, cut off flow of water up stems, causing curling	Use pasteurized soil (mentioned above). Avoid overwatering, especially in plastic, glazed, or ceramic containers. Give good drainage.
	Aphids	Control with commercially obtained lacewing larvae. Spray with nicotine sulfate or soap and water (1 teaspoon [5 ml] soap to 2 quarts [19 l] water).
	Mites	Use commercially available mite predators, or spray with soap and water every several days. See CAUSE: Mite damage, under SYMPTOM: Yellow leaves.
Cupped leaves (mainly at growing tip)	Aphids	See SYMPTOM: Curling of leaves.
	Mites	Use commercially available mite predators. Dip plants in soapy water or use buttermilk-flour spray. Increase humidity.
	Unburned gas injury	When lighting greenhouse gas heaters, light match first. Have good ventilation.
	Leaking gas	Have utility company check stoves and incoming gas lines in your greenhouse. Sometimes "onion smell" or "rotten egg" odor can mean fuel tank is running low. Check fuel gauge.
Brown leaves	Fertilizer burn due to soluble salts	Avoid overfeeding. Remove plant from pot and rinse soil from roots and repot in new soil. If browning is caused by leaves touching salt buildup on rim of pot, scrub rim of pot.
	Hot dry air	Use humidifier in winter. Set potted plants on trays of moist pebbles. Try double potting. Can syringe foliage of smooth-leaved plants, but those with hairy leaves will show water spots.
	Overwatering and poor drainage, shutting off oxygen from roots, causing suffocation	Cut down on water, especially in glazed or plastic pots. Provide good drainage; use perlite and/or sand in potting mix.
	Crown or root rot	Check roots. If brown, peel off and dust ends with sulfur. Repot in fresh mix.

SYMPTOM	CAUSE	TREATMENT
White material on leaves	Could be mealybugs (insects)	Put cotton swab on toothpick, dip in alcohol or hydrogen peroxide and touch each cottony mass. Immerse in soapy water and wash with soft toothbrush; commercially available lacewing larvae also very effective.
	Powdery mildew, identified by thin layer of white fuzzy growth on stems and leaves; later causes foliage to turn brown and drop off	Don't syringe foliage or splash water on plants. Give good air circulation (can use small fan). Dust with sulfur. Move plant to sunnier location.
Root or stem rot	Overwatering or poor drainage which brings on diseases such as *Pythium, Rhizoctonia, Verticillium, Xanthomonas,* and others	Repot plants, cut out dead spots. Replant in fresh pasteurized soil mix and clean pot.
	Pot too large	Repot in smaller container.
Lanky or leggy plants	Lack of light makes plants stretch for it	Move to brighter spot or use fluorescent lights.
	High room temperature	Causes fast growth. Cut temperature to 68°F (20°C) during day and 60°F (16°C) at night.
	Excess nitrogen; overfeeding causes "soft" lanky growth	Cut down on feeding. If overfed, knock soil ball out of pot, flush soil away from roots and repot.
	Lack of pinching	Many species of *Begonia, Coleus, Fuchsia,* and *Geranium* need to have growing tips nipped back to induce growth of more branches.
	Overcrowding causes competition for light and nutrients	Leave space between plants in planters and between pots in groupings.
New leaves tiny, off-color, spindly, pale green	Lack of light	Move to brighter window.
	Lack of nutrients	Give balanced plant food oftener.
Roots showing above soil of container	Dry soil (checks growth)	Keep soil moist, not soggy.
	Lack of organic matter	Add compost or peat moss, 1/3 volume to soil.
	Nematodes	Check roots for lumps; no control, discard plant.
	Pot too small	Repot in larger container.
Green "mold" on soil	Algae or fungi	Not serious. Due to poor air circulation, sometimes to heavy soil. Add sand or perlite to soil mix to encourage air circulation and water drainage. Use tines of fork to loosen surface of soil once a week. Also check to be sure lighting is adequate.
White crusty salts on surface of soil and pots (mainly clay types)	Fertilizer salts or magnesium or calcium carbonates in hard water	Not serious if from hard water. Loosen soil with fork and water thoroughly and repeatedly from top to flush out salts. Do not allow unabsorbed water to remain in saucer.
	Chlorine in tapwater	Let water stand overnight or boil and cool before using.

(chart continued on next page)

SYMPTOM	CAUSE	TREATMENT
Sticky leaves, coated with sooty coal-dust-like material	Plant lice (aphids), whiteflies, mealybugs, and scale insects; pump out sap from plants and secrete a sticky substance which nourishes spores of sooty mold	Inspect leaves for these insects. Spray, covering tops and bottoms of leaves. Wash leaves with mild detergent or soap solution regularly (1 teaspoon [5 ml] soap to 3 quarts [2.8 l] water). Control with commercially available lacewing larvae.
Holes in leaves	Snails and slugs	Look for slimy trails, or check plants at night. Handpick; place inverted citrus skins in area; use stale beer in shallow pan; sprinkle lime or wood ashes around plants; stalk them with a salt shaker and sprinkle few grains on each one.
	Earwigs	Check under pot rims or under leaves and inside blossoms. Handpick and destroy.
Rotted or brown spots on foliage	A fungous infection	Dust with sulfur.
	Bacteria	Keep surface of leaf clean.
	Fluoridated water may cause spots on leaves of sensitive plants	Add 2 teaspoons (10 ml) of limestone to each 6-inch (15 cm) pot, on soil surface and water to leach lime into soil.
Quick defoliation	Insects	Check plant with magnifying glass to identify insect; treat with recommended remedy.
	Extreme changes in temperature, drafts, too much heat, dry air	Move out of drafts; keep plants away from radiators, heaters, TV sets.
	Dry soil	Keep soil uniformly moist.
	Shock, such as when potted plants have been summering outdoors and roots are broken off when returned indoors	Prevent by giving pot a twist each week to dislodge roots growing through pot. Slip nylon stocking up over pot to keep roots from growing into ground.
	Cats using plants as a litter box	Repot immediately and keep out of reach of cats in future; hang plant from wall bracket, etc.
Slow defoliation	Insect attack	Check for insects and use proper remedy.
	Soggy soil	Avoid overwatering; use well-drained soil mix; take into account whether glazed, plastic, or porous container.
	Dry soil	Increase water.
	Lack of light	Some plants need more light than others or they will lose foliage.
	Certain diseases such as crown and stem rots, *Fusarium,* and *Verticillium*	Use pasteurized, well-drained soil mix.
	Excess feeding; fertilizer salts burn feeder roots, especially if soil is dry	Feed less or at longer intervals; flush roots and repot if fertilizer burn is suspected.
Stunted plants	Too much plant food burns roots; symphyllids, other insects such as fungus gnat larvae, springtails, or sowbugs	Flush off root ball and repot. Use fresh soil with application of nicotine sulfate. (Nicotine sulfate is very toxic. Handle carefully and do not get it on your skin.)
	Nematodes (some cause small lumps on roots; others do not)	No control. Discard entire plant by burning or refuse collection. Do not use in compost pile.

SYMPTOM	CAUSE	TREATMENT
Wilting of entire plant	Look for grubs or aphids in soil or on roots	Drench soil with nicotine sulfate.
	Too little water	Set plant in pan full of warm water for half an hour and mist foliage. Move to cool place.
	Too much water	Knock plant out of pot and let soil ball dry for several hours, then repot.
	Excess fertilizer	Flush root ball for 3 or 4 minutes.
	Exposure to cold	If plant is not completely frozen, trim it back to live tissue and permit regrowth.
	Crown rot, stem rot, or wilt rot	Knock plant out of pot and cut out diseased portions, then dust with sulfur.
Browning of tips	Pollutants; overexposure to sun; fluoridated water adversely affects sensitive species of *Chlorophytum, Cordyline, Dracaena, Maranta, Yucca,* and others	See SYMPTOM: Browning of leaf tips. Use unfluoridated water; add 2 teaspoons (10 ml) of limestone to each 6-inch (15 cm) pot, if fluoride is suspected. (Lime is not recommended for plants needing an acid soil, such as azaleas.)
Sudden blackening of new growth	Excess plant food	Flush soil from roots.
	Hot or cold drafts	Keep plant away from radiators, doorways, open windows and the like.
	Freeze injury	Draw draperies at night. Move plants away from glass panes.
	Sunburn	Place plant behind curtains for shading. Note that sun moves and can be too hot at certain seasons or times of day. Move plant to different location and cut off damaged growth.
Spotted foliage	Sun's rays too hot	Move plant to other location.
	Cold water on foliage	Take care in watering; use room temperature water.
	Bacterial or fungous infection	Avoid splashing water on leaves.
	Air pollution	Not much that can be done except fight for clean air.
Torn or chewed leaves	Cats	Provide a pot of catnip or grass (especially couch grass). Put orange peels in other pots as a repellent. Keep out of cats' reach.
	Sweepers, carts, curtains, or people brushing against them	Give plants plenty of growing room.
	Snails	Check plants with a flashlight at night as snails hide during daytime. Handpick or treat as recommended under SYMPTOM: Holes in leaves.
	Earwigs	See SYMPTOM: Holes in leaves.

(chart continued on next page)

SYMPTOM	CAUSE	TREATMENT
Failure to bloom	Not enough light	Move to brighter window; provide artificial light in winter.
	Excess fertilizer	Withhold feeding; remove plant from pot and flush roots with water.
	Failure to give short day-long night treatment as in Christmas cactus, poinsettia, and species of *Kalanchoe* and others that need shading at night	For Christmas bloom, shade these items from artificial light at night from 6:00 P.M. to 8:00 A.M. from September 1 to November 15. Removal from this light regime will inhibit blooming.
	Too constant watering of cacti or plants in dormant period	Allow drying-out period.
	Too high temperature	Hardy spring bulbs need winter cold period to bloom.

Diseases of Flowering Plants

The house plant boom has brought with it many disease problems. For easier reference we have divided the diseases into two groups: (a) flowering plant and (b) foliage plant. Although we have mentioned some diseases in previous charts, the following information should be more helpful for disease identification.

CAUSE	SYMPTOM	TREATMENT
Alternaria **blight**	Causes dark brown to black lesions, small and circular.	Keep foliage dry. If you wash plants do so early in the morning in an airy place so they can dry during warmer hours.
Anthracnose	Pink pustules or light brown rotted areas, especially on cacti and various foliages.	Cut out and destroy affected areas.
Botrytis **blight**	Fungous growth that causes buds and blooms to turn brown and dry up. Some blooms become mushy first (e.g., *Pelargonium*). Especially susceptible to drying are species of *Gardenia* and *Sinningia*.	Avoid splashing water on foliage. Provide good drainage and good air circulation.
Brown fungal leaf spot	Causes tiny lesions that turn yellow. Prevalent on *Dieffenbachia* but attacks other foliages also.	Dust plant with sulfur. Cut out and destroy diseased parts. Keep foliage dry.
Cercospora **leaf spot**	Causes ¼-inch (6 mm) spots on leaves, resembling frogs' eyes. Common on rubber plants (*Ficus elastica*).	Avoid overwatering. Cut affected leaves into a sealable bag and place in trash can or burn.

CAUSE	SYMPTOM	TREATMENT
Crown rot or stem rot	Plants usually wilt and die (as with African violets); foliage turns yellow and stems rot at soil level or below.	Avoid overwatering; provide good drainage. Discard badly infected plants; sterilize pots.
Damping-off	Certain fungi attack seedlings and young plants at soil level, causing them to topple over. Or plants may rot before emergence.	Start seeds in loose "soilless" medium or pasteurized soil mix. Do not sow seeds too thickly, or as deeply as for outdoor plants. Give good air circulation.
Fusarium leaf spot	Causes small pinpricks on foliage; entire leaf turns brown and drops.	Keep water off foliage.
Leaf and stem blight fungi (See *Botrytis* blight and others) Note: Dieback of *Ficus benjamina* has spread lately and is caused by *Phomopsis* fungus.	Causes black, watery, or charred-looking areas; dry brown rot; or drying up of leaves and stems.	Cut out dead leaves and twigs. Burn or seal in plastic bag and discard. Never leave any infected parts that may cause reinfection. Avoid overwatering.
Mosaic virus	Causes mottled foliage, stunted abnormal growth.	No control. Destroy entire plant. Propagate only from healthy plants.
Oedema (pronounced Eh-dee-muh)	Causes blisters on leaves, later turning to a corky texture. Especially prevalent on begonias during dank, cloudy weather.	Give good ventilation. Take care not to overwater. Space plants so air can circulate between them. You may need to add artificial light.
Phytophthora leaf spot	Spots appear as mushy, shiny, water-soaked areas. Worse on *Dieffenbachia*, *Peperomia*, and *Philodendron* species.	Cut off worst leaves and seal in plastic bag for discarding. Avoid getting water on leaves.
Powdery mildew	White, fuzzy growth on leaves and stems; eventually causes leaves to turn brown and fall. Can be bad on African violets, indoor roses, and begonias (especially Rieger).	Give good air circulation even if you must use a small fan.
Ramularia, *Septoria*, and others	Whitish, yellowish, or brownish spots on leaves.	Avoid wetting foliage.
Rhizoctonia foliar blight	Causes brownish wet rot, with reddish brown threads.	Keep foliage dry.

(chart continued on next page)

CAUSE	SYMPTOM	TREATMENT
Rhizoctonia root rot	Wilting of tips followed by entire plant collapsing at soil line. Slow growth, yellowing of foliage; root discoloration and decay.	No control. Discard entire plant. Use pasteurized potting soil and disinfect pots.
Ringspot virus	Causes small leaf spots, each surrounded by a definite ring.	No control. Destroy entire plant. Propagate only from healthy plants.
Rusts: *Glomerella, Puccinia,* and others (Can be caused by both fungi and bacteria)	Causes brown, black, orange, yellow, red, or gray spots on foliage.	Avoid wetting foliage. Remove diseased plant parts. A fan will help control most fungous leaf diseases.
"Shotgun fungus" disease	Causes leaf spots or tiny holes, as if hit by birdshot.	Keep foliage dry. Remove diseased leaves and seal in plastic bags to discard.
Verticillium	May cause sudden wilting of tips, as with *Rhizoctonia,* but roots are not rotted. Discolorations (streaks) appear inside stems.	No control. Discard entire plant. Use pasteurized soil mix and disinfect pots.

Soilborne Diseases of Foliage Plants

CAUSE	SYMPTOM	TREATMENT
Fusarium wilt	Causes stems and roots to rot, then wilt. Worse on *Dracaena* species.	Keep foliage dry. Discard if badly affected.
Phytophthora	Causes soft, often mushy stem rot and foliage blight. Look for stem lesions on species of *Dieffenbachia, Dracaena,* and *Peperomia.*	Seal badly affected plants in plastic bags and discard in trash or burn.
Pythium	Causes roots to turn watery, then blacken and rot. Plants collapse suddenly. Affects species of cacti, *Dieffenbachia, Gardenia, Raphidophora* (Pothos), *Schefflera,* and many others.	Seal badly affected plants in plastic bags and discard in trash or burn.

CAUSE	SYMPTOM	TREATMENT
Rhizoctonia	Believed to be the No. 1 soilborne disease of foliage plants. Attacks at or near the soil line. May spread to leaves, causing entire plant to wilt slowly and collapse, especially on species of *Aglaonema, Aphelandra, Gardenia, Gynura, Philodendron, Raphidophora* (Pothos), and others.	Use pasteurized soil mix. Avoid overwatering.
Sclerotium or *Sclerotinia*	Look for white fungous growth on soil surface and affected plants. Produces many small, dark, structures the size of mustard seed or a little larger. Black bodies are called sclerotia.	Very little can be done. Seal plant and soil in plastic bag and discard or burn.

CHAPTER 10

Foliage Plants

While almost all indoor plants will flower under the right conditions, some do so with varying levels of difficulty in the home because of the more or less limiting environmental conditions offered there. Certain plants bloom only rarely indoors; others produce flowers that are inconspicuous or few in number. In a wonderful demonstration of the economy of nature, many of these indifferent bloomers have been endowed with singularly interesting foliage that compensates handsomely for the absence of eye-catching flowers. Grown primarily for the characteristics of their leaves, they are known as foliage plants, or green plants.

Often of tropical origin, foliage plants were long of limited interest and grown only casually indoors. In recent decades, however, there has been a dramatic change; according to a foliage plant census done by the United States Department of Agriculture, sales figures for green plants increased by more than 1,000 percent from 1959 to 1977, climbing from $24.1 million to over $271 million. The reasons for this soaring popularity are not hard to find.

Unlike flowering plants, which regularly lose their *raison d'être* with their petals, foliage plants usually remain eminently presentable year-round. They are, moreover, generally easier to maintain in peak form than plants valued for their flowers, for many of them can get by with less light and lower temperatures — and consequently with little food other than that present in their potting medium. Also, because the primary interest in growing these plants is to develop and maintain the vegetative growth of leaves and stems rather than to coax forth flowers, it is rarely necessary to increase or decrease natural daylength as is sometimes required to initiate flower buds. Less prone to insect and disease problems than flowering types, green plants suited to home growing also tend to be less vulnerable to dehydration, for their leaves are often relatively thick and tough and designed to store and retain water.

APPRECIATING FOLIAGE PLANTS

In addition to offering significant ease of culture, foliage plants boast numerous aesthetic

Tropical Jungle: Many of our popular foliage plants hail from natural habitats like the one depicted in this engraving. This type of environment, with soil rich in organic matter, warm, humid air, and bright, dappled light serves as a good guideline for the sort of conditions you should provide for your tropical house plants.

Opposite, close-up of Coleus *foliage.*

aspects that are not found in flowering plants or pass largely unnoticed in them because of the distraction created by a profusion of bright blooms. These subtle attractions range from a palette full of leaf colors through intriguing leaf patterns to the texture, aroma, shape, and arrangement of the foliage.

Not all foliage plants are green, nor is the green they offer of a single shade. The range of greens found in nature offers surprising scope for low-key but pleasing contrasts even in a group of solidly colored plants — contrasts abetted by the deepening of colors when foliage is bold and thick, thus absorbing light and casting dramatic shadows, or, when

The Subtleties of Green: A grouping of green foliage plants need never be monotonous, thanks to a wide variety of possible leaf shadings and patternings. Two dieffenbachias share center stage here, showing different degrees of variegation.

leaves are delicate and thin, radiating a vibrant spring green as light shines through them. Sometimes these "plain green" plants are highlighted by white, red, silver, or gold veining. As the elegant tracery on fittonias, jewel orchids, and silver-veined anthuriums attests, the effect can be spectacular. Also splendid when used alone as the focal point of a room or judiciously in plant groupings are the more flamboyant plants having foliage of more than one color. Sometimes the variegation takes the form of an exquisite and often elaborate pattern, as in the begonia treebine *(Cissus discolor), Maranta* species, and various calatheas, including those so aptly called peacock plants *(Calathea makoyana).*

Perhaps the most common mode of variegation is a green leaf with a narrow or broad margin of creamy white or yellow — an effect found, for example, in certain ivy, *Sansevieria,* and *Peperomia* cultivars. Sometimes the leaves have a vertically striped appearance, as in the variegated cast-iron plant (*Aspidistra elatior* 'Variegata'), or horizontal "bands" as in the variegated *Sansevieria trifasciata* 'Laurentii' and the stunningly cross-banded *Dracaena goldieana.*

In other, "painted" types of multicolored plants, such as *Coleus,* aluminum plant *(Pilea cadierei),* polka-dot plant *(Hypoestes phyllostachya)* and the very popular cultivars of *Aglaonema, Codiaeum, Dieffenbachia,* and *Epipremnum* having *picta* or *pictum* in their names, there are daubs, splashes, or marblings of one or more colors on the basic green of the foliage. Yet other plants have essentially green foliage overlaid with another color, as in *Philodendron* 'Burgundy' and purple heart (*Setcreasea pallida* 'Purple Heart'). Or the ornamental color may come in the form of an iridescent sheen, such as the metallic blue-green glint given off by the indoor oak *(Nicodemia diversifolia),* or as hairs that give the plant an iridescent quality (as in *Gynura* spp.). Occasionally added color is present only on some leaves of the plant (as in *Codiaeum* cvs.), or flashes forth from the

(continued on page 174)

The Sensation of Textures: There is more to foliage plants than simply the color and shape of leaves. Texture adds another dimension, appealing to both the visual and tactile senses. One glance at the feathery, graceful lines of a *Cycas*, upper left, and it's easy to imagine the tickling sensation that comes from running the palm of your hand along the frond tips. The cloudlike masses of soft, tiny leaves, upper right, belong to *Soleirolia*, baby's tears. The center image is not a close-up of some reptile's scaly skin, but rather the clearly delineated ridges and valleys of a puckery *Pilea* 'Moon Valley'. The *Marsilea*, or water clover fern, lower left, offers a daintier image with its arrangement of thin, delicate, slightly ruffled leaves. The sleek, glossy leaves in the photo at lower right belong to a member of the ivy group.

More on Variegation

In plants with white or yellow variegation there is little or none of the pigment chlorophyll, which absorbs the red and blue wavelengths of light. The presence of other nongreen hues in foliage is due to pigments other than chlorophyll which either conceal it or become visible in its absence. When variegation is caused by abnormal cells resulting from a viral infection or other genetically damaging injury, it cannot be perpetuated through propagation by seeds. Sometimes, however, a variegation is "normal" and consistent in nature and therefore transferable through sexual propagation. (When this trait is the basis for a plant's species name, the descriptive word, such as *marginata, picta,* or *variegata,* is not capitalized and does not have single quotation marks around it.)

In other instances, normal variegation persists only in cultivation, when transmitted by vegetative methods of reproduction such as division or leaf cuttings. Variegated cultivars of this kind named for their coloring are designated by capitalized nonitalicized names surrounded by single quotation marks. In some vegetatively perpetuated cultivars with variegated margins — *Sansevieria trifasciata* 'Laurentii', for example — division is the only sure way to insure the passing on of variegation, for new plants derived from leaf cuttings will form from the unvariegated cells in the center of the leaf and revert to species.

To maintain the patterned variegation and/or bright blend of colors that make them so ap-

Contrasting Variegation: Lots of light will insure that this *Alternanthera bettzickiana* retains its lovely deep green and pink foliage coloration. These colors, along with a compact, low growth habit, make this a handsome plant to include in a group display.

Coleus Colors: You should have no trouble finding a pleasing color combination among the many coleus hybrids available. Shown here are just two possibilities: coppery red leaves that look like they've been dipped in mint green paint, and pastel pink leaves rimmed with green.

preciated, most multicolored cultivars need higher levels of light than the solid green members of their species or genus. The reason for this is that chlorophyll is essential to a plant's manufacture of food, and under low-light conditions plants already low in this pigment must necessarily make more of it so they can make the most of what light there is to maintain an acceptable rate of photosynthesis. The result will be a loss of much of their variegation as the pigment becomes or reverts to green. In relatively bright light, however, the chlorophyll in the green por-

The Radiance of a Croton: All the splendor of Nature's palette is evident in the striking coloration of these leaves. These bushy plants require lots of light to maintain the brilliance of their colors.

The Regal *Cordyline:* A graceful, upright form combines with slender, deep green leaves marked with red to create a handsome foliage plant.

tion of such plants is sufficient to maintain the plant in health, and the other-colored areas of the foliage will remain distinct and bright. In addition to creating a need for stronger light, the relatively smaller amount of chlorophyll pigment in variegated plants causes them to need less water and food than related plain green plants, for their more limited ability to make food means that they grow more slowly. For the same reason, variegated cultivars within a genus may prefer cooler temperatures than green ones; cro-

tons *(Codiaeum variegatum* var. *pictum)* are an example of this. Perhaps in compensation for the comparatively lesser amount of water needed around their roots, variegated forms also may require a higher humidity, and smaller types (such as *Ficus pumila* 'Variegata') sometimes need to be in terraria to do really well. There are, of course, exceptions to the foregoing generalizations. For example, variegated or not, woody-stemmed plants like crotons need a fair amount of water to retain their leaves; redmargined dracaena *(Dracaena*

marginata) and cultivars of *Cordyline terminalis,* particularly need ample water in winter.

Clearly, multicolored foliage plants call for extra attentiveness; they are more sensitive to extremes of temperature, moisture, and light, generally less vigorous than all-green cultivars, and sometimes susceptible to disease if their special needs are not met. For foliage plant aficionados, however, the splendid color accents and intriguing patterns offered by these striking oddities guarantee the admiring care they should have.

undersides of the foliage, as in variegated Moses-in-the-cradle (*Rhoeo spathacea* 'Variegata'), saffron pepper *(Piper crocatum),* and rosary vine *(Ceropegia woodii).*

In addition to offering subtle to pronounced color and patterning, foliage plants delight the eye and hand with a considerable variety of textures. The tapestried look of fairy carpet begonia *(Begonia versicolor)* is enhanced by a pile of fuzzy red hairs that invite touching, as do the lush downiness of the gynuras and the appealing roughness of the piggyback plant *(Tolmiea menziesii).* At the other extreme lie the extraordinarily glossy and smooth leaves of the lacquered pepper tree *(Piper magnificum),* the cool waxiness of sansevierias, and the delicately thin succulence of German ivy *(Senecio mikanioides).* Then there is the rich, velvety look of the black-gold philodendron *(Philodendron melanochrysum),* the satinlike luster of the quilted taffeta plant *(Hoffmannia roezlii),* and the crinkly, puckered appeal of the seersucker plant *(Geogenanthus undatus).* Other foliage plants are grown primarily because their leaves please the nose. Examples are the various scented foliage geraniums sweetly redolent of apple, ginger, lemon, lime, nutmeg, orange, and peppermint.

More dimensions of foliage plants that offer rewards to the close observer are the shape of the leaves and the manner in which they are arranged — matters of greater interest here than in flowering plants because the foliage itself is the premier attraction. Leaf contours can vary greatly within a single genus; crotons *(Codiaeum variegatum* var. *pictum),* for example, can have lancelike, straplike, ovate, or oakleaf-type foliage, while leaves among the exceptionally popular *Dracaena* species range from fearsome-looking, massive rosettes of spikey, yuccalike foliage *(D. arborea)* to the small oval leaves of the gold-dust dracaena *(D. surculosa).* The marvelously diverse leaf forms of foliage plants beguile the imagination and have given rise to many of the more descriptive popular names — bird's foot ivy (*Hedera helix* 'Pedata'), for example, and the heartleaf, fiddle-leaf, and spade-leaf philodendrons (*Philodendron scandens* subsp. *oxycardium, P. bipennifolium,* and *P. domesticum,* respectively). As even these few examples suggest, leaves may be entire or lobed (having deep indentations). Sometimes, as in philodendrons, the same plant may exhibit both whole and split foliage (unlobed leaves are sometimes associated with a plant in its juvenile stage and perforated leaves with a mature plant).

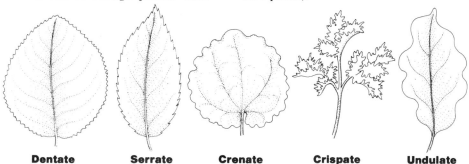

Dentate   **Serrate**   **Crenate**   **Crispate**   **Undulate**

Leaf Margins: A distinguishing feature among plants is the manner in which their leaves are edged. Presented here, from left to right, is an assortment of leaf margins which are found on many common house plants. The toothed leaf at left is called dentate and is found on strawberry begonias and piggyback plants. Serrate leaves are notched, as on the kangaroo vine or flowering maple. Crenate or scalloped leaves are very common, appearing on Swedish ivy, coleus, and florists' gloxinia plants. Crispate leaves are not as common; examples of this curly type are parsley and Ming aralia leaves. Undulate leaves are those which are wavy both along the margin and across the leaf; fiddle-leaf fig and elephant's ear plants display this form.

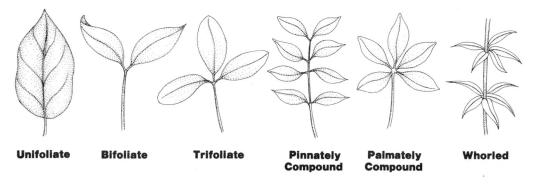

Unifoliate   Bifoliate   Trifoliate   Pinnately   Palmately   Whorled
Compound   Compound

Leaf Arrangements: Leaves can be arranged on a plant in any number of ways, ranging from one simple leaf growing off the main stem to more complex whorls of leaves rising the length of the stem. A unifoliate plant has a single undivided leaf blade on a petiole emerging from a main stem. Two leaves on two petioles off a main stem signify a bifoliate plant, while three leaves coming off one stem are called trifoliate. Pinnately compound foliage features leaves comprised of leaflets running along both sides of a petiole. Foliage which is palmately compound displays leaflets radiating from a single center point. A whorled arrangement presents a starburst of leaves in a circle around the stem.

There are also many kinds of leaf margins; some of the more common are dentate (having coarse indentations that are perpendicular to the margins), denticulate (finely dentate), serrate (saw-toothed, with teeth pointing forward), serrulate (finely serrate), crenate (scalloped), crenulate (finely crenate), crispate (curled), sinuate (strongly waved), and undulate (wavelike along the margin and across the leaf). As a rule, plants coming from the tropics tend to have smooth or rounded edges, whereas those native to temperate areas often possess notched margins.

Whatever their shape, leaves can be arranged in a host of ways. In the simple leaf plan found on many popular foliage plants, there are one or more simple leaves coming off the base of the main stem, or from the rootstock. *Narcissus* species and pineapple plants *(Ananas comosus)* are two plants which have this sort of simple leaf arrangement. In compound arrangements, a leaf is made up of separate blades or divisions (leaflets) on a single petiole. When foliage is pinnately compound, as in feather palms and ferns, the leaflets are arranged on both sides of the stem. In palmately compound arrangements — found in schefflera *(Brassaia actinophylla)* and false aralia *(Dizygotheca elegantissima)* — leaflets emanate from a sin-

gle point, somewhat like splayed fingers from the palm of a hand. There are a number of subdivisions within these compound categories and other categories as well, all relating to the number of leaves or leaflets and their position on the stem and relative to each other. For example, leaves can be opposite each other or alternate on different sides of the stem, or they can be arranged in spirals of various kinds or whorled in a circle around the stem.

The terms pinnate and palmate can refer to venation in leaves, as well as to leaf arrangements. Pinnately veined leaves have small veins arranged along both sides of a central vein running the length of the leaf. In palmate venation, the veins emanate from a single point at the base of the leaf.

Leaf shapes and arrangements aside, foliage plants also appeal aesthetically and practically by virtue of their wide range of sizes and growth habits. One or another of these infinitely varied plants can be trained up moss totem poles or logs, allowed to cascade from plant poles, coaxed around a window frame, used to enhance terraria or dish gardens, placed on tables of any height virtually anywhere, or set up on the floor to provide a magnificent room accent. Many of the larger, woody-stemmed foliage plants are dis-

(continued on page 178)

Those Amazing Aroids

A structurally unique and often weirdly beautiful assortment of plants, the aroids or arums, includes formerly undervalued food plants now believed critical to the diet of many southeast Asians, flowering ornamentals as diverse as anthuriums, calla lilies, and Jack-in-the-pulpits, and a surprising number of many of our longest-lived and best-loved indoor foliage plants. The Arum family (Araceae) also includes some downright oddities, such as the fastest-growing plant in the world, which is also endowed with the largest inflorescence. (This is the awesome-looking and evil-smelling *Amorphophallus titanum,* a specimen of which flowered all too memorably at the New York Botanical Garden in 1937, sending forth a morning-glory-like inflorescence that was found to be nearly 13 feet/ 3.9 m in diameter. The overpowering "flower" gave off an equally immense stench that stunned the curious and may or may not have attracted the carrion-fly pollinators for which it was intended.)

Like the gigantic *Amorphophallus,* all Araceae are characterized by an inflorescence made of a fleshy, rodlike spike called the spadix. Covered with the true flowers of the plant, the spadix is surrounded by a large green, white, or color-specialized leaf, or bract, termed a spathe. The spathe forms a funnel-shaped tube, which along with a sometimes unappealing odor, like that exuded by *Amorphophallus,* facilitates pollination by insects — especially flies. In addition to their striking inflorescences, aroids are distinguished by their bitter sap, which in most species contains sharp crystals of calcium oxalate. Literally exploding on impact, these crystals imbed themselves in the tender mouth tissues of animals attempting to eat aroids. The pain and swelling caused by this mechanical irritation are a lesson apparently remembered the next time the forager looks for food.

Hungry humans also have learned to know the burning sensations imparted by raw aroids. Called raphides, the crystals are responsible for the inflammation and temporary speechlessness that result from eating the leaves of *Dieffenbachia,* a well-known aroid house plant which, because of this effect, is called dumb cane. (An antidote for such pain and swelling is to rinse the mouth or skin with vinegar, which will dissolve the imbedded crystals.)

Ranging in habit from terrestrial herbs that often have tubers or rhizomes to climbing epiphytes, to swamp-dwellers or even aquatic plants, the aroids are monocots living mostly in the wet parts of the tropics but sometimes in temperate or semi-arid regions. The approximately 105 genera and up to 2,000 species of the Arum family evolved over a long period, diverging early from other flowering plants. Although they are not closely related to any other plant group, they are believed to have ances-

A Study in Green: These *Dieffenbachia* leaves display an eye-catching arrangement of dark green daubs of color on a yellow-green background, rimmed with dark green. Children and pets should be kept from chewing on these attractive leaves, for they can cause a burning sensation and temporary loss of speech.

tors in common with the palms.

Aroids often have showy foliage. Leaves are usually pinnate or palmate and in many species — notably among philodendrons — look markedly different during the plant's juvenile stage than they do in maturity.

Economically valuable aroids include the fast-growing "elephant ears" of the *Colocasia* genus, which produce large corms that become edible when they are boiled, baked, or dried thoroughly to destroy the calcium oxalate crystals in them. Known as tropic taro, *C. antiquorum* is a staple starch in parts of south-

Tropical Showpiece: The genus *Caladium*, a member of the Arum family, encompasses many cultivars with exquisitely colored foliage. The contrasting venation and different leaf shadings have a dramatic impact, making these appealing plants to feature in a foliage grouping.

east Asia, while *C. esculenta* is the green taro, or dasheen, of the South Pacific and the source of the well-known Hawaiian food *poi*. The corms of *Colocasia* and other aroids such as *Alocasia, Xanthosoma,* and *Amorphophallus,* together with their greens, form a vital part of the slender native food supply of Bangladesh, and the roasted or boiled corms of *Caladium* have been eaten in South America and the colorful leaves of that plant consumed in the West Indies. The rhizomatous native North American aroid known as sweet flag or calamus root *(Acorus calamus)* yields a spicy-flavored aromatic oil that is added to perfumes and to beer and gin. The leaves and root stalks of sweet flag also are used in sachets and as a folk remedy — indeed, the boiled roots and rhizomes have been made into a candy valued in the Middle East and Asia for its purported curative powers.

Flowering ornamentals of note in the Arum family include the largest genus, *Anthurium,* numbering perhaps 550 species; the calla lily (*Zantedeschia* spp.); water arum *(Calla palustris);* and the much-loved North American wildflower Jack-in-the-pulpit *(Arisaema triphyllum)*. One of the more curious, if less appealing, aroids is the eastern skunk cabbage *(Symplocarpus foetidus),* which is able to utilize the starch in its large root to increase its metabolism and respiration and thereby maintain an internal tempera-

ture of from 60° to 90°F (16° to 32°C) for several weeks in late winter — a unique characteristic that allows skunk cabbage to bloom in late February while other plants are still deep in dormancy.

The aroids of greatest aesthetic and economic value most likely are those that are grown and appreciated for their outstanding foliage. Imposing decorator plants that convey the exotic warmth of the tropics, they offer variously shaped and textured leaves of generous size and are generally tough enough to survive being overlooked — or over-pampered, which can prove equally fatal to more delicate plants. Frequently tolerant of relatively low temperatures, aroids as a group live longer

than any other indoor plants. Their luxuriant growth under good conditions adds to their appeal; in nature, the spectacular climbing or rambling vine known as *Monstera deliciosa* generates attractively split and perforated leaves up to a meter in length. Aroid expert Dr. Michael Madison of the Marie Selby Botanical Gardens calls monstera "probably the finest foliage plant introduced in horticulture." Other vigorous and richly colored foliage aroids include the aglaonemas, silver-veined anthuriums, caladiums, epipremnums, philodendrons, spathiphyllums, syngoniums, and xanthosomas. For cultural specifics on many of these handsome plants, see the Encyclopedia section.

cussed in chapter 20, and families of such outstanding foliage plants as bromeliads, cacti and other succulents, carnivorous plants, and ferns have required whole chapters in this book to do them justice.

Still remaining, however, are an abundance of genera exhibiting splendid foliage in a myriad of forms. Many of these plants are upright and self-supporting, like *Codiaeum, Dieffenbachia, Dracaena,* some peperomias, trunk-forming philodendrons, and sansevierias. Such upright foliage plants may be entirely herbaceous; subshrubs (woody-stemmed plants with more or less herbaceous branches); bushes (woody, thickly branched plants that grow as tall as 3 or 4 feet/0.9 or 1.2 m); shrubs (woody plants with no central stems that grow to 3 to 15 feet/0.9 to 4.6 m), or trees (trunk-forming plants that branch near the top).

Like *Asparagus densiflorus* 'Sprengeri',

Tendril Climbing Vine: The upward growth habit of plants like the one shown here is most effectively displayed when trained along a trellis, stake, or any type of wire frame. Some highly developed tendril climbers develop sucking disks on their tips that cling tenaciously to vertical surfaces.

other plants prized for their foliage are of an arching or weeping disposition, while a considerable number are weeping plants with stems too weak to permit self-support; these lengthened stems move upward, outward, or downward toward possible sources of support, resulting in plants that climb, creep, or trail. In horticulture all such woody or herbaceous plants are rather loosely termed vines, although true vines such as certain *Hoya* species, Madagascar jasmine *(Stephanotis floribunda),* and German ivy climb either by clambering or by stem-twining — that is, by revolving on their stems as they rotate around a support. As Charles Darwin suggested in his 1875 study on *Climbing Plants,* twining is an adaptation that allows a plant to climb within one season to a height where it can compete with surrounding vegetation for light and air. Some twiners move from left to right, but the majority curl around a support from right to left. The higher the temperature, the faster the growing tip of a twining plant can make a complete circle around a support. In nature some tropical vines can make a circle up to five feet (1.5 m) wide to move around a tree, but twining plants from more temperate places are usually capable only of moving around supports a few inches (approximately 5 cm) in diameter. In the home, twiners such as hoyas may be happily trained up strings or wires.

In more highly evolved vining types of plants, such as gloriosa lily *(Gloriosa* spp.), the leaf tips are adapted into tapering structures that can coil around a support; sometimes it is the leaf stalks — or even the flower stalks — that are elongated and flexible and curl around anything within reach. In woody vines that are even more advanced, parts of the stems or leaves or the tip of the inflorescence are modified into slender, elongated structures that often are threadlike and herbaceous. Like adapted petioles, these tendrils respond to touch, and if rubbed gently with a matchstick on one side will begin to curl in that direction within minutes. Popular foliage vines with tendrils are the *Cissus* species, particularly grape ivy *(C. rhombifolia)*.

On the most highly evolved of the tendril-climbing plants, the tips of tendrils swell into suction-cup-like disks several days after they come in contact with a supporting surface. These remarkable sucking disks, as they are called, exude a cementlike substance that alllows the plant to cling with astonishing tenacity to a wall, tree, or other vertical surface. Growing thicker and stronger after they become attached, the adhesive disks of such familiar foliage plants as Virginia creeper *(Parthenocissus quinquefolia)* and Boston ivy *(P. tricuspidata)* are said to resist a pull of ten pounds (4.5 kg) of pressure even after a decade of exposure to all kinds of weather. Tendril-climbers in general do well trained up a trellis, room divider, wire frame, or a stake, and those with sucking disks can climb up a window frame or brick or other wall.

Perhaps the majority of the most widely grown climbing foliage plants adhere to a support by means of adventitious roots growing from their stems. These aerial root climbers, which do well on a moss pole, a pillar of tree fern, a slab of bark, or even a stake, include all the vining philodendrons, English and Canary Islands ivies (*Hedera* spp.), creeping fig *(Ficus pumila)*, ornamental peppers *(Piper* spp.*)*, golden pothos *(Epipremnum aureum)*, and wax plant *(Hoya carnosa)*.

Still other plants with long, flexible stems neither twine nor climb by means of tendrils, disks, or aerial roots. Tumbling handsomely over pot rims or cascading from hanging containers, these can be trailers like peperomias, Swedish ivy *(Plectranthus* spp.*)*, and gynuras, or runner-forming types that root at the nodes if given the opportunity; examples include spider plant *(Chlorophytum comosum* 'Vittatum'*)*, decoratively leaved episcias such as *Episcia cupreata* and *E. dianthiflora* cultivars, and strawberry begonia *(Saxifraga stolonifera)*. Creepers such as the striped inch plant *(Callisia elegans)*, nerve plant *(Fittonia verschaffeltii)*, pellio-

A Versatile Vine Support

This easy-to-build, versatile support allows a vine plant to be viewed from all sides. The 1 inch by 1 inch (25 by 25 mm) post to which the joined 1 inch (25 mm) thick crossbars (of optional length) are screwed may be 20 inches (508 mm) long, or longer by increments of 8 inches (203 mm), and more crossbars may be added for taller plants.

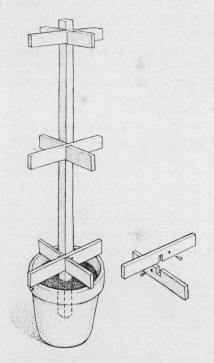

The bottom 4 inches (101 mm) of the post are placed into the pot before soil and plant are added. The lower crossbars rest on top of the pot for added support. You can either use the wood as it is, or paint or stain it. The assembly can be removed and placed in almost any pot of average size or larger.

nias, certain peperomias, and baby's tears *(Soleirolia soleirolii)* hug the ground, sending down roots where the stem touches soil. Sometimes, as with *Callisia fragrans* 'Melnickoff', a plant both creeps and sends out plant-bearing runners.

As the development of tendrils in climbing plants suggests, many of the more interesting characteristics of foliage plants are evolutionary adaptations. Often the leaves themselves are modified in either structure or arrangement to perform functions in addition to the essential one of making sugars or starches. Sometimes they are thickened, as in sansevierias and other succulents, to store water; sometimes they are arranged to overlap in a whorl so as to form hollows that can catch and hold moisture (this is the case with bromeliads — often called vase plants because of the shape and capacity of their reservoirs — and is also true of rosette-forming foliage plants such as certain species of *Dracaena* and *Pandanus*).

On the other hand, some green plants — often those with broad, thin leaves which are especially vulnerable to rot — have foliage with so-called drip tips (that is, pointed ends that curve downward so excess water runs off quickly rather than pooling on leaf tops or standing along leaf edges where it could create an inviting point of entry for bacteria or fungi). Other foliage plants are protected from heavy rains by hairs off which the rivulets of water roll. (Fuzz is also a deterrent to insect pests looking for succulent leaf tissue.) Leaves also may be adapted into food-trapping devices as they are in the fascinating carnivorous plants (see chapter 23). Another way foliage can be instrumental to a plant's survival is by assuming a form that offers minimum resistance to high winds; many plants originating in locations that experience frequent hurricanes have long, narrow leaves or deeply lobed foliage that can ride out gale-force winds without serious damage.

Yet other plants grown primarily for their foliage show leaves adapted to ward off the effects of too much light. For example, anthuriums growing in a very open, scrubby habitat in the interior of Brazil have foliage that is stiff and so severely undulated that the halves of each leaf are bent virtually parallel to each other — a modification that shades most of the leaf top for much of the time and allows the plant to survive in a very unlikely setting. Conversely, jungle-growing foliage plants often have deeply lobed leaves which allow light through to the lower levels; sometimes only foliage at the top of the plant is split. Another adaptation intended to maximize light is the progressive lengthening of petioles on leaves toward the bottom of the plant — the effect is a cone shape.

The very way in which leaves are disposed may reflect a foliage plant's effort to receive as much light as possible. Responding to auxins that regulate the way in which leaves bend toward light, the leaves of ivy, certain figs (*Ficus* spp.), and other plants with broad, flat foliage arrange themselves in a kind of mosaic so they overlap each other as little as possible. Often the upper leaves on an upright plant remain horizontal while those moving down the plant become increasingly slanted toward the vertical to expose their tops to a maximum of light.

Leaves even may be adapted to help keep plants from overheating when they are in full sun. Botanist Michael Madison of Marie Selby Botanical Gardens in Sarasota, Florida, believes that the holes in *Monstera deliciosa* leaves increase convective cooling by breaking up the layer of still air next to the leaf.

CREATING GOOD GROWING CONDITIONS FOR FOLIAGE PLANTS

Environmental factors such as light, temperature, humidity, water, and food are interrelated and should keep pace with one another. For example, at high levels of light and warmth, a plant needs more water and nourishment than it will when light is less intense and temperatures lower. Generally speaking, the most limiting factor is what will hold back a given plant's development. In the case of foliage plants, however, there are some special considerations. If the temperature, for example, were increased without increasing light and all the other environmental factors, the result would be weak stems and small foliage, thereby defeating the purpose of growing such plants in the first place. For foliage plants as well as flowering ones, a proper balance of all environmental factors must be achieved to develop the most healthy plant possible.

The temperature range within which most foliage plants will grow best is from 65° to 75°F (18° to 24°C). Fortunately, this is also the temperature range found in most homes for most of the year. Although many green plants can tolerate temperatures below or above this range, temperatures below 45°F (7°C) can be expected to result in injury to the foliage of tropicals such as *Aglaonema* and *Dieffenbachia*. If maintained for long periods, temperatures over 85°C (29°C) also can result in poor growth, as was previously mentioned.

Humidity is generally more difficult to control than temperature, but for some plants it is a critical factor. Most foliage plants ideally prefer a humidity of at least 40 percent, but many with thick leathery or hairy leaves can tolerate a drier atmosphere, although their growth and appearance may suffer somewhat. There are, however, many stunning and exotic foliage plants that need only moderate light and can succeed in the home if a humidity of 50 percent can be maintained around them.

Misting foliage and vine plants is commonly recommended as an effective way to increase humidity. Be aware, though, that when foliage is repeatedly misted it offers an ideal environment for the development of foliage disease organisms. Also, hand-misting will not increase humidity enough to make a substantial difference in the overall moisture in the air surrounding the plants. At best it creates only a very temporary increase in humidity and generally applies too much water for too short a period of time. It is therefore not recommended for large-leaved plants, which are particularly vulnerable to bacterial leaf spot disease. When used with other plants, misting should be done early in the day so the foliage dries before nightfall. Do not mist plants on dull, overcast days or when light is otherwise dim. Supplementary atmospheric moisture for humidity-loving climbing foliage plants such as pellionia and Canary Islands ivy *(Hedera canariensis)* may be provided by growing them on a sphagnum moss totem pole (described in chapter 3) and keeping the moss constantly moist. Other efficient methods for increasing home humidity to encourage good plant growth are discussed in chapter 2.

Chlorinated drinking water can be used on foliage plants with no detrimental effects. However, do not use chlorinated water from a swimming pool to water your plants, for the higher concentration of chlorine in such water can be extremely harmful. One of the most common problems with water quality *vis-à-vis* foliage plants is damage caused by the excessive fluoride and boron found in the water supply in some areas of the country. Excess boron is more of a problem in the western United States; if you suspect high levels in your water, have it tested and ask your county agricultural agent to interpret the results relative to foliage plant growing. Fluoride is added to most municipal water supplies and toxicity symptoms linked to water or other sources commonly show up on plants in the genera *Aglaonema, Chlorophytum, Cordyline,* and *Dracaena*. Species and cultivars in the families Agavaceae, Liliaceae, and Marantaceae are also suspected to be sensitive to fluorides. One of the most commonly grown plants exhibiting tip burn from excess fluoride is the spider plant. Here are some suggested ways to minimize fluoride injury to sensitive foliage and vine plants:

1. Avoid excessive phosphorus in the soil.
2. Use soil components that contain low levels of fluoride. (Avoid perlite and German peat moss, which contain relatively high amounts of fluoride.)
3. Add ground limestone if you are making up your own potting mix. An approximate relative amount is given in the potting mix formula for foliage plants that follows shortly.
4. Avoid raising fluoride-sensitive plants in environments which accelerate the rate of plant water loss and subsequent uptake of fluoride — that is, in situations featuring high light intensities, excessive air movement, and extremely high temperatures.

Plants differ in their light needs. Those plants native to shaded, low-light places will, of course, require less light to grow. This is the case with most foliage plants, although many of them prefer bright, diffused light or even full sun if they are to make their strongest growth and attain their best appearance. Indeed, often plants liking bright, indirect light in general because their foliage tends to scorch in intense sun can be given full sun during winter months. Frequently, however, growers reserve their best-lit windows for flowering plants and seek to use foliage plants in positions farther back in the room. As light levels are reduced, less and less growth will occur until the foliage plant's "light compensation point" is reached. This is the light level at which no, or very little, growth will occur but the plant will continue to maintain itself in a healthy condition. For some plants such as *Aglaonema* and *Aspidistra* it can be as low as 10 footcandles. With a gradual reduction in

Low-Light Plants: African violets and other blooming plants would not fare well in this dimly lit corner, set back as it is from a window. But this light limitation doesn't rule out the presence of plants altogether, for there are many foliage plants, such as the sansevieria and philodendron shown here, which can be grown in dim light.

light to this level, the foliage of these genera shows no ill effects. Don't try this technique indiscriminately, however, as certain plants cannot tolerate the reduction of light to low levels, no matter how slowly it is done.

If light levels drop below the light compensation point, plants will register their protests in various ways that will affect their good looks and their well-being. Foliage may turn limp and become scantier and smaller and duller in color. In upright plants, stems and leaf stalks may become elongated, and the overextended plant may begin to lean to one side. Vining plants may start to produce rank growth, while the tendrils of climbers may move off supports in quest of more light. Light-starved plants also may begin to lose their leaves. To treat such symptoms, consider lighting the dim corner and its inhabitant with a 150-watt incandescent spotlight at a distance of at least 36 inches (91 cm) for a few hours or more each day. Evenings spent at least 12 inches (30 cm) below a lighted 75-watt table lamp can also serve the purpose. Other options are to move the plant to a brighter location for several weeks every now and then to rejuvenate it, or to replace it temporarily or permanently with another species having a lower light requirement.

As implied earlier, research has shown that there is a direct correlation between light intensity and a plant's need for fertilizer. A plant growing under 200 to 500 footcandles of light needs much less fertilizer than the same plant growing under 500 to 1,000 footcandles. The increased fertilizer requirement is mainly a result of the plant growing faster at the higher light level. Therefore, because foliage and vine plants generally require and get less light than flowering house plants, they also generally need less fertilizer. Another factor to consider is that in northern areas during the winter, days are shorter and the light levels are usually lower than at other times of the year. This means that foliage and vine plants generally require very little food during the winter months.

In feeding foliage plants, choose or make fertilizers somewhat richer in nitrogen — which promotes leaf growth — than in phosphorus and potassium, which are more related to successful flowering and fruiting. Fish emulsion or another high-nitrogen material is a good choice. Keep in mind, though, that if your foliage or vine plant is not doing well, more fertilizer is not necessarily the answer. In fact, it can compound the problem by burning the plant roots. If a foliage plant shows rapid but too-soft growth and the plant droops, you should reduce the frequency of feedings or cut them to half strength. On the other hand, yellowing foliage toward the bottom of a plant, a general fading of color, or a decrease in the size of new leaves suggests more food is needed. (See chapter 7 for more on making organic fertilizers and rates of application.) Sometimes foliage plants being grown in low light are sufficiently nourished from one potting to the next by the nutrients in a well-made growth medium.

Just as foliage plants generally require less light and food than flowering plants, they also generally will not require as much water. Indeed, the most common cause of foliage plant failure is overwatering. When growing plants like the bamboos *(Arundinaria, Bambusa,* and *Sasa), Calathea,* and *Xanthosoma,* which crave even moisture year-round, never allow the surface of the soil to dry out. The medium should always be moist to the touch without being kept in a wet condition. That is to say, grains of the medium should be damp enough to adhere to a fingertip, but the soil should not be water-soaked. Some plants, of course, like to be kept evenly moist only during periods of active growth and respond well to partial drying out during winter (and sometimes autumn) when days are shorter and dimmer and temperatures cooler. In the case of plants needing such alternately moist and dry conditions seasonally (examples are foliage begonias and geraniums) or all the time (examples are *Sansevieria* and *Ceropegia woodii)* the soil surface should be dry to the touch before the plant is watered again. With plants preferring a dry situation, allow most of the soil mass in the pot to dry out completely before watering again. Note: When you do water plants of *any* category, water thoroughly — that is, until 10 percent of the water applied runs out of the bottom of the pot. Consult the Encyclopedia section to determine the specific water requirement for each plant you are growing. Then set up a watering schedule based on your unique growing conditions — not on those of the store or greenhouse or friend's house where the plant formerly grew, for the environment there may have required more frequent or less frequent watering.

Many popular foliage and vine plants are from the moister parts of the tropics, and need a growing medium with excellent drainage and superior water-holding capacity. One good mix for foliage and vine plants can be made from 1 bushel (35.2 l) of Canadian sphagnum peat moss, ½ bushel (17.6 l) of vermiculite, 5 tablespoons (75 ml) of ground limestone, and 10 tablespoons (150 ml) of bone meal. (For another humus-rich mix based on garden soil and for all-purpose potting mixes adequate for foliage plants requiring less constant moisture, see Potting Mixture Recipes in chapter 6.)

DIAGNOSING FOLIAGE PLANT PROBLEMS

No matter how good a grower you are, you will eventually have to do some troubleshooting in regard to one or more of your foliage plants. Over half of the problems you encounter will probably be related to such cultural matters as overwatering or underwatering, insufficient or excessive light, and inadequate humidity. To identify problems related to culture, begin by asking and answering the seven general questions that apply to any ailing plant. These are given in chapter 9. Further diagnostic help is provided by the House Plant Clinic in chapter 9.

If insects are a problem on your foliage plants, diagnosis is usually relatively easy, for most pests can be readily seen and identified. The most common ones found on foliage plants are aphids, mealybugs, scale insects, spider mites, and whiteflies. Any one of these insects can cause extensive damage to leaves. The best way of preventing this unsightly injury is to identify and destroy the insects as early as possible.

Some foliage plants that are particularly susceptible to aphid injury are Swedish ivy, *Fittonia* species, and baby's tears. Baby's tears, together with *Coleus,* is also very susceptible to whiteflies, which will attack nearly all foliage and vine plants. If you suspect these insects are in residence, gently rustle the leaves and the adults will fly out. Certain foliage plants such as English ivy *(Hedera helix)* and Vinca vines are particularly vulnerable to two-spotted spider mites. If you think mites are present but see very little foliage injury and no webs, place a piece of white paper under the plant and gently shake the plant. If two-spotted spider mites are in hiding they will fall onto the paper, where they can be easily identified with the naked eye. These mites got their name from the two distinct spots on their backs that become visible when you look at them with a magnifying glass or hand lens. Especially susceptible to mealybugs are croton *(Codiaeum variegatum* var. *pictum), Coleus, Dracaena,* strawberry begonia, and the piggyback plant. Scale is especially fond of croton, *Dracaena,* ivy cultivars, and *Philodendron.* (For a complete discussion of pest identification and control, refer to chapter 9.)

Diseases are not as much of a problem with foliage plants as insects. Some that do occur occasionally are powdery mildew, bacterial leaf spot, root rot, *Botrytis,* rusts, and virus.

All foliage plants are more or less susceptible to virus problems and to powdery mildew, but large-leaved specimens are more likely to come down with bacterial leaf spot, a disorder primarily caused by getting an excessive amount of water on the foliage during watering, and by periodic misting of the foliage. Foliage plants that are especially prone to root rot include *Dieffenbachia, Peperomia, Sansevieria,* and *Tradescantia.* Along with the piggyback plant, wandering Jew *(Tradescantia fluminensis)* is also particularly susceptible to *Botrytis.* For details on house plant diseases and their control, see chapter 9.

GETTING PLANTS TO RUN AND VINE

Generally, the more runners and vines you get to develop on climbing, creeping or trailing foliage plants, the more beautiful they are. Encouraging these plants to perform in this way can sometimes be a frustrating experience, but if you provide the proper growing conditions and use some helpful techniques, you should not have a problem. Effective techniques usually involve one or all of the following: adjusting the amount of light, warmth, and water, and pruning.

One of the most common foliage plants to develop runners is the spider plant. A common misconception is that spider plants must be potbound to develop runners. This popular idea has been discredited by a researcher at the University of Illinois, who demonstrated that the critical factor influencing the growth of runners by plants with that capability is not whether they are potbound but how much light they receive. Spider plants develop runners after they bloom, and they have been found to send out flower stalks most readily when given short-day light conditions of only eight hours of light per day for 12 weeks. Therefore, you might temporarily growing spider plants under a short-day regimen to elicit more runners. Slightly reduced temperatures and less watering and feeding also will be required during this treatment; otherwise, you could very well end up with an overwatering problem and/or spindly plants.

Vine plants will vine as a normal part of their growth habit. There are times, however, when you might wish to produce more vines on a more compact plant. If this is the case, pruning the plant periodically is the answer. For example, with support, vining philodendrons can be grown straight up like a small tree; or they can be encouraged to develop more vines through regular pruning. For more details on how to prune a plant, see Pruning, in chapter 3. Once the desired number of vines has developed, they can, of course, be encouraged to grow faster by applying fertilizer at rates slightly higher than those normally recommended. Be careful, however, not to overfeed. Remember, you just want to encourage growth — not create a junglelike appearance.

Depending on how you want to display vining house plants, you may wish to provide them with some support for more upright growth. Supports such as short wooden slabs or compressed fiber stakes are available at garden centers, or you can build your own vine plant support as described in A Versatile Vine Support earlier in this chapter. Most vining plants must be artificially fastened to any such support with paper-covered wire or string, or by hand-weaving the vines around the support.

GROOMING

Housekeeping practices essential to both leafy good looks and good health include pruning, foliage cleaning, removing dead leaves, and periodically turning plants.

Pruning can be used not only to force out additional branches and vines but also to keep plants in proper proportion to the rest of the room. Vining plants are usually fast growers and can soon outgrow their location. They should be pruned back occasionally as described in chapter 3 to prevent the straggly, overextended look of unchecked growth.

Foliage plants with dirty leaves must be cleaned periodically to enhance their beauty and to permit the leaves to accomplish transpiration and respiration. Large-leaved foliage plants such as *Aglaonema, Dieffenbachia, Monstera deliciosa,* and *Philodendron* are big dust collectors. One of the simplest ways to clean their foliage is simply to wash the leaves off with a damp sponge that has been soaked in warm water to which a few drops of mild dishwashing detergent have been added.

Propagation Tips for Some Foliage Favorites

Single- or double-eye leaf-bud cuttings are the best way to propagate popular vining aroids such as *Monstera deliciosa,* and *Philodendron scandens* subsp. *oxycardium,* and can also work well with *Dieffenbachia* and most other Araceae — especially if you house the cutting in a plastic tent to assure the warmth and humidity that will cause the dormant buds to sprout quickly. Single-eye cuttings consist of a short stem section with an attached leaf. Stem sections about two inches (5 cm) long root better than longer or shorter lengths, and cuttings taken from the center of a vine plant usually root faster than sections from the tip or base. The single-eye cutting should be stuck into the rooting medium to a depth slightly below or at the level of the eye on the cutting, since new roots will come from that point. Double-eye leaf-bud cuttings, which have

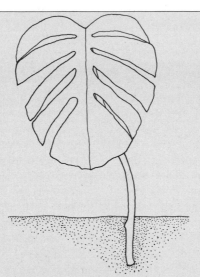

Single-Eye Cutting: Vining aroids, such as the *Monstera* shown here, respond well to propagation by leaf-bud cuttings. A single-eye cutting involves only one attached leaf on a section of stem; the double-eye cutting has two leaves on the stem section.

two leaves attached to the piece of stem, are sometimes used as specimens intended for plant totem poles, for they grow at a faster rate than single-eye cut-

tings. Both single- and double-eye cuttings are propagated in the same way; any aerial roots on them should be retained if space permits to aid the new plant in absorbing moisture from the air.

Some upright foliage plants such as *Dieffenbachia, Cordyline terminalis,* and certain dracaenas (*Dracaena fragrans* 'Massangeana' and *D. deremensis* 'Warneckii', for example), are perpetuated readily from cane sections. The soft cane portion of the *Dieffenbachia* is usually cut with one eye or bud per section; pieces taken from the upper part of the stem and planted shallowly will grow the largest plants. *Cordyline* likewise may be propagated from short, two-to four-inch (5 to 10 cm) sections containing one eye or from larger pieces with more than one eye. Dracaena stem sections of up to one to four feet (30 to 120 cm) can be used. For more on these and other methods of propagation used for foliage plants, consult chapter 8.

If dead leaves appear on your foliage plants, diagnose the problem first and then physically remove the leaves and destroy them. Nothing looks worse than dead leaves dangling forlornly on a plant or lying where they fell in desiccated array on the soil around its base. Moreover, dead leaves atop the planting medium can decay and cause more trouble by harboring diseases.

The leaves of plants usually grow and bend toward the strongest source of light. To prevent foliage from bending and becoming lopsided, give each plant a quarter-turn weekly.

DISPLAYING LEAFY AND VINING PLANTS

SHOWING OFF RUNNERS OR PLANTLETS

One of the best ways of displaying plants that develop runners and plantlets is to place them in hanging baskets. You can purchase attractive hangers that screw into a wall, or use simple metal hooks in the ceiling for overhead plants. Be very careful in selecting the particular spot to hang a planter. For example, proper light conditions for a given plant must be considered. Also remember that plants hung high in a room are usually in a much warmer location than those grown at floor level or table height. This means they may have to be watered and fertilized more often for best results. The light requirements of several vining and trailing plants are specified in the House Plant Encyclopedia later in this book.

GROUPING VINES AND UPRIGHT FOLIAGE PLANTS

Where space and room decor permit, several green plants with similar light needs may be massed together. Basic criteria for any plant arrangement should be kept in mind: these are color, texture, and size. The object is to vary these elements to achieve eye appeal.

Color is the most obvious aspect of any grouping. Foliage and vine plants present many shades of green and up to three or four additional colors if they are variegated. Don't mix too many variously colored plants together. Crotons, for example, have differently colored leaves on a single plant, while other plants have a live mix of red, pink, cream, and green or other colors on all their foliage. Avoid the use of too many such multi-hued plants in a grouping. Perhaps a single croton, caladium, *Cordyline terminalis* 'Tricolor', or *Zebrina pendula* 'Quadricolor' placed in the center of a mass of all-green foliage is all that is necessary to serve as the focal point. Be sure, though, that the surrounding plants do not intercept the bright light the brightly colored standouts need to retain their vivid hues.

Foliage plants also add interest to a plant grouping through the size and shape of their leaves. The long, narrow leaves of the white-striped Japanese sweet flag (*Acorus gramineus* 'Variegatus') or the slender umbrella plant *(Cyperus alternifolius),* for example, have a delicate, soft-textured look,

Colored Foliage Accent: This foliage grouping, with its mix of leaf color, shape, and texture, affords plenty of visual variety. The focal point is a croton with its spectacular multi-hued foliage. A verdant framework is formed by the lacy leaves of a false aralia, the broad, heart-shaped expanse of *Aglaonema* leaves, a glimpse of strikingly banded prayer plant foliage, and the spiky fronds of a palm.

whereas the large, broad leaves of the fiddle-leaf fig *(Ficus lyrata)* or *Monstera deliciosa* create a bold, strong appearance. Avoid juxtaposing fine-textured foliage and the emphatically coarse-textured kind by separating such plants with one or more of the many upright or vining plants presenting a texture somewhere in between these two extremes. For more ideas on how to use foliage plants to best advantage in decorating, see chapter 30.

CHAPTER 11

Ferns

Indoor gardeners are discovering what fern fanciers have known all along—that ferns offer varieties and challenges enough to try the keenest horticultural skills. Gardeners have always been attracted first by fruits and colorful blossoms, and the more subtle beauties of the fern were slow to be noticed. But when they were, horticultural history was made.

Nonnative ferns were grown in a few English rockeries as early as the mid-1600s, but plants that died were not easily replaced. Collecting live specimens was a hazardous venture for both people and plants, shipping space was costly, and shipping methods were risky for delicate live tropical specimens. Collecting plants was a rich man's hobby.

Some observations of the reproductive cycle of the fern were recorded as early as 1699, but it was not until John Lindsay, a Jamaican surgeon, reported to the Linnaean Society of London in 1794 his successful experiments in raising ferns from spores that there was an alternative to the costly and chancy handling of live plants. Though several eighteenth century naturalists and botanists at least skirted the very simple notion of an enclosed glass case for growing plants, Nathaniel Ward's name is firmly associated with it. In 1830, Ward's chance discovery of young plants, one of them a fern, in moist debris in a loosely covered jar containing a moth chrysalis he had collected and forgotten, nudged fern growing nearer to the British parlor. Ferns, once collected and shipped in open moss- or soil-filled boxes, were now safely shipped in closed glass cases.

By the mid-1800s these scattered discoveries by Lindsay, Ward, and other amateur growers and professionals made fern collecting an affordable pursuit for the Victorian-era Britisher who found that the fern particularly appealed to his or her taste for intricate decoration. Glasshouses and conservatories protected the plant collections of the wealthy from factory fumes, and decorative Wardian cases and bell jars graced parlors all over Britain.

The fern-collecting tide was carried along by the publication of new books on fern identification, the availability of microscopes, and cheaper, duty-free glass which made greenhouses and cases available to more and more people devoted to the fashionable search for the fern. What became generally available finally became common and then unfashionable, and the craze ended after about 30 years.

A hundred years later, with the experience of decades supported by sophisticated tools and technology, the best beginning for the indoor gardener with a yen for ferns is still the same as that of his Victorian counterpart—a plant and dirty hands. Today the Wardian case is often a used aquarium with a new life and the Victorian bell jar a mass-produced apothecary jar. Chances are the fern will be a *Nephrolepis* species or cultivar (a relative of a longtime favorite parlor plant, the Boston fern), a *Cyrtomium falcatum* (holly fern), one of the many *Pteris* (brake fern) species, or even an *Adiantum* (maidenhair fern) simply because all these ferns are mass produced in greenhouses and sell well, and therefore are most often available.*

FERN BOTANY

In the best gardening tradition, the indoor grower will first choose a fern that appeals— then take it home and get acquainted. To

---

*The asparagus fern, another favorite, is not considered a true fern. Information on it can be found in the Encyclopedia section of this book.

Opposite, close-up of maidenhair fern, Adiantum *species.*

make this experience more rewarding, it is helpful to know, at least generally, how the plant functions—what the parts are and the role of each. Besides, fern plants sold by dealers and growers are sometimes identified incompletely or not at all, and mastering a few terms will enable you to make at least a general identification of your purchase from more technical literature.

STRUCTURE

The rootstock or stem is the permanent part of a fern from which new leaves or fronds grow. It may grow erect or horizontally. If

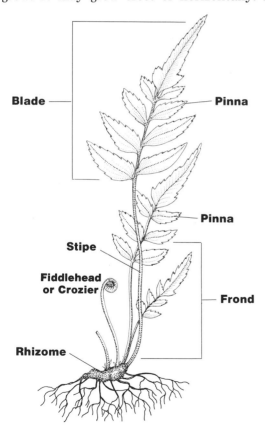

Fern Structure: Becoming familiar with fern structure will help you to identify unlabeled and newly purchased plants. The shape of the frond, type of rhizome or rootstock, and growth habit are all keys to identification. This illustration shows the parts of a typical fern.

the stock grows erect, it may form a single crown or it may develop several crowns on the same stock, as the *Nephrolepis* does. Tree ferns *(Sphaeropteris, Dicksonia)* the largest members of the Fern family, have decidedly upright stems, understandably called trunks.* A horizontal stem, called a rhizome, may creep just above (or occasionally just below) the soil surface, across rocks, and into trees with roots attaching to soil or to bits of organic debris in tree and rock crevices. The very slender, horizontal, creeping stems of the Boston fern are called stolons. Rhizomes may or may not branch and may be almost smooth and green, as in *Polypodium lepidopteris,* or they may be covered with golden brown, scaly structures giving the appearance of feet or paws and leading to the popular common identification of such plants as "footed ferns." Fern stocks or rhizomes serve to produce and support the fronds, to absorb, carry, and store water and nutrients, and even to produce new plants. They will produce roots to serve as anchors, allowing a fern to climb. Stolons and runners will form new crowns or plants at nodes or tips only after roots form while the stolon is still attached to the parent plant.

Fern roots grow from the stock or rhizome and, like all roots, absorb water and minerals from the soil or other material in which they are anchored. At least one common species, *Nephrolepis cordifolia,* has fleshy tubers on the roots for water and food storage (not reproduction). Most fern roots are fine, dark brown or black, dense and many branched, fibrous, and able to fill a container quickly.

Fern foliage is what most growers find appealing, and a fern leaf is called a frond. Croziers, or young fronds, are commonly

---

Sphaeropteris cooperi, the Australian tree fern, and *Dicksonia antarctica* are two frequently cultivated tree fern species. They are *not* easy for anyone without a large, humid greenhouse.

called fiddleheads because as they uncurl they resemble a shepherd's crook or the scroll of a violin. Most simply, the frond has two parts, the stipe and the blade. The stipe (or petiole) grows from a stock or rhizome and supports the wider, leafy blade. The stipe may be dark and polished, as in the maidenhair fern *(Adiantum);* covered with hairs or scaly structures, as in *Polystichum tsussimense;* long, as in bird's nest fern *(Asplenium nidus)* and *Polypodium coronans;* or even absent, as in *P. meyenianum.* The rachis is that part of the stipe that continues into the blade. Fern blades may be simple, or undivided, as in the hart's tongue fern *(Phyllitis scolopendrium),* or they may be compound, or divided once or more, as in most ferns. Various terms are used to describe the frond as a whole. They refer to the number of times the frond is divided or cut, and to a description of those divisions.

When single leaflets or pinnae (singular, pinna) are arranged laterally on each side of the rachis, the frond is pinnate, or once divided (featherlike). If the pinnae are themselves divided, the fern is bipinnate (twice divided) and the divisions are called pinnules. The pinnules also may be pinnate or bipinnate. The edges of any division, or leaflet, may be smooth, wavy, cut, notched, or curled.

Also, if the blade is so constructed that the leaflets join at the same point on the stipe and there is no rachis, the frond is palmate like a clover leaf, as in the *Marsilea* species. If the blade is divided into two or more sections, the frond is pedate, as in the common American maidenhair fern.

Roots growing at intervals under the creeping rhizomes of some fern species (*Davallia* and *Polypodium* spp., for example) enable them to secure a footing in bits of organic matter on rocks and trees where they may live as epiphytes, drawing water and nutrients from their mossy tree trunk. The popular staghorn ferns (*Platycerium* spp.) are perhaps the most obviously epiphytic ferns,

and bear specialized fronds which form a base to protect the roots which attach the plant to a supporting tree or some other structure. Epiphytic ferns, with their fleshy rhizomes and sturdy foliage, and preference for treetop perches, require good light and can tolerate moderately dry conditions. A few aquatic ferns also are grown by amateurs. *Salvinia,* a tiny floating plant, requires an aquarium, and *Marsilea,* the water clover fern, may be grown in an aquarium or in always-wet soil in a pot. Most fern species are terrestrial, or soil-growing plants. Many species classified as epiphytic may be grown in loose, quick-draining soil mixes in pots or baskets.

No matter what the size or form of a fern, it is a sporophyte, or spore-bearer. All ferns reproduce by means of spores which are usually produced on the undersides of the fronds. In some ferns, notably *Pteris cretica* 'Albo-lineata', the spore-bearing, or fertile, frond has a different shape than the nonfertile frond. The dustlike spores are borne in spore cases called sporangia, which are grouped together in clusters called sori (singular, sorus). The sorus in turn may or may not be covered by a small piece of protective tissue known as an indusium. The sori may be arranged on the underside of the frond in round clusters or in a linear pattern sometimes located along leaflet margins or arranged or positioned along veins. They also may cover the entire underside of a frond. The shape and location of the sori are characteristics often used to identify genera.

THE LIFE CYCLE OF A FERN

It is likely that spores are produced in such enormous quantities because so few of them manage to complete the growth cycle from spore to mature plant. When the single-celled spore falls on a lighted, moist place, it grows and produces a cell to anchor it and then others to produce food. The food-producing cells form a thread which divides to become a fragile ribbon, and then becomes a tiny, flat, fan-shaped plant called a prothallus. The under-

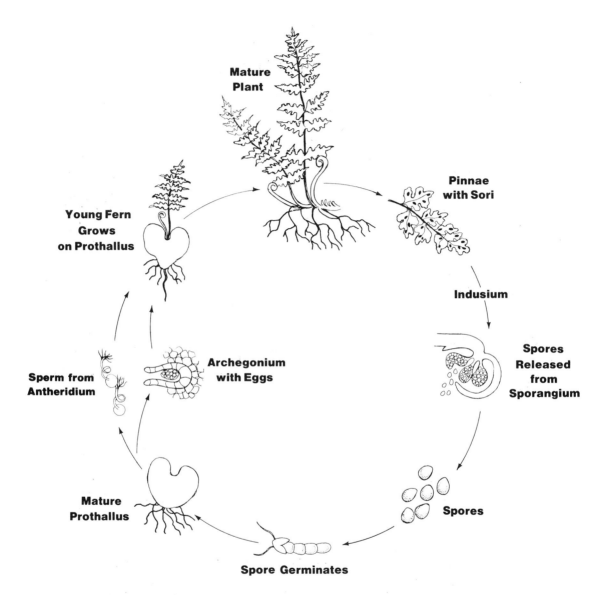

Life Cycle of a Fern: All ferns reproduce by means of spores. The cycle begins when a ripe spore is deposited in a lighted, moist environment and begins producing cells to form the prothallus, on which the new fern will grow.

side of the tiny plant has both male and female reproductive organs and special cells that act as roots to collect moisture and nutrients. A drop of water enables sperm to swim to the egg, fertilization occurs, and a young sporophyte begins to grow. It grows on the prothallus, which provides nourishment and then withers after the young fern can support itself.

The first few fronds of a sporophyte have some characteristics of the typical adult, such as a shiny stipe or a certain shape of pinna.

In less than a year, some new plants may be mature enough to produce spores themselves and the cycle is completed.

Ferns evolved in the Carboniferous Age in places where the sun shone weakly through heavy mist, so it is not surprising that most ferns flourish in warm, moist conditions. Most of the ferns readily available to indoor growers—and those varieties most suited to indoor gardening—are tropical and semitropical. Many are evergreen but some are partially deciduous. Though we can't handily re-create the age of dinosaurs on a windowsill, we can grow such ferns quite successfully indoors—if we know their requirements.

CULTURE

SOIL

Every gardener seems to have a favorite potting mix to suit his or her own particular habits and available growing conditions. As long as the mix furnishes plant and root support, retains water but allows ample air movement around the roots, and has a pH between 6 and 7.5, the majority of ferns will grow well. The popular "1-1-1," one part each of peat, perlite, and vermiculite, with perhaps the addition of one part pasteurized loam, is a good mix, although some gardeners prefer a higher proportion of organic matter. Supplementation with crushed oyster shells and/or crushed eggshells provides extra lime and aeration for lime-loving species such as *Adiantum. Polystichum tsus-simense,* on the other hand, requires an occasional application of a solution of two tablespoons (30 ml) vinegar to a quart (946 ml) of water to increase soil acidity. (For further information on potting mixes, see chapter 6.)

The effects of overfeeding ferns are quickly evident, for roots damaged by excess salts will result in browned pinnae and wilted fronds. However, ferns do need fertilization, for continuous proper watering of ferns in quick-draining soil mixes typically results in loss of the essential, but easily leached, nitrogen. The beginner can most safely use a balanced liquid or water-soluble fertilizer applied at one-quarter strength every three or four waterings *when the fern is actively growing.* If a fern shows evidence of overfeeding, excess liquid fertilizers can be leached easily; dry fertilizers applied to the surface must be scraped away, or the potting mix containing dry food must be replaced by a fresh unfertilized mix and leached thoroughly. Fertilizer should *never* be applied to plants in or approaching dormancy, nor to a dry root ball.

CONTAINERS

A grower's imagination devises countless containers for ferns. As long as it furnishes adequate drainage and aeration and is not made of material detrimental to the plant, any attractive container proportioned to the plant may be used.

To approximate the native habitat of most epiphytic ferns, line a wire or Lincoln-log basket with uncut or sheet sphagnum and fill with a loose mix further aerated with fir bark chips. The oxygen-loving roots of terrestrial ferns are most often shallow, so a squat clay bulb pan can meet their needs. Evaporation through the porous sides assures cool roots on hot days and allows excess salts to escape. Such clay pots should be scrubbed clean often and discarded when heavily encrusted. Water-retaining plastic pots are more effective when using capillary matting.

Ferns of all kinds are well suited to casual, natural plantings, and to wood, stone, and earthenware containers. Containers need not be costly. Before tossing a fruitwood log in the fireplace consider it as a possible fern planter. With a chisel or router, hollow out a section large enough to plant one fern or a grouping. Pour boiling water through the hollowed-out area to eliminate pests. Lining it with uncut sphagnum, fill the log with the

(continued on page 197)

How to Care for 10 Favorite Ferns

NAME		SOIL	LIGHT	WATER/HUMIDITY
Adiantum raddianum (maidenhair fern)		1 part each: peat, perlite, vermiculite.	Subdued light; northern exposure.	Constant moisture (but not soggy); high humidity.
Asplenium nidus (bird's nest fern)		1 part each: peat, perlite, vermiculite.	Subdued light; northern exposure.	Constant moisture; house humidity.
Cyrtomium falcatum (holly fern)		1 part each: peat, perlite, vermiculite.	Bright filtered light; northern or eastern exposure.	Let soil dry slightly; house humidity.
Davallia fejeensis (rabbit's foot fern)		1 part each: peat, perlite, vermiculite.	Subdued light; northern or eastern exposure.	Let soil dry slightly; house humidity.
Nephrolepis exaltata 'Bostoniensis' (Boston fern)		1 part each: peat, perlite, vermiculite.	Filtered sun; eastern exposure.	Let soil dry slightly; house humidity with daily misting.
Pellaea rotundifolia (button fern)		1 part each: peat, perlite, vermiculite.	Subdued light; eastern or western exposure.	Nearly dry between waterings; high humidity.
Phyllitis scolopendrium (hart's tongue fern)		1 part each: peat, perlite, vermiculite.	Subdued light; northern exposure.	Constant moisture; high humidity.
Platycerium bifurcatum (staghorn fern)		1 part each: peat, sphagnum moss.	Filtered sun; eastern or western exposure.	Nearly dry between waterings; house humidity.
Polystichum tsus-simense (shield fern)		1 part each: peat, perlite, vermiculite.	Filtered light; eastern exposure.	Constant moisture; high humidity.
Pteris cretica and **P. spp.** (brake fern)		1 part each: peat, perlite, vermiculite.	Subdued light; northern or eastern exposure.	Constant moisture; house humidity.

TEMPERATURE	BEST METHOD OF PROPAGATION	SPECIAL TIPS
Day: 80°- 85°F (27°- 29°C) Night: 62°- 65°F (17°- 18°C)	Division.	Frequent misting may help humidity needs.
Day: 80°- 85°F (27°- 29°C) Night: 62°- 65°F (17°- 18°C)	Plantlets which may appear at base of older plant. Propagation by spores difficult.	Cold drafts and underwatering are enemies.
Day: 68°- 72°F (20°- 22°C) Night: 60°- 65°F (16°- 18°C)	Division of older plants; spores easy.	Very hardy fern; can stand more neglect than others.
Day: 68°- 72°F (20°- 22°C) Night: 60°- 65°F (16°- 18°C)	Root rhizomes on moist sphagnum partly covered with clear plastic.	Does very well in the home.
Day: 68°- 75°F (20°- 24°C) Night: 50°- 60°F (10°- 16°C)	Pin runners in soil; new plants will develop.	Some fronds generally turn brown in winter; mist twice daily with distilled water.
Day: 68°- 75°F (20°- 24°C) Night: 50°- 60°F (10°- 16°C)	Rhizome division.	Does not tolerate wet roots.
Day: 55°- 60°F (13°- 16°C) Night: 40°- 45°F (4°- 7°C)	Rhizome division; spores easy.	Can be difficult indoors because of cool temperatures needed.
Day: 70°- 75°F (21°- 24°C) Night: 55°- 65°F (13°- 18°C)	Small plants develop at base of older plants; or spores.	Usually wired with osmunda fiber to tree fern or bark slab and mounted on wall. Fiber must be kept moist.
Day: 68°- 75°F (20°- 24°C) Night: 50°- 60°F (10°- 16°C)	Division of older plants; or spores.	Fronds bruise easily. Do not allow water to come in direct contact with fronds of young plants. Prefers acid soil.
Day: 68°- 75°F (20°- 24°C) Night: 50°- 60°F (10°- 16°C)	Division; spores easy.	Likes to be potbound.

Creating an Airborne Fernery

You can transform commercially made wire baskets such as those used for epiphytic ferns and various patio plants into a floating fern garden. Line two wire baskets with a 1-inch (2.5 cm) layer of tightly packed uncut sphagnum moss. Adding a 2-inch (5 cm) layer of fern potting mix, fill the basket centers with more packed sphagnum. Moisten both containers and let them drain. Place open sides of the baskets together and wire them securely at the rims to form a sphere. Wet the ball of wire with a gentle warm spray, turning constantly to moisten the entire sphere, soil mix, and sphagnum. Plant three or four small walking fern (*Adiantum caudatum*) plants having three or four fronds each at even intervals between wires on the top half of the sphere; then hang the globe below the end of a four-tube fluorescent fixture so the tops of the plants are about 10 inches (25 cm) from the tubes.

The sphere may be hung with ¼-inch (6 mm) chain cut to length from the spools of chain readily available at hardware stores. Use a hook bent in this way:

Painting both chain and hook flat black will make the mechanics of the sphere disappear into the background, and enhance the effect. About a week later (or when the mix is firm and plants are established), turn the sphere over, suspend it, and plant the other half. Rotate the sphere 180 degrees every week, and pin the end of each bud-bearing frond securely to the sphere to promote "walking" and even foliage distribution. When firmly established, the floating topiary may be displayed in a window admitting bright indirect light but no sun. Water and fertilize it with a gentle spray. The sphere can be maintained for more than a year with consistent care and grooming, the key to the care of any fern.

Step 1: Line the two baskets with sphagnum and add potting mix and a core of sphagnum.

Step 2: Wire the baskets together.

Step 3: Plant the top of the sphere.

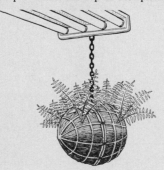

Step 4: Hang the sphere under lights.

Step 5: Turn the sphere and plant the other half.

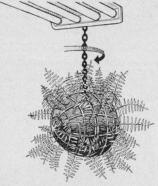

Step 6: Rotate the sphere every week.

Pin down the ends of the fronds.

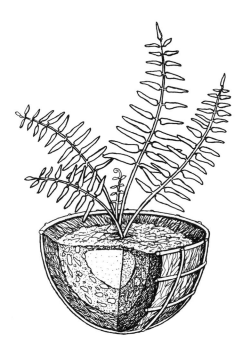

Planter for Epiphytic Ferns: A wire basket lined with sphagnum and filled with a loose, airy growing medium makes an attractive hanging planter for epiphytes such as rabbit's foot fern or polypody fern.

a wider variety of shapes is available at a mill. Be sure any wood you buy is untreated. Hollowed-out pieces of oak or maple burl suspended by leather thongs through drilled holes make excellent fern planters. Add a drain hole or a layer of drainage material to the container bottom; plant and water just to moisten.

Almost every planter will be outgrown in a year and the fern should be replanted. Choose immature plants or slow-growing types such as *Asplenium daucifolium, Doodia media,* or *Polystichum tsus-simense.* Also recommended are *Adiantum* cultivars with small pinnae such as *A. raddianum* 'Micropinnulum' and 'Pacific Maid'.

proper mix, then moisten and plant it with one or more small or slow-growing species. Or, select a section of log with a branch or two. With a chisel or router, hollow out several areas, then sink one end of the log in a large, squat stone- or gravel-filled clay pot to provide a sturdy base, and plant as above. Every day moisten the plants thoroughly with a hand mister.

Volcanic or "feather rock," available at rock shops and building supply stores, may be chiseled or routed and planted in the manner described above. The lacy walking fern *(Adiantum caudatum)* makes an especially effective planting. Display the planted stone on a tray of moistened small stones or gravel.

Bark slabs left from sawmill cuts make attractive plaques for mounting *Platycerium* varieties. Slabs are sold in garden centers, but

Log Planters for Ferns: Hollowed-out logs lined with sphagnum and filled with growing medium make interesting planters for terrestrial ferns such as the maidenhair fern.

POTTING

Potting and repotting ferns is relatively simple and may be done at any time of year indoors, though it is usually undertaken when new croziers are beginning to emerge. Choose a pot just large enough to comfortably accommodate the roots. To pot up young plants correctly, follow the directions for potting given in chapter 6. And remember that good drainage is crucial for ferns.

Moving an established plant from one pot to a larger one calls for the same potting procedures, and a pot one size larger, except with pots eight inches (20 cm) or more, when a two-size change is acceptable. Often a fern's root system will fill a pot completely and roots will attach to the container, making removal from larger pots a test in tugging. If tapping fails to remove a rootbound plant, run a sharp knife blade around the inner surface of the pot. In stubborn cases, such as when footed types have sent rhizomes over the pot edge, the pot should be broken to avoid injury to the fern. Remember, the plant is usually more valuable than the pot.

LIGHT

Many ferns will thrive in gently filtered natural light, such as the light filtered through the sheer curtain on a nearby window—roughly the equivalent of an overcast day outdoors. Ferns grown with insufficient light—in a too-dark corner that a decorator might want to brighten with a green plant—will have spindly, tired foliage, and generally be short-lived. Ferns that receive too much light are often compact but smaller plants, with pale green foliage despite proper nutrients and water. If direct sun is the light source, greater harm can result, for while some species, such as the footed ferns which climb into treetops, will tolerate and even enjoy a bit of dappled sun, full middle-of-the-day summer sunlight through glass will quickly burn leaflets and full fronds of plants in or near windows. To prevent such accidents, keep ferns away from

Ideal Environment for Ferns: A spot in front of a window where sunlight is gently filtered through a sheer curtain is perfect for many ferns, such as this Boston fern.

south-facing windows. A north window with little or no outdoor shading is ideal; a tree-shaded east or west window can be equally good. Greenhouse-grown ferns should be shaded or grown under benches.

Fluorescent tubes are an ideal light source. They may be used to supplement natural light, or a two-tube, four-foot (1.2 m), 40-watt fixture with reflector will provide all the light necessary for any fern you choose. Usually ferns should be placed with the top of the foliage no further than 14 inches (36 cm) from a two-tube fixture; most ferns grow best 8 inches (20 cm) from the tubes. Fluorescent light-grown ferns have firm, lush, bright foliage with none of the leaflet burn that is possible from the heat of the sun. Also, artificial lighting makes it possible to grow ferns virtually anywhere indoors, for space is the fluorescent light gardener's only limitation. However, you may wish to experiment with different locations: in or near windows, in the greenhouse, or under fluorescent lights to find the situation that best suits a particular plant's needs.

The effect of light, especially sunlight, is partially tempered by the temperature and by the moisture content of both the surrounding air and the soil.

TEMPERATURE

The tropical and semitropical beauties that most of us grow are happy in much the same temperatures that we prefer—60° to 80°F (16° to 27°C). Tropical ferns generally stop growing below 60°F (16°C), but temperatures above 80°F (27°C), especially coupled with the usual low household humidity, may result in wilted, scorched fronds and dried-out croziers. Immature growth and newly transplanted ferns suffer most from temperature extremes—and ferns are generally intolerant of *all* extremes. These plants are said to prefer a quiet atmosphere.

HUMIDITY

Most ferns grow best at a relative humidity of 60 to 80 percent, which is uncomfortable for the grower, injurious to furnishings, and generally impractical—except in the immediate area of the plant. A lower humidity of 50 percent is generally adequate for most species, however, and many ferns will tolerate even less moisture in the air if the temperature is 70°F (21°C) or below, and the soil is kept moist. Plants suffering from a lack of humidity will have a grayish green, slightly papery appearance, rather than the fresh, crisp foliage of plants grown in relative humidity of 60 percent or more. Humidity is of the utmost importance to fern culture, so if your indoor environment is low in humidity, increase the level by one of the techniques described in chapter 2.

But don't overdo it. Even in the driest areas of the country excessive humidity around a fern may stimulate growth of algae and fungus diseases. As a precaution, decrease humidity at night and when temperatures are lower, and assure gentle air movement through plant groupings under artificial light with a small, slow-moving fan. (In heavily used parts of the house, the constant coming and going of people should provide adequate air circulation for plants grown there.)

WATER

Moisture—too much or too little in the air and in the soil—accounts for most fern failures. A well-known gardener, Shirley Hibberd, wrote in *The Fern Garden* in 1881: "However many lessons you may learn of the habits of the several kinds of ferns, there should be one lesson impressed on your mind more deeply than any—it is this, that, much as they love moisture, it is a most rare thing to see a fern growing with its roots naturally in water. When they congregate, as it were, to drink of the brook that passes by, they keep their feet clear away from the current. . . ."

Most indoor ferns grow best in soil that is *constantly* moist, but not so wet that water puddles around a finger pressed into the mix. Even the few exceptions usually will tolerate constantly moist soil long enough to signal another preference to the grower. The aquatic water clover fern *Marsilea,* and *Salvinia,* also sometimes grown in aquaria, will tolerate moist soil, but both prefer to live in water. *Selaginella kraussiana* and *S. emmeliana* grow best in very moist soil. (*Selaginella* is not a true fern, but belongs to a related group called "fern allies.") The genus *Adiantum* is an excellent example of those ferns which require constantly moist, but not soggy, soil. Other commonly available genera requiring consistently moist soil are *Asplenium* (spleenwort), *Dryopteris* (shield fern), *Lygodium* (climbing fern), *Phyllitis, Polystichum,* and *Pteris.* Most epiphytic ferns such as *Davallia, Platycerium,* and *Polypodium* (polypody fern), grow best when wa-

Proper Watering Techniques Are Important:
Nephrolepis (top), *Cyrtomium* (bottom), and *Pellaea* (right) all grow best when they are allowed to dry out slightly between thorough waterings. Other genera, such as *Asplenium,* need constant moisture.

that cause any plant to lose water either rapidly or slowly. In general, water all terrestrial ferns from the top, at soil level, with a gentle flow of water at room temperature (60° to 68°F/16° to 20°C). Gentle top watering lessens soil erosion around the shallow roots and rhizomes and prevents the prolonged wetness on foliage which encourages rot and disease, especially among those ferns with fine foliage or plants in crowded conditions. Thoroughly drench the root ball and allow water to run freely through the drainage holes in the pot to leach any excess minerals accumulated from water and fertilizers. Moisten thoroughly with each watering and avoid incomplete daily "sips," which increase surface mineral buildup. See the Encyclopedia section for more information on specific ferns.

A fern that is habitually underwatered, but not to the obvious point of wilting, will have pale green, less luxuriant foliage, looking much the same as that resulting from too little humidity. A consistently overwatered plant with oxygen-starved roots rotting in soggy soil is unable to absorb nutrients, and will show poor growth and yellow-green foliage. Seemingly healthy fronds will rot and break at soil level, or the entire plant may suddenly appear to "wilt." Tap such a plant from the pot and gently remove damaged roots and excess soil, then repot the root ball in barely moist, fresh, well-drained potting mix. Excess moisture around the remaining undamaged roots will be distributed throughout the mix through capillary action, and after a day or so you should again just moisten the soil ball. Survival of a damaged plant is not assured, however.

Capillary mats have proved a boon to indoor fern growers. The mats resemble carpet padding and assure constant, even moisture and effectively raised humidity—just what ferns want. Watering from below encourages accumulation of fertilizer salts, and each pot should be removed from the mat regularly and thoroughly leached with clear water in an amount that is five times the pot's vol-

tered thoroughly and then allowed to dry out a bit—the same cycle they experience in their native habitats. *Cyrtomium, Nephrolepis, Pellaea* (cliff brake fern), *Pityrogramma* (silver-back or gold-back fern), and *Rumohra* (leather fern) thrive in similar conditions. *Pityrogramma* likes drier circumstances than most ferns and does not tolerate water on the foliage.

There is really no satisfactory answer to the popular question, "How often shall I water my ferns?" other than experience, which is really a learned awareness of conditions ume. Set up a capillary-mat system for ferns according to the method described under Wick Watering in chapter 2. Capillary matting should make it unnecessary to water your ferns from the top unless the mat is allowed to dry out. The loose, porous soil that ferns prefer is ideal for use with capillary matting.

PESTS AND DISEASES

Cleanliness is the first and best line of defense against pests and diseases. Aphids may feed on tender new fiddleheads and young foliage, and can be removed easily with a gentle spray of warm, soapy water. Conspicuously destructive are slugs and snails that leave a slimy trail and a swath of nibbled foliage and fiddleheads. Both are night feeders and hide in damp, dark crevices, in drainage holes, under pot rims, and deep in thick fern foliage. These pests may be handpicked and squashed with a certain satisfaction; or you can bait them with slices of raw potato placed in, around, and under pots. You must inspect the underside of the potato each morning and remove the slugs that congregate under it. This technique is time-consuming, but effective.

Scale insects are the bane of fern growers. These sucking insects attach themselves to any above-ground, smooth, edible part of a fern—especially to veins in pinnae and crevices in the stipe—and they sometimes secrete sticky honeydew which can harbor a black mold in damp areas. Observation of the sticky mess and the random arrangement of scale insects should keep you from confusing the pests with the orderly pattern of spore cases. Scale can be eliminated as described in chapter 9.

Fungus gnat larvae can destroy a fern's shallow roots, rhizomes, and rootstock and weaken the plant. As they are especially destructive to tender prothalli, the prudent grower will cover containers used for spore propagation. The tiny black gnat—which may be mistaken for a fruit fly—will fly around when an affected plant is disturbed. Though less common, mealybug species may attack fern foliage and roots. See chapter 9 for control measures.

PROPAGATION
SPORE COLLECTION

With just a bit of care, even the most casual fern grower can gather more than enough spores to start a propagation project and to supply several friends. As the spore cases ripen they change from a very light green to a brown or black, or in some species to a bright yellow-orange. Use of a 10x hand lens can assure that spores are gathered at the proper time. At the proper stage for collection the sporangia, which are minute spheres borne on short, thin stalks, should be plump and round; open, tattered sporangia indicate that the spores have already been shed. Pick a frond while the spore cases are still closed and colored a shiny, light brown. After washing the frond under a faucet to remove debris or hitchhiking pests, dry it on paper towels, and then place it in a smooth, white envelope for a day or two until the spores have fallen. As an alternative, the entire frond may be laid, spore side down, on a sheet of white paper. If left undisturbed for a day or two, then removed, it will leave behind a tracing of itself in millions of spores. Sift the accumulation through a very fine sieve to separate spores from spore cases and debris and store the spores in a clean, smooth envelope on which you have noted the species and date. (Do not use plastic; spores adhere to it.) Some spores may be viable for years if stored in your refrigerator (40°F/4°C); others are viable for only a couple of days. *Todea barbara* and *Osmunda* spores, which are green colored at maturity, are viable for only a short period of time. It is always safest to sow spores as soon as possible, by one of the methods described in chapter 8.

Spore Patterns: The distribution of spores on fronds occurs in a variety of unusual and interesting patterns. Shown here are the spores of *Adiantum concinnum* (top), *Polypodium formosanum* (bottom), and *Asplenium nidus* (facing page, top).

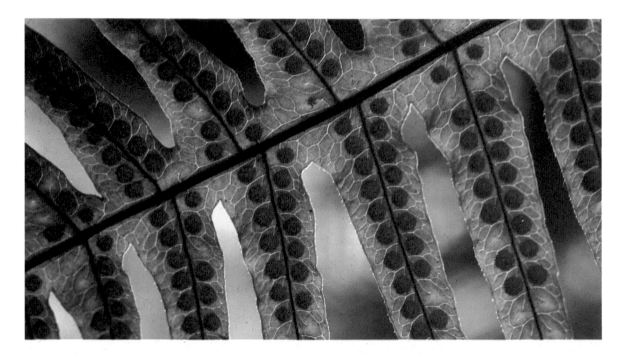

VEGETATIVE PROPAGATION

Repotting affords the logical opportunity to divide and rejuvenate mature ferns, and a discussion of how to refurbish and repot ferns of three specific growth habits also will serve to illustrate the simplest form of vegetative propagation, division.

When several crowns grow from an erect rootstock, as in the genus *Nephrolepis,* use a clean, sharp knife to divide the multiple crowns, taking care to retain some roots with each piece. Avoid damaging new growth, but trim dead roots and remove as much of each dead or damaged frond as possible. Position the well-tidied division in the center of a clean pot, carefully spread the roots and add potting mix just to the base of the crown. Then firm the soil and water thoroughly. Often three or four inches (8 or 10 cm) of stipe bases (the points at which the fronds are attached to the plant) must be trimmed from a rapidly growing *Nephrolepis* and the entire

trimmed stem and healthy, active roots may be successfully maneuvered into a pot and covered with fresh soil. If necessary, anchor the new plant with a soft cloth strip tied across the plant and pot. Some other genera that may be similarly divided are: *Cyrtomium, Phyllitis, Pityrogramma,* and *Polystichum.*

In other types, rhizomes that creep above or just below soil level may spread and form clumps, or they may branch and crawl, forming fronds at intervals. Both the clumps and pieces of rhizome will form new plants. When the rhizome is very short, as in *Asplenium bulbiferum* and *A. daucifolium* and *Pteris* varieties, it may be divided as described above. Plants like *Adiantum* with rhizomes creeping mostly at soil level may be divided with ease despite the plant's fragile appearance. Decide where natural divisions occur in rhizome and foliage and cut down completely

Division of *Nephrolepis*: To divide a fern in which several crowns grow from an erect root, as is the case with Boston fern, first divide the crowns, retaining some roots with each piece.
Next, trim off any dead roots and damaged fronds.

Then, position each new plant carefully in the center of a clean pot. Gently spread out the roots, and add potting mix only to the base of the crown. Keep the fronds out of the soil.

through rhizome and root ball. Remove damaged and spent fronds, neatly trim stipe bases close to the rhizome, and position the division, off-center if necessary, so the main growing tip has ample space to creep. Filling the pot with soil mix, cover all roots but leave the rhizome at least partially exposed. Then firm and water the soil.

Rhizomes that creep on soil, rocks, and trees may be similarly divided, but often present a greater challenge in handling. Vigorous specimens of *Davallia* and *Polypodium* will completely cover a container with their tough, hairy "feet" and defy division even with a sharpened shovel. Division of a mature footed fern produces a lopsided plant and propagation is best performed by severing a piece of an actively growing rhizome—with a few roots if possible to hasten what is often a slow process. Choose a rhizome with at least one characteristically lighter colored growing tip and several developing buds (buds feel like bumps at intervals along the rhizome), and cut a two- to three-inch (5 to 8 cm) piece. Anchor the cutting at half its

depth in a well-drained rooting medium (½ medium perlite and ½ screened peat), making certain the growing tip is neither damaged nor buried. Keep the setup *barely moist,* warm, and humid, but do *not* cover it, and be patient. When roots and a frond have formed, leave as much rooting medium as possible on the new roots, and plant the cutting at the same depth in fresh mix. Long, hanging rhizomes need not be severed but instead may be successfully air layered and nourished by the parent plant while rooting.

The small plants or "pups" sent out by *Platycerium* species are best severed from the parent after they have produced four or five of the round shield or base fronds which provide a spongy cache for water and nutrient collection. The young plant division may be mounted directly on a piece of board or tree trunk, or if necessary, with a bit of uncut sphagnum underneath to hold additional moisture. Secure the plant with strips of cloth or other soft material until it attaches naturally.

Any instrument used to divide ferns or

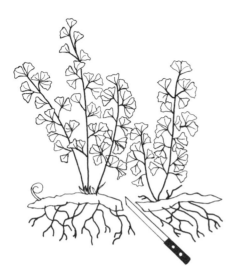

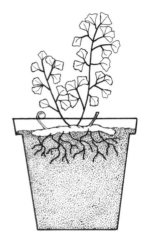

Division of _Adiantum:_ To divide ferns like the maidenhair, with rhizomes that creep at soil level, cut through the rhizome and root ball where divisions naturally occur in rhizome and foliage.

Place the division in a pot so that the main growing tip has room to creep. Add potting mix to cover the roots, but leave the rhizome partly exposed.

Division of _Davallia:_ To divide rabbit's foot and other footed ferns, cut off a 2- to 3-inch (5 to 8 cm) piece of rhizome which has a lighter colored growing tip and several buds.

Anchor the cutting in a porous growing medium, being careful not to damage or bury the growing tip. Repot the cutting when roots and a frond have formed.

Mounting *Platycerium* Pups: Young divisions of a staghorn fern can be mounted directly on a piece of board or bark. A bit of sphagnum can be placed underneath the plants to help retain moisture.

to cut sections of rhizome should be sharp and clean. Wounded parts of roots and rhizomes are susceptible to fungus invasion, so keep the cuts as small and clean as possible.

Some ferns produce buds or little plantlets on the fronds or roots. Both *Adiantum caudatum* and *Camptosorus rhizophyllus* bear a bud on the frond tip which produces a small plant when it touches moist soil, accounting for the name, walking fern. Buds on other species such as *Asplenium bulbiferum, A. daucifolium, Polystichum setiferum,* and *Woodwardia orientalis* may be removed and planted at half their diameter on a fine rooting medium (½ screened peat and ½ fine perlite will do), and partially covered with clear plastic until small plants form. For best results wait until plants are two inches (5 cm) tall before transplanting.

If buds are not removed, sometimes they drop off. (*Tectaria cicutaria* buds fall easily and plants develop in the pot, humidity tray, and any nearby hospitable areas, making it nearly a weed.) More usually, though, small plants form on the frond. The entire frond may be anchored to the soil while still attached to the plant, then severed and divided after the small plants root. (Outdoors, the weight of many small plantlets on an *Asplenium bulbiferum* [mother fern] combine with dew and rainfall to bend fronds to the soil, where the plantlets root and form a dense mat.) Small plantlets also may be removed and anchored individually to a moist soil surface, though the rooting process is somewhat slower than when the parent plant provides sustenance.

In the case of the hart's tongue fern *(Phyllitis scolopendrium),* small plantlike structures form not on fronds but on stipes; pieces of stipe from a young frond will form plants if barely pressed into a warm, damp rooting medium.

At the present time, fern propagation by meristem or tissue culture is practical only in laboratory or other controlled conditions, but many plants are produced in this way for the popular market. A microscopic group of cells is cut from fern tip or runner and grown in a nutrient-containing agar-type solution, then divided and redivided to form many hundreds of genetically identical, disease-free plants from one parent.

GROOMING

Fern housekeeping is a year-round task indoors, and far and away more fun than regular household chores. Fronds yellow naturally with age and should be cut close to the soil or rhizome to make room for new fiddleheads. Bits of foliage and debris on the soil surface make excellent habitats for pests and breeding places for disease organisms. Weeds are unsightly and compete with the potted plant for water and food. Repeated watering washes soil from the base of plants. Coupled with the natural loss of fronds and with shallow roots, soil loss eventually may cause some species to begin to wobble. So, add fresh mix to the surface occasionally. Dust and shedding spores and chaff may be washed away with a fine spray of water, and you can wash away ugly water and fertilizer spots from fern fronds with a soft cloth or cotton swab moistened with a solution of one tablespoon (15 ml) white vinegar to a cup (236 ml) of warm water. This solution also can be used in a hand sprayer, but several applications may be necessary for stubborn spots.

WHERE TO GET FERNS

Every fern grower has an active "want list." A species easy to obtain in one area may be a collector's item in another. Fern societies in the United States and other countries publish journals that include sources for live plants; these groups also encourage round-robin correspondence and feature spore stores and exchanges, and the grower willing to propagate from spores can increase his collection steadily with patience and effort. See the Appendix for the addresses of fern societies.

Native ferns may not be suited for indoor growing, especially if the mature plant is a rampant grower or if it is completely deciduous. (Tropicals such as *Davallia* species may also be deciduous. However, at warm indoor temperatures new fiddleheads appear as fronds fall.) Fern collecting in any location should be undertaken only after thorough study of literature on local flora. Rare varieties should not be taken unless threatened by bulldozers or other similar tools of progress, and in any case, permission should be obtained from the landowner or from the responsible agency if you are on public land. Collect from small mature plants, preferably dividing them and taking only enough of the crown and roots to start a new plant. Better yet, collect only spores. Label all collecting envelopes with an accurate description of the plant and the immediate area where it was collected. In the United States, transporting plants into the country or from one state to another requires permission from the USDA. Readers outside the United States should contact the appropriate agencies in their country.

The selection of live plants available from local nurserymen depends on their interests and skill, facilities, the season (in North Temperate zones, winter weather restricts the shipping of plants), simple economics, and pure chance. The fern plants sold by vendors are usually the kinds best able to withstand minimum care—such as Boston fern, brake fern, holly fern, and polypody fern. All are excellent for beginners and remain favorites of experts. If purchasing directly from the grower, ask for cultural tips and a fertilizing schedule to avoid possible overfeeding.

CHAPTER 12

Flowering Plants

Plants thrived for millions of years on earth before their greenery was relieved by the gay forms and colors of flowers. Those early land plants, the seedless ferns, reproduced as sea plants had, scattering minuscule single cells called spores. These germinated when exposed to moisture, forming an organ which was both male and female. After the male sperm fertilized the female egg, however, weeks and months went by before the incredibly small structure could take hold as a new individual. What were needed, evolutionarily speaking, were seeds — masses of cells containing their own food reserves and capable of establishing themselves with greater rapidity. Eventually the first step in the evolution from spores to seeds occurred: dissimilar spores came into being. Other changes followed, such as the reduction of the female spore case to one or a few female spores which could no longer be released, the evolution of the male organ into a pollen tube, and the replacement of spores and eggs by male and female nuclei. Forests of seed ferns sprang up and eventually pollination occurred — that momentous event in which male spores were transferred to female spores in place on the parent plant.

To facilitate this process and the creation of many seeds and their dispersal and growth into vigorous offspring, flowers evolved. These agents of attraction made vegetation palatable to animal pollinators and disseminators by virtue of their color, shape, scent, and the food of their pollen and nectar. It was perhaps 120 million years ago that the vegetative buds on certain plants that were descended from seed ferns evolved into reproductive buds. Gradually the spaces between the leaves disappeared, and the lowest leaves on the leafy shoot became bracts, while the next highest became the sepals.

The leaves above the sepals evolved into the petals of the flower, and the highest (now the innermost) groups of leaves developed into the male and female sexual organs.

Plants producing these highly diversified reproductive structures as a prelude to the production of seeds in a dry or fleshy structure (an ovary fruit) are called angiosperms, whereas nonflowering plants producing naked, or exposed, seeds are called gymnosperms. Angiosperms may be divided into dicotyledonous and monocotyledonous types. The dicots are quite different from the monocots; they have two seed-leaves, net-veined leaves, and flower parts commonly occurring in fours or fives. (Examples among house plants are woody plants such as azaleas, citrus, and gardenias, and herbaceous plants such as African violets, begonias, coleus, marigolds, and pileas.) Monocots, on the other hand, have one seed-leaf and usually have leaves with parallel veins and flower parts occurring in threes and sixes. (Monocotyledonous house plants include amaryllis, bromeliads, lilies, and orchids.)

There are numerous flower variations possible in the structure of both monocotyledonous and dicotyledonous flowers. If sepals, petals, and both male and female parts are present, the flower is described as complete. If any of these are absent, it is termed incomplete. The inconspicuous nature of some flowers is due to their being incomplete. A flower with both reproductive structures present and functioning is bisexual or perfect, while a blossom with only one structure is unisexual or imperfect. Unisexual flowers with male reproductive organs (stamens) are termed staminate flowers; those having only female organs (pistils) are pistillate. Staminate and pistillate flowers may occur on one plant, in which case the flowering plant is

Opposite, close-up of passionflower, Passiflora *species.*

Basic Classes of Flowering Plants: A flower which has evolved with four or five parts is characteristic of the dicotyledonous class of plants, represented at left by an African violet. A plant with flower parts occurring in threes and sixes, as seen on the lily at right, belongs to the monocotyledonous class.

monoecious, or on separate plants, making the plant dioecious.

The earliest angiosperms probably evolved in climates marked by alternating dry and wet periods or short growing seasons, where greater pressures existed to shorten the reproductive cycle. In such challenging environments, those plants in which structures related to fertilization were more evolved and the growth of endosperm and embryo development had been speeded up would certainly be the plants most likely to perpetuate themselves. Probably fertilized by beetles, these most primitive of flowering plants were low-growing shrubs with simple leaves and bisexual, rather simple magnolia-like or buttercuplike flowers. They probably had comparatively large numbers of each part, the parts were separate, and the members of each part were separate from each other. Most likely, the petals and reproductive organs of these least efficient of flowers were not elevated above the ovary, and all of their petals had the same shape and served the same function. As time passed, these ancestral angiosperms were superseded in seasonal environments by more highly advanced

flowers in which the flower parts had become increasingly specialized to better assure the plant's perpetuation. That is, the pistils began to fuse and the petals to unite, while the corolla became elevated and certain petals began to evolve into a landing platform for insects, or a porch or spur capable of holding larger amounts of nectar.

The movement, then, was from simple, wide-open, upright, vaselike flowers producing plenty of pollen and catching it in their cuplike forms (examples are the wild rose and the poppy), toward two quite divergent lines of evolution. One of these led to the development of flowering plants with many small flowers in clusters, a development culminating in the sometimes sizable flower heads and spikes of the umbellifers, composites, and palms. The presence of so many tiny florets in composite or massed flowers such as those of the aster, chrysanthemum, daisy, dandelion, and hydrangea means that insect visitors scatter pollen over many flowers at the same time, and this aids the setting of seeds.

The other line of development from the simple, pollen-bearing flowers led to the evolution of plants bearing relatively few large and showy flowers that were more suited to large insects approaching from one direction. Many of these highly evolved flowers are wonderfully intricate in design and function. In addition to producing nectar, some droop or fold up at night to maintain the warmth needed for the viability of ovules, pollen, and nectar, and to keep pollen dry or concealed from night-flying insects. Many light-colored flowers open wide only when the sun sets, for they are pollinated by moths or wasps. Some flowers have even more complicated means to safeguard their pollen or nectar from all but preferred pollinators. For example, often bell- and funnel-shaped flowers have nectaries so recessed that only insects with a requisitely long tongue can reach them.

To the same end, the "jaws" of snap-dragon flowers cannot be forced open by in-sects weaker than a bee, and the *Calceolaria* hides its nectaries inside a pouched flower that snaps closed when the satiated bee lifts off from the bloom's lower lip. In other rela-tively advanced flowering plants — *Salvia,* for example — self-pollination is prevented by the production of ripe pollen before the stigma is ready to receive it. The most sophis-ticated of the line of flowering plants bearing relatively few flowers that are highly special-ized in form — and often in color and scent as well — are the extraordinarily insect-adapted blooms of the lobelias, orchids, snapdragons, and tropical gingers.

Today, flowering plants are in the major-ity all over the world, comprising close to 300 plant families and approximately 234,000 species. Existing even in the inhospitable aridity of the deserts and among the glaciers and snow fields of the Arctic and Antarctic, flowering plants grow most lavishly in rainy tropical areas. Because such rain and cloud forests provide stable conditions so favorable to plant life, they have become living muse-ums containing relics of relatively primitive flowering plants that came into existence and later died out in more rigorous climes.

Plants that flower have sustained the

(continued on page 214)

Cloud Forest: Each morning this forest is blanketed with clouds which serve to moderate the climate, eliminating extremes of hot or cold. This very humid environment is the perfect haven for many flowering plants such as orchids and bromeliads.

Composite Flower: A close-up view of an *Agapanthus* flower reveals that what we might think of as one bloom is instead a mass of small florets.

Flower Fragrances and Fragrant Flowers

Stirring vague but powerful feelings and associations, the scents given off by plants have added immeasurably to their symbolic value. Fragrances are also of economic worth, for the aromatic oils exuded from the epidermis of the leaves and stems of herbs and other plants have provided us with material used in medical and cosmetic preparations, in waxes and paints, and in chemicals. In fragrant flowers, the scented oil is secreted not by every epidermal cell but by oil glands. These special organs have been created to dispose of the by-products of plant metabolism, and in the process of making oil are said to generate both heat and electricity. An aroma is created when chemicals in the oil break down — something that happens when the oil passes into the outer cells of a flower's petals or sepals and is vaporized on exposure to the air. The resulting scent is most noticeable in flowers with thick, waxy petals or with many petals ("doubles"), and when given off in warm, still air.

Although they originate from metabolic leftovers, many flower fragrances have evolved — much as flower colors, structures, and shapes have — to attract the most suitable pollinator. It is no accident, for example, that the most vividly colored flowers are often disappointingly lacking in scent; often these showy blooms are pollinated by bees or hummingbirds, which are attracted by sight rather than by smell. More often, it is the wide-open white, pale pink, or yellow flowers that are most rewarding to the human nose, for such blooms — of-

ten opening at night — make themselves conspicuous to pollinating butterflies and moths by wafting a fragrance through the dark as well as by displaying their broad, light-colored surfaces. In some scented flowers, the petals have patches of scent that constitute an even more explicit guide to the nectaries.

Flower fragrances defy scientific classification because their appeal — and often how they are perceived — varies with the pigmentation of the nasal mucosa exposed to them and also may be influenced by how strong or diluted the fragrance is and how near or far away. The oil of flowers such as the aroids and certain members of the Lily family and other plants having inflorescences of a brownish, purplish, or chrome yellow cast is appealing to flies and midges but noxious to humans, for it is high in indol, a chemical which is also present in the breakdown of animal tissue, and which conveys the smell of rotting flesh. Almost as unpleasant are the flowers of *Pyracantha* and other blooms with fishy-smelling oil containing trimethylamine, another chemical associated with rot, and flowers containing acid-alcohol compounds, which create an aroma of animal fur or musk.

Happily, there remain vast numbers of flowers that delight the nose. These include the heavily scented lilies and narcissus, which have a fairly low concentration of indol and are generally perceived as pleasant although they can become oppressive if there are several plants with fading flowers in a warm, poorly aired room. There are aromatic flowers giving off the scent of clove (carnation), balsam (hyacinth), or vanilla

(sweet pea). Also appealing are the violet-scented types — including violets, certain irises, and mignonette; rose-scented blooms, such as certain tulips, peonies, irises, and, of course, roses; and lemon-smelling flowers such as lily-of-the-valley. Still other blooms float the refreshing scent of fruits such as apples or bananas, while some offer the enticing smell of honey.

To add the intriguing dimension of fragrance to your environment, consider featuring one or more of the following lusciously scented plants in each room. Some belong to the richly scented indol-containing group, others are of an aromatic, fruity, or delicately musky persuasion. All are wonderfully pleasing.

> *Bouvardia longiflora* (sweet bouvardia). White flowers in spring, possibly late fall.
>
> *Carissa grandiflora* (Natal plum). White flowers intermittently year-round.
>
> *Cestrum nocturnum* (night jessamine). Greenish or creamy white flowers in summer and intermittently year-round.
>
> *Coffea arabica* (Arabian coffee plant). White flowers, late summer.
>
> *Daphne odora* (winter or fragrant daphne). Creamy white to pink flowers winter into spring.
>
> *Dendrobium moschatum.* Orchid blooming late winter through summer.
>
> *Epidendrum phoeniceum* (chocolate orchid). Orchid blooming in

Fragrance to Fill a Room: These waxy white flowers of *Jasminum polyanthum*, above, belie their delicacy and size by filling the air with a cloud of distinctively sweet scent. This slow-growing, climbing shrub blooms from spring to fall, and will flower when still quite young.

Scented White Stars: As pleasing to the nose as they are to the eye, the waxy white blooms of *Stephanotis floribunda* are a delight to the senses. Glossy green, oval leaves serve as a backdrop to these heavily scented blooms. This climbing shrub can be trained up a trellis or along a frame for an attractive display.

summer, fragrance of chocolate cake.

Epiphyllum oxypetalum (Dutchman's pipe). A white-flowered cactus blooming freely in mid to late summer.

Exacum affine (German or Persian violet). Bluish lilac flowers summer into autumn.

Gardenia jasminoides (gardenia, cape jasmine). White or cream-colored flowers with a sweet, heavy fragrance produced early spring to early summer.

Gelsemium sempervirens (Carolina yellow jessamine). Yellow flowers in summer or later. All parts poisonous.

Heliotropium arborescens (common heliotrope).

Purple flowers with vanilla fragrance from late winter to summer.

Hylocereus undatus (night-blooming cereus). Large, white flowers opening for one night, anytime from summer to fall.

Jasminum sambac (Arabian jasmine). Sweet-scented white flowers turning purple, early spring to late autumn.

Lycaste aromatica. Orchid flowering spring to fall, cinnamon aroma.

Maxillaria tenuifolia. Orchid blooming summer through winter, coconut fragrance.

Neomarica gracilis (walking iris) and *N. northiana* (apostle plant). White and blue

or violet flowers in late winter.

Nicotiana alata "Grandiflora' (jasmine tobacco) and *N. ×sanderae* (flowering tobacco). Summer bloomers, *N. alata* with white and yellow flowers, *N. ×sanderae* with yellow flowers flushed with deep rose or red.

Osmanthus fragrans (sweet olive). White flowers in fall, strongly jasmine scented.

Reseda odorata (mignonette). Small, honey-scented, yellow-white flowers in winter indoors.

Stephanotis floribunda (Madagascar jasmine or wax flower). White, waxy blooms in late winter.

Eye-Catching Form and Color: The tubular yellow flowers of this *Heliconia* seem to jump out of the fiery red bracts which surround them. This unusual flowering plant is related to the bird-of-paradise, which also bears flowers with showy bracts and projecting tubular flowers.

world's billions with food and other necessities derived from their seeds, leaves, stalks, roots, and fruits. The many angiosperms producing flowers conspicuous for their beauty also have nourished man's spirit and kindled his imagination. Symbolizing the realm of the ideal, the images of the rose (which often stands for all flowers) and of the lily permeate Western culture even as the lotus flower and the chrysanthemum represent the spiritual essence of the East. Throughout history, flowers have been prized and perpetuated by monarchs as diverse as Charlemagne, Montezuma, Louis XIV, and the Empress Josephine. Writers such as Shakespeare, Herrick, Herbert, Blake, Keats, and Shelley have cele-

brated flowers in plays and poetry of undying beauty, and artists like Van Gogh and Monet have painted them with an almost obsessive fervor. As a reminder of the astonishing beauty and fragility of the natural world, flowering plants speak powerfully to all of us, and thanks to the unceasing efforts of plant hunters and breeders, there are now multitudes of cultivars capable of producing magnificent blooms even under the constraining conditions of an indoor environment.

SOME FLOWERING FAVORITES FOR INDOOR GARDENS

Flowering plants vary in the length of their life cycles. Those which produce stems and leaves, then flowers, fruits, and seeds in one outdoor growing season (or in about one year or less when grown indoors), and die afterward are called annuals. Germinating in about 1 or 2 weeks and flowering in anywhere from 5 weeks from seeds (dwarf marigolds) to 16 to 24 weeks (such dawdlers as annual carnations, cigar plant or *Cuphea ignea,* and annual Canterbury bells or *Campanula medium*), annuals cram their entire life into 6 months or so. During this brief span, the energy of the plant is not stored in its roots but is directed toward the creation of as many seeds as possible. To the delight of the gardener, this biological imperative translates into a profusion of flowers, which the plant strives mightily to replace when they are removed for enjoyment in floral arrangements. This abundance of brightly colored flowers produced rapidly by shallow-rooted plants provides an excellent return for a modest investment of time, space, and effort on the part of the indoor gardener. Just a handful of the annuals that can succeed handsomely when brought or started indoors if given the bright light they require are dwarf and full size varieties of *Alonsoa warscewiczii* (mask flower); *Browallia speciosa* 'Major' and

A Flowering Annual for Indoors: This explosion of color can grace your windowsill from midsummer to fall, the blooming period for *Salpiglossis sinuata*. The velvety petal texture and contrasting venation and flower centers heighten the appeal of these flowering plants. Since they are annuals, enjoy them for one season, then discard after blooming.

B. viscosa 'Compacta'; *Clarkia; Coleus; Cuphea* (cigar plant); *Heliotropium; Lantana camara* (common lantana, shrub verbena, or yellow sage) and *L. montevidensis* (trailing lantana); *Mimulus × hybridus* 'Grandiflorus' (monkey flower); *Reseda odorata* (mignonette); *Salpiglossis* (painted tongue); *Tagetes tenuifolia* 'Pumila' (dwarf marigold); and *Torenia fournieri* (blue wings).

Flowering plants known as biennials usually make only vegetative growth during their first season, then die back, going on to flower, set seeds, and expire in their second year. Under good conditions, however, bien-

nials such as hound's tongue *(Cynoglossum amabile),* gloriosa daisy *(Rudbeckia hirta* 'Gloriosa Daisy'), and black-eyed Susan vine *(Thunbergia alata)* will flower during their first year from seeds. Sometimes this early flowering is achieved through hybridization, as with the 'Foxy' cultivar of foxglove *(Digitalis purpurea).*

When the vegetative and reproductive phases of a plant take two years and continue after that time, it is a perennial. Most of the blooming plants grown indoors are either true perennials or very tender perennials such as carnations, chrysanthemums, cyclamens, early flowering dwarf dahlia hybrids, flowering maples, gazanias, geraniums, impatiens, and wax begonias. Many of these plants are grown as annuals outdoors in most parts of the temperate zone but can live on, escaping winterkill, when raised or brought indoors. Often taking three years to flower, perennials are mostly sold already well started in containers or as bare-rooted speci-

(continued on page 218)

A Popular Flowering Perennial: *Cyclamen* is but one example of a flowering perennial which will bloom for you indoors, season after season. After flowering is completed, to insure lovely flowers the next time around, give *Cyclamen* a cool, dark rest period, then repot when new shoots appear.

A Roomful of Begonias: Expert begonia grower Jack Golding set aside a basement room for the sole purpose of raising these beautifully varied plants. Ample artificial lighting, controlled temperature, and good ventilation allow these begonias to thrive and put on a showy display of foliage and flowers.

Begonias: Imitative, But Never Duplicated

A frequent companion to the geranium on the windowsills of many countries is the begonia. Mostly tropical and succulent, these favorite pot and garden plants are much prized for their versatility of size and appearance, compatibility with other plants, and suitability for growing under lights. Anywhere from several inches (approximately 5 cm) to six feet (1.8 m) in height, begonias usually have asymmetrical, alternate leaves varying greatly in color and form. Foliage often imitates that of other plants, such as ivy, elm, or maple. Flowers are slightly irregular, usually made up of two pairs of joined petals and sepals (tepals) in shades of red, pink, yellow, or white. Like begonia foliage, the blossoms can be reminiscent of those of other species, and hobbyists can enjoy

cultivars with flowers that look like camellias, carnations, fuchsias, gardenias, or rosebuds. Somewhat unusually, begonias have male and female flowers on different plants (female flowers can be recognized by their five tepals and by three wings, or stipules, at their base). The monoecious nature of these plants explains why they are usually propagated vegetatively. As this trait encourages cross-pollination, it also is probably the reason why the genus *Begonia* is so huge; at present it is believed to include as many as 1,200 species and well over 4,000 hybrids and cultivars.

Like many other well-loved flowering tropical plants, the begonia was discovered by Europeans during the seventeenth century, which was a period of intense botanical exploration by amateurs. The plant was collected by Michel Begon in the

French West Indies, where the natives supposedly used it to treat fever. Adapting well to life in France (where it was presumably given the humidity, lime, and well-drained soil begonias need), the begonia became popular rapidly because of its wonderful variation, color, and ease of propagation both outdoors and indoors.

By 1717, the English began importing from Jamaica the begonias they had seen their French neighbors enjoying. Toward the end of the eighteenth century, plant hunters working for the English firm of Veitch and Sons discovered tuberous begonias in Bolivia and Peru, and in 1858 the famous rex begonia, discovered in Asia, reached England via the East India Company. Around 1880, begonias found their way into the hearts and gardens of North Americans through a community of French Huguenots in Flushing, Long Island, and enthusiasm for them has burgeoned ever since.

Although the well-known *Thompson Begonia Guide* (see Bibliography) organized begonias into eight groups in a classification based on that suggested for show begonias by the American Begonia Society in 1969, these very diverse plants are traditionally divided into three major types, according to root structure. The largest grouping — and the one containing the best house plants — consists of begonias with fibrous roots. Prized for their ability to bloom year-round, the fibrous-rooted members of the *B.* × *semperflorens-cultorum* hybrid complex, called wax begonias, are quite often the first begonias in a beginner's collection, and their round, crisp, waxy green, bronzy, or reddish leaves and single to double flowers of white, pink, or red are a familiar sight. Large-flowered cultivars of this easily pleased pot and bedding plant include 'Caravelle', 'Danica', 'Fortuna', 'Red Butterfly', and 'Stratos Rose'. For Christmas flowering, wax begonias such as the compact, red-flowering 'Scarletta' can be grown from seeds planted in mid-July, and plants for Valentine's Day can be started from seeds September 1. Also favored as house plants — though they tend to become

A Dramatic Begonia for Indoors: There are begonias grown especially for their blooms and others grown especially for their foliage, but this one, the angel-wing begonia, is equally prized for both. The distinctive wing-shaped leaves are speckled with white and tinged with red at the edges. The reddish pink flowers appear in drooping clusters from summer to fall.

large and must be pinched back regularly — are the various species and cultivars of the cane-stemmed begonias, often called angel-wing begonias because of the shape of their foliage. Having arching stems that produce drooping blooms at intervals, these fibrous-rooted types make good hanging basket plants, but need more moisture than most begonias. Good cultivars include the venerable 'Corallina de Lucerna' and 'Alzasco', 'Orange Rubra', and 'Pink Rubra'. Certain fibrous-rooted begonias are called hairy (or hirsute) types because of the hair on their shiny or leathery leaves; those with shorter hairs are termed felt-leaved. These begonias are fast growers and tolerate low humidity; some worthwhile species are the old favorite *B. scharffii,* and *B. ×alleryi, B. ×drostii, B. ×prunifolia,* and *B. ×viaudii.* There are also branching, small-leaved fibrous-rooted begonias; two charming, free-blooming ones are 'Preussen', with coppery olive, silver-spotted, ovate leaves and big pink blooms, and 'Sachsen', with rosy red flowers and small angel-wing leaves.

The second major group of begonias has rhizomatous roots and blooms in spring, usually requiring a slight rest with a decrease in watering in winter. Often grown for their splendidly ornate foliage, many of these begonias are too large for house plants; however, there are some adorable dwarf forms (see chapter 22). These creeping rhizome types can fill a pot or hanging basket handsomely and those with rhizomes that grow erect

(examples are the easy-to-grow rex cultivars 'Baby Rainbow' and 'Calico') or upright and branching (such as the readily raised rex cultivars 'Lavender Glow', 'Peter Pan', and 'Silver Sweet') can climb up a moss totem pole. The most popular and probably the easiest of the rhizomatous begonias to grow indoors are the *B. ×rex-cultorum* hybrids. Sometimes called painted leaf or fan begonias, they have broadly oval, pointed leaves up to a foot (30 cm) long that are richly brocaded in metallic green, silver, and purple. Rex begonias need lots of water during their growth season and, unlike some begonias, should never be exposed to direct sun. Similar in their cultural requirements are the colorful *B. ×erythrophylla* and *B. ×erythrophylla* 'Bunchii' cultivars — the so-called beefsteak begonias, with leathery, dark green leaves that are red on their undersides. Offering pointed leaves that have given them their common name of star begonias are such favorites as the pink-flowering *B ×ricinifolia* (bronze-leaf begonia); *B.* 'Joe Hayden' (black begonia), which has black-green leaves and red blooms in winter; and *B. ×sunderbruchii* (finger-leaf begonia), which has bronze-green leaves with silver netting and pinkish flowers. More challenging to grow are the extraordinarily beautiful *B. masoniana* (iron cross begonia) and the striking, stitch-leaved *B. boweri* cultivars, which have purple or blackish brown markings on their foliage.

Generally speaking, tuberous **(box continued on next page)**

Begonias: Imitative, But Never Duplicated (continued)

begonias (B. ×tuberhybrida) are least suited to life as house plants, usually needing a cool winter rest period. Many, however, are gorgeous basket plants and can be brought into profuse summer bloom if they can be placed in a lath house or dappled shade and given the cool night temperatures (65°F/18°C), light, evenly moist soil, and moist, moving air they need. Unfortunately, high temperatures and direct sun will result in scorched leaves and bud drop. Somewhat easier to grow indoors are the semituberous species and hybrids, many of which bloom in autumn and winter. The novel B. bogneri is grown for its long, slender, grasslike leaves and tiny pink flowers, and does best in a terrarium under either indirect light or fluorescents, which can sometimes keep it from going dormant. Capable of producing hundreds of pink flowers, B. ×cheimantha (Christmas begonia) needs 60° to 65°F (16° to 18°C) nights, steady temperatures, and no drafts, and will drop its flowers in a warm room. An improvement over the Cheimantha hybrids, from which they are derived, the very popular new 'Rieger' or 'Elatior' strain consists of vigorous, very floriferous plants blooming in vivid new colors for eight to ten weeks in autumn and winter. The 'Schwabenland' cultivars offer single flowers of pink, red, red-orange, or orange on upright plants, while the 'Aphrodite' Riegers boast double blooms of cherry red, red, rose, and pink and are well suited to hanging baskets. Although these spectacular plants sometimes bloom continuously for as long as a year, they are susceptible to mildew and therefore should never be misted and should be assured of good air circulation.

For greatest success with these premier house plants, remember to pinch back the stem tips next to the blossoms when the buds have developed beyond them. If begonias of show quality are your goal, take the suggestion of experienced amateur grower Corliss Engle: "Watch them! Prune and pinch often, and turn the plants regularly to achieve symmetry."

mens during their dormancy. These longer-lived plants generally flower less exuberantly than annuals, for part of their strength goes into the building of roots and stems that can sustain them for years and there is not the same evolutionary imperative to generate vast numbers of seeds in a single growing season. Indeed, flowering perennials can live to astonishing ages: in 1972 horticulturist James Crockett was told of a still-thriving deep red peony plant that dates back to at least 1846, before which it was probably brought to the United States from China on a clipper ship! Although they are technically perennials, most bulb plants and certain other flowering plants such as miniature pansies (Viola tricolor) and the winter-blooming blue sage (Eranthemum pulchellum) lose their vigor or looks after their first flowering season and are usually treated as annuals even indoors. (Gardeners with limited space and patience and sufficiently hard hearts also consider as disposable perennials such as poinsettias, calceolarias, and indoor primroses, which require extra care, are difficult to grow on, or lack interesting enough foliage to warrant keeping them around until they bloom again.) Remaining, however, is a legion of outstanding and long-lived perennials well worth nurturing through the slight or pronounced rest period they require after blooming. Many of these splendid plants are discussed in the specialty chapters that follow — particularly those on bromeliads, gesneriads, orchids, and miniatures.

HERBACEOUS FLOWERING PLANTS

During the life cycles of a flowering plant, its vegetative portions may remain soft, watery, and green. This is the case with most flowering annual house plants and is also true of some of the popular perennials. Such plants are called herbaceous. Many perennials, however, are woody: their nonflowering parts become hard and relatively dry and change from green to a color often ranging from brown through gray. Certain woody perennials are evergreen, keeping their foliage around the year. Others are partly or entirely deciduous, dropping some or all of their leaves during a dormancy brought on by low temperatures. The herbaceousness or woodiness of a given plant tends to influence the way(s) in which it can be vegetatively propagated and its habit of growth.

Relatively small and more or less upright herbaceous flowering plants that are delightful indoors include the summer-blooming *Acalypha hispida* (chenille plant) and *Anemone coronaria* (poppy anemone) which can be forced to produce its large open blooms with colorful sepals from February into spring; *Catharanthus roseus* (Madagascar periwinkle), which offers very showy, phloxlike, pink, white, or rose flowers from spring to fall and may be summered outdoors and used as a source of buds that will continue to open in a vase; *Chrysanthemum × morifolium* cultivars in a vast range of sizes and colors that can be forced into bloom during the winter and at practically any time of year; the free-flowering *Exacum affine* (German or Persian violet); *Gazania ringens* (treasure flower), which is drought and heat resistant and has a long blooming season; *Myosotis sylvatica* 'Compacta' (dwarf forget-me-not), with charming sky blue flowers with yellow eyes in winter, from seeds sown in summer (the 'Sunshine' hybrids flower from June to October); *Nicotiana alata* 'Grandiflora' (flowering tobacco), producing a profusion of two inch (5 cm) wide flowers in a host of available colors, including such unusual shades as burgundy and chocolate; *Primula sinensis* (Chinese primrose), a winter-blooming primrose available in various flower shades such as mauve, scarlet, pink, or white; and *Rivina humilis* (rouge plant), which generates sprays of pinkish white blooms followed by red ber-

Long Blooming Season: *Gazania* sports blooms with black centers and daisylike petals ranging in color from orange to yellow. This perennial bears many flowers from spring through summer.

Bountiful Flowers: The small but plentiful violet flowers of *Exacum affine* will continue to appear for months once blooming begins. The plant is technically a biennial, but is usually treated as an annual, being discarded when flowering is done.

220

Ornamental Berries: *Rivina humilis*, a perennial, bears white or pink flowers in racemes which are followed by shiny red berries that will remain on the plant as long as the soil is not allowed to dry out.

Deep Sea Look-Alike in a Pot: The curving bracts of *Justicia brandegeana,* the shrimp plant, are reminiscent both in color and in shape of the sea-dwelling crustacean. The cream and salmon-colored bracts are papery thin, and nestled between them (for the most part out of sight) are tiny white flowers.

ries in fall and winter. A favorite gift plant is *Justica brandegeana* (the shrimp plant), better known by the name of *Beloperone guttata.* It features graceful, pendulous bracts of salmon to rose, surrounding creamy white flowers with red spots on the lower lips.

FLOWERING SHRUBS

Quite spectacular for larger areas are a host of woody, mostly evergreen flowering shrubs and trees. *Acacia armata* (kangaroo thorn) obligingly thrives in a small pot and puts forth vivid yellow flowers in March and April if it is given just moderate light and allowed to dry out somewhat between waterings. *Rhododendron* species (azaleas) sold as gift plants are often hybrids offering single or double flowers in shades of white, pink, red, or orange. *Brunfelsia pauciflora* 'Floribunda' (yesterday, today, and tomorrow) will generate its white-eyed purple flowers from January to July. *Ardisia crenata* (coralberry) is an appealing, waxy-leaved little tree which pro-

duces fragrant white flowers in summer that are followed in winter by decorative waxy red berries that may linger for up to six months until flowering resumes.

The magnificent *Camellia japonica* has been bred to develop no less than six different flower shapes, ranging from a single to a rose-form double and peony forms; it will bloom well indoors winter through spring if properly cared for. Also much loved are the deliciously fragrant, white or creamy-flowered *Gardenia jasminoides* cultivars, mostly flowering in the long days of spring and summer.

A truly elegant flowering shrub belonging to perhaps the showiest genus of the tropics is *Hibiscus rosa-sinensis* 'Plenus' (double rose of China). Hibiscus can bloom in winter and spring as well as summer if the light is strong enough and the plant is fed and watered generously. *Hydrangea macrophylla* cultivars are often forced into bloom for Easter or Mother's Day. The large flowers are

A Flowering Shrub for the Indoor Garden:
Although tricky to bring into bloom indoors, *Gardenia jasminoides* is a true showpiece with its hauntingly fragrant, waxy-petaled, cream-colored flowers. These exquisite blooms are framed effectively by the glossy, deep green leaves of this woody, evergreen plant.

available in shades of white, pink, red, blue, and purple.

Also splendid is the spring- to summer-blooming *Ixora coccinea* (flame of the woods), producing clusters of star-shaped rose to red flowers from an early age and capable of flowering intermittently if branchlet tips are pinched back. Valued for its fernlike foliage in its juvenile stage as well as for its silky blue-violet flower panicles in spring, *Jacaranda acutifolia* (mimosa-leaved ebony) is a semievergreen tree which loses some leaves before putting forth its large flower clusters.

Further information on these and other flowering shrubs can be found in Flower Fragrances and Fragrant Flowers and Plants for Chilly Rooms, and also in the Encyclopedia section.

FLOWERING VINES

If floor space is limited, indoor gardeners can choose from a vast number of lush flowering vines that can be coaxed around window frames, or trailing types that can lend great beauty to a hanging basket. A lovely cascading variety of flowering maple is *Abutilon megapotamicum* 'Variegata' (trailing abutilon), which offers creamy white to yellow, variegated, arrow-shaped leaves and highly decorative, lemon-shaded flowers with red calyxes which appear from May to October. If primed with lots of sun, food, humidity, warmth, and water, the impressive-looking *Allamanda cathartica* 'Hendersonii' (golden trumpet) will send forth golden blooms up to seven inches (18 cm) across in summer and fall.

A traditional favorite in greenhouses, *Bougainvillea* will bloom in spring and intermittently year-round if given the place of honor in a sunny window, kept somewhat on the dry side, and provided with warm temperatures. An excellent trailing basket plant, *Browallia speciosa* 'Major' (sapphire flower) is also capable of blooming almost continuously and will flower at the end of winter if started in July. The twiner *Ipomoea alba* (moonflower) is a night-bloomer offering large, sweet-smelling white flowers.

Very attractive even when not flowering and gorgeous when it proliferates red flowers with creamy white sepals in spring and summer and perhaps again in fall, *Clerodendrum thomsoniae* (glorybower or bleeding-heart vine) can be trained around a picture window. A climbing shrub that can produce beautiful, funnel-shaped, rose-pink flowers with a yellow throat year-round is *Mandevilla* ×*amabilis* (Mexican love vine); a good cultivar for indoors is the hybrid 'Alice Du Pont'.

The rather voluptuously beautiful *Fuchsia* was a heavy-blooming favorite in the Victorian conservatory, and in recent years hanging basket types bred to be somewhat tolerant of dry air and hot sun have enjoyed cycles of popularity as house plants. Fuchsias are capable of blooming year-round, although

(continued on page 224)

Geraniums on the Windowsill: These lovely blooming plants are long-time favorites, and deservedly so, for they bloom readily indoors, producing numbers of brightly colored clusters. Geraniums bloom at different times throughout the year, and their cheerful colors are especially welcome in winter. In this particular setting they enhance the springlike feeling created by the use of vivid, vibrant pink and greens— all in contrast with the snow-covered scene outdoors.

A Geranium by Any Other Name . . . Is a Pelargonium

Perhaps the most durable and enduring of flowering house plants, geraniums are affectionately nurtured and exchanged around the world, everywhere embodying the spirit of comfortable domesticity and neighborliness and endearing themselves by their ease of culture and propagation and variety of effect. There are as many as 8,000 cultivars of these herbs and shrubs, all belonging to the Geranium family (Geraniaceae) but divided among the genera *Pelargonium* and *Geranium*. Derived from the Greek word for crane, the term geranium was used by Pliny the Elder in the first century A.D. to identify a European plant with long, pointed seed cases resembling that bird's bill. The crane's bill geranium which Pliny named grows wild in the temperate zones of the Northern Hemisphere, and is cultivated annually, biennially, or perennially in Europe and North America. Variously called "herb Robert," "Robin redshanks" and "meadow crane's bill," the cultivated varieties of this wild geranium are used today in rock gardens. Like other "true" geraniums, it has flowers with five petals that are about the same in size. Authentic geraniums are in most locations herbaceous rather than woody, and are often able to withstand freezing temperatures. Many of the plants popularly called geraniums do not share these characteristics; they are more or less woody subshrubs that die if subjected to more than light frost and have irregular flowers with two upper petals usually wider than the three lower ones. More definitively, members of the genus *Pelargonium* differ from *Geranium* species in having flowers with nectaries lodged inside distinctive tubular spurs reaching from the calyx down to the pedicel. (Established by the French scientist L'Heritier, who claimed to have assembled 45 geraniums by 1789, the genus *Pelargonium* takes its name from the Greek word *pelargos,* which means stork, and the name stresses the relationship of these plants to the European crane's bill.)

The perennial evergreen *Pelargonium* cultivars we grow on windowsills, in hanging baskets, in urns or tubs, or massed to stunning effect in borders or gardens are natives of South Africa that began their far-ranging travels when an English sailing vessel made a stop for repairs in that part of the world. While waiting for his ship to be made seaworthy, the captain explored the coastal forests and plateaus of the area. He brought back to his vessel a woody herb covered with bright flowers and scented leaves that filled his quarters with a pleasant fragrance all the way home. In England, the geranium was given the usual royal welcome accorded exotic plants, and it grew well in the damp, mild climate. From then on, the English as well as Dutch colonists, traders, missionaries, and sea captains brought infinite variations of this plant from South Africa. Unfortunately, the Dutch — who claimed the territory and all things in it — accused the British of invasion, and the geranium caused an international rift that lasted almost a century.

In America, the first mention of geraniums appeared in a 1760 letter to the famous nurseryman John Bartram of Philadelphia; the English associate who wrote it enclosed seeds. The geranium was to become the most popular colonial flower, for it was readily reproduced through cuttings or would flower in five to eight months from seeds tucked in a letter, and had sufficient toughness to survive a westward trek and put forth a brave flash of color in the dust by the door of a new homestead. Over the past century, these plants have come to represent hospitality as well as home, and the exchange of geranium slips between enthusiasts has become customary in the more rural areas. Geraniums have had a utilitarian season in America, too: their cinnamon-, nutmeg-, or lemon-scented leaves often have been used in place of expensive spices to flavor roasts, jams, and preserves.

Today's geranium fanciers can choose from three major kinds (including some spectacular subdivisions) and from a host of interspecific hybrids and miscellaneous plants, many of which are both novel and curious. Known for its ability to flower year-round in bright sun, the very popular *Pelargonium* ×*hortorum,* called garden, cannon, or fish geranium, or even zonal geranium (a term more correctly applied to *P. zonale*), offers globular clusters of scalloped, roundish leaves. The Carefree series of hybrids — in

white, pink, red, and bicolors — are grown from seeds and accept high summer temperatures; *P.* ×*hortorum* 'Carefree Deep Salmon' was an All-America selection. Some of the most prized garden geraniums are those with colored leaves, such as the famous tricolor geranium *P.* ×*hortorum* 'Miss Burdett Coutts'. There is also a plethora of wonderfully appealing dwarf and semidwarf forms (see chapter 22) and a group of fancy-flowered types with blooms resembling carnations, rosebuds, poinsettia flowers (with narrow, twisted petals) or "bird's eggs" (bird's-egg cultivars have petals flecked with small dots).

Usually trailing types that can grow up to six feet (1.8 m) in a temperate climate (twice as far in the subtropics), *P. peltatum* cultivars are known as ivy geraniums because of their growth habit and their shiny, ivylike leaves with lighter-colored veins. Several ivy types introduced in the 1880s and still much in demand are 'Charles Turner' (double blooms of deep rose-pink); 'Galilee' (large doubles of light, clear pink); and the very respected 'L'Elegante' (white singles tinted with lavender and having dark throat markings and waxy leaves of gray-green edged in cream). Newer favorites include the striking Mexican 'Rouletta' (white double flowers broadly bordered with dark crimson); and the well-known 'Sybil Holmes' (a slow grower with large double blooms of deep, silvery pink resembling the flowers of the 'Sweetheart' rose). Also worthwhile is the Deacon series of floribundas —

new hybrids of the ivy and miniature geranium. Available in shades such as scarlet, orange, coral, and neon pink, the Deacons are almost spherical plants of self-branching, large, upright habit, which offer numerous globes of flowers at a time.

The third major grouping of geraniums embraces *P.* ×*domesticum,* known variously as the show or regal or Martha or Lady Washington geranium (often called the Martha or Lady Washington pelargonium). Derived from as many as 20 species in pure or hybrid form, regals are larger than garden geraniums, attaining up to three feet (90 cm), and generate larger flowers of white or in the pink to purple range and dark green serrated leaves of heart or kidney shape. Generally boasting three to five shades or colors, flowers are splashed, "washed," lined, veined, or feathered with darker colors, creating a rich, velvety pansylike look. Needing low night temperatures in order to bloom indoors in March, regals are not as dependable as other geraniums when grown indoors under average conditions. A few of the most popular of the more compact and easy-to-grow regals best suited to life indoors are 'Earliana' (blooms primarily orchid with upper petals maroon, rose, and white margined); 'Edith North' (shades of salmon-pink with dark brown splashes); 'Madame Layal' (white, rose-tinted and veined bottom petals, with upper petals violet and white edged); 'Marie Vogel' (single red blooms flushed with salmon, wavy petals); and 'White

(box continued on next page)

A Geranium by Any Other Name . . . Is a Pelargonium (continued)

Champion' (huge, pansy-shaped flowers of glistening white).

The scented-leaved geraniums so popular with herb gardeners include various species, hybrids, and cultivars available in a surprising range of flower, fruit, and spice fragrances, including apple-mint, coconut, and old spice! The aroma is released when the lobed foliage is rubbed between the fingers. Most of these plants have unimpressive flowers; their foliage, however, is quite varied in shape and texture. A few of the more attractive and smaller cultivars are 'Pretty Polly' (very compact; almond scented with pink flowers); 'Lemon Crispum' (strong lemon scent and lavender flowers); and 'Prince Rupert Variegated' (lemony, parsleylike leaves and orchid-lavender blooms).

Geranium lovers with a taste for the unusual enjoy the more striking cultivars of the zonal geranium such as 'Double New Life', which proudly waves red and white striped petals and is often called 'Stars and Stripes'. Among the regal geraniums are the extraordinary "black-flowered pelargoniums" such as the vigorous, compact 'Black Magic' and 'Black Lace', a superb hanging basket plant having spectacular red-black flowers with orange stamens. There are also many curious species of pelargoniums that make novel house plants. *P. echinatum* and *P. fulgidum* are tuberous "cactus geraniums" having succulent, spiny stems and waxy leaves which they lose during summer dormancy, usually sending forth their small flowers in winter. Also deciduous is *P. gibbosum*, called the "gouty geranium" because its yellow-green flowers appear in spring on stems grossly swollen at the nodes.

they flower most exuberantly during the long days of spring to fall.

A lovely accent plant with pleasant foliage and vivid, handsomely stamened lily flowers that change in color as the blooms age, *Gloriosa rothschildiana* (climbing glory lily) will flower on a support or in a hanging basket.

Offering myriads of charming little tubular red and yellow flowers in winter, the twining *Manettia inflata* (firecracker vine) thrives in a small pot and likes warmth.

The many species of the popular twiner *Passiflora* (passionflower) are prized for their large, showy blooms and sometimes for edible fruits; a fragrant, free-blooming hybrid that can be grown around a window and produces multicolored, intricate flowers in summer even when young is *P.* ×*alatocaerulea*.

A good basket plant that can flower almost continuously, *Russelia equisetiformis* (coral plant) needs maximum light and copious water. In a bright, cool window, the stem-twiner *Thunbergia alata* (black-eyed Susan vine) will provide cheerful yellow to orange, funnel-shaped flowers with a black-purple throat. The everblooming *Tripogandra multiflora* (Tahitian bridal veil) with its tiny white flowers is another splendid trailer. (For the names of more exquisite climbing or trailing flowering plants, see Flower Fragrances and Fragrant Flowers.)

SPECIAL CULTURAL CONSIDERATIONS FOR FLOWERING PLANTS

Successful flowering requires somewhat more humidity than does foliage production; indeed, bud drop or drying can frequently be traced to inadequate relative humidity. The best relative humidity for most flowering plants is from 40 to 50 percent — a range in which flowers also often last longer.

Another difference between plants grown for their flowers and those valued for their foliage occurs in light requirements. As a general rule more natural or artificial light is needed for flowering plants. An unobstructed southern exposure is necessary for optimum blooming of many, but not all, flowering

Trailing or Climbing Flowering Vine: *Manettia inflata* will adapt itself to your particular space either by dangling gracefully from a hanging basket or by climbing up a support. Along its vining branches appear myriads of bright red, yellow-tipped tubular flowers which have given *Manettia* its common name of firecracker plant.

plants. Certain flowering plants, such as African violets and other gesneriads, can succeed in an eastern exposure, as can some orchids.

Where feeding is concerned, it is possible to make a distinction between flowering plants and those grown only for foliage. Generally, flowering plants should be fertilized more often than foliage plants because they are growing at higher light levels. Also, nitrogen should be decreased and phosphorus increased as the time for flowering approaches, for too much nitrogen at this time favors vegetative over reproductive development. One way to insure an adequate initial supply of phosphorus is to incorporate a tablespoon (15 ml) of bone meal in each quart (1.1 l) of growing medium. Later applications of phosphorus can be provided by a water-soluble organic fertilizer rich in phosphorus. During

the nonflowering or vegetative growth phases of flowering plants they may be given the same kind and amount of food as foliage plants.

Adequate ventilation is also needed for sturdy, vigorous flowering plants. Unventilated areas with plants tend to develop carbon dioxide depletion and excess water vapor around the plants. Low carbon dioxide reduces photosynthesis and thereby limits growth, and too much moisture favors disease. Movement of people nearby will help keep the air circulating, as will providing occasional fresh air via a window opened in an adjoining room. Avoid direct drafts of cold air on plants during the winter.

Many flowering plants in their natural habitats undergo a period of decreased growth or rest known as dormancy. In some cases this dormant period is necessary if flowers are to be produced again. With other plants, long-term vigor and good blossoming are enhanced when dormancy is initiated indoors. In the home there is an absence of environmental cues for dormancy such as cold (for temperate zone plants) or decreasing rain and/or temperature changes (for plants of tropical origin). Therefore the grower must supply these stimuli by lowering the temperature (and perhaps light, if the plant is being grown under artificial illumination) or decreasing water as indicated. Any plant in a dormant condition should have less water and fertilizer. (See the Encyclopedia section for details on dormancy requirements for specific plants.)

House plants are often pruned from time to time to control size or improve appearance. In many woody house plants the use of pruning may improve flower or fruit production. Some general rules when pruning woody flowering shrubs and vines are to remove dead or dying shoot growth, to prune back to just above a bud, and to remove rapidly growing soft shoots (watersprouts). Older shoots are cut back to encourage new shoots to take their place.

Winter and Early-Spring-Blooming Plants for Chilly Rooms

All of the following plants can thrive and flower handsomely at temperatures as low as 50°F (10°C). Some of them will accept even colder locations, as indicated, while those marked with an asterisk prefer temperatures of 55° to 60°F (13° to 16°C), but will tolerate 50°F (10°C). For information on popular bulb plants that do well in cool rooms, see chapter 18 and the Encyclopedia section.

Abutilon spp. (flowering maple)

Calceolaria spp. (pocket book plant or slipperwort)

Calendula officinalis (pot marigold)

Camellia japonica hybrids (camellia); 40°F (4°C) or higher.

*Carissa grandiflora (Natal plum)

Chrysanthemum frutescens 'Chrysaster' (Boston yellow daisy)

*Cyclamen persicum (Alpine or Persian violet)

Cytisus canariensis (genista); keep cool and dry at 40°F (5°C), raising temperature slightly to force for Easter bloom.

Daphne odora 'Marginata' (variegated winter daphne)

Hermannia verticillata (honey bells)

Jasminum polyanthum (pink jasmine)

Lachenalia aloides and L. bulbiferum (Cape cowslip)

*Lantana camara (yellow sage) and L. montevidensis (weeping lantana)

Lotus berthelotii (parrot's beak or coral gem)

*Malpighia coccigera (miniature or Singapore holly)

*Ornithogalum umbellatum and O. arabicum (star of Bethlehem)

Osmanthus fragrans (sweet olive)

Oxalis spp. such as O. braziliensis, O. pes-caprae, O. purpurea, and O. regnellii

*Pittosporum tobira (Australian laurel, mock orange)

Primula malacoides (fairy or baby primrose)

Prostanthera rotundifolia (round-leaf mint bush)

Rhododendron hybrids (azaleas)

Senecio × hybridus (cineraria)

Veltheimia viridifolia (veltheimia); 45°F (7°C) or higher.

For one way to assure the consistently cool root temperatures that keep cool-growing plants at their best, see the project, Build Your Own Cold-Air Window Box, in chapter 28.

WHEN PLANTS DON'T FLOWER

Sooner or later some flowering plant will fail to show off its beauty, even though you think you did everything right. If so, there are a number of questions to consider.

1. Is the plant in too large a container?

Some plants, such as many gesneriads or bulbs like the amaryllis, bloom better when potbound. These plants appear to direct activities mostly to the growth of roots and shoots until the restriction of space signals a change to flower production.

2. Has the plant been repotted lately?

Certain species or genera such as *Clivia* respond to transplanting by failure to bloom for some time afterward — a phenomenon that may be related to the need for being potbound. Plants of this type should have the top third of their soil mix replaced in lieu of transplanting until repotting becomes absolutely necessary.

3. Is the reluctant bloomer getting enough phosphorus?

If the soil pH is below 6.0 or above 7.5, phosphorus forms chemical complexes which make it unavailable to plants; as a result, it is often a limiting nutrient in pot culture. Shy bloomers may be encouraged by a pH change or perhaps simply by adding supplemental phosphorus.

4. Might a change of temperature induce flowering?

Bulbs such as tulips and hyacinths need a month or two of cold conditions before they will bloom; the same is true of some cool-growing orchids, such as odontoglossums from high altitudes. Cacti often bloom after exposure to temperatures of 45° to 50°F (7° to 10°C) for several weeks. Other plants such as African violets may bloom after exposure to warmer temperatures.

5. Does the plant have special day-length needs?

Some plants will bloom only when subjected to darkness for a certain number of hours each day. Examples include poinsettias, kalanchoes, Thanksgiving cactus, and Christmas cactus. In some cases this need can be eliminated by changing the temperature. In others the only course is to artificially darken the plants by shading them with black cloth or putting them in a closet each night for the required number of hours. Even an incandescent bulb turned on briefly can disrupt this procedure.

6. Could the plant be too young to flower?

Certain plants, particularly woody-stemmed perennials, will not bloom until they reach several years of age. In recognizing whether this is the problem, it helps to know what the earliest blooming age is for the plant. It is wise to inquire about blooming age when you purchase the plant.

If none of the above information seems to apply to your problem plant, bear in mind that if cultural conditions are favoring too much leafy growth, flower clusters may be suffering. The answer just might be to raise or lower the humidity or to cut back the plant rather severely or cut way back on watering to curb the growth of vegetation (withholding water is often very effective with impatiens, for example). With certain plants such as bromeliads, the gases released from an apple may help (see chapter 14).

CHAPTER 13

Gesneriads

To many people, gesneriads mean African violets. Discovered by Baron Walter von St. Paul in Usambara (now Tanzania) in 1892, these now-famous plants and their seeds were sent to the baron's father in Germany where they were shared with the Director of the Imperial Botanic Garden near Hanover. The flowering response of the genus *Saintpaulia,* as it came to be called, was to revolutionize house plant growing, for these tropical perennials could bloom throughout the year at relatively low levels of illumination. They also have proved to be ideal subjects for light gardening.

In recent years, however, indoor gardeners have been discovering that a host of other plants in the Gesneriad family share the beauty, floriferousness, and ease of culture of the African violet, while offering an astonishing diversity of habit, of interestingly colored and textured foliage, and of flower shapes and shades. For sheer variety of appearance and appeal, perhaps no other plant family has the range of this one, which embraces plants as different as the elegant florists' gloxinia *(Sinningia speciosa),* the graceful and versatile *Streptocarpus saxorum,* the dazzling, multicolored *Episcia,* the cheerfully flashy *Aeschynanthus,* the succulent *Chirita,* and the strangely beautiful *Nematanthus.*

A medium size family of plants, the Gesneriaceae were named in 1693 in honor of the celebrated naturalist Konrad Gesner, who lived from 1516 to 1565. There are about 120 genera and over 2,000 species of gesneriads. Perhaps 300 species are in cultivation, together with a substantial and constantly increasing number of cultivars and hybrids. Most members of the Gesneriad family come from the tropics of the world, but a few originate in the temperate zones.

SOME GESNERIAD BOTANY

Gesneriad flowers feature a corolla with a short to long tube usually consisting of five partially united petals (lobes), and can be divided symmetrically along one plane. Found singly or on short stems emerging from an elongated axis (a raceme) or on floral axes terminating in a series of single flowers, each of which arises from a single point (a cyme). Often the gesneriad flower is two lipped, having two smaller, upper lobes and three larger, lower lobes. Certain forms of the florists' gloxinia and all *Sinningia cardinalis* 'Kalmbacher' plants are the exception, for they have circular flowers with five or more lobes roughly equal in size. Gesneriad flowers have from two to five stamens fused in pairs or joined together in a ring or square.

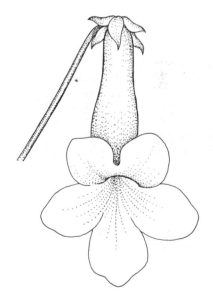

Gesneriad Flower Structure: This illustration shows how the elongated tube flares out at the end to form an upper lip of two smaller lobes and a lower lip composed of three larger lobes.

Opposite, cape primrose, Streptocarpus *hybrid, in full bloom.*

Stems are simple or branched, and leaves are simple and basically oval or spatulate, broadening toward the tip. They can be positioned on the stem opposite one another, alternate, or whorled in a basal rosette. In some species true leaves are lacking; instead only one seed-leaf (cotyledon) continues to grow after germination, looking and functioning like a leaf. Blades are simple, usually toothed and sometimes unequal in each pair. Some gesneriads bear small vegetative reproductive structures (propagules) in their leaf axils or inflorescences. These shoots can be removed and rooted to propagate new plants. Roots can be fibrous, tuberous, or of a scaly rhizomatous nature, with stolons sometimes present.

Although some members of this plant family are trees and shrubs, the house plants of the group are terrestrial herbs or epiphytic subshrubs or vines. The Gesneriad family is divided into two subfamilies. The Old World subfamily (Cyrtandroideae) is characterized by flowers having superior ovaries (that is, the entire ovary is above the base of the corolla). It includes five tribes, one of which—Didymocarpeae—includes the very popular *Saintpaulia* and *Streptocarpus* genera. Most of the remaining genera discussed in this chapter belong to the ten tribes comprising the New World subfamily (Gesnerioideae). In these plants, the ovary is inferior, much or all of it being located in the stalk below the bottom of the corolla.

GROUPS OF GESNERIADS

Botanist Henry Teuscher has divided gesneriads into five groups according to their root structure and/or growth habitats. These are the rock-dwellers, the tuberous types, the scaly-rhizomed gesneriads, the terrestrials with fibrous roots, and the epiphytic gesneriads with fibrous roots. Here is a closer look at some of the more widely cultivated plants belonging to these classifications and their differing cultural requirements.

ROCK-DWELLERS

Saintpaulia

African violets have come a long way in the United States since the firm of Armacost and Royston first secured seeds from Germany and England in 1927. Bred extensively to obtain a wider and richer selection of flower colors and to heighten intriguing variations in foliage, saintpaulias began to achieve public favor in the mid-1940s. In the years since, these hairy tropical perennials have become the most popular of gesneriads, for the genus is easy to grow, can flower year-round on a windowsill, and is a seemingly inexhaustible cornucopia of blossom forms and colors and leaf shapes and shadings.

The *Saintpaulia* species from which today's full size and miniature plants have been bred may be divided into two groups, based on growth habit. Some of the more commonly hybridized species such as *S. diplotricha, S. ionantha, S. orbicularis,* and *S. tongwensis* take the form of an open rosette, whereas species like *S. goetzeana,*

Open Rosette: This African violet shows the characteristic rosette form. Although there are also trailing and upright violets, the rosette type is most commonly seen in indoor culture.

S. grotei, and *S. magungensis* have a trailing or creeping habit, with a stem that roots at the nodes and leaves growing alternately on the sides of the stem. Recently hybridizers seeking perfection of form and improved performance have begun to cross these distinctly different types. Their object is to combine the better characteristics of creepers like *S. grotei,* which has attractively thin leaf blades and advantageously wiry leaf stalks, with the shiny or interestingly patterned leaves or the more appealing growth habit and flowers of various rosette-shaped saintpaulias.

African violet leaves run a gamut of shapes. They can be narrow to broadly ovate, sometimes slightly oblong, heart shaped, round, or rhombic. Species plants of the rosette type have rather oval, somewhat pointed leaves, while trailing species have roundish leaves. To add to the forms possible, leaves of these shapes can be unruffled and plain green in color (the so-called "boy" foliage), or notched or scalloped and with a white area at the base of the leaf ("girl" foliage). Leaves also can be bent, wavy, or spooned (that is, curled upward more or less sharply along the sides), and variegated or even albino.

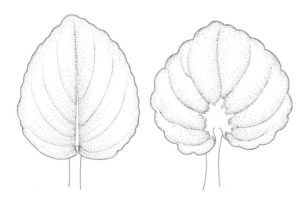

"Boy" and "Girl" Foliage: There are two basic variations on leaf edging and color which appear in African violet foliage. The "boy" foliage on the left is solid green and smooth along the edges. In contrast, the "girl" foliage on the right features a white spot at the leaf base, and has notched or scalloped edges.

The flowers of African violets occur singly or in small clusters on axillary peduncles. They range in color from a deep, intense purple through blue-violet, wine red, and pink-violet, to pink, bluish, and white. Usually the blooms are of a single color, but they can be two-toned (featuring two shades of one color) or multicolored (having two or more different colors). There is also great variety in flower structure. Blossoms can be single (that is, having two upper lobes and three lower ones), semidouble (having more than five petals but not ten), double (having at least two layers of petals), or star shaped. The so-called "Geneva" cultivars have flowers edged in white. Fringed blossom types are deeply serrated or have fringed outer petals, whereas Amazon-flowered violets are distinguished by thicker petals with a rather firm texture.

The key to successful African violet culture is consistent care. Since these plants are rock-dwellers in their native habitats, they need a porous, well-drained soil which retains moisture well. Preferring a temperature of 65°F (18°C) or higher year-round, the genus *Saintpaulia* is one of the few that tolerate temperatures above 85°F (29°C).

African violets can thrive in east, west, or southeast or southwest windows, though the strong midday sun pouring into south windows in late spring and summer should be countered by moving plants away from the glass somewhat, or by using a thin curtain or a venetian blind with the slats angled upward during the brightest hours. Plants under lights can be placed from six to ten inches (15 to 25 cm) below a fixture with two 40-watt fluorescent tubes; the closer distance is best handled by younger plants being coaxed into bloom. Actually, the higher the light level African violets can tolerate without bleaching, the richer their colors will be and the more profusely they will flower. Although these plants can bloom with 600 footcandles of light or less, the optimum range is 1,000 to 1,500 footcandles.

Both sufficient intensity and adequate

Saintpaulia Varieties: Choosing the Best from All the Rest

Each year more versions of America's favorite house plant make their debut in the already crowded benches and catalogs of gesneriad dealers. And each looks more tempting than the last. Amid this effusion of saintpaulias, how is the new—or even the experienced—enthusiast to separate truly outstanding African violets from the novelty plants destined to be passing fancies?

The answer to this nagging question lies with Madeline Gonzalez, a dedicated Californian who from 1970 to 1978 compiled yearly lists of the best in African violets. Sidetracked for a while by a heart attack, Mrs. Gonzalez now is back doing what she loves—"helping with African Violet Society of America work." As this interest implies, the saintpaulias featured on her lists are not just personal favorites—they are consensus choices emerging from a poll of members of the society, who each year are asked to submit a list of 25 favorite African violets. Approximately 2,000 growers respond, and Mrs. Gonzalez places all cultivars receiving at least 50 votes on a Best Varieties list, which is duly published in *The African Violet Magazine.*

Those violets which rank among the Best Varieties for five consecutive years are elevated to the Honor Roll. Obviously highly selective, this ultimate list is a broad-based, impartial record of saintpaulias of enduring appeal, and growers who want to collect plants of excellent quality might do well to concentrate on members of the Honor Roll.

According to Madeline Gonzalez, the highest scorers to date on the Honor Roll are 'Tommie Lou', which appeared on the select list in 1969, and 'Miriam

One Expert's Favorites: This selection of *Saintpaulia* cultivars comes from Anne Tinari, a well-known authority on African violets. Clockwise from the front, the plants are 'Tommy Lou', 'Poodle Top', 'Eternal Snow', 'Tina', and 'Wisteria'.

Steele', which is among the 12 most recent introductions to the Honor Roll. Favored primarily for its unusually beautiful variegated foliage, 'Tommie Lou' also offers creamy white, double blossoms tinged with lavender. 'Miriam Steele' has green leaves and is prized for its exceptionally large, white semidouble flowers.

In addition to 'Miriam Steele', the latest additions to the African violet Honor Roll include 'Garnet Elf', with pansy-faced, deep red, single flowers with white edges; 'Like Wow', having large, semidouble, royal purple, star-shaped blossoms with white edges; 'Mary D', a double, dark red, star-flowered type with plain tailored foliage; 'Ballet Lisa', a frilled, bright pink single with plain foliage; 'Cordelia', offering big, double, pink blooms with variegated foliage like that of 'Tommie Lou'; 'Granger's Pink Swan', a plant with huge, shell-pink, semidouble flowers; 'Pocono Mountain', a semidouble, purple, star-shaped flower with darker purple edges and tricolored foliage; 'Richter's Step-up', with large, deep blue, semidouble blooms and smooth ovate leaves; 'Starshine', which is considered the best of the saintpaulias with single white flowers; 'Whirlaway', with huge, double-blue blooms with white edges and dark foliage; and 'Wisteria', which sports double lavender blooms and plain glossy foliage.

duration of light must be provided for regular and plentiful flowering. When natural light is being used this means at least 6 to 8 hours of light a day that is bright enough to produce a faint shadow when a hand is held just above the plant. Plants growing under artificial lights need from 12 to 18 hours a day. (Note: African violets with dark green leaves need slightly more light than variegated types or those with lighter green foliage.)

If a saintpaulia is receiving too much illumination, it will react promptly by displaying drooping yellow leaves with burned margins; if it is not getting enough light, foliage will be dark green and ascending and flower count will be poor. Many variegated violets will turn all green if given insufficient light and also will become less variegated at temperatures above 70°F (21°C). The cultivar 'Nancy Reagan', for example, will lose its white coloring in summer. Other African violets with variegated foliage, such as the white-flecked 'Lillian Garret', keep their variegation during the high temperatures of summer. Changes in variegation are probably linked to yearly cycles rather than to temperature; however, the variegated violets will not grow well in relatively low light and high temperatures.

To promote the symmetry so prized in rosette-type saintpaulias, remove the scraggly leaves at the bottom of the plants and give their pots a quarter-turn daily, or at least weekly. Offsets marring the cartwheel shape of a plant may be removed and potted up separately, and plants beginning to tilt because they are planted too high may be repotted somewhat lower. When a violet becomes too "long necked" for this remedy, it may be rejuvenated as described later, under Propagation.

When repotting violets, you can help the plants reestablish themselves more quickly by removing all buds and blooms and not applying fertilizer. The transplants will take from six to eight weeks to flower again. *Saintpaulia* plants prefer small pots, thriving in containers that are one-third as wide as the plant's diameter.

African violets are easily killed by overwatering, and if you are not using an automatic watering setup, water the plants only when their topsoil is almost dry. A high humidity of 50 to 60 percent is desirable if your plants are to flourish at relatively low light

Display of Flower Forms: Whether your taste runs to the plain or fancy, the infinite variations possible in flower color and form insure that there will be an African violet that appeals to you. Shown here is just a sampling of the possibilities, starting clockwise from the top with a single, two-toned lavender blossom. The relative simplicity of that bloom contrasts with the fringed petals and white edging on the neighboring flowers. The next violet is an Amazon-flowered type, with thick, firm-textured, deep purple petals. 'Geneva' cultivars are easy to spot, with their white edging that offers a crisp contrast to the rich petal shades. Completing this panorama of violets are the double, fringed pink blooms on the plant at the left, which create a luxurious, full appearance.

levels. They can, however, flower abundantly at a humidity as low as 30 percent if given at least 500 footcandles of light.

Ease of propagation is one of the characteristics that have endeared African violets to indoor gardeners. The plants are renewed readily by taking leaf cuttings, and by crown division and offsets—the two surest ways to pass on variegated foliage. Trailing plants may be multiplied from stem cuttings, and all types may be grown from seeds, which should be planted atop a fine-textured medium like sand or perlite and kept continually moist in a warm and humid (but occasionally ventilated) environment. Seeds will germinate in two or three weeks but may take up to a year to become flowering plants.

Streptocarpus

Including both rock-dwellers and some epiphytic plants from moist forests, such as *S. kirkii* and *S. caulescens, Streptocarpus* is a genus of showy, low-growing perennial herbs with tubular, two-lipped or irregularly lobed flowers of violet, blue, white, pink, or crimson. This genus is native to South Africa and Madagascar, and features two distinctly different kinds of plants, which have been designated as the subgenera *Streptocarpus* and *Streptocarpella.*

Plants of the subgenus *Streptocarpus* are unifoliate—that is, one seed-leaf continues to develop and the second one withers away. In species such as *S. dunnii,* this is the only leaf the plant will ever produce. In other species, leaves develop on the petiolode, which is the root-initiating section of the short stalk connecting the seed-leaves with the anchoring roots. These leaves are some distance below the inflorescence of the first leaf and produce their own roots in turn. A third form, represented by *S. rexii,* is produced by elongation of the petiolode, from which individual leaves arise, each capable of generating a series of flowering stalks. Commonly called the cape primrose, *S. rexii* is a parent of many cultivars and hybrids currently widely grown in the United States and recommended for their ease of culture.

Plants of the *Streptocarpus* subgenus are easy to grow so long as their four basic requirements are met: cool temperatures, plenty of light but no direct sunlight (dappled sun is acceptable), perfect drainage, and ample moisture. During the active growth of summer the night temperature should be between 60° and 65°F (16° and 18°C) and the daytime temperature between 75° and 80°F (24° and 27°C). In the semidormant growth phase during the winter a range of 50°F (10°C) at night to 65°F (18°C) during the day, and reduced watering are desirable.

The 1:1:1 Cornell soil mix described later under Growing Media and Fertilizers is satisfactory if two to four tablespoons (30 to 60 ml) of ground eggshells are added to each quart (1.1 l). *Streptocarpus* species do not respond well to mixes high in peat moss, and their soil should be kept less acidic than that of many other gesneriads.

Plants should be kept slightly potbound and should never be watered directly into the crown. A moderately high humidity is necessary to keep leaf margins from browning.

The *Streptocarpella* subgenus features plants of a different structure requiring slightly different care. The streptocarpellas are not unifoliate, but display a more usual pattern of leaf growth. Unlike the unifoliate types, they are caulescent (having stems), and they develop as regular short-stemmed rosettes or as regular branched herbs with normal leaves issuing from vegetative buds on the petiolode. Plants of the *Streptocarpella* subgenus include the exceptionally beautiful hanging basket plant *Streptocarpus saxorum, S. caulescens, S. holstii, S. kirkii,* and *S. stomandrus.* Such plants are easier to grow than the unifoliate types, for they do not rot as readily.

Preferring a rich blend of 3 parts peat moss, 2 parts vermiculite, and 1 part perlite, they thrive in high temperatures of 65° to 80°F (18° to 27°C) and constant moisture. Streptocarpellas can be propagated readily by stem cuttings.

S. saxorum requires natural light to flower decently, but other "streps" of both kinds are good light garden subjects. Plants of this genus have been hybridized extensively. A very colorful strain of hybrids was developed by Carl Fleischmann of Wiesmoor, West Germany. Boasting flowers with fringed or wavy edges that reach up to five inches (13 cm) in diameter, the Wiesmoor hybrids have been grown from seeds by many home gardeners.

Contributing even more to the spiraling interest in "streps" as house plants is the chain of events growing out of work done at the John Innes Institute in England. In 1946, horticulturists there developed the prize-winning S. 'Constant Nymph'—the culmination of nearly 15 years of plant breeding. Twenty years later in the Netherlands, vegetatively produced plantlets arising from single cells of a 'Constant Nymph' leaf were irradiated with X rays to produce mutant plants having a flower color different from the intermediate blue of 'Constant Nymph'. Plants also were treated with a chemical called colchicine to increase their chromosome count. The resulting 'Nymph' cultivars have flowers in rich hues of blue or purple and are among today's favorite *Streptocarpus* hybrids. So is the natural mutant 'Maasen's White', which was developed in Holland.

Vying with those cultivars is a series of John Innes hybrids bearing women's names. Available in a spectrum of flower colors, the

Prolific Bloomer: *Streptocarpus* 'Maasen's White' is considered by many growers to be one of the best white cultivars for the indoors. A real powerhouse of a bloomer, it will produce many blooms over a long period of time without pause, and does especially well in light gardens.

The Inspiration for a Hybrid Series: *Streptocarpus* 'Constant Nymph' is the most popular hybrid, prized by gesneriad fanciers for its profusion of medium blue to purple flowers. From this plant has been bred a series of hybrids, fast becoming as widely grown as their forebear. These hybrids have characteristically wrinkled leaves and bloom throughout the year, with each flower lasting for several days.

Innes cultivars are smaller and more compact than the older Wiesmoor hybrids. They flower almost year-round under broad spectrum fluorescents and although they are descended from the cool-growing subgenus *Streptocarpus,* they do well at relatively high temperatures, in the range of 62°F (17°C) at night to 75°F (24°C) during the day.

In growing *Streptocarpus* species or cultivars, plants identical to the parent may be gotten through the vegetative propagation of leaf cuttings or sections or by suckers or crown division. However, the name "streptocarpus" means "twisted fruit," and the long and twisted seed pods of these plants unwind

Breeding a Plant for the Future

To a growing number of plant breeders and amateur plant enthusiasts, as well as professional horticulturists, the genus *Streptocarpus* represents an exciting potential for future development. One such dedicated researcher is Christian Hopka, a horticulturist and greenhouse curator with the Department of Horticulture at the University of Wisconsin in Madison.

Throughout the four years in which he has been working with *Streptocarpus*, Chris feels he has been moving steadily toward his goal of an improved flowering pot plant.

What constitutes improvement? Cape primroses have several major drawbacks that professionals and amateurs both complain about. Many of the current cultivars produce very large and often brittle leaves. Also, plants frequently have an undesirable growth habit, being

In Search of the Perfect Cape Primrose: University horticulturist Christian Hopka breeds *Streptocarpus* hybrids, seeking the plant which will combine desirable growth habit with floriferousness and a less brittle leaf texture.

composed of few-leaved rosettes which often lack symmetry and are displeasing to the eye. Lastly

but most importantly, many cape primroses simply don't produce enough of their beautiful flowers. Hopka's goal as a breeder deals with these major problems. His ideal plants should be vigorous and compact with a lot of attractive foliage combined with a profusion of colorful flowers.

But the breeding process is long and arduous. Four years ago, Hopka and colleagues collected all the available hybrids and species and crossed the most promising plants. The resulting offspring (F, or first filial generation) of approximately 1,000 seedlings were reduced to the 10 "best" plants. These 10 selections were "selfed" (that is, self-pollinated to get another generation of plants, the F_2 generation) and approximately 5,000 plants were grown and screened, and narrowing his collection to 25 advanced selections. These plants are his "base" plants for breeding, and he uses them to

when dry and release seeds, from which new plants can be grown readily. Lightly cover the seeds with an equal mixture of fine sand, leaf mold, and loam and keep moist and shaded at 55° to 65°F (13° to 18°C). Propagating new plants from the seeds of 'Nymph' cultivars can result in especially intriguing and original specimens.

Other Rock-Dwelling Gesneriads

A very appealing rock-dwelling species is the Chinese, or silver, chirita *(Chirita sinensis),* a splendid-looking representative of the only truly succulent genus among the gesneriads. This chirita comes from Hong Kong and is a rosette plant growing to a height of about six inches (15 cm). It has quilted, deep green,

fleshy leaves to eight inches (20 cm) long, generously marked with silver. The funnel-shaped flowers have lavender lobes and white corollas with touches of yellow in the throat. The blooms appear in large clusters during the summer. Bright but diffused or dappled light is needed to assure flowering, and plants thrive on frequent watering (the foliage should never be wet, however), generous humidity, temperatures of 60°F (16°C) or above, and a humus-rich soil blend. Chiritas can be propagated from seeds or from tip or leaf cuttings.

Called the hidden violet, *Petrocosmea kerrii* is an especially worthwhile close relative of the African violet and needs the same general culture. In addition, though, it re-create new hybrids by, among other things, crossing them with wild *Streptocarpus* species native to Africa.

Perhaps the hardest part of any breeder's job is selecting the few superior seedlings which exhibit the characteristics he wants out of large populations, and ruthlessly eliminating the others. Chris can make 16 crosses in an afternoon, which can easily yield over 1,000 seedlings. Large numbers are necessary to see all the possible genetic variations and combinations. Fortunately, initial discards often have obvious defects or fail to meet certain objective, measurable standards. However, after that the process becomes more difficult. The final selections, or survivors, are often chosen by very subjective and intuitive decisions because horticultural beauty and a plant's overall effect cannot be easily quantified or scientifically measured.

How did a university horticulturist become involved with the breeding of a not-too-widely-grown gesneriad? Chris's interest began, he recalls, when he read that *Streptocarpus* was a popular indoor plant in Europe, where homes have traditionally been kept cooler than homes in the United States. The idea of a flowering plant that required less heat to bloom seemed awfully attractive in light of increasing energy costs. Until recent years, the need for cool temperatures made *Streptocarpus* difficult for amateur indoor gardeners to grow, and warmth-loving plants like African violets have been great favorites. Now that soaring heating costs are pushing thermostats lower, perhaps it is time for *Streptocarpus* to come into its own.

In 1946 the development of the hybrid 'Constant Nymph' revolutionized over 100 years of *Streptocarpus* breeding. This popular, medium blue hybrid,

developed at the John Innes Horticultural Institute in England, is freely flowering and very tolerant of cultural extremes. Since its development, Dutch scientists have x-ray treated the original "Nymph" and produced a series of mutation hybrids. The original 'Constant Nymph' and the subsequent mutations renewed interest in *Streptocarpus* breeding both in Europe and America, resulting in numerous new cultivars.

Some cultivars which Chris favors and which he feels would be good choices for home growers with a cool, bright environment, include the Innes 'Helen' and 'Margaret' hybrids, and all the plants in the "Nymph" series. Particularly recommended are 'Maasen's White' and the more recently introduced American hybrid 'Essue'. Generally, the blue- and purple-flowered plants are easiest to grow and flower, while the red and pink cultivars offer the greatest challenge.

quires a period of cool or intermediate temperatures to bring on flower bud formation. Growing on the floor of forests in southeast Asia, this aptly named plant has a low-lying rosette emerging from a thick rhizome and fleshy, quilted, pleasantly hairy leaves. The small flowers, which are usually concealed by the foliage, have white lower lobes and upper lobes that are white spotted with yellow. Plants can be propagated by division or from leaf cuttings.

GESNERIADS WITH SOLID, FLESHY TUBERS

Tuberous gesneriads are found in lateritic soils—that is, in the stony, clay, iron oxide-containing soils of Central and South America. As the formation of tubers suggests, these plants are native to regions that experience dry spells and they are able to endure drought for a period in their growth cycle. Many tuberous gesneriads go into dormancy for several months of the year, and water should then be withheld until the tubers send forth new shoots.

Sinningia

Containing over 75 species originating in the American tropics, the tuberous genus *Sinningia* is fast becoming one of the most appreciated gesneriads. Known as florists' gloxinia, the widely grown *S. speciosa* has been commercially available since 1817. This dramatic plant ranges from nearly stemless to 12 inches (30 cm) in height, having opposite, long-stalked, fuzzy leaves which are oblong or oblong-oval, toothed, and up to 8 inches (20 cm) or more long and 6 inches (15 cm) or more wide. The tubular or bell-shaped flowers attain a width of 3 to 6 inches (8 to 15 cm). *S. speciosa* plants have been divided into three convarieties (groups of cultivars). The Speciosa Group includes only the short and hairy wild plants native to Brazil, which have small, usually white or purple flowers. These tubular blooms are somewhat swollen on one side and droop downward, or "nod." Members of *S. speciosa* (Maxima Group), improved plants that are often called slipper gloxinias, have similar—but larger—flowers. This strain has been widely hybridized and is available in a host of flower colors. Plants in

The Florists' Gloxinia: This plant with its glorious, bright red blooms is also a *Sinningia speciosa*, but is a hybrid belonging to the Fyfiana Group. The spectacular, trumpet-shaped blooms are a familiar holiday sight, since this is the plant commonly sold under the name gloxinia by florists.

S. speciosa (Fyfiana Group) are derived from hybrids of the first two groups. They have been bred extensively and boast generous size, funnel-shaped flowers having from 5 to 12 equal lobes instead of upper and lower lobes of different size and shape. These trumpet-shaped flowers are held erect—an ornamental advantage which helps account for this group's great popularity as gift and holiday plants. The strong appeal of Fyfiana plants is also explained by the fact that they have been successfully bred to develop large clusters of flowers in the center of the crown.

There are numerous high-quality hybrids in the Speciosa and Fyfiana Groups available in flower colors ranging from white to dark blue and red. Sometimes the blooms are solid colored with white borders or cen-

The Native Gloxinia: In nature, the species form of *Sinningia speciosa* is short and bears small white or purple flowers which have a pouchlike underside. This plant grows wild in Brazil.

ters; they also can be speckled or streaked and sometimes are "doubles," having two layers of petals.

S. speciosa was first named *Gloxinia speciosa,* but under the International Rules of Botanical Nomenclature, the plant's name was changed to *S. speciosa.* Today the word gloxinia is often used as the common name for *S. speciosa* (in this book the phrase "florists' gloxinia" is used instead), and as the generic name for a group of completely different gesneriads. To complicate matters further, the former ×*Gloxinera* (members of a hybrid genus derived from crosses between *Rechsteineria* and *Sinningia* plants) and *Rechsteineria* species have been reclassified in the genus *Sinningia.*

One of the most noteworthy of these new sinningias is the cardinal flower, *S. cardinalis* (formerly *Rechsteineria cardinalis*). This compact but imposing plant has velvety green leaves and in late winter and spring puts forth vivid scarlet blooms covered with white down. The brilliant flowers have purple on their throats and projecting red filaments. To the untrained eye, the cardinal flower and other plants just added to this genus do not look like the more familiar sinningias. Nevertheless, they hybridize freely with them, giving a far wider diversity to the genus than there is among the African violets. As a result, these plants have the potential to become even more popular in the future.

Perhaps the most important developments in *Sinningia* breeding are the interspecific hybrids of the smaller species. In the 1950s, Dr. Carl D. Clayberg—then at the Connecticut College of Agriculture—crossed the much-loved miniature *S. pusilla* and the medium size *S. eumorpha* and produced *S.* ×*pumila* 'Tetra'. This hybrid was a fertile tetraploid (that is, it had four times the number of chromosomes usually found in the germ cell), and it subsequently bred true from seeds. Inspired by Dr. Clayberg's work, in 1963 Ruth Katzenberger produced *S.* 'Dollbaby', the first fertile sinningia dip-

loid (a plant having double the usual number of chromosomes). *S.* 'Dollbaby' also came true from seeds, and it continues to be the biggest favorite of all the smaller sinningias.

Since then a host of small hybrids have been developed from various species—particularly from *S. pusilla,* which is the only gesneriad that has no dormancy at all under optimum conditions. Therefore, despite their tubers, many hybrids such as *S.* 'Dollbaby' will bloom around the year under fluorescent lighting if they are consistently kept evenly moist and given 60 to 70 percent humidity, 12 to 16 hours of illumination every day at a distance of six to ten inches (15 to 25 cm) from the lights, and temperatures in the 65° to 85°F (18° to 29°C) range. Beware of overwatering or too-dry air, either of which can cause bud blast.

The culture of *Sinningia* species and hybrids is easy—even if you choose the larger plants that are not everblooming. When dormant tubers start to sprout, pot the entire tuber or a piece of one containing a bud in an all-purpose blend of equal parts of peat, perlite, and vermiculite. The pot should be two to three inches (5 to 8 cm) larger across than the maximum diameter of the tuber. Partially fill the pot, then place the tuber inside with its sprouted end up and cover it lightly with potting mix. Water the soil well and place the plant in a brightly lit area, but protect it from strong sun. Keep it moist but not waterlogged. As the shoots grow, remove all but one (you can propagate the others as tip cuttings); water sparingly until good root and leaf growth is established. During bloom and afterward, the plants may be given light of lower intensity.

After flowering, allow the plant to grow for four to six weeks to give the tuber time to store up food. Then gradually withhold water as the plant begins to go dormant. During dormancy, keep the tuber in the pot (barely moistening the soil every few weeks) or store it in a plastic bag with dry vermiculite. Keep it at a temperature of 60° to 65°F (16° to

Palm Size Charmer: Many diminutive hybrids have been bred from the lovely miniature species, *Sinningia pusilla.* A perfect specimen is one that is symmetrical and full in leaf, yet measures barely two inches (5 cm) in width. It should bloom freely, having as many as five flowers in bloom at once, with another five in bud, ready to open.

18°C), preferably in a dark, damp location.

When growth resumes in anywhere from several days to ten weeks, repot the tuber in fresh mix and put it back into light at a temperature of 68° to 75°F (20° to 24°C), and repeat the cycle. Well-cared-for tubers can maintain their vigor for up to 30 years or more, blooming profusely once or even twice a year. (Note: Smaller species and hybrids grown under lights as pot plants or in terraria should not be dried off and stored. In such miniatures as S. 'Bright Eyes', S. concinna, S. pusilla, and S. 'White Sprite', new crowns replace old ones nearly continuously.)

Plants of this genus are most easily propagated from whole or divided tubers or from leaf cuttings or sections, but also can be started from seeds. Any method should include shade, moisture, and heat.

Chrysothemis

The lesser-known tuberous genus *Chrysothemis* comes from Central and upper South America and the West Indies. The large leaves of this plant are sometimes as long as the plant is high—that is, about 12 inches (30 cm). Not unusually attractive, the foliage is in the form of opposite, equal leaves that are bronze or green, oval, pointed, and toothed. Rather small flowers, which are yellow with red stripes, are borne in small clusters in the leaf axils.

Perhaps the most interesting characteristic of *Chrysothemis* is the colorful, ribbed, tubular calyx enhancing its flowers. This part of the plant is yellow-green in *C. friedrichsthaliana* and a flamelike orange-red in *C. pulchella* and in *C. villosa,* which is a small species well suited to indoor growing. The vivid, relatively large calyxes are evident long before flowers become evident in the spring, and remain showy even after the flowers drop.

The cultural requirements of this genus are the same as those of *Sinningia,* though chrysothemises prefer a richer soil mix. These plants can be propagated readily from the offsets that sometimes develop in leaf axils. It is also possible to take off and pot up growths on the tubers.

GESNERIADS WITH SCALY RHIZOMES

Some gesneriads have underground rhizomes with modified leaves (scales) growing from the base of the stem. (In a few genera, scaly runners also appear aboveground and tiny scalelike reproductive structures emerge in the axils of leaves or in the inflorescence or at the tips of branches.) Looking much like miniature pine cones, scaly rhizomes serve as storage organs during dry rest periods. All plants having them can be propagated by breaking their rhizomes apart into as many or as few pieces as desired. Sometimes the scales can be sown individually on a moist medium. Tip stem cuttings also can be used for propagation.

Most gesneriads with scaly rhizomes go dormant and can be treated the same as *Sinningia* tubers at that time, though the period of dormancy is usually longer. Food, humidity, and temperature needs also resemble those of *Sinningia*. The native habitat of these plants is usually in hollows at the foot of wooded slopes—places rich in humus where some moisture remains even during the dry season. Hence, the most satisfactory potting medium usually is a rich blend of 3 parts sphagnum peat, 2 parts vermiculite, and 1 part perlite, although a blend of equal parts of these media also gives good results.

Achimenes

Native to tropical America, *Achimenes* species were first mentioned by Patrick Browne in his *Civil and Natural History of Jamaica* in 1778. Having roots or rootstocks that are more or less tuberous, these plants can be upright or trailing in habit. They have opposite or whorled leaves tinted on their undersides and flowers with curved tubes, emerging from leaf axils singly or in groups. *A. erecta* was introduced in England in 1778. This heavy-blooming, scarlet-flowered species became increasingly favored by hybridizers up to about 1875, when interest peaked. It revived around 1940 and has continued ever since. Those species of *Achimenes* under cultivation (primarily *A. erecta, A. grandiflora,* and *A. longiflora*) have been hybridized so extensively that the botanical names now in use probably indicate horticultural forms rather than true species.

The summer blooming season of achimenes makes them highly desirable as porch or patio plants. In habit they range from compact to tall, erect types or trailers. The trailing strains are especially well suited to

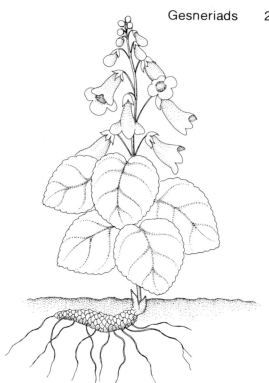

Scaly Rhizome: This underground structure serves a special function during the gesneriad's rest period by storing up enough vigor while the topgrowth dies back to produce a whole new set of stems and leaves for the following season. The rhizome can be broken into pieces for propagation purposes, with each piece generating new growth for another plant. In some cases the scales (which are actually modified leaves) also can be used for propagation. The small nubbins seen emerging from around the base of this plant are two propagules which can be removed and planted like rhizomes to produce new plants.

hanging basket culture on a moderately shady porch, where they can contribute cascades of pansylike flowers, which come in a rainbow of colors from white through pink, yellow, orange, red, lavender, purple, and blue. Achimenes can be brought indoors to continue blooming until late fall, at which time they may be treated the same as sinningias that go dormant. The length of dormancy for *Achimenes* species is variable, and plants should be checked regularly for signs of sprouting.

Good cultivars include the Michelssen series and Cornell-developed plants such as

Promoting Year-Round Bloom: Through extensive breeding, *Achimenes* grower Klaus Neubner has come up with hybrids which can be kept in bloom throughout the year under artificial light. With this exciting breakthrough, the possibility exists that a new genus may be added to the ranks of gesneriads brought to flower under lights by amateur growers.

A. antirrhina 'Red Cap', *A.* 'Cornell Jewel', *A.* 'Pink Lady', and *A.* 'Yellow Mist'. Other standouts are *A.* 'Peach Blossom', *A.* 'Purple King', *A.* 'Vivid', *A.* 'Wetterlow's Triumph', and *A.* 'Yellow Beauty'. Good-looking and compact species capable of blooming in three-inch (8 cm) pots are *A. andrieuxii* and *A. ehrenbergii.*

Especially promising for year-round indoor growing are the new hybrids originated by Klaus Neubner of the George W. Park Seed Company. Although this genus formerly was nearly impossible to bring to bloom under artificial light, Neubner has been able to keep his hybrids flowering throughout the year under fluorescent lights set at 13 hours a day. If his success can be duplicated by amateur growers with cultivars of exceptionally high quality, achimenes seem destined to become widely grown as house plants.

Unlike some gesneriads with scaly rhizomes, *Achimenes* species thrive on an all-purpose mix of equal parts of peat, vermiculite, and perlite. During active growth, they do best with a daytime high of 80° to 85°F

(27° to 29°C) and a nighttime low of 62° to 65°F (17° to 18°C) coupled with moderately high humidity and evenly moist soil. They can go into dormancy if their soil is allowed to dry out and are prone to bud blast at temperatures above 85°F (29°C). Achimenes are easily perpetuated by planting propagules arising in leaf axils and on inflorescences.

Gloxinia

The genus *Gloxinia* used to be rather nondescript; it also has been obscured by the confusing application of its name to *Sinningia speciosa,* the florists' gloxinia. The true gloxinia grows from rhizomes rather than tubers, and in recent years some attractive forms have become available.

The long-cultivated *Gloxinia perennis* offers spikes of downy, bell-shaped purple-blue flowers with darker throats. They exude a refreshing peppermint fragrance. This fall-blooming species with its heart-shaped, waxy-topped leaves is popular despite the fact that it can reach 30 inches (76 cm) and tends to sprawl as it ages.

The Botanical Gloxinia: One glance reveals that the genus *Gloxinia* bears little resemblance to the plant commonly sold as the florists' gloxinia (*Sinningia speciosa*). *Gloxinia* blooms are tubular, slightly pouched, and flare out at the ends into five tiny lobes. The delicacy of these flowers contrasts with the arresting, bell-shaped form of the florists' gloxinia, which features bolder, slightly ruffled lobes.

Purplish pink flowers with lighter specklings are found on *G. gymnostoma. Gloxinia* 'Chic' is a constantly blooming Lyndon Lyon hybrid that offers cherry red flowers. Well suited to either pot or hanging basket culture, this plant was developed from further crosses of the *G. gymnostoma* × *G. latifolia* hybrid produced by Iris August in 1968.

Gloxinias can be propagated and grown like achimenes, but they like a richer soil and do best if overpotted or direct-planted, for their roots need to range freely. They grow well when placed four to six inches (10 to 15 cm) beneath fluorescent lights.

Kohleria

Kohleria species have been under cultivation since their original introduction in 1848, but the first plants did not become available in the United States until the 1940s. Of the 65 species found from Mexico south through northern South America, only a handful have been extensively grown.

"Fuzzy" is the best one-word description of kohlerias, for these terrestrial herbs are generously endowed with the pilosity that characterizes many gesneriads; their leaves, stems, and even their flower tubes are covered with short hairs. Green or mottled, kohleria leaves are opposite or whorled, with flowers occurring alone or in little groups in leaf axils or clustered on a short flower stalk in leaf axils or in a raceme. Blossoms have corollas that are either cylindrical or swollen toward the throat, and the upper two lobes are bent backwards and are often of a different hue than the lower lobes.

The care of kohlerias is basically the same as that of achimenes, but they prefer the richer soil mix of 3 parts sphagnum peat, 2 parts vermiculite, and 1 part perlite. For taller species in this genus, the best method of culture involves the regular propagation of tip cuttings, an activity which will assure reasonably compact plants and forestall dormancy. If you handle kohlerias under lights in this manner, you can have plants that will

not go dormant at all unless they are allowed to become quite dry. Plants that do go dormant need temperatures during winter of 50° to 60°F (10° to 16°C), and during spring in the 60° to 80°F (16° to 27°C) range.

Kohleria rhizomes are white to pink to pale green and vary in thickness from quite small to about the width of an earthworm. If a plant does go into a dormant period, the rhizomes can be stored right in the pot, or in a plastic bag with dry vermiculite. Before growth resumes, you can break long pieces into smaller segments and pot up each one individually.

Some of the more attractive *Kohleria* species include the low-growing *K. amabilis,* which has pink flowers and becomingly mottled foliage; and the tall *K. eriantha,* a beautiful plant with rich, orange-red blooms and red hairs on green leaves. (It can be maintained well below its potential height of four feet/1.2 m by underpotting.) *K. lindeniana* has white flowers tinged with purple which are borne on long, erect flower stalks. The inside of each bloom is yellowish with a lavender to violet zone at the base of the throat. Appealing hybrids include the striking *K.* 'Rongo', which has mottled leaves and brilliant magenta flowers and is everblooming under lights. The bigger *K.* 'Longwood' offers large, strawberry red flowers.

Koellikeria

A delightful little plant from Colombia, *Koellikeria erinoides,* was taken to England in 1845. Known as dwarf bellflower, it made its North American debut in 1951 when Dr. Henry Teuscher of the Montreal Botanical Garden brought back plants from Venezuela. The hairy leaves of this species (which may be the only one in its genus) are oval, toothed, and concentrated at the base of the plant. They are covered with tiny spots which can be mistaken for insects at first glance. *Koellikeria* flowers grow in a raceme, in the axils of small alternate bracts. During spring several flower stalks from 9 to 12 inches (23 to 30 cm) tall are borne at a time. These have very tiny, bicolored white and deep pink flowers on 1 inch (2.5 cm) long pedicels.

If grown in a small pot, dwarf bellflower can be maintained as a miniature; at the most, flower spikes will reach 12 inches (30 cm) in height. If the rhizomes are allowed to spread out, more plants will form. The 1 inch (2.5 cm) long, ⅛ inch (3 mm) wide scaly rhizomes of *Koellikeria* need a three-month dormancy. They should then be repotted in an all-purpose gesneriad mix of 1 part peat, 1 part vermiculite, and 1 part perlite, and fed lightly with each watering.

The light and temperature needs of this plant resemble those of achimenes, but its need for a humidity of over 80 percent and for room for root clusters to develop makes *Koellikeria* an ideal specimen for a terrarium made from a five-gallon (18.9 l) fish tank. Plants may be propagated by division or from cuttings or rhizomes.

Smithiantha

A small but gorgeous genus from the American tropics, *Smithiantha* was formerly called *Naegelia,* but is best known and loved as temple bells. Having upright single or branched stems and attractive, heart-shaped leaves of velvety green sometimes mottled with red or purple, the plant takes its popular name from its spires of nodding, bell-shaped flowers ranging in color from red, pink, orange, and yellow to a soft, creamy white. Outstanding for its plush garnet red foliage and bright scarlet and cream flowers, *S. cinnabarina* grows to 12 or 24 inches (30 or 61 cm) high, flowering heavily in fall. The somewhat taller *S. zebrina* has deep green foliage handsomely patterned with red-brown, and bright scarlet and yellow flowers with a light yellow throat flecked with red. The first species to be cultivated, *S. zebrina* has been much hybridized. The charming result of one cross with the ivory-flowered *S. multiflora* was *S.* 'Zebrina Discolor', an easily grown and flowered

cultivar with dramatically multicolored leaves and red and yellow blooms spotted inside with brown. Other zebrina hybrids with beautifully colored flowers include *S.* 'Orange King', *S.* 'Rose Queen', and the low-growing *S.* × *hybrida* 'Compacta', which has flowers of lemon yellow grading into red at their tops. Also notable are *S.* 'Abbey', *S.* 'Carmel', *S.* 'Cathedral', and *S.* 'Santa Barbara'. *Smithiantha* requires the same culture as *Sinningia* species and should be kept cool and barely moist during the winter dormancy after blooming is finished. Generous amounts of humidity, warmth, and light should be given when new growth appears in spring. Propagate these plants from dormant rhizomes, from cuttings of young shoots, from leaves (without petioles), or from seeds.

Other Gesneriads with Scaly Rhizomes

Plants in the *Diastema* genus look like some of the smaller *Achimenes* species. A relatively

Flowers for the Terrarium: If you want to add some color to your terrarium, include a petite *Diastema*. Shown here is *D. vexans,* an appealing plant with fine hairs covering the leaves. The white tubular flowers seem to have been touched by an invisible hand dabbling with watercolors, which left behind lovely shadings of color on the lobes and throat.

popular pot plant from this group is *D. quinquevulnerum.* Dwarf and branching, this species grows up to five inches (13 cm) high and can bear loose clusters of small, tubular white flowers (with a lavender spot on each lobe) throughout the summer. Ideal for terrarium growing is the white-flowered miniature *Phinaea multiflora.* Another good, relatively small plant for a high-humidity environment is the six inch (15 cm) high *Niphaea oblonga* species from southern Mexico and Guatemala. This plant has serrated, glossy leaves as long as five inches (13 cm), and one inch (2.5 cm) wide white flowers with yellow centers that are produced several to the leaf axil. All of these plants are readily propagated from scaly rhizomes.

TERRESTRIAL GESNERIADS WITH FIBROUS ROOTS

Frequently, fibrous-rooted gesneriads are found in nature on river banks in humus-filled depressions. They can be propagated easily from tip cuttings and from seeds. This group of gesneriads is wide ranging in form. Many are upright growers like the more popular species of *Alloplectus* and *Nautilocalyx;* some are shrubby, like *Gesneria* plants, which tend to be stiffly erect. Others are vinelike or clambering, like *Besleria,* or rosette forming, like the lovely, blue-flowered *Boea hygroscopica,* or low-growing stoloniferous plants, like the highly popular episcias.

Episcia

In addition to about ten species of *Episcia* endemic to southern Mexico, Brazil, and the southern island of the lesser Antilles, there are dozens of hybrids. These beautiful plants have been termed the peacocks of the gesneriads because of their many-colored leaves and rainbow of flower colors. *Episcia* leaves are elliptic to ovate in shape and are arranged in opposite pairs or in three-leaved whorls on short petioles. The tubular, bell-shaped flowers are borne in the angle between leaf stalk

Fibrous-Rooted Gesneriads: The diversity of growth habit and variation in flower form and color among fibrous-rooted gesneriads can be seen in this group. Clockwise from the lower right are a creeping *Codonanthe,* with a scattering of small white tubular flowers, and a *Columnea* with spreading stems carrying red tubular flowers. Dominating the upper portion of the display is *Aeschynanthus speciosus,* with its bold clusters of yellow and orange tubular flowers. Peeking out from behind a drooping *Aeschynanthus* bloom in the center are the colorfully veined leaves and pendent red flower of an *Episcia* cultivar. Directly to the right of this plant, in the background, is a *Nematanthus,* covered with tiny, pouchlike, reddish yellow flowers.

and stem; they grow singly or in pairs or in four-flowered clusters.

The most familiar and popular member of the genus is *E. cupreata,* the flame violet, which features slightly hairy leaves with a puckered surface, in hues ranging from coppery red to bright green, at times displaying silvery variegations. Dainty red flecks may appear on the inner surface of the red and yellow flowers. Some other striking selections include E. *cupreata* 'Tropical Topaz', E. 'Cygnet', E. *lilacina* 'Lilacina', and E. 'Moss Agate'. E. 'Cleopatra' is also special, and the spectacular E. 'Tricolor' has been found outstanding for performance and effect. For a different-looking episcia, consider the very compact and clustering rosette plant E. *dianthiflora,* which has scalloped, dark green leaves and deeply fringed white flowers. (This episcia should be given somewhat more light than the cultivars with colored leaves.)

Episcias thrive on warmth, preferring a daytime temperature of 75° to 80°F (24° to 27°C) with a slight drop at night. A day range of 65° to 75°F (18° to 24°C) is acceptable, but for best results, night temperatures should not fall below 65°F (18°C). Episcias will collapse fatally at temperatures below 55°F (13°C). High humidity—50 percent or more—is a foremost need of this genus, with even moisture being another important requirement. The latter can be assured by using the loose but moisture-holding potting blend of equal parts peat, vermiculite, and perlite. Bright light is a must for optimum growth; so is steady fertilization during active growth, for episcias are heavy feeders.

Many *Episcia* species are suited to terrarium culture, although they may eventually outgrow that environment. They can be propagated from the tips of stolons (these can grow in water for several months), from stem cuttings that have at least one node, from leaf cuttings, or from seeds.

Alloplectus

The diverse genus *Alloplectus* includes about 70 tropical American species. Frequently characterized by paired leaves of unequal size and by vivid red or red-orange calyx lobes, these plants do well in a hot, humid location but eventually tend to become too large for house plants. For this reason and because they become unattractive as they age, specimens are best replaced each year or so with new plants. These can be started easily from stem cuttings. Recommended upright types include the yellow-flowered, fall-blooming A. *capitatus* and the similarly flowered A. *vittatus,* which has beautifully patterned leaves. A. *calochlamys* is said to perform well under lights.

Adding some appeal to the genus are two species that were formerly classified as *Hypocyrta* species—A. *nummularia* and A. *teuscheri.* The first is a creeping vine with green or reddish leaves that can be rooted at the pealike nodules forming at joints on its stem. It has a helmet-shaped flower with a pouched vermillion corolla that becomes deep purple where it flares out to form yellow lobes. Several plants potted together make an attractive display, blooming for six to eight weeks. A. *teuscheri* has a four-sided stem reaching a height of 24 inches (61 cm), and velvety green leaves marked with gold or silver veining. The yellow, pouched flower tubes flare out into small red lobes and are enclosed at the base by brilliant scarlet, leafy, toothed sepals.

These plants do well if kept in relatively small pots of lightly packed mix and given warm temperatures, high humidity, and moderate light. They can be propagated from stem or leaf cuttings or from seeds.

Gesneria

Some of the plants now classified in the genus *Sinningia* were once called gesnerias, but the true members of this genus are characterized by alternate rather than opposite leaves and by fibrous (not tuberous) roots. There are about 60 species of these upright, often large, woody-stemmed plants. Plentiful in Puerto Rico and other islands of the West Indies and also found in northern South America, gesnerias are mostly known to North American gardeners through the charming and diminutive *Gesneria cuneifolia.* The cylindrical, 1 inch (2.5 cm) long fiery red flowers of this shiny-leaved, 6 to 12 inch (15 to 30 cm) high beauty have earned it the sobriquet of firecracker plant. Beginning life as a low-growing and compact bright green rosette, the firecracker plant eventually develops a short, branching, woody stem. Its wedge-shaped leaves are about 4 inches (10 cm) long.

Preferring a very high humidity, species plants of G. cuneifolia do best in a terrarium but can succeed under lights with moderate humidity. At high levels of humidity these plants need bright, diffuse light to flower well, but they will perform better at lower light levels if the humidity is less than ideal. The soil must always be kept wet, however, to prevent flower drop. The soil mixture should be a mix of 1 part peat, 1 part vermiculite, and 1 part perlite with up to four tablespoons (60 ml) of lime added to each quart (1.1 l). Propagation is from seeds, from cuttings of longish branches, or from underground runners that sometimes develop.

Nautilocalyx

The showy foliage plants of the genus *Nautilocalyx* are usually upright (less often, trailing) and are found in South America near the Amazon River. These succulent-stemmed plants have leaves that are roughly embossed between depressed veins. The foliage changes from dark green in youth to an olive or bronze appearance when the plant ages or when it is placed in bright light. Flowers are small, tubular, and hairy, and either creamy or pale yellow in color.

Nautilocalyx species should be pinched back regularly to promote fullness of growth (the tip cuttings obtained this way may be propagated). Notable species include *N. forgetii*, which has shiny, bright green leaves patterned with red or a darker green around the veins, and light yellow flowers. Even more dramatically colored is *N. lynchii* (called the black alloplectus), which has relatively smooth and unhairy bronze to blackish red leaves, and stems that turn from purple and fuzzy to brown and smooth. The rather subtle ivory flowers with purple down bloom in summer. *Nautilocalyx* species thrive under the general culture suggested for gesneriads, later in this chapter.

More Terrestrials with Fibrous Roots

Well suited to culture under lights, the Oriental streptocarpus *(Boea hygroscopica)* is one of the East Asian gesneriads. Its blue flowers just under ½ inch (13 mm) wide look like those of African violets, and the resemblance is strengthened by this plant's rosette of deeply veined, light green, quilted leaves covered with white hairs. A perennial reaching a height of perhaps six inches (15 cm), the Oriental streptocarpus needs to be kept evenly moist to prevent its leaves from curling up. It is a lovely species and may be propagated by division of crowns (new ones form at the base of the plant and also in leaf axils) or from leaf cuttings or seeds.

Like *Saintpaulia* and *Streptocarpus,* the genus *Chirita* shares the distinction among gesneriads of having only two fertile stamens. In addition to the rock-dwelling *C. sinensis* discussed earlier, a good species for indoor gardeners is the fat-stemmed *C. micromusa,* a native of Thailand having brilliant yellow, orange-throated flowers about 1 inch (2.5 cm) long. Unusual seed capsules which look like bunches of bananas have given this plant the common name of little banana. It is succulent and a fast grower that will reach a height of about 12 inches (30 cm). Cultural needs are like those of *C. sinensis.*

TRAILING GESNERIADS WITH FIBROUS ROOTS

Including the genera *Aeschynanthus* and *Codonanthe,* and certain species of *Columnea* and *Nematanthus,* the trailing gesneriads with fibrous roots are mostly epiphytic. These plants grow best in baskets containing the rich blend of 3 parts peat, 2 parts vermiculite, and 1 part perlite and can do well with their tops from 12 to 24 inches (30 to 61 cm) below fluorescent lights. All of them can be propagated from tip cuttings after flowering or from seeds.

Aeschynanthus

About 170 species of *Aeschynanthus* may be found in jungles from the Himalayas south to Borneo at elevations up to 5,000 feet (1,500 m). Most of them are spreading, climbing, epiphytic vines. Their leaves are fleshy or leathery, equal and opposite, and lie on the same plane. All of these plants have tubular flowers that emerge from the calyx like lipstick from a tube. For this reason, the common name of lipstick plant has been given to red-flowered species such as *A. radicans* and *A. pulcher.*

Most *Aeschynanthus* species have clusters of 10 to 15 flowers at the growing tips, though newer species on the market produce blooms all along the trailing stems. These plants are seasonal bloomers, and often specimens bought in brilliant and profuse bloom

Lipstick on a Vine: With a little imagination, these brilliant red, tubular *Aeschynanthus* flowers can be thought of as opened tubes of lipstick, as they protrude from their green calyxes.

may not flower again for a year. Flower colors range from dark red (on the compact *A. micranthus*) to orange (*A. evrardii*) to bright yellow and orange (*A. speciosus*) to green (the mottled-leaved species *A. marmoratus*).

The attractive *A. marmoratus* has marbled leaves—the handsomest in the genus—and green flowers splashed with chocolate brown (these form in the leaf axils rather than at the stem tips). Another likely choice is the hybrid *A.* 'Black Pagoda', developed by breeder Lyndon Lyon. Unlike most *Aeschynanthus* species which bloom sometime between spring and fall, this cultivar produces lots of burnt orange flowers at intervals over the winter. Another good performer is *A. ellipticus,* which has salmon-colored blossoms, flexible stems, and small leaves. For its spectacular flowers and good performance, *A. speciosus* is highly recommended to gardeners with ample space.

The former name of this genus was *Trichosporum,* which means "hairy seed," and all *Aeschynanthus* seeds have a hairy appendage which serves as an anchor until germination takes place. Because of their generous size and need for warm 75°F (24°C) daytime and 60°F (16°C) nighttime temperatures, these plants are more suited to greenhouse culture than to a light garden environment. They can, however, thrive under lights if space can be made for them, and also will grow quite well in a southeast or southwest window.

Codonanthe

Codonanthe is a small genus of evergreen climbers or creepers growing naturally from Mexico to southern Brazil and Peru. Known as the Central American bellflower, this fibrous-rooted trailing plant is not epiphytic. In fact, it is found growing on ant hills shaded by trees in low-altitude forests. There or anywhere, this genus can be identified quickly and surely by the red spots on the undersides of its shiny, thick, ovate leaves. These are the nectaries, which attract ants to carry off the seeds. Unlike the seeds of any other gesneriads, those of *Codonanthe* are enclosed by a cover (aril). The flowers of this plant are small white tubes borne in the leaf axils. They grow in a horizontal position so that ants can carry on the function of cross-pollination.

Codonanthe flowers generally remain open only briefly—for up to several days. Lightly scented, they are scattered over the whole plant and are positioned well above the foliage.

The most commonly cultivated species of this small but sprawling plant include *C. crassifolia* and *C. macradenia*. Also worthwhile for hanging basket culture is a hybrid called *C.* 'Gena', which was developed by gesneriad breeder Gary Hunter.

Codonanthes are as easy to grow as the more popular columneas. They may be divided when they become woody at the base, and can also be propagated readily from tip cuttings.

Columnea

Named by Linnaeus in 1753 for the Italian botanist Fabium Columnea, these plants had little impact on the world of horticulture for two centuries because their flowers were small and bloomed only once a year. Over the past several decades, however, some of the more floriferous species and hybrids of the trailing forms of *Columnea* have become quite popular, and at present they are probably the most widely grown and hybridized of all the trailing gesneriads.

Either of shrubby habit with stiff upright or spreading stems, or vinelike and creeping or trailing, columneas have two-lipped tubular flowers found clustered or singly in leaf axils. Flower colors range from red to yellow with some pinkish shades, and the velvety green, narrowly elliptic to ovate-oblong leaves are sometimes covered with purple hairs.

There are more than 150 species of this genus with new ones still being recorded. Dr.

Robert E. Lee and Dr. Harold E. Moore, Jr., of Cornell University, in Ithaca, New York, developed the first hybrids in the 1950s, and Cornell hybrids such as *C.* 'Ithacan' and *C.* 'Othello' offer plentiful and almost continuous blooms if they are grown under lights. Other excellent cultivars are the compact *C.* 'Mary Ann' and *C.* 'Joy'; *C.* 'Yellow Dragon'; *C.* 'Early Bird'; and *C.* 'Katsura', which has variegated foliage. Noteworthy species include *C. erythrophaea, C. jamaicensis, C. mortonii, C. raymondii,* and *C. zebrina.*

As epiphytes which live on trees in the West Indies and Central and South America, the trailing columneas are best suited to hanging basket culture in a light, porous medium. They do well four to six inches (10 to 15 cm) below 40-watt fluorescents or in an

Goldfish on a Vine: Cascading stems of this *Columnea* bear orange-red flowers with overhanging upper lobes which resemble fantail goldfish.

east, west, or lightly shaded south window. In winter a few hours of direct sun each day can be beneficial. Do not overwater, for columneas like their soil barely moist. Most trailing columneas prefer daytime temperatures of between 65° and 85°F (18° and 29°C) with a drop of 7° to 8°F (4°C) at night. Some of them (such as *C. microphylla, C. hirta,* and *C.* 'Stavanger') require a cool or short-day period before they will flower and are best suited to the cool greenhouse.

Nematanthus

Rather similar to *Columnea* species in appearance and cultural needs, *Nematanthus* plants differ in having waxier foliage and flowers that have a top-shaped rather than a cylindrical calyx and tube and a more open and swollen, somewhat funnel-shaped corolla. The pouchlike flowers of some species hang by long, thin, dangling stalks.

The shape and red and yellow color of *Nematanthus* flowers have caused these plants to be popularly known as either the guppy flower or the candy corn plant. This epiphytic genus includes climbing and trailing plants that are attractive when grown in hanging baskets; plants having leaves with variegated or reddish undersides create an especially pleasing display. Nonvining forms of *Nematanthus,* however, can be trained into erect and handsome bushes.

Nematanthus flowers are tiny but abundant and can be enjoyed year-round if plants are given the choice light of a south window or kept no less than ten inches (25 cm) below fluorescent lights. (Less light is advisable for variegated types.) For good flower production and retention, these plants should have temperatures not much higher or lower than 65° to 75°F (18° to 24°C) and a humidity of around 50 percent. Allow the plants to dry out between waterings, and water them much less frequently when they are taking their frequent rests. Propagation is best accomplished by division, stem cuttings, or seeds.

Guppy Flower: These *Nematanthus* blooms, with their swollen belly and small protruding lobes, do indeed resemble their underwater namesake. The red and yellow coloration has also given rise to another common name, the candy corn plant.

A marvelous group of plants too long overlooked, the genus *Nematanthus* is beginning to achieve a measure of well-deserved recognition. This growing appreciation is largely the result of the work of professional and amateur hybridizers who discovered that members of the genus *Hypocyrta* could be easily crossed with *Nematanthus* species. As a result of such efforts, many hypocyrtas have been reclassified by botanists into the genus *Nematanthus* and a plethora of cultivars suited to various indoor situations are now available. (For more on some outstanding cultivars and the amateur who developed them, see Creating New Gesneriads.)

GENERAL CULTURE

Gesneriads are no different from other house plants in their essential needs. Like all plants, they require support, food, water, light, a certain amount of warmth, and air. They also should be scrutinized for signs of insects or disease and may be propagated by some special methods.

GROWING MEDIA AND FERTILIZERS

The primary criterion of a medium for gesneriads is good drainage. This is linked to porosity, for few gesneriads will grow in hard-packed soil. A simple yet satisfactory all-purpose blend for gesneriads is the original Cornell mix, which consists of equal parts of milled sphagnum peat moss, vermiculite, and perlite. If you want to include more organic matter in the medium, add two parts of pasteurized compost. To partially neutralize the acid in the peat moss, eggshells ground in a blender can be mixed in at the rate of two to four tablespoons (30 to 60 ml) per quart (1.1 l) of mix. Beware, though, of raising the pH too much, for most gesneriads do best in a slightly acidic mix with a pH of 6.8.

Over the years, many growers have tried varying the above blend with other ingredients such as fir bark, cat litter, or coarse sand. Experiment with these materials if you wish, but avoid cat litters treated with deodorizing chemicals, for these can be harmful to plants.

Actually the basic mix has proved to be all that is necessary for many award winners. Some growers prefer a richer mix of 3 parts peat, 2 parts vermiculite, and 1 part perlite. Its greater water-retaining capacity is a characteristic that makes this variation useful for fibrous-rooted genera. According to gesneriad authority Iris August, however, it may be wiser to use plastic containers and to provide higher humidity and more frequent waterings than to change the basic mix too greatly.

Use the Cornell mix in conjunction with a good organic fertilizer such as fish emulsion. These products work well on gesneriads if they are applied with each watering at the rate of $\frac{1}{4}$ teaspoon (1 ml) per gallon (3.8 l) of water. If you prefer, you can use a slightly stronger solution of $\frac{1}{2}$ teaspoon (3 ml) per gallon (3.8 l) of water once a week. Never fertilize dry gesneriads with a solution that is at 100 percent of the strength recommended on the label. Foliar feeding has not been proved to be helpful with many gesneriads, so leave it to the experts for further study.

CONTAINERS

It is important to consider the type of root growth, growth habit, and cultural requirements of a gesneriad when selecting its container. Both clay and plastic pots are suitable for many plants, but hanging baskets of hardware cloth, wooden slats, or open-weave plastic are a better choice for the smaller tu-

G–B–S Growing Mix

A soilless growing medium especially suited to gesneriads has been developed by nurseryman and plant breeder Michael Kartuz. The "G-B-S" stands for *Gesneriad-Begonia-Saintpaulia,* but Kartuz recommends his blend for a wide variety of house plants. It has the advantage of holding moisture well, while still providing excellent drainage.

To make the G-B-S mix, remove the lumps and small twigs from 2 quarts (2.2 l) of sphagnum peat moss by rubbing it through half-inch (13 mm) mesh hardware cloth. Thoroughly mix the peat with 1 quart (1.1 l) of horticultural grade vermiculite, 1 quart (1.1 l) of medium or coarse perlite, and 2 tablespoons (30 ml) of ground limestone. Store the mix dry until you are ready to use it. Then moisten the amount to be used with a weak fertilizer solution.

Creating New Gesneriads: An Expert Amateur's Story

Hybridizing. The very word conjures up images of sophisticated crosses, complicated trait information systems, and years of formal genetic training. Not something an amateur with an interest in plant genetics could possibly hope to tackle—right? Wrong. An amateur hybridizer living in Brewster, Massachusetts has been working with gesneriads for the past 15 years, with stunning results. As a result of William Saylor's efforts, most members of one gesneriad genus have been officially reclassified, and a host of brilliant hybrids of a once obscure genus are exciting much interest in the gardening world.

This significant outcome grew from a humble beginning. "I didn't even know what a gesneriad was," Saylor said, discussing his early work with the compact, gracefully trailing plant with pouched blooms that was then called *Hypocyrta*. He thought, however, that hypocyrtas were "interesting looking" and decided to use his newly built lean-to greenhouse to hybridize these neglected

An Expert Amateur: Not all work relating to botanical classification belongs in the realm of the professionals. William Saylor's hobby of working with gesneriad hybrids contributed to the official reclassification of most species of *Hypocyrta* into the genus *Nematanthus*. Saylor is shown here holding a member of a new genus he has bred, × *Codonanthus*.

plants. Bringing to bear some 30 years of interest in plant genetics, by the late 1960s Saylor had created the first two *Hypocyrta* hybrids: 'Rio', which has attrac-

tively dense foliage and vivid, cardinal red flowers, and the very floriferous 'Tropicana', which sports handsome yellow and maroon striped blooms with russet calyxes.

In the meantime, Dr. Robert Lee of Cornell University was working with *Nematanthus*, a trailing gesneriad characterized by long dangling flower stalks and tubular flowers. Crossing *Nematanthus longipes* with *N. fritschii*, Dr. Lee obtained a hybrid he named 'Stoplight' because of its red blooms.

Saylor happened to read of Dr. Lee's work and the resulting hybrid. By this time he was aware that both *Nematanthus* and *Hypocyrta* were gesneriads and in addition had the same number of chromosomes. He also knew the plants shared the same natural environment. Pondering this information, Saylor decided to cross *Hypocyrta wettsteinii* (called the candy corn plant because of the look of its small flowers) with Dr. Lee's hybrid, 'Stoplight'. The result of that cross was five seedlings. One of these was an attractive plant with very dark green leaves and red flowers. Saylor dubbed this first successful *Nem-*

berous or scaly-rhizomed gesneriad species. Low-growing fibrous terrestrials like episcias are well suited to terraria, since they thrive in high humidity and moist soil during the time of year when they are in active growth. African violets still in their pots also can be placed in a terrarium, snifter, or glass or plastic bowl and surrounded with live sheet moss. (The container should be kept covered part of

the time to boost humidity and kept in bright light but out of direct sun.)

LIGHT

A strong case can be made for controlling the amount of light gesneriads receive, for although plants given 50 to 70 percent humidity can get by on somewhat less light, no atanthus × Hypocyrta 'Black Magic'.

The existence of this cultivar and several other fertile Nematanthus-Hypocyrta crosses accomplished by Saylor caused botanists to conclude that most Hypocyrta species were really members of the genus Nematanthus, for when plants are categorized in different genera they usually are very difficult (or impossible) to cross and fertile seedlings are rarely obtainable. Saylor had proved that despite the quite different appearances of Nematanthus and Hypocyrta, these plants were genetically similar.

The early hybrids bred in Saylor's Massachusetts greenhouse remain popular, and a rainbow of such Saylor achievements as the compact N. 'Castanet' (pink and orange striped flowers), the very dwarf N. 'Bambino' (orange and yellow flowers), and the trailing, spreading N. 'Bijou' (deep pink blooms year-round) may be ordered through Kartuz Greenhouses, Lauray of Salisbury, or W. B. Richardson Gesneriad Growers.

But Saylor is not content to rest on past laurels, and his fascination with the plants now called Nematanthus continues. He is now involved with intergeneric crosses between Nematanthus and Codonanthe—a genus usually having all-white blooms. To date, this gifted amateur has produced five primary hybrids (first-generation crosses) and coined the hybrid generic name ×Codonatanthus to show the Codonanthe-Nematanthus relationship. Saylor's favorite hybrid from this first group is called 'Fiesta'. It is distinguished by bright red flowers that are creamy white at their multi-lobed mouths (limbs) and "seems to be an everbloomer" like a good many gesneriads.

If Mr. Saylor's achievements have gotten you interested in trying your luck with hybridizing, he offers some suggestions for beginners. First, read all you can about genetics and hybridizing, especially in books devoted especially to amateur hybridizing and plant breeding: he recommends the handbooks on Propagation and Breeding Ornamental Plants from the Brooklyn Botanic Garden Record Series, published by the Editorial Committee of the Brooklyn Botanic Garden. Also, you might want to do a little research to see if the plants you want to cross have been determined to have the same number of chromosomes—if they do not, a successful cross is unlikely. (The chromosome numbers of many of the gesneriads are listed in the Brooklyn Botanic Garden's handbook on African-Violets, Gloxinias and Their Relatives.)

Saylor stresses that hybridizing is mostly trial and error and believes it should always remain fun and challenging. He adds, though, that patience is required in working with these gesneriads. For example, from three to five years may elapse before you see the first bloom. (Saylor has found that the average time from one generation of Nematanthus to the next is about two years.)

The most important tools Saylor uses and recommends are really quite simple. One is a jeweler's loop (about 3-power magnification) employed to examine flower parts; another is a fine probe usually used to transfer pollen. Saylor made his probe by grinding down a crochet hook until it had a fine point. He also finds useful a small pair of scissors and tweezers with a fine tip.

amount of care can compensate for insufficient light. Most gesneriads seem to flower most readily and profusely with a daylength of at least 12 hours. Exceptions may be the kohlerias and certain species of other genera such as Sinningia and Smithiantha. In one experiment conducted at a nighttime minimum of 70°F (21°C), Sinningia speciosa and Smithiantha zebrina flowered more quickly and abundantly when given short days and relatively low light levels (produced by filtering light through two layers of cheesecloth) than they did when given long days and high light.

Where only artificial lighting is used, gesneriads will thrive under a mix of 40-watt warm white and cool white or natural white and daylight fluorescents. Regular or Wide-

Spectrum Gro-Lux tubes used alone or in combination also give good results; so does Tru-Bloom Verilux. For gesneriads being grown under lights in the northeastern part of the United States and in Canada the optimum in winter is 12 to 14 hours of illumination per day. To keep pace with more rapid growth in the higher temperatures of summer, 14 to 16 hours of light is preferable. Such seasonal variations in growth and light needs may be less apparent in plants grown in homes located in western or southern states.

Generally speaking, seedlings and newly sprouted tubers and rhizomes (especially those of *Achimenes*) need to be closer to fluorescents than do adult plants. Placing such plants so their foliage tops are four to six inches (10 to 15 cm) below the center of the tubes is not too close; however, the lights must be raised gradually—or the plants lowered gradually as they grow. Cuttings require less light when rooting but should be treated as seedlings thereafter. Among full-grown plants, miniature gesneriads require less light than standard size ones and can do well under the ends of tubes or between sets of fixtures where they can thrive on peripheral light from both directions. Nonminiature species of *Sinningia; Chirita sinensis;* and all *Kohleria, Smithiantha,* and *Achimenes* species also may be given less light during and after flowering than before they bloom.

Gesneriads receiving too much illumination will have leaves that turn down and curl around the pot in an effort to get away from the light source; their foliage also may bleach out. Too little light is indicated when leaves reach up toward the light source and when leaf stalks and stem internodes are exaggerated in length.

The same indicators of light preferences may be used to evaluate plants being grown in natural light. In general, such gesneriads do best in locations that provide from six to eight hours of bright light daily, but direct sun only early in the morning in all seasons but winter.

TEMPERATURE

Gesneriads that are raised as house plants require intermediate to warm temperatures, for most of them come from the tropical regions of the world. Species originating in higher altitudes even near the equator (such as *Petrocosmea* spp. and many species of *Columnea* and *Streptocarpus*) usually require relatively cool temperatures of 55° to 65°F (13° to 18°C) at night, but other gesneriads need at least 65°F (18°C) at night. All gesneriads benefit from a nighttime drop of 8° to 10°F (4° to 6°C), and most are at their best when daytime temperatures are at least between 70° and 75°F (21° and 24°C).

With the coming of summer, all gesneriads except those that have fine hairs on their leaf tops will thrive outdoors if you remember to bring them back indoors when the night temperatures begin to approach 50°F (10°C). Among gesneriads that stay indoors (the warmth-loving episcias are a notable exception), a very hot summer spell may be followed by a period of few blooms and the appearance of stem rot. Fortunately, this period coincides with the general housecleaning and relandscaping of the indoor garden in preparation for bringing in plants that have grown larger during a summer outdoors.

WATER AND HUMIDITY

Most failures with gesneriads can be traced to improper watering. The majority of plants in this family prefer even moisture. (Special requirements were mentioned in the discussions of individual genera, earlier in the chapter.) Water always should be at room temperature, for cold water creates characteristic "burn spots" on leaves and shocks roots. If you use a tepid mist-spray occasionally to remove dust and wash off insects or their eggs, keep plants out of direct sunlight until their leaves dry. Keep in mind that plants consume water at different rates depending on light, temperature, humidity, soil mix, containers, and their stage of growth. (If you water by hand, you can make your job easier by grouping plants with similar water requirements in the same tray.) By making sure that the soil is never allowed to dry out, you can compensate for low humidity that would otherwise impair the growth of these moisture-loving plants.

Watering can be done from above or below, though occasional top-watering is essential to prevent the accumulation of fertilizer salts on the surface of the medium and on the pot rim. Such deposits can burn leaves or petioles that touch them. (Another way of minimizing the salt problem is to plunge potted plants into peat moss, then top-dress them with sheet moss.) If you water from above, be especially careful not to water too often, lest your plants develop "wet feet"; soggy roots coupled with little or no drainage are a sure way to encourage root rot.

Perhaps because it lets the plants themselves control water uptake and thereby assures adequate but not excessive soil moisture relative to humidity, automatic watering is highly recommended by some gesneriad growers. Various methods of wicking are possible. Basically, all consist of a reservoir of water below the pot with a wick of some durable material such as nylon or fiberglass (or even burlap or rolled cheesecloth) inserted into the bottom of the pot to draw up the water by capillary action just as wicks in old-fashioned lamps take up kerosene. Wick-watering methods are discussed in chapter 2.

If you prefer to top-water, a watering wand is excellent, or, if you have many shelf-feet of gesneriads, it may be worthwhile to use a ½ inch (13 mm) diameter hose attached to a laundry room or kitchen faucet. Use a shut-off nozzle at the watering end and a fertilizer proportioner between it and the rest of the hose. However you top-water, you can increase humidity by standing plants on a pebble layer or grid suspended over a drainage saucer or tray. Remember, however, that although watering plants promptly when the topsoil is almost dry can help offset low humidity, gesneriads with soft leaves are apt to develop brown edges on their leaf tips if there is too little moisture in the air. Stunted flowers can be another symptom of low humidity.

Humidity needn't be a problem if you have a large number of wick-watered plant trays. You also can use a room humidifier of some kind during the winter; for example, a two-gallon (7.6 l) vaporizer may be turned on at night during cold spells when indoor heat is especially drying. According to Virginie and George Elbert, who are successful with gesneriads at a humidity as low as 30 percent, if you are unable to increase humidity to ideal levels, you can compensate by giving gesneriads extra light. African violets, for example, need at least 500 footcandles if they are to bloom at a low humidity. On the other hand, if you can offer high humidity your plants will be able to produce more and larger flowers at lower light levels than would be possible at a low humidity. At 60 percent humidity, for example, some African violet cultivars will flower with just 150 footcandles. If the temperature drops while the humidity remains high, cutting back on water can help counteract the relatively excessive amount of moisture in the air.

AIR

The final requirement for growth for gesneriads, as for other plants, is air, which is vital for the oxygen and carbon dioxide it contributes. The degree to which air moves also affects the well-being of plants, for circulating air acts to prevent temperature buildup at leaf and root surfaces. The gentle movement of the atmosphere is beneficial at high temperatures when the humidity also is way up, for stagnant, moist, hot air around plants favors the growth of disease organisms. On the other hand, brisk air circulation can be lethal to warmth- and humidity-loving plants such as gesneriads if the temperature is low, and dangerously dehydrating if humidity is below par. To counter excessive heat coupled with high humidity during the hottest time of year, you can place an oscillating fan eight to ten feet (2.4 to 3 m) from your plants or use a window fan positioned so it blows away from the garden to pull air over it. Never, however, expose gesneriads to drafts of either cold or hot air.

INSECT AND DISEASE PROBLEMS

The major insect pests affecting gesneriads are leaf mealybugs, scale, cyclamen mites, blossom thrips, aphids, and whiteflies.

Cyclamen mites cannot be seen without a hand lens, but the signs of their damage cannot be mistaken in advanced stages. New leaves are gray, hard, hairy and twisted; flowers are streaked and distorted and pedicels are stunted. These mites are extremely difficult to get rid of without using strong insecticides, and even if the insects are killed, the leaves are permanently damaged. Thus, it is best to discard affected plants rather than treat them.

Blossom thrips cause premature flower drop, streaking of flowers, and distortion of flowers in advanced infestations. The young insects are yellow and threadlike; mature insects are tan and $1/8$ inch (3 mm) long. They attack the pollen sacs.

Mealybugs, scale, aphids, and whiteflies are all described in chapter 9.

Needless to say, the best way to handle pests is never to get them. The most important sanitation practice in preventing insect problems is to isolate all new plants for four to six weeks while you watch for signs of insects. Follow this policy even with plants given to you by your best friend or mail-ordered from reputable sources. For more detailed information on insects and organic remedies, see Controlling Insects and Mites, in chapter 9.

Diseases most likely to beset gesneriads include root and crown rots, *Botrytis* blight, powdery mildew, and viruses. Proper watering, good air circulation, and good sanitation practices will prevent most disease problems, and rot-infected plants can sometimes be saved by propagation of uninfected parts. Viruses, however, are carried by insects, and by tobacco smoke and on smokers' fingers, and since there is no cure for virus infections of house plants, the infected plants should be destroyed immediately. For more specifics on diagnosing and responding to plant ailments, see Plant Diseases, in chapter 9.

PROPAGATION

Most gesneriads can be propagated by a number of common methods. These include seeds, leaf and stem cuttings, division of crowns and offsets, stolons, tubers, and rhizome sections. Generally speaking, if a gesneriad has soft, dull-colored leaves with prominent veins, it can be multiplied readily from leaf cuttings; usually such plants are fibrous rooted. Though tuberous gesneriads have fewer leaves, sometimes they, too, can be propagated from leaf sections—a method that yields one or two plants directly, whereas removing the little tubers that form on the roots necessitates a delay, since the minitubers should be kept moist or in moistened vermiculite in a plastic bag until they sprout and only then planted.

In starting gesneriads from seeds, sow the seeds as quickly as possible, for viability is limited. Stem tip cuttings should be salvaged immediately if a gesneriad with a reasonably developed stem develops stem rot as a result of inadequate drainage, overwatering, and/or high humidity. For details on all these methods of propagation, see chapter 8.

Several additional techniques of propagation are particularly relevant to gesneriads. These are the rejuvenation of a necky *Saintpaulia;* the special treatment of leaf cuttings of tuberous gesneriads to generate extra tubers; the division of leaf sections of *Streptocarpus, Sinningia speciosa,* and possibly *Episcia;* and the planting of propagules emerging from the leaf axils or elsewhere on

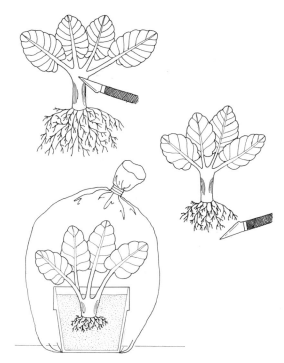

Restoring a Necky African Violet: An unsightly plant can be beautified by this simple method. Let the plant wilt a bit before removing it from the pot. With a sharp knife, scrape away the stem until you reach the green area just below the outer surface. Clean most of the dirt from the root ball and trim away a portion of the root system. When repotting the plant, make sure to bury most of the necky stem and then water thoroughly. Enclosing the plant in a plastic bag for a month will help the root system to develop, and all you need to do is open the bag occasionally to reduce the chance of mildew forming.

species of *Chrysothemis, Achimenes,* and *Gloxinia.*

The restoration of African violets becomes almost mandatory as these plants age, for as the outer leaves die, they leave stubs on the stem, which eventually comes to resemble the neck of a plucked chicken. On a show plant, judges will subtract as much as three points for a "neck," depending on the specialty status of the competition. You can remedy the situation and keep a plant going indefinitely by one of two methods.

The easier way is to allow the plant to become slightly wilted, then remove it from the pot. Scrape the stem only down to the cambium (the green growing area just below

the surface). Next, cut part of the root system off the bottom, removing as much soil as possible from the root ball. Then repot the plant low enough to bury most of the elongated stem and water it thoroughly. Put the newly potted saintpaulia in a plastic bag for about a month until the plant has developed a new root system; check it often and air it once in a while to prevent mildew.

The second method of rejuvenating a necky violet involves treating the whole plant as a tip cutting. Leaving about an inch (2.5 cm) of neck below the last row of healthy leaves, slice through the stem, scrape the stem of the cutting as described above, and put the tip cutting in a propagation box to

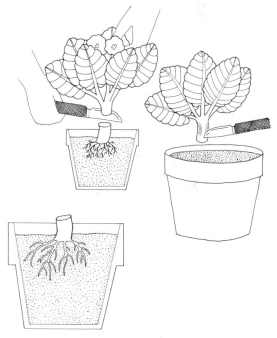

The Tip-Cutting Method of Rejuvenation: An older African violet with an elongated neck can receive a face-lift of sorts by being handled as a tip cutting. Cut through the stem an inch (2.5 cm) below the last row of healthy leaves. Scrape the stem until you reach the green layer, then place this cutting in propagating medium where it will root. The original stem can be left in the pot and cut back until 1 inch (2.5 cm) remains. With an application of mild fertilizer, leaves can begin to emerge from the stem sides in a matter of weeks.

root. Trim the stump remaining in the pot so about one inch (2.5 cm) protrudes above the soil and apply some mild liquid fertilizer. In a few weeks leaves should start to emerge from the sides of the truncated neck.

In propagating gesneriads with solid tubers (such as *Sinningia* and *Chrysothemis*), two tubers instead of one can be gotten by wounding the petiole of a leaf cutting. If the petiole is not injured, a single tuber will form on the base of the leaf-petiole cutting. Extra shoots from recently sprouted tubers can be removed and rooted easily.

Streptocarpus or *Sinningia speciosa* leaves can be propagated in two ways. The first approach is to cut triangular sections and plant them as described under Leaf Cuttings, in chapter 8. Or you can remove the main vein and place the two halves cut side down in the propagation medium as shown in the illustration.

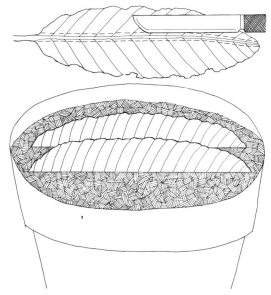

Leaf Section Propagation: *Streptocarpus* species or *Sinningia speciosa* respond well to this method, which is relatively easy to perform. Take the leaf you have removed, lay it flat, and slice along both sides of the main vein. Then, take both halves and place them in the propagating medium with cut sides down. Plantlets will appear along the edges of the leaf halves, and can then be removed and potted up to mature further.

Propagules occur not only at the base of all gesneriads with scaly rhizomes, but in the leaf axils of *Achimenes, Chrysothemis,* and some *Gloxinia* species, and less frequently on inflorescences. These may be removed and propagated as rhizomes.

BREEDING GESNERIADS

Gesneriad flowers contain both stamens (male parts) and pistil (female part). Self-pollination does not always occur in gesneriads, however, because the pollen is sometimes shed before the stigma is receptive. Depending on the genus, three days or more may elapse between the occurrence of those two events within a single flower. This time lag may make successful pollination difficult, for the pollen that reaches the stigma must be fresh (used shortly after the flower opens or after being stored properly as described in chapter 8), and the stigma must be receptive to it (that is, open and sticky).

Because both parts of a gesneriad flower are not always ready at the same time, cross-pollination between flowers on the same plant or on different plants may be necessary. To carry on the same strain, you may wish to work with two flowers on the same plant or on separate plants of the same variety. To be more adventurous, use flowers on two different varieties or cultivars or try crossing two gesneriad genera to obtain a bigeneric hybrid. (This has been done quite successfully: for example, ×*Stroxinia* is a hybrid cross of *Streptocarpus* and *Gloxinia* and ×*Eucodonopsis* is an intergeneric hybrid of *Achimenes* and *Smithiantha*.) Whatever the origin, the parent flower that furnishes the pollen is called the pollen parent; the one that bears the seeds is called the seed parent.

EQUIPMENT AND TECHNIQUES

The materials needed in plant breeding are probably already on hand or are inexpensive to purchase. They also are easy to use. Items required are a magnifying glass (10 or 15 power), tweezers, small sharp-pointed scissors, camel-hair brush or toothpicks (optional), small vials or containers, alcohol, rubber bands or soft wire, paper or plastic bags, paper clips, tags, notebook and pen, and two colors of thread.

The steps in breeding are simple:

1. Mark blossoms serving as parents with different color threads.
2. Protect the flower to be used as the seed parent from unwanted pollen by emasculating it (removing the stamens) before the anthers split open and before the stigma gets ripe (becomes sticky). To do this, just before or soon after the corolla has opened, use scissors to make a circular cut around the petals near the base, leaving the petal stubs still attached to the calyx. You will see the pollen sacs at the top of four thin filaments. Remove them and the filaments with tweezers.
3. Cover the emasculated flower of the seed parent with a protective bag.
4. When the stigma of the seed parent is sticky and the pollen parent is ripe and fertile (the anthers usually split open, releasing the pollen), it is time to remove the stamens from the pollen parent and uncover the seed parent.
5. Use tweezers to split the pollen sac if you are working with plants such as *Saintpaulia, Petrocosmea, Boea,* and others where pollen is not readily shed. (With *Columnea, Aeschynanthus, Sinningia,* and *Streptocarpus,* there is no need to slit the sac.) Next, remove an anther with your fingers or tweezers, wipe it across the recep-

tive stigma and discard it and wash your hands. If you prefer, you may use then throw away a toothpick. Some hybridizers employ a small brush to transfer the pollen to the stigma, but fingers are just as effective and eliminate the possibility of contaminating a new flower with pollen from the last cross. (Clean any tools you do use in alcohol after each use to keep this from happening.)

6. Replace the protective bag over the flower with the treated stigma. If a cross has taken, the remaining portion of the corolla will drop from the calyx within 48 hours and the ovary will begin to swell. It is best to pollinate several flowers at the same time to increase chances that at least one will be fertilized; if all the flowers produce seed pods, you can easily snip some off.
7. Label the seed parent with a small string-tag that includes the botanical name of the seed and pollen parents and the date on which the cross was made. Attach the label to the flower stalk just below the blossom which has been pollinated.
8. Record each cross and subsequent information on resulting offspring on a separate page of a notebook.

Gesneriad seed pods vary in size, shape, number of seeds produced, and rate of development. The pods of *Sinningia* mature in six weeks whereas *Saintpaulia* pods require six to nine months. Leave the pod on the plant until the pod is brown and dry and cracked. Then remove the stem, label and all, mark the date on the label, and record it in your notebook. Put the stem in a warm, airy (but not drafty) place to continue drying.

If the fruit of your plant is a berry (e.g.,

Sample Notebook Page

Kind of Plant

Seed parent

Pollen parent

Date cross made   Year, then number to be assigned offspring
                         (example: 80-1, 80-2)

Traits of seed parent

Traits of pollen parent

Traits desired of offspring

Offspring notes:

Date planted	Date of first flowering	Traits			Date of pollination		Harvesting information	
		Size	Color	Etc.	first	last	date	no. of seed

Recording Data for Effective Gesneriad Breeding: Once you have successfully pollinated and fertilized a flower, it is to your advantage to keep careful records of information (such as physical descriptions and significant dates) relating both to parent plants and their offspring. Keeping a well-documented notebook will assist you in refining your breeding process until you have arrived at the desired traits.

from *Columnea, Episcia,* or *Codonanthe*), allow it to remain on the plant until the flower stalk is dry and the berry has begun to shrivel. Then mash the berry on a piece of smooth paper, smearing it around. Allow it to dry. Then carefully remove the seed.

If you plan to introduce a new cultivar, you must continue crossing your seedlings to the third sexual generation, eliminating the poorer ones carefully. Should you pursue gesneriad breeding for any length of time, you will learn that some genes (cells that determine genetic traits of a plant or animal) are dominant and others recessive. Hybridizers study such matters very carefully and plan all crosses with the goal of eventually attaining a plant with specific, sought-after characteristics. It sometimes requires many years to achieve the desired end.

For information on introducing and registering a new cultivar in any gesneriad genus except *Saintpaulia,* you can write to the registrar of the American Gloxinia and Gesneriad Society, Inc.; *Saintpaulia* information and registration materials are available from the registrar of the African Violet Society of America, Inc. (see Appendix for addresses).

SHOWING GESNERIADS

The variety and versatility of the Gesneriaceae makes this plant family an ideal choice for the flower show enthusiast. Indeed, the rapid rise in popularity and the availability of many types of gesneriads is testimony to the appeal of the striking displays hobbyists and commercial growers have provided for the public.

Generally, gesneriads are exhibited in three major horticultural classifications: those grown primarily for bloom; those grown primarily for foliage; and those species or hybrids new to cultivation. Classes may also be offered for miniatures, terraria, artistically grown specimens, or for cut flower arrangements. In addition, some shows may provide special classes for novice exhibitors, juniors, or commercial exhibits.

The classes available are determined by the Show Committee and will vary according to the size of the show and degree of specialization. The judging system may vary as well, though the standard one employed is that termed Competitive-Merit. Under this system each plant in the class is scored numerically on a scale of 100 points. The highest-scoring plant (over 90 points) wins First in the class, the next highest wins Second, and so forth. When the first-place plant in each class has been determined, the judges select from these specimens the Best in Show and, if any special awards are to be presented, designate their recipients as well.

POINT SCALES

The categories of Gesneriads in Bloom and Gesneriads Grown for Foliage are the major horticultural sections in which your plants are likely to compete. Under Gesneriads in Bloom you will find subdivisions for tuberous, rhizomatous, and fibrous gesneriads and, under each of those headings, classes for specific genera (such as *Sinningia, Achimenes,* and *Columnea*). There may even be further specialization of classes (for example, *Sinningia speciosa,* single-flowered; *Sinningia speciosa,* double-flowered). In the foliage category you probably will be offered a class specifically for episcias, and another for "Any Other" foliage plant (*Chirita sinensis, Nautilocalyx,* and so forth).

Familiarity with the Point Scales and the criteria judges use in evaluating your plant should help you to select plants worthy of being shown, and to show them to their best advantage. That should insure success, even if you have never shown a plant in competition before.

The Point Scales total 100 points, the "perfect specimen" in the eyes of the judging team. While this ideal of perfection exists only conceptually, it is a concept worthy of respect, for all qualified judges are trained to envision that 100-point paragon of perfection,

Growing for Show: When raising a plant for show (like this African violet), you should strive for a symmetrical, compact rosette and an abundance of flowers in good condition held nicely above the foliage.

and to assess your plant accordingly. Plants competing in the Gesneriads in Bloom category are given up to 40 points for cultural perfection, a maximum of 35 for quantity of bloom, and up to 25 points for condition. Entries in the foliage category can earn the same top scores of 40 and 25 for cultural perfection and condition, but derive the up to 35 points remaining from their score for ornamental value. (In the New Cultivar class of either category, the emphasis on horticultural perfection is expanded to include distinctiveness and desirability of the new plant.)

It might be helpful to think of expanding your role from grower to critic, for the greatest competitive advantage you can acquire is the ability to evaluate your own plants objectively as they grow under the unique combination of cultural techniques and environment you can offer them.

Following is an explanation of the criteria judges use in evaluating show plants. Used as a guide, it may help you grow and exhibit your plants to best advantage. Do so with confidence and enjoyment, remembering that your judges are also your fellow growers. They are personally familiar with the problems inherent in growing, timing, and transporting show gesneriads. They volunteer time and effort to acknowledge plants of merit, and approach this task with respect for you and your well-grown plant.

The score attained for Cultural Perfection indicates how well you have grown your plant throughout its entire cycle. Judges note its overall appearance and vigor to determine if it has been consistently healthy and culturally sound.

They look for indications of proper growing conditions (appropriate light, temperature, humidity) and careful management (the best use of water, fertilizer, bench space and pot size, pruning and shaping)—all factors which affect your plant and contribute to its show potential.

Also noted is foliage which is crisp, uniformly colored, glowing with a sheen of health, lacking blemishes of any sort, and devoid of symptoms of pests or disease. The judges observe petioles (leaf stems) and internodes (distance between successive sets of leaves); here, lankiness could indicate an underlit or underfed plant, or one grown too quickly in too warm a temperature. They note absence of intermittent growth spurts, as would occur with sporadic care. On plants in bloom, the length and strength of pedicels (flower stems) are examined. These should support their blossoms securely and distribute them evenly and visibly.

Those judging note a well-established plant, securely centered in its pot, mature enough to exemplify the characteristics of its type. On a rosette-type plant they look for flat, evenly spaced leaves, indicating proper lighting, and the absence of foliage stretching upward or curling downward, indicating improper culture. Also desirable are strong, straight stems on an upright cultivar; supple and evenly layered strands on trailers; leaves

intact the entire length of the strands, lack of bare patches, and the absence of mechanical damage.

Penalty for mechanical damage to plants depends on its extent, and on whether it is recent enough to have happened at the show, or is due to past carelessness. Since accidents do happen, mechanical damage is less severely penalized than that caused by pests, disease, or improper culture.

Whereas the points given for Cultural Perfection indicate how well you have grown your plant, the score obtained for Condition evaluates how well you have shown it. Condition, simply, is grooming: this may be a perfunctory quick shower and change of pot, or involve decisive camouflage techniques.

Judges note a clean, well-watered plant, centered in a clean container which is in proper proportion to plant size. They notice the absence of stale, damaged, or unbalanced growth, stubs, seed pods (though decorative seed pods and showy calyxes may remain), or residues of sprays, mud, or dust. Looking for the absence of crusts, algae, or debris on pot or potting mix surfaces, the evaluators note the absence of faded, limp blossoms and generally check pistils and stamens, which begin to darken and shrivel when the flower is past its prime.

Condition may well be affected by the location and duration of the show. Transporting show plants and maintaining their pristine, fresh appearance is a challenge to even the most experienced showman. Temperature and humidity fluctuations at the show site may contribute additional problems. Nevertheless, judges can base their critique only on the condition of the plant before their eyes. They can imagine neither how it looked yesterday, nor how it might look after tomorrow's shower. Your skill in showmanship is of importance here, and a wise exhibitor travels to the show with an array of grooming tools, ready for last-minute repairs or primping.

The point score awarded for Quantity of

Bloom takes into account open flowers, buds, and showy calyxes. There is no particular number of flowers which is "right," rather a total effect to consider: the portrayal of a plant in full bloom, with its mass of flowers in good proportion to its mass of foliage. Quantity of Bloom should, in all cases, be representative of the particular cultivar being judged. Therefore, you would not be penalized for showing a plant with a sparse bud count if that were recognized as typical for that cultivar. Likewise, some gesneriads produce flowers which remain on the plant in good condition for quite some time; these cultivars would be expected to be exhibited with a greater accumulation of bloom than would a cultivar having blossoms that quickly fade and drop.

While buds showing color are counted nearly as heavily as open flowers, plants having only buds cannot be credited and should not be shown until further developed.

Gesneriads grown and shown primarily for foliage are evaluated for Ornamental Value rather than amount of bloom. They must possess distinctive enough foliage and growth habit to command attention without the advantage of bloom, though the presence of flowers is acceptable on plants entered in this category. Judges note foliage color, texture, and patterning, the growth habit of the plant, and the grower's skill in capitalizing on both to show it to full advantage.

A class for New Cultivar, Hybrid, or Species is generally offered at larger specialty shows, and is designed to introduce new plant material to judges, commercial growers, and the public. The point scale is as follows:

Cultural Perfection	25
Desirability of Plant	25
Quantity of Bloom	15
Condition	15
Distinctness	15
Educational Labeling	5

Cultural perfection, quantity of bloom, and condition are evaluated as described above.

The score for Desirability of Plant reflects the ornamental value of the new plant. Judges note its size and growth habit, its floriferousness, and the color, texture, and size of its leaves and flowers. However, the paramount consideration is whether the new introduction is an attractive, manageable, worthy addition to the Gesneriaceae.

Points garnered for Distinctness are based on an evaluation of whether the new plant differs sufficiently from others in its genus to warrant encouragement on its own merits.

For maximum point value, Educational Labeling should include information pertinent to the origin of the plant and, if a hybrid, its parentage.

In the Horticultural Division miniatures will be judged for the same qualities as their larger relatives. Technically, miniature gesneriads measure six inches (15 cm) or less in diameter. They tend to respond poorly to temperature and humidity fluctuations and are often displayed in a glass case supplied by the Show Committee. If one is not available it is usually permissible to show your miniature in a spotless glass container.

In summation, showing gesneriads is a challenging, rewarding experience, but there are only two requirements important to your success: the first is to grow healthy, robust plants; the second is to recognize the role of, and techniques for, grooming. Then, you have only to travel carefully to the show, and enjoy it.

CHAPTER 14

Bromeliads

Since their discovery by Columbus in 1493, bromeliads have had a fascinating history. Columbus first found the fruit of the edible pineapple (*Ananas comosus*) growing on the island of Guadalupe in the West Indies. He brought the pineapple, a bromeliad, back to Queen Isabella and soon after an appetite for its fruit spread throughout Europe. Explorers and fortune hunters set out for the New World in hopes of locating new species to delight the palates of their patrons. By the 1500s, the pineapple was popular worldwide. European botanical gardens began to send collectors to Central and South America, as did commercial nurseries and wealthy indi-

viduals. By the 1850s, hundreds of species of bromeliads could be found in European gardens and hothouses.

Further interest in the Bromeliad family grew. Propagation and hybridization of these plants had begun in commercial nurseries where the "inedible value" of the bromeliad as an ornamental house plant was discovered. Although early New England colonists had used the pineapple as a symbol of hospitality for West Indian rum-runners, bromeliads as ornamentals were not commercially marketed in the United States until the late 1800s.

In the 1930s Americans began to collect and cultivate bromeliads in quantity. In

Natural Habitat: At low altitudes, epiphytic bromeliads cluster in the trees of a lush tropical rain forest.

Opposite, inflorescence of variegated pineapple, Ananas comosus *'Variegatus'.*

1935, Mulford Foster from Florida, known by some as the modern-day father of the bromeliad, made a landmark voyage to Brazil and returned with over 200 previously unidentified species. Foster's remarkable success, along with the keen interest of a small group of enthusiasts, led to the establishment of the Bromeliad Society in Los Angeles in 1950. The Bromeliad Society was formed to promote the exchange of plants, cultural hints, and experiences.

Plants in the huge Bromeliad family are nonwoody, or herbaceous, and are usually characterized by long, stiff leaves, often in the form of stemless rosettes. Approximately 45 genera and 2,000 species of bromeliads are known and named to date. These dramatic plants range from 1 inch (2.5 cm) to 30 feet

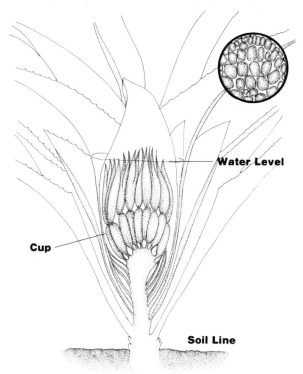

Bromeliad Structure: This cross section of a typical bromeliad rosette shows the inflorescence in the center of the rosette, in the cup formed by the plant's overlapping leaves. Detail shows the arrangement of scales on the leaf surface.

(9.1 m) in height, and some of the larger ones attain the form of subshrubs. Most are epiphytes, that is, they are found growing in organic debris trapped high up in the various angles and crotches in the limbs of trees and shrubs. Others, however, are terrestrials, living in soil and organic litter at ground level.

Except for one species native to the rocks and cliffs of West Africa (*Pitcairnia feliciana*), bromeliads are found in the subtropics and tropics of Central, South, and North America. Their habitats within this area are extremely variable. At low altitudes they may be found in rain forests on trees and on the ground, on desert sands and on cacti, or on seashore sands and rocks. Bromeliads also may exist at great elevations, to 14,000 feet on the rocky slopes of inhospitable mountains. Humidity in these diverse environments varies from desert dryness to the constant wet stickiness of a lowland tropical rain forest, and the water supply may be anywhere from almost nonexistent to abundant, ranging from an occasional rain or fog to frequent daily downpours. The temperatures where these plants grow range from the sharp cold of a mountainside to the steamy heat of a jungle, but most of the bromeliads used as house plants are found in the warm, humid rain forests of the tropics.

SOME BROMELIAD BOTANY

The leaves of these distinctive-looking plants are usually long and stiff, and are most commonly arranged in a stemless rosette. Like corn leaves, bromeliad leaves, with the exception of those of some *Pitcairnia* species, have no leaf stalk (petiole). The leaf bases overlap to form a continuous sheath, which gives the interior of the rosette a cuplike or tubular appearance. A few bromeliads, such as those in the genus *Puya*, have stems.

The upper and/or lower surface of the bromeliad leaves is covered with scales. These are specialized structures which absorb water and nutrients through the leaves much as the roots of terrestrial plants absorb these substances from the soil. If present in sufficient numbers, scales give a silvery cast to the leaves. Sometimes their distribution is such that they give the appearance of silver bands. All bromeliads have scales, although some species have so few that they are not readily visible. Leaves can be colors other than green or silvery green; dramatic bands, splotches, or variegations of red, pink, purple, yellow, black, cream, or white are also possible, especially in hybrids. Leaf texture varies from soft and delicate to tough, leathery, and spiny.

Flower stalks arise from the center of the rosette. Sometimes, as with *Cryptanthus* and *Neoregelia*, these are so insignificant as to be unnoticed, and the flowers appear to sit in the cup of the rosette. In other bromeliads (such as *Aechmea* and *Guzmania*), the flower stalks are taller—in certain *Billbergia* and *Tillandsia* species, they are so tall that they are pendent, or leaning over. Bromeliad flowers vary considerably. There may be as few as one or as many as a few thousand flowers on a plant. The inflorescence (flower spike or cluster) on the stalk can assume several forms: heads, panicles, racemes, or spikes (see illustration). Blooms are found in varying shades of yellow, red, blue, purple, or white. However, it is often not the flowers, but the bracts (modified leaves found at the base of the flowers) that make the inflorescence attractive. These bracts are brilliantly colored in hues of red, rose, white blushed with pink, orange, yellow, yellow-orange, purple, and even two-tone combinations. The fruits produced by the plants can be dry and leathery (capsules); separate, fleshy, and colorful (berries); or collective masses of individual fruits (multiple fruits). The pineapple is an example of a bromeliad that bears a multiple fruit.

Roots of epiphytic bromeliads serve more for anchorage than for water and nutrient absorption. It is sometimes possible to distinguish an epiphytic plant from a terrestrial one in that the first has a less pro-

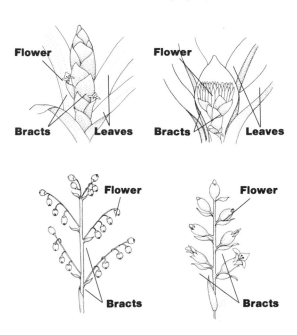

Bromeliad Inflorescence: The four possible forms of bromeliad inflorescence are (clockwise from upper left) spike, head, raceme, or panicle.

nounced root system. Though scales can be found on both forms, the rosette cup is associated mostly with epiphytes. In terrestrial bromeliads, the rosette is often lower and only a slight cup—or no cup at all—is apparent. These are not absolute differences; some exceptions do exist, such as in certain species that can exist in either epiphytic or terrestrial habitats. But observing the roots and leaves can serve as a general guide to differentiating between the two bromeliad forms.

NOMENCLATURE

There are about 45 genera in the Bromeliad family (Bromeliaceae), and they can be grouped into three subfamilies. The first is Pitcairnioideae, which contains the less attractive, more primitive genera. Of these, *Deuterocohnia, Dyckia, Fosterella, Hechtia, Pitcairnia,* and *Puya* are seen in cultivation. Plants of all these genera, except for *Fosterella* and *Pitcairnia,* have a rosette of stiff, succulent, spiny leaves which are usually drab shades of green, gray, or blue-green. Except for a few climbing and spiny species, pitcairnias have a rosette of smooth, grasslike leaves. Leaves of all pitcairnias have silvery scales on the undersides. Most are terrestrial, though very few species of *Pitcairnia* may be epiphytic. Their tubular flowers are found in shades of yellow, red, orange, or white. Each floret opens for a single day, but the tall stalk will produce an inflorescence that can provide color for several months. Some *Pitcairnia* species are quite decorative, but they are not among the most beautiful bromeliads. While over 260 species are described, only a few are known in cultivation. Some plants in this subfamily, especially *Dyckia* and *Hechtia*, will take on brilliant shades of red when exposed to bright light.

Bracts and Flowers: The brilliant red bracts of *Tillandsia flabellata* give the inflorescence its striking appearance. The actual flower can be seen extending outward near the top of the bract.

Another subfamily is Tillandsioideae. It contains the following genera seen in cultivation: *Catopsis, Guzmania, Tillandsia,* and *Vriesea.* The less common *Catopsis, Glomeropitcairnia,* and *Mezobromelia* are usually found only in the collections of bromeliad specialists. These genera are primarily epiphytic, with minimal roots and spineless leaves. *Tillandsia* is a variable genus with forms ranging from rosette to bulbous to lichenlike. Some are covered with silver scales. The well-known Spanish moss (*T. usneoides*) is found in this genus, and it and other species of *Tillandsia* are the predominant bromeliads of North America. Over 400 species are known and listed to date.

Vriesea and *Guzmania* add to the beauty of the Tillandsioideae subfamily. *Vriesea* is probably the bromeliad genus that has been hybridized the most due to its beautiful form and showy inflorescence. Many of its species have a rosette form.

Vriesea hieroglyphica and *V. fosterana* 'Red Chestnut' are probably the most sought-after members of the *Vriesea* genus, but unfortunately, they are not abundant commercially at this time. However, the genus *Vriesea* includes over 200 other recognized species and innumerable hybrids to delight the home grower. The inflorescence usually bears an erect, two-ranked spike of flowers. The bracts are both brilliant and showy and will last in color for many months. They are smooth edged and easy to handle and their adaptability to indoor conditions makes them a highly desirable house plant. *V. splendens,* often referred to as the flaming sword, is probably the most available *Vriesea* on the commercial market, popular because of its beautifully marked foliage and striking, swordlike inflorescence. However, it is not always the easiest *Vriesea* to grow in the home. *V. incurvata* 'Poelmanii' and other *Vriesea* hybrids are equally beautiful and may give the beginner a more successful start.

The genus *Guzmania* also is becoming a house plant favorite and *G. lingulata* has

Tillandsioideae: Three members of this subfamily are shown here (left to right): *Guzmania lingulata* var. *cardinalis,* *Vriesea splendens,* and *Tillandsia flabellata* 'Rubra'.

long been cultivated by bromeliad collectors. The increasing popularity of this plant is making it more widely available in plant shops than it has been in the past.

The last subfamily, Bromelioideae, contains the most genera (25), the most widely cultivated species, the greatest variety of form, and undoubtedly the most attractive bromeliads. The edible pineapple is a member of this group. Genera seen in cultivation include *Acanthostachys, Aechmea, Ananas, Billbergia, Bromelia, Canistrum, Cryptanthus, Fascicularia, Hohenbergia, Neoglaziovia, Neoregelia, Nidularium, Ochagavia, Orthophytum, Portea, Pseudananas, Quesnelia, Ronnbergia, Streptocalyx,* and *Wittrockia.* Many are epiphytic, but some (*Ananas* and *Bromelia*) are terrestrial with

no cup. Members of the Bromelioideae are often rosette in form and many do have the typical bromeliad cup. Bromelioideae are easily distinguished from the other two subfamilies by their berry fruits and the presence of marginal spines which may grow quite large. The most commonly found genera in this subfamily are *Aechmea, Ananas, Billbergia, Cryptanthus, Neoregelia,* and *Nidularium.*

Certainly the most famous of this subfamily is the edible pineapple (*Ananas comosus*), but *Aechmea fasciata,* often referred to as silver king, or sometimes mistakenly called Foster's favorite, is the most popular indoor ornamental house plant of the entire family.

The genus *Aechmea* is prized primarily for its long-lasting blooms. *A. fasciata* will bloom for three months and the blooms of

Bromelioideae: Six members of this large and varied subfamily are shown here (clockwise from front): *Cryptanthus fosteranus* 'Elaine', *Neoregelia carolinae, Ananas comosus, Aechmea fasciata, Billbergia pyramidalis* 'Striata', and (center) *Nidularium bilbergioides.*

some species may last for a year. Every stage of the *Aechmea* bloom is magnificent to watch. The flower spike (inflorescence) will appear gradually over the months in an assortment of colors and will reach its berrying stage without special prodding. The berry colors vary from species to species.

The genus *Billbergia* is noted for its unusual appearance and assuredly has the most intricate and delicate of all bromeliad blooms. Though the flowers are beautiful, the flowering period is short, but this should not dis-

courage you. *Billbergia* is generally an excellent breeder and will cluster readily. A cluster of billbergias will often bloom two or three times a year.

Species of the genus *Cryptanthus* (often called earth stars) are common in cultivation and have been used widely in dish gardens and terrarium planters. They are low-growing, terrestrial members of the Bromeliad family and are characterized by their starlike leaf formation. Their blooms, for the most part, are simple, but their foliage can vary in color from bright red and pink to a deep fudge with silver-frosted banding. Probably the two most prized and widely grown earth stars are *Cryptanthus* 'It' and *C. bromelioides* var. *tricolor*. Both of these plants are variegated, and may be striped with pink, white, or green.

Another popular bromeliad genus found in cultivation is the *Neoregelia*. The two most widely found neoregelias are *N. carolinae* and *N. carolinae* 'Tricolor'. Neoregelias, in general, are characterized by a rosette of leaves forming a cup. When in bloom, these plants have an inflorescence deeply set in the cup, with small blue flowers. The most attractive quality of the *Neoregelia* species is not the flowers, but the central leaves, which will blush in an array of colors ranging from pink, violet, or purple, to red. The central leaves will maintain their color for months after the plant has finished blooming, provided the plant is given bright light. Most neoregelias reproduce readily, but the center of the cup of the *Neoregelia* must be kept fairly dry during the blooming period to prevent rot. Neoregelias are a favorite for indoor gardens and are frequently grown outdoors in the southern parts of Florida, Louisiana, Texas, and California. Many gardeners enjoy experimenting with their neoregelias by changing light and humidity factors to bring out different pigment colorations. Because of the variations possible in pigmentation and the ease of growing these plants, they have become popular with hybridizers.

The genus *Nidularium* has been in favor with Europeans for centuries, and in the last few years has come to the attention of plant lovers in the United States. *Nidularium* species are often confused with *Neoregelia*, because both genus names begin with the letter "N" and also because there are similarities in their blooming habits. But the leaves of *Nidularium* are generally softer than those of *Neoregelia* and their central leaves are more defined and expressive. The leaves of *Nidularium* can be indescribably subtle in their beauty. *Nidularium innocentii* var. *innocentii* and *Nidularium burchellii,* two very intriguing species, are characterized by subtle and frosted purple iridescent leaves. They will maintain their color in medium light, and make excellent house plants. They are easy to grow, and can take a fair amount of abuse.

HYBRIDS

Many genera of the Bromeliad family are used in hybridizing. These hybrids may be intergeneric crosses between species of two genera, or crosses between species within one genus. There are three intergeneric crosses seen frequently in cultivation: × *Cryptbergia,* a cross between a *Cryptanthus* and a *Billbergia;* × *Neomea,* a cross between a *Neoregelia* and an *Aechmea;* and × *Neophytum,* a cross between a *Neoregelia* and an *Orthophytum.* Genera frequently used to create hybrids between two species within a genus include *Aechmea, Billbergia, Canistrum, Cryptanthus, Dyckia, Guzmania, Neoregelia, Nidularium, Tillandsia,* and *Vriesea.* An example is the well-known hybrid *Aechmea* 'Foster's Favorite', which is a cross between *A. victoriana* var. *discolor* and *A. racinae.*

Another group of bromeliads listed as hybrids are simple crosses within one species between two differing varieties or clones. They are mostly obtained from varieties and clones of *Guzmania lingulata* and *Vriesea splendens.* An example is *G. lingulata* var. *intermedia,* which is a cross between *G. lingulata* var. *cardinalis* and *G. lingulata* var. *splendens.*

Intergeneric Hybrid: The hybrid *Cryptbergia* (foreground) represents a cross between two genera, *Cryptanthus* (left) and *Billbergia* (right).

CULTURE

Since bromeliads can tolerate a reasonable deviation from natural habitat conditions in regard to light, temperature, and other factors, they are excellent choices for use in the home with either natural or artificial light, or in the greenhouse. The species in the subfamily Bromelioideae have slightly more tolerance than the others, so these would be the best choice for homes where conditions are less than good for house plants. As with any house plant, optimal results with bromeliads are best obtained by creating an indoor environment similar to their natural habitat. In this respect organic gardeners will have an edge, since a basic in the bromeliad habitat is a growing medium richer in organic matter than the standard house plant mixes.

POTTING

Epiphytic and terrestrial bromeliads can be grown in similar media, with the ingredients mixed in varying proportions. The potting mix may consist of any of a number of different materials, but must always possess excellent aeration, good drainage, and organic matter to retain some moisture and fertility and to hold the plant erect. The organic matter can be peat moss, leaf mold, osmunda fiber, shredded fir or redwood bark, or even two- or three-year-old sawdust. Adding an equal volume of coarse builder's sand, perlite, or crushed gravel about ¼ inch (6 mm) in diameter improves aeration and drainage. (One good mixture is leaf mold plus sand.) The use of these materials usually produces a medium with the correct pH, which is slightly acidic to neutral.

In general, epiphytic bromeliads need a looser potting mix than terrestrial types. Because epiphytes feed through their leaves and use their roots primarily for anchorage, the roots are adapted to being exposed to air and need a mix that is extremely well aerated. Terrestrial bromeliads need a higher proportion of organic matter because of their greater number of feeding roots. Many epiphytes will thrive in a terrestrial mix (and usually will develop some feeding roots), but terrestrial species usually cannot get enough nourishment from an epiphytic potting mix.

Epiphytic and terrestrial bromeliads both can be grown in conventional pots of clay or plastic. Success is likely with either kind of pot, as long as the differences in watering and fertilization indicated for each are recognized. When potting, never set the leaf bases much below the surface of the medium. If a young plant or offset has not yet developed its root system, it can be staked until roots form that can hold it up. Use wood or bamboo for stakes—never use copper or galvanized wire, which can burn bromeliad leaves.

Epiphytic species, especially small plants such as tillandsias, can be grown in and on a wide range of unusual containers and mounts, in addition to pots. For example, with their roots enclosed in a ball of sphagnum moss tied securely with nylon fishing line, they may be suspended from a small tree branch or dowel to form a living mobile.

Eye-catching wall displays can be worked up using cork wall paneling, natural cork bark, driftwood, a piece of tree fern trunk, a weathered board, or any piece of wood providing a rough surface to which the bromeliad can cling.

If the backing material you choose has natural hollows, like driftwood, plants should be set into them. Wrap plant roots in a ball of sphagnum moss bound together with fishing line or plastic-coated wire. Then, with additional lengths of fishing line or coated wire, fasten the plant securely to the backing using tacks or a staple gun.

If plants are to be mounted on a board or other flat surface, a perch can be constructed for them. Mold a small pocket from chicken wire and staple or tack the outer edges to the backing. Line the basket with approximately an inch (2.5 cm) of dampened sphagnum, and insert the plant. If further support is necessary, use fishing line or plastic-coated wire to attach the plant to the wire pocket.

WATER AND NUTRIENTS

Water requirements of bromeliads vary extensively. Some species can withstand so much drying that they are xerophytic like cacti—that is, they can adapt, live, and grow with a limited water supply. Others need constant moisture. Appearance can often aid in

Mounting Techniques for Epiphytes: Top, *Tillandsia bulbosa* (left) and *T. argentea* on a driftwood mobile; bottom, *T. fasciculata* mounted on a piece of wood for a wall display.

determining water requirements. Epiphytes with soft, green leaves, few silvery scales, and a cup require more water than most other bromeliads. Some water should be left in the cup at all times (although it's a good idea to change it occasionally) and the growing medium ought to be kept moist, but not soggy. If the epiphyte has a slight cup or none at all, many silvery scales, and stiffer leaves, it will need less water, and moderate drying between waterings is suggested. Terrestrial types extensively covered with scales and having stiff, leathery leaves require even less water and can be watered like cacti (*Bromelia* species and some of the genera in the Pitcairnioideae subfamily fit into this category). With the xerophytic tillandsias, spray-misting every few days may be enough. Softer-leaved terrestrials with few scales can tolerate moderate drying between waterings. *Dyckia, Hechtia,* and *Puya* prefer to be kept fairly dry at the roots. Saxicolous (rock-loving) species, including some *Pitcairnia* species, need to be kept moist.

Water can be sprayed on bromeliad foliage and allowed to drip into the growing medium, especially with those plants containing many scales. Spraying also helps to wash off accumulated dust particles which may clog leaf pores and scales. If you are in a hurry, water can be applied directly to the growing medium.

Bromeliads have adapted to do well without a lot of food. In nature, the only nutrients they absorb come from stray dead leaves or bird droppings that fall into their cups or nearby and an occasional insect that wanders into a water-filled cup.

Fertilization is relatively simple and the same for all types of bromeliads. Very weak manure tea makes a good bromeliad food, or use any good organic liquid fertilizer, diluted to one-half or one-quarter of the usual strength. It is a good idea to alternate fertilizers in order to provide varying N-P-K ratios. Fertilizer solutions can be sprayed on the leaves at monthly intervals. At six-month in-

Assembling a Bromeliad Tree

Bromeliad Tree: A striking way to display a group of epiphytic species.

Mounting several bromeliads on a tree limb makes for a striking display. The first step is to find the right "tree" for your bromeliads. Several types of wood are suitable. You might, for instance, choose a weathered, decay-resistant piece of oak, maple, or redwood. Avoid pieces with flaking bark or small holes which indicate termite activity. Look for a large branch with smaller lateral branches, or a weathered stump which may be inverted so that the roots become branches. If the wood you select is green, season it for a year in a dry location. The ocean carves stray branches into interesting shapes; if you comb the beach for a suitable driftwood planter, always soak the wood in fresh water to draw out the salt before you use it. The best specimens from either land or sea are those which provide crevices and a rough surface for your bromeliads to cling to. The size of the piece will depend on its intended location—whether it's to be set on a tabletop or placed on the floor.

When you have selected the wood, cut the bottom of the piece so it will stand flat. For more stability, larger pieces need to be anchored in a container, such as a redwood tub or small wooden barrel. To do this, mix 3 parts sand, 1 part cement and water as needed, pour into the container, and stand the tree upright, anchoring its base in the mortar. If you like, make an indentation in the mortar before it dries, to accommodate a terrestrial plant at the base of the tree. Allow the mortar to dry for 24 hours.

Next, using wood chisels or rotary files on an electric drill, scoop out planting spaces in the lateral branches or deepen natural hollows to about 1 inch (2.5 cm). Also, drill a few holes in the bottoms of these cavities for drainage.

Plants well suited to growing on a bromeliad tree include aechmeas (these larger plants should be placed at the base or on the lower branches), *Billbergia nutans, B. zebrina,* and small *Neoregelia* species. The smaller varieties of *Tillandsia* and *Cryptanthus* are also good candidates.

Anchor small plants without roots on the tree with a dab of silicone glue applied to the base of the plant. Encase the roots of larger plants in dampened sphagnum moss. Tie the sphagnum ball with plastic-coated wire, nylon fishing line, or thin strips of nylon stockings, then attach it to the tree, nestling in the planting spaces you've prepared. A small plastic-coated tack embedded in the branch can serve as an anchor for the wire, fishing line, or nylon stocking. Always position plants upright, so the vase can be kept filled with water. Finally, fill the hollow in the mortar base with bromeliad growing media. Some good plants to fill this ready-made spot are *Aechmea fasciata, Ananas comosus,* or *Billbergia nutans.*

Place the completed "tree" in a place where there is plenty of light, but where frequent mistings and dripping water will not do any damage to the floors or to furniture.

tervals, you can use an aqueous spray of sea-weed extract or any chelated fertilizer to supply trace elements to prevent micronutrient deficiencies. Fish emulsion, because it is oil-based, may clog the scales.

Take care never to feed a dry plant—always give it a little water first. And never pour any full-strength fertilizer directly into the plant's dry cup, or severe burning of new growth and leaves will occur. Metals and metallic salts are deadly to bromeliads.

With regular feeding, do not be surprised if your epiphytes soon develop as many feeding roots as the terrestrials. These plants respond to the environmental conditions created by consistent watering and fertilization, which are often lacking in their natural habitat.

LIGHT

As would be expected from their different habitats, bromeliads need varying amounts of light. The kinds with thick or stiff leaves require bright light and indirect sun, as do those covered heavily with scales. In the home a southern exposure would be best. Softer, more brightly colored, more strongly patterned leaves or few scales indicate the need for a more moderate level of light, such as that entering an eastern or western window. High light levels may actually lighten the leaf color of these types. Bromeliads with solid, dark leaves such as *Aechmea* 'Foster's Favorite' will bleach out in bright light. Others, like *Neoregelia carolinae* 'Tricolor' and *N. marmorata* will heighten in color with bright light.

If you see evidence of leaf burn, reduce the light exposure. Should the color of leaves appear drab, first try lowering the light level. If this fails, increase it. If you are using fluorescent lights (two 40-watt tubes per fixture are recommended), you might place the bromeliads requiring the higher light about six inches (15 cm) below the tubes and others about eight inches (20 cm) beneath. Change

the distance if leaf burn or poor coloration result. Most bromeliads will thrive if lights are on for 16 hours of the day and off for 8.

HUMIDITY

Epiphytic bromeliads require higher levels of humidity than the terrestrial types, which will tolerate the relative humidity of the average home. Epiphytes can tolerate these levels, too, but their appearance and well-being (as well as your own well-being) will improve over the years with a relative humidity of 40% to 60%. (Techniques for raising humidity levels are discussed in chapter 2.)

Good air circulation is another important key to healthy bromeliads. The epiphytes, in particular, which are found perched on tree-tops and limbs, are always exposed to fresh air in their natural habitat. (It is often thought that the most likely place for a bromeliad is in the bathroom, where there is higher humidity. However, many bathrooms have poor light, and poor air circulation, and growing an epiphyte in this environment may result in failure.)

TEMPERATURE

Nighttime temperature drops have become more commonplace in our homes since the energy crunch developed. A night temperature of 60°F (16°C) is fine for most bromeliads, and most of them can even tolerate night temperatures between 45° and 50°F (7° to 10°C). Daytime indoor temperatures (68°F/20°C or higher) pose no problems, although temperatures may be magnified by direct light through a window.

PESTS AND DISEASES

Pest and disease problems are minimal for bromeliads. Some trouble may occur with scale insects. These usually appear as brown or black hemispherical or oval structures on the upper or lower leaf surfaces. They are the same types of scale found on other common foliage plants. They may appear at any time, as bromeliads are suitable host plants, but they usually can be sponged off with soapy water. Red spider mites sometimes attack thin-leaved bromeliads and seedlings. See chapter 9 for further information on pest controls.

FLOWERING

Patience is indeed a virtue when it comes to coaxing blooms from a bromeliad. As a general rule the minimum time for flowering is three years from seed or about two from vegetative propagules (pups). If your bromeliad is mature and still not showing a flower bud, a change of environment is in order. First apply an organic fertilizer rich in phos-

The Apple-in-the-Bag Trick: To encourage a reluctant bromeliad to bloom, enclose a ripening apple and the plant in a clear plastic bag for a week. The ethylene gas given off by the ripening fruit may stimulate the bromeliad to bloom.

Don't Waste That Pineapple

Next time you buy a fresh pineapple, save the leafy crown with about an inch of attached fruit. Let this air dry for 36 to 48 hours until the fruit has callused over. Bury the crown cutting up to the bottom of its leaves in the growing medium suggested for bromeliads. Then place it in a sunny spot and spray it with water and fertilizer as suggested in the text. (Some indoor gardeners prefer to let the crown root in fertilized sand, leaving it in a warm, dark place until it does, then transplant it to the growing medium.) The growing medium should be kept moist, but never soggy. Water near the sides of the pot so the crown does not rot. Give the plant lots of light, and evenly warm temperatures of 75° to 85°F (24° to 29°C).

Fruit should appear after about two years. If it does not, try the apple-in-the-bag trick suggested under Flowering. If you are successful, you might have to support the developing fruit by staking it as it matures.

In any event, a vigorous pineapple may put forth as many as 80 leaves from 3 to 5 feet (0.9 to 1.5 m) long.

Propagating a New Plant from a Pineapple Fruit

Step 1: Cut off the crown with an inch (2.5 cm) of fruit attached.

Step 2: Bury the crown cutting in growing medium, taking care not to cover the bottom of the leaves.

Staking: As the pineapple fruit develops, it will need to be staked for added support.

phorus. If this doesn't work, try putting the plant into a brighter and/or warmer spot.

Should all these techniques fail to produce flowers within a year, it is time for the apple-in-the-bag trick. First pour off any water in the bromeliad cup. Obtain a fragrant ripening apple and enclose it and the bromeliad in a sealed, clear plastic bag. Keep the bagged plant out of the sun, but in a warm place. After one week remove the bag and apple and return the bromeliad to its former location.

This method can be used to force a pineapple or any other bromeliad to produce flowers and fruit within one year. The apple while ripening produces a gas called ethylene, which stimulates bromeliads to flower. Most cases of failure occur because the apple is way underripe or overripe, at which point ethylene production is minimal. Chemicals are available which produce ethylene, but they are explosive and/or flammable, and are best left alone. If this trick doesn't work the first time, wait a few months and try it again. (Note: Forced blooming may produce imperfect blooms or premature blooming in young offsets not yet detached from the parent plant. If you should decide to attempt to force blooming, be sure your plant is at a mature stage and well-established on its own.)

PROPAGATION

Completion of flowering signals the death knell for most bromeliads. They are monocarpic, that is, they flower once during their life cycle and then die within a year or two after the blooming period is over. Fortunately, most plants produce offsets that look like miniature rosettes during this time. These arise either in the leaf axils (as with most species of *Cryptanthus* and *Orthophytum,* and some *Tillandsia* species), or at the base of the plant (as with most species of *Aechmea, Billbergia, Neoregelia, Nidularium,* and *Quesnelia*). The offsets should be allowed to develop until they assume the characteristics of the parent plant, such as color and pattern. At this stage, they can be gently pulled away, or cut if resistant, making sure to get the complete rosette and as much of the stem as possible. If a wound is visible, allow the offsets to air dry for 24 hours out of the sun.

Then place each offset in a small pot of growing medium. Water and fertilize by foliar spraying at least until roots develop. Rooting may be very slow compared to other house plants, but this poses no problem since the leaf scales serve to absorb nutrients from the water.

Propagation of Offsets

Offsets that form in leaf axils come off easily with a gentle pull or twist. To remove stoloniferous offsets growing at the base of the plant, cut the stolon about 1 inch (2.5 cm) from the parent plant. If the stolon is long, trim it from the offset before planting. To remove an offset growing close to its parent, slide a sharp knife in between the offset and the parent, and carefully cut them apart so that neither plant is damaged.

Vriesea splendens and some related species must be treated a little differently from the norm. These species usually form just a single offset next to the old flower stalk. As the young plant grows, it eventually replaces the parent. The offshoot should be allowed to grow with the parent for several years before it is severed with a sharp knife or razor blade. Be sure to cut off a small piece of the old plant along with the youngster. Then discard the parent plant.

Bromeliads also can be grown from seed with good results. Commercial seeds are available, but you also might try producing your own. Most bromeliads have bisexual flowers, which have both a functional male (stamen) and female (pistil) reproductive structure. This makes self-pollination possible for individual plants. To facilitate it, as soon as the flower opens, remove the pollen grains (yellow granules) with a forceps or brush and place them on an open dish or wax paper to air dry for about two hours at room temperature. The pistil becomes receptive (looks moist) about two hours after the flower opens. At this time a small watercolor brush can be used to transfer the pollen to the sticky or moist top of the pistil (stigma). Depending on the species, seed will be produced in one to six months. Winged seeds usually form in dry pods within the subfamily Pitcairnioideae; winged, slow-germinating seeds with silky fibers are produced by Tillandsioideae; and plump seeds develop in the berries of Bromelioideae.

Seeds can be germinated on milled sphagnum moss or even on a wet paper towel in good light (but not direct sun) at 65° to 70°F (18° to 21°C). Use a glass or plastic cover to keep the humidity high. Some dilute organic fertilizer (about one-quarter of normal strength) may be needed before the seedlings are large enough to transplant into growing media.

GROOMING

Like all plants, bromeliads should always look their best. Glossy-leafed types like the pineapple are most attractive when their leaves are kept clean. Wipe the leaves gently with a damp cloth to remove dust and spots, supporting the underside of each leaf with your other hand to keep it from cracking. To impart a higher sheen to the leaves, wipe them with a dry cloth when they are dry.

Examine your plants regularly and strip off all dead and yellowing leaves. Any such leaves that cling tenaciously to the plant can be removed by splitting them down the middle and pulling the halves apart until they strip away from the plant. It is not a good idea to strip off too many leaves at once and leave several inches of the soft, white part of the stem exposed. Such practice weakens the stem and makes the plant more vulnerable to fungus invasions. When you need to remove several leaves at the same time, it is better to cut them off close to the stem than to strip them away completely.

Brown leaf tips can be simply trimmed off. Trimming the leaf to match its original shape will make the surgery less obvious than lopping off the brown tip straight across the leaf.

After plants have bloomed, remove dead flowers and stalks when they have dried out. It is also good practice to remove with a soft brush or cloth any debris that has collected between leaves or in the cups of plants having cups. Change the water in the cups from time to time to keep it fresh.

Removing Stubborn Leaves: Damaged or dying leaves that cling stubbornly to the plant call for special measures to remove them. First split the leaf lengthwise down the middle. Then pull the two halves apart until they strip away from the rosette.

CHAPTER 15

Cacti and Other Succulents

Often formidable, sometimes bizarre, but always intriguing, cacti and other succulents may justly be called the survivors of the plant world. Inured to hardships, these astonishingly rugged specimens thrive under indifferent care and reward the most casual attention with their unique symmetry and spination and sometimes with a blaze of silky, vividly colored flowers. Although they are rightly valued for being extraordinary to look at and easy to grow, succulents are also worth cultivating and understanding because

of their unparalleled ability to endure through adaptability and self-discipline in environments where many other living things have perished.

Not a biological category, the term "succulent" is derived from the Latin *succos*, meaning juicy, and is used to describe some 10,000 plants which are adapted to store and conserve water and thereby survive drought. There are more or less succulent plants in over 44 plant families — including such favorites as the Geranium family (Geraniace-

Victorian Cactus House: Cactus collections became the vogue in Europe in the late nineteenth century, when glass houses such as the one shown here were filled with an exotic assortment of plants. To meet the demand of European fanciers, cacti were snatched up in huge numbers from North America and shipped across the ocean, while Americans remained oblivious to the delight of raising these intriguing native plants. Eventually laws were enacted to prohibit the plundering of cacti, and Americans finally awoke to the wealth of plant life within their own borders, with the result that the cactus's popularity has been growing steadily.

Opposite, inflorescence of crown of thorns, Euphorbia milii *var.* splendens.

281

ae), Gesneriad family (Gesneriaceae), and Orchid family (Orchidaceae) — but an extreme modification of physiology is most prominently exhibited in the Cactus family (Cactaceae) and in the 7 other families of succulents discussed in this chapter.

Highly succulent plants often have short, thick shapes which contribute to the ability to store water and minimize transpiration by greatly reducing the plant's surface area relative to its volume. Other water-conserving characteristics are thickened sap, which is less readily evaporated, and a reduction in the number of pores through which precious moisture can be drawn out into the dry air. In some succulents, tubers or tuberous roots are adapted to store water. The so-called stem succulents are those in which leaves are reduced or absent and water is stored primarily in an enlarged stem; cacti and other plants of this kind are dicotyledonous. In the leaf succulents, water is stored primarily in thick, fleshy foliage. Often the extent of the fleshiness is a clue to the severity or length of the drought the plant endures in its natural habitat, and reveals whether the plant needs a more or less dry rest period in cultivation. Leaf succulents often are rosette formers or clustering plants; they may or may not have stems, which may be either woody or succulent, and they are usually monocotyledonous.

Many succulents live in semiarid or arid regions; some, like yucca, sagebrush, and mesquite actually prefer the hardship of prolonged dry spells. These are called xerophytes — the Greek word for dry plants. More surprisingly, some succulents are epiphytic, living on trees or rocks in South American forests, where they experience drought during the summer. Still others actually live in bogs, but need reserves of water to compensate for the fact that the soil they live in lacks oxygen and therefore prevents them from absorbing the water around them. Yet other succulents of an alpine nature depend on their water-saving traits to withstand the intense sun and drying winds found on rock faces at high altitudes.

CACTACEAE (CACTUS FAMILY)

Even more than most succulents, the cacti have made quantum biological leaps in their struggle to survive. Found almost entirely in the Western Hemisphere, this redoubtable family has managed to find niches for itself in one unique form or another at every altitude and in a surprising range of habitats. Cacti can be found growing under the winter snows of western Canada, in the dry heat of the Sonoran Desert, and even in the rain forests of South America, which are home to the tree-dwelling types.

Cacti are distinguished from other succulents by several characteristics. The most obvious is the spine-cushion, or areole, a kind of large pore found at the nodes of the plant stem. From the areoles arise small, usually short-lived leaves (in some cacti) and flower and vegetative buds. The bases of these pores also give rise to silky or woolly hairs, barbed bristles called glochids, or spines in various forms and combinations. The form these outgrowths take is used in classifying the various cacti. The Cactaceae also have distinctive flowers. The petals are variable in number, usually blending into the sepals with little difference in appearance. There are many stamens and the stigma is divided into several lobes. With or without stalks, cactus flowers are often silky, large, and fragrantly scented. Most bloom during the day, but some open at night, among them the famous cacti of the night-blooming cereus group.

Cacti are relative newcomers on the face of the earth, making their fantastic adaptations to adverse conditions during a short geological time period. One of the rare fossil cacti that has been found is from Utah and lived about 50 million years ago in the Middle Eocene period. The ancestors of that fossil cactus — probably small leafy trees with

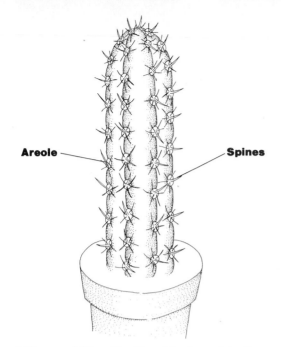

Areole —   — Spines

A Means of Classification: Members of the Cactus family are classified according to the form of the outgrowths along their surface. Shown here is a cylindrical cactus covered with spine-laden areoles. Areoles are large pores from which flowers and other vegetative growth may emerge. These pores are also dubbed spine-cushions since spines appear around their bases. In some cacti, variously textured hairs or barbed bristles called glochids are found clustered around the areoles.

woody trunks — began adopting their unusual shapes and growing habits in the Americas as geological uplifts left their environment progressively drier. While less adaptable plants failed to evolve, the early relatives of today's cacti apparently migrated into tropical grasslands and even up into trees. Their success there set the stage for the adaptation of later cacti to the more extreme conditions of the North American deserts.

One of the most useful evolutionary changes in the history of the cactus was the emergence of the spines that continue to exasperate would-be admirers. Some botanists contend that these were once the tips of growing twigs; others say they are a highly altered leaf. But regardless of their origin, cactus spines are one of the most versatile and effective design features in the plant world. Besides providing the plant with obvious physical protection from potential marauders, they absorb and reflect a great deal of intense desert sunlight. Like the shade of a miniature lath house, streaks of spine shadow keep the body tissue of the cactus in its natural environment 20°F (11°C) cooler than it would be without them. At the same time the spines, hairs, and fine bristles that cover the bodies of many cacti trap a thin layer of air next to the stem, serving as an insulation device similar to the fishnet underwear worn by a hiker. In this way the cactus is kept cooler by day and warmer by night.

On larger cacti, spines act as a windbreak by diffusing the force of the desert wind, and there is even a theory that they aid the cactus in pumping water up high stocks by acting as an ion generator. The wind passing through the spines, so the theory goes, creates a charge differential between the upper reaches of the cactus and the surrounding ground (including the free ions in the groundwater). The differential causes the water that is absorbed by the roots to be drawn up the body of the cactus, much as a magnet picks up iron filings from a piece of paper.

On young and smaller cacti, spines act as drip-tips, collecting mist, dew, fog, and light rain, and channeling the moisture in downspout fashion to the ground where developing roots can most readily pick it up. In some of the driest natural locations water collected this way can be a plant's major source of moisture.

As another creative response to an increasingly dry environment, cacti evolved cellular water-storage tissue, which gives the plants a spongelike interior. Cactus sap also became a mucilaginous substance that is not easily drawn out of the plant by the hot, dry winds of the desert (or the hot, dry winds of forced air heat). Obviously, it is only a figment of the imagination of some would-be Zane Grey that a cowboy or prospector, dying of thirst in the desert, need only split open a barrel cactus to get his fill of fresh water. How many old barrel cacti, one wonders,

Intriguing and Mysterious Spines: There is no consensus among experts as to how these menacing but eminently useful features evolved. There's no doubt that they serve as self-defense, for what creature would dare accost a soft, succulent plant body, fairly bristling with needle-sharp spines? There is a wide diversity of spine shapes and arrangements among cacti and some other succulents, ranging from a dense cover of thick barbs to several scant rows of slender, toothlike projections. Spines serve as moisture collectors, and also as a heating and cooling system to temper the effects of blazing midday sun and cooler night temperatures.

have survived the rigors of their desert environment, only to have their tops lopped off by someone who has heard the story of their water-storage abilities and wants to test the theory personally? Nowadays impromptu experiments or removal of native desert species without a valid permit will land the cactus butcher or thief in jail. At least in Arizona and California almost all desert plants are protected by endangered species laws.

Today, of course, these curiously evolved natives of America are found throughout the world, mostly transported to new environments by man. Even prickly pears, which are such a characteristic part of the Mediterranean landscape, are descended from plants brought from America centuries ago. According to one story, no less an ancient scholar than Pliny the Elder speculated that prickly pears might have been carried by birds to the Mediterranean from some as yet undiscovered land. This speculation dates from about 1,500 years before the discovery of the New World, and possibly marks the beginning of a fascination with cacti among Europeans that still exists today. The very name of the genus *Opuntia,* to which prickly pears belong, is derived from the town of Opus in Greece; and in Israel, the Hebrew word for the fruit of the prickly pear, *sabra,* is also a nickname for a native-born Israeli (both are said to be tough on the outside, but sweet beneath the surface).

CLASSIFYING CACTI

Including over 1,300 known species in more than 100 genera, the Cactus family has been divided into three tribes. The *Pereskia* tribe (Pereskieae) consists of one genus, *Pereskia,* and of several species of the genus *Maihuenia.* The stems of these terrestrial cacti are not very succulent, and their alternate, broad, flat, deciduous leaves are much like those of other woody, flowering dicots. Spines occur in leaf axils (there are no small, barbed bristles on the areoles), and the flowers have stalks of varying length. The *Opuntia* tribe (Opuntieae) features terrestrial plants having rounded woody stems; small and short-lived, usually cylindrical leaves; and more often than not, glochids on the areoles. Flowers are wheel shaped and have short tubes. Having variously formed stems and branches, the Opuntieae have been divided into several subdivisions of genera: *Opuntia* subgenus *Cylindropuntia, Opuntia* section *Tephrocactus,* and *Opuntia* subgenus *Platyopuntia.*

The third major grouping of cacti is the Cereus or Cactus tribe (Cacteae). Featuring plants with very rudimentary leaves and no glochids, the Cacteae have flowers consisting of an elongated tube. This vast tribe includes better than 75 percent of all cacti and the overwhelming majority of those grown as house plants, and its members exhibit a great range of stem and flower forms. The Cacteae is divided into eight huge subtribes, each containing many genera. Six of these subtribes are entirely or primarily terrestrial and usually have areoles that bear spines; they are the Echinocereanae (hedgehog cacti), which usually have one or a few short joints and produce flowers at lateral areoles; the Hylocereanae (climbing cacti), which are partial epiphytes having thin stems and aerial roots; the Cereanae (torch cacti), which have several to many long joints and are eventually bushy or arching; the Cactanae (melon cacti), which are short and single jointed, having flowers and spines at different areoles and flowering at a central terminal mass; the Coryphanthanae (pincushion or fishhook cacti), which differ from Cactanae in having flowering areoles at the bases or sides of small rounded swellings; and the Echinocactanae (including various genera popularly grouped as living rocks and barrel, star, chin, and ball cacti), which are similar to Echinoceranae but having flowers emerging from central areoles. The two remaining subtribes of the Cacteae feature completely epiphytic plants that have mostly spineless areoles. These are the very popular Epiphyllanae, which have many long, flat joints and usually funnel-shaped flowers, and the Rhipsalidanae, which have stems with few segments and many slender joints, and round flowers.

The discussion which follows is organized according to tribes and subtribes and will highlight selected genera, species, and hybrids that make outstanding house plants. More detailed information on many of them can be found in the Encyclopedia section.

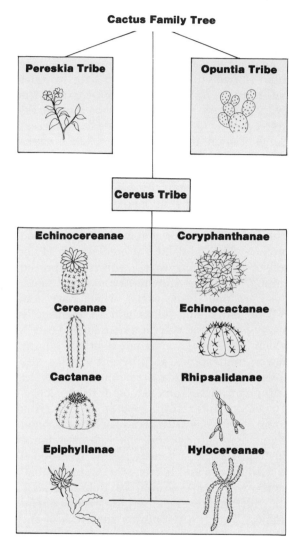

This schematic presentation of the Cactus family shows the three main tribes and further breaks down the Cereus Tribe into eight subtribes.

THE PERESKIA TRIBE (PERESKIEAE)

Pereskias are thought by many botanists to be living fossils, surviving ancestors of the type of plant from which modern cacti are derived. The pereskias are leafy, thorny plants which look more like young citrus trees than like the cacti we know today.

As house plants, pereskias make good conversation pieces and are sure winners in any friendly wager as to what kind of plants they are. They do, however, tend to grow long and shrubby, and aren't likely to be a first choice unless you've got plenty of room, or a particular desire for this uncharacteristic cactus. An attractive species is *P. grandifolia* (rose cactus), which is a shrub or tree having a very spiny trunk, waxy, oval leaves, and end clusters of pink flowers like wild roses.

THE OPUNTIA TRIBE (OPUNTIAE)

Found in nature from northern Canada to the cold southern tip of South America, members of the tribe of prickly pears are well protected from animal predators by their tufts of bristles. They have stems or branches that generally have either flat and padlike segments, as in the popular plants called bunny ears, or cylindrical segments, as in the cholla cactus types. Nomenclature varies, and plants sometimes listed as species of *Opuntia* section *Tephrocactus, Opuntia* subgenus *Platyopuntia,* or *Opuntia* subg. *Cylindropuntia* may be included in the genus *Opuntia.*

An outstanding pad-type *Opuntia* species for even novice growers is the low-growing, rounded *O. microdasys* (bunny ears), a pale yellow-flowered plant which comes in a host of pleasant cultivars: *O. microdasys* var. *rufida* is called cinnamon cactus because of its reddish glochids; *O. microdasys* 'Ora-spina Montrose' has twisted yellow glochids; *O. microdasys* 'Polka Dots' has thick pads "dotted" with white tufts; while *O. microdasys* 'Angel Wings' also has white spines. Other worthwhile opuntias with flattish pads are the purple-flowered *O. basilaris* (beavertail cactus) and *O. schickendantzii* (green donkey ears).

Cylindrical in form and small enough to make a good pot plant is the Bolivian *O. verschaffeltii,* which is attractive and offers orange to red flowers. *O. fulgida* var. *mamillata* (the boxing glove cactus) is another popular

Opuntia Tribe: There are two growth habits of note among members of this tribe. Plants may have either flattened or cylindrical segments, with each form bearing the characteristic tufts of bristles called glochids. The *Opuntia* on the left, middle row, is an example of cylindrical growth, and all the rest are flat shaped, with the exception of *O. linguiformis* 'Maverick', in the lower right corner, which is an amalgam of the two forms. The glochids vary in color from white to yellow to red, and some species may even produce spines, as seen on the plant in the upper right corner.

cylindrical form with one or more "fists" at its stem ends. Though spectacular in their native habitats of the Southwest, where they are among the few cacti that grow completely unshaded in the hottest, brightest places, most cholla cacti require very high levels of light when grown indoors. Chollas generally grow too large for indoor culture, and will not flower until they reach a large size.

THE CEREUS TRIBE (CEREEAE)

Subtribe Echinocereanae

The Echinocereanae are an important group of cacti to house plant fanciers, for as potted plants these various genera are ideal. They have highly ornamental spines which form a thick pattern over the entire body of the plant and large, often sensational flowers, some as big as four inches (10 cm) across. The plants in this group are low-growing globes or cylinders, usually deeply ribbed. Known as the hedgehog cacti, they're easy to grow, and if treated to ample sunshine are capable of producing some stunning flowers which range from shades of yellow to day-glow purple and often last for several days. Hedgehog cacti are also better suited to cold weather than many of the other smaller succulents of the desert, tolerating Fahrenheit temperatures down to the 20s.

Some house plant favorites among this group are *Echinocereus engelmannii,* and the rainbow cacti *E. pectinatus* var. *neomexicanus* and *E. pectinatus* var. *rigidissimus,* which are valued for their multicolored spines.

Good beginning cacti for a collection are the small barrel-shaped *Echinopsis* species, known as Easter lily cacti because they yield beautiful trumpet-shaped flowers. These prolific bloomers also remain popular with experienced collectors. Without a doubt it is the spectacular flowers of *Echinopsis* species that make them so popular. The blossoms are often up to eight inches (20 cm) long and come in shades of white, pink, or red. Mostly they open at night and then last for only a day. *Echinopsis* species are tough, can take more cold than many cacti (even snow in some cases), and, indoors, can adjust to either direct or indirect lght. They tend to prefer a rich potting mixture and ample watering and feeding during the growing season.

Lobivia, a genus of smaller, day-blooming hedgehog cacti, also makes a fine house plant and produces beautiful flowers under the right conditions. If planted in a medium of half sand and half all-purpose potting soil, and given an occasional watering, lobivias are among the easiest of cacti to cultivate. They may also reward the gardener with large, showy flowers that often look as large as the plant itself. Flowers appear in shades of purple, red, yellow, and orange, and last only a day or two, but are replaced quite often. Because of their ease of propagation from seeds, *Lobivia* species have been much hybridized. Their compact bunching growth habit makes lobivias good windowsill plants. Recommended species include *L. arachnacantha* and *L. torrecillansensis.*

Other good candidates for the window garden are the related *Rebutia* cultivars, which are as easy to grow as lobivias. Members of this genus produce their beautiful flowers in a circle around the base, and for this reason are known as crown cacti. Rebutias are hard to damage and have been known to bloom prolifically. They prefer some sphagnum in their soil, partial shade, and cool temperatures of 40° to 50°F (4° to 10°C) over the winter for better flowering in the spring. The plants do well outdoors in summer in a protected but partly sunny place.

Some of the best species for beginning or augmenting a collection include *R. kupperana, R. minuscula,* and *R. senilis.*

Yet another appealing hedgehog cactus for beginners is *Chamaecereus sylvestri,* the scarlet-flowered peanut cactus. This finger-shaped Argentinian cactus needs partial shade and a cool, dry, bright winter followed by increased humidity and watering as the red buds develop in spring.

Subtribe Hylocereanae

Members of the hylocereus group distinguish themselves by being some of the few cacti suited for cultivation in hanging baskets. *Aporocactus flagelliformis,* the rattail cactus, is a particular favorite and is recommended for beginners. Its inch (2.5 cm) wide, trailing stems (which are responsible for its unfortunate nickname), can grow up to six feet (1.8 m) long if the plant is left unpruned and in a sunny location. Covered with fine, reddish spines, aporocactus puts forth its crimson flowers in spring, and, unlike many of the nocturnal flowering plants in this subtribe, it blooms during the day.

Several of the best known of the night-blooming cacti among the Hylocereanae are *Hylocereus undatus,* which is enjoyed as a hedge plant in Hawaii; and the various "moon cerei" of the genus *Selenicereus,* which produce the largest of all cactus flowers — fragrant blooms up to 13 inches (33 cm) across. These beauties may be coaxed up a wire or trellis in a bright window or sun porch and will bloom in summer if given humusy soil, humidity somewhat higher than most cacti, ample water when buds are setting (even moisture otherwise), and temperatures above 62°F (17°C).

Subtribe Cereanae

Named torch cacti for their splendid blooms, the Cereanae are divided into four groups according to their forms: candelabra types, organ pipes, columnar types, and slender torches. One of the so-called candelabra cacti suited to the novice grower is *Cereus peruvianus,* which is among the fastest growing of all cacti. This prickly, columnar plant blooms reluctantly in a pot, and may or may not branch until it is quite sizable.

Among the hairy, usually massive organ-pipe cacti, smaller or slower-growing plants that can be grown indoors include *Lemaireocereus beneckei* and *L. stellatus;* and the lovely, multi-flowered *Trichocereus spachianus,* which attains four feet (1.2 m) in height and clusters with age.

The columnar, so-called "old man cacti," named for their woolly heads, are among the most popular specimens in indoor collections. Favorites include the slow-growing *Cephalocereus senilis* (the old man of Mexico), and the silky-haired *Espostoa lanata* (the South American old man).

Among the slender torches, which are prized for their vivid, tubular blooms, good house plants are *Monvillea spegazzinii* 'Montrose', which is dark green to black with white-haired edges, and the slumping *Cleisto-cactus strausii,* which has a pale yellow center spine and red flowers.

Subtribe Cactanae

Sometimes called melon cacti, the chiefly West Indian Cactanae are relatively short but wide in stature. They are distinguished by a headlike, woolly central mass called a cephalium, from which red or brown bristles and flowers emerge. Spines develop from lateral areoles. Probably the most interesting and popular indoor species in this group are the slow-growing plants known as Turk's heads — *Melocactus caesius,* a pink-flowered, globular to oval plant that grows to eight inches (20 cm); and *M. matanzanus,* which develops an attractive cephalium as it ages, has rosy pink blossoms, and is the smallest *Melocactus* species, reaching an approximate height and width of only four inches (10 cm).

Subtribe Coryphanthanae

Collectively known as pincushion or fishhook cacti, the Coryphanthanae include 16 genera, the most outstanding of which are *Coryphantha* and *Mammillaria.*

Widespread in the wild from southern Canada to Mexico, the coryphanthas are covered with knobs (tubercles) from which spines grow. Producing eye-catching yellow, red, or purple flowers from summer to autumn, they need a dry winter rest period at 45° to 50°F (7° to 10°C), but otherwise should not be kept excessively dry. These pincushion cacti do well in sandy soil with a little added bone meal. One species recommended for indoor cultivation is *C. cornifera* var. *echinus,* a globelike to conical plant up to two inches (5 cm) in diameter which bears heavy spines and yellow flowers. A purple-flowering type that clusters handsomely with age is *C. macromeris* var. *runyoni. C. erecta* is distinguished by pronounced knobs, weak spines, and large, narrowly segmented yellow blossoms.

Much better known and more widely available are the fishhook cacti of the huge genus *Mammillaria.* Numbering over 400 species, these are among the most widely grown and easily recognized of cacti. Because of their compact size and ease of cultivation they are sometimes sold in supermarkets, airports, and other places where plants are not usually available. Mammillarias are characterized by a neat, geometric ordering of spines and flowers which are produced from

Fishhook Cacti: As the common name suggests, these members of the genus *Mammillaria* are known for their luxurious growth of spines. Spine forms vary from long, menacing hooks (upper left), to the dense, lacy patterning on *M. elongata* (lower left), and all stages in between. The spines are geometrically arranged, and project from knobs on the surface. Widely available, these cacti are very willing to flower if a cool, dry winter rest is provided. Other species shown are *M. spinosissima* (upper right), *M. mystax* (lower right), and *M. rhodantha* (center left).

From Tomatoes to *Mammillaria*: Vegetables yielded to cacti as Archie Deutschman began to explore another gardening hobby. The walls of his homemade greenhouse have been expanded three times to make room for his collection of 4,000 cacti, most of which belong to the genus *Mammillaria*.

It Started with Tomatoes

"I got bored with growing tomatoes in the winter in Tucson and asked myself: 'What does a man do with an empty greenhouse in the desert when he gets tired of raising winter vegetables?' "

With this modest explanation Archie Deutschman, of Tucson, Arizona, swings open the frame door of his homemade greenhouse, revealing one of the world's outstanding cactus collections. Crowded together on three wide, wooden benches, often several plants to a pot, are some 4,000 cacti.

After starting his collection with many kinds of cacti, Deutschman, who is a Ph.D. and a chemist at the University of Arizona, decided to specialize in raising the genus *Mammillaria* — a group which has more than 400 clearly defined species, all small but varied in appearance and offering numerous types of flowers. Deutschman now has 500 named plants in his collection and 50 to 75 more which he has not yet positively identified. "There are better overall cactus collections," the ex-vegetable grower concedes, "but I don't know of anybody in the world who has a better *Mammillaria* collection."

As his collection expanded, so did the greenhouse, which Deutschman built himself in four different installments. He estimates that he spends about one hour a day there tending the plants and enjoying them, and about 5 percent of his time bouncing over back tracks and roads of the Sonoran Desert with his wife and sometimes

or between the spirally arranged knobs. These flame-bright blossoms seem to radiate a stored-up burst of desert sunshine. *Mammillaria* is also one of the cactus genera most likely to bloom in captivity, offering halos of small white, yellow, pink, or red flowers in spring and summer.

Like other hardy North American cacti (they are found as far north as Colorado), mammillarias respond well to a cool (50° to 55°F/10° to 13°C), dry winter rest. During this time they should be watered only every six weeks, but need as much light as you can give them.

Modest size makes mammillarias suitable potted plants for lath house, greenhouse, and windowsill, and makes them perfect candidates for miniature desert landscapes contained in tabletop dish gardens. Mammillarias grow well in a blend of half sand and half potting soil (add some calcium in the form of ground limestone for those with white spines). They need bright light, but don't need the full exposure to sun required by some cacti and in fact must be watched for scorching when the summer sun shines directly on them through a windowpane. Keep them somewhat moist in the spring and summer when buds are forming.

For starters in a mammillaria collection, or in a general collection of indoor cacti, try a redheaded Irishman (*M. spinosissima*) or a with one or more of his five children in search of cacti.

"The challenge of this thing is collecting and identifying, putting the whole story together," Deutschman explains.

The treasure-hunt aspect of finding and identifying a plant, he adds, can become particularly exciting when one is searching for a plant that has become known only in very recent years. "And sometimes," Deutschman says with a contagious kind of enthusiasm, "the plant may be found only in an area of a hundred yards or so in some remote Mexican mountain range. Imagine what it's like to drive for days in some unmapped region of Mexico just looking for an area of a few yards. Then imagine that what you're looking for in that tiny area often has to be in bloom in order for you to see it at all — some of these cacti are buried and only send their bright flowers aboveground for a few days each year.

"And how do you find this one place?" he asks. "It's a game you play with yourself. The idea is to go and find a plant described in a book — to confirm the find for yourself." Deutschman "the sleuth" then tells how he once resorted to finding a particular plant pictured in a book by looking at the skyline in the photo of the plant while driving along slowly and carefully in the area where it supposedly was growing. Eventually he was able to match the skyline in the book with the one he saw out of the window of his car, and after a little more matching of picture and reality, he spied the sought-after plant. (This kind of plant collecting must be done carefully, of course, for many states have laws governing the collection of plants from the wild. Beginners will do better to purchase plants from a reliable nursery.)

Even though publishing details of their own finds isn't of significant interest to the Deutschmans, their collection is known internationally. Deutsch-

man says that "cactus collectors are a close-knit group of people," and that he receives requests for seeds and plants from around the world. "Surprisingly," says Deutschman, "Europeans are more nuts about cacti than Americans." Apparently this has always been so, because many names of cacti are of German or Dutch or other European origin, and Deutschman estimates that 15 to 20 percent of his own *Mammillaria* collection came from Europe. Nevertheless, it's not unusual for him to get a request from there for seeds of a particular plant.

It seems a long way from growing tomatoes in a makeshift greenhouse to sending seeds of an unusual cactus to Europe, but Archie Deutschman is casual about the whole thing. "It's still only a pastime," he insists, and one that centers on the fun rather than the seriousness of maintaining one of the world's outstanding cactus collections.

silk pincushion (*M. bombycina*). Some other outstanding mammillarias for beginners are powder puff (*M. bocasana*), old lady cactus (*M. hahniana*), owl's eyes (*M. parkinsonii*), *M. wildii,* and *M. zeilmanniana.*

Subtribe Echinocactanae

Cacti in the Echinocactanae group are quite spiny and generate their flowers from an undeveloped place in the center of the plant. This subtribe includes perhaps the greatest variety of appealing house plants for amateur growers and is commonly subdivided into five groups organized around plant shapes or markings.

Some of the smaller plants of this sub-

tribe belong to the genus *Gymnocalycium.* These are the chin cacti, which got their nickname from the chinlike bumps located just below each cluster of spines. Spherical in shape, these plants are among the easiest of cacti to grow indoors. They are a particularly happy choice because they can be coaxed into bloom when still small, they have a long spring-to-fall blooming season, and their long-lasting flowers of red, pink, white, or yellow remain open for several days. Several noteworthy *Gymnocalycium* species are the miniature but heavily blooming *G. bruchii,* which has lacy white spines and clusters freely; *G. baldianum,* which has unusual wine red flowers; *G. denudatum* (spider cactus), which has soft spines close to the plant's body; and *G. mihanovichii,* the tangerine size, multicolored "plain cactus," which can produce high-standing blooms larger than the plant several times each year.

Also recommended is the obliging dwarf chin cactus (*G. quehlianum*), which will flower as a young plant. If you have the room on a sunny porch, you can cultivate the dwarf's big brother, the giant chin cactus (*G. saglione*), which is the largest member of the genus, growing up to 12 inches (30 cm) wide with pink or flesh-toned flowers ringing the crown. *Gymnocalycium* species do well in a blend of half sand and half potting soil, with plenty of water during the growing season. They need protection from strong sunlight, but if kept dry are more tolerant of low temperatures than many cacti.

Other valuable echinocactanae include the genera *Notocactus* and *Parodia,* known as ball cacti. Both are suggested for the novice because of their ease of culture, fine form (including spine patterns), and attractive flowers. Indeed, editors of the *Cactus and Succulent Journal,* Charles Glass and Robert Foster, recommend "species of *Notocactus* as undoubtedly the best plants for the beginner"; they particularly prefer *Notocactus haselbergii,* which has soft, silvery white spines and rather small, crimson flowers that last for up to three weeks. Other splendid candidates for a sunny breakfast table are *N. magnificus* and *N. scopa* (particularly the cultivar 'Cristata', a crested version of the silver ball cactus). Having colorful spines and/or silky hairs, notocacti are particularly popular because of the large, translucent flowers they bear (usually yellow, although sometimes peach, cerise, or purple) — flowers that first emerge in spring of the plant's second or third year and last nearly a month. Equal parts of sharp sand and potting soil and a free circulation of fresh air in a brightly lit location are needed along with a cool, dry rest period in winter to keep these plants looking their finest. Repot them every second year.

Parodia species are similar to *Notocactus* in appearance and growing requirements. Shaped like flattened globes, parodias have spiraled ribs and hooked spines which climb the plants like miniature versions of the steps on spherical water tanks. They flower freely in the summertime in shades of orange, yellow, or red. In his *Exotic Plant Manual* (see Bibliography), Alfred Byrd Graf describes these plants as "amongst the most beautiful of cacti." Outstanding cultivars are the Brazilian *P. aureispina,* a tiny plant with dense, vivid yellow spines and golden flowers, and the twice-as-large, yellow-green *P. maassii,* which reaches a width of almost six inches (15 cm) and has deep ribs and orange-red flowers.

The most sensationally spined members of the Echinocactanae are the "barrel cacti" found in the *Ferocactus* and *Echinocactus* genera. These plants are generally too large for indoor culture, often reaching 12 feet (3.6 m) in height. A hint of their potential, though, is revealed in such common names as eagle claw, mule crippler, fire barrel, and fishhook cactus. Some immature members of these large-growing genera are sometimes seen as indoor plants, particularly the beautiful golden barrel (*Echinocactus grusonii*), which has long yellow spines. The shallow-ribbed *E. horizonthalonius,* formidably named devil's head (or eagle claw), is a relatively small form. *Ferocactus* species that make handsome specimen plants include *F. glaucescens,* with its light green body and golden spines; the widely ribbed *F. histrix;* and the purple-flowering Mexican species *F. latispinus.*

A much more favored subgroup of the Echinocactanae subtribe among cactus gardeners is the "star cacti" of the genus *Astrophytum.* The common names of bishop's cap (*A. myriostigma*), sea urchin or sand dollar (*A. asterias*), and goat's horn (*A. capricorne*) do more to characterize these sought-after species than any detailed botanical description. *Astrophytum* species resemble no other plants on earth. Often freckled and spineless, sometimes covered with woolly hair, and frequently looking like a scale model for a geodesic dome, they are among the most popular of cacti. Some aficionados have large collections consisting only of cultivars of a single species of *Astrophytum.*

These cacti will tolerate all but very strong sun and like a fair amount of moisture in summer, although constantly wet roots will soon rot. In the summer they flower from the top in shades of yellow, with the blooms often having red throats. The bishop's cap is a unique specimen and a popular species for beginners and experienced collectors alike.

The "living rock cacti" of various genera are other unusual but popular members of the Echinocactanae subtribe. As their common name implies, these cacti have adapted to their surroundings by hunkering down close to the earth and displaying wrinkled, leathery skin that enables them to avoid bird and animal predators by camouflaging themselves as rocks. They are slow growing and can be rapidly turned into a pile of pulp by overwatering and/or a slow-draining growth medium. For this reason, they are not the easiest cacti to cultivate, but because of their unique appearance they're well worth the effort. Although plants of the genera *Aztekium, Pelecyphora, Obregonia,* and *Strombocactus* are considered living rocks, they are not readily available; somewhat easier to find but a little more expensive than more common cacti are *Ariocarpus* species such as the warty, gray rosette plant *A. fissuratus,* a native of Texas and Mexico with pleasant pink flowers.

Living rocks like a warm and sunny location as well as infrequent waterings through their well-draining potting mix, which should have a high percentage of sand or gravel.

Subtribe Epiphyllanae

Often called leaf cacti, Epiphyllanae have broad, flat branches that look like fleshy foliage. Completely epiphytic, these cacti grow on the bark or branches of trees in the tropi-

cal jungles of South and Central America and into Mexico. Like the Hylocereanae, these cacti can be grown in hanging baskets. Predictably, epiphytic cacti have cultural needs significantly different from those of terrestrial genera. Instead of the usual fast-draining potting mix, they require a very loose growing medium high in humus, and they benefit from light shade, high humidity, and frequent watering and feeding. As experts Glass and Foster point out, this is a subtribe of cacti that is "virtually a field of its own," one in which the fern grower is probably more at home than the cactus collector. Nevertheless, these unusual plants are not hard to grow and are very ornamental, producing many showy flowers.

Of the 9 genera in this subtribe, the most spectacular is *Epiphyllum.* Named orchid cacti for their large and brilliantly colored flowers, the 12 species have been bred extensively with each other and with *Hylocereus* and other epiphytic genera. These produce iridescent blooms of every shade except true blue. Flowers are arranged in clusters of 3-inch (8 cm) blooms or appear as individual trumpet, plate, or cup-and-saucer shapes up to 10 inches (25 cm) wide. Just a few of the many outstanding *Epiphyllum* hybrid cultivars are the delicate, red-flowered *E.* 'Ackermannii'; the dwarf *E.* 'Elegantissimum', which boasts large flowers of vivid crimson; the longtime favorite 'Hermosissimus', offering tricolor petals with a central orange stripe edged in violet; 'Nocturne', with flowers purple outside and whitish inside; and 'Royal Rose', with blooms of rose and deep yellow.

Epiphyllums should be potted in a rich blend of equal parts of sand (or perlite), loam, and peat moss, to which a teaspoon (5 ml) of bone meal has been added for every four inches (10 cm) of pot. For lavish blooms, feed the plants every two weeks from March through October and provide ample moisture during that time. They will thrive outdoors in summer provided temperatures go no lower than 55°F (13°C). During the winter rest

The Orchid Cactus: These lovely bursts of color are assured if you pay attention to proper year-round culture for your *Epiphyllum*. A vast selection of hybrids is available in a host of flower colors.

they should be kept barely moist and given cool nights of 50°F (10°C). Keep these plants in relatively small pots, for their roots like crowding. Let small-flowered types with drooping branches trail from a hanging basket; low branching types with long branches such as 'Hermosissimus' and 'Padre' may be espaliered. For fuller growth, pinch back the plants regularly; such cuttings are easily rooted.

Once considered epiphyllums but now classified as *Schlumbergera truncata* and *S. bridgesii* are the familiar Thanksgiving and Christmas cacti. These winter-blooming epiphytes require the same culture as *Epiphyllum* species but require short-day conditions or a carefully regulated cool period to set blossoms. Also needing the same treatment as epiphyllums are the very compact Easter cacti (*Rhipsalidopsis* spp.), which generate star-shaped blooms of red or pink in March and April if given a cool rest period in winter. (See the Encyclopedia section for details.)

Subtribe Rhipsalidanae

Another group of Central and South American epiphytic cacti are the Rhipsalidanae, which have dangling, ropelike, jointed, many-branched stems with bristles but without spines. Intriguing hanging basket plants that should be cultivated like epiphyllums, the *Rhipsalis* species are slow growing and shy bloomers. They are nicknamed mistletoe cacti because their small flowers are followed by tiny sticky berries like those of the mistletoe.

OTHER SUCCULENTS

While members of the Cactus family exude a clear liquid when cut, the more or less succulent plants found in over 44 other plant families tend to ooze a milky sap, a characteristic that is sometimes reflected in their botanical or common names. Some of these structurally varied plants store water in underground tubers, bulbs, or corms. More often, however, it is aboveground parts that are thickened to hold water. In stem succulents leaves are relatively small or absent and the stem is enlarged. On the other hand, in leaf-succulent types — which are usually very short and squat — the foliage is fattened and the stem, if present at all, is short and a secondary storage site. The plant families, genera, and species featured here, then, as the most popular succulent house plants, are more diverse physically than the stem-succulent cacti. As a result they sometimes have different cultural needs. They often grow in arid or semiarid environments where their growth cycles are keyed to rainy seasons rather than to warm periods (as those of hardy cacti are). As a result, in nature many of these succulents grow and flower in winter (that is, they are short-day plants) and rest during the long, dry days of summer.

EUPHORBIACEAE (SPURGE FAMILY)

Most of the succulents not belonging to the Cactus family are found in the Spurge family, which flourishes primarily in the Eastern Hemisphere (particularly Africa), where its fantastic forms create effects similar to those obtained by cacti in the Americas. Many of the plants of the diverse genus *Euphorbia,* which includes over 1,600 species, look more like cacti than any other succulents, differing in their lack of areoles and true spines (euphorbias may have persistent, modified leaf bases). Euphorbias also have less showy inflorescences, in which male flowers surround one central female flower. The bracts are sometimes petallike and colorful, as in the poinsettia (*E. pulcherrima*).

A third characteristic of the genus is its milky sap. This latex flows freely in certain euphorbias. In fact, the abundant sap of larger, treelike species such as *E. lactea* and *E. tirucalli* contains hydrocarbons and as a result, euphorbias are now being investigated as a possible source of fuel. Unfortunately for indoor gardeners, the potentially valuable latex in euphorbias can cause rashes or blisters on the skin and swelling of the mucous membranes. Exposed areas should be washed immediately with soap and water. (Interestingly, the juice from the leaves of another succulent — *Aeonium lindleyi* — is an antidote to euphorbia poisoning and can stop the burning sensation almost immediately.)

The more succulent euphorbias are not grown for their flowers but for their almost limitless variety of form and size, and many of these uniquely shaped, colored, and textured plants can be as decorative in the home as a welded sculpture or modern wood carving. Euphorbia species suitable for indoor growing include *E. canariensis,* which devel-

Family Portrait: This assemblage of seemingly unrelated plants fools the eye since all are members of the same genus, *Euphorbia*. Starting clockwise from the front is *E. obesa*, nicknamed the baseball plant. This spineless sphere even has markings which resemble the stitches on a ball, but as it ages the shape changes subtly until it resembles a pear. To the left is *E. lactea*, a succulent plant with milky sap harbored within its scalloped branches. Statuesque in form is the spine-laden *E. canariensis*, which is a good indoor specimen and can bloom while still young. To the right is *E. milii* var. *splendens*, the crown-of-thorns, a shrub bristling with spines, which belies its fierce appearance by producing delicate, salmon-pink to yellow flowers throughout the year. In addition, that holiday favorite with the colorful bracts known as poinsettia is also a *Euphorbia*.

ops branches like a saguaro and flowers while still small, and the well-known *E. milii* var. *splendens* (crown-of-thorns), which offers long, climbing, thorny stems and salmon-red to yellow bracts at Easter time and through much of the year. A study in contrasts is *E. obesa,* the baseball plant, which is a spineless globe that elongates into a pear shape as it grows, and which requires the same cultural conditions as cacti. Attractively mottled and freely branching but compact is *E. trigona,* the African milk tree, which does well in a dish garden when small. Another easy-to-please euphorbia that thrives in night temperatures of 62°F (17°C) or higher is *E. lactea* (mottled spurge or dragon bones), which has scalloped branches and a candelabralike form.

With the exception of the African milk tree, most euphorbias are slow growing, and are fairly tolerant of indoor conditions such as partial shade. In general they may be potted in a mix of equal parts of sand, leaf mold, and soil. Water generously during the blooming season and let them dry out in winter.

CRASSULACEAE (STONECROP FAMILY)

The succulents other than cacti most familiar to house plant fanciers belong to the Crassulaceae — a more or less leaf-succulent family including such delightful genera as *Aeonium, Crassula, Echeveria, Kalanchoe, Sedum,* and *Sempervivum.*

Among the *Crassula* species, a superbly durable and traditionally favored house plant is *C. argentea,* the jade plant. This thick and woody-stemmed plant with its shiny, turgid leaves is grown upright as a tree form in a pot or dish garden. It is tolerant of light levels as low as 25 footcandles, but if older specimens are given bright light during the autumn, they may bloom.

Another interesting and easy-to-care-for crassula is *C. lycopodioides,* called watch chain because of the close-set, symmetrical leaves on its narrow, dangling, or climbing stems. Other charmers are *C. perforata* (necklace vine), which responds well to underpotting and cool winters, and a number of oddly formed miniature species from the deserts of South Africa. These can thrive separately in two-inch (5 cm) pots, or together in dish gardens in a mix of 2 parts coarse sand, 1 part potting soil, and 1 part leaf mold. Some of the more picturesque of these small, structurally fascinating plants are the pagoda-shaped types such as *C. cornuta* and *C. deceptrix;* the

Bringing Your Jade Plant into Bloom: If older jade plants are given bright light during autumn, they will burst forth in clusters of small, starry, pinkish white blossoms that can linger up to eight weeks. A plant grown in a windowsill can be encouraged to bloom if it is given supplemental daylight in the form of a 60-watt incandescent bulb and supplied with at least 300 footcandles of light as buds form.

conelike *C. teres;* and the wide-leaved *C. barbata,* which proffers an upturned rosette edged with long, white hairs.

Within the genus *Echeveria,* much hybridization has created plants of spectacular size and unique color and geometrical shape. The symmetrical rosettes of these plants, made of waxy, velvety, or frosted leaves sometimes touched with blue, purple, pink, or chalky white, are almost as decorative as the tall stalks of small, white to orange or red flowers the plants send up in summer and fall. A few of the many worthwhile *Echeveria* species and cultivars are the felt-leaved *E. pulvinata,* which has scarlet flowers; *E. crenulata* 'Roseo-Grandis', which forms a maroon-edged rosette up to 10 inches (25 cm) wide; *E. derenbergii,* offering plump, tightly stacked rosettes of red-margined leaves; *E.* 'Doris Taylor', with shiny, red-tipped

A Collection of Crassulas: Members of the genus *Crassula* exhibit a diversity of fascinating forms. At left is the familiar jade plant, *C. argentea*, which features woody, branching stems and thick, firm leaves. *C. teres*, the central plant, is an interesting addition to any collection, noteworthy for its tightly overlapping geometric arrangement of leaves. *C. perforata* earned its common name of necklace vine by the way in which its pointed leaves are strung like so many beads along the stem.

leaves covered with velvety white hairs, and *E.* 'Black Prince', a striking hybrid that turns black when grown in bright sun. Found in the wild from Mexico to northern South America, these plants thrive on bright sun and ample water in summer, and reduced water and temperatures no lower than 50°F (10°C) in the winter.

Originally from Africa and Madagascar, *Kalanchoe* species and cultivars have opposite leaves that can be scalloped, arrow shaped, or of numerous other shapes, and either smooth or downy. The long-stalked flowers are profuse and often long lasting, ranging in hue from white and yellow to red and purple. One particularly desirable cultivar is *K. blossfeldiana* 'Tom Thumb' (dwarf Christmas kalanchoe), which may be summered outdoors and which requires short days in autumn to bloom in December. Another favorite that may flower toward the end of the year is *K. tomentosa* (panda plant), which has

an upright branching stem with white-felted leaves edged with brown teeth. Some other curious kalanchoes are *K. pinnata* (or *Bryophyllum pinnatum),* called air plant or miracle leaf because it can generate plantlets in the scallops of its leaves even after the leaves are removed from the plant; and *K. marmorata,* known as the pen wiper plant because its broad, waxy, bluish or pinkish green leaves are splotched with purple. Easy to propagate from cuttings or plantlets, kalanchoes thrive in sun, warmth, good air circulation, and sandy soil that is allowed to dry out between waterings.

The sizable genus *Sedum* includes over 350 species of plants very diverse in their foliage and growth habits and often reluctant to bloom indoors. One enjoyable plant that will dangle tassels of spindle-shaped leaves from a hanging container is *S. morganianum* (burro's tail). This curious plant was first found under cultivation near Vera Cruz, Mexico, and despite considerable effort it has never been traced back to its original location in the wild. In recent years, the prestigious Huntington Gardens in San Marino, California, has introduced a dwarf cultivar named *S. morganianum* 'Burritos', which holds its leaves better than the old form. There is also a large hybrid with huge leaves called *S. morganianum* 'Super Giant Donkey's Tail', and another named 'Giant Burro's Tail', which has large, well-spaced leaves that do not drop off readily.

A dainty, creeping sedum often planted in rock gardens but suitable for a small hanging basket is *S. dasyphyllum.* The woody-stemmed dwarf, *S. multiceps* (dwarf Joshua tree), resembles a yucca — it has rosettes of needlelike leaves and may bear star-shaped yellow flowers in winter. *S. pachyphyllum,* invitingly called the jelly bean plant, has plump, glossy leaves with red tips.

Sedums are at their colorful best in bright sun, with cool nights and sandy soil that is allowed to dry out between waterings when the plant is resting.

Cacti in Their Natural State: The desert collection at Huntington Gardens in California is one of the largest of its kind in the world. Breeders at Huntington introduced the *Sedum morganianum* cultivar, 'Burrito'.

Sempervivum cultivars are rosette formers that bear a host of common names based on their tendency to be surrounded by a group of offsets. (Like sedums, they are also called stonecrops for their ability to thrive in poor soil and with little fertilizer.) The hardy *S. tectorum* var. *calcareum,* which is called hen-and-chickens or sometimes houseleek (because it grows on thatched roofs in Europe), has leathery leaves which are red-brown on their tips. The smaller form, *S. arachnoideum,* is called cobweb houseleek because white hairs cover and connect the leaf tips and new growth. Both of these plants like cool nights and sparse watering in winter, and prefer full sun and to be kept barely moist in summer. They can, however, get by in partial shade and do not respond well to rich soil and to fertilizers that are high in nitrogen.

Another pleasant genus in the Stonecrop family is *Aeonium*. These plants from North Africa, Madeira, and the Canary Islands proffer rosettes of flat, rounded leaves on small, branching stems. They are not hard to grow, needing bright light, cool temperatures, and limited water in winter but ample moisture and bright, indirect light during periods of active growth. Clusters of white, yellow, or red flowers sometimes appear in spring. Popular species include *A. lindleyi,* a small plant with medium green leaves that as mentioned earlier are an antidote to euphorbia poisoning; *A. haworthii* (pinwheel), which has wide, red-margined, blue-green leaves and which reaches 18 to 24 inches (46 to 61 cm) in height; and *A. arboreum* cultivars, dramatic specimens that can lift their flaring, fringed rosettes to a height of 36 inches (91 cm), some with leaves turning purple or black in full sun.

AIZOACEAE
(CARPETWEED FAMILY)

More difficult to cultivate than the crassulas, but rivaling the euphorbias in uniqueness, are the extraordinary plants of the Carpetweed family within the supergenus *Mesembryanthemum.* Popularly called flowering stones, or living stones, because of their astonishing ability to mimic stones or pebbles ranging from iron ore through limestone, quartz, and sandstone, these plants are also sometimes known as midday flowers, for the large, often quite fragrant blooms of most species open in the morning and close in the afternoon. Although many "mesembs" are diminutive plants that are found in nature within a few hundred miles of each other in arid South Africa, these remarkable leaf succulents take emphatically different forms and have been divided into over 122 genera and about 2,300 species. Only a handful are readily available through plant dealers — notably *Lithops, Fenestraria, Faucaria, Pleiospilos,* and *Conophytum* species.

Perhaps the most intriguing of the mesembs is *Lithops,* one of several genera that bury themselves in the ground, admitting light through patterened, translucent windows at the tips of their buried leaves. Each of these small living stones is made of two fat leaves wedged together to form inverted cones. The cleft across the flattened top is the place where new leaves and the attractive, many-petaled white or yellow flowers emerge.

Another windowed genus in the supergenus *Mesembryanthemum* is *Fenestraria* (baby's toes), which has light green, club-shaped leaves and white or yellow flowers. These small plants should be watered sparingly in summer and even less in winter. The

Dazzling Variety of Form: These succulents belong to the supergenus *Mesembryanthemum,* which encompasses more than 122 genera. Scattered in the left foreground are *Lithops,* the living stones. These pebble look-alikes produce new sets of leaves and daisylike flowers through the cleft in the middle. The plant to the rear, a member of the genus *Fenestraria,* has earned the epithet baby toes due to its clump of stubby, rounded leaves which have light-filtering windows at the tips. In the center are clumping, stemless dwarf plants belonging to the genus *Conophytum.* New fleshy leaves and flowers emerge from the cleft, much like the living stones. At right is *Faucaria,* christened tiger's jaws because of the ferocious appearance of the spreading, tooth-lined leaves.

more assertive-looking genus *Faucaria* (tiger jaws) has opposite keeled and toothed leaves ("jaws") sometimes dotted with white. They may reward the gardener with large yellow flowers, and in fact are relatively easy to bring into bloom from the end of summer to midwinter. When given optimum conditions of bright light but little moisture in late winter, the leaves turn pleasantly purple. *Faucaria* species are more tolerant of overwatering than are many mesembs.

Leaves similar in shape to those of *Faucaria,* although toothless and gray-green and often marked with dark green spots, are found on several species of *Pleiospilos,* usually referred to as split rocks. Like *Lithops* and *Faucaria* species, these succulents usually bloom in summer and rest in winter, when they should be kept very dry.

A Potful of Pebbles: If you look closely, you can spot the imposters, those members of the genus *Lithops* that are known as living stones. Interspersed among smooth pebbles are these mimicking plants, which can be distinguished by the cleft across the top. Aside from this cleft, the coloration and form of the living stones make them blend right in with the surroundings.

The clump-forming species of *Conophytum,* nicknamed coneplant, can put forth yellow, purple, or pink flowers from summer into spring and require less light than many flowering stones. Quite small but relatively easy to grow, they usually rest in June and July.

Flowering stones have unusually succulent leaves and need a well-draining soil mixture of half sand and half all-purpose potting soil, with a pinch of bone meal added. They should be fertilized only rarely. Liking bright light and good air circulation, these plants need cool winter temperatures of around 50°F (10°C). Because mesembryanthemums are less endangered by the complete drying out of their roots than are most other succulents, it is far better to err by underwatering than by overwatering. During their first year of life, however, living stones need a little more water and less direct sun than older plants.

Knowing when to observe dormancy in order to bring on proper flowering (which usually begins in the second year) can pose

some problems for indoor growers. The seasons in South Africa are the reverse of those in the North Temperate Zone, and some plants adapt partially or completely to the short- and long-day seasons of their new home, whereas others do not. The best course is to watch mesembs carefully, letting them experience dormancy after flowering, which may occur once or twice a year. At this time new leaves will come forth from inside the old.

The plant will not need watering until the new foliage has withdrawn all the water from the old leaves and left them desiccated and papery. Only then should the old leaves be removed. The plant may then be watered whenever the soil dries out until the new leaves are grown and their color begins to dull.

Although many flowering stones grow below ground in their natural habitat, in cultivation the leaves are kept above the soil to prevent rot. A top-dressing of gravel or pebbles is helpful, and if the stones are chosen to match the colors and markings of the plants, this mulch can demonstrate how effectively these little plants camouflage themselves from birds and animals in the wild.

LILIACEAE (LILY FAMILY)

Although many members of the succulent Lily family are too large for house plants, certain species in three genera have won a place in many indoor gardens. A familiar sight are members of the genus *Aloe,* plants from the African veldt with stiff, toothy leaves usually in a rosette and often attractively patterned. Aloes enjoy a summer outdoors in bright sun. *Aloe barbadensis* (better known as *Aloe vera,* unguentine cactus, or medicinal aloe) is handy to have on the kitchen windowsill. The pulp of this attractive, easy-to-raise plant eases the pain of minor burns, cuts, and ulcers. Other distinctive *Aloe* species are *A. ciliaris* (climbing aloe); the dark green *A. distans,* with leaves edged with gold teeth; the white-splotched *A. harlana,* with long, tapering leaves having reddish edges; *A. striata,* with thin white lines running the length of light green leaves; and the very popular *A. variegata,* which is crossbanded with white spots.

Tolerating partial shade, aloes prefer day temperatures of 70°F (21°C) and night minimums of 55°F (13°C) and need sandy soil allowed to dry out between waterings. They are rather reluctant bloomers indoors in most locations, although if given bright enough light their pink or white flowers will appear.

Haworthia is another genus of succulent African plants that includes very desirable house plants; haworthias are compact and relatively tolerant of shade. *H. fasciata,* or fairy washboard, is especially picturesque. With its zebra-striped rosette, it looks like a child's fantasy plant.

Various truncate forms within this diverse genus have a different but also novel appeal. *H. truncata,* for example, features two ranks of leaves positioned on top of each other; the outer third of the foliage appears to have been cut off by a knife and the "cut" edges are translucent windows admitting light. The modest light requirements of this and other windowed haworthias are the result of their being grown above ground in cultivation, whereas in the wild only the windows show and absorb sunshine.

The stemless genus *Gasteria* offers other succulents of relative toughness that are good plants for beginners. Sometimes called lawyer's tongue or ox tongue cactus, these plants are somewhat similar to aloes but the flatter, broader leaves appear randomly around the center rather than symmetrically. Some *Gasteria* species grow to 12 or 24 inches (30 to 61 cm) high. These hearty plants require moderate amounts of light and twice-monthly feedings in spring and summer.

Some species well suited to indoor culture are *G. verrucosa* (warty aloe), which has deep green leaves that are long, narrow, and tapering, with little white warts; *G. liliputana,* a miniature with thick, short, dark

green leaves, mixed with lighter green leaves; and *G. maculata,* a thick, fleshy plant with tongue-shaped leaves mottled with white and growing in a spiral twist.

Perhaps the most durable and omnipresent of the succulent lilies are the virtually indestructible *Sansevieria* species, which are discussed in chapter 10. Almost as tolerant and making extraordinary decorator plants for those who can provide the ample space they require are the large, dramatic *Yucca* species, which are included in chapter 20.

ASCLEPIADACEAE (MILKWEED FAMILY)

House plant succulents from the Milkweed family are found mostly in the genera *Stapelia, Ceropegia,* and *Huernia.* Although the large, fleshy, beautiful five-pointed flowers of *Stapelia* are pollinated by flies and are rather unpleasant smelling, these angular and knobby, leafless stem succulents are among the easiest of succulents to grow, for they are hardy and accept limited sun. Species with spectacular flowers that are a good introduction to the genus include the popular *S. variegata* (spotted toad), of medium size with toothy notches on its stems and spotted flowers; *S. gigantea* (giant starfish), with fingerlike erect green stems; *S. nobilis,* with branching, finely toothed, velvety, light green stems; and *S. hirsuta* (hairy starfish), which is relatively large, with smallish flowers covered with long, purple hairs. All heavy feeders, *Stapelia* species need to be kept almost completely dry from November to March. They will thrive in a light, sandy, slightly alkaline soil mix containing a small amount of rock phosphate.

Also rugged African plants that tolerate moderate light and cool temperatures, *Ceropegia* species can be leafless semishrubs or twiners with opposite leaves. Often they have tuberous or cormlike roots. Ceropegias are called lantern flowers because the lobes of their blooms may be attached at the tips.

Trailing types do well in hanging baskets on porches, in entryways, or outdoors in warm areas, as they tolerate hot and dry conditions.

Especially recommended is the woody-rooted *C. woodii* (rosary vine, or string of hearts), which has succulent, heart-shaped leaves on a slender trailing stem and which puts forth small purple flowers almost continuously in fall and winter if it receives enough light. Other worthwhile species include *C. ampliata, C. haygarthii,* and *C. stapeliiformis.* For best results, give these plants good light and well-draining, humus-rich soil; do not let them dry out too much between waterings.

Called dragon flower, the African genus *Huernia* contains tiny plants with spiny, columnar stems up to four inches (10 cm) high. The charming *H. pillansii* has soft maroon spines and is a good bloomer, offering yellow, crimson-spotted, star-shaped flowers. Somewhat larger is the robust and rapid-growing *H. macrocarpa.* Huernias thrive in bright sun and temperatures of 62°F (17°C) or over. They should dry out somewhat between waterings.

AMARYLLIADACEAE (AMARYLLIS FAMILY)

Containing over 300 species, the best-known succulent genus in the Amaryllis family is *Agave,* the Western Hemisphere's equivalent of the African *Aloe.* Often large to quite huge, the so-called century plants need anywhere from 10 to upward of 60 years to produce tall inflorescences above their rosettes of straplike leaves. Young or smaller species of *Agave* make good container plants, for although they glory in full sun, they can get by on as little as 100 footcandles of light, and will tolerate drafts and air conditioning. Some good prospects for indoor gardens include *Agave americana* 'Marginata' (variegated Caribbean agave), with compact rosettes of stiff, upright, blue-gray leaves with white margins; the small-growing *A. parviflora,* a pygmy

form with a stemless rosette up to eight inches (20 cm) wide and green to olive gray leaves with white threads on the margins; and *A. victoriae-reginae,* with a dense rosette of dark green leaves striped with white. Agaves should be kept on the dry side in light, well-drained soil.

COMPOSITAE (SUNFLOWER FAMILY)

Including perhaps one-ninth of the world's flowering plants, the huge Sunflower family features several genera of succulents. The most notable are the plants of the former genus *Kleinia,* now included in the physically

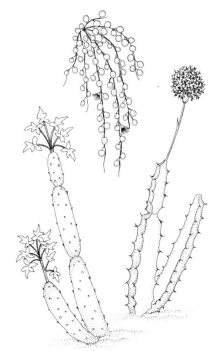

Assortment of Senecios: Dangling down like beads on a string are the leaf-laden stems of *S. rowleyanus,* a natural for potting in a hanging basket. At lower left is *S. articulatus,* composed of jointed stems with bursts of fleshy leaves at the top. During dry spells these leaves are shed, and the remaining stem joints resemble candles, hence the common name candle plant. To the right is the candy stick plant, or *S. stapeliaeformis,* which features deep green or purple stems marked with silver.

varied genus *Senecio,* which in addition to the succulents contains a popular vining foliage plant, *S. mikanioides* (parlor ivy) and a favorite flowering gift plant, *S.* × *hybridus* (the cineraria).

One of the best known of the succulent species is *S. rowleyanus* (string of beads), which offers spherical green leaves on a long, green stem, and which makes a very adaptable hanging basket plant. Extraordinarily different in appearance is *S. articulatus* (candle plant), which has fleshy, deeply lobed leaves which it loses during a dry period, and thistlelike flowers of yellowish white. A third succulent species of yet another growth habit is the attractive creeping *S. macroglossus* 'Variegatum' (variegated wax ivy), which has ivylike leaves variegated with cream. The upright, branching *S. stapeliiformis* (candy stick) is painted with silver between the ribs of its dark green to purple stems. Another of the trailing types is *S. radicans,* which is a cylindrical, vining plant with plump, pointed leaves. These succulent *Senecio* species grow best in moderately dry soil, temperatures about 50°F (10°C), and full sun to partial shade.

INDOOR CARE OF CACTI AND OTHER SUCCULENTS

There is no fail-safe magic formula for growing succulents, only some hints to work with while you let your plants teach you about their needs in your climate, and on your windowsill, under your skylight, or on your sun porch. According to Charles Glass and Robert Foster, editors of the *Cactus and Succulent Journal* and authors of the indispensable book *Cacti and Succulents for the Amateur* (see Bibliography), "There are no rules concerning good culture which may not be and occasionally should not be broken; there are only principles and guidelines which, when followed with interest, common sense, and love will be of help."

GETTING SUCCULENTS TO FLOWER

The key to flowering succulents is an annual rest, for if most cacti and other succulents are forced to continue growing throughout the year, they probably won't flower, and they may rot off at the base.

Where terrestrial cacti are concerned, flowers are by no means certain, for many of these plants need many hours per day of sunlight to bring on flowering, and in some climates and some locations this is simply not available. Even in the same house a cactus facing a northern exposure may not flower, whereas the same plant would bloom if allowed to face south. Also, not all cacti flower as young plants. Experimentation and patience are what is needed if it's flowers you're after; it will also help if you select genera that bloom readily, such as *Echinocereus, Echinopsis, Lobivia, Mammillaria, Notocactus,* and *Rebutia.* If you are especially eager for flowers on your succulents, you might concentrate on epiphytic orchid and holiday cacti and also collect other succulents such as crown-of-thorns *(Euphorbia milii* var. *splendens),* Christmas kalanchoe *(K. blossfeldiana),* haworthias, and huernias.

WATER

Water — usually too much of it — is the cause of the untimely demise of the majority of indoor succulents, for when the roots are wet, pathogens can thrive. It cannot be emphasized too often that these plants must not be overwatered, and the only way not to overwater is to carefully examine the soil to see if it has dried out sufficiently between waterings. No schedule will ever substitute for becoming familiar with each plant and each pot to determine just how much water it needs and how much time must elapse before it is dry again.

When you do water, be sure to do it completely. In watering their large collection in Santa Barbara, California, Foster and Glass

(continued on page 306)

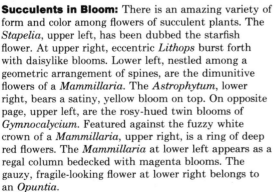

Succulents in Bloom: There is an amazing variety of form and color among flowers of succulent plants. The *Stapelia*, upper left, has been dubbed the starfish flower. At upper right, eccentric *Lithops* burst forth with daisylike blooms. Lower left, nestled among a geometric arrangement of spines, are the dimunitive flowers of a *Mammillaria*. The *Astrophytum*, lower right, bears a satiny, yellow bloom on top. On opposite page, upper left, are the rosy-hued twin blooms of *Gymnocalycium*. Featured against the fuzzy white crown of a *Mammillaria*, upper right, is a ring of deep red flowers. The *Mammillaria* at lower left appears as a regal column bedecked with magenta blooms. The gauzy, fragile-looking flower at lower right belongs to an *Opuntia*.

make three passes with the hose to be sure the plant is thoroughly watered, and then they let it go almost dry before repeating the process. On the other hand, horticulturist Frank Horwood needs to water only half as much at Abbey Gardens nursery, which is only a few miles from the Foster-Glass collection. (A slight difference in elevation puts Abbey Gardens closer to sea level, and thus in a cooler, more humid location.)

Clearly, the only rule in watering is that there are no rules, and even experienced growers usually will not presume to give anyone living out of their specific location an exact formula for successful cultivation of cactus.

As a general rule, however, cacti need less water than other succulents. During spring, summer, and fall you might water cacti in pots with drain holes anywhere from once every two or three weeks to as often as three or four times a week (more frequent watering is likely to be needed when temperatures are very high, if your cactus is outdoors in summer, or if it is in a very quick-draining mix containing relatively large amounts of sand, gravel, or perlite).

In winter water very sparingly — just enough to keep cacti turgid and unshriveled. Don't water so often that the plants start growing in the dim winter light. This will result in elongated growth, or in a pinheaded look. The best plan in winter is to mist plants needing moisture on comparatively warm days that are sunny (misting is especially preferable to watering if the plants are in a cool, damp location).

Hardy cacti can go with almost no water at all in the winter months, and some growers keep them dry from October until March, giving them temperatures of 41° to 53°F (5° to 12°C) at night, with four or five hours of bright sunlight during the day. Without this winter rest, many temperate zone cacti will not be healthy and most will refuse to bloom. (Examples are *Chamaecereus, Echinopsis, Mammillaria, Notocactus,* and *Opun-*

tia.) Artificial lighting can be used to fulfill the light requirements during this period or even in summer if the plants' location doesn't provide enough.

Epiphytic cacti, leaf succulents, and cacti not native to temperate zone deserts should not be allowed to dry out completely. Plants of this type include *Melocactus,* and *Lithops* and other mesembryanthemums. These non-hardy plants also need nighttime temperatures in winter no cooler than 50°F (10°C). If the root system of a succulent has been allowed to go bone dry in winter or at any other time, the first waterings should be given cautiously. The fine root hairs need time to reestablish themselves. About every three months, place each plant on a drainboard and pour water into the medium until it trickles out of the drain hole. This will flush excess salts from the soil.

Pots without drain holes are not recommended for cacti or other succulents, but if you use them, take the advice of Arizona Growers, a Tucson nursery specializing in native Arizona and Mexican cacti, and never give such plants moisture by pouring water on the soil. Instead, mist them every two weeks or so until the top inch (2.5 cm) of the medium is moist.

Although some books advise to the contrary, do not set a cactus in a pan of water to soak, or allow water to collect in the bottom of the planter. Where succulents with turgid leaves are concerned, a softening of the lower leaves will warn you that you have overwatered the plants.

VENTILATION

Cacti can withstand quite intense heat because of the insulation provided by their spines, and their ability to close their pores during the day to reduce the loss of precious moisture. This characteristic, together with their preference for low humidity, makes these plants ideal for carefree greenhouse culture, for they can get through summers under

Grafting Cacti

With cacti in particular, grafting is a commercially used technique that can also be practiced at home. It is relatively easy because the propagator is cutting through soft rather than woody tissue and does not have to be too exact about lining up the cambiums (inner growth rings) of the two plants. When vigorous and fast-growing genera such as *Opuntia* or *Harrisia* or other members of the Cereus tribe are used as rootstock, the effect can be striking and the result will be faster growth and earlier flowering of the top part of the graft, which can be cut off later and rooted if so desired.

In addition to being used to speed development, grafting of cacti and succulents is done sometimes to save the uninjured top of a diseased plant; to prolong the growth and survival of crestate cultivars; to create a standard, or tree, form by using a columnar rootstock and a weeping cultivar as the scion; or to elevate orchid cacti or other epiphytic types to achieve a better display of their flowers.

Grafting is preferably done in spring and summer on a hot, sunny day when sap is on the move. The kinds of grafts often used with cacti are the side graft (which can be practiced with plants of any shape), in which

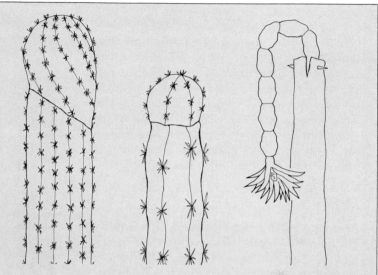

Cactus Grafts: There are three main types of grafts, and the one you use is determined by the shape of the plant you're working with. At left is a side graft, which involves cutting on a slant and is suitable for plants of various shapes. In the center is a flat graft, best for fat, spherical plants; the cuts are made horizontally. At right is a cleft graft, the best type to use for flat or thin-stemmed plants. The root stalk is cut horizontally, then slit in the top so the wedge-shaped scion can be slipped into place.

both the scion and the rootstock are cut on the slant; the flat graft (which is often used on fat, spherical plants), in which both parts are cut horizontally; and the cleft graft (which is preferred for flat or thin-stemmed plants such as epiphytic cacti), in which a slit is made in the top of the horizontally cut rootstock and the scion is cut in a wedge shape so tissue on both sides is in contact with that of the rootstock next to it. In grafting, the plants should be sliced cleanly — never cut with a sawing motion — and the parts fitted together immediately. Any exposed surfaces remaining should be dusted with powdered sulfur. Rubber bands or string or wooden toothpicks or cactus spines can be used to assure the close contact of the grafted parts, and a paper bag should be placed over the plant for several days to keep the graft clean and moist. Care should be taken never to get water on the graft site or rot may result.

glass without the aid of expensive cooling equipment and constant wetting-down. Similarly, their acceptance of summer heat means cacti and other succulents are good choices for non-air-conditioned apartments or homes in areas where plants cannot be summered outdoors to obtain the benefit of cooler night-time temperatures.

Indirectly, however, high temperatures coupled with the higher humidity of summer can make succulents vulnerable to rot. The preventive measure needed year-round, but especially when temperatures rise above 80°F (27°C), is good air circulation. Fresh air in gentle motion not only helps to lower the temperature around plants by evaporating transpired water, but also works against fungal rot, for dried-off plants do not provide an inviting breeding ground for disease spores. The need for good ventilation is one reason why cacti do well when plunged into beds of sand outdoors for the summer. Bring them in around the beginning of September.

LIGHT

Although cacti and many succulents are desert dwellers, many contrive in their native habitats to grow in semishade by growing in clusters or near rocks or beneath taller plants. It follows that plants being grown in an unshaded glass greenhouse or on a windowsill in the full glare of summer sun can be burned by such intense, powerfully focused light. The danger of sunburn is particularly great in spring, when plants may too suddenly be subjected to glass-focused glare after long weeks of weak winter light. Therefore, exposure to direct sun in spring should be gradual.

In late spring and summer, succulents will need shade in a glass greenhouse (fiberglass glazing casts sufficiently diffused light). If grown on a windowsill, they should be moved back from the glass or placed behind a sheer curtain on intensely bright days.

Young succulents, in particular, must be shaded from direct sun; so should tender ones such as *Epiphyllum* and *Rebutia* species. As a rule of thumb, give intensely green plants without spines or hairs (that is, jungle types) shaded light; succulents covered with hair or spines (desert dwellers) are self-shading and can take more direct sun. Also, nonepiphytic flowering succulents usually need high levels of light if they are to bloom.

Generally, south, southeastern, or perhaps eastern window exposures, or from 14 to 18 hours a day of fluorescent light, are best for indoor succulents.

Cactus House: Cacti are among the least demanding of plants to grow under glass. In hot summer weather, you don't have to worry constantly about the plants baking or drying out, because by their very nature cacti can keep themselves cool and don't demand constant moisture. During the cold days of winter, there is no need to heat the greenhouse as you would for tropical plants, since a cool rest period is just the thing to bring cacti into spectacular bloom.

Although cacti and succulents need to be grown slowly, virtually the only essential regarding light is that they must be watched for signs of becoming pale in color and elongated (etiolated is the world professional growers are apt to use) or pinheaded — both indications of too little light. One danger to watch for in the winter windowsill garden is the presence of a frost pocket between curtains and the window. When curtains are pulled, if there is a collection of succulents on the windowsill, the curtains should be between the plants and the glass.

POTTING MIXES AND REPOTTING

Just about everyone who is a serious succulent grower has his own potting mix and swears it is the only one that works. As a starting point, try the cactus mix suggested in chapter 6. But as you become more involved in cultivating cacti and succulents, you will probably develop your own variations. Noted *Mammillaria* collector Archie Deutschman uses equal parts of mortar-wash sand and all-purpose potting soil for plants from various sources and never pasteurizes the medium, although he admits to losing some plants when he transplants or propagates. The cactus nursery Arizona Growers suggests two different mixes. Their formula for plants in pots with drain holes consists of equal parts of coarse sand, peat moss, and potting soil; plants in pots without drain holes are given a blend of equal parts coarse sand and potting soil. K & L Cactus Nursery of Galt, California, suggests potting plants in equal parts of loam, medium-coarse sand, and leaf mold, and adding "a little peat moss and ground bone meal."

Actually, the climate where you live should be taken into account in formulating a potting mix if it is markedly different from the climate where the plant was grown. If you live where there is a fair amount of rain and fog (that is, high humidity) and mild summer temperatures, add an extra half-part of sand to your mix. In very hot, bright, and dry locales you might put in extra leaf mold or peat moss to keep plants from drying out very quickly. (Extra sphagnum can also be a good idea for South American cacti such as *Rebutia* species, which like somewhat acid soil.)

Plants bought locally as well as those arriving bare-rooted by mail should be transplanted into one of these dry mixes on arrival, then watered lightly and kept out of bright light for a few weeks. Move them into bright light gradually.

Most cactus growers advise repotting in spring and only when necessary, and since most cacti and succulents grow slowly, this may be only every two to five years — longer if plants are planted in groups in roomy boxes

or bowls. Again, this is where common sense and careful observation count.

To protect these spiny plants — and your hands — at repotting time, don old leather gloves or fold a newspaper page accordion fashion into a long, narrow "collar" that can be curved around the cactus and pinched closed with the fingers of one hand while the pot is removed and a new one supplied with the other hand. Or you can use wooden salad tongs or metal ice tongs to hold the cactus. With this method, protect the spines by inserting wads of crushed tissue paper or newspaper between the tongs and the plant. Small plants can be picked up with chopsticks.

Repotting Painlessly: A prickly cactus is no treat to work with, but when it comes time to repot there are measures you can take to protect the plant and your hands. Leather gloves guard against inadvertent contact with the spines. While switching pots a length of newspaper folded in accordion pleats can be used as a collar to securely grasp the cactus.

Most cactus growers seem to prefer clay pots, using plastic or glazed ceramic pots (if at all) only for smaller plants which dry out very rapidly in tiny clay pots. The pot should be about one inch (2.5 cm) larger than the diameter of the root ball of the succulent. Another rule of thumb, suggested by Judith Nelson, a horticultural writer and author of *Money-Saving Garden Magic* (see Bibliography), is to select a pot half as wide as the plant is high for vertical forms and to use a pot that is an inch (2.5 cm) wider than the diameter of the plant for plants with rounded foliage.

Cacti and other succulents also look very good in bowl or dish gardens, and some growers take great delight in making complete miniature desert landscapes in large bowls, complete with a few stones, interesting pieces of wood, and other accessories. The only requirement for a bowl garden is that all of the plants must have more or less the same growing period and cultural requirements. Cacti that look fine in bowl gardens include species of *Mammillaria, Notocactus, Parodia,* and *Rebutia* — in other words, any of the globular types. Some of the smaller species of *Opuntia* such as *O. microdasys* can be added with good effect.

Another handsome, culturally sound way to grow these plants is in rectangular wooden boxes that are up to 18 inches (46 cm) wide and 30 inches (76 cm) long and 6 to 8 inches (15 to 20 cm) deep. Such setups give plants the root room they like, making repotting unnecessary for long periods of time, and if necessary can accommodate heating cables for a collection requiring warm temperatures in winter.

Plants in pots or large containers can benefit both aesthetically and practically from a top-dressing of white stones. In addition to enhancing the form of the cactus or other succulent, this mulch reflects added light on the plant, delays drying out, keeps a surface crust of salt from building up, and facilitates the slow, thorough uptake of water.

FEEDING

Most succulents can grow satisfactorily without additional nutrients, provided their soil is rich enough and they are repotted every two years or so. Although some food can be helpful to encourage growth and flowering, these plants are so well adapted to hard times that potting them too richly or feeding them too often can be fatal.

The organic answer is to add bone meal to the potting mix (1 teaspoon/5 ml per six-inch/15 cm pot). To encourage bloom, some gardeners periodically apply a liquid fertilizer that is low in nitrogen, medium in potash, and high in phosphorus. Older plants might be given a small amount of rotted manure in their potting soil and cacti with white hairs, such as *Mammillaria* and *Astrophytum* species can benefit from a half cup (118 ml) of ground limestone added to each bushel (35.2 l) of growing medium.

Provide some supplemental feeding every four to six weeks during the plant's active growth season, usually in spring and early summer. Monthly feedings can be given at half the usual strength recommended for flowering plants.

CONTROLLING INSECTS AND DISEASES

Aphids, mealybugs, and cactus and woolly cactus scale, as well as thrips and red spider mites, are sometimes found on cacti. Watch out for these and use the remedies described in chapter 9. Root-knot nematodes can also threaten succulents and can be thwarted by pasteurizing the growing medium and disinfecting used pots.

Fungal diseases are best dealt with by avoiding them. This means paying special attention to not overwatering, not bruising the plants, and taking proper precautions if offsets or other plant material is removed for propagation. If infection does occur, the damaged areas may be carefully cut away with a clean knife and the infected wound dusted with sulfur.

Because succulent seedlings are especially prone to damping-off fungus, which even pasteurizing the medium sometimes fails to prevent, when growing these plants from seeds you may want to use as a medium chunks of polyester fiber, which is also said to result in faster and better germination than other media. If seeds are started this way, the fiber can be sprayed once each week with a half-strength solution of fish emulsion and kept under glass until most of the seeds have germinated.

PROPAGATION

As plants adapted to surviving and perpetuating themselves under inhospitable conditions, succulents are efficiently designed for successful propagation. Many of them, such as agaves, aloes, ceropegias, the flowering stones, and stapelias, may be readily started from seeds; this is particularly true of single-stemmed succulents which do not produce offsets (*Aeonium nobile,* for example).

The list of succulents that can be started very easily from stem cuttings is long indeed, and includes plants of the Compositae, Crassulaceae, and Euphorbiaceae, and many cacti such as opuntias. With cacti, one can actually cut off and root the top of the plant or a branch (a practice called decapitation, which encourages the plant to put forth many plantlets at the wound). With fleshy succulents, it is vital to let the cut part dry out for up to ten days so a callus is formed; otherwise the prospective new plant will rot instead of root. The cutting should then be placed in dry sand, vermiculite, or a blend of equal parts of sand and potting soil. Highly succulent cuttings such as those from *Euphorbia* species should not be watered at all until they have rooted.

Various leaf succulents such as kalanchoes, gasterias, and haworthias may be propagated by rooting all or part of a leaf. This too must be allowed to form a callus before it is placed in a rooting medium. Clustering or rosette-forming succulents like aloes and sempervivums often form plantlets or offsets that may be allowed to root, then detached and planted, or severed with a knife and treated as unrooted cuttings. See chapter 8 for more information on various methods of propagation.

CHAPTER 16

Edibles

Yes, it is possible to vegetable garden indoors—summer and winter. It takes the proper containers, space, a good soil mix, enough light, the right temperatures, some sense about how much to water and feed, and, perhaps most important, the human ingredients of patience, skill, and careful observation—and a little luck. To grow healthy indoor edibles you must be as competent as an outdoor gardener and as skilled as an expert on house plants, for indoor production is really a blend of the two activities.

No matter how productive your outdoor plot and beds and how diligently you preserve your harvest by freezing, canning, drying, pickling, or storing in ground or cellar, there will, at least in northern areas, be a dreary and housebound period of the year when your whole body seems to yearn for something truly fresh, newly sprung from soil. The indoor garden serves its highest calling in offering that "something" to you.

Of course, there are many other reasons for gardening indoors. Vegetable plants can be just as decorative as more conventional house plants. Indoor gardening transforms a seasonal activity into a year-round avocation; and, because all indoor plantings must be comparatively small, they offer an intimacy with individual plants not found in family size plots. With the coming of spring, the knowledge gained by such daily close observation can be transferred outside to the mutual benefit of plants and growers.

Then there are people—more and more of them all the time—who just don't have access to the outdoor earth. Apartment dwellers and other city folk, people in wheelchairs, and those with strong allergies to ragweed and other weed pollens—none should be denied a chance to produce part of their own food supply.

The important thing to remember is that you will never be able to fill a freezer and wave a final goodbye to the vegetable market by growing edibles indoors. For all the undependableness of nature—its unexpected frosts and its plagues of cutworms—the out-of-doors is still the natural place to grow food. The minute we dig up a plant and bring it inside we have removed it from its natural environment.

Outdoor gardeners sometimes make graph-paper plans before they lift a spade, setting hypothetical spinach on the shady side of hoped-for corn. Indoor gardening takes even more careful planning because it is less natural and more confined. List what you want to grow, and calculate what you have to offer in terms of the temperature, light, humidity, and space requirements discussed in this chapter.

Vegetables from the Past: Leaf lettuce has been a favorite among gardeners for years and is one backyard crop that can be grown indoors as well.

Opposite, midget tomatoes, Lycopersicon lycopersicum *'Tiny Tim', ready for picking.*

Indoor arrangements should be planned for people as well as the plants. It's handy to keep herbs within reaching distance of the stew pot for *bouquets garni,* for example, and scraggly carrot tops in an expanse of soil will do less for a living room's decor than will a carefully trained European cucumber. For public areas of your house, emphasize the decorative—use marigolds to mask the base of a long-stemmed pepper plant, for instance, or train peas to cover a divider screen.

Vegetable plants do well in private areas like a spare bedroom, a study, or a bathroom—just make sure they are not out of sight and therefore out of water. The extra heat and humidity in bathrooms can do wonders for moisture-loving crops such as cucumbers, green peppers, strawberries, and tomatoes—if adequate light is available, which is most likely during the summer.

MEETING THE NEEDS OF VEGETABLES INDOORS

CONTAINERS

Any container that will confine soil and roots, retain the right amount of moisture while providing drainage, and offer space for growth is as acceptable for a vegetable as for an ornamental plant. Review what you learned in chapter 4 about pots and trays, and think big. A 20-gallon (75.7 l) plastic garbage can with small holes drilled in the sides and bottom may not be the stuff of art or romance, but two large tomato plants will live happily there. The holes are important for drainage, and drainage in turn demands that there be a lower vessel or tray to catch excess water. Block large holes with pot shards or coarse gravel to keep the soil from washing out. Waterlogging due to inadequate drainage can lead to root rot and other sorrows. If you have your eye on an antique copper boiler or large crock, and drilling holes would be an impossibility or an affront, fill

the container with several inches (approximately 5 cm) of coarse gravel and a little charcoal into which water can drain from the upper soil. Or use the antique piece as a decorative holder for a less attractive but more functional tub.

Containers come in all sizes and shapes. You might consider stone sinks, wooden or metal tubs, kitchen pots and pans, wooden troughs, plastic-lined baskets, photographic developing trays, casks, kegs, and tea chests. Other recyclables include old aquaria, sand pails, retired refrigerator crispers, dishpans, plastic or metal wastebaskets, large size shortening tins, and plastic-lined produce boxes. Even a child's old wagon or some discarded bureau drawers can serve the purpose of germinating seeds or growing leaf crops with shallow root systems. With the exception of dwarf fruit trees, which need containers 14 to 18 inches (36 to 46 cm) deep as they mature, most plants can get by with containers that have a soil depth of 9 inches (23 cm). As far as diameter of containers is concerned, bushy plants such as peppers and eggplants need at least 12 inches (30 cm), though more compact plants such as dwarf tomatoes and herbs can get by with 6-inch (15 cm) pots. These also will do perfectly well for a few leaves of lettuce or several radishes. For more tips on sizing edible plants to containers, see Other Containers, in chapter 29.

To avoid buying or recycling a container as such, you can make your own "grow-bags" by laying down a large bag of lightweight, all-purpose potting soil and making holes in the top (front) of the bag. You can plant directly into the holes one or two dwarf tomato, eggplant, or pepper plants, or plenty of leaf lettuce. These "containers" can be reused, but should be replaced yearly. And because of their extremely utilitarian appearance, they are best used in a greenhouse or a garden in a study, workroom, or other "nonshowy" part of the house.

If space is a problem for you but money is not, give some thought to buying some of

Vertically Potted Garden: Stacked pots with side pockets make it possible to garden indoors in limited space.

the stack pots so popular among European apartment gardeners. These pots have side pockets for plants and fit atop each other to provide vertical growing room. Another vertical setup particularly suited to strawberries is a plastic, potting mix-filled sleeve which is suspended from a clip; the plants poke out of holes along the sides of the sleeve.

SOILS AND FEEDING

As a rule, indoor edibles will thrive in a light, well-drained soil mix such as equal parts of peat moss, vermiculite, and potting soil with ¼ cup (59 ml) each of rock phosphate and dolomitic limestone added to each peck

(8.8 l). Another good blend would be a combination of 2 parts topsoil, 1 part coarse sand, and 1 part thoroughly decomposed compost, with ½ cup (118 ml) of bone meal mixed in per peck (8.8 l) of medium. Preferably the soil and sand should be pasteurized for 30 minutes at 180°F (82°C).

When growing plants for which pollination and early fruit set are desired, be careful to feed very lightly until after flowers and fruits have begun to form. Thereafter, in bright, warm conditions heavy feeders like tomatoes, peppers, and squash may be fertilized weekly with dilute manure tea or with fish emulsion or liquid seaweed fertilizer applied at half the usual recommended rate. Or plants may be top-dressed with an inch (2.5 cm) of sieved compost and fed only every two weeks. If temperatures are high and light is strong, leaf vegetables too may be fed as often as once a week, but every two weeks should suffice for root crops. (For more on potting soils and plant foods, see chapters 6 and 7, respectively.)

HUMIDITY AND WATERING

Most American homes are a little too dry for many edibles to flourish in them. Pollination, fertilization, and early fruit set in plants such as peppers, tomatoes, eggplants, and some beans are affected by humidity in addition to temperature and soil-related factors. For best results, these vegetables need a humidity level between 40 and 60 percent. To counteract the desertlike air in heated interiors, you can grow your crop in a brightly lit bathroom or the space near a sink, or you can group plants atop a layer of pebbles that is half-submerged in water. (Other strategies for heightening humidity are discussed under Humidity, in chapter 2.)

Edible plants can be watered in the same way as other house plants unless their particular culture demands exceptional treatment. Remember, however, to keep the soil of fruiting plants moist to encourage maximum productivity, and monitor vegetables and fruits in hanging containers quite often, for the warmer air currents up high coupled with restricted root space will cause them to dry out faster. On the other hand, if you are growing vegetables in a cool location in low light, water them sparingly and only in the morning, for damp soil at night is an invitation to disease.

HEAT

Vegetables are no different from conventional house plants in their temperature needs; those with tropical background and ancestry will prefer a torrid location, while more northern types will do better in a cool place. It's the crops that you would otherwise be braving cold winds to plant outside in early spring or harvesting after the light fall frosts that do best in cool indoor sites—that is, lettuce, peas, radishes, and spinach.

Though requiring heat for germination, early growth, and setting fruit, most cool weather plants grow stockier when heat is kept down, especially at night. They thrive on daytime temperatures of between 65° and 77°F (18° and 25°C) accompanied by nighttime lows of 50° to 60°F (10° to 16°C). Such plants grow best when cloudy days are followed by relatively low nighttime temperatures and sunny days by higher ones. For example, greenhouse tomatoes bred to set fruit at low temperatures have been found to grow fastest when 77°F (25°C) nights follow sunny days or when much cooler nights of 46°F (8°C) succeed overcast days offering only 8 percent sun.

Suppose you are blessed with sunny days and want to grow tomatoes or other fruiting vegetables without subjecting your household to unhealthy and fuel-consuming nighttime heat? There are ways of keeping your tomatoes or other crops warmer than you keep yourself. One way is to use an inexpensive heating cable in or near the containers you use for tender plants. Or you can construct a cable-heated, plastic-covered night greenhouse box for the heat lovers. Encasing plants in plastic bags or surrounding them with propped-up sheets at night will enable them to use their own "body heat" the way you do under the blankets. Even if you prefer to use a small heater with its own thermostat and a fan for circulation in the plant-growing area, it's still less expensive than unnecessarily heating your whole house. Remember also that heat rises. Spots on the floor may be cold, while hanging baskets up by the ceiling are catching warm air currents.

Finally, bear in mind that drafts as well as light can come through windows. You can protect window-shelf plants with drapes that close between them and the panes, or use cardboard screens on cold, windy nights when you cannot move the containers to a warmer spot.

LIGHT

Light, or the lack of it, can play tricks on plants. In a warm house buds on flowering plants will shrivel up when light is not strong enough. The temperature may say, "bloom," but the light intensity says, "not yet." As this suggests, if light levels are low, temperatures should be kept down also, or if this is impossible, a fan may be used to help cool plants. Duration of light (daylength) also can have significant effects on plant development. For example, short days may encourage the top growth of onions to the detriment of bulb formation.

Many outdoor vegetables flower as the days grow longer. If you are trying to grow them indoors in fall and winter, you must deceive them with supplementary artificial light. Beans and peas fall into this category. In *The Indoor Garden* (see Bibliography), Edward H. and Margaret Hunter recommend a minimum of 4 hours of sun plus 8 hours of artificial light daily for such long-day fruiting plants. Other long-day flowering plants, such as beets, carrots, Chinese cabbage, radishes,

Vegetable Gardening without Soil or Sun

Sprouted seeds or beans are so easy to grow, and so fast, that generating sprouts seems more a part of cooking than of gardening. It can be done any time of year without the help of soil or sun—all that is required is a dark or dimly lit place that is fairly warm but not hot. Each cook seems to have a different way of sprouting—the options range from using mason jars with metal or plastic mesh or cheesecloth lids to setting up a system of self-rinsing tiered pans. Some sprout growers prefer to cover seeds lightly with soil in the oriental way. Almost any untreated seed can be sprouted, from the plebeian but multi-form bean to exotics like fenugreek and almond. The list of favorites includes barley, corn, flax, rye, sunflower seeds, and triticale. Sprouting such seeds enhances their nutritional value, for the carbohydrate content is lowered while the amount of protein, minerals, and niacin and vitamin C is increased.

If you're a beginner, start with untreated mung bean seeds—that is, those bought at a natural foods store or described in a catalog as specifically for sprouting. Soak seeds or beans overnight, drain them, and place a large spoonful in a quart (946 ml) jar. Cover the jar with a thickness of cheesecloth, securing it with string or a rubber band, and set the jar in a warm, dim place. Two or three times a day—more with soybeans—remove the covering and put the jar under a tap to fill it with lukewarm water. Shake it and drain off the water, using your fingers or the cheesecloth as a sieve. After replacing the cheesecloth cover, you may find it a good idea, especially with tangly sprouts like alfalfa, to tilt the jar sideways and distribute the rinsed seeds evenly over the side by shaking gently. Then set the jar on its side in a shallow pan or dish, the jar tilted slightly downward to allow any remaining water to drain off. Flat-sided jars make this extra aeration easy to provide; do so after each rinsing and aim at making one even layer of sprouts. A temperature of 68° to 75°F (20° to 24°C) works best for most seeds, but pumpkin seeds, soybeans, and mung beans sprout best at 86°F (30°C), and cress and peas at below 68°F (20°C). If you are careful never to let the seeds dry out and to keep them warm, sprouts should appear on the second or third day. After this you can give them more light to add a bit of greenery—and more vitamins—if you wish. Use mung bean sprouts when they are 1½ to 3 inches (4 to 8 cm) long; alfalfa and lentil sprouts are better shorter. Sprouts taste good raw in salads or sandwiches or added to stir-fried dishes or to soups, breads, and casseroles. They also excel as a meat extender or served as a hot buttered vegetable.

Sprouting Beans and Seeds: Sprouts make a nutritious and tasty addition to salads and sandwiches, and can be grown in a few days without soil or sunlight—all you need is a mason jar or other container.

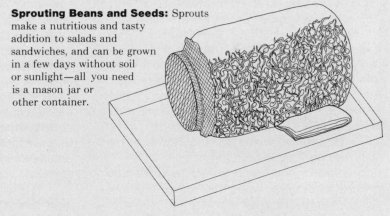

and spinach, do not set fruit from their flowers and so do not need long days when grown for food. In fact, it is desirable to keep these plants from flowering and setting seed stalks. To do so, time their indoor culture so that most of their growth occurs as the days are getting shorter. Or be sure the plants get no more than 12 hours of light a day.

Fortunately, some of the favorite flowering vegetables—tomatoes, cucumbers, and peppers, for example—are day neutral. They will flower and set fruit almost regardless of daylength.

The length of the daylight period gives

cues for sexual changes, but the more well-known function of light is its contribution to photosynthesis and therefore to year-round plant growth and health. The effectiveness of any light source in promoting plant growth is linked not only to its daily duration but also to its quality and intensity—concepts defined at length in chapter 25. In growing edibles under natural light, the rule of thumb is that leaf and root crops need at least four hours (preferably six hours) a day and that they can get by with the minimally intense and mostly indirect sunlight entering an east window in the morning or the somewhat brighter light coming in a west window in the afternoon. Fruiting crops, on the other hand, require strong, direct sunlight for at least eight hours a day, so they ideally need a sun porch or a south windowsill, although a west one can sometimes serve.

If you cannot provide this duration and intensity of light, you can opt to grow crisp, leafy vegetables during short, dull winter days and to confine indoor growing of tomatoes, peppers, and cucumbers to spring through early fall. (To make the most efficient use of natural light, start fruiting plants around January 20 and transplant them to containers around the end of February when the days are becoming as long as the nights. In bringing started plants indoors in late summer, make sure they are large enough to become well established by October 21, since after that time daylength and sun strength begin to decline critically.)

Another possible response to brief, dim winter days is to boost and extend natural light. Where intensity is concerned, the idea is to provide at least 600 footcandles for germinating seeds, at least 200 to 500 for leaf crops, and at least 1,000 footcandles for flowering vegetables. Note that even close to the brightest window, winter daylight tends to average below 1,000 footcandles, compared to up to 5,000 footcandles in the summer. If you add 500 to 1,000 footcandles of artificial light by suspending two 40-watt fluorescents six inches (15 cm) or less above plant tops, you can double or more than double winter light levels and provide somewhere near the 2,000 footcandles desired by fruiting vegetables like tomatoes, peppers, and cucumbers.

Duration is as important as intensity when it comes to supplementing natural light. The general rule is to supply two hours of fluorescent light for each hour of required sunlight that is not being provided. That is, if your lettuce or spinach is getting only two hours a day of low-intensity light, you must add at least four hours a day of fluorescent light to obtain the equivalent of the minimum four hours per day of sunlight required for good growth.

To be on the safe side, you can choose instead to operate two 40-watt fluorescent tubes for 16 hours a day during short or dark days; cool white lights will do for leaf and root crops, but Wide-Spectrum Gro-Lux or Agro-Lite tubes may give better results with fruiting plants.

If you are growing low-light vegetables and don't want to install a special supplementary fixture, you can move them under a table lamp or bathroom fixture for several hours at the end of the day. If even this supplementation is impractical, try boosting total room light by using some of the measures discussed under Window Exposures, in chapter 28. Or you can increase the yield of individual plants like tomatoes by mulching them with aluminum foil. Harvest leaf crops immediately if there is a succession of cloudy days and they begin to droop.

Should you choose to substitute artificial light for natural light more or less completely, success is most likely if you grow leaf vegetables under standard fluorescents in a cool location, taking care never to let the plants dry out and to thin them adequately. 'Bibb' lettuce and the new cultivar 'Chesibb' are said to do very well under lights. They and other salad greens will need 12 to 16 hours at about five to ten inches (13 to 25 cm) below the lights.

If food plants are to make the fullest use of available light to produce good yields, they also must have an adequate supply of carbon dioxide. To provide this, maintain good air circulation in areas where plants are growing and admit fresh air to nearby rooms even in winter, leaving connecting doors open so the raw air will gradually reach plants after it is somewhat warmed.

TIME TO MATURITY INDOORS

Short days and low light levels coupled with less than ideal temperatures often extend time to harvest significantly when edibles are grown indoors. For example, vegetables forced out of season in a heated greenhouse with supplementary light can take up to twice as long to mature as the same varieties raised in season outdoors. The lag will definitely be on the long side if you are growing food crops in northern latitudes, in an overcast climate, in the dimmer, unidirectional light coming in a window, or in a place that has a temperature at or below the low end of the recommended range (50° to 68°F/10° to 20°C for leaf vegetables and 60° to 78°F/16° to 26°C for fruiting vegetables).

Because of such variables, it is impossible to give more than a "guesstimate" of time to maturity for edibles grown indoors, and the figures given in this chapter should be interpreted relative to growing conditions. Crops affected by poor light and low temperatures usually do not die, but they do slow down, and fruiting kinds will bear few if any flowers and fruits. Feed and water such plants less if they have been forced into relative dormancy. When spring comes, they will catch up.

BRINGING GARDEN PLANTS INSIDE

There are several sources for edible house plants, but your easiest hunting ground is likely to be the rows of a seasonal outdoor garden. Bringing outdoor plants indoors involves almost the reverse logic of putting house plants out for a summer vacation. It's a cure for the "end-of-season blues" for you and a blessed commutation of a frosty death sentence for the plants. Cabbage, carrots, lettuce, onions, peas, and spinach, among other crops, do not transplant well, are comparatively easy to start from seeds and, in some cases, mature quickly and require frequent transplanting. Digging up these plants to bring them indoors makes little sense. On the other hand, long-season crops like cucumbers, eggplants, melons, peppers, and tomatoes both take a long time to germinate and benefit from a healthy outdoor start. These plants are better candidates for autumn transplanting. Peppers, tomatoes, and eggplants are perennials and can go back outdoors in spring.

Look for healthy specimens free from insects and disease. Dig up as much of the root ball as possible, set it in an appropriately sized pot, and supplement the earth clinging to the roots with an all-purpose potting soil. Gently hose or rinse the plant to remove any insects and insect eggs that may be present.

Do your transplanting about four weeks before you turn on the heat inside so your new guests will have time to adapt. For a gentle transition, bring outdoor plants in gradually during late August and September. Leave them out in the daytime, even in soft rain, but bring them in at night. This is a sort of reversed hardening-off; perhaps one could call it "softening-in." You will almost certainly lose some of these plants. It is hard to tell when an established vegetable plant is too large or mature to transplant well. Certain varieties do better than others, too. Indeed, the choice of variety is so important for indoor success that rather than just enlisting any volunteer you may do better to plan ahead and plant varieties amenable to being brought indoors at season's end. Or go a step further and deliberately start selected seeds outdoors in containers in midsummer, moving plants to progressively larger pots (preferably keeping the pots plunged in soil) until it is time to bring them in. Tomatoes also may be propagated easily by taking tip cuttings from vigorously growing shoots in the middle of summer. These root quickly in pots of soil if they are covered with plastic. The new plants should be kept out of direct sun until rooted. Before bringing in any tomato plants from outdoors, check them carefully for whiteflies.

Among the more common vegetables most suitable for "transplanting-in," the following plants also can be started indoors from seeds or grown there from purchased plants.

EGGPLANT (Solanum melongena var. esculentum)

Eggplants, like peppers, have seeds that are hard to germinate—they require at least 75°F (24°C) to do so and prefer 80° to 90°F (27° to 32°C). Since eggplants also require a long season, transplanting them indoors after a midsummer start is a good idea. Eggplants make attractive house plants with their handsome leaves and bushy growth, and they come in miniature varieties. The plants need ample food and water: never let them dry out. They also need as much light and warmth as peppers and tomatoes and sometimes even more if they are to mature in nine to ten weeks after transplanting. Two full size plants can fit in a 24-inch (61 cm) container, and lettuce and radishes can be grown around the eggplants while the plants are still small. When the plants bloom, you can help self-pollination by shaking the plants to scatter pollen, or by transferring pollen from one flower to another with a small brush or paper twist. Fruits can be harvested when they reach 8 inches (20 cm) long and turn the characteristic shiny purple-black color.

MELONS (Cucumis melo vars. and Citrullus lanatus)

If anything could possibly be more difficult to grow indoors than squash, it would probably be melons, which require nighttime temperatures that remain above 70°F (21°C) and a daytime temperature of 80° to 85°F (27° to 29°C). The cantaloupe, or muskmelon (Cucumis melo var. reticulatus) is just a shade easier than the full size watermelon (Citrullus lanatus), though both are often impossible for all but the most experienced indoor gardeners. Like squash, these fruits must have pollen transferred by hand from the male flower to the female blossom. If you are ready for a challenge and want to try your hand at growing melons indoors, the best one to attempt is a midget watermelon started outside in its own bushel-capacity container. 'Sugar Baby' is one small cultivar that bears well, matur-

Melons for Advanced Gardeners: Melons present a challenge for indoor gardeners because of their size and their need for light soils, high temperatures, and hand pollination. When fruit does develop, it can be supported by enclosing it in a mesh bag until ready for picking.

ing in about 11 weeks. Keep it warm, well lighted, wet, and fed enough to want to go on living—and that won't be easy. But if you do succeed you will have something to brag about for years.

PEPPER *(Capsicum annuum)*

Among edible sweet peppers, both bell and banana types make decorative container plants when transplanted from outdoors. One excellent cultivar called 'Sweet Banana' bears tapered yellow fruit which turns red when ripe. Though compact, the plant needs staking because of its brittle stems. Other good container peppers are 'Bell Boy', 'Burpee's Tasty Hybrid', 'California Wonder', 'Canape', 'Jalapeno', 'Keystone Resistant', 'Long Red Cayenne', 'Sweet Cherry', 'Tokyo Bell', and 'Yolo Wonder'. All of these require eight- to ten-inch (20 to 25 cm) pots, but usually need no staking. Ornamental peppers are often called Christmas peppers and sometimes Christmas cherries (just don't confuse them with the poisonous Jerusalem cherry of the *Solanum* genus). Started outdoors or indoors, cultivars such as 'Christmas Candle', 'Nosegay', 'Pinocchio', and 'Red Chile' make good-looking pot plants in autumn and winter. They provide showy but edible miniature fruits that add a pleasant tang to salads or vegetable soup.

Peppers have about the same temperature and light requirements as tomatoes, and like tomatoes, they often require supplementary heat and light in winter. If anything, peppers like it even hotter than tomatoes in the daytime—up to 90°F (32°C)—and they are challenging to grow even in a warm greenhouse. Peppers yield more with hand pollination by shaking or brush, though even that will not result in the development of every blossom. Indoors, pepper pods will never grow as large as they do under natural conditions, but some people prefer the small pods for salads and garnishes. Start two transplanted peppers in a 16-inch (41 cm) tub set

Peppers Growing Indoors: Ornamental chili peppers can be used fresh from the plant or dried for use later on.

in the brightest spot in the house. Feed and water them frequently and the plants will reach maturity in ten weeks or so. Harvest the peppers when the fruits are either green or beginning to turn red or orange, depending on the variety.

SQUASH *(Cucurbita* spp.)

If you are lucky enough to find a late-developing squash plant in the garden in early fall and it survives transplanting, you may persuade it to produce indoors by giving it lots of heat and light and feeding it heavily. The various kinds of summer squash *(C. pepo)* are your best bet indoors, maturing in about 7 weeks compared to 13 weeks or more for winter squash (*C. maxima, C. mixta,* and *C. moschata*). Two plants can fit in a five-gallon (18.9 l) tub. 'Burpee's Hybrid Summer Squash' is a good cultivar and 'Golden Crookneck' can be made to grow in a sturdy sphagnum moss-lined wire hanging basket, although it requires several waterings each day for good growth. Other summer squashes for containers include 'Aristocrat', 'Hybrid Zucchini', and 'Patty Pan'. 'Kindred' is a smaller bushlike squash with dry yellow fruit. Among winter squashes, 'Banana', 'Ebony', 'Gold Nugget', and 'Table King', will sometimes grow in containers indoors. In the Squash family, male flowers and female flowers are separate, and hand pollination with a brush is necessary.

TOMATO (*Lycopersicon lycopersicum*)

The best varieties for indoors are those bred for greenhouse use and requiring less heat and light than outdoor kinds, or those of miniature size or compact, short-vining "determinate" habit which are therefore quicker to ripen and/or easier to find space for. Greenhouse cultivars include 'Kindford Cross', 'Michigan-Ohio Forcing', 'Michigan State', 'Spartan Red 8', 'Stakeless', 'Tropic VF', 'Tuckcross 520F', and 'Vendor'. Among the small, faster-bearing "outdoor" tomatoes are 'Epoch Dwarf Bush', 'Fireball', 'Patio', 'Pixie', 'Red Cherry', 'Small Fry', 'Sugar Lump', 'Tiny Tim', and 'Yellow Pear'. Some varieties like 'Sub-Arctic Cherry' fit into both groups.

In a taste evaluation of eight tomato varieties developed for container growing, *Sunset* magazine's *Joy of Gardening* (1979) rated the comparatively large plant 'Small Fry' best (it also was the most productive), the early-bearing 'Pixie' second best, and the sprawling 'Toy Boy', another early bearer, third. The handsome, late-ripening 'Patio', which produced the largest fruit, placed

Harvest from a Windowsill: Dwarf and cherry tomato cultivars such as 'Tiny Tim' (shown here) will grow well indoors if supplied with enough light and space to spread out.

fourth. Cascading decoratively, the sixth-place 'Tumbling Tom' is excellent for hanging baskets, as is the seventh-place 'Tiny Tim', but they require frequent watering. 'Sweet 100' is a tall-growing plant that bears one-inch (2.5 cm) fruits in profusion. It is also suited to container growing.

Large plants like 'Patio', 'Pixie', 'Small Fry', and 'Sweet 100' must be staked, given a lattice to climb on, or propped with a wire pen just like outdoor tomatoes. It is best to transplant them in late summer and give them ample water—enough to keep the soil evenly moist (some indoor growers recommend daily shower baths for housebound tomatoes). Monthly feedings of fish emulsion in water or one tablespoon (15 ml) of bone meal dug into the soil of each pot will help tomatoes bear better. Increase both feeding and watering when plants are blooming. Some varieties need pinching back to control heavy topgrowth. Though midget plants such as 'Salad Top' or 'Tiny Tim' can be grown in 10-inch (25 cm), or even 6-inch (15 cm) pots (with careful feeding), large ones require a 12- to 18-inch (30 to 46 cm) diameter container and do well in wooden tubs. Keep room temperature around 60°F (16°C) at night and up to 80°F (27°C) in the daytime, or use heating cables or other local heat. Use two hours of supplementary artificial growing light for every hour short of the minimum six hours of sunlight received in a day. If proper heat, light, and moisture levels are maintained, most container varieties will mature in seven to ten weeks from transplant size. You can help pollinate blooming plants by gently shaking them or flicking the flowers with your fingers when they are dry and the sun is out. Or use a paint brush or cotton swab as described under Producing Your Own Seeds, in chapter 8. If whiteflies become a problem, use a soapy water spray or one of the other remedies suggested in chapter 9. Pick the tomatoes when they are slightly underripe, but turning red. Though popular among indoor gardeners, the tomato is not an easy plant to grow for heavy production indoors.

STARTING PLANTS FROM SEEDS

Almost any indoor edible can be grown from seeds and almost anyone with gardening experience knows the basics of seed germination. There are, though, several schools of thought in matters of transplanting, depth of planting, proper temperature, and other phases of the operation.

Helga and William Olkowski, authors of *The City People's Book of Raising Food* (see Bibliography), make open-ended cubes from milk cartons sliced into thirds and set these into trays made by slicing larger cartons lengthwise. They pack a dry sand, soil, and peat moss mixture into the cubes, wet it, and make one depression in each corner, into which two or three seeds are dropped and covered lightly with clean sand. Lettuce seeds are left uncovered because they need light to germinate. The Olkowskis make sure the soil surface does not dry out but they never flood it, and when seedlings first push through they transfer the cartons to a windowsill. When the first leaves appear, all seedlings but the healthiest in each corner are removed by snipping them off with a small scissors. The surviving seedlings are kept damp but not wet as they grow. When the second, or true, leaves appear seedlings may be transplanted to larger containers or to their permanent pots, but it also is possible with this method to move them when they are a little further along.

While germinating, seeds should be kept in a dim and warm place—70° to 75°F (21° to 24°C) is right for most vegetable plants. Some gardeners cover flats of seeds with newspapers or glass or slip them into plastic bags. These methods conserve needed moisture and cut off unwanted light, but they may also encourage growth of fungus if the flats are not checked and aired frequently. (Shredded sphagnum moss in flats also holds in dampness and discourages damping-off organisms.) For flats, it's possible to use egg cartons, wooden or plastic boxes, or even the indentations of deeply sculptured damp carpet padding. Or you can build the seed flats described in chapter 8.

To assure higher and faster germination rates, you might want to stratify the seeds of cool-weather greens in the refrigerator as described under Special Pretreatments, in chapter 8. Or you can presprout seeds before sowing by soaking them or sprinkling them on a wet paper towel and then enclosing them in a plastic bag and leaving the bag tied closed in a dim spot for two days. Sprouted seeds should be planted less deeply than unsprouted ones. They are fragile and difficult to handle, but they do save time.

Where short-season crops like salad greens are concerned, you might want to practice succession planting to guarantee a steady supply. Beginning in late summer, you can plant lettuce seeds on top of the soil in flats every three weeks until it is time to plant the outdoor crop in spring.

Many indoor vegetable gardeners use either inexpensive 40-watt cool white fluorescent or horticultural fluorescent lights for seed germination and claim they work better than natural light when seedling flats are set three to four inches (8 to 10 cm) from the light source and lights are left on for 14- to 16-hour periods. After seedlings appear, such light gardeners adjust the distance from the light to ten inches (25 cm), but continue the same light period. (For information on selecting fluorescent lights, see Choosing the Right Bulbs and Tubes, in chapter 25.)

For depth of planting, follow instructions on seed packets, erring always on the shallow side. Larger seeds generally go three times deeper than their own diameter. For seedling flats, use a soil mix that is not too rich, and increase humus content when you transplant. Sometimes more than one transplanting may be desirable. Some delicate plants, like lettuce, cannot tolerate a lot of rich soil all at once, and you may have better results if you transplant the plants into gradually richer soil mixes. Most plants benefit from being sunk lower into the soil when transplanted than they were in their original flats.

Ironically, the best seeds to plant for indoor crops are generally the ones found in a package that specifies "sow directly in the garden as soon as soil can be worked in the spring." Usually these seeds produce short-season, hardy plants that are the very easiest crops to grow indoors, require little space, and can do with less light and heat than long-season crops. They are especially well suited to homes where the thermostat is turned down at night or where unused rooms are not kept as warm as the family living space. With these cultural tips in mind, here are some vegetables that can succeed from seeds in an indoor garden.

SNAP BEAN AND LIMA BEAN (*Phaseolus vulgaris* and *P. limensis*)

Beans require much root room and are generally not grown indoors other than in a greenhouse because of limitations of space, temperature, and light. But if you can give them lots of room and wish to give them a try in your indoor garden, plant bush-type varieties of snap or lima beans for best results. Sow in early spring or give the plants increasing amounts of supplementary light so the plants can enjoy the lengthening days so important to their flowering and fruiting. If you can supply large tubs, extra heat, and ample light, your indoor bean crop can be planted the same as your outdoor plants. When the plants bloom, shake them gently or transfer pollen by hand to help along pollination. Bush snap beans will need at least 6 to 9 weeks to mature and limas require 8 to 11 weeks. Bush snap beans amenable to container culture include 'Burpee's Brittle Wax', 'Greensleeves', 'Tender Crop', and 'Topcrop'. Likely limas include 'Fordhook 242', 'Henderson Bush', and 'King of the Garden'.

BEET (*Beta vulgaris*)

Some indoor-adaptable beet cultivars are 'Burpee's Golden', 'Detroit Dark Red', 'Early Red Ball', 'Early Wonder', 'Little Egypt', 'Ruby Queen', and 'Tokyo Cross'. For greens, try the excellent 'Golden', 'Green Top Bunching', or 'Sugar Beet'. Sow soaked seeds in succession so you can use the tops for greens, or harvest the whole plant when it is 4 inches (10 cm) high and eat it raw in salads. If you want mature beets you will have to allow at least seven weeks and provide an 8 to 12 inch (20 to 30 cm) deep container into which seeds are sown directly. Thin plants to 2½ inches

(6 cm) apart when they are 2 inches (5 cm) high. Beets have the same temperature and light requirements as carrots. They can thrive even in straight sphagnum moss if it is well limed.

CHINESE CABBAGE (*Brassica rapa,* Pekinensis Group)

For an unusual indoor plant, you might try this snappy-flavored vegetable. After germination, set seedlings in a cool but bright place. A cool environment is important to produce the best flavor; too much warmth may cause the leaves to develop an unpleasantly strong taste. Later thin or transplant the young plants to allow 12 inches (30 cm) of container space for each one. Keep soil close to each plant's roots and fertilize every two weeks with liquid seaweed or manure or compost tea. This vegetable takes at least 9 to 13 weeks to mature after transplanting, but you can cut the cylindrical heads while they are still immature. Discard the tough outer leaves or use them for soup, and use the blanched inner leaves in salads. Chinese cabbage also can be stir-fried for Chinese dishes or cooked like cabbage. Cultivars to try indoors include 'Burpee Hybrid', 'Crispy Choy', 'Michihli', and 'Springtime Stokes Hybrid'.

CARROT (*Daucus carota* var. *sativus*)

'Baby Finger', 'Little Finger', 'Nantes', 'Short N' Sweet', 'Sucram', and 'Tiny Sweet' carrots are all 4 inch (10 cm) long Belgian-type carrots that do well indoors in pots 6 to 8 inches (15 to 20 cm) deep. For larger carrots allow up to 16 inches (41 cm) of depth. Plant seeds directly in the container and thin seedlings at six weeks to stand 3 inches (8 cm) apart (as little as 1½ inches/4 cm for the smallest varieties). Fertilize and water well until they are almost mature. Once they have germinated, carrots like a moist soil, cool air, and temperatures ranging from 40° to 75°F (4° to 24°C). They need more light than lettuce, and a

Carrots from a Pot: Round or small-rooted carrots are more practical for indoor culture than long-rooted types, although larger carrots can be grown successfully in deeper pots.

longer growing season. Germination alone can take up to three weeks and succession plantings at three-week intervals are recommended for a continuous crop. Harvest the smaller carrots in a little under two months, just before they are mature.

CELTUCE (*Lactuca sativa* var. *asparagina*)

This two-crop plant is cultivated like lettuce, but takes somewhat longer to mature. Plant seeds ¼ inch (6 mm) deep and 12 to 15 inches (30 to 38 cm) apart. You can begin picking the younger outer leaves about seven weeks after sowing, or when plants are 5 inches (13 cm) high. When they reach 8 inches (20 cm) in height, cut off the plant about an inch (2.5 cm) above the base, and use the succulent green core in salads, as you'd use celery. Be sure to first peel off the outer skin, to avoid the bitter, milky liquid carried in sap tubes there. The stump of the plant may produce a new crop of leaves.

CORN SALAD
(Valerianella locusta)

This delicately flavored salad crop is a good choice for a warm room—it grows better than lettuce in warm temperatures. Start corn salad seeds directly in permanent containers, sowing heavily since germination is not the best, and thinning later to ten inches (25 cm) between plants. Except for temperatures, provide the same growing conditions as for lettuce. Cut off the plant at its base when it has matured in seven or more weeks, or pick individual leaves as you need them after they have had a month to mature.

GARDEN CRESS
(Lepidium sativum)

Thriving in bonsai trays, pots, or flats in an east or south window, cress needs a temperature below 68°F (20°C). In a warmer environment, the leaves will develop a too-peppery flavor and the plant will go to seed. Sow three to four seeds per inch (2.5 cm) of growing space, and thin seedlings to stand one inch (2.5 cm) apart. This fast-growing vegetable may be cut off and consumed a week or ten days after sowing, or you may remove leaves from more mature plants which will then continue to grow. Garden cress makes a tangy addition to soups, salads, and sandwich spreads.

CUCUMBER (Cucumis sativus)

Cucumbers are a long-season crop, taking seven to nine weeks under ideal conditions. They would do best inside if moved in after a good garden start; unfortunately, the shallow-rooted, top-heavy cucumber is even

harder to transplant than squash. For indoor growing, plants of small, compact habit are essential. One possibility is to start such plants outside eight to ten weeks before planting in permanent pots, and bring them in when blossoms have appeared. With careful feeding and watering, the cucumber 'Pot Luck' does well in a hanging basket, producing short vines and regular size slicing fruit. If supported by trellises, the compact 'Minicu', 'Park's Bush Whopper', and 'Patio Pik' will grow in six-inch (15 cm) pots or three plants to a five-gallon (18.9 l) container. Larger pots are required for 'Lemon' and 'Victory'. All of these cucumbers require high temperatures,

Even Cucumbers Are Possible: Compact, short-vining cucumber varieties such as 'Pot Luck', shown here, are the best to grow indoors. Cucumbers make attractive hanging basket plants for sunny windows.

Try European Cucumbers in Your Indoor Garden

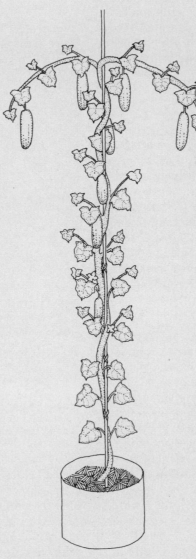

For another solution to the cucumber problem, you might consider growing the European greenhouse variety of cucumber in a south-facing window. Recommended by Clayton R. Oslund in the November, 1978, issue of *Flower and Garden,* European cucumbers produce 12 to 16 inch (30 to 41 cm) long, slender fruits on plants grown from seeds in as little as two months. The plants produce fruits without pollination, and the fruits are seedless. European cucumbers also require less heat and light than other types, though you may still need to supplement their light on cloudy days. Varieties include 'Farbio', 'Femdan', 'Femfrance', 'Fertila', 'LaReine', 'Pandex', and 'Toska'. 'Fembaby' grows 8-inch (20 cm) fruits on more compact vines. Oslund uses 4-inch (10 cm) peat pots for germination, one seed to each. When the seeds sprout in four to five days he transplants the peat pots to permanent 5- to 10-gallon (18.9 to 37.8 l) containers, sinking them ½ to 1 inch (13 to 25 mm) below the soil line, and watering and fertilizing

Training Cucumber Vines:
Train the plant to twine up a vertical support with only two side branches hanging down from the top. Pinch off all unnecessary flowers so that the cucumber fruits are concentrated in the upper half of the plant.

thoroughly. Thereafter, the cucumbers are fed weekly.

The training of European cucumbers is essential to good bearing. A knotted plastic cord stretched from ceiling to container will give the vine something to wind itself around. Anchor it with ties as necessary. To assure a balance of foliage and fruit, remove all lateral growth and axillary buds that develop up to a height of 36 inches (91 cm). Above 36 inches (91 cm), remove the tip of side stems beyond the first well-formed leaf, continuing this practice above 4 feet (1.2 m), but also leaving one blossom to develop in every alternate leaf axil on the main stem. At ceiling height nip off the central tip while allowing two side branches to grow downward. Support these and trim them in the same alternating manner as the main stem. At points where the vines are weak, remove buds. A well-trained plant will produce up to 15 fruits, but bright light is essential for the rapid growth that results in vines of 4 feet (1.2 m) in eight weeks or less.

generous watering, strong light, and hand pollinating with a brush. Fertilize the soil before planting and again when plants are five to six inches (13 to 15 cm) high. Pinch back the vines so they will not overwhelm the support you provide.

ESCAROLE AND ENDIVE
(Cichorium endivia)

The cultivar of escarole called 'Full Heart Batavian' does well under lights in a cool place. So does 'Green Curled' endive, which is basically the same plant with fancier leaves. Seeds of both are sown ¼ inch (6 mm) deep where they are to grow, and maturing plants require about 12 square inches (77 sq cm) of space. Time to maturity is about 12 weeks. Use the inner leaves or tie plants 2 weeks before harvest to blanch the leaves and reduce bitterness.

LETTUCE (Lactuca sativa cvs.)

All lettuces take longer to mature indoors than outside, so leaf lettuces make a better crop than the slower-developing head lettuce. You might, however, want to try some relatively short-season heading varieties likely to grow inside such as 'Buttercrunch', 'Summer Bibb', and 'Tom Thumb', or the new variety 'Chesibb', which reportedly heads at a relatively low light level (800 footcandles) if it is maintained for a 15-hour day. Start seeds in a cool place at 65°F (18°C), preferably toward spring or under lights. For winter growing in natural light, you might seek out the 'Bibb' type called 'Deci-Minor', a European cultivar developed to mature in seven to eight weeks under short-day, dim light conditions. It is available from Stokes Seeds, Inc. (Buffalo, New York, and St. Catherine's, Ontario, Canada). The other varieties mature in ten weeks, so in any case two plantings should be started in the course of a winter. Transplant each seedling to an 8- or 12-inch (20 or 30 cm) pot, or group them 10 inches (25 cm) apart in a larger container. Fertilize frequently using

Indoor Lettuce: A few lettuce plants on a cool, bright windowsill can provide the basis for a fresh, homegrown salad in the middle of winter.

liquid seaweed or fish emulsion. Check often for signs of rot, but keep the soil surface slightly damp, as lettuce can become tough and bitter if it is allowed to dry out.

Although lettuce needs less sun than fruiting crops (from four to six hours a day) and will do well in an east or west window, some supplementary light may be needed during cloudy weather or short days. The greatest difficulty in growing lettuce indoors is managing to provide both adequate light and cool enough temperatures. A range of 50° to 68°F (10° to 20°C) is ideal for head lettuce.

Leaf lettuce is generally easier to grow than the heading types—especially on a windowsill. Ready to pick as little as six weeks after planting, it matures two or three weeks more quickly than head lettuce. Follow the same cultural guidelines, but plant leaf lettuce every two or three weeks for a continuous crop. Planting in six-inch (15 cm) pots or six to seven inches (15 to 18 cm) apart in flats will provide the plants with adequate space. Some good cultivars for the indoor garden are 'Blackseeded Simpson', 'Grand Rapids Forcing', 'Greenhart', 'Green Ice', 'Oak Leaf', 'Ruby', 'Salad Bowl', and 'Slobolt'. You might want to try several for variety. Pick the leaves of maturing plants from the outside, so inner growth will continue.

MUSTARD (Brassica juncea)

Needing cool temperatures, short days, and ample watering to keep its leaves from growing too hot and peppery, this vitamin-rich green matures in about four weeks but seedlings can be snipped off a week or less after planting to be enjoyed along with tender young cress in delicate sandwiches made with very thin bread. Mustard seeds can be sown on the surface of a light, rich soil mix in flats or pots. Spray lightly, and cover the container with plastic until the seedlings are 1½ inches (4 cm) tall. Keep them out of direct sunlight during this time, but give them lots of bright, indirect light. Thin the young plants to stand 6 inches (15 cm) apart in a tub, or place each plant in a 6-inch (15 cm) pot.

EDIBLE-PODDED PEA (Pisum sativum var. macrocarpon)

As thermostats are set lower in many American homes, the plant known variously as the Chinese, sugar, snow, or edible-podded pea is becoming an increasingly popular house plant. The seeds will germinate at 40°F (4°C), but will benefit from presprouting and should be planted 1½ inches (4 cm) deep, and about 6 inches (15 cm) apart. Peas can stand low night temperatures as long as they are kept at 60° to 65°F (16° to 18°C) during the

day. Try to maintain as little temperature fluctuation as possible, and make sure peas receive good light. Shake the plants when in bloom to assure pollination, or use a cotton swab or small brush to transfer pollen from one flower to another. Don't expect a crop in less than about 12 weeks, but if you are lucky, you may get two short harvests. Peas climb trellises which may take the form of unused window screens or of room dividers with peas climbing from troughs on both sides of them. Window boxes mounted on the inside of sills make excellent containers, and the vines can climb strings tied to a curtain rod overhead. You could build the indoor window box described in chapter 28 to grow peas near a bright, cool window. Pinch back growing tops to encourage higher yields. 'Mammoth Melting' is one good cultivar for the indoor garden. Others are 'Dwarf Gray Sugar' and, for smaller plants, the short, bush-type 'Little Sweetie'. Midget-type non-edible-podded peas like 'Mighty Midget' and 'Tiny Tim' can be planted, too, but may yield poorer harvests. A new type of sugar pea, 'Burpee's Sugar Snap', needs a trellis or stake but is higher yielding and matures earlier outdoors than other regular size snow peas. Moreover, its fleshy pods remain edible even after the peas inside are full size.

RADISH (Raphanus sativus)

Radishes are the easiest of all root crops to grow indoors. They also are one of the quickest-maturing crops, and can be ready to eat in as little as five weeks. Germination takes one week, and is best achieved at temperatures near 60°F (16°C). Sow a dozen seeds, lightly covered, in a 10- or 12-inch (25 or 30 cm) pot. Thin seedlings to six or seven per pot or to stand an inch (2.5 cm) apart. Keep the room temperature above 50°F (10°C) but no higher than 70°F (21°C). Water regularly and thoroughly whenever the soil seems dry. Good cultivars for indoor growing include 'Cherry Belle', 'Icicle', 'Scarlet Globe Forc-

Quick and Easy Radishes: This is one indoor crop that only takes up a small amount of space and is ready to perk up wintertime salads in five to six weeks.

ing', and 'Sparkler'. When you pull up a mature radish, plant a new seed in its place for a continuous crop.

ROCKET (Eruca vesicaria subsp. sativa)

A chardlike plant, rocket is challenging to grow because it needs full sun as well as cool temperatures and constant moisture. Sow seeds ¼ inch (13 mm) deep, then thin seedlings to one plant to a 6-inch (15 cm) pot, or in tubs to stand 6 inches (15 cm) apart. The leaves may be harvested about six weeks after sowing and will add a memorable touch of spring to salads and soups, or you can cook rocket along with other greens for an inter-

esting side dish. The distinctive sharp, spicy flavor of rocket has been likened to horseradish, and is a favorite with many temperate-zone gardeners.

SPINACH (Spinacia oleracea)

Spinach can be a tricky crop indoors or out. Begin by soaking the seeds for 24 hours. Then plant them ½ inch (13 mm) deep in 4 inches (10 cm) of sandy soil, allowing 4 inches (10 cm) between plants. For best results, sow seeds in the pots or flats where plants are to grow—spinach does not take well to transplanting. Water and fertilize the plants frequently, and keep them in a cool place. Spinach can grow at temperatures as low as 32°F (0°C) but will thrive at from 50° to 68°F (10° to 20°C). To prevent bolting, grow your spinach crop when the days are getting shorter, or restrict daylength by covering the plants. Spinach takes six to nine weeks to reach full maturity. The outer leaves can be picked individually for salads, or you can pull every other plant while the plants are still young and the leaves are tender. Spinach cultivars suitable for indoor gardens include 'Avon Hybrid', 'Bloomsdale Long-Standing', 'Cleanleaf', and 'Cold-Resistant Savoy'. Also recommended for container culture are 'America' and 'Melody'.

Spinach substitutes such as Malabar spinach *(Basella alba)* and New Zealand spinach *(Tetragonia tetragonioides)* withstand heat better than regular spinach, although they take a few more weeks to mature. Both these vegetables have a milder flavor than spinach, and many gardeners prefer them in their favorite spinach dishes. If your growing space is rather limited, try Malabar spinach, which is a vining plant and can be trained on a trellis. Each plant requires a 12-inch (30 cm) pot and a 36-inch (91 cm) trellis to climb. New Zealand spinach is more spreading and bushy in its growth habit. Chard *(Beta vulgaris,* Cicla Group) is another good leaf crop for warmer rooms, although it does best with sunny days followed by cool nights. Grow 'Red Swiss', 'Rhubarb', or 'Ruby' in an attractive 6- to 8-inch (15 to 20 cm) pot for a handsome living (and edible) centerpiece.

Kale (*Brassica oleracea*, Acephala Group) is probably the best leafy vegetable to grow in cold locations. It can tolerate temperatures of 40°F (4°C) or less, and will do well indoors in low-heat places with lots of natural light. Temperatures for kale should never exceed 70° to 75°F (21° to 24°C), so an unheated room or sun porch with a southern or eastern exposure would be ideal for a winter kale crop. The best indoor cultivars are those of the Vates strains—'Dwarf Blue Curled', and 'Dwarf Blue Scotch', which are ready for harvest of individual leaves in eight weeks or more.

WATERCRESS
(*Nasturtium officinale*)

Even if you don't live near a clear running brook you can enjoy fresh watercress in soups, salads, and sandwich spreads throughout the year. This small, peppery-leaved plant can be grown from seeds in a plastic flat in a two inch (5 cm) deep blend of peat moss and sand. Scatter the seeds on top of the growing medium, and keep the medium moist until the seeds germinate. Then raise the water level to a depth of one inch (2.5 cm) as the plants grow. Fertilize occasionally and let fresh water trickle through weekly to avoid stagnant conditions. If you prefer, you can plant watercress seeds in a shallow clay pot lined with sphagnum moss. Be sure to provide good drainage. Cover the seeds lightly with sandy soil and set the pot and tray in a northeast window, never in full sun. Reseed often, preferably with sprouted seeds, or seed heavily, for not all seeds will sprout. It is a good idea to add one tablespoon (15 ml) of ground limestone to each quart (1.1 l) of potting mix. Seeds germinate in ten days to two weeks, and plants can grow to their mature height of about ten inches (25 cm) in

approximately seven weeks. Plants will need frequent thinning (harvesting) when they start to branch.

FLOWERS FOR FOOD

A scattering of *Calendula* (pot marigold) petals adds éclat to any salad. Or try nasturtium leaves or blossoms—or the seeds, which can be pickled like capers. Perhaps the most widely eaten flower is the edible chrysanthemum. The leaves of this Japanese favorite are harvested before blossoms form and added to hot vegetable or pork dishes, stews, or clear broth. (See the Encyclopedia section for culture of *Calendula* and *Nasturtium*.)

GROWING STARTED PLANTS

Whether you are inexperienced and timid, or wise and properly cautious when dealing with finicky seedlings, it is often well for you to let someone with better facilities and know-how see your prospective edibles through their "touch-and-go" infancy, especially if they are ones that may go if you touch them. Among seedling plants and stock available from nurseries are broccoli, cabbage, cantaloupes, cauliflower, celery, celtuce, chicory, eggplant, onions, sweet and hot peppers, strawberries, and tomatoes.

Since the main business of nurseries is to produce plants for outdoor gardeners, you may find plants difficult to obtain out of season. Write to a large, dependable company and explain your needs, or talk with a local greenhouse nursery. They may be willing to start plants for you. Here are some worth buying and trying that have not been discussed previously.

CABBAGE (*Brassica oleracea*, Capitata Group)

Cabbages, especially early ones, do better than their temperamental relatives, cauliflower and broccoli, when grown indoors, but the best indoor brassica is still the more primitive nonheading kale. Cabbage prefers cool temperatures, needs six hours of sun daily and requires a large, 10- to 12-inch (25 to 30 cm) pot and frequent feeding and watering. Small-headed early cultivars taking as little as eight weeks to mature from transplant size are 'Baby Head', 'Dwarf Morden', 'Early Greenball', and 'Little Leaguer'. Cabbage odor may pose a problem in living areas as the outer leaves mature.

CELERY *(Apium graveolens var. dulce)*

Celery is hard to grow, indoors or out, for it requires a very long, cool growing season and tends to be disease prone. The best solution is to grow celtuce instead, but should you locate healthy celery plants for sale in the fall, give them a try. Celery requires frequent watering and feeding because it has shallow roots. Give this plant an eight- to ten-inch (20 to 25 cm) pot and keep it cool, providing six hours of sun a day. Blanching by covering is not necessary unless you insist on pure white stalks. Besides, green celery is more nutritious. If your plants survive, harvest stalks one by one to keep them going—though celery takes at least 15 weeks to mature fully from seeds (at least 5 weeks if grown from bought plants three inches/8 cm high), it is edible at any stage. A good early green cultivar is 'Summer Pascal', while the early cultivar 'Golden Self-Blanching' is bred to produce yellow stalks.

STRAWBERRY *(Fragaria* spp.)

Strawberry plants can be made to grow indoors in plastic pots with side pockets, which can be stacked vertically, in transparent plastic vertical sleeves, and in small barrels and hanging baskets, but they will never bear as well indoors as out. To help along self-pollination, shake flowering plants or flick the blossoms with a finger. Easiest to grow are the miniature Alpine strawberries, or *fraises de bois,* such as 'Baron Solemacher' or 'Alexandria'. These runnerless plants are most gener-

ally raised from seeds and may produce fruit in August if sown in March. Just sow the seeds on top of soil (don't cover them) and keep the flat at 70°F (21°C) until they germinate, transplanting seedlings to individual pots when they are large enough. These charmers do well in strawberry jars, producing a handful of berries once in a while from late summer through the winter and perfuming the air with their wonderful fragrance. When you order regular strawberry plants, try to select ones that are compact and bear early and therefore need less heat. 'Darrow', 'Earlidawn', and 'Earliglow' are possibilities. These will produce fruit during their first warm season. But avoid the "everbearing" and "climbing" strawberries advertised in Sunday magazine supplements. The claims made for such plants are usually misleading, so do not be seduced by them. However, patio tubs, pyramids, hanging baskets, or strawberry jars that have been preplanted make good sense for indoor use. Plants need rich soil, plenty of water, abundant sun and frequent feeding. (For more information on vegetable and fruit varieties or cultivars suited to indoor growing and on their minimum times to maturity, see Some Food Cultivars for Greenhouse Growing, in chapter 29.)

FORCING VEGETABLES

Forcing is the practice of inducing plants to mature or bloom at times other than those evolutionarily advantageous for them. In a sense, all indoor growing is forcing. But the term is more widely used to refer to radical manipulation of the sequence toward maturity in a few special vegetables and fruits which produce roots, crowns, stools (a clump of adventitious roots induced by pruning the lower part of the plant), or bulbs. To force these crops you need an area that is carefully temperature controlled and thoroughly darkened. This can be a cellar, a cupboard, or space under a stairway or beneath a sink.

WITLOOF CHICORY, OR BELGIAN ENDIVE (*Cichorium intybus*)

The Witloof strain is less bitter than other leaf chicories and its forced shoots are a gourmet treat raw or braised. Plants intended for forcing should be sown from seeds outdoors. Dig or pull the roots after the first hard frost when the dandelion-shaped leaves have wilted. Choose roots about eight inches (20 cm) long, and trim off the tops, leaving a two-inch (5 cm) stub above the crown. Lay the roots in sand and/or peat moss, covering them with some of it and/or with black plastic. Store them like rhubarb in a 40°F (4°C) place for at least a month. To begin forcing,

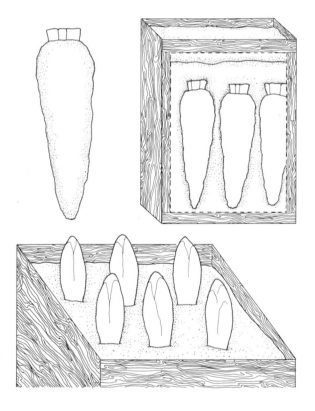

Forcing Belgian Endive: To produce this succulent winter vegetable, set the trimmed roots together in a large box or pot, cover with soil, and keep in a dark place until the young heads emerge from the soil.

first trim the roots to equal length. Then fill a large orange crate or other forcing box or a large flower pot or bucket with equal parts of moist sand, loam, and composted manure or peat moss. Set the roots upright in this material, close together but not touching, and water them thoroughly. Cover them with sand or damp burlap to exclude light. Keep the forcing medium moist but not wet at an even 50° to 60°F (10° to 16°C). In about three weeks check to see if endive heads, called "chicons," are poking through the sand. They can be harvested by twisting or cutting when they are five to eight inches (13 to 20 cm) long and weigh three or four ounces (84 to 112 g). Sometimes you can obtain a second, though smaller, harvest by covering the roots again and repeating the waiting process. A red-leaved cultivar of chicory called 'Rouge de Verone' produces small, self-blanching heads when forced in the same manner.

GINGER (*Zingiber officinale, Z. zerumbet*)

Ginger is not forced in quite the same way other roots are, partly because it is the root, not the shoot, that we eat, but it shares with other forcing crops the attraction of the truly exotic. It's less tricky to force than endive. Select a gnarled but plump, firm, unblemished, shiny-skinned rhizome at a Spanish or oriental market, or a natural foods store. Fill a 6-inch (15 cm) container with a mixture of equal parts soil, sand, and humus, or 3 parts potting soil and 1 part sand. Bury the entire rhizome or a section with a bud horizontally just ¼ inch (6 mm) below the surface, and soak the potting mix with warm water. Place the container in a warm, dimly lit spot and keep the humidity high and the room warm. Water regularly, but do not soak the soil or let water stand in the saucer. When shoots appear, move the plant to bright light and feed it with an all-purpose liquid fertilizer.

Spring and summer are the best times to grow ginger, and during the three months of winter it is advisable to let the plant become half dormant by reducing the heat, keeping it rather dry, and suspending feeding. Actually, the spiky shoots will grow (slowly) in good light even at low temperatures. If you provide a good size container, tropical temperatures, and partial shade, the shoots may grow long enough to be ornamental, and with real luck white flowers will open at the spike ends. When the root has filled the container, unpot the plant, cut off a section of rhizome with a growing tip or live bud to start a second crop, and keep the rest for eating. The spicy flavor of fresh ginger root adds zing to oriental dishes and to desserts such as pumpkin pie.

ONION AND SHALLOT (*Allium* spp.)

The onion *(Allium cepa)* takes many months to grow from seeds indoors. When you grow onions from bulbs or sets, indoors in winter, you are in a sense forcing them. They will probably never reach storable size, but they will grow large enough to make acceptable scallions and you also can snip their tops like chives. The stems of white onions are best for cutting this way. Plant a group of sets in an eight to ten inch (20 to 25 cm) deep pot and fertilize lightly, or plant them around larger plants. Keep the soil slightly moist and provide about six hours of sunlight a day. In five weeks you can begin harvesting green onions. Pull every other bulb and the remaining ones will grow a little larger.

The shallot *(A. ascalonicum),* which is the aristocrat of the Onion family, can be grown indoors in a pot of sandy soil, from a shallot clove planted to half its depth. Cover the clove with compost after four or five shoots have emerged. You can cut small amounts of this topgrowth anytime for use like chives (but do not injure the central shoot). Shallots are not difficult to grow indoors, but they do require at least four months to mature, and like onions, they need six hours of sunlight a day, and moderate moisture. If waiting almost half a year for ful-

ly formed bulbs exceeds your store of patience, you can harvest plants when the bulbs have reached the size of green onions.

RHUBARB (*Rheum rhaponticum*)

In the late autumn lift a few well-developed rhubarb roots that are two years old or older from an outdoor patch, or order some from a nursery. Expose the roots to frost by laying them on top of the ground. Then, for a month or more, store the roots covered with soil or compost in an area kept dark by black plastic. The place should be dark and cool, but not freezing. If you have nowhere else, use your refrigerator and omit the soil. If it's more practical, you can dig up rhubarb in late winter and omit this indoor cold storage. When the simulated or real winter dormancy period is over, the rhubarb is ready to force either all at once or at intervals. Set the roots in soil in pots or flats in a dark cellar or hotbed, or place a cardboard box with ventilation holes in it over the forcing unit. Start the forcing at 44°F (7°C). After ten days, increase the temperature to 50°F (10°C), and then by small increments to 60°F (16°C). During forcing keep the roots moist, but not saturated. In four to six weeks after the start of forcing you will be able to pull the sprouted rhubarb sticks and use them in pies, breads, puddings, and sauces as you would garden-grown rhubarb. Suitable cultivars to use include 'Prince Albert', 'The Sutton', 'Timperly Early', and 'Victoria'.

SEA KALE (*Crambe maritima*)

Sea kale is a large, coarse plant with blue-green leaves, but its blanched shoots are tender and succulent when they are 5 to 8 inches (13 to 20 cm) long. The nutty-flavored shoots may be savored raw in salads or prepared like asparagus. To force this perennial, select established plants which have been grown 20 inches (51 cm) apart outdoors and kept free of flower heads all season. Roots should be 4 to 5 inches (10 to 13 cm) long and plants should have been mulched since May. Dig the plants in November when the tops have died back, bringing in only the crowns and roots. Following the general instructions given for rhubarb, start forcing at 50°F (10°C) and over a period of four to six weeks slowly increase the temperature to 60°F (16°C). When the shoots are long enough, harvest them individually by snapping or cutting them off at ground level.

Fast, dependable sprouts, lush greens on windowsills, and splashy small tomatoes in pots—these are the bounty and benefits of growing edibles indoors. Compared to gardening outdoors under the unobstructed sky, the cultivation of edible plants indoors may seem a scaled-down activity, the rewards of which are few in proportion to the effort invested. But like other forms of specialized art, indoor vegetable gardening has its devotees and its trophies.

CHAPTER 17

Herbs

To some people, herbs are simply those plants which find their way into small jars on the spice shelf, to be sprinkled into various cooking pots. The more you find out about herbs, though, the more vast and bewildering a conglomeration of plants they become. According to the botanical definition, the one often found in dictionaries, an herb is "a flowering plant whose stem above ground does not become woody and persistent." In the strict botanical sense, then, rosemary, with its woody stem; bay, which is a tree; and sage, which is a shrub, are not herbs.

However, we are speaking here of a special group of plants which are not classified on the basis of their biological characteristics. For our purposes, an herb is a plant which is valued for its culinary, aromatic, cosmetic, or healing qualities. That seems to be a workable definition, true enough to the spirit of things to include not only the hundreds of herbs in use today, but also the many hundreds more waiting in the wings of history for a recall.

Herbs, more than any other plants, can be regarded as a link to antiquity. Seeds of the coriander have been found in Egyptian tombs, for example, and we recognize the delicate and arresting form of the Egyptian onion in wall frescoes painted thousands of years ago. That onion still looks the same in our kitchen garden as it did growing in ancient Egypt! The bay leaf of ancient Greece, the garlic, the rosemary, and many other less familiar herbs have been in use, in the same form, for thousands of years.

In the early days of Western medicine, herbs were called "simples," which meant that simply one herb could be used for an effective cure. And today, though herbs do not make the front page of the newspaper, they are still the basis of many modern medi-

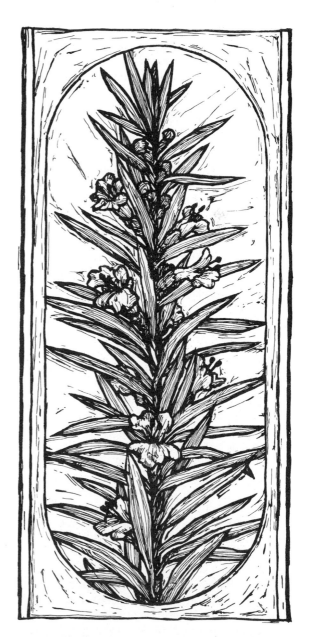

Ancient Herbs: Some of our favorite herbs of today, such as rosemary, have been used by cooks and healers for thousands of years.

Opposite, close-up of flower head of dill, Anethum graveolens.

cal preparations, and are still lovingly used in cooking, for baths that are either relaxing or rejuvenating, as a part of preparations for the hair and skin, and to add delightful fragrance to the house and garden. In fact, with the rise and expansion of the holistic health movement and the growing concern for learning self-health care, herbs as healing medicines are truly enjoying a popular comeback.

From all this, we can gather that herbs are potent, interesting, and mysterious plants. Their delicious array of fragrances, which ranges from the arresting scent of sweet basil through the delicate fragrance of lavender to the refreshing smell of rose geranium; their subtle and often very nutritious contributions as foods and seasonings; and their many healing applications all make herbs very worth cultivating indoors.

CULTURE

In general, herbs grow best in moderately rich soil with good drainage and plenty of sun. Many herbs are so hardy that in their natural settings they can grow in very poor soil, but this ascetic treatment of them is not appropriate in the indoor garden. Given a bit of consideration, though, most herbs are quite easy to grow indoors. Often, herb nurseries and growers use one type of soil for nearly all their herb plants. This shows how easy herbs are to please. A good soil mix for many herbs consists of equal parts of sphagnum moss, ground granite, and aged, screened compost. Some people prefer to use equal parts of potting soil, sand, and peat moss. Still others use 2 parts loam, 1 part compost or leaf mold, and 1 part sand, with a tablespoon (15 ml) of bone meal added to each quart (1.1 l) of soil mix. Feed the plants with liquid fish emulsion or compost tea every two or three weeks, except during the winter months when they are resting.

Herbs love humidity, and many of today's homes are much too hot and dry for their liking. Average temperatures of 65° to 68°F (18° to 20°C) are best for herbs. If your indoor environment is dry (as most are), herbs should be misted frequently and grown near windows where they can get some air circulation. Herbs should be watered thoroughly from the top of the pot, rather than from the bottom. Of all the herbs in the indoor garden, the mints in the genus *Mentha,* such as peppermint and spearmint, require the most water. (Lemon balm, basil, catnip, lavender, marjoram, oregano, rosemary, sage, and thyme are also members of the Mint family, Labiatae, but have varied growing habits and cultural needs.) In fact, they like to be wet all the time, so much so that they are the only herbs whose pots do not require good drainage. Sage, on the other hand, will languish and wilt with too much water. Some of the really humidity-hungry herbs, like tarragon, may do a whole lot better in the bathroom than in the kitchen, providing you can give them enough light there. Try the humidity-raising techniques discussed in chapter 2 to create the optimal environment for these plants. If you match the desired high humidity with good air circulation your herbs should be sturdy and display a genetically built-in resistance to diseases and pests.

If pests should appear—perhaps overlooked hitchhikers on plants or plant parts brought in from an outdoor garden—they can be controlled by the techniques described in chapter 9. Needless to say, never use any pest or disease remedy that will affect the flavor or wholesomeness of herbs you intend to consume.

One commercial herb grower, Mary Ann Borchelt, suggests that a higher natural humidity coupled with artificial lighting can make the basement the best place to grow herbs indoors. Certainly, the direction in which your windows face will dictate whether you can naturally place an herb garden there, or whether you might better choose to light your plants with fluorescent tubes instead of relying on insufficient sunlight. As a rule of thumb, herbs like 4 to 5 hours of direct sun

A Commercial Grower Talks about Herbs

"When I was just a little girl, I remember going with my grandmother into her herb garden. Somehow, it was magical to me. You know how things are when you are a child. Well, she really loved her herbs. She would tell me about them and she often said, 'Now, be careful how you walk here. You don't want to hurt any of these living things.' So I grew up with a great love of herbs, and it was from her, from those times in her garden."

Today, Mary Ann Borchelt is a handsome woman with graying hair whose fascination with herbs has remained undimmed over the years. If anything, it has flourished. The Borchelt Herb Gardens have been in business for 14 years now. The first commercial garden was in Texas. Then, in 1970, the Borchelts moved back east to Massachusetts, to ten acres of land inherited from Mrs. Borchelt's grandparents.

The Borchelt gardens, which began "just as a hobby," today attract visitors from all over the United States and Europe, who walk slowly through the luxuriant, fragrant display beds with obvious appreciation for the care and attention that went into making them. Today, the Borchelts grow over 200 varieties of herbs.

The beautiful display gardens and the little herb plants visitors come to buy are all the result of much earlier work underground. Underground? Yes, that's right—actually, in the basement. The Borchelts' whole basement has been transformed into an indoor herb garden and nursery. Mrs. Borchelt has found that the cellar can be a great place to grow herbs.

"Herbs really do like humidity, and so many people's homes are too dry for them, so I think basement gardens suit herbs," she says.

In the cold Cape Cod winters, the Borchelts close in their basement from inside with large sheets of plastic, to ensure a warm enough climate for the plants. They use large fans to circulate the air. Potted in a soil of homemade, aged compost mixed with bone meal and vermiculite, the small herb plants are placed on long tiered benches. There are aisles between them for easy access to all parts of the garden. Above each tier, fluorescent tubes with reflectors provide growing light. Mrs. Borchelt's experience has persuaded her that ordinary fluorescent tubes are every bit as good as lighting specially designed for growing plants indoors.

"You don't have to go out and buy those expensive setups," she declares. "It's easy to construct these layered herb shelves, buy fluorescent tubes and build your own reflectors for them."

The Borchelts use the same soil mix for all their herbs, except for *Aloe barbadensis,* which they give a heavier blend. "We fertilize all our herbs every three weeks with a fish emulsion mixture," she notes. Asked her opinion of the popular notion that herbs are so hardy that they love poor, sandy soil, she laughed. "Some people do like to say that. But why subject them to that if there is something better possible? I think my herbs thrive on good soil." Looking around, you'd have to agree.

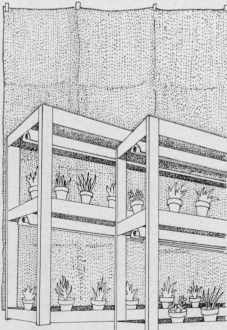

Basement Herb Garden: In winter, the Borchelts insulate the walls of their basement with sheets of plastic and grow many kinds of herbs on long, tiered benches under fluorescent lights. Aisles between the benches allow ready access to all parts of the garden.

every day. Windows with a southern or western exposure will please most sun-loving herbs. Plants grown under fluorescent lights should be placed so the plant tops are four to six inches (10 to 15 cm) from the tubes, and should receive 14 hours of light daily.

Some herbs, though, thrive on indirect light, or in shade, and will do better in an east window. This group includes lemon balm, bay, chervil, lovage, and mints.

CONTAINERS

A wide variety of containers can be used to grow herbs, so long as they have drainage holes in the bottom and offer ample room for root growth. Unglazed clay pots, wooden planters, and terra cotta strawberry jars are all good choices. If you plan to grow caraway, comfrey, dill, parsley, or other herbs with long roots, select a deep container that will allow the roots to grow downward.

There are many ways in which to arrange your indoor herb garden. One of the simplest setups is a window box inside a sunny kitchen window. You can construct one yourself from pine or cedar, and place in it five-inch (13 cm) pots of sun-loving culinary herbs, such as basil, chives, marjoram, oregano, parsley, and thyme. To embellish your kitchen window garden, or add a touch of fragrance to other sunny locations indoors, try planting some herbs in hanging basket planters. Herbs which do well and look wonderful when handled in this manner include burnet, chives, mints, prostrate rosemary, and creeping thymes. You can hang parsley this way, too. Another nice way to plant herbs indoors is in a strawberry jar, which makes a conversation piece that adds a bright decorative touch to house, porch, or patio. The strawberry jar is most suitable for plants which do not have large root systems or a great desire to spread. The top of the jar can be used to plant deep-rooted herbs, such as chives, scented geranium, parsley, or tarragon. In the little side pockets, small rose-

Kitchen Garden: Sun-loving herbs like (left to right) thyme, mint, chives, parsley, and basil will thrive in a simple homemade window box built in a sunny kitchen window.

Strawberry Jar Garden: A strawberry jar full of herbs adds a decorative touch to a bright spot in the house, and provides easy access to your favorite herbs. Plant deep-rooted types, such as chives, in the top. The side pockets can hold small specimens of (clockwise from upper right) rosemary, dwarf basil, mint, sage (center), and thyme.

mary, sage, thyme, or dwarf basil plants can be placed. Make sure the drainage hole is left open if you decide to use the strawberry planter.

Some people enjoy planting their herbs in a tray garden, allowing them to grow luxuriantly close together in a way which proffers a full, rich panoply of form, color, and fragrance. Select plants with similar light and water requirements but avoid the mints, as they are too invasive and will choke out other herbs. You can begin your tray garden with a metal barrelhead 24 inches (61 cm) in diameter. If you'd like to paint the outside, you can simply use flat green paint, or you can add folk art patterns to that basecoat as a decorative touch. This garden requires about half a bushel (17.6 l) of sphagnum moss and one quart (1.1 l) of good loam (and a flat stone as a base if you decide to feature a miniature statue or some other object as a center-

piece). Cover the bottom of the tray with the moss, and add a layer of garden loam. Then plant some well-rooted small herb plants around the central rock, making sure that the tallest plants are closest to the center, and that the more creeping plants are planted toward the edge of the tray. Basil, chives, rosemary, and sage can be grown near the center, with marjoram, oregano, parsley, and thyme moving out toward the rim of the tray. This arrangement makes a very handsome garden.

For large plants such as bay, comfrey, coriander, and dill, you can build a shallow floor tray of wood. After lining the bottom with polyethylene, pour in a layer of pebbles. Then set in the potted herbs.

A GUIDE TO HERBS THAT GROW INDOORS

ANISE (*Pimpinella anisum*)

Anise is one of the most ancient herbs, mentioned in early Egyptian records. The Romans used it in a rich cake favored at feasts and weddings. Anise is grown for its leaves and seeds, both of which have a pleasing licorice flavor. The seeds are used in cheese, cottage cheese, beet salad, and applesauce, and are much loved in baked goods such as cakes, cookies, breads, and soda bread. The finely chopped leaves enliven green salads and soups, and make an attractive garnish. Anise is used commercially in toothpaste, soap, perfume, and liqueur. The seeds make a good addition to potpourri.

This slow-growing herb is started from seeds, which must be fresh for good results. Seeds sown ¼ inch (6 mm) deep in fine soil should germinate in two weeks or less at a temperature of 55°F (13°C). Transplant only when small, as the long taproots resent being disturbed. Plants like a fairly rich, well-drained soil and should have four hours of sunlight daily.

Tray Garden: A small tray garden of herbs can be conveniently located on a table or counter top. Plant taller herbs toward the center and smaller plants toward the rim of the container. Chives are growing in the center of this garden, with sage to either side, bay in front, and thyme creeping out toward the edges of the tray.

LEMON BALM *(Melissa officinalis)*

Lemon balm is a deliciously scented perennial herb which is part of the Mint family, Labiatae, and like its minty cousins it is hardy, likes shade, and spreads rapidly. The plant can be propagated from seeds or from either root divisions or rooted stem cuttings. It will grow to about 12 inches (30 cm) indoors, and like all mints, it enjoys a very moist soil. The medium should also be fairly rich and loose. Because lemon balm does not require a lot of sun, it can be placed in an east, south, or west window and do well. Regularly pinch back the plants to keep them bushy and healthy.

In Shakespeare's time, lemon balm was strewn on pathways and on the floors in public meeting places and churches. As people walked on the herb, its tangy fragrance was released into the crowded rooms, refreshing the air. Lemon balm can be used in teas, and to make wine as well. Fresh, it is good in salads and soups, and with lavender and a little orange peel, it makes a nice decoration for an herbal bath. During summer's hottest days, you can make a good "sun tea" by putting some sprigs of lemon balm and some fresh comfrey leaves in a green glass jar with spring water. Set the jar out in the summer sun until the herbs are nicely infused—about six to eight hours. Then refrigerate and serve with lemon and honey for a cooling drink.

BASIL *(Ocimum basilicum)*

Basil is a beautiful, richly green herb with leaves that give off a sharply pungent fragrance when rubbed or crushed. This member of the Mint family is an annual plant that is easily grown from seeds. Common, or sweet, basil and the variety known as Dark Opal for its gorgeous purple foliage both grow well indoors in rich, well-aerated soil with plenty of sun—at least three to four hours daily. A miniature variety, *O. basilicum* var. *minimum,* grows only six to ten inches (15 to 25 cm) tall, and is especially well suited to container culture. Basil seeds germinate in four to seven days at 70°F (21°C), and once past the seedling stage, the little plants can be replanted in four- or five-inch (10 or 13 cm) pots. You can keep the plants compact and at a height of about eight inches (20 cm) by pinching off the growing tips frequently. This will also prevent flowering, and this lengthens each plant's lifetime.

Fresh basil leaves are very tasty in salads, in vegetable and egg dishes, in Italian tomato sauce, pesto sauce, soups, and salad dressings. This versatile herb can even be steamed and served much like spinach, topped with butter or sauce. Basil tea has been used for hundreds of years against rheumatism, and decoctions of basil—that is, extracts obtained by boiling it—are recommended by herbalists for use in treating nervous disorders such as headaches and nausea.

Basil gets its name from the Greek word *basileus,* or king. Sweet basil is favored in French kitchens, where it is called *herbe royale.* The sacred basil native to India (*O. sanctum*) is revered in Hindu homes as the plant of Krishna and Vishnu. Throughout history basil usually has been considered a fragrant protector of the home. In the Middle Ages, however, European herbalists thought that basil had an affinity to poison, and that scorpions were drawn to it and were even bred mysteriously by it!

Basil is a hearty and delightful herb; in your kitchen it will unerringly offer a fragrant and healthy green beauty.

BAY *(Laurus nobilis)*

The sweet bay laurel, a member of the Lauraceae, is definitely one plant which can be called "an herb revered of old." The shiny, deeply fragrant branches of the bay were once woven into crowns to honor the noble heads of Greek and Roman poets, artists, victors, and statesmen. Bay was associated with Apollo, the sun god; bay growing near one's

Aromatic Herbs: The herbs shown here (clockwise from right front), anise, lemon balm, burnet, basil, and bay, exhibit an interesting diversity of distinctive scents and flavors, ranging from the fresh, cucumberlike quality of burnet to the tang of lemon balm, the aromatic fragrance of bay, the licoricelike flavor of anise, and the pungency of basil.

home has always been considered a beneficent influence.

This aromatic tree can grow from 30 to 60 feet (9.1 to 18.3 m) high outdoors, but indoors, and over some years' time, it will reach a height of from 3 to 6 feet (0.9 to 1.8 m). Bay is one of the few herb plants that is very difficult to propagate from either seeds or cuttings. Seeds are just about impossible for all but the most skilled gardeners to germinate, and cuttings take about six months to root. Many home gardeners prefer simply to go to a reliable nursery and purchase a healthy bay tree of one or two years' growth. If you do decide to try rooting a cutting of the bay, however, root it in a pot of moderately rich soil with good drainage, mist several times each day, and allow it to establish itself in that same container.

In the indoor garden the stately bay needs some sunlight—but not a lot. Unless you can supply direct overhead sun from a skylight or window greenhouse, it is best to allow bay to grow in indirect light and even shade. An established bay tree demands good drainage and evenly moist soil. During the winter it will do best in a cool room (45° to 60°F/7° to 16°C). The tree can be trimmed into a topiary shape, or left unpruned. Either way, it is very handsome and sweet smelling; its leaves can be plucked continuously for culinary and medicinal uses.

Bay leaves, fresh or dried, can be used to flavor soup stocks, stews, meat, fish, and other dishes. Crushed bay leaves may be sewn into either a collar or pillow to help rid pets of fleas or lice. The plant is insect repellent and will protect other nearby plants from insect pests. Placed in containers with flour or cereals, bay leaves will keep away moths and bugs. As a tea, bay leaf has been used to help relieve flatulence; it is also good for relieving cramps. An oil made from the leaves is good for sprains and bruises.

BURNET *(Poterium sanguisorba)*

A native of the Mediterranean regions (as are many familiar herbs), burnet is a pretty perennial plant with deep green, delicately serrated foliage. Burnet belongs to the Rose family, Rosaceae, likes dry, rather sandy soil, and needs about four hours of sun daily. It is low growing, and the plant looks especially fine planted in a hanging basket in a kitchen window garden. It can be grown easily from seeds, which germinate in about ten days.

The refreshing cucumberlike flavor of this herb makes it popular in salads—in fact, it is sometimes called salad burnet—and if you'd like to grow enough to satisfy your salad bowl, you will want to plant two flats, at least. Burnet is also good in herb butter and in cream cheese spreads. It is very fragrant, and mixed with mints and wild thyme was once used as a "strewing herb" scattered freely about to freshen the air in public places.

CALENDULA (Calendula officinalis)

The calendula, also known as pot marigold, is a sweetly old-fashioned plant which came originally from southern Europe. A hardy annual, it belongs to the Sunflower family, Compositae, and sports light greenish yellow leaves and large, showy flowers of either yellow or gold. Its flowers rise and open with the sun, and close as the sun goes down. This habit immortalized the little calendula in the verse of more than one poet, among them John Keats. In a poem titled "I Stood Tiptoe Upon a Little Hill," Keats wrote, "Open fresh your round of starry folds,/ Ye ardent marigolds!/ Dry up the moisture from your golden lids,/ For a great Apollo bids/ That in these days your praises should be sung . . ."

The calendula has an impressive history not only as a beloved garden flower, but also as a cooking ingredient, a bath additive, and a medicinal agent. Its pungent flowers, like those of the peppery nasturtium, make a tasty and beautiful addition to fruit and vegetable salads, and a handsome garnish for special dishes. Dried flower petals are used as a saffron substitute in rice, sauces, and custards. Calendula petals, fresh or dried, can be used in tea or bathwaters. Some people swear by calendula in a footbath as a remedy for sore feet and sprained ankles. Mixed with vinegar and applied as a poultice, the plant's leaves are good for reducing swellings. Calendula is also used in treating chronic ulcers, varicose veins, hemorrhoids, toothache, and headache.

Calendulas can be grown from seeds in moderately rich soil, and, of course, they like the sun! Plants do best in a cool room—try an unheated room with a sunny south or west window. Remove fading flowers to prolong the plant's life and encourage new blooming.

CARAWAY (Carum carvi)

Caraway is a tall, fragrant herb of the Parsley family, Umbelliferae, to which anise, chervil, coriander, dill, and lovage belong. Caraway is a biennial plant whose seeds are often used in breads, soups, cheeses, sauerkraut, meat dishes, and pickles. The licorice-flavored foliage can be chopped and added to tossed salads and soups. But if you intend to grow it only for its seeds, make sure it has a great deal of sun in order for the seeds to mature properly. Actually, as with other umbelliferous plants, you should have a real liking for the plant itself, or growing it for the few seeds it will offer may seem like a bother.

Caraway can be grown from seeds, which should be sown directly into the container in which you expect the plant to remain, as it does not transplant well. It prefers a fairly heavy soil, on the dry side.

CATNIP (Nepeta cataria)

Once upon a time, before trade with the East brought Chinese tea to Europe, catnip tea was the ruling domestic beverage among the English. Of course, we already know how the leaves affect cats, who will roll and roll in catnip greens until they are simply delirious from the volatile essence. (Keep your catnip plant in a cat-safe place and avoid bruising its leaves, or you may find an overturned plant and a satisfied cat.) Interestingly, the leaves are known to have a calming effect on people and are even said to dispel headaches caused by nervousness. Catnip root, however, has the legendary reputation of making even gentle people quarrelsome.

Catnip is a member of the large and varied Mint family, Labiatae. Thriving in rich soil, it does not need direct sunlight, and can be grown in indirect light. The plant has green-gray, heart-shaped leaves which are rather furry. Indoors, this perennial will reach 12 to 18 inches (30 to 46 cm) in height. You can grow it from seeds, or by dividing at the roots a large clump from an outdoor garden. Cut back the plants to encourage branching.

If you decide to make catnip tea, make sure that you infuse the tea by gently simmering the leaves in water for about ten min-

Cultural Requirements: All herbs do not grow best under the same conditions, and it is important to become familiar with the needs of each. The plants shown here (clockwise from front), chives, caraway, catnip, calendula, and chervil, will serve to illustrate this point. Although all of them prefer moderately rich soil, chives, caraway, and calendula need lots of sun, while catnip and chervil thrive in moderate light.

utes, then straining the brew. Do not boil this herb, as boiling will dissipate its volatile oil. Catnip tea is regarded as a good general tonic, and is specifically used for coughs, headaches, hysteria, nightmares, and to break fevers.

CHERVIL *(Anthriscus cerefolium)*

Chervil is a delicately beautiful annual herb growing about 12 inches (30 cm) tall, that was originally found in the Levant and Mediterranean regions. Throughout history, chervil has always been regarded as a great rejuvenator and tonic. Like parsley, it belongs to the Umbelliferae. In fact, chervil is often called gourmet parsley and can be used interchangeably with that herb in salads and soups, and meat, egg, fish, and vegetable dishes of all kinds. It is definitely best when fresh.

Chervil will grow in moderately rich soil without a lot of sun (an east window is fine), but it does need moisture. Mist it often, and make sure the plant has good drainage so that it does not get waterlogged. Do not overwater. Start chervil from seeds pressed into a furrow one inch (2.5 cm) deep. Light is needed for germination, so don't cover the seeds. Be sure to keep them constantly moist until the seedlings emerge, at which time the small plants should be given partial shade until they are several inches or centimeters tall. Transplant chervil only when it is small; older plants do not like to have their roots disturbed.

You may want to keep several of these lovely plants in your kitchen, and pinch them regularly to use in cooking or in brewing a gentle tea.

CHIVE *(Allium schoenoprasum)*

This sturdy, 12 inch (30 cm) tall perennial of the *Allium,* or onion, genus of the Lily family, Liliaceae, hails originally from Europe and Asia. Chives need moderately fertile soil, good drainage, and lots of sun. They can be started from seeds (just be patient, as the slow-growing plants take a year to reach maturity), or propagated from bulbils or from divisions. Just dig up a clump from your outdoor garden and gently pull it apart, making sure that there is a good root system in each division. When bringing a pot of chives indoors for the winter it is necessary to force them. Just allow the pot to remain outdoors for a month after cold weather sets in to let the roots freeze. (Plants also can be forced in the refrigerator.) Then bring the plant inside and place it on a sunny windowsill.

In cooking, chives add a delightful flavor to fresh salads, potato and tomato dishes, omelets, and fish. Their onion-y tang is very good in herb butter, a classic with sour cream, and a welcome addition to cream cheese and other cheeses, too. Chives lose their flavor when dried, so keeping fresh ones available in the kitchen will insure the best flavor. When clipping the long, hollow leaves with scissors, make sure that you snip them at least two inches (5 cm) above the soil surface, so the plant has enough body left to resume healthy growth. You may like to have two chive plants in your kitchen; it is a very pleasant and versatile culinary herb.

COMFREY (Symphytum officinale)

Comfrey is a widely used and well-loved herb which has acquired an array of nicknames, among them knitbone after its reputed value in healing bones and wounds, and donkey-ears for the shape of its long, furry, fleshy leaves.

Comfrey is a member of the Borage family, Boraginaceae. It is a hardy perennial which can easily be propagated from root cuttings of a large, established plant or from crown cuttings having buds. Although comfrey can reach a height of 36 inches (91 cm) in the garden, container-grown specimens remain much smaller. Plant root or crown cuttings several inches or centimeters deep in an eight-inch (20 cm) or larger pot. Place pots in an east or west window, giving plants a moderate amount of water. Comfrey enjoys a sweet, liberally limed soil, with a pH of 6 to 7.

This rather amazing plant contains large amounts of calcium, potassium, phosphorus, and vitamins A and C. Comfrey may also be the only land plant that contains vitamin B_{12}. It also offers allantoin, a soothing substance used in hand creams to relieve dry skin. Allantoin is known to reduce swelling—an effect that may explain comfrey's reputation

for speeding the healing of broken bones and wounds. In both dietary and medicinal uses, the fresh plant is to be preferred over the dry.

Comfrey leaves can be served fresh in salads, or steamed and served like spinach. (The smaller leaves are more tender.) As a tea, comfrey provides a rich source of nourishment and tastes good, too, either alone or mixed with chamomile or nettles or alfalfa. Macerated comfrey leaves can be applied as a poultice over sores, boils, open wounds, and broken bones. And comfrey root has a reputation as an internal healer—an ounce (30 ml) of comfrey root mixed with a quart (946 ml) of milk and heated for 30 minutes in the top section of a double boiler has been used to cure dysentery and diarrhea. The root also has been used in the treatment of intestinal and stomach ulcers.

CORIANDER (Coriandrum sativum)

Coriander, a member of the Parsley family, Umbelliferae, is a delicately beautiful annual herb which yields a fragrant and delicious seed often used in cakes, pastries, custards, soups, meats, broths, rice dishes, pickling spices, and salads. The dried seeds, which become more aromatic with age and which have a clean lemon scent, make a delightful potpourri ingredient. Coriander seeds have a soothing effect on the stomach, and they may be chewed as a digestive aid and a natural breath sweetener. The distinctive-tasting fresh leaves of this herb are a must in Mexican and Chinese cuisine but are just about impossible to buy in many areas—another good reason to grow your own.

The plant will thrive in a moderately fertile, well-drained soil. Coriander loves the Moroccan climate, a fact which gives an indication of its climatic preferences, which include lots of sun and a rather arid environment.

You can sow coriander seeds directly into the container where the plant will remain. Plant the seeds in drills ½ inch (13 mm) deep to allow them to germinate in darkness.

One thing you should know about coriander—just before its umbels go to seed, the usually delightful coriander becomes what the historian Pliny termed "a very stinkinge herb." If you can stand the offense, which is temporary, the coriander is a beautiful and aromatic herb for the home garden.

DILL *(Anethum graveolens)*

The feathery blue-green leaves and aromatic seeds of this member of the Umbelliferae are another wonderful addition to the kitchen herb garden. Dill is usually grown from seeds which are sown directly in the intended pot, in drills ¼ inch (6 mm) deep. Seeds will germinate in a week or less when the temperature is kept at 65°F (18°C). Dill likes full sun and loose, rich soil. Indoors, this annual will grow to about 12 inches (30 cm) high.

Both dill weed, as the foliage is called, and the seeds are used in cooking many different foods. Dill weed is wonderful in potato or chicken soup, stews, fish dishes, or potato salad. Fresh, it is delightful in salads and their dressings, too. You can make dill vinegar by placing a dill branch in a pint (473 ml) jar of white wine or apple cider vinegar. Of course, dill weed is most famous for its part in making dill pickles. The weed is also said to increase milk in nursing mothers, to relieve flatulence, and to ease swellings and pain. Dill seeds are often added to breads, soups, stews, bean salads, baked apples, and baked fish.

GARLIC *(Allium sativum)*

Another herb with an incredibly long list of medicinal uses is the humble and often unappreciated garlic, another member of the *Allium,* or onion, genus of the Lily family, Liliaceae. The substance that makes garlic smell so strong is also responsible for its healing qualities. It is called allicin, and it makes garlic useful in curing colds, sore throats, intestinal worms, earache, toothache, and other maladies. Garlic is a natural antibiotic; it can

Herb Botany: The group of plants we know as herbs is amazingly diverse, and encompasses plants from many different botanical families. Shown here (clockwise from top) are scented geranium, a member of the Geranium family, Geraniaceae; garlic, which belongs to the Lily family, Liliaceae; comfrey, of the Borage family, Boraginaceae; and coriander and dill, both of which belong to the Parsley family, Umbelliferae.

be used as an antiseptic and blood cleanser and liver tonic as well. It is a good insect-repellent plant, too, as you may have already guessed—bugs like its pungent odor as little as many people do. Of course, the culinary value of garlic is very well known. In Italian cooking, Chinese vegetable and meat dishes, and East Indian cuisine, garlic is indispensable. For an herb about which so many jokes prevail, it is really quite popular!

Garlic likes a moist, sandy soil and lots of

sun. Plant individual garlic cloves one inch (2.5 cm) deep in small pots—one clove in a three-inch (8 cm) pot is fine. Work a little well-aged compost into the topsoil about a month after planting. Feed with fish emulsion every two to three weeks and provide ample water. After about eight months of sunny growing time, the bulbs should be ready to harvest. In the meantime, you can also clip off just the tops of the garlic greens and use them as you would chives or scallion tops.

SCENTED GERANIUM (*Pelargonium* spp.)

The many varieties of scented geranium, which had their heyday as house plants during the Victorian era, originally came from the Cape of Good Hope, where they grow as tall as bushes. Though these geraniums flower prettily, they are prized for their fragrant leaves. All varieties of the scented geranium belong to the Geranium family, Geraniaceae, and need at least four hours of sun daily, a fertile soil high in humus, and pots with good drainage. Pots can be three to five inches (8 to 13 cm) in diameter, and the plants will profit from a potting depth of more than five inches (13 cm). Plants need to be pinched back often to encourage bushiness.

This perennial is easily propagated from stem cuttings about six inches (15 cm) long. Insert the cutting into sterilized sand, water it, and keep in the shade. Mist often. After three weeks or so, you can transplant the cuttings to pots, and gradually introduce the new plants into sunlight.

The rose geranium, *P. capitatum,* is the best known of all the scented geraniums. Its leaves, when crushed, emit a lovely roselike aroma that enlivens any room. And the leaves can be used in rose geranium tea and jelly, or as an ingredient in potpourris or sachets. New cuttings should be taken annually, as established plants lose their strength and become too large after about a year.

LAVENDER (*Lavandula* spp.)

This wonderfully sweet-smelling evergreen shrub has been cherished over the centuries for its delicate, calming fragrance. Pre-Christian Greeks and Romans used it for soaps and in bathwaters, and the herb still is used for those purposes, as well as in sachets, potpourris, and perfumes. It is less well known that oil of lavender is a good antiseptic for wounds and can be used for treating sore joints and toothaches, or that tea made from lavender flowers and leaves is good for calming the nerves. Of the several species, English lavender (*L. angustifolia*) is the most fragrant.

Lavender can be grown from cuttings or seeds. To help germination of the tiny seeds, place them in the freezer for 24 hours prior to sowing. Press seeds firmly into soil and lightly cover them with fine soil to a depth of 1/8 inch (3 mm). This member of the Mint family does best in a neutral to alkaline soil that is coarse or even sandy. Indoors, the plant needs at least four hours of sunlight. If grown from seeds, it will not bloom until the second year. Keep the soil slightly moist, make sure the temperature range is 40° to 70°F (4° to 21°C), and mist your lavender often. When the blossoms begin to fade, clip them off and cut back the plant by about one-third.

LOVAGE (*Levisticum officinale*)

Lovage is a hardy perennial member of the Umbelliferae, native to the Balkans and the Mediterranean region. Its leaves and stalks were used extensively in the past as a cure-all as well as for stomach disorders, colic, jaundice, urinary problems, and eye troubles. Considered to be a natural body deodorant, it has been favored as a mouthwash and gargle and can be added to bathwaters. Lovage also can be used to season salads, soups, and gravies, and both the bright green leaves and the hollow stem have a pungent fragrance, which has been likened to curry or celery.

Outdoors, lovage produces yellow flower umbels followed by brown seeds, and is very attractive to birds. The plant may grow to six feet (1.8 m) tall and last 20 years. Indoors, it should reach a height of about 12 to 16 inches (30 to 41 cm) if it is pinched back often. Lovage is easy to grow. Avoid too much sun—it does not need several hours of direct sun as

Medicinal Herbs: The herbs shown here (clockwise from front), lovage, lavender, and mint, have been used for many years by folk healers and practitioners of herbal medicine. Lovage is considered to be a natural deodorant, and can be used in mouthwashes and gargles, as well as to cure stomach disorders. Lavender tea is said to calm the nerves; its antiseptic oil has been used to treat wounds, toothaches, and sore joints. Mint tea is a time-honored remedy for indigestion, and oil of peppermint rubbed on the forehead can soothe the pain of a headache.

do some herbs. After sprouting the seeds, transplant the seedlings to a fairly fertile, well-drained soil, with some manure compost and lime added, or use a fish emulsion solution every three weeks.

MARJORAM *(Origanum majorana)*

Marjoram's name comes from the Greek; it means "joy of the mountains," a phrase that gives some notion of the spirit of the plant. Marjoram is a fragrant and beautiful perennial of the Mint family, which looks very attractive indoors in a hanging basket near a sunny window. (When grown inside, marjoram forsakes its usual upright and clumpy habit and tends more toward a trailing form.) It will reach a height of 8 to 12 inches (20 to 30 cm). This herb needs good sunlight, lots of humidity, and moderately fertile soil.

The lovely, round, gray-green leaves of marjoram have many delicious uses in the kitchen—meat dishes, Italian tomato sauces, roast lamb, soups, white sauces, egg dishes, and the green vegetables all profit from some marjoram. It is also a pleasant addition to potpourris. Dried, it maintains its fragrance well.

Marjoram can be grown from seeds, but watch for damping-off during germination. When the plant is mature, leaves and shoots can be continuously pinched back. And when its seeds, which are contained in green, ball-like spheres, appear, the whole plant can be cut back halfway to the soil and a second, even more luxuriant growth will occur.

MINT *(Mentha* spp.)

Mints are all rollicking, rampaging perennials of the Labiatae which love to spread rapidly across the outdoor garden. Indoors, in pots, they are much more tidy and manageable. All *Mentha* species like constantly moist soil; they will thrive in a soil that is moderately rich to a little sandy and prefer a shady location to full sun. The rapidly spreading roots cause the plants to quickly become potbound, so mints should be divided and repotted several times a year. Keep plants shapely by frequent pinching.

Of the more than 100 species of mints and their many mysterious crossbreeds, the two most common are spearmint (*M. spicata*) and peppermint (*M. ×piperita*). Today, peppermint oil enjoys many commercial uses in cosmetics, candy, medicines, and even cigarettes. This oil is also very soothing when rubbed on the forehead to relieve headaches and nervous tension. A tea made from peppermint leaves is often used for relieving indigestion, breaking fevers, and treating colds.

Spearmint is less strong than peppermint; it is the mint used most often in jellies, sauces, and lamb dishes. Both peppermint and spearmint, as well as the apple mint (*M. suaveolens*) and orange mint (*M. ×piperita* var. *citrata*), named after their scents, can be grown from cuttings or from the runners, which are called stolons.

NASTURTIUM *(Tropaeolum minus)*

With their lovely, bright flowers of gold, orange, and pink, and their pretty round leaves, nasturtiums make a beautiful addition to the indoor herb garden. The low and compact dwarf varieties, which reach 12 inches (30 cm) or less in height, are especially suited for growing inside. Native to South America, this annual member of the Nasturtium family, Tropaeolaceae, has leaves and flowers with a sharp, peppery flavor like cress, which are delightful in vegetable salads and sandwiches, and which are distinctive as a special garnish, or as a decoration floated on punch. The Chinese eat pickled nasturtium seeds, which can be used like capers. To try this delicacy, pick half-grown seed pods and pickle them in boiled rice vinegar.

When planting nasturtium seeds, presoak them for a day to soften the seed hulls. The plants like sun, and a very fertile, well-drained soil. Give them plenty of sun but not too much water or they will develop much foliage but forget to flower. Their spectacular large blossoms and habit of trailing make them attractive choices for hanging baskets.

EGYPTIAN ONION *(Allium cepa)*

Usually, onions send up festive-looking seed heads that flower in purple-pink balls. This beautifully elegant and unusual onion, however, instead sends up tiny clusters of onion bulbs at the ends of its top stalks. Left alone long enough, the stalks will sway under the growing weight of these bulb clusters, and bending to the ground, will seed new onion plants. This herb is easily started by planting its little bulbs in a moderately rich soil. Avoid fertilizing it with manure; it does best fertilized with a compost not too rich in nitrogen. Egyptian onions require a sunny south window and plenty of moisture.

Indoors, several of these onions make a striking pot plant, and can serve many useful purposes as well. Like all onions, the Egyptian onion belongs to the Lily family, Liliaceae. It is fine for any recipe calling for onions; both its bulb and stalks can be used in cooking. Besides that, it is useful in treating asthma and colds, in killing intestinal worms, and as an antiseptic.

OREGANO *(Origanum* spp.)

Native to the Mediterranean countries, oregano is a hardy, spreading perennial in the Mint family, with rounded leaves and a flat-topped inflorescence. *O. vulgare* is often considered to be wild marjoram. Having white, pink, or purple flowers, it is used medicinally, the oil as a liniment or as a toothache remedy, and the leaves in poultices to reduce swelling or in an infusion said to speed eruption of measles and to ease nervous headaches. The more flavorful *O. heracleoticum* has white blossoms only and is frequently described as "true" oregano. Beloved in Italian cuisine, it contributes a rich nuance to spaghetti sauce, tomato sauces, pizza, salads, omelets, cheese dishes, meats, soups, and vegetable dishes.

Growth Habits: The great variety of forms and growth habits among herbs is apparent in this photo of five well-loved herb plants (clockwise from left rear): rosemary, Egyptian onion, oregano, sage, and parsley.

Oregano responds well to sun and moderately rich, well-drained soil. Because of its long flowering period and its graceful way of spreading, this herb is a good choice for an indoor rock garden of herbs. It may be propagated from seeds, cuttings, or division. After blooming, cut back the entire plant by half to encourage new growth.

PARSLEY *(Petroselinum crispum)*

The ancient Greeks wore crowns of parsley to absorb the fumes of wine at banquets and thereby help prevent drunkenness. The herb was considered the plant of Hercules, and crowns of parsley adorned the heads of victors in the athletic games. When people were very sick in those days, it was said that they were "in need of parsley."

Sound judgment, that, for we now know this biennial member of the Umbelliferae is very high in both vitamins A and C, as well as in calcium, thiamine, riboflavin, and niacin. This very nutritious food is more usefully

---

Old-Fashioned Herb Bread

  2 cups (473 ml) warm water
 ¼ cup (59 ml) honey
  2 tablespoons (30 ml) dry baking yeast
  1 teaspoon (5 ml) salt (optional)
 ⅓ cup (79 ml) dry milk powder
 1½ tablespoons (22 ml) dried and crumbled
    herb or 3 to 4 tablespoons (45 to 60 ml)
    fresh herb, chopped fine*
 ½ cup (118 ml) soy flour
  5 cups (1.2 l) whole wheat flour
    (approximately)

Stir honey into warm water. Sprinkle yeast onto water and let stand 5 to 10 minutes. Add salt, milk, and herbs and blend well. Sift in half of flours and stir. Add part of the remaining flours (according to the coarseness of the flour more or less than 5 cups [1.2 l] may be needed). Knead 5 to 10 minutes. Dough should be elastic. Allow to rise in oiled bowl until double in volume. Knead again, shape into two loaves and place in oiled bread pans to rise again until double in size. Bake at 350°F (177°C), 45 to 50 minutes.

---

*Select any herb or a combination of several: anise seed, sweet basil, caraway seed, chervil, chives, dill seed or weed, sweet marjoram, oregano, parsley, sage, savory, tarragon, or thyme.

employed when added generously to vegetable and fish dishes and to sauces rather than used merely as a garnish. Parsley also excels when blended into salad dressings, tossed into salads, and made into tea. A cleansing herb, fresh parsley is a good remedy for bad breath and stomach trouble.

You might want to plant more than one kind of this superbly useful herb. Common or curly-leaved parsley, *P. crispum,* is the ancient form and was at one time classified as a variety of *P. hortense.* This many-branched parsley grows to 10 to 15 inches (25 to 38 cm) high under optimal conditions and has crisp edges on its curled leaves. *P. crispum* var. *neapolitanum* (Italian parsley) has flat leaves that are not crisped and is preferred by many cooks; *P. crispum* var. *tuberosum* (Hamburg or turnip-rooted parsley) has flat leaves and thick roots that can be cooked like parsnips.

Propagate parsley from shallowly planted seeds. Soak them overnight in warm water before planting to overcome any resistance to germinating. This herb likes sun and prefers rich, humusy soil that is well drained. Plants do best in a cool room and benefit from misting. Work in some well-aged compost occasionally.

ROSEMARY
(Rosmarinus officinalis)

Rosemary is a perennial evergreen shrub belonging to the Mint family and native to the Mediterranean region. It is hard to grow from seeds, and is usually propagated from cuttings of the six inch (15 cm) long tips of new growth. After stripping off most of the foliage (leave some on the tip), bury the lower half in sand or vermiculite. Keep the rooting medium moist, mist frequently, and keep out of direct sunlight. In two or three months, the cutting will be ready to transplant. Favoring well-drained, slightly alkaline soil, rosemary also responds to a cool growing place, with light and a little sun. Indoors, it may be susceptible to red spider mites if the air is too

---

Moth Repellents

Many herbs that smell good to people will repel moths. These herbs include bay, lavender, rosemary, and thyme. Place lavender leaves and blossoms in a tiny handkerchief, tie securely with a piece of yarn and place among woolen blankets and sweaters. Mix 2 parts each rosemary and thyme with 1 part crushed bay leaf, add a small amount of orris root powder and sew the dried herb mixture into small decorative bags to place in drawers or closets. Extra bags make thoughtful gifts.

---

dry. Mist it often, and water it daily to prevent drying out, which can be fatal. You can cover the top of the pot with sphagnum moss to help keep the roots moist.

With its beautiful blue flowers and fragrant, spiky leaves, rosemary has long been regarded as the plant of the Virgin Mary, and associated with the quality of remembrance. Traditionally, it has been used at both weddings and funerals.

In cooking, rosemary is delicious with roasts, poultry, omelets, peas, and in soups, stuffings, and sauces. Oil of rosemary may be rubbed directly on the scalp as a cure for dandruff. A tea made from the herb is good for both insomnia and headaches.

SAGE *(Salvia officinalis)*

Salvia literally means "health" or "salvation," and from this name we can correctly infer that sage has been used for many years as a medicine. This hardy perennial of the Mint family, with its hairy, gray-green leaves and stems and beautiful purple flowers, makes a lovely indoor plant. It does best in a sunny window and moderately rich soil. Do not allow plants to set seeds or they may die. Propagate from stem cuttings or seeds, which germinate readily. Germination takes about a week at a temperature of 68°F (20°C).

Sage is believed to be a great blood cleanser and purifier. It has been used in treating palsy, for cleaning and whitening teeth, for strengthening the stomach, and for clearing the memory. It aids in digestion, especially of fatty meat dishes. As a culinary herb, sage can be mixed into cheeses or soups, and used to season meat and poultry. The flowers look and taste beautiful in salads. Cosmetically, a very strong distillate of sage tea can be used as a rinse to darken graying hair.

SUMMER SAVORY
(Satureja hortensis)

WINTER SAVORY
(Satureja montana)

A touch of savory in cooked green beans, bean soups, or legume dishes adds a zesty, peppery flavor. Because of savory's affinity for beans (it is an excellent companion to beans in the garden, as well as in the kitchen), it has earned the nickname of bean herb. Savory also enlivens egg dishes, soups, poultry, meats, and green salads. The French call it *sarriette* and add a sprig when cooking new peas; often savory is included in mixtures of *fines herbes*. Crushed fresh leaves of summer savory may be applied to beestings to relieve the pain. A bunch of sprigs tied in cheesecloth and added to bathwaters creates a pleasant herbal bath.

Summer savory is an upright annual with numerous woody stems branching towards the top. Because of its growth habit, plants become top heavy and prone to toppling unless they are kept clipped back. The quickly germinating seeds are up and growing in less than two weeks. They sprout best in light, well-drained soil.

While summer savory is the variety most people prefer to use in the kitchen, the perennial winter savory makes a more handsome pot plant. Winter savory has narrow leaves which somewhat resemble those of rosemary, but the savory plant is more prostrate and its foliage is a darker green. Plants are propagated by stem cuttings or by seeds which are quite slow growing. Both savories belong to

the family Labiatae, thrive in well-drained, rich soil and do best in a sunny south or west window.

TARRAGON
(Artemisia dracunculus)

Tarragon, which once was cultivated only in the beautiful and complex herb gardens of the nobility, is an ancient herb, one of the "simples" used by Hippocrates. The plant can be grown from cuttings or root divisions. Take care that you choose the variety known either as French or German tarragon, rather than the Russian kind, which has a less fragrant oil.

Tarragon, a member of the Compositae, likes a fertile, well-drained soil, moderate sun, and lots of humidity. It does not usually require daily watering. You can water it one day, skip a day, then water again. Success in

Herb Vinegar

Herb vinegars serve a dual purpose—they come in handy in the kitchen and are also a beauty aid. You can add herb vinegars to homemade salad dressings or use them to marinate meat, poultry, or game. Vinegar splashed on the face after washing renews the skin's natural acidity and tightens skin pores. Several tablespoons of vinegar added to a pint (473 ml) of pure rain water or spring water makes an excellent after-shampoo rinse to restore the hair's natural acid mantle. Besides the traditional tarragon vinegar, try basil, salad burnet, dill, lavender, mint, nasturtium, rose, rosemary, savory, thyme, or lemon verbena.

Use either apple cider vinegar or white wine vinegar. For each pint (473 ml) of vinegar use 1 cup (236 ml) of fresh herb, placing both in a tightly sealed glass jar. Keep on a sunny windowsill and shake daily for two weeks before straining and rebottling in pints for the kitchen or fancy bottles for your bathroom. For faster results, heat the vinegar to 150°F (66°C) and pour over herbs, cool to room temperature and strain.

growing tarragon indoors lies in giving it a large pot to allow for its extensive root system. Give each plant a 12-inch (30 cm) pot all to itself to avoid crowding. Every several years plants must be divided and repotted after the roots are carefully untangled.

This mellow-flavored herb is used in making tarragon vinegar, Béarnaise sauce and white sauces, and to flavor green vegetables, fish, and cheese or egg dishes. Tarragon's fragrance stays stronger if you freeze rather than dry the herb. Of course, it is best fresh.

THYME *(Thymus* spp.)

There are many varieties of this perennial member of the Labiatae, ranging from French thyme, which is most commonly used in cooking, to the more exotic caraway thyme and lemon thyme. Indoors, French thyme, which is the variety most gardeners may be inclined to choose, needs a fairly large pot to accommodate its root system. It will reach a height of 8 to 10 inches (20 to 25 cm) and needs three to four hours of sun each day for proper growth. Thyme loves high humidity, and should be misted frequently. But it needs watering only when dry. Thyme will not tolerate a heavy soil, so be sure to plant it in a light, well-drained potting mix. Clip the foliage often to encourage spreading and bushy growth. Plants are heavy feeders, requiring twice-monthly applications of fish emulsion or compost tea. French thyme is a fragrant and beautiful plant—narrow-leafed and grayish in color. Rudyard Kipling loved it so much he called it "dawn in paradise." It looks pretty in a hanging basket and imparts a wonderfully pungent flavor to red meats, poultry, fish, egg dishes, soups, stews, and vegetables. Another culinary favorite you might try indoors is the green and low-growing English thyme. The creeping thymes are well suited to hanging planters.

Lemon thyme, also a popular variety, emits a dazzling scent of lemon when rubbed.

Culinary Herbs: These four herbs deserve a place in every kitchen (clockwise from front): tarragon, winter savory, summer savory, and thyme.

The several cultivars of lemon thyme are delightful for teas, and for making sachets and potpourris. All lemon thymes need a maximum of sun and do best in a south window.

LEMON VERBENA *(Aloysia triphylla)*

Lemon verbena is appreciated for its long, pointed, lemon-scented leaves which are used in potpourris and sachets. Sprigs may be placed in drawers to give them a refreshing, clean smell. Leaves, either fresh or dried, can be steeped into a delightful herb tea, added to fruit compotes, and used to garnish iced tea or fruit drinks.

In its native South America and other frost-free areas, this member of the Verbena family can attain a height of 10 feet (3 m), but when container grown it usually remains under 24 inches (61 cm). Since seeds are quite slow to germinate, propagation by cuttings is best. Provide lemon verbena with

Potpourris and Sachets

Potpourris consist of coarsely broken bits of scented herbs, flowers, and spices. For sachets the ingredients are finely ground. Potpourris are displayed in decorative glass jars with tight-fitting lids which are opened on occasion to let the mellow scent pervade the room. Sachet blends are put in small bags made from pretty fabrics and can be used to scent linens, closets, drawers, or purses. Mix your blend of ingredients in a ceramic bowl using a wooden spoon. Place the mixture in a large glass bottle with a tight lid for two months. Once the scents are blended and fixed, transfer the mixture to clear potpourri jars or if intended for sachets, grind fine before filling fabric bags.

Lemon Essence

2 cups (473 ml) lemon verbena leaves
1 cup (236 ml) rosemary
½ cup (118 ml) rose geranium
6-8 drops lemon oil
½ ounce (15 ml) orris root (fixative)

Herbal Scent

1 cup (236 ml) lavender
1 cup (236 ml) rosemary
1 cup (236 ml) lemon balm
½ cup (118 ml) thyme
½ cup (118 ml) spearmint
6-8 drops lavender oil
½ ounce (15 ml) orris root (fixative)

HARVESTING AND PRESERVING HERBS

If you have a large indoor herb garden, or if herbs "grow on you" (as they tend to) and you find yourself seeking out wild herb plants in fields, on hills, and by creeks, you may like to know some good methods to harvest and preserve herbs.

Herbs should be harvested before they flower and in the early morning, just as the dew leaves them. This is when they have the most fragrance, flavor, and oil content. In indoor gardens, where plants are usually kept from flowering by pinching back, and where dew does not fall nightly, it still is good to follow these rules of nature to get optimal benefit from herbs.

Of course, the most picturesque way of drying herbs is to tie them in bunches and hang them from rafters, or from hooks on the walls, out of direct sunlight in a warm room. They will dry within a week, and meanwhile, lend a pleasant, cozy feeling to the room. Some herbs, those with woody stems, dry best if their leaves are stripped off before drying. Most herbs, however, can be dried whole, and leaves can be stripped off afterwards, taking care to keep them as whole as possible for best fragrance and oil retention.

If you are harvesting the plants for their seeds, you may wish to try the paper bag method of drying. Harvest seed umbels or pods just as they are turning from green to gray or brown, and hang them inside a paper bag with the seed head down, as illustrated here. Tying the top of the bag with string or wire, hang it in a warm place with indirect light where the whole bag can have air circulating around it. In two to three weeks, the seeds will drop onto the floor of the paper bag, and can be collected easily later.

One herb-growing family in Oregon has put a wooden molding around the ceiling of their warmest room, and strung thin-gauge wires from one side of the room to the other, fastening the wires to the molding with

rich soil, good drainage, and lots of sunshine in the summer. A deciduous plant, it loses all of its leaves and does not look too pretty for a few months in midwinter. During this period move the plant to an east window in a cool room and continue to water it as before. Legginess is its natural form, so pinch and prune often to form a compact, bushy plant.

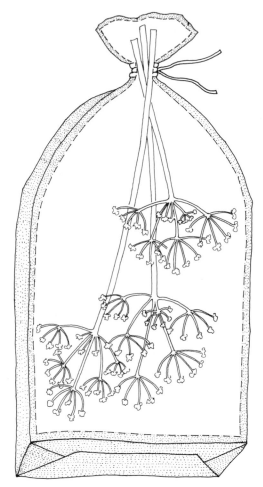

though, that some attics don't get enough air circulation, and herbs may not dry well.) If you decide to use the screen method of drying, just lay the plants or stripped-off leaves in thin layers on the screen in a warm, dim place with good air circulation, and cover them with cheesecloth to keep off bugs or dust. Those whose living space is too limited or who prefer a fast drying method can dry herbs in the oven. Place your herbs on cookie sheets in an oven set at 150°F (66°C) or less. Leave the oven door open to let moisture out. In three hours or so, your herbs will be dry. Basil and chervil are very sensitive to heat, so if you decide to dry them this way, make sure the oven temperature stays down at 90°F (32°C).

Harvesting Seeds: If you are harvesting plants such as dill for their seeds, the paper bag method is the best way to dry them. Tie the stalks with seed heads down inside a paper bag, and hang the bag in a warm, dry place. When dry the seeds will fall into the bottom of the bag, where they can be collected easily.

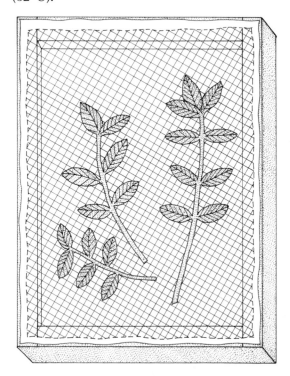

screws. When they collect large amounts of wild herbs, they place a small bunch of herbs in each of many paper bags, and suspend the bags with clothespins from the wires. This approach keeps the herbs from getting dusty. It does take longer than the free-hanging method, though.

Some gardeners dry mints and other light herbs on screen racks, placing them high on the rafters in sheds or in the attic for warmth and indirect light. (It must be noted,

Screen Rack: A convenient way to dry herb plants is on a simple screen rack placed in a warm, dimly lighted location with good air circulation. A shady outdoor spot or a well-ventilated attic are good possibilities. Lay the plants in thin layers on the screen, and cover them with cheesecloth to keep them clean. When dry, strip off the leaves and store in airtight containers.

After drying your herbs, by whatever method you choose, discard the stems, if you haven't already done so, and store the leaves in airtight containers. Check them after a few hours, and again a few days later, to make sure that they are really dry and no moisture has condensed on the glass or plastic. If moisture does appear, take the herbs out and dry them some more. (When using herbs in recipes and in other ways, keep in mind that usually 1 part of dried herbs is equivalent to 2 to 3 parts of the same herb in fresh form.)

Freezing is another good way to preserve some culinary herbs. Chervil, chives, dill weed, sweet marjoram, mints, oregano, parsley, and tarragon all keep well when frozen. (Tarragon, in fact, is much better frozen than dried, retaining more of its fragrance and volatile oils that way.) Place the herbs in plastic bags and seal with wires. When you want to use some of the frozen herbs, just take them out and chop them before they thaw.

SOME SPECIAL THINGS TO DO WITH YOUR HERBS

HERB OILS

You can extract the oil from sweet flowers such as the rose, jasmine, lavender, honeysuckle, lilac, and geranium, and from herbs such as mint, rosemary, sage, and marjoram. If you plan to use flowers, collect the most perfect flower petals early in the morning. With herbs, collect the best leaves.

There are several ways to collect oil from plant parts. Perhaps the easiest is to place the herbs or flowers from which you wish to extract oil in a clean ceramic crock and just cover them with rain or spring water. (Keep the herbs from floating by weighting them down beneath a jar of water with its top screwed on tight.) Let the crock stay in the sun for several days or until a scummy foam appears. This is the oil. Once it begins to col-

lect, carefully absorb it into a small cotton ball, squeeze it into a small jar, and seal. This method yields a strong oil that can be used in fragrant and healing preparations.

As a second option, you might use an oil/alcohol base to take up the oil from your herbs. Place 1 quart (946 ml) of a light oil such as safflower oil in a glass jar, together with ½ cup (118 ml) of alcohol. Next, pack the jar with herbs or flowers. (The plant material should first be chopped coarsely so it will release its oil more readily.) Let the jar sit in full sun for several days, and check it every six hours or so. Make sure you monitor smell as well as appearance so you catch the mixture before it becomes rancid. When the oil is suffused in the larger mixture strain out the chopped herbs using cheesecloth. Be sure to twist the cheesecloth around the removed material tightly or to press the herbs against the cloth to force out any remaining oils. This method makes pleasantly aromatic oil—not as potent as the oil produced by the first method, but fine for cosmetic uses and for massage.

HERBAL WATERS

Herbal waters are pure waters that have been infused with fragrant herbs and are used as skin toners and tonics, body washes, light perfumes, hair rinses, and soap scents. Use distilled or spring water when making herbal waters. In a stainless steel or enamel saucepan place 1 to 1½ cups (236 to 370 ml) fresh herbs. Cover with 2 cups (473 ml) water. Bring to a simmer and gently simmer several minutes. Remove from heat and steep 15 to 20 minutes before straining.

HERBAL SOAPS

To create soaps with distinctive herbal scents (mint, lavender, lemon verbena, and rosemary are favorites), chip pure blocks of castile or Ivory soap into 1 gallon (4 l) glass jars. Add just enough herbal waters or oils to cover the cut-up soap—the idea is to incorporate a strong enough scent but as little additional liquid as possible, to shorten the time it will take the soap to set and harden. Then allow the chips to liquefy at room temperature until well blended with the scented water or oil. While your soap is turning to a liquid, you can be preparing molds to shape it. Molds can be as simple or as fancy as you wish, and can be made from materials already available around the house. For example, you might recycle the plastic trays that hold cookies. If you don't happen to have any, they can gen-

erally be had free for the asking from bake-shops and from friends and relatives who purchase boxed cookies. In selecting molds, it is usually best to choose flexible containers that will let you remove the finished soap by pushing inward on the bottom or base of the mold. If you prefer, though, you can also pour the liquid soap into wooden flats with removable sides, then cut the soap slabs into small squares with a length of thin wire before they have completely hardened.

When the soap chips in the jars have completely liquefied and blended with the scented water or oil, pour the mixture into the molds you have selected. Then set them aside to dry and harden. While the soap is drying, do not allow the temperature to drop below what it was when the soap was poured. Ideally, you should place the molds outdoors during the summer in a very warm spot. Cover them with cheesecloth to keep debris from falling into the soap. Do not allow the cheesecloth to touch the soap, or it will harden right into it. If you must bring your molds inside due to cool weather, dry the soap in the warmest part of the house. Do not, however, use the oven, for the smell of soap drying in a hot oven is unpleasantly sharp. Exactly how many days it takes for your soap to set will depend on how much herbal water or oil you added to it.

THE HERBAL BATH

This particular recipe for "magic waters" comes down to us from the memoirs of the famous French beauty Ninon de l'Enclos. She says, "Take a handful of dried lavender flowers, a handful of rosemary leaves, a handful of dried mint, a handful of comfrey roots, and one of thyme. Mix all together loosely in a muslin bag. Place in your tub. Pour enough boiling water to cover and let soak for ten minutes. Then fill up the tub. Rest fifteen minutes in the 'magic waters' and think virtuous thoughts."

As you learn more about the various

Using the Herb Harvest: Many herbs are best preserved by drying. There are a multitude of uses for herbs in dried form — they can be part of decorative dried arrangements, fragrant potpourris and sachets, hot or iced teas, soothing medicinal preparations, and of course, they are indispensable in the kitchen for seasoning sauces, soups, stews, breads, butters, casseroles, and a host of other dishes.

qualities and strengths of herbs, you can begin to concoct your own herbal bathing mixtures. (Since they contain highly aromatic herbs, many herbal bathing mixtures also can be used as sachets, potpourris, and even incense.) Comfrey and parsley in baths will have an invigorating effect on the skin; sage and marjoram help with aching muscles; marigold is good for circulation; lavender and mints are calmative. You can put dried lemon or orange peel or blossoms, rose petals, or jasmine blossoms in the bath, too. To make a decoction for bath use, simmer the desired assortment of herbs, either in a muslin bag or loose, in a pot of water for 10 to 15 minutes. Then take out the herbs, pour the decoction into the bathing waters, step in, and relax. For a more concentrated herbal bath, a few drops of an herbal oil can be added to a hot tub.

HERBED BUTTERS AND CHEESES

Ordinary bread, muffins, omelets, vegetables, meats, and fish taste extraordinarily good served with herb butters and herb cheeses. These treats are easy to make, and you can be as imaginative as you like with them,

using one or several herbs, depending on the desired taste. For a garlicky herb butter, cream together ½ cup (118 ml) softened butter, 2 mashed garlic cloves; 2 tablespoons (30 ml) chopped chives; 1 tablespoon (15 ml) fresh dill weed; ½ teaspoon (2.5 ml) lemon juice; and 2 tablespoons (30 ml) chopped parsley. Reshape and refrigerate this blend for several hours before serving so the flavors are well mixed. A variation is a chive butter made with ½ cup (118 ml) softened butter, 1 tablespoon (15 ml) chopped chives, 1 tablespoon (15 ml) parsley, and ¼ teaspoon (1.3 ml) rosemary.

To create a tangy herb cheese, you can blend any combination of chives, parsley, sage, dill, thyme, oregano, and marjoram into soft cheeses like cream cheese or cottage cheese. Add 1 tablespoon (15 ml) dried herb or 2 to 3 tablespoons (30 to 45 ml) fresh herb for each 12 ounces (360 ml) of cheese. With hard cheese like cheddar, herbs like sage, dill weed, or caraway seed can be added as the cheese is melted. For each 4 ounces (118 ml) of cheese, stir in 1 teaspoon (5 ml) dried herb. Of course, you can add fragrant herb seeds and leaves to your favorite bread recipes, too.

CHAPTER 18

Forcing Spring Bulbs

Despite what many people think, there is no great mystery about forcing bulbs. Forcing is a simple procedure used to make spring-flowering bulb species bloom ahead of their outdoor schedules in order to provide springtime color and fragrance indoors during winter.

The wonderful thing about forcing bulbs is that anyone can do it — whether in a large house or in an apartment. You can force only one bulb or as many as you have room for and the desire to try.

There are many places where you can force bulbs: in a ground pit, in a cold frame, in a cold cellar or unheated garage (providing the temperature does not drop too low), or even in a window box. In fact, one of the best places for forcing bulbs is in a refrigerator.

If you are a beginner, do not try to aim for exhibition dates in flower shows, or for any dates for that matter. Just consider that you want some colorful flowers from bulbs in the house well ahead of when you might expect to have them outdoors. It takes a great deal of experience to know how to get bulbs to bloom on an exact date. With practice, however, it is possible to target specific dates or come close enough if, beginning with your first experience, you keep detailed time records and exact information about ingredients of your potting mix, watering schedules, temperatures, and light.

SELECTING BULBS

All kinds of spring-flowering bulbs can be forced. Probably the most popular are hyacinths *(Hyacinthus orientalis),* daffodils and narcissus (*Narcissus* hybrids), and tulips (*Tulipa* hybrids), but you are not limited to these. Providing their own special charm, *Amaryllis* (belladonna lily), *Anemone, Crocus, Freesia, Hippeastrum* (amaryllis), *Iris*

reticulata, and *Muscari* (grape hyacinth), among others, may be readily forced. There are two primary categories of bulbs commonly available for indoor forcing: hardy bulbs and fragile or tender bulbs. Hardy bulbs all require a cold period before they can be forced, while fragile bulbs require no cold period. Both types need a period of darkness before forcing. Essentially, all the bulbs in each group require the same care. Some, however, take longer than others to force into bloom.

Your selection of bulbs will depend on the colors and shapes of flowers you prefer. Garden centers and catalog firms usually have color reproductions of most bulbs, and a wide range of colors is available. For example, if your favorite color is yellow, there are crocuses, daffodils, *Iris danfordiae,* ixias, narcissus, ranunculus, sparaxis, and tulips from which to choose. You can also select blooms in varying shades of red, pink, white, orange, blue, and purple. Some cultivars of *Crocus, Ranunculus,* and *Tulipa* are bicolored. There are many possibilities for combining colors in dish gardens and arrangements.

SOME BULB BOTANY

Before you buy and plant bulbs you should understand what a bulb is. First of all, a bulb is a living entity — at all times. Even before it is planted it is very much alive, containing embryonic stem, leaves, and flower.

Botanically, a bulb is a short stem with fleshy leaf bases known as scales. There are two kinds of bulbs: tunicate and scaly. In a tunicate, or layered, bulb, the scales extend completely around the bulb. When the bulb is sliced down the middle and examined in cross section, the scales appear as a series of compact concentric rings, as in an onion.

Opposite, flower of an amaryllis, Hippeastrum *hybrid.*

361

Bulb Structure

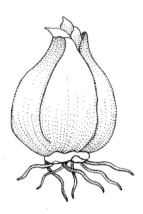

Tunicate Bulb: A tunicate bulb has scales which extend all the way around the bulb.

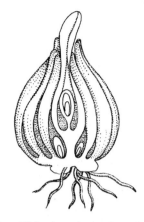

Cross Section: This view of a tunicate bulb shows the position of the embryonic flower. Note how the scales appear in cross section as a series of concentric rings.

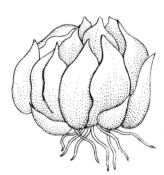

Scaly Bulb: This bulb has a number of narrow scales which do not completely encircle the stem.

Amaryllis, daffodils, hyacinths, narcissus, and tulips are some examples of plants having tunicate bulbs. Scaly bulbs, such as the bulbs of the Easter lily *(Lilium longiflorum)* have a series of narrow scales which do not totally encircle the stem.

All bulbs have a basal plate (at the flat end), which is the point from which the bulb puts forth its roots. If the basal plate is dam-aged or diseased the roots will not be healthy and chances that the plant will thrive are slim. The brown outer skin of the bulb is known as the tunic.

Some bulb plants, such as crocuses and ixias, do not form true bulbs, but instead produce corms. The two structures are similar but corms are solid, lacking the fleshy leaves that bulbs contain.

Colors of Spring Bulbs

White	Pink	Red	Orange	Yellow	Blue	Purple
Anemone	*Anemone*	*Anemone*	*Anemone*	*Freesia*	*Anemone*	*Anemone*
Crocus	*Crocus*	*Hippeastrum*	*Crocus*	*Hyacinthus*	*Hyacinthus*	*Crocus*
Hippeastrum	*Hyacinthus*	*Hyacinthus*	*Freesia*	*Iris danfordiae*	*Iris reticulata*	*Iris reticulata*
Hyacinthus	*Ixia*	*Ixia*	*Ixia*	*Ixia*	*Muscari*	*Sparaxis*
Ixia	*Ranunculus*	*Ranunculus*	*Ranunculus*	*Narcissus*	*Tulipa*	*Tulipa*
Narcissus	*Tulipa*	*Sparaxis*	*Tulipa*	*Ranunculus*		
Tulipa		*Tulipa*		*Sparaxis*		
				Tulipa		

Treat bulbs as you would treat anything that is alive, and handle them gently at all times. They are sensitive to their environment and react accordingly. Left in the sun, they will shrivel. Left out in the rain, they will rot. If you keep them closed in a plastic bag, they will suffocate — as you would in an airless room. Besides visible damage, in cases such as these the greatest harm is done to the basal plate and the preformed bud found inside the bulb. The flower buds are formed during the summer to bloom the following spring. With that bud and the root base, you are assured success insofar as the grower is able to provide it. If the bud or basal plate is damaged, you will wait in vain for colorful, fragrant spring flowers.

BUYING AND STORING BULBS

It is important to select bulbs carefully from a nursery or a reliable catalog firm. Nurseries and greenhouses generally sell two sizes of bulbs. There is a top-quality grade, often called "exhibition" or "first" grade, which is reserved for large bulbs that produce the best blooms when forced indoors or planted outside. Some dealers also market smaller bulbs which are not as old and which will yield a poorer flower than top-grade bulbs. These "second" bulbs are most often found in "bargain" bulb mixes and special offers. They are acceptable for naturalizing and outdoor growing, but are not recommended for forcing.

Although most growers take great care in producing the bulbs, do not forget that various things could happen to them during shipping. Just as you pick over fruit and vegetables in the supermarket, it is good practice to gently pick over the bulbs. But be careful not to damage any bulbs by groping anxiously for the largest, plumpest one. Always select bulbs that are firm. A small nick is not important, but do not pick a bulb that is soft or bruised; it is probably damaged or diseased. Check all bulbs to make sure the basal plate is firm. Blue mold on bulbs is not usually cause for rejection, unless the mold is on the basal plate. Problems with bulbs are minimized because of the strict regulations under which bulbs are produced. Nevertheless, select bulbs with care, so that the results will live up to your expectations.

It is advisable to plant bulbs as soon as you purchase them, but this is not always possible. The best plans can go awry. Or you may want to stagger plantings for a succession of blooms. Whatever the cause for delay, treat your bulbs kindly while they wait. Spread them out where they can be well aerated, for example, on slatted wood or hardware cloth. Mesh shopping or beach bags also can be used for storage. Do not store bulbs in a greenhouse where they will receive too

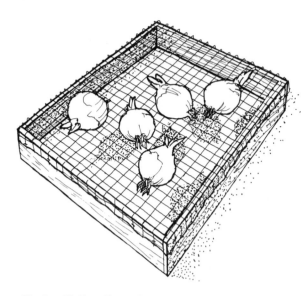

Storing Bulbs: If you find it necessary to store bulbs before you are ready to force them, spread them out where they will get plenty of air circulation but no sun. One good method of storage is to stretch a piece of hardware cloth across the top of a box or a wooden frame, and lay the bulbs on top.

much moisture. Wherever you store bulbs temporarily, the location you choose should be cool and out of the sun. Cool does not mean cold, however. *Never put bulbs in a freezer,* or you will kill them.

POTTING

The best planting medium for bulbs is a well-drained, loamy soil, neither so porous and thin that it fails to hold the bulbs in place (which is the soil's main function), nor so heavy with clay that it holds too much moisture. A pasteurized all-purpose soil mix is ideal. Packaged, pasteurized planting soil, which is heavier than potting soil and intended for outdoor garden use, can be combined with peat and perlite or vermiculite in equal parts for a suitable potting mix. Whatever soil you use, be sure it is fresh. You do not need to mix manure or compost with the soil; in fact, you do not need to use any kind

of fertilizer. Bulbs contain within themselves all they need in the way of food to carry them through for their first performance.

Bulbs can be planted in any container, as long as it has a drainage hole to insure that the bulbs will not rot. Most ceramic containers, while decorative, have no drainage hole. A layer of pebbles on the bottom of such a pot will not provide sufficient drainage. Ask a local nurseryman to drill a hole in the pot, or use ceramic containers as attractive showpieces to hold bulb pots. Plant bulbs in wooden boxes, if you can find them. Better yet, use plain, unglazed clay flower pots; you will want what are called "azalea pots," or bulb pans. They are shallower than the usual flower pots.

Be sure to scrub all pots before planting the bulbs. Soak clay pots overnight. After immersing them in water, put your ear near the sink. If you hear a hissing sound, the pots are absorbing water. Leave them in the water until the hissing stops. By soaking up excess moisture from the soil when you water, clay pots help prevent bulbs from rotting.

Generally speaking, the earlier you start to pot up bulbs, the earlier they will bloom. In colder areas of the country, spring-blooming bulbs appear on the market at the end of August or beginning of September. By staggering plantings from September first to November first, you can have a wealth of bulb flowers in bloom well ahead of spring and their outdoor show. If you are working with hardy bulbs, bear in mind that the first and longest stage, called cold treatment, must last about 13 weeks, with an additional 2 or 3 weeks necessary for some *Tulipa* cultivars.

For example, by starting bulbs in early September you will have flowering plants in January. October plantings bloom in February; November potting brings flowers in March; bulbs started in December bloom in April.

When potting, make sure you have all the necessary materials assembled: bulbs, pots, soil mix, clay shards or small stones, and labels. First, cover the hole at the bottom of the pot with shards or stones as described in chapter 4, to insure good drainage. Fill the pot with soil to within about two inches (5 cm) of the rim. Set bulbs on the soil, pointed ends up. Do not press them down, or you might injure the basal plates. The tips of the bulbs should be even with the pot rim.

The number of bulbs planted per pot varies with the size of the pot. The size of the bulbs, especially daffodils and narcissus, varies, too. A six-inch (15 cm) pot normally holds six tulips, three hyacinths, or three double-nosed daffodils (double-nosed means having two growing tips instead of one, therefore producing more flowers).

Set tulip bulbs with their flat sides against the side of the pot. This way, the first flowers to bloom will turn out from the pot, making a more attractive display and allowing for easier watering. If tulips are not planted this way, large leaves will turn inward, crowding the center of the pot. Watering is difficult and the plant becomes prone to disease.

Plant bulbs close together, but not touching each other. Sprinkle soil around and between the bulbs, bringing it to ½ inch (13 mm) below the edge of the pot. Leave the tips of the bulbs exposed. Do not pack the soil beneath the bulbs when potting or the bulbs' roots, being unable to grow down through the compacted soil, will push the bulbs up and out of the pot.

Number and label each pot, indicating the kind of flower, cultivar, color, and planting date. You can write all the information on a label stuck into the soil, or even on the side of the pot. For convenience and accuracy, keep a duplicate record in a notebook. If you also record the date of blooming, this record will prove very useful in planning next year's blooming schedule.

Water each pot slowly and gently, making sure the soil is thoroughly soaked. A long-necked watering can is good for watering pots from the top. If the settling soil causes bulbs

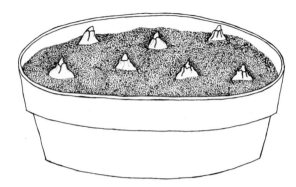

Planting Bulbs Correctly: After filling the pot with soil to within 2 inches (5 cm) of the rim, set the bulbs on the soil with pointed ends up. The tips of the bulbs should be even with the pot rim. Next, sprinkle soil around and between the bulbs, bringing it to a level about ½ inch (13 mm) below the pot rim. The tips of the bulbs should remain exposed.

to tilt, straighten them immediately and add more soil to firm them into position. Another suitable watering technique is to place pots in a large container two-thirds full of water until the soil surface is moist, allowing the water to be absorbed into the soil by capillary action. Check from time to time to make sure the bulbs are not tilting, and add more soil as needed.

A single tulip or daffodil alone in a pot looks awkwardly spare, but a single hyacinth planted in a four- or five-inch (10 or 13 cm) pot is effective. One hyacinth provides enough perfume to scent a whole room. (It also can be used to add temporary color when set in a dish garden among foliage plants.)

A COLD PERIOD FOR HARDY BULBS

Unlike fragile bulbs, all hardy bulbs require a cold period before growth can be forced. This means putting them in a dark location where the temperature is between 35° and 48°F (2° and 9°C) for between 10 and 13 weeks. There are many spots that will meet this tempera-

Dish Gardens of Dutch Bulbs

Besides having pots containing one kind of flowering bulb, you can try combining different bulbs in a single eight-inch (20 cm) azalea pot to make a Dutch garden. Though you can devise any combinations you like, it is more fun to plant different types of bulbs that will bloom at different times and prolong the life of the garden.

For example, in an eight-inch (20 cm) pot you might plant six white crocuses, six blue or purple *Iris reticulata* corms, one yellow daffodil, one pink hyacinth, and three red tulips. Set the taller-growing bulbs to the back of the pot and the shorter ones to the front. Because the shorter-stemmed flowers are apt to be the earlier-blooming ones, flowering will progress from front to back.

In the center rear, set three tulip bulbs in a triangle so that they almost touch. Coming forward on the left, set a double-nosed daffodil bulb ½ to 1 inch (13 to 25 mm) from the tulips. In similar position on the right, set the hyacinth. In front, set the group of six *Iris reticulata* corms on one side and the six crocuses on the other. If you wish, you can make the dish garden with all hyacinths and crocuses, or tulips and daffodils. Cold treatment of such pots will be the same as for pots of one kind of bulb. Try this, especially if you live in an apartment and do not have space for many pots of different flowers.

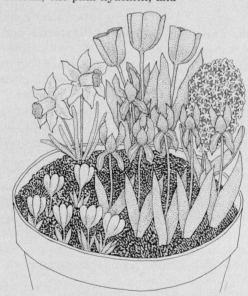

Planting a Dish Garden: An 8-inch (20 cm) pot can hold 6 crocuses, 6 *Iris reticulata* corms, 1 daffodil, 1 hyacinth, and 3 tulips. For an attractive display that will provide a succession of flowers, place the tulip bulbs in a triangle at the center back of the pot. Slightly forward and to the left, set the daffodil bulb ½ to 1 inch (13 to 25 mm) from the tulips. Place the hyacinth in a similar position on the right. Toward the front of the pot, set the crocuses on one side and the iris on the other. Blooming should progress from the front to the back of the garden.

Dish Garden: A group of bulbs can be planted together for an attractive dish garden. Dish gardens can contain all one kind of flower in different colors, or a number of different flowers like the garden shown here, which displays tulips, daffodils, crocuses, hyacinths, and *Iris reticulata*.

ture requirement, depending upon the climate where you live: an unheated garage or shed, a cold frame, a pit in the garden or yard, a wide outdoor windowsill, a closet with an outside wall, even a Styrofoam cooler or ice chest set on a deck or balcony against a wall of the house or apartment. If you live where winters are mild, you can use your refrigerator to give hardy bulbs the necessary cold period.

No matter where bulbs are placed for outdoor cold treatment, plan to insulate the pots when winter temperatures drop below the minimum requirement. Never allow the bulbs to freeze. Suitable insulation materials include multiple wrappings of newspaper, burlap, shredded Styrofoam or styrene, earth, hay, evergreen boughs — anything that helps retain warmth and is easily removed when you periodically check the progress of the bulbs.

Bulb soil should remain moist to the touch, which may mean watering about once a week. If they receive rain, bulbs stored outdoors will probably not need watering.

Since the weather in all but southern climate zones will grow increasingly cold and unpleasant for outdoor activities, try to locate your cold storage area as close to the house as possible. Be sure you can get the pots out of storage when the forcing period is over. Window wells are ideal and among the most accessible locations for a small number of pots. However, even though window wells provide ready access and the necessary cold, you must still mulch the pots to protect bulbs from freezing. Leaves you rake in the fall are fine for this because they are lightweight and allow penetration of air and water.

If you have only a few pots, they can be stored in a deep box placed on the ground or on a deck against a wall of the house. The box should be deep enough to allow several inches or centimeters of mulch on top and around the pots.

For a large number of pots, a cold frame serves beautifully. If you do not have one,

Starting Bulbs in a Cold Frame: If you are forcing several pots of bulbs, an outdoor cold frame is a good place to provide the cold period. Spread a layer of gravel on the bottom of the frame, set in the pots, and fill in around them with several inches or centimeters of sand, coarse bark, or Styrofoam for insulation. Cover the glass top of the frame with tarp, burlap, foil, or a board to insure darkness for the bulbs.

you can buy one ready made or build one yourself. Ideally, the frame should be located in a cool, shady spot. Loosen the soil at the bottom of the frame, or, better yet, spread a couple of inches (approximately 5 cm) of gravel. Set taller pots at the back of the frame, shorter ones to the front, and fill in between them with three to four inches (8 to 10 cm) of sand or coarse bark or eight inches (20 cm) of Styrofoam for insulation. You also can cover pots with inverted pots, burlap, or evergreen boughs. Though not widely available, shredded Styrofoam is a most efficient insulator because it is lightweight, porous, does not freeze, and is easily removed when you wish to check the progress of the bulbs. Cover Styrofoam with screening, netting, or chicken wire to keep it from blowing away when you have to open the glass top of the cold frame to check the bulbs.

To insure darkness at all times for bulbs, (in order to simulate underground conditions), cover the glass with a board or tarp, tape it with foil, or coat it with greenhouse shading paint. Water regularly until severe cold sets in. Pots also can be covered with inverted pots taped so they will not fall off. This not only keeps the bulbs in darkness, but also protects the emerging shoots.

THE "TRENCH" METHOD

The traditional way to provide cold treatment is by leaving pots in a pit dug in the garden or under a roof overhang. This method comes closest to simulating natural conditions of growing bulbs outdoors. It entails more physical work at the beginning but less concern when the forcing process is under way.

Dig a pit wide enough to accommodate

The Trench Method: The traditional way to give hardy bulbs the necessary cold treatment is to place the pots in an outdoor pit or trench. The trench should be dug wide and deep enough to accommodate all the pots. Loosen the soil in the bottom of the trench, and spread a layer of gravel and sand to improve drainage. Set the pots on the gravel, water them, and cover with several inches or centimeters of sand or vermiculite. Cover with a layer of soil, and mulch with a thick layer of straw or leaves. Dig a small drainage ditch around the bed, driving stakes into the corners to mark the location of the forcing pit.

all the pots you intend to treat and six inches (15 cm) deeper than the tallest one. As you dig the soil, break it up as much as possible. Once you have prepared a pit of the required dimensions, loosen the bottom soil of the pit, especially if it is a heavy clay. You might have to spread a two-inch (5 cm) layer of gravel and sand to improve drainage.

After setting all the pots close together in the pit, water them well and cover them with three to four inches (8 to 10 cm) of sand or vermiculite. Make sure the material settles down between the pots to provide as much insulation as possible. Sand and vermiculite are loose enough to improve soil drainage. Then, on top of the sand or vermiculite, add six inches (15 cm) of loosened soil. Here again, shredded Styrofoam would be an ideal substitute because it is so lightweight. Mulch the pit with coarse straw or thick layers of recently raked leaves to prevent freezing and to equalize the ground temperature. Water the bed regularly until the first freeze occurs.

When you have set all the pots, dig a small trench around the bed to further improve drainage and facilitate removal of pots. Drive tall stakes at the four corners of the pit as a reminder of the pit's boundaries. Should snow drift over the pit, clear it away as soon as possible. Keeping the pit uncovered in this way will make your job easier at the end of the cold treatment period when you must dig down to pry out the pots.

After no more than 13 weeks (December first if you started September first), dig down carefully into the side of the trench with a digging fork. Loosen two or three pots on the outer edge of the bed and check for roots and green shoots that have reached two to three inches (5 to 8 cm) in height. Roots begin to develop in the fall as soon as bulbs are planted. After 13 weeks of cold storage, roots should be coming out of the bottom of the pot. If, by chance, some shoots are frozen, do not touch them. Move the bulbs to a moderately warm spot (about 50°F/10°C) where the roots and shoots can thaw slowly.

COLD STORAGE IN APARTMENTS

There are still other ways to provide the cold treatment. One of the best methods is to use the refrigerator, which normally ranges in temperature from around 36° to 38°F (2° to 3°C). With a little perseverance, you undoubtedly can clear enough space to make room for two or three pots of bulbs for three months. Cover them with aluminum foil or inverted pots to block out light and help keep soil moist. Check periodically to make sure the soil does not dry out.

A GUIDE TO FORCING HARDY BULBS

Up to this point your potted bulbs have been doing the same thing as bulbs planted in the outdoor garden. The latter will continue to grow slowly until their normal flowering time in spring. But you are hurrying along your potted bulbs by forcing them to speed up their activity and bloom two to four months ahead of their outdoor counterparts. In a sense you are providing spring weather earlier.

The procedure is simple. When the cold period is over, bring the potted bulbs to a place where the temperature ranges from 55° to 65°F (13° to 18°C). The area should be well ventilated without exposure to direct sunlight. Some artificial light for brief periods is acceptable.

This period of forcing lasts from two to four weeks, depending on the kinds of bulbs used. Some *Tulipa* cultivars take longer than others for stem elongation and coloring. It is a good idea to give bulbs newly brought in from the cold half-light for a week until the shoots turn green. The flowers will stay in bud form longer if the temperature remains at 50° to 55°F (10° to 13°C). A five-degree rise in temperature during the day encourages slow opening of the flowers and is perfectly acceptable to the well-being of the bulbs. But temperatures above 70°F (21°C) will reduce overall plant quality and duration of flowering. Keep the bulbs away from radiators, stoves, and other heat sources, and out of drafts.

During the forcing period check pots frequently to make sure the soil is moist. If you notice that any shoots have pulled up the tunic (brown skin) of the bulb, remove it carefully to allow the foliage to open naturally.

When the flowers begin to open, always keep them away from any heat sources. The cooler you keep flowers, the longer they will last.

Continue to keep the pots well watered. You have flowers in full bloom with an extensive root system in a confined space, both demanding moisture. Water when the soil surface starts to dry out. Do not wait for the flowers to wilt, which is too drastic a signal for watering. Feed the plants only if you intend to plant the bulbs outside the following fall. The nourishment contained within them will carry bulbs through their first season, but is inadequate for future growth.

If clay pots do not please your aesthetic sense, place them inside decorative ceramic containers as described earlier.

When the flowers fade, cut off blooms, but leave the stems and leaves to help feed the bulb. If you plan to plant the bulbs outdoors for the following season, fertilize them when you first pot them up and again in the spring when you transplant them to the garden. They will bloom again in a year or two, but the flowers will be smaller than the first time around. Hardy bulbs cannot be forced indoors a second time.

SOME POPULAR HARDY BULBS TO FORCE

Here is a summary of the color, flowering time, and special requirements of some of the more popular hardy bulbs available on the market. All have been tested at Michigan State University for suitability for forcing.

The lists are by no means complete; you may enjoy experimenting with some of your own garden favorites.

TULIPS

Tulipa hybrids are available for early, midseason, and late bloom. Because midseason varieties generally overlap the early and late ones, you can have continuous blooms over a period of several weeks. Early-blooming tulips generally are shorter stemmed than late-blooming types.

Tulips for Forcing

Cultivar	Color	Flowering Time
Bing Crosby	Red	Early and late
Charles	Red	Early
Danton	Red	Early and late
Olaf	Red	Early and late
Paul Richter	Red	Early
Prominence	Red	Early to midseason
Stockholm	Red	Early
Bellona	Yellow	Early and late
Hibernia	White	Early and late
Christmas Marvel	Pink	Early
Peerless Pink	Pink	Late
Preludium	Pink	Early
Invasion	Red, edged white	Late
Golden Eddy	Red, edged yellow or cream	Late
Karel Doorman	Red, edged yellow or cream	Early
Kees Nellis	Red, edged yellow or cream	Early
Madame Spoor	Red, edged yellow or cream	Early
Thule	Yellow with red	Early

Tulips: *Tulipa* cultivars are available in a wide range of colors and color combinations. If tulip bulbs are planted with the flat sides against the side of the pot, the leaves and flowers will turn out from the pot as shown here, to make a more attractive display.

DAFFODILS AND NARCISSUS

Although daffodils and narcissus are very similar in appearance, narcissus flowers are usually considered to have a shallower cup than daffodils. *Narcissus* cultivars are forced best at about 63°F (17°C). At this temperature, stems remain short enough not to require staking. Since daffodil bulbs are large, use pots no smaller than six inches (15 cm). Be sure to select double-nosed bulbs for the most effective display.

Daffodils and Narcissus: *Narcissus* hybridize in nature, and there are hundreds of named cultivars available in varying shades of white, yellow, and orange. The flowers take a number of different forms — there are trumpet types, large- and small-cupped types, double-flowering blooms, and unusual hanging blossoms.

Narcissus for Forcing

Cultivar	Color	Flowering Time
Trumpet Type		
Dutch Master	Yellow	Early and late
Explorer	Yellow	Early and late
Gold Medal	Yellow	Early and late
Joseph MacLeod	Yellow	Early
Unsurpassable	Yellow	Early and late
Magnet	Yellow trumpet, white perianth	Early and late
Mount Hood	White	Early and late
Large Cupped		
Carlton	Yellow	Early
Yellow Sun	Yellow	Early and late
Flower Record	Yellow and orange cup, white perianth	Late
Ice Follies	Cream cup, white perianth	Early and late
Small Cupped		
Barrett Browning	Orange cup, white perianth	Early and late
Double		
Van Sion	Yellow	Late
Cyclamineus		
February Gold	Yellow	Early and late

HYACINTHS

Hyacinthus is the easiest of the hardy bulbs to force into bloom. Pot several bulbs singly in four-inch (10 cm) pots to perfume different parts of the house, or plant them in groups of three or five in larger pots. Space them about ½ inch (13 mm) apart—farther apart than tulips.

You also can grow hyacinths in water in special glasses that resemble cut-off hour-glasses. They are available at most places that sell bulbs. If you can find treated bulbs, no cold storage is necessary, but they are gen-erally found only at wholesale bulb suppliers. Treated bulbs have been harvested early and stored under cool temperatures so they are ready to bloom when purchased.

For bulbs that have not been treated, fill the glass with water to barely touch the basal plate of the bulb, and set the bulb in the top half of the glass. Put glass with water and bulb in a cool closet. If no such place exists in your home, put the glass with water and bulb in a foil ice cream bag, tie the top to keep the bulb in darkness, and put it in the refrigera-

Hyacinths: Noted for the pervasive fragrance of their flowers, *Hyacinthus* cultivars are the easiest hardy bulbs to force into bloom. They can be forced in a pot, as shown here, or in water in a specially shaped glass. Hyacinths bloom in varying shades of red, pink, blue, white, and purple.

Hyacinths for Forcing

Cultivar	Color	Flowering Time
Jan Bos	Red	Early
Amsterdam	Pink	Early and late
Anne Marie	Pink	Early
Lady Derby	Pink	Early
Marconi	Pink	Late
Pink Pearl	Pink	Early and late
Bismarck	Blue	Early
Blue Giant	Blue	Late
Blue Jacket	Blue	Late
Delft Blue	Blue	Early to midseason
Marle	Blue	Late
Ostara	Blue	Early and late
Perle Brillante	Blue	Midseason
Carnegie	White	Midseason to late
Colosseum	White	Early
L'Innocence	White	Early
Madame Kruger	White	Early and late
Amethyst	Violet	Late

Some Other Hardy Bulbs for Forcing

Cultivar	Color	Flowering Time
Crocus		
Flower Record	Purple	Midseason to late
Remembrance	Purple	Early and late
Victor Hugo	Purple	Early and late
Joan of Arc	White	Early and late
King of the Striped	Striped	Early and late
Pickwick	Striped	Early and late
Yellow	Yellow	Late
Iris reticulata		
Harmony	Blue	Early and late
Hercules	Purple	Early and late
Muscari		
Early Giant	Blue	Early and late

tor. Check it after a few weeks. When the sprout is roughly four inches (10 cm) high, bring the glass into any part of the house that is out of direct sun. Roots will curl around the bottom of the glass. At all times, the water in the glass should barely touch the bottom of the bulb.

MINOR BULBS

Miscellaneous, or minor, bulbs are so called simply because they defy categorization. The varieties are too few to be discussed separately, like tulips, daffodils, and hyacinths. They are, however, extremely colorful in their fascinating diversity of form. In many cases they are more appealing than the larger and more commonly forced bulbs. This group

Branches Can Be Forced, Too

Bulbs are not the only available source of spring flowers in winter. Branches of spring-blooming shrubs and trees can also be made to bloom indoors from one to two months prior to their normal blooming time.

Pick branches you would normally prune anyhow, and cut those with plump flower buds — the fatter the buds, the better the blossoms will be. Remember that if you cut the branches too early, the flowers will be small and could even die; if you cut too late, though, you will not have blossoms until the branches would normally bloom outside.

Pussy willows are the easiest, and they can be forced in January, during a thaw. February, after a mild rain, is a good time to force forsythia and cornelian cherry. In March you can force a May-blooming lilac, or clip some flowering crab apple and you will have lovely pink blossoms in only three weeks. Try to cut branches during mild weather at about noon, when they are filled with sap.

Slit and scrape the cut ends of branches to about three inches (8 cm) up the branch. Or you can split the ends with a hammer. Then put the branches into water at 70° to 75°F (21° to 24°C) for 24 hours. Following this, they should go into a container of cool water and be placed in a shady location, such as the basement or garage or anywhere that the temperature is 60° to 65°F (16° to 18°C). Put some charcoal in the water to keep it fresh.

Three or four days later, move the branches to a lighter, warmer area (but not in direct sunlight), like a north windowsill. Once a week, change the water and cut about an inch (2.5 cm) off the stems. Charcoal should be readded, too. To simulate spring rain and humidity you can mist the branches with water at least three times a week — preferably every day. This will keep the buds full.

When blossoms begin to open, move the arrangement into bright sun. This will give the buds, and finally the flowers, good color. If you find your flowers blooming sooner than the date you had planned for, they can be retarded by moving them to a cool (55° to 65°F/13° to 18°C) place. To speed the process, place the branches in warm (100° to 110°F/38° to 44°C) water each day; let the water cool with the branches in it. Misting with warm water will speed growth, too.

Shrubs that blossom before the leaves appear (like forsythia) will force more readily than those with leaves that grow before blossoms. Remember, too, that the later the plant blooms outdoors, the longer it takes to force indoors; and the closer your branch-forcing approaches blooming season, the less time you will need for indoor forcing. Fall and early winter are too soon for forcing. The branches need a cold period before they will bloom.

Branches that can be forced fairly readily include apple (*Malus* spp.), azalea (*Rhododendron* spp.), beach plum (*Prunus maritima*), flowering cherry (*Prunus serrulata*), flowering dogwood (*Cornus florida, C. florida* 'Rubra'), forsythia (*Forsythia* spp.), and pussy willow (*Salix discolor*).

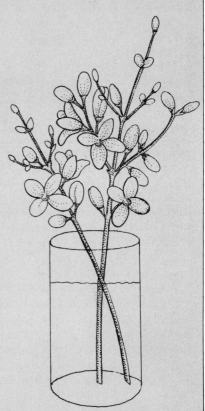

Forcing Branches: Branches of many spring-flowering trees and shrubs can be forced into early bloom indoors in a container of water. But timing is important — if branches are cut too early the flowers will be small; if cut too late, branches will not bloom any earlier than their normal outdoor flowering time.

Spring Comes Early: The graceful, short-stalked *Iris reticulata* can be forced into bloom to interject a welcome touch of color into the gray days of winter.

includes such traditional favorites as crocus, *Iris reticulata,* and grape hyacinth *(Muscari).*

Use at least a five-inch (13 cm) pot for the best show with these smaller blooms. It will hold about ten bulbs. Choose the largest crocus and grape hyacinth bulbs you can find because they will produce the most flowers. The procedure for planting these bulbs differs slightly from that recommended for major bulbs. Whereas the tips of the major bulbs are left exposed, minor bulbs must be covered entirely with one inch (2.5 cm) of soil.

A GUIDE TO FORCING FRAGILE BULBS

Fragile bulbs such as paper-white narcissus, amaryllis, freesia, ixia, sparaxis, ranunculus, and florists' anemone must be forced and kept indoors away from extreme heat and freezing temperatures. Fragile bulbs do best when given a rich potting mix and constant cool temperatures. The best blooms are produced when plants grow slowly.

PAPER-WHITE NARCISSUS

The easiest fragile bulbs to grow are *Narcissus tazetta,* the paper-white narcissus (which is pure white), a yellow cultivar of the same species called 'Soleil d'Or', and the Chinese sacred lily *(Narcissus tazetta* var. *orientalis).* You can force these blooms in soil in regular pots, but they are much more interesting and quicker to flower when grown in water. Use any ceramic or glass container that suits your fancy, providing it is at least three or four inches (8 or 10 cm) deep. Fill the container with pebbles (available wherever plant supplies or bulbs are sold) to within ½ inch (13 mm) of the top. The pebbles will hold the bulbs in place. Do not be concerned that the bulbs are sitting in water; it will not hurt this type of bulb. In fact, the opposite caution applies here — never allow the bulbs to dry out.

Set the bulbs about ½ inch (13 mm) apart and use as many as your container will accommodate. For best results put the container in a dark closet, check the water periodically, and remove the pot when some sprouts are up three or four inches (8 or 10 cm).

Paper-white narcissus grows fast. If your bulbs are planted during the third week of October, you should find them sprouted by mid-November, ready to be brought into light. Soon after they are moved into bright light, the pale sprouts will turn rich green. Within another two weeks, some of the bulbs will flower, emitting their special hypnotic fragrance. Because the paper-white narcissus performs so quickly, plantings should be staggered in order for you to enjoy blooms throughout the winter. After the flowers fade, discard the bulbs; they cannot be forced again. If you live in a warm climate, however, you can plant them outside in semishade, and they will multiply for years.

AMARYLLIS *(Hippeastrum)*

Another bulb easily grown indoors is the

Cure for Winter Doldrums: You don't have to wait for warm weather to enjoy a profusion of blooming bulbs. The fragrant paper-white narcissus is an easily forced fragile bulb, which sprouts quickly.

flower most people know as amaryllis (of the genus *Hippeastrum),* and the closely related belladonna lily (of the genus *Amaryllis).* To force these large bulbs into bloom, choose a pot twice the diameter of the thickest part of the bulb. Put an inch (2.5 cm) of broken crock or gravel in the pot to aid drainage. Bury two-thirds of the bulb in any rich and porous potting mixture. Water well, leaving the soil moist, but not soggy.

Keep the bulb in a cool, dark place and water sparingly for six weeks to two months to allow roots to develop. When the flower stalk appears, give it the brightest light possible, even morning sun, but do not subject the plant to high temperatures. As the shoots grow, increase the amount of water. It is best to place the pot in a dish of water and let the water soak up through the bottom. These plants are heavy feeders, and respond well to applications of compost or bone meal. You can expect the amaryllis to flower six to eight weeks after potting. There's no telling exactly how tall the stalk will grow.

All amaryllis bend sharply toward the light. Since you will not be able to keep up with them by just turning the pot, stake the tall stems to prevent them from breaking.

To prolong the life of the bloom, remove the anthers before they shed pollen and place the plant in a cool, but not freezing, spot.

What many people do not realize is that amaryllis bulbs will flower for many years. Do not discard them! After flowering has ceased, cut the stalk to about two inches (5 cm) above the bulb, making sure not to

Amaryllis: These big bulbs will produce large, striking flowers year after year if you treat them properly. When blooming has ceased, cut the stalk back to 2 inches (5 cm) above the bulb. Let the foliage grow until it yellows. Then cut off the leaves, stop watering, and store the bulb for 3 months. The forcing procedure can then be started again.

disturb the foliage. Stake foliage if necessary. Fertilize with bone meal and water regularly.

When the leaves begin to yellow, cut them off, stop watering, and store the bulb in a small container of vermiculite. After three months of storage, pot it up again. The amaryllis is as unpredictable as it is regal and majestic. If the foliage does not wither, do not cut it. Until the foliage does yellow and wither, keep watering and feeding the plant as if it had not stopped flowering.

Most likely, the bulb will not bloom twice in one year, but will open in early spring of the following year. Around late April when the ground is sufficiently warm, you can plant the bulb (neck exposed) outdoors. It should flower in midsummer. Feed the amaryllis once a month for the remainder of the season. Bring it indoors before frost and repeat storage care for indoor bloom.

FREESIAS

Although freesias are somewhat more difficult to force than amaryllis, their spicy-sweet fragrance and flashy orange and yellow hues are a delight.

Plant the bulbs close together, approximately eight to ten in a five- or six-inch (13 to 15 cm) pot. Set bulbs with their pointed ends up and cover with an inch (2.5 cm) of soil. You can start planting freesias outdoors in pots in September, or even August if bulbs are available. Plant them as early as possible because freesias need about five months to grow. Bring pots inside before the first frost, leaving them where the temperature does not rise above 50°F (10°C).

When growth appears, move the pots into bright light (morning sun is fine), water regularly, and feed every two or three weeks with mild all-purpose fertilizer. Because freesia stems are generally weak, they need staking. Continue to water regularly, even after the flowers have faded, until the foliage dies back. Reduce the amount of water, and set the pots in a cool, dark place where they can dry out until September. Shake soil from the bulbs' roots and repot them in fresh soil to start a new season.

IXIAS, SPARAXIS, RANUNCULUS, AND ANEMONES

Ixia, Sparaxis, Ranunculus, and *Anemone coronaria* (florists' anemone) are all handled the same way as *Freesia,* but each one has some characteristics of its own.

Ixias are so small that you can have a miniature garden in a five-inch (13 cm) pot. Though the stems look fragile, they are wiry

Ranunculus: These showy, long-lasting flowers bloom in many shades of yellow, white, red, pink, and orange, and look like large double buttercups.

and strong. Blooming in a vibrant array of red, orange, white, yellow, and pink, blossoms will close one night only to reopen the next day and stay open for several days. Ixias make lovely cut flowers, too.

Sparaxis could almost be called the "clown of the flower world." The blooms are multicolored, predominantly purple, lavender, red, white, and yellow, usually with a black band at the base of the petals and a contrasting yellow eye. Stems may need staking. They make beautiful cut flowers, but do not stay fresh as long as ixias.

Ranunculus with its waxy petals looks like a large double buttercup (to which it is related). The flowers bloom in yellow, white, red, pink, orange, and bicolors. Flowers are long lasting, both on the plant and in the vase. Because the flower heads are heavy, stems need to be staked.

Before planting, soak the tubers, which resemble masses of claws, in tepid water just long enough to soften them slightly. When you can dent them with your fingernail, they have been soaked sufficiently. Leaving them in water any longer might cause them to rot.

The florists' anemone produces red, white, or blue poppylike single or double flowers. No two of the warty tubers are alike, which sometimes makes it difficult to know which way to plant them. Some have a small point that indicates up; others have vestiges of old roots that indicate down. But no matter how you plant them, these tubers will sprout. Soak them before potting as you would ranunculus bulbs.

CHAPTER 19

Orchids

Truly the royal family of the plant kingdom, orchids stand at the pinnacle of development of the monocotyledons, the immense grouping that includes all those plants in which a germinating seed gives rise to only one seed-leaf. These highly evolved and astonishingly diverse plants are found on every continent except Antarctica and comprise the largest class of plants in the world, accounting for well over 10 percent of all the flowering plants in existence. The Orchidaceae number almost 1,000 genera and anywhere from 20,000 to 35,000 species. Because these desirable plants hybridize freely (the Orchid family is one of the few in which one genus may be crossed with another), there are also more than 45,000 registered hybrids. Despite this huge number of orchids, only about 60 genera are cultivated extensively; they are grown by an estimated 400,000 orchidists throughout the world.

This great plant family includes plants growing anywhere from a splash away from the sea to elevations of above 15,000 feet (4,500 m). Orchids may be less than ¼ inch (6 mm) tall—or over 20 feet (6.1 m) high. Their flowers may be as miniscule in width as ¹⁄₁₆ inch (2 mm) or as extravagantly broad as 10 inches (25 cm). They may, moreover, bloom in perfection in any or every season of the year, and for anywhere from a fleeting two or three days to a remarkable six or seven months. (Those genera or species that have flowers that are relatively small and short lived or which for other reasons are unsuited to commercial cultivation and are little used in hybridization are called botanical orchids.)

The Orchidaceae are wonderfully varied in all aspects of appearance and in their growth habits as well. Though most of the more widely grown orchids are prized for their glamorous blooms, about 15 genera—the so-called "jewel orchids"—are valued for their beautifully marked foliage. On the other hand, some African forms are without any leaves or stems. There are also several very rare Australian orchids that are almost entirely subterranean, and even a few semi-aquatic types.

Perhaps 80 to 85 percent of all the orchids in the world are found in the cooler rain forests and on the mountain slopes of the tropics and subtropics. The locales richest in these striking plants are the country of Colombia and that part of Asia stretching from the Himalayas south through New Guinea.

Orchids may have been cultivated in China as early as 2800 B.C. Collected by the royal families and nobility of both China and Japan, they were mentioned in the writings of Confucius, who was born in 551 B.C., and their culture was described in a book written in Chinese around A.D. 1000.

The first orchid from the New World is believed to have reached Europe in 1698, when a plant from the southern Caribbean island of Curacao was taken to Holland. Orchids proved difficult to grow from seeds, and by the second decade of the nineteenth century European horticultural firms were sending orchid hunters to the tropics, where they risked their health and their lives to bring back plants that were eagerly sought by wealthy and sometimes royal patrons. Interest in these magnificent plants continued to grow although (or perhaps because) orchids that did not perish in transit usually expired promptly in the overheated or underheated, badly ventilated greenhouses of that time, which were warmed by the burning of solid fuel and/or by underground flues. The advent of the cleaner, more even heat provided by hot water circulating through cast-iron pipes, the gradual accumulation of cultural

Opposite, lady slipper orchid, Paphiopedilum *species.*

information on orchids, and the discovery that they could be hybridized readily to create even more beautiful specimens gave impetus to the orchid-hunting craze, which reached its feverish zenith in the interval from the mid-1850s to World War I. During those years new orchid varieties became status symbols among wealthy Victorians, and to meet the demand intensely competitive agents from such famous orchid dealers as James Veitch and Frederick Sander engaged in elaborate strategies of foreign intrigue and espionage to outwit and outrace their rivals.

Scouring the jungles for new orchids, these collectors returned to England with as many as 30,000 plants of a single species—plants that were sold at auction within hours of their arrival.

The wholesale despoliation of orchids and their habitats inevitably depleted the supply of plants and helped end the heyday of orchid hunting by World War I. In recent years international laws have been drafted with the intent of protecting orchids from the excesses of collectors. (See Orchid Hunters: Lost in the Jungle.) New species continue to

Growing in the Wilds of El Salvador: Securely perched high in a tree, with its roots clinging to a limb, this *Epidendrium* thrives under the light, temperature, and moisture conditions of its tropical locale.

Orchid Hunters: Lost in the Jungle (of Red Tape)

"I'm 62 years old, and ready to go to the jungle again anytime," boasts orchid fancier Elvin Faust, an Allentown, Pennsylvania, native whose hobby has taken him to some pretty exotic locales. In 1971, it took him to the Peruvian wilderness.

Faust's party flew from Lima to Iquitos, on the Amazon River, then went by river steamer down the winding estuary to a crude riverbank shelter. Early each morning, they set out in small flat-bottomed boats in search of wild orchids.

"We'd head up one of the little tributaries, and as soon as we'd land, everybody would scatter into the jungle looking for orchids," he recalls. "Some people thought they'd find them hanging around everywhere, but you've got to search for them in the trees. The humidity and heat were incredible; as soon as we got out of the boats we were soaking wet."

Faust's reward for his sweaty adventure was several fine additions to his growing collection of orchids and a new understanding of the natural habitat of the brightly colored epiphytes. He also made a friend, professional orchid hunter and guide Fred Fuchs, who calls his Naranja, Florida, orchid business "just an overgrown hobby," but speaks with pride of his long association with Latin American horticulturists and orchid fanciers. His ability to take neophytes like Faust into the jungle and "bring 'em back alive," with orchids, has turned his hobby into a thriving business. In recent years, though, government regulations have made his job a bit tougher.

In accordance with a decision

be discovered in little-explored places—often by professional expeditions sponsored by scientific institutions and governments.

ORCHID BOTANY

As intricate as they are appealing, orchid plants vary widely in growth habit and in structure, both of which furnish direct clues to the environment an orchid comes from and to its cultural needs and preferred modes of propagation. Because individual orchids ex-

hibit such a high level of adaptation to incredibly wide-ranging locales, they can be classified and described in terms of any or all of several different characteristics. They may, for example, be epiphytic or terrestrial—or somewhere in between.

Nearly all orchids originating in the temperate zone are ground growers, but most tropical species are epiphytic; that is, they are nonparasitic plants which grow above the ground, taking nutrients and moisture from the surrounding environment instead of from the soil. Containing storage organs to sustain

---

of the 49-nation Convention on International Trade in Endangered Species of Wild Flora and Fauna, implemented in this country by the Endangered Species Act of 1973, orchid importation has been greatly restricted. Although traffic in only seven certified endangered species has been banned outright, the law states that all orchids brought into this country must be accompanied by a permit from the country of origin, stating that the specimens are not members of an endangered species. The resulting snare of red tape has enraged Fuchs, who sees orchid fanciers as preservationists, bringing rare species from the hazardous jungle environment to propagate and protect them. Fuchs admits that a few "armchair naturalists" have in ignorance actually lessened some species' chances of survival, but he insists that orchids are most threatened by the Latin American natives themselves, who are destroying the habitats as they strip and burn the land for farming. Because he and other plant hunters take only mature, well-

formed plants and leave seedlings and inaccessible specimens to grow in the wild, they claim they are not threatening any species.

On the other side of this controversy are scientists such as Dr. William Brown, Executive Secretary of the Endangered Species Scientific Authority, an umbrella committee comprised of representatives of various government agencies.

Although Dr. Brown concedes that private collectors are "probably right" in their assertion that they are preservationists rather than exploiters, he adds that conserving orchids in the wild is a more worthwhile goal than keeping them in greenhouses. "If what we're doing can aid that, it's worthwhile. I'm not really convinced that safari collecting does no harm."

Ironically, however, the regulations that were designed to protect orchids have resulted in the destruction of many thousands of impounded plants at quarantine stations. Late in 1978, United States Department of Agriculture inspectors who

had previously winked at documentless orchids passing through their ports of entry suddenly clamped down. In a few months, tens of thousands of orchids perished because there were insufficient facilities for their care. The *New York Times* reported in January of 1979 that 5,000 Guatemalan orchids had died in one day at the Miami station from lack of water. No one knows whether those plants were indeed members of an endangered species, though everyone is sure that they had no permits.

Waste like that angers conservationists on both sides of the issue, and may result in the adoption of a more workable system when the Convention next revises the list. Until then, professional and amateur collectors must hack their way through a jungle of red tape nearly as impenetrable as their quarry's native habitat, and even though fanciers like Elvin Faust are "ready to go . . . anytime," they may find that locating orchids is the easiest part of the trip.

them through short or long dry spells, epiphytes are accustomed to nearly drying out before they receive moisture. They attach themselves to their perches with adventitious roots arising from nodes on their stems. Some epiphytic orchids also put forth aerial roots which extend into the air and play an important role in the absorption of dew and rain and of minerals carried in such water. Contributing greatly to the absorptive power of the epiphytic orchid's roots is a thick, loose, spongy outer membrane called the velamen. The cells of multiple-layered corky outer tissue also furnish a habitat for a highly specific beneficial fungus, which in return provides a nourishing substance to the orchid. (These root fungi, or mycorrhizae, are present in most, perhaps all, orchids in their native environment and are believed necessary to germination and growth. It is not known, though, whether mycorrhizae are essential to the health of mature orchids.) As their root structure suggests, although epiphytic orchids may "roost" on trees or shrubs or even on rocks (in which case they are more correctly called lithophytic), they derive virtually no direct nourishment from the supporting object.

Terrestrial orchids, on the other hand, grow with their roots in soil or in the loose layer of humus which covers the floor of tropical jungles; the roots so housed range in structure from thin and fiberlike to fleshy and tuberous. Terrestrials often lack organs for the storage of water and nutrients and cannot survive drying out. A ground-growing orchid usually has a stem that is upright or ascending and one or more leaves which, like those of the epiphytes, can vary greatly in shape and texture although they almost always have parallel veins. Foliage is often folded or plicate (folded in a fanlike way) and frequently in the form of a basal rosette.

There are intergrades between epiphytic and terrestrial, and orchid specialists often make reference to semiterrestrial or semiepiphytic plants. Moreover, a single genus may include species ranging from quite epiphytic to emphatically terrestrial.

The members of this diverse family also may be evergreen or somewhat or completely deciduous. Some orchids from low altitudes near the equator grow apparently uninterruptedly year-round, whereas species native to higher elevations in the tropics or to cooler regions farther from the equator periodically lose some or all of their leaves.

Some of the most culturally significant variations within the Orchid family have to do with vegetative structure. In a minority of orchid genera—primarily those originating in Asia and Africa—the main axis of the plant is vertical, and growth takes place more or less continuously at the tip of the main stem (and sometimes in the form of offshoots usually arising from lateral buds at the base of the plant). These so-called monopodial, or single-footed, orchids come from places where moisture is relatively constant; therefore they grow continuously rather than seasonally and lack organs for the storage of water and food. Tending to be natural climbers with vining or vinelike stems, epiphytic monopodials often have aerial roots along the full length of their stems. When present, these roots grow from the junction of leaf and stem, as do the flower stalks. The leaves of monopodial orchids are arranged in two opposite ranks on the main stem and in an alternate fashion. Monopodials growing in shade may have relatively broad, succulent leaves and virtually no stems, whereas sun-dwelling types may be identified by their thick, narrow, moisture-conserving foliage and tough stems. Eventually the lower leaves of monopodials fall off; the plant may be given a new start by the propagation of a top cutting. Certain monopodials are also perpetuated from their offshoots. Orchid genera of monopodial habit include *Aerides, Angraecum, Phalaenopsis, Renanthera, Rhynchostylis,* and *Vanda.*

The vast majority of the Orchidaceae have the creeping growth habit so common among the monocots; having many "feet,"

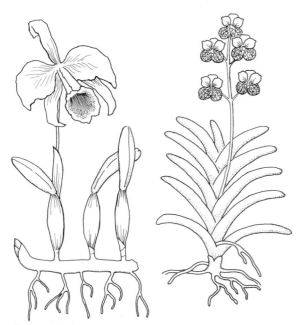

Basic Growth Habits: The sympodial orchid at left (a *Cattleya*) exhibits the characteristic lateral growth, whereby the plant seems to walk across the pot as it ages. The horizontal ground stem, called a rhizome, has a growing tip which sends up a new stem each season that will mature within the same season. Most epiphytic sympodials have pseudobulbs or swollen stem bases which store food and water for dry rest periods. The monopodial orchid at right (a *Vanda*) grows vertically, often producing aerial roots along the main stem. Lacking pseudobulbs for storage, this type generally grows year-round without a rest period.

these orchids are described as sympodial. They have a main axis in the form of a horizontal, rootlike, short to long ground stem called a rhizome. Actually a primary stem, this structure produces adventitious roots that grow downward and sends up secondary stems often termed branches. The vertical stem growing from the rhizome matures in a single season of growth, and one or more new sections of rhizome and stem (called leads) arise seasonally from one or more lateral buds, or eyes, on the growing end of the rhizome. In this way, sympodial orchids "walk" across a pot.

Though the stems of some terrestrial sympodials from shady, moist places are long, slender, and leafy (or very truncated, giving the plant a rosettelike appearance), most sympodials have stems of a markedly different character. Usually epiphytic, but sometimes terrestrial, these are the plants that dominate most orchid collections. They come from environments that experience dry intervals, and they possess stems in which the aboveground, green part is enlarged into a solid, often ribbed, specialized organ used to store water and food. Called pseudobulbs, these modified stems can be short and quite round or long and shaped like a pencil or spindle, or even jointed and canelike. Growing either along the length of the pseudobulb or from or near its top is one leaf, or less often, two or even three. These leaves are usually tough or fleshy, and have a waxy surface and recessed leaf pores that help to slow the loss of water. Sometimes, though, as in cymbidiums, the leaf blades in pseudobulbous plants are almost grasslike in form.

The flower sheath from which the flower bud emerges develops where the bulb and leaf meet, so inflorescences can be either terminal (arising from the apex of the plant) or lateral (coming from the base or side of the pseudobulb or from the rhizome). The pseudobulbous sympodial orchid sends forth its leads from buds at the bottom of the front, or lead, pseudobulb. In the great majority of these plants, a bulb will flower just once. In any case, in perhaps four years the old pseudobulbs at the rear of the plant—known as back bulbs—will cease to produce flowers, then leaves. Eventually they will shrivel up and die. Younger back bulbs are very often used in propagation by division.

The sympodial orchids are much greater in number and in variation of form than the monopodial group and include orchids that are native to the Americas, Asia, and Africa. Some of the more frequently cultivated sympodial genera include *Cattleya* and its allies, *Coelogyne, Cychnoches, Cymbidium, Dendrobium, Epidendrum, Odontoglossum,* and *Paphiopedilum.*

As complicated and variable as the vegetative parts of orchids may seem, their floral

(continued on page 386)

A Gallery of Orchids: Considering that within this single family, there are up to 30,000 species and countless hybrids, it is no wonder that there is a myriad of flower shapes and a rainbow of colors associated with the orchid. No other flowers catch the imagination quite the way orchids do, running the gamut from insectlike forms to the flouncing ruffles on a woman's dress. Assembled here are a smattering of flower forms, which can only hint at the fascinating variety which exists. Appearing on this page, starting at upper right and moving clockwise, is *Miltonia*, known as the pansy orchid for its flat, open-faced flowers reminiscent of the common garden plant. Along the same lines, *Anguloa clowesii* produces blooms which mimic another popular spring flower, the tulip; hence the common name of tulip orchid. *Brassavola* 'David Sander' juxtaposes stark, starfishlike petals and sepals against a frothy edged lip. On the opposite page, clockwise from upper left, is *Neofinetia falcata*, the samurai orchid, with its distinctive, spidery, arching spurs. One glance at *Oncidium*, the dancing lady orchid, and images of calypso dancers, swirling in brightly colored, full skirts come to mind. Contrasting with that image is the simple elegance and porcelainlike beauty of *Lycaste virginalis*.

parts are even more so. The glory of the plant world, orchid flowers are as unrivaled in their botanical complexity and variety as they are in their splendor. As the most sophisticated of blooms, they have a myriad not only of forms but also of aromas, which range from inexpressibly sweet to sharply unpleasant. Such diversification springs from adaptations made to accommodate many modes of pollination and to heighten appeal and accessibility to a host of pollinators such as moths, butterflies, bees, wasps, mosquitoes, ants, flies, and even hummingbirds and snails. But despite differences in appearance great enough to inspire such popular names as dancing lady or butterfly orchid *(Oncidium),* moon orchid *(Vanda),* moth orchid *(Phalaenopsis),* necklace orchid *(Coelogyne dayana),* nun's orchid *(Phaius),* and swan orchid *(Cychnoches),* all orchids share a group of unusual features related to their flowers and reproductive organs that are the defining characteristics of the family.

Orchid flowers are usually perfect (having both male and female organs) but are occasionally unisexual. They differ from those of most other plants in that they do not have male parts (stamens) separate from the female organ (pistil); instead the male and female parts are more or less fused to form a column, which can look like a cylinder or even like a bird or insect. There is one fertile anther, or less commonly two, at the top of the column or occasionally projecting above it. When there is one anther it is opposite the largest petal (a characteristic that makes orchids bilaterally symmetrical); when there are two anthers, one is on each side of the column. The stigma consists of three joined lobes, one of which often is in the form of a flaplike structure that hangs in front of the anther. This rostellum, as it is called, is covered with a sticky substance which picks up pollen grains from the hairs or fuzz of a visiting insect and helps assure transfer of pollen from the pollinator to the anther. (In most orchids, the grains of pollen are fused by a

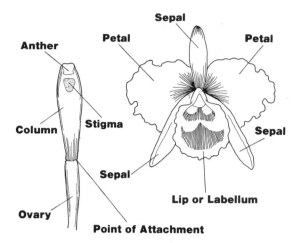

Orchid Flower Structure: The appealing orchid flower is composed of three sepals and three petals. One of these petals, modified into a lip, is usually larger and often showier and exhibits a form that differs from the others. The sepals (plus, in some cases, the petals or lip) are attached to the column at the area labeled Point of Attachment. The column is comprised of the fused male and female organs, joining together both pistil and stamens. A fertile anther appears at the top of the column, and contains the sticky mass of pollen grains known as the pollinium. Three joined lobes make up the stigma which is located below the anther. The ovaries lie beneath the Point of Attachment, in the upper part of the plant stalk.

clear, sticky fluid into an aggregate mass called a pollinium—another defining characteristic of the family.)

Orchid flowers usually consist of three sepals and three petals, which are usually separate. Ordinarily one of the petals is modified into the lip, or labellum, which is generally of a more vivid color and larger than the others, varying in form from a pouchlike shape to a flat or lobed structure, and possibly fringed or spurred—in short, a highly visible landing platform for a pollinator. In a process called resupination, which occurs in many orchid flowers, the lip twists into a downward position by the time the flower opens. The sepals of the orchid flower are often attached to each other, and they, or the petals, or just the lip, may be attached to the column. The ovary is inferior (that is, within the upper portion of the plant stalk below the petals and sepals), and the ovules do not develop into ripened seeds until several months to a year or more after fertilization.

Orchid seeds are phenomenally tiny—it has been estimated that up to 4.5 million of them are present in a single one of the capsules that are the fruits of the orchid. Disseminated by wind when the ripened capsule opens, only a relative few of the seeds make their way to the highly specific conditions needed for germination and growth. The odds against their survival must be increased enormously by the fact that the miniscule outcasts are completely lacking in stored food that can be used for the development of the embryo. This absence of an endosperm is another in the combination of unusual features that distinguish the Orchid family.

THE ENVIRONMENTAL REQUIREMENTS OF ORCHIDS

The complex botany of orchids underscores the fact that these sophisticated plants are very highly adapted to unique conditions. Unlike the members of less specialized families, which flourish in a variety of soils and can adjust to a wide range of climatic conditions, each orchid species thrives within a narrow set of parameters. Fortunately, these environmental limits are well known, and the gardener who wishes to grow a few orchid plants has only to get an idea of what to look for in the way of suitable orchid environments, to research available conditions that may be within the necessary limits, and then to select an orchid plant with compatible environmental needs. Of course, we gardeners sometimes fail to do this. We see a plant that is irresistible. We buy it and rush home with it, and then, while it languishes, we move it from pillar to post hoping to find conditions under which it will thrive. That's not the way to do it, especially with orchids. Define your conditions first, and then select plants which will grow in the environment you can supply.

Right away, as an indoor gardener you can exclude the North Temperate Zone species. Quite a large number of orchid species are native to areas where winters are cold and snowy; probably there are several kinds of orchids growing wild in every state of the United States. None of these make suitable house plants, however, for they need total winter dormancy brought on by cold soil, cold air, and short days.

The orchids most suitable for indoor culture are from the vast number of genera native to subtropical and tropical zones. Just because these grow where there is no true winter dormancy does not mean that they all thrive on high temperatures or that they all can adapt to commonly available indoor conditions. It is luckily true, however, that a surprising number of splendid orchids can prosper under conditions fairly different from those they experience in nature. For example, the large-flowered cattleyas and their relatives are apt to be found wild in Venezuelan or Colombian Andes rain forests at altitudes from 4,000 to as much as 7,000 feet (1,200 to 2,100 m). Close to the equator, such places have a daylength that stays at about 12 hours throughout the year. Night temperatures hover between 55° and 62°F (13° and 17°C), while days are about 10°F (6°C) warmer, and the sunlight, like all mountain sunlight, is intense (these orchids often grow just under the leafy canopy of the uppermost twigs of trees, receiving dappled sunlight). While the humidity remains high day and night, there is a brief daily shower at midday, which sends it even higher. The air is very fresh.

There is no way to duplicate this sort of environment indoors, but amateur orchidists in increasing numbers are discovering that a home greenhouse set up to approximate the needs of this group of large-flowering orchids can produce plants which often flower better than their wild counterparts. A host of orchid groups in addition to the cattleyas are well suited to life in the greenhouse, though ideal conditions there vary for each group.

If growing orchids in a plant room, or even on a windowsill or in a basement, is more to your liking (or necessity), that too is possible if you select plants carefully. You have only to confine your collection to the species and hybrids able to adapt to conditions inside the home. Indeed, respectable success in the house can be achieved even with cattleyas, though the number of spikes and flowers will be fewer than what is obtainable in a greenhouse.

TEMPERATURE

The ideal temperature ranges for the culture of various orchids have traditionally been defined in terms of greenhouses intended to provide the most suitable conditions for growing and flowering them. These orchid houses are described and differentiated in terms of the ideal minimum nighttime temperature to be maintained in a structure located in the North Temperate Zone. Three categories are commonly recognized, but all have in common night temperatures at least 5°F (3°C) and preferably 10°F (6°C) lower than those reached during the day. Maintaining this diurnal difference is critical to success with the great majority of orchids, and growers should, if necessary, turn down heat at night to assure that the temperature differential is maintained during any extended periods of cloudiness when daytime temperatures do not rise as high as usual. The fourth greenhouse category is an exception to this rule and is intended solely for orchids in the genus *Odontoglossum* and its close relatives.

In the warm, or East Indian, house, sometimes called a stove house, night temperatures in winter ought not to fall below 65°F (18°C), and there should be a winter daytime rise of at least 5°F (3°C) even on cloudy days. In summer, this house should have a night temperature of 65° to 70°F (18° to 21°C). It will heat up, perhaps to 85°F (29°C) by early afternoon on a sunny day. (Measures described under Keeping Cool in Summer, in chapter 29, may be required to keep the temperature from going much higher when outside temperatures soar.) Orchids which grow in the warm greenhouse originate in tropical climates no great distance above sea level. At first glance, it would seem that these are the orchids for the average home, but humidity, fresh air, and light requirements create problems. Some orchid genera for the warm greenhouse are: *Aerides, Angraecum, Catasetum, Cychnoches, Haemaria,* many *Phalaenopsis* species, *Renanthera, Rhyncostylis, Stanhopea, Vanda,* and some species of *Dendrobium* and *Coelogyne.* (Generally speaking, those species with mottled leaves prefer warmer locations in the greenhouse than those with solid-colored foliage; the rule does not apply to *Phalaenopsis* plants, however, as they all do best in warm temperatures.) The greenhouse growing of such heat-loving orchids is of course most feasible where winters are very mild—that is, in subtropical areas of the United States such as Florida, the Gulf Coast, southern California or along the southeastern seaboard as far north as North Carolina.

The intermediate, or temperate, greenhouse, has come to be synonymous with the old "Cattleya House." Orchids growing in this greenhouse are those that come from altitudes below 5,000 feet (1,500 m) in the milder parts of the tropics. They thrive at nighttime winter temperatures ranging from 55° to 62°F (12° to 17°C), and growers concentrating on plants suited to this range hold a night temperature of 55° to 60°F (12° to 16°C). Midsummer daytime temperatures ought to be in the 65° to 80°F (18° to 25°C) range—certainly below 85°F (29°C) if possible. For temperate as well as warm- and cool-growing orchids, temperatures that fail to achieve a relative drop at night cause plants to use up food reserves that should be saved for use in forming flowers. To assure good bloom, if the intermediate house is 58°F (14°C) on a winter night, through the day it should rise to 66° or 68°F (19° or 20°C). The same sort of day/night temperature shift is important in summer.

Orchids growing in the intermediate temperature range are, by and large, those most suited to the home grower, for this is the easiest range to maintain year-round in areas that are neither as warm in winter as Florida, other parts of the South, and lower California, nor as cool in summer as the Pacific Northwest or New England. One way to manage the summer temperature problem in extreme environments where very hot weather is common is to move plants from the greenhouse to an outdoor lath house with mist nozzles mounted overhead and connected to a timer-operated solenoid valve so that every few minutes through the strong-light hours a fine mist is produced to lower the temperature and raise the humidity. Orchids which thrive in the intermediate house include *Paphiopedilum* species with mottled leaves, some phalaenopsis, some coelogynes, and also *Brassavola, Cattleya, Dendrobium, Epidendrum, Laelia, Schomburgkia,* and *Sophronitis.* The last seven genera named here can grow in an epiphytic medium (as can *Cymbidium* and *Paphiopedilum* spp.) as long as plants are fed regularly. The flowers usually are showy, and mostly large. Plant breeders have worked with these groups to produce intergeneric hybrids such as ×*Brassocattleya,* ×*Brassolaeliocattleya,* and even ×*Potinara,* which is *Sophronitis* × *Brassavola* × *Laelia* × *Cattleya.* (Hybrids created by crossing four or more genera are given names ending in -ara.) The lists of named cultivars are endless, and prices range from very low to astronomical. Even the rankest beginner with an intermediate house can make a selection from this group of genera and produce acceptable blossoms on vigorous plants.

Warm Orchid House: Reveling in the warm temperatures are genera representative of those orchids which require ample heat to grow. In the foreground is a golden *Dendrobium,* in the middle a lilac-colored *Vanda,* and to the rear, a single white *Angraecum.*

The cool house maintains a winter minimum of 45° to 50°F (7° to 10°C) at night and 50° to 60°F (10° to 16°C) during the day. That sounds appealing when you are catching up on your horticultural reading during chilly winter evenings. There's that saving in fuel consumption, after all. The catch comes when you realize that these plants, which come from tropical mountain elevations of 5,000 to 8,000 feet (1,500 to 2,400 m) also want it cool in summer (they need 60°F/16°C, both day and night, although a selected few can tolerate a daytime temperature rise of a few degrees). Now, although cold winters can be countered by many heat-conserving measures (see chapter 29), noth-

Intermediate Orchid House: The conditions in this house are the easiest to maintain, and by seeing that the temperature drops during the night, you can be greeted by as rich a display as this during blooming season. Included in this house are *Cattleya, Epidendrum, Dendrobium,* and *Phalaenopsis.*

ing is more difficult or expensive than artificially cooling a greenhouse. This means, of course, that a cool house for orchids is most economically feasible in locations where summer temperatures are on the cool side, such as the New England states or the Pacific Northwest. Many of the species thriving under cool greenhouse conditions come from the higher altitudes of South and Central America. There is a variety of cool temperature ranges accepted by various orchids. Some *Cymbidium* species; all green-leaved members of genus *Paphiopedilum* and all species of *Phragmipedium* and *Selenipedium* (formerly grouped by horticulturists under the umbrella genus *Cypripedium*); all *Maxillaria* species; some *Oncidium* species; and others thrive at a winter nighttime minimum of 55°F (13°C) and a daytime rise of 5° to 8°F

(3° to 4°C), while some species and hybrids of *Cymbidium, Laelia, Odontoglossum* and *Oncidium* (Mexican kinds only), will tolerate a night minimum of 45°F (7°C). Daytime temperatures again need to be 5° to 8°F (3° to 4°C) higher. Most of the cool house orchids will tolerate intermediate house summer temperatures and, fortunately, most grow well in full summer shade, making it easier to give them a cooler-than-outdoor air temperature, especially in a lath house with daytime intermittent misting as described above.

The problem comes with odontoglossums and a few of their close relatives. To do really well, most of these absolutely beautiful Andean orchids must have a year-round, day/night temperature of 60°F (16°C), and a house maintaining that steady temperature is the fourth type of orchid house. Needless to say, holding such a precise temperature year-round is quite difficult. Fortunately, many of the more popular odontoglossums can tolerate some variations in temperature. Species such as *O. pulchellum* are capable of succeeding in a cool greenhouse, and more adaptable strains such as *O. bictoniense, O. brevifolium, O. grande, O. hallii, O. insleayi,* and hybrids (including bigeneric ones) can even be grown by somewhat experienced orchidists in cool plant rooms.

Growers who cannot locate more adaptable odontoglossums can grow their physically similar relatives, the miltonias. Although the more popular miltonias come from the mountains of South America and require cool house conditions, many of the lower-growing *Miltonia* species, such as the very beautiful *M. roezlii,* can succeed in the intermediate greenhouse if given excellent ventilation and kept out of direct sun.

If you want a widely varied collection of orchids, you can compartmentalize your greenhouse into two or more sections maintaining different temperatures. In larger greenhouses, partitions can be built in during construction or erected later by stapling plastic film to both sides of a lath frame made to follow the inside profile of the greenhouse. If separate thermostats for the different sections are impossible, heat can be boosted in temperate and warm areas by the use of electric space heaters or plastic-covered, mineral-insulated heating cables attached to the greenhouse side(s) with ceramic cleats.

For best results in northern latitudes, if a greenhouse has a north-south axis, divisions should be made from east to west; if the structure runs from east to west, it should be divided only once down the center to create a south-facing section that should be shaded in summer and a north-facing compartment that probably will not have to be shaded.

Even if you cannot provide the temperature ranges and shifts associated with an intermediate, warm, or cool greenhouse, don't count yourself out as an orchidist. Although

Cool Orchid House: The temperature is held down in this greenhouse year-round, to provide the coolness reminiscent of the tropical mountains where these orchids originated. Daytime temperatures should not rise much above 60°F (16°C); 45°F (7°C) is the minimum on winter nights and 60°F (16°C) is proper summer night coolness.

it is hardly a boon to greenhouse growers, the energy crisis has altered conditions in many American homes in a way that makes them increasingly suitable for growing orchids. Lowered thermostats mean that night temperatures in at least some rooms of many homes now dip into the lower 60s and upper 50s (Fahrenheit) during part of the year. Nighttime temperatures of 55° to 62°F (13° to 17°C) in the winter are ideal for such popular beginners' orchids as paphiopedilums and cattleyas. Consistently higher temperatures can result in weak, flaccid growth and delayed or skipped flowering. Although the equally popular phalaenopsis prefer night temperatures somewhere between 60° and

65°F (16° and 18°C) for rapid growth, a few weeks of 55° (13°C) nights will do them no harm if they are not kept too wet.

Daytime temperatures should be a bit higher, but few of the plants amenable to house culture need the stifling heat people usually associate with tropical plants. The genera just mentioned do fine in daytime temperatures between 70° and 85°F (21° and 29°C), depending upon the availability of light.

A Massachusetts gardener who cultivates orchids in several rooms of his city apartment, Joseph Levine accomplishes this desirable day/night temperature fluctuation economically in two different growing setups. In his upstairs living room, a large bank of south-facing Thermopane windows allows passive solar heating to control the temperature. On dark, gray days the temperature rises little above nighttime levels, allowing the plants on the windowsills to manufacture food slowly instead of forcing them into rapid growth when little light is available. On bright, sunny days, however, the temperature in the room can rise to over 80°F (27°C) with no help from the electric baseboard heating system. Following such bright, warm days, the temperature drops slowly back toward the thermostat setting of 55° to 60°F (13° to 16°C), aided when necessary by the judicious opening of a window or two at a respectable distance from tender plants.

In a smaller room downstairs are located several banks of fluorescent lights which provide the radiant energy for about half of the grower's collection. To put the heat generated by the lights and ballasts to work, the doors to this room are closed early in the morning, shortly after the plants have been watered and the lights have been switched on for the day. Small fans blowing along the length of the tubes keep air moving gently while distributing the heat throughout the room. The heat produced by eight 8-foot (2.4 m) tubes and twelve 4-foot (1.2 m) tubes (and their ballasts) is sufficient to raise the temperature

of the 9-by-15-foot (2.7 by 4.5 m) room to 80° to 85°F (27° to 29°C) by midday. The doors to the room are opened at about 6:00 P.M., at which time the same fans and convection currents quickly disperse the warm air to other parts of the house where it is greatly appreciated. In the spring, as the outside temperature moderates, the windows of the room are gradually opened—first at night and then in the daytime—to help regulate the room temperature. Even in a setup of this type temperatures vary from one part of the room to another, and the observant grower can place his or her plants in a manner which uses this situation to advantage. For example, paphiopedilums—which prefer slightly cooler temperatures than phalaenopsis—are placed on lower tiers of the plant carts, while the phalaenopsis grow on warmer, upper shelves.

Many growers help assure orchids of the beneficial nightly drop in temperature in summer by moving them outdoors to a lath house—a measure that also provides the dappled shade and moving air so vital to moderating the strong light and excessive heat of summer. Those orchids requiring cold periods can be left outside until autumn so they can enjoy lower temperatures than can be provided indoors at that time of year.

As Joe Levine's success with orchids in New England suggests, intermediate or even warm-growing types can be grown satisfactorily wherever the appropriate nighttime minimums can be maintained in conjunction with suitably higher day temperatures and where partial shade and excellent ventilation can be supplied in summer. In general, however, this type of environment can be most economically and easily achieved in homes in southern areas where less fuel is required to maintain relatively high day and nighttime temperatures in winter, and where orchids can be grown outdoors for much of the year. Living-room orchidists in colder areas who lack storm windows or double-pane windows, extensive artificial lighting setups, or other

Orchids under Lights: Depending on their temperature preferences, coolness-loving plants can be placed on the lower shelves of a light garden and plants needing warmer temperatures can grow on the upper levels, to take advantage of the natural temperature variation within a growing room.

ways of boosting daytime heat in winter will probably be more successful growing cool-climate Mexican orchids such as certain oncidiums, laelias, and odontoglossums and their primary hybrids.

AIR QUALITY

In growing many plants, the gardener's concern with the air around them centers on making sure that it is warm or cool enough. With orchids, however, there is a lot more to air management than just temperature. In their native environments, the air either sweeps across vast ocean areas or else is filtered and purified by jungle vegetation on tropical mountains. As collectors have discovered at sometimes great expense, orchids in captivity must have clean, fresh air.

Certainly air in the average dwelling, which may be polluted with everything from aerosol spray-can propellants to fumes from pilot lights and imperfectly vented stoves and furnaces, is not the best for orchids. Even greenhouses warmed by unvented heaters generally grow poor plants. Ideally orchids prefer clean, fresh, preferably outdoor air that is brought to the right humidity (and heated in winter to the correct degree)—the kind of refreshing air occuring in nature after a thunderstorm. It is certainly possible, however, to grow orchids successfully in a city or suburban environment, provided your air is not contaminated by leaking gas. The worst culprits are ethylene and a sulfur-containing odorizer added to propane; both these gases cause flower drop and other kinds of damage.

In addition to being relatively fresh and unpolluted, air for orchids must be in motion. To simulate the constant breezes which in nature help orchids to combat high temperatures and fungus diseases, and which provide ample carbon dioxide for use in photosynthesis and plentiful oxygen for the use of root fungi, many orchid enthusiasts install air circulators. These slow-moving fans keep the air gently stirred. In a plant room a cold water humidifier often produces about the same results, adding essential moisture to the air at the same time. Good air circulation for plant tops and roots also is promoted by keeping orchids about one inch (2.5 cm) apart and elevating potted specimens on some form of grid or mesh over trays.

HUMIDITY

Humidity is another factor that must be closely regulated in orchid growing. Orchids grow best when the air around them is rather dry at night and moderately dry in the morning, becoming much moister as the light intensity peaks about midday. While each species has its own optimums, most growers providing intermediate house conditions shoot for a night humidity of about 55 percent in winter and about 80 percent in summer; in the morning, humidity will tend to drift upward as the light increases because the plants themselves will give off a bit of water and the increasing warmth created by added light will step up evaporation slightly. In early morning, humidity can and should be held slightly above the nighttime level by admitting fresh outside air—without allowing any drafts to reach the plants. In late morning a light misting of foliage—and in greenhouses, of staging or benches and walks—raises the humidity.

A humidity of 80 to 100 percent while you are actually misting the plants or surroundings is practical for a sunny day. More water may be applied later, just after noon. The humidity is allowed to slip back down gradually as light declines in late afternoon, and the air allowed to dry out even more as darkness approaches. The drop in humidity overnight is particularly important in greenhouses so that condensation does not form on overhead glazing and drip onto the orchids, which cannot tolerate cold, wet conditions and water standing on their leaves. Such dripping can be a common problem, especially in the southern United States, and most greenhouse growers have fans or evaporative coolers to help combat it. It also is desirable to install drip gutters to catch and carry off condensation and/or to stretch a layer of plastic film far above the plants to intercept falling drops of water.

Managing humidity during winter months is not difficult if you have a lot of automation in your greenhouse or plant room, or a lot of time to devote to your plants. For windowsill gardeners, however, maintaining an optimum daytime humidity of 50 percent or more without steaming the wallpaper off the walls, warping furniture, or entertaining mildew can be a considerable problem. Many have found, though, that grouping plants on wire racks set over rust-proof pans or trays from which drainage water is allowed to evaporate creates an acceptable humidity of around 40 percent, which is usually adequate for orchids receiving the lower light levels common to windowsills or artificial light gardens. Another possibility is to place the potted plants directly upon layers of pebbles in trays. (Such setups will probably have to be at least partially emptied occasionally to prevent the large amounts of water draining from the plants from rising to the level of the pot bottoms. Also, the pebbles should be flushed occasionally with a weak solution of household bleach to prevent the growth of algae.)

LIGHT

Where orchids are concerned, light is a far less formidable problem than fresh air. Once you are aware of the light needs of a given plant, your job is simply to meet the requirement with natural or artificial illumination—or a combination of both. Most orchids grow relatively near the equator and therefore are accustomed in nature to roughly 12 hours of alternating light and darkness on a year-round basis to maintain a balance between the taking in of carbon dioxide and manufacture of food that occurs only in the light, and the cell respiration and multiplication which takes place primarily in the dark. The ideal of at least 10 hours of darkness every day becomes harder to reach as distance from the equator increases. But then, many other obvious and subtle environmental changes come into play when orchids are grown indoors and in regions other than those where they thrive in nature. Given the impact of such variables, which can be difficult or impossible to control, it is believed that in addition to diurnal changes in temperature and seasonal changes in temperature and watering, anywhere from 8 to 14 hours of darkness must be provided if orchids are to grow and flower properly.

Information as to photoperiodic requirements of the thousands of species and hybrids is far from complete, and prospective growers would do well to inquire on this score before buying seldom-cultivated plants that may have exacting light requirements. It also can be fruitful to experiment with short-day or long-day conditions (depending on the flowering season of the plant in question) if an orchid fails to bloom after it has completed its vegetative growth cycle. In cultivating orchids when days are being lengthened by nature or by artifice, remember to give plants relatively higher temperatures both by day and by night (always maintaining the critical diurnal temperature change, of course). Similarly, orchids experiencing short-day conditions should be given somewhat lower temperatures. These shifts occur more or less automatically for orchids grown in natural light, but more attention may be needed when artificial light or black plastic is employed to extend or shorten the days.

Gardeners relying on natural light to grow orchids in a greenhouse or home in the North Temperate Zone, where winter days are short and dim and nights are long, usually keep their plants on the dry side over the winter at temperatures toward the minimums for the species. As a result, the plants tend to rest. This is fine, except for the very desirable winter-blooming types that need shortening days as a cue for flowering. These should be covered with black plastic at dusk in the fall and winter if they are being grown where artificial light of any kind is present after dark. Needless to say, the farther north the location, the greater the problem in this respect and in regard to dim daylight with short-day orchids which make their flowering growth during the late winter and early spring months. Gardeners in such latitudes who prefer to work with natural light soon learn to concentrate on summer- and fall-blooming orchids.

Vandas and related species can be grown

Pebble Trays to Boost Humidity: The parched air of most homes can interfere with the raising of healthy, attractive orchids on windowsills. To counteract the dryness, set your plants in trays filled with pebbles and water, making sure the water never touches the pot bottom.

in greenhouses successfully as far north as the Great Lakes area across the United States. They do not do well in home culture north of the Carolinas. The exception to this is the West Coast, where almost anything can be grown almost anywhere. Phalaenopsis and paphiopedilums can be home grown reasonably well in just natural light at least as far north as Massachusetts, although protected summers outdoors do them a world of good. The crucial factor in natural-light-growing of orchids is not latitude but the number of sunny versus cloudy days during the fall, winter, and early spring. In central parts of the United States characterized by bitter cold but clear and sunny winter weather, there is no reason why home growers cannot do well with certain plants farther north than in the Northeast, where at least half of a typical winter is fogbound.

Growing orchids under lights is a satisfactory alternative for indoor gardeners in dim northern latitudes who want to grow winter-blooming orchids. Indeed, fluorescent lights will assure more consistent results with light-hungry types (such as cattleyas, most oncidiums and odontoglossums, and miniature and dwarf species and hybrids of many genera) in any location where days are often overcast and dim. Artificial lighting also makes orchid culture possible even in an ordinarily gloomy basement or in a room on the north side of a home or apartment. Whenever it is feasible, though, plants under lights should be placed near a window for optimum health and good looks.

Orchids depending primarily or entirely on artificial light seem to do best under a minimum of four 40-watt fluorescent tubes, preferably mounted in one fixture (though a two-tube fixture is adequate for low-light types like paphiopedilums). Tubes that are $2\frac{3}{8}$ inches (6 cm) from center to center are not too close to provide the flood of light that orchids require. The lights used can be either Wide-Spectrum Gro-Lux or a 2-2 combina-

Time for a New Pot: This *Laelia* has been well tended, receiving plenty of light and the proper care. It has responded with rampant growth, and in fact has outgrown its container. This can be remedied by repotting the plant after it is finished blooming.

tion of the less expensive warm white and cool white fluorescents. Such a setup should be arranged to provide the flood of multidirectional light that orchids and other plants receive outside but are deprived of on the windowsill and even in most plant rooms. Fluorescents are said to give best results with orchids preferring light of modest intensity—examples include paphiopedilums, some *Phalaenopsis* and *Cattleya* hybrids, ascocendas, and epidendrums and dendrobiums of smaller size. Used as the sole light source for basically shade-loving orchids, such lights should be between 12 and 20 inches (30 and 51 cm) above the plant tops; cattleyas and others liking strong light should be placed so their leaves almost touch the tubes, for such pseudobulbous orchids need 1,500 to 4,000 footcandles in order to flower. A distance of 6 inches (15 cm) or more from the lights is appropriate for plants also receiving natural light. Lights should be on at least 12 hours a day; better results with pseudobulbous plants have been obtained with up to 16 hours per day (the longer daylength helps compensate for the lower intensity of artificial light). To maintain some seasonal variations that help in controlling flowering, some orchid light-gardeners change their timers every two weeks to reflect the gradual increase or decrease in daylength occurring outdoors. A simpler approach that assures ample light periods/intensity but enough periodic increases to encourage blooming is reported by Gloria Jean Sessler in her book *Orchids and How to Grow Them* (see Bibliography). The idea is to provide 15 hours of light in January and February, 16 hours from March to August, 15 hours in September and October, and 14 hours in November and December.

Where electric lighting is not used, light management depends on the time of year and on what material the daylight passes through to reach the plants. In a glass-glazed greenhouse where the light-loving cattleya group of orchids is growing in the brightest area, and perhaps congenial lower-light species or hybrids are growing on the north side or partly under benches, all shading should be removed by late summer and the glass should be kept clean through winter to get maximum benefit from what light there is. But about mid-February, as days lengthen and the sun swings northward, shining down more directly, a bit of shading is needed. Where roller slat shades are used, they can be rolled down on sunny days about midmorning and rolled up again in late afternoon. An alternative to roller shades is to build and attach an ecliptic shade as described in Build Your Own Ecliptic Shade, in chapter 29. Designed to provide the dappled shade orchids love, this device may be left in place throughout the year and is self-operating.

The greatest need for shade comes with or shortly after the vernal equinox (March 21) when days become as long as nights and the sun is often at its brightest. Theoretically, as daylength declines and the sun slips southward, the shading ought to be removed gradually. As a matter of practice, it usually is maintained through July and August because it is needed to help reduce the temperature, but eliminated from September on to assure the higher light levels needed to harden the new growth and bring on flowering.

Many (but not all) orchid species destined for a greenhouse take kindly to the light transmitted through fiberglass and other plastic materials. (Exceptions tend to be the rare botanicals.) The quality of the light is considerably different from that transmitted by glass, for some of these materials admit at least some ultraviolet light, whereas glass is largely opaque to such rays. The results, however, are good in most cases. With plastic glazing, less winter shading is required, but more shading is needed through the brightest period of late spring.

Orchids growing in houses or apartments blessed with large, bright, draft-free windows should be placed according to their light needs and, if necessary, moved with the seasons. Plants with hard pseudobulbs, such as cattleyas, should be grown in south-facing windows for most of the year, although sheer curtains might be necessary to protect them from the midday sun during late spring and early summer. Softer-tissued plants such as phalaenopsis and paphiopedilums require less light and will grow reasonably well in bright north or east windows. If yellowing foliage signals too much light, transfer plants to less bright windows or install a very sheer white curtain between the plants and the glass. In no case pull them back into the room. The light is too one-sided as it is, even right in the window (which means that plants ought to be turned frequently), and light farther back in the room is even more directional. If the light in a given situation seems to be basically adequate except during the darkest part of the winter, the use of incandescent plant lamps can add enough extra energy to help the plants flower better.

Regardless of whether orchids are in a greenhouse, plant room, or living room, if there is one thing that orchid research has brought to the fore, it is the importance of giving these plants all the light they will tolerate. The stronger the light, within tolerance, the tougher the specimen and the better the quality of its flowers. But as the grower pushes his orchids out on the knife-edge of strong light, he or she also has to raise the humidity during bright light hours and supply additional nutrients. It also may be necessary to water more frequently.

In attempting to judge the intensity of light your orchids can tolerate, keep in mind this is correlated to some extent with temperature. For example, many of the cool-growing orchids, including green-leaved paphiopedilums, some oncidiums, and certain odontoglossums and their hybrids require considerably less light than orchids commonly grown under intermediate house conditions. On the other hand, some of the warm-growing sorts—especially the reed-stemmed epidendrums, and some Asiatic vandas and phalaenopsis—thrive in stronger light. Growers attempting to cultivate cool or warm orchids in the intermediate greenhouse adapt according to lighting conditions within the house. Paphiopedilums, for instance, may be placed partially beneath the bench (where it is cooler and dimmer), whereas epidendrums and phalaenopsis might hang near the glass, where it is warmer and much brighter. However, the strength of light needed varies not just among genera and species, but may differ for a single species at different times in its growth cycle. *Cymbidium* species, for example, ordinarily need cool house temperatures, but need even chillier night lows before flowering. On the other hand, *Cattleya* hybrids having *C. labiata* in their genetic background need warmer than usual night temperatures to initiate flower buds.

As orchids vary so widely in the amount of light they welcome, it is wise to monitor not just flower production but also leaf color to check on the appropriateness of your lighting arrangement for a given plant. As has been mentioned, bleached-out, yellowish foliage is an indication of too much light, whereas deep green, lush-looking leaves reveal that growth and flowering are being limited or prevented by too little light. If an orchid flowers regularly and displays light to medium green leaves which are shiny when new, you can be confident that it is getting the right kind and amount of light.

WATER MANAGEMENT

Watering orchid plants properly is made simpler when you have an understanding of their stem and root structure—matters discussed earlier under Orchid Botany. In greenhouse culture, where humidity is high, most orchid plants should be watered around the roots only infrequently. On dull, short, cold winter days epiphytes may go up to three or four weeks without water being added to the pot. If the approximate schedule for watering

comes around and the weather is gloomy, watering is put off until a bright, sunny day. Terrestrials need somewhat more moisture, but they, too, are watered only in bright weather, and only often enough so the medium never goes bone dry.

For neophytes raising orchids in the home, learning to water them properly may prove to be the most difficult aspect of indoor culture. The problems arise from the unfamiliarity of new growers with potting mixes used for epiphytic orchids, combined with the widely varying moisture requirements of various genera and the varying watering practices needed by different potting media. The low relative humidity in most home growing situations adds to the difficulty in estimating exactly when plants need a thorough watering (meaning that the entire pot should be totally drenched so that water runs copiously out of necessarily large drainage holes in the bottom). Growers with only one or two orchids can accomplish this by carrying the plants to the sink and rising them well with room-temperature water for a minute or so. As the collection grows, however, this method quickly becomes too time consuming. Because of the relatively large amount of water which goes right through the pots, standard pebble trays fill up rapidly and must be emptied, for orchids can *never* stand in water.

One way to assure doing this chore less frequently is to group plants on plastic or aluminum grids (old refrigerator shelves also work well) placed over rustproof trays or pans, where runoff water may be allowed to evaporate to provide more humidity or emptied when it nears the top of the tray. If you have a large collection of orchids, it may be worthwhile to install drains in the empty trays or those containing pebbles when they are set up. Flexible plastic tubing can be made to run from the trays into rubber buckets tucked out of sight under or behind light carts. Buckets of the right size will hold the runoff from at least one complete watering, and can be emptied at the grower's convenience. Since it is generally best to water orchids early in the morning—when most of us have schedules to keep—self-draining trays are more than worth the little extra effort it takes to set them up. With a little practice, you will find that you can even use a hose to water your plants. Just attach a good quality hose to the kitchen faucet and attach a shut-off valve to the business end, together with one of a wide choice of gentle mist and watering nozzles. To protect surfaces below your plants from splashes, overlap the lips of adjoining trays as best you can and place plastic sheeting on the shelves below. If necessary, more plastic may be taped to the very bottom of any windows near plants and arranged so any condensation forming on them after watering will run down into the trays or pans.

If you have reasonably humid conditions, you may choose to alternate a thorough flush-watering of the type described above with a heavy misting designed to wet the top layer of the potting mix well. The misting helps to maintain even moisture throughout the pot despite the fact that the top inch or so (approximately 3 cm) of loose bark mixes dries out almost overnight while the bottom remains wet for much longer.

A word of caution is necessary here in regard to misting: the water supplies in many major metropolitan areas contain large amounts of dissolved mineral salts. Repeated light mistings using water of this type lead to a gradual buildup of mineral salts on plant leaves and roots and on the surface of the potting mix. Although the leaves of orchids do not usually suffer from this treatment, their tender root tips are easily burned. Regular flush-watering will help to prevent this problem. Another aid in this regard—in addition to annual repotting—is a periodic drenching by a natural rainstorm whenever outside temperatures permit. The naturally soft and acid rainwater helps to neutralize and dissolve alkaline salts commonly found in city water supplies.

Depending on the combined effects of temperature and humidity at any particular time, most home-grown orchids in four- to eight-inch (10 to 20 cm) plastic pots do well on one thorough watering and one or two heavy mistings per week. Smaller but well-established plants in two- to three-inch (5 to 8 cm) pots have to be watched more closely, and may need watering or heavy misting every other day, depending on the nature of the potting media used. Generally speaking, plants without pseudobulbs need more water than those with them.

As previously mentioned, orchids do differ somewhat in their moisture requirements. Like most terrestrials, paphiopedilums like to be kept "evenly moist but not constantly wet" in a fine to medium grade of bark according to pot size (the smaller the container, the finer the medium). True epiphytes, such as cattleyas, on the other hand, need to be thoroughly watered and then allowed to approach dryness. That is, if the surface of the medium feels cool and moist, wait a few days, for the medium should be dry almost to the bottom of the pot before you water. There are exceptions, however. For example, phalaenopsis are epiphytes but lack pseudobulbs—they therefore prefer even moisture year-round, combined with a coarser potting mix than is used for "paphs" and other terrestrials. Also, epiphytes being grown with their roots entirely or mostly uncovered may need to be misted up to several times a day in very hot, sunny weather.

The watering practices just described are for orchids in active growth. Species and hybrids having storage organs above or below ground take rest periods at certain times in their growth cycles. The end of this inactive time is signaled by signs of new roots and growth. Depending on the structure of the orchid and growing conditions, watering either should be curtailed or stopped completely during rest, and humidity—and often temperatures—lowered somewhat. (Note: Hybrids generally take lighter rest periods than species orchids—especially when grown under lights—and all orchids growing in natural light will experience rest periods virtually automatically, since during the shorter, dimmer days and cooler days and nights of winter, photosynthesis and transpiration will naturally decrease and, as a result, fertilizing and watering will be done much less often. Growers relying partially or entirely on artificial light, however, may have to cut back on watering—and perhaps light and temperature—quite deliberately at a specific time or times in a plant's growth cycle.)

In some evergreen orchids with stems aboveground, the nongrowth period comes before flowering and is necessary to promote the satisfactory initiation of flower buds. Examples of orchids going into a prolonged rest and requiring little or no water during this two- or three-month stage are brassavolas, catasetums, coelogynes, cymbidiums, dendrobiums (especially the deciduous ones), pseudobulbous epidendrums, and oncidiums. The vandas, which are Asiatic monopodials with climbing stems, do not require a rest period, but will benefit from cooler and drier conditions before flowering. Other evergreen orchids having aboveground stems need a short to long rest period after their flowers have faded; these include cattleyas, laelias, certain odontoglossums such as *O. grande* and *O. pendulum*, and schomburgkias. Deciduous types sending stems above the ground take a complete rest after their foliage begins to die back, losing their leaves and sometimes their roots. These orchids need to be kept dry and on the cool side for several months and should not be watered from the time they put forth spikes of flowers until new growth starts. Plants in this category include the cooler-growing and more deciduous kinds of dendrobiums. These orchids (and cycnoches as well) actually lose their leaves up to six months before flowering and also need less water—in addition to cool temperatures—during that time to assure blooming. Other species requiring a cool rest from flowering to

the beginning of new growth are the deciduous forms of *Calanthe,* as well as the lady's slipper orchids native to the North Temperate Zone.

Certain stemless orchids such as paphiopedilums and phalaenopsis are without storage organs of any kind; during their brief rest period after vegetative growth stops, they should continue to be watered. Usually native to tropical Asia, such plants do, however, require less water and lower humidity at cooler times of the year.

POTTING MEDIA

The potting medium for an epiphytic orchid plant is intended largely for support, but it also gives the thick, brittle orchid roots a suitably aerated, humid habitat which will help root fungi to function effectively and also supply some nutrients to the plant. Most semiterrestrial orchids are highly specialized botanicals and they, too, can grow in an epiphytic medium (as can cymbidiums and the tropical kinds of Asian paphiopedilums and their American relatives) so long as a regular scheme of fertilizing is carried out. Orchid growers once largely used chunks of the tangled, wiry roots of the various *Osmunda* ferns, called osmunda fiber or osmundine, in the pots holding their epiphytic orchids. Some people still prefer this medium, and many orchid species which grow best with roots almost completely exposed are simply wired to a slab of osmunda fiber so that some roots penetrate while others grow outward into the air. Osmunda holds moisture longer than other media and has nutrients lacking in fir bark, which has come into favor more recently. Epiphytic plants potted in osmunda need little additional feeding and the medium remains in good condition for about two years. It does, however, hold considerable moisture and requires experience (and substantial amounts of drainage material) to support vigorous, healthy growth. If you repot a plant grown in osmunda to a bark-based medium, remember never to pack fir bark around a root ball containing osmunda, for watering practices geared to fir bark will rot the parts of the roots in osmunda.

Cheaper than osmunda and requiring less skill to use, modern potting mixes are based largely on chopped fir bark or shredded tree fern fiber, mixed with loose, inert mineral products such as perlite and vermiculite, sometimes with bits of osmunda. The idea is to have a coarse, friable, nondecaying medium which holds moisture with no trace of sogginess, and which allows free movement of air. For epiphytes such as ascocentrums, angraecums, brassavolas, cattleyas, dendrobiums, and phalaenopsis, you might be successful with a particularly airy medium consisting of fir bark of fine, medium, or coarse grade (the smaller the plant, the finer the bark), possibly mixed with chopped tree fern root. For coelogynes, miltonias, and oncidiums, try tree fern fiber or osmunda.

Choosing and blending your own ingredients for a satisfactory potting medium for epiphytic orchids requires an intuitive understanding of plants' requirements. For that reason, beginning growers usually purchase a prepared mix from a local garden shop or orchid specialist, or by mail.

Unlike epiphytes, terrestrial orchids can grow in a multiplicity of media. Many of them will prosper in the same fiber mixes used for epiphytes, especially the newer blended media, although supplementary fertilizing at fairly frequent intervals is required. Paphiopedilums also can grow well in the medium suggested earlier for cattleyas. It is also possible to work up a slightly denser potting medium for these or other terrestrials. Begin with 2 parts of a bark-based potting mix, and add 1 part of coarse compost and 1 part of old, decayed cow manure. Such natural ingredients really should be pasteurized as described in chapter 6, so again, you may find it easier to go to a local orchid grower and buy a prepared mix for terrestrials. The terrestrial

mix is handled much like the epiphytic mix. Plenty of broken crockery is used in the pot. It is topped by a layer of very coarse, fibrous compost, and finally the plant is placed in the pot, and the potting medium worked between and around the roots.

CONTAINERS

Commercial orchid growers tend to grow all orchid plants in top-quality, hard-fired, unglazed terra-cotta flower pots with large drainage holes or slots. Epiphytes do well in these when the pot is half filled with broken crockery for fast drainage and the potting medium is amply coarse. Terrestrials grow quite well in clay pots, too. If you cannot find terra-cotta containers with sufficiently large holes to assure good drainage and air circulation, you can enlarge the holes in standard pots by tapping away carefully with a hammer and chisel. For a more attractive effect, add your own holes to the sides of such pots by using an electric drill with a ½- or ⅝-inch (13 or 16 mm) masonry bit. As an alternative, evenly spaced slits extending from the bottom of a pot halfway up its sides can be made with a 10- or 12-inch (25 or 30 cm) hacksaw equipped with a tungsten carbide rod.

Because drainage so often can be a problem, amateur growers often cultivate their orchid plants in rather shallow redwood, cypress, or wire baskets or in the airy plastic baskets used to serve bread and rolls. Phalaenopsis often seem to do exceptionally well in baskets and species of *Stanhopea* always are grown in baskets with a coarse bottom grid because they produce their flower stalks downward, through the medium and the underside of the container.

Epiphytic orchids preferring some or all of their roots to be exposed also can thrive if placed on a rough-barked section of a tree limb or on weathered barnboard, cork bark, or slabs of tree fern root. For species needing moisture and nutrients, a handful or pad of potting material should be placed around or

Choose Pots with Plant in Mind: The blooming habit of this *Stanhopea tigrina* dictates the type of container that must be used. Because the flower stalks emerge from the bottom of the growing medium and project through the bottom of the pot, a basket with a bottom grid is needed.

under the roots. The orchids may be attached to the mounting and hung, if desirable, using nylon fishing cord and eye screws.

REPOTTING

Orchid plants are repotted only when they completely overgrow the pot or when there is evidence that the potting medium has deteriorated. The rate at which the mix breaks down is controlled by its composition, by the amount of water it gets, and by other environmental factors. This means, of course, that it is difficult to generalize about how often to repot. Usually, though, plants in fir bark should be repotted yearly, preferably in

spring, while those in osmunda can go for up to two years without deterioration. Also, monopodial orchids such as phalaenopsis may go without repotting much longer than sympodial types if the potting medium is in good condition.

Try to repot a given plant at the beginning of its growth cycle, when new growth is about an inch (2.5 cm) high and new roots are just starting to be seen above the potting mix. This usually happens in spring or early summer. If you must repot during a plant's rest period because of souring of the mix, new growth may be delayed. Well-established terrestrials like paphiopedilums may, however, be repotted just before new growth starts. Multiple-stemmed (sympodial) orchids grow more or less in one direction like an iris plant, and in potting them, the oldest part of the plant is backed against the rim of the pot so the growing end of the rhizome is about in the middle of the pot, and successive vertical growths can travel across the container. The pot is filled one-third to one-half with coarse, broken crockery and then almost filled with the potting mix, with the plant positioned so the top of the root crown is level with the top of the rim. Until new roots extend down into the medium to hold the plant upright, it is either staked or fastened down with bent pieces of wire. Single-stemmed (monopodial) orchids, which grow vertically on an upright stem, should be placed squarely in the center of the new pot; otherwise they are treated like sympodial types. In potting all orchids, tamp the mix down very firmly so it provides support for the plant.

In the greenhouse, newly potted orchid plants do best in slightly reduced light and increased humidity. Their foliage should be sprayed several times a day, but they should not be watered directly for seven to ten days. Watering should then be done lightly for two weeks or more—until active root growth is apparent. At that time, humidity can be reduced to usual levels, and artificial light can be used to give the transplant a strong start.

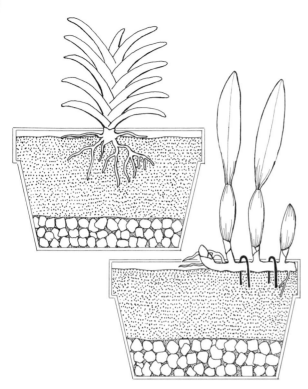

Repotting Orchids: Symapodial orchids with several stems should be placed with the oldest section up against the pot rim so the growing tip of the rhizome has plenty of room to spread and send up new leads. A monopodial orchid, which will add new growth vertically, can be set in the center of the pot. Both types of orchids require an ample layer of drainage material, on top of which can be added the appropriate potting mix. Plants should be set with the top of their root crowns level with the rim.

PROPAGATION

Repotting provides the perfect occasion for vegetative propagation. Cleanliness is critical to success in this matter, for disturbed orchid plants are subject to decay. Therefore, use only scrubbed and clean pots and broken crockery, and make sure clippers, knives, and other tools are shining clean. Many growers dip tools in alcohol after making each cut.

Methods of propagating orchids asexually are varied and most are readily used by amateur growers. The vast majority of epiphytes are sympodial and pseudobulbous; they and sympodial terrestrials with pseudobulbs develop many branches, or leads, from lateral buds on the base of the pseudobulbs.

Connected by rhizomes, these may be separated into divisions having from two to four or five pseudobulbs each. The larger the bulbs in each division and the greater their number, the stronger the new plants will be and the sooner they will flower. It can be a good idea to cut halfway through the rhizomes before new growth begins; the dividing can be completed later during repotting after new shoots have grown and put forth their own roots. This method will yield many divisions from large plants.

Some sympodial epiphytes or terrestrials (such as cattleyas, cymbidiums, and more problematically, odontoglossums) are propagated by removing leafless "old" back bulbs (pseudobulbs). The younger these bulbs are, the better; with cymbidiums just one back bulb may be potted up, but at least three are desirable to start a new cattleya. Back bulbs may be coaxed to send forth shoots and roots while still attached to the plant by partially cutting through the connecting rhizomes; when they are under way, they can be treated like divisions. Or the dormant back bulbs may be taken off at repotting and kept warm, humid, and shaded in either a new pot or a propagation box or in a plastic bag containing slightly moist vermiculite or sand and peat moss. They can be potted up after new growth appears. Some orchids generate adventitious growths, or bulblets, from their pseudobulbs; when these have developed their own roots, they, too, can be separated and grown on as new plants. The same is true of the buds that sometimes form on the tuberous roots of many terrestrial orchids.

Crown-forming sympodial terrestrials—that is, nonpseudobulbous kinds—may be pulled or cut apart into single rosettes after they have developed clusters; with paphiopedilums especially, chances of success are greater if you make sure such crown divisions feature at least three growths and their roots. Sympodials lacking pseudobulbs also can be multiplied from stem cuttings. The stems of reed-stemmed epidendrums and certain den-

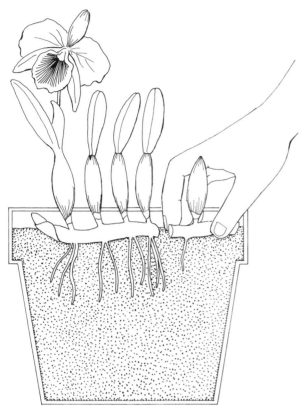

and will flower during their third year. Sometimes keikis can be induced to grow by removing the tip of the plant; the tip cutting itself can be rooted and grown on as a new plant—a procedure especially desirable as the plant loses its lower leaves with age. Sometimes phalaenopsis and related types produce keikis on old flower spikes; in fact, hormone paste can be used to stimulate keikis at dormant nodes on phalaenopsis spikes. Air layering is another method that is sometimes successful with vandas.

Certain sympodial and monopodial orchids may be propagated from adventitious growths that emerge from their flower stems. With *Phaius* orchids the piece of stalk with the latent bud can be cut off and laid in moist sand under a glass or plastic cover. Pieces without growths may be treated the same way in the hope of eliciting them. The same procedure can be followed with phalaenop-

Orchid Propagation: One method for gaining two plants from one calls for the removal of one or more back bulbs. These bulbs are the older leafless pseudobulbs from which new leads have appeared in successive seasons. To stimulate root and top growth while the back bulb is still attached to the plant, slice partially through the rhizome. Once this growth has started, the back bulb can be severed the rest of the way and potted up on its own.

drobiums break at the joints, and these sections can be placed horizontally on moist sphagnum; the long stems of climbing orchids may be cut into four- to six-inch (10 to 15 cm) segments and propagated the same way.

Given optimum conditions, monopodial orchids such as vandas, as well as the sympodial *Dendrobium nobile* and its hybrids, will generate plantlets with roots from latent lateral buds on the main stem. These side-shoots are called keikis. They can be cut off and repotted when they are about a year old

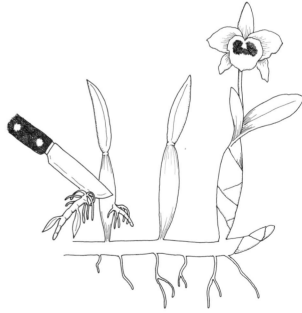

Propagation by Side-Shoots: The Hawaiian term for babies, *keikis*, has been incorporated into orchid terminology to signify side-shoots that develop from lateral buds on the main stem of some orchids. These little plantlets can be cut off and potted up when they are a year old; you can expect blooms in their third year.

sis, although, after blooming, plantlets may form at the nodes of flower stalks on these plants without such measures.

As the foregoing material suggests, good results are often had by amateurs using traditional methods of vegetative propagation. Also, the limited number of plants obtained in this way, and the fact that they can come to flower in two or three years or less and are sure to be genetically identical to the parent plant, make asexual reproduction the best avenue for almost all home growers.

FERTILIZING ORCHIDS

Feeding an orchid is just as important as fertilizing any other growing, flowering plant—perhaps more so for several reasons related to orchid structure and to the conditions under which these plants grow in nature. Most orchids are epiphytic, and although this means they are not parasitic, it does not mean that they derive no nutrition from their host plant. Orchids do not grow willy-nilly on any species of tree, but are actually rather selective in their choices. On the "right" kind of trees, there are often certain kinds of fungi living in the bark of the host that decompose cellulose into various nutrients that the orchids can utilize. Additionally, there is the phenomenon of nutrient-rich "leaf wash." Water that runs off the leaves of many kinds of trees is rich in nitrogen and other essential plant nutrients. This leaf wash often runs down the trunks of trees or splashes down onto epiphytes on middle and lower branches.

When an orchid is being grown in a pot of fir bark, however, the situation is completely altered. Not only are the proper fungi and the leaf wash missing, but also there are usually microorganisms in the bark that compete with plant roots for nitrogenous substances. For this reason, it is of more than usual importance to use a relatively high-nitrogen fertilizer that includes all the necessary trace elements as well in order to insure proper growth and flowering. To assure these

high levels of nutrients, major growers and most amateur enthusiasts with large collections use special feeding formulations intended for orchids. Fish emulsion is highly recommended as a periodic supplement to such inorganic products. Because this organic fertilizer also contains important salts in a readily usable form, it also can be used as the sole fertilizer on a monthly basis (twice a month if plants are potted in fir bark). The terrestrial orchids—cymbidiums, phalaenopsis and related genera, and others—can thrive on dilute manure tea (and on the nitrogenous fumes from compost or manure) if they are *not* being grown in fir bark, although the source and type of manure that is given as food should be changed from time to time to insure a more balanced supply of essential minerals.

As a rule, orchids are fertilized only when in active growth, and the more vigorous the growth, the more fertilizer may be applied. As this also is true of water, it follows that including a constant, minimal amount of fertilizer solution in an orchid's water supply is a reasonable way to balance fertilizer application against growing needs. The quantity of fertilizer to be used in a constant-feed program or the frequency of occasional fertilizings will vary from one genus to the next. So will the rest periods, during which fertilizing should be stopped.

Feeding requirements also are affected by where orchids are being grown, for light (and therefore, growth) levels vary in different environments. For example, windowsill plants are likely to need only half as much food as greenhouse orchids, and plants growing under fluorescent lights need perhaps half as much as those in a window. Plants summering outdoors usually need more frequent feeding than those indoors to help them cope with high night temperatures and the flushing out of fertilizer caused by showers.

Nutrients also can be applied as a leaf spray, for orchids have been proved to absorb nine times more of the nutrients in mist applied to their foliage—especially to the thin undersides of their leaves—than they do of the nutrients in fertilizer solutions applied directly to the growing medium. Be wary, however, of letting water with fertilizer in it pool in the crowns of crown-forming orchids. The presence of such fertilizer will increase the danger of fungal and bacterial rot, and the problem is especially acute with organic fertilizers. Used judiciously, however, and done only in the morning when temperatures are rising, foliar feeding is especially helpful with plants under fluorescents, with those summering outdoors, with young seedlings, and with just-repotted orchids that have not yet formed extensive roots.

Signs of overfertilization in orchids include soft growth, and in sympodial types the start of new leads that fail to develop properly. The accumulation of fertilizer salts is another possible indication of excessive food in the medium.

DISEASES AND PESTS

Orchids suffer from various ills, but generally their hard, tough leaves make these elegant plants more resistant to diseases and insect parasitism than many other plants used for indoor culture. Of basic importance is the plant source. Reputable dealers grow and maintain their stock in a spotlessly clean environment, and plants gotten from such growers are not likely to be contaminated with viruses, infected with foliage, stem, or root diseases, or infested with parasites. Nevertheless, examine plants closely when you are buying in person and avoid selecting any with black or brown spots, streaks, or mottling on the leaves, or with flowers that are mottled in color, deformed, bruised, or punctured, or which have light brown or pinkish spots or dots. All of these symptoms may indicate bacterial, fungal, or viral infection or insect damage.

When clean, new stock reaches your premises, a high level of sanitation coupled with correct cultural practices is necessary to keep plants disease and pest free. Plants grown in a close atmosphere, such as in the basement under fluorescent lighting, occasionally contract leaf diseases, probably because the plant tissues are too soft and succulent, a result of several more or less wrong environmental factors adding up to poor-quality plants. Diseases are less likely to gain a foothold in a strongly sunlit and adequately ventilated greenhouse.

The same cannot always be said of insect pests. Sometimes snails, slugs, and similar animal pests manage to get in, and it takes constant vigilance to keep them under control. Orchid root conditions are ideal for these pests, and they remain in the dark containers, gnawing root tissues by day and coming out at night, usually to attach themselves to flowers and buds. Probably the most serious insect pests are the various scale insects, their relatives the mealybugs, and occasionally, whiteflies. These do sneak in, even into plants growing in the house or under lights in the basement. The best control is to inspect your plants minutely at frequent intervals. Watch especially the crevices where leaves (and sometimes bud-sheaths) join together and unite with the pseudobulbs, and look within the papery sheaths which surround new growths. (Remove these sheaths as quickly as they dry, to reduce insect hiding places.) Other likely places for insect infestation are the crevices in the rough portions of the rhizome. If signs of disease or pests are present anywhere on your orchids, act quickly, using the organic remedies described in chapter 9.

Sometimes environmental diseases show up. In summer, leaves may develop strange spots that can be traced back to scorching due to a combination of heat, too-bright light, and perhaps water droplets on the foliage. Roots may deteriorate or decay as the result of overwatering; of the wrong potting medium; of deteriorated potting medium; of wrong, too concentrated, or too much fertilizer; or of a buildup of toxic chemical salts from water. To combat problems with potting media, fertilizer, or salts, repot the affected plant in fresh potting medium or when feasible, flush the plant repeatedly to wash out excessive salts. Where high levels of salts have encrusted a clay pot, a new one should be used—or the old one scrubbed clean of its whitish deposits or crusts in vinegar and water, then soaked thoroughly in several changes of water before reuse.

SELECTING THE BEST ORCHIDS FOR YOU

In choosing which genera to buy, begin by determining the light levels and temperature ranges you can provide both winter and summer, and narrow the field accordingly to appropriate genera—or, with wide-ranging genera, to species coming from a suitable altitude and climate. You also will want to take into account growth habit relative to available space. If you are a windowsill grower, the most sensible choices are dwarf or smaller sympodials and monopodial types, which are fairly compact—ascocendas are particularly good. Keep in mind that some plants, such as most cattleyas and some of the larger dendrobiums, are just too big for sill culture.

Other variables to consider before you buy are ease of culture, time to flowering, and cost. These three considerations are related not only to a plant's genus and species, but also to its age and original mode of propagation. In general, hybrids are easier to grow than species orchids. You can, of course, buy established hybrids or species plants of blooming size, but they can be quite expensive and the culture shock will be great—especially if you plan to grow such orchids in the house; the setback possibly could delay the flowering of a mature plant for up to three years. If you are a beginner who wants mature plants, you would do better to start with those raised in a greenhouse than with more costly jungle-collected specimens. On the other hand, two or three inch (5 or 8 cm) high seedlings tend to acclimate to indoor conditions better than mature plants reared in a greenhouse. These young plants can be purchased out of a community pot or flat to which they were transferred from a flask. (You can also buy seeded flasks or flasks with seedlings ready to transplant—but the problem then becomes one of raising or disposing of hundreds of almost-identical plants.)

Seedlings just a few inches or centimeters high need more tender loving care than older specimens and may take two to five years to bloom, but they are attractively low priced, often costing as little as one-fifth or even one-tenth as much as a full-grown plant in which a dealer has invested considerable money or time and space. At such low prices you can afford seedlings of new hybrids—experimental crosses that would be prohibitively expensive as mature specimens. The risk is, however, that a given seedling may be strong, weak, or middling, and that its eventual flowers may be good, bad, or of indifferent quality.

Also available are mericlones. These are vegetatively propagated plants that have been generated from the tip of new growth (that is, from a plant's meristem tissue) in a sterile growth medium. At present meristem culture is being used only with genera having pseudobulbs or with those that put forth new growths each year, such as paphiopedilums. Unlike seedlings, mericlones are sure to grow up identical to the presumably superior plant from which they are generated and are virtually guaranteed to be virus free. They generally take from two to three years to bloom.

The task of selecting beautiful orchids specifically suited to your growing conditions at reasonable cost has become easier of late, for orchids can be hybridized freely, and there is now a huge variety of available species and hybrids, particularly of the beginners' orchids that have been widely grown for years and are now particularly popular with the "new breed" of amateur orchid growers.

The reason for the great proliferation of *Cattleya, Paphiopedilum,* and *Phalaenopsis* hybrids, among others, may be traced to the phenomenal growth in the number of home growers over the last five to ten years. Formerly, the output of commercial orchid hybridizers was destined almost exclusively for the cut-flower trade, so that flowers were selectively bred for size and longevity as cut flowers, and for blooming times synchronized with Mother's Day and other holidays. Today's amateur orchidists, however, have created an entirely new kind of market: one keyed to compact growth, extended blooming periods, and diversity in colors, shapes, and patterns. In order to satisfy the new growers, hybridizers have used the large, flat, white, pink, or red standard florists' types in crosses with numerous species within each genus and among related genera, providing a veritable wonderland of new hybrid types. Furthermore, many previously rare species have been propagated commercially and are available for the first time at approachable prices.

A GUIDE TO SOME ORCHIDS FOR BEGINNERS

Several "groups" of orchids are especially suitable for novices to grow either in the greenhouse or in the home, and confining a collection to these types should not prove seriously limiting, for better than 90 percent of all orchids under cultivation belong to this handful of allied groups. The plants included in each category share similar cultural requirements and can be hybridized readily with one another.

CYMBIDIUMS

Cymbidium hybrids derived from various geographically based groups (Burmese, Japanese, and Chinese) are among the easiest orchids with which to start. Having straplike, evergreen leaves and gracefully arching stems covered profusely with appealing flowers,

these orchids are much loved and widely hybridized by orchidists. These sympodial plants grow reasonably well in a potting mix made by adapting an epiphytic orchid potting medium obtained from a garden shop or commercial grower. To 4 parts (by volume) epiphytic mix, add 1 part dehydrated cattle manure or sterilized old barnyard manure, plus 1 part sandy garden loam. Mix well. In frost-free climates where there is a greater than 20°F (11°C) day/night differential, terrestrial cymbidiums make good garden subjects. Because of this need for a large daily temperature differential, experts used to say cymbidiums were not suitable for home growing; actually, the temperature span works to the advantage of the amateur grower. Potted plants are moved to a lath house or to bright shade in the garden over summer, where pots may be plunged into the ground or left aboveground, and they stay out in the fall until nights drop near frost for two weeks or longer, while days warm up nicely—typically Indian summer conditions. Then, plants come indoors to the coolest part of an intermediate greenhouse, and usually they will bloom in 6 to 12 weeks. Cymbidiums also will grow on in a cool, bright room or plant room, provided the daytime humidity is kept at 50 percent or more. Nighttime temperatures should be in the 48° to 58°F (9° to 14°C) range. Small cymbidium hybrids are suitable for growing in 6- to 8-inch (15 to 20 cm) pots, while the larger types do well in 12-inch (30 cm) pots to 24-inch (61 cm) tubs. A single, well-grown plant may produce a dozen or more spikes, each with from 15 to 50 or more blossoms that will last for two or three months. In evidence from fall to spring—depending on the cultivar—cymbidium flowers are white, creamy, straw colored through reddish brown, or pinkish or green. Hybrids may display a combination of colors.

PAPHIOPEDILUM GROUP

The tropical forms of the Asian paphiope-

Cymbidium Hybrid: If you are new to orchid growing, there is no better introduction than this orchid which is easy to raise, and once established will reward you with a flurry of blooms. Cymbidiums pour a great deal of energy into flowering, and each flower stalk can be laden with up to 30 blooms. The process of opening takes several weeks, and once opened, each bloom lasts for over a month in good condition.

dilum and its North and South American relatives of the *Phragmipedium, Selenipedium,* and *Cypripedium* genera were formerly classified together as cypripediums. Do not, however, confuse the popular and easy-to-grow "paphs" with the *Cypripedium* species native to North America, for the native lady's slippers are extremely difficult to grow indoors unless they are exposed to freezing temperatures during the winter, then forced. The tropical paphiopedilums so widely grown indoors may be divided into two groups: those with entirely green leaves, and those with mottled leaves, which generally are cultivated under slightly warmer conditions. Mostly winter bloomers, these evergreen or-

chids are sympodial (although lacking pseudobulbs) and mostly terrestrial. All are in the mold of the lady's slipper as far as flower form is concerned; the blooms appear to have only two sepals instead of the usual three, for two have become fused through evolution.

All paphiopedilums grow in relatively reduced light, like that at the fully shaded end of a greenhouse. This can be an intermediate house, but a cool one is even better, especially for green-leaved types. Keep these terrestrials moderately moist always—less so just after flowering. Grow them in a medium that drains well but retains moisture. Possibilities are soft brown osmunda, or finely chopped fir

Creator of a Tropical Paradise: Orchid grower Joseph Levine, seated in his Massachusetts apartment and framed by part of his collection, has succeeded in raising a multitude of healthy, floriferous orchids far from their native climes.

A Luxuriance of Orchids Where the Snow Blows

The atmosphere and "furnishings" of Joseph Levine's Massachusetts apartment in February stand in total contrast to the icy winds and stark, gray-white tones of the harsh New England winter. The warm, moist air, circulated gently by fans, fogs the eyeglasses of newcomers entering from the subzero cold. Profusely flowering *Phalaenopsis* species and hybrids display from one to several dozen flowers per spike in shades of yellow, green, white, pink, and purple, in every conceivable combination of stripes, spots, and flushes of one color on another. Golden yellow oncidiums seem to glow with a light all their own as they bask in the late afternoon sun. Perky miniature *Cattleya* hybrids, in shades of scarlet and crimson, gleam from the same sunny windowsill, often adding fragrance to the bouquet of visual delights. *Paphiopedilum* flowers—which vary in character from dainty pink and white "elves" to gigantic purple-striped creatures of the night—perch primly, lurk menacingly, or simply stand proudly on their tall stems in the north windows. Beneath the windowsill plant trays, banks of fluorescent lights nurture hundreds of tiny seedlings toward maturity. After taking in all this, the newcomer usually glances surreptitiously out the back window, looking for a hidden greenhouse or a florist's delivery truck, unwilling to believe that all these plants actually grow in a downtown apartment.

What's the secret? This amateur orchidist does not "talk" to his collection. Neither does he restrict the musical environment to either an endless succession of harpsichord variations and or-

bark used alone or with dried oak leaves. Plants in osmunda will need little feeding, and those in other media need only a weak solution of manure tea or fish emulsion once or twice a month. It is said that mutation of these orchids can be prevented by mixing small amounts of fertilizer such as lime, bone meal, or blood meal into the planting mix.

"Paphs" also can be grown in a north or east window in a heated porch, spare room, or a cool place where the daytime humidity holds at 50 percent and the night humidity does not drop below 30 percent. Plants being summered outdoors should be brought in when night temperatures begin to edge below 50°F (10°C). At the first sign of a flower bud, stake the plant immediately so the slender flower stems will be able to hold the heavy blooms erect.

The unusual shape and markings of this genus's flowers have made it tempting to hybridizers; indeed, an 1872 cross of *P. barba-*

gan fugues or a steady diet of punk rock. He does devote considerable effort to the care of the plants, and has spent long periods in study and experimentation to determine the best growing methods for his particular situation. Joe is convinced that there is no real secret involved at all—that an ability to grow orchids in the home depends on common sense in selecting the proper genera for home cultivation and on a willingness to make certain minor adjustments in lifestyle to accommodate the plants. In general, he says, "It is safe to say that anyone who can successfully cultivate African violets and begonias stands a good chance of managing well with carefully chosen orchids."

Many of the techniques Joe Levine uses to cultivate orchids in his plant room and living quarters are incorporated in the text of this chapter. He insists, however, that choosing the right plants "is crucial," and urges novice growers to get started with phalaenopsis, paphiopedilums, and cattleyas—three genera that have cultural

Loving Care: A sunny room with proper moisture and temperature levels and plenty of space certainly seems to be an environment conducive to luxuriant, healthy plant growth. But there is one more essential ingredient—human care. Successful orchid growers combine all these elements, complementing an ideal growing environment with a life-style which allows much time for tending the plants.

requirements not too difficult to meet in the average home and that can adapt remarkably well to a number of different growing practices. Will confining first plant purchases to these genera restrict the choice of flower shapes, sizes, or colors? "Not much at all," says orchidist Levine. "The selection of species and hybrids within these genera is so large that it would take the average grower at least five years to sample the best of each." If more variety is desired by a home grower, Joe suggests miniature cymbidiums; if a summer outdoors is possible for the plants, he also recommends dendrobiums and oncidiums.

tum and the still popular *P. insigne* yielded the second successful hybrid in the orchid world, and *P. insigne* figures in the ancestry of many contemporary cultivars. The *Paphiopedilum* hybrids that are available today can be divided into two basic classes: complex and primary.

Complex hybrids can be green, maroon, ox-blood red, pink, or near white, with various combinations of spotting, striping, and flushes of colors on the petals and dorsal se-

pals. Good-quality flowers—which are usually produced one to a stem—are large, rounded in shape, and have heavy, waxy, long-lasting flower parts.

Primary hybrids involve crosses between two species and offer astonishing variety in size, shape, color, and flowering habit. Crosses involving species like *Paphiopedilum rothschildianum* produce flowers with long, pointed petals and tall dorsals, with colors ranging from dark purples to maroons and

Paphiopedilum: An outstanding choice for the beginning indoor grower, these orchids are generally tolerant and will flower readily if given the appropriate care. Easily distinguished by their pouchlike lips and waxy-textured flowers, paphiopedilums have been widely hybridized for various types of markings and colors.

green. The flowers are borne in groups of three or more on 24- to 36-inch (61 to 91 cm) stems, and are often boldly striped. The additional attraction of mottled foliage makes these plants real eye-catchers in any collection. Hybrids of other species like *Paphiopedilum concolor* produce smaller, rounded flowers in shades of white and pink with red spots. These flowers are usually borne singly or in pairs close to foliage mottled in green and silver.

Closely resembling paphiopedilums and sharing their cultural requirements, *Phragmipedium* species are somewhat deciduous terrestrial sympodials native to South America, which tend to be evergreen in cultivation. Some flower in summer, some all year round, producing unusual multiple blooms of unique color and shape on a single flower stalk that can be up to 40 inches (102 cm) long. All require less water and cooler temperatures in winter than in summer, when their roots must be kept warm and moist at all times. One flamboyantly attractive species is *P. caudatum*—the mandarin orchid. Having about six strap-shaped yellow-green leaves to 24 inches (61 cm) long growing at the base of its stem, this orchid has the largest flowers in the genus. These are green-brown, and crimson, boasting a slipperlike lip over 2 inches (5 cm) long and incredibly elongated, taillike petals as much as 30 inches (76 cm) in length. The mandarin's flower stalk bears from two to six blossoms and the plant blooms from April to August.

Novel in a different way, the selenipediums are the towering giants of the Orchid family. The true members of this terrestrial genus were little known and cultivated until fairly recently, for the name formerly was erroneously used to designate certain phragmipediums. From the lowlands of Panama, the mammoth *Selenipedium chica* is a bamboo-like plant with a reedy stem and leaves folded lengthwise like a fan. It is best tried in a greenhouse, for it can grow as tall as 15 feet (4.5 m). The yellow, pouched flowers are rather inconspicuous and displayed at the top of the plant in a terminal raceme.

CATTLEYA GROUP

Plants sharing cultural needs similar to those of the *Cattleya* species and hybrids include the *Brassavola, Dendrobium, Epidendrum, Laelia, Schomburgkia,* and *Sophronitis* genera and their hybrids. Large flowered and dramatic, these orchids are similar in flower structure and with the exception of *Dendrobium,* are often interbred. As mentioned previously, they are suited to intermediate house conditions. They thrive on strong light, 50 percent humidity (higher on sunny days), and 65° to 72°F (18° to 22°C) room tempera-

Orchids for an Intermediate House: While each is strikingly unique in appearance, these genera do share common cultural needs, and (with the exception of *Dendrobium*) are often interbred for exciting combinations of color, form, growth habit, and frequency of bloom. Beginning clockwise from upper right is a magenta-hued *Cattleya* type, with delicate frills. The elongated sepals and softly curving petals of *Laelia autumnalis* create an elegant line, enhanced by shadings of rosy purple. Each blossom of *Dendrobium aggregatum* 'Majus' is in itself a sunburst of color; a cluster of these flowers on a spike becomes a glorious, shimmering, golden yellow cloud. At upper left, the dramatic red-orange coloring and fringed lip of *Epidendrum ibaguense* suggests fiery tongues of flame.

tures that drop about 10°F (6°C) at night. These epiphytic plants should be grown in osmunda fiber or bark mix in pots with a lot of drainage or in hanging baskets (including the special ones for orchids, called rafts). They also do well on slabs of fiber. In the absence of a greenhouse, members of this group may prosper in a steamy room such as a bathroom or kitchen if you can provide a south window that is curtained lightly only during the longest, brightest days. Foliage benefits from frequent misting under any safe greenhouse conditions, and the potting medium must be kept on the dry side, especially in winter months. (Taken outdoors in summer to bright shade, plants in the Cattleya group may be watered and fed more often until new growth matures, at which time it is desirable to cut back until buds swell.)

When these orchids are grown under fluorescent lights, their leaves must almost touch the lamps; a vertical bank of lights will give far better results than fixtures placed just overhead. Plant-room gardeners also have fair luck with many plants in this group—especially with epidendrums, which are very adaptable.

One of the largest genera in the Orchid family, *Epidendrum* includes over a thousand species and cultivars, embracing sympodial plants quite diverse in foliage, flowers, structure, size, and growth habit. Members of the Encyclium group of epidendrums have prominent pseudobulbs (it is these that generally share the cultural requirements of cattleyas) and rest after new growth is completed, whereas the reed-stemmed types of the Epidendrum group are usually vinelike in habit and do best if their roots are kept moist at all times. The reed-stemmed plants prefer a little more sun than the pseudobulbous types and flower more profusely—and almost constantly—if they are fed often. One of the best known and most intriguing epidendrums is the clamshell, or cockleshell, orchid *(E. cochleatum)*. Blooming almost all

year, this pseudobulbous plant produces clusters of flowers which hang upside-down at the end of flower stalks 8 to 10 inches (20 to 25 cm) long. The yellowish green petals are set off by a violet-black, shell-shaped lip that is striped yellow or green.

Considered the archetypal orchid by those who have seen their magnificently shaped and colored flowers in corsages, cattleyas are thought by some gardeners to be the easiest of all orchids to grow. The genus is sympodial and may be divided into unifoliate and bifoliate types. Coming mostly from Colombia or Brazil, the single-leaved cattleyas have one leaf on each fleshy pseudobulb. The psuedobulbs are swollen into a spindle or club shape and just one or several flowers are on each inflorescence. Usually having two leaves per pseudobulb, the bifoliate "catts" have cylinder-shaped pseudobulbs that frequently look like stems. Their blooms are smaller, of heavier texture, and more abundant than those of the single-leaved sorts.

Recent developments in breeding are yielding *Cattleya* hybrids dramatically different from their forebears. The blooms of old-time florists' "catts" were produced on huge, ungainly plants that were simply hideous when not in bloom. In addition these plants often required full sun, were too tall to grow well under lights and usually bloomed only once a year (during an appropriate holiday). They were also quite sensitive to changes in temperature. Concerted efforts in breeding with smaller, related genera like *Laelia* and *Sophronitis* have changed all that. A new line of delightful small "Sl" *(Sophrolaelia)* and "Slc" *(Sophrolaeliocattleya)* hybrids produces bouquets of diminutive but well-shaped and brilliantly colored flowers on plants that can be grown to specimen size in five-inch (13 cm) pots. Names like 'Pixie Gold' aptly describe the diminutive size and shining colors of these perfect under-light subjects. Other, slightly larger plants like the various progeny of *Sophrolaeliocattleya* 'Jewel Box' provide clusters of medium size flowers on relatively compact specimens that can bloom two to three times a year when given proper culture. Still other lines of breeding have emphasized the development of the so-called "art shade" cattleyas, which range in hue from yellow and orange to peach and multicolored types.

Also containing species and hybrids easily raised by beginning orchidists, the *Dendrobium* genus is mammoth, including over 1,500 sympodial, mostly epiphytic species spread over a wide area in Southeast Asia and South India in habitats ranging from jungle lowlands to Himalayan peaks. Dendrobiums vary greatly in appearance and requirements; a favorite suited to living room culture is *D. aggregatum,* a dwarf with arching sprays of yellow, orange-centered flowers appearing for several months in early spring. Also often grown is the deciduous *D. nobile,* which generally accepts intermediate conditions but requires cool, dry treatment in fall and winter to bring on flowering, and the many evergreen *D. phalaenopsis* hybrids, which exhibit a canelike type of growth.

VANDAS AND PHALAENOPSIS HYBRIDS

Some of the vandas, which normally are considered warm house orchids, will grow under intermediate house conditions, as will the very beautiful, allied *Phalaenopsis* hybrids. Found at various altitudes in Asia and Australia, vandas need stronger light than other orchids suited to temperate house conditions, and so are grown very close to the glass (hanging or on raised staging) in a greenhouse or close to a bright window in the plant room. They also do best in the warmest part of the greenhouse.

There are three types of vandas: the terete (cylindrical)-leaved, the semiterete forms (including hybrids), and the strap (flat)-leaved types. All are evergreen monopodial epiphytes and are easily grown and brought to flower if given plentiful water,

weekly feedings, high humidity, an unusually coarse medium, and good air circulation. Large in size, vandas boast tall flower spikes crowded with blooms from two to four inches (5 to 10 cm) across. Flowers are often round and flat and can be white or various combinations of pink, purple, blue, brown, and green. Individual vandas grow and bloom continuously throughout the year, though some species peak in spring and early summer. The popular *V. coerulea*—famous for its blue flowers, an unusual color among orchids—flowers better if given cool autumn temperatures of 57° to 61°F (14° to 16°C) and less water before flowering in January. Those vandas blooming in late winter need slightly higher temperatures and less water before flowering, and all vandas are said to be stronger and more floriferous if watered less during nongrowth periods. Growers who want large vandalike flowers on a small plant are trying miniature types called ascocendas. These are hybrids obtained by crossing vandas with small-growing *Ascocentrum* species such as *A. curvifolium,* which is an attractive plant native to Thailand. (For more information on various outstanding miniature orchids, see chapter 22.)

Commonly called moth orchids because their flowers resemble that insect and thereby attract pollinators, phalaenopsis are monopodial like vandas and share most of the vandas' cultural requirements, but prefer a slightly more shaded position—especially during the summer when they are in active growth. Their foliage will burn if the light intensity goes above 1,000 footcandles. These orchids thrive on warm temperatures and frequent misting in the summer, and should never be allowed to dry out between waterings as they lack pseudobulbs. But "phals" need somewhat less water than vandas during the nongrowth period. Of modest size and easy cultivation, these epiphytic beauties can do well on a slab of bark or on a handsome piece of driftwood with a small amount of

Phalaenopsis: This orchid produces airy sprays of flowers which are a delight to behold, and because the blossoms resemble the outspread wings of a moth, it has been dubbed the moth orchid. Several of the plants shown here represent certain trends in hybridization, namely delicate pink striping on a white flower, and reddish bars on a yellow flower.

duce their cascades of waxy blooms in spring, although some flower year-round and hybrids can bloom at any season.

Phalaenopsis breeders are still working to "gild the lily" with more and more refinements on the solid white and solid pink hybrid "phals," but have simultaneously made excellent progress in other lines of breeding. It is now possible to obtain excellent semialbas (white with colored lip), stripes (pink or red strips on white, often with colored lips as well), and numerous spotted and barred types. Many of these new hybrids sport strikingly mottled foliage which makes them attractive even when out of bloom, and some

Vanda: Popular and easily grown, this orchid bears long-lasting flowers which inspire the nickname of moon orchid with their flat, round shape. Much hybridization has been done within the genus and with other orchid genera.

sphagnum for the roots. These beginners' orchids are especially suited to plant room growing; indeed, African violet enthusiasts are surprisingly successful at raising phalaenopsis under fluorescents under *Saintpaulia* conditions, fostering plants with long sprays of pink, white, yellow, or purple flowers which are fully as beautiful as professionally grown specimens from greenhouses.

Distributed widely through the equatorial Far East, the plants are stemless, having shiny, fleshy, evergreen leaves rarely over 12 inches (30 cm) high, and arching flower stalks to 4 feet (1.2 m) long. Most phalaenopsis pro-

Bountiful Blooms: It would be hard to rival the sheer delight of entering a greenhouse full of orchids in bloom in the middle of winter, offering up their colors as respite from the general drabness of the season.

even have fragrance—something missing from the older florists' hybrid lines. "Desert shade" phalaenopsis can produce flowers in any color from tan to orange, beige, or apricot and with unexpected stripes, spots, and flushes. Excellent progress also has been made in efforts to produce good, solid yellow "phals." A particularly exquisite species, *Phalaenopsis violacea,* has been used to infuse vibrant purple flushes into the flower parts of its progeny, although these plants are somewhat slower growing than most other cultivars.

OTHER ORCHIDS

Where there is a will, there is a way, and amateurs determined to grow and to flower miltonias from higher elevations or even the more difficult of the allied *Odontoglossum* hybrids and species (for example, *O. crispum,* which is intolerant of heat in summer as well as in winter) have managed in such unlikely places as the cool alpine greenhouse or a chilly guest bedroom with cold vapor humidifiers going full blast. Although these plants may be grown successfully in east windows where there is air conditioning or in east windows in northern climate zones with relatively cool summers, they cannot be recommended for general growing because too often their stringent environmental limitations result in failure. The gardener determined to grow a few orchids first ought to analyze the environmental conditions available and then make the necessary adaptations to create suitable temperature, light, and humidity levels. The next step is to buy, from an orchid specialist, healthy, vigorous plants of a few easy sorts—epidendrums, phalaenopsis, cattleyas—and make every effort to follow simple but specific cultural instructions. Orchids are not all that difficult. They just have special requirements and grow under environmental conditions that challenge the indoor gardener. The rewards of accepting that challenge, however, can be glorious.

CHAPTER 20

Trees and Shrubs

When it comes to filling large spaces indoors, the decorative advantages of trees and shrubs are far greater than those of smaller house plants—even an untrained eye notes the disproportion between a foot-high (30 cm) clivia or fern and a lofty cathedral ceiling. In addition to offering outstanding design potential, many species of trees and shrubs provide flowers and fruit, often on a grand scale. You need only think of the ponderosa lemon (*Citrus limon* 'Ponderosa') with its melon size fruits to understand this. Beyond the possibility of such indoor beauty and productivity, there is a final economic consideration. One hundred and twenty dollars for a ten-foot (3 m) Norfolk Island pine *(Araucaria heterophylla)* seems a considerable amount. But if you are willing to pay that much for an imposing specimen, you'll be less likely to neglect it and have to buy a replacement later.

Both shrubs and trees can be of impressive size, and differentiating the two forms can sometimes pose problems. It is generally agreed that a tree is a single-stemmed woody plant that grows over ten feet (3 m) high, while a shrub is a multi-stemmed woody plant that tends to be smaller. Trees increase in size by producing new branches and usually by expanding the girth of the main stem; shrubs, on the other hand, expand by sending new shoots up from the ground. The most obvious distinction, however, is often height, for it is usually possible to readily distinguish a mature shrub from a venerable tree in a natural habitat.

On the other hand, these generalizations seem useless in discussing specimens grown as house plants because trees and shrubs cultivated indoors may develop quite differently than they would in the wild. Consider, for example, the schefflera *(Brassaia actinophylla).* Indoors, you often see a decoratively potted plant having a cluster of three or more shoots—a truly shrublike characteristic. Yet in its Australian homeland, a schefflera will develop one trunk and will grow in excess of 100 feet (30.5 m). Similarly, the popular avocado *(Persea americana)* in the living room never seems to want to exceed 10 feet (3 m) in height, the usual limit of the ceiling. Consequently, it is tempting to assume the plant must be a shrub. But at least one botanist, who fell out of a 50-foot (15.2 m) specimen in

Norfolk Island Pines, *Au Naturel:* Indoors, *Araucaria* sits demurely in its pot, a diminutive, delicately branched, rather slow-growing specimen. However, in its natural habitat, it switches identity to become a towering, handsome, and sturdy tree.

Opposite, leaves of a weeping fig, Ficus benjamina.

419

the tropics, learned the hard way that the avocado is definitely a tree. Given such confusion, it is best not to worry about the definitive characteristics of trees and shrubs. What's important is to concentrate on how the growth and well-being of a specimen alters when it is brought indoors and subjected to changes in environment that might seem quite subtle. For example, in the natural dappled shade of a tropical forest the weeping fig *(Ficus benjamina)* will lose and replace an insignificant number of leaves at a constant rate. But when the tree is suddenly brought indoors to low light, it can lose a hundred times as many leaves. Moreover, growing plants in containers provides a contrived and artificial environment that must be carefully controlled. Without the possibility of surface runoff, pots must have good drainage so that surplus water will run out the bottom. Lacking this, a touchy shrub like a camellia will rot.

THINK BEFORE YOU BUY

When you consider the possible variations in light, heat, and humidity in the home, numerous microclimates emerge, any of which may help or hinder the growth of indoor trees and shrubs. Before investing in trees and shrubs, which can be quite costly, you should evaluate the available growing conditions to determine whether you can provide locations in which plants can survive and retain a healthy appearance.

Proper illumination is, of course, a primary concern. If you plan to use only natural light, you will have to study the various exposures in your home and determine which plants are best suited to each location. Some trees and shrubs, such as those in the *Citrus, Yucca,* and *Pittosporum* genera, either prefer or require the bright light of a southern exposure. Others, like *Araucaria* species, will do better in subdued northern light. Since artificial illumination can give plants most of the wavelengths they need, light is an adjustable quantity in the interior environment. (For more information on fluorescent and incandescent lighting for plants, see chapter 25.)

One factor of growth that is not as easily manipulated is heat. Plants can tolerate reasonable shifts in temperature, but extremes of hot or cold, especially sudden changes, will kill plant tissue. Some trees and shrubs need cool air, from 50° to 60°F (10° to 16°C)—this group includes species of *Araucaria, Jasminum,* and *Podocarpus,* and the silk oak *(Grevillea robusta).* On the other hand, the fiddleleaf fig *(Ficus lyrata)* and the avocado are unlikely to survive such chilly air. It is important, moreover, to provide sufficiently warm air around the bottom of a plant. Although we are aware of the temperature in the upper two-thirds of a room, we often overlook the critical floor area, which can be a good 10°F (6°C) colder. This can be a hazardous difference for plants, for roots will not tolerate chilly soil as easily as foliage will adjust to cool air. As a simple thermometer will show, containers that sit in drafty hallways, near an unlit but breezy fireplace, or next to poorly insulated windows often have soil that is 15° to 20°F (8° to 11°C) cooler than the air. Because the soil temperatures of tropical house plants should not fall below 65°F (18°C) during periods of active growth, a new position inside may be necessary for a plant with chilled roots. If a change is not feasible, heating cables, double glazing on windows, better insulation, or insulated shades or curtains may be indicated if larger plants in tubs at floor level are to remain healthy.

A reasonably high level of humidity within the home also is of primary importance. Many of our indoor plants are natives of the tropics where naturally humid conditions moisten their foliage daily—an effect that can be simulated most easily indoors in a bathroom where people shower often or in a greenhouse that is "hosed down" frequently. To approximate this cleansing effect in other locations, keep the plant stomata, or pores, free of dirt and grease by regularly wiping both the upper and lower sides of the foliage with a damp cloth. For hard-to-reach leaves—those on the uppermost branches of a mature fig tree, for example—adjust the nozzle of your sprayer to give leaves a steady and direct shot of water. For more information on increasing atmospheric moisture, see chapter 2.

Microclimates are a combination of the above variables, and creating suitable ones involves manipulation of the environment. By using natural and/or artificial illumination you can regulate the amount of light various trees and shrubs receive; by controlling temperature you can provide them with optimum heat; and by increasing relative humidity you can insure adequate moisture.

A final consideration in choosing large plants is the amount of vertical and horizontal space available. If you plan to use natural light from living room windows and the crown rosette of the yucca you like exceeds the height of those windows, think again. If you wish to utilize a moisture-rich but heavily traveled bathroom or kitchen for growing a large coffee plant *(Coffea arabica),* which happens to have leaves that will turn brown when brushed against, you may have to reconsider the location you have in mind for the plant (or settle for a smaller specimen or a less touchy genus).

Yet another factor to consider is whether a tree or shrub goes into a complete dormancy in which it loses its looks and requires special care. For example, *Hydrangea macrophylla* produces beautiful, long-lasting blooms that can attract any indoor gardener, but the plants are also deciduous. Each winter these shrubs must lose their foliage and enter a period of dormancy in order to flower the next summer. The bare bush is a stark sight, and inducing and facilitating dormancy in such deciduous plants can be tricky. Dormancy requirements vary greatly from one plant to the next, and the degree of success you attain then often affects the floriferousness of flowering trees and shrubs and indeed, the basic well-being of the specimen whether

Wrong Plant for This Window: A statuesque yucca with crown rosettes that rise above and beyond the window should be relocated where ample light will fall on its foliage.

it flowers or not. For this reason it is important to be sure you are aware of and can accommodate any special needs of the tree or shrub you buy.

As a final criterion in buying trees and shrubs, it is advisable to take into account the safety quotient of the plant. Think twice about the spiny thorns of the grapefruit or lime or about the fact that all parts of the oleander *(Nerium oleander)* are poisonous if eaten, before you bring such a plant into a home with young children or pets.

SELECTING AND CARING FOR TREES AND SHRUBS

Once you have decided upon a type of tree or

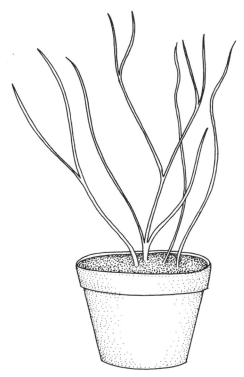

Dormant before Flowering: This hydrangea reverts to a barren, stark look during its winter dormancy. If the proper care is given during this critical period, the plant will reward you with attractive, abundant blooms later on.

shrub for your home, you will be ready to select and purchase a particular specimen. (Propagation is a reasonable alternative to the expense of a full-grown tree, but the time you must wait and the setbacks that may occur before a plant reaches treelike proportions may not suit your needs.) Remember to choose any tree or shrub with care. First of all, check a promising specimen to see if it is well rooted by gently shaking the trunk just above soil level. If it moves easily, don't buy the plant. If the plant passes that test, go on to ask yourself some additional questions. Does the plant have well-proportioned growth? How fast does it grow? Will it need repotting soon? Will it require frequent pruning? Is it disease and pest free? How much care are you willing to give it? Most impor-

tantly, is this tree or shrub something you want to have in your home for a number of years?

When you have chosen your plant, consider whether you want to repot it straightaway in a more decorative container. If you buy a pot or tub elsewhere and bring it with you, the nursery often will do the labor for you at no cost, although you may have to buy the soil. Nurseries charge varying amounts to deliver trees. If a plant is under six feet (1.8 m) tall, they will most likely try to fit it into your car. But larger specimens require larger vehicles—usually the company truck. Some firms deliver for free, provided the tree is very costly; for less expensive specimens there is a delivery charge. Other nurseries have a standard fee unless the tree is excessively large, in which case a truck may have to be rented. In such situations you should plan to pay an extra fee, perhaps even up to 100 dollars in special cases.

After the plant is home and in its place, proper care will assure its health. As a general rule, trees and shrubs should be fed lightly once a month while they are in active growth. Use fish emulsion fertilizer applied at the half-strength rate of ½ tablespoon (7.5 ml) per gallon (3.8 l) of water. Fruiting plants may require more feeding, while low-light types, like palms, require much less.

Given the large volume of soil needed to accommodate trees and shrubs, watering them neither too much nor too little poses special problems. Overwatering can all too easily debilitate or kill specimens in large pots, but underwatering is just as bad. As the moisture in the soil is used, the drying root ball will become more compact, often shrinking away from the sides of the container. When you next apply water, much of it can escape down the sides of the soil ball without being absorbed by the soil. In such instances, a bath or shower is the recommended practice. If the plant is small enough, simply submerge it in a tank of water—a bathtub will do—until the air bubbles stop rising from the medium. With larger plants, however, a bath can be a sizable chore. To circumvent the dilemma of trying to jostle a ten-foot (3 m) tree to the work area, you can try the following, all of which can forestall the need to move a plant to water it and some of which will reduce the chance of overwatering.

First, you can employ the probe of a moisture meter to determine the wetness of the soil. This instrument will save you from having to scratch through several inches (approximately 5 cm) of dry soil and will prevent you from underwatering or overwatering.

With huge plants that are not double-potted, you can test for moisture at the bottom of the root ball by inserting a plastic or aluminum tube so it extends from above the soil level down into the drainage layer at the bottom of the container. Do this at the time you pot the plant. Thereafter a thin dowel or other stick can be slid into the tube when you want to check moisture levels. When it comes out dry it is time to water.

When such preventive measures are not enough to prevent drying out of the root ball, you should move your tree or shrub to water it or give it a bath as described earlier. When this becomes necessary, you can employ any of several methods to relocate the plant outdoors or over a floor drain in the laundry room (see Strategies for Moving Heavyweight Trees and Shrubs). Then water the plant until water drips from the drainage holes. Repeat this process one or two more times at intervals of several minutes, to completely rehydrate the root ball. Such repeated watering also can be used to flush away accumulated salts deposited by water or fertilizer.

If a plant in a pot without drainage holes has been allowed to dry out so much that the root ball is pulling away from the pot, you can rehydrate it *if* you proceed cautiously and slowly and use less water.

Watering problems aside, it could become necessary to transport a large specimen outdoors for pest control purposes. If mealybugs, mites, or scale have attacked your weeping fig, for example, a vigorous washdown from the garden hose will be in order to blast off these pests. Also, you'll want to rinse off the sticky "honeydew" secreted by some of these insects, for it not only makes a sticky mess but also gums up the feet and antennae of the predators you may wish to introduce to fight your house plant pests. Spraying with water is also beneficial as a simple cosmetic for dusty trees and shrubs. A third reason for moving potted trees and shrubs is aesthetic as well as practical. When summer comes around, the natural beauty that trees like acacias can give to your yard or patio makes mobility a must. Besides, trees and shrubs taken outdoors in their pots for the summer will profit from the increased humidity, extra water, and better air circulation. To assure success, however, you must take measures that will help house plants being moved outside or brought back indoors to adjust to a different environment.

ACCLIMATING TREES AND SHRUBS

The process of preparing a plant to survive the transition to a new environment is called acclimation. It is necessary to ease the shock a plant undergoes in being moved from bright outdoor sunlight in the summer (8,000 to 12,000 footcandles) into less intense interior light in the fall (150 to 800 footcandles), and from high levels of humidity outdoors to the low moisture of the home, or vice versa. Dr. Charles Conover of the Agricultural Research Center in Apopka, Florida (associated with the University of Florida at Gainesville), has made a comprehensive study of the acclimation of plants. He found that when weeping fig trees were placed in outdoor shade for five weeks before being brought inside, the specimens dropped fewer leaves than when grown in full sun and abruptly moved indoors. But Dr. Conover also noted that sungrown trees developed thicker trunks than those grown in shade. Consequently, he sug-

Strategies for Moving Heavyweight Trees and Shrubs

Never strain yourself trying to lift a gargantuan decorator plant; there are easier ways to move it. Before purchasing such a hefty specimen you may find it worthwhile to locate a ready-made decorative container already mounted on heavy-duty casters; some manufacturers offer rolling planters that can support a weight of up to 180 pounds (81.7 kg). It is also possible to mobilize a stationary planter by attaching sections of 2 × 4 to its underside, then drilling holes in the added wood and inserting four casters on stems. If you prefer, you can fasten a pair of 2 × 4s along the sides of a planter by their narrow edges. You can then run axles through holes made at each end of the 2 × 4s and attach small rubber or wooden wheels.

To move a planter that doesn't have its own wheels, you can build a simple dolly by at-

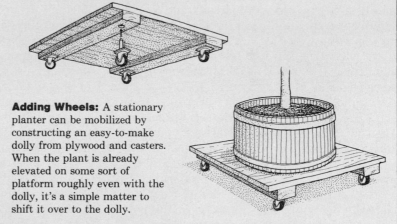

Adding Wheels: A stationary planter can be mobilized by constructing an easy-to-make dolly from plywood and casters. When the plant is already elevated on some sort of platform roughly even with the dolly, it's a simple matter to shift it over to the dolly.

taching two sets of stem- or plate-type casters to two pieces of 2 × 4 screwed to a rectangle or square of thick plywood. If the plant is displayed on a brick pedestal of equivalent height, it can be maneuvered onto such a dolly with moderate effort.

In a pinch, you can transport a heavy tub plant without wheels of any kind—provided the terrain is reasonably smooth and level. The idea is to jockey the plant, preferably already in an elevated position, onto three or four 1½ inch (4 cm) wide dowels. These should be at least

12 inches (30 cm) or so longer than the planter is wide and positioned so they are parallel to each other and will roll in the desired direction. The plant can then be pushed slowly. As the container moves off the rear dowel, that wooden roller should be lifted and placed under the front end of the planter so progress can continue. If the surface is somewhat bumpy, it can be helpful to lay parallel 2 × 4s underneath the dowels and at right angles to them so the itinerant plant can travel in style on its own special tracks.

Built-In Casters: A container with its own set of casters already attached can be a boon when moving a weighty tree.

The No-Wheel Method: In a case where wheels aren't feasible or available, dowels are a possible substitute. Several dowels of the appropriate size are all you need, as well as plenty of muscle and energy to push the planter along and to bring the rear dowel around to the front.

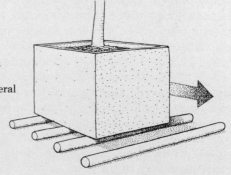

gests that trees be grown in sun during the summer but brought into the shade for at least five weeks prior to their reintroduction to the house in the fall.

The transition period also is important because when trees and shrubs such as *Pittosporum tobira* are grown in full sun, they develop foliage with less chlorophyll, a factor that decreases the plant's ability to produce food when placed indoors in low light, and which also modifies the color of the leaves somewhat. All of these findings make the point that your trees and shrubs should not be placed in full sun during the summer months unless you can properly acclimate them. A screened-in porch or a lath house, though, could serve as an excellent halfway house for your plants, both before you expose them to the summer sun and before you bring them back indoors.

MEETING DORMANCY NEEDS

In their native environments trees and shrubs experience a periodic dormancy that is brought on by changes in temperature or moisture. During this time, a plant's life processes slow down so it can survive the stress of drought or of significantly lower or higher temperatures. When the environment again becomes more hospitable, the plant resumes growth with renewed vigor. Because the stimuli that induce this rest period do not usually occur naturally indoors, many indoor trees and shrubs show few or no signs of dormancy. A watchful eye, however, may discern that a plant is not putting forth new leaves, or note increased leaf drop or deterioration. At such times it is desirable to help the plant rest more completely. If you lack highly specific information on how to do this for your particular plant, it is a good idea to reduce watering and feeding substantially, and to lower light levels if the plant is being cultivated under artificial light.

If even subtle signs of decreasing activity are absent, you can contribute to the vigor and longevity of your plants if you induce dormancy by cutting back on light, water, and food. The most appropriate time to do this with trees and shrubs from the temperate zone is usually from mid-December through January, when natural light is at its briefest and dimmest. Plants of tropical and subtropical origin also may be rested then, but if they show symptoms of dormancy at other times of the year, they also should be watered and fed less at those times until active growth begins again.

PRUNING

Indoors or out, trees and shrubs need periodic pruning. Most horticulturists caution against the fear of pruning, and rightly so, because many trees and shrubs that have not been groomed and trained will soon get out of hand. Moreover, the drastic surgery that may be called for after prolonged neglect can make a plant unsightly for many years.

The best time to prune your indoor trees and shrubs is while they are in a period of active growth. Do not feed them afterward until they have had time to adjust to the shock of being pruned. Waiting is especially important if a plant is also being subjected to the stress of being moved shortly after it has been pruned.

In deciding how to prune, the structure of the plant should be considered first. Azaleas and pittosporums are shrubs that look best when bushy; to strive for such fullness you will need to pinch back branch tips so that the axillary buds, which are dormant leaf buds lying where the leaf stem meets the stalk, may become activated, forming two stems where there was one. On the other hand, many trees often grow like shrubs indoors, producing new shoots instead of branches. Do not hesitate to cut out these woody shoots if they do not meet the plans you have for the tree. Slow-growing *Podocarpus* species, the so-called yew pines, are mostly bushy if left alone, but in time they

Prune for the Desired Effect: To encourage bushiness, as with *Pittosporum* (left), pinch back the branch tips. To promote a treelike form in plants like *Podocarpus* (right), remove the longer, trailing lateral branches.

also can be trained as trees. In the Orient they grow to be 100 feet (30.5 m) high. If you want a tree, clip the longer, weeping branches and stake the main stalk of the plant so it can be trained to grow in an upright manner. But you must have patience, since the process will take years.

Although dusting cuts with sealing compounds is unnecessary, you may want to sterilize your clippers with rubbing alcohol to prevent contaminating the plant with diseased material you may have been working with elsewhere. Sometimes repeated pruning may be needed to attain the branching pattern you want. But by keeping the eventual form in mind and pinching terminal buds, trimming sideshoots at the base, taking out interior leafless wood, cutting back errant branches or bushy sides, and fostering the growth of blossoms and leaves by grooming and clipping, you should be able to shape

compact shrubs, tall, bold trees, or spreading canopies of foliage that will highlight any room. Just remember to work with the basic growth pattern of the tree when pruning.

CONTAINERS

Indoor plants naturally work toward the obsolescence of their current pot, a phenomenon that only repotting and root pruning will remedy. But with large trees and shrubs, either method becomes a task looked on with trepidation and accomplished with relief. Just as there are methods to help you move large trees when necessary, there are also sensible steps to take when choosing pots. Consider the aesthetics of the pot, for what good are indoor trees and shrubs if they do not give visual satisfaction? Match the pot to the plant, and make sure both complement their setting in your home. You can choose plain or

A Gallery of Tree Shapes: The diversity of forms and growth habits among trees makes them interesting additions to indoor decor. Some examples are, upper row, from left to right, a bushy gardenia, a sculptural bunya-bunya, and a sculptural yucca. Lower row, from left to right, presents a delicate false aralia, a canopied weeping fig, and a bold fiddle-leaf fig.

ornate terra-cotta, plastic of various hues and molds, octagonal pots of redwood, light but solid ferroconcrete, stoneware, metal, or any of a dozen other types of containers. But the design of the pot should reflect the feeling you wish to impart with the shape and placement of your indoor tree or shrub.

There are, of course, practical considerations to weigh as well. Needless to say, the larger the tree or shrub, the more vital it is that the container be equipped with drainage holes (and several inches or centimeters of drainage material) to help prevent overwatering. Plastic containers are inexpensive and easily found; they also retain moisture better than clay pots. But being lighter, they are more likely to tip as a top-heavy tree sways

in the wind. Furthermore, if you have a hardy plant that can withstand frosty temperatures before coming inside, plastic pots, which insulate the roots poorly, can sometimes crack from the cold. Some wooden, plastic, or stone pots are straight sided. When the need to transplant arises, you will find it difficult to remove the root ball from them, as the friction will be greater than in tapered pots. Wooden containers, regardless of their shape, are notorious for decaying slightly as the expanding roots rub against the surface. Prevention involves a coat of wood preservative (the nontoxic Cuprinol), inside and out, as well as an emulsion to hinder decay. The cure is to slice around the perimeter, loosening roots that have become embedded. If you

A Ferroconcrete Pot for Trees or Shrubs

Interesting pots add to the special feeling trees and shrubs can bring to a house or apartment. To mask a peat or plastic pot with the decorative handiwork of your own design, you might try adapting these basic instructions for a cement pot so the resulting container is sized and shaped to accommodate your favorite plant.

Begin by assembling your tools and materials. You will need a bag of Portland cement, a trowel and a trough in which to mix cement, a 6-foot (1.8 m) length of fine-mesh chicken wire or porch screening (width to be determined by the height of the pot to be made), enough rigid but pliable wire to outline the shape of the pot (coat hangers will do), and some 4-inch (10 cm) strands of wire (sandwich bag twist-ties are fine).

Bend the pliable wire into the crude but recognizable form of a pot: it can be oval, square, hexagonal, or any shape that will suit the configuration of your plant and the design of the room. (You also might consider the size and shape of casters or dollies if you plan to use them.) Mold the screening around the

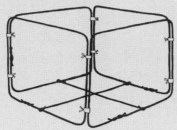

The pliable wire is bent to form a square and fastened with wire strands.

Screening wrapped around five sides of the frame is attached with wire.

bottom and sides of the wire frame, as you would wrap a present, leaving only the top open. (If the screening is rigid enough, you can forego the frame.)

If you're confident, at this stage you can decide to make the pot into a direct planter. To do this, simply cut a few drainage holes in the bottom of the screening. Then plug the holes with paper, which can be burned out later.

After securing the screening to the frame with the short strands of wire, mix the cement to a firm consistency. Turn the frame upside down and have someone hold it while you use the small trowel to apply the cement to the outside of the frame, beginning with the bottom of the pot-to-be and working down the sides. As you spread cement with the trowel, press against the inside of the screening with a piece of cardboard to keep ex-

cess cement from dropping off. Don't worry about irregularities; just make sure the cement adheres. Once you have coated the screening so it is covered on both sides, let the cement begin to harden. Check it periodically until you feel you can shape it without causing it to drop off the screen. Now you can smooth out rough spots, build up low spots with extra cement, or lightly carve in any relief that will help enhance your design. When the cement becomes even firmer, look at the areas on the container's rim or bottom on which it rested while drying and repair any places where the frame may be showing. Allow a week or so for your new decorative pot or planter to dry thoroughly, then you can take pleasure in it as something that has grown from your hands as surely as the tree or shrub it complements.

Cement is applied to the inverted frame.

Once the cement has firmed up enough, you can begin the shaping of it.

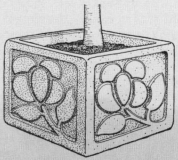

The finished project, once it has completely hardened, is ready to receive a tree or shrub.

Complementary Pots: The handmade pots for the weeping fig and the jade plant on the windowsill blend in with the muted, earthy tones and simplicity of this room.

REPOTTING AND ROOT PRUNING

When your tree or shrub doesn't grow well during its active season, when leaves are smaller and scarcer and roots appear in drainage holes, and when the plant needs watering more than ever before, it is time to repot. (Top-dressing is an effective way to replenish worn-out soil, but it will not help the tree or shrub that has outgrown its pot.)

If you welcome the idea of an even bigger specimen, at repotting time buy a new container that is at least two inches (5 cm) in diameter larger than the old one, collect new soil, and prepare a system of drainage that will benefit the plant. The typical rock, gravel, and shard drainage beds have been

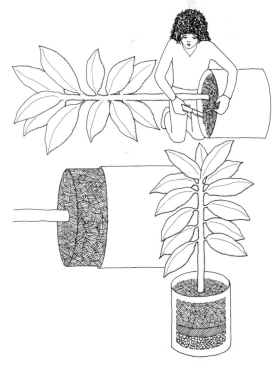

Room to Grow: A potbound tree or shrub will appreciate a roomier pot and will reward you with more vigorous growth. Carefully lay the old pot on its side and run a knife along the inside to loosen the root ball, then slide the pot away from the soil. Set the plant into a new pot at least 2 inches (5 cm) wider, filled with layers of drainage material.

are handy and like the look of wood, it may be worthwhile to construct a cube-shaped cedar, cypress, or redwood planter that is equipped with hinges so it can be partially disassembled for easy plant removal.

To avoid any chance of carpets or floors being ruined by water overflow or leakage from trees and shrubs, the use of a double pot is worth considering. As long as the drainage in the interior pot is excellent so that it doesn't store excess water, using two pots can be decorative and practical. Standing water in the outer pot should be emptied promptly after watering; it can be drawn out with a siphon. Finally, tall, cylinderlike pots dry out faster than shorter, wider ones of the same volume and therefore can help prevent root rot, a problem that is hard to diagnose in large plantings. Recent research has shown that taller pots have better aerated soil and such containers are quite stylish.

found in some cases to collect soil particles, and may clog drainage holes with mud and silt. To avoid this problem you can place a separator of fiberglass wool or a layer of sphagnum or coconut fiber on top of the gravel to filter out the soil. When the root ball of the tree to be transplanted has dried out somewhat, lay the plant on its side and, after loosening the root ball from the pot by working around the perimeter with a long knife, pull the plant out of the pot. (You may need to knock the pot with a mallet to separate it from the roots. Sometimes it is necessary to break the pot.) At this point, you may need help to lift and position the tree in its new container, but once in place and surrounded with new soil, your tree will thrive again.

If your plant needs repotting but you do not want it to grow larger for reasons of space or aesthetics, you have two choices. It is possible, of course, to take and propagate a cutting, in effect starting all over with a small version of the same plant. However, if the tree or shrub can be pruned (that is, if it is a many-branched type that has growing tips at the ends of single stems), you can maintain it in a container of the same size by using a combination of root and top pruning.

To do this, after removing the plant from its pot, pick off any crockery adhering to the roots, then use a sharp knife sterilized with rubbing alcohol to cleanly cut off the sides and bottom of the root ball. Trim off ½ inch (13 mm) all around if the plant is in a pot 10 inches (25 cm) or less in diameter; if the container is larger than that, you can safely remove 1 inch (2.5 cm) or even more of the root ball. Never, however, remove more than a third of the root system. The next step is to reposition the plant in its old pot, which has been scrubbed clean, or in a new container of the same size, in which the washed drainage material and soil separator have been placed. Placing new soil under and around the trimmed root ball, remember to keep the soil surface a few inches (approximately 5 cm) below the rim of the pot to accommodate pools of water that briefly flood the surface when plants are watered.

The newly root-pruned tree or shrub should be covered with polyethylene or polypropylene plastic to heighten humidity and thereby slow down loss of water through the leaves until the truncated roots once again can take up enough water to support a high rate of transpiration. After a week or so, the plastic cover can be opened gradually. When the plant looks recovered from any wilting it may have experienced, you should prune its top to reduce the demands on the smaller root system; remove about the same percentage or fraction of the topgrowth as you cut from the root system.

Limits to Growth: A plant that needs repotting but can't afford to grow too large can be kept from becoming unwieldy by a combination of root and top pruning. The roots are pruned at the time of repotting, and the top is pruned only after the plant has recovered from any wilting.

A GUIDE TO SOME CHOICE TREES AND SHRUBS FOR INDOOR GROWING

ARALIA FAMILY

As araliads the schefflera (*Brassaia actinophylla,* which formerly was classified in the genus *Schefflera*), and the false aralia *(Dizygotheca elegantissima)* share certain characteristics. These related species are trees in their native habitats, but when confined to pots and grown indoors, they resemble shrubs, forming numerous small trunks. Both plants, moreover, have a common pattern of leaf growth. The false aralia produces from 7 to 11 leaflets in clusters at the ends of slender branches; as the plant matures, it produces leaves that are two to three times the size of the former ones. The schefflera also has clusters of leaflets, but they increase in number, rather than size, as the specimen matures, with up to 16 leaflets per cluster on the older plants.

To stretch the similarities further would do injustice to both these popular species. Schefflera is also called the umbrella tree, for its glossy, oblong, bright green leaflets arise from the top of stems which radiate from more elongated stems like the spokes of an umbrella. False aralia, however, has delicate, long, serrated, lacy leaflets that are copper-red in bright light. While the false aralia needs partial sun, moderate warmth, and constant moisture, and can tolerate relatively wet soil, schefflera, which also prefers at least three hours of bright light daily, likes a slightly cooler room and should dry out between waterings. False aralias are most often propagated from cuttings, scheffleras by air layering. Both trees do well in a blend of 2 parts loam, 1 part compost (or leaf mold), and 1 part sand, and enter a dormant period from October to February when the air temperature around them should drop to the high 50s (approximately 13° to 15°C).

Another appealing decorator plant in the

Aralias: From left to right, schefflera, false aralia, and Japanese aralia represent the Aralia family. Although sharing a common leaf growth pattern, these three plants exhibit a diversity of leaf shapes ranging from oblong and bright green to long, serrated, and copper-red to large, glossy, and maplelike.

Aralia family is the Japanese aralia *(Fatsia japonica).* The only species in its genus, this little-branching shrub will reach a height of four to ten feet (1.2 to 3 m) indoors, putting forth large, glossy, maplelike leaves having as many as nine deep, broad lobes. Tolerating temperatures down to 40°F (4°C), Japanese aralias like moist, sandy, peaty soil and can get by on fairly dim light, although they do best with ample light—even full sun. The cultivar 'Variegata', which has white-edged leaves, needs diffused light and less water than the species, and the compact 'Moseri' makes a particularly manageable house plant. Fatsias benefit from occasional thinning and spring pruning to prevent legginess. They are best propagated from suckers or cuttings.

The popular tree ivy or aralia ivy ($\times$*Fatshedera lizei*) is an intriguing cross of *Fatsia japonica* 'Moseri' and *Hedera helix* var. *hibernica.* With support this woody-stemmed shrub grows to six feet (1.8 m) high, displaying mammoth, leathery, English-ivy-like leaves that may reach eight inches (20 cm) in length and ten inches (25 cm) in width. Liking diffused moderate to bright light and even moisture, the tree ivy tolerates a wide range of temperatures, accepting anywhere from 70°F down to 55°F (21° to 13°C) in the daytime, and from 55° to 40°F (13° to 4°C) at night. The variegated form prefers low light and needs to dry out somewhat between waterings. Fatshederas are perpetuated by air layering or stem cuttings.

Also among the more attractive genera in the Araliaceae is the Polynesian genus *Polyscias.* Many-branching shrubs with picturesquely crooked stems and feathery, aromatic leaves, polyscias like some shade and should be watered when the soil surface is dry. A delightful species for indoors is the willowy Ming aralia *(P. fruticosa),* which has plentiful lacy leaves clustered toward its branch ends and which reaches a height of six to eight feet (1.8 to 2.4 m). The cultivar 'Elegans' grows perhaps half as tall; given moderate to high humidity, evenly moist, loamy soil, and temperatures above 65°F (18°C), it makes an easy-going and aristocratic-looking container plant. Propagate it from tip or root cuttings or by air layering.

Araucaria Species

Evergreens belonging to the Araucaria family, Araucariaceae, araucarias have found their way from the South Temperate Zone into many an outdoor ornamental planting in mild regions of the United States. They also are much loved as house plants. Of the three *Araucaria* species most often grown in the home, *A. heterophylla,* the Norfolk Island pine, is the most well known. Although *A. araucana,* the monkey-puzzle tree (a native of Chile with stiff needles and asymmetrical, seemingly disjointed branches), and *A. bidwillii,* the bunya-bunya (an Australian

An Evergreen for Indoors: Symmetrical and graceful enough to accent any decor, Norfolk Island pine is a slow grower that requires even moisture, cool temperatures, and filtered light to do well.

tree having tiered, spokelike, spiny branches that also grow with little direction), are both less symmetrical in shape than the Norfolk Island pine, all three are appealing indoors and are cared for in much the same way. The most illustrious of the three is a native of Norfolk Island, which is approximately 900 miles (1,448 km) northeast of Sydney, Australia. There the related *A. columnaris* grows over 200 feet (61 m) high. Toward the end of his second expedition to the South Pacific islands, Captain James Cook described the tree in his logbook: "We found tall trees to be a kind of Spruce Pine, very proper for spars, of which we were in want. We were no longer at a loss to know of what trees the natives made their canoes. On this little island there were some which measured 20 inches diameter and between 60 and 70 feet in length and would have done well for a foremast to the *Resolution* had one been wanting."

Even though *Araucaria* species will never make masts when grown as indoor trees, they have many advantages. They do well in cool rooms with low light—a southern exposure can burn the tips of the branches—and they will grow slowly but steadily in the same pot for many years, benefiting from a dry period in the winter. By misting the foliage and providing evenly moist, but not waterlogged, soil high in humus, you can nurture small, well-proportioned or asymmetrical plants (depending on the effect you wish to achieve) into ten-foot (3 m) specimens over the years. Propagation is by seeds, air layering, or from the tip cutting of the terminal leader. Be cautious about removing the tip of the terminal leader or other branches of the Norfolk Island pine, though, for pruned branches won't grow back and the tree may lose its graceful symmetry.

Citrus and Related Species

Citrus trees are by far the most prominent members of the Rue family—a group of mostly woody, often evergreen plants characterized by pungent or aromatic oil. The re-

wards of growing citrus are probably greater than those derived from any other group of related plants, for such trees can provide the threefold pleasure of lush foliage, fragrant flowers, and edible fruit. Bear in mind, however, that propagating grapefruit or lemon seeds will only rarely yield the coveted results, although it will save money. Plants grown from such pips often develop into scrubby, overly thorny shrubs that flower infrequently and fruit almost never. On the other hand, it is quite possible to start fruiting lime, orange, and kumquat trees from seeds. The alternative is to buy dwarf citrus varieties or cultivars; under ideal conditions some of these can grow to 8 feet (2.4 m), but indoors they easily can be maintained at heights as low as 24 inches (61 cm) or less—especially if both top pruning and root pruning are done.

Likely choices for indoor pot culture include *Citrus aurantiifolia* 'Bears', a dwarf

Dwarf Lemon Tree: Abundant glossy green leaves, sweetly scented flowers, and large, tasty fruits are the rewards to be savored when raising *Citrus limon* 'Ponderosa'.

lime; *C. limon* 'Meyer', a dwarf lemon which looks its best in midwinter; *C. limon* 'Ponderosa', another dwarf lemon much prized for its large, fragrant flowers, distinctive leaves and huge, flavorful fruits; × *Citrofortunella mitis,* the widely grown, highly ornamental calamondin—a hardy, easy-to-grow hybrid yielding small, well-flavored fruits like acid tangerines, which keep well on the tree and make an excellent fruit drink; and *Citrus* × *limonia,* the very decorative Otaheite orange, much favored as a dwarf pot plant.

Once included in the genus *Citrus*, the closely related genus *Fortunella* also includes pleasing plants for container growing. *F. margarita,* the Nagami kumquat, looks much like a miniature orange tree. It is sweetly scented all over and yields completely edible, bright orange fruits the size and shape of olives that ripen in late spring.

Citrus-type trees need bright light year-round and require soil that is rich in humus but exceptionally well drained. A planter 14 to 18 inches (36 to 46 cm) square will provide many years of ample root room for a dwarf specimen, although a smaller pot may be adequate for two to four years or for trees being kept small by root pruning. A key requirement is moisture, and citrus plants should be grown where the humidity can be kept high and should never be allowed to dry out between waterings—an oversight that can result in excessive fruit and leaf drop. (Note: Some so-called "June drop" of fruit and leaves is considered normal during hot, dry weather and will often occur despite adequate watering.)

The growth of orange and lemon trees slows greatly when the temperature drops to 50°F (10°C), and that of limes and kumquats decreases at around 55°F (13°C), but the trees can be rested in winter in a well-lighted location at temperatures as low as 40°F (4°C). During such a rest they should be watered much less than in summer. If the trees are being grown not in a cool greenhouse but in the home, nighttime temperatures in winter should be at least as low as 55° to 60°F (13° to 16°C).

Spring temperatures for citrus should be no lower than 50°F (10°C), rising to 70°F (21°C) by May, with a midsummer high of 80°F (27°C) for oranges and 85°F (29°C) for lemons and limes. Ventilate the trees well in hot weather, and shade them somewhat from very intense sun. When it is warm, the foliage should be mist-sprayed daily, although very high humidity should be avoided.

Citrus trees can be fed monthly with fish emulsion fertilizer applied as directed on the package. The trees can be fertilized lightly year-round.

When flower buds open, hand pollinate them as described in chapter 8 unless you have placed the trees outdoors where insects can effect pollination. (Actually, many citrus flowers can set fruit without being pollinated; the fruits not pollinated will simply be seedless.) During fruiting, high temperatures and moderate watering and humidity are needed to create fruits of a good size and flavor.

Oranges and lemons can be propagated from leafy semihardwood cuttings rooted in sandy soil under good light in July. The Meyer lemon is one of the easiest citrus trees to perpetuate in this way. Oranges also can be propagated by layering branches into sandy soil in summer, while lemon shoots can be layered in October.

Ficus Species

Their attractiveness and durability have made fig trees among the most ubiquitous of house plants. Belonging to the Mulberry family, members of this genus vary greatly in appearance, but generally share the need for warm temperatures of up to 80° or 85°F (27° or 29°C) during the day and a nighttime minimum of 60°F (16°C). Thriving in loamy soil and moderate to bright light, figs prefer a humidity of 40 to 50 percent and do best if surface soil is allowed to dry out between thorough waterings. These plants enter a dormant period in early winter, and from the time they stop growing (and perhaps drop some leaves) until growth resumes, they should not be watered before the soil is bone dry. Otherwise root rot may result. As they quickly lose any shape you may strive to create, figs need to be well pruned. This should be done just above the leaf nodes before spring growth starts. Fig trees are propagated by air layering.

The so-called weeping figs, with drooping branches, include *F. stricta* and the popular *F. benjamina,* a two- to five-foot (0.6 to 1.5 m) tree with smallish, pointed, ovate leaves that are quite profuse if the tree is given ample light. An outstanding cultivar is *F. benjamina* 'Exotica', with leaves that are somewhat twisted at their tips.

Having large, thick leaves, the supremely adaptable rubber plant *(F. elastica)* is hard to kill unless you give it too much water or move it suddenly from partial shade to full sun. To make a rubber plant send forth branches, it is necessary to cut off the straight stem at the uppermost node when the plant is about 24 inches (61 cm) tall. One slow-growing and good-looking cultivar is the wide-leaved 'Decora', which needs bright light, and the most attractive variegated form is 'Doescheri'.

A third handsome species is *F. lyrata,* the fiddleleaf fig—a vigorous, woody-stemmed plant with glossy, dark green, generously sized leaves shaped like violins. Unlike the light-loving weeping figs and rubber tree, this fig prefers partial shade; its leaves scorch readily in bright sunlight.

Other fig trees suited to indoor container culture include the mistletoe fig *(F. deltoidea),* which bears pseudo-fruits, and the 'Celeste' cultivar of the common fig *(F. carica),* which can yield delicious fruits when cultivated properly. Not requiring hand pollination, the common fig bears small green fruits that quite suddenly plump to the size of walnuts and turn bronze-purple on ripening. Two-year-old stock may fruit during the second summer after planting. Fruit usually

Fig Trees: Although not commonly called a fig, the hardy rubber tree at left, with its bold, glossy leaves, is indeed a member of the genus *Ficus.* More readily identifiable is the weeping fig *(F. benjamina)* at center, with its drooping branches. The fig *(F. lyrata)* at right displays large, glossy, fiddle-shaped leaves, from which its common name is derived.

ripens in June or July outdoors and in the autumn when grown indoors. When you first receive a fig tree from the nursery, expose it to strong sun gradually. It will generally do best in diffuse rather than direct light. Set it outside in summer if possible and feed it frequently with manure tea. Pinch off the growing tips of all strong shoots when they have produced four or five leaves and you will create a bushier, heavier-bearing tree — sometimes one with as many as four trunks. Some people find that fig trees in pots live longer and bear better if given a winter dormancy period in a cool basement where the temperature can be maintained at 40° to 45°F (4° to 7°C). During this winter period soil should be kept from drying out entirely, but less water is required. Inside, fig trees grow to five feet (1.5 m) tall.

PALM FAMILY

Equally suited to swaying on a tropical island or lending their graceful lines to an apartment or office, palms are unique among trees: they belong to the monocotyledonous class of plants, and their trunks are tubular stems with spongy centers and lack the central core of hard wood ringed by growth cells that characterizes most trees. As a result, palm trunks do not grow in width as hardwood trees do. They increase only in height, usually growing from a single terminal point. If this bud is removed, the stem will die. As this suggests, palms cannot be pruned; they can, however, readily be limited in size by confinement in pots that are quite small relative to the height of the plant. This characteristic, coupled with the facts that palms are slow growing, lack taproots, and prefer—or at least tolerate—low light, makes these stately plants excellent choices for indoor container culture.

Highly ornamental, palms are usually classified in two groups according to their foliage. Those with long fronds divided into many segments from the midrib are called feather palms, whereas genera with broad leaves shaped much like a hand with fingers spread are termed fan palms. During the Victorian and Edwardian eras, huge-leaved fan palms such as *Livistona chinensis* dominated many a parlor, but contemporary decorators increasingly favor the more upright and compact feather types. Some popular genera are *Chamaedorea, Howea, Caryota,* and *Phoenix.*

Often chosen for their oriental ambience are reedy feather palms such as the very durable, dwarf, cluster-forming bamboo palm *(Chamaedorea erumpens),* the Costa Rican, or showy, bamboo palm *(C. costaricana),* with handsome green canes and long-lasting, attractive fronds; the lacy-looking reed palm *(C. seifrizii);* and the comparatively fast-growing parlor palm *(C. elegans),* or its miniature slow-growing cultivar 'Bella' (sometimes called neanthe bella). Except for this small

Blooming Palm: Most palms grown indoors are not likely to bloom; however, a mature plant, four to five years old, grown under optimum conditions may surprise you with tiny, round, yellow flowers borne on slender stalks rising from a leaf stalk cluster.

cultivar, which grows to about 36 inches (91 cm), *Chamaedorea* species reach 8 to 10 feet (2.4 to 3 m) in height. Prized for their excellent growth in subdued light, they prefer warm temperatures, a humidity of 40 to 50 percent, and a blend of 2 parts loam, 1 part coarse compost or leaf mold, and 1 part sand, kept evenly moist.

Caryota and *Howea* species prefer bright indirect light, but they, too, require moist conditions. The well-known, easy-to-please curly sentry palm *(Howea belmoreana)* attains heights of 30 feet (9.1 m) with relative speed on its native soil of Lord Howe Island in the Pacific; cultivated indoors, however, this palm matures slowly, usually never reaching half of its potential height. On the other hand, the kentia, or paradise, palm *(H. forsterana)* can grow to an enormous size indoors, but its weak stem can snap easily. As a young plant, however, the kentia palm has

Haven for a Palm: Through daily use, this bathroom provides ideal humidity levels for palm growing. In order to make room for plants, the original window was extended outward by 36 inches (91 cm), and clouded glass was used in the lower third to insure privacy.

shade, and regular watering, but can adjust even to air conditioning.

Like other palms, most of which need constant moisture, all of the species discussed here make excellent plants for the humid microclimate of the bathroom. For best results, help new palms adjust to growing conditions in the house by starting them off in a bright location. If a plant appears to be field-grown, replace light brown or clayey soil with a lighter, better-draining soil mix. At the very least, scrape off any extra fertilizer on the soil surface, since high levels of fertilization will cause root burn (and browning of the leaves)

(continued on page 440)

A Touch of the Tropics: A brightly colored pet lorikeet adorns the graceful fronds of this palm tree. The overall coloring, frond shapes, and growth habits of palms tend to create a verdant, junglelike effect, which helps to soften a stark decor or fill in barren spaces.

been a parlor favorite since its introduction to Europe in 1871. Like *H. belmoreana,* this is a good plant for beginners, for it will live on for years, enduring dry air and changes in temperature. Howeas are nonsuckering and for a fuller look, several different size specimens of a species can be planted in the same pot.

Unlike *Chamaedorea* and *Howea* palms, *Caryota* species like soil kept constantly wet rather than just evenly moist. *C. mitis* (the clustered, or dwarf, fishtail palm), and the nonsuckering *C. ureus* (the fishtail palm) are highly decorative but challenging to grow indoors, for they must have good light and plenty of warmth and humidity, and cannot tolerate drafts or air conditioning.

The pygmy date palm *(Phoenix roebelenii)* offers a single rough trunk topped by arching, dark green, feathery leaves. This prototypical palm will reach eight or nine feet (2.4 or 2.7 m) indoors and prefers warmth,

12 Popular Palms for the Indoors

Included in this chart are several popular and easy-care palms,
as well as some that are less well known but equally enjoyable to grow.
All palms do well in an all-purpose potting mix, with normal room
temperatures. Daily mistings and high humidity help them thrive and
keep frond tips from turning brown. These palms can be fertilized
every 2 weeks during active growth with mild manure tea,
except for *Chamaerops* and *Rhapis* species, which should be fed once a month.

NAME		DESCRIPTION	LIGHT	MOISTURE	COMMENTS
Caryota mitis Dwarf fishtail palm		Fan-shaped fronds with wedge-shaped, ragged-edged, deep green segments; mature plant measures up to 8 feet (2.4 m) tall.	Bright light, no direct sun; eastern or southern exposure.	Constantly moist; decrease watering during winter rest.	A popular choice for the home, with undemanding culture; the striking shape of the frond segments makes this palm a good showpiece when featured against a bare wall.
Chamaedorea elegans Parlor palm		Feathery fronds borne on slender, canelike stems; mature plant measures up to 10 feet (3 m) tall.	Low light, no direct sun; eastern exposure.	Evenly moist; keep soil barely moist during winter rest.	The palm most commonly found indoors due to ease of culture and wide availability; popular choice to fill in dimly lit corners with greenery; group several smaller plants in a pot for bushy effect.
Chamaedorea erumpens Bamboo palm		Feathery fronds on tall stems, resembling bamboo; mature plant measures to 10 feet (3 m) tall.	See *C. elegans*	See *C. elegans*	See *C. elegans*
Chamaerops humilis Fan palm		Fan-shaped fronds with stiff, gray-green segments; trunks are black and rough textured; mature plant measures to 6 feet (1.8 m) tall.	Bright light, some direct sun; eastern or western exposure.	Evenly moist; let surface dry during winter rest.	Pale green immature fronds sport a covering of fine, silvery hairs; the growth habit adds dramatic vertical accent to room design.

NAME		DESCRIPTION	LIGHT	MOISTURE	COMMENTS
Chrysalido-carpus lutescens Butterfly palm		Feathery fronds with pale green leaflets, borne on clusters of yellow, canelike stems; mature plant grows to 5 feet (1.5 m) tall.	Bright light, no direct sun; eastern or western exposure.	Evenly moist; keep soil barely moist during winter rest.	Tight stem clusters with graceful arching fronds create a fountain shape that is very effective in enhancing room decor.
Howea belmoreana Curly sentry palm		Feathery fronds with dark green, waxy, drooping leaflets; mature plant measures up to 8 feet (2.4 m) tall.	Bright to low light, no direct sun; any exposure.	Evenly moist; keep soil barely moist during winter rest.	This palm with its canopy of green fronds adds freshness to low-light areas; several plants combined in a pot create a lush, full effect; tolerates a degree of neglect.
Howea forsterana Kentia or paradise palm		Feathery fronds with flat, rigid, waxy leaflets; mature plant grows to 8 feet (2.4 m) tall.	See *H. belmoreana*	See *H. belmoreana*	See *H. belmoreana*
Livistona chinensis Chinese fan palm		Fan-shaped fronds with shiny green segments that droop at the tip; mature plant measures from 4 to 10 feet (1.2 to 3 m) tall.	Bright, filtered light, no direct sun; eastern or western exposure.	Evenly moist; decrease watering during winter rest.	The fountain shape provides an attractive tropical backdrop for groupings of other plants.
Phoenix roebelenii Pygmy date palm		Feathery, arching fronds; dark green leaflets are covered with fine layer of white scales; mature plant grows to 6 feet (1.8 m) or more in height.	Bright, filtered light, no direct sun; eastern or western exposure.	Evenly moist; decrease watering during winter rest.	A more dramatic display can be created by grouping several smaller plants in the same container; a hardy palm that tolerates some neglect while adding a graceful and elegant accent to room design.

(chart continued on next page)

NAME		DESCRIPTION	LIGHT	MOISTURE	COMMENTS
Rhapis humilis Lady palm		Fan-shaped fronds with broad and rounded segments; rigid stems arranged in clumps, covered with rough brown hairs; mature plant measures 5 to 8 feet (1.5. to 2.4 m) tall.	Bright, filtered light, no direct sun; eastern or western exposure.	Water when soil is slightly dry; decrease watering during winter rest.	The numerous reedlike stems create a bushy, compact effect, just the right touch to fill in empty space in a room.
Washingtonia filifera Petticoat palm		Fan-shaped fronds with gray-green segments bearing thin fibers along the edges; mature plant measures 6 to 8 feet (1.8 to 2.4 m) tall.	Bright light, several hours direct sun; eastern or western exposure.	Evenly moist; decrease watering during winter rest.	An easy plant to tend in the home, this palm has a stark, rugged look which lends a bold accent to decor.
Washingtonia robusta Thread palm		Fan-shaped fronds with stiff, bright green segments bearing thin fibers along the edges; mature plant measures 6 to 8 feet (1.8 to 2.4 m) tall.	See *W. filifera*	See *W. filifera*	See *W. filifera*

in the dimmer light of the home environment. Make sure palms are never chilled by direct cold drafts from open doors or windows, for afterward the leaves are likely to turn brown and drop. If possible, water palms from below, but never allow them to sit in stagnant water. Try to use deep containers rather than wide, shallow ones, for palm roots grow more vertically than horizontally, and provide at least three inches (8 cm) of drainage material in the bottom. Repot these plants only when absolutely necessary, transferring them to pots of the next larger size either in spring or early summer. Fertilize palms very lightly and infrequently unless they are growing in strong light.

Most palms are propagated from fresh seeds sown in peat at 70°F (21°C) under very humid conditions. A few can be reproduced by division. For more cultural information on members of some popular genera in the Palm family (Palmae) see appropriate entries in the Encyclopedia section.

Yucca Species

Succulents forming rosettes of rugged leaves, yuccas can be stemless herbs or treelike in structure. These distinctive-looking plants belong to the Agave family, Agavaceae, which used to be classified as part of the Lily family, Liliaceae. The long, slender, lancelike

The Rugged Yucca: These succulent plants are easily raised indoors — just provide lots of sun, warmth, and thorough watering when needed. Because they are highly tolerant and nearly immune to pests, you can count on their dramatic presence for a long while.

leaves of yuccas, which sit erect atop rough-barked trunks, are quite dramatic, and the stark, bold quality of these trees makes them a striking choice for a modern or southwestern decor. Somewhat surprisingly, given their scabrous hide and sharp foliage, yuccas blossom in spring or summer, producing cup-shaped, waxy, white flowers. (The inflorescence is really a raceme that arises from the center of the leaves.)

Since their native habitats tend to be arid regions of the southwestern United States *(Yucca brevifolia)* or Mexico *(Y. elephantipes),* you can treat yuccas as you would cacti: that is, give them plenty of light, direct if possible (they can, however, survive in light as low as 20 footcandles); low humidity; and thorough watering whenever the soil has be-

come quite dry. The growing medium for these plants can be sandy and must drain freely; yuccas should never be allowed to stand in water. Preferring hot days and cool nights, these tolerant trees can adjust to somewhat cool temperatures—even to air conditioning. Stemmed yuccas are propagated from seeds, stem cuttings, or offsets. Unlike many house plants, they are rarely attacked by diseases or insects. A particularly handsome species is *Y. gloriosa* (palm-lily), which has a short, crooked trunk, pointed gray-green leaves with reddish margins, and fragrant flowers that open at night.

As Shakespeare wrote in *As You Like It,* there are "tongues in trees." What they say in terms of space and mood can rival the poetry of any great writer. They not only have unlimited appeal in color, shape, and size, but thanks to their dimensions, their potential for creating balance and symmetry in a room far exceeds that of most house plants. An interior landscape is kinetic when filled with trees and shrubs, for they alter their shape over the years, filter sunlight in continually different patterns, and change color during growing seasons, sometimes offering fragrant blooms. In a city apartment trees and shrubs can replace those found in the traditional suburban or rural lawn. But such islands of greenery do more than impart a feeling of nature to a room in the city or the country.

At the Isabella Gardner Museum in Boston, Massachusetts, the central courtyard holds the most precious art on view in the halls. There, jasmine bushes droop with yellow blossoms, highlighting the works of Monet and Sargent; miniature white blossoms of heather set off the mosaic of Medusa's hair; and podocarpus trees delicately balance the sturdy Grecian urns. Your home may never match the beauty of this Renaissance palazzo, but as you grow in ingenuity and understanding of your interior space, the art of trees and shrubs holds such a promise for you.

CHAPTER 21

Bonsai

Literally, bonsai denotes any dwarfed plant or tree grown in a shallow pot or tray. Producing bonsai is a careful process of pruning new growth and old roots and attaining a delicate balance of branches and twigs on a trunk that tapers gently to the top of the plant. But the spirit of bonsai goes much deeper than the techniques involved; the planting and growing of that tree is an ancient art of oriental derivation. It is an art of form and design, the ultimate goal of which is to produce an impression in miniature of a tree as it exists in nature. Bonsai is judged on the shape of its branches, the flow of its trunk, and the way it stands beside other trees of its kind. The growing of the bonsai plant, from its very beginning to its repotting, its training and shaping, and to its display, is a long process that requires great patience and perseverance. It is an art form that has been passed from father to son for many years in Japan. It is not unusual in that country to see a bonsai tree that has been in cultivation for several hundred years in the same family. Such is the process of this gentle but steadfast oriental art.

Bonsai is a symbolic art, which aims to create a "little nature." The bonsai practitioner seeks to focus on one part of the forest, perhaps one tree that appears to be drifting with the wind, or a small clump of trees that grow together around cliffs or near streams. By capturing a detail of nature, the grower strives to create a feeling of *wabi,* the sense of quiet, dignified simplicity associated with a place, or *sabi,* the sense of simplicity and quietness associated with something that is old and used over and over again.

The origins of bonsai are a bit cloudy. Some scholars claim that it began in China about 1,500 years ago, but the earliest evidence we have is a Japanese scroll painting from 700 to 800 years ago that pictures a dwarfed tree in a ceramic pot.

The fashions of bonsai have changed over the course of its history. At first, the aim was most often to produce plants that assumed grotesque shapes; a more natural flow of branches and trunks became prevalent in the mid-nineteenth century. Since World War II, flowering trees and informal styles have become more popular in Japan.

The first bonsai displayed in the West was shown at an exhibition in London in 1909. Bonsai was brought to the United States by Japanese-Americans who settled on the West Coast. The art soon spread, and today people from all regions have taken it up. In fact, the United States, with its wide range of climates, soils, and geographical characteristics, has produced specimens not seen in Japan.

The goal of indoor bonsai as it is practiced in the West today is to grow small-leaved, woody-stemmed evergreen, deciduous, or flowering plants in very small containers. Plants are kept small by frequently pinching off the growing tips, by cutting off all leaves that exceed the desired size, by wiring branches to control the direction of growth, and by yearly root trimming.

CHOOSING PLANTS

Successful bonsai begins with choosing the right plant. The western definition of bonsai encompasses any woody-stemmed plant that is grown in a complementary container and trained to a miniature size and a decorative shape. Trees, shrubs, and some vines, both hardy and tropical, all can be trained as bonsai. The best bonsai candidates are plants that have some character to begin with. Look for plants with small leaves, interesting bark,

Opposite, Japanese five-needle pine, Pinus parviflora, *correctly wired for training.*

and a branching growth habit. The style in which you wish to train the plant also influences the choice of a likely specimen. The formal upright style, for example, requires a symmetrical plant with a straight trunk and heavy branches near the base of the trunk. On the other hand, slanted or cascading styles and root-over-rock plantings work quite well with trees that are gnarled and twisted into irregular shapes.

For indoor bonsai it is important to choose a plant, such as a jade plant, that will grow well indoors. Tropical types are often good choices, although some hardy evergreen and deciduous plants will do well if they are given a dormant cold period each year. You need not feel bound to using the pines and maples with which the Japanese have traditionally worked. If you do wish to take a traditional approach, junipers and cypress are two classic bonsai plants that are well suited to indoor cultivation.

In general, beginners may find broadleaf evergreens and deciduous trees easier to work with than conifers. The Kingsville Dwarf Boxwood (*Buxus microphylla* 'Compacta'), for example, is an excellent bonsai candidate. It is naturally petite, with tiny leaves and aged-looked bark. Pruning and pinching are usually all that's necessary to train this small tree — wiring is not needed. The common myrtle *(Myrtus communis)* is another beautiful and easy-to-grow subject. If your taste runs to flowering and fruiting plants, you might try azaleas, or trees such as crab apple, orange, persimmon, or pomegranate. For best results, these plants should be grown as house plants for several months before training begins to allow them to adapt to the indoor environment.

Other good plants for novice growers include the dwarf powder puff *(Calliandra surinamensis),* confederate or star jasmine *(Trachelospermum jasminoides),* and small-leaved *Ficus* species such as the mistletoe fig *(F. deltoidea).* Miniature gardenias and camellias also work well. See the chart on Plants for Beginners for a list of plants which the American Bonsai Society recommends for novice growers.

Plants for Beginners

The American Bonsai Society has recommended these plants for beginning bonsai growers.

Alpine Plants (require a cold period in winter and cool growing conditions)

Ficus neriifolia var. *regularia*—(briefly deciduous)

Picea glauca var. *albertiana*—Alberta spruce (evergreen)

Picea pungens and varieties—Colorado spruce (evergreen)

Pinus mugo—Swiss mountain pine (evergreen)

Temperate Plants (require a cold period in winter)

Acer ginnala—Amur maple (deciduous)

Acer palmatum—Japanese maple (deciduous)

Acer rubrum—native swamp maple, red maple (deciduous)

Buxus microphylla var. *japonica,* and other varieties—Japanese boxwood (evergreen)

Buxus sempervirens and varieties—English boxwood (evergreen)

Ilex crenata 'Convexa' and other cultivars—Japanese holly (evergreen)

Juniperus chinensis, and cultivar 'Robusta Green'—Chinese juniper (evergreen)

Juniperus chinensis 'Nana'—dwarf spreading juniper (evergreen)

Juniperus squamata 'Prostrata'—prostrate juniper (evergreen)

Pieris japonica—andromeda (evergreen)

Pinus parviflora—Japanese white pine (evergreen)

Pinus peuce—Balkan pine (evergreen)

Pinus thunbergiana—Japanese black pine (evergreen)

Podocarpus macrophyllus, and var. *maki*—yew pine (evergreen)

Rhododendron spp., especially low-growing varieties—azalea (evergreen, semievergreen, or deciduous, depending on species)

Taxodium distichum var. *distichum*—bald cypress (deciduous)

Temperate Plants (continued)

Ulmus crassifolia—cedar elm (deciduous)

Ulmus parvifolia—Chinese elm (semievergreen)

Ulmus pumila—Siberian elm (deciduous)

Zelkova serrata—Japanese gray-bark elm (deciduous)

Tropical and Subtropical Plants (need no cold period)

Carissa grandiflora, including dwarf varieties—natal plum (evergreen)

Ficus benjamina—weeping fig (persistent-leaved)

Ficus deltoidea—mistletoe fig (persistent-leaved)

Gardenia jasminoides—gardenia (evergreen)

Grevillea robusta—silk oak (evergreen)

Olea europaea—European olive (evergreen)

Quercus agrifolia—California live-oak (evergreen)

WHERE TO GET PLANTS FOR BONSAI

Plants for bonsai may be started from seeds, although some grow so slowly that several years would be needed for the plant to be mature enough for training to begin. In some cases it is desirable to begin with seedlings, but more often it is better to purchase a plant that is old enough to train. Woody-stemmed house plants and many kinds of trees and shrubs suitable for bonsai culture can be purchased at local nurseries, garden marts, and even plant shops. There are a number of nurseries in the United States which specialize in bonsai plants. It is best to choose your bonsai candidates on the spot — ordering plants or seeds by mail does not guarantee that you will receive a plant that is well suited to training. However, if you are unable to purchase suitable plants from nurseries in your area, you might check the *Journal of the American Bonsai Society*. The society screens all advertising accepted for the journal, and you can be sure that the dealers listed there are reputable.

You also may be able to find some good bonsai specimens in the wild. Dwarfed plants may sometimes be found in nature, where they have been stunted by climatic extremes and a harsh environment. Often their battle for survival has increased their resilience, and they are extremely rugged plants. Nature itself has distorted their shapes, often creating wild beauty that the home gardener is hard pressed to produce in domestic plants.

You can hunt in wooded areas or parks for these highly prized specimens, but do so only with great care. Such trees have been sought for so many years in Japan that it is rare to find them there outside of protected areas. Since the art of bonsai is relatively new in the United States, the chances of finding them here may be better. But it is of the utmost importance to be cognizant of the delicate balance of nature. Abide by any local regulations that may govern the removal of plants from public parks and wooded areas. Be aware of private property, and seek the permission of the owner of the land you are hunting on. And check to make sure you are not collecting a rare, threatened, or endangered species.

The best season for collecting such plants is early spring, before the new buds have opened. Transplanting too late in the season will shock the plant's system and possibly kill it.

When a suitable plant has been found, it is best to retain as much of the original surrounding soil as possible. It is also best to dig out the tree without cutting the taproot. If this is not possible, cut the taproot as far down as possible. The earth and the roots should then be well covered with wet sphagnum moss and secured in a cover of paper or plastic sheeting. As the tree is being transported to its destination, it must be secure and not allowed to be jolted unnecessarily. In addition, it should be kept in the open air, and not closed into any small space for any length of time. The tree must be kept damp by misting with a sprayer.

Once home, the tree should be planted as soon as possible. If its roots are short near the trunk, it can be planted in a deep training pot, retaining the original soil. Do not try to begin training the young tree until it has formed new roots, which usually takes three or four months or more. During this period, the soil around the tree should be kept moist, and its leaves should be misted several times daily, depending on the heat.

GROWING AND CARING FOR BONSAI

Bonsai plants are dwarfed by a careful process of pinching back the growing branch tips and pruning the roots. Root pruning encourages the development of a shallow system of fine feeder roots, rather than a large, deep taproot. It also helps to keep the plant small, and combined with top pruning, causes the trunk and branches to grow thicker instead of taller or longer. Getting started with bonsai will be easier with the help of some special tools. You will need:

> Trimming shears: One size for branches and roots, a smaller set for buds, twigs, leaves, roots
>
> A brush, for topsoil
>
> Pruners, for cutting branches
>
> A watering can with a long nozzle
>
> A sprayer, for misting leaves
>
> Wire cutters, for use with wire needed to tie roots

These tools are available from bonsai nurseries and mail-order firms which specialize in bonsai accessories.

The soil mixture for bonsai should have excellent drainage but enough weight to anchor roots. The mix should be so open in texture that when you water the excess will flow through the medium and drain out the holes in the bottom of the container. Drainage is especially important in shallow pots because they are not deep enough to permit the force of gravity to pull water down and out of the

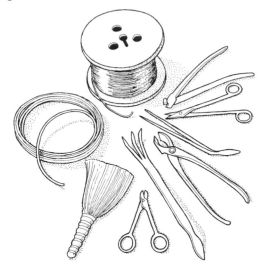

Bonsai Tools: Clockwise from the spool of wire at top are wire cutters, a large pair of trimming shears, tweezers for any delicate work, a pruner, a pronged stick to loosen soil ball, a small pair of trimming shears, a brush for soil, and string for binding rock plantings.

soil. The mix should not be overly rich, but may contain some peat or screened compost. A blend of 1 part all-purpose potting soil and 1 part coarse sand or fine pebbles is usually suitable. Some growers prefer to add extra sand for coniferous plants and extra humus for acid-loving plants like azaleas.

POTTING, REPOTTING, AND ROOT PRUNING

As the bonsai plant grows and matures, it will require replanting and root pruning. Most older bonsai will have to be repotted every two to four years; some plants require yearly root pruning. One sign that a plant needs repotting is when the soil appears to be rising over the rim of its present pot; normally, the soil level should remain just below the edge. If the level is rising, it means that the plant's roots have spread out too far, pushing the soil toward the top. Another sign that a plant needs repotting is the appearance of roots through the drainage hole at the bottom of the pot — this should not be allowed.

Generally spring is the best time for re-

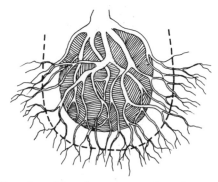

Root Pruning: After the outer roots have been untangled from the root ball, gently work away at least one-third of the soil to free the roots. Trim carefully, leaving 1 inch (2.5 cm) or so of growth outside the root ball.

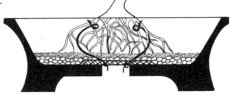

Repotting: Two strands of flexible wire are anchored by twisting one end around a piece of wire mesh set over the drainage hole. These wire strands, which extend upward into the pot, will be used to tie down the plant's roots. Before placing the plant in the pot, spread a layer of gravel on the bottom, followed by a thin layer of soil. After the plant has been tied down, gently add more soil until the surface is even with or slightly lower than the top of the pot.

potting, when the buds on the plants have begun to appear and the plant is strongest.

If you plan to do the repotting outdoors, wait for an overcast day, and pick a spot that is protected from winds.

Gently remove the plant from the pot, taking care not to disturb the soil around the roots. A mature specimen may be returned to the same pot after trimming, but it should be placed in the same spot in the container that it occupied before. When you take the plant out of the pot, be sure to remember how it was positioned.

Next, carefully untangle the roots from around the root ball. With a tapered dowel or a small stick, brush away some of the soil from the roots on the outer edges (sides and bottom) of the root ball. At least a third of the soil around the roots should be removed.

As you work, be careful not to disturb the soil around the stem (or trunk) of the plant.

Now the exposed roots are ready for trimming. The objective of root pruning is to create a small, shallow system of fine roots. What you will do, essentially, is cut back the main root (taproot) and thin out the surface roots. But care must be taken to avoid drastically cutting the taproot; this could kill the plant. With a pair of sharp shears, trim back the roots until they extend only an inch (2.5 cm) or so beyond the ball.

If you are repotting the plant in a new pot, the container must be prepared.

For the new pot, you will need stainless steel mesh and some flexible copper or aluminum wire. A U-shaped piece of wire is inserted through each of the drainage holes in the pot and held in place by a piece of the mesh placed across the holes, around which the wire is twisted. This wire will be used to tie the roots and hold the plant in place.

Spread a layer of gravel in the pot, and then cover it with a thin layer of potting soil. Place the trunk into the soil, but avoid placing it directly in the center of the pot. Then tie down the roots with the wire. They should be rather loosely tied, to allow them to grow in diameter, and excess wire should be cut off. Next place soil in the pot. Gently tap the side of the pot to fill in any spaces between the roots. Excess soil should be brushed away, until the soil surface is slightly below or even with the top of the pot. Water the plant until water comes out of the drainage hole. The plant then can be placed in indirect sunlight for several days before acclimating it to full sun.

For three or four days, watering of the plant should be limited. Wait until the topsoil is dry. For several weeks the new leaves may grow quickly, and will need to be trimmed. After about two months, depending upon the type of plant, the leaves will cease to grow so quickly. This is a sign that the plant has stabilized, and normal care can be given from this point.

TRAINING THE BONSAI PLANT

Training of the bonsai should begin even before the plant is potted for the first time, by removing extraneous branches and up to two-thirds of the root system. One primary root should be left for every branch. Sometimes, the plant is initially shaped by simply cutting it back to the lowest limb. The goal is to remove all but the main branches which form the basic shape you wish the tree to assume. Some growers put the young plant in a regular pot and let it strengthen for six months to

Formal Upright Style: A trident maple tree exhibits the earmarks of this traditional style — a straight trunk with symmetrical, horizontal branches distributed equally on both its sides, with one bottom branch lower than the one opposite it.

Informal Upright Style: The essence of this style is exemplified by the branches of this maple tree *(Acer ginnela)*. A slightly bent trunk bears three major branches, one each extending to the left, to the right, and to the rear to create a dimension of depth.

Slanting Style: A tree bowing before the wind is evoked by the dwarfed form of this apple tree *(Malus sylvestris)*. Two graceful lower branches and an angled trunk are essential elements of this style.

Semi-Cascade Style: In reality an exaggeration of the slanting style, but not as extremely angled as the cascade style, this form requires that the uppermost point of the plant (here, *Hedera helix*) be brought down until it lies on the same plane as the rim of the pot, or extends slightly below it.

Cascade Style: In full bloom, this azalea appears to float on a gentle breeze. This style embraces an extremely slanted trunk, and is best displayed where the trunk can extend downward freely. A twisted, irregular form is created by removing branches from the back of the trunk, and by training the uppermost tip to extend away from and below the bottom of the container.

a year before proceeding with the training. This is almost mandatory for plants started from seeds, because the seedling must be allowed to become strong before regular root trimming and pruning is begun. Some experts recommend waiting until the second repotting (two years) to begin pruning and shaping the tree.

The style of your bonsai tree should follow the natural lines of the plant you select to train. Of course, you can train most plants into any of the following styles, but your task will be easier if you work with the natural shape of the plant. There are five traditional styles into which bonsai can be trained.

The formal upright style is vertical, with the tip of the tree positioned directly in line with its base, and requires an equal number of symmetrical branches on each side of the trunk.

Informal upright is the most commonly used style, because it requires only minimal training. Most plants and trees need only root and branch trimming and little wiring to assume this shape. The informal upright style is characterized by a slightly curved trunk, with one major lower branch to the left, one to the right, and one to the back for depth.

A leaning trunk and two lower branches are required for the slanting style. The lower branches are needed to balance this composition. This style creates the impression of a tree bowed by prevailing winds.

The last two styles are not usually recommended for beginners, as the necessary wiring is rather complicated and requires much patience. But for the more accomplished grower, these dramatic and beautiful styles can be challenging and rewarding.

Semi-cascade is an exaggerated slanting style, in which the tree is trained so that its apex is level with or slightly below the rim of the pot.

The cascade style features an extremely slanted trunk, almost flat against the container. No branches are left on the back of the trunk, and the apex of the tree extends below and beyond the container. Both cascading styles give the feeling of a tree growing on a steep slope or a ledge of rock. Some experts recommend fruiting trees, junipers, and small-leaved azaleas for training in these styles.

As an additional option, trees in the slanting or cascade styles are sometimes trained in the "windswept" form, in which all branches are trained to grow in the same direction, giving the appearance of the tree being buffeted by the strong winds on a mountainside or seacoast.

Wiring the trunk and branches is the usual method of training plants. One basic rule to remember is never to wire the plant

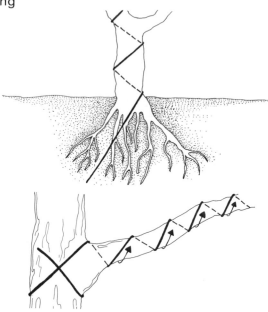

Training through Wiring: To train a bonsai specimen, the trunk and branches are carefully wrapped with wire so they can be gradually bent and held in the desired position. For trunk wiring, secure the wire in the soil by pushing it through the root ball to the bottom of the pot. Wrapping should proceed diagonally up the trunk, in even, 45-degree turns. For branch wiring, take one turn around the trunk to anchor the wire, then continue the spiral wrapping along the branch. Branches on the right side of the trunk are wired in a clockwise direction, as shown here; branches to the left are wrapped counterclockwise.

Windswept Bonsai: This form is meant to evoke the image of a tree bending before gusty winds. To achieve it, all the branches are trained to grow in the same direction.

during its budding season. At that time it is easy to cause permanent damage to the developing tree. Another rule is to wire only as much as is absolutely necessary. Overwiring is one of the two most common mistakes made by bonsai novices. (Overwatering is the other.) Learning how to wire correctly takes time and practice. You must train your hands to "feel" when the wire is being placed properly, and that takes patience.

Two kinds of wire can be used for the operation. Copper wire is good, as is aluminum wire. Wire that has been heat treated, or annealed, is best to use because of its flexibility. You can anneal it yourself by heating it over the flame of a candle until it glows red, and allowing it to cool before bending it. The thickness of the wire should be no more than one-third the thickness of the branch to be wired, and the length should equal the length of the branch. Number 8 copper wire is often used for wiring the main trunk, while the lighter gauge Number 16 is preferred for thinner branches. After training has been completed and the branch has reached the desired shape, all wire is removed.

Before wiring, it is best not to water the tree for one day. This assures that the tree will be flexible enough to withstand the necessary bending of its limbs into the desired shape.

When wiring from the trunk, the wire should be anchored by pushing it into the soil and right through the root ball, toward the bottom of the pot. The wiring is done diagonally around the trunk in even, 45-degree turns upward. Wire firmly enough to allow a stable grip on the trunk, but not so tightly that the wire cuts into the branches. Continue the wire from the trunk to the desired branch, carefully beginning to shape the limb. Once it has been wired it can be moved into position to form the desired style. When wiring only a branch, wrap the end of the wire around the main trunk to anchor it, and then proceed with the spiral wrapping. Wrap the wire in a clockwise direction around branches to the right of the trunk; counterclockwise for branches to the left.

Branches also can be tied into new shapes by a guy wire anchored around the trunk or around another branch. This should be done gradually. The branch can be bent part of the way (if the desired new shape is drastically different), tied for two months, and then bent further, until the new position has been achieved. Attaching several judiciously placed guy wires and pinching and pruning carefully are sometimes all that's needed to train a plant.

After wiring has been completed, the tree will need special care. Keep it out of direct sunlight for two to four days and water it generously. The length of time that the wire should be left on the tree varies from about

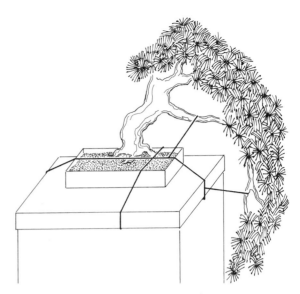

Shaping with Guy Wires: Sometimes a plant can be trained into a new form through the use of guy wires attached in strategic spots on trunk or branches. Used in conjunction with careful pinching and pruning, it can be an effective method. If the tree is to be trained into a shape quite different from its natural one, it is best to proceed in stages, rather than bending the tree into the desired shape at the outset.

three months to a year. When removing the wire, start at the furthest point away from where it is rooted and uncoil the wire slowly and gently so as not to damage the branches.

SOME SPECIAL TECHNIQUES FOR PLANTING AND DISPLAYING BONSAI

Much of the striking effect of a mature bonsai depends on the way it is displayed. Selecting the proper container is very important. The pot should suggest the natural setting of the plant, enhance its beauty, and actually become a part of the bonsai composition. Subdued, earthy colors and subtle forms are most appropriate. The pot should harmonize with the plant and not attract attention to itself. If viewers of your bonsai remark on the beauty of the pot instead of the tree, you have probably chosen the wrong pot. Plants trained in cascading styles are planted in deep containers, but for upright and slanting styles shallow pots just wide enough to allow for maintenance of the root system are used. Containers also must have adequate drainage holes. Since bonsai require constant moisture (sometimes up to four waterings a day in summer), good drainage is a must.

Display your bonsai at eye level, against a light, neutral background which will not interfere with viewing the intricate patterns created by the trunk, branches, and foliage. Some bonsai enthusiasts build special shelving and cases to display collections.

ROCK PLANTINGS

There are various ways to plant bonsai for maximum effect and desired beauty. One popular method is rock planting, which consists of two basic styles: "root over rock," in which the plants are grown on rocks placed on soil (with the plant roots curling around the rock and into the soil), and "clinging to a rock," in which the roots adhere to a layer of peat placed over the rock.

Both aim to re-create a mountain landscape. Rock plantings have certain advantages in that young trees can be more readily used here than in upright and formal styles. A finished-looking bonsai can be made in a relatively short time. Also, unusually shaped trees that are too asymmetrical to use for a more traditional formal upright or slanting style lend themselves to the dramatic beauty of rock planting. Azaleas, junipers, pines, and other evergreens are well suited to rock plantings. You may also wish to include moss or other small, creeping plants.

For clinging-to-a-rock plantings, the best stones to use are those with rough surfaces that can hold pockets of soil. Or holes can be drilled into the rock to accommodate the growing medium. Differently shaped stones will produce varying effects in these plantings. For instance, a large rock with sharply vertical sides and jagged edges may produce

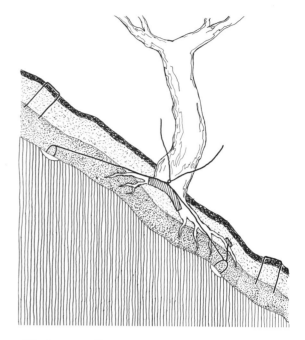

Clinging-to-a-Rock Planting: One way to design a planting reminiscent of a mountain landscape is to provide the tree with a secure foothold on the surface of a rock. The rock shown here lacks natural crevices into which supporting wires can be anchored, so small holes are drilled or chiseled into the surface. Two wire anchors are cemented in place, allowed to dry, then covered with a thin layer of the appropriate peat-based growing medium. The tree is set gently in place, and a thin piece of rubber is laid across the tender roots to prevent the wire from damaging them as it is wrapped around. After the roots are secured, the final covering layer of peat is added, then topped with a layer of living green moss. For additional support until the tree has established itself, wire clips or string can be employed to help bind all the layers together.

the feeling of a steep cliff, with the tree growing on and over it.

Rock planting is similar in effect to a repotting procedure; thus, it should be done in the same season. To form the growing medium, mix equal amounts of peat and soil with enough water to produce a sticky texture. Place a thin layer of the peat mixture on the rock. Then remove the bonsai from its pot and carefully wash most of the soil from its roots. Place the plant on the rock, and

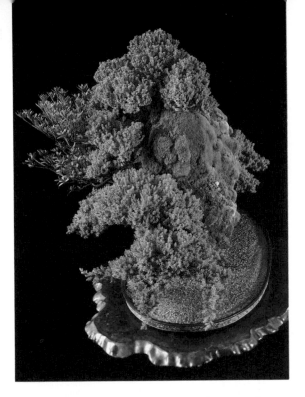

Clinging to Rock: This arrangement, incorporating dwarfed juniper, azalea, and rocks, mimics on a small scale a clump of trees growing on a mountainside. Holes drilled into the rock to cradle soil, along with strategically placed wires can help plants establish themselves in their elevated perches.

Root-over-Rock Planting: The exposed roots of this trident maple have become gnarled and twisted during the course of the tree's growth — wherein lies the appeal of this style. This look is achieved by partially burying a rock, setting a plant over it, then draping the roots down to the soil.

gently cover its roots with a thin layer of the peat mixture.

Until the bonsai can establish itself, the roots must be gently wired to the rock. Thus, as already mentioned, rough-surfaced rocks are very good: the wire can be firmly placed into crevices that will hold it down. If the rock you have chosen is very smooth, you can make some chips in the surface. Place the wire under these chips and cement it down, and completely cover with peat to prevent the wire from being seen. A thin piece of rubber may first be placed over the roots to prevent any damage from the wire. Finally, cover the peat with a layer of living green moss to help hold it in place. The finished planting can be bound together with string until the moss begins to grow. Place the rock planting on a tray covered with a layer of damp sand.

If the rock planting is to be of the root-over-rock type, fill a pot three-quarters full of soil, and place the stone on top. Then fill in with topsoil, until a quarter of the rock is buried. Place the bonsai on the rock, gently spreading its larger roots over the rock and leading them down into the soil. The twisted, gnarled growth of the roots over a period of years is perhaps the most interesting and appealing aspect of this type of planting.

GROUP PLANTINGS

Another very striking way to plant bonsai is in groups. The purpose of such a method is to try to present the bonsai trees as they might appear naturally in a forest or grove. Forest plantings may be created in a number of different ways. One method is to raise several fast-growing seedlings together in a standard

Forest-Style Group Planting: This group of *Serrisa foetida* imitates a dense cluster of trees found in the forest. The simplicity and understated elegance of the art of bonsai is implicit in this planting.

clay pot for a year or two, constantly pinching, pruning, and shaping the topgrowth. At the end of that time, when strong, thick roots have developed, the clump can be planted in a bonsai pot, with the upper roots to be exposed. The trees can be kept in place at first by wrapping a string around the main trunks and tying it under the bottom of the container, or by running wires through the drainage holes in the pot and wrapping them around the root balls. Wrap the roots in damp sphagnum to protect them, and expose them gradually to the air and light. As this type of planting ages, the roots take on an interestingly twisted and weathered appearance. Seedlings of the Japanese maple are especially effective in this sort of planting.

Sometimes a forest is made from a single tree by removing all the branches from one side of the trunk, planting the tree on its side in the container, and training the now upright branches into the desired tree forms. This is called raft-style bonsai.

The most formal of the group plantings is the clustered style. In this style the trees are planted very close together. Their appearance is that of a dense forest, so closely do their leaves intermingle. Composition is most important in this type of planting. Trees are usually grouped in circular or triangular patterns. The pot in which they are placed should be related to the shape of the cluster, to complement it without distracting from the style.

GENERAL MAINTENANCE

Care given to bonsai depends upon the type of plant, manner of planting, and depth of container. However, there are several general considerations to keep in mind as a starting point.

As a rule, bonsai should be watered from above with a fine spray of water that will not wash soil out of the container or away from the roots. Water once for the moss (or soil surface, if no moss is present) and once again for the plant itself. The reason for this double watering is that if the surface soil has been moistened it will more readily absorb greater amounts of water. Passing over the bonsai container several times with a gentle spray of water will allow water to sink deeper into the soil than if the same plant is watered just once whenever watering is necessary.

Continue watering until water drips out the bottom of the pot. Daily watering is usually essential, for the soil in shallow pots dries out quickly. Frequency must be determined by the type of plant and its location, so keep a close watch on all your bonsai and treat each plant individually.

Here are some general guidelines for seasonal watering:

Spring: Once or twice a day, preferably in the morning or afternoon.

Summer: Two or three times daily, depending on how hot and dry the weather is.

Autumn: Once a day on sunny days; less water may be needed during prolonged stretches of cloudy weather.

Winter: Water in the morning every other day, depending on weather conditions, whether plant is in its dormant period, and other factors. As a rule, deciduous trees need less water during the winter than evergreens.

Growing very fine moss on the surface of your bonsai will insulate it against extremes of temperature and protect it from wind and driving rain when it is summering outdoors.

Fine moss such as that growing between sidewalk cracks, so long as it is clean, is about the best moss to use, and the sidewalk is about the best source of moss for urban gardeners. Country dwellers can gather moss from woodland sites.

Bonsai may be fed occasionally during periods of active growth with a mild, all-purpose fertilizer. Some growers prefer to feed plants by top-dressing with compost. Trees growing on stone (clinging-to-a-rock plantings) may be fed several times during the growing season with weak manure tea. They

The Splendor of "Little Nature" on Display:
These various examples of traditional styles using miniature bonsai show the wide range of effects which can be created through training and pruning. The beauty of the forms and designs is enhanced by the selection of sleek containers in muted tones which are in harmony with the shape and color of the bonsai itself. The neutral background highlights the exquisite patterns created by the foliage and branches.

The Bonsai Villages of Japan

Embodying the discipline, patience, and symbolic view of nature that are at the heart of Japanese culture, when practiced properly the art of bonsai is more than a hobby or even a cherished avocation. Like the tea ceremony and the many other philosophically based pursuits valued in Japan, the painstaking culture of these small trees can be a way of life.

Well to the north of Tokyo in the relatively small city of Sendai, bonsai growing has been a vital tradition since the sixteenth century, when the activity was encouraged by a feudal lord. A long series of gifted amateurs in that area have furthered bonsai from that day to this, working with cryptomeria, Japanese white pine, juniper, and even the deciduous zelkova, but perhaps most often with the hybrid pine that is a cross between the Japanese red pine *(Pinus densiflora)* and the Japanese black pine *(P. thunbergii)*. This tree grows on the small islands in Sendai Bay.

The major city of Nagoya and its environs are another stronghold of bonsai-growing families. So is Niigata, the "snow country" of northwest Japan immortalized in Nobel prize-winner Yasunari Kawabata's famous novel of that name. Bonsai also are cultivated widely on the southern Japanese island of Kyushu in the vicinity of Kurume — a city renowned too for the fine cloth made there. A favorite bonsai subject in this area is the native Kirishima mountain azalea *(Rhododendron kiusianum)*. Not far from Kurume is the huge ironworks at Yawata; many of the 40,000 people who work there also work seriously at bonsai culture.

For some of the people in the above places, growing bonsai is not only a way of life but also a way of earning a living. The two ways have merged completely at the two best-known centers of bonsai culture and research in Japan — Bonsai Village, which is an hour north of Tokyo by train, and the older community of Kinashi, located to the south of Osaka on the Inland Sea.

Kinashi's involvement in bonsai began around the beginning of the nineteenth century for economic reasons. The land around the village was not well suited to growing rice and barley, but the nearby mountains and coastal areas did boast many wild pines, and the little town was protected to the north and west by mountains, and so enjoyed a moderate climate favorable to grafting and cultivating trees. Beginning by uprooting and potting naturally dwarfed or wind-shaped trees and seedlings of unusual shapes, the villagers gradually learned the special techniques of grafting, pruning, and trimming that have given true bonsai their distinctive appeal. By 1878, little black or white pines were being sold to surrounding areas; much greater prosperity was assured in 1894, when specimens of a distinctive variety of black pine were found. Soon named *nishiki-matsu* (brocade pine) because of its extraordinarily thick and richly patterned bark, this handsome tree was propagated by grafting to get seedlings. Demand for these plants sparked the sale of bonsai in urban areas such as Osaka and Hiroshima, which were just a short Inland Sea voyage away from Kinashi.

Bonsai culture reached its prewar peak in this community by 1937, when 99 acres (40 hect-

---

are never repotted or root pruned, but every few years the moss cover should be lifted and more soil added around the roots. Root-over-rock plantings also need periodic renewals of soil. Roots are never separated from the rock, but the roots growing down into the soil are pruned like those of container-grown bonsai.

Pests which are likely to attack bonsai plants include aphids, spider mites, and scale insects. See chapter 9 for recommended ways to get rid of these pests. If the pests have nested in the soil, the plant must be repotted. The old soil should be completely removed from the roots, which may then be soaked for a short time in a weak solution of pyrethrum.

DORMANCY

Bonsai plants from tropical climates may be kept indoors all year, but trees from northern ares) were under cultivation by 105 bonsai farmers. Although World War II drove half these growers out of business, Kinashi had regained its prewar acreage by 1966, and since 1975, 131 acres (53 hectares) have been devoted to the small trees.

As a traditional skill, the art of bonsai continues to appeal to the youth of Kinashi, and young people in their twenties have organized a club and hold seminars to improve their knowledge and skills. To learn the techniques by which each cultivator can express an aesthetic idea of his own, students also undergo a long apprenticeship in which they work under their seniors' instruction. Today, about 200 families grow pine bonsai in this area, which is now part of the city of Takamatsu. Visitors can walk a labyrinth of footpaths around nursery fields and see potted trees from 10 to 100 years of age in various stages of training on benches in the growers' front yards. Auctions take place twice a month.

Given the great amount of time and labor required to produce a truly perfected bonsai, mass production is impossible.

In recent years, the bonsai farmers of Kinashi have concentrated increasingly on using an efficient mass-production and mass-sale system to turn out seedling or grafted bonsai intended as gardening material. Amateurs often buy these relatively inexpensive plants and train them into artistic bonsai. Because of this adaptation to modern conditions, the term bonsai — once synonymous with artistic bonsai — has taken on a wider meaning, and the perfected specimens that are the culmination of decades or even centuries of care are now regarded as belonging to a special category.

The other leading bonsai center in Japan came into being after the disastrous Tokyo earthquake of 1923. Concerned about the problems of poor air and limited space in Tokyo, three bonsaimen decided to locate elsewhere so they and other growers would have ample room to live and work and the better conditions needed to produce bonsai scions of top quality. The site chosen was a 2½-acre (10,000 sq m) plot in a relatively undeveloped area just north of Tokyo where the soil and water

were judged suitable for bonsai.

When the first small group went to live on this rented land in Omiya in the summer of 1925, there was no electricity — and no housing. Gradually, however, more nurserymen and growers came to the new community, and by 1935 there were 20 working families. Before the outbreak of war, the small village in Omiya had become known throughout Japan and was much visited by "outside" bonsai growers and amateurs interested in learning cultural techniques. During the war years, the village was virtually destroyed as a bonsai center, but in the postwar period it was revived by the determined efforts of people dedicated to the art. Working hard to improve nursery techniques through research, such growers have reestablished the town as the foremost bonsai center in the country. Officially known as Bonsai-cho (-village), the Omiya site now features 15 nurseries, with one belonging to the very prominent Saburo Kato, who is a son of one of the original founders and the president of the Bonsaimen's Association of Japan.

climate zones need a cold dormant period during the winter. These types are generally placed outdoors for the winter, but must be protected against freezing temperatures.

For winter care, a packing crate can be used to create a shelter for the bonsai. The greatest danger to the plant is frost, which may destroy it. The crate can be insulated to help prevent frost, with one side left open. If

the weather is extremely cold and the temperature is constantly below freezing, the bonsai plant should be placed in a cold frame, closed porch, or other shelter that is covered on all sides. The shelter should be made of wood so air can penetrate it. Plants also can be covered with a thick layer of mulch. Plants need little or no watering during their dormant period.

CHAPTER 22

Miniature Plants

Miniatures fix the gardener's attention as perhaps few other plantings do, if only because it is difficult to take anything so small for granted. Miniatures invite *looking;* they beg to be studied. There is wonder in the perfect functioning of living things in a space so small.

Diminutive plants also can be supremely practical, for there are few gardeners for whom space does not eventually become a problem. For the indoor hobbyist, space limitations may seem to dictate curtailing the number of plants under cultivation, or restricting the range of genera to those for which a very few different environments need to be provided. It is unfortunate to limit your collection in such ways, for plant diversity is part of the attraction of gardening. It is also unnecessary, because of the availability of a wonderful spectrum of miniature plants.

Miniatures can enable you to grow 10 or 12 individual specimens on the same windowsill or shelf which would house only 3 or 4 standard varieties. In addition, many outstanding miniatures from different plant families are culturally compatible, lending themselves to varied closed-environment plantings in which entirely different climates are created within a few feet of each other. Enthusiasts who enjoy hybridizing plants will find that most smaller varieties have briefer reproductive cycles, allowing for a more rapid succession of generations so that desired traits may evolve in a shorter time.

Light gardeners can save money and energy simply by growing more plants under the same wattage and number of lamps they would have used for smaller collections of larger plants.

Although many plant fanciers might consider it one of the novelty areas of indoor gardening, there is nothing especially "new" about the cultivation of miniature plants. While it is true that many varieties of miniatures have been developed recently, and that American gardeners have shown strong interest in these tiny specimens only during the past ten years or so, their propagation and use in indoor gardens dates back for centuries among growers preoccupied with economy in the use of gardening space. This has been especially true in Japan, although most people associate the Japanese way with small plants with the practice of bonsai. These dwarfed trees are not true miniatures, but rather standard varieties deliberately dwarfed by training their roots and stems—a practice detailed in chapter 21.

The popularity of miniature plants has increased along with that of terraria and bottle gardens, which entered the realm of possibility some 140 years ago. The discovery at that time that plants could flourish in closed glass containers coincided happily with the seeking out and hybridizing of miniatures by Western horticulturists—although most experts now recommend that terraria and bottle gardens not be hermetically sealed, but have some opening, however small. No doubt the nineteenth-century exploration of the tropics, which are the natural habitat of many miniature species, also furthered enthusiasm for these plants.

DEFINING AND SELECTING MINIATURES

What is a miniature plant? There is little agreement on an exact definition, and the question is further complicated by use of the terms "dwarf" and "semidwarf." Some growers consider a dwarf to be under 12 inches

Opposite, miniature Crassula *species in a toothpaste cap.*

459

Standard and Miniature Sinningias: Both flowers are members of the genus *Sinningia*, yet the miniature cultivar 'Dollbaby' on the right is about one-quarter the size of the standard 'Talisman Cove'.

from overrapid growth by root confinement and a moderate feeding schedule. *Begonia suffruticosa* and other small begonias can achieve unwieldy growth if they are not confined.

Miniatures are developed in a number of ways. As is the case with *Sinningia pusilla* (also called miniature gloxinia, or miniature slipper plant), some occur in nature. Other strains begin as "sports"—that is, individual specimens which for no apparent reason differ from other specimens of the same cultivar. These mutants are then selectively bred to continue their accidental but desirable traits; in this case, their small size. Sometimes a sport will take the form of a plant with shorter internodes or smaller leaves than others of its species. A sport usually must be propagated vegetatively—by leaf, root, or stem cuttings—in order to reproduce the effect; less frequently, it will yield seeds from which similar seedlings will grow.

(30 cm) in height and a miniature to be under 6 inches (15 cm). But there are almost as many sets of criteria as there are growers—and as many as there are miniature species and cultivars, since each must be compared against the standard for its genus or species. Obviously a scaled-down version of a plant which commonly reaches a height of several feet (approximately 91 cm) need not fit in a thimble to earn the designation "miniature."

Miniatures may be considered to be those plants which generally meet at least two of the following three requirements:

1. The specimen should have small leaves and flowers. One inch (2.5 cm) is a figure commonly mentioned by growers, although this, too, is relative.
2. Stems must have short internodes; that is, there must be only a small space between leaves.
3. The plant should be slow growing. This is a particularly important requirement; however, if it cannot be met, plants can still be kept

Difference in Leaf Spacing: The internode areas between leaves are always very much smaller on miniature plants than they are on standard size ones. This is one of the ways to identify miniatures.

Thimble Size Miniature: Minuscule plants invite the use of unusual containers. This one-inch (2.5 cm) thimble provides just the right amount of growing area for *Crassula spathulata* 'Capo Blanco'.

Select miniature plants with the same care and attention to practical considerations that you use in choosing specimens for a standard size indoor collection. That you should buy healthy stock from reputable growers goes without saying; you may even wish to deal directly with a specialty greenhouse that does a large part of its business with miniatures. Many of these firms will ship mail orders.

With regard to your choice of cultivars, there are a number of considerations to keep in mind. If you are new to miniatures, it makes sense to begin with varieties having larger relatives with which you already are familiar, or with those that require less special care. African violets (members of the genus *Saintpaulia,* which belongs to the Gesneriad family) are likely to fit both parts of this description, as are the little begonias. What's more, these two genera get along well

together and make good starting stock for a terrarium or bottle garden.

What plants should you avoid at first? Most professional growers warn against approaching miniature orchid cultivation without some experience, partly because orchids take a long time to bring to flower. Tiny roses also can be tricky, for they come from the temperate zone rather than the tropics or semitropics, and require cool temperatures as well as full sun. Roses also are vulnerable to leaf mildews if subjected to the still air of a terrarium offering a desirable high humidity. Miniature evergreens also can present problems, as they prefer a cooler environment in winter than can be provided by indoor gardeners lacking an unheated sun porch.

The second consideration is compatibility with the growing media and with the light and humidity conditions you intend to provide. The limits of compatibility can be surprisingly accommodating. For example, such visually different plants as begonias, small spring-flowering or tropical bulbs, certain miniature succulents in the *Crassula, Echeveria, Kalanchoe, Pachyphytum,* and *Stapelia* genera, and petite orchids and gesneriads that can tolerate night temperatures down to 60° or 65°F (16° or 18°C) all can be grown in close proximity, though generally in separate pots. (For a first-hand account of growing these seemingly unlikely but effective combinations, consult the wide-ranging work by Charles Marden Fitch, *The Complete Book of Miniature Roses,* listed in the Bibliography.) Do not, however, attempt to combine such varied plants until you are more practiced as a miniature plant grower.

It is best to begin your experience with miniatures less ambitiously, by selecting or creating one environment and stocking it with plants of just a few compatible genera. Of course, this rule applies to plants of any size, but the miniatures are so inviting that there is a temptation to pick them out at random, like penny candy, so the caveat bears repeating.

SPECIAL CULTURAL CONSIDERATIONS FOR MINIATURES

The small root balls of miniatures and the limited amount of soil surrounding them pose challenges for the grower. For one thing, their soil is likely to dry out much more quickly than that of standard size plants of the same genus. Plants in small clay pots under bright light may require more than one watering per day, especially if temperatures are high and air circulation is good. Drying out is especially threatening if plants are being culti-vated under fluorescent lights. Although fluorescents do not generate nearly as much heat as incandescent bulbs, their proximity to the plants as they provide up to 16 hours of artificial light daily will tend to dry the growing medium.

To lessen the chance that your minia-tures will be injured or fatally affected by in-advertent underwatering, you may want to put those types demanding even soil mois-ture (gesneriads and roses, for example) atop pebbles, aggregate gravel, or moss kept con-stantly moist, or on wood, wire, or plastic lou-ver grids placed over a tray filled with water.

Groupings of Miniatures at a Glance

The following suggested combinations are based upon the compatibility of plants within each environment and on aesthetic considerations. Use the information in this chapter as your guide in adding other harmonious plants to these groups or to put together your own arrangements.

ENVIRONMENT	PLANTS	CULTURAL SPECIFICS
A warm, humid situation such as that provided in a terrarium or bottle garden located in a moderately sunny window or under fluorescent lights.	*Sinningia pusilla* and its variants (examples are *S.* 'White Sprite', *S.* 'Star Eyes', *S.* 'Bright Eyes', and *S.* 'Snowflake'); *Sinningia concinna* and hybrids; dwarf or miniature *Saintpaulia* cultivars such as *S.* 'Mini-fantasy' and *S.* 'Small Change'; smaller begonias such as *B.* 'China Doll', *B. acaulis*, and slow-growing *B. boweri* 'Nigromarga'. As groundcovers: plants listed for the following environment.	Temperature: 62°-80°F (17°-27°C). Humidity: 50% or higher.
Hanging baskets in humid, moderately to well-lit areas.	Miniature forms of *Peperomia, Pilea,* and *Selaginella*, the small and slow-growing miniature creeping fig (*Ficus pumila* 'Minima'); *Sinningia pusilla* and *S.* 'White Sprite', which will self-sow, germinate, and become a groundcover in this situation if desired.	Temperature: 60°-80°F (16°-27°C). Humidity: 40-60%
The cool, well-lit windowsill.	Miniature ivy cultivars; diminutive geranium cultivars such as *Pelargonium* 'Arcturus', *P.* 'Dopey', and *P.* 'Volcano'.	Temperature: 45°-70°F (7°-21°C) or higher. Humidity: 40-50%.
The cool, airy light garden.	Separately potted miniature roses, and begonias tolerating cooler temperatures, such as *Begonia boweri* and the semituberous Rieger hybrids.	Temperature: 50°-65°F (10°-18°C) or higher if humidity is raised by misting. Humidity: 50% at temperatures of 65°F (18°C) or lower.

Keeping Miniatures Moist: The tiny amount of soil needed to pot up miniature plants will dry out quickly unless the plants are kept near a source of moisture. Set moisture-loving miniatures on wet pebble trays or some surface that can hold water.

Other cautionary measures include the use of capillary mats below tiny pots, or tighter terrarium closures above them. For plants requiring somewhat drier soil, such as geraniums, the simple use of plastic pots should be sufficient.

Unhappily, overwatering also can cause problems, for the danger with all miniatures lies in the rapidity with which their soil can reach either extreme of aridity or supersaturation. As a result, the very methods used to combat drying out tend to encourage root rot. The answer to this dilemma is the use of soil mixtures that have particularly good drainage, and perhaps some extra attentiveness to the petite plants from you.

When potting or repotting any miniature, avoid the problems that accompany extremes in pot size. Overpotting can cause too-vigorous growth and may sometimes result in a specimen twice as large as the dainty miniature you were led to expect. Underpotting, of course, can keep plants at a more manageable and perhaps more appealing size, but it also will increase the possibility of losing miniatures to dehydration or rot.

Where fertilizing schedules are concerned, miniatures that are heavy feeders generally do better if given a very dilute application of fertilizer with every watering as opposed to a full-strength feeding every two or four weeks. On the other hand, light feeders such as geraniums should be fed less often than full size plants of the same genus and at half the strength. Salt buildup in these small plants can be rapid if they are fed heavily. It therefore may be necessary to flush the soil occasionally by top-watering thoroughly several times in immediate succession, and to change the top layer of soil one or more times a year.

A GUIDE TO SOME POPULAR MINIATURES
GESNERIADS

The Gesneriad family is lush with many of the most popular miniature species and cultivars. For example, horticulturist Elvin McDonald has called *Sinningia pusilla* the "perfect" miniature, while the *Saintpaulia* genus includes a host of diminutive cultivars in a panoply of flower colors. Pocket size gesneriads also offer the advantage of thriving at even lower light levels than their larger relatives, and if an indoor miniature garden were to contain plants from only one family, these tiny beauties would be a most likely choice.

Sinningia pusilla, S. concinna (which offers larger blossoms than the better-known *S. pusilla*), and their related cultivars are moisture-loving plants which seldom exceed three or four inches (8 or 10 cm) in breadth. Both bloom almost constantly. The flowers of *S. pusilla* are pale lavender, spreading from an elongated white throat into five petals. Identical in habit and size is this plant's mutant counterpart, *S.* 'White Sprite', which has pure white blooms offering fine color contrast. Variations in flower color, size, and number, along with slight refinements in the oval, furry, dark-veined leaves are found in a myriad of available *S. pusilla* hybrids, all of which attest to the ease with which this little plant may be crossbred. Somewhat larger than *S. pusilla, S. pusilla* × *eumorpha* 'Doll Baby' boasts lavender-blue flowers with a purple eye and a pale yellow throat. Also appealing is the quite small *S.* 'Bright Eyes', which has purple and white flowers. Another minuscule treasure is *S.* 'Tom Thumb', which offers erect, velvety red, bell-shaped flowers almost two inches (5 cm) across while growing in a pot only a little wider. Writing of this plant in his classic *Exotic Plant Manual,* Alfred Byrd Graf describes it as "the most charming little baby gloxinia that ever appeared for the pleasure of the gesneriad fancier."

Miniature gloxinias, or slipper plants, are tuberous, and may be propagated from tubers or from seeds. Although they have tubers, many small hybrids can be everblooming if given the proper care as described in chapter 13. Tubers can be revived from dormancy after as long as several months, provided that the soil holding the dormant tuber has been kept moist enough to keep the tuber from drying out, but dry enough to prevent rotting. At no time should tubers of these miniature plants grown under lights or in terraria be allowed to dry off. Seeds are germinated on the surface of a moist, pasteurized growing medium (milled sphagnum is good), kept in warmth and shade, and preferably covered with glass or polyethylene or polypropylene plastic (which are permeable to carbon dioxide and oxygen) until seedlings are well developed.

Gesneriads in general, and sinningias in particular, respond well in a soilless potting medium. An excellent one is the "G–B–S" mix developed by greenhouseman Michael Kartuz. Directions for this blend, named for its suitability for begonias and gesneriads (*Saintpaulia* species in particular), and for the also effective Cornell gesneriad mix, may be found in chapter 13. Some sinningia fanciers have found that a mixture of 3 parts of a

African Violet in Miniature: *Saintpaulia* 'Pixie Blue' blooms in profusion at a height of scarcely three inches (8 cm).

soilless mix and 1 part rich compost is ideal.

These plants are native to humid regions of South America; consequently, sufficient moisture is important in their cultivation. All miniature gesneriads do well in closed (but slightly ventilated) quarters, and a popular means of raising them, aside from actual terraria and bottle gardens, is in individual small pots nesting within a transparent plastic box such as those used in clothing stores for storage of dress shirts. If you use this sort of container, keep the lid slightly ajar, as plants placed in direct sun in a closed box will "cook" and turn mushy. Watering will be less frequent when plants are raised in such enclosures, and humidity can be easily maintained, both in "closed" spaces and in open benches, by use of a capillary mat or a layer of aggregate stone that is kept half-submerged in water beneath the pots.

Miniature gloxinias will easily tolerate low light intensity, although flowers may be fewer and less frequent. Strong, direct sunlight is not recommended; filtered light is

Streptocarpus: In addition to sinningias and African violets, the Gesneriad family produces some charming miniature species of *Streptocarpus*, the cape primrose.

best. Most growers prefer fluorescent lighting, as the symmetry of a plant's development and its frequency and generosity of bloom are more easily controlled with a measured allotment of light. Twelve to 14 hours is frequently recommended. Of course, plants this size are economical users of lighting energy, and will fit easily under a small fluorescent unit in an out-of-the-way spot. They also can be kept happy under a regularly lit incandescent lamp on an end table.

The miniature African violets are as varied and as beautiful as the standard plants from which they have been developed. Like the petite slipper plants, they are easy to care for and bloom profusely when given proper lighting.

Although miniature African violets, like the larger varieties, are grown as much for the patterns and texture of their foliage as for their blossoms, many cultivars have been bred especially for their beautiful flowers; the white-blossomed *Saintpaulia* 'Icicle Trinket',

and *S.* 'Small Change', with its large purple blooms, are two fine examples. Other popular small saintpaulias include *S.* 'Dancing Doll', a heavy-blooming semiminiature with bright pink, open double flowers, and *S.* 'Mini Fantasy', which garnered a top prize at the 1979 convention of the African Violet Society of America for its extraordinary double blooms marked with purple, pink, and lavender.

Miniature African violets share with sinningias the ability to thrive equally well on a windowsill or in a fluorescent-lit environment. Remember, however, that water on the foliage of these plants in direct sun will cause "burn" spots, whereas this is not a problem under artificial light. Like sinningias and larger violets, the small ones prefer daytime temperatures above 62°F (17°C), preferably 70° to 75°F (21° to 24°C), with a 5° to 10°F (3°to 6°C) drop at night. Avoid day/night extremes and adjust humidity to temperature—higher when warmer, lower when cooler. Thus, small violets growing in winter sunlight at an east, south, or west window—provided the house is not overheated—will get by with less humidity than a warmer environment would require, or than most homes can offer during cold-weather months. In summer, when temperatures are higher, humidity can be increased by means of semi-enclosed plantings, such as those described for sinningias. In winter, remember to protect violets from low temperatures that prevail around single-pane windows after dark. Move the plants farther away from windows, or shield them from the glass with a heavy curtain or shade. Likewise, keep them away from intense, direct sunlight in summer. Fluorescent tubes are best kept eight inches (20 cm) away from plants, and left on to provide at least a 12-hour "day."

Miniature African violets or their offsets can be propagated by cuttings of leaves from middle rows of the plants. These should be rooted in moist vermiculite. Beware, however, of uprooting or tearing the tiny main plant when dividing suckers to start new

Propagating African Violets: Start leaf cuttings by taking leaves from the middle rows of the plant and rooting them in moist vermiculite.

plants by division or from leaf cuttings. (See Leaf Cuttings, in chapter 8, for more information.) High humidity is especially important during the early stages of growth, and plastic- or glass-covered trays are advisable.

The soilless "G–B–S" mix referred to earlier makes a good potting medium for miniature saintpaulias. So do the other mixtures described in chapter 13 or the commercially sold African violet mixes, which are, or may be, lightened with perlite or vermiculite. While keeping miniature violets in small pots under three inches (8 cm) is necessary to retard unwanted growth, many experts recommend repotting in fresh soil and in the same pot or one of identical size about three times per year. At this time, the unproductive outer rows of leaves may be removed.

BEGONIAS

Along with small slipper plants, begonias are perhaps the easiest miniatures with which to begin a collection. A shelf of tiny forms of this easily grown household favorite can be a delightful center of attention. Or, as mentioned earlier, many begonias have temperature and humidity requirements similar to those of *Sinningia* species, and some of the rhizomatous and semituberous begonias (which are actually tuberous begonias with smaller tubers) can be grown together with slipper plants with little difficulty. Some begonias

are difficult to grow outside terraria, since their humidity requirements often exceed 50 percent, but these can be cultivated in clear containers. One such species is the popular two inch (5 cm) tall *Begonia prismatocarpa,* a yellow-flowered rhizomatous species from Africa. It may be the most widely grown begonia in the United States. Another is *B. bogneri,* an infrequently blooming semituberous begonia. Even begonias that thrive in closed containers need air circulation, however, so remember to leave lids ajar.

Soil, water, and fluorescent lighting requirements for miniature begonias are generally the same as for miniature gloxinias and African violets, but remember when combining genera that rex and other rhizomatous begonias should be given lower levels of light, less water, and no food during dormancy, which is heralded by lack of new growth, and sometimes by loss of leaves. For this reason, they should be potted separately and perhaps even removed during dormancy from plantings shared with gesneriads. (If you are not sure whether such plants are resting or rotting, squeeze a rhizome; if it is firm, the plant is healthy, but dormant. Resume normal culture when new growth appears.) In general, rhizomatous begonias such as *B. prismatocarpa* and *B. boweri* (the miniature eyelash begonia), are more tolerant of drier soil than are the tuberous and semituberous types. Indeed, the rhizomatous *B. mazae* (sometimes called the miniature begonia), which has pink flowers spotted with red, actually prefers fairly dry soil, though it does require perfect drainage. Another begonia that needs to be kept fairly dry is the charming fibrous-rooted, double-flowered cultivar *B.* × *semperflorens-cultorum* 'Curli Locks', called the petite thimble begonia, and the summer-blooming hybrid known as the Lilliput tuberous begonia, which puts forth rich yellow, double flowers.

Some appealing moisture-loving types include the hybrid known as the dwarf tuberous begonia and the semituberous *B. dregei,* the miniature maple leaf begonia, which has

Tiny Begonias: Like a miniature forest, small-scale begonias rise from the soil to about two inches (5 cm) high.

white flowers and leaves the size of a fingernail.

Another variable to keep in mind when planning a terrarium or other group planting of miniature begonias is the likely eventual size of your plants. Miniatures of this genus generally reach a greater size than other miniatures. So if your plantings are not readily accessible for removing and repotting, choose from among the slower-growing miniature begonias, like the dark-leaved, winter-flowering cultivar *B.* 'China Doll', the hybrid *B.* 'Bebe', or *B. boweri* 'Nigromarga', which will creep in shallow quarters and can even be planted next to roses in pots of six inches (15 cm) or larger.

The list of choice miniature begonias is long and varied. Little rexes suited to a terrarium, small Wardian case, dish garden, or as edging in a light garden or in pots of roses include *B.* 'Baby Rainbow' (with multi-hued, iridescent leaves), *B.* 'Black Diamond', *B.* 'Lucille Closson', and *B.* 'Pansy'. Other intriguing rhizomatous types include the various *B. boweri* hybrids, all of which are small and pink flowered; *B. rotundifolia;* and the

Mexican *B. hydrocotylifolia,* a pink-flowered, winter-blooming creeper with six-inch (15 cm) stems that is suitable for terrarium growing. An unusual but especially beautiful rhizomatous begonia also preferring terrarium conditions is the Chinese *B. versicolor,* which has thick round leaves of silver-bronze and emerald-green, and salmon-pink flowers. For vividly colored flowers that appear in fall and winter and will be long lasting in cool locations, consider the smaller, semituberous Rieger hybrids derived from *B.* ×*hiemalis* and *B. socotrana.* Wax begonias, which are fibrous rooted (as are the angel-wing and the hairy types), offer the advantage of flowering around the year; good small cultivars in the *Begonia* Semperflorens-Cultorum hybrid complex include the hybrid *B.* ×*semperflorens-cultorum* 'Carefree', and the previously mentioned thimble-type *B.* ×*semperflorens-cultorum* 'Curli Locks'. For a more complete and descriptive list of begonias, consult *The Thompson Begonia Guide,* which is available in larger libraries. (See Bibliography.)

Begonias offer numerous alternatives for propagation. These apply to the miniature varieties as well as to the standards, but remember that hybrids, which comprise a large proportion of the smaller strains, do not always reproduce identically when grown from seeds. It can be exciting, however, to pollinate a hybrid begonia, then plant the seeds to see the resulting motley plants, which will exhibit all kinds of variations, and can then, if desirable, be reproduced vegetatively. If true reproduction of hybrids is sought, rely on leaf and stem cuttings—or, in the case of rex and other rhizomatous cultivars, leaf or rhizome cuttings.

If seed propagation is feasible, which is usually the case with fibrous-rooted begonias, germinate seeds in a moist growing medium located in a warm environment. Vegetative propagation from rhizome, leaf, or stem cuttings is accomplished in the same moist soil and high humidity that the mature plants prefer.

Miniature begonias will respond favorably to a 12-hour fluorescent light cycle. One Massachusetts begonia fancier follows a monthly pattern, in which she starts her begonias with a 9-hour light period, which she gradually builds up to 12 hours. She has found that this procedure imitates the lengthening day in nature, forces blooms—and saves electricity. The miniature gesneriads which share this regimen suffer no adverse effects. It seems likely, however, that a positive response to such treatment may depend upon the geographical origin of the plants involved.

WARMTH-LOVING MINIATURE FOLIAGE PLANTS

Excellent choices for filling in a hanging basket, dish garden, or terrarium are the smaller forms of plants in the *Peperomia, Pilea,* and *Selaginella* genera, all of which thrive in high humidity and temperatures no lower than 55°F (13°C). The miniature, or dwarf, aluminum plant (*Pilea cadierei* 'Minima') is slow growing and picturesque, with quilted deep olive and silver foliage and pink stems. It prefers bright shade, but can survive in dim light. Where a lower-growing plant is desired, such as for groundcover in a terrarium, consider creeping pilea (*P. depressa*), which has succulent, shiny, pea-green leaves. This plant roots at nodes, and reaches four to six inches (10 to 15 cm) across. The artillery plant (*P. microphylla*) is named for the puffs of pollen given off from its flowers. It has appealing fernlike foliage and makes a pleasant four to six inch (10 to 15 cm) high contribution to a terrarium. All three of the foregoing plants may be propagated by cuttings, and the creeping pilea also by division. Keep these pileas barely moist, but not wet, at all times.

Their attention-getting variegated or pointed leaves make peperomias deservedly popular foliage plants. Many of the rosette-forming or clustering species are compact. Especially interesting is a dwarf cultivar of the variegated baby rubber plant. This little plant has light green leaves variegated with milky green and areas of creamy white extending inward from the margins. Its imposing name is *Peperomia obtusifolia* 'Albomarginata Minima'. Like all peperomias, it does best in bright indirect light, and when allowed to dry out somewhat between waterings; otherwise it is prone to stem rot. Propagation is by cuttings or division.

Allied to the ferns, the bright green, low-growing, many-branched selaginellas can be used to great effect as a cushiony ground-cover in terraria. Cultivars of the self-rooting creeper called club moss (*Selaginella kraussiana*) include the dwarf forms *S.* 'Aurea', *S.* 'Brownii', and *S.* 'Variegata'. Selaginellas can tolerate temperatures somewhat lower than pileas and peperomias (down to 50°F/ 10°C). They also need partial shade, getting by on as few as ten footcandles of light, and should not dry out between waterings. Propagation is from stem cuttings, layering, or spores.

GERANIUMS

Miniature geraniums (*Pelargonium* spp.) offer the bright foliage and hardiness of their larger counterparts, without the tendency toward unwieldiness that big geraniums sometimes show. There are many pocket size cultivars, with the majority being hybrids of the zonal geraniums so favored for their ability to bloom around the year on the windowsill. Ranging from about three to seven inches (8 to 18 cm) in height, geranium miniatures have relatively large flowers, and many plants bloom when they are still quite tiny. One of the more popular miniatures is *Pelargonium* ×*hortorum* 'Black Vesuvius', which boasts dark green leaves zoned with blackish brown, and large, vivid, scarlet-orange single flowers. This old, very dwarfed cultivar was bred in Victorian England. It grows anywhere from four to ten inches (10 to 25 cm) tall, depending on how much light it gets. A very dramatic miniature is *P.* 'Anta-

Pelargonium Cultivar for a Small Space: Fancy pink blossoms emerge from a dwarf trailing geranium plant, 'Sugar Baby'.

res', which creates a rich effect with dark leaves and single flowers of deep scarlet. Other standouts are the unusually minute *P.* 'Tiny Tim Pink', which puts forth single, light pink flowers when it is little more than an inch (2.5 cm) high, and the appealing *P.* 'Brownie', which grows to five inches (13 cm) and features clusters of single red blooms and chocolate-zoned foliage, with new leaves golden brown in color. Also memorable is the steady-blooming *P.* 'Pygmy', which has light green, scalloped foliage and exquisitely small, red, double flowers. *P.* 'Minx' is a dense and very compact plant with deep red, double blooms; it has been described as "an almost perfect miniature" by *House and Garden* contributor Richard Langer.

All geraniums do well in cool environments. They are among those plants most capable of acclimating to lower winter temperatures in our homes, and can easily pass their winter rest period in a 45° to 50°F (7° to 10°C) cellar, where they should be watered sparingly.

Although larger pelargoniums are being increasingly cultivated from seeds, the most common method of propagating the minia-ture varieties is by taking stem cuttings, generally from the tips. These may be rooted either in moist sand or in a regular potting soil. Be careful not to position cuttings too deeply, for this seems to encourage a fungus causing deformed basal growth that is especially common among tiny geraniums. After they are rooted, geraniums do best in good garden loam mixed with a generous proportion of clean sand. Keep new cuttings away from direct sunlight.

Despite their small size, miniature geraniums are not terrarium plants. They do not thrive in the humid environment that begonias and sinningias crave, although it is also a definite mistake to include geraniums among plants that can get by on a minimum of water. They require soil which is well drained, and which is allowed to dry slightly between waterings. During their winter rest they need little water.

Although little geraniums can thrive under horticultural fluorescents, windowsill shelves are an ideal place to grow these easy-to-please plants. They will bloom with as little as three hours of unobstructed (but not overly strong) sunlight per day. Avoid north-facing windows, particularly in winter, for although temperature will be no problem, the light will be too weak to induce blooming.

Miniature geraniums are seldom troubled by root-binding if 2½- or 3½-inch (6 to 9 cm) pots are used. They may remain potted in containers of that size for several years, although an annual or twice-yearly changing of the top layer of soil is beneficial. Given the small volume of soil per pot, Lilliputian geraniums should be fed only every three weeks during active growth (less during winter). They do well in fish emulsion fertilizer applied at half the usual recommended strength.

IVIES

The small ivies, all cultivars of the parent species *Hedera helix,* meet all of the criteria

An Elfin Ivy: A number of lilliputian cultivars have been bred from the dependable English ivy, *Hedera helix*. Miniature ivies make attractive hanging basket plants.

for miniature plants: they are small-leaved; their leaves are close together; and they are slow growing. As with large indoor and outdoor ivies, the foliage is the attraction. A few among many appealing small ivy cultivars are the very compact *H. helix* 'Pixie'; *H. helix* 'Jubilee', the smallest variegated ivy, having half-inch (13 mm) leaves of light green, gray, and white; *H. helix* 'Walthamensis', a white-veined type called baby ivy because it's the tiniest of typical English ivies; and the slender-vined Italian strain *H. helix* 'Gold Heart', with foliage tinted yellow at the center.

Most miniature ivies begin as sports, and are then vegetatively propagated. Cuttings of tips or stems will root in moist sand, or in a peat/sand mixture, provided that the cutting contains at least one leaf node lying beneath the surface of the potting medium. To conserve humidity, cover with glass, or with polyethylene or polypropylene plastic. Then place the cuttings in bright light.

Ivy, like geraniums, welcomes the lowering of American thermostats. Indeed, if kept too warm and dry, it becomes especially vulnerable to infestation by red spider mites. The small ivies are just as hardy, in the face of frigid windowsill conditions (or drafts or air conditioning), as the standard varieties; but they are likewise as susceptible to both overwatering and underwatering. Ivy roots will rot if allowed to stand in water in a poorly drained pot, and the plant will die. On the other hand, allowing soil to dry out will cause leaf drop, and several days of bone-dry soil will kill ivy.

Since moisture retention and drainage are crucial to miniature ivies, a potting medium of 3 parts sphagnum and 1 part perlite is recommended.

During warmer months, ivy does best in a shady window. In winter, full sunlight is weaker and is beneficial to ivy. If indoor winter humidity is low, water more frequently.

BULB PLANTS

Miniature bulbs can be forced and grown in much the same way as the big daffodils, tulips, and hyacinths. They are at the opposite end of the spectrum from the terrarium plants, spending much of their cycle in temperatures barely above freezing, with only enough moisture to dampen the medium in which they are being forced. Even after the bulbs have begun to produce foliage, the plants are most at home in cool sunlight and moderate humidity.

Their compactness, however, enables a considerable collection to bloom in a minimum of space, and also eliminates the need for large areas in basement, garage, or cold frame in which to store standard size bulbs while they are being forced. In fact, a city apartment dweller with an unheated room—perhaps a pantry or sun porch—might be able, using miniatures, to experiment with bulbs for the first time.

The secret of success with bulbs indoors lies in planting them in autumn in earthenware bulb pans having numerous drainage holes, then giving them two months in a quite cool location in complete darkness. During this period the bulbs should be kept moist but not soggy or they might decay. This time in darkness builds strong root systems, and when you expose the bulbs gradually to increasing light and warmth they will respond promptly and vigorously. When the plants are in bloom, water them generously—but only when the soil beneath the surface is drying out. This is the case when the clay container gives off a hollow, ringing sound rather than a dull tone when it is tapped. After blooming, store your bulbs or replant them outside immediately for outdoor enjoyment the following year.

Bulbs in a Bonsai Dish: Miniature bulbs only a few inches high will brighten up a cool area of the home. This dish garden includes diminutive irises and narcissus.

An interesting collection of miniature bulbs might feature three to six inch (8 to 15 cm) high dwarf *Narcissus* cultivars such as the cream-colored angel's tears (*N. triandrus* var. *albus*) and the hoop petticoat daffodil (*N. bulbocodium* var. *conspicuus*), a fine yellow daffodil that can be planted six to a five-inch (13 cm) pot; the delightful Persian squill (*Scilla tubergeniana*), which sends up several stalks per bulb with star-shaped, one inch (2.5 cm) wide blue and mauve blooms; *Tulipa tarda,* a three-inch (8 cm) tulip with tricolor flowers of white, yellow, and green; the large-flowered, warmth-tolerant tulip hybrids *T. kaufmanniana* and *T. fosterana;* and winter aconite (*Eranthis hyemalis*), a perennial tuber with tiny blossoms resembling buttercups.

Miniature bulbs noted for their ability to flower for a prolonged period in relatively cool indoor settings include *Erythronium dens-canis* (the dog-tooth violet) and *E. californicum* 'White Beauty'; and the orange- and purple-flowered crocus *Crocus candidus* 'Subflavus'. Petite and long-lasting hyacinthlike flowers worth trying are the amethyst-hued *Brimeura amethystina,* which flowers in late spring or early summer, or some of the multi-flowering types that bloom in March. These have the advantage of producing several stalks from a relatively small bulb.

ORCHIDS

There are a great many miniature species, varieties, and cultivars of orchids. To a greater degree than the miniatures of any other family, such plants should be cultivated like their full size counterparts. Orchids are somewhat more difficult to grow than most plants, and the miniature types are orchids first, miniatures second. Their cultivation is best learned, then, through a study of orchids rather than a study of miniatures.

Still, a few points can be made about the small orchids, which usually range in height from three to eight inches (8 to 20 cm). For the most part, their ranks do not include the more culturally demanding kinds of epiphytic orchids, which in their natural habitat derive much of their nourishment from the air and

Epiphytic Orchids: The Orchid family puts on a spectacular show of miniatures from many genera. Perched on this "tree" are some examples from the genus *Oncidium*. From the top, moving clockwise, are yellow *Oncidium* 'Midas', dark pink *O.* 'Katherine Wilson', and light pink *O. osmentii* × *pulchellum*.

from precipitation. Most epiphytes have to be grown on slabs of osmunda or in baskets, and kept dry at the roots though surrounded by ambient moisture. Less fussy epiphytic plants can, however, be potted in a loose mix of 2 parts osmunda fiber and 1 part coarse peat. The miniature orchids available to amateur growers are more often among the less difficult epiphytes or are from the terrestrial groups, which do well potted in humusy soil containing osmunda fiber or shredded pine bark together with peat or sphagnum. Temperature needs vary greatly among miniatures, as they do among larger orchids. Generally, however, they can respond well to being grown under slightly warmer conditions than full size plants of the same genus.

The number of appealing small orchids is staggering, for in recent years there has been much work in interspecific and intergeneric hybridization resulting in profusely blooming

Dwarf Vanda Hybrids: Intergeneric breeding has produced small hybrid orchids in a variety of lovely colors. From left to right are × *Renantanda* 'Seminole', × *Ascocenda* 'Meda Arnold', and × *Ascocenda* '50th State Beauty'.

dwarf or miniature plants that are easily brought to flower under fluorescent lights. Some of the most adaptable of these new hybrids include those from the *Oncidium-Odontoglossum* group of related genera. Among the finest of all orchids are the multi-generic hybrids involving the diminutive genus *Sophronitis,* which bears scarlet to mauve flowers from winter to spring. Also outstanding are the ×*Ascocenda* cultivars, petite hybrids combining the large, single-color or variegated flowers of the *Vanda* genus with the small growth habit of the Thai species *Ascocentrum curvifolium.* Other prized small hybrids include those of *Phalaenopsis lueddemanniana* and other tiny moth orchids; dwarf cattleyas; *Cymbidium* hybrids such as *C.* 'Minuet'; and the more compact *Paphiopedilum* crosses.

Some favorites among the more minuscule species of orchids are the astonishingly floriferous *Mystacidium distichum* and the excellent terrarium plant *Haemaria discolor,* one of the so-called jewel orchids cultivated primarily for their outstanding variegated foliage. This representative offers lush, dark leaves dramatically veined with bright red. It does well in a wide, shallow container that can accommodate its creeping, horizontal growth. The miniatures in the genus *Oncidium,* the dancing lady orchids, are also much loved. Of special interest are the lemon-scented, yellow-flowered *Oncidium cheirophorum* and several lovely, lavishly blooming little equitant oncidiums, which have duplicate leaves standing inside each other in two ranks. These are *O. triquetrum, O. pusillum,* and *O. pulchellum*—all of which can be grown successfully under lights if given sufficiently high humidity and moisture. The relatively small "paph" *Paphiopedilum bellatulum* is another miniaturist's delight, as are *P. concolor* and *P. niveum.* Also worthwhile is the Caribbean native *Epidendrum tampense,* the particularly good-smelling *E. fragrans,* and the splendid *E. mariae,* which responds beautifully to the gradual introduction of bright light and warm temperatures. Valuable miniature *Phalaenopsis* species include the pink-flowered *P. lindenii* and the white-flowered *P. maculata.* The *Dendrobium* genus offers the very popular evergreen, dwarf plant *D. aggregatum,* a honey-scented orchid with yellow, orange-centered flowers which needs low night temperatures (down to 50°F/10°C) to induce bud formation for spring flowering.

In growing the aforementioned small orchids or any others, remember that each plant must be potted separately, even if the plants are to inhabit a terrarium, which is a practical way of assuring the humidity of 55 to 70 percent that is required by many of them. Do not, however, confuse providing adequate atmospheric moisture with watering too frequently; orchids succumb easily to "wet feet." They also will not flourish if grown in still or impure air.

Members of the Orchid family vary widely in their temperature, light, and seasonal care requirements, and this variability occurs not only from genus to genus but often from species to species within the same genus. The orchidist's challenge—and pleasure—lies in learning through study and experimentation what each specimen must have to create the extravagant blossoms for which these spectacular plants are prized. (For more extensive information on orchid culture, see chapter 19.)

ROSES

Miniature roses are descended primarily from crosses of hybrid tea and floribunda types with the China rose (*Rosa chinensis* 'Minima'), which has been grown in China since ancient times. These diminutive beauties fall into three groupings: bush, climbing, and tree-form roses. Although many of the little roses are true miniatures, reaching a height of just 6 to 9 inches (15 to 23 cm), some can grow to 12 or 15 inches (30 to 38 cm). This is hardly a point over which to quibble, considering the dimensions of some full size standard rose bushes; but it is important to cultivators who wish to confine plants in a small area. Another point to remember is that the truly petite miniatures should be grown separately from the larger ones if possible. Unfortunately, buyers are sometimes sold "miniature" roses which eventually grow to anything but miniature proportions. Therefore, it is most important to deal with a local grower you trust, or else to order plants by mail from a miniature rose specialist. Be sure to buy pot-grown plants and to plant them slightly lower than they were positioned at the nursery. Newly purchased plants also should be soaked before planting (for up to 12 hours if their leaves are yellowed). Use plastic or clay containers at least five inches (13 cm) deep—squarish ones will allow more root room.

Favorites among the lower-growing miniature cultivars include *Rosa* 'Red Imp', with its clusters of double, deep red blooms; low-spreading, bush-type (multiflora) *R.* 'Pixie', which offers double white flowers (similar to cabbage roses) suffused with pink; the brassy *R.* 'New Penny', with semidouble blooms that are a blend of orange and salmon-pink; and the perennially popular, free-flowering *R.* 'Cinderella', which boasts shell-pink, double flowers fading to white at their edges. (Usually classified as growing to six to nine inches/15 to 23 cm, *R.* 'Cinderella' can double that height if it is fed lavishly and given ample root room.)

Other quite petite miniatures worth considering, in part because of their historical significance, are two cultivars of *R. chinensis* 'Minima'. (By convention, *R. chinensis* 'Minima' is often referred to as a species, *Rosa roulettii,* though it has never been found growing in the wild.) Discovered growing in a window garden in Switzerland in 1917, this plant is everblooming with rosy pink flowers. It usually grows to eight or nine inches (20 to 23 cm)—taller if its roots are unconfined. The smaller, bushy *R.* 'Pompom de Paris' has fragrant, emphatically double, bluish pink

Potting Up Miniature Roses: Soak newly bought roses in their original pots, then repot them in spacious containers, setting the plants lower in the soil than they were in their original pots.

blooms. Also found in Europe, this cultivar was registered in 1839 and is the oldest miniature hybrid on the market.

Of interest among the taller miniatures are the flame-and-gold-flowered *R.* 'Baby Masquerade' (a hybrid descendant of *R. chinensis* 'Minima') the yellow *R.* 'Baby Gold Star', with semidouble, hybrid tea-type flowers; and *R.* 'Coralin', which offers semidouble coral and orange blooms. Other worthwhile intermediate to tall miniatures are the venerable and enduring polyanthas (primarily a number of crosses between *R. multiflora* and *R. chinensis*), which do well indoors or out. Commonly started from seeds rather than from budding, grafting, or cuttings, the fairy or fairy moss rose (*R. multiflora* 'Nana') is a small bush type proffering clusters of small flowers in all seasons.

Charming polyantha cultivars such as *R.* 'Margo Koster', which has cup-shaped, light orange flowers with salmon-red centers, and *R.* 'Mothers-day', with crimson-red globular blooms, make superb pot plants that can be forced readily. Many fanciers grow polyanthas in pots outside during the summer. (Sinking the pots into the ground will make it less likely that the roots of your summering roses will dry out if you forget to water them. Surrounding the pots with moist peat moss provides further insurance.) Polyanthas summered outside may be brought indoors when cold weather threatens. The hybrids, especially, can be forced for Easter bloom if they are allowed to experience frost before being trimmed slightly, and forced starting in January. (Begin the forcing procedure in full sun at 50°F/10°C, misting the canes until shoots emerge. Then increase the warmth and water generously.) Other potted roses can be forced, too.

At the very least, miniature roses grown indoors should be treated to an enforced dormancy around January. This can be done by withholding water for about four weeks, then pruning the plants back to a height of perhaps three inches (8 cm). They should then be watered thoroughly several times and the early new growth that will follow should be pinched back. It is likely, however, that these temperate-zone plants will do better if you can manage to give them a cold period. In January roses (still in pots) can be stored on their sides in a cold frame or other protected cold place and covered with hay. At signs of new growth they can be brought out in early spring. Plants cut back in October but denied a cold period and encouraged to bloom in winter and spring under lights have been known to do well for a couple of years. Roses subjected to this demanding regime probably should be moved outdoors permanently or rejuvenated by winter rest in a cold frame.

Cultivation of miniature roses indoors is most successful if evenly moist roots, 50 percent humidity, and temperatures in the mid to upper 60s (Fahrenheit) can be maintained. Temperatures of above 65°F (18°C) become acceptable only if even higher humidity is provided by misting and covering with plastic at night. (Note: When misting or using a water spray to wash off spider mites, be sure roses are dry before nightfall.) Although the high humidity of a terrarium poses no problem, roses, like orchids, will suffer if air circulation is poor. If uncovered regularly, roses can do well in terraria, preferably potted individually in a soil-based growing mix. (Equal parts of loam, leaf mold, sand, and cow manure is one good mixture.) In basements, garden rooms, or other places with little air movement, it can be advisable to run a fan up to 24 hours a day.

It is easy to remember the lighting preferences of small roses: full sun in winter, indirect light in summer, and close proximity to the source (as close as four inches/10 cm) if horticultural fluorescents are used. (Such lights should be run for 14 hours a day. For substantial increases in the number of blooms, provide both natural light and 18 hours a day under lights.)

Roses growing in natural light should be moved from a south window in winter to an eastern or western exposure during the summer. Unless they are sharing space with plants that benefit from a similar light regimen (all potted individually, of course), it is best to keep a separate terrarium for your small roses.

Keep the soil damp, never muddy, when plants are in bloom. They will need less water when growth and flowering stop and the plants are in dormancy. The dormant period is also the time to repot, although a root-bound plant in bloom also can benefit from repotting. Trim the tips of miniatures back in the spring as buds swell but before fresh growth begins. During active growth, take off weak shoots and cut back unusually long ones to give the plant an attractive shape. Miniature roses may be propagated from stem cuttings at any time.

CHAPTER 23

Carnivorous Plants

"Death flowers" that are large enough to engulf a man, seductive enough to stupefy him with their fragrance, and potent enough to consume him with burning acid; vines that suck the blood out of living animals; trees whose leaves and branches reach out to devour birds, monkeys, and men — these are all popular fantasies perpetuated in lurid stories and illustrations. As outrageous as these tales are, they nevertheless have some factual basis. Carnivorous plants do exist, and indoor gardeners will find their cultivation as spellbinding as any storyteller's tale.

Carnivorism, the habit of eating flesh, is not something we expect from plants. We in the animal kingdom are accustomed to being preyed upon by the members of three other kingdoms, the bacteria, the protozoa, and the fungi, but not by members of the plant kingdom. Animals are supposed to eat plants, not the other way around, since animals depend on plants for their nourishment, and most plants in turn get their energy from the sun. Many of us, upon learning of the existence of such carnivorous plants as bladderworts, butterworts, pitcher plants, sundews, and Venus' flytraps, share the sentiments of an anonymous poet who wrote:

What's this I hear
About the new Carnivora?
Can little plants
Eat bugs and ants
And gnats and flies?
A sort of retrograding;
Surely the fare
Of flowers is air
Or sunshine sweet:
They shouldn't eat
Or do aught so degrading.

A plant cannot be termed carnivorous simply because animals are injured by it.

When Winnie-the-Pooh fell into the spiny gorse bush he was woefully assaulted, but it would be improper to call the gorse a carnivorous plant. To be considered carnivorous, a plant must fulfill three conditions. First, it must be able to lure, trap, and hold onto prey. Second, it must possess a means to digest complex organisms and molecules and to absorb the by-products into its own tissues. And third, these absorbed materials must ul-

Natural Habitat: The yellow flowers rising above the surface of this lake in Madison, Wisconsin, are the only visible indication that bladderworts are growing there. The plants grow just below the water surface and send up their bright flowers in midsummer. The leaves and traps of the bladderwort plants are not visible in this photo — the vegetation on the water surface around the flowers is duckweed.

Opposite, "pitchers" of the common pitcher plant, Sarracenia purpurea.

timately be used by the plant for growth and development. Under this strict definition there are 14 genera of carnivorous plants: *Aldrovanda, Byblis, Cephalotus, Darlingtonia, Dionaea, Drosera, Drosophyllum, Genlisea, Heliamphora, Nepenthes, Pinguicula, Polypompholyx, Sarracenia,* and *Utricularia* (see the table, Carnivorous Plant Families).

Confusion may arise because in many advertisements and articles the term insectivorous is used. When these plants were first discovered, the most commonly observed prey were insects, and hence the term insectivorous was coined. Subsequently, however, some carnivorous plants were found to consume fish, frogs, and on some occasions even mice, as well as a host of noninsect invertebrates. Therefore the more appropriate term carnivorous, which encompasses the eating of all kinds of flesh, has been substituted.

The 14 genera of carnivorous plants are distributed in six different plant families, a number of which are only distantly related to one another. This is an indication that carnivorism among plants is a fundamental evolutionary adaptation that has appeared again and again; it cannot be dismissed as a one-time freak occurrence. If we wish to explore the conditions that have favored the evolution of carnivorism, we cannot simply look among the plants on our windowsills, but must go to the plants' native habitats.

Most green plants get their energy from the sun, their carbon from the atmosphere, and their minerals from the soil. Carnivorous plants, however, live in mineral-poor localities such as bogs, heaths, savannahs, or on crumbly clay marl. Many plants could not

Carnivorous Plant Families

Family and Genus	Common Name	Number of Species	Native Range	Trap Type
Droseraceae				
Dionaea	Venus' flytrap	1	North and South Carolina	Active/Bear
Aldrovanda	Water-wheel plant	1	Warm areas of Eastern Hemisphere	Active/Bear
Drosera	Sundew	±150	Worldwide	Passive/Flypaper
Drosophyllum	Dew-leaf plant	1	Western Mediterranean	Passive/Flypaper
Nepenthaceae				
Nepenthes	Tropical pitcher plant	±75	Borneo and vicinity	Passive/Pitfall
Sarraceniaceae				
Sarracenia	Pitcher plant	8–10	Eastern North America	Passive/Pitfall
Heliamphora	Marsh pitcher	6	Venezuela, Guyana	Passive/Pitfall
Darlingtonia	Cobra lily	1	California, Oregon	Passive/Pitfall
Cephalotaceae				
Cephalotus	Australian pitcher plant	1	Southwest Australia	Passive/Pitfall
Lentibulariaceae				
Pinguicula	Butterwort	±50	Northern Hemisphere	Passive/Flypaper
Genlisea	....	±14	Brazil, West Africa	Passive/Labyrinth
Utricularia	Bladderwort	±170	Worldwide	Active/Suction
Polypompholyx	Bladderwort	2	Australia	Active/Suction
Byblidaceae				
Byblis	....	2	Western Australia	Passive/Flypaper

survive under such conditions, but carnivorous plants, having evolved a direct means of obtaining nutrients from living organisms rather than relying on the decomposition of organic matter to replenish the soil's fertility, are able to prosper in these environments. Animal prey provides these plants with supplemental nitrogen and phosphorus, and freed from competition from other plants that cannot tolerate the harsh conditions, carnivorous plants can build up large populations. In bogs in the mountains of northern New England, for example, there are nearly pure stands of *Sarracenia purpurea,* the common pitcher plant, an acre or more (approximately 0.5 hectare) in extent.

Faced with nearly 500 species of carnivorous plants, the novice or would-be grower can easily become intimidated. By dividing the plants according to their type of trap, however, a measure of order can quickly be imposed.

For our purposes, the first distinction may be made between active and passive traps. Active traps involve a rapid movement of a plant part that results in the prey's capture. Passive traps may exhibit movement but the movement occurs after the prey has been captured. Each of these two divisions can in turn be divided into two more.

The active traps consist of bear traps and suction traps. The bear trap is typified by the Venus' flytrap, with the opposing halves that suddenly clamp together. Less well known, but operating in the same manner, is the water-wheel plant *(Aldrovanda vesiculosa),* a diminutive aquatic version of the Venus' flytrap. The second type of active trap, the suction trap, is found in the bladderworts *(Polypompholyx* and *Utricularia* spp.). Bladderworts have a trapdoor sealing off a chamber, and when the door is triggered open, water rushes in, carrying the prey along with it.

The passive traps consist of the pitfall and the flypaper traps. The pitfall traps, represented by pitcher plants (*Cephalotus, Dar-*lingtonia, Heliamphora, Nepenthes, and Sarracenia spp.) consist of leaves that form hollow, watertight pitchers into which the prey falls and is unable to crawl out. The flypaper traps are represented by two groups, the sundews (*Byblis, Drosera,* and *Drosophyllum* spp.) and the butterworts (*Pinguicula* spp.). The sundew leaves are covered with stalked glands, each of which secretes a droplet of sticky mucilage in which insects quickly become mired. The butterworts have similar glands on the surface of flat leaves that also secrete sticky material. In sundews there is movement of the stalked glands once prey has become stuck to them, and in butterworts the edges of the leaves roll inward, creating what Charles Darwin called a "temporary stomach." In both of these plants, however, the movements are slow, occur after the prey has been captured, and are associated with digestion. Hence the term passive seems more appropriate to describe their trapping mechanisms.

Once prey has been captured it must be broken down. Most carnivorous plants possess glands on the inside of the traps that secrete digestive enzymes to break down the proteins, fats, and starches in the animal's body. The pitcher plants contain populations of bacteria in the liquid held in their pitchers, and these serve to digest the prey, whose byproducts are then absorbed by the plant.

A persistent question is whether animal prey is really necessary for the survival of carnivorous plants. Skeptics point to greenhouse-grown specimens that have lived for years without consuming a single item of prey. It is important to recognize that there are degrees of survival, however. Charles Darwin, one of the first people to seriously study carnivorous plants, along with his son Francis, showed that sundews that were fed an insect diet were more vigorous, produced more flowers, and set more seed than those that received no insects. Recent research has confirmed this to be true for butterworts and bladderworts as well.

How Carnivorous Plants Trap Insects

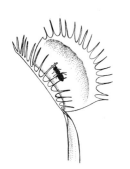

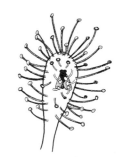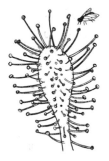

Venus' Flytrap: One type of active trap, typified by Venus' flytrap, works like a bear trap — its halves clamp together when an insect touches a trigger hair.

Sundew: *Drosera rotundifolia* (shown here) and other sundews all have flypaper-type traps. Stalked glands on the surface of sundew leaves secrete a sticky "dew" in which insects become stuck. When an insect is trapped, the glands begin to move slowly — a motion that is associated with digestion of the captured prey.

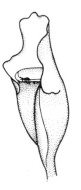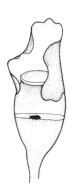

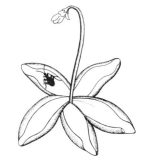

Pitcher Plant: *Sarracenia purpurea* (shown here) and other pitcher plants provide examples of passive pitfall traps. Pitchers contain digestive fluids, bacteria, and sometimes rainwater. Insects are attracted by nectar and crawl inside the pitchers, where they become trapped and eventually fall into the fluids below.

Butterwort: *Pinguicula* species have flypaper traps in which insects are caught in sticky material on the surface of the leaf. Leaf edges roll inward to create what Darwin called a "temporary stomach" and digestive fluids are secreted by leaf glands.

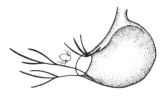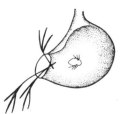

Bladderwort: The diminutive *Utricularia* and other bladderwort genera have active suction traps. Trapdoors are triggered to open by the touch of a passing aquatic organism and water rushes into the bladder, carrying the prey along.

Carnivorous Seeds

Shepard's purse *(Capsella bursa-pastoris),* in the Mustard family, is a roadside weed common all over the United States. Its tiny pinhead size seeds are so small that it takes about two million to make up a pound (454 g).

Moisten one of these seeds and it produces a sticky covering. This is not unusual, but when one of these seeds is put in water containing mosquito larvae, as many as 20 larvae will become stuck to the tiny seed.

Even more surprising, the mosquito larvae soon die. Studies have shown that the seeds attract the mosquito larvae, produce a toxin, secrete a protein-digesting enzyme, and absorb the resulting amino acids which the seedling uses when the seed germinates. This seed appears to fulfill all the requirements of a carnivorous plant, except the seeds do not ordinarily germinate in water filled with mosquito larvae.

John T. Barber, a biologist from Tulane University, has investigated the effects of these seeds on nematodes, protozoa, and bacteria. Reporting his findings in a 1978 issue of the *Carnivorous Plant Newsletter,* he found that the seeds attract all three organisms and there is clear evidence that they kill the nematodes they attract.

Shepard's purse seeds are so small that there is very little nourishment contained within them for the developing seedling. By attracting, killing, and digesting small organisms, the seed may be creating a locally nutrient-rich environment in which to germinate.

CULTURE

Many species of carnivorous plants can be grown successfully indoors if we remember that the plants are newcomers to the house plant world and have not been specifically selected or bred for life away from their native habitats. As indoor gardeners, then, we must try to re-create the plants' natural environment in the home. Obviously, this is easiest to do in a greenhouse, and certain plants such as tropical *Nepenthes* species with their giant dangling pitchers are best grown there. Most other carnivorous plants, however, can be grown successfully in a bright windowsill or under artificial light.

Our aim as carnivorous plant growers should be to maintain plants that are growing vigorously enough to flower and reproduce. Too often, plants are purchased, kept for a few months, and allowed to succumb to inadequate conditions. To grow carnivorous plants well there are first a few basic requirements that must be met.

POTTING

Most carnivorous plants are harmed by salt in the soil, and for this reason a clay pot which has been previously used for a heavily fertilized plant should not be used. Even the salt that progressively builds up as water evaporates from a pot can be toxic, so it is best to use pots with drainage holes. This will permit the salt remaining from previous waterings to be flushed out the bottom. Pitcher plants in the genus *Sarracenia* like their roots very wet, and they can be grown in undrained pots provided the entire pot is submerged in fresh water and drained every six months or so to remove any salts that have built up. Although plastic pots may appear slightly less attractive than clay, there is no danger of salt being absorbed by their walls. Some plastic pots, however, may give off toxic materials to the water (which is usually acidic) that passes through them when the plant is watered.

The potting medium preferred by most growers is live, green sphagnum moss. This may seem like an unusual "soil," but its unique water-holding ability and the way it maintains a high acid level and a low level of nutrients and salt make it an ideal choice. If you cannot obtain live sphagnum locally, you can order some by mail from the suppliers listed in the Appendix. Since it is a living plant, sphagnum moss will grow and spread and you will be able to use the extra in other pots. If you have only a small amount of live sphagnum initially, you can fill the bottom of the pots with dried, dead, long-fiber sphagnum. But do not use the so-called milled sphagnum, which is a dusty powder — it tends to cake up, and it adds no texture to the potting mix.

Carnivorous plants are very susceptible to mold and fungus invasion, and keeping the growing medium acidic will help to deter fungus growth. Tea leaves, because of the tannic acid they contain, can be added to a sphagnum moss medium every two months to keep acid levels suitably high. Add the equivalent of one tea bag of wet tea leaves (either used or fresh) to the growing medium for every seven to eight inches (18 to 20 cm) of terrarium or pot space occupied by your plants.

An alternative potting medium is one that mimics the sandy coastal soil of the southeastern Atlantic states, the richest locality in the United States in terms of the number of species of carnivorous plants occurring there. Donald Schnell, co-editor of the *Carnivorous Plant Newsletter,* recommends the following formula:

  1 part fine, washed silica sand
  1 part fine peat (German or
    Canadian, neither of which has
    added fertilizer)
  1 part small perlite

Mix the ingredients well, moisten thoroughly, and allow to stand for a week or two before using.

FEEDING

Obviously the most natural means of feeding these plants is with live animal prey. If you cannot move your plants outdoors, you can bring the insects to them. An entomologist's aspirator is a handy device for capturing small insects outdoors to feed to your plants (see illustration). Basically it consists of a small glass jar with two tubes running into it through a two-hole stopper. One tube has a small screen covering the end inside the jar; the other tube has both ends open. By sucking on the tube with the screen-covered end you can deftly pick up small insects at which you point the end of the other tube. Although we tend to think of flies as food for carnivorous plants, ants are actually more commonly eaten and they are easier to collect.

Some gardeners recommend feeding plants with seaweed emulsion, diluted to one-tenth of its prescribed strength and lightly sprayed on the foliage.

A 1 percent solution of plain gelatin in water (1 part gelatin to 99 parts water) is another acceptable fertilizer for carnivorous plants. It is administered with an eyedropper, one drop at a time, to individual leaves.

Beware of overfeeding your plants. Although they grow better with some feeding, feeding too much or too often will have adverse effects. For example, Venus' flytrap will eat bits of hamburger, but the food is really much too rich and is likely to cause the trap to rot. A growth of blue-green algae on the surface of the sphagnum moss is an indication of overfeeding.

In general, the appearance of the leaves is the best guide to follow in determining when carnivorous plants should be fed. Healthy-looking leaves that are turgid and upright can safely be fed. Leaves that are limp and unhealthy cannot absorb nutrients and should not be fed.

LIGHT

Most carnivorous plants are accustomed to large amounts of sunlight, which are most easily provided in a greenhouse. Sunny windowsills are a suitable alternative, and if you don't have any of those, then fluorescent lights can be used. Fluorescent lights work best with plants like Venus' flytrap, sundews,

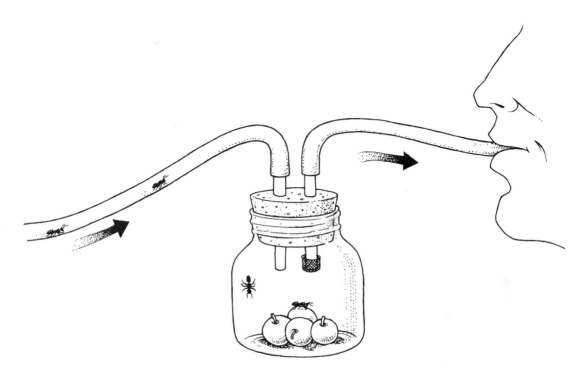

Entomologists' Aspirator: You can make one of these handy devices for capturing live prey for carnivorous plants. Basically all you need are a small glass jar with a 2-hole stopper to fit the top, 2 small pieces of glass tubing, 2 lengths of rubber tubing, and a small piece of screening. Assemble the aspirator as shown here; to use it, place the end of 1 tube over the insect you wish to catch and suck in on the tube that has the screen on 1 end. The suction will draw the insect into the jar. If you plan to keep the bug for a day or 2 before feeding your plant, you may want to put a few bits of fruit or other food into the jar for the insect to eat.

and butterworts, which have a low-lying rosette of leaves, all of which are equidistant from the lamp bulbs and thus will receive the same amount of light. Smaller pitcher plants will thrive under lights as well, but with some of the taller specimens there will be dramatic differences in the intensity of light striking the top of the pitchers and the developing bud at the bottom of the plant. This may be compensated for by using additional lamps arranged to provide more uniform illumination. Fluorescent lights are an excellent accompaniment to a terrarium, since they will not cause the air inside to heat up excessively. There are electric timers now available that can be set to exactly duplicate the hours of daylight outdoors. See chapter 25 for more information on selecting and installing lights.

TEMPERATURE

Carnivorous plants prefer to have the temperature drop 9° to 18°F (5° to 10°C) at night. A daytime temperature range of 60° to 80°F (16° to 27°C) is ideal during the growing season for most carnivorous plants. The cobra lily, *Darlingtonia californica,* is one exception. It likes to be kept cool and shady with a nighttime temperature of 68° to 72°F (20° to 22°C). *Drosera* and *Sar-*

racenia also prefer cooler temperatures. When the plants are dormant, some carnivorous plants, especially those from the temperate zone, will withstand frost.

MOISTURE

The water used for carnivorous plants should be low in dissolved salts. It is possible to use tapwater in some cities, but this certainly should be allowed to stand for 24 hours to allow the chlorine to evaporate before it is used. It is much safer to use rainwater or distilled water for your plants. If you can get your water analyzed, the water you use should have less than 50 parts per million of dissolved solids in it. During the growing season the soil should be kept constantly wet but not dripping.

Carnivorous plants come from bogs and swamps where they are accustomed to wet roots and high humidity. Few of us would choose to live in a bog, and hence the necessary humidity is most welcome in a greenhouse where there are few personal belongings to mildew or warp. If you are growing a larger number of plants in the house, a humidifier will raise the room's humidity very nicely, offsetting the excessive dryness brought on by central heating and air conditioning.

The most convenient way to create a microhabitat of high humidity for carnivorous plants is to use a terrarium. Terraria, however, must not be exposed to full sunlight for long periods of time or the plants inside will be dangerously overheated. It is best to remove or at least open the cover of the terrarium when sunlight is shining on it, to permit air to circulate inside.

PESTS AND DISEASES

Yes, carnivorous plants have insect pests, too. As in all indoor gardening, prevention is the best protection. Use clean pots and tools and be cautious when introducing a new plant to your collection. There are some specialized pests such as the small yellow and black moth, *Exyra,* whose larvae feed on the tissue of *Sarracenia* pitchers. In fact, there are a large number of insects that have managed to find homes in the seemingly inhospitable environment of a pitcher plant. But the most common pests you will encounter in your collection will be aphids, mealybugs, and scale.

Techniques for eliminating these pests are discussed in chapter 9. One caution to keep in mind, though, is that alcohol should not be used to kill pests on *Sarracenia* species. This pitcher plant can be damaged by coming in contact with alcohol, which takes away the waxy coating on its leaf surfaces.

Carnivorous plants are very susceptible to mold. Giving them intermittent fresh air will help to prevent the growth of molds and fungi. If plants are potted in sphagnum moss instead of soil, keeping the acid content high as described under Potting is also important.

DORMANCY

All temperate-zone carnivorous plants require a resting period, and many tropical ones do also. During this period the plants cease growing, and some species of bladderworts, butterworts, and sundews form a hibernaculum, a winter bud from which new growth will emerge when dormancy is over. Formation of this winter bud, or cessation of growth and a dying back of foliage, are indications that it is time for a plant to enter its dormant period, a period that must be respected. You should reduce watering until the soil is only slightly damp, and place the plant in a protected, cold outdoor location, in a cool basement, or in the refrigerator. When plants are in the refrigerator it is important to remember to water them occasionally to keep them from drying out. Three months of dormancy is adequate for most carnivorous plants and will generally take place during the winter months, when daylength is short.

A Beginner's Terrarium

The easiest way for a beginner to start growing carnivorous plants is in a terrarium made from a rectangular fish tank. Line the bottom with an inch (2.5 cm) of gravel to hold the pots above any excess water. Then buy plants of such easy-to-cultivate species as Venus' flytrap, *(Dionaea muscipula)*, the sundews, *Drosera binata* and *D. capensis* (which require no dormancy), and the orchid-flowered butterwort, *Pinguicula moranensis*. These should be put into individual plastic pots with live sphagnum serving as soil. The pots can then be set on top of the gravel and additional sphagnum packed in around them to hide the pots.

A pane of glass covering the terrarium will hold the moisture. Two 40-watt fluorescent bulbs suspended 12 inches (30 cm) above the plants will provide adequate light. By growing the plants in their own pots it is easy to replace them if necessary and the Venus' flytrap and the butterworts can be removed easily when they go into dormancy.

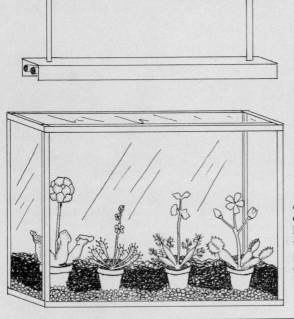

A Carnivorous Plant Terrarium: Probably the easiest way to provide carnivorous plants with the humid environment in which they thrive is to grow them in a terrarium. Growing the plants in individual pots makes it easy to remove those that need a dormant period. A layer of sphagnum moss over and between pots will effectively hide the pots.

A GUIDE TO GROWING SOME CARNIVOROUS PLANTS

VENUS' FLYTRAP
(Dionaea muscipula)

This is usually the first plant that comes to mind when you are asked to name a carnivorous plant. For a plant of such unprepossessing stature, fitting neatly into a two-inch (5 cm) pot, the Venus' flytrap has received an enormous amount of attention. Linnaeus, the father of modern taxonomy, called it a "miracle of nature" and wrote, "though I have doubtless seen and examined no small number of plants, I must confess I never met with so wonderful a phenomenon." Charles Darwin was later to declare the plant to be "the most wonderful plant in the world."

Considering that the Venus' flytrap is now so commercially ubiquitous, it is surprising to realize how restricted its natural distribution is. It grows only in scattered savannahs of southeastern North Carolina

Venus' Flytrap: This tiny plant with its clam-shaped traps is found in the wild only in a 60- to 75-square-mile area of North Carolina. Insects are attracted to the traps by the red color and sweet nectar. When the unwitting prey brushes against one of the trigger hairs located on the inside of the trap, the halves clamp quickly together and the insect is caught.

and northeastern South Carolina in an area with a radius of 60 to 75 miles (97 to 135 km) around Wilmington, North Carolina.

Named after Dione, the mythological mother of Venus, the goddess of love, the Venus' flytrap grows in a rosette, the leaves arising from a fleshy white rhizome called a bulb. The leaves, which may be up to 5 inches (13 cm) long, consist of a flattened petiole and a leaf blade that is modified into a trap that may be as much as an inch (2.5 cm) or so long. The trap, shaped like a clam with stout, hairlike projections along the margin, is normally opened at an angle of 40 to 60 degrees. The interior of the trap may vary in color from green to red. Plants grown in insuffi-

cient light have long petioles, with small green traps. Along the margins of the trap are nectar glands and perfume glands that serve to lure insects, while the inner surface of the trap is covered with digestive glands. Finally there are three trigger hairs (more in unusual specimens) on the inside of each half of the trap.

When an insect, attracted to the trap by the red color, the sugary secretions, and the pleasant odor of the nectar glands, bumps against the trigger hairs, the halves of the trap clamp together quickly, some in a fraction of a second, the hairlike structures preventing any but the smallest insects from escaping. This rapid closure is followed by a more gradual one in which the halves press even more tightly together and digestive enzymes are secreted, stimulated in part by the struggles of the prey inside. The trap remains closed for a week or so, after which it opens to reveal the dry remains of the insect.

By touching one trigger hair twice, or two hairs in succession, the trap can be made to close, but if there is no prey inside, the trap will reopen in a day. The reopening is the result of differential growth, one side of the trap growing faster than the other. Consequently, the number of openings and closings is limited. If triggered but provided no prey, traps will open and close about a dozen times; when capturing prey, traps function only three or four times before dying.

Although the mechanism of trap opening is well understood, that of trap closing is not. The best current explanation is that the open trap is in a state of unstable osmotic equilibrium. Slight changes in turgor pressure brought on by touching the trigger hairs cause rapid closure. Tiny electric currents, or action potentials, have been found within the leaf when the trigger hairs are touched. These action potentials have been found to effect water movement and turgor in the plant cells.

When you order a Venus' flytrap from a company, you will receive a rhizome about the diameter of a dime that has been stored in a refrigerator to simulate dormancy. The rhizome should be placed just below the surface of the sphagnum moss. The first few leaves will be small and then, if the rhizome is big enough, a flower cluster will appear with anywhere from 2 to 15 flowers on it. The attractive white flowers can be hand pollinated. When the tiny black seeds ripen they can be sown immediately on the surface of a mixture of finely chopped live sphagnum and silica sand. As your plant continues to grow, larger trap leaves will be produced until the plant enters dormancy. A dormancy period is extremely important for Venus' flytrap.

Plants that appear to be dying are most likely just going into dormancy. Reduce the water, allow the foliage to die back, and store the rhizomes in the refrigerator for two to three months (do not freeze them). If you wish to propagate Venus' flytraps asexually, leaf cuttings laid flat on a bed of sphagnum moss in warm shade will produce plantlets at the cut ends.

SUNDEW (*Drosera* spp.)

While there is only one species of Venus' flytrap, whose distribution is extremely restricted, there are nearly 150 species of sundews distributed worldwide. Their name comes from the Greek word meaning dewy and refers to the tiny drops of sticky liquid secreted by the stalked glands that cover the leaves. Although all the plants form a rosette, the variation in leaf shape is enormous. The common *Drosera rotundifolia* has tiny spatulate leaves only ⅓ to ½ inch (8 to 13 mm) in diameter, *D. filiformis* has narrow leaves up to 20 inches (50 cm) long, and *D. binata* has leaves that are forked. *D. binata* var. *multifida* has leaves that fork again and again, producing numerous points on each leaf.

There are two types of glands on a sundew leaf, the stalked ones which secrete the sticky material, and the sessile digestive glands, which secrete enzymes to break down the trapped prey. When an ant stumbles onto a leaf of a sundew it quickly becomes trapped in the sticky secretion of the stalked glands at the edge of the leaf. These glands then slowly begin bending in toward the prey, carrying the trapped insect into contact with the digestive glands.

The culture of sundews is similar to that of Venus' flytrap. The more temperate species, such as *D. anglica, D. intermedia, D. linearis,* and *D. rotundifolia,* require temperatures close to freezing and low light intensities for three to four months after they form winter buds in the fall.

With the enormous range of species, there is an opportunity for adventurous indoor gardeners to try hybridizing. Most seeds can be sown immediately, although seeds of a few species, such as *D. anglica* and *D. linearis*, will require stratification.

The Australian genus *Byblis* and the western Mediterranean *Drosophyllum* are also sundews. *Byblis* has long, thin leaves. *Drosophyllum* is an unusual carnivorous plant, because it grows on semiarid gravelly hillsides in Portugal and Morocco.

Sundew: There are almost 150 species of sundews native to various parts of the world. Most familiar are those such as *Drosera rotundifolia* and *D. capillaris* (shown here), both of which have small round or spatulate leaves. But other types of sundews such as those in the genus *Byblis* have long, thin, threadlike leaves. Sundew leaves have two types of glands — stalked ones that secrete tiny drops of the sticky material that lures and traps insects, and sessile digestive glands which secrete enzymes to break down captured prey.

PITCHER PLANTS (*Sarracenia* spp., *Darlingtonia californica*, *Nepenthes* spp.)

There are five genera of carnivorous plants with passive pitfall-type traps. All are known as pitcher plants. The three most commonly cultivated are *Sarracenia* species from eastern North America, the cobra lily, *Darlingtonia californica,* from the Pacific Northwest, and species of *Nepenthes* from the vicinity of Borneo.

The fleshy trap leaves of *Sarracenia* vary in height from 8 inches (20 cm), as in the parrot pitcher plant, *S. psittacina,* to about 36 inches (91 cm), as in the white-topped pitcher plant, *S. leucophylla.* Tubular in shape, each leaf has a wing that runs up the side facing the center of the plant. At the top of each pitcher is a hood that may arch over the pitcher to prevent water from falling into it, as in the huntsman horn, *S. flava,* or not, as in the common *S. purpurea* which has rainwater-filled pitchers.

Nectar-secreting glands are located on the outside of the pitchers. Some plants may actually have a "guide-trail" for ants, leading them to the lip of the pitcher. When an unwitting insect walks into the mouth of the pitcher, it is prevented from walking out by down-pointing hairs on the inside and a very thick, waxy cuticle along the inner pitcher surface. Just below the hairs is a highly polished area where the digestive enzymes accumulate in the pitcher below. The insect tumbles into this liquid and is digested. Some insects (such as midge larvae), however, are not digested and are impervious to the digestive enzymes.

The flower of *Sarracenia* is complex enough so that even when the petals have fallen the resulting seed pod is sometimes mistaken for a flower. Hand pollination of the flower will lead to seed formation, a more reliable method of propagation than leaf cuttings. Rhizome cuttings, however, also will produce additional plants. Plants should be

Common Pitcher Plant: The 5 genera of pitcher plants include plants of a wide range of sizes and forms. The most familiar, *Sarracenia purpurea,* grows low to the ground and has rainwater-filled pitchers.

given a three- to five-month dormancy period with temperatures at 38° to 45° F (3° to 7°C).

The cobra lily, *Darlingtonia californica,* is the only pitcher plant native to the western United States. These pitchers have a hood that almost completely covers the opening, leaving only a small entrance on one side. From the lip of the pitcher a forked tongue projects. The resulting snakelike appearance of the pitchers earns the plant its common name. While the pitchers of *Sarracenia* species open toward the center of the plant, each pitcher of the cobra lily is twisted 180 degrees so that the openings face away from the center of the plant.

The small entrances to the pitchers would ordinarily make the interiors too dark to attract insects, but translucent sections in the hood, known as windows or fenestrations, let light into the pitcher. An insect attracted to the nectar glands located at the top of the pitcher and on the tongue walks inside and then attempts to escape through the windows; ultimately exhausted, it falls into the liquid below. Cobra lilies are believed to have no digestive enzymes of their own and rely on populations of microorganisms in the liquid to digest the prey.

Cobra lilies like to be kept cool. Water them with cold water and grow them in clay pots so that evaporation will cool the roots. The plant can be propagated by seeds or rhizome division. The plants should be given three to six months of dormancy at temperatures near freezing.

Nepenthes species are tropical pitcher plants. Each leaf consists of a blade, an elongated midrib that can twine around branches for support, and an expanded hollow end that forms a pitcher. New pitchers are covered by a hood, but as the pitcher matures the hood opens. *Nepenthes* pitchers can be very large; some may contain several quarts or liters of liquid, and in these have been found the remains of small vertebrates.

Nepenthes are easiest to grow in greenhouses. Such species as *N. maxima* and *N. rafflesiana* are best suspended from the roof in sphagnum-filled baskets and provided with shading that cuts out about half the light. Smaller species such as *N. gracilis* may be grown in a large terrarium by setting the

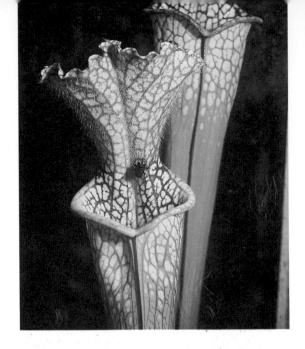

White-Topped Pitcher Plant: The slender, tubular pitchers of *Sarracenia leucophylla* can grow as tall as 36 inches (91 cm). Each graceful pitcher is topped by a white hood streaked with red veining and having wavy or ruffled edges.

Cobra Lily: The hood of this exotic-looking pitcher plant almost completely covers the opening of the pitcher, leaving only a small entrance on one side. Translucent windows in the hood let light into the interior of the pitcher. Insects attracted by nectar glands walk up the tongue and into the pitcher, then try to escape through the windows. Eventually the insects tire and fall into the liquid below, where they are digested by microorganisms.

pot containing the plant on top of a second upside-down pot. The latter should be standing in a few inches or centimeters of water that is kept warm and slowly evaporating by an aquarium heater.

Although *Nepenthes* are not the easiest carnivorous plants to grow because of their gangly size, they are readily propagated from stem cuttings, and their pitchers are truly spectacular.

BUTTERWORTS (*Pinguicula* spp.)

Butterworts are widely distributed in nature but uncommon in cultivation. The plants have a rosette of stubby leaves that taper to blunt points and lie flat on the ground, although the edges of the leaves curl upward slightly. The surface of the leaves has a greasy feel and *Pinguicula* comes from the Latin word for fat. The plants have two types

Tropical Pitcher Plants: The spectacular pitchers of some *Nepenthes* species can grow large enough to hold several quarts or liters of liquid. Each pitcher, which is actually the hollow end of the leaf, is connected to the leaf blade by a long midrib that can twine around tree branches for support. *Nepenthes* are best grown in a greenhouse because of their large size and high humidity needs, but they provide a truly striking display.

Butterworts: *Pinguicula* species are most likely to bloom in summer and early fall, and will produce graceful, violetlike flowers on long, slender stalks. The flowers range in color from lavender to pink and white, purple, or bright yellow, depending on the species. It is sometimes possible to produce seeds from indoor plants if you pollinate the flowers by hand. When the seeds ripen, sow them on a bed of fine, moist sphagnum moss.

of glands — stalked glands which secrete a mucilagenous, sticky fluid and sessile glands responsible for digestion. When an insect lands on the surface of a leaf it becomes mired in the sticky material and is soon awash in secretions from the digestive glands. The upcurled edges of the leaf prevent the pool of digestive juices from spilling off the leaf. In some species the edges of the leaf may roll inward and envelop the prey as well. This brings the maximum number of digestive glands in contact with the prey, making the process of digestion and assimilation more effective. Individual butterwort leaves may last only five days, and a species such as *P. grandiflora* may produce a total of 62 square inches (400 sq cm) of trapping surface a season.

Butterworts are accustomed to being slightly shaded in later summer, so indoor gardeners should provide less light and water late in the season. Butterworts are slightly unusual in that they do best when the soil is allowed to dry out between waterings. The soil should be kept only slightly damp in the winter when the plants are dormant.

When they flower, butterworts produce only a single flower on a long stalk. It somewhat resembles a violet, and may be lavender and white, as in *P. pumila;* purple, as in *P. vulgaris;* or yellow, as in *P. lutea.* Indoors the flowers can be pollinated by hand and the ripe seeds sown immediately on fine sphagnum. Butterworts also can be propagated asexually by pulling off leaves and laying them on the surface of moist sphagnum.

Students of economic botany (uses of plants) may be interested to know that in Europe in the nineteenth century *P. vulgaris* was used to curdle milk in the preparation of a yogurtlike dish.

BLADDERWORTS (*Utricularia* spp.)

These carnivorous plants are hardly ever grown indoors, partly because many of the species are aquatic, and partly because the traps are so tiny. The delicate threadlike plants lack true roots, and there is little distinction between stem and leaves.

The traps are tiny egg-shaped bladders no larger than ⅕ inch (5 mm) in diameter, filled with air, and attached to the plant by a stalk on one side. At the mouth of the bladder are hairs that form a funnel leading to an entrance sealed by a trapdoor with trigger hairs on it. The trap, when set, has concave sides. When a tiny animal brushes against the trigger hairs, the door swings inward. At

Bladderworts: Although seldom grown indoors, the bladderwort with its tiny traps is a fascinating aquatic plant. The bladders grow just below the water surface and are attached to the plant by a stalk on 1 side. Each egg-shaped bladder is no bigger than 5 mm in diameter, so the chief prey of this plant are microscopic creatures such as rotifers and cyclops. The rather sophisticated traps operate by sucking in water and prey, then pumping out the water after the prey has been digested.

the same time the walls of the bladder spring outward, sucking water and the hapless animal into the bladder. Specialized glands then digest the animal and pump water out of the bladder, setting the trap again. The principal prey are microscopic animals such as rotifers and cyclops, but the plant also will feed on mosquito larvae and baby fish. If only a portion of a fish is sucked into a bladder, the plant will digest that portion, then suck in another section and digest it, much like a snake swallowing its prey.

The aquatic species of *Utricularia* can be grown in a small pool of pure water with peat on the bottom. Let it stand for a week before putting in the plants, which can be propagated simply by breaking them apart. The flowers are often the most conspicuous part of the plant. They look much like butterwort flowers except that there may be as many as 15, depending on the species.

THE FUTURE OF CARNIVOROUS PLANTS

The realization that many carnivorous plants occur in small populations in habitats that are easily disturbed by draining or filling has brought on a concern for carnivorous plant conservation. This includes attempts to prevent both the destruction of habitats and the wanton collecting of wild plants. Carnivorous plants are now protected by law in some parts of the United States, and individual collection in the wild is prohibited.

Purchasers of carnivorous plants should try to ascertain whether the plants for sale have been collected in the wild or grown by the nursery. At present there are only a few nurseries that can claim that they propagate all their stock.

It will be easier for growers to propagate their own material when faster methods have been developed. Experiments continue to test techniques to hasten germination, including such exotic ones as lightly burning the seeds of some species. Tissue culture is also being developed as a means of propagating carnivorous plants.

While carnivorous plants require certain special conditions, indoor gardeners growing them in the greenhouse or on the windowsill will find them fascinating. They are, after all, an example of fantasy that is fact.

CHAPTER 24

Aquatic Plants

Aquatic plants suffer from an identity crisis. Most people assume that to be an aquatic means that the plant must be found in an aquarium — a pale green twig tucked in a corner, to be nudged and nibbled by the fishes. While it is true that plants and fishes make for a properly balanced system within a tank, aquatic plants also may be found growing in wooden tubs, indoor pools, and ponds. Exciting possibilities exist for creating "aquascapes," with or without fishes, in which a rich variety of sizes, shapes, and colors of plants can be used to enhance the indoor environment.

What sets aquatic plants apart from other plants is that they can live entirely or partially submerged and supported by water, and in addition have the ability to draw in nutrients from all their surfaces, not just the roots. There are all sorts of variations on these growth habits: the slow-growing water trumpet (*Cryptocoryne* spp.) can spend most of its life completely underwater; fanwort *(Cabomba aquatica)* rises to the surface of the water, and then trails; and the water lily (*Nymphaea* spp.) grows partially submerged with a buried root stalk which produces flowers and leaves that float on the surface of the water.

Aquatic plants are traditionally included in fish tanks, where they serve as a natural means of maintaining the proper environmental balance in the water, precluding the need for chemical treatment. Submerged plants are called oxygenators, meaning that they liberate oxygen which is taken in by the fishes. In turn, fishes release carbon dioxide which is used by the plants. The waste material from the fishes sinks to the tank bottom, where after decomposition it is absorbed by the plants' roots and serves to stimulate growth.

Aquatic plants are stylish and functional tank accessories, providing a natural cover and habitat for fishes and also performing the necessary job of hindering algae growth by competing for the available light and nutrients. Some people raise aquatic plants without ever owning a single fish, finding that the plants merit consideration as gardening specimens in their own right. Many water gardeners choose to grow aquatic plants because they find them equally as attractive as the more commonly grown kinds of house plants.

Victorian Water Garden: The amphibious and aquatic motifs of this ornate stand highlight the watery scene it supports. The water garden incorporates fish, submerged plants, a rock arch, and moisture-loving ferns within a nicely proportioned design.

Opposite, close-up of a small-flowered water lily, Nymphaea daubeniana.

The Varied Splendor of Aquatic Plants: A lush green underwater panorama is created by including a wide range of foliage textures and colors. In this aquascape, clumps of feathery, slender, and broad-leaved aquatic plants complement each other in varying shades of green.

The anemic-looking, spindly plants usually encountered in fish tanks are not truly representative of the broad spectrum of aquatic plants. Far from being a uniform shade of green, the foliage of these water-dwellers can be a sparkling emerald color, bear yellow or white markings, or become tinged with red. Certain plants feature leaves arranged along a single, slender stem in feathery, dense, or bushy whorls. Others have a bunch of long leaf stalks, each bearing a single leaf which sways gracefully in the water. These leaves may be lance or heart shaped, often with crinkled edges. One plant, *Vallisneria spiralis,* earns its common name of corkscrew val by the manner in which its slender leaves twist along their length. Members of the genus *Aponogeton* exhibit a wide variety of leaf forms, many with crisped or wavy edges. The showiest species, *A. mada-*

gascariensis, is called the Madagascar lace plant because of the delicate lacy effect created by the openings between the vein network in the leaves. In contrast to these leafy-stemmed plants are the freely floating duckweed (*Lemna* spp.), and fairy moss (*Azolla* spp.), both of which carpet the surface of the water like moss carpets a wooded glen, appearing in varying shades of green.

Aquatic plants also produce flowers, with the blooms of the water lily the first to come to mind. A plant called the water hyacinth (*Eichhornia crassipes)* has lilac and blue flower spikes that remind some observers of the blooms of the popular spring bulbs in the genus *Hyacinthus.* Outdoors, water hyacinth is a troublesome weed which is causing serious problems in the waterways of the southeastern United States. But indoors its growth can be contained, and it makes an attractive addition to an aquarium, tub garden, or indoor pool. Other plants produce blooms which aren't as showy but are nonetheless charming. For example, swamp spoon *(Ludwigia natans)* bears yellow flowers which contrast with the reddish brown of its foliage, and frog's-bit *(Hydrocharis morsus-ranae)* features tiny, light blue, star-shaped blooms. There are also curiosities among the aquatics, such as the banana plant *(Nymphoides aquatica)* with a rootstock closely resembling the familiar bunched fruit found on the tropical banana plant.

Apart from their varied and intriguing appearance, aquatic plants offer further enticement to the indoor gardener — they are relatively self-sufficient and undemanding. Once properly established in a suitable environment, they can be left unattended for longer periods than most house plants.

There is an added bonus to keeping a tank or deep glass bowl full of aquatics in your home. This water garden will work along the same lines as a tray filled with pebbles and water to increase the humidity level in the air around it. This proves to be a boon to neighboring house plants which might be suffering in the parched air of a centrally heated home.

In addition, aquatic plants enable adventuresome gardeners to broaden their horizons. Plants such as the water lily or water hyacinth, when grown in wooden tubs set in sunny locations, expand the realm of indoor gardening by allowing the indoor gardener to simulate a pond environment on a scale that is manageable in the home.

TYPES OF AQUATIC PLANTS

Aquatic plants are divided into three types according to the way they are oriented in the water: rooted, bunch-type, or floating. All three may be found in a typical pond, where

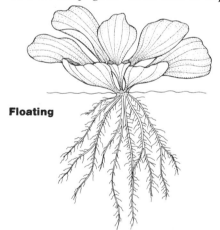

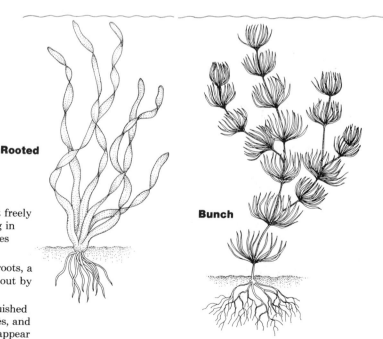

Floating

Rooted

Bunch

Floating Plants: Plants of this type may float freely on the water's surface with short roots dangling in the water as shown here, or may root with leaves and flowers that float.

Rooted Plants: Characterized by submerged roots, a crown, stems, and leaves, these aquatics spread out by producing runners.

Bunch-Type Plants: These plants are distinguished by submerged roots, long stems with many nodes, and leaves and flowers which may be submerged or appear above the water.

you might find rushes (rooted), hornwort (bunch-type), and duckweed (floating).

Rooted plants are distinguished by having the following parts: roots, crown, stem, and leaves. The crown produces runners, leaves, and, in some cases, a flower spike. Rooted plants spread by sending out these runners and by producing new stems, which can make them competitive aquarium inhabitants because they tend to crowd out their neighbors. These plants generally stay entirely submerged, and when planting them it is important not to bury the crown. Some popular rooted aquarium plants are arrowhead (*Sagittaria* spp.), eelgrass (*Vallisneria* spp.), lace plant (*Aponogeton* spp.), and sword plant (*Echinodorus* spp.).

Bunch-type plants have no crowns, appearing instead as long stems with nodes. These nodes are the points of growth for the roots, leaves, and flowers. The roots always remain submerged, but leaves and flowers may break the surface. The tendency for bunch plants is to grow taller rather than produce new stems. Fanwort *(Cabomba caroliniana),* goldfish weed (*Elodea* spp.), hornwort (*Ceratophyllum* spp.), swamp spoon (*Ludwigia* spp.), and water hyssop (*Bacopa* spp.) are all bunch-type plants.

There are two types of floating aquatic plants. Freely floating plants appear on the surface or just below it, with their abbreviated roots dangling free, never rooting in the bottom mud. Examples of these are duckweed and fairy moss. Others root, but are still considered floating aquatics because their leaves and flowers appear on the surface of the water. Water hyacinths belong to this category.

EQUIPPING AN UNDERWATER GARDEN

Since aquatic plants are most commonly grown in an aquarium, a discussion of the types of materials and maintenance techniques involved is helpful because the same procedures can be followed with any other suitable container. Equipment needed to maintain the proper heat, light, and aeration can be found in an aquarium supply store, along with some plants and many kinds of fishes. For the more exotic types of plant and animal life, you may have to look beyond the local aquarium shop and make your purchases through one of the larger mail-order suppliers.

Select as your container a tank or watertight bowl at least eight inches (20 cm) deep. Containers may be glass, acrylic, or Plexiglas. Tanks range in size from 5 to several hundred gallons (18.9 l and up). A 5- to 10-gallon (18.9 to 37.8 l) tank is suggested for a first underwater garden. A 5-gallon (18.9 l) tank comfortably accommodates 5 plants; a 10-gallon (37.8 l) tank, 6 to 10 plants; a 15-gallon (56.7 l) tank, 12 plants; a 20-gallon (75.6 l) tank, 12 to 15 plants. Tanks are available with glass covers which are handy for keeping out debris that can foul up the water, and with hood and light attachments.

Artificial light may be provided by incandescent or fluorescent bulbs. Fluorescents are the best choice, because they are less costly to run and don't generate as much heat as incandescent lamps. Gro-Lux lights specifically made for the aquarium also are available. To provide sufficient light for many aquatic plants, either two fluorescent tubes or one tube with some supplemental daylight is necessary. Make sure you take into consideration the light preferences of any fishes in your tank; some prefer shade and would be harmed by long periods under intense light.

Aquatic plants are flexible in their temperature needs and will generally adapt to a range of 65° to 78°F (18° to 26°C). This means that if you are including fishes in the tank, you can accommodate their specific temperature needs without being overly concerned about how the plants will fare. A heater and thermostat will allow you to pro-

A Habitat for Fishes: Iridescent fishes darting in and out of gently undulating aquatic plants add color and movement to this scene. The plants and fishes exemplify a symbiotic relationship, where two unlike organisms living closely together benefit each other. The plants give off oxygen to be used by the fishes, which in turn release carbon dioxide to be utilized by the plants. Fish waste material also serves as a fertilizer.

warm, you will not need to heat a tank that receives some sunlight since the water at room temperature will be sufficiently warm for the plants. Just be careful that the temperature does not fall drastically at night. During the cooler part of the year, you will need to enlist the aid of a heater and thermostat to keep the temperature at a constant level. This is especially critical during winter nights, when temperatures in the home drop sharply.

A pump and filter are a must for larger tanks stocked with fishes. Together, this apparatus aerates the water and keeps it free of decayed food and rotted plant parts which tend to create cloudy water conditions. To insure best results, clean the filter at regular intervals.

GROWING MEDIA

The purpose of the growing medium in an underwater garden is to provide support for aquatic plants with roots. The best choice is a 2-inch (5 cm) layer of medium size aquarium gravel, or coarse sand ($\frac{1}{16}$- to $\frac{3}{16}$-inch/2- to 5-mm particles). This sand is available in various colors and can be used to create interesting effects in aquascapes. If you collect your own gravel, make sure you sterilize it just as you would pasteurize garden loam for your house plants. Bake the gravel you have gathered in a foil tray for 30 minutes in a 200°F (93°C) oven. Avoid using crushed marble in the tank, as it is too high in harmful calcium salts. Purchased gravel should be thoroughly rinsed under running water, or allowed to soak in a pan of water. Besides cleaning items that go into the tank, scrub out the inside of the tank itself with warm, soapy water and then rinse thoroughly to get rid of any traces of soap.

For topographical interest you might consider adding some stones, shells, coral, or driftwood to your aquascape. The stones should be of the hard variety, not soft like pumice stone which dissolves quickly. Lime-

vide the proper degree of warmth and prevent wild temperature fluctuations which could harm both plants and fishes. Avoid heaters that are placed underneath the gravel or below the tank, for the same reason that you should never set a tank over a radiator — the plants' roots must always be kept cool.

In an underwater garden which contains only plants there is no need to artificially maintain the temperature, depending on the season and the location of the aquarium in your home. On summer days when the air is stone and gypsum are much too alkaline to be included in a tank. If you decide to use coral and shells, keep in mind that there will be an increase in the alkalinity of the water, and check to see that your plants will tolerate slightly alkaline conditions. Most common aquarium fishes will not tolerate the hard, alkaline conditions caused by the inclusion of shells and coral in the aquarium, so be careful. Slate, sandstone, or smooth riverbed stones are all good candidates for the underwater garden, but avoid any rocks containing iron or copper veins. These elements are leached out by the water and can upset the chemical balance in the tank. Before you include any of these decorative materials in your aquascape they should be boiled clean, except for saltwater driftwood, which should be allowed to soak in fresh water for a week or more to draw out the salt.

Larger rooted plants such as lace plants, sword plants, and water trumpets do best when they are grown in organic material. If they are to be cultivated in aquaria without fishes, they can be potted individually in a mixture of garden loam, sand, and bone meal instead of being planted directly in the gravel. Keep in mind, however, that when plants and fishes are to be grown together, this organic material can have adverse effects on the fishes. Use small clay or plastic pots, two to three inches (5 to 8 cm) in diameter, and spread a layer of gravel or coarse sand on top of the soil after the plant has been potted. This final layer serves to hold the soil in place when the potted plant is being submerged and anchored in the gravel layer in the tank.

The acid or alkaline condition of the water will be determined by the types of fishes and plants involved and their specific needs. As far as the plants go, they generally do well in soft, slightly acid water with a pH of 6.5. However, arrowhead, eelgrass, fanwort, goldfish weed, and sword plant can adapt to more alkaline conditions. When you take water from the tap to add to the tank, let it stand for at least 24 hours to allow the chlorine to dissipate. You can eliminate this waiting period by using distilled water in place of tapwater, but be sure whatever water you use is at room temperature.

PLANNING AND PLANTING AN UNDERWATER GARDEN

When you have assembled all the ingredients for the aquarium, the fun can begin. Give your creativity full rein in planning your submarine garden, just keeping in mind the general pointers mentioned here.

Prepare the tank right at its intended location — you are asking for trouble when you attempt to move an aquarium full of water. The first step is to spread a layer of prepared gravel or sand to a depth of two inches (5 cm). Shape the gravel terrain of your aquascape and incorporate the rocks, shells, and wood you have collected. Experiment with different combinations until you achieve an effect that pleases you. Don't be afraid to attempt multi-level constructions by building a pyramid of rocks or by creating an archway. You can plan an arrangement that imitates a real underwater scene, a forest glen, or a jungle. Or you can take an abstract approach and avoid mimicking nature by simply working with the colors and shapes of your materials in a sort of free-form underwater sculpture.

Once the growing medium is in place, add six inches (15 cm) of water. This is accomplished with minimal disruption to your arrangement by using a spouted water container. The idea is to let the water gently trickle in, aiming it at the side of the tank to break the force of the flow.

Now you are ready to add the plants. You should have a scheme in mind that includes no more than four different species of plants, because any more would make it difficult to meet all their growing requirements. Make sure they are compatible in their needs for temperature, light intensity, and alkaline

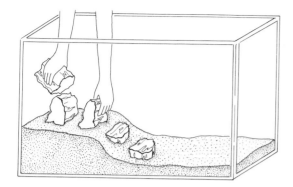

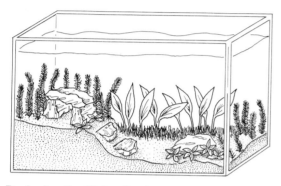

Designing the Water Garden: Contouring the sand or gravel and building a rock archway transports a humdrum underwater garden to the realm of the imagination, as it becomes a druid's wooden glen. Adding differently textured plants, while keeping the bold-leaved ones to the back, creates variety within a controlled sense of proportion.

or acid water. (For information on individual plants, see the chart on Plants to Make an Ordinary Water Garden Extraordinary, and the Encyclopedia section later in this book.) When you are selecting plants for a new aquarium which lacks any accumulated organic material and hence has a low level of natural nutrients, it is wise to stick to bunch-type plants for the first several months. Rooted plants are heavier feeders, and will do better when introduced into an established aquarium where there are reasonable amounts of natural nutrients available to the plants.

Pay as much attention to the selection of these plants as you would when choosing cut flowers to adorn the center of your table. Al-

though aquatic plants are surrounded by a watery medium, their color and form are not dulled one bit. Choosing a variety of foliage colors, forms, textures, and heights adds beauty and drama to the garden. For example, you can create striking effects by contrasting the feathery, arching shapes of such plants as fanwort and water hyssop with the sturdy-looking bunches of swamp spoon and water star. Once you begin collecting these plants, you will realize that there are any number of variations possible which allow you to play up each plant's particular characteristics to the best advantage.

As you position the plants in the tank, keep in mind their light requirements. Don't set a shade-loving plant where it will receive lots of sun and, conversely, don't put a sun-worshipper in the dimly lit background. Set taller plants like goldfish weed and milfoil (*Myriophyllum* spp.) in the rear corners where they can hide a heater or filter, then balance their height by grouping several medium to small size plants around them. *Echinodorus tenellus* as well as small species of *Sagittaria* and *Cryptocoryne* are likely choices for these groupings. Even tall-growing plants can be used in the foreground as long as they are kept judiciously trimmed. Work with the entire tank in mind, not leaving any gaping, awkward spaces. For the best appearance, two inches (5 cm) of clear space should be left between the front surface of the tank and the closest plants.

When planning an interesting, well-proportioned water garden, it is wise to give some thought to the creation of a focal point, by strategically placing an eye-catching plant. This center of interest may be the largest plant in the tank, or the one having the showiest foliage, and it need not be plunked directly in the center of the aquarium. Placing it slightly off-center, where it stands alone, will draw viewers' attention to it.

Before setting any plant in the tank, check it over thoroughly, removing any snails or visible eggs and yellowed leaves; then rinse

(continued on page 504)

7 Plants to Make an Ordinary Water Garden Extraordinary

The aquatic plants featured here all have some characteristic that sets them apart, whether it be unique foliage, striking flowers, an interesting growth habit, or an eccentric root formation. You may have to search a little harder for some of these plants, but the character they add to an underwater garden makes the extra effort worthwhile.

NAME		DESCRIPTION
Azolla caroliniana **Fairy moss fern**		A free-floating plant; tiny, buttonlike leaves form a green carpet; may be tinged with red.
Cryptocoryne cordata **Water trumpet**		A rooted plant with lance-shaped leaves and shrublike form; yellowish to dark green leaves are borne on red stems; leaf underside is purple; flower consists of purple spathe with yellow throat, encircling a rosy-pink spadix.
Hydrocharis morsus-ranae **Frog's-bit**		A free-floating plant; small, bluish flowers are borne above the surface on a stem; leaves are kidney shaped, appearing in a rosette.
Marsilea quadrifolia **Water clover**		A rooted aquatic fern with tall, erect stalks bearing four cloverlike leaves which float on the water.
Nitella flexilis		A free-floating alga that drifts at all levels within the tank, not just on the surface; appears as a dense mass of blue-green branching stems.
Nymphoides aquatica **Banana plant**		A rooted plant with floating flowers and leaves; broad, yellow-green foliage appears on purple stems; flowers are white; rootstock resembles a bunch of bananas.
Riccia fluitans **Crystalwort**		A free-floating liverwort, appearing as a mat of many light green branches; seen in the water it resembles a floating piece of coral.

LIGHT	TEMPERATURE	GENERAL CHARACTERISTICS
Indirect, filtered sun	50° to 80°F (10° to 27°C)	A rapid grower; propagate by division.
Shade	78° to 84°F (26° to 29°C)	Should be potted individually in a mix of garden loam, sand, and bone meal; propagate by division.
Indirect, filtered sun	65° to 80°F (18° to 27°C)	A rampant grower that blooms readily; lowers alkalinity in the tank, creating a more favorable acid condition; propagate by cuttings.
Shade	60° to 82°F (16° to 28°C)	Propagate by division.
Indirect, filtered sun	65° to 78°F (18° to 26°C)	A rapid grower; indicates condition of water by thriving when conditions are fine, and dying as soon as water is fouled and balance is upset; propagate by division.
Shade	64° to 86°F (18° to 30°C)	Propagate by division.
Indirect, filtered sun	50° to 80°F (10° to 27°C)	Increases acidity of the water; many fishes enjoy nibbling on its branches; propagate by division.

Well-Designed Aquarium: An attractive display of aquatic plants requires attention to proportion and the creation of a focal point. Too many plants tend to create a crowded, busy effect. Plants of the same height, same color, and same shape create a monotonous display. Instead, use a wide variety of sizes and shapes, juxtaposing different leaf types. Here, the focal point is slightly off-center to the right, where the eye is drawn toward the reddish plant nestled against a backdrop of green.

the plant under lukewarm running water.

Always be sure to handle rooted plants gently, to avoid injuring the delicate crown. To plant a rooted specimen, make a hole in the gravel or sand with your finger or a spoon, insert the plant just to the point where the white roots meet the green stem, then push the gravel back in place, making sure the crown is not buried. Since these plants tend to spread out, do not crowd them. Larger plants, such as lace plants and sword plants, need a buffer of six inches (15 cm) for growing space, and should be potted individually so their growth doesn't run rampant.

With bunch-type plants, trim off the lower inch (2.5 cm) of roots before inserting the plant into the gravel. Set individual plants ¼ to ½ inch (6 to 13 mm) apart, since they are visually more attractive as a clump rather than as scattered and solitary specimens. Some bunch-type aquatics have relatively undeveloped roots, which makes anchoring them difficult. Aquarium shops carry lead weights which can be attached to the plants, preventing them from floating to the surface. These weights are thin, flexible and about 2 inches (5 cm) long; they may be twisted around the lower portion of the bunches the same way you would close a plastic bag with a coated wire twist-tie.

When the plants are in place and the aquascape is arranged to your satisfaction, dechlorinated water can be added to fill the tank nearly to the top. At this point, the

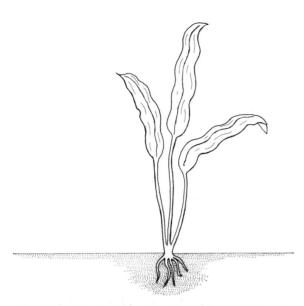

Planting a Rooted Aquatic: The crown, or thickened part at the base of the plant, should never be covered by gravel or sand. Poke a hole in the gravel, and gently insert the plant no farther than the point where the white roots join the green stem. The gravel can then be patted back around the roots for support.

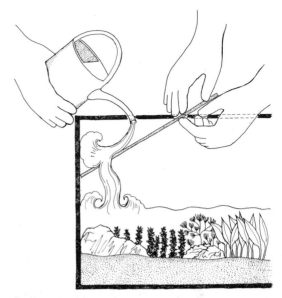

Final Addition of Water: A stiff piece of cardboard, held at an angle against the glass, breaks the force of the water as the aquarium is filled. By using this method, you avoid extensive repair work, since the gravel will not be churned up and the plants will not be dislodged by a full, unbroken flow of water.

floating plants can be dropped in. This final addition of water is tricky and you must work carefully so that a torrent of water doesn't wipe out all your efforts. It is best to enlist another pair of hands, to hold a stiff piece of cardboard at an angle against an inner side of the tank. Then you can pour the water from a spouted container onto the cardboard, which will break the initial flow. In this way, the plants and gravel already in the tank will suffer a minimum of dislocation. If your aquarium is filled with tapwater, it may appear cloudy for five to ten days. This is a normal condition caused by the growth of algae, and bacteria should die out once their nutrient supply is depleted. If the cloudiness persists longer than ten days, you might consider installing a filter if you do not already have one, or you can reassemble the tank using distilled water.

When selecting fishes and plants to go in your aquarium, make sure their general requirements are compatible. It is best to wait one week after planting before adding any fishes. Do not cram the tank full, because both plants and fishes will suffer. Consult a local aquarium shop for the fishes best suited to your specific tank size and conditions. Species which bear live offspring are generally more hardy, and popular types include swordtails, mollies, and guppies.

MAINTAINING AN UNDERWATER GARDEN

Aquatic plants are basically hardy and will adapt to a wide range of conditions, within reason. The temperature should be kept in the recommended range at all times, without any extreme fluctuations.

In general, aquarium plants need 8 to 10 hours of light each day from natural sources, boosted with 4 to 6 additional hours of artificial light. Most plants thrive on 14 to 16

Paludarium: This exotic variation on underwater gardening includes plants and animals in both dry land and water zones. A small body of water and ample humidity create a marshlike atmosphere that benefits both aquatic and moisture-loving plants. A soilless mix is contoured to form dry areas that jut out above the water, which can then be attractively landscaped with rocks or other natural objects. Mosses, ferns, and carnivorous plants can be added to create a lush green effect. Surprisingly, the Chinese evergreen and some palms have a latent amphibious nature which allows them to adapt to such a moisture-laden environment. Within the water itself, emersed, submerged, or floating aquatic plants, such as duckweed, can be added. A nice finishing touch is the inclusion of some tropical fishes or amphibians.

hours of combined natural and artificial light daily, with floating aquatics needing a little more. Do not set the tank where direct midday sun will strike it, because the intensity and heat are liable to harm your plants. Instead, the gentle rays of early morning and late afternoon sun will provide beneficial light without the damaging heat.

Foliage is the best indicator of whether or not plants are receiving adequate light. With too much light, algae quickly forms on the sides of the container and on plant leaves. Rooted and bunch-type plants may lean over and flatten out on the sand; their leaves may yellow and rot. Overabundant light also may trigger a growth spurt, causing plants to quickly outgrow their allotted space. On the other hand, with too little light, plants and water turn an unappealing brown and the plants either may become spindly or may not grow at all.

Aquatic plants derive most of their nourishment from the water, and in a tank which includes fishes, the droppings are adequate fertilizer. When plants are grown in an aquarium without fishes, periodic feedings can be given. Avoid overdoing it though, since heavy-handed feeding creates too rich a growing medium, which in turn fosters harmful bacterial growth.

Bone meal/clay pellets or weak manure tea are suitable fertilizers for any aquatic plant with roots set in a growing medium. Rooted plants potted separately in organic material may be lifted out of the tank in their pots and given an occasional shot of manure tea. The bone meal/clay pellets can be used with these plants, as well as with any that are growing in the layer of gravel on the tank bottom.

To make the pellets, mix coarse bone meal with enough wet clay to bind it together. This mix then can be shaped into small balls, and one may be inserted in the growing medium next to each plant's roots. This is usually done at the initial planting, but pellets also may be given to established plants which seem to be drooping. Always remember that in all probability there are other reasons why your plant is ailing — and proper light and temperature are more critical than feeding.

The grooming routine for aquaria includes checking plants for any dead leaves or roots, and removing spotted or discolored foliage. Bunch-type plants are notorious for growing too tall and spindly, and must be pinched back regularly to retain a compact, bushy shape. Healthy prunings may be inserted in the gravel to root.

Algae growing on the sides of the tank should be scraped away with a razor blade. Algae appearing as a brown or green scum on the foliage can be easily rubbed off with your fingers without removing the plant from the tank.

Once a month the water in a tank full of plants should be freshened. With a cup remove about one-third of the water, and gently add distilled or dechlorinated water to fill the tank. Allow any new water to sit out for several days and come to room temperature before adding. The water in the tank should always be kept clean and free from dust and debris.

PROPAGATION

Propagation is a simple matter with aquatic plants. Rooted plants reproduce by runners, or they can be propagated by crown division. Arrowhead and eelgrass are two plants which send out runners across the tank floor with new plants appearing every few inches or centimeters along these horizontal branches. Leave the runners attached to the parent plant until the foliage and roots of the new plants are fully developed. At that point, the individual plantlets may be removed and pushed into the gravel. Overgrown lace plants, sword plants, and water trumpets may be propagated by crown division. With your fingers, gently pry apart the crown of a mature plant, making sure to include some roots with each section.

Bunch-type plants can be propagated by cuttings. Take a section of the stem with several nodes on the end that is to be inserted in the gravel, as well as three or more leaf-bearing nodes above gravel level. Pluck the leaves from the lower nodes before planting, and when these growing points are set in the gravel, they will work at producing roots.

Free-floating plants such as fairy moss and duckweed reproduce rapidly and will eventually blanket the water surface with their prolific growth. Most free-floating aquatics can be propagated by simply separating the clump into two or more sections. Water ferns (*Ceratopteris* spp.) are viviparous aquatics, meaning that they produce offspring right on the leaf edges. These young plantlets then replace the older plants which die off. If allowed to root in shallow water, *Ceratopteris* species will produce aerial fronds like other ferns. Under proper conditions these fronds will produce both viviparous plantlets and spores, both of which can be used for propagation. Other plants which are rooted and have floating leaves and flowers, such as the water lily and water hyacinth, are propagated by rhizome division.

PESTS AND DISEASES

Aphids and mealybugs aren't likely to plague your plants, but aquatic plants are attacked by pests and diseases. Fishes themselves may be considered pests when they nibble and even defoliate such plants as duckweed and goldfish weed. Also, if fishes are overfed the excess food will collect on the bottom where it can cause rotting at the base of the plants.

Ram's head snails, which are small, brown, and spiral shaped, are common pests in the aquarium, where they multiply rapidly and may eat plants. They are inadvertently introduced into tanks on plant foliage, so it is a good idea to check over any new additions to the water garden for mature snails, and rinse thoroughly to dislodge any eggs. If, despite these precautions, snails do appear, you will simply have to pick them off by hand.

Growth of algae is a potential problem often resulting from too much light. If algae growth appears in your aquarium, cut back on the amount of light. "Mystery snail" and algae-eating catfish provide a natural method of algae control.

If you spot a white residue on the leaves in the morning which disappears later in the day, there may be a pH imbalance in the water. A complete change of water can help to eliminate this imbalance.

At times, even though most of the tank water is clean, there may be a murky cloud hovering above the bottom, along with dark, smelly patches in the sand. This indicates the presence of harmful bacteria, which can cause plants to become translucent, decompose, or float to the top. If this condition arises, ask yourself if you have been overzealous with the fertilizer or fish food; if the plants are cramped; if the tank needs a filter or, if it already has one, whether it is working correctly; and if the light and temperature are appropriate for the plant species in your tank. A thorough cleaning of the bottom combined with partial water changes will usually correct this condition.

TUB GARDENS

There's more than one way to raise an aquatic plant, and tub gardens provide an opportunity to experience growing some unique species with showy flowers and emersed foliage (leaves which appear above the surface of the water) which are too large to do well in aquarium tanks. Tub-grown aquatics may be seen as the intermediate step between the relatively simple aquarium and the greater investment of time and money represented by an indoor pool.

Many striking effects can be created by combining an aquatic plant featuring a flower that floats on the surface with a rooted plant adding vertical interest with leaves emerging from the water. For example, you might grow a brilliant crimson water lily in a tub with a bog rush *(Juncus effusus),* with its deep green,

Tub Garden: For a unique departure from the traditional plant-in-a-pot, try growing aquatic plants in a tub of water. A blooming water lily adds a soft pink touch to the green background formed by the lily pads and a delicate-leaved *Cyperus.*

emersed leaves. The possibilities are limitless, and these tub gardens are easy to prepare and relatively maintenance free.

For our purposes here, the word "tub" refers to any watertight container which is at least 20 inches (51 cm) deep and at least 12 inches (30 cm) wide. Old wooden barrels sawed down to half their height, washbasins, ceramic pots, even geometric-shaped acrylic or Plexiglas containers, all can be used for "tub" gardens. Containers that are not watertight may be used as decorative containers when the actual planting is done in a plastic tub, which can then be set inside the more decorative container.

Wooden barrels which held tar or any oily substance are likely to carry a residue which will foul the water, so barrels used for storing wine, vinegar, or beer are your best choices. To insure that the barrel is watertight, keep it full of water until the wood is sufficiently swollen. Any container which you choose should be scrubbed thoroughly without detergent, to avoid leaving any traces of soap which would cloud the water in your garden.

WATER LILIES

Prime candidates for tub gardens are water lilies. Their attractive flowers in a wide range of colors appear above or on the water. Each blossom lasts from three to five days, and as soon as one fades there is a fresh replacement. The floating oval leaves, called lily pads, extend from the rhizome which is set in soil, and are kept from floating away by flexible leaf stalks. There are two types of water lily, hardy and tropical.

The hardy lilies are perennials, and may be distinguished from the tropicals by their flowers, which float on the surface of the water. You can expect blooms from spring through fall, opening in the morning and closing around dusk. There is undoubtedly a color to suit your fancy, ranging from pink, white, and red to yellow and peach. When

Water Lily: A prolific bloomer available in a wide range of colors, *Nymphaea daubeniana* is the perfect accent of color in a tub garden. This tropical lily opens during the day, releasing a lovely fragrance, then closes by late afternoon. Each flower lasts for several days, and there are continual replacements for faded blooms from early spring to late fall.

lilies are grown outdoors, the pads die off in the fall, and the rhizome enters a dormant period. Indoors, these lilies require a resting period, too, and it should begin in the fall.

Tropical lilies produce highly fragrant flowers which are borne above the water on thick stems 6 to 18 inches (15 to 45 cm) tall. You can select either day or night bloomers; the daytime blooms open with the sun and close by late afternoon, while the nighttime blooms open in late afternoon, last through the night, and close by midmorning. Tropical lilies offer a wider range of colors than do hardy types; you may choose among white, pink, rose, red, yellow, orange, purple, or blue. Tropical lilies bloom from early spring through late fall. Although the tubers may be stored following the growing season, tropical lilies are difficult to overwinter in the temperate zone without the aid of a greenhouse, and are usually discarded after blooming.

Both hardy and tropical water lilies are available in miniature forms which are well suited to indoor tub culture. Smaller specimens such as *Nymphaea* 'Daubeniana' or any of the hybrid cultivars of *N. pygmaea* also can be grown peeking out of deep glass bowls, set on sunny windowsills.

PREPARING A TUB GARDEN

Water lilies need ample room to grow, so no more than one lily should be grown per tub. Including one submerged oxygenating plant and one emersed plant will round out your garden, but don't add many more than that or you will overcrowd the space. Good oxygenators include arrowhead, eelgrass, fanwort, and goldfish weed. Suitable plants with emersed leaves are bog rush, elephant's ear *(Colocasia esculenta),* and the papyrus plant (*Cyperus papyrus* 'Nanus'). Each plant should be provided with an individual pot, which can then be positioned in the tub of water.

To plant a mature water lily with pads and leaf stalk, select a plastic or clay pot, 3 to 5 inches (8 to 13 cm) wide and 8½ inches (22 cm) deep. Fill the pot with pasteurized garden loam which has been sieved to remove any large pieces of organic matter which could rot and foul the water. Avoid using peat moss, compost, or manure. Hardy water lilies benefit from a small amount of bone meal added to the soil, while tropical lilies prefer a handful of sand mixed in. Insert the plant carefully into the soil, working gently with the slender, threadlike roots. Hardy tubers should be set at a 45-degree angle against the side of the pot; tropical tubers should be centered in the pot. Keep the crown of both types above the soil. At this point, a bone meal/clay pellet (see Maintaining an Underwater Garden, earlier in this chapter, for directions on how to prepare these pellets) can be pressed into the soil near the roots. Top-dress with a 1-inch (2.5 cm) layer of sand or gravel. Next, thoroughly water the lily in the pot to get rid of any air pockets and to pack down the soil.

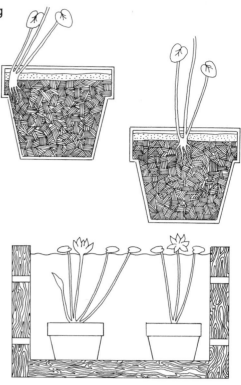

Planting Water Lilies: The pot on the left shows correct placement of the tuber of a hardy lily, where it is set at a 45-degree angle against the side of the pot. The tropical tuber can be set in the center of the pot, as shown on the right. Keep the tuber crowns above soil level when potting, and add a finishing layer of sand to keep the soil in place when the pot is submerged. The water level should always be high enough to allow the leaves to float on the surface, as shown in the lower illustration.

The potted plant is now ready to be set in a tub of water. Allow this water to sit for at least 24 hours before adding any plants, so the chlorine can dissipate, or use distilled water. Water lilies need six to eight inches (15 to 20 cm) of water above the soil level at all times, and if there is only a limited amount of sunlight, water depth should never exceed six inches (15 cm). The leaves should

Tub Gardening: A water lily, a floating plant, and several emersant plants are featured in this water garden. Plants are set into pots of garden loam, then top-dressed with a layer of sand which holds the soil in place underwater. Water lilies must always have 6 to 8 inches (15 to 20 cm) of water above the soil line, enough so that their leaves can float. The height of the emersant plants, center and left, has been adjusted by stacking bricks so that the leaves and inflorescences emerge from the water.

be able to float on the water, so adjust the level of the pot within the tub by using bricks or inverted pots. As the plant grows and the water evaporates, you will have to top off the tub occasionally to keep the water at the appropriate level.

Tubers without foliage and stems can be potted in the same manner as established plants. When you set them in the tub, add just enough water to cover the crown, raising the level as the leaf stalk lengthens.

MAINTAINING A TUB GARDEN

When choosing a site for your water lilies, keep in mind that they require sunshine — and lots of it. If the tub can be set outdoors on a balcony, in a southern exposure, your water lilies will thrive and respond with beautiful blooms. If you are unable to provide adequate sun, your lilies can get the light they need by artificial means. Fluorescent bulbs suspended several inches or centimeters above the water can be kept on for 12 to 14 hours to promote blooming.

The water in the tub should be kept warm, from 65° to 75°F (18° to 24°C). Tem-

peratures below 65°F (18°C) will make your water lily a reluctant bloomer. An aquarium heater with a thermostat can insure an adequate, constant temperature.

Water lilies aren't heavy feeders, and need to be fertilized only twice a year, with bone meal/clay pellets. (See Maintaining an Underwater Garden.) All this involves is pushing a single pellet down into the soil around the roots in spring and summer.

As far as pests and diseases are concerned, a tub garden set on a balcony may attract gnats and mosquitos which are more annoying to humans than they are damaging to the plants. Older lily pads may yellow; these can be removed by pinching, and new, healthy ones will appear. Algae growth can pose a problem, but by including snails or

A Miniature Lily in a Bowl

If you would like to grow water lilies, but just don't have the room for a tub garden, don't despair. You can scale the project down to a manageable size by using miniature water lilies and a 6 to 10 inch (15 to 25 cm) deep glass bowl or brandy snifter. Any of the following plants are good choices because of their diminutive size: *Nymphaea* 'Daubeniana', *N.* 'Margaret Mary', *N. odorata* var. *sulfurea*, cultivars of *N. pygmaea*, or *N. tetragona*. Plant the tuber in a 3-inch (8 cm) layer of sieved garden loam, making sure the crown is not covered. On top of this, layer ½ to 1 inch (13 to 25 mm) of gravel or sand. Add enough water to cover the crown, then increase the level as the leaf stalk lengthens, so that the leaves are floating on the surface.

Aquatic Plants for Tub Gardens

NAME	DESCRIPTION	LIGHT	TEMPERATURE	SPECIAL CHARACTERISTICS
Colocasia esculenta Elephant's ear	A rooted plant with broad, emersant leaves; foliage is dark green and purple; flowers are yellow.	Full sun	65°F (18°C)	Many cultivars are available as ornamental plants; provide 2 inches (5 cm) of water above soil level; goes dormant in winter; propagate by division.
Hydrocleys nymphoides Water poppy	Fleshy, floating leaves and large flowers are borne on stems above the water; foliage is olive green, flowers are golden.	Full sun	65°F (18°C)	Stem and leaves carry a milky sap; a rapid grower, vigilance is required to keep it from overgrowing the tub; provide 5 to 6 inches (13 to 15 cm) of water above soil level; treat as an annual; propagate by cuttings or division.
Juncus effusus Bog rush	A rooted plant with emersant leaves which are dark green and pointed.	Indirect, filtered sun	70°F (21°C)	Plant is a prolific grower, tends to take over space; provide 2 inches (5 cm) of water above soil level; propagate by division or seeds.
Nelumbo nucifera Sacred lotus	Leaves and flowers are borne above the water on long stems; foliage is wavy and green; fragrant flowers come in shades of pink and white.	Full sun	65°F (18°C)	Provide 6 to 8 inches (15 to 20 cm) of water above soil level; goes dormant in winter; propagate by division or seeds.
Pistia stratiotes Water lettuce	Leaves and flowers float freely on the surface; foliage appears in a small, velvety, light green rosette; flowers are white.	Indirect, filtered sun	65°F (18°C)	Goes dormant in winter; propagate by division.
Trapa natans Water chestnut	Leaves and flowers float on the surface; dark green leaves tinged with red appear as a rosette; flowers are off-white.	Indirect, filtered sun	65°F (18°C)	Provide 5 to 6 inches (13 to 15 cm) of water above soil level; treat as an annual; propagate by seeds.

oxygenating aquatic plants the algae will be deprived of carbon dioxide and soon die off.

SEASONAL CARE

Fall is the time when tubs should be drained and cleaned. Remove the potted lilies and empty the tub, then scrub it thoroughly so it will be ready for replanting in the spring. Hardy water lilies should be allowed to dry out in their pots in the fall. Once the foliage has withered, knock the tuber out of the pot, and store it in a container of damp sand or peat moss in a cool location.

In early spring, check for any new shoots. Split the tuber so that each piece has some roots and new shoots, then pot each section individually and place in the prepared tub. As the plants mature, you can choose the more vigorous grower and discard the other, or prepare a second tub. Either way, you're set for another summer's enjoyment of beautiful blooms.

Tropical water lilies are much harder to overwinter successfully, and are usually discarded in the fall after blooming has ceased. If you want to try your hand at storing them, after the tub has been drained take the potted tuber and set it in a cool, dark site for two weeks, keeping the soil barely moist. At that point, remove the tuber from the soil and let it soak in room-temperature water for two more weeks. Next add one inch (2.5 cm) of damp sand to a lidded container, add the tuber, then cover with enough sand to completely fill the container. Store the covered container in a cool, dark site. In the spring, remove the tuber from the sand and set it in a jar with enough water to cover the tuber, then place in full sun. When sprouts begin to appear, the lily may be repotted in fresh soil.

OTHER PLANTS FOR TUB GARDENS

You need not limit yourself to growing just water lilies in a tub garden. The chart on Aquatic Plants for Tub Gardens offers a selection of blooming and foliage aquatic plants which are equally attractive and easy to maintain. The general care and preparation procedures for water lilies apply to these plants: pot individually in garden loam mixed with bone meal; avoid overcrowding; adjust the height of the pot in the water so that flowers and leaves float on the surface; fertilize occasionally with bone meal/clay pellets; treat in the same manner as hardy water lilies during winter dormancy, or discard if the plant is an annual.

CHAPTER 25

Gardening under Electric Lights

Light is the fundamental source of energy in the vegetable kingdom. With it, plants turn air, water, and nutrients from the soil into food. Without it, they die of starvation. Light is necessary for the development of the whole plant structure — for the production of flowers and seeds and for the formation of bulbs. If it is not provided in sequence with a certain number of hours of darkness, apparently healthy plants may fail to bloom. For no reason other than inadequate lighting, flowering species drop their buds, germinating seeds develop into pale, spindly seedlings, and gift plants collapse and die.

When it comes to providing the right light for plant growth, many homes fall far short of the ideal. Plants placed in the center of a room probably receive only about one-tenth of the illumination they would receive outdoors. Although philodendrons, aspidistras, and other foliage plants accustomed to growing in dark forests may thrive in these surroundings, few other plants will.

Even the light pouring through the proverbial "sunny south window" is fairly dim by outdoor standards. Plants set on that windowsill receive less than one-quarter of the illumination they would get outside. But given the brightness of summer sunlight, which may be up to 30 times greater than the light shed by a 100-watt incandescent bulb, the reduced light just inside a window is adequate for even flowering plants in summer. However, in winter, when the sun may be less than one-tenth as bright as it is in summer and when its rays do not enter the window until later in the day, lower light levels may be insufficient for many plant genera. So, although seasonal dips in light intensity and duration may be acceptable or even desirable for African violets, begonias, and certain ferns and ivies, other plants such as summer annuals, bromeliads, cacti, gesneriads, and orchids may refuse to flower if they must rely solely on a steadily diminishing source of light.

At one time, an indoor gardener needed a greenhouse to provide many house plants with sufficient light year-round. Although Liberty Hyde Bailey showed as early as 1893 that plants could use electric light for growth, no one at that time seemed to consider the practical implications of his discovery. Then, years later, scientists learned that length of day controls the flowering of some plants. Florists subsequently began to use lights in the greenhouse to extend the daylength for chrysanthemums and poinsettias and to force other plants as well to blossom or form bulbs out of season. And plant scientists began using incandescent and fluorescent lights in their research projects.

In the late 1940s, amateur gardeners Frederick and Jacqueline Kranz started applying scientifically established principles of light gardening in the home. Experimenting with electric lights in their New York City apartment, they discovered that an ordinary 60-watt bulb gave their house plants just enough extra light to bloom on the windowsill. The Kranzes began to experiment with incandescent and fluorescent lamps of all kinds, sharing their promising results with other home gardeners in a 1957 book, *Gardening Indoors under Lights* (see Bibliography). Electric light gardening caught on, and other house plant enthusiasts discovered that, with the right lights, they could grow healthy, flowering plants anywhere in the home. Whether in the basement, attic, or a

Opposite, Dieffenbachia *species under fluorescent lights.*

sunny living room, electric lights could supply as much illumination as plants needed to grow.

In recent years, gardening under lights has become a specialty science. Researchers have made great strides in understanding the relationship between plants and light, and the formation of the Indoor Light Gardening Society of America, Inc. (ILGSA) in 1965 enabled amateurs to exchange cultural and construction ideas and trade seeds suited to growing under lights. Special tubes and bulbs have been developed for illuminating plants. Special furniture has been designed so that plants can be attractively displayed as they grow. There are even growth chambers in which all the environmental factors — light, humidity, and temperature — are controlled by the turn of a dial or flip of a switch.

If the use of these mechanical devices seems like an artificial way to grow plants, remember that house plants are, by definition, growing in an environment that is "unnatural" to them. No plants can grow unattended indoors. Placed in our homes, they must rely upon us to supply all their basic needs. If the right temperature, moisture, humidity, and soil are provided, the right lighting should be supplied, too.

The aim of gardening under lights, like that of greenhouse gardening, is to create conditions as close as possible to those of the plants' native habitats. Just as heat is added in the greenhouse, so light can be added in our homes. Given this necessity, plants meant to bloom will do so — and produce fruits and seeds as well. Grown indoors under lights, they may be even healthier than they would be in some greenhouses where lighting may be inconsistent or even sparse. Unlike sunlight, electric light is available every day of the year — winter as well as summer. Daylength can be controlled exactly for each plant and light intensity can be regulated easily by moving plants closer to or farther from the fixtures.

If the energy costs of light gardening seem prohibitive, consider the personal and environmental expense of a traditional greenhouse. Most traditional glass houses are notoriously inefficient structures which lose heat rapidly at night and in cold weather. Therefore, much of the solar, electric, or fuel-generated energy that goes into heating the building is wasted. Greenhouses also need to be cooled in summer. Moreover, the construction and maintenance costs of greenhouse gardening can be high.

Fluorescent lights, on the other hand, are relatively efficient energy converters which change 20 to 24 percent of their wattage into usable light. They are set up in an already heated house and they contribute to household illumination. Lit an average of 12 to 14 hours each day, one standard 40-watt, four foot (1.2 m) long tube consumes some 480 to

---

Figuring Electricity Costs for a Light Garden

To calculate the operating costs of your light gardening setup(s), multiply the total wattage required by the hours of use per day to get the daily wattage. Since 1,000 watt-hours equal one kilowatt-hour (kwh), divide your first total by 1,000. Multiply that result by the number of days in a month (30) to arrive at the kwh used per month by the light gardening fixture(s). Next, multiply that total by the amount charged per kwh by your electric company. The resulting figure will be the cost per month that your light gardening activities are adding to your light bill. For example, a standard four-foot (1.2 m) fluorescent fixture uses a total of 100 watts. Multiplied by 14 hours of use per day, the 100-watt fixture uses 1,400 watts per day. When this total is divided by 1,000, the result is 1.4 kwh per day. Assuming 30 days per month, the fixture uses a total of 42 kwh per month. By multiplying 42 by a typical unit cost of $.04, you can see that in a locality where kwhs are priced at $.04, it will cost roughly $1.68 a month to run a two-tube setup 14 hours a day.

Energy-Saving Tips for Light Gardeners

Whenever possible, use artificial light to supplement natural light rather than as a sole light source, turning on lights only for several hours in the early morning or evening from October to February and on overcast days.

If your garden receives no natural light, grow plants with low or moderate light intensity requirements or short-day flowering types so you can run your lights for fewer hours per day and/or buy fewer lamps or lamps of relatively low wattage.

Limit your light gardening activities to young plants, which make the most efficient use of light and take up less space than mature specimens.

Summer plants outdoors.

Clean your lamps and reflectors often.

Avoid long life or soft white incandescents, and consider using PS-30 incandescents rather than the less efficient standard types.

Where space permits, always use fluorescent tubes rather than incandescent bulbs.

Always use external reflectors with fluorescent setups, or purchase special reflectorized fluorescent tubes. (Though slightly lower in lumens than untreated tubes, these lamps direct up to 50 percent more light downward than do standard types.)

Never buy deluxe fluorescent lamps.

Use preheat fluorescent tubes, or at least use a starter with rapid-start types.

If you plan to use cool or warm white fluorescents, consider buying the new, energy-saving equivalents. Some of these ultraefficient lamps have more lumens at the same wattage and/or lose fewer lumens as they age. Others produce more light than standard tubes of the same length even though they have a lower wattage.

In large room-gardens or growth rooms, bypass standard fluorescents and install the more efficient very-high-output (VHO) types. For greatest economy, select VHO-equivalent energy-saving tubes such as General Electric's Lite-White Power Groove lamps. When equipped with lead-circuit high-power-factor rapid-start ballasts, these eight-foot (2.4 m) tubes shed more light than standard VHO eight-foot (2.4 m) lamps, while allowing for a reduction of 41 watts per lamp. Other economical options for large gardens are high-intensity discharge lamps or a low-pressure sodium/incandescent combination. (Both of these setups produce about twice as much light as regular fluorescents for about the same wattage.)

For high-intensity-discharge installations featuring mercury vapor lamps, substitute 150- or 215-watt E-Z Lux lamps for the standard 175- or 250-watt kinds. Even greater cuts in energy costs are possible if you replace 400- or 1,000-watt mercury lamps with General Electric's "I-Line" Multi-Vapor equivalents.

---

560 watts per day (plus one-third that amount to power the single-lamp ballast). When two tubes are used in a fixture, the energy cost is 960 to 1,120 watts per day, with about one-quarter of that amount to be added for the operation of the two-lamp ballast. For about 640 watts, therefore, a 40-watt standard tube will provide 12 hours of light for plants growing in an area over four feet (1.2 m) long and at least six inches (15 cm) wide, and for 1,200 watts, a two-tube fixture will light an area at least twice as wide. If natural daylight can be used as a supplement, fewer hours of electric lighting and therefore fewer watts will be needed. And if some plants can be placed on the porch or in a lath house during the summer, the wattage required over the course of the year will drop even more dramatically. For other ways to conserve electricity in light gardens, see Energy-Saving Tips for Light Gardeners.

With reasonable attention to cost-cutting techniques, chances are the price of setting up and operating a fluorescent light garden or even an entire "growth room" will not be excessive.

Whatever the costs, if you are an enthusiastic and dedicated gardener who is willing to take the time to care for an indoor garden, the investment is well worth it. With electric lights, you can raise almost any plant grown in the greenhouse or on the windowsill. Given cool but bright lighting that keeps pace with warm indoor temperatures, cuttings develop roots very quickly and seeds germinate into compact, healthy plants that compare favorably with greenhouse-grown stock. However, in order to succeed as a light gardener, you first must understand the principles involved. It's necessary here to discuss the properties of light in more detail than we did in chapter 2.

WHAT IS LIGHT?

In layman's terms, light is a visible form of energy. Generated by the sun, it travels to our planet at a rate of 186,300 miles per second. It warms the earth, provides plants with the energy needed to grow, and stimulates our eyes so we can see.

Like infrared rays, radio waves, X rays, and cosmic rays also transmitted by the sun, light travels in waves. It differs from these invisible forms of radiation only in regard to the distance between the crests of each wave. This length is measured in nanometer units — one nanometer (nm) being equal to one one-thousandth of a micron or one one-billionth (10^{-9}) meter. In some books, particularly older ones, wavelengths are cited in angstrom units. One angstrom (A) is ten times longer than a nanometer.

Among known wavelengths, the distance between the crests is greatest in radio waves, which are therefore the longest known type of electromagnetic radiation. They travel at very slow rates and apparently have little effect on plant and animal life.

Infrared radiation waves are slightly shorter than radio waves and travel at a higher frequency. These rays are primarily heat waves of the sort generated by a sunlamp or a stove. Although necessary to warm the earth and important to some aspects of plant growth, infrared energy can harm plants and animals if it is too intense.

Cosmic and gamma rays are the shortest of the known waves and have the highest frequency. Together with waves associated with so-called "far ultraviolet" radiation, cosmic and gamma wavelengths usually are considered fatal to plants and animals when present in large amounts. Since the outer atmosphere absorbs most shortwaves, they seldom reach the earth. However, at high altitudes, where the air is thinner, these waves are fairly abundant. Alpine plants can withstand large dosages of some shortwave radiation, particularly the ultraviolet kind. According to at least one scientist, certain plants may even utilize ultraviolet waves in flowering and seed germination.

Some people can "see" into the ultraviolet range of wavelengths, but most of us are blind to all radiation that does not fall between 380 nm (3,800 A) and 780 nm (7,800 A). This is the range of visible light. The shortest of these visible waves looks purple to us. In order of increasing length, they appear blue, green, yellow, orange, and finally red, which at from 580 to 780 nm represents the longest visible radiation. These colors are called the qualities of light. They are the colors of the rainbow we see when a prism bends and separates the light coming in a window.

Like the various lengths of invisible radiation waves, each quality of visible light affects living things in a different way. The human eye is most sensitive to green and yellow wavelengths. Bees and other insects react to red and even far-red and infrared radiation and are unable to see some blue waves. Plants, on the other hand, are most responsive to the blue and red ranges. The very fact that they appear green to us shows that they are absorbing the other colors of light and reflecting the green waves.

Healthy growth and development of plants and animals depend not only on the quality of the available light, but also on its intensity or luminosity. Our eyes can be damaged by exposure to extremely bright light and our skin can be burned. Plants also be-

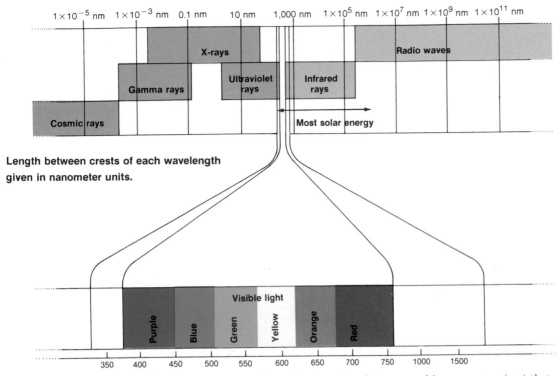

Electromagnetic Spectrum: This chart presents the various wavelengths (measured in nanometers/nm) that comprise the electromagnetic spectrum. The enlarged portion of the spectrum represents light which is visible to the human eye, lying between 380 and 780 nm. The colors of these visible waves, ranging from shortest to longest, are: purple, blue, green, yellow, orange, and red. The outer brackets of this enlarged section signify the nm range of most solar energy.

After *Photoprocesses, Photoreceptors, and Evolution* by Jerome J. Walken (New York: Academic Press, 1975).

come "sunburned" in bright light. Under certain circumstances, they may even exhaust themselves as a consequence of being overstimulated by light.

Light intensity is measured by several different techniques and devices and described in many terms. Usually a light meter such as General Electric's Model 213 is used, with the results given in footcandle (fc) units. It also is possible to use a camera with a built-in light meter to determine footcandles (see box). One footcandle equals the amount of light produced by one standard candle on a surface one foot (0.3 m) away. A match struck in a dark room produces 1 footcandle; a 100-watt incandescent light bulb sheds about 400 footcandles on a surface four inches (10 cm) beneath it. Two somewhat used 40-watt cool

white fluorescent lamps produce about 700 footcandles three inches (8 cm) beneath them, and at noon on a sunny summer day, there may be up to 12,000 footcandles of sunlight in a given area of your front yard.

These numbers measure visible light without regard to quality. They tell the gardener nothing about the amount of red or blue waves being shed or about the amount that plants actually are using. For this reason, many plant scientists feel that footcandle measurements are useless in horticulture. Since such readings measure only visible light without indicating the presence or absence of light specifically useful to plants, it is logical to question how they can be used to determine the amount of light plants needed to function. Indeed, footcandle measurements

Using a Camera to Measure Footcandles

If your camera has a built-in light meter, you can use it to provide approximate footcandle readings in your light garden. Set shutter speed to $\frac{1}{60}$ second and ASA dial to 25. Point the camera toward a piece of white paper that you have placed where your plant top(s) would be, and adjust the f-stop until the meter is correctly set for picture-taking. If the f-stop reads f/2, then light intensity is about 100 footcandles; f/2.8 indicates 200 footcandles; f/4, 370 footcandles; f/5.6, 750 footcandles; f/8, 1,500 footcandles; f/11, 2,800 footcandles; and f/16, 5,000 footcandles.

should not be taken for special plant lights, which are high in the less visible red and blue waves light meters do not register. But, if you know the quality of the sunlight or electric light you are measuring, and if you understand how much red, yellow, blue, or green light plants need, then the measurement can be very helpful indeed.

Suppose, for example, that the listing of suitable growing distances from cool white fluorescents for various plants that appears in this chapter does not include a plant you want to grow. Or suppose you want to choose plants that will do best under the lighting equipment you already have. By using a footcandle reading for your growing site, together with the chart on Optimum Light Intensities for Various Groups of Decorative Plants, in chapter 2, you can put together combinations of lighting setups and plants that are likely to work especially well.

Nevertheless, it is regrettably true that any two light meters may give readings for the same site that vary by as much as several hundred footcandles. If this imprecision troubles you, you may prefer to use light meter readings as a relative measurement of visible light. To do this, record a plant-top-level reading where plants are doing well and also

note the plant species, the kind of lamps, their age, their distance from the plants, and the hours per day the lamps are lit. You then can approximate these conditions in growing other plants of the same species or other species with similar lighting needs. (For an example of the relative use of meter readings, see the chart on Light Intensity at Different Locations under Various Fluorescent Fixtures, later in this chapter.)

In addition to the amount of light reaching the plants, another measurement useful in gauging light intensity is the amount of visible light being emitted by the light source. This light is measured in units called lumens. A lumen is equivalent to the amount of light given off in a solid angle from a uniform point source of a single candle. Like a footcandle reading, the lumen rating of a lamp does not take into account the invisible radiation that is so valuable to plants. Unlike footcandles, however, lumens are directly and accurately related not just to the strength of the light source, but also to the spectral quality of its visible light. For example, if two lamps of the same wattage have different lumen ratings, you can be certain that the lamp with the lower score is giving off more of its energy in the less visible parts of the spectrum — as violet or red light, for example, rather than as green, yellow, or orange. As long as the kind of light emitted by two lamps is different, lumen ratings may seem virtually meaningless. It is necessary to keep in mind, however, that differences in spectral quality that do not significantly affect plant growth can be accompanied by great differences in lumens; deluxe versions of fluorescent tubes, for example, give off roughly 35 to 40 percent less total light than their nondeluxe counterparts. This light loss is compounded by a relatively greater drop in lumens when deluxe tubes reach 40 percent of their rated life. As this suggests, gardeners can do both their plants and their pocketbooks a favor by evaluating a lamp's light output as well as its light quality.

HOW PLANTS USE LIGHT

Light of various qualities plays a significant role in nearly all aspects of plant growth and development. It stimulates certain growth hormones, influences seed germination, causes flowers to open and close, and makes plants move in what time-lapse photography shows to be a kind of dance. Light even determines the shape of many plants. Most important of all, it provides the energy every green plant needs in order to perform one of the most significant of life processes, photosynthesis.

The amount of photosynthate (food-for-growth) produced by a plant is largely determined by the amount and quality of available light. If the light is properly balanced between the red and blue and green wavelengths, then most foliage plants can survive with an intensity of only 100 footcandles. Flowering plants generally need at least 1,000 footcandles of balanced light in order to grow properly. This minimum luminosity needed for the plant to maintain itself is called the compensation point. It is the level at which food production (photosynthesis) can keep abreast of food consumption (growth and development). If light is below the compensation point, then plants exhaust their stored food. They grow taller, but their leaf area does not increase and flowers do not form: cells are dividing, but there is no *new* plant matter being created. The plant looks pale and lanky and, as soon as the stored food is exhausted, it may die.

If the light intensity is increased beyond the compensation point, most plants will grow and develop at an increasingly rapid pace. When they reach their saturation level of light intensity, their growth rate stabilizes. This point varies from species to species, but it generally occurs at around 600 footcandles for foliage plants and near 3,000 for flowering species.

Thus, although on a sunny day there may be a luminosity of 12,000 footcandles, even the most sun-loving plants probably are benefiting from no more than 25 percent of that light, or 3,000 footcandles. The lower the light intensity, the more efficiently the green pigments in the uppermost cells of the plant leaves work to capture it. Under lamps supplying 100 to 2,000 footcandles, virtually all plants can get the light they need to grow at a fast, healthy rate.

While photosynthesis provides the energy required to keep plants alive and growing, the actual flowering, seed production and germination, formation of bulbs and tubers, and onset of dormancy often are controlled by another light reaction — photoperiodism. This is the plant's response to the relative lengths of day and night periods. It has nothing to do with the intensity of the light present, but only with the duration needed to trigger a certain phase of the plant's development. Under the right conditions, a chemical stimulus is sent from the leaves to the stem tips where it "tells" the plant to begin forming flower buds instead of leaf buds. A similar stimulus might be sent from the leaves to the roots, initiating tuber or bulb formation, or from one part of a seed embryo to another, stimulating germination.

In some plants, such as tuberous begonias, lettuce, petunias, and snapdragons, this change is initiated by the transition from long winter nights to the shorter nights of spring and summer. Though the temperature and moisture may be right in spring and fall, these plants refuse to flower during these months. They will not flower, or in some cases germinate, unless the night is shorter than 12 hours. They are called short-night or long-day plants.

Other plants, including Christmas cacti, chrysanthemums, kalanchoes, certain orchids, poinsettias, and zebra plants, are strictly short-day bloomers. In their native habitats, they flower in spring, fall, or winter when the nights are longer than a certain critical period. If they do not receive a sufficiently long, uninterrupted dark period, they will not flower, or, as the case may be, produce tubers or enter dormancy. Sometimes, just an electric light shining for one minute of the "night" is enough to inhibit flowering, particularly if the lamp is turned on in the middle of the dark period and is sufficiently intense. Florists who want short-day plants to blossom out of season must cover them with tarps to protect them from extra hours of daylight. At home, these plants can be set in a closet or darkened room where their crucial night period will not be interrupted by electric lights or daylight.

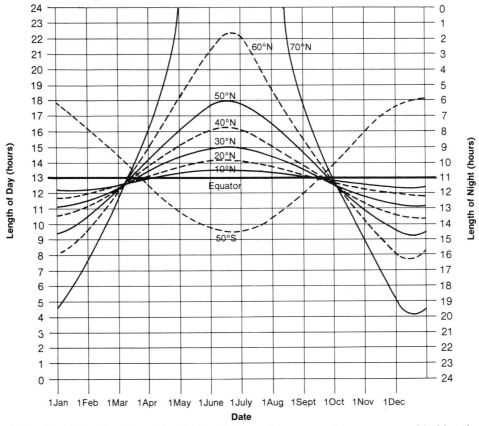

Variation in Daylength by Month and Latitude: The time of year, as well as your geographical location, are the factors which determine the amount of darkness vs. light your plants receive. Their photoperiodic needs can be met by providing artificial lighting to lengthen the day, or by providing an uninterrupted dark period to lengthen the night. The latitudes of some North American cities are given to help plot the changes in daylength during the course of the year.

25°N:	Miami
29°N:	Daytona Beach, Houston
30°N:	Jacksonville (FL), Mobile, New Orleans
32°N:	Charleston (SC), Columbus (GA), Dallas, Jackson (MS), Tucson, San Diego
34°N:	Greenville (SC), Little Rock, Los Angeles
36°N:	Las Vegas, Nashville, Tulsa
38°N:	Charleston (WV), Colorado Springs, Sacramento

40°N:	Lafayette (IN), New York City, Salt Lake City
42°N:	Boston, Grand Rapids, Sioux City
43°N:	Toronto (Canada)
44°N:	Bangor (ME), Eugene (OR), Minneapolis
46°N:	Bismarck, Duluth, Montreal (Canada), Walla Walla (WA)
47°N:	Quebec City (Canada), Seattle
48°N:	Vacouver (Canada)
50°N:	Winnipeg (Canada)

After *Artificial Light in Horticulture* by A. E. Canham (Eindhoven, Holland: Centrex Publishing Company, 1966), p. 36.

Some plants flower well only when days and nights are about equal in length. Among these intermediate-day types are *Bougainvillea* and *Impatiens hawkeri* 'Exotica' — the popular New Guinea strain.

Other plants are affected by daylength in a rather complicated way: the Lady Washington geranium *(Pelargonium ×domesticum)* requires short days succeeded by long days to bloom. Sometimes daylength and temperature factors interact. For example, if temperatures are relatively low, some species will set buds even if their photoperiod requirements are not being met. The Christmas cactus *(Schlumbergera bridgesii)* is known for this trait, flowering at 55°F (13°C) despite long days, but requiring short days at 65°F (18°C). The fairy primrose *(Primula malacoides)* behaves similarly, being day neutral below 60°F (16°C) and short day at higher temperatures. Yet other plants, the petunia included, lose their responsiveness to daylength as they grow older.

Many, in fact most, plants are day neutral. Although they may prefer certain schedules, they are unaffected by changes in the lengths of days and nights. Such plants also are called indeterminate or indifferent. Their development depends upon temperature or moisture stress or upon some innate, genetically determined pattern of growth. Popular indeterminate house plants include African violets and other gesneriads, wax begonias *(Begonia ×semperflorens-cultorum* hybrid complex), and geraniums.

The reasons for these different photoperiodic effects on plants are complex and not entirely understood by plant scientists. In recent years, scientists have linked sensitivity to nightlength to a blue pigment called phytochrome which, like chlorophyll, is present in plant leaves. Acting as an enzyme, it triggers not the formation of food, but the beginning of growth changes in the plant's stem tips.

Phytochrome occurs in two reversible forms, one which absorbs red light (about 669 nm) and another which absorbs far-red light (735 nm). If red light is used to interrupt a long night, the phytochrome undergoes a molecular change from one form to the other. This change promotes flowering in plants accustomed to shorter nights (long-day plants) and inhibits flowering in plants accustomed to the long night (short-day plants). The effect can be reversed by applying far-red light.

The implications of this phenomenon are obvious. Unless you provide plants with the daylengths they need, they probably will not flower. Under lights, long-day plants must be separated from short-day plants as the plants mature if either group is going to be given the proper lighting sequence. And the lights themselves must provide sufficient quantities of red and infrared light. Regardless of the photoperiodic habits of the plant, it will not flower unless it receives these wavelengths.

Red and infrared light have other important effects on plant growth and development. Besides taking roles in photosynthesis and photoperiodism, they also are associated with seed germination. Some seeds, such as those of lettuce, will not germinate unless they are exposed to red light. But when far-red light is present, germination is inhibited.

Orange and yellow light are considered useless to plants though they are absorbed to a certain extent by some pigments. Green light generally is reflected by plant cells and also is ineffective. It may even be harmful to plants in large doses.

Blue and violet light are very important to plant growth and development, not only in photosynthesis, but also in phototropism. Discussed in detail in chapter 2, this is the light response which causes a plant to "grow toward" the source of light.

Slightly shorter wavelengths that fall in the ultraviolet or black-light range usually are considered harmful to plants. However, the recent experiments of Dr. John Nash Ott at the Health and Light Institute in Sarasota, Florida, have shown that although very short waves of less than 290 nm are harmful,

Light Color and Light Shields

Depending on the quality (color) of their lighting, plants take on different appearances. Under the white light of an incandescent bulb, they tend to look the same as they would outdoors. Pink and reddish hues are particularly brilliant. In fluorescent lighting, foliage plants are most enhanced, with green and blue pigments looking very dark and rich. Horticultural fluorescent tubes enhance all plant colors — pinks and reds as well as greens — but this lighting lends a rather unnatural coloring to rooms and gives people and furnishings a purplish glow. If you want to use fluorescent lights on a large scale, try installing Paracube or ParaWedge louvers over the tubes. These shields allow 85 to 90 percent of the light energy to reach plants, but they eliminate annoying eye-level glare. They can be purchased from most large lighting supply houses and often come as a part of indoor gardening units.

As an alternative, wooden light shields of your own design can be installed on fluorescent fixtures in living areas. Painted, stained, or covered with adhesive-backed paper, such shields decorate a light garden handsomely, but of course the side facing plants must be painted flat white or lined with foil or another reflective substance. The most effective use of wooden valances is set forth in the *Light Garden Construction Manual* published by the Indoor Light Gardening Society of America, Inc. The society recommends that shields masking 4 inch (10 cm) high commercial fixtures be 4½ inches (11 cm) high if the lights are 36 inches (91 cm) or less above floor level. The shield will then extend ½ inch (l3 mm) below the bottom of the tubes. For fixtures from 36 to 48 inches (91 to 122 cm) off the floor, the shield should be 5 inches (13 cm) high and reach 1 inch (2.5 cm) below the lights. Units from 4 to 6 feet (1.2 to 1.8 m) above ground level need a 6 inch (15 cm) high shield that comes down 2 inches (5 cm) below the tubes.

One Plant, Four Different Light Sources:
A daylight fluorescent bulb enhances the green coloring of this pothos while muting red tones.

Under a horticultural fluorescent tube, the red and blue colorings are heightened, creating a characteristic pinkish tone.

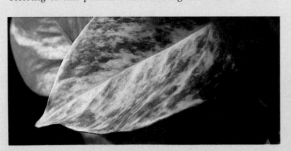

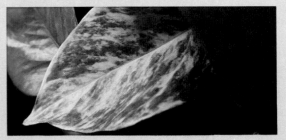

With an incandescent bulb, the foliage colors don't differ much from their appearance outdoors, although the yellow tones are slightly enhanced.

The pothos, as it appears in the full spectrum of natural light.

longer ultraviolet waves may benefit plants. Some species may even require "black" light of 290 to 400 nm in order to produce flowers.

No electric light emits all of these different wavelengths of light in exactly the same proportions as the sun. A few fluorescent lights come quite close, but these are not always the best lights for growing plants. And why should they be? Green plants have their own "action spectrum," which is not at all the same as the sun's emission spectrum. In fact, plants cannot use most sunlight since it falls in the green and yellow ranges. They absorb and use only the far-red, red, blue, and violet waves. As long as they must get their light from a broad-spectrum source such as the sun, they require thousands of "extra" footcandles. The advantages of electric lighting for plant growth is that these unused portions of the spectrum can be eliminated. Bulbs and tubes can be designed to produce almost all of their light in the far-red, red, blue, and violet ranges with little wasted as yellow or green waves. When the quantity and timing as well as the quality of these electric lamps is closely controlled, plants can be grown with very few footcandles and, hence, relatively little energy.

CHOOSING THE RIGHT BULBS AND TUBES

There is a mind-boggling variety of electric lamps available to the home gardener. A scientific report or advertising brochure can be found to recommend just about any lamp or combination of lamps, and different gardeners always will swear by different setups. The relative merits of the various types of lamps are described and discussed in the following pages. Let this coverage serve as a brief guide to light gardening equipment, but before buying anything, read other books, talk to indoor gardeners, and if necessary seek the advice of the ILGSA (see Appendix for address). The trick to successful plant lighting is to find lamps that can supply just the kind of light your plants need at minimal expense.

INCANDESCENT BULBS

Incandescent or filament bulbs are the most widely used form of electric lighting. They are rated 110 to 120 volts and come in a variety of wattages. For plant lighting, 60- to 500-watt bulbs usually are selected. They screw into metal or porcelain sockets (porcelain should be used with bulbs of 75 watts or more). Ordinary incandescents are fitted easily with an appropriate reflector that directs the light downward at the plants. Depending upon the width of the area to be lit, the dome can be deep, standard, shallow, or of the inexpensive aluminum pie-pan type — used mostly for protection from condensation in greenhouses. Incandescent bulbs are the cheapest types of electric lamps to purchase and the simplest to install.

In its most basic form, the typical incandescent bulb consists of a tungsten wire sealed in a glass bulb which has been filled with nitrogen or argon gas. Like the sun, it provides light through a heat reaction. Electricity heats the tungsten wire to 5,000°F (2,760°C), a temperature which is almost twice that of molten steel. Since there is no oxygen present, the wire continues to emit light for an average of 1,000 to 2,000 hours before it is consumed.

The light emitted by this hot wire is very rich in red and far-red radiation. These waves are absolutely essential for the flowering and dormancy (and in some cases, the seed germination) of many plants. They are particularly important to summer field crops. Before the development of wide-spectrum horticultural fluorescents, fluorescents and white and warm white standard incandescent bulbs were the only electric lamps that supplied large amounts of red light, and they were used widely by researchers and amateur light gardeners in combination with cool white fluorescents at the rate of one watt of incan-

Some Lamps Used in Light Gardening

LAMP TYPE	WATTAGE, LENGTH	QUALITY	USE
Incandescent R Incandescent PS-30 Incandescent PAR Incandescent	30 to 1,000 75 to 500 150 to 300 75 to 500	High in red, low in blue; excessive infrared. R types available in broad-spectrum plant lights.	Extending daylength in the greenhouse or fluorescent light garden. R and PAR types also are used as spotlights to enhance plants. External reflectors needed with standard bulbs.
Preheat Fluorescent Rapid-Start Fluorescent	15 (18 in./46 cm) 20 (24 in./61 cm) 30 (36 in./91 cm) 40 (48 in./122 cm) 30 (36 in./91 cm) 40 (48 in./122 cm)	Cool white, deluxe cool white, daylight, white, warm white, deluxe warm white. Also available in various standard and wide-spectrum plant lights.	Preheat types are standard economical choice for general plant growing and are used with a starter in industrial or channel fixtures or in growth chambers. Quieter but more costly, rapid-start types are used with or without a starter in industrial or channel fixtures for general plant growing. Rapid-start high-output (800 MA) or very-high-output (1,500 MA) tubes are available in higher wattages per inch in many lengths for plants needing intense light but require different fixtures and wiring. Slimlines are used for greater intensity and in larger gardens and need special fixtures but no starter. Slimlines also are available in HO and VHO forms. Reflectorized lamps available in preheat 4-foot (1.2 m) length, slimline 8-foot (2.4 m) length and in VHO tubes. Otherwise external reflectors are needed.
Instant Start Slim-line Fluorescent	55 (72 in./183 cm) 75 (96 in./244 cm)	Cool white, deluxe cool white, daylight, white, warm white, deluxe warm white. Natur-Escent and Vita-Lite plant lights available in 8-foot (2.4 m) length.	
Low-Pressure Sodium	35 to 180	Monochromatic yellow	May be used in large growth rooms or greenhouses in combination with incandescents to grow large, early-blooming plants. This combination is more efficient than fluorescents used alone. Reflectors needed.

High-Intensity Discharge
 	
  Mercury vapor
 	
  High-pressure sodium
 	
  Metal halide
	
	40 to 1,000
	
	150 to 1,000
	
	400 to 1,500
		
		White or warm white (wide spectrum but high in violet and red)
		
		Warm white (wide spectrum but high in yellow and orange)
		
		White (wide spectrum and moderately high in violet, blue, green, and red)
			For supplementary lighting or as sole lighting in growth chambers and growth rooms where high intensities are needed. HPS and metal halide work well together as a light source. External reflectors are necessary.

Compiled primarily from *Plant Growth Lighting*, published by General Electric Company.

descent light to three to five watts of fluorescent light. It is still true that this combination will result in better growth of fruiting vegetables or certain low-light flowering house plants needing red and blue light than will the use of cool white fluorescents alone. However, ordering special fixtures that hold both incandescent bulbs and fluorescent tubes can be avoided by instead using a 1 to 1 ratio of cool white and warm white tubes, or teaming regular and wide-spectrum Gro-Lux lamps. Both of these options have proved superior to the old tandem of incandescents and cool white fluorescents. Nowadays, incandescent bulbs are employed more often by seedsmen, commercial growers, agriculturists, and florists who wish to control special photoperiodic responses in greenhouse-grown plants.

There are a number of inherent disadvantages which limit the use of these bulbs. For one thing, they heat up and will break easily if accidentally splashed by water in the moist conditions of a greenhouse or indoor garden. Also, although incandescents are an excellent source of crucial red light waves, they come nowhere near to supplying all the light waves plants need. They emit virtually none of the blue radiation so necessary for enzyme and hormone action, photosynthesis, and other growth and developmental processes. Plants that must depend on incandescent bulbs for all their illumination tend to be poorly formed, tall, lanky, and almost leafless. What's more, only 6 to 8 percent of the energy emitted by the bulb is light. Over 90 percent is heat radiation, which scorches plants. Then too, incandescents do not distribute light very evenly over the flat surfaces beneath them and lose 15 percent of their light when they have reached 70 percent of their rated life.

Because of these problems, incandescent bulbs have only limited uses in the indoor garden. Their small size enables them to be used conveniently in the home and their light is much less objectionable than that of some fluorescent types. Low-wattage bulbs (15 to 40 watts) can be used to spotlight plants as long as they are placed at least 24 inches (61 cm) above them, although they will not help the plants grow. (Note: Long life incandescents and soft white types may make maintenance easier and cast more attractive light, but they yield less light than the standard bulbs.) Breakage problems can be solved by covering bulbs with suitable reflectors or shields or by selecting silicone-coated bulbs that resist moisture.

Excessive heat radiation can be reduced by suspending a glass or clear plastic screen between the lamp and the plants or by using several low-power incandescent bulbs to diffuse heat buildup instead of one strong one that radiates a great deal of heat in one spot. Some gardeners recommend using special incandescent bulbs which are supposedly cooler at plant level than standard types. Called reflector (R) lamps, these are available from most electrical suppliers as either floodlights or spotlights in various sizes, including 75 and 150 watts. Light emerges from the end of the bulb, which is frosted. The remaining inside surface is aluminized so it acts as a built-in reflector. Thus, the light is directed downward to the plant and the heat is transmitted through the sides of the bulb. Because of the great heat they generate, R lamps should be used only in porcelain sockets. In addition to ordinary incandescents, plant lights such as Agro-Lite and Gro-and-Sho are purchasable as R lamps. So-called PS-30 lamps are reflectorized much like R types, but their different shape eliminates the "hot spot" created by R lamps. The 150- and 200-watt PS-30s are much more economical to use than standard 100-watt bulbs with reflectors, and cast a wide, uniform beam of light. Porcelain sockets should be used with PS-30's.

Similar to reflector lamps in shape but slightly more efficient and more costly are parabolic aluminized reflector (PAR) lamps, which have a protective envelope of Pyrex glass and metal which prevents breakage and keeps the lamp clean and the reflector bright. These lamps, too, should be used only in porcelain sockets and in addition require a special fixture with a well-ventilated back to dissipate heat. Available in spot, narrow-beam, flood, or wide-flood distribution, they are not made in plant lights. Like ordinary incandescents, non-plant-light R lamps and all PS-30 and PAR lamps do not "grow" plants; they merely maintain and highlight them and as a sole light source at best can be counted on to provide adequate light for foliage plants requiring only very low levels of illumination.

There is, however, a 160-watt combination incandescent/mercury vapor bulb now on the market which can keep plants growing slowly and induce flowers as well. Called Wonderlite, this hybrid sheds more light than incandescents at the cost of less energy. It can be used in a standard screw base porcelain fixture and needs no special wiring or attachment, but it is unpleasantly bright and rather expensive.

FLUORESCENT LAMPS

Most of the lamps used for plant growth are fluorescent tubes. Although installation and replacement are somewhat more costly and complicated than that of incandescent lamps, fluorescents burn up to 15 times as long and produce much more light per watt. In the long run, they are about 3 times cheaper to operate. In addition, fluorescent lamps tend to have more uniform light distribution and, since their light is in the violet end of the spectrum with no infrared waves, they produce far less heat than incandescent bulbs. The heat that is emitted is not radiated by the tube itself but by a separate electrical box or ballast which, if necessary, can be moved away from the light garden; the tubes themselves are so cool that they will not burn plants even an inch or two (2.5 or 5 cm) away and will not break if hit by a stray water drop.

Light Quality of Fluorescent Tubes: The difference in the quality of light emitted from various types of fluorescent tubes is evident in this photo of, from top to bottom, warm white, which emits predominantly yellow waves; cool white, which gives off yellow and green light; horticultural fluorescent, which is rich in red, blue, and violet waves; and daylight fluorescent, which emits light in the violet to red range.

Fluorescent lamps work on much the same principle as X-ray machines. They consist of a glass tube coated on the inside with phosphorous materials and filled with mercury vapor and argon gas. At each end of the tube are a tungsten filament or electrode and one or two prongs which fit into a special electrical lamp fixture. When heated by an electrical current, the electrodes send off electrons which travel back and forth from one end of the tube to the other, colliding with mercury vapor and argon gas. This collision produces short ultraviolet waves which, in turn, cause the phosphorous coating to glow. Thus, the invisible ultraviolet waves are changed to slightly longer, visible light waves.

The spectral quality of the light produced depends mostly upon the kind of phosphorous material that is used. Different materials produce light of slightly different wavelengths and the tubes are classified accordingly. The ordinary cool white fluorescent tube, for instance, emits mostly yellow and green wavelengths but does produce significant amounts in the violet range as well. Deluxe cool white has basically the same spectral distribution but offers an added boost in the red ranges that makes for warmer, softer light. Warm white has more yellow and less red than deluxe cool white and deluxe warm white has very high amounts of both red and yellow. Like deluxe cool white, the deluxe warm white sheds light more like incandescent light while providing extra far-red. Little used nowadays, white and deluxe white stand between deluxe cool white and warm white in amount of red and yellow light. The daylight fluorescent is very rich in the violet to blue range with less red light than the other lamps. It is balanced to simulate north light. The daylight tube has no deluxe version. All the others do, however, and — as sources of illumination, though not necessarily as sources of light promoting plant growth — the deluxe options are considerably less efficient than the more basic lamps, emitting less visible light. Even more inefficient in total light output than deluxe fluorescents are the numerous tubes designed especially for horticultural use, which give off up to more than 40 percent less total light than cool white tubes. Sold under the trade names Gro-Lux (Sylvania), Gro-and-Sho (GE), Plant-Gro (Westinghouse), Vita-Lite and Natur-Escent (Duro-Lite), Agro-Lite (Westinghouse), and TruBloom (Verilux), these lamps emit slightly more waves in the 600 to 700 nm range (red light) as well as some in the blue and violet ranges. Wide-

spectrum grow lights such as Wide-Spectrum Gro-Lux (Sylvania) even contain some far-red radiation (700 to 800 nm). The pinkish color emitted by some of these grow lights intensifies certain pigments in leaves and flowers, imparting an unusual glow. Partisans claim that plants look much healthier and more attractive under the lamps, but others detest the pinkish tones common to most. (Vita-Lite and TruBloom approximate noon sunlight and so are least objectionable in living areas.)

Of course, the manufacturers of these special agricultural lamps are always quick to claim that plants raised under their fluorescent tubes not only look healthier but actually *are* healthier than those grown under ordinary tubes. This may well be true, but there is no really solid experimental proof available and indoor gardeners have mixed opinions of the tubes.

Since such grow lamps emit less yellow and green light and much more red and blue light than regular fluorescents, they are undoubtedly more efficient for plant growth even though they produce less total light. According to a number of gardeners, plants grow more rapidly and produce many more flowers under horticultural lights. Cuttings also are said to take root faster and certain seeds are reported to germinate more successfully. Some users say the lights are particularly effective with azaleas, begonias, and primroses, as well as African violets, gloxinias, and other gesneriads. Gro-Lux and others emphasizing red rays are supposedly good for perennial and annual seedlings, while Vita-Lite is believed especially helpful to bromeliads, cacti and other succulents, geraniums, and orchids. Both Agro-Lite and TruBloom are wide-spectrum types that encourage compact growth — a real benefit if you have limited space. Wide-Spectrum Gro-Lux benefits a wide assortment of low-light tropicals such as African violets and other gesneriads, begonias, orchids, and succulents.

On the other hand, many other gardeners find that the foregoing claimed advantages are outweighed by the lamps' high costs, for some of them sell for nearly twice as much as standard tubes (the cheapest grow lamp is Wide-Spectrum Gro-Lux, which costs little more than standard tubes). Too, grow lamps lose more lumens than regular tubes as they age, and must be replaced sooner to maintain high light levels. Also, since a smaller percentage of their light is in the green and yellow range (making up the most visible wavelengths), grow lights do not contribute much to the total brightness of their surroundings.

Unless a particularly high emission in the 600 to 700 nm range is desired for lettuce-seed germination, for the setting and ripening of fruit on vegetable plants, for seed production, or for certain house plants such as those named above, ordinary fluorescent lamps probably will be satisfactory for the beginning light gardener. This is true even when more red light is desired, provided that plants are receiving several hours of natural light every day. Members of the ILGSA recommend using cool white, deluxe cool white, or a combination of cool white and warm white (one or two tubes each). Some amateur growers claim a cool white/white blend gives particularly good results with seedlings, tender plants, and cuttings, while researchers at Texas A & M University suggest teaming warm white and plain white fluorescent tubes to get taller plants instead of the short, stocky ones linked to cool white alone — obviously a good idea if you are growing roses or carnations instead of pot plants like chrysanthemums. Other gardeners recommend combining cool white and daylight fluorescents.

Fluorescent lamps are available in lengths of 15 to 96 inches (38 to 244 cm) and in 14 to 72 watts. (High-output and very-high-output types offering more watts per inch or centimeter also are sold. They require different fixtures and wiring.) By far the most commonly used lamps are the 4-foot (1.2 m), 40-watt tubes and the 8-foot (2.4 m), 72-watt

ones. The most economical choice is definitely the cool white 40-watt tubes, which discount stores feature in a two-tube workshop fixture. Also, cool white 40-watt tubes are frequently on sale at one-fifth or one-sixth of the cost of a horticultural fluorescent. Though lamps of smaller sizes are desirable for small garden areas, they often are not stocked by electrical supply stores. These off-sizes include: 33-inch (84 cm), 25-watt; 18-inch (46 cm), 15-watt; and 15-inch (38 cm), 14-watt tubes. Also available are 25-inch (64 cm), 33-watt self-contained tube-and-fixture combinations complete with a 6-foot (1.8 m) cord and a feed-through on/off switch. Unfortunately, these disposable units are costly, have a shorter life, and project much less light than standard tubes of similar length. Usually, wattages are marked directly on a fluorescent tube along with the spectral quality and the starter requirements (see discussion of the metal cylinders called starters, later in this chapter).

There are also circular fluorescent tubes called circline lamps. These are quite uneconomical, but they can be very useful in table-lamp type fixtures or in small niches. Having diameters of 6 inches, (15 cm), 8¼ inches (21 cm), 12 inches (30 cm), and 16 inches (41 cm), circlines are available in most sizes in cool white, deluxe cool white, daylight, warm white, and deluxe warm white. The most realistic choices for gardening are the 12-inch (30 cm), 32-watt and 16-inch (41 cm), 40-watt sizes, used in conjunction with reflective surfaces.

Depending upon their wattage, length, and quality, fluorescent tubes emit different amounts of visible light. A four-foot (1.2 m), 40-watt cool white fluorescent tube may have a rating of 3,150 lumens while a deluxe cool white of the same size and wattage will have only 2,200; a grow light will have still fewer. If two lamps have the same spectral qualities but different lumen ratings, remember that plants can be placed at a greater distance from the stronger tube. To increase the amount of light that reaches plants without increasing lumens, consider buying cool white tubes in which part of the glass has been met-allized to form a built-in reflector. Such tubes are more expensive and actually have fewer lumens than regular cool whites, but the re-flector causes up to 50 percent more light to reach plants.

LOW-PRESSURE SODIUM VAPOR LAMPS

Tubular like fluorescents, but U-shaped and filled with sodium vapor instead of mercury vapor, low-pressure sodium (LPS) lamps can be a good alternative if you have a large area to light. According to work done by the Agri-cultural Research Service (ARS) of the United States Department of Agriculture, LPS tubes in combination with incandescent bulbs are 51 percent more efficient than cool white fluorescents used alone and promote growth just as well for at least 100 plant spe-cies. Available from 35 to 180 watts, LPS lamps have the same voltages and cycle re-quirements as fluorescents (if the suitable ballast is used) and their substitution for fluo-rescents translates into less power and less wiring (and less shading where lights are being used to supplement natural light). Un-like other lamps, LPS setups do not suffer a decline in lumens as the lamps age. They are not suited to display gardens in living areas, however, for the light they cast makes foliage look almost white and gives flesh a gray tint. Also, every precaution should be taken to prevent breakage, for a fire could result.

HIGH-INTENSITY DISCHARGE LAMPS

Expensive but powerful, so-called high-inten-sity discharge (HID) lamps used in plant lighting are of three types: metal halide, mer-cury vapor, or sodium vapor. The sodium-containing lights also are called high-pressure sodium (HPS) lamps. Although bulb shaped, all HID lamps work in a manner similar to

fluorescent lamps except that their vapor is more pressurized. HID lamps require all sorts of special wiring, fixtures, and switching equipment. Since they emit considerable amounts of heat, they must be used with proper exhaust fans. On the other hand, HID fixtures are moisture-resistant and the better ones have improved reflectors. The lamps last 20 to 50 percent longer than fluorescent tubes, and require half as much wattage to produce the same light. Professional growers and plant researchers have found that the cost of the special fixtures can be recouped through lower operating expenses, less shad-ing, and substantial increases in plant yields. For example, when the ARS used high-pres-sure sodium and incandescent setups as sup-plemental lighting in growing geraniums from seeds, the time to flowering was short-ened to just 9 weeks, whereas geraniums lit with fluorescent/incandescent light of the same intensity took 15 to 20 weeks to bloom. The high-pressure sodium vapor/incandes-cent combination also worked well for the ARS in photoperiod control, producing heavi-er plants.

High-pressure vapor lights are not for most amateur gardeners, but in large room-gardens, greenhouses, or growth rooms where lamps can be placed far above growing plants, HID lamps can be very successful, and in cool locations the heat they radiate can be beneficial. Their light is fairly well bal-anced for plant growth, and the mercury types offer high amounts of red and far-red (and infrared) radiation. HID lamps are available in wattages ranging from 40 to 1,500 watts (each size lamp requires a differ-ent fixture) and produce 60 to 150 lumens of light per watt.

FLUORESCENT FIXTURES

Incandescent bulbs are easy to install, since they require nothing more than the familiar screw-in socket, but fluorescent lighting is a bit more complex. The typical fluorescent fixtures are designed to hold one, two, three, or four fluorescent tubes of a certain length. The size selected depends primarily upon the growing area you wish to illuminate. Basically, 15 to 20 watts of fluorescent light are needed to illuminate 1 square foot (929 sq cm) of indoor garden space. Therefore, one 40-watt tube will light 2 square feet (1,858 sq cm) or a space 4 feet (1.2 m) long and 6 inches (15 cm) wide. Two 40-watt tubes will serve a growing area approximately twice as wide and four tubes will adequately light a space 4 feet by 2 feet or 8 square feet (1.2 m by 0.6 m/7,433 sq cm). Keep in mind, though, that the intensity of illumination reaching this growing space will vary greatly from one setup to another, depending upon the distance from the lights to the plants, whether the fixtures have reflectors, and how much space there is from the center of each tube to that of another. In a booklet entitled *Light Garden Primer,* published by the ILGSA, expert light gardener Jack Golding recommends that a working garden with young plants be set up under a standard industrial four-tube strip fixture with 2-inch (5 cm) centers and a reflector. The lamps should be 12 inches (30 cm) above the table surface and the plant tops just a few inches or centimeters below the tubes. For a show garden featuring larger plants, Golding suggests assuring an even more uniform distribution of light by using two two-tube fixtures with 6-inch (15 cm) centers, suspended 18 inches (46 cm) above the tabletop. For best results in such a setup, plants should be within a 16 inch (41 cm) wide area with their tops 6 inches (15 cm) or more away from the lamps. (For more data on levels of light at various distances and widths, see the chart on Light Intensity at Different Locations under Various Fluorescent Fixtures.)

As a general rule, to reduce the amount of light being converted to heat and to get more even light distribution, try to use basic fixtures with 6-inch (15 cm) centers (place them 6 inches/15 m apart) or strip fixtures with 3-inch (8 cm) centers with 8 inches (20 cm) between fixtures. Separate double-tube units will allow you to keep the light source up to 20 inches (51 cm) away from the plants instead of the maximum 12 inches (30 cm) recommended for flowering plants under a single two-tube fixture. Golding claims that the good distribution, valuable "stray light" from adjacent fixture(s), and ample intensity possible with such equipment is perhaps even more important than which fluorescents you use. By putting more and more tubes side by side, you can create a situation where there is less and less difference in intensity at various levels under the lights.

Fluorescent tubes tend to give off less light toward their ends and more in the center — that is, light intensity begins to drop sharply 12 inches (30 cm) from the center. For that reason, place plants needing the most light toward the middle of tubes, and select the longest possible tubes and fixtures to light a given area. If your indoor garden is to be 100 inches (254 cm) long, use 8-foot (2.4 m) tubes rather than 4-foot (1.2 m) tubes laid end to end. Of course, the 8-foot (2.4 m) tube is initially more expensive than the shorter one, but most gardeners agree that, in spite of the high replacement costs, longer tubes are more economical. The same point can be made for longer fixtures: although there may be a cost differential between 2-foot (0.6 cm), 4-foot (1.2 m), and 8-foot (2.4 m) sizes, it is minimal considering that you are getting from two to four times more lighted area with the lengthier types. If you should choose to boost intensity by going to fixtures and tubes of high or very high output, that is, 800 or 1,500 milliamperes (MA) fluorescents, do not assemble more than five such tubes under a compact canopy without providing cooling via fan ventilation. If you do, the lamps will operate at above their normal temperature and their light output will be cut by one-third.

Light Intensity at Different Locations under Various Fluorescent Fixtures

TYPE OF FIXTURE (ALL WITH COOL WHITE 40-WATT LAMPS)	DISTANCE BELOW LAMP (INCHES/ CENTIMETERS)	MAXIMUM INTENSITY METER READING*	WIDTH (INCHES/CENTIMETERS) OF AREA WITH INTENSITIES GREATER THAN:			
			90% of Max.	70% of Max.	Meter Reading* of 500	Meter Reading* of 250
2 in./5 cm centers	12 in./30 cm	1,000	4 in./10 cm	8 in./20 cm	12 in./30 cm	16 in./41 cm
	18 in./46 cm	800	8 in./20 cm	12 in./30 cm	13 in./33 cm	20 in./51 cm
	24 in./61 cm	630	4 in./10 cm	9 in./23 cm	7 in./18 cm	16 in./41 cm
3 in./8 cm centers	18 in./46 cm	680	8 in./20 cm	10 in./25 cm	9 in./23 cm	17 in./43 cm
	24 in./61 cm	560	8 in./20 cm	13 in./33 cm	8 in./20 cm	20 in./51 cm
	30 in./76 cm	445	9 in./23 cm	16 in./41 cm	—	20 in./51 cm
3 in./8 cm 8 in./20 cm / 3 in./8 cm centers	18 in./46 cm	400	12 in./30 cm	18 in./46 cm	—	18 in./46 cm
3 in./18 cm 6 in./15 cm / 3 in./8 cm centers	18 in./46 cm	440	8 in./20 cm	14 in./36 cm		18 in./46 cm
3 in./8 cm 4 in./10 cm / 3 in./8 cm centers	18 in./46 cm	560	6 in./15 cm	14 in./36 cm	8 in./20 cm	18 in./46 cm
6 in./15 cm centers	12 in./30 cm	340	18 in./46 cm	20 in./51 cm	—	23 in./58 cm
	18 in./46 cm	320	16 in./41 cm	22 in./56 cm	—	19 in./48 cm
	24 in./61 cm	300	14 in./36 cm	18 in./46 cm	—	16 in./41 cm
3 in./8 cm centers	18 in./46 cm	420	6 in./15 cm	12 in./30 cm	—	14 in./36 cm
3 in./8 cm centers	18 in./46 cm	360	6 in./15 cm	12 in./30 cm	—	12 in./30 cm

*Readings are determined by a photometer and are not in footcandles. They should be used only as a relative indication of light intensity. Generally speaking, flowering plants such as African violets, begonias, and gloxinias thrive at a photometer reading of 250, and seedlings and young plants do well at above 500. Adapted from the *Light Garden Primer,* published by the Indoor Light Gardening Society of America, Inc.

Unless HID lamps or slimline fluorescents are used, the fixtures selected for the fluorescent light garden will operate on 115-volt, 60-cycle house current, just as ordinary lamps and appliances do. To figure total wattage used by a fixture, add the wattage ratings of the tubes. As a rule of thumb, for every 40 watts, add another 10 watts for the part of the fixture that controls the flow of current. This will give you the total amount used by the setup. If your garden consists only of one two-tube four-foot (1.2 m) unit, its 100-watt consumption can be handled adequately by the usual 15-ampere household circuit, provided the total demand on that circuit does not exceed 1,500 watts. But before you install additional fixtures, consult an electrician to be sure your home's electrical system can support the load you have in mind. You may need a separate circuit for your light garden. It is also wise to use a grounded plug and a cord with three wires that are at least 18-gauge to avoid any chance of electrical shock or malfunction.

Although there are some premounted types of fluorescent fixtures which operate without sockets or ballasts, most units consist of the same basic parts: the lampholder, the ballast, the starter, and the reflector. Low-pressure sodium and high-intensity discharge lamps also have ballasts and should be used with reflectors. The average light gardener need not know each component in detail, but it is important to understand generally how each part functions. The following explanation will focus on fluorescent fixtures, which are those most widely used.

LAMPHOLDER

The metal box which holds the fluorescent tubes is called the lampholder. At each end, it has plastic discs called mounts. The pins on the ends of fluorescent tubes fit in the holes of the mounts.

BALLAST

On the upper surface of the lampholder is a rectangular metal box called the ballast. This component regulates the flow of current from the house wires to the fluorescent tubes. Without it, current would build up and destroy the tube. When the lamp is in operation, the ballast produces the high-pitched hum so characteristic of fluorescent lighting units. It is specifically designed to fit certain tubes and house currents so, before changing to energy-saving tubes in a given fixture, check with an electrician to make certain that the ballast is sufficient.

Since the ballast is the heat-producing part of the fixture, some gardeners remove it and install it several feet or meters away from the garden. However, a small portable fan will blow off most heat radiation and unless a great many lamps are being used in a small area, there is usually no need to move

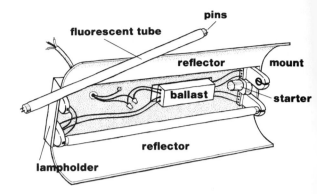

Parts of a Light Fixture: Mounts in the ends of the lampholder receive the pins on ends of fluorescent tubes, holding the tubes securely in place. The ballast controls the flow of current into the tubes, and in the process builds up heat and produces a high-pitched hum. The starter insures more efficient functioning of the fixture by reducing the amount of voltage required to keep the light on. So that the light generated is put to most effective use, reflectors attached to the lampholder channel the light into the growing area.

the ballast. If this should seem desirable, by extending its wires, a ballast can be relocated up to 12 feet (3.6 m) away. If such a ballast is being used with instant- or rapid-start tubes and no starter, the fixture must be grounded in order to start. That is, the lamp must be within 1 inch (2.5 cm) of a grounded metal reflector or fixture. In any case, a remoted ballast should be inside a metal container or an enclosed metal area to keep heat away from other wiring.

Ballasts usually last 10 to 12 years. If the fixture seems to hum more loudly than usual or if the lamp begins to smoke, the ballast probably needs to be replaced. Be sure to select the right size and type for the fixture.

STARTER

The starter is the metal cylinder which fits in a hole at one end of the lampholder. When the fixture is turned on, the starter preheats the electrodes in the lamp and cuts down on the amount of voltage that must be used to run it. Although they usually last a bit longer than the tubes themselves, starters do wear out every year or so. In fact, when a young tube fails to light, it is almost always because of a worn-out starter in the fixture. When purchasing replacements, select the size appropriate to the tube and fixture; for example, 15- and 20-watt lamps require FS-2 starters; 30- and 40-watt lamps need FS-4 starters.

Available in 15, 20, 30, and 40 watts, among other sizes, only the so-called "pre-heat" tubes need starters. The common "rapid-start" types can be used with them, but since their filaments are continuously heated at a low voltage, these tubes swing into full operation without the extra push provided by a starter. Rapid-start tubes can be used with smaller, quieter ballasts than preheat lamps. They are particularly valuable in living rooms, where the steady hum of a larger ballast can be annoying. However, rapid-start lamps are less economical and tend to have a shorter life when used without a starter. (To maximize life span, make sure you align the crease at the end of the tube with the socket opening of the fixture so that full contact is made.) Rapid-start tubes are available only in 40- and 30-watt sizes (a 22½ inch/57 cm long U-shaped type with 6 inches/15 cm between "legs" is available in 40 watts).

If you are willing to install special wiring and fixtures, you also can buy high-output (800 MA) rapid-start tubes in various lengths in various tones. The four-foot (1.2 m) high-output tube is a 60-watter, with the cool white yielding 4,300 lumens after 100 hours of life versus 3,150 lumens for a standard 40-watt cool white tube. Very-high or super-high-output (1,500 MA) tubes of the same length consume 110 watts and produce 6,900 lumens after 100 hours.

Another type of lamp that does not use a starter is the "slimline instant-start" tube. Because these tubes operate at a high voltage, they need special fixtures and ballasts and cannot be interchanged with rapid-start and preheat tubes. Instead of the standard

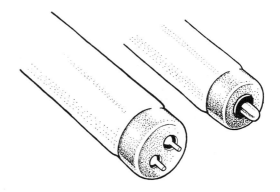

Two Types of Tube Ends: Tube on the left is a standard fluorescent type with two pins. Tube on the right shows the single pin end of a slimline tube.

two-pin bases, slimline tubes have only one pin on each end. This makes for quick, easy insertion.

Available in various wattages, slimlines usually are bought in the six-foot (1.8 m), 55-watt or eight-foot (2.4 m), 75-watt sizes because standard fluorescents are not available in those lengths. The popular eight-foot (2.4 m) tube also is available in high-output (110 watt) and very-high-output (215 watt) versions, which require still different fixtures. (A cool white eight-foot/2.4 m high-output tube yields 9,200 lumens after 100 hours of use, while the very-high-output tube offers 15,500 lumens.)

Slimlines are more expensive than preheat and rapid-start tubes and, according to many gardeners, they are less efficient than standard tubes. Their main advantage is instantaneous response which, in the indoor garden, is of little importance. However, since the tubes are the only type that fit six- or eight-foot (1.8 to 2.4 m) fixtures, they are sometimes useful in large home gardens.

FIXTURE STYLES AND REFLECTORS

Because of their tubular shape, fluorescent lamps that are not reflectorized send much of their light away from the growing area.

Therefore, some kind of reflecting device is needed to direct all of the light down toward the plants — indeed, veteran light gardeners claim that fluorescents are almost useless without the extra light such a reflector provides. (They also garner free light whenever possible from white walls and from white drainage pebbles or egg crate diffusers under the plants.) Industrial fixtures are equipped with white-enameled metal reflecting hoods that are attached to the lampholders. The most effective ones have a parabola-shaped curve to them and are made of aluminum. Open-end, closed-end, turret, and slimline industrial fixtures all come with this type of reflector already assembled and attached. Although some gardeners repaint them with a flat white paint, most prefer to use reflectors as they are.

Strip fixtures or "channels" do not have attached reflectors. Somewhat thinner than industrial fixtures, they usually are installed in or under cabinets and shelves where there is a flat surface to serve as a reflector. Of course the surface must be painted white or, if desired, covered with mirrors in order to be an effective reflector. Strip fixtures also can be fitted with metal hoods of the kind used with industrial fixtures. These can be purchased from manufacturers or home-made by simply cutting a piece of the required size from a sheet of aluminum, shaping it, and painting it white. Use screws to attach it to the lampholder. Similar to strip fixtures but even simpler are the thinner but wider basic fixtures, which have six or eight inches (15 or 20 cm) between tubes instead of two or three inches (5 or 8 cm).

ASSEMBLING THE FIXTURE

Fixtures can be purchased in almost any stage of assembly, from a box of loose wires and metal parts to a completely assembled unit that is ready to plug in. The self-contained, premounted types which operate without a ballast or socket have the advantage of being completely silent, and since the wiring is concealed in their plastic stripping, they are very neat and attractive. However, they are short lived, unecological, and very expensive.

In most cases, the only assembly needed for other types of fixtures is to install the cord and plug, attach the ballast wires, screw on the reflector hood, and hang the unit. Clear instructions usually are given with the unit and the only problem that may arise is in realizing which wires to connect. The wiring diagram for each kind of fluorescent-lamp circuit is given on the ballast. If the directions are at all unclear to you, ask the advice of an electrician.

Fixtures have several holes in different places along the top and ends of the lampholder. These can be used to attach hooks (which come with industrial fixtures) or to screw the unit to the undersurface of a shelf. Use an electric drill to make additional holes if necessary.

Starters are installed by pushing the points in one end of the starter into the larger part of the socket hole in the fixture. Twist the starter slightly to the right to lock it in place. It will not fit tightly and may seem to wobble a bit, but this is perfectly normal.

There are two kinds of tube sockets that hold the standard two-pin lamps in the unit. One kind has a triangular impression in the mount with an opening at the top. The tube is inserted with the two pins at an angle. When the upper pins snap into contact, the tube is turned.

The other type of socket is a simple vertical slot into which the pins are inserted. The tube is turned on its own axis and locked easily into place.

Single-pin, slimline tubes use slightly different sockets that are spring loaded. Insert one end of the tube in the spring-loaded socket and line up the other pin in the rigid socket. Push the tube into place.

No matter what kind of socket is being used, always make sure that the pins are properly lined up in both mounts. Do not try to turn the tube until it is aligned, for you may connect it incorrectly or even break the pins.

SWITCHES AND TIMERS

The only pieces of equipment needed in addition to the fixture itself and the tubes are the switch and timer. Many gardeners find that a switch is unnecessary, since the time-clock can be set to turn the unit on and off. However, it is little trouble to install one and it may come in handy.

There are two types of switches, the in-line switch and the direct switch. The in-line switch simply is installed in the unit's cord. It can be purchased from a hardware store

Light Garden with Timer: The plants in this working light garden receive the amount of light suited to their photoperiodic needs, thanks to a timer, pictured in the foreground.

along with instructions for slicing the cord and connecting the necessary wires.

Switches that are installed in the fixture itself are called direct switches. These fit in special knockout holes in the ends of units. Their installation is a bit more complicated, but when a timer is being used in addition to a switch, they are probably more useful than in-line switches.

A timer is a special electric clock into which the fixture is plugged. It is then plugged into the house outlet so that it can turn the current on and off as directed. On the time-clock's dial are two small levers which can be set for any time of the day or night. If the "on" lever is set for 7:00 A.M., the lamp will switch on at 7:00 in the morning. If the "off" lever is set for 10:00 P.M., the lamp will turn off then.

In selecting a timer, make certain that it carries at least 1,500 watts, or about 10 to 20 percent more than the total wattage of the units to which it is attached. The most reliable timers bear an Underwriters Laboratory (UL) label and are made by a major manufacturer such as Tork, GE, or Paragon.

LIGHT GARDEN ENVIRONMENTS

An electric light garden can be built anywhere there is electric power and sufficient amounts of humidity, warmth, and ventilation. Gardeners who want a strictly utilitarian light garden may select a basement corner, an empty closet, or a seldom-used guest room for their lights. Since these places are well off the beaten track, they need not fit into any sort of decor. Industrial fixtures suspended from the ceiling or propped upon benches, old tables, discarded cabinets and shelves, and old, unmatched pots can be used to create a kind of hodgepodge garden site. Such no-frills setups make fine propagating places, "intensive care" areas, and just plain working gardens. Plants raised under the

Working Light Garden: Much propagation and grafting activity goes on in this basement corner, as well as other routine care. A bank of four lights is suspended from the ceiling by a chain and pulley, for easy raising and lowering. A piece of aluminum-coated insulation paper, shiny side down, is draped across a wooden cross bar frame covering the fluorescent tubes. The paper serves as a reflective surface, and the ventilation space between paper and tubes prevents buildup of heat.

lights can be removed as they begin to flower and placed elsewhere in the home for display and enjoyment.

Other gardeners prefer to design at least some of their light gardens so that they fit into and even enhance their living rooms, bedrooms, dining rooms, and kitchens. They build light gardens in bay windows, under cabinets, in bookshelves, under stairs, in fireplaces, and on tables. Instead of using the standard industrial fixtures, artful growers select slimline fixtures for which they can design their own, attractive reflectors. They may purchase prefabricated units which rest on tables or serve as multi-shelf garden spaces so plants live and grow right in the most lived-in rooms of the house.

Whether you choose a garden site that is to be decorative or strictly utilitarian, it is im-

portant to consider environmental factors such as humidity, temperature, and ventilation as well as lighting. Choose your site with these factors in mind. As in any garden, all environmental conditions must be controlled if the plants are to grow. Here is a brief summary of the best ways to measure and control these factors.

HUMIDITY

Creating adequate humidity is one of the most difficult problems confronting the indoor gardener. Our homes are dry to begin with and the heat from electric lights makes the situation even worse, reducing moisture in the air by up to 5 or 10 percent. To measure the relative humidity of your prospective garden site, purchase an industrial humidistat or hygrometer. Set it near the garden site, away from any water that might be splashed on it. If your home is typical, during the heating season it will be drier than the Sahara Desert, registering a humidity as low as 13 to 20 percent.

Increasing household humidity levels 20 or 30 percent to reach the minimum 35 percent acceptable to most plants can be done in several ways. A central humidifier or a portable room humidifier easily can raise the moisture in the air to that level, providing a humidity you will enjoy as much as your plants. (In living areas, however, use a humidifier judiciously; at about 40 percent humidity windows may begin to "sweat" and furniture could warp or mildew.)

Unless your light garden is in a specially designed, windowless "growth room" or in a basement, you will have to rely on other methods to raise the humidity beyond 35 or 40 percent. Fine misting, which both lifts humidity and mimics dew, is particularly beneficial to all plants growing under lights as long as the lights are kept on for at least two hours afterward. The gentle light dries the leaves slowly so there is no danger of spotting or rotting foliage — even leaves as notori-

A Working Light Garden

A working light garden in a basement, little-used room, or other out-of-the-way place provides an extremely practical space for a multitude of indoor gardening activities. The working garden is built from standard size utility shelving units, which can be bolted together in whatever combination best suits your needs. These sturdy units are relatively simple to assemble and can be set up without a lot of expensive tools.

The first step is to erect the shelving according to the manufacturer's directions, allowing from 12 to 28 inches (30 to 71 cm) between shelves to accommodate plants and light

Working Light Garden: This unit may not be extremely stylish, but it is eminently functional. You need look no further than a hardware store for the basic materials—standard industrial shelving units. These sturdy shelves provide ample room for starting flats of seeds and carrying out other propagating activities. The light is just right for getting flowering and foliage plants into top shape to assume their places in show gardens and/or home decoration.

fixtures, and allow access to the plants. Two or more units can be bolted together to form longer shelves if you wish. You may also want to paint the units white to increase light reflection.

Next, mount a two-tube fluorescent fixture to the underside of each shelf. Use stove bolts to

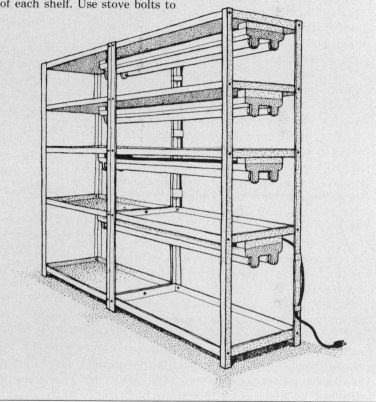

mount the fixtures securely. Be sure to use a cable with a ground when wiring the fixtures. For convenience, wire the fixtures to one another and have a single power cable from the bottom light fixture to the source of power.

ously susceptible as those of the African violet. (For more on humidity and how to boost it, see chapter 2.)

Of course, the best solution for plants which need high levels of humidity (70 percent or above) is the terrarium or Wardian case. These can be used attractively throughout the home and supplied with their own, separate electric lighting fixture designed to fit the case exactly. Circline lamps can be suspended above round terraria, and standard

fluorescents may be used above rectangular terraria or over very large breeders' aquaria and the like. Care must be taken, however, to prevent heat buildup in an enclosed terrarium. For example, the gardener converting a breeder tank is likely to find that the fluorescent tubes attached are too dim and too hot. It is far better to use clear glass or plastic as a top and to suspend a four-foot (1.2 m), two-tube fixture several inches or centimeters above the top. A standard 10- to 15-gallon

(37.8 to 56.8 l) tank needs a two-tube fixture for good lighting. Incandescents have been tried and found unsuitable for enclosed terraria; they are simply too hot and not conducive to good, compact growth.

TEMPERATURE

Temperature is rarely a problem in the fluorescent light garden, for average household temperatures are perfect for many plants and fluorescent lamps seldom cause any significant alteration.

If your garden site has temperatures higher than 60° to 85°F (16° to 29°C) during the day with a 10°F (6°C) drop at night, you might consider installing a small portable fan or, in extreme cases, an air conditioner that will reduce the heat of lights. During extremely hot summer days, consider cutting back the daily lighting period to as little as seven to ten hours to let plants "rest." You also can cut back on lighting when you go away on vacation to reduce the plants' rate of water consumption.

If temperatures are too low, which may be the case for tropical plants being grown in a basement light garden, check to be sure that all possible heating vents or radiators are open and "on." If the temperature is still too low, you probably will have to select plants that can be grown successfully at those temperatures. (For a list of plants that prosper in cool places, see chapter 2.) Bottom heat supplied by a water-heater top or by a soil-heating cable or a special heating coil built into your plant bench may help somewhat. Germinating seeds that do not require light for germination can be given the warmth they need by simply placing them on top of the light fixture, where the ballast will give them bottom heat.

VENTILATION

Ventilation affects both humidity and temperature and is one factor which light gardeners tend to overlook. It is extremely important in preventing the development of disease organisms, mold, and mildew, and in supplying the carbon dioxide so necessary for photosynthesis. However, too much ventilation — whether it be a slight draft or a cold wind blowing across your garden site — can devastate plants and lower the efficiency of fluorescent lights.

In the average size indoor garden which includes just a few fixtures, ventilation other than that which naturally occurs in the room is probably unnecessary. As long as air is continually coming in from some outside source, plants should fare pretty well. If the garden site is very humid, you can use a small portable fan (or even one of the miniature fans sold to cool electronic equipment) to evaporate moisture collecting in plant axils and to circulate the air. But do not create a strong air current that causes leaves to shake, and do not direct the fan at the plants.

Under drafty conditions, it is wise to lessen ventilation by surrounding the garden space with a plastic or even a cheesecloth curtain. A white bedsheet, which helps reflect light from the fluorescent fixtures, may be a good idea. If light gardens are built in or near a window, make sure storm windows have been installed and that there is a heavy curtain or insulated shutters or shades to be drawn on cold nights.

SETTING UP THE LIGHT GARDEN

How you choose to arrange your garden is largely a matter of personal choice, available space, and environmental conditions. Basically, there are three different kinds of light gardens: those built on tabletops, in shelves and cabinets, and into fireplaces and "nooks."

TABLETOP GARDENS

Gardens set up on tabletops or benches are probably the easiest to maintain and arrange. They can be simple basement structures built

Tabletop Light Garden: This attractive unit features a wooden canopy which houses the fluorescent tubes and easily blends in with the interior decor. This selection of foliage and flowering plants rests on a layer of drainage material.

on old carpentry benches or on sawhorses topped by plywood or elegant living room types laid out on a favorite sideboard or bureau. The standard industrial reflectors can be suspended on chains from the ceiling or, for a fancier arrangement, a wooden canopy can be built to hold the tubes and serve as its own reflector. Or pieces of angle aluminum can be fastened to the ends of an industrial fixture to serve as legs, with the whole setup resting on the table. A similar fixture can be designed for a circline tube by cutting a square of plywood the appropriate size, painting the underside flat white, covering the outside with Formica, and attaching four wrought-iron legs of the appropriate length. Mounts for the circline tubes are easily screwed onto the board. Tabletop units of

this sort also are available from commercial dealers.

Before buying any tabletop unit, consider whether it will fit in the available space. The setup you choose should be made of rust-resistant material and should be easy to assemble and, if necessary, to move. Some units have adjustable lights. If you plan to grow plants of different sizes under one unit, however, it may be simpler to raise or lower individual plants.

SHELF AND CABINET GARDENS

Shelf gardens can be created from already standing cabinets, bookshelves, or room dividers or purchased as separate units specifically designed for light gardens. To create a

A Custom Cabinet Garden: This cabinet was especially designed and built to brighten up a dim basement corner with plants. The rock arrangement is made of lightweight volcanic rocks, and the inside of the unit is painted pale blue to blend with the decor while still allowing for a high degree of reflection. For a finished effect, pots in the foreground are sunk in pine bark. The unit does not provide enough light to initiate blooms on flowering plants, but once plants have begun to bloom elsewhere in the house, they may be transferred here to provide a colorful accent, then moved back to brighter spots when they begin to droop.

shelf garden from an existing piece of furniture, be sure there is a space of at least 12 to 16 inches (30 to 41 cm) between the upper surface or shelf where the lamps will be attached and the lower platform which will hold the plants. If the distance is less than this, it still may be possible to design an attractive and successful light garden, but you will be limited to growing small plants and you may experience some problems with overheating.

To convert an entire bookcase, or just one section of it, into a garden, begin by painting the underside of the upper shelf (or shelves) with flat white paint. Or instead, you might coat the sides and bottom of the unit with rubber cement and line it with mirror tiles or rice paper, velvet or other fabric, or wallpaper in order to enhance the plant material. Purchase appropriately sized fluorescent lamps and fixtures and remove the bottom plate which fits around the sockets.

By putting screws through the small holes in the upper surface of the metal ballast box, you can attach the lampholder to any overhead surface. If you prefer, you can recess the ballast to the back of the case to reduce heat buildup inside. After the holder is in place, the bottom plate can be screwed on again. There are also two holes at the top of either end plate which can be used to attach the fixture in other ways. Actually, fastening the lamp directly to the underside of the shelf may result in harmful heat buildup if there is not sufficient air circulation, and allowing

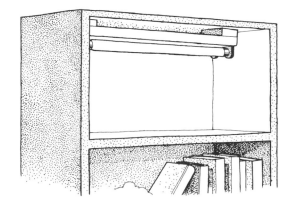

Adding Greenery to the Shelves: A bookshelf can easily be converted into a light garden by adding fluorescent light fixtures. It is a good idea to cover the shelf with waterproof material or to set the pots on saucers to guard against water stains. The inside of the shelf can be painted or lined with a material that will complement your arrangement of plants.

½ to 1 inch (13 to 25 mm) of air space between the shelf and the fixture is prudent. (If air cannot cool the ballast adequately, the lights may go off, as the ballast has a built-in safety shut-off.)

By using hooks and chains, the unit can be hung from the upper shelf. Helping circumvent overheating, this arrangement also has the advantage of being adjustable. Even easier, though a bit more expensive, is simply to choose the premounted fluorescent units which "stick" onto the upper shelf and do not require any special wiring, unscrewing, or complicated fixtures. Keep in mind, though, that at least two of these new "instant" fixtures must be used side by side about two inches (5 cm) apart to even approach the recommended light intensity for plant growth.

The same basic methods also can be used to convert empty cabinets, small chests-of-drawers, end tables, kitchen cabinets, china closet tops, and secretaries into usable light gardens. The shelf below the lights always should be covered with plastic sheeting and provided with greenhouse bench trays or other suitable drainage devices if really hardcore gardening is going to be done in the space. Gardens can be planted directly in the tray, if desired, and plants treated as if they were growing in a large dish garden. By adding glass panels, you can convert the entire area to a kind of semiterrarium. For a simpler setup, just place individually potted plants on saucers and arrange them beneath the lights.

Movable, multi-shelf gardens can be purchased from manufacturers at no small price. These usually consist of a supporting structure built of metal tubes with two to five shelves and reflectors. Sometimes, the shelves or lights are adjustable so that plants can be moved farther away from or closer to the tubes. There may be room for incandescent bulbs as well as fluorescent tubes, and the units often are equipped with plastic shelf trays to hold the plants. However, many of these units do not supply enough light for flowering plants. If you want to *grow* plants and not simply display them, make sure the stand supplies 15 to 20 watts of light per square foot of growing area.

Although some manufacturers have attempted to make such structures attractive as well as useful, most of the units are not at all appropriate for most living areas. Even the "early American" models that have been designed are rather clunky looking and have little appeal in the home. Steel and aluminum multi-tier units, the so-called Floracarts or Gro-Carts which can be moved about on casters, and the round-shelved plant stands are all best suited to basements or other rooms used more for growing than for living. More capacious and space-efficient working gardens that are cheaper per square foot of growing space can be built at home (see Build Your Own Plant Display Cart).

If you have an old television set with a wooden cabinet that is too handsome to discard, you can devise your own indoor gardening show if you remove the picture tube and parts. Paint the inside of the set white, glue on light-colored burlap or other fabric, or use mirror tiles to get maximum reflection of the light from a two-tube 24-inch (61 cm) fluorescent fixture mounted overhead. (To prevent undesirable heat, mount the ballast on the exterior back of the set.) The perimeter of the screen will conceal the lighting unit somewhat, but for a finished look that will make your plant show worth viewing, nail or screw on an appropriately sized and styled wooden picture frame that you have stained to match the cabinet. Potted plants with similar humidity requirements can be grouped in a plastic tray, their containers disguised by an overlay of vermiculite or long-grain sphagnum moss.

Bromeliads, orchids, and other moisture-loving, hard-to-grow plants also thrive in commercially manufactured growing cabinets. Sold under the names Dewpoint, Klima-Gro, Phyto-Gro, and Phytarium, these sophisticated and expensive chambers are

(continued on page 546)

Build Your Own Plant Display Cart

This cart provides a movable display area for plants. The concealed fluorescent fixtures provide light for both growth and display of plants. Because the cart is movable, there is easy access to the plants from all sides to make watering, feeding, and grooming chores easier. The wheels also allow the cart to be moved in front of a window for supplemental natural light.

Materials:

Item	Quantity	Description
Bins:		
A. Ends	4	$\frac{3}{4} \times 5\frac{1}{2} \times 24\frac{5}{8}$-inch #2 pine
B. Ends	2	$\frac{3}{4} \times 9\frac{1}{4} \times 24\frac{5}{8}$-inch #2 pine
C. Sides	4	$\frac{3}{4} \times 5\frac{1}{2} \times 49\frac{1}{4}$-inch #2 pine
D. Sides	2	$\frac{3}{4} \times 9\frac{1}{4} \times 49\frac{1}{4}$-inch #2 pine
E. Bottoms	3	$\frac{1}{2} \times 23\frac{7}{8} \times 49\frac{1}{4}$-inch A-C plywood
F. Corner supports	4	$\frac{3}{4} \times 2\frac{1}{2} \times 54$-inch select pine
G. Corner supports	4	$\frac{3}{4} \times 1\frac{3}{4} \times 54$-inch select pine
H. Castor blocks	4	$1\frac{3}{4} \times 1\frac{3}{4} \times 4$-inch #2 pine
I. Castors	4	$2\frac{1}{4}$-inch stem-type castors with castor sockets
Glue	—	White vinyl glue
Nails	—	5d box nails
Nails	—	4d finish nails
Screws	48	$1\frac{1}{4}$-inch #10 flat-head wood screws
Screws	16	$\frac{5}{8}$-inch #10 pan-head sheet metal screws
Finish	—	Urethane finish
Lights	4	2-tube fluorescent fixtures
Caulk	—	Clear silicone caulk

Special Tools: Router (optional)

Procedure:

1. Cut pieces A through H according to the dimensions in the materials list.
2. Cut a $\frac{3}{8}$-inch-deep $\times$ $\frac{3}{4}$-inch-wide rabbet in both ends of all the end panels (A and B).
3. Cut a $\frac{3}{4}$-inch-deep $\times$ $\frac{1}{2}$-inch-wide rabbet along one edge of the top and bottom bin sides (C).
4. Cut a $\frac{3}{8}$-inch-deep $\times$ $\frac{1}{2}$-inch wide groove in all four members of the middle bin (B and D) 4 inches from one edge.
5. Assemble all three bins by gluing the rabbets and nailing through the ends with 5d box nails.
6. Rout a $\frac{1}{4}$-inch radius on all edges of the bins or break the edges with a sanding block.
7. Glue and nail corner supports (F and G)

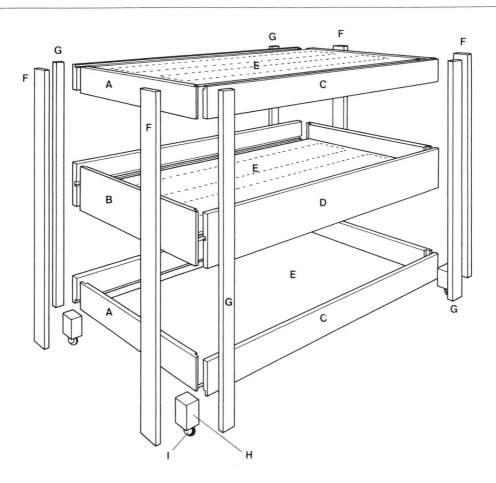

together by nailing through F with 4d finish nails.

8. Rout a ¼-inch radius on all edges of the corner supports (F and G) and castor blocks (H), or break the edges with a sanding block.

9. Drill a ⅜-inch-diameter × 1 ½-inch-deep hole in the center of one end of the castor blocks (H). This is for a ⅜-inch castor shaft.

10. Glue and nail the castor blocks (H) flush with one end of the corner supports with 4d finish nails.

11. Assemble the bins and the corner supports. Screw from the inside of the bins into the corner supports. The top bin will be flush with the top of the corner supports, the bottom bin will sit on top of the castor blocks (H), and the third bin will be positioned in the middle.

12. Finish by sanding all surfaces of the cart.

13. Apply three coats of urethane finish.

14. Install castor sockets in the holes and insert the castors.

15. Install two fluorescent fixtures side by side underneath the top and middle bins. They are screwed in place through the top of the fixture. Be sure the cords are lined up to plug in at the same end.

16. Caulk the inside corners of both bins with clear silicone caulk.

17. The unit is now ready for your plants.

Fireplace Light Garden: A collection of low-light, humidity-loving plants is ensconced within a fireplace, with fluorescent tubes suspended out of sight by chains from the damper. The interior of the fireplace is lined with black cardboard, and a black cardboard strip conceals the pots in the foreground. The designer of this light garden has found the best performers to be rex begonias, streptocarpus, and anthuriums. Blooming African violets can be tucked in for colorful accents, but after a month must be relocated to a brighter spot.

special enclosed boxes with controls that can be set to turn lights on and off, supply carbon dioxide, add water, or open vents according to schedule. Growing cabinets are available from specialty manufacturers and horticultural supply houses.

FIREPLACE AND NOOK GARDENS

During the off seasons, fireplaces make excellent locations for portable electric light gardens. A lighted terrarium of the right size may be perfect in an unused fireplace as long as the upward draft can be cut off and the temperature kept sufficiently high or low.

A fireplace that is no longer in use can be converted permanently to a light garden by simply sealing the chimney opening with brick or plywood and painting the surface white or even flat black to display the plants dramatically. An industrial fluorescent light unit can be suspended the appropriate distance above the hearth from chains in the damper mechanism or attached to angle irons fastened to the firebrick or hung from a heavy-duty tension curtain rod. Or, shelves can be installed and several fixtures used. To mask pots, you can spray-paint a six inch (15 cm) high piece of cardboard to match the fireplace interior and lay it across the opening of the firebox. Leafy spreading plants also can hide pot rims. A freestanding fireplace with a metal smoke cone also can be temporarily or permanently converted to a charming light garden by hanging a circline fixture inside and running the electric cord out of the small damper opening. Good choices for fireplace gardens are low-light plants with interesting colors and veining — genera such as *Anthurium, Begonia* (especially the rex and angel wing types), *Bromelia, Caladium, Calathea, Coleus, Fittonia, Maranta, Peperomia,* and *Rhoeo* species.

Other nooks and niches can be converted to light garden sites in similar ways. By installing triangular platform shelves in almost any corner, a small corner cupboard garden can be built. The space beneath an open staircase makes an excellent growing area and closets of all shapes and sizes, with or without their doors, can be converted into shelf gardens. So can decorator pieces such as an old bourbon barrel sanded and lightly coated with urethane finish. (When the barrel is purchased, have the cooper place the bands so there will be a large center opening. The staves should be located high and low but not in the center.) With a two-lamp circline fixture attached to the top of the barrel and a pleasantly curved opening in one or two sides of the barrel to frame cacti and other succulents (or other plants) placed inside, such a piece can be used to grow plants over an extended period. Daily misting is advisable.

Another distinctive display nook for plants can be created inside an old upright piano. Like the foregoing barrel, this idea was executed by the Philadelphia, Pennsylvania, chapter of the ILGSA and the result exhibited to great effect at a recent Philadelphia Flower and Garden Show. The piano garden can be created by removing all the instrument's insides except the sounding board and the harp and strings and taking off the front

wooden panel above and below the keyboard. Plants can be exhibited in these two areas (lined with 4-inch/10 cm plastic) beneath two-tube 4-foot (1.2 m) fixtures. For a high-humidity terrariumlike display, 1/4 inch (6 mm) thick glass finished on all sides can be mounted behind both openings and provisions made for opening and closing each area to control humidity.

Clearly, the choices for light garden locations are as limitless as your imagination and as unique as the furnishings and out-of-the-way nooks and crannies of your home. The ILGSA has published an informative booklet detailing the construction of a variety of light gardens. To obtain this helpful 56-page guide, write to the ILGSA librarian (see Appendix).

SELECTING PLANTS FOR THE LIGHT GARDEN

Before selecting plants to grow under lights, it is necessary to know which plants have compatible temperature, moisture, and light requirements (see the Plant Selection Guide in chapter 28 for such information), and which plants will respond best to electric lighting conditions. Since almost every plant will respond to the miracle of continuously "sunny" days, this second consideration may seem a bit silly. However, where light gardening space is limited, it would be a shame to grow plants that could do perfectly well on the windowsill or beneath a single incandescent bulb.

Many light gardening books and publications contain long lists of plants and their specific light requirements, including the distance they must be from a typical fluorescent light source, such as two 40-watt cool white bulbs, and the number of uninterrupted hours of light they need in order to flower. This information is undoubtedly important, for plants placed too far from tubes may not flower or may display the overlong and weak stems symptomatic of too little light, while

(continued on page 550)

Custom-Made Places for Plants

One beauty of light gardening is that special garden spaces can be set aside in any area of the house without altering the existing structure of the building. To make a greenhouse part of your home, you'd have to take down a wall; a plant room necessitates the installation of a waterproof floor or the construction of special beds. But a light garden requires none of these major alterations. Fluorescent lights can be used to provide illumination for plants in any number of places where natural light is not available, or they can be used to supplement the natural light from a window. A light garden can be set up wherever you would like a bit of greenery to brighten the area — in a dark corner of the living room, along an empty bedroom wall, in a den or a basement workroom. Many indoor gardeners find that adding some fluorescent lights helps them to make more effective use of their homes to provide garden space for their favorite ornamental and edible plants.

Herb and Ann Speanburg's house in upstate New York has many of the simple, thoughtful touches through which the home environment can be adapted to meet the needs of plants. At the time their house was being built in 1969, the Speanburgs' interest in growing plants indoors was just beginning to take shape. As their involvement grew, they began to recognize that their new home had great potential for indoor gardening projects. They realized that they had inadvertently included such features as

Therapeutic Light Cabinet: Herb lowers the plastic sheet that will enclose this light garden, creating a humid atmosphere to help rejuvenate some flagging plants. A bank of lights hangs directly above the unit, shining down through the glass diffuser which serves as the top of the cabinet.

a bay window in the living room with a generous window ledge and Thermopane glass, a basement with ample space for light gardening units, and a platform off the back of the house that could be enclosed to be used as a working window garden.

Now, as you walk through their home, you can see how Herb and Ann have made room in their lives and in their surroundings to actively pursue various aspects of indoor gardening.

Downstairs, in the basement, a sizable portion of the available space has been devoted solely to light gardening, with a small greenhouse added on to the end of the room. Herb began gardening under lights in 1970, and has put his years of experience as a self-employed carpenter to good use in the design and construction of light garden units. These hold, among other plants, his fa-

vorite rex and other rhizomatous begonias. Extending down the center of the room are several large shelf units under banks of lights, alive with abutilons, African violets, crossandras, cyclamens, sinningias, and streptocarpus. Along one wall are two wooden cases with light fixtures that Herb designed and built, which he jokingly refers to as the "sick-bay." These cases are enclosed with either sliding glass panels or plastic sheeting which can be rolled up and down, as needed. These allow him to provide a more constant level of humidity, to rejuvenate any ailing begonias. Also scattered about in different areas under the fluorescent lights are glass-bowl-type terraria which house several species of begonias that will thrive only in this kind of enclosed environment. As a less expensive alternative to these glass terraria, Herb has found that the domed plastic bowls used to ripen fruit are just as effective. He also uses aquaria fitted with glass tops to create the warm, moist environment beloved by begonias and fittonias.

Along the outside wall, opposite the sick-bay, Herb keeps his working paraphernalia. Here is located a 15-gallon (56.8 l) can, which was a gas station grease barrel in its former life, and which has since been painted fire engine red and fitted with a spigot. It is filled with a fertilizer/water solution, which is always at room temperature, ready for application. Alongside this barrel is a small, tabletop-

Herb Speanburg's Light Garden: A colorful assortment of gesneriads rests on rows of wooden slats set above a layer of damp sand. To the right of the fluorescent light fixture is a domed fruit-ripening bowl that Herb has transformed into a terrarium for humidity-loving begonias.

The "Sick Bay": Sliding glass panels help maintain a constant, high level of humidity, a boon to ailing begonias. A single fluorescent tube provides the steady light inside. Glass shelves hung on pegboard behind the cabinet bring smaller plants closer to the two fluorescent tubes suspended from above, while other potted plants and a glass terrarium sit on top of the cabinet.

sized oven, past its prime as far as use in the kitchen is concerned, but just right for pasteurizing compost.

Over the years, Herb has evolved a basic rule of thumb for adjusting the height of lights over the plants. For flat growth in African violets, it is important to keep the light source no more than 12 inches (30 cm) from the top of the plant. For other plants he advises keeping the lights at a level where you can reach easily beneath them and work comfortably, which translates to about 20 to 24 inches (51 to 61 cm). This way, he says, you will not have to be forever raising and lowering the lights to get at the plants in the course of the daily maintenance routine.

Herb and Ann, who both are retired, have the luxury of enough time and optimal indoor gardening conditions to experiment with growing flowering annuals under lights and bringing

them to bloom in winter. Ann plants her seeds in the beginning of September in order to brighten up a normally dreary February with fresh flowers. The Speanburgs also try their hand at forcing tulip and daffodil bulbs in this basement area. In addition, they have had much success with raising lettuce under lights in the winter. Their secret to success is snugging the flats of seedlings right up under the lights, only a few inches or centimeters away.

Coming up the stairs from the basement light garden, you find the enclosed platform extending from the back of the house, which has been transformed into a working window garden. As you enter, you cannot help but see how all the plants benefit from the sun that pours in from the south and west windows. It is in this room that Herb and Ann do a lot of their mainte-

(box continued on next page)

Custom-Made Places for Plants (continued)

nance work, and they consider this to be almost another greenhouse, since it benefits from its proximity to the heated garage. In the dead of winter, the door leading from this room to the garage can be left open to take the chill out of the air.

In this room you will find plants hung from the ceiling for display, as well as flats of seedlings and cuttings resting on a table made from a board set on two sawhorses, and covered with white reflective cloth.This room is also the way-station for an-

nual flowers which have been started from seeds under lights in the basement, and then are moved up to this area to be acclimated to natural light before they are assigned their places in the garden outdoors.

Moving back into the main part of the house, you come to the bay window in the living room, which faces east. In summertime, there will be no plants here, but come winter, right around the holiday season, this area comes alive with lush greenery and colorful blooming plants. A fluorescent light fixture installed overhead behind a valance and the Thermopane

window help to create a healthy environment for the plants on display, so they don't suffer any side effects from winter's subdued natural lighting and New York State's intense cold.

If you've been wanting to create an environment for plants without going to the expense of adding a greenhouse or plant room, you might want to consider setting up a light garden in addition to or instead of making use of the space near your windows. With a little imagination, you can adapt distinctive places in your home just like the Speanburgs did for growing plants all year-round.

plants placed too close may remain too compact or have small, pale leaves that curl under. And obviously, a short-day plant cannot be grown under the same lighting conditions that a long-day plant requires. If both are going to be brought to flowering, integration simply does not work.

However, it is easy to become so involved with the dicta of other gardeners and so caught up in a ritual of measuring and timing that all common sense is lost. There can be no rule that says you always will succeed with a certain plant if you place it so many inches or centimeters beneath the lights and give it so many hours of darkness and so many of light. Photoperiodism is closely related to humidity and temperature as well as light. It is a complicated phenomenon that scientists do not understand entirely. What's more, depending upon the temperature in your home, the quality of the lights you select, how many hours they have been burned, how near or far a plant is from the center of the tube, and the kind of reflecting surface you provide, plants will need to be farther from or nearer to the lamps than even the most authoritative gardening books suggest.

Indeed, the widely varying footcandle figures given for various distances under lights are confusing and apparently contradictory unless you remember that such charts are based on diverse assumptions about the age of the tubes, the position of the plants, and so forth.

Because of such variables, it is advised that the chart Artificial Lighting Requirements of Popular House Plants be used only as a provisional guide to culture under lights. This cautious approach is particularly indicated where only the family or genus name is given, for there can be a wide variation in lighting needs among genera in the same family and among species in the same genus. Always begin by placing plants at the maximum recommended distance from the lamps. Gradually move the plants closer if they seem to be shooting upward instead of spreading out and developing their correct habit. If you cannot seem to get them close enough, then more lamps are needed, or perhaps your lamps must be replaced or dusted. (Remember, if four lamps are used instead of two, plants can be placed almost twice as far beneath them.)

Follow the photoperiodic suggestions

presented more closely than the distance suggestions and be sure to separate short- and long-day plants, at least during flower initiation. Plants listed as short-day need 6 to 8 hours of light and 16 to 18 hours of uninterrupted dark during the one to two months before their blooming period. They will not do their best if subjected to short days year-round. Long-day plants need 16 to 18 hours of light prior to flowering. Day-neutral types prefer 14 to 16 hours during flower initiation, but they can stand up to 18 hours of light.

THE ECONOMICS OF PHOTOPERIODISM

If the strategy is carefully planned, long-day and short-day plants can be brought to flowering (or kept from flowering) by giving them *very low* levels of light at crucial times. What's more, lighting used to extend day-length need not be continuous. Long-day plants such as pansies or snapdragons can be made to flower by giving them just one hour's light in the middle of their night. Short-day plants such as chrysanthemums and poinsettias can be kept from flowering by the same methods. Thus, simply interrupting a plant's period of darkness for 60 minutes, with as little as 40 watts of incandescent light, may be enough to produce the same reactions as a long day of continuous light. Rather than running your fluorescent lamps continuously for up to 18 hours a day, it would be worthwhile for you to experiment with this night-break system of lighting. It not only will save money, it also will help to conserve up to 95 percent of the energy that otherwise would be used to supply the long hours of light needed to initiate blooming.

MAINTAINING THE LIGHT GARDEN

In most respects, maintenance of an indoor light garden is no different from that of any other garden — indoors or out. Plants must be watered and pruned, insects controlled, and nourishment provided. However, the fluorescent lighting fixture does add a few mechanical tasks which must be carried out if the garden is to function properly.

Most important and most often overlooked is the fact that lamps must be cleaned and dusted fairly often or they will not provide adequate light. Dust lamps and reflectors every few weeks and clean the entire fixture each time tubes are replaced.

REPLACING TUBES

Although manufacturers say plant growth lights have a life span of about 7,500 hours and that standard white fluorescents such as cool white and daylight last for about 12,000 hours, their actual service life is somewhat different. First of all, light intensity is gradually decreasing so that the lamps become less valuable in the light garden and therefore should be replaced before they actually expire. (Within just a few hours after installation, fluorescent lights begin to dim. During the first 2,000 hours after the initial 5 or 6 hours of use, they may lose some 5 to 10 percent of their intensity. In the next 10,000 hours of use, they lose from 20 to 40 percent.) Secondly, manufacturers rate a lamp's longevity on the assumption that the tube will be burned for 3 hours each time it is started. Since light gardeners usually burn the lamps for 12 to 18 hours, lamps may last slightly longer, but this benefit is usually outweighed by the declining illumination.

As a general rule, replace lamps at about 80 percent of their rated service life or as soon as dark rings appear at the ends of the tubes. (These indicate that the electrodes are beginning to deteriorate.) It may be a good idea to date the tubes with a grease pencil or felt-tip marker (put the date on the metal cap at the end of the tube) so that by multiplying the hours they burn each day by days of use you can determine when they should be replaced.

(continued on page 554)

Artificial Lighting Requirements of Popular House Plants

PLANT	PHOTOPERIOD NEEDS	DISTANCE IN INCHES/CENTIMETERS FROM 2 40-WATT COOL WHITE FLUORESCENT TUBES
Abutilon	Day neutral	4 to 6 in./10 to 15 cm
Achimenes	Day neutral	4 to 6 in./10 to 15 cm
Aglaonema	Day neutral	10 to 12 in./25 to 30 cm
Alternanthera ficoidea 'Amoena'	Day neutral	4 to 6 in./10 to 15 cm
Anthurium scherzeranum	Day neutral	6 to 10 in./15 to 25 cm
Aphelandra	Day neutral	4 to 10 in./10 to 25 cm
Araucaria	Day neutral	4 to 10 in./10 to 25 cm
Ardisia crispa	Day neutral	6 to 10 in./15 to 25 cm
Asparagus	Day neutral	6 to 10 in./15 to 25 cm
Asplenium	Day neutral	6 to 10 in./15 to 25 cm
Azalea	Day neutral	6 to 10 in./15 to 25 cm
Beaucarnea	Day neutral	4 to 15 in./10 to 38 cm
Begonia metallica	Day neutral	8 to 12 in./20 to 30 cm
Begonia rex	Short day	4 to 10 in./10 to 25 cm
Begonia × semperflorens-cultorum	Day neutral	6 to 10 in./15 to 25 cm
Begonia tuberosa	Long day	6 to 10 in./15 to 25 cm
Bromeliaceae	Day neutral	10 to 12 in./25 to 30 cm
Browallia	Day neutral	3 to 4 in./8 to 10 cm
Cactaceae	Short day	3 to 6 in./8 to 15 cm
Caladium	Day neutral	4 to 10 in./10 to 25 cm
Calceolaria	Day neutral	6 to 12 in./15 to 30 cm
Capsicum	Day neutral	4 to 6 in./10 to 15 cm
Chamaedorea elegans	Day neutral	6 to 10 in./15 to 25 cm
Chlorophytum	Day neutral	6 to 10 in./15 to 25 cm
Chrysanthemum	Short day	4 to 6 in./10 to 15 cm
Cineraria	Day neutral	4 to 6 in./10 to 15 cm
Cissus	Day neutral	6 to 12 in./15 to 30 cm
Citrus	Day neutral	4 to 6 in./10 to 15 cm
Coleus	Day neutral	4 to 6 in./10 to 15 cm
Columnea	Day neutral	4 to 6 in./10 to 15 cm
Crassula	Day neutral	4 to 10 in./10 to 25 cm
Cyclamen	Day neutral	6 to 10 in./15 to 25 cm
Davallia	Day neutral	6 to 10 in./15 to 25 cm
Dieffenbachia	Day neutral	6 to 10 in./15 to 25 cm
Dizygotheca	Day neutral	4 to 10 in./10 to 25 cm
Dracaena	Day neutral	4 to 12 in./10 to 30 cm
Episcia	Day neutral	6 to 10 in./15 to 25 cm
Erodium	Day neutral	4 to 6 in./10 to 15 cm
Euphorbia fulgens	Short day	4 to 10 in./10 to 25 cm

PLANT	PHOTOPERIOD NEEDS	DISTANCE IN INCHES/CENTIMETERS FROM 2 40-WATT COOL WHITE FLUORESCENT TUBES
Euphorbia pulcherrima	Short day	6 to 10 in./15 to 25 cm
Exacum affine	Day neutral	6 to 8 in./15 to 20 cm
Ficus	Day neutral	10 to 12 in./25 to 30 cm
Geogenanthus undatus	Day neutral	6 to 10 in./15 to 25 cm
Gesneriaceae	Day neutral	4 to 8 in./10 to 20 cm
Gynura aurantiaca	Day neutral	4 to 6 in./10 to 15 cm
Hedera helix	Day neutral	8 to 10 in./20 to 25 cm
Heliotropium	Day neutral	4 to 6 in./10 to 15 cm
Hibiscus	Day neutral	6 to 8 in./15 to 20 cm
Hippeastrum	Day neutral	8 to 12 in./20 to 30 cm
Hoya	Day neutral	4 to 10 in./10 to 25 cm
Impatiens	Day neutral	4 to 10 in./10 to 25 cm
Justicia brandegeana	Day neutral	4 to 8 in./10 to 20 cm
Kalanchoe	Short day	3 to 6 in./8 to 15 cm
Lantana	Day neutral	6 to 8 in./15 to 20 cm
Malpighia	Day neutral	6 to 10 in./15 to 25 cm
Maranta	Day neutral	8 to 10 in./20 to 25 cm
Mimosa pudica	Day neutral	6 to 8 in./15 to 20 cm
Nematanthus	Day neutral	4 to 8 in./10 to 20 cm
Nephrolepis	Day neutral	6 to 10 in./15 to 25 cm
Orchidaceae		
(some fall-flowering)	Short day	4 to 8 in./10 to 20 cm
(some spring-flowering)	Long day	4 to 8 in./10 to 20 cm
Oxalis regnellii	Day neutral	6 to 10 in./15 to 25 cm
Pelargonium	Long day	2 to 6 in./5 to 15 cm
Peperomia	Day neutral	6 to 12 in./15 to 30 cm
Philodendron	Day neutral	6 to 12 in./15 to 30 cm
Platycerium	Day neutral	6 to 10 in./15 to 25 cm
Plectranthus	Day neutral	6 to 12 in./15 to 30 cm
Polyscias	Day neutral	6 to 12 in./15 to 30 cm
Rosa (miniature)	Day neutral	4 to 6 in./10 to 15 cm
Saintpaulia	Day neutral	6 to 10 in./15 to 25 cm
Sansevieria	Day neutral	10 to 15 in./25 to 38 cm
Saxifraga stolonifera	Day neutral	6 to 8 in./15 to 20 cm
Schefflera	Day neutral	6 to 12 in./15 to 30 cm
Schlumbergera	Short day	4 to 10 in./10 to 25 cm
Scilla	Day neutral	10 to 12 in./25 to 30 cm
Setcreasea pallida 'Purple Heart'	Day neutral	6 to 8 in./15 to 20 cm

(chart continued on next page)

PLANT	PHOTOPERIOD NEEDS	DISTANCE IN INCHES/CENTIMETERS FROM 2 40-WATT COOL WHITE FLUORESCENT TUBES
Sinningia speciosa	Day neutral	4 to 6 in./10 to 15 cm
Solanum	Day neutral	4 to 6 in./10 to 15 cm
Tolmiea	Day neutral	10 to 12 in./25 to 30 cm
Tradescantia	Day neutral	6 to 12 in./15 to 30 cm

Never replace all the lamps in a multi-tube fixture at one time. The sudden increase in intensity could be a serious shock to the plants and they might even show some damage. If you exchange a single standard tube with a horticultural lamp, you might take the special precaution of doubling the former distances from the lights, then gradually moving plants back to where they were over a period of 10 to 14 days.

WHY LAMPS MAY FAIL TO START

Several factors could cause lamps to refuse to start when the timer switches on the current. First of all, the problem could be related to the lamp itself, particularly if it is nearing the end of its expected life. If the tube is black at the ends or *very* dark down its entire length (some darkening is normal), then it could very well be that it needs to be replaced. If it tends to flash on and off it also may be near the end of its life.

However, if the lamp is fairly new, chances are that the problem is either in the starter, the ballast, or even in the timer wiring. Replace the starter first and, if this does not correct the problem, consider replacing the ballast if it is more than ten years old.

Rapid-start lamps and, occasionally, preheat types, may start very slowly under certain conditions. High humidity causes moisture to build up on the glass and interfere with the insulating effect of the glass tube. By spraying tubes with dusting and furniture polish sprays that contain silicone, you can lessen the problem. Temperatures below 50°F (10°C) also might cause fluorescent tubes to start slowly or not light to their full capacity. In very cold rooms where hardy plants are being grown, cover lamps with plastic safety lamp covers.

USING INDOOR LIGHT GARDENS FOR OUTDOOR GARDEN PROJECTS

Probably the best, most practical application of the electric light garden is in propagation. It is not only an excellent environment for growing house plants from seeds and cuttings, but it is also the best place for starting vegetable crops and annuals that will be moved outdoors in spring and summer. Fluorescent lamps provide intense but cool illumination that stimulates growth but does not scorch plants or dry out soil. Under lights, cuttings develop roots rapidly and seedlings grow into healthy young transplants.

STARTING SEEDS

Although a few seeds need light in order to germinate, most need only moisture and warmth. However, as soon as they have germinated and emerged from the soil, all plants need light of the right quality, intensity, and duration to stimulate proper growth and development. Anyone who has ever raised seedlings on a windowsill knows what weak or imbalanced lighting can do to plants: stems are elongate, leaves small and pale, and the entire plant tends to bend toward the light.

Under fluorescent lamps that provide even, intense lighting of the correct quality, seedlings will be stocky, green, and upright.

The majority of seeds do not require light for germination and simply can be placed on top of a fluorescent fixture where they will receive heat emitted by the ballast.

If seeds need light for germination, place their trays about three inches (8 cm) beneath two 40-watt lamps. This will keep the soil fairly warm and will speed germination. After germination, all vegetable and summer annual seedlings should be placed three or four inches (8 or 10 cm) from the tubes, where they will grow into stocky plants. Provide them with 12 to 16 hours of light per day until flower initiation is wanted, when they should be lit according to their photoperiodic needs. (According to light gardening expert Charles Marden Fitch, plants receiving 12 or more hours of light per day should receive a weak feeding with every watering.) Tropical house plants can be given 8 to 12 hours of somewhat dimmer light.

CUTTINGS

Light levels for cuttings are even more important than for young seedlings, for if a cutting cannot carry on photosynthesis, it will not be able to form roots, and it soon will die. Warmth, moisture, and ventilation are also very crucial to root development. The environmental conditions needed by cuttings are discussed in more detail in the section on Vegetative Propagation, in chapter 8.

Again, the fluorescent light garden can provide ideal lighting without the excessive heat radiation that would cause the cutting to dry out. Since most cuttings tend to root readily in low intensities of artificial light, they can be placed 6 inches (15 cm) beneath a single 20-watt tube or 12 inches (30 cm) beneath two 20-watt tubes. With two 40-watt tubes, cuttings can be placed up to 24 inches (61 cm) below the fixture. Always maintain a humidity of at least 50 percent, but not over 70 percent, for under most circumstances that could lead to rotting. The clear plastic shoeboxes sold in variety stores make excellent containers for rooting cuttings, but be sure the medium you use has excellent drainage. You may even want to puncture some drainage holes in the bottom of the box with a heated ice pick. See chapter 8 for additional information.

USING ELECTRIC LIGHTS IN THE GREENHOUSE

Incandescent, high-intensity discharge, and fluorescent or low-pressure sodium vapor lamps all can be used in the greenhouse. For controlling photoperiodic responses such as seed germination and flowering, standard or R incandescent bulbs usually are used. They are inexpensive and easy to install. To speed propagation or to extend daylength in small greenhouses, fluorescent lamps may be used. These can be mounted under benches or under shelves lining the opaque wall of an attached greenhouse, thus expanding the growing space. Low-pressure sodium and HID lamps are used for these purposes and simply to supplement natural daylight. Depending upon the plants being grown and the desired results, lamps are used and set up in different ways. Growers of China asters, begonias, chrysanthemums, poinsettias, and roses all rely heavily on incandescent and fluorescent lighting to control flowering. Tulips and other bulbs can be forced under low light intensities and, with supplemental fluorescent or HID lighting, can be made to develop long, attractive stems. Written material describing photoperiodic applications of fluorescent and incandescent lighting in the greenhouse usually is available from United States Department of Agriculture extension agents or from the extension service of state agricultural colleges.

CHAPTER 26

Terraria, Bottle Gardens, and Dish Gardens

By definition, terraria and bottle gardens are completely or partially enclosed miniature environments, similar to small greenhouses. Varying the soil mix, types of plants, and amounts of heat and light will let you recreate under glass a bit of the tropics, a moist woodland, or even a tiny bog. A miniature landscape also can be created in a dish garden. Planted in an open container, the dish garden is subject to the changeable, year-round atmosphere of the home.

The first recorded glass gardens were made in Greece around 500 B.C., for the annual festival of Adonis. Small plants in bell-shaped jars were cared for under statues of Aphrodite's slain lover. After eight days, the little plants were neglected until they withered, then were thrown into the Aegean Sea as a symbol of the death and regeneration of the earth's plant life.

In the early nineteenth century, the English physician Dr. Nathaniel Ward "discovered" the modern terrarium while he was trying to get a hawkmoth chrysalis to develop in a closed bottle. He saw that a fern had sprouted in a small amount of soil in the base of the bottle and was fascinated that such a thing could happen. Dr. Ward began

Wardian Case: Nathaniel Ward's inadvertent discovery that plants would thrive inside glass containers opened up a whole new range of indoor gardening possibilities. These gardens under glass were first in vogue during the 1800s and have retained their popularity ever since.

Opposite, view through the panes of a leaded glass terrarium.

experimenting with growing plants inside glass containers, and in 1832, he tried shipping ferns and grasses under glass from England to Sydney, Australia. The plants arrived unharmed, and a blossoming of world trade in plants began. "Wardian cases," as those first terraria were called, were the means for the introduction of Chinese bananas to Fiji and Samoa, Brazilian rubber trees to Ceylon, and quinine to British India from South America. European gardeners began to use the cases to grow ferns and tropical plants that otherwise were unable to tolerate the cold winters outdoors or in drafty parlors.

In addition, Victorian homemakers came to use terraria extensively as decoration in their households. As time went on, the simple Wardian cases became elaborate constructions, built into tabletops, sometimes with stained glass insets and often multi-sided.

But regardless of the size and shape of a terrarium container, the environment inside remains fundamentally the same, and understanding how this small world functions will give you a better appreciation of how to care for it.

TERRARIUM ENVIRONMENTS

The environment inside a terrarium is a self-sustaining system that needs a minimum of care. Water is taken up by the plant roots and transpired as vapor through the leaves into the air. The water vapor creates a humid atmosphere and condenses on the sides of the glass, eventually settling back into the soil where it again can be taken up by the plant roots.

Air is "recycled" by two chemical processes in the plants, so that plants do not exhaust the air in the terrarium container. During photosynthesis, water from the soil and carbon dioxide from the air are combined to form carbohydrates (starches and sugars), and oxygen is released as a by-product. In respiration, plant leaves take in oxygen from

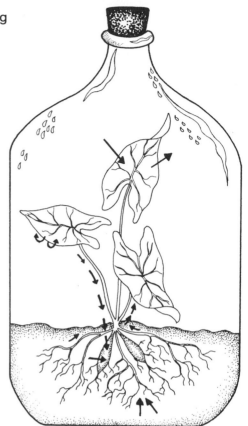

Recycling Air in a Terrarium: The root structure and leaf on the left show photosynthesis at work, a process which converts carbon dioxide from the air and water from the soil into sugar which is stored in the roots. Oxygen, as a by-product of this conversion, is given off by the leaves. As shown by the leaf on the right, the plant respires by taking in oxygen from the air in exchange for carbon dioxide. In this way, the two processes are interdependent, for respiration uses the oxygen freed by photosynthesis and in turn provides the carbon dioxide necessary for the continuation of photosynthesis.

the air and give off carbon dioxide. Since both chemical processes use the side products of one another's reactions, the closed terrarium environment allows both gases to be recycled, thus eliminating the need for additional air.

The variety of possible terrarium environments is practically as great as the range of environments that exists on earth. Within the confines of the container you can create tropical, temperate, woodland, bog, semidesert, and alpine landscapes. Each of these environments is re-created by supplying the appropriate soil mix, amount of moisture and light, sufficient temperature and air circulation, and by planting specific types of plants in the terrarium.

A tropical forest, for example, is normally moist, with rich, humusy soil, warm temperatures, low to moderate air circulation, low levels of light, and specifically tropical plants.

Temperate or woodland conditions are cooler, with humusy soil, average moisture, filtered light, and moderate air circulation. The woodland plants that you will be able to grow most successfully are native to the temperate parts of the world.

Bog environments are highly specialized, needing peat moss, sphagnum moss, lots of water, acidic conditions, low air circulation, and plants from swampy habitats, such as sundews, pitcher plants, and other carnivorous types.

Semidesert terraria need more moisture and somewhat less light than cactus bowls and dish gardens. Epiphytic and tropical cacti and other succulents that can tolerate slightly moist conditions will do well in this environment.

Alpine environments require cool to cold temperatures year-round and good air circulation to simulate high-altitude conditions.

Each of these environments calls for a slightly different set of growing conditions, and you will need a variety of materials to create them.

CONTAINERS

Any size or shape of container can be used for a terrarium as long as it is transparent, easy to open and close, and able to hold water. The range of possibilities is limited only by your imagination. Goldfish bowls, brandy snifters, apothecary jars, canning jars, salad oil bottles, perfume bottles, and old aquaria all can make interesting and unusual terraria. Clear plastic or acrylic is unbreakable and

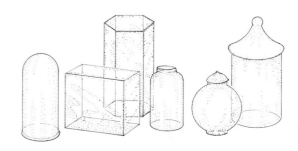

An Array of Terrarium Containers: A variety of bottles, bowls, and jars are suitable for terraria, as long as they are watertight, transparent, and can be readily opened and closed.

less expensive than glass, but has the disadvantage of being easily scratched. Do not use tinted containers — even very lightly colored glass reduces light intensity.

Bottle gardens can be defined as terraria in bottles rather than open-mouthed containers. The chief difference is that bottle gardens are planted with long-handled tools (such as those listed under Terrarium Tools). Plants, too, must be tailored to narrow bottle necks.

As with other terrarium containers, the best bottles to use are those made of clear glass, to allow plenty of light inside. The large bottles used to store springwater, decanters, salad oil bottles, and old-fashioned glass cider jugs all can make wonderful bottle gardens. They can stand upright or rest on one side if supported to keep them from rolling.

TERRARIUM TOOLS

In order to reach into the container to plant and maintain a terrarium, you will need to buy or make some specialized tools.

While a tablespoon is the best all-around tool for landscaping a brandy snifter or similar shallow, wide-mouthed container, bottles and other containers with necks too narrow to accommodate your fingers require slender planting aids. These tools must be smaller in diameter than the bottle opening and have handles longer than the bottle's depth.

(continued on page 564)

Make Your Own Miniature Greenhouse

Attractive and Functional: This glass structure encloses your plants to provide the proper terrarium environment, and is striking enough in design to be featured prominently in your home.

Utilizing the copper foil technique that is employed to create "Tiffany" type lamp shades and intricate stained glass window designs, you can construct an attractive terrarium resembling a miniature greenhouse. As few as seven pieces of glass can be used to build the terrarium. However, more pieces may be used if you wish to better represent the many individual panes of glass that are found in a large greenhouse.

A terrarium made up of 60 pieces of glass is shown in Figure 1. You can simplify the project by using single pieces of glass for each of the six side sections and for the top, reducing the total number of glass pieces to seven. The size of the terrarium can be varied to suit your preference—the dimensions appearing on Figure 1 are shown merely for purposes of this project.

Tools and Materials Required

Glass cutter

Small soldering iron—60 or 80 watts

Adhesive-backed copper foil—a single roll is sufficient for the terrarium shown in Figure 1.

Solid wire solder—60% tin–40% lead type

Soldering flux—nonacid, paste or liquid type

Single weight clear glass—approximately 6 square feet (54 sq m) are needed for the terrarium shown in Figure 1.

Paste brush—for applying soldering flux

Razor-blade knife

Ruler or straightedge

Small sharpening stone

Plastic soil tray—15½ in. × 10½ in. × 4 in. (394 mm × 267 mm × 101 mm) deep for the terrarium shown in Figure 1. Size of tray is dependent upon terrarium size, and should measure at least ½ inch (13 mm) smaller than outside dimensions of terrarium.

(The first five items can be purchased in a hobby shop specializing in stained glass supplies. The plastic tray may be obtained in the housewares section of a department store.)

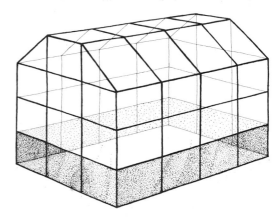

Figure 1: The finished terrarium, measuring 16½ in. (42 cm) long, 11 in. (28 cm) wide, and 12¼ in. (31 cm) tall at the highest point, is composed of 60 sections of glass.

Cutting the Glass

If you are not familiar with cutting glass, it is a good idea to practice on some scrap glass to get the feel of the cutter before attempting to cut the glass to size. Place the glass to be cut on a level surface covered with soft material such as felt, a smooth rug, or a blanket. Hold the glass cutter with your thumb on the bottom and your index and middle fingers on the top sides of the cutter, as shown in Figure 2.

To score the glass, place the cutter about ⅛ inch (3 mm) from the top far edge of the glass and pull it toward you while you apply even

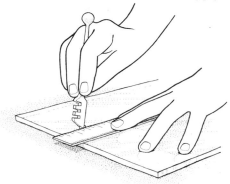

Figure 2: Correct way to hold glass cutter when preparing to score a piece of glass.

downward pressure (about 15 to 20 pounds/7 to 9 kg) along the entire length of the glass being cut. It is a good idea to use a ruler or straightedge to guide the cutter when making a straight cut. After the glass has been scored, snap it apart by placing your thumbs on top of the glass about ½ inch (13 mm) away from the scored line and firmly pressing down and away until the glass snaps, as shown in Figure 3. Another way to break the glass after it has been scored is to tap it lightly with the end of the cutter (a cutter with a ball on its end must be used), beginning beneath the far edge of the

glass and tapping toward the middle and then to the near end. This will cause the glass to crack or break along the score line as the tapping progresses.

When cutting the glass to size, it is desirable to make a full size diagram of the terrarium sides; this can be used as a guide for cutting the glass pieces by placing the diagram beneath the glass while you score it. The diagram also may be used to check the accuracy of the cut glass pieces and the assembled sections.

Copper Foil Wrapping

After all the pieces of glass have been cut to size, wash them to rid them of any dirt or oil that may inhibit the adhesion of the foil to the glass. At the same time, remove any rough edges with a small sharpening stone. Be careful to avoid getting the pieces mixed.

Next, wrap each of the pieces of glass along its edges with the ¼ inch (6 mm) adhesive copper foil, overlapping the starting end of the foil by about ¼ inch (6 mm), and allowing an even overhang on both sides of the glass (see Figures 4 and 5). Press the two overhangs against the sides of the glass, thus forming the foil into a "U" shape, by using the back edge of a pair of scissors. Any unevenness in the width of the foil on the sides of the glass can be trimmed off with a razor-blade knife.

Assembling the Sections

After you have wrapped with foil all the pieces of a particular section of the terrarium, place them on the full size diagram and fasten them together with solder. Brush soldering flux on

(project continued on next page)

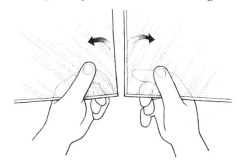

Figure 3: Proper position for hands when snapping apart scored glass.

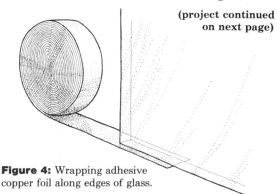

Figure 4: Wrapping adhesive copper foil along edges of glass.

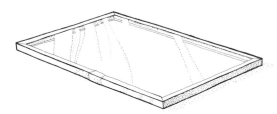

Figure 5: Section of glass wrapped with copper foil with allowance for ¼ inch (6 mm) overlap of starting and finishing edges.

the edges of the copper-foil-wrapped pieces of glass and "tack" the pieces together on one side of the section, using about ¼ inch (6 mm) of wire solder. Press the hot soldering iron directly on the solder and hold it there until the solder melts and flows evenly over the copper foil on the seam between the two pieces of glass being connected. Make sure the two pieces of glass being tacked together are pressed together tightly during the tacking operation. Do not allow the solder to flow onto any of the outside edges of the section being assembled, as it will make it difficult to line up the sections when connecting them. Figure 6 shows the tacking points for an end section of a terrarium employing 12 pieces of glass.

Turn over the assembled section (carefully—it is quite fragile at this stage) and solder it together on the opposite side, placing the solder along the entire length of all the interior seams instead of tacking—again being careful not to get any solder on any of the four outside edges of the section. Allow the solder to flow smoothly on all of the interior seams of the section. The section now can be turned over again

and solder placed along all the interior seams of the other side. A cross-sectional diagram of a soldered seam is shown in Figure 7.

(Note: If you are using only one piece of glass for each of the seven sections, the above soldering procedure is not necessary.)

Figure 7: Cross section of soldered seam showing how solder is applied to both sides of seam.

Assembling the Terrarium Sections

After the seven sections have been assembled by soldering, the four sections comprising the two ends and the two bottom sides are ready to be soldered together. Hold each section vertically on a flat horizontal surface and tack together the connecting vertical edges, while making sure all the four inside corners are at 90-degree angles (see Figure 8). Next, place the two slanting side sections in position and tack them to the ends and to the vertical sides of the terrarium, leaving only the top horizontal section to be inserted and tacked in place. After the seven sections have been tacked together, carefully turn over the terrarium and place solder evenly on the entire length of all the seams on the inside of the terrarium, covering all the exposed copper foil. Following this operation, turn

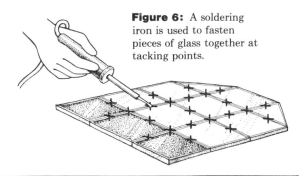

Figure 6: A soldering iron is used to fasten pieces of glass together at tacking points.

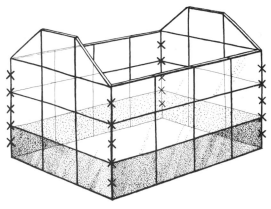

Figure 8: Tack along vertical edges where indicated when assembling ends and sides.

the terrarium over again and repeat the soldering procedure for all the seams on the outside. The soldering operation is complete only when all the copper foil on the inside and outside is completely covered with solder. At this time you will find the completed terrarium to be an extremely rigid structure.

Variations

A number of variations may be used to enhance the terrarium's appearance and utilization. Some suggestions follow.

Colored Glass: The extensive use of colored glass in a terrarium is not advisable because it cuts down the light entering the growing area. However, using colored glass along the base of the terrarium will enhance its appearance, as it will hide the soil tray inside the terrarium. Several pieces of colored glass also may be inserted in the end section (see Figure 9).

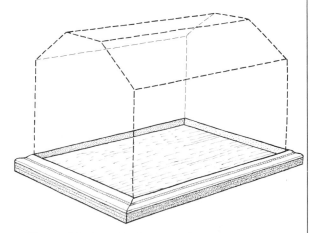

Figure 10: A wooden base may be used to support glass structure and to hold soil liner.

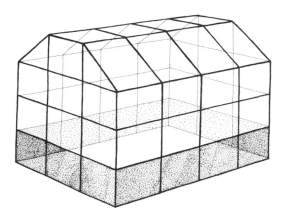

Figure 9: Sections of colored glass may be used along the base.

Wood Base: Use of a wood base for the terrarium not only adds to its appearance, but makes it more convenient to move without disrupting the plants. It also provides added protection for the surface on which the terrarium is placed because it prevents the soil liner from coming into direct contact with the surface. A wood base can be constructed using ¾ inch (19 mm) plywood and picture frame molding (see Figure 10).

Top Vent: By having it possible to remove one

of the top horizontal panes of glass, the terrarium can be vented or watered when necessary without lifting the entire structure.

If this variation is desired, three of the four panes of glass on the top surface must be soldered into place separately rather than being installed as a unit of four. The fourth pane of glass is left loose so it can be removed for venting and watering. Solder two small strips of copper sheeting beneath the adjacent panes to hold the removable panel in place, as shown in Figure 11. The removable pane should be wrapped in copper foil and covered with a thin film of solder so it will appear to be part of the terrarium when it is inserted in place.

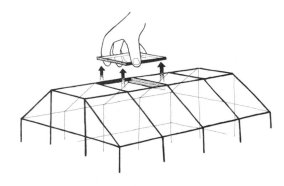

Figure 11: Top vent allows for ease in watering and in providing air circulation.

Especially helpful are:

A wooden dowel, pointed on one end, for poking moss and plants into place and covering roots.

A length of sturdy but pliable wire that is easily bent into a hook for pruning and extracting plants. Bent to the contour of the bottle, the wire also can be used for cleaning glass or wiping out insect pests (by snapping an elastic band over a tissue or cotton wad wrapped around one end of the wire).

A small funnel with its spout inserted into a large plastic drinking straw or piece of garden hose (if you are planting a multi-gallon/multi-liter container), for depositing the growing medium, adding decorative gravel patches, and watering plants in deep containers.

Equally handy are:

Narrow-bladed, long-handled digging trowels.

Iced tea spoons.

Small cork taped to a dowel for tamping.

Razor blade inserted in the split end of a dowel for pruning.

Percolator brush or small paint brush taped to a dowel for cleaning foliage.

Rubber bulb laundry sprinkler.

Flexible mechanical finger, kitchen tongs, or long-handled forceps for placing or planting spiny cactus.

GROWING MEDIA

After a container has been chosen, the first step in making a terrarium is to assemble the substrate, or growing medium. Drainage ma-

terial, which forms the bottom layer of substrate, can be made up of clear glass marbles, pebbles, coarse sand, aquarium gravel, crushed pumice stone or other volcanic rock, broken glass, or other porous materials. This layer of material is extremely important to the terrarium; it permits excess moisture to drain away from the plant roots, allowing air to get to the roots and preventing rot.

On top of the drainage material is placed a layer of hardwood charcoal (not the kind used in barbecue grills, but the kind available at plant stores) which is able to absorb acids produced by plants and soil bacteria. If left unchecked, these acids can destroy a closed terrarium system. In open systems, the acids are ordinarily flushed away as excess water drains from the pot.

The terrarium's upper layer of substrate consists of the growing medium for your plants. The soil mixture is determined by the type of environment you wish to create and the kinds of plants you will grow there. The basic planting mixture consists of 1 part sand, 1 part peat moss, and 1 part garden or potting soil. (If you decide to use garden soil, bear in mind that unless it is pasteurized it may carry insects or disease microorganisms harmful to house plants. For information on how to pasteurize soil, see chapter 6.) Variations on the basic mixture for specialized environments include varying amounts of peat moss, humus, sand, or lighteners like perlite or vermiculite. For example, carnivorous plants in a bog environment will need a higher percentage of acid organic matter than woodland or tropical plants. Recommended soil mixtures for each of the environments are as follows:

For Tropical Plantings
Mix 1 —
  2 parts garden or unenriched potting soil
  1 part peat moss
  1 part perlite
  1 part sand

Mix 2 —
- 2 parts sandy soil
- 1 part peat moss
- 1 part perlite

For Woodland Plantings

Mix 1 —
- 2 parts humus
- 1 part sand
- 2 parts perlite

Mix 2 —
- 1 part sphagnum moss
- 2 parts humus
- 1 part perlite
- 1 part peat moss

For Semidesert Plantings

Use the soil mix recommended for desert dish gardens, later in this chapter.

For Alpine Plantings

Use Mix 1 recommended for woodland plantings.

For Bog Plantings

Mix 1 —
- 3 parts peat moss
- 2 parts unenriched potting soil
- 1 part charcoal
- 1 part sand

Mix 2 —
- live sphagnum moss on a bed of peat moss

CHOOSING PLANTS

Whichever environment you choose, plant selections must be compatible. Because a terrarium mimics a specific kind of outdoor environment, you need to plant in each one the kinds of plants that are native to that habitat outdoors. A plant's adaptability to the environment is a more important consideration than its size. Although most terraria are small and thus require small plants, choosing a plant just because it is a dwarf or miniature often proves disappointing. Providing they are the right size for the growing space at the time of planting, many moisture-loving plants make suitable terrarium candidates, regardless of the height they attain at maturity. Growth can be restrained by planting in shallow, unenriched soil and by regular pruning. And overgrown plants can always be replaced with new ones. Of course, some plants, such as Venus' flytrap *(Dionaea muscipula)*, are so small that they can grow to maturity in a terrarium.

Bottle garden plantings are somewhat more specialized. The small openings limit plant choices to those with pliable stems and leaves that will not break easily. Young specimens of such plants as dwarf creeping fig *(Fi-*

Tropical Terrarium: The plants shown here offer a variety of foliage colors and forms while sharing common growing needs of warmth, moisture, and high humidity. Arranged clockwise from the rear are *Dizygotheca elegantissima, Peperomia, Pellionia, Selaginella, Pila,* and *Ficus pumila.*

cus pumila 'Minima'), Buddhist pine
(*Podocarpus macrophyllus*), and some *Dracaena* species lend themselves to bottle garden culture.

The three most popular types of terraria are tropical, temperate or woodland, and bog environments. Semidesert conditions will be discussed along with the desert environment under Ornamental Dish Gardens, later in the chapter.

The tropical areas of the world are, for the most part, warm and very moist with high humidity. Vegetation is lush, and there is a wide diversity of plant species.

Plants for a Tropical Terrarium

Botanical Name	Common Name
Aglaonema commutatum	Chinese evergreen
Asparagus	Asparagus fern
A. densiflorus 'Myers'	
A. densiflorus 'Sprengeri'	
A. setaceus	
Begonia boweri 'Nigromarga' (and other miniature cvs.)	Miniature begonias
Chamaedorea elegans	Neanthe bella, parlor palm
Cissus antarctica 'Minima'	Dwarf kangaroo ivy
C. striata	Miniature grape ivy
Coffea arabica	Arabian coffee plant
Cordyline terminalis 'Lilliput'	Dwarf ti plant
Cryptanthus bivittatus 'Minor'	Dwarf rose-stripe earth star
Dizygotheca elegantissima	False aralia
Dracaena	
D. sanderana	Belgian evergreen
D. surculosa	Gold dust dracaena
Ficus	
F. deltoidea	Mistletoe fig
F. pumila 'Minima'	Dwarf creeping fig
Fittonia verschaffeltii	Mosaic plant
Maranta leuconeura var. *kerchoviana*	Prayer plant
Nephrolepis exaltata cvs.	Boston fern
Pellionia	Trailing watermelon begonia

Botanical Name	Common Name
P. daveauana	
P. pulchra	Rainbow vine
Peperomia spp.	Peperomias
Pilea	
P. cadierei 'Minima'	Aluminum plant
P. depressa	Miniature pilea
P. microphylla	Artillery plant
P. nummulariifolia	Creeping Charlie
Pteris spp.	Brake or table ferns
Saintpaulia cvs.	Miniature African violets
Selaginella	Club moss, moss fern
S. kraussiana	Creeping club moss
S. pallescens	Sweat plant
Sinningia pusilla (and other miniature cvs.)	Miniature gloxinias
Syngonium	Arrowhead vine, *Nephthytis*

The following temperate plants also can be grown in tropical terraria:

Botanical Name	Common Name
Asplenium nidus	Bird's nest fern
Chlorophytum bichetii	Dwarf spider plant
Pellaea rotundifolia	Button fern
Podocarpus macrophyllus	Buddhist pine, Japanese yew
Saxifraga stolonifera 'Tricolor'	Variegated strawberry begonia

Temperate areas on earth are moist, cooler for a greater part of the year, and are less diverse in species than the tropics. As a rule, temperate zone plants do well in a cooler environment. The list includes hardy garden and woodland plants, as well as house plants. Because many native ferns and other wild plants are becoming endangered species they should be used with discretion and collected only in accordance with local regulations, or purchased from reliable wildflower specialists. The following temperate zone plants thrive in temperatures in the range of 50° to 65°F (10° to 18°C).

Plants for Temperate and Woodland Terraria

Botanical Name	Common Name
Adiantum raddianum	Maidenhair fern
Ajuga reptans	Bugleweed
Araucaria heterophylla	Norfolk Island pine
Asarum europaeum	European ginger

Woodland Terrarium: This container is a showcase for several native plants from eastern Pennsylvania which thrive in cool and moist conditions.

Botanical Name	Common Name
Asplenium resiliens	Ebony spleenwort
Brachythecium salebrosum	Common sheet moss
Buxus microphylla var. *japonica*	Japanese boxwood
Chimaphila maculata	Spotted wintergreen
Climacium americanum	Tree moss
Cornus canadensis	Bunchberry
Dryopteris spp.	Wood ferns
Epigaea repens	Trailing arbutus
Goodyera pubescens	Rattlesnake plantain
Hedera helix	Miniature English ivies
H. helix 'California Gold'	
H. helix 'Garland'	
H. helix 'Green Feather'	
H. helix 'Itsy Bitsy'	
H. helix 'Star'	

Botanical Name	Common Name
Linnaea	
L. borealis	Twinflower
L. borealis var. *americana*	
Lycopodium	Club moss
L. lucidulum	Shining club moss
L. obscurum	Tree club moss
Mitchella repens	Partridgeberry
Oxalis	
O. acetosella	Irish shamrock, white wood sorrel
O. hedysaroides 'Rubra'	Fire fern, red flame
Polypodium	Polypody fern
P. virginianum	Rock cap fern
P. vulgare	European polypody
Polystichum acrostichoides	Christmas fern
Pyrola elliptica	Shinleaf

Botanical Name	Common Name
Selaginella	Club moss, spike moss
S. densa	
S. douglasii	Douglas's spike moss
S. rupestris	Dwarf lycopod, rock spike
Thuidium delicatulum	Common fern moss
Viola	Violet
V. affinis	Common blue violet
V. sororia	Confederate violet

Bog or swampland plants are highly specialized for specific conditions of high acidity, low nitrogen, and an abundance of water. As you may expect, there are only a small number of plants that you can use successfully in this type of terrarium, but they are also among the most interesting. Many of them are carnivorous, digesting prey in front of your eyes. Flies and other small insects will find their way into your terrarium if you leave the cover ajar. Otherwise, you can feed carnivorous plants as suggested in chapter 23.

Plants for a Bog Terrarium

Botanical Name	Common Name
Acorus calamus	Sweet flag
Arisaema triphyllum	Jack-in-the-pulpit
Calla palustris	Wild calla
Caltha palustris	Marsh marigold
Claytonia virginica	Spring beauty
Coptis trifolia	Goldthread
Cypripedium calceolus var. *parviflorum*	Small yellow lady's slipper
Darlingtonia californica	Cobra lily
Dionaea muscipula	Venus' flytrap

Bog Terrarium: This dramatic bog garden, with its assortment of moisture-loving plants, conjures up images of a mysterious, dimly lit swamp. The layers of peat and sphagnum moss in the bottom of the terrarium imitate the layers of organic matter which accumulate naturally in swamps and bogs.

Botanical Name	Common Name
Drosera	Sundew
D. filiformis	Thread-leaved sundew
D. rotundifolia	Round-leaved sundew
Equisetum	Horsetail, scouring rush
E. hyemale	Common horsetail
E. scirpoides	Dwarf scouring rush
Hydrocotyle sibthorpioides	Water pennywort
Ludwigia natans	False loosestrife, swamp spoon
Myosotis scorpioides	Forget-me-not
Nasturtium officinale	Watercress
Onoclea sensibilis	Sensitive fern
Pyrola asarifolia var. *purpurea*	Bog wintergreen
Vaccinium macrocarpon	American cranberry
Viola	Violet
V. blanda	Sweet white violet
V. lanceolata	Lance-leaved water violet
V. palustris	Marsh violet

The following tropical plants can be grown in a warm bog environment:

Acorus gramineus 'Pusillus'	Grassy-leaved sweet flag, variegated grass
Aglaonema modestum	Chinese evergreen
Cyperus alternifolius	Umbrella plant
Dracaena sanderana	Belgian evergreen
Hydrocleys nymphoides	Water poppy
Philodendron	
P. ornatum	
P. scandens	Common philodendron
Spathiphyllum cannifolium	Peace lily, spathe flower

ASSEMBLING THE TERRARIUM

When you are preparing to assemble your terrarium, have your container and materials for the substrate ready, since they will be the first to be used. Make sure your container is clean (hot water and chlorine bleach will do the job). After rinsing away all traces of chlorine, dry the inside of the container thoroughly (by wiping or inverting over bottom heat); otherwise the glass will become muddy when the terrarium is assembled.

For a more attractive appearance, conceal the substrate with a lining of moss that

Terrarium Assembly: Before you begin, have the clean container, appropriate growing medium, necessary tools and suitable plants assembled on a surface that provides adequate room to work.

is approximately one-fifth the total height of the container. Use sphagnum moss, sheet moss *(Brachythecium salebrosum),* or dried decorator moss that has been moistened and squeezed nearly dry. Place the green side against the glass, overlapping the edges so no soil will show through. Line only the sides of the container; a layer of moss on the bottom decreases drainage and could cause plant roots to rot.

Bottles can be lined by cutting the moss into small strips and poking them through the narrow neck, then pressing them side by side against the glass with the end of a dowel. Next you are ready to add the drainage material. Use a funnel and tube to direct the pebbles, gravel, or other material into your

Preparing the Substrate: A funnel is helpful in guiding drainage material into the container. Here, gravel is being poured into the moss-lined bottom through a funnel extended by a piece of tubing.

around. If the garden will be viewed on only one side, then your point of interest need be visible only from the front. Prior to planting the terrarium, sketch out a plan of how you will arrange the plants. Trace the circumference of the bottom of the container on a piece of paper, and plan your arrangement to allow room for side and top growth.

The primary rule of terrarium planting is: Do not use too many plants. Remember, this is a miniature garden where each plant is chosen for a specific effect. Carefully plan the central focal area, or point of interest — it can be a single plant or a group of plants chosen for their interesting color, texture, or shape. Unless the container opening is large enough to permit easy trimming, the tallest plant should be several inches or centimeters shorter than the shoulder of the glass.

Focal Point: A well-planned terrarium will include enough plants for a luxurious, but not overcrowded, display of greenery. Here, the point of interest is the tallest plant, which is correctly proportioned for the bowl, measuring several inches beneath the curving glass shoulders as indicated by the dotted line.

container until they form a layer one-third the height of the moss. Then, funnel a layer of charcoal over the drainage material and a layer of peat moss over the charcoal to keep the soil from filtering down into the drainage material.

The soil should be moist and finely textured enough to flow through the funnel and tube. A few taps with your hand will help keep it flowing. Fill the container up to the top of the moss with the appropriate soil mixture, using the blunt end of a dowel to push the soil into the container and pack it down.

Now for the plants. If your terrarium is to be viewed on all sides, plants must be arranged so that a point of interest is visible all

Before you assemble the plants inside your terrarium, you need to be aware of possible insect or disease problems. Obviously, only healthy-looking, disease-free plants should be selected in the first place, and any visible insects should be washed off thoroughly or picked off before planting. Plants procured from reliable growers are usually pest free, but slips taken from house plants and material you dig outdoors should be carefully inspected. Aphids, mealybugs, scale, slugs, red spider mites, whiteflies, spiders, crickets, springtails, sowbugs, centipedes, millipedes, daddy longlegs, and earthworms are some of the creatures that could damage or destroy your terrarium plants.

Aphids or mealybugs can be wiped out of bottle gardens with a few drops of rubbing alcohol on a cotton wad impaled on the pruning wire. Better still, catch a ladybug or two and drop them into the container. Uncork the bottle when the job is finished so they can satisfy their appetites elsewhere. Slugs can be lured to the top of a bottle planter by soaking

Grooming: Use a razor blade and cork extended on dowels to remove dead leaves and to trim a plant that has grown too tall. The cork provides a solid surface for the razor to slice against. Any plant material that falls to the bottom can be pulled out with tongs.

the cork in beer. The pest control methods described in chapter 9 also can be used in terraria and dish gardens.

Using either a tablespoon or a pointed dowel, make holes in the soil where each plant is to go. Then, tap moistened root balls from their pots, trimming and molding so the base of each plant's stem is at soil level.

Push bottle-garden plants through the opening root first with the blunt end of a dowel pressing against the base of the plant. Plants are easier to place when they are weighted with some soil (firmed to the size of the opening). Tilting the bottle slightly will help direct plants and hold them upright until you can pack soil around their roots with the dowel.

Positioning the Plant: Wooden tongs are helpful when setting a healthy, pest-free plant into the prepared hole.

Bottle necks may become muddy during the planting process, but are easily wiped clean with a percolator brush or wire and a small piece of tissue.

After the plants are in place, fill in any gaps in the soil surface with small pieces of sheet moss, live sphagnum, or gravel accents tapped through the funnel and tube.

If you are interested in adding decorative accessories to your terrarium, this is the time to place them among the plants. It can be fun to hunt your own accessories. For the most natural effect, use stones of unusual shapes and sizes, snail shells, or bits of driftwood. Acorns, lichens, and pine cones are attractive

Cleaning: A wire form covered with tissue and attached to a dowel makes it easy to keep the sides of the glass free of smudges and dirt.

but should be avoided because they will mold unless displayed in open semidesert gardens or well-ventilated bowls. Nonceramic metal or plastic figurines and miniature garden ornaments also may mold unless coated with liquid plastic or clear nail polish.

In addition to being scaled to the miniature landscape, these decorative objects must be measured carefully so they will fit through the opening of the container. Figurines weighted by rubber cementing them to galvanized shingle nails drop readily into place and (with some prodding from a dowel) usually stand upright.

If you are using a fairly large container, planting procedures can be greatly simplified by setting the plants in place in their original pots and covering the pots with soil. This method offers the advantage of easier replacement of overgrown or ailing plants.

After planting, brush any loose soil from plant leaves with a small paint brush, and wipe smudges of dirt and bits of moss from the glass with the tissue and wire.

Unless soil and root balls are already moist, direct about a teaspoonful (5 ml) of water to the base of each plant through the funnel and tube. Retain this moisture in the container with a cork or a cover of glass or plastic that fits tightly enough to prevent evaporation.

If water droplets begin beading the inside glass in small patches within 24 hours, the self-contained rain cycle is functioning and further watering is unnecessary.

You may wish to set the new terrarium in a cool, shady place for a couple of days to allow it to make temperature and moisture adjustments. Then the container can be placed where it will receive bright light but no direct sun. Remember that tropical terraria need more light and higher temperatures than woodland or bog gardens. Watch the terrarium for a few days to make sure it is not too wet. If you notice a lot of condensation on the sides, remove the top and let the garden stand uncovered for a day to allow some of the water to evaporate. You can wipe the inside of the container if necessary. When the amount of moisture has stabilized and a slight haze is visible on the sides of the container, close the top.

TERRARIUM MAINTENANCE

Now that you have finished putting together your terrarium, do not make the mistake of thinking that it will never need any upkeep. When the plants become too large, they will need to be pruned or replaced with smaller ones. And do not forget to pick off any dead leaves. Leaves can be pruned by twisting stems and letting them dry enough to snap off. Extract the leaves from deep or narrow-necked containers with a hooked wire. Remove hopelessly overgrown and unwanted plants entirely, root first (with the hooked wire). You can vary the landscape by replacing an old plant with temporary flowering material or seasonal figurines, or you can substitute a new plant.

It is not advisable to fertilize a terrarium because the plants would quickly outgrow the container. Also, the soluble salts in the fertilizer would be unable to drain off, and could cause serious damage to the plants.

The right light exposure and temperature will help maintain the proper moisture balance. Most terrarium plants do best when temperatures are in the range of 60° to 70°F (16° to 21°C) during the day and 55° to 65°C (13° to 18°C) at night. Nine to 16 hours of indirect light from the north or northeast each day is sufficient for most tropical and woodland gardens.

African violets and other flowering plants, however, will benefit from some filtered sunlight or additional exposure to artificial light. Desert gardens and carnivorous bog plants need a little direct sunlight each day.

If there is not enough light, the plants can become spindly and susceptible to fungus attack. When window light is unevenly distributed, give the container an occasional turn so plants continue to grow straight.

When your environmental conditions are not quite correct, signs of distress may become apparent to warn you of potential problems. If the foliage becomes brittle and the moss turns brown, the terrarium badly needs watering. In such a case, water lightly, just enough to renew the moisture cycle.

On the other hand, overwatering encourages mold and leaf decay, a condition that can be corrected by uncovering the container until the excess moisture evaporates. Cloudy glass caused by sudden temperature fluctuation can be cleared by wiping or temporarily ventilating the container.

Semidesert gardens and other plants growing in partially open containers will require light weekly watering. Many species of cacti rest during the shorter days of winter, and less moisture is needed during this season. Some cacti should not be watered at all in winter, so it is important to become familiar with the needs of the individual plants you are growing.

You also may see stunted growth, yellowing of the leaves, or leaf drop in terrarium plants. For information on treating these symptoms, see the House Plant Clinic in chapter 9.

SOME SPECIAL USES FOR TERRARIA

After you have become adept at creating the basic types of terrarium and bottle garden environments, you may wish to put your glass gardens to some more interesting, unusual, and practical uses. Following are some ideas for making creative use of a terrarium.

VIVARIA: BOTH PLANTS AND ANIMALS

A terrarium complete with small, live animals is known as a vivarium. It provides an opportunity for indoor nature study and can

Dress Up a Terrarium with Sand Design

An attractive and easy way to accent your terrarium with a dash of color is to try your hand at sand designing. You can create geometric or free-form designs, seascapes, and landscapes with a bit of ingenuity and a few materials and tools.

The principle of sand designing is to invent colorful pictures by pouring variously colored layers of sand on top of one another in various thicknesses, sometimes mixing them with tools to create special effects.

You will need:

Colored, fine-grained sand, and covered jars to store it in

Small containers for the sand you are working with

Bent iced tea spoon

Small paint brush

Knitting needles of various sizes

Glass container for terrarium

Turntable such as a modeling wheel or lazy Susan

Masking tape

Funnel and plastic tubing

Wax or paraffin

Pour the colors of sand that you want to use from the covered

Layering Sand: A funnel and attached plastic straw direct the flow of colored sand into the container placed on a turntable for easy access to all sides.

jars into the smaller containers for easier use during your sand designing. Make sure the glass container for your terrarium is clean and dry before you begin.

The geometric design is the easiest type to start with if you are a beginning sand designer. Place your terrarium container in the center of the modeling wheel and turn it around as you spoon or pour with the funnel and tubing your first color of sand so that you have an even level of sand all the way around. If you find it difficult to make an

even line, put a piece of masking tape around the container so that you can line up your sand with it. Continue to spoon on different colored layers of sand, punctuating them with jabs of the knitting needles as your artistic taste dictates. You can create a scalloped, rolling pattern

Designing: Pressing the tip of a knitting needle through one layer of sand into another layer allows the top color to trickle down and create an attractive pattern. When removing the needle, pull it back toward the center away from the side, instead of pulling straight up and out of the sand. This avoids dislodging the sand against the front surface and keeps the pattern edges neat.

be a source of endless fascination for adults and children alike.

Tailor the type of animal you use to the environment of your terrarium — desert creatures will thrive best in a desert situation, and woodland animals will do best where

there is more moisture. Do not be afraid to give your animals space. Remember that even though you are dealing with a terrarium, the creatures need a container that is large enough for their comfort. A small pond can be made from a dish or cup sunk into the by varying the thickness of the sand layers, allowing the sand to pile up at some places, and keeping it thinner at others.

Free-form designs are just what their name implies—unplanned, spontaneous creations. Spoon the sand into the container as you choose, and experiment until you are happy with the results.

Seascapes and landscapes are more complex than the geometric and free-form designs. With

they do not turn out well, use the paint brush to sweep that bit of color out of the way toward the center of the container. Experimentation and patience will develop your skill at sand designing.

After you have completed your design, carefully pour hot wax or melted paraffin over the top of the sand, making sure it is completely covered. After the wax cools, you are ready to assemble a terrarium on top.

Protecting Your Sand Design: When the design is complete, pour a small amount of melted paraffin on top. This hardened layer will serve as a base for the terrarium substrate and prevent the sand from being disturbed when you water and groom the plants.

practice, you can learn to arrange the sand with your bent spoon to form mountains, water, sky, and other features around the outside of the container, making sure that you continue the color in a layer across the inside to lend stability to the uneven designs. Birds, grass, and other small decorations can be formed with small jabs of a knitting needle into the sand against the walls of the container. If

Cleaning and Repairing: A paint brush can be used to whisk away sand particles on the front surface or to sweep away part of the pattern that you want to try again.

The Finished Terrarium: The colorful free-form sand pattern combines with the attractively arranged plants to create an eye-catching display.

soil mixture, and food can be obtained from a pet store.

A desert garden might provide a home for Texas spiny lizards, fence lizards, horned toads, Mediterranean geckoes, or gopher tortoises. Woodland gardens can accommodate American chameleons, Texas spiny lizards, Mediterranean geckoes, Eastern glass lizards, salamanders, toads, frogs, turtles, newts, and brightly colored insects. Tree frogs, toads, salamanders, newts, and mud turtles will do well in a bog situation. As many of these

Vivarium: Small toads thrive in the environments provided by woodland and bog terraria. In addition to the plants, be sure to include a small body of water and a rock or piece of wood on which the toad can bask.

creatures enjoy a basking place, provide a rock, driftwood log, or sturdy-branched small tree for them to climb on.

A STARTING GREENHOUSE

You also can use a terrarium as a miniature greenhouse or nursery to start flowers, foliage plants, and vegetables from seeds and cuttings any time of the year. To start plants from seeds, cover the bottom of your terrarium with moist pebbles and set small flats of finely ground, moist peat moss on top. Soak the seeds in water for 12 hours before you plant them in a furrow made with a pencil. Small seeds can be sown on the surface of the soil, while larger ones should be covered with soil to twice the depth of their diameter.

Since the peat mixture is moist when you plant the seeds and you will cover the terrarium immediately afterward, watering is not necessary until the seedlings sprout. If you give them too little water, they will become spindly or die, and if you water them too heavily, they will become susceptible to fungus and may rot. When the seeds sprout, uncover the terrarium for ventilation, and

give them as much light as is available (without direct sun). The seedlings will instinctively grow toward the light, so rotate the terrarium frequently to prevent them from becoming bent.

If you have saved some of last year's garden seeds and wonder if they are still viable, you can plant a number of them in a terrarium to see whether or not they will grow. Carefully labeling each kind, spread seeds thinly over the top of the thoroughly moistened, firmly packed shredded sphagnum. Depending on the type of seeds, some will respond more quickly to darkness than light. See chapter 8 for further information. Seed testing saves time and disappointment when you are starting a garden.

Another nonornamental use for your terrarium is as a nursery for propagating plants by cuttings. Detailed information on cuttings is available in chapter 8.

A TRAVEL CASE FOR PLANTS

Dr. Nathaniel Ward's nineteenth century discovery that plants travel well inside terraria can benefit you today. If you have occasion to move plants any distance, it is a good idea to keep them in a closed container instead of an open pot. They will withstand temperature and moisture fluctuations much better in an enclosed environment.

Expect some cloudiness on the glass from temperature variations (a temporary condition which can be prevented by uncovering the containers before moving them). Using tissues to cover loose gravel and insulate plants and ornaments against shock will help hold miniature landscapes in place during transit. Bottle gardens travel well in sectioned cardboard liquor boxes; multi-gallon/multi-liter planters can be transported in metal milk bottle cases.

Similarly, an instant terrarium made from a closed plastic bag makes a good plant sitter when you are away on vacation. Just be sure the bag is large enough to permit exchange of oxygen and carbon dioxide, and prop it up with pencils or chopsticks to keep it from collapsing.

ORNAMENTAL DISH GARDENS

Dish gardens differ from terraria in that the plants are grown in open, flat containers fully exposed to conditions of the surrounding atmosphere instead of being enclosed.

Dish gardens are usually grown in containers from two to four inches (5 to 10 cm) deep. Any container will do, but the more interesting a dish you have, the further ahead you are toward an attractive dish garden. Always remember that you should gear your choice of plants to the type of container you have. For example, larger, bold-leaved plants should be grown in solid, heavy containers, while soft, delicately shaped plants such as ferns or miniature roses look better grown in appropriately fragile or delicate bowls or cups.

DISH GARDEN ENVIRONMENTS

Like terraria, different kinds of dish gardens with tropical, woodland, oriental, or desert plants need their own specific soil mixtures and amounts of moisture in order to grow successfully.

The basic formulas for dish garden soil mixtures are the same as for corresponding terrarium mixtures; use the woodland terrarium mix for both woodland and oriental dish gardens, and the tropical terrarium mix for tropical dish gardens. A desert or semidesert dish garden will need more sand, specifically:

3 parts sandy soil

2 parts humus

1 part perlite

1 part charcoal

1 part grit (very coarse sand)

If you are planning to grow orchids and bromeliads, particularly epiphytic species, you may have best results if you forget about the soil mixtures and simply use fir or osmunda bark.

The needs of the tropical garden are similar to those of the oriental and woodland gardens, except that the plants prefer temperatures of approximately 78°F (26°C) by day and 68°F (20°C) at night, slightly warmer than the other two. Only a few hours of bright, indirect sunlight are needed each day. Choose from one of the recommended tropical terrarium soil mixes.

Plants for a Tropical Dish Garden

Botanical Name	Common Name
Acorus gramineus 'Pusillus'	Grassy-leaved sweet flag, variegated grass
Anthurium scherzeranum	Flamingo flower, painter's palette, tailflower
Asplenium nidus	Bird's nest fern
Begonia	Small-leaved begonias
B. *aridicaulis*	
B. *dregei*	Grape leaf or maple leaf begonia
B. *dregei* 'Macbethii'	Dew drop or maple leaf begonia
B. *foliosa*	Fern leaf begonia
Carissa	
C. *grandiflora*	Natal plum
C. *grandiflora* 'Nana'	
Chamaedorea elegans	Neanthe bella, parlor palm
Cissus	
C. *antarctica* 'Minima'	Dwarf kangaroo ivy
C. *striata*	Miniature grape ivy
Cryptanthus	Earth stars
C. *bivittatus* 'Minor'	Dwarf rose-stripe earth star
C. *fosteranus*	
C. 'It'	
C. *zonatus* 'Moon River'	
Epipremnum aureum	Golden pothos
Exacum affine	Arabian violet, German violet
Ficus	
F. *pumila* 'Minima'	Dwarf creeping fig
F. *pumila* 'Quercifolia'	Oakleaf creeping fig

Botanical Name	Common Name
Fittonia verschaffeltii var. *argyroneura*	Nerve plant
Hedera helix cvs. (see Plants for Temperate and Woodland Terraria)	Miniature English ivies
Malpighia coccigera	Miniature holly
Maranta leuconeura var. *kerchoviana*	Prayer plant
Masdevallia spp.	Orchid
Oncidium pulchellum	Orchid
Oxalis	Lucky clover, shamrock plant
O. hedysaroides 'Rubra'	Fire fern, red flame
O. rosea	Old-fashioned shamrock oxalis
O. rubra 'Alba'	White-flowering shamrock oxalis
Pellaea rotundifolia	Button fern
Pilea depressa	Miniature pilea
Punica granatum 'Nana'	Dwarf pomegranate
Sansevieria trifasciata 'Hahnii'	Miniature snake plant
Saxifraga	
S. stolonifera	Strawberry begonia
S. stolonifera 'Tricolor'	Variegated strawberry begonia
Syngonium	Arrowhead vine, Nephthytis

The woodland dish garden is well suited to growing native plants, including grass and small trees, but they need to be species that can grow under lower moisture conditions than can be provided in the woodland terrarium. Average indoor temperatures (68° to 70°F/20° to 21°C by day, 60°F/16°C at night) are fine for a woodland garden that receives indirect, filtered sunlight and that maintains a relative humidity of approximately 50 percent. The soil mixture recommended for woodland terraria is also suitable for woodland dish gardens.

Plants for a Woodland Dish Garden

Botanical Name	Common Name
Ajuga reptans	Bugleweed
Asarum shuttleworthii	Wild ginger

Botanical Name	Common Name
Bryum argenteum	Silver moss, silvery thread moss
Buxus microphylla var. *japonica*	Japanese boxwood
Crocus kotschyanus	Crocus
Cyclamen hederifolium	Baby cyclamen
Dianthus barbatus	Sweet William
Dryopteris spp.	Wood ferns
Euonymus	Spindle tree
E. japonica 'Microphylla'	
E. japonica 'Variegata'	
Fragaria vesca 'Alpine'	Alpine strawberry
Gentiana farreri	Gentian
Hedera helix cvs. (see Plants for Temperate and Woodland Terraria)	Miniature English ivies
Juniperus communis 'Depressa'	Prostrate juniper
Narcissus 'February Gold' (and other miniature cvs.)	Miniature narcissus
Oxalis acetosella	Irish shamrock, white wood sorrel
Polypodium virginianum	Rock cap fern
Polystichum	Shield fern
P. acrostichoides	Christmas fern
P. tsus-simense	
Primula vulgaris	English primrose
Rhododendron, kureme hybrids	Azaleas
Saxifraga virginiensis	Early saxifrage
Selaginella kraussiana 'Brownii'	Dwarf club moss, Irish moss
Sisyrinchium spp.	Blue-eyed grass
Viola	Violet
V. affinis	Common blue violet
V. odorata	Garden violet, sweet violet
V. sororia	Confederate violet

The oriental garden is known for its simplicity and sparse beauty. All of the components must be in proportion, so plants, accessories, and the container must be chosen with great care. The oriental garden is characterized by its style rather than its environment. For best results, treat it as you would a woodland dish garden. Many kinds of plants can lend themselves to oriental gardens.

Plants for an Oriental Dish Garden

Botanical Name	Common Name
Acorus gramineus 'Pusillus'	Grassy-leaved sweet flag, variegated grass
Begonia dregei	Grape leaf or maple leaf begonia
Gasteria liliputana	Miniature gasteria, miniature ox-tongue
Juniperus	
J. chinensis 'Pfitzerana Compacta'	Compact Chinese juniper
J. chinensis var. sargentii	Japanese cushion juniper
Laelia pumila	Orchid
Picea orientalis	Oriental spruce
Punica granatum 'Nana'	Dwarf pomegranate
Sedum multiceps	Miniature Joshua tree
Tillandsia ionantha	Sky plant

If you find you enjoy the elegant simplicity of a basic oriental dish garden, you may wish to explore the ancient Japanese arts of *bonkei* and *saikei,* miniature tray landscapes. The aim is to create a tiny replica of nature by combining live plants with clay, colored sand, and other materials in a carefully molded landscape that re-creates and idealizes a natural scene.

In the Japanese home, the tiny landscape is usually displayed in the alcove *(tokonoma),* the place reserved for very valued items. The Japanese also hand-carry their landscapes to friends and relatives to wish them well. But the art of *bonkei* easily crosses cultural lines and can be equally at home on your dining room table or living room mantelpiece.

The desert dish garden is generally easy to maintain, and is well suited to the dry atmosphere that exists in many homes as a result of central heating systems. Give the garden bright light, and keep the soil mixture on the dry side, watering only when necessary. The unusual sculpturesque forms of many succulents make a well-planned desert dish garden an interesting addition to a room

environment. A wide variety of cacti and other succulents can be grown in open terraria and dish gardens.

Plants for a Desert Dish Garden

Botanical Name	Common Name
Adromischus	Calico hearts, leopard spots
A. alveolatus	
A. festivus	Plover eggs
A. maculatus	Calico hearts
Aloe	Medicine plant
A. aristata	Lace aloe
A. brevifolia	Short-leaved aloe
A. variegata	Partridge-breasted aloe
Astrophytum myriostigma	Bishop's cap
Cephalocereus nobilis	Cylinder cactus
Cereus peruvianus 'Monstrosus'	Curiosity plant
Crassula	Jade plant, silver dollar, string of buttons
C. cooperi	
C. lycopodioides	Toy cypress, watch chain cactus
C. rupestris	Rosary plant
Echeveria	Painted lady, plush plant
E. derenbergii	Painted lady
E. elegans	Mexican snowball
E. secunda var. glauca	Hen and chickens
Echinocactus grusonii	Golden barrel cactus
Echinocereus	Hedgehog cactus
E. pectinatus var. neomexicanus	Rainbow cactus
E. reichenbachii	Lace cactus
Epithelantha micromeris	Button cactus
Euphorbia lactea 'Cristata'	Crested euphorbia, frilled fan
Faucaria tigrina	Tiger's jaws
Gasteria liliputana	Miniature gasteria, miniature ox-tongue
Haworthia	Pearl plant, wart plant
H. angustifolia	
H. fasciata	Zebra haworthia
H. jonesiae	
H. margaritifera	Pearl plant
H. subfasciata	
H. tenera	
H. tessellata	
H. viscosa	
Lithops spp.	Living stones

(continued on page 582)

Make a Miniature Tray Landscape

Even though the arts of *bonkei* and *saikei* are not widely practiced in the West, most of the essential materials and tools can be found at any arts and crafts or department store. The tools you will need to create your landscape are spatulas, spoons, brushes, tweezers, a wedge, and a shallow tray.

The tray is usually 18 inches by 6 inches (46 cm by 15 cm) and no deeper than 1 inch (2.5 cm). Because water is almost always used in *bonkei* construction, the tray should be waterproof. The standard *bonkei* tray is round or oblong and should not compete with the landscape for attention.

Spatulas are used to smooth mountains, to apply thick pastes, and to build up surfaces. One medium size spatula will be sufficient for the beginner. When you are more advanced, you may want to purchase other sizes.

The wedge, called an *Ate-ita* in Japan, should be about 3½ inches (9 cm) wide. It is used for support when shaping *Keto* (a natural vegetable peat traditionally used in *bonkei*) or clay to form mountains or hills. The wedge can be made of plywood, plastic, metal, or even heavy cardboard, as long as it is rigid.

Spoons in two sizes are used to pour sand or remove excess water from the landscape. A bulb syringe is also handy to withdraw water.

Brushes in several sizes are employed to sweep away any unwanted clay or to paint hills and mountains.

A long pair of tweezers with a loose spring can be used time and time again to position trees, moss, and cuttings.

You also will want to have on hand a mister to keep the landscape fresh looking.

Keto is the material traditionally used to form mountains and hills in *bonkei*. Do not be disappointed if you are unable to purchase *Keto* in your area. An adequate substitute and one that is often used in Japan is a mixture of wet newspaper and clay. Tear old newspaper into strips and put them in a large pot. Pour boiling water over the paper and let it cool. When the paper has cooled, knead it to form a solid mass. Pour off any excess water. Add to this mass some dried clay, and mix until you have a pliable, doughy product. You also may want to experiment with different kinds of peat available at nurseries and plant stores. When the peat is mixed with water and kneaded, you may find a type that is elastic enough to use for the landscape. Furnace cement is another possible substitute.

The Japanese also use several types of dried powders, all in neutral earthy colors to suggest lifelike mountains, soil, and rocks. Powders and dry paints can be purchased in arts and crafts stores.

Dried and fresh moss and small plants or cuttings will be used often in the landscape. Cuttings can be obtained from your house plant collection, and moss can be purchased from most nurseries.

Miniature ornaments such as small houses, bridges, and animals may be used to complete the landscape. These can be purchased at an arts and crafts store, or you can be really creative and make your own from flexible wood or other materials.

Rocks, pebbles, and small seashells also add a lifelike appearance to the tray landscape.

Before you assemble any of the tools necessary to create your *bonkei,* it is important to select a theme. If you are a beginner, it would be wise to start with a simple landscape and one that is familiar to you. For instance, you could start with a scene from the mountains or the seashore or a hilly area near your home. When you have a clear idea of what you want your *bonkei* to represent, make a rough sketch on plain paper. Now study the sketch to determine near, middle-distance, and far-distance areas. If your sketch is of mountains, for example, your near area might be a valley, your middle-distance area would be the foothills, and your far area would be the snow-capped peaks. It is important to figure out these three areas because *bonkei* by custom is three-dimensional with clear distinctions. You also might want to make paper cutouts of the landscape features you want to represent and arrange them on the shallow tray, keeping in mind the three spatial areas.

Now you are ready to begin modeling the clay mixture or peat to resemble your picture or sketch. Use the wedge for support as you shape with the spatula. Start with the tallest point of interest, which will predominate and be the focal point of your landscape. Never place the tallest point in the middle of the tray, or you will risk splitting the landscape in half and losing the harmony of your finished *bonkei*. For best results, position the tallest point off center, to either the right or left.

After the tallest point has been created on the tray, begin working with the adjacent areas, remembering that symmetry, proportion, and perspective are vitally important in creating the image.

If water will be represented in the landscape, begin by molding waves, ripples, or waterfalls from clay or peat to achieve the desired effect. Then completely cover the clay with blue sand to represent the water. If the water is to be peaceful and still, pour the blue sand directly on the tray and water it well. Shake the tray so the sand is smooth. Remove any surface water with the bulb syringe or kitchen spoon. White or beige sand can be used to create foam-capped waves or waterfalls.

Remember that the landscape should suggest its season by its colors and textures. For instance, late fall and winter scenes might have snow-capped peaks, fading grass, bare trees, and swollen rivers. Spring and early summer can be suggested with flowers in full bloom and thick moss.

The last step is to cover the clay or peat mountains with fresh and dried moss. Set the living grass, miniature trees, or plant cuttings in place. It is a good idea to wrap the roots of miniature trees and plants in wet newspaper before incorporating them in the *bonkei*. Cover them with a layer of soil for protection. Add any ornaments, but remember that too many will clutter the landscape and make it appear artificial.

It is oriental custom to title a *bonkei*. However, making the title too specific may invite unnecessary comparisons. If, for instance, your landscape represents the Rocky Mountains, "A Mountain Range" is an adequate title.

Place your tray landscape where it can be viewed and enjoyed. Mist it often to retain its freshness and trim or replace plant cuttings when necessary.

A Seascape: As an example of the versatility of *bonkei*, here the Japanese art form translates into a scene at the shore. Near, middle, and far distances are represented respectively by the waves and beach, lighthouse compound, and hills. To enhance the harmony of the whole arrangement, the lighthouse, as the tallest point, has been set off-center to the right. In such a scene, a variety of colors can be featured, ranging from blue to white to green to brown. An assortment of textures can be employed also, from gritty sand through rough wood to smooth rock. Interspersed throughout are miniature plants, adding a touch of greenery.

Botanical Name	Common Name
Mammillaria	Pincushion cactus, powder puff cactus
M. bocasana	Powder puff cactus
M. compressa	
M. elongata	Golden star cactus
M. fragilis	Thimble cactus
M. fragilis 'Minima'	
M. heyderi	Coral cactus
M. hutchisoniana	
Opuntia	Beavertail, bunny ears, prickly pear cactus
O. erectoclada	Dominoes, pincushion cactus
O. humifusa var. *austrina*	
O. microdasys	Bunny ears
O. vilis	Dwarf tree opuntia
Portulacaria	
P. afra	Elephant bush
P. afra 'Variegata'	Rainbow bush

Botanical Name	Common Name
Rebutia	Crown cactus
R. kupperana	Scarlet crown cactus
R. minuscula	Red crown cactus
Rhipsalidopsis rosea	Brazilian cactus
Sedum	Stonecrop
S. acre	Golden carpet, gold moss
S. adolphi	Golden sedum
S. dasyphyllum	Golden glow
S. lineare 'Variegatum'	Carpet sedum
S. morganianum	Burro's tail
S. multiceps	Miniature Joshua tree
S. pachyphyllum	Jelly beans
S. ×*rubrotinctum*	Christmas cheer
S. stahlii	Coral beads
Sempervivum	Hen and chicks, houseleek
S. arachnoideum	Cobweb houseleek
S. tectorum var. *calcareum*	Hen and chicks

A semidesert environment calls for a bit less light and slightly more moisture than a desert garden. Because air circulation is important, these conditions are best created in a dish garden or a terrarium that is left uncovered part of the time.

To add ground cover and fill in gaps between plants in a semiarid garden, you can use pincushion moss (*Leucobryum glaucum*) or other mosses and lichens that can withstand some dryness.

Plants for a Semidesert Dish Garden

Botanical Name	Common Name
Ceropegia	
C. barkleyi	Umbrella flower
C. woodii	Rosary vine
Crassula	
C. argentea	Jade plant
C. argentea var. *variegata*	Rainbow jade
Epiphyllum spp.	Orchid cacti
Euphorbia milii	Dwarf crown of thorns
Hoya bella	Miniature wax plant
Kalanchoe	
K. blossfeldiana 'Tom Thumb'	
K. eriophylla	Angora plant
K. ×'Houghtonii'	Coconut plant, palm trees
K. pinnata	Air plant
K. tomentosa	Panda plant

Desert Dish Garden: The cacti and succulents shown here are compatible in a dish garden, for they all need plenty of light, little moisture, and low humidity.

Botanical Name	Common Name
Schlumbergera spp.	Christmas cactus, Thanksgiving cactus
Senecio	
S. herreianus	Gooseberry plant
S. mikanioides	German or parlor ivy
S. rowleyanus	String of beads
Stapelia decaryil	Miniature starfish flower

ASSEMBLING A DISH GARDEN

After you have selected a dish garden container, pour in the appropriate soil mixture, creating hills and valleys for interest. The soil and drainage material should fill no more than a quarter of the container. Dig small holes for the plants and make sure their roots are well covered with soil mix. As in a well-designed terrarium, there should be a central focal point in every dish garden that attracts attention through color, texture, or shape. When the plants are in place, you can sprinkle aquarium gravel, small pebbles, or pieces of lichen on top of the sand for decoration.

DISH GARDEN MAINTENANCE

It is necessary to add water regularly to your dish garden since it is open and moisture will evaporate from the soil. Desert gardens should be kept on the dry side, but the tropical, woodland, and oriental gardens should be evenly moist. As they grow, you may have to prune the plants, or eventually replace them with smaller ones if they become too large for the container.

CHAPTER 27

Indoor Gardens: Garden Rooms, Solaria, Atria, and Skylights

Even a few plants haphazardly lined up on a windowsill can bring cheer to a room, but a carefully designed indoor garden can become the heart of a home, magnetically drawing occupants and guests alike into close proximity to its quiet vitality for relaxing conversation, an *al fresco* meal, or moments of delicious solitude. Aesthetically, masses of greenery and flowers unified by built-in or movable beds will look far better than an assortment of disparate pots; such a garden can add warmth to a formal room and soften the hard, angular lines of contemporary furniture.

Integrating plants into living space to an extent that a traditional greenhouse cannot, indoor gardens are also less expensive to create (and often to maintain) while offering the same advantage of organizing plants in one place so that watering, pruning, and other plant-keeping tasks become easier. Like greenhouses, indoor groupings are beneficial to plants, for a canopy of plant foliage coupled with moist peat packed around pots, or layers of moist pebbles or sand, will create a humid microclimate in which moist air lingers around the plants instead of rising promptly to the ceiling as it is warmed. The people living around this green oasis in a once-dry home also will reap the benefits of healthfully increased humidity — and the added moisture will enable them to live more comfortably with the thermostat turned back. Moreover, higher levels of oxygen and of refreshing negative ions are created by masses of plants. An indoor garden also can help to remove pollutants from the air.

Spotlighted Garden Bed: A minimum outlay of cash and a minimum investment in time yielded maximum impact with the creation of this informal tropical scene. Tucked away in an unused corner of the living room is a grouping of foliage plants, set at various heights for an effective composition. Included in this bed are a dracaena, monstera, rubber tree, and Boston fern.

Aesthetic pleasure and a heightened sense of well-being can be yours whether your garden is a simple grouping of potted plants created at little or no extra cost, a delightful bonus obtained by enclosing or remodeling a little-used area to create more living space, or the dominant feature of a cus-

Opposite, garden room with orchids, begonias, ferns, fruiting citrus, and other plants.

Light Box Show Garden: This elegant show garden was designed especially to fit into an entryway nook. The backdrop is a wooden frame housing fluorescent bulbs, covered with light-diffusing material. In front of the box is a low-lying movable planter made of oak and lined with a metal tray. A layer of pebbles forms the base into which individually potted plants are set, and a piece of driftwood is included as a roost for an epiphytic orchid and bromeliad.

tom-built home or addition. Easiest of all, and surprisingly effective, is to meld randomly placed plants into an imposing formal garden simply by bringing them together on a slightly raised platform of brick, slate, or tile. Such an indoor terrace is particularly effective if placed in the geometric shapes of light cast by sliding glass doors or a bay window, or in an entryway area that can be artificially lit. The platform doesn't even need to be mortared together, although it should be constructed upon a layer of thick plastic to protect the floor. The sides of this floor covering should be curved upward between the outermost and adjacent rows of the material used. Bricks are particularly attractive and may be laid down in a host of easily changed

patterns. About 4½ bricks will be needed per square foot (0.09 sq m) of platform; designs in which the bricks are not parallel and directly lined up require some half-bricks.

Also relatively simple to construct are gardens in which plants are direct-planted or placed as individually potted specimens in built-in or movable beds, which function as a unifying frame. These may be boxes, troughs, planters — or even raised benches as described in chapter 29. The containers should be leakproof, large enough to hold a good number of plants, and deep enough to conceal pots (or, more craftily, vases holding cut flowers to be used as seasonal accents). For convenience, good air circulation, and insurance against mildew, these units should be mounted on casters if they are not built in. They can look first-rate by a window-wall, under a skylight, as a floodlit welcome garden inside an entrance, or as holders for climbing foliage plants comprising a wall garden. Such setups also can be placed atop blocks on a radiator top (where damp pebbles and frequent misting during the heating season will be needed for all but cacti and other succulents), or used to divide living areas in large rooms or between adjoining rooms. Beds built into even small alcoves such as the space between a bathtub and a window also can create an effect out of proportion to their size.

Indoor gardeners with more money and space to spare can fashion more all-encompassing green retreats. One possibility is a garden room. Sometimes called an indoor-outdoor room or a Florida or plant room, such a structure is a place where plants complement family activities. Lower in humidity than a greenhouse, the garden room is not so crowded with plants, for it favors the needs of people, offering a more or less Mediterranean climate throughout the year. Garden rooms are enclosed and attached to the house; one may be designed into a house when it is built or added later. Usually at ground level, garden rooms also may be erected on a broad

Cactus Garden: These movable beds, made watertight and filled with vermiculite, are positioned to receive optimum sun beneath north-facing skylights. Each cactus pot is buried in the vermiculite, and the desertlike mood is further enhanced by a scattering of rocks on the surface.

balcony or flat roof if building codes permit.

Although these plant rooms have some glass (or plastic) in their walls and ceilings, they have less of this than a greenhouse in order to prevent excessive heat gain in summer and extensive heat loss in winter. Often about 40 to 50 percent of the ceiling admits light, allowing for enough illumination to grow almost any kind of plant. Ideally, garden rooms are well insulated so that supplemental heat is needed only in the winter. They feature an adequate ventilation system, a floor that cannot be damaged by water, and some provision for drainage. Materials are mostly natural (wood, brick, stone, and so forth), and there is space for furniture, which is made of bamboo or wicker, or is otherwise resistant to dampness. Usually there are elec-

trical outlets and a sink, or at least a faucet or hose bib.

Locations for garden rooms are many. Some possibilities are to enclose a deck or a patio or remodel a garage; an often practical option is to put a garden room between the house and the garage. With some imagination, spacious bathrooms can be converted into magnificent garden rooms. Garden rooms — or at any rate, alcoves — also can flourish in such apparently unlikely locations as a stair tower, which can be effectively enlarged by the use of deep casements and shelves. Then there are other additions of various kinds — a curved bay, for example, built with or without a foundation.

Although a converted screened or unscreened sun porch may lack one or more of

Garden Room: Design a room like this and you, too, can step into a garden of heavenly scents and gorgeous colors, even during the deepest, darkest days of winter. Differing in form and function from a greenhouse, this room seeks to integrate human activity with the growing of plants in an environment comfortable to both.

the defining features of a garden room, it is by far the most realistic place for one in many dwellings — particularly if the porch has a southern exposure and if a wide doorway links it to the house. The screened or open sides of the porch can be covered temporarily or replaced permanently by glass or plastic panels, or even by window greenhouses, and additional light provided by a skylight. Built-in or movable beds or benches may then be added. Such a porch may be left unheated in many climates and, with a minimum of concern about insects and maintaining sufficient humidity, may be used to grow a wide array of flowering plants that take temperatures down into the 40s. In colder regions a bright but unheated enclosed porch makes an excellent garden site for hardy evergreen shrubs or for spring-flowering ones that will bloom early there. Intermediate-temperature plants can often be grown on a sun porch with the benefit of only a small supplemental heat source if the porch opens

into a heated area or if nighttime insulation is used.

Unlike the garden room, a solarium is usually on the top floor or an upper floor of a house and is primarily for plants. Traditionally the solarium has an all-glass roof, but in contemporary versions often only part of the ceiling admits light; the walls, however, are largely of glass to provide the day-long flood of bright light that characterizes solaria and makes them suitable for flowering plants requiring the highest levels of illumination. Almost like a greenhouse in the home, the solarium must have provisions for excellent air circulation and a relatively high humidity to complement the intense light. Ideal temperatures there are a maximum of 85° to 90°F (30° to 32°C) during the day and a minimum of 65° to 70°F (18° to 21°C) at night.

Although a solarium may be added to a home or condominium, an atrium is virtually always part of the original design. The Latin word *atrium* means central court, and this version of the indoor garden is usually at the center, or hub, of the house, dividing a single large room into several separate living areas. Usually a square or rectangle surrounded by glass walls that allow it to be viewed from adjacent rooms, the atrium is lit from above through skylights or a ceiling of fiberglass or another material admitting ample light. It can, however, be open to the elements from above, although this perforce narrows the selection of plants that can be grown in hot or cold climates and restricts the use of the atrium as a comfortable and weatherproof passageway from one room to another.

Intended to be the focal point of the home, an atrium should have especially attractive flooring and be furnished with well-groomed plants trained into tree shapes (standards) and otherwise dignified and compactly formed topiary or specimen plants. These should be displayed in ornamental containers and selected and arranged to create a restrained, somewhat subdued and har-

Lush Tropical Atrium: This enchanting enclosed courtyard beckons you to enter and enjoy the bath of sunlight pouring in from above. The tranquility of the scene is enhanced by stately palms arching overhead and other tropical plants scattered on ground level.

monious effect that is rather formal. Ample space should be left for strolling.

SITING THE INDOOR GARDEN

An indoor greenery should be centrally placed so it becomes an integral part of home life and invites the involvement of all family members in its care. Bringing pleasure and relaxation to home dwellers as they go about their daily routines, it should also be a place to linger and feel closer to the natural world — a happy reminder of woods and fields or perhaps of the elegant formal gardens, or desert landscapes or jungle habitats of one's fantasies.

In addition to taking into account the life-styles and comfort of a home's occupants, the siting of a garden must reflect such realities as plant growth requirements and the need to conserve energy.

A most critical factor influencing how

bright and how warm your garden will be is its position relative to the sun. Ideally, it should have an exposure that takes optimum advantage of the sun in winter; this would be south to southeast or southwest in a cold climate (assuming some overhang or shading is available for protection from the hot summer sun); and east to northeast in a warm climate where much light is reflected, such as a home in the desert or one in the South surrounded with light-colored pavement. Nevertheless, indoor gardens can thrive even in northern exposures if techniques are used to optimize natural light or if low-light plants are selected (see chapters 2 and 30 for specifics on these options) or if artificial lighting is employed (see chapter 25). Given this fact, if there are several possible locations for a garden, family habits and interests should be given considerable weight. A garden room off a living room can be wonderful, but so can a green alcove in the kitchen, or in the bathroom, or off a family room or bedroom.

PLANNING THE INDOOR GARDEN

In designing your green space, be practical and work with what you have, weighing the kind of environment you would ideally like to create against the conditions you can now offer. Then decide whether your budget will permit you to add any necessary light, flooring, ventilation, heat, and so forth; if not, change your design and settle for a less ambitious, perhaps smaller garden in the same location or perhaps in another, more feasible site that might be adapted more inexpensively.

Size is a key consideration. First, think carefully and realistically about how much time you can spend planting, watering, feeding, grooming, and otherwise caring for the greenery. Certainly it would be a mistake to construct a garden so big or complex that you can't keep it constantly tidy and fresh looking. Think also about how you want your garden to function in your life. Gardens opening off kitchens or bathrooms, for example, are intended mostly for viewing and can be tucked into relatively shallow alcoves and watered easily by hand. On the other hand, a garden room off the dining room or living room in which you plan to dine and relax and entertain must be adequately sized to nurture both people and plants without crowding either; for true comfort, such a garden should measure at least 16 by 20 feet (4.8 by 6.1 m). If your garden is to be on an upper floor, its weight should be taken into account when planning its size, for large plants in pots, planters, boxes, concrete beds, or what-have-you filled with moist soil can add up to an astonishing load.

Once you have decided on the suitable location and dimensions of your indoor garden, you must make some very specific choices as to the best ways to provide essentials such as light, heat, ventilation, and humidity, and the best materials to use given your tastes, purposes, and finances.

LIGHT

Natural light is about twice as effective as cool white fluorescents in facilitating plant growth. By providing about 160 footcandles of fluorescent light you would otherwise use, you can lower maintenance costs and make the garden more inviting by avoiding the somewhat unnatural and distracting effects associated with artificial illumination. According to Richard L. Gaines of the American Institute of Landscape Architects, interior landscapes should receive a minimum of 50 to 75 footcandles at ground level and about 150 footcandles five feet (1.5 m) above the ground for 10 to 12 hours per day. (Light levels at prospective garden sites can be measured with a camera or light meter as described in chapter 25.)

Obvious sources of natural light are windows or window-walls. Bear in mind that traditional windows are sized and placed to give a pleasant view of the outdoors and are not designed to bring much light to the room in general; light entering the bottom of the usual window will illuminate only a small area on the floor. On the other hand, long horizontal windows high in a wall, or vertical windows extended above the usual 80-inch (200 cm) height can allow light to penetrate to the very back of a room; if small in area these more light-efficient windows also can greatly reduce heat loss in winter.

One way to benefit from the advantage of relatively small windows set high in the wall is to install a clerestory, which is a high-rising structure punctuated by windows that because of their height let in a good deal of diffused light (and air, too, if desired).

If such a window is installed in the roof and is other than vertical in position, it becomes a skylight. Long associated with artists in garrets, for whom they were a necessity, skylights have a strong appeal, which seems based on an irresistible blend of practical and romantic considerations. Thomas Jefferson liked the idea of these windows to the sky so much that he had 14 of them installed at Monticello, and this design feature has never been more in vogue than it is today. Skylights are able to flood a room with natural light even on overcast days at no sacrifice of privacy. Eliminating the need for drapes or other light-hampering materials, they may be installed with a minimum of construction. Affording the luxury of a glimpse of blue sky, or of stars, or perhaps trees or hills, these light sources are supremely compatible with indoor gardens, highlighting their colors dramatically while offering the kind of ample, overhead light that encourages plants to grow straight up and compactly instead of leaning lankily toward light that is inadequate because it is one-directional.

Often used in attics, entry areas, bathrooms, and hallways, skylights can enhance any room you select as the site of your indoor garden. They can illuminate the garden of a

Letting the Sun Shine In: A skylight is just the thing to illuminate a room naturally, so that plants and people benefit. A well designed and installed fixture in no way interferes with the decor or use of the room, and the increased light level will be a boon to plants growing nearby.

converted porch beautifully and at the same time raise light levels in the formerly dim room adjoining the porch. In weighing where to position such a light source, keep in mind that it should be accessible for cleaning, repairing, and possibly also for opening and closing it or installing shading in the summer and putting up and taking down heat-conserving devices in the winter. An outdoor deciduous tree near a skylight also can be a plus, for it will help block hot summer sun while interfering little with weaker winter sun, and it can also provide an attractive vista. To allow a clearer view of trees or even nearby hills, a skylight should be located close to an outside wall. In any event, it should never be placed too high above the

garden area you intend to illuminate or light levels there at floor level will be too low; a distance of 10 to 14 feet (3 to 4.2 m) is considered best for good light. It also might be well to consider carefully before placing a skylight in a humid room such as the bathroom, for the natural moisture there coupled with that given off by an indoor garden will encourage condensation.

The best size for a skylight over a garden depends partially on factors such as how large the garden is to be, how much light the plants in it require, how much light is being transmitted by the glazing and how many layers of it are being used, and how reflective the walls of the room and of the light well (if there is one) are. As a rule of thumb, however, if the opening is 10 to 14 feet (3 to 4.2 m) above the floor, it should be sized at 7 percent of the floor area to be illuminated. Should there be frequent smog or cloudiness in the area, or if other factors related to the structure of the skylight limit the light entering, then the size of the opening should be increased to 10 percent of the floor area to compensate. If necessary, of course, two or three skylights may be used to brighten the whole of an average size room. (Before getting under way, however, be sure to determine whether you need a building permit, and check local building codes, which may limit the size of skylights, or require that there be a certain distance between them.)

The types of skylights are many indeed, and choices range from having a skylight custom made, to buying one of a host of prefabricated units, to making one. Skylights may be made of wired or tempered glass or of plastic. Usually acrylic, the plastic ones tend to be more airtight and watertight than glass skylights and are also easier to install. They are available in clear plastic (skylights of this material admit 85 to 92 percent of outdoor light versus the 22 percent coming through a window); in white translucent plastic (which reduces glare and diffuses light at ceiling level); and in various tints (which are most satis-

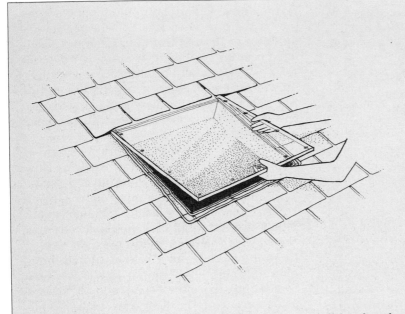

A Simple, Leakproof Skylight

An easy-to-make skylight has been designed by architect Alex Wade. Wade feels mounting a skylight on the traditional curb is an invitation to leakage. His has no curb and needs no flashing but is nonetheless leakproof. Installation is simplified in yet another way, for shingles and felt are not stripped off the roof beyond the perimeter of the skylight opening.

To make this skylight you will need a piece of clear, rigid plastic sized 4 inches (10 cm) larger all around than the perimeter of the roof opening. (Note: For this and other home-constructed plastic skylights, use plastic 3/16 inch/15 mm thick for units meauring over 9 square feet/ 1.9 sq m and 1/8 inch/13 mm thick for smaller ones.) The top of this rigid plastic is slipped under existing roofing just like a big shingle. The plastic is then sealed in place over the regular roofing around the sheet's sides and bottom with clear silicone caulking. It should then be secured with roundhead screws and washers spaced at 12-inch (30 cm) intervals around its perimeter and the screwheads subsequently sealed with silicone.

factory where light is very intense and must be moderated considerably). For indoor gardens, the bright light coming through clear plastic or glass is usually the most desirable, and such skylights should be placed somewhat closer together than those which diffuse light; maximum distance between them should be no more than half the height from the floor to the ceiling.

Regardless of the glazing material used, double glazing of some kind is important to discourage condensation from forming and help compensate for the insulation lost by removing roofing material. Ideally the air space between layers should be vented to the outside through small holes so the humidity in the air space is similar to that outdoors. The holes should not be large enough, however, to leak air. (Features like these can be seen on cross-sectional diagrams of the better prefabricated skylights.)

Skylights may be cut straight through a roof — the simplest kind in terms of installation time and cost — or may involve cutting through both a roof and a ceiling. In the latter situation a comparatively long light well or shaft is created between the skylight and the ceiling. That opening must be framed out and covered with wallboard, paneling, foil-faced foam, or burlap so it harmonizes with the room. A straight shaft is a possibility if the ceiling opening can be directly beneath the roof opening; if not, the shaft can be tilted so light enters at an angle. If possible the well should be angled outward as it descends so the opening into the skylit room is larger than that of the skylight itself; this will help reflect stray light downward and

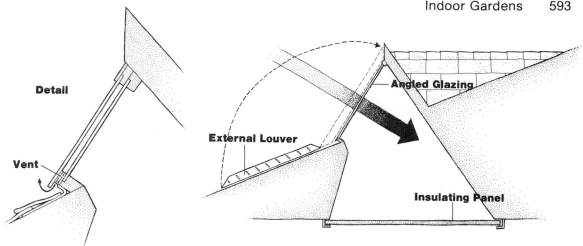

Detail

Vent

External Louver

Angled Glazing

Insulating Panel

Best Features for a Skylight: This cross section reveals features which can be incorporated for an efficient, problem-free skylight. An external louver can be opened in winter (as shown here) and closed in summer for protection from the sun. Angled glazing also helps capture as much of the winter sun as possible, while tempering the effects of intense summer sun. The movable insulating panel can be opened during the day but slid into place at night to reduce heat loss. Detail shows a vent in the air space between glazing layers which avoids condensation problems by insuring that the moisture content of the trapped air approximates that of the outdoors.

help compensate for hourly and seasonal changes in the position of the sun; it also will disperse light over a wider area and permit a view of the outdoors from more places in the room. To optimize light for plants and people, a light shaft should be painted white or a light color or covered with foil or perhaps light-colored burlap. If you should need to reduce light coming through the shaft in summer, you can place a transluscent, light-diffusing dome or panel where it intersects the ceiling of your plant room.

Skylights are of varied shapes. They can be simple squares or rectangles; these types are favored by do-it-yourselfers and often are mounted atop a frame (called a curb) and either caulked or surrounded by metal flashing to prevent leakage. Prefabricated skylights (sometimes self-flashing) usually come in frames, and may or may not require curbs; they may be flat topped, or rectangular or circular domes, or pyramid or dormer shaped.

These overhead windows can be installed horizontally or at a slope. Angled glazing is most desirable because it is self-cleaning and facilitates the runoff of precipitation and condensation. Just as importantly, a skylight angled fairly steeply from the horizontal

transmits more light and therefore more warmth in winter when the sun is low, and less burning light and unwelcome heat in summer when the sun is higher in the sky. For example, for optimum winter light and warmth, the best position for a skylight facing south at a latitude of 40°N would be an angle of 65° to the horizontal. (For a fuller discussion of how the angle of glazing affects

65°

Effective Angling: An angle 65 degrees to the horizontal is the ideal position for a south-facing skylight at 40°N latitude. This angling lets as much heat and light as possible enter in the winter, while lessening the effects of the strong summer sun.

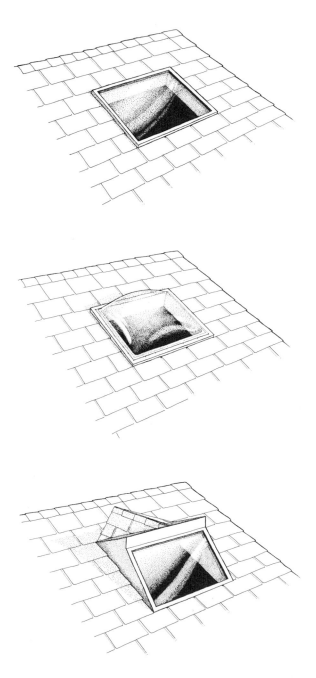

Skylight Shapes: These windows to the sky come in a variety of forms. Some examples given here, from top to bottom, are flat-topped, rectangular-domed, and dormer-shaped skylights.

light transmission, see Siting Your Greenhouse, in chapter 29.) Unfortunately, angling a skylight steeply on a shallowly sloped roof requires building a superstructure that makes the skylight that much more noticeable. To maintain a good view through a skylight when angling it to receive more winter light, the skylight should be enlarged, or the north wall of the light well should be cut deeper as the skylight is tilted upward, for visibility is best when the line of sight is perpendicular to the opening.

Skylights may be permanently closed or constructed so they open. The capability of opening slightly is particularly desirable in a hot climate, if the skylight is located at the top of a light well, or if the unit has louvers inside, since heat will get trapped between them and the glazing. If the open unit is screened and keeps out rain, it can be left that way all summer and will function as an excellent cooling and ventilating device for the garden room.

For garden rooms or other sizable garden areas, the best source of natural light may be a sun roof. This should be sloped to shrug off snow, leaves, or other light-blocking debris; a generous slope is particularly necessary if the roof is of corrugated fiberglass — otherwise condensation may drip into the garden room below. With so much light being admitted, heat buildup can pose problems — especially if the garden area faces south. Such setups require provisions for shading in the summer, and the use of fans, windows, or doors to ventilate hot air and promote cooling via air circulation. (For an evaluation of the various rigid plastics that may be used for a sun roof and suggestions on materials for shading, see Glazings, in chapter 29.)

HEAT

In many locales and situations, supplemental heating for an indoor garden is unnecessary. Temperatures on winter nights will dip lowest on sun porches or in other garden spots surrounded by large expanses of glass or plastic that is not double glazed and not insulated after dark. On the other hand, garden rooms warmed by adjoining house space and incorporating heat-conserving materials or measures may need little or no supplemental heat, even in a fairly rigorous climate, especially if the plants grown are coolness-loving types rather than heat-loving tropicals.

If extra heat is indicated, it can sometimes be provided by extending the home heating system or by using some of the passive or passive/active hybrid solar heating strategies outlined in chapter 29. If the garden is to involve new construction or extensive remodeling, other possibilities are to install radiant hot water heating in concrete overlaid by a slate, tile, brick, or other masonry floor. Water sprinkled on such a floor will raise the humidity quite pleasantly. It is also possible to run greenhouse-type pipes under windows, disguising them under slat-topped benches on which plants can rest. The heat supply can be controlled by a separate thermostat in the plant room. Other solutions that have worked for indoor gardeners are electric panels in the ceiling, a small gas-fired heater attached to roof beams, or a fireplace nearby. Oil heat is not a good idea for a garden area, for each gallon (3.8 l) of oil burned creates an equal amount of water vapor, and the unhappy result may be condensation drip that makes the garden site unpleasantly wet. (For more on heating options and on ways of conserving heat by providing night insulation, see chapter 29.)

VENTILATION, HUMIDITY, AND WATERING

Fresh, gently moving air is essential to an indoor garden. Plants should not, however, be exposed to frequent blasts of hot or cold air from open doors or windows or from the ducts of heating and cooling systems. Indoor plants are more sensitive to such climate changes than outdoor ones. Good air circula-

Passive Heating for an Indoor Garden: Just beyond this built-in garden bed you can glimpse the stacks of black, water-filled drums which serve as a thermal mass in this passively heated solar home. At night or during periods of cloud cover, the stored heat is slowly released to insure a comfortable temperature for both people and plants.

tion can be provided with such stylish devices as an old-fashioned ceiling fan and fostered by leaving space between plants and by elevating big plants on platforms or casters. Humidity, too, must be adequate — especially when light is intense and plants are growing rapidly. Indoor gardens geared to the comfort of people as well as plants are not kept as humid as greenhouses and floor areas need not be dampened. Nevertheless, a humidity of 40 to 50 percent should be maintained; in winter, this will be welcomed by those near the garden, for high humidity makes lower house temperatures seem more comfortable. Watering of modestly sized gardens can be done with a large watering or sprinkling can.

If the garden is large, cold water should be piped to a hose bib there. A small in-line heater can be installed, with a thermostatic control to moderate temperature.

MATERIALS TO USE

For practicality's sake, all parts of the garden area should be tolerant of humid conditions and resistant to water damage. Needless to say, all electrical outlets and fixtures should be waterproof. Masonry walls of rock or perhaps light-colored, underbaked brick are desirable, for they will absorb heat on sunny days and release it slowly when the sun goes down, and may be wetted down so they slowly release moisture for a sustained increase in humidity. Such walls also make a handsome display area for climbing plants lodged in a trough, box, or built-in bed, or for hanging plants suspended from hooks driven into the masonry. Other good choices for walls are panels made of rough-hewn cedar or of teak, cypress, or redwood, all of which offer natural good looks and hold up well under humid conditions. Pine protected with polyurethane varnish is another possibility. Ceilings should be of wood (preferably lacquered), plywood painted white, or plaster.

Floors in particular should be water- and stain-resistant and should not support the growth of fungus or mold, or buckle or warp with high humidity. Again, masonry is best. Poured concrete, concrete aggregate, or concrete brick will absorb and hold heat and may be provided with a built-in drain. Other good bets are flagstone or slate or earth-colored quarry tile, or brick laid on a layer of sand leveled over black tar paper. Concrete may be covered with vinyl tile or with cork tile sealed with polyurethane. If a wood floor is desired, teak is best because it repels water. Other woods should be sealed with a plastic finish. Less rugged floors can be protected from water by the use of watertight containers or plastic or glazed clay saucers. If a floor covering is wanted, best buys are plastic matting

Functional Flooring Material: For a garden room to be practical, it should have a floor that is waterproof, won't stain easily, and isn't prone to buckling or warping. The brick floor in this entrance garden is attractive, and at the same time can handle the demands of indoor gardening. In addition, it has the advantage of being heat retentive, an attractive feature during cool nights or cold spells.

or polypropylene carpet, for rush matting is likely to mildew in a humid garden area.

Garden space can be enclosed by a host of materials. Stainless steel is excellent, for it is permanent, nontoxic to plants, and is easy to clean. Interesting plant troughs may also be fashioned of 8 foot (2.4 m) long steel culvert. Copper also can be used, but it is softer and joints must be carefully soldered to be strong and hold their shape. Also, minerals in your water supply may cause salts to form around the edges. The commercial fiberglass boxes sold for outdoor pools can be used for indoor ponds or water gardens as well, and are obtainable from manufacturers of fountains or from places that sell aquatic plants. Also suitable for indoor garden pools are cattle troughs, which can be framed with wood or flagstone or built-in at ground level. (All of the foregoing materials can be cleaned with soap and water.)

Decorative portable beds might also be

Indoor Gardens for Special People

Indoor gardening can be a delightful shared experience for parents and children and a way of conveying values as well as knowledge and skills related to the natural world. Toddlers who watch plants change and grow can readily be taught that they are living things and helped to develop a caring, nurturing attitude. Interest and a sense of responsibility can be heightened by giving a child a small part of the garden — perhaps a single plant — to care for. Youngsters particularly enjoy water gardens (for they are usually fascinated by water), flowering plants, and performing plants such as carnivorous species and plants that respond to touch, as does the sensitive plant *(Mimosa pudica).*

Handicapped and elderly people often respond very positively to the quiet therapy provided by green and growing things, but they gain most from gardens that take into account their special needs. The blind will be most stimulated by gardens rich in tactile differences, where they can feel the varying textures of rocks, moss, sand, tree bark mounts, and leaves that are smooth, puckered, or downy. Fragrant plants will also be appreciated. Appealing scents can also add to the pleasure of a garden for the deaf, as will a variety of colors, and contrasting forms, textures, and growth habits that speak to the eyes.

For easy access, gardens for the physically or visually handicapped or the elderly should be waist-high to eliminate the need to bend. If people in wheelchairs are to work in them, the bottom of the raised beds should be at least 30 inches (76 cm) high and there should be knee space underneath so the gardeners can be right next to the plants. It is also possible to raise beds higher so they can be worked in comfortably at about elbow height by gardeners standing up. Special

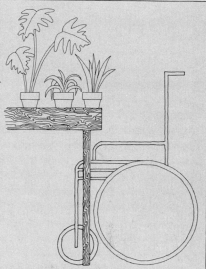

Gardening at Arms' Reach:
A raised garden bed allows for wheelchair access and places plants within easy reach.

people also appreciate bay window gardens and light gardens that concentrate plants in one easily accessible spot. For patients confined to a bed and wheelchair, a light garden can be installed in a bedroom closet or corner.

made of wood that is sealed and waterproofed, then stained or painted to match the room decor. These also can be lined with sheet metal trays. (For step-by-step directions for building such large planters, see Customized Planters, in chapter 28.)

Concrete beds are too weighty and immovable for some situations but can make handsome built-in gardens, as can brick. Loose particles may be scrubbed off with water and a brush. If the concrete or brick is very dirty it may be washed with a strong solution of vinegar and water.

Some of the most effective gardens are those planted directly into a recess in the floor holding drainage layers topped by deep soil — a possibility usually realized when the concrete foundation for a home is poured around the square or rectangle intended for the garden, or limited or even eliminated when an addition is constructed. After drainage layers are laid down but before they are topped with growing medium, the bed should be filled to one-fourth its depth with water to test drainage. If drainage is good, the water will be completely gone in half an hour. If it is not, it will be necessary either to loosen the compacted subsoil or to install drain tile before adding growing medium. (For more on providing drainage for direct-planted beds, see Ground Beds and Terraces, in chapter 29.)

CHAPTER 28

Window Gardens

For over a century window gardening has grown in popularity as people have left rural areas to seek employment in industrialized cities. With the decline of the old-fashioned notion that living plants rob oxygen from the human inhabitants of a room, and the introduction of evergreen tropical plants that adapt to indoor conditions, enthusiasm for window gardening has grown so rapidly that today almost every home has at least one potted plant on a windowsill.

Perhaps the appeal of window gardening lies in a basic need to work the soil, in the quiet therapy derived from caring for other living things, or in the pleasure and pride of watching a thriving window garden grow and bloom. Whatever the reason, this most basic of indoor gardening options is here to stay. It is hoped that this chapter will help you avoid some of its pitfalls and solve some of its most common problems, as well as select appropriate plants, and create an imaginative, eye-pleasing garden.

What is a window garden? Quite simply, it is plants growing in a window. Basically, there are two types of window gardens—the working garden and the show garden.

The functional working garden is not always beautiful, but it is necessary for growers who start seeds, propagate cuttings, experiment with unusual plants, and perform other fundamental tasks of gardening. The decorative show garden, on the other hand, functions as part of a room's decor. Show gardens are carefully planned and stocked with well-grown specimen plants to create a decorative addition to a room.

WINDOW EXPOSURES

Before you begin to make any plans for a window garden, it is wise to evaluate the in-tended window's exposure. The term exposure refers to several conditions; duration and intensity of light, temperature, and humidity are all variables that together make up a window's exposure. Determining that exposure is essential before suitable plant material may be selected.

Both the intensity and the duration of light are of prime importance to plant growth. Evaluating light exposure for a win-

Window Garden from the Past: Areas for window plantings used to be built with graceful conservatory windows, fountains, pools, and planters, creating a much more elaborate effect than is popular today.

Opposite, Aloe barbadensis *and other plants thrive in a south-facing window garden.*

dow can be difficult because light varies a great deal with the seasons and the latitude, and of course is affected also by altitude and by regional weather patterns. As a consequence, the average yearly percentage of possible sunshine varies tremendously from place to place. Here are the figures for a sampling of North American cities:

Quebec	45%
Vancouver	45%
Portland, Wash.	47%
Seattle	49%
Montreal	50%
Toronto	50%
Albany, N.Y.	53%
Detroit	54%
Winnipeg	55%
Chicago	57%
Houston	57%
Louisville	57%
Washington, D.C.	57%
Indianapolis	58%
Boston	59%
New Orleans	59%
New York City	59%
Atlanta	61%
Kansas City	64%
Miami	66%
San Francisco	67%
Denver	70%
Salt Lake City	70%
Los Angeles	73%
Phoenix	86%

Geographical location of your house aside, available light also is determined by the compass direction of the window in question. In addition, other circumstances will moderate the amount of light a window receives. Some of the variables to consider include curtains, shutters, or shades that are frequently closed; a large overhang, porch, or awnings outside the window; screens on the window; and nearby trees, shrubs, or buildings. On the other hand, bright reflective surfaces just around the window help increase the amount of light received by the plants. White stone mulches under house overhangs; solar panels or large convex reflector screens mounted outside; and white walls, mirrored surfaces, and Mylar wall coverings inside reflect much light to the windowsill area, while dark painted surfaces or wood paneling absorb much light.

The Light Evaluation Chart included here can help you calculate light exposure for any location, for it gives a point value to all the above-mentioned variables. By starting with the basic score determined by a window's compass direction, then adding or subtracting points for pertinent variables, you can rate each window you have on a number scale from one to ten. Next you can determine suitable species for that particular window by looking for the corresponding number in the Plant Selection Guide featured in this chapter.

An evaluation of two windows will illustrate the use of the chart and guide. Located where the average yearly percentage of sun is 56 percent, the first window faces south, is just four feet (1.2 m) wide and has no screens. A five-foot (1.5 m) overhang above a sidewalk is immediately outside and shades the window. Inside walls painted white and white linings on floral drapes serve as reflective surfaces. If one uses the Light Evaluation Chart, the window rates a 4, or is in the low-perfect range:

South window	+9
Bright, reflective surfaces (includes white walls and cement in walkway outside)	+1
5-foot (1.5 m) overhang (deduction of 2 points for each foot over 2 feet/0.6 m)	−6
(Total Value)	4

Light Evaluation Chart

10		
9	SOUTH	Provide for some shading
8	SSE - SSW	Provide for some shading
7	SE - SW	High perfect growing conditions
6	EAST	Near-perfect growing conditions
5	WEST	Near-perfect growing conditions
4	NW - NE	Low perfect growing conditions
3	NNW - NNE	Minimally acceptable growing conditions
2	NORTH	Minimally acceptable growing conditions
1		

After finding the number above that corresponds to the compass orientation of your window, add or subtract the appropriate number of points for the following variables. The final score will then express one of the growing conditions described above.

Small window (less than 3 ft./0.9 m wide) −1

Large window (more than 4 ft./1.2 m wide) +1

Extra large window (over 6 ft./1.8 m wide, but not a bay or corner window) +2

Bay window or corner window +2

Dirty window, city smog (deduct ½ point for each) Maximum of −1

Bright, white, or reflective surfaces either inside or outside the window (includes frequent or extended snow cover in winter or large cement areas outside) Maximum of +1

Dark surfaces around window inside the house (wood, dark paint or paper, drapes) or outside the house (do not deduct for usual surfaces such as grass, soil, or asphalt) Maximum of −1

Sheer curtains between plants and window −2

Screens on window −½

Shading trees or structures (other than a porch or roof overhang) outside window −1

Shade outside (deduct 1 point for dappled shade, 2 points for dense shade) Maximum of −2

Porch outside window (deduct 5 points for porch up to 6 feet/1.8 m deep and 6 points for porch 6 to 10 feet/1.8 to 3 m deep) Maximum of −6

Roof overhang or awning (a 2-foot/0.6 m overhang is normal, but for each foot over 2 feet/0.6 m deduct 2 points) Maximum of −6

Average yearly percentage of possible sunshine:
Check this for your locality with the local weather service and if it is:

46% or lower	−2
47-48-49%	−1½
50-51-52%	−1
53-54-55%	−½
56-57-58%	0
59-60-61%	+½
62-63-64%	+1
65-66-67%	+1½
68% or above	+2

(—deduct or add—)

To be successful, a garden in this window must have a selection of plant material that requires an equivalent level of light. According to the Plant Selection Guide, appropriate choices would be *Clivia, Hoya,* and *Neomarica* species, and *Ceropegia woodii,* for these plants can tolerate a light exposure of 4 and also share similar temperature and humidity requirements.

The second window is a bay window facing north which has no roof overhang and is unshaded by outdoor trees. Indoors the window is shaded by neither screens nor curtains, and the walls surrounding the window are painted white. In addition, the house is located where there is a reasonably high average percentage of sun (60 percent). It is also in a heavy snow area, and snow reflects light into the window from December to March.

While a northern exposure would seem to indicate a poor plant window, all the moderating factors combine to earn this window a 5½, which translates into near-perfect conditions for a good number of plants:

North window	+2
Bay window	+2
Bright, reflective surfaces (includes snow cover)	+1
Average yearly percentage of sunshine	+ ½
(Total Value)	5½

One good warm-growing grouping for this ex-

posure would be *Saintpaulia, Aeschynanthus,* and *Episcia* species, while a cooler window with the same light and low humidity could accommodate *Geranium* and *Aloe* species and *Euphorbia milii* var. *splendens.*

Evaluate the light quality of your windows with the help of the Light Evaluation Chart. The resultant number values will be a great aid in the selection of appropriate plants.

If it is more convenient, you can instead measure the amount of light coming in a window with an incidental-light meter. Such meters often express the amount of light in footcandles—or the instruction booklet supplies a formula for converting the reading into footcandles—and you can then select

Window #1 Facing South: Even though this is a southern exposure, usually considered ideal for a number of plants, the rating of this window is a low one (4) because of the overhang and curtains that serve to obstruct the sunlight.

Window #2 Facing North: This northern exposure earns a relatively high rating (5½) because of the bay window unobstructed by an overhang, curtains or screens, and unshaded by trees.

The Working Garden: Since its functions are mainly utilitarian, the working window garden is best located in a den or workroom away from the main family living areas. The working garden is a good place for attending to propagation chores, nursing weak plants, and bringing flowering plants into bloom for display elsewhere in the home.

Maximizing Light: To make the most of the light admitted by a dark or small window, use reflective surfaces such as white walls or mirrors to bounce more light back onto plants growing in a dim corner.

plants accordingly. It is also possible to use a camera with a built-in light meter for footcandle readings as described in Using a Camera to Measure Footcandles, in chapter 25. For a chart listing light needs of various plants in footcandles, see Optimum Light Intensities for Various Groups of Decorative Plants, in chapter 2.

It is possible to moderate a window's light exposure if it is not satisfactory. A window that is too bright can be shaded easily by adding sheer curtains, venetian blinds, shutters, or shades, and closing them during the brightest part of the day. Adding light to a window that is too dark is more difficult, although much can be done by removing curtains and other obstructing objects, or adding reflective surfaces inside the garden. Mirror tiles, Mylar wall coverings, or even aluminum foil placed on the walls facing the window or below the plants will reflect a great deal of light back on the plants. Using a plant spotlight or fluorescent fixtures to extend daylength and/or heighten the intensity of the natural light received is also a possibility. If supplied for four or five hours at sundown and during dark winter days, the additional light will aid the plants as well as spotlight the garden. (See chapters 25 and 29 for more information on using natural and artificial lighting.)

Evaluating a window for heat or cold is simple. Just take thermometer readings at several spots in the window area to identify the cold and warm areas. Some methods of avoiding problems during critical times such as summer heat waves and winter cold spells are suggested later in the chapter.

The ideal temperature for most indoor plants falls in the range of 60° to 80°F (16° to 27°C), with a 5° to 10°F (3° to 6°C) drop at night. Occasional cold or heat spells will cause temperatures outside this range, but most plants can adapt to these infrequent excesses. Fortunately, most windows provide acceptable temperatures for the balance of the year. If a window area is consis-

(continued on page 607)

Plant Selection Guide for Window Gardens

The following list of choice plants for window gardens has been compiled through practical experience, for all of them have been grown successfully in different windows and in different parts of the country under varying conditions. Most have proven tolerant and hardy given average care under average home conditions.

Those plants that deserve a star for service above and beyond the call of duty because of their decorativeness, ease of cultivation, and adaptability have been singled out with an asterisk (*). Plants that flourish in cool windows (that is, those that drop to 50°F/10°C at night) are indicated by a C, and those that are choice plants but temperamental (and therefore a challenge for green thumbs) are marked with an exclamation point (!).

Genera preferring a humidity of 35 percent or over are noted with a +H, and those tolerating a humidity of 20 percent or lower are identified with a −H. Plants not marked with +H or −H should be grown where the humidity is between 20 and 35 percent. The preferred light exposure range expressed in numbers derived from the Light Evaluation Chart is provided for each plant, and species are arranged alphabetically, according to the lowest number of their light ranges. Although some of the plants can adapt to more or less light, the range given will result in best growth. Of course, it is always possible to grow a plant liking low light in a bright window simply by placing that plant behind another or to the side of the window, where it will be shaded somewhat.

Light Exposure Numbers	Botanical Name	Common Name	Special Remarks
1-6	*Aglaonema* spp. and hybrids	Chinese evergreen; silver king; silver queen; pewter plant	*
1-6	*Aspidistra* spp.	Cast iron plant	*, C, −H
1-8	*Sansevieria* spp.	Snake plant, mother-in-law tongue	C, −H
2-5	*Peperomia obtusifolia* and *P. caperata*; others	Pepper plant; emerald ripple	
2-6	*Epipremnum aureum*	Devil's ivy	*, −H
2-6	*Schlumbergera bridgesii* and *S. truncata*	Christmas cactus; Thanksgiving or crab cactus	*, C
2-6	*Spathiphyllum* spp.	Spathe flower	!, +H
2-6	*Syngonium* spp.	Nephthytis, arrow plant	*
2-7	*Cissus rhombifolia* and *C. antarctica*	Grape ivy; kangaroo vine	*, C
2-7	*Dracaena deremensis* 'Warneckii'	Warneckii dracaena, striped dracaena	*
2-7	*D. fragrans* 'Massangeana'	Corn plant	*
2-7	*D. marginata*	Red margin dracaena	*
2-7	*Epiphyllum* spp.	Orchid cactus	
2-7	*Hedera helix* var.	Ivy	C, +H
2-7	*Philodendron* spp.	Philodendron	*
2-7	*Rhipsalidopsis gaertneri*	Easter cactus	C
2-8	*Asparagus setaceus* and *A. deflexus*	Plume asparagus; sprengeri or asparagus fern	*, C
2-8	Bromeliaceae: *Neoregelia carolinae* 'Tricolor', *Aechmea fulgens*; others	Blushing bromeliad; coralberry	
2-8	*Ficus benjamina*	Weeping fig	*
2-8	*F. elastica*	Rubber plant	
2-8	*F. lyrata*	Fiddleleaf fig	
2-8	*Rhoeo spathacea*	Moses in the cradle	*, C
2-9	*Beaucarnea recurvata*	Pony tail palm	*, C, −H
3-6	*Asplenium nidus*	Bird's nest fern	C, !, +H
3-6	*Begonia masoniana*	Iron cross begonia	!, +H
3-6	*Begonia* spp.	Angel wing begonias	
3-6	*Begonia* spp.	Rhizomatous begonias	!
3-6	*Cyrtomium falcatum*	Holly fern	C, !, +H
3-6	*Davallia fejeensis*	Rabbit's foot fern	C, !, +H

Light Exposure Numbers	Botanical Name	Common Name	Special Remarks
3-6	*Maranta leuconeura* var. *kerchoviana*	Prayer plant	
3-6	*Nephrolepis exaltata* 'Bostoniensis'	Boston fern	C, !, +H
3-6	*Platycerium bifurcatum*	Staghorn fern	!, +H
3-6	*Polypodium aureum*	Bear's foot fern	C, !, +H
3-6	*Tradescantia* spp.	Inch plant, others	C
3-6	*Zebrina* spp.	Wandering Jew	C
3-7	*Araucaria heterophylla*	Norfolk Island pine	C
3-7	*Chlorophytum* spp.	Spider plant, airplane plant	*, C, −H
3-7	*Crassula argentea*	Jade plant	C, −H
3-7	*Dieffenbachia* spp.	Dumbcane	
3-7	*Dracaena surculosa*	Gold dust dracaena	
3-7	*Hippeastrum* spp.	Amaryllis	C, −H
3-7	*Saxifraga stolonifera*	Strawberry begonia	C
3-8	*Brassaia actinophylla*	Schefflera, umbrella tree	C
3-8	*Dizygotheca elegantissima*	Thread-leaf false aralia	!
3-8	*Plectranthus* spp.	Swedish ivy	*, C
3-8	*Polyscias balfouriana*	Balfour aralia	!
3-8	*P. fruticosa*	Ming aralia	!
4-6	*Clivia* spp.	Kafir lily	C
4-6	*Hoya* spp.	Hindu rope; wax plant	C, −H
4-6	*Rhododendron* spp.	Azalea	C, !, +H
4-7	*Hemigraphis* spp.	Waffle plant	+H
4-7	*Nematanthus tropicana*	Goldfish vine	!, +H
4-7	*Neomarica* spp.	Apostle plant, walking iris	C
4-7	*Senecio rowleyanus*	String of pearls, bead cactus	C, !
4-8	*Ceropegia woodii*	Rosary vine, string of hearts	C
4-8	*Myrtus communis*	Myrtle	C, !
4-8	Palmae	Palms	C, +H
4-8	*Podocarpus* spp.	Buddhist pine	C
4-8	*Rosmarinus officinalis*	Rosemary	C, !, +H
4-9	Cactaceae	Cacti	*, C, −H
5-6	*Begonia cucullata* var. *hookeri*	Wax begonia	*, C
5-6	*Erodium chamaedryoides* 'Roseum'	Alpine geranium	!
5-6	*Oxalis regnelli*	Shamrock plant	C
5-6	*Paphiopedilum* spp.	Lady slipper orchids	!, +H
5-6	*Phalaenopsis* spp.	Moth orchids	!, +H
5-7	*Abutilon* spp.	Flowering maple	!, C
5-7	*Aeschynanthus* spp.	Lipstick vine	!, +H
5-7	*Episcia* spp.	Flame violet	!, +H
5-7	*Saintpaulia* spp.	African violet	!
5-8	*Aloe* spp.	Burn plant	C, −H
5-8	*Chrysanthemum* spp.		C
5-8	*Citrus* spp.	Calamondin orange; meyer lemon; others	C, +H
5-8	*Codiaeum* spp.	Croton	C, !
5-8	*Cyclamen* spp.		C, +H
5-8	*Cyperus alternifolius*	Umbrella plant, umbrella grass	C, !, +H
5-8	*Euphorbia milli* var. *splendens*	Crown of thorns	C, −H
5-8	*Impatiens* spp.	Every day bloomer, busy Lizzy	*, C
5-9	*Coleus* spp.	Coleus	*, C
5-9	*Echeveria* spp.	Desert rose; others	C
5-9	*Pelargonium* spp.	Geranium	C
5-9	*Sedum morganianum* and *S. lineare* 'Variegatum'	Burro's tail; variegated sedum	C
7-9	*Hibiscus* spp.		C, !

Build Your Own Cold Air Window Box

While attending a Cleveland chapter meeting of the Indoor Light Gardening Society of America, Inc., Wade and Edith Dill played a practical joke that turned into an even more practical idea. It seems the Dills had recently purchased a blooming cyclamen plant at a nursery. Being fun-loving people, they brought it along to show off at the meeting.

"We had pretty well fooled most of the members into believing we had grown the plant from seed," recalls Wade, "until an experienced (and therefore skeptical), member asked, 'How did you apartment dwellers get the 50°F (10°C) nighttime temperatures necessary to bloom cyclamens?!?'

"Well, the joke was over and we had to 'fess up'—but the incident got me to thinking and experimenting with ideas to provide cool conditions for plants without freezing out the other occupants of the room."

Wade is in the construction business, and his solution to the problem involves a variation of an energy-saving heating technique he has been promoting for factories—a strategy based on the fact that air in factories, apartments, and homes cools first near the outside walls and windows. Being heavier than the warmer air in the rest of the room, this cooled air drops down the windows and walls and rolls out on the floor. The usual result of this phenomenon is cold feet for occupants of the rooms. But, Wade reasoned, if this cold air could be trapped and held around plants that prefer "cold feet," the result should be vigorous, blooming specimens.

So Wade and Edith built a plywood shelf that rests on the east windowsill of their apartment living room and extends the sill area to make room for a sizable window garden. During the warm months of the year, this shelf garden holds the overflow of plants from their adjacent light garden. In autumn the shelf is enclosed by a three-sided structure to make a flower box.

Here are directions for constructing a version of the cold air box designed to fit an aluminum-framed apartment window. Adjust the dimensions as necessary to fit the window you choose.

Plants that do well in a cold air window box include azaleas, calceolarias, Christmas cacti, chrysanthemums, cinerarias, forced daffodils, hyacinths, and tulips, hydrangeas, primroses, and miniature roses. Many others are suggested in the Plant Selection Guide in this chapter.

Adapted from an article in *Light Garden,* published by the ILGSA.

Materials:

Item	Quantity	Description
A. Sill	1	$\frac{3}{4} \times 9\frac{1}{4} \times 31$-inch #2 pine
B. Sill hold-down	1	$1 \times 1 \times 29\frac{3}{4}$-inch aluminum angle
C. Box back	1	$\frac{3}{4} \times 11\frac{1}{4} \times 30\frac{1}{2}$-inch #2 pine
D. Box sides	2	$\frac{3}{4} \times 11\frac{1}{4} \times 8\frac{1}{2}$-inch #2 pine
E. Dowels	2	$\frac{3}{8} \times 1$-inch dowels
Screws	5	$1\frac{1}{4}$-inch #6 flat-head wood screws
Nails	—	6d finish nails
Glue	—	White vinyl glue
Finish	—	Polyurethane varnish

Special Tools:

Table saw
Router (optional)

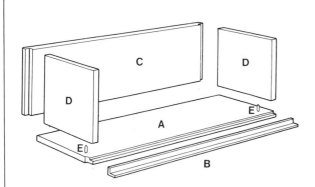

Procedure:

1. Select window to be fitted with the cold air box.
2. Decide how to support the additional windowsill (A) (bottom of the unit) if it is needed. The window we used was an aluminum sash and frame with a 6-inch-wide windowsill.
3. Cut pieces A, C, and D according to the dimensions in the materials list.
4. Cut a ¼-inch-deep × ½-inch-wide rabbet along one edge of the sill (A). Our aluminum window had a lip on it as a place to grip for opening and shutting the window. It may not be necessary for your application.
5. Cut a 1 × 1 × 29¾-inch piece of aluminum angle for the sill hold-down (B).

6. Screw the aluminum angle (B) to the edge of the sill (A) which has the rabbet. Leave the angle extending below the bottom of the sill.
7. Fit the sill to the window, closing sash down on the angle. This will hold the sill in place.
8. Rout a ¼-inch radius on the other three edges of the sill or break the edges with a sanding block. Rout or sand both sides for a clean end grain.
9. Cut a ⅜-inch-deep × ¾-inch-wide rabbet on both ends of the box back (C).
10. Glue and nail the box together, nailing through the back (C) into sides (D). This section is removable from the additional sill (A) and held in position by two dowels.
11. Rout a ¼-inch radius on all edges of the box or break the edges with a sanding block.
12. Cut two dowels (E) and sand the ends to a point.
13. Lay out and drill two ⅜-inch-diameter holes for positioning dowels (E) in the sill.
14. Drill corresponding holes in the bottom edge of the box.
15. Glue the dowels (E) into the holes in the sill.
16. Finish sanding all parts of the sill and box.
17. Finish the unit with two coats of polyurethane varnish.

tently over 70°F (21°C), steps should be taken to reduce the temperature in the room (especially at night), or to grow heat-tolerant plants. Windows that register temperatures consistently below 65°F (18°C) are not a serious problem since there are many plants that prosper at low temperatures. Building a cold-air box may be the remedy for a window that is too warm or a means of maintaining a cool garden for the many beautiful flowering or foliage plants that require relatively lower temperatures.

Humidity is the final condition to consider while evaluating a window and is of concern mostly to gardeners in parts of the West and in cold northern areas that require a great deal of winter heating. Alas, the average heated home has a humidity as low as 13 percent (even the Sahara Desert has a humidity of 25 percent), whereas a reading of 30 to 40 percent relative humidity on a humidistat is the minimum for good plant growth.

A large window garden will maintain a satisfactory level of humidity because of the proximity of many plants and the evaporation from moist soil and drainage pebbles. However, if more humidity is needed, it is added easily by running a cool-mist vaporizer or an ordinary humidifying unit among or near the plants for a few hours of the day. In some circumstances—if, for instance, you have a bay window—it is possible to make a roller shade of clear plastic that can be drawn down over the garden during dry periods to preserve the humidity. A shower curtain can serve the same function, although less attractively. And if these solutions are not feasible, it is always possible to create an attractive window garden with plants tolerating low humidity levels—for example, cacti and other succulents.

PLANNING A WINDOW GARDEN

As is true of all home projects, creating a window garden requires thinking ahead. The location of the garden should be planned carefully to coincide with the habits of the family. A large, showy window garden in an unused back room is not recommended because it cannot be seen and admired. Consequently, occasional lapses in watering and care are sure to occur because the garden is not part of the living pattern of the family. The same garden, located in the kitchen or family room in full view of everyone, can be appreciated and quickly tended whenever plants in need of water or care are noticed. Such a garden is sure to thrive.

On the other hand, consider installing a working garden in that unused back room. It is a good, inconspicuous place to start seeds, propagate cuttings, and resuscitate ailing plants, provided someone is making a daily check on their progress. Whether it's for ornamental or propagating purposes, a garden not attended regularly will not prosper and will bring only disappointment and ultimate failure.

It is fun to design a show garden to match the decor of the room it occupies. A formal French living room can look splendid with a formal, matched garden in the window. Such an arrangement would be reminiscent of a traditional European garden and include bushy and leafy plants, perhaps some standard forms (that is, plants trained into tree shapes), other examples of topiary, and traditional plants such as azaleas, citrus, ivy, and myrtle. Plants would be arranged symmetrically to balance each other. In the formal garden all the elements work together, and no plant looks out of place. On the other hand, a rustic, paneled family room will benefit from an informal arrangement in front of the window. This more casual garden could be a less balanced grouping of dramatically shaped plants such as the *Yucca* species or *Dracaena marginata* and perhaps barrel and columnar cacti—all in terra-cotta pots or baskets. The working paraphernalia of gardening (such as seed flats) definitely does not add to

Formal Window Garden: A formal room can be enhanced by a symmetrically arranged window box.

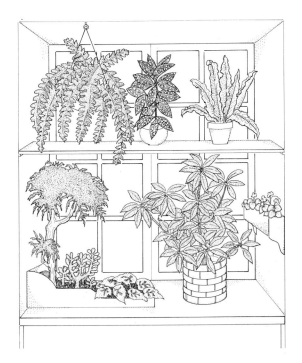

Informal Window Garden: A casual grouping of plants would be most effective in an informal room.

the appearance of a show garden and should be cleverly hidden or kept in a less formal room.

If a window garden is in a position to be enjoyed from the outside, plan a scene that is rewarding to view from both directions. There is nothing so pleasing on a cold winter's day as the sight of fresh garden tropicals and bright blooms laughing through the window at winter's gloom! With some lighting nearby, perhaps just a table lamp, even at night the plant silhouettes will create a pleasant tableau.

After determining the location of your window garden, consider the various ways in which window space may be used effectively. A row of potted plants lined up on a windowsill is rather boring—and impedes the opening of the window. Instead, think about using plants at all levels. Hanging plants have become quite popular and have the advantage of being out of the way of cats, children, and window mechanisms. Several large floor

plants placed to each side can frame a window effectively. Consider boosting large plants up on decorative pedestals of overturned clay pots or log rounds so the foliage receives sufficient light. Beware of standing or hanging plants far below sill level, as foliage will not prosper when shaded by the wall.

Shelving units create an orderly look in a window garden and provide a means to use the full height of the window effectively. The use of glass shelving is especially recommended as it allows more light to reach through to lower plants and the room beyond. Clear glass shelves installed across the window on brackets can be positioned to allow access for opening windows. Sill space frequently is unusable because it is too narrow. Widening the sill is done easily by installing shelf brackets just beneath the sill and placing a shelf or window box on the brackets. Shelf brackets may be purchased in a variety of widths, so it is possible to vary the width of the shelf from 8 inches (20 cm) for smaller plants all the way to 14 inches (36 cm) or more for larger specimens.

Movable planters that roll on large casters also are useful. Very simple plant stands can be made from rolling tea carts and TV stands. The advantage of these is apparent if a sink is available nearby and watering and

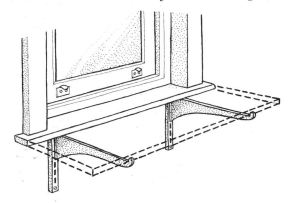

Extending a Windowsill: Brackets supporting a glass or wooden shelf can add width to a narrow windowsill.

Build Your Own Indoor Window Box

If you'd like to grow plants in the natural light from a window but your windowsills are too narrow for pots, this indoor window box will let you take advantage of the sun and provide an attractive display place for plants. The shelves below offer space for low-light plants, books, or storing gardening supplies. The unit is free-standing, so it does not require any mechanical attachment to the window trim or walls and is easy to move.

This window box was designed for a window that is 40 inches from the floor and 38 inches wide. The measurements may be adjusted to accommodate the size of your window.

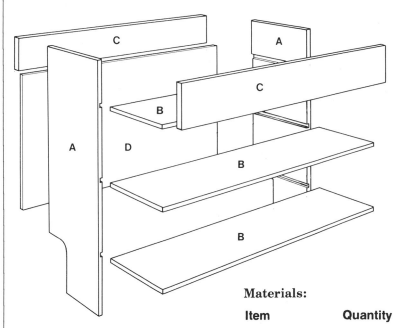

Special Tools:

Table saw
Router

Materials:

Item	Quantity	Description
A. Ends	2	$\frac{3}{4} \times 9\frac{1}{4} \times 39\frac{3}{4}$-inch #2 pine
B. Shelves	3	$\frac{3}{4} \times 9 \times 37\frac{1}{4}$-inch #2 pine
C. Box sides	2	$\frac{3}{4} \times 5\frac{1}{2} \times 36\frac{1}{2}$-inch #2 pine
D. Back	1	$\frac{1}{4} \times 37\frac{1}{4} \times 30$-inch plywood
Nails	—	6d finish nails
Glue	—	White vinyl glue
Finish	—	Polyurethane varnish
Caulk	—	Clear silicone caulk

Procedure:

1. Cut pieces A, B, and C from #2 pine according to the dimensions in the materials list.
2. If you have a baseboard heating system, the back bottom corners may have to be cut out of the end pieces (A) to fit over the baseboard heater.
3. Lay out and cut dadoes in the end pieces (A) for the shelves (B) and rout a $\frac{1}{4}$-inch-wide × $\frac{3}{8}$-inch-deep rabbet along the back

edge of the end pieces (A) to receive the plywood back. Note that this second step does not carry a rabbet all the way up the back where back piece (D) meets sides (C), therefore a router must be used.

4. Assemble all of the above pieces with glue and nails. Note that all pieces are nailed in place through ends (A) except back (D), which is held by nails through its back.

5. Cut a ¼-inch plywood back (D) to fit, and glue and nail it in place.

6. Rout a ¼-inch radius on all edges or round off the edges with a sanding block.

7. Finish-sand all the edges and all the surfaces.

8. Finish the unit with three coats of polyurethane varnish on top of any stain you select, to protect it from moisture.

9. Caulk the inside edges of the window box with clear silicone caulk to make it watertight.

plant washing can be accomplished by rolling the stand to the sink. However, a large group of potted plants is a heavy load, and more often than not, rolling a plant cart across carpeting will only cause pots to tip. An inexpensive stationary plant stand can be made from a wooden stepladder. Stained or painted to match the room, the steps become useful plant shelves, and the rungs are handy for hanging plants.

PROBLEM SOLVING

Good planning for a window garden will take into account certain problems and find ways to surmount them. Already mentioned is the common mistake of blocking access to the window. To avoid frustration and falling plants, keep plants a few inches or centimeters away from any window that is opened frequently, and free the sash area entirely.

If drapes or shades are frequently drawn, you should also leave an unblocked area to accommodate them. Curtain rod bracket extensions may be purchased to extend drapes farther into the room. Hanging plants installed from ceiling hooks placed about 12 inches (30 cm) from the wall should not interfere with closing the curtains. Since the plants curtain the window to some extent, perhaps it will not be necessary to close the drapes nightly. An alternative to drapes is a roller shade, but if this is used, space must be left at the back of the garden to allow for the shade movement. As easier method of shading the window is provided by venetian blinds, especially the new, thin, matchstick styles. These are operated by a cord at the side of the window and are not as troublesome to open and close as curtains or shades.

Frequently the family cat causes problems by insisting on sunning in the window garden and snacking on the plants. Perhaps the cat will be less destructive if a soft bed is left among the plants in her favorite spot and a pot of sprouted bird seed or grass seed placed nearby. In other words, make your cat part of the garden decor!

Dogs are usually larger and therefore more vigorous and destructive. They are also more difficult to keep out of the garden if they have already developed the habit of entering it. Other than closing a door to keep them out of the garden area, there seems to be no simple solution to this problem.

With time and patience, children can be trained, and unless the garden happens to be located in the end-zone of their indoor football field, they should quickly learn to respect the green things growing in the window.

You can keep winter cold from damaging plants in a window by making sure their leaves are several inches or centimeters away from the glass. On extremely cold nights, leave the curtains open to allow warm air to circulate in the window (or stand or tape sheets of newspaper or cardboard against the glass).

Avoiding heat sources is a common window gardening problem, as registers are generally located right below the window. If it is at all feasible, shut off the heat source under an overheated garden, even if this is possible only part of the time.

Many older homes are heated by radiators fitted with radiator covers. When a waterproof planter is placed on a radiator cover and moist drainage material is maintained in the planter, almost all potted plants of tropical origin grow surprisingly well, for the beneficial humidity created by the constantly evaporating water in the drainage material compensates for the drying radiator heat. (Plants that will *not* do well atop a radiator include species of *Azalea, Calceolaria, Cyclamen, Fatsia, Fuchsia, Lilium,* and *Primula;* some *Hedera* varieties; coolness-loving members of the Orchid family; and plants of the Cactus family.) If the planter is warmed excessively by the radiator, it may be possible to cool the plants by placing a pad of Styrofoam or other insulation between the radiator cover and the planter.

Summer heat can be moderated by shading the window when the sun shines in. You can use venetian blinds or simple, inexpensive roller shades for this purpose.

Frequently window gardens are designed around large planters into which the plants are set directly. This practice often leads to problems as one vigorous plant takes over and chokes out the others. This "survival of the fittest" syndrome can be avoided by placing individually potted plants in the planter and filling in around them with long-grain sphagnum moss or vermiculite until none of the pots show. Remember, unless drainage material has been placed in the bottom of the planter, watering will have to be done with care so the concealed bottoms of the pots are not habitually standing in a small pond.

The last pitfall to avoid is heralded by strange symptoms: loud crashes in the night—and sometimes even during the day! This problem of falling plants or shelves is

Using Window Space Creatively: This window gardener has used every available inch of space to create a pleasingly ordered arrangement of greenery. Even the space below sill level is put to good use with the installation of fluorescent fixtures above shelves that hold still more plants.

avoided easily by hanging plants securely from sturdy brackets or from ceiling hooks firmly supported by toggle or Molly bolts. Plant shelves also should be sturdy and securely fastened to the wall with heavy-duty brackets. It is best to nail the brackets into the studs of the wall. Potted plants are heavy, especially after being watered—for example, a large cactus in a ten-inch (25 cm) clay pot can weigh in at a surprising 15 pounds (6.8 kg), so plan any building projects accordingly.

BAY WINDOW GARDENS

Bay windows offer such excellent potential as window gardens that they deserve special mention. Such windows offer the advantage of large size and a curved design that allows light to reach plants from three sides. Bay windows are also usually part of the decorated living areas of the house, and therefore are more likely to be lavished with the attention that is necessary to make them show-places.

There are some negative aspects of bay window gardens, and these stem from the fact that the window bows out from the house walls and is more fully exposed to the weather. In winter such a window can become quite cool—a fact that can be turned to advantage if you assemble a collection of blooming plants that prefer cool conditions. In summer, a bay window that receives much sun will need to be fitted with shades, venetian blinds, curtains, or other shading during the hottest part of the day.

But such drawbacks are merely minor inconveniences; anyone blessed with a bay window should use it to good gardening advantage, for it offers almost all the possibilities of a small window greenhouse, plus the extra benefit of being a decorative focal point of the room.

CREATING SHOWY WINDOW GARDENS

When planning a decorative window garden, you can assure a pleasing result by using some designer tricks.

The techniques of placing plants at all levels in the window have been discussed, but the aesthetic importance of doing this should be stressed again. Good designers always use height, width, and depth to create a full, flowing design.

Modern styles lean toward a more informal look, and so formal, carefully matched arrangements are rarely used today. Instead, contemporary designers tend to vary the size and height of their material and choose plants with varied leaf shapes and colors. The resulting arrangement usually mimics a natural garden scene. Taller plants act as sentinels to the back and sides, medium size specimens (including some eye-catching plants with spiky leaves or bright foliage or flowers) make an attractive central emphasis,

and low-growing bushy plants or vines serve as the front border, hiding the pots behind and softening the front edge of the whole scene.

Achieving a completely natural look sometimes involves artificial means. For instance, plant heights may be varied by raising plants, pots, and saucers on inverted pots, wood blocks, or clear plastic cubes. If an entirely natural appearance is desired, it is possible to construct a waterproof planter than is deeper than the plant pots you plan to use. Add some drainage material to the box and then sink the pots completely in vermiculite or long-grain sphagnum. These two materials are recommended because they are light-weight, sterile, and not terribly messy. Vermiculite looks a great deal like sand and makes an excellent foil for a cactus and succulent garden. Both materials allow for the easy turning, removal, and replacement of plants and pots.

If a planter box is not used, some thought should be given to coordinating plant pots to achieve a unified look. Natural terra-cotta is a classic, and always a good choice. Plastic pots in darker shades of green, brown, or black are also good as they persuade the eye to focus on the plant rather than the subdued pot. Many effective window gardens feature plants in unusual containers. When the pots and plants are matched imaginatively this approach can be a real show-stopper! For example, animal effigy terra-cotta pots from Mexico and Guatemala can be the basis of some superb displays. The effigy wire baskets often sold as lettuce dryers or egg baskets also have fine potential: a four- or five-inch (10 or 13 cm) pot of ivy, Swedish ivy (*Plectranthus australis*), or wandering Jew (*Tradescantia* spp.) slipped into the open back of a high-necked swan basket makes a pretty and interesting planting. The foliage which cascades over the body of the swan provides a topiarylike look achieved with little effort.

In designing such pot-and-container

(continued on page 616)

Customized Planters for Windowsill Gardens

Planter boxes with waterproof liners are a real plus for window gardeners. They allow for a natural arrangement of plants while hiding the plant pots, and the moist material filling the planter provides beneficial humidity. (For reasons stated in the text, it is preferable to keep the plants in their pots instead of planting directly into the planter.) These planters are especially useful in large bay windows. Here are suggestions for two different waterproof planter liners, one of which is sturdy enough to be used without a supporting frame.

Aluminum liners may be manufactured to your specifications at a local roofing company or sheet metal shop. These shops have machines that can bend and seal a solid sheet of aluminum into a tray shape. The shop should use a solid sheet of aluminum the length and width of your planned garden box plus enough extra to turn up sides all around. For instance, if a liner with the final dimensions of 3 feet by 4 feet (0.9 m by 1.2 m) with 6-inch (152 mm) sides is needed, then it is necessary to start with a sheet of aluminum 4 feet by 5 feet (1.2 m by 1.5 m), so a 6-inch (152 mm) edge may be turned up on each side of the liner. Ask the metal worker to seal and waterproof the corners of the liner just as he would a roof gutter. For a sturdy liner it is necessary to use aluminum at least 0.025 mil thick.

Aluminum has the advantage of being lightweight, rustproof, and inexpensive, but if the surface it is to be placed on cannot support it firmly, it must be used as a liner inside a supporting planter to prevent bending.

Galvanized sheet metal also may be ordered made up as a plant tray, although it is somewhat more expensive than aluminum. Again, ask the metal worker to construct the tray to be waterproof. Unlike an aluminum tray, as added protection the finished sheet metal tray must be painted with a basecoat of rustproofing paint and then painted to match the room decor. A tray made from 22- or 24-gauge steel is rigid and can serve as a planter alone, without the support of a planter box.

Metal liners have a tendency to sweat as condensation forms on the underside of the tray. To provide the air space necessary for evaporation, an aluminum or steel liner should rest on top of wood or plastic slats. A finished surface covered with a sheet of plastic over which slats of wood or plastic are laid provides a safe, waterproof base to support a metal planter.

Garden boxes designed to surround a waterproof liner are not difficult to build. Adding a decorative touch to any liner, they are essential with aluminum liners, which need firm support. To make such a frame, build a wooden, bottomless garden box from lumber wide enough to hide the pots (usually 1 × 8s). Next, nail or screw support ledges of 1 inch by 1 inch (25 mm by 25 mm) for boxes 2 feet by 4 feet (0.6 m by 1.2 m) or smaller, or 1 inch by 2 inches (25 mm by 51 mm) inside the box about ½ inch (13 mm) above the bottom edge of the long sides. Place some 1-inch by 2-inch (25 mm by 51 mm) pine support slats across the box so their ends rest on these ledges. For a custom-built look, mitre the corners of the garden box, hide nail heads with wood putty, and carefully sand and stain or paint the frame to match the

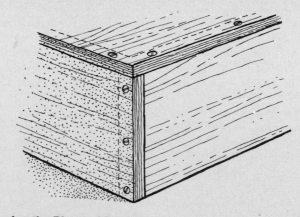

Cornering the Plywood Box: This illustration shows how the sides of the box are first attached to one another, then how the bottom is attached to the sides.

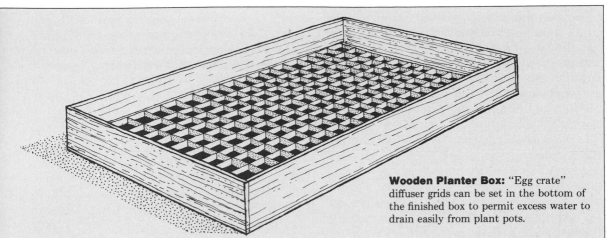

Wooden Planter Box: "Egg crate" diffuser grids can be set in the bottom of the finished box to permit excess water to drain easily from plant pots.

room decor. For a one-piece window planter that is less costly and perhaps more attractive than one made of 22- or 24-gauge steel, you might want to construct a waterproof wooden planter in your home workshop. Either ¾ inch or ½ inch (19 mm or 13 mm) thick exterior grade plywood may be used. Choose the thinner plywood for planters 2 feet by 4 feet (0.6 m by 1.2 m) or smaller.

First cut plywood sides, making the edges as high as needed, from 2 inches (51 mm) for working gardens to 6 inches (152 mm) or more for show gardens where it is desirable to hide the pots. Glue the joints with a waterproof glue, and while the glue is still wet screw the sides together with flat head #6 brass wood screws either 1 inch or 1½ inches (25 mm or 38 mm) long, depending on whether the plywood is ½ inch or ¾ inch (13 mm or 19 mm) thick.

Next, cut a full plywood bottom, deriving the measurement from the outside dimensions of the planter sides. Glue and screw the bottom to the sides, using about two #6 screws every 12 inches (305 mm), and placing them closer together at the corners.

Countersink the screws, then sand the edges of the planter and paint or stain it.

Waterproof the planter by coating the tray inside with a waterproof epoxy resin available at marine paint and specialty stores. All epoxy paints harden quickly after mixing, so it is advisable to mix a small amount at a time. Coat the entire tray and carefully fill all cracks and openings. After the first coat hardens, add a second coat to the inside of the tray, forming narrow concave strips, or fillets, along the edges and corners to provide a better seal. These coats of epoxy paint will form an impenetrable plastic barrier and no plastic sheet liner is needed to protect the planter or window seat from any water that may drain from plants. Drainage holes also are unneeded since the small amount of water reaching the bottom of such a planter will evaporate in a day or two.

Once the garden box and waterproof liner or waterproof planter is complete, do, however, remember to add a couple of inches or centimeters of drainage material to make absolutely certain the plants will never be standing in excess water. Frequently pebbles are used as drainage material, but they are heavy, difficult to clean and disinfect, and sometimes a nuisance on which to balance plant pots. Instead, consider using "egg crate" diffuser grids as a drainage layer. Made of white plastic, these grids are designed for use as light diffusers in fluorescent ceiling fixtures. They are sold at hardware and lumber stores in 2-foot by 4-foot (0.6 m by 1.2 m) sheets, are lightweight, easily cut with a saw, easy to clean in soapy water, and provide a sturdy, flat support for plant pots while permitting excess water to drain away from plants. "Egg crate" is not a suitable drainage material when plants are set directly into a planter filled with soil mix, but it is quite appropriate when plants are left in their pots or when potted plants are sunk in vermiculite or sphagnum moss.

combinations, particularly pleasing results come from using natural materials such as wicker, basketry, clay, rock, and driftwood rather than painted ceramics and plastic. Also, low-spreading or bushy plants are better candidates than tall plants, which don't need special pots as one's attention is always drawn to the statuesque plant anyway.

A garden scene sometimes is not considered complete until some nonplant interest has been added. Garden ponds are always interesting and are easy to duplicate indoors with a small bowl of goldfish placed among the plants. Or consider a mobile for moving interest, either the hanging variety or a movable statue that features birds flying on the ends of long, gracefully swaying metal rods.

Garden statues have long been popular and an attractive object or two added to an indoor garden adds a pleasing touch. Possibilities include natural objects such as driftwood or articles made from it, cactus wood, and interesting rocks (including lava rock). Primitive art is also very appropriate since it is usually made from natural materials. Informal gardens also are enhanced by sculptures of appropriate animals such as squirrels or birds or by Japanese garden statues and lanterns. More formal arrangements can be completed by a typically European garden artifact—perhaps a bronze cherub or sundial or a mythological figure. Be wary, though, of anything distracting; a garden is a living thing and statuary should be in harmony with its naturalness and sized proportionately to the plants and the garden as a whole.

Recently, attractive rooting jars made of clear glass have come on the market. Manufactured in interesting animal shapes, these rooters add pleasing interest to a garden while serving the practical purpose of rooting cuttings. Indeed, any attractive vase with cuttings makes an unusual focal point in a garden of potted plants.

Seasonal changes also can add much to a garden. A pot of poinsettias at Christmas; a vase of forced forsythias or pussy willow in spring; vases of cut garden flowers in summer; and dried flowers, chrysanthemums, pumpkins, or Indian corn in autumn all change the scene and help to keep the garden interesting.

PUTTING IT ALL TOGETHER

The art of decorating a window garden is probably best communicated by describing both in words and sketches the steps taken to decorate some typical home windows.

A bay window is a good beginning since its bright spaciousness makes this the most favored site for a window garden. Whether the window faces south, east, west, or north has little bearing on the decoration scheme, since appropriate plants can be selected to use in each exposure. In the traditional bay window garden, decoration begins with the placing of some taller background plants at the back and sides of the scene. The plants are placed so foliage does not touch the glass and spreads naturally. Hanging plants make excellent backdrop plants and help prevent crowding by using empty air space.

The center of the garden can feature eye-catching medium size accent plants. Some favorites include plants with interestingly shaped, colored, or variegated leaves, and flowering plants. Often chosen are bird's nest ferns, bromeliads, dramatic spike-leaved dracaenas, or rhoeos. Leafy medium size plants can fill in the scene with lush greenery. Finally, the front edge of the garden should be softened with full, draping plants. Some outstanding ones for the purpose are the Boston fern (*Nephrolepis exaltata* 'Bostoniensis'), grape ivy *(Cissus rhombifolia),* spider plants (*Chlorophytum* spp.), or Swedish ivy. For a colorful focal point, a glimmering bowl of goldfish may be placed just off-center on a block of wood which raises it for easier visibility. When the bowl is surrounded with foliage plants, the garden pool effect is complete.

Although it is not necessary, it is helpful

The Show Garden: A well-planned window garden is a visual delight. For the best appearance, give careful consideration to placing plants at all levels in the window and using attractive, complementary containers.

to have an aluminum (or sheet metal) liner and wood planter box made to fit the dimensions of the window seat. The waterproof liner makes watering easier by preventing water spills from spoiling the window seat and permits moist drainage material to add beneficial humidity to the garden area. The planter box should be about six inches (15 cm) deep to hide the front of most standard pots. The box may be stained or painted to match the woodwork of the window. (See box on Customized Planters for construction details on liners and boxes.) A good alternative to a wooden window box is simply made by positioning a six inch (15 cm) wide stained or painted board across the front of the garden. This will serve to hide the front pots and also an aluminum liner, if one is used. If fill-

ing in around the pots with vermiculite or long-grain sphagnum is not desirable, washed river gravel makes good drainage material and an attractive base for the plant scene. Some of the background plants may be raised on wood blocks or overturned pots, but these supports usually can be hidden by placing a bushy plant such as a Boston fern or grape ivy in front of them.

Decorating a full-length window or patio-door glass wall offers both opportunities and challenges. Doorway passages must be left free of plants during any part of the year when the door is used. Plants also must be arranged so as not to interfere with normal room activities.

Standard windows of average size, usually three to four feet (0.9 to 1.2 m) wide and three to four feet (0.9 to 1.2 m) high, offer several possibilities for limited window gardens. Installing some shelves across a small window creates space for a collection of smaller plants. Shelf brackets of any width from 8 to 14 inches (20 to 36 cm) may be securely fastened to the window frame or the wall next to the frame. Glass shelves may be ordered from a local glass company. They should be cut to exact size from heavy-duty glass and the edges sanded smooth (tell the glass cutter their intended use). Wooden shelving also may be used, but glass is preferred because it allows light to pass through and is impervious to water. The shelving should be installed so it will not interfere with window openings, and brackets for curtains or hardware for other means of shading should be provided if necessary.

Gardens for Small Windows: Installing clear glass shelves across small or narrow windows provides space for a collection of small plants.

Small sculptured plants, especially cacti and succulents, look particularly dramatic on glass shelves as their exotic shapes are silhouetted against the window. A collection of small colored glass items placed among the plants can add a touch of brightness, and the edges of the garden may be softly disguised with draping plants such as smaller specimens of spider plants or grape ivy. Pots and saucers of the same dark color should be used for a unified look.

Another good choice for a shelf garden is a display of plants potted in unusual containers. Animal effigy pots, shells, and household objects such as shoes and teapots all make interesting planters. Growing plants in novel containers is an art and poses some difficulties (mainly watering), but if creative good taste is exercised, the result can be an outstanding window garden. By matching plants to pots either by size, style, or theme, a sensitive gardener can fashion combinations that are always interesting and often witty. For instance, a ceramic baby carriage of the kind that florists like to send to new mothers may be planted with baby's tears *(Soleirolia soleirolii),* a "praying hands" planter with a lush rosary vine *(Ceropegia woodii),* and a brown toad with the succulent *Faucaria tuberculosa,* which is known for its very warty leaves.

Another idea for a small window garden allows for easier closing of sill-length curtains. In this garden a hanging plant or two occupy the upper area of the window, and a widened sill, described earlier, holds several plants. A mobile statue adds nonplant interest to the garden. The sill-length curtains will close easily behind the plants on the broadened sill, provided plants are arranged toward the front.

Long, narrow windows must be fitted with vertical gardens. A hanging macrame planter featuring two plants could fill a long window effectively. Rejuvenated bird cages and/or their stands make interesting hanging plant holders. They are fairly stable, as the base of the stand is weighted to compensate

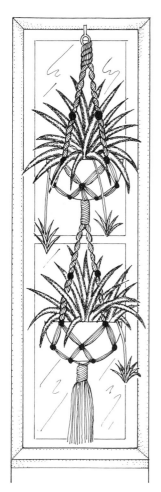

Vertical Gardens: Long, narrow windows need plants arranged vertically for the best effect.

Designing and maintaining a handsome, living scene is not difficult, and the guidelines to success may be summarized briefly as six steps:

1. Evaluate all aspects of the window's exposure, and choose only plants appropriate to that exposure.
2. Take into account the working parts of the window when planning the garden. Allow for opening the window, closing the curtains, and providing shading if required.
3. For show gardens, choose plants for their decorativeness and ease of culture. This kind of garden is intended to be an aesthetic experience—not an experimental laboratory for different plants.
4. Give the garden regular loving care. Use good cultural practices: water carefully when necessary, rinse dust and dirt from the foliage monthly, fertilize regularly during the spring and summer months, pinch and prune for attractive bushy growth, remove dead and broken foliage and flowers, and give plants a quarter turn every week.
5. If a plant becomes diseased or develops insect problems, remove it immediately and treat it elsewhere so the problem cannot spread to other plants or detract from the general appearance of the garden.
6. Enjoy your garden! No one knows if talking to plants really helps them grow, but the fact remains that gardens that are appreciated and lovingly cared for usually flourish!

for the weight of the bird cage. A tall floor plant combined with a single hanging plant is another possibility for a long window.

An old-fashioned coat tree makes a most effective vertical hanging garden—provided the coat hooks extend far enough from the pole to allow a plant to hang freely. Installing swinging brackets at alternate levels down both sides of a long window also can provide a pleasing effect.

The possibilities for window gardens are endless and are limited only by the creativity of the gardener. A flourishing garden is possible in any window as long as the limitations of the location are recognized and respected.

CHAPTER 31

Greenhouse Gardening

Through the ages humankind has been fascinated by translucent structures that make it possible to coax plants into life and growth independent of the seasons. History tells us one of the first to benefit from this magic was Tiberius Caesar, who enjoyed a physician-prescribed cucumber a day year-round thanks to a gardener with the wit to cover manure-heated beds with thin plates of translucent stone such as talc or mica.

Lost for a while during the Dark Ages, the art of growing plants in enclosures re-emerged in Italy toward the end of the thirteenth century and seems to have been fostered by the wealthy traders of Venice and Genoa, who imported exotic fruits. To the north, the expansion of French, Dutch, and English trade and exploration from the late 1500s to the 1800s was accompanied by much experimentation with forcing frames glazed first with oiled paper and then with glass. Built to produce early fruits and vegetables, some of these structures featured a second layer of glazing, thick masonry walls, and canvas curtains pulled at night—all heat-saving ideas being reapplied today. Heat was provided first by hidden flues, which usually drew with difficulty, wasted much fuel, and often leaked noxious fumes and smoke. Other warming devices included smoking smudge pots or iron stoves that distributed heat very unevenly. Obviously the plants in these working greenhouses had to struggle to survive. So did the gardeners, who must have alternately choked and frozen.

While servants and market gardeners toiled in such practical surroundings, the aristocracy of Europe and colonial America was bringing to perfection the so-called wintering galleries or orangeries, planned as much for architectural elegance and pleasant strolling as for the competitive pastime of growing superior fruits. Often unheated, the glassed-in gardens intended primarily for protecting citrus trees were the predecessors of the elaborate conservatories that reached their zenith in Victorian England. Heated by steam or hot water, these elegant plant display areas were often combined with a game or music room. The ostentatiousness of such English plant rooms was rivaled and often exceeded by the immense plant palaces built by American millionaires during and after the Gilded Age in the nineteenth century.

Reminder of a Bygone Era: This elaborate and elegant glass palace at the Botanical Garden of Berlin exemplifies the architectural spirit that reigned during the Victorian and Gilded Ages. The conservatories built during those extravagant eras were the forerunners of today's scaled-down, energy-conscious, eminently functional greenhouse.

Opposite, blooming annuals thrive on a greenhouse shelf.

Over the past hundred years, mass technology and an increasing willingness to "build-it-yourself" have made home greenhouses available to the not-so rich, and slowly but surely people who love gardening have been discovering the special kind of re-creation that happens only inside a greenhouse. A quiet place suited to a host of activities such as renewing tired house plants and propagating new ones from cuttings, starting transplants for outdoors, raising vegetables to harvest, wintering-over tender plants, sheltering early bloomers, forcing bulbs, and growing specialty plants year-round, the greenhouse also is beginning to come into its own as a rewarding live-in environment for dining, entertaining, playing, working, or just taking some sun. As we will see, this expanding concept of the greenhouse's role is linked to comparatively recent changes in its form.

TYPES OF GREENHOUSES

Something like a golden age of greenhouses has come into being over the past 15 years, and the gabled glass houses once serenely ensconced at the center of the indoor gardening scene are being challenged by a flashy montage of new shapes. These have been made possible by recent developments in glazing materials and made desirable by new discoveries about plant needs and the increasing costs of supplemental heating. From A-frames right on through geodesic domes, many-planed hyperbolic paraboloids, and beautifully functional solar structures, potential greenhouse gardeners now have an unprecedented array of choices. Whatever your situation and inclination—whether you long for a leafy attic skyroom, an enclosed patio shaded by fruit trees and vines, a working greenhouse to grow your own orchids or your own food, or just a peaceful nook to start some seeds—now more than ever there is likely to be a greenhouse out there that is meant for you.

TRADITIONAL GREENHOUSES

Attached Greenhouses

Attached greenhouses are far and away more popular among homeowners than the free-standing kind, for they can be built more easily and cheaply, and the protection of a solid, often warm north wall means they are less costly to heat. Built against a house, garage, shed, fence, or any walled structure that can support them, attached greenhouses also can be designed for direct entrance from a dwelling as well as from outside, an important convenience in cold or bad weather. Attached plant shelters are also convenient in a more important way. By leaving connecting doors or windows open or building upper and lower vents in the common wall, it is possible to use house air to help warm the greenhouse at night, while excess heat from the plant room sent into the dwelling on bright days in fall, winter, and spring can reduce heating bills in the home by up to 50 percent.

Just about the smallest of attached structures is the window greenhouse. Available in many prefabricated sizes or easily crafted from a plan, a window greenhouse can be mounted on a south-facing window near the ground. One quick and easy approach is to screw a vertical shelf track to each side of a window frame—on the outside, of course—then lay acrylic or glass shelves atop parallel brackets inserted in the track. Plastic film then can be stretched over the entire arrangement and nailed down around the outside of the window frame beneath strips of lath.

You also can encase a window well with glass sash or a plastic bubble. Often 2 to 2½ feet (0.6 to 0.8 m) wide and 2 to 4 feet (0.6 to 1.2 m) from front to back, window wells at or below grade level make nice little plant nooks.

Another type of window greenhouse is possible if you have a first-floor window opening to the ground. Dig a rectangle 12 inches (30 cm) deep in the ground outside, lining the bottom of the hole with 2-inch (5 cm) boards

A Simple Window Greenhouse

One of the easiest window greenhouses to install is designed around a wooden storm window. The storm window used can be the one made for the window — in which case the greenhouse will have to be built up from the windowsill — or it can be somewhat longer than the window (as shown here) so that when it is slanted outward the bottom of the storm sash will be even with the windowsill.

To construct the greenhouse, begin by assembling your materials. You will need a good size sheet of ¾-inch (19 mm) exterior plywood, two 1 × 1 or 1 × 2 boards of equal length, glue, some 2½-inch (64 mm) #10 screws, six 2-inch (51 mm) #8 screws, two hooks and eyes, and several 3d and 6d finishing nails.

Prop or hold the storm window out from the window frame at about a 30-degree angle. Measure the right triangle created by the storm window and the window casement (labeled A in the illustration). Then measure the width of the window.

Lay out the measurements for three parts of the greenhouse on the sheet of plywood. There will be two triangular pieces (A) to fit between the window casement and the storm window. There will also be a shelf (B) that is as deep as the baseline of the triangles, and 1½ inches (38 mm) narrower than the width of the window (so the triangles can overlap the ends of the shelf).

Attach a 1 × 1 or 1 × 2 wood strip (C) along both top sides of the shelf with glue and 3d finishing nails.

Slip the baseboard/shelf assembly into position. The baseboard should fit snugly against the windowsill and the sides of the casement. Tack the assembly into place with 3d or 6d finishing nails. Then position both of the triangles, attaching each to the window casement with four or five 2½-inch (64 mm) #10 wood screws. Drive three 2-inch (51 mm) #8 screws through the baseline of each triangle into the edge of the shelf.

Hang the storm window in place and secure it with a hook and eye at each side near the bottom, attaching the hook to the inside of the storm sash and the eye to the plywood triangle.

For best results in fall, winter, and spring growing, caulk all the joints, although to use the greenhouse through the summer, you might want to use a removable sealant so that in hot weather you can replace the glass sash with a screen of the same size. Drill a few holes in the bottom shelf so that rain can drain off harmlessly. In any case, cover the unit with a coat of primer, and house paint to match your home's trim.

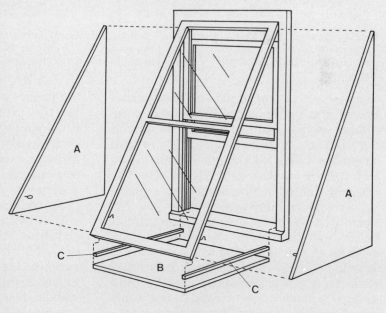

Window Greenhouse: This unit provides the benefits of increased space and light available for gardening on the windowsill, without the sizable investments of space and money a full size greenhouse requires. Although a window greenhouse shares to a large extent the environmental conditions of the home, many plants can be raised satisfactorily there.

or other material for insulation, then build a wooden framework out from each side of the window so you can place a storm window on top of it at a 45-degree angle. (If you stuff newspaper where the frame meets the house and seal the works with artist's clay, the structure can be removed without a trace.)

Though window greenhouses are too small to maintain an environment much different from that inside the house and can overheat quickly if venting to the dwelling or outside is not provided, they can be a pleasing introduction to greenhouse gardening and make it possible to grow light-loving plants indoors without artificial lighting.

The most popular kind of attached greenhouse is the lean-to, which has one solid side. Perhaps the easiest way to fashion this type of greenhouse is to close in a south-fac-

ing porch or a condominium terrace with fiberglass panels or recycled storm windows, using supplemental lighting if necessary to compensate for the porch's extra framing. By fitting a porch with removable panels, you can convert it to a screened patio during the summer.

A very popular standardized lean-to consists of half of a traditional gabled even-span structure. These greenhouses can have vertical or outward-sloping sides, curved or regular eaves, and glazing that goes right to the ground or stops at a knee wall. It is also possible to build a three-quarter-span attached house, which will be wider and brighter than a half-span and offer the great advantage of allowing vents on both sides of the ridge. The three-quarter-span type is useful on a hill that slopes away from the adjoining building.

By putting an end instead of a side against another structure, you can attach an entire even-span greenhouse—or any other freestanding model with a flat end wall. This approach affords almost the same benefits as the usual lean-to while allowing for twice as much growing space, better light, and increased ventilation.

The "half of a house" type of lean-to also may feature a variable pitch, as in the curvilinear, or mansard-shaped style, or consist of half of a Gothic Arch or Quonset house. Half an A-frame is another easy-to-build option.

By sinking a lean-to structure four or five feet (1.2 or 1.5 m) into the ground, you can save a good deal of money (especially if you do your own labor) and create an indoor growing space that will not deprive your dwelling of light or cut off your view. Such attached-pit greenhouses are fairly easy to erect because you need provide only enough glazing for a one-sided 45-degree roof over a concrete block retaining wall. Warmer than detached pits, they can be used even for growing tropicals if you let in some heat from the basement or put in a small electric heater.

Freestanding Greenhouses

Freestanding greenhouses may be sited to best advantage, are easier to enlarge than attached types, and usually receive more and more evenly distributed light since they are exposed to the whole of the sky dome rather than to just half of it. For the simplest of separate greenhouses, you can rig up a simple frame tent of plastic film over planting rows in the garden to extend the growing season in fall or to get an early start in spring. This structure can be as wide as you like and anywhere from two to six feet (0.6 to 1.8 m) high at the ridge (keep the sides at about a 45-degree angle). Make a simple wooden tent frame by bolting one inch (2.5 cm) square crosspieces to uprights at three- to four-foot (0.9 to 1.2 m) intervals, then drape a sheet of 6-mil polyethylene over the frame, anchoring

down the sides with soil, cement blocks, stones, or other heavy material. To ventilate and water, open the end flaps of the tent. In fairly temperate regions you can use the same kind of unheated, freestanding structure to grow rugged, mildew-resistant greens from the first frost until spring, though it is a good idea to provide a more substantial frame of wood and fasten the plastic to the frame with staples or with strips of lath nailed over it at intervals.

Another simple but more enduring and heat-conserving kind of plant shelter is the pit greenhouse. Sunk below ground level, this simple nonfreezing unit is a kind of walk-in cold frame that relies on earth-stored heat to buffer winter air temperatures overnight, maintaining temperatures above freezing by means of movable insulation placed over the glazing at night and on cold, dull days. For protection in frigid weather, some pit gardeners use a total of 300 watts of light bulbs under the bench or run electric heaters—also a good idea if you want the pit to maintain 40° to 45°F (4° to 7°C) so it can be used as a cool greenhouse. Serious indoor gardeners often use pits as an adjunct to a heated greenhouse, since bulb plants from the pit can be put in the greenhouse for forcing and greenhouse blooms can be prolonged into summer by transferring them into the cooler, shaded pit.

Traditional pits are made of cinder block and often feature hotbed sashes of three by five feet (0.9 by 1.8 m) angled at anywhere from 45 to 60 degrees on the south-facing side. In A-frames, the lesser angle is used and there is glazing on the north side as well, but some pits have a solid north wall with a shingled roof pitched less steeply than the glazing to leave more space inside for tall, woody plants like camellias (*Camellia japonica*) or for two- or three-step staging. Nowadays, pits are taking on a new look. Concrete and stabilized earth or railroad ties and conduit are being used as foundations and framings. Sometimes the roofs and glazed areas are rounded, with gracefully arched wooden

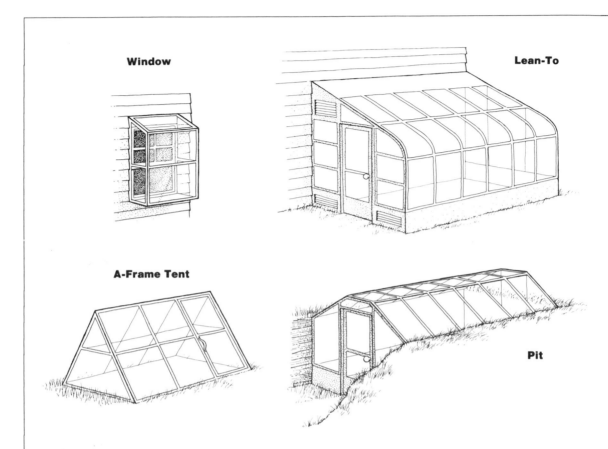

Window

Lean-To

A-Frame Tent

Pit

A Gallery of Greenhouse Styles: An attached window greenhouse affords the convenience of gardening on an extended windowsill which receives an increased amount of light. The lean-to style shown here shares a common wall with the adjacent dwelling and has glazing that stops at a knee wall. The A-frame tent is a simple setup which can be used right in the outdoor garden to extend the growing season. The pit greenhouse, through its design, conserves heat by utilizing the insulating qualities of the earth to maintain an even temperature. Individual "lights" (or panes of glass) in wooden frames joined to a framework comprise the Dutch light greenhouse, which is a temporary, bolted-together structure. The even-span, a popular style, can be altered in various ways to insure that adequate light enters in winter and early spring. The Gothic Arch greenhouse is a sound choice in regions receiving heavy snow and rainfall, since its sloping sides keep precipitation from collecting on the roof and putting stress on the structure. While the curved walls of a Quonset-style curved roof greenhouse may not accommodate tall plants, smaller flowering, fruiting, and bedding plants can fare very well. Inherent in the design of the geodesic dome are such qualities as strength without internal support, maximum light transmission, and large interior volume. Solar-style greenhouses are designed to collect and store the sun's energy, which can then be released as needed.

struts covered with plastic film or flexible fiberglass. It is even possible to build a double-eave pit with two adjoining sashes angled in parallel fashion to admit twice as much light from the south.

A variation on the completely excavated pit is the trench-pit greenhouse, called a Bijou greenhouse in British indoor gardening books of a century ago. In this kind of house—which is less difficult to build than a

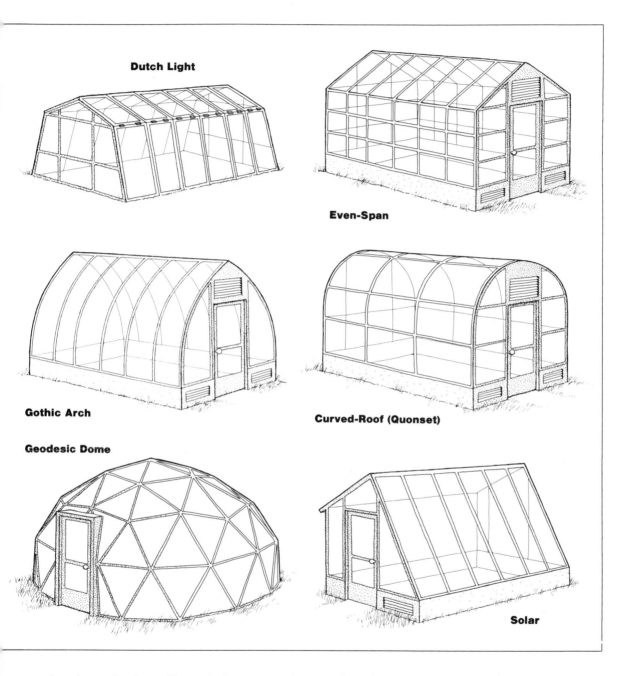

Dutch Light

Even-Span

Gothic Arch

Curved-Roof (Quonset)

Geodesic Dome

Solar

regular pit—only the walkway is dug out, and the ready-made waist-high benches next to the glazing on either side are used for direct planting or container gardening. Such pits tend to be colder and damper and are more vulnerable to pests and diseases than completely dug out pits, since they really cannot be insulated. As with all pits, a site providing or facilitating good drainage is a must. (See Floors and Walks, later in this chapter.)

Another freestanding option is the Dutch light greenhouse, a structure somewhat resembling a large cold frame which consists of comparatively few parts which are easy to join together and dismantle. In the authentic type, each "light" consists of a 56- by 28¾-inch (142 by 73 cm) piece of glass which is held in grooves within a wooden frame. The panels are then bolted to a framework to form a temporary and removable structure on top of a low wall. The glazing is usually at a 20- to 25-degree angle, which makes this style best suited for spring and summer growing, but there are also mansard shapes. Some greenhouses on the market with large glazing panels have a similar shape and look, but are not made of individual lights.

The venerable span-roofed greenhouse offered by so many manufacturers is still the favorite type of freestanding structure among those gardeners who buy their greenhouses rather than build from plans. Developed in the Low Countries of Europe in response to low levels of rather diffuse light in winter, the traditional gabled or even-span greenhouse provides a good setting for propagation activities and pot plants, although its shallow roof pitch reflects away a lot of light during the winter and the large proportion of glazing means that tremendous amounts of heat are lost by conduction, convection, and radiation.

High sides on even-span houses can help boost the amount of light admitted in winter and early spring. If these sides are slant legged rather than vertical, a little more winter light will enter, but vertical growing room near the greenhouse sides will be cut back unless a high ridge modifies the slope. Another way to get more light into a traditional even-span is to choose a model with curved eaves.

The mansard (or curvilinear) greenhouse is more costly to build than the span-roofed type, and it, too, loses a lot of heat. To compensate, however, it admits an extraordinary amount of light, for it is constructed to provide a range of angles so that in a house that runs east to west, the sun is almost always hitting part of the glazing at the 90-degree angle that allows the most light to enter and the least to be reflected away. This means that the mansard is ideal for most crops, although it tends to be hot in summer and hard to heat in winter, especially when the glazing goes to the ground.

Usually requiring fan-and-louver equipment for ventilation, curved-roof greenhouses such as the barrel vault are structurally stronger than the gabled types—which means they increase the load-carrying capacity of fiberglass panels—and are said to transmit more light and heat than span-roofed houses. Because of the curvature of the side walls, however, Quonset greenhouses (also called part-circle, arch, or tunnel greenhouses) are not very suitable for growing tall plants or for placing raised benches along the glazing. They therefore offer somewhat less growing space than other styles. Nevertheless, they are well suited to growing flowering and fruiting plants in winter and to producing bedding plants at or slightly above ground level.

The Gothic Arch style of curved house can provide adequate height at the sides without loss of strength if it is properly designed, and the arch shape shrugs off snow and water and tends to keep the plastic film often used in glazing it pressed against the supporting frame even in a stiff wind. Very sound structurally, the Gothic Arch has proved capable of withstanding heavy snow, hail, and sleet, and winds above 70 miles (112.6 km) per hour.

Circular greenhouses such as gazebos have obvious advantages in regard to heat and light transmission, but they are more costly than more conventional styles with the same amount of growing space, and can pose ventilation problems. However, the geodesic dome gives the largest possible interior volume for the space it occupies, requires no interior supports, provides maximum light transmission, and is one of the strongest shapes known. In addition to dome-shaped greenhouses made up of glass or rigid plastic panes in a framework, there are also air-supported "bubble" houses using plastic film.

SOLAR GREENHOUSES

Unlike traditional attached and freestanding greenhouses, solar structures are designed to use the sun's heat as well as its light to retain and store the extra solar energy that accumulates inside on bright days, then release it to keep the greenhouse warm during nights or cloudy days, or to help heat an adjoining building. Balancing the need for light during the shorter, dimmer days of winter against the goal of relying mostly, if not completely, on sun power to grow plants year-round, solar enthusiasts bend all their ingenuity to developing design strategems and management techniques that let in adequate light without letting out that precious heat. The aim of the

Heat Collection in a Solar Greenhouse: The form of a solar greenhouse, whether active or passive, is suited to its function of collecting and storing solar energy for heating purposes. The south-facing glass exposure is angled so that light can enter, where it is absorbed by plants and other surfaces. Through this absorption, light is transformed to heat. Some form of storage mass, either rock, water, or masonry wall is required to hold the heat for subsequent release during the night or during overcast weather.

game is to use sunlight to minimize the natural temperature swings from day to night—a goal that makes sense when you realize that even the coldest part of the United States receives a full 50 percent of the total annual amount of solar energy that falls on the warmest part of the country.

Actually, solar greenhouses have a long history. It is known, for instance, that growing houses complete with an insulated north wall and a south-facing glass roof dotted the landscape of seventeenth- and eighteenth-century Europe. These were eclipsed by all-glass houses when coal and glass became cheap and plentiful, and most greenhouse operations ever since have relied unquestioningly on fossil fuels to maintain minimum temperatures. But all that is now rapidly changing.

Traditional forms of energy have become not only astonishingly expensive, but also inconsistently available, and this is happening at a time when the amount of energy used in food production is increasing faster than that used in other sectors of the economy. Aggravated by longer, harsher winters and drought-stricken summers, this reality is pushing the prices of vegetables and fruits out of sight, and professional growers and inflation-devastated consumers alike are looking for ways to extend the growing season at both ends without being bankrupted by fuel bills. All these converging needs have caused an explosion of solar greenhouse research in recent years, work that also is proving the practicality of using an attached greenhouse to provide up to half of the heat needed by an adjoining home or building.

As we will see, the different purposes, and sometimes self-imposed limitations, of solar experimenters have dictated wonderfully varied approaches to the challenge of using solar heat to the fullest. But many of the design and management basics that together embody the theory are present in the simplest kind of solar greenhouse—the passively heated type.

The Passive Solar Greenhouse

By definition, a purely passive solar greenhouse derives all its heat from the sun, using no conventional energy sources to transfer heat in or out of storage. Some passive structures use solar collectors outside and below the greenhouse, and the heat moves to storage or directly inside the greenhouse by natural circulation. More often, though, the house itself is a collector. Often it is attached to a heated structure (usually the owner's home) to make stabilizing greenhouse temperatures and maintaining minimum temperatures easier. It also makes possible the use of interconnecting vents so the extra radiant energy can lower fuel bills in the home, for if it is well designed, the greenhouse will deliver more heat to the dwelling during the day than the home returns to it at night.

Passive solar greenhouses are capable of storing heat for only one or two days at a time, gathering it during the day and releasing it when the sun goes down. For this rea-

Passive Solar Greenhouse: The plants in this greenhouse reap the benefits of warmth and bountiful light, and respond with lush growth. Access to this extension of the home is through a sliding glass door, and once inside a table and chairs offer an invitation to sit back and enjoy the display.

son they are most successful at maintaining temperatures above freezing in rigorous climates when they are situated at high altitudes, or anywhere else where days tend to be clear and sunny.

Like all solar greenhouses, the passive types store heat in water, in rocks, or in masonry walls; exposed earth also retains heat, but not as well as the other materials. The heat collected through the glazing is necessarily low-grade to make it tolerable to plant life, and a large volume of storage mass is needed, for water and rocks store heat inefficiently when the temperature differential is low, as it is in this case. Moreover, masonry and even water are slow to give and take heat when they are not receiving direct light, which will be the case during the spring in a typically designed and oriented solar greenhouse.

All this means that considerable storage mass is necessary. The rule of thumb to keep the temperature inside 30° to 40°F (17° to 22°C) above that outside is to supply 2 gallons (7.6 l) of water or 75 pounds (33.2 kg) of rock for every square foot (0.09 sq m) of south-facing glazing. Moreover, this material should be distributed widely so there is a large surface area to absorb and release heat. Often it is placed on or under the ground, or against walls, or actually used as walls.

Able to hold twice as much heat in a given volume as rock, water also can pick up and release heat faster. It is often used for storage, either in an insulated pool with dark container walls or in the widely used 55-gallon (209 l) steel drums. (For best results, the drums should be insulated on their backs and tops where they are not directly exposed to sun and stacked upright on top of each other.) For even less heat waste, water can be held in 1- to 5-gallon (3.8 to 18.9 l) squarish metal or plastic containers stacked for fullest contact with each other: 5-gallon (18.9 l) square metal cans stacked on their sides are just about ideal.

These containers are painted black—or the water in transparent plastic bottles is colored black with fabric dye. The cans or bottles are then arranged at one or two thicknesses against one or more walls or even under raised benches, although they should be kept away from glazing. With metal containers it is important to add a small amount of motor oil or another rust inhibitor.

Quart (0.9 l) jars under the floor also store heat effectively. Another place to keep water is in 5 foot (1.5 m) high fiberglass "solar battery collector storage tubes" that hold 300 pounds (136 kg) of water mass each and are commercially available.

Masonry walls are not particularly effective as a thermal mass, and because they pick up only 30 to 35 percent of the heat in the air

Solid Wall for Heat Storage: Black metal cans filled with water are stacked against the north-facing wall in this passive solar greenhouse to serve as thermal mass. A sheet of plastic separates these cans from the gardening area of the greenhouse.

after ten hours of direct illumination, they can contribute to overheating. To help overcome such limitations, one greenhouse owner in the northeastern United States painted black the concrete block wall between his solar greenhouse and attached dwelling and installed an aluminized Mylar curtain over it. This is closed at night and during cloudy weather to cut heat losses through the glazing and is also drawn during very hot weather so it reflects light instead of absorbing and storing unwanted heat.

Adequate thermal mass of whatever kind has a moderating effect on the temperatures in both freestanding and attached solar greenhouses and is essential to prevent extreme temperature swings from near freezing at night to around 100°F (38°C) during the day. In fact, inside temperatures of over 90°F (32°C) in winter indicate that more storage mass is needed, for there should be no need to vent the greenhouse in cold months.

In addition to making themselves known by the water and rock masses they incorporate, greenhouses designed for optimum solar performance can be recognized by a variety of other characteristic design features. These include:

—Southern glazing sloped so it reflects away much of the light from the high summer sun but admits as much light as possible during January and February, the time of year when the combined effect of low outside temperatures and reduced solar radiation is most severe. Actually a wide range of angles meets this requirement, with various experts suggesting that the pitch of glazing be determined by adding anywhere from 20 to 50 degrees to the latitude of the greenhouse location, letting the final decision be influenced by practical considerations such as the desired height of the greenhouse and on-site obstructions to sunlight (such as nearby trees and hills).

—An orientation in which the long axis of the greenhouse tends to run east-west versus the north-south orientation preferred for fully glazed, conventional houses. A north-south orientation has been found to admit up to 12 percent less light than an east-west setting. Here again, however, there is room for variation, for it also has been found that houses with roof slopes of 35 to 60 degrees at orientations as much as 20 degrees off true south will receive only 4 to 5 percent less total daily radiation through the glazing than a greenhouse oriented due south. In fact, a shift of up to 20 degrees to the southwest may actually work out better in coastal areas and other locations where morning clouds are often followed by afternoon sun.

—A north wall that is opaque, insulated, and reflective in order to reduce heat losses significantly with comparatively little loss of light. Depending on orientation, all or part of the end walls may also be opaque.

—Self-shading calculated to keep out the sun when it is at its highest and hottest. Shading may take the form of an overhang or a south-facing roof with up to a third or even half of the upper part opaque.

—Many heat-conserving design and construction aspects. Solar greenhouses are thoroughly insulated and well sealed in winter so that energy losses through walls, roof, floor, and cracks are reduced to a minimum in cold weather. Foundation perimeters are insulated to the frost line; in small greenhouses or those with water in pools, insulation is placed under the floor. Also, vents are insulated and sealed in winter and there is usually a double layer of glazing and/or removable insulation is used on glazing at night. Such insulating measures are crucial since skimping here means more heat storage is needed, and that takes up precious growing space. By reducing air exchange in all these ways, heat requirements are kept to a minimum.

The Active Solar Greenhouse

Active greenhouses ideally share many of the design characteristics of their passive counterparts—unless, that is, a conventional greenhouse has been retrofitted (meaning a solar heating system has been added to an already existing greenhouse). The difference is that active heating systems contain moving parts and use mechanical means powered by conventional sources of energy to collect, store, and circulate the sun's heat, which is pumped or moved by fan from one place to another to stabilize greenhouse temperatures rather precisely. Active setups can be used for short-term storage, as passive systems are, or to stockpile heat for extended storage of several days or more, transferring it as needed when the greenhouse thermostat falls below a preset level. At this stage of active solar technology, extended storage seems to work best with some sort of backup heating system and when the greenhouse is maintained at below 60°F (16°C).

As researchers are only too aware, gathering and storing enough solar energy to meet all the heating needs of a moderate to warm greenhouse in most areas of the United States and Canada requires a huge collection area (often external auxiliary collectors and reflectors can take up as much space as the greenhouse), a corresponding increase in the amount of thermal storage, and extra fans or pumps to transfer the heat from storage to the greenhouse air.

As all this suggests, active systems can be complicated and costly. Work done at Cornell University suggests that at present a passive system used with a highly insulated night cover offers greater benefits than an active collector system, and can provide a large fraction of night heating needs even during cold weather in a climate providing only modest solar radiation. Obviously, to be cost effective now or in the near future, active systems of any sophistication require a higher threshold of winter radiation than is available in most parts of the United States and Canada.

Though still experimental and geared toward large-scale commercial situations, the research into active solar systems involves concepts and methods that are being adapted for use in smaller greenhouses and are worth looking at for that reason. There are various kinds of collectors used in active setups. Some systems collect heat inside the greenhouse (as passive systems do), while others use either flat-plate or concentrating collectors placed outside.

Despite the extra cost of the collector and heat transfer equipment, and the substantial space requirements, external collectors have advantages. For one thing, they can be much more efficient than the greenhouse glazing itself, which can transmit only the low levels of heat tolerable to plants, whereas high temperatures or vast amounts of storage are necessary to obtain large amounts of solar energy. Moreover, it is possible to optimize the size and orientation of the collector even in retrofitting, and to use water more readily in collection and storage.

Concentrating collectors use mirrors or an acrylic lens to focus light on, for example, a pipe containing a moving fluid. These devices can create very high temperatures, but they must be moved to track the sun and since they can use only direct sunlight, they don't perform well on hazy days or in overcast climates.

Far more feasible operationally for smaller greenhouses are flat-plate collectors made of a glass or plastic sheet through which light passes to be absorbed by a dark surface beneath. The amount of heat collected depends upon the size of the collector and on the angle at which it is tilted. Plate-type collectors can use water in tubes or water flowing freely and evaporating and condensing against the cover to collect heat. Or they can use air, which removes heat from metal plates or surfaces beneath the glass or plastic. The metal can be in the form of a corrugated metal strip with both sides exposed to the airstream, or metal fins, screens, or cans cut in half and fastened to a dark lower surface.

Flat-plate collectors mounted outside the greenhouse are being used in some relatively small-scale greenhouse projects despite the fact that they are expensive and require lots of space in order to gather enough heat to counteract low winter temperatures. As fuel costs continue to climb, build-it-yourself collectors are beginning to look increasingly feasible to commercial growers and more adventurous amateurs.

For the present, it seems most realistic to use external collectors in conjunction with a well-designed and thoroughly insulated solar setup to provide a modest amount of heat for a relatively small area.

At a prototype greenhouse-residence built at Colorado State University, hot-air collectors are used together with air-to-water heat exchangers not to warm the greenhouse air at night, but to meet the lesser heating needs of warm soil and irrigation water—an approach which has been found to reduce nighttime heating needs significantly, since plants with warm roots can tolerate much cooler temperatures. The researchers have found that this efficient use of solar heat combined with lowering heat losses through the use of a common wall, thorough caulking, and perimeter insulation 16 to 22 inches (41 to 56 cm) below ground is very effective in reducing heat demand.

Another approach to indoor collection is to heat the air in the unused ridge of the greenhouse and move it into storage. Most effective in growing foliage plants which need partial shading year-round anyway, this method involves placing clear polyethylene from eave to eave of a preferably double-glazed greenhouse, thereby creating a sealed-off attic. A layer of black polypropylene shadecloth providing from 25 to 50 percent shade (as much as the plants will tolerate) is then stretched immediately above the clear polyethylene to serve as the collector. The superheated air is moved by fan-and-duct into an 18 inch (46 cm) deep bed of ½-inch (13 mm) gravel under the benches. At night or during cloudy periods the air from the greenhouse is sent through the heated gravel, warmed, then recirculated. Developed by scientists at the University of Florida and Rutgers University, this system lowers the cost of collectors dramatically—in fact, the clear polyethylene more than pays for itself by acting as a thermal curtain that reduces 30 to 40 percent of the greenhouse heat losses at night.

If the modes of collection in active solar heating are markedly different from those in passive systems, the storage media are still water and rocks, although these are often used in greater quantities and more sophisticated ways since active technology allows for more effective heat transfer devices and makes possible long-term storage. In an overcast climate like that of the northwest United States, a heat siphon makes it possible to send heat from a nearby wood-heated sauna into a greenhouse fish tank and the stored

The Heated Attic: Based on the idea that air heated in the unused greenhouse ridge can be moved into storage and drawn upon as needed, this method requires sealing off the ridge to create an attic. Stretch clear polyethylene from eave to eave, then add a layer of black polypropylene shadecloth to act as the collector. A fan-and-duct system moves the heated air into a layer of gravel under the benches, where it is stored. When supplemental heat is necessary, air from the greenhouse can be moved through the warm gravel and recirculated.

heat can support the fishes. On a more ambitious scale oriented to long-term storage, researchers in Ohio have been testing a solar pond that will double as a collector and storage system and be capable of heating a rural home or greenhouse. The idea is to trap solar energy in a dense layer of brine at the bottom of a pool—thus preventing heat from being lost at the surface. The warm brine is then pumped to a brine-to-air heat exchanger.

Rock storage systems of an active kind often involve many tons of fist size rocks or gravel; the larger these materials are, the longer it takes them to pick up and give off heat. When located under the floor of a greenhouse or perhaps in an insulated basement, such storage beds can supply heat for several days in the absence of sun, provided the storage and collection areas are large enough.

The modes of distributing or transferring heat in active solar greenhouses vary from simple exhaust or circulating fans, through fan-and-tube or fan-and-duct setups, to somewhat more unusual heat exchangers. For example, since collectors are more efficient to operate at low temperatures, it makes sense to use them that way, providing you can furnish the larger surfaces necessary for equivalent heat transfer. Working along these lines, researchers have discovered that it is possible to use low-efficiency, low-cost, wood-and-plastic collectors to heat water merely to 80° to 90°F (27° to 32°C), put it into storage in an insulated bed of loose gravel, then use minimal horsepower to pump it out at night so it trickles over a large vertical sheet of black vinyl draped over structural members of the greenhouse or a clothesline.

The heated plastic then warms the air, with the water rolling back down to the storage beds through the porous concrete floor. When used in combination with black polyethylene curtains to keep in heat at night, such a large, warm lake of water under the floor has successfully maintained nighttime temperatures of over 70°F (21°C) when it was 30° to 35°F (-1° to 2°C) outside.

Hybrid Solar Heating Systems

Some of the solar entrepreneurs who use a minimum of mechanical aids to collect, store, and distribute the sun's heat wince at the rigid definitions of active and passive solar heating, since approaches using a lot of expensive technology and equipment as well as strategies using only a little are both considered "active." Those systems using a minimum of technology might more fairly be called hybrids. Like passive setups, the hybrids use glazing as the solar collector, but they seek to avoid the common passive problems of overheating and underheating by using fans, blowers, and active thermal storage systems designed for optimum efficiency. In short, hybrid systems attempt to make the active approach cost effective by using efficient, reasonably economical live-in collectors.

Proponents of hybrid systems claim that a double-glazed or night-shuttered greenhouse that is properly designed, oriented, and insulated will create a temperature differential high enough to yield an operating efficiency greater than that of most medium-temperature active collectors. That being the case, they say, all that is necessary is to provide enough active control to regulate fluctuations in temperature and get the most value from the glazing's performance.

CHOOSING THE GREENHOUSE THAT IS BEST FOR YOU

Choosing from among the wealth of prefabricated greenhouses and intriguing plans is no easy task, but you will find that your options will narrow quite naturally and inevitably when you come up with the answers to some very specific questions:

1. What are the limitations imposed by your situation regarding the size of a greenhouse, its permanence, and its location in regard to climate, the amount of light that will be available, protection from wind, and drainage? Obviously, the multi-faceted answer to this question will help you decide whether to build an attached or freestanding house and will suggest appropriate styles as well.

For example, if you rent your home or live where your tax assessment will go up substantially if you construct what is considered to be a permanent addition to your property, you might want to choose a style that requires no foundation and can be erected and dismantled easily and inexpensively. This would rule out traditionally shaped glass-glazed houses.

Or, for instance, if your greenhouse is to be sited in an exposed area where winters are cold and blustery and hailstorms occur, you will probably want to rule out a freestanding glass-to-ground gabled house—unless you are willing to pay monstrous heating bills in winter (or to shut down during the coldest months) and to pay extra for tempered glass.

On the other hand, if you live where the climate is mild and the air calm but the sun very intense, a glass-to-ground even-span house may be ideal since the heating bills will be low and the nonplastic glazing will be impervious to ultraviolet degradation. If you live where winters are frigid but where there is a high level of solar radiation in midwinter, clearly an energy-hoarding solar greenhouse would be preferable to a traditionally glazed one—especially if you have little money to spend for supplemental heating.

2. How much do you want or need to trade off labor for money in building, equipping, running, and maintaining your greenhouse? The answer to this will help you clarify many points that bear on greenhouse shapes and styles—for example, whether you want to buy a prefabricated house or build from scratch with local, possibly recycled materials; whether you

might want to put up a solar house or a pit in order to eliminate or greatly reduce the cost of buying and running a heating system and the need for automated forced-air cooling or venting systems; or whether you prefer to pay more for a house with glazing and framing that will last longer and require less maintenance.

3. What kind of greenhouse environment do you want to create? If a no-frills working greenhouse that can hold a maximum of plants, give you plenty of puttering pleasure, and perhaps yield some part-time income is your goal, you will give priority to getting a maximum of growing space for your investment, and you might choose to retrofit a porch with scrounged-up materials, or put up a curved shape covered with fiberglass or film that sacrifices appearance to economy and performance.

On the other hand, if you want to put a greenhouse off a kitchen or at the end of a breezeway and use it as a sun/work/play room that provides a restful background of tidy pot plants and rejuvenating house plants, you may find that one of the more handsome attached glass span-roofed or mansard houses is well worth the extra cost to you. After all, you will be getting an extra room for relaxing, entertaining, enjoying breakfast, or even doing some desk work, and be boosting the market value of your home in the bargain.

4. What types of plants do you intend to grow? Obviously, their light and heat requirements interacting with your budget and the limitations of your situation will have some influence on the style and shape of greenhouse you choose. Foliage plants, for example, will thrive in the cheaper warmth that can be provided by an attached house and will tolerate the uneven light of modest intensity delivered for a limited number of hours per day. If you plan to specialize in hardy flowers and

bulbs such as cyclamens, narcissus, and tulips, or other plants that can tolerate wide temperature fluctuations, a detached-pit greenhouse will serve admirably. On the other hand, cut flowers such as carnations (*Dianthus caryophyllus*) and roses, flowering pot plants, and fruiting vegetable plants like to be bathed in the kind of bright, diffused light provided, for example, by a freestanding curvilinear or curved-roof house covered with self-shading fiberglass.

5. When do you plan to use your greenhouse? If you merely want to extend the growing season at both ends, a simple half or whole A-frame of plastic over wood or one of the small ready-made portable-panel greenhouses may be adequate. Remember that Dutch light and span-roofed houses have a roof pitch primarily designed for spring and summer growing, and solar designs and pits are geared toward winter and in some climates may overheat seriously in summer and have to be shut down. For year-round vegetable and flower production, a freestanding, glazing-to-ground, span-roofed, curved-roofed, or curvilinear greenhouse would be the most desirable. To hold down heating costs in cold climates it will be important to choose a type like the Gothic Arch or Quonset that can be double glazed easily, or perhaps a double-glazed even-span or mansard type with a knee wall which can be insulated. For summer use, such a high-light-intensity house should have plenty of vents or be amenable to forced-air cooling to keep the temperature below 90°F (32°C).

6. Is there any possibility that you will want to enlarge your greenhouse later? If so, you might want to avoid domes, film-covered types, and most attached greenhouses, and instead consider a freestanding even-span or mansard house glazed with glass or fiberglass, since it will be relatively easy to add sections to such a structure.

Once you have a particular style of greenhouse in mind, if you have any choice in the matter, it is important to give some thought to whether the attached or freestanding version is preferable in your case. Both have their good and bad points. Detached greenhouses are available in a greater variety of shapes and sizes, and they may be located and oriented to get a maximum of light and protection from wind and snowloads falling off other nearby structures. They also are usually easier to enlarge. If lightweight, they can be built without the costly foundation often recommended for attached greenhouses to keep them from separating from the adjoining structure when the ground heaves. All else being equal, gabled freestanding houses also are easier to keep cool in summer and air successfully in winter since they have vents on both sides of the ridge; this means there is more adequate air exchange in summer and that there will always be vents away from the wind that can be opened in winter.

In addition, a separate greenhouse at a distance from the house can provide a quiet place to retreat from the world for a few hours. And where cost is concerned, if you consider initial expense relative to growing space, ease of installation, and economy of upkeep, freestanding units give more value per dollar than attached units do. The lowest cost per square foot of growing space is provided when you buy a high-sided freestanding house 17 to 18 feet (5.1 to 5.4 m) wide, which can accommodate a bench along each side, two walkways, and a wide center bench.

On the other hand, the lowest total cost honors go to a lean-to house from 7 to 12 feet (2.1 to 3.6 m) wide with benches on either side of a center path. Much more convenient for enjoyment (provided they are built over a connecting door), attached houses lose a lot less heat than nonsolar freestanding types. According to one source, an 8- by 12-foot (2.4 by 3.6 m) lean-to requires one-fifth less heat to maintain 50°F (10°C) than an equivalent separate structure when the outside temperature is 0°F (-18°C). And, if needed, supplemental heating can often be provided without investing in any additional equipment, by extending pipes or ducts from the home furnace at a relatively low cost. Well-designed lean-tos also can contribute heat to your home in bright, cold weather.

But although they have great advantages in retaining heat and lowering fuel bills, attached greenhouses suffer a great reduction of light from April to September. Structures attached to a two-story house are at a particular disadvantage in overcast weather, since they are exposed to little more than half of the sky dome at any time. In very humid areas, adjoining greenhouses also can make a home uncomfortable in the summer and even encourage mildew on furnishings. On the other hand, the added moisture can add healthful humidity to homes in dry areas in the summer and to homes everywhere during winter.

In juggling all the variables that will lead you to choose an attached or separate greenhouse of whatever kind, remember to consider size. For example, the smaller a greenhouse is, the more heat it loses per unit of volume. Therefore, if you live in a severe climate and are contemplating a greenhouse smaller than 100 square feet (9 sq m), you really should attach it to offset this disadvantage. If you live where winters are mild, do the same for a greenhouse less than 200 square feet (18 sq m) in size.

In sizing your greenhouse-to-be, it is a good idea to think ahead and put up a structure big enough to meet your future needs—especially if you choose a type of greenhouse that is difficult or impossible to enlarge. By all means, try to avoid the mistake of letting a lower purchase or building price persuade you to put up a tiny box of a greenhouse, for the cost per square foot of growing area tends to drop with larger greenhouses and, more importantly, the higher surface area-to-volume ratio of very small houses causes them to lose heat faster than larger ones. As a result,

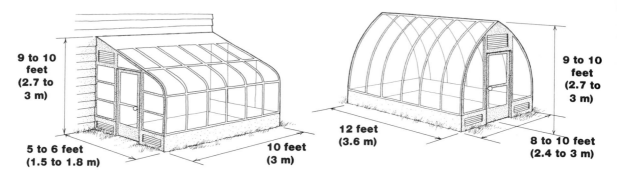

Minimum Greenhouse Dimensions: The measurements for two styles of greenhouses (lean-to on the left and freestanding on the right) given here represent the minimum dimensions at which they provide efficient growing area and stable temperatures.

temperatures in a tiny greenhouse will fluctuate drastically.

As far as length and width are concerned, the absolute minimum for a lean-to should be 5 or 6 feet by 10 feet (1.5 or 1.8 m by 3 m), with the preferred width between 8 and 10 feet (2.4 to 3 m) regardless of length— a span that provides good growing space and allows the glazing to contribute substantial heat to the greenhouse, but limits the surface through which heat is gained in summer or lost in winter. To function properly, separate greenhouses should be at least 8 or 10 feet by 12 feet (2.4 or 3 m by 3.6 m) in size. Long, rectangular, south-facing shapes will give your plants a longer period of daylight than more squarish houses.

Actually, the vertical dimensions of the greenhouse are perhaps even more critical in stabilizing temperatures. The height at the eaves should be at least five feet (1.5 m) and preferably as much as seven feet (2.1 m) to provide ample air circulation above the plants and generous head room for plants and people. The ridge should be nine or ten feet (2.7 or 3 m) high to provide a cushion of air that will buffer the plants from sudden temperature changes outside and keep them from cooking in the hotter air that rises and stays trapped at the greenhouse peak. Remember, though, that unless you recirculate air in a high ridge with a fan, you will lose a lot of heat through the ridge via conduction and ra-

diation in the winter, and the temperature difference between outside and inside will be higher than it would be in a greenhouse with a lower profile. A high ridge also means a greater distance between the plants and the glazing, which translates into less light at plant level. It also increases the volume of air that must be heated. One rule of thumb holds that the ridge height should equal the height at the eave, plus one-quarter the width of the greenhouse.*

BUILD IT OR BUY IT?

Once you have determined the style of greenhouse and the framing and glazing materials you'd like (see The Greenhouse Exterior, later in this chapter), you must decide whether to build from a plan or buy a prefabricated structure from a manufacturer. Just to make this decision more challenging, there are many appealing plans and prefabricated kits on the market and several pros and cons to sort through regarding each course of action.

---

*Note: For glass-glazed houses the roof pitch should be at least 6 inches (15 cm) of rise per foot (30 cm) of wall to keep condensation from dripping on plants, whereas a greater roof slope of 7 to 8½ inches (18 to 22 cm) of rise per foot is required for fiberglass and film-covered houses.

The most obvious advantage of building yourself is the money you will save, which can range anywhere from a third to half or more of what you would pay for a roughly equivalent manufactured house if you buy all new materials, and much more if you are willing to let your greenhouse take shape around materials you can salvage or scrounge, such as old window sashes, discarded doors, or used lumber.

In comparing manufacturers' prices with what you would have to pay for the raw materials, keep in mind that the cost of the foundation (which in any event you will have to build) is not included in the price of a prefabricated house and that often such essentials as vents are listed as options that will drive the true cost up further. The same is true of solid knee walls, which you can build of brick, stone, wood, or aluminum. As all this suggests, depending on the model you want, even a prefab house can require a surprising amount of preparatory labor on your part, in addition to from hours to many days of time spent putting up the greenhouse itself, for most manufactured houses are not preassembled. Unless you buy from one of the few manufacturers that ship partially preassembled sections of walls, roofs, and doors, what you'll get will be precut pieces requiring complete assembly during installation. You will find, too, that the less expensive prefabs are often somewhat more difficult to erect.

On the other hand, manufactured houses offer some genuine advantages in return for their price tag. For one thing, commercial structures are designed by competent engineers who use their skills to provide maximum structural strength and light, pitch the roof properly for condensation runoff, and design roof bars or rafters with drip grooves to carry off water that would otherwise plop into plants. The components of a manufactured house also have been selected to work together to best advantage, and have been chosen and pretreated to withstand the high humidity of the greenhouse environment.

What's more, these materials are engineered to fit together tightly, thereby saving you money on heating bills. Reputable dealers provide step-by-step directions for every aspect of construction for the greenhouse, and usually for an appropriate foundation as well. It is also true that certain framing materials like aluminum and steel or iron are hard to purchase to specification and maddening to work with "from scratch." For example, it just doesn't make any sense to try to put together your own aluminum-and-glass English-style greenhouse.

In addition, manufacturers are catching up with the importance of offering models designed to conserve heat, many of which now have double glazing and other energy-saving features unavailable commercially until recently. Some kindly dealers will even allow you the option of buying local lumber to somewhat reduce the cost of your frame.

In general, you will do well to buy if you're long on money and short on construction skills or time. If you do go this route, you might want to advertise in the newspaper in hopes of locating a used manufactured house which you can buy inexpensively and move piece by piece to your location. Meanwhile, send away for a generous sampling of manufacturers' catalogs and peruse them carefully, comparing the models offered and their prices in reference to the minimum heights, widths, and lengths recommended for satisfactory gardening results (see Choosing the Greenhouse That Is Best for You), and guarantees on framing and glazing.

Given present and projected problems in regard to costs and availability of fuel, you would also do well to try to obtain and compare the Btu heat loss figures for models which you are seriously considering. Some manufacturers are already providing this information in their brochures and it is worth serious attention. When you have narrowed down your choices, ask the manufacturers still in the running to give you the location of one of their models nearby and *go see it.* One look is worth a thousand pictures. You also might try to get the names of several owners to talk to; a responsible dealer should be willing to make them available to you.

Building might be the better choice for you if your first priority is to keep costs down and if you like carpentry and have confidence in your skills. It is also the sensible choice if you want to put together a simple freestanding greenhouse, such as Dutch lights hinged at a 120-degree angle with simple, triangular ends framed in wood and covered with plastic (that can be moved aside for ventilating and watering). Other greenhouses which lend themselves to home construction include the plastic-over-wood structures resembling glorified cold frames that are described under Types of Greenhouses, earlier in the chapter, or traditional pit houses.

Building it yourself, with or without a professionally designed plan, also can be the best solution if you have a promising site for a retrofitted structure; such attached greenhouses are often the cheapest and simplest of all to construct. To keep such a retrofit as easy and basic as possible, consider the advice of Bill Yanda, a no-nonsense solar greenhouse designer and builder who encourages people to build lean-tos with straight or slant-legged sides. Shed roofs, says Yanda, save money, time, and complications by making it easier to work with standard lengths and angles. They also have fewer intersecting planes (which makes sealing the greenhouse easier) and simplify applying movable insulation since you are working with large, flat surfaces. See the Appendix for a list of some sources of greenhouse plans.

SITING YOUR GREENHOUSE

In judging the best place to build your greenery, again it is important to weigh many factors. Your first order of business should be to check local zoning laws, since few experiences are more agonizing than having to dismantle a lovingly completed structure for purely le-

galistic reasons. You will also want to locate your greenhouse for convenient access—not just to you, but to a water line and probably to electric current as well, which should preferably run underground to the greenhouse.

Next, take into account both air and land drainage conditions. The way in which air moves around a greenhouse can have quite an effect on the temperatures inside, and if possible you will want to place your structure so it is not in a low-lying pocket, valley bottom, or other closed-in spot where cold air, frost, and fog will settle in over it, causing the house to warm up late and cool off early—and to cost more to heat. Low ground at the bottom of a slope is also bad for water drainage, especially if you will grow plants in the ground or under benches, or if you plan a pit greenhouse. And if you build on the side of a slope you may have to put drainage on the higher side to keep rain from seeping in.

If the greenhouse will be attached to or located near your home, it is important to consider what's overhead. Beware of gutterless roofs that will roll rivers of rain onto the greenhouse or nearby, compounding drainage problems, or of sloping roofs that will dump snowloads on the greenhouse in winter.

Whenever possible, site your greenhouse so it is sheltered from strong prevailing winds by a building, hedge, or fence. This is almost as important to greenhouse warmth as orientation, for in cold weather the temperature inside an exposed greenhouse will drop about $\frac{1}{2}°$ for every mile-per-hour of wind speed over 15 mph (km-per-hour over 24). And in summer, a hot, dry wind will make it hard for you to provide enough humidity to protect your plants from dehydration.

Consider also the character of the land where you build. There should be no tree stumps or organic fill that will cause the greenhouse to sink or shift as the material decomposes, and fresh-filled land should have at least two to four weeks to settle before construction.

Locating your greenhouse so it gets as many hours a day as possible of the strongest possible light is, of course, of paramount importance. This is trickier than it might seem, since a site that gets brilliant light from a sun relatively high in the sky from March to October might be blocked off from the weaker, more oblique rays of the lower winter sun. To anticipate whether this will be a problem for a potential site intended for winter growing, you should determine what altitude the sun reaches at noon in your area on December 21 (the time when the sun is at its lowest angle). Then use two pieces of wood to make up a siting angle, making the angle between them the same as that figure. By putting one leg of the device on the ground at your prospective site and looking up the other piece of wood, you will be able to tell whether trees, buildings, hills, and other surroundings will be a problem at the time of year when natural light is at its briefest and dimmest.

Another highly important aspect of siting is orienting the greenhouse ridge so that a maximum of light enters. This obviously is more of a given and less of a choice when the greenhouse is to be attached. If the long sides of the dwelling face true north-south, the greenhouse is best placed anywhere on the south side, while if your home faces east of south by less than 45 degrees, the greenhouse should go on the southeast corner of the

south face. If the house is exactly 45 degrees southeast, the greenhouse can go on either the southeast corner or on the southwest face at the corner nearest south. When the home is more than 45 degrees east of south, the greenhouse definitely should be on the southwest face.

Actually, if obstructions to light or lack of space prohibit such optimum siting, which maximizes morning light, it might still be worthwhile to put an attached greenhouse even on the north side of a house, for many plants can be grown with only three hours of sunlight, and though many flowering plants will not do well in a northern exposure without supplemental lighting, you can still grow lower-light plants like ferns, African violets, tuberous-rooted begonias, achimenes, and some orchids.

The best orientation for a freestanding house depends somewhat on the latitude, on the shape and length of the greenhouse, and on the time of year it will be most used.

THE GREENHOUSE EXTERIOR

FOUNDATIONS

Not all greenhouses require a foundation. For example, if you live where winds are no problem and where the winter climate is distinctly

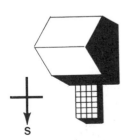

Four Orientations for Maximum Light: Here are the optimum siting angles for a greenhouse attached to a dwelling with its long sides facing in each of the given directions, from left to right: for a dwelling facing true north-south, site the greenhouse on the south side; for a dwelling facing east of south by less than 45 degrees, site on southeast corner of the south face; for a dwelling facing southeast at 45 degrees, site on southeast corner or on southwest face at corner nearest south; for dwelling facing east of south by more than 45 degrees, site on southwest face.

mild, or if your greenhouse is to be a free-standing, lightweight model made of plastic film or fiberglass panels that go all the way to the ground, you might be able to set it up directly on a level, well-drained site. To hold down such a house, you can use rot-proof buried anchors or even treated wooden stakes, although these are less reliable.

Some of the commercially available free-standing or attached houses made of aluminum and plastic or fiberglass can be erected on flat earth, on a slate, concrete, or wooden patio, or on an apartment roof or terrace with no underpinnings. However, a wooden sill is sometimes recommended. One very workable idea for a temporary structure is to lay redwood ties on leveled earth covered with two inches (5 cm) of sand, then screw, nail, or bolt down the ties every three to four feet (0.9 to 1.2 m) with yard-long (0.9 m) metal or wooden stakes (be sure wooden stakes are treated with copper naphthenate).

Usually, though, attached greenhouses built on soil need a solid foundation to keep them from separating from the adjoining house or garage. Indeed, local building codes may require a sturdy foundation. And the heavier freestanding houses with side walls of brick, stone, concrete, or even wood or cement-asbestos panels demand a foundation of some kind to prevent them from gradually sinking. Although in balmy settings glass-to-ground houses may get by on a simple redwood sill, any kind of glass house needs a firmer foundation where the ground thaws and freezes, for this heaving can crack the glazing and twist the frame. Harsh winters may do the same to fiberglass-paneled houses.

So-called "full foundations" made of stone, brick, concrete or pumice blocks, or poured concrete are recommended for such houses whenever the primary vertical parts of the frame are four feet (1.2 m) apart. Though double wood with an air space in between was once commonly used as a cheap and easily installed perimeter foundation, it

is not as stable and protective as masonry and not nearly as durable. Poured concrete is a popular option, for it is easy and economical and can bear the weight of continuous concrete or masonry foundation walls.

Side or base walls of wood or aluminum are offered as options by many greenhouse manufacturers. If you are building your own greenhouse from a plan, you can make these simply an upward extension of a poured concrete or concrete block foundation wall. Or you can top a full foundation with a handsome structure of redwood, brick, or fieldstone that will complement your home. Recommended wherever winters are cold and long, side walls can make up for less light under the benches by protecting glazing from heaped-up snow, by acting as a buffer against infiltration of the especially cold air at ground level, and by reducing the amount of glazing in the greenhouse, thereby lessening heat loss and lowering fuel consumption.

Obviously, insulating side walls optimizes the amount of heat they can keep in. In fact, side walls covered with insulating board to a depth of 12 to 24 inches (30 to 61 cm) underground save 5 to 10 percent on fuel bills. If you live in a cold climate, avoid aluminum side walls unless they are insulated, for aluminum by itself conducts 250 times as much heat as glass of the same thickness, and will actually lose heat as fast as single-layer glass and a lot faster than double-glazed rigid or film plastic.

If you're interested in trading off some heat savings for extra light, you can always build a side wall on the side of your greenhouse where you plan to use raised staging—perhaps the north side, which will admit little light through lower glazing anyway—and omit the knee wall on the light-gathering south side, perhaps growing border plants there.

The Solar Option

Since solar greenhouses aim to store heat during the day for gradual release during the cooler nights, their design tends to maximize the heat-retaining potential inherent in insulated foundations and side walls. Clearly, the advantages offered by a full size ready-made side wall by way of either storing heat or reflecting light help make attached solar houses more workable in this respect, and even free-standing kinds feature a massive, completely opaque wall as their steeply sloped north side, since a glazed surface on that side tends to lose more in heat during the winter months than it gains in light. For superior heat storage these full north walls are often quite thick, usually requiring a poured concrete foundation, and are made of concrete, brick, adobe, or concrete or hollow pumice blocks. (When blocks are used, the center holes in the top course should be filled in with poured concrete for added strength and mass.)

Since the end walls of both solar and conventional houses are completely vertical, it also may be desirable to make one or both of them opaque and massive.

Needless to say, however, end walls that face southeast or southwest should almost always be glazed since they might make a solid contribution to the amount of light and heat admitted. Also, it is best to avoid solid end walls in really small houses since they might cast too much shade relative to the amount of light coming in through a short span of southern glazing.

FRAMES

In choosing the frame for your greenhouse picture, you must juggle the factors of initial cost, durability, the time and money involved in maintenance, and the material's ability to transmit light, keep in heat, and keep out cold. Long favored by people building their own greenhouses because of its low cost and workability, wood has other solid advantages. Because of its natural insulating ability (redwood, for example, transmits heat 1,400 times more slowly than aluminum), wood makes for houses that stay considerably warmer

than metal structures and is for that reason a sensible framing choice for solar greenhouses and other types having a relatively high proportion of frame to glazing.

Needless to say, the advantage of wood as a material that conducts heat slowly holds only if the greenhouse is tightly glazed to prevent air leaks, but that is easier to do with wood than with metal. Wood is also much simpler to caulk, weatherstrip, and otherwise insulate than metal and has less tendency to "sweat" and cause condensation problems, since it changes temperature more slowly.

But if wood scores high on economy, heat retention, and a warm, natural look, it gets lower marks when it comes to admitting light. Light transmission is a more important factor than you might guess in frame selection, for the supporting structure of the greenhouse can account for 60 to 70 percent of the total light loss. Since wood has a much lower strength-to-bulk ratio than just about any other framing material, in a greenhouse made of any but the flimsiest glazing wood members will have to be thicker and/or more closely spaced than metal ones, and might work against the use of larger panes and panels that can maximize light gain. There are, however, differences from wood to wood in this respect: redwood boards, for instance, can support more weight than the same volume of Western red cedar.

Wood also demands more preparation and maintenance than metal does. For maximum durability it should be pressure-treated or dipped in a slowly heated preservative, then allowed to cool in it. Penetration varies considerably among timbers, with redwood said to absorb preservative at about the rate of one inch (2.5 cm) of depth per week of soaking. Pine or fir soaked in copper naphthenate at home is said to last from 7 to 15 years, which is the life span of untreated, top-quality redwood or cedar heartwood. Pressure-treated redwood lasts 25 years or more.

To get more protection and reflect more light inside the house, most authorities suggest painting treated wood. Since paint made with white lead is more vulnerable to mildew, it is best to lay on one or two coats of a good white primer made with a titanium base and tung oil, then to add a top coat. This can be white greenhouse paint, which with a matte finish will reflect 75 to 90 percent of the light that strikes it, or aluminum paint, which is more resistant to moisture but reflects only 60 to 70 percent of the light. Depending on the quality of the paint job and the climate where you live, wooden greenhouses may have to be repainted as often as every three years, although red cedar frames may instead be "painted" yearly with a thin mineral oil that will penetrate the wood but allow it to breathe.

More maintenance is required if you glaze with putty, which is awkward to use and in time will crack and let in moisture and need replacing. To forestall this unhappy day, it is desirable to get a tight seal by glazing with nonhardening mastic or with a plastic compound applied with a gun. The rigid glazing can be held on with brass nails or clips. Or you can cover your wooden sash bars with aluminum bar caps. These will minimize deterioration of paint and putty, give a tighter seal, and hold down glass vibration in windy locations. On the other hand, if winters and winds are not very troublesome, you can choose a Dutch light type of house in which the glass simply rests in grooves. Although this so-called "dry glazing" allows a little rattling, it calls for no maintenance and can be a good choice in a benign climate and wind-sheltered spot.

What kind of wood should you choose? If you are willing to take pains to preserve and paint it, you can do fine with relatively inexpensive construction grade pine or fir timber that is straight, has few knots, and gives off a firm and full sound when tapped against something. More long-lasting woods offered as part of prefabricated houses and by greenhouse building suppliers include first-grade Western red cedar (which is the best of the

Wood-Framed Greenhouse: The warm, natural tones of the wood are readily apparent in this finished greenhouse. Aside from appearance, wood has the added advantages of being relatively inexpensive and easy to work with, as well as acting as a natural insulator.

soft woods but inclined to expand and contract a lot), heartwood of swamp-grown cypress (which is costly but most durable of all for rafters and gutters), and clear heart California redwood that has been properly kiln-dried for greenhouse use.

An increasingly popular framing material is aluminum. Although this material has a high initial cost and squanders heat through its surface and through the spring clips often used with lapped glass in this kind of frame, aluminum is virtually maintenance free. Moreover, because of its superb strength-to-bulk ratio, when aluminum is used with a lightweight glazing like fiberglass, it is possible to use large panels that can admit light with a minimum of interference from sash bars. (Sash bars, by the way, can be insulated so they do not act as a thermal bridge, and the condensation problems that can occur with aluminum can be offset

Aluminum Framing: This lightweight metal is highly desirable because it is maintenance free, long lasting, and suited for use with large, light-admitting panels. Aluminum frames can be used in conjunction with various types of glazing to provide the greenhouse with those features best suited to your temperature, light, and maintenance needs.

by choosing a frame with built-in drip grooves that will carry off drops to the side before they fall onto plants.)

Often used in prefabricated houses with small spans, aluminum with lightweight, rigid plastic glazing can make the expense and effort of a foundation unnecessary, although a wooden sill is required to keep such frames from direct contact with soil. Mill-finish aluminum is highly resistant to weathering, but it does tend to darken gradually and pit somewhat with time, particularly in salty coastal air or in areas with heavily polluted air. But aluminum covered with a baked-on enamel finish makes the most trouble-free and long-lasting kind of frame (albeit the most expensive).

Moreover, to lessen heat losses and weathering, some greenhouse manufacturers offer houses designed to expose a minimum of

frame and to capitalize on the ability of aluminum to be shaped so as to allow groove glazing. Combined with spongelike elastic gasketry, groove glazing can reduce air leakage considerably.

The best bet for framing an exceptionally strong, maintenance-free hobby greenhouse nowadays is hot-dipped galvanized steel. Keep in mind, though, that when galvanized steel is used for the entire frame or as the substructure, stainless steel or galvanized bolts or fastenings must be used, for aluminum glazing clips and bar caps will react chemically with galvanized coatings to create rust.

Another kind of greenhouse frame becoming more and more popular among do-it-yourself builders, as the costs of other structures rise, is pipe. Easy to put up quickly, pipe frames use very few framing materials relative to the area covered, but are best suited to Quonset or other curved types of greenhouses to be covered with plastic film. The idea is to use a bending frame or roll jig to make bows or arches of conduit stabilizers. The ends of the bows or arches are held inside larger pipes driven into the ground. Wood is used to make a pressure-treated sill and to help frame fan openings and support the plastic film at the vertical ends of the greenhouse. Pipe framing works particularly well under a double-glazed plastic film house that is air-inflated (see Double Glazing, under Glazings).

GLAZINGS

The paramount concern in choosing a glazing material is to let in as much light as possible while letting out as little heat as possible. In selecting the best bet for your unique greenhouse situation, you also will want to consider durability; resistance to breaking, tearing, and scratching; cost; ease of installation and maintenance; and any relevant characteristics of your climate or location.

Glazing may be divided into three

types—rigid, semirigid, and flexible. The classic rigid glazing is glass, which continues to be the choice of almost half of all home greenhouse owners. Creating a beautiful see-through setting, clear glass transmits about 91 percent of the available light under ideal conditions and is immune to deterioration caused by sunlight, which affects most plastics sooner or later, in the process increasing the amount of light they absorb and decreasing the fraction that reaches the plants.

Glass panels will last indefinitely (or until they break), weathering only under such unusual conditions as sandstorms. Thanks to their rigidity and resistance to abrasion, the traditional glass panels can be hosed down or scrubbed with a long-handled mop without harm—an important consideration if you live in a sooty or dusty area, since dirt on glazing can reduce light transmission quite a bit.

In addition to letting in substantial amounts of light, glass of greenhouse thickness does a good job of holding in heat to create the well-known "greenhouse effect." That is, since it is 98 percent opaque to long-wave radiation, glass lets in and out only 2 percent of the warming long infrared rays, whereas polyvinylchloride (PVC) film transmits 21 percent and polyethylene transmits 55 percent. This tendency of glass (and of fiberglass) to keep out much of the total incoming heat can be a disadvantage on cold, dull winter days but is on the whole considered a plus since it means glass will screen out burning rays on hot summer days and will keep in heat radiated by the soil and plants much longer during cold weather, thus keeping the greenhouse temperature from plunging rapidly as soon as the sun disappears.

But though glass houses lose less heat through conduction and radiation, they tend to compensate by losing more by convection—that is, by infiltration of air through glass laps, doors, and fan and vent openings. Glass is also expensive, difficult to work with if you're building your own greenhouse, and because of its heaviness requires a much sturdier and potentially more expensive frame than the much lighter plastics. It is also costly to replace if it gets broken. What's more, the expense and disappointment can be multiplied many times by the total loss of plants inside should the catastrophe happen in frigid weather.

If you do decide on glass panels, you would do well to pay extra for tempered glass, since it has been made highly resistant to breakage through a process of reheating and sudden cooling, and can withstand the impact of an eight-ounce (227 g) steel ball dropped from 10 feet (3 m). Tempered glass is also a lot more comfortable to have overhead than annealed glass—which is what easily broken, conventional double-strength window glass is—because if it does happen to break, it will crumble into very small, rough-edged pieces rather than shatter into threatening, knifelike shards. Actually, the building codes where you live may require you to use tempered or wired glass overhead or for the first 16 inches (41 cm) aboveground in fully glazed houses. So it is best to check before you purchase glazing materials. Remember, too, that it is impossible to recut tempered glass after it has been processed. To improve the heat-retaining characteristics of glass by about 30 percent, you might want to consider buying the double-pane kind called Thermopane.

If you work with impact-resistant glass, you can go to ⅛ inch (3 mm) thick 34- by 76-inch (86 by 190 cm) size panes to maximize light entry. But if you choose double strength glass, it is best to stay with smaller, old-fashioned, standard size panes since they will be less expensive to replace. And stick with a factory-cut edge, which gives more resistance to thermal stress than home-scored glass. Secure and seal your glass with mastic or, better yet, plastic compounds, which last much longer than putty and are easy to apply with a glazing gun. Also, don't make the amateur's mistake of butting two pieces of glass together or of making your frame too tight. If you do, the glass will break if the frame moves ever so slightly because of changes in temperature and humidity.

For a shatterproof kind of rigid glazing, you might consider polycarbonate plastic, which is several times more expensive than glass. Available in a transparent form called Lexan, which is offered as an eye-level option in some prefabricated greenhouses, polycarbonate is also available in an acrylic formulation called Acrylite SDP. In Swedish tests this glazing had a higher light transmission rating and greater heat retention score than fiberglass, glass, and double plastic. Polycarbonate is also available in an extruded translucent double-wall form called Tuffak-Twinwal, which has a light transmission rate of 80 percent, holds heat 50 percent better than single-pane glass, and is 300 times stronger while being very fire resistant and light enough (four ounces per square foot/118 ml per 0.09 sq m) to make a foundation and heavy framework unnecessary.

Like other kinds of rigid, ice-clear plastics, polycarbonate glazing eliminates the shadows, glare, sun-shafts, and hot spots associated with glass and makes additional shading unnecessary. The light waves hitting this material are bent so they strike plants at various angles. The result is a diffused light that permeates the greenhouse evenly. Polycarbonate is ultraviolet stabilized and reportedly has considerable resistance to the weathering effects of sunlight, rain, air pollution, and so forth. Significantly, though, guarantees on it run only to about five years.

A third rigid glazing—the thick acrylic sold as Plexiglas—has a performance profile that almost parallels the polycarbonates. It is slightly less expensive, but somewhat more likely to scar or pit when you to try to remove dust and dirt, which it unfortunately tends to attract. Ornamental foliage plants and many of the more popular orchids are said to do especially well under the bright but more diffuse light provided by these translucent rigid acrylic glazings.

Like polycarbonate, however, Plexiglas (along with other similarly formulated acrylic resins popularly called plexiglass or fiberglass) has a much higher coefficient of expansion than glass does. That means it expands and contracts through daily and yearly temperature swings, creating stress and movement where the material joins the frame. This characteristic can result in buckling and other problems in areas where there are great differences between high and low temperatures over the course of a year, for a 4 foot (1.2 m) wide piece of Plexiglas will move $\frac{1}{3}$ inch (8 mm) over a 150°F (84°C) thermal cycle. To ease the strain, if you screw down any of the thick, rigid plastics, do so through an oversized hole so they will not buckle.

Thick acrylic comes in clear or translucent forms. The clear kind is sometimes used overhead in glass houses since it is five times lighter than glass and much more impact resistant. Acrylic is also available either flat or corrugated. Flat acrylic is easier to use in crafting the end walls of a gable house. Although corrugated acrylic is stronger, which makes it lighter and allows you to leave more space between frame supports, it also has from one-tenth to one-fifth more surface area, which means more heat loss. The problem will be compounded if you fail to seal the exposed ends with foam strips to prevent wind infiltration. Corrugated fiberglass also can contribute to condensation dripping on your plants. And the troughs tend to collect dirt and debris.

The life of any good-quality sheet plastic can be extended by scrubbing it with steel wool and painting the outside with liquid acrylic every five or six years. Another approach is to buy acrylic panels to which a thin skin of ultraviolet-resistant Tedlar (a polyvinylfluoride film) has been chemically bonded.

Simply by opting for thinner acrylic you can move from a rigid to a semirigid glazing which will be somewhat cheaper, a little more difficult to install and maintain, and which will lose a little more heat than thick fiberglass. Even so, thin acrylic ranks ahead of the thicker kind and before glass as a desirable outer glazing.

One of the best outer glazings of all is called fiberglass-reinforced plastic (FRP), which incorporates from 15 to 20 percent nylon fiber for added strength and durability. Cheaper than polycarbonate, FRP products tend to expand and contract about a third less than polycarbonates and acrylics do, and they have the best impact-resistance record of all. When clad with Tedlar, reinforced fiberglass has been found to have a respectable length of life.

One company selling prefabricated houses features a double-wall, acrylic-fortified fiberglass that consists of two rigid panes bonded onto an aluminum I-beam grid to give ½ inch (13 mm) of dead air space while admitting over 90 percent of the available visible light. The panels also let through enough ultraviolet rays to help control viral and bacterial populations, but reportedly screen out the harsher ultraviolet responsible for stem elongation, collapse, and discoloration. This glazing material also conserves 145 percent more heat than double-insulating glass and is coated with special resins to last 20 to 25 years.

Another FRP formulation is Sol-Light, featured in Gothic Arch greenhouses, boasting a light transmission of 92 percent but recommended in Tedlar-coated form. Tedlar-treated material is also advisable when purchasing Filon, which admits 85 percent of the light after coating and is used by many commercial greenhouse owners. Available corrugated or flat, in grades guaranteed for 5, 10, 15, or 20 years, Filon is also sold "Filoplated"—that is, with an acrylic-modified gel coating which reduces light transmission to 76 to 78 percent. Quite similar to Filon is another FRP called Lascolite.

Yet another reinforced fiberglass is Kalwall, which admits anywhere from 85 to 90 percent of the available light and which has a life expectancy of 7 to 20 years, depending on whether you choose the regular type or one of the premium grades. Kalwall has the greatest tensile strength of any of the rigid or semirigid glazings discussed so far and the lowest coefficient of expansion of any except glass. It is suspected, though, to lose a significant part of its ability to transmit light as it ages.

Semirigid vinyl sheeting is another quasi-flexible covering, second only to fiberglass-reinforced plastic and semirigid acrylic in its overall acceptability as a single outer layer of glazing (see the chart on Rating the Glazings).

If you are looking to put up a rather temporary, inexpensive, lightly framed greenhouse, you might want to pass by rigid and semirigid glazing materials in favor of flexible plastic film. Having a tendency to break down quickly in places with intense solar radiation such as in the southwest United States, or at high altitudes, thin plastics work best in cloudy coastal climates where the atmosphere filters some of the ultraviolet rays. Regardless of where you use these films, it is always advisable to choose the "UV-treated" or stabilized versions to delay the onset of "ultraviolet bloom" or the beginning of the brittleness that leads to bending fatigue along the rafters or at original fold lines. (One way to fight this kind of stress weathering is to buy film in the widest unfolded widths available and use lath to hold it down outside at seams and at as many contact points as possible so high winds cannot whip at the expanded plastic until it tears.)

If you live in a damp climate, keep in mind, too, that single-glazed plastic greenhouses tend to have a relative humidity about 10 percent higher than that in glass houses. Unless sprayed with a wetting agent or double glazed, they also are linked to lots of condensation and dripping—great for tropical foliage plants, azaleas or certain orchids, but not advisable for gesneriads and many cut flowers. And besides, such conditions can encourage molds, mildew, and rots.

Rating the Glazings

Single-Layer Glazing Materials		A	B	C	D	E	F	G	T₁	T₂
Rigid 125-mil	Glass	4	5	1	5	4	2	3	24	15
	Thick Acrylic	4	5	1	4	4	2	3	23	15
	Polycarbonates	4	5	1	4	5	1	3	23	14
Semirigid 25 to 40-mil	Reinforced Fiberglass	4	5	1	4	5	3	5	27	18
	Thin Acrylic	4	4	1	4	4	3	5	25	17
	Vinyl Sheets	4	4	1	3	4	3	4	23	16
Flexible Film 4-mil	Polyethylene	3	1	1	1	2	5	5	18	15
	Vinyl	4	3	1	2	3	4	5	22	17
	Mylar	4	4	1	3	3	3	5	23	17
	Acetate	4	5	1	1	2	4	3	20	17
	Tedlar	5	3	1	3	3	2	3	20	14
	Teflon	5	3	1	3	3	1	3	19	13

1 Bad
2 Poor
3 Good
4 Very Good
5 Excellent

A Solar Transmittance
B Infrared Absorption
C Reduction of Heat Flow
D Weatherability (UV, Ozone)
E Resistance to Tear, Fracture and Scratching
F Low Cost
G Installation and Maintenance
T₁ Total of A through G. Evaluates materials as an outer glazing.
T₂ Total of T₁ minus D and E. Evaluates material as an inner glazing.

(In bright, cold, dry climates, however, condensation can be advantageous, for while it lowers light transmission by about 5 percent, it helps insulate at night and adds needed humidity.)

Perhaps the least recommended of all the thin plastics is the cheapest: untreated polyethylene, which can have a life as short as three months if you put it up at the beginning of the summer. Hastening the end of polyethylene through ultraviolet degradation is the fact that it expands and contracts an astonishing 61 times as much as glass and almost 10 times as much as rigid acrylics and polycarbonates. This means that it sags during the day, when it can be whipped by wind, and gets drum tight at night, cracking from brittleness in cold weather. Polyethylene is best suited to calm, mild, cloudy locations where temperatures do not fluctuate widely. Mild daily temperature swings are helpful for yet another reason; since this plastic lets heat waves in and out readily, it does very little to buffer the changes in outside temperature.

Possibly the greatest advantage of polyethylene is that it is permeable to carbon dioxide, which along with light and temperature is a limiting factor in plant growth. Costing about 40 percent more than regular polyethylene, the treated kind will last anywhere from 6 to 24 months. A copolymer of polyethylene, Monsanto 602, is also said to last up to 2 years.

Other thin plastics are polyvinylchloride and polyvinylfluoride. Polyvinylchloride is soft and pliable but available in much narrower widths than polyethylene. Offered in 3- to 12-mil thicknesses, vinyl films have a lifetime of two to four years. Heat loss is not as serious with PVC or polyvinylfluoride film as with polyethylene, for the characteristics are similar to those of single-pane glass. Moreover, the expansion rate of vinyl film is less than one-thirtieth that of untreated polyethylene.

Highly resistant to ultraviolet damage, 4-mil Tedlar, a polyvinylfluoride, transmits 92 to 94 percent of available light and in tests has continued to transmit 95 percent of that original figure after five years of exposure. Costing perhaps five times as much as untreated polyethylene, Tedlar is available in either clear or translucent form. It dirties rather easily and becomes brittle at -5°F (-21°C).

Polyester plastic, called Mylar, lets through 85 percent of the light and is perhaps the best of all the flexible plastics for an outer or inner layer of glazing. Because it is very thin—from 1 to 5 mils—Mylar requires a stronger, more supportive framework than the other films. It is structurally durable, however, holds heat slightly better than glass, and has a coefficient of thermal expansion that is remarkably low for a plastic. The weatherable Mylar is slightly yellowish and available in rolls that are four feet wide.

Duplicating Tedlar's profile, though slightly more expensive, Teflon is a slightly better bet than polyethylene as a single outer glazing but least preferable of all the films as an inner glazing. Though acetate loses less heat at night than any other plastic film—transmitting only 8 percent of thermal infrared rays—it is not often used for greenhouse glazing because it weathers very badly and is fragile, having little resistance to wear and tear.

Double Glazing

Because of the added protection from ultraviolet rays, plastic films have increased life and effectiveness when they are used as the inside layer of a double-wall greenhouse, although they can be and sometimes are employed as both layers or even on the outside of more rigid glazings (see the chart on Rating the Glazings for information on the best use of various coverings).

In recent years there has been a great deal of academic and commercial research confirming that such double glazing can save anywhere from 30 to 60 percent of heating bills in a conventional greenhouse, and this measure—combined with movable insulation at night—is definitely advisable if you are north of Washington, D.C., and hope to use little or no supplemental heating.

The payoff in double glazing depends very much on what materials are used. In one study done with otherwise-identical houses, double-pane insulated glass required 47 percent less heat than single-pane glass, while a double layer of film needed 37 percent less heat, and double-paned, fiberglass-reinforced plastic required fully 60 percent less heat than single glass. In addition to holding in heat, double glazing in a film house is usually beneficial since it reduces condensation.

Much of the insulating effect attributed to a second skin on the greenhouse is due to the 3/4 inch to 4 inches (19 to 102 mm) of dead air space left between the glazing layers. This buffer conducts heat poorly, providing a resistance to heat transfer that cannot be offered by single glazing at the thicknesses used. There are several ways to provide this valuable air space.

One approach is to make a bubble or air-inflated greenhouse. This is done by using two layers of film—a procedure that need not cut down critically on light transmission. In using the air-inflation method of double glazing, both layers of film are placed over the outside of the greenhouse frame, which preferably should be smooth and of a rounded shape and designed to be fan ventilated. It is possible to just drape both sheets over the frame, using a 4-mil layer on the outside and a 2-mil layer inside. Then the double skin is nailed at 12-inch (30 cm) intervals to boards which travel around the base of the greenhouse. The plastic is nailed alternately over one board and under the next.

With double-film houses, constant air inflation can be a good way to protect fragile expanding and contracting plastic from wind stress, since you are meeting the force of the wind with some degree of countering air pressure. The method can be surprisingly cheap to operate, too.

It is also feasible to create air space without a fan, simply by putting both layers of film outside the framework and putting a two- by two- inch (5 by 5 cm) spacer between them where you fasten them to the rafters. Just nail the spaces through the inner layer and into the frame to keep it in place. Or staple the inner film to the rafters. Then put on the second sheet of film, top it with a batten strip and drive double-headed nails all the way through the spacer and at least an inch (2.5 cm) into the rafter.

UV-treated plastic film also can be applied over fiberglass or glass already in place. The film can be rolled down from the ridge and attached under bar caps at sizable intervals. Or the over-layer of film can be held down by fastening a long Fastak or Snap-Lock bar to the greenhouse footing bar by self-tapping screws, then draping the plastic over the base and clicking in the "tongue" of the extrusion fastener to lock the film in place. A small air pump is then used to inflate the second layer several inches (approximately 5 cm) above the first.

In most cases, though, it is easier to add a second layer of glazing on the *inside,* perhaps by stapling film to the bottom of wooden glazing supports or stapling or gluing film to wood frames, then nailing the frames to the main supports. A simpler solution is to forego the air space and apply an inner skin directly to the inside of the glazing. Applied with water, these convenient films let in 90 percent of the light, including beneficial ultraviolet rays, and the viscosity of plastic and glass is said to bond them in place for up to a year.

In a somewhat more elaborate insulating system, Styrofoam beads are pumped up into the air space between the two layers of glazing at night. During the day the beads are stored in a bin. The pump can be activated by hand, timer, or photoelectric cell. The system, which is marketed in the United States under the name of Beadwall, is said to reduce nighttime fuel consumption by as much as 90 percent.

If you live in a very cold area, you might be tempted to install more than two layers of glazing. Be wary, though, for while a second layer reduces light by only 5 to 10 percent, each layer beyond two will cut down the light admitted by about 13 percent while you will not increase the resistance of your greenhouse to heat flow very significantly. For example, assuming your second layer cuts heat loss to 50 percent of what it is with one layer, a third layer will give you a saving of only 17 percent more, and a fourth layer will add just 8 percent.

Triple glazing can work, however, if you live where there is a full winter snow cover, since the added light reflected will help to compensate for the dimming caused by multiple layers.

THE GREENHOUSE INTERIOR
GROUND BEDS AND TERRACES

Direct planting in the greenhouse floor can be a good idea if you have a greenhouse with little head room, a yen for giant tropical plants, or if you want to avoid the expense and relative permanence of raised benches. Ground beds will add extra humidity to the greenhouse and allow you to water less often. They also provide more soil depth for plants with ambitious root systems and make it easier to tend tall flowering plants, vine plants like cucumbers, and staked, full size tomatoes. Moreover, the soil microorganisms living in the greater volume of decomposing organic material will contribute carbon dioxide to the atmosphere. It is also true that although cold air entering the greenhouse immediately settles over plants at ground level, the continuous soil mass acts as a buffer against extreme changes in soil temperature. Such changes are more likely to occur in pot plants, which follow the temperature outside the soil ball rather closely.

Nevertheless, direct-planted ground beds tend to be cold in the winter—especially during overcast periods—and the reduced air circulation and poorer drainage coupled with inability to closely control watering make problems with root and foliage diseases and insect pests more likely than they are with raised benches. And even if succession planting is practiced, ground beds do not use space as wisely as raised setups which allow for multi-level growing, though they can be used fairly efficiently in combination with lots of trailing plants in overhead hanging baskets.

Also, ground-level planting just is not very convenient for the gardener, though it becomes quite comfortable if you're doing it along the side walls of a pit house where only the center walk has been excavated. In such a situation, low-growing plants can be nurtured in a soil border between the glazing and the tiered concrete blocks that make the inside walls of the greenhouse. However, the soil will probably remain chilly because of lack of insulation between the inside and outside soil masses. To warm up these or other border plantings, you can always dig up the soil, put down a polyethylene liner, then put in some layers of drainage material before replacing the original soil.

To do away with ground chilliness and some of the other disadvantages of direct planting at ground level and still get that prized vertical growing space, you can always put pots on the soil or on a layer of pea gravel, turning them often to prevent plants from rooting through bottom holes.

If you prefer direct planting, one way to

Ground Beds: Direct planting at ground level requires close attention to watering, drainage, and temperature, especially during chilly winter weather. In return for this attention, the beds provide ample vertical space for growing tall tropical plants as well as a host of vining plants, both vegetable and flowering varieties.

fight potential problems is to improve drainage before you get your gardening under way. At the very least, work in lots of organic matter to lighten and aerate your natural soil if it is heavy and compacted. (Make sure any homemade compost you use has heated up sufficiently to kill weeds and bugs.) If poor drainage is a problem where your greenhouse is sited, take the extra trouble to put in an under-layer of gravel topped by sand. Or you could build slightly elevated closed beds, lined with polyethylene and covered with a few inches (approximately 5 cm) of gravel before soil is added.

Realistically, plan to make such closed-ground benches or borders less than a full armspan wide to make working in them from a crouched or kneeling position tolerably comfortable. If you prefer, however, it is possible to work with low-growing or widely spaced plants in much wider plywood-enclosed beds, if you stretch a working plank over or between plants from the aisle side, perhaps resting the board on the wooden sill under glazing that goes to the ground. For this purpose you might use an extra wide piece of lumber as a sill, extending it a few inches (approximately 5 cm) into the greenhouse and using it between times as a shelf for potted plants.

To combine the advantages of warmer air for plants with the benefits of a large soil mass, you might try terracing one or more greenhouse borders, a move that also will let you use soil more vertically so it can absorb more solar heat. Terracing is an especially good idea for the north side of the greenhouse, since this area is often shaded in winter by plants growing in ground beds between it and the low-angled sun. Stacking handsome fieldstone or concrete blocks (painted dark brown on the side facing the sun) to support such terracing or a single-level raised bed is a completely functional way to get more heat-storage mass in your greenhouse. You might even put rocks under your layer of growing soil.

RAISED STAGING

Whether you choose to plant in soil-filled benches or opt for the greater flexibility of container culture, elevating your plants on benches will result in warmer roots and fewer disease problems because of improved drainage and air circulation. In most situations, setting plants higher will make it much easier to care for them, inspect them, and display them attractively. Moreover, the closer you bring plants to the glazing, the more light they'll get.

Though you can make raised benches as low as 12 to 18 inches/30 to 46 cm (for bedding plants or others needing little care) or as high as 48 inches/120 cm (to allow you to grow shade-loving plants below), most greenhouse gardeners choose a height that feels

good to them for working in a standard position. This is usually about waist high, anywhere from 30 to 36 inches (76 to 91 cm). If your greenhouse has solid side walls, it is a good idea to have benches at around the same height so plants on them get a maximum of light, yet leave ample space overhead for hanging baskets. Make sure, too, that benches near the sides of the house are low enough so plants to be grown there will not touch the sloping overhead glazing. (In calculating bench positions, remember that you ought to leave from 6 to 12 inches/ 15 to 30 cm of space between benches and walls so air can circulate and so plants are away from the cold zone right next to the glazing.)

Bench width is another variable, this one depending primarily on the length of your reach. Usually benches accessible from one side are no more than 36 inches (91 cm) across. In smaller houses, benches between two aisles are often from 3½ to 4 feet (1.1 to 1.2 m) wide, and it is feasible to make them as wide as 6 feet (1.8 m).

In determining the dimensions of benches to make or buy, consider how you plan to arrange them. The usual setup in commercial houses is to run benches the length of the greenhouse to make supplying water, heat, mist, and plant support simpler and cheaper. But if you don't have to be concerned about such matters and want as much growing space as possible, you may prefer to run a fairly wide center aisle down the length of your house, intersecting it with narrow, 18-inch (46 cm) paths. These slender paths will parallel the benches, which extend from the long walls to the center aisle. This so-called "peninsular" arrangement will increase your bench-to-walk ratio, partly by replacing some or all of the usually recommended space or aisle next to the glazing by benches in which you place plants that will tolerate the cooler temperatures there.

Raised benches may be either flat and tablelike or built like steps, and they can be either open or closed bottomed and with or without sides. You also have the choice of making them fixed or movable.

Closed-bottomed flat benches intended for direct planting or to hold sand for cuttings or heavy aggregate material are often built of redwood, white oak, cypress, or pine (listed in order of their durability). All of these woods should be pretreated with copper naphthenate; never use creosote or any other oil-borne preservative, since the toxic fumes given off can kill your plants. If possible, weather your treated wood for six months to a year before using it if plants are to be direct planted, to be sure there is no danger at all of toxicity to plant roots. And in making wooden benches with raised sides leave ⅛ to ¾ inch (3 to 19 mm) between the boards for drainage, lining the bench if necessary with burlap. Where there is little drainage space, you also will want to leave ⅛ to ¼ inch (3 to 6 mm) between the bottom and the 6 inch (15 cm) high sides, which you should attach with galvanized steel or aluminum corners and angles measuring ⅜ by 5 by 5 inches (10 by 127 by 127 mm). An increasingly popular material for closed benches is flat or corrugated cement-asbestos board (called Transite) which cannot be destroyed by water or insects and is virtually as permanent as concrete. Lasting a lifetime, benches topped with this material can be readily bought or made (with matching or wooden sides, if desired). Again, drainage space should be left between the flat bottom and sides. Ordinarily, flat Transite benches are not strong enough to be filled with soil. Corrugated Transite is, however, and it allows far better drainage off the sides of the bench (provided any sides are attached with galvanized bolts and straps so the corrugated "dips" are not covered). To give smaller pots firm footing on rippled Transite without sacrificing air circulation, you can cover it with wire mesh. A bottom layer of gravel or coarse sand is desirable in direct planting.

Though some container gardeners like to

Raised Benches: These benches alleviate constant bending and stooping while tending plants, and allow you the choice of direct planting or the use of individual containers. Plants benefit from being elevated by increased air circulation and better drainage.

place pots on moist pebbles or sand in closed benches to delay drying out, this practice can provide an inviting host medium for insects and disease organisms in a greenhouse. Pot gardeners usually would do better to use open benches, which give a lot of ventilation, thus cutting back on moisture-induced diseases and on insect woes by making it harder if not impossible for slugs and other creatures to migrate from pot to pot.

If you plan to garden only in containers, you can save much space by using step-type benches, which hold about a third more plants than a single-deck flat bench taking up the same amount of floor space. Suited to sideless and open-bottomed construction, step benches display plants to fine advantage, offer plenty of air circulation, assure plenty of light and heat for the plants in back, and make all plants especially easy to reach and look over carefully. The light and airiness these structures encourage make them especially good for orchid culture, provided the steps are made of wide mesh hardware cloth or widely spaced slats.

One disadvantage, as you might guess, is that step benches demand more materials and labor. More importantly, depending on where you site such benches, plants on them will get uneven light or might cast shade on one another. If you run one- or two-sided step benches from north to south, perhaps using them as part of a peninsular bench arrangement in an east-west greenhouse, the plants will get equal light, will not shade each other, and will not have to be turned regularly. One-sided step benches will do well facing south, perhaps set against an opaque north wall. But if two-sided step benches run longitudinally in an east-west house, the plants on the north side will get much less light in winter when the sun is lower unless you help them out by covering the north wall with reflective material or painting it white.

You can improvise step benches by stacking bricks horizontally every four feet (1.2 m) or so down the middle of a flat bench and resting strips of lath or boards atop them. Or you can build two-sided portable steps of lumber to set in the center of a flat bench, or a one-sided step setup to get at the back of a regular bench along the north wall.

To allow more light beneath a step bench for shade plants, and to make excellent use of space to show off medium and small pot plants, you can start your steps a little above ground level and let them climb to shoulder height, making them 10 to 12 inches (25 to 30 cm) wide with a 6-inch (15 cm) rise. If you prefer, you can change the dimensions to accommodate larger plants on the bottom shelves, graduating to smaller pots or seed trays at the top. Just narrow the steps from 12, to 10, to 8 or 6 inches (30, to 25, to 20 or 15 cm) or whatever and adjust the rise relative to the height of the pots and plants you expect to have. You can mount the steps on boards and make them of pressed steel mesh or hardware cloth, cement-asbestos board, or evenly spaced wooden boards. Paint the structure white to avoid any possible toxicity problems linked to treated wood and to reflect more light on plants grouped below on the ground or on a low bench.

Step Benches: All the benefits gained by elevating container-grown greenhouse plants, plus the saving of precious space, can be yours by utilizing this type of bench. Any number of variations are possible on the basic design, allowing the bench to fit your exact space and growing needs.

Build Your Own Lightweight Greenhouse Benches

These greenhouse benches were designed to be lightweight, easy to move, and inexpensive to build—yet sturdy and long lasting. There are four bench options—differing only in the construction of the bench bottom. One is solid plywood while the other three—wood slats, ½-inch hardware cloth, and turkey wire — are open for ventilation and drainage.

The use of ¾-inch galvanized pipe for legs (as described in Build Your Own Greenhouse Bench Supports) was intended as a means of support that wouldn't rot. They involve a little additional effort in construction now, but the result will be a long-lasting, rust-free support system. Treated 2 × 4s, cable, and turnbuckles are used for extra stability.

TO MAKE THE BASIC BENCH FRAME

Materials:

Item	Quantity	Description
A. Sides	2	1 ½ × 3 ½ × 96-inch construction grade spruce
B. Ends	2	1 ½ × 3 ½ × 27-inch construction grade spruce
Nails	—	16d galvanized common nails

Procedure:

1. Cut sides (A) and ends (B) according to the dimensions in the materials list.
2. Nail together through sides (A).

TO MAKE THE PLYWOOD BOTTOM

Materials:

Item	Quantity	Description
C. Bottom	1	½ × 30 × 96-inch exterior sheathing grade plywood
Nails	—	6d galvanized common nails
Preservative	—	Cuprinol wood preservative
Bottom liner	1	36 × 103-inch polyethylene plastic

Procedure:

1. Cut bottom (C) according to dimensions in the materials list.
2. Nail bottom (C) in place.
3. Coat all surfaces (including basic frame) with preservative.
4. Line inside of bench with polyethylene plastic.

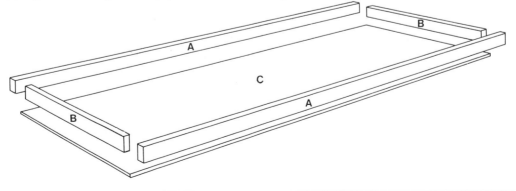

TO MAKE THE WOOD SLAT BOTTOM

Materials:

Item	Quantity	Description
Bottom members	29	$\frac{3}{4} \times 2\frac{1}{2} \times 30$-inch furring lath
Nails	—	6d galvanized common nails
Preservative	—	Cuprinol wood preservative

Procedure:

1. Cut bottom members according to the dimensions in the materials list.
2. Nail the lath to the bottom of the frame, leaving a $\frac{3}{4}$-inch space between each lath member for drainage.
3. Coat all surfaces (including basic frame) with wood preservative.

TO MAKE THE HARDWARE CLOTH BOTTOM

Materials:

Item	Quantity	Description
Cross supports	3	$1\frac{1}{2} \times 3\frac{1}{2} \times 27$-inch construction grade spruce
Bottom	1	30×96-inch, $\frac{1}{2} \times \frac{1}{2}$-inch hardware cloth
Retaining rail sides	2	$1\frac{1}{2} \times 1\frac{3}{4} \times 96$-inch construction grade spruce
Retaining rail ends	2	$1\frac{1}{2} \times 1\frac{3}{4} \times 27$-inch construction grade spruce
Nails	—	16d galvanized common nails
Staples	—	$\frac{3}{4}$-inch, 14-gauge staples
Preservative	—	Cuprinol wood preservative

Procedure:

1. Cut the cross supports and retaining rails according to the dimensions in the materials list.
2. Nail the cross supports equal distances apart inside the basic frame with 16d galvanized common nails to provide support for the bottom.
3. Cut the hardware cloth to size and staple it to the top of the basic frame.
4. Nail the retaining rails on top of the hardware cloth with 16d galvanized nails.
5. Coat all surfaces (including basic frame) with wood preservative.

TO MAKE THE TURKEY WIRE BOTTOM

Materials:

Item	Quantity	Description
Cross supports	3	$1\frac{1}{2} \times 3\frac{1}{2} \times 27$-inch construction grade spruce
Bottom	1	30×96-inch, 1×2-inch mesh turkey wire (14 gauge)
Nails	—	16d galvanized common nails
Staples	—	$1\frac{1}{4}$-inch, 9-gauge fence staples
Preservative	—	Cuprinol wood preservative

Procedure:

1. Cut the cross supports according to the dimensions in the materials list.
2. Nail the cross supports equal distances apart inside the basic frame with 16d galvanized nails to provide support for the wire bottom.
3. Cut the turkey wire to size and staple it to the bottom of the basic frame.
4. Coat all surfaces (including basic frame) with wood preservative.

Build Your Own Greenhouse Bench Supports

These bench supports were designed to support the greenhouse bench with legs made from materials that will not rot or decay. The use of ¾-inch galvanized pipe provides lightweight, sturdy, and rust-free support. Treated 2 × 4s, cable, and turnbuckles are used to improve the stability of the unit.

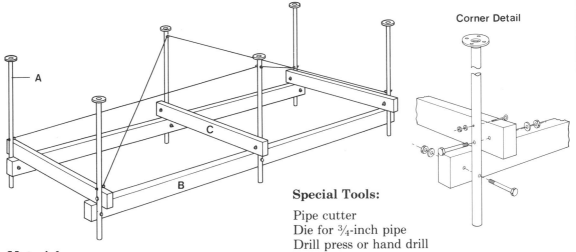

Corner Detail

Special Tools:

Pipe cutter
Die for ¾-inch pipe
Drill press or hand drill

Materials:

Item	Quantity	Description
A. Legs	6	¾-inch inside diameter × 32-inch galvanized pipe
B. Stretchers	2	1 ½ × 3 ½ × 96-inch construction grade spruce
C. Cross stretchers	3	1 ½ × 3 ½ × 30-inch construction grade spruce
Bolts	12	¼ × 20 × 3-inch machine bolts with washers and nuts
Eye bolts	6	3/16 × 1 ½-inch eye bolts with washers and nuts
Pipe flanges	6	¾-inch pipe flanges
Cable braces	20 feet	1/8-inch stranded cable
Turnbuckles	4	3/16-inch turnbuckles
Screws	12	¾-inch #8 flat-head wood screws
Wood preservative	—	Cuprinol wood preservative

Procedure:

1. Cut six pieces of pipe according to the dimensions in the materials list for the legs (A). Thread one end of each leg.
2. Drill a 9/32-inch hole in the six legs (A) 6 inches from the bottom of the leg for the wooden stretchers (B).
3. Perpendicular to the holes in step 2, drill a 9/32-inch hole 9 ½ inches from the bottom of the six legs (A) for the bolts to hold the cross stretchers (C).
4. Parallel to the holes in step 3, drill a 13/16-inch hole 12 ¼ inches from the bottom of the four corner legs (A) for the eye bolts to hold the cable braces.
5. Drill a 13/16-inch hole 2 inches from the top of the center legs (A) for the cable braces so that the eye bolt will align with the eye on the inside of the frame. Each eye bolt will accommodate two wires.
6. Cut the wooden stretchers (B) and cross stretchers (C) according to the dimensions in the materials list.

7. Lay out and drill one ⁹/₃₂-inch hole centered at each end of all the stretchers.

8. Bolt the stretchers to the pipe legs with 3-inch machine bolts.

9. Install the six eye bolts for the cable braces.

10. Screw the pipe flanges onto the top of the legs.

11. Screw the assembled legs to the bottom of the greenhouse bench.

12. Cut cable into four 5-foot lengths. Splice an eye on one end of each cable brace

through one eye of the turnbuckle, or clamp with wire rope clips. Fasten two turnbuckles to each eye bolt on center legs. You will need to open the eyes to slip in the turnbuckle ends, then close them again.

13. Install the cable braces on opposite outside corners. Trim to length and splice an eye through the eye bolts. Tighten the turnbuckles until the bench legs are square and true.

14. Coat all the wood stretchers with wood preservative.

OTHER CONTAINERS

Though specialized plants like carnations, chrysanthemums (*Chrysanthemum* × *morifolium*), lettuce (*Lactuca sativa* cvs.), snapdragons (*Antirrhinum majus*) and spinach (*Spinacia oleracea*) are often grown in soil-filled benches, many greenhouse gardeners find it easier to keep their houses clean and disease free if they confine their plants to flats, pots, tubs, and hanging baskets. Perhaps most important of all, gardening in portable units makes it easier to rearrange plants to best advantage. When they are looking peaked, it will be the work of a moment to elevate them for more light and heat, pop them under a bench for needed shade and coolness, or perhaps move them farther apart for better air circulation.

Even if you like to do some direct planting in borders or benches, it can be pleasant to renew house plants in the greenhouse from time to time and to have the option of borrowing attractive potted flowering plants for a few hours to add richness to a winter dinner table. And, of course, movable containers make transplanting to the outdoor garden a lot quicker and a lot less messy.

If you plan to grow your own bedding plants or vegetable seedlings or to propagate cuttings, you may want some flats. Cardboard and plastic trays are now on the market for this purpose and you may want to consider them, since the old-style larger wooden flats may set you to staggering when they are filled with wet sand. On the other hand, you can easily put together your own wooden flats, making them as small as eight by ten inches (20 by 25 cm) and six inches (15 cm) deep. (Directions for building a simple wooden flat can be found in Build Your Own Basic Flat, in chapter 8.) For large-rooted crops like carrots and radishes, you might want to make especially deep flats and dismantle them later. If you want to work with traditional flats, be aware that sizes vary. It may be worth your while to check with some commercial greenhouses to see what dimensions are used in your area so you can size your benches accordingly. To restrict the roots of seedlings so they transplant more readily and successfully, you can separate plants in flats with rectangular pieces of rot-resistant material called plant bands. You also can use strips of veneer, plastic, or three-inch (8 cm) bands cut from milk cartons for this purpose.

Containers for the Greenhouse: Hanging pots are only one possibility out of many for your greenhouse-grown plants. Tubs, pots, plastic or wooden trays, and hanging baskets are other options. Also, pieces of bark or logs may be used for epiphytic plants, as shown here. Recycling containers opens up a whole new range of possibilities, and as long as they provide adequate room and drainage there is no limit to what can be used.

Again, though, it is satisfying and quite feasible to use recycled items in a working greenhouse even for good size plants. You can grow herbs, leaf lettuce, radishes, spinach, or strawberries (*Fragaria* spp.) to maturity in quart (0.9 l) size cottage cheese or ice cream containers, and dwarf tomatoes, carrots, chard, eggplants, peppers, and other crops will thrive in half-gallon (1.8 l) bleach bottles. For full size tomatoes or vining plants like cucumbers, potatoes, and squash, you can use holders over 12 inches (30 cm) in diameter. Or line fruit baskets with plastic and coax the plants up homemade redwood-lath trellises. You also can press used metal drums or plastic garbage cans into service, though you

must punch drainage holes in the lower sides of such large containers as well as in the bottom. Just be sure to clean containers thoroughly before you use them.

If you are willing to put together boxes from scrap lumber, you will get fine results with vegetables like beets, carrots, kohlrabi, onions, turnips, and zucchini in boxes that are 24 by 36 by 8 inches (61 by 81 by 20 cm), while cucumbers, peas, pole beans, and tomatoes can thrive in narrow boxes 12 by 48 by 8 inches (30 by 122 by 20 cm) with a trellis inserted.

Ideas for larger plants you might want to show off in wide aisles include wooden butter tubs or half kegs, which will last for three years or so if you treat them with copper naphthenate. You also can hammer together handsome wooden planters, using galvanized nails and five nine-inch (23 cm) squares of treated redwood. Along the Eastern Shore of Maryland some greenhouse professionals are now offering larger containers called "Baltimore urns." These popular planters are made from a discarded tire and wheel and hold heat nicely. (Remember the gardener's trick of placing a rubber tire around heat-loving plants to keep them warm after sundown?)

You can accommodate semiterrestrial or epiphytic orchids, ferns, and bromeliads on bark or logs, provided you water and spray often. Or hang these exciting plants in open teak or cedar baskets.

FLOORS AND WALKS

There are choices aplenty when it comes to deciding what will be underfoot in the greenhouse, but here you will be guided most by how you want to use this special environment. If you plan to display potted plants in a "green room" adjoining a kitchen or den—the kind of place you'll retreat to for *al fresco* breakfasts, sunning, and entertaining—then a full tile or concrete floor with drainage might look good to you, for though it will be somewhat costly to install, it is the easiest of all to keep tidy and free from weeds and slugs. But there is a hidden price for that degree of cleanliness: that much concrete probably will not drain well and will store heat readily, which is hardly desirable unless summers are cool and brief. Just as important, concrete cannot absorb moisture and release it into the atmosphere as needed to add humidity and help cool overheated air on really hot days.

A better full-floor choice for such a versatile greenhouse setting might be old bricks set in mortar or in a deep sand bed. In addition to being easy to clean and good looking, this porous flooring will contribute moisture when it is needed and help disperse it when it's not.

If you plan a working greenhouse that is to be more concerned with plants than people, a greenhouse that's likely to harbor wheelbarrow traffic and maybe even a compost heap, permanent flooring is not the best answer. You probably will want to keep the area under raised benches "rough" to catch dripping water. Rammed-down earth, cinders, or pebbles can do nicely, though the hands-down favorites seem to be crushed rock or pea gravel, which are inexpensive, maintenance free, and "breathe" to help control temperature and humidity. Another idea is to set flagstones in sand or ashes so you can fasten down their edges with cement. If elevated slightly under benches, such stones will dry quickly, and you can rinse them easily with a hose. Be careful, though, when using such a setup under benches or just as a walkway; too much water running about can dislodge sand or ashes and cause the slabs to sink or tilt. Slab stepping-stones also can be embedded in the soil in wide-bed plantings.

For paths between permanently located raised benches, many people favor a 2-inch (5 cm) thickness of concrete. This can be as narrow as 19 inches (48 cm) wide—the no-frills width commercial greenhouses use—24 inches (61 cm) wide for a more spacious, gracious look, and 36 inches (91 cm) wide if more than one person plans to putter at a time or if you want to negotiate a wheelbarrow inside. (You can always line a wide aisle with tub plants.) If you choose concrete walks, make sure you avoid the mistake of the gardener who carefully laid water pipes beneath, only to kick himself later when the pipes froze and the walk had to be taken up to reach them.

If you prefer, you can lay flagstones, brick, slate, or tile in concrete or sand. But be sure the finished walk is level so you aren't condemned to stand in post-watering puddles. Gravel or crushed rock make the simplest paths of all, though they can be unpleasantly uneven and a bit sloshy unless you raise and slope the material slightly to encourage quick runoff of water (a wise prac-

A Baltimore Urn

Here's how to convert an all-American eyesore into a handsome, heat-storing planter suitable for nonedible plants of all kinds.

1. Start with a worn tire-and-rim sized to suit your purpose. (But don't use a snow tire, a radial, or a belted tire.)

2. Place the tire on the ground with the inside of the rim facing upward, and chalk a wavy line around the tire about 3 to 4 inches (76 to 102 mm) from the rim, leaving about 12 inches (305 mm) from the peak of one "wave" to the next.

3. Cut along this line with a linoleum knife.

4. Turning the tire over, put your foot in the wheel and pull up the outside of the tire, turning the top part of the tire inside out to form a vase-shaped urn.

5. Paint the tire and rim if you wish with an outdoor latex paint having a matte finish, remembering that a dark color will help the urn absorb heat, while a light shade will add to reflected light. (Note: Avoid oil-based and glossy paints, as they will rot the rubber.)

6. Put some screening or large rocks over the axle and lug holes to keep gravel and soil from leaking out.

7. Fill the bottom third of the urn with gravel and the upper two-thirds with a blend of equal parts of good soil, peat, and vermiculite. Then plant flowering annuals or perennials, shrubs, or even a dwarf tree.

tice for every kind of walk). Raised gravel or just flagstones in earth make good choices for aisles when there is exposed soil under the benches or a direct-planted border adjoining the walkway.

Another option is to lift yourself above it all on a traditional deck of slatted wood. You can hammer some of these walks together easily using treated boards and, although they are harder to clean, wear out in a few years and can be slippery at times, they yield most pleasantly underfoot. An easily removable walk of this kind over a rammed-earth floor is particularly good if you direct plant in borders, since you can take it up instantly to pasteurize or cultivate the soil.

A Few Words about Drainage

Depending on where your greenhouse is sited and what kind of structure it is, you may have to provide for drainage in addition to that offered by the few inches (approximately 5 cm) of crushed rock or pea gravel you may put down as a floor. A drainage setup is especially important where the water table is high or when the greenhouse is an attached or freestanding sunken (pit) type. In their classic book, *Winter Flowers in Greenhouse and Sun-Heated Pit* (see Bibliography), Taylor and Gregg suggest that pits on top of a hill or on very sandy or gravelly soil contain a foot-deep (30 cm) drainage layer/floor consisting of stones graded from fist size (at the very bottom) to pea gravel. For pits on level ground or on a slope or in clay soil anywhere, they suggest drainage tile at the bottom of the excavation leading to nearby lower ground or to a pump—perhaps already functioning in an adjoining basement—or to a dry well filled with stones.

If your greenhouse is an aboveground, attached type, make sure the gradual slope away from your dwelling for runoff is still operative after you've added the greenhouse. And try to connect with or at least follow existing lines of drainage established by drains and gutters. Take special care if you plan to plant in ground beds, since water pooling beneath your greenhouse can disturb the balance of your greenhouse ecosystem, especially in winter, and increase your heating needs.

THE POTTING AREA

It is traditional to put a potting shed on the north end of a north-south running greenhouse, and in the case of an east-west ridge, you might put your workspace at the west end or perhaps off an opaque north wall. In any event, a separate area for a workbench, pots, soil mix components, and tools remains a good idea—especially for small greenhouses—since it leaves a maximum of the precious warm space within for plants. Also, if the potting place provides entry to the greenhouse on the side from which prevailing winds come, you can prevent significant heat loss through drafts in the winter just by installing a second door between it and the greenhouse proper. An adjoining shed also can double as a convenient place to store your lawn or garden equipment and might feature a sink with a faucet which mixes hot and cold water so you can scrub off pots conveniently.

If you are severely strapped for building space, of course, you can leave a few square feet in the least well-lit corner of the greenhouse for potting purposes, working at a portable or collapsible potting bench and using quite small containers for sand, peat moss,

and other media and refilling them from a larger cache kept in the garage or basement. And you can always hang tools on an adjacent peg board on a north or west wall.

Ideally, your potting bench should be topped with galvanized sheet metal to keep the wood from warping from moist soil and to spare your fingers from splinters. Depending on the quantities of soil you plan to blend at one time, the sides and back should be anywhere from 4 to 48 inches (10 to 122 cm) high. The best height for potting is usually around 40 inches (102 cm)—or whatever lets you work from a standing position without back strain. A 40-inch (102 cm) depth will let you deal with fairly efficient amounts of soil at one time and a width of 60 inches (152 cm) will accommodate some pots within easy reach and leave room for flats on your left and right, with space directly in front for potting activities.

For convenience, beneath the bench you might want to build in bins that tip forward to give you ready access to compost, peat, sand, and other materials. These should be a few inches (approximately 5 cm) off the floor and made of rot-resistant but untreated wood. On the other hand, you can get by nicely keeping potting components in plastic garbage cans or galvanized cans with covers. (If you wish, you can put larger containers on swivel casters.)

The styles of potting benches are many. You can put in sturdy fixed types with shelves on brackets to one side to hold pots or with a high, solid back featuring several shelves behind your potting space. Or you can make do in a small setup with something as simple as a portable wooden box-type affair that you balance on two raised benches over an aisle or a collapsible dropleaf workbench with or without sides that you can hinge to the side or end of a plant bench.

INTERIOR DESIGN POSSIBILITIES

If plants are to take precedence in your

Potting Area: Whether it's in a separate shed or tucked away in a corner of the greenhouse, this workspace serves an important function, as an area where basic potting activities are carried out and where pots, tools, and various soil media can be stored.

Live-In Greenhouse: A greenhouse incorporated into the home provides an oportunity to share your living space with plants. This solar-heated oasis includes a rattan chair and various straw accessories interspersed among the plants to suggest a tropical setting. The masonry walls and floor store heat collected through the glazing on sunny days.

greenery, and if you plan to do much of your gardening on raised benches, arranging them to best advantage in regard to light and space will be the controlling factor that shapes your greenhouse interior (see Raised Staging, earlier in this chapter). But by sacrificing a scant few feet of bench space at the north or west end of the greenhouse—a corner if you like— you can create a place for people as well. This can be as simple as a rattan chair or a wooden bench on a patch of brick flooring—with a hanging plant or two or a fragrant, potted camellia or gardenia or perhaps a dwarf fruit tree nearby as the restful accompaniment to a leisurely cup of tea. Or you might save a corner for a petite table or even a handsome slab of redwood that can serve as a desk and also hold a few favorite foliage plants.

Another idea which is especially feasible for greenhouses opening off a kitchen, living room, or den, is to arrange growing benches around the sides of the greenhouse (or do all border planting), leaving the center area open to create a festive patio atmosphere with plenty of head room for tall tub plants.

With a little more imagination you can create a downright luxurious tropical setting fit for fantasizing by in a lounge chair. You might, for instance, pour waterproof cement into a wire mesh-reinforced hole to create a pond. Using stones to fashion a natural-looking watercourse, you could conceal a small submersible electric pump in an area about 14 inches (36 cm) deep under the waterfall, where foaming white water will hide it. To complete this jungle oasis, arrange creeping plants and foliage plants in the ground or pots and train some vines overhead. Tree ferns like *Cyathea* and *Dicksonia* species as well as smaller tropical ferns thrive when landscaped into such a setting, and the planted area will hold enough moisture to make caring for tropical or cool-temperature ferns much simpler. (You can always grow more ferns on benches to replace or supplement those in the landscape as they mature.)

If your greenhouse is cooler, you might prefer to create the austere serenity of a Japanese rock garden with raked gravel in which you can winter-over potted alpine plants. In a low-humidity situation, you could sculpture a sandy desert scene to taste-fully display your collection of cacti and other succulents year-round.

Somewhat more general suggestions bearing on interior design are to:

—Take advantage of the naturally oc-curring microclimates in greenhouses dur-ing cold weather by placing cool-temperature plants near the glazing and toward the floor, near the north side (of a freestanding even-span house), and at the dead center of the greenhouse; and by put-ting heat-lovers at higher levels where warm air will naturally rise and toward the southern side of the house or near an insu-lated and reflective north wall or a com-mon wall. Light-loving plants should always be placed closer to the glazing in hanging pots or on higher shelves or benches.

—Consider partitioning the greenhouse when you build (it will be cheaper then) so you can have the pleasure of growing some warm-temperature plants by special-heat-ing just a small area.

—Arrange to have the interconnecting door in an attached greenhouse either slide open and closed or open into the dwelling so it doesn't limit your design possibilities inside the greenhouse.

—Paint the greenhouse frame and all in-sulated walls that cannot store heat flat white if you plan winter growing.

—Paint heat-storing walls flat white if you are growing light-loving plants or fruiting or rooting types since you will gain more from the extra light than you would

from stored heat. On the other hand, in an unheated greenhouse used for leaf crops in winter, paint masonry walls black, dark brown, or green (or even red or dark blue) so they will absorb and release heat in-stead of add to the light supply. To have matters both ways, you can paint a ma-sonry wall on the north side of the green-house a dark shade and cover it with a reflective curtain in the summer and on dull winter days.

CULTURAL PRACTICES

Greenhouse growing techniques may be di-vided into practices borrowed from the out-door garden and others suggested by the challenge of nurturing plants in an enclosed space. Though some greenhouse gardeners feel that mulching in the greenhouse might attract rodents and snails, others, like the very experienced "Doc" and Katy Abraham of upstate New York, favor the use of hay, straw, wood chips, bark, or sawdust to hold in moisture, fight weeds, help stabilize soil tem-perature, and ultimately improve soil tex-ture—just as these materials do in an outdoor garden.

The Abrahams particularly recommend mulching raised benches, which tend to dry out fast. They like to mulch with biodegrad-able black, wax-coated paper or black poly-ethylene plastic, which in effect collects solar energy as it strikes the soil. With the air space under the mulch helping to seal in this heat at night, soil temperatures remain mod-erate even in colder weather, and extreme fluctuations are avoided.

Given the recent discovery that higher temperatures in soil and irrigation water make it possible for plants to tolerate signifi-cantly lower air temperatures at night, using black plastic mulch in tandem with soil ca-bles in an unheated or cool greenhouse could make it possible to grow a greater variety of plants and harvest them earlier. Aluminum foil or aluminized plastic sheets used as mulch will not do as much to warm the soil but can offer the gift of more, and more evenly distributed, light in dull winter climates, increasing yields of light-loving plants such as tomatoes by up to 15 percent.

Another outdoor cultural technique that can be brought inside the greenhouse is companion planting, or intercropping, to thwart insects and diseases which are more likely to take hold in monocultures of such crops as tomatoes or chrysanthemums. To help safeguard your favorite plants, you might try growing some highly scented flowers and herbs. Chives, garlic, and onions are good companions for all crops, while marigolds repel soil worms, and pyrethrum (*Chrysanthemum cinerariifolium*) and feverfew (*Chrysanthemum parthenium*) will kill or drive away many insects. Rosemary and sage may be tucked in alongside any cole crops to keep away aphids and cabbage moths. Certain combinations of plants also have been found to spur one another's growth because they complement each other in size, shallow versus deep root structure, need for light, or in other, more mysterious ways. Some of these "good buddies" are carrots and peas, kohlrabi and beets, tomatoes and parsley, radishes and lettuce, and turnips and peas.

If you are using your greenhouse for intensive wintertime vegetable production, you might even find it worthwhile to renew the soil in beds and benches by rotating your crops, and by occasionally using the summer growing season to plant and turn under soybeans or even cover crops like alfalfa, which you can let bees in to pollinate. It is also possible to make compost right in an unused portion of a greenhouse bed by turning under modest amounts of organic wastes such as leaves, eggshells, coffee grounds, and vegetable and fruit scraps. Be sure to also include high-nitrogen material to make the pile heat up during decomposition, so that disease pathogens are not harbored in the finished compost.

One of the most intriguing and important techniques unique to the cultivation of plants in artificial environments is the practice of adding carbon dioxide to the air. Work done at the Ohio Agricultural Research and Development Center has established that an inadequate supply of this gas is a primary factor limiting plant growth and development at all levels of light intensity except perhaps the very lowest. The problem is especially acute in midwinter and in tightly sealed detached solar houses, since fresh air is not being let into the greenhouse. As a result, plants very often quickly exhaust all available carbon dioxide in the early morning and for the rest of the day can make little photosynthetic use of even bright light. Carbon dioxide enrichment is also useful in northern areas from October to March and in the south from December through February as a way of boosting photosynthesis by helping to compensate for reduced light.

Indeed, with all else being equal, researchers have found that levels of from 1,000 to 1,500 parts per million (ppm) of carbon dioxide in greenhouse air can raise yields anywhere from 10 to 70 percent, depending on species and varieties. On the other hand, when the ambient carbon dioxide drops to a third of the 300 to 350 ppm found in normal outside air, photosynthesis in tomatoes has been found to drop from 15 to 40 percent. Adding carbon dioxide also can reduce heating bills, since it enables you to greatly reduce ventilation. And it cuts down on watering since stomatic openings on plants are reduced, causing them to lose less water vapor.

There are several ways to add this efficacious gas to your greenhouse. In attached houses, you can leave interconnecting doors, windows, and vents open regularly to admit air from your dwelling, which contains carbon dioxide exhaled by you and your family. You won't get much carbon dioxide this way, though, or from keeping rabbits or chickens on the greenhouse premises as some people do.

Some other, possibly more effective but hard-to-measure, sources include earthworms and actively decomposing compost heaps, for carbon dioxide is provided by the respiration of local soil organisms and can be markedly increased by fermenting manure and other organic materials. (According to waste reclamation expert Dr. Clarence Golueke, a compost heap will lose one-third to one-half its weight over three weeks and 95 percent of this lost weight is carbon given off as carbon dioxide.) For small greenhouse setups, it is easy and inexpensive to save and melt down old, used candles in large tin cans, then add a wick. When lit on cold, sunny days, such candles will use up extra oxygen and through combustion give off carbon dioxide.

For larger greenhouses, you can set out dry ice at the rate of 28 ounces (794 g) per day per 100 square feet (9 sq m) of floor area, putting out a quarter of the amount in the early morning and the remainder in two or three equal portions (the last no later than 3:00 P.M.). More conveniently, you can buy compressed carbon dioxide in cylinders and set a solenoid valve-operated timer so the gas is released from sunrise to 30 minutes before sunset at a flow rate of 1½ to 2 cubic feet (0.4 to 0.6 cu m) per hour per 100 square feet (9 sq m) of greenhouse floor. Like the dry ice quantities mentioned above, this will yield about 2,000 ppm of carbon dioxide.

Setting forth the wealth of detailed information in greenhouse literature on the culture of specific flowers, foliage plants, vegetables, and fruits is beyond our scope here, but you owe it to yourself to scan some of the rewarding books on that subject. See the Bibliography for a list of recommended publications.

WATERING GREENHOUSE PLANTS

Watering setups in the greenhouse can be as simple or elaborate as you care to make them. As usual you can spend time, effort, and ingenuity, or you can spend money for a partially or completely automated system. You also get to choose between watering your plants from above or from below.

The simplest kind of surface watering can be done with a large watering can (which is fine for potted plants in a small greenhouse) or with a hose. Either should be equipped with a rose attachment that releases fine streams of water instead of a torrent that can cause compacting or washing out of soil, not to mention splashing on foliage, which can encourage and spread leafborne diseases and rot tomatoes and other crops. Between uses, keep the hose and its rose attachment off the ground to foil the spread of disease.

If your greenhouse is small and convenient to your home, you might very easily be able to use water from an indoor faucet that mixes hot and cold water. But don't stretch your luck—or your hose—too far. If you cover much distance with long lengths of small-bore hose, friction will reduce the pressure of the water immensely by the time it reaches the greenhouse, and you may have to settle for an exasperating trickle.

A better alternative is to run a water pipe into the greenhouse—usually 1-inch (2.5 cm) supply pipe is adequate—and to install a mixing faucet to which a hose can be screwed. If you have well water, which is less chemicalized than municipal water but can be 10°F (6°C) colder, without such a faucet you may have to use a tempering tank, for plants dislike chilly water and are said to do much better if the temperature of the water given is 70°F (21°C). For greenhouses over 12 feet (3.6 m) long, consider placing several mixing faucets along the aisles under the benches and using several short hoses. If you work with just one hose, you can always put snap-on hose attachments on faucets to make life a little easier.

Work done at the University of Georgia suggests that you also can use concrete blocks in a waterbath to provide a constant moisture level that yields excellent results in germinating and growing vegetables and flowering plants. To germinate seeds or to grow bedding plants, you can fill peat pots with moist soil and stand them directly on top of lightweight 4- by 8- by 16-inch (10 by 20 by 41 cm) concrete blocks. Or the pots can be put into flats with hardware cloth bottoms that are pushed down on a layer of sand spread over the blocks. For fruiting plants, it is possible to set a 1- by 6-inch (2.5 by 15 cm) frame on top of the blocks, fill it with a soil-based medium and grow plants right in the soil at a rate of one or two per block.

The recommended starting water level for this approach is one inch (2.5 cm) below the top of the blocks, but it should be lowered to the middle of the blocks after two days or when the soil surface appears wet. Never let water stand above the top of the blocks, for it would oversaturate the growing media.

Researchers at Georgia claim excellent yields of cucumbers, eggplants, bell peppers, and tomatoes with this method, and it can sustain plants for several days even if you forget to add water or if you use an automated setup that fails.

A somewhat more elaborate way of watering from below is the capillary bench, which you can buy in kit form or improvise for yourself. The idea is to line a very strong, level bench having raised sides with polyethylene (sometimes fiberglass sheeting is put on top of the plastic), then fill the bench with ¼ inch (6 mm) of coarse sand, followed by a layer of fine sand to a total depth of 2 to 3 inches (5 to 8 cm). Below the sand—or sometimes on top of it—a perforated plastic tube or hose-pipe runs down the center of the bench, releasing water kept at a level from ½ to 1 inch (13 to 25 mm) below the surface of the sand. To maintain the water height you can use a ball-cock tank or a float controller or valve. It is also possible to use a slow-dripping hose or to top the bench with a hose once in a while, but beware of letting the bench get too dry, or the plants in plastic pots atop the sand will not be able to take up enough water by suc-

Cement Block Watering Method: This form of watering from below may be used for vegetables and flowering plants, during both germination and later stages of growth. Individual pots or flats can be set directly on the blocks. Add water until it stands 1 inch (2.5 cm) below the top of the blocks, and as soon as the soil surface feels wet, lower the water level until it reaches the middle of the blocks, as shown here.

tion and will extend their roots into the sand and suffer when they are lifted.

REGULATING HUMIDITY

To reach a working balance between the water taken up by roots and released by leaves, the air in a greenhouse should have a relative humidity of from 30 to 80 percent, depending on the species being grown. Cacti and other succulents need the least humidity; certain foliage plants like dieffenbachias, dracaenas, peperomias, pothos (*Epipremnum aureum*), snake plants (*Sansevieria* spp.), and ti plant (*Cordyline terminalis*) need an intermediate amount; many other foliage plants, as well as flowering plants such as camellias, chrysanthemums, gardenias, and poinsettias (*Euphorbia pulcherrima*) need high humidity.

In areas used for germinating seeds and propagating cuttings, the humidity should be about 75 percent. That is, the air should be holding 75 percent of all the moisture it is possible for it to absorb at that time.

What makes maintaining appropriate humidity levels an ongoing challenge is that

Capillary Bench: A bench with raised sides, lined with plastic and filled with layers of sand, forms the basis for this type of watering from below. Water is supplied by a tube or pipe that is buried or lies on top of the sand. If the sand and the soil in the pots are ever allowed to dry out, you must moisten the soil in the pots as well as the sand to get the capillary action going again. A small circle of nylon stocking or wire mesh set over the drainage hole in each pot before soil is added will keep roots from extending into the sand.

the amount of moisture the atmosphere can hold varies with the temperature: the warmer the air, the more moisture it is capable of absorbing—indeed the capacity of the air to hold moisture about doubles with each 20°F (11°C) increase in temperature. This means that as the temperature rises in a greenhouse, the relative humidity will drop unless more moisture is introduced. And, of course, as the temperature goes down, the relative humidity will increase even though the same amount of moisture is present.

This basic relationship between temperature and relative humidity is a direct guide to when you can expect humidity problems in the greenhouse—and to how you can solve them. Too much humidity, for example, is often a problem in spring and fall, when there is often a great change in temperature during a 24-hour period. High humidity also can strike in the summer during a stretch of dull, overcast days if you fail to cut back on watering and damping down. It also can happen at sunset when the plants and greenhouse cool rapidly, or during warm, muggy nights. In winter, excessive humidity is often a problem

in solar greenhouses because they are kept tightly sealed to avoid heat loss.

Remedying high humidity is much easier when the air outside the greenhouse is cooler than that inside, for when this drier air is admitted through vents or doors, in warming it picks up water vapor, thus lowering humidity and reducing the danger of moisture condensing on slightly colder plants. Then the warmed air rises and leaves the greenhouse through open escape vents.

The effect of such cold, dry air is significant. For example, a pound (0.45 kg) of outside air with a relative humidity of 60 percent and a temperature of 40°F (4°C) that leaves the greenhouse at the same relative humidity but at 70°F (21°C) will have picked up 0.0053 pounds (0.002385 kg) of water. So lowering relative humidity in cold weather is easy if you have a supply of cold, dry air and enough heat to warm it to the greenhouse temperature. One way of handling condensation problems at sundown is to turn on the heat just before sunset and gradually close the ridge vent until it is just barely open. This time-honored technique is known as "night-firing."

By using an exhaust fan, which can expel humid greenhouse air very quickly, it is possible to lower the relative humidity in the greenhouse even if it is raining outside (that is, at 100 percent humidity). Of course, the lower the temperature of the outside air, the more heat is required to maintain the greenhouse at the desired temperature. In the event that a greenhouse suffers from poor heat distribution or from air currents caused by infiltration of wind, a circulating fan with a waterproof, plastic-covered cord can be used to prevent the excessive humidity that can easily develop in cold spots. For example, if the temperature drops just 9°F (5°C) in a greenhouse at 65°F (18°C) and 75 percent relative humidity, the humidity in the affected place will be 100 percent. As this example reveals, it is important to avoid wide variations in temperature within a greenhouse, since they will directly affect relative humidity.

Alas, it is harder to control high humidity in summer since there is much less temperature differential to help out. During dull periods with no air moving it is best to cut down on sprinkling greenhouse walkways and under the benches and to make sure you don't overwater. Otherwise you will be introducing unnecessary extra moisture that cannot be taken up by an already saturated atmosphere.

As an added help, exhaust fans can remove the hottest, most humid air. For best results, an exhaust fan should be able to change the air in your greenhouse once a minute (see Forced-Air Cooling, later in this chapter, for information on sizing and placing fans).

Too little humidity can be as destructive to your plants as too much, and plant wilt is a real threat on burning hot summer days when you open the vents in the hope of cooling off the house—especially if your locale is arid, for the moist air you have painstakingly created will quickly escape. Moreover, since the outdoor air is not much cooler, it will be able to bring down inside temperatures by only a few degrees. Low humidity also can occur in winter during bright, clear, intensely sunny periods, because the sun heats the air, driving down the relative humidity.

The cures for dry air are many and vary with the season. For help in humidifying and heating in winter, you can introduce steam as water spray, using a humidistat if you like to control the pump or valve action supplying the moisture. (Unfortunately, humidistats lose their accuracy quickly and must be calibrated once a month or so.)

One way to boost low humidity is to leave patches of open soil. You might do some direct planting in borders or leave the original soil exposed under raised benches. Or you can sprinkle a few inches or centimeters of peat moss or loam on top of gravel flooring.

Another remedy for low humidity suitable in early spring and late fall or perhaps year-round in a mild, arid climate is keeping active compost heaps inside the greenhouse. One Oregon man has found that two ten-cubic-foot (0.3 cu m) bins add enough moisture to protect the leafy vegetables in his unheated greenhouse from killing frost. Rather than freezing the plants, the cold freezes the moisture on them. This hoarfrost and the ice on roof and walls also have an insulating effect.

Be cautious about composting inside, though, if you live where cloudiness is common, for in an already humid environment added moisture in the absence of supplemental heat can send the relative humidity up to 90 or even 100 percent, creating condensation and dripping that only rain forest plants or mildew-resistant greens like endive, oakleaf lettuce, and romaine may be able to tolerate.

During the summer, too little humidity is linked to hot, bright, clear days when stronger light and rapidly climbing temperatures in the greenhouse create the need for a corresponding gain in moisture. At such times the cheapest and most effective approach is to dampen walkways and the areas under benches frequently with a hose equipped with a mist nozzle. Or you can set a lawn sprinkler on a path or under benches, moving it often so no area gets oversoaked.

If you live in a very hot, dry climate and/or like to go away sometimes, it may be worth your while to consider more sophisticated setups, for they will reduce your plants' watering requirements and enable them to get by for a few days on their own. Such arrangements can be operated manually or hooked up to a humidistat. Use this triggering device carefully, though, for the actual humidity on the surface of plant leaves is higher than the reading a humidistat will give. So try to keep the recorded humidity under 70.

If a year-round humidifying system sounds good to you, you might want to look into the compact units sold by some greenhouse manufacturers. Many of them can be mounted overhead on a structural member, and can be operated with a hand valve or automatically with a time clock or electric valve. Intervals of 1 minute on and 5 to 10 minutes off are commonly used for general humidification. If you are using such an arrangement over cuttings or some germinating seeds which need constant misting, employ a higher ratio of 1 on to 60 off. For example, 6 seconds on to 6 minutes off.

The ideal for humidifying and cooling is a high pressure system which fogs rather than mists, filling the air with moisture without wetting the foliage. Most efficient in a high greenhouse and located high overhead to cool the hottest air in the house, this setup can bring down temperatures with the greenhouse vents nearly closed and also improves air circulation. Together with intense light it will spur incredibly fast plant growth.

Humidity also can be raised effectively through the use of an evaporative cooling system in which a fan precools air entering the greenhouse by causing it to evaporate water from a wet pad. (See Forced-Air Cooling, later in this chapter.)

Even if the general humidity in your greenhouse tends to be readily raised by hosing down, hand misting, and other methods, you will want to maintain an especially high humidity of 75 percent whenever and wherever you germinate seeds and root cuttings. A misty atmosphere cools the plant leaves by as much as 10° to 15°F (6° to 8°C), which encourages root growth to zoom ahead of top growth, thereby producing more rugged plants. At the same time, the lowered temperature makes it possible to propagate rootless cuttings in full light with little loss of water through transpiration—a condition resulting in quicker rooting since the leaves can continue to make food. In some mysterious way, misting also seems to protect rose cuttings and other touchy cuttings from disease.

In the case of seeds, providing extra humidity can be as simple as covering a watered flat with polyethylene or polypropylene plastic, which will not have to be removed after germination and during the rooting period since it is permeable to both oxygen and carbon dioxide. Or you can cover seed flats with panes of glass topped with newspaper, partially removing or raising them if too much condensation develops and lifting them completely as soon as the seeds germinate. In a bottom-heated bench for rooting, you can sprinkle or syringe by hand, keep your cuttings in polyethylene bags, surround the bench with polyethylene curtains, or use plastic domes that fit over plastic seed trays. It is possible also to buy or build a propagation case.

TEMPERATURE CONTROL

Keeping Warm in Winter

Depending on the kind of plants you are growing, the kind of greenhouse you have, and where you live, it is more than likely that you will need to resort to a heat source other than the sun during the coldest months. If you have an attached greenhouse built over a basement or first-floor door or window, you can simply let the warm air from the house flow naturally into the greenhouse. Or you can help matters along with a fan in the doorway or window, or with a small circulating fan placed in the coolest part of the greenhouse to eliminate cold spots.

Lacking an interconnecting door or window, you can help heat your greenhouse—and your house—by installing high and low vents in the common wall. On winter nights or overcast winter days you can let warm air flow from the house through the top vents, perhaps providing mixing with a small fan in the greenhouse, and on bright, cool days in the spring and fall you can pull cool air from the house into the greenhouse through the lower vents and vent warm air into the house through the upper vents. (Upper vents should be at least six feet [1.8 m] above lower vents to assure a good circulating pattern.)

To use your home heating system more

(continued on page 675)

Build Your Own Mist Chamber

A mist chamber is an enclosed area which is designed to provide high levels of humidity to plant cuttings and minimize the evaporation of the water within the chamber.

Our mist chamber is made of a wood frame covered with polyethylene. Sliding doors have been provided for easy access to the inside of the chamber. This chamber was made to fit an existing greenhouse bench, and all material dimensions are based on that unit. Adjust the measurements to fit your benches.

Three mist nozzles have been provided so that the water is sprayed in a uniform pattern throughout the chamber. A time clock is used to activate the solenoid water valve. The clock cycles every six minutes and can be adjusted to vary the amount of spraying time. This arrangement provides a semiautomatic system. A fully automatic system can be built by putting a second time clock in series with the first clock. The second clock would be adjusted to turn on the mist chamber water system during certain periods of the day.

Materials:

Item	Quantity	Description
Chamber:		
A. End panels	2	$3/4 \times 27\,1/4 \times 28$-inch exterior plywood
B. Bottom rails	2	$1\,1/2 \times 3\,1/2 \times 94\,1/2$-inch construction grade spruce
C. Top rail	1	$1\,1/2 \times 1\,1/2 \times 94\,1/2$-inch construction grade spruce
D. Support post	1	$3/4 \times 1\,1/2 \times 28$-inch #2 pine
E. Hoops	3	$1/8 \times 3/4 \times 48$-inch aluminum
F. Cover–front	1	54×96-inch polyethylene
G. Cover–end	1	28×30-inch polyethylene
H. Door track	16 feet	$1/4$-inch sliding door track
I. Doors	2	$1/4 \times 22\,3/4 \times 48$-inch acrylic
Screws	6	2-inch #12 flat-head wood screws
Screws	6	1-inch #8 flat-head wood screws
Paint	—	Exterior paint
Glue	—	White vinyl glue
Plumbing:		
J. Manifold	1	$3/4 \times 81$-inch plastic pipe
K. Nozzle saddles	3	$3/4 \times 3/8$-inch plastic saddle

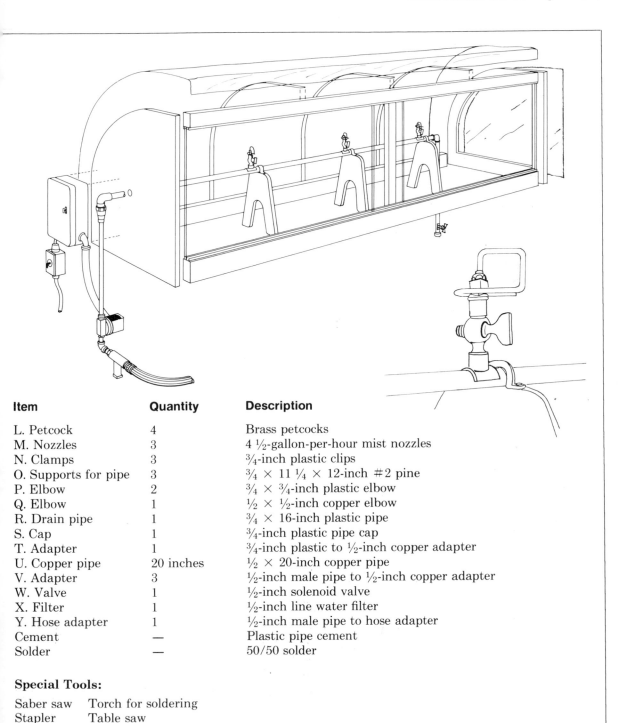

Item	Quantity	Description
L. Petcock	4	Brass petcocks
M. Nozzles	3	4 ½-gallon-per-hour mist nozzles
N. Clamps	3	¾-inch plastic clips
O. Supports for pipe	3	¾ × 11 ¼ × 12-inch #2 pine
P. Elbow	2	¾ × ¾-inch plastic elbow
Q. Elbow	1	½ × ½-inch copper elbow
R. Drain pipe	1	¾ × 16-inch plastic pipe
S. Cap	1	¾-inch plastic pipe cap
T. Adapter	1	¾-inch plastic to ½-inch copper adapter
U. Copper pipe	20 inches	½ × 20-inch copper pipe
V. Adapter	3	½-inch male pipe to ½-inch copper adapter
W. Valve	1	½-inch solenoid valve
X. Filter	1	½-inch line water filter
Y. Hose adapter	1	½-inch male pipe to hose adapter
Cement	—	Plastic pipe cement
Solder	—	50/50 solder

Special Tools:

Saber saw   Torch for soldering
Stapler   Table saw

(project continued on next page)

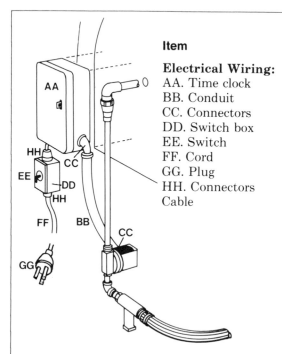

Item	Quantity	Description
Electrical Wiring:		
AA. Time clock	1	6-minute cycle time clock
BB. Conduit	1	20-inch waterproof conduit
CC. Connectors	2	Waterproof connectors for conduit
DD. Switch box	1	Cast aluminum bell box
EE. Switch	1	Waterproof switch and plate
FF. Cord	25 feet	14-gauge, 3-wire cord
GG. Plug	1	Grounded male plug
HH. Connectors	3	Waterproof connectors
Cable	As needed	Waterproof cable

Procedure for the Chamber:

1. Cut pieces for the wooden frame, A, B, C, and D, according to dimensions in the materials list.
2. Lay out and cut the middle portion out of one end panel (A), leaving about a 2-inch-wide frame. Use a saber saw.
3. Lay out and drill a ⅞-inch hole for the water supply pipe in the center of the other end panel (A).
4. Cut grooves ⅛ inch deep and ¾ inch wide in the back of the rear bottom rail (B) and the top of the top rail (C), for the support hoops (E).
5. Glue and screw the end panels (A) onto the rails (B and C) with 2-inch #12 screws.
6. Cut three aluminum support hoops (E) and bend to fit.
7. Drill a hole in each end of the three support hoops for screws and countersink all the screw holes for flat-head screws.
8. Paint the frame with two coats of exterior paint.

9. Install the support hoops with 1-inch #8 flat-head wood screws.
10. Cover the frame with a piece of polyethylene (F), pulled tight and stapled to the frame.
11. Cover the cut-out end panel (A) with a piece of polyethylene (G), and staple it.
12. Install the ¼-inch aluminum sliding door track on top of the front bottom rail (B), and on the bottom of the top front rail (C).
13. Cut two pieces of clear acrylic to fit in the door opening, making sure they overlap an inch, and install them.
14. Install the mist chamber on the greenhouse bench.

Procedure for Plumbing the Mist Chamber:

1. Cut a piece of plastic pipe for the mist nozzle manifold (J).
2. Lay out and drill three ⅜-inch holes for the mist nozzle saddles (K) in the manifold (J) and glue the saddles in place, centering them around the holes.
3. Lay out and cut three pipe supports (O) from ¾ × 11 ¼ × 12-inch pieces of pine. (See illustration for shaping.)
4. Screw the petcock valves (L) and the mist nozzles (M) into the mist nozzle saddles (K).

5. Install the mist nozzle manifold (J) in the mist chamber, slipping one end through the hole in panel (A), and fasten it to the pipe supports (O) with ¾-inch plastic pipe clamps (N).
6. Glue a ¾ × ¾-inch plastic elbow (P) to each end of the manifold (J) so each is pointed down toward the floor.
7. At the exhaust end of the manifold (J) install a drain pipe (R) down through the greenhouse bench with a drain petcock (L) and cap (S) positioned below the bench.
8. At the feed end of the manifold (J) attach a ¾-inch plastic to ½-inch copper adapter (T).
9. Solder a piece of ½-inch copper pipe about 20 inches long (U) between the solenoid valve (W) and the manifold (J) so that the valve part of the solenoid is under the bench.
10. Pipe between the solenoid valve and the in-line filter (X). You may have to cut the 20-inch pipe (U).
11. Attach the water supply to the filter (X) either with a female hose connector or piping directly into the water supply.

Procedure for Electrical Wiring:

1. Mount the time clock (AA) on the solid end panel (A) of the mist chamber.
2. Run waterproof conduit (BB) between the solenoid (W) and the time clock (AA) using two waterproof connectors (CC).
3. Put the wire through the conduit (BB) and connect it to the proper terminals in the time clock (AA).
4. Mount the switch box (DD) on the end panel of the mist chamber (A).
5. Run waterproof cable between the switch and the time clock.
6. Run waterproof cable from the switch to the power supply.
7. Wire the switch and time clock.
8. Turn on the power supply and test the system.

efficiently, you can extend it right into the greenhouse, providing it has a sufficient heating capacity. Otherwise you may need a booster pump. Some manufacturers sell kits that enable mechanically inclined people to make this change themselves, but if you have a hot air system, you will have to let a dealer do it. (Actually, hot air heat is very drying and is not usually recommended for a greenhouse. Unless you have a plastic house or problems with high humidity, you will have to compensate for hot air heat by wetting down frequently or using a humidifier.)

Supplemental Heating

If you need or want to heat your greenhouse independently of your home, you can choose from among electric heat or that provided by steam, hot water, or hot air systems fueled by coal, oil, natural gas, or electricity, or even burning wood. If you have a small green-

house, or have partitioned a larger house for different temperatures, or if you have a very well insulated unit—perhaps a pit or solar greenhouse—you will probably be able to get by with the simplest of heating devices.

You may just want to provide bottom heat under benches devoted to seed germination or propagation from cuttings. This can be done with a soil-cable heating system that requires just 10 watts for each square foot (0.9 sq m) of space.

To heat small areas from above, you might choose to suspend radiant heat lamps by a chain. A 150- to 200-watt heat lamp suspended 32 inches (81 cm) above a planting bed will warm a 3- by 3-foot (91 by 91 cm) area 15° to 20°F (8° to 11°C) above the outside air temperature. Lamps can be controlled by a thermostat that will turn off the setup when the temperature hits 45° to 50°F (7° to 10°C). In tests conducted in a double-glazed plastic 8- by 12-foot (2.4 by 3.6 m) greenhouse in Connecticut, four 2-watt infra-red heaters hung 20 inches (51 cm) above the soil proved more economical than any other source of electric heat, costing just $45 to keep the greenhouse at 60°F (16°C) for a year.

It is also possible to hang electric or gas-heated panels over benches or ground beds. Or you can put mineral-insulated heating cables covered with polyvinylchloride along the side(s) of a greenhouse, using ceramic cleats.

Another approach popular for green-houses under 25 feet (7.5 m) long is space

Estimating the Maximum Heating Requirements of a Greenhouse

Though the following procedure does not factor in heat lost through solid walls or framing (which will be minimal if you insulate properly), it will give you a reasonably good idea of how many Btu's per hour will be needed to maintain the desired temperature in your greenhouse at night and on overcast days during the coldest time of the year. You will find this figure essential in choosing and sizing an auxiliary heating system, and in these days of astronomical fuel costs, it also would be prudent to project your heating needs before you commit yourself to build or buy a specific kind and size of greenhouse and before you decide what kinds of plants to grow. Here's how to go about it.

1. Determine the difference between the lowest outside temperature likely in your area and the lowest temperature you plan to maintain in the greenhouse. For instance, if you want to keep your greenhouse temperature no lower than 45°F and the coldest it ever gets outside is 0°F, your temperature difference is 45.

2. Find the number of square feet of glazing in the greenhouse, being careful to include exposed sides and ends as well as roof.

3. Multiply the temperature difference by the total square feet of glazing.

4. Multiply your total from step #3 by the number of Btu's per hour per square foot per °F that your glazing material loses. You'll find this figure—called the U value—listed below:

Glass	1.13
Polycarbonate plastic	
Lexan	1.10
Tuffak-Twinwal	.48
Acrylic	
0.187-inch-thick	
Plexiglas	1.09
FRP plastics	
Filon and Lascolite	.95
Kalwall	.45
Polyester film (1-5 mil)	
Mylar	1.05
Polyethylene film (4 mil)	1.60
Solar Polyvinylfluoride	
film	
Tedlar	1.16
Double-glazed plastic film	
or glass	.80

Your total from step #4 will be the number of Btu's per hour that your heating system should be able to provide. If you live where the average wind speed in winter exceeds 15 mph, increase that total by 4 percent for every 5 mph over 15. And if your house is not tightly sealed by weather-stripping or caulking or if your glazing is lapped, add another 12 percent.

To get some idea of the comparative cost of providing the heat you will need with various fuels, keep in mind that in order to supply 100,000 Btu's, you will need 1.02 gallons of #2 oil, 11.3 pounds of coal, 125 cubic feet of natural gas, 1.36 gallons of propane, or 29.3 kwh of electricity. (These figures take into account the typical efficiency of heating systems, which ranges from 65 percent for coal and 70 percent for oil to 100 percent for electricity.) By finding out the unit costs (i.e., gallon of oil, pound of coal) of these fuels where you live and multiplying each by the 100,000-Btu figure given above, you can assess which is most economical to use, though of course you must also consider the initial expense of buying and installing the system you choose.

heaters, which are of various kinds and many sizes. Kerosene heaters will do for really small houses or lean-to's needing little heat. In a 6- by 9-foot (1.8 by 2.7 m) house a 5,000 Btu unit will burn about one gallon (3.7 l) of kerosene per day to winter-over such plants as azaleas and camellias, although there are fumes to which more delicate plants like cucumbers, fuchsias, roses, and tomatoes are sensitive.

Although they are vulnerable to power failure, electric heaters have many advantages. They are clean, efficient, easy to control, need no venting, and are inexpensive and simple to install. Electric heaters are worth considering where winter temperatures stay about 20°F (-7°C) or where the heaters are used only to maintain a minimum temperature of 45°F (7°C), or just as a backup in extremely cold weather. (The amount of electricity needed just about doubles with every 5°F/3°C of heat maintained in the greenhouse.) To be hooked up with a moisture-proof plastic cable, electric heaters are available in sizes providing from 1 to 4 kilowatts, with 3,414 Btu's per hour being generated for every kilowatt. Like all space heaters, electric ones work best when they have a fan to help distribute the heat and should release heat from the sides rather than the top, unless you have a high greenhouse. A single heater can be placed beneath a bench at one end of the greenhouse to encourage the circular flow of air across and up, over, and down again. Two heaters may be positioned at opposite corners of the greenhouse.

Whatever your heating choice, if your system is at all elaborate you really must automate it, for failure here can wipe out your entire stock of plants within hours. (Instructions for a simple temperature control system made from standard thermostats and power relays are available from the Cooperative Extension Service at Pennsylvania State University. See the Appendix for details.)

Use an alcohol-filled thermometer to trigger your thermostat and place it at eye level midway in the greenhouse, where masses of plants are. Shade the thermometer from direct sun with a hood, and make sure it is not near a vent. To save on fuel, consider using an aspirated thermostat, which works by circulating air over its thermometer, thereby measuring average air temperature rather than the lower temperature of the dead air immediately around the thermometer. To get something of the same effect, you might use a small circulating fan near the thermometer or a heat siphon near the ridge, which will funnel warm air toward the floor of the greenhouse, thereby keeping the air in circulation and helping to equalize temperatures throughout the greenhouse.

For much-needed protection against temperature fluctuations caused by calamities like broken glass and electrical failures, you might invest in a thermometer that also serves as a temperature alarm. These minimum/maximum thermometers not only show actual temperature, but also have two movable hands that can be set, for example, at 40°F (4°C) and 90°F (32°C). An alarm bell run on dry-cell batteries can be rigged to go off in your dwelling if the temperature goes below or above these critical levels.

Keeping Cool in Summer

The long days and high sun angles of summertime allow a maximum amount of light to penetrate the greenhouse, where it is transformed into heat as it is absorbed by the plants and other surfaces. Luckily for them, plants have a built-in cooling system, for 50 percent or more of the radiant energy they absorb is lost through transpiration. But transpiration takes water, and when the light is intense and the temperature is high, plants may be forced to give off water faster than they can take it up. The result? Pitiful drooping despite all your efforts to mist and water frequently and to boost humidity by hosing down. When this happens, you must take steps to cool the greenhouse by providing shade and ventilation.

28 Ways to Bring Down Fuel Bills

There are many steps you can take to lower your greenhouse heating needs and costs to rock bottom. Indeed, if getting by without fossil fuels is your top priority, you stand a healthy chance of succeeding. For starters, ponder the strategies and techniques evolved by solar greenhouse pioneers and see if you can adapt some of them to gain and store as much solar heat as possible in your location. Next, work to minimize the loss of solar and other forms of heat by making use of the following tips on greenhouse design, building, and management practices:

1. Try by all means to build a pit greenhouse and if possible to attach your greenhouse to a heated building, since both of these structures help lower heat losses by reducing the temperature difference between the inside and outside of the greenhouse.

2. Put up a good size greenhouse. The smaller the volume is relative to exposed surface area, the more heat the house will lose relative to its volume, and the more the air temperature inside will be affected when a door is opened.

3. Avoid aluminum greenhouses—or at least insulate aluminum side walls and glazing bars—for an aluminum frame can lose heat as fast as most single layers of glazing.

4. Make the north wall of an east-west running greenhouse opaque since the small light gain from this direction is offset by large heat losses. In new construction, an insulated, reflective north wall can reduce heating bills up to 28 percent if 3½ inches (9 cm) of fiberglass is used. To convert a glazed north wall to a solid one, either replace the glazing, or build an insulated wall inside the glass, or simply attach aluminum building paper or sheeting inside, leaving a dead air space if possible. It also may be feasible to cover the north end wall of a north-south greenhouse.

5. Assuming you don't have plentiful groundwater or a high water table, take advantage of the insulating qualities of dry earth (24 inches/61 cm equal 1 inch/2.5 cm of fiberglass) by making an earth berm next to opaque walls.

6. Choose a sheltered location for your greenhouse or plant open hedges or fences around it to break the force of the wind. (Wind promotes the loss of warm air by convection and also encourages leakage of air in from outside through any cracks when a lower air temperature is created inside by strong winds. In a five-year study done in England, wind increased fuel consumption by from 38 to 57 percent.) All else being equal, a shelter belt of evergreens to windward can cut fuel usage by about 25 percent, and sheltering a greenhouse on all sides but the south will save about 40 percent. Ideally the windbreak should be at a distance of about four times the height of the greenhouse, and it should be 30 to 40 feet (9 to 12 m) longer than the width of the greenhouse.

7. Build a foundation wall that extends at least 24 inches (61 cm) into the ground and cover it on the inside with insulation board. This is especially important with concrete, which conducts heat more rapidly than soil.

8. Make a small room off the outside entrance of the greenhouse to create an air lock that will seal out gusts of cold air and lessen infiltration around the door. At the very least, position the door on the side of the house away from prevailing winds.

9. Build as tightly as you can and use long-lasting silicon caulking and weather stripping (especially around vents) to seal all openings, since heat leaks from infiltration at such places can amount to anywhere from one-tenth to one-twelfth of your total heat losses.

10. For tremendous savings in heat, look to your glazing, which will account for about 60 percent of your overall heat waste even under the best of conditions. Consider one of the new double-wall polycarbonate or reinforced fiberglass glazings, or double-glaze glass or plastic film houses.

11. Beware of single-layer clip-type glass and stapled plastic films, which can promote air loss and drafts. If not sealed with special sponges, corrugated fiberglass will do the same. In any case, it loses more heat than flat fiberglass because it has 10 to 20 percent more surface area.

12. Since over 75 percent of the supplemental heating in greenhouses is needed at night when radiation heat losses are highest, you can reduce glazing and overall heat losses most effectively by using indoor or outdoor movable insulation at night and even during periods of extremely low temperatures and low light intensity. If your average outdoor winter temperature is 30° to 35°F (−1° to 2°C) or below, you should do this even if you have double glazing to make sure the glazing is bringing in more heat than it is losing.

You can if you like use canvas-covered batts or rolls outside (one idea is to buy or rent roll-down blankets of flexible insulation covered by black polyethylene—the kind used by cement companies). Or you can hinge insulating shutters with reflective inner surfaces to the outside of glazed areas so they open downward and/or outward to reflect added light inside during winter days and protect and insulate when closed at night. To insulate from the inside, you can clip panels of Styrofoam or styrene backed by Masonite or plywood onto the glazing. However you do it, if you provide insulation equivalent to 3 inches (8 cm) of fiberglass or 1½ inches (4 cm) of Styrofoam for 14 hours each night, you will cut heat losses through double glazing by a minimum of 50 percent.

Recent research done at Cornell University and elsewhere suggests savings of up to 55 percent are possible with a new form of movable indoor insulation called thermal blankets. These are actually night curtains of black 4-mil polyethylene or polyester/aluminum foil that are drawn around the inside walls of the greenhouse and from eave to eave or eave to ridge. Eave-to-eave installations give the best results, but the curtains must be tight to be effective since convection accounts for 60 percent of glazing heat loss versus 30 percent from conduction and 10 percent by radiation.

13. Run exhaust stovepipes from oil, gas, or wood heaters the length of your greenhouse to extract a maximum of heat before it leaves the premises.

14. Put aluminum foil or other reflective insulation between your heater and any nearby wall or glazing so the heat is bounced back into the greenhouse.

15. Tack skirts around the bottoms of open benches and hang black cloth or polyethylene horizontally above plants as close to them as possible on winter nights to hold in warm air.

16. Arrange plants near heat storage masses so the released heat is efficiently used at night. One technique is to alternate black containers full of water with white ones in which tomatoes are growing.

17. Grow "cool" rather than "warm" plants. For example, in midwinter grow root crops, lettuce, endive, kale, or other plants that can tolerate night temperatures as low as 40°F (4°C). Save crops like tomatoes, which need a 60°F (16°C) night temperature in order to flower, for fall and spring.

18. Plant earlier in the fall or later in the spring, working with short-season varieties of vegetables and flowers.

19. If you want to grow some moderate- to warm-temperature crops or need heat for propagating, compartmentalize your greenhouse to minimize the heat needed or create a small plastic-surrounded area and heat it with soil cables. (If you're germinating seeds, you can put this setup under a raised bench, which will also benefit from the heat as it rises.) Or just suspend a low-kilowatt radiant heat lamp over a bench or bed.

20. If you have moderate-temperature plants, consider setting your thermostat lower at night, then warming up roots and soil with 75°F (24°C) water applied in the morning as the thermostat is turned up. In research done in Connecticut, chrysanthemums and lilies grown with the night temperature dropped to 45°F (7°C) were no different in size and quality from those given a constant night temperature of 60°F (16°C). Plant physiologist John Thorne claims this late-night lowering is not harmful because plants finish metabolizing, transporting, and using products formed during the day within the first few hours of darkness and after that are not affected by a moderate drop in temperature. But this tolerance to night cold varies from species to species and even among cultivars. Also, the lower temperatures may result in slower growth and in a longer time to flowering.

21. Do not set your thermostat at a temperature your heating system isn't capable of maintaining. You'll squander heat in relatively mild weather and encourage active soft growth that will be stopped abruptly during a cold snap.

22. Use a small circulating fan to cut down on heat losses

(continued on next page)

through the ridge of the greenhouse.

23. Guard against misleading temperature readings that can cause your thermostat to kick on unnecessarily. For example, at 60°F (16°C) a fluctuation of 2°F (1°C) can result in 10 percent greater fuel consumption. Ways to prevent this include using an aspirated thermometer or situating a fan near the thermometer so it registers the temperature of moving air instead of dead air. Or you could use a heat siphon.

24. Keep the contact points on your thermostat clean to maintain accuracy, and clean and adjust your heater yearly.

25. If you have automated vents controlled by a separate thermostat, set it 5° or 10°F (3° to 6°C) higher than your heating thermostat so the vents don't open when the heater turns on.

26. Close down a greenhouse having a large exposed surface from December 1 to March 1—a practice that will cut your yearly fuel needs by half and give you time for cleaning and making repairs. Attached solar greenhouses afflicted by wild temperature fluctuations in the winter also may be shut down during the coldest months and used to reduce fuel needs in the adjoining house. The idea is to close and seal all outside vents, then vent air from the floor level on the cold far north side of the dwelling under the house between insulated floor joists and into the bottom of the greenhouse where it will be warmed by the sun, rise, and flow back into the house through open vents in the common wall near the ridge of the greenhouse. Close both sets of interconnecting vents at night and on dull days when the greenhouse may be losing more heat than it is gaining.

27. For some free heat and humidity, vent your electric clothes dryer into the greenhouse.

28. Mulch the soil in raised benches to keep plant roots warmer by preventing soil heat from escaping into the air.

When it comes to shading, your choices are plentiful. Most solar greenhouses are built with an overhang that automatically shelters plants when the sun is at its highest and hottest, and since solar houses usually have a minimum of glazing, often the overhang and the natural screening provided by morning glories (*Ipomoea* spp.), silverlace vines *(Polygonum aubertii),* or other vining plants on trellises or by a nearby row of sunflowers (*Helianthus* spp.) furnish all the shade needed during the hottest part of the year.

Traditionally shaped houses not covered with the light-diffusing translucent plastics usually need more thorough seasonal shading to effectively bring down leaf temperature and transpiration. When used together with a humidifying setup or wetting down, proper shading can lower the greenhouse temperature from 10° to 15°F (6° to 8°C).

You can, if you like, paint or spray on shading substances. Choices include commercially sold powders or liquids thinned with water or paint solvents; whitewash (not to be used on aluminum houses because it contains lime, which is corrosive to aluminum); and cheap white latex paint diluted with water at a ratio of 8 parts water to 1 part paint. All of these shadings are temporary and will weather unevenly, sometimes wearing off on cue by fall or winter.

Shading compounds or tinted vinyl or fiberglass are good choices if you are growing plants that like shade with plenty of diffused light, for example, carnations, chrysanthemums, and many annuals. But never paint, spray, or daub shading compounds on fiberglass houses. They really don't need this treatment and the compounds are hard to scrub off fiberglass surfaces.

For a more formal look, you might prefer rollup shades of slatted wood, aluminum, or bamboo with rust-resistant couplings—rope-operated devices that also can protect your house from hail.

Another option is flameproof shade fabric. Lumite shade cloth made of mildew-proof woven Saran gives uniform shade in densities from 6 to 92 percent (the standard weave gives 63 percent shade) and can be purchased with reinforced taped edges and brass grommets. Polypropylene mesh is 150 percent stronger than Lumite, weighs half as much, and is said to last 15 years. Either kind can be attached to the ridge and rolled up and down or even supported two feet (0.6 m) above the house on a redwood frame so vents can open and close underneath.

There are also fixed, flat types of shading that can be put on in spring or summer and removed in fall. These include tinted fiberglass panels that are clipped to the roof bars or fastened to the sides of the greenhouse, or aluminum laths that fit into slotted wood or metal frames attached to the roof bars (these metal strips may be moved closer or farther apart to regulate the width of the sun stripes in between). For light and cheap flat shading that will reflect away summer sun and also serve as movable winter insulation, you can glue Styrofoam tiles to the underside of 36 inch (91 cm) wide unpainted aluminum roofing panels. Obviously all of the rollup and flat types of shading must be cut or spaced so any vents can be opened.

It is also quite acceptable to provide shade inside the greenhouse by placing shade cloth, reed mats, a wooden lattice, cheesecloth, or even muslin over the rafters. Indoor shading is especially feasible if ridge vents cover a large part of your greenhouse roof— and necessary, too, since the plants below will be in even brighter light than before should you open the vents wide on clear days. For a natural and beautiful solution to the problem, you might consider training vining plants like gloriosas up posts or other supports. They will provide a canopy of dramatic flowers and mottled shade when you need it most, then die back in winter. For emergency shade indoors, you can simply cover propagation benches and seed flats with newspapers, or tape big sheets of butcher's paper to the glazing.

Actually, new developments in shading research soon may make scrubbing off whitewash or fussing with shades or panels unnecessary. Working to get the maximum usable daylight into the greenhouse without automation or manual effort, scientists are perfecting self-shading roofs. Designed to remain transparent when the temperature is below 70°F (21°C), thus admitting the beneficial early morning and late afternoon sun, one such roof features double glazing of glass or Plexiglas that is roughened on the inner surface of the outer layer. Next to the roughness is an inner space filled with a vapor. At lower temperatures the vapor condenses and the surface becomes transparent. As it does, a partial vacuum is created which helps insulate the greenhouse at night. The other approach to self-fogging uses a liquid mixture in the inner space. This liquid becomes milky white at 78°F (26°C) when large clusters of molecules are formed, and reverts to transparency when the temperature drops.

In addition to shading, you can cool down the greenhouse by letting out some of the hottest air and admitting somewhat cooler air from outside. This is quite often done by vertical ventilation through a system of vents along the ridge of the house, though greenhouses longer than 12 feet (3.6 m) also usually need vents in their sides or small sliding vents in the foundation. These are often used in conjunction with a screened door for horizontal as well as vertical ventilation.

Often sold as extras by greenhouse manufacturers, vents are essential unless you plan to use a forced-air cooling setup, and generous venting is especially critical in little greenhouses, since the smaller the house the harder it is to steady the temperature. Sadly enough, the cheaper ready-made houses usually need more vents than the manufacturers provide. As a rule of thumb, the square footage of the ridge vents in a greenhouse should be at least one-fifth to one-sixth of the floor area, and lower vents should be proportionate in size. Roof vents work best at catching wind

Build Your Own Ecliptic Shade

This greenhouse ecliptic shade was designed to provide shade during the summer months and maximum light penetration during the late fall and winter months. This shade was inspired by a similar structure designed by orchidist Milan Fiske of New York.

The angles and width of the slats are oriented, in this shade, to work at 40°N latitude, and in a greenhouse with a 47-degree sloped front, facing south. This greenhouse was designed with nine glazed segments each having $20 \frac{3}{4} \times 43 \frac{1}{2}$-inch openings. Each ecliptic shade is mounted into one of the openings. Adjust the dimensions as needed to fit your greenhouse.

To determine the angle of the slats and their spacing for your own window, you have to take your location into consideration. Once you know your latitude, and the tilt angle of your window, you can use the following simple calcu-

lation to determine these two measurements and maximize your shading in the summer and the amount of light you admit in the winter.

To determine the angle for cutting the slats:

1. Measure tilt angle of window (angle A).
2. A + (66.5 − latitude) = B
3. B = the cut angle for your slats.

Special Tools:

Table saw
Dado head for saw
Router (optional)
Drill

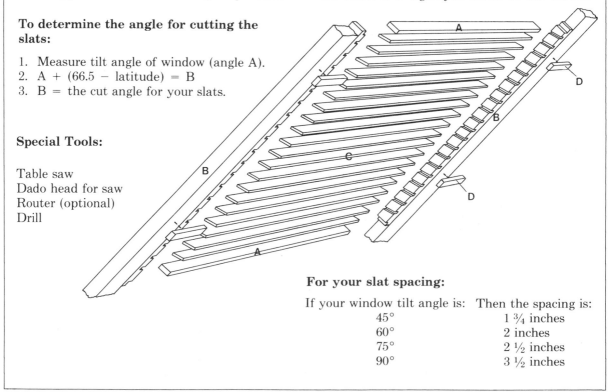

For your slat spacing:

If your window tilt angle is:	Then the spacing is:
45°	1 ¾ inches
60°	2 inches
75°	2 ½ inches
90°	3 ½ inches

Materials:

Item	Quantity	Description
A. End pieces	2	$\frac{3}{4} \times 2\frac{1}{2} \times 20$-inch #2 pine
B. Side pieces	2	$\frac{3}{4} \times 2\frac{1}{2} \times 43\frac{1}{2}$-inch #2 pine
C. Slats	20	$\frac{5}{16} \times 2\frac{1}{2} \times 20$-inch #2 pine
D. Latches	4	$\frac{3}{4} \times 1\frac{1}{4} \times 3$-inch #2 pine
Screws	4	$1\frac{1}{2}$-inch #10 round-head brass screws
Washers	4	$\frac{1}{4}$-inch flat brass washers
Nails	—	3d finish nails
Glue	—	White vinyl glue

Procedure:

1. Cut pieces A, B, C, and D according to the dimensions in the materials list.
2. Cut a $\frac{3}{8}$-inch-deep $\times$ $\frac{3}{4}$-inch-wide rabbet on each end of both side pieces (B).
3. Cut $\frac{3}{8}$-inch-deep $\times$ $\frac{5}{16}$-inch-wide slat dadoes across the side pieces (B) at the angles you have calculated for your location as instructed above. Be sure to make a right- and a left-side piece.
4. Glue and nail the shade components together.
5. Rout a $\frac{1}{4}$-inch radius on all the corners, or break the edges with a sanding block.
6. Drill a $\frac{3}{16}$-inch hole through the center of each latch (D).
7. Mount the latches with $1\frac{1}{2}$-inch #10 round-head brass screws and flat brass washers.
8. Install the shade.

and letting warm air out if they open to an angle of 55 degrees, which is well above the horizontal and usually enables them to form a straight line with the slope of the other roof. Needless to say, don't open vents this wide against a strong wind or if rain is expected—unless only water-loving foliage plants are positioned beneath!

As far as placement is concerned, in lean-to's or in other situations where they are to be put on only one side of the ridge, vents (and doors) should be located on the side away from prevailing winds. In a freestanding even-span house, vents should run the whole length of both sides of the ridge, or at least 12 or 24 inch (30 or 61 cm) wide vents should alternate from side to side. In attached houses, which are the most difficult of all to ventilate, vents ideally should run the whole length of the ridge, and there should be at least one box or panel vent in a side wall, placed below bench level to minimize drafts on plants. Low-down vents are also a good idea in glazing-to-ground situations.

In a house ventilated by vents alone, cooler air will flow in through the lower side vents as warmer air leaves the ridge vents by convection. To assist this process, the usual practice is to open the east-side vents just a couple of inches (approximately 5 cm) in the morning while the west side is opened wide. At noon the east vents should be opened wide and those on the west side shut a little. By midafternoon the west vents are lowered so the sun cannot penetrate until late afternoon. At nightfall the ridge vents are closed enough to let rain or dew run off on the roof.

For cross-ventilation, open a screened door and vents at the other end, keeping the highest vents opened just sufficiently to let out hot air. This is also a good practice if you plan to be away all day, but make sure the greenhouse is thoroughly wetted down if the weather is hot, bright, and clear.

Vents can be operated by hand with a push rod, chain, or handcrank, but they are so vital to managing temperature in smaller houses that you can lose your plants in just a

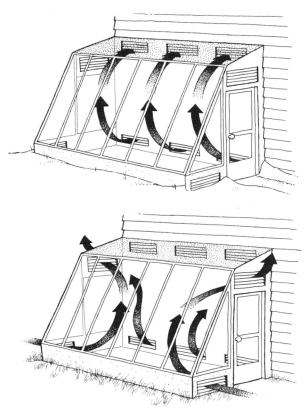

Seasonal Use of Vents: In winter when the air in the attached greenhouse needs to be warmed, heated air from the adjoining structure enters through the lower vents and is recirculated through the upper ridge vents. In summer, to clear the greenhouse of excess heat, open the lower vents to allow cool air to enter. Through the process of convection, the warmer air will leave by the upper vents.

day if you forget to adjust them. For this reason many greenhouse gardeners feel that an automatic ventilation system is second in importance only to automatic heating if you ever intend to be away from home for more than a day at a time. It is also a good precaution if you are using an automatic gas heater.

The simplest way to automate vents is to hook them up to a thermostat, but they can also be included in a costly, completely integrated system that takes into account temperature, wind, humidity, light, and rain. Energy-conscious greenhouse owners are now

discovering and using automatic vent openers that do not require electric power. For example, you can buy a fairly inexpensive solar-powered vent that activates at from 68° to 75°F (20° to 24°C) and lifts up to nine pounds (4 kg). (It is manufactured by Dalen Products Company of Knoxville, Tennessee.)

Forced-Air Cooling

Though many owners of hobby greenhouses make do using just vents and doors for summer ventilation, for greater control over temperature with a minimum of labor, some kind of forced-air system is required. Perhaps the simplest is an exhaust fan at one end of the house opposite a door, vent, or automated inlet louvers at the other end. (To reduce drafts on plants and cool most effectively, both the fan and the air inlet should be as high up as possible—over a door in tall enough houses.)

Used together with regular damping down, such a setup can cool your greenhouse substantially. If the fan and louvers are wired to a thermostat and sized to meet your seasonal requirements, they can keep your greenhouse within 3° to 10°F (2° to 6°C) of the outside temperature. For optimum cooling, the Northeast Regional Engineering Service recommends an air exchange rate of at least 12 cubic feet (0.36 cu m) per minute per square foot (0.09 sq m) of floor area for small greenhouses with an air volume of 5,000 cubic feet (150 cu m) or less. (To find your approximate volume, multiply your floor area by 7.) If you don't live in a terrifically hot area, however, you can get by with a fan handling enough cubic feet (cubic meters) per minute to provide one change of your greenhouse air volume per minute.

A more sophisticated cooling system uses a fan to draw outside air continuously through a wet pad. The air is cooled as it picks up and evaporates the water in passing. Known as evaporative or fan-and-pad cooling, this approach is the contemporary version of an old technique used in India in which mats of fresh straw or fiber called "tatties" were hung in doorways or window openings and kept sprinkled with water. (Temperature records made in India in 1792 documented a temperate 87°F/31°C inside a tatty-cooled house when it was 110°F/44°C outside in the shade and a blistering 118°F/48°C in the sun. The evaporative agent was a strong, hot, western wind.)

In today's commercial greenhouses, entire walls are often covered with aspen pads used as tatties once were. In a small house you can improvise evaporative cooling by hanging strips of burlap from lower vents into pans of water. As hot air leaves ridge vents, cooler air will be drawn through the burlap below, which will take up the water like a wick and cool the air further. Or spray water in front of a fan through a mist nozzle to cool a greenhouse down by 10°F (6°C) in ten minutes. It is also possible to buy small, self-contained units in which a fan is surrounded by three pads kept moist by a recirculating pump.

Since it humidifies as well as cools and can reduce greenhouse temperatures up to 30° or 40°F (17° or 22°C) in very hot, dry places, evaporative cooling is thought of as most feasible for the southwest United States, where it is obvious that using vents for cooling steals precious humidity. Actually, however, the effectiveness of this method is directly linked to the outdoor bulb temperature—that is, to the temperature you get when you evaporate moisture into air until it becomes 100 percent humid. Fan-and-pad cooling can bring the temperature of a greenhouse down to within 3°F (2°C) of the wet bulb temperature outside, and so is quite workable in any region with a relatively low summer wet bulb reading—a definition that applies to parts of New England and much of the continental United States west of the Mississippi River. This method is also worth considering anywhere that summer heat might shut down the greenhouse. It also makes it possible to grow cool-weather, high-light-intensity crops like chrysanthemums all summer, for the lower temperatures mean that little or no shading is needed.

To select a fan-and-pad system of the right size, find the cubic feet (cubic meters) of your greenhouse by multiplying the length by the width by the average height. Adding 50 percent to this total, select a unit which can handle at least that many cubic feet (cubic meters) per minute.

YEAR-ROUND AIR CIRCULATION

As the growing use of fan-and-tube systems suggests, ventilation is useful for reasons unrelated to cooling. Actually, fresh air is essential to good growing conditions no matter what the time of year. For one thing, exchanging old air for new assures plants of adequate carbon dioxide. Present at about 0.03 percent in normal outside air, this gas is a plant's only source of carbon, which makes up half its total dry weight, and is just as essential to photosynthesis as sunlight and water are. On hot, bright days plants may use up the carbon dioxide in the greenhouse in the early morning, and fresh air is one way of restoring it. To maintain normal levels of this valuable gas, the air in a greenhouse should be changed at least every ten minutes.

Supplying such ventilation in warmer weather and other sources of carbon dioxide in colder periods is particularly important in freestanding greenhouses, for they will lack the more dependable supply entering attached greenhouses in the air coming from a house and its inhabitants. To maximize air exchange in attached houses, some people leave connecting doors or windows open constantly or open floor and ceiling vents in a common wall during the day in spring, fall, and winter, switching over to outside vents in summer. This approach can add needed humidity to a dwelling during the winter but should be used sparingly in warmer weather or with greenhouses having high humidity, since it can cause mildew problems in the home. Ventilation is a particularly good way to add carbon dioxide to the greenhouse since vents and fans are usually not needed overnight, which is when plants are producing carbon dioxide themselves. (For other means of introducing carbon dioxide, see Cultural Practices, earlier in this chapter.)

In addition to bringing in a beneficial gas, the steady circulation of air also removes unwanted gases linked to heating systems which burn gas, coal, or oil. The culprits here, which can scorch leaves and kill buds and flowers, are carbon monoxide, propylene, ethylene, and the sulfurous odorizer at the bottom of propane tanks.

The air movement that redistributes gases in the air also helps plant pollination, and by discouraging humidity buildup around plants helps lessen the condensation or drip problems linked to single-glazed plastic houses. Excellent air circulation also acts to break up the layer of air which adheres to leaf surfaces and works against the transference of carbon dioxide and water vapor. And air movement helps make up for a poorly designed heating system by preventing pockets of stagnant hot or cold air. (You can check your greenhouse for such "dead spots" by introducing a metal can containing smoldering bits of paper, and observing where the air flow carries the feather-light fragments.)

Owners who rely on vents to meet their air circulation needs should remember to crack their ridge or side vents even in cold weather. This practice is not advisable if the temperature is below freezing, but if it is sunny and above freezing, wait until the greenhouse has warmed perhaps 20°F (11°C) above its night low, then open vents away from the wind one or two inches (2.5 or 5 cm).

In larger houses and those with poor heating or insufficient vents, circulating fans are desirable. At a very low energy cost a standard fan or a turbulator type designed to prevent high humidity and stabilize temperature can help keep drafts off plants in plastic houses in winter and provide vital air move-ment in dampish pit houses during moist, overcast periods when they are especially vulnerable to mildew and other fungus woes. On hot, dry days such a blower can create cross-circulation to spread around available moisture.

Circulating fans also are highly suited to solar houses (usually kept tightly sealed in winter) since they help to remove solar radiation from overheated air in daytime and put it into storage in water tanks and masonry masses which release it slowly at night when it's wanted.

LIGHTING

For fastest, healthiest growth, you should select plants for your greenhouse taking into account their light requirements as well as their temperature needs. For example, shade-loving tropical foliage plants should be grown with orchids and begonias rather than with light-loving companions like tomatoes, roses, and carnations. Always group and situate your plants so they get the maximum amount of light they can take, remembering that plants in strong light will grow slowly if temperatures are low, that plants need more light when temperatures are high, and that more watering and humidification are called for as the light intensity increases.

To help compensate for the dimmer, shorter days of autumn and winter or for a less than ideally situated greenhouse, choose a glazing that will admit—and keep admitting—a high percentage of the available light. Instead of double glazing, consider using movable nighttime insulation, which is just as effective at keeping in heat and which will not reduce the transmission of already limited light during winter days. You also should take pains to keep your glazing clean, since dirt and soot can screen out up to 10 percent of the available light. Another way of maximizing the light reaching your plants is to build a greenhouse with low profile and use raised benches, for the farther plants are from the glazing, the less solar radiation they

Light-Compatible Plants: The plants in this south-facing greenhouse share the same general need for ample light. Those plants which can tolerate direct sun are located closest to the glass, while those which prefer medium light are placed farther away. Shown here are a cyclamen, reichsteineria, anthurium, and orchid in bloom. Some light-loving ferns are also included — namely an *Asplenium* and a *Nephrolepis* cultivar.

For example, about 91 percent of the light hitting clean glass glazing at an angle perpendicular to the surface is admitted, with most of the rest being reflected. But when the sun's rays strike the glazing at a greater or lesser angle, the amount of light lost by reflection increases. The loss is particularly great at angles of over 50 or 60 degrees.

You can help counter this reality by angling south-facing glazing so it admits a maximum of light when the sun is lowest during the winter and by limiting the amount of glazing which lets in little light but tends to reflect some of the entering light back outside the greenhouse. An excellent way to do this is to make your north wall opaque and paint it flat white or cover it with aluminum foil so it reflects light back onto plants. Combined with painting the inside of the frame, this simple measure was found by the Brace Institute of Montreal to increase the amount of light in the greenhouse by as much as a third, and to bring plants to maturity faster. You also might try aluminum foil mulch to ricochet light on the plants from below. If all this additional reflected light is not enough for your situation or your special gardening interests, you may want to consider installing direct lighting fixtures.

Most people don't bother to illuminate a greenhouse just for the sake of convenience, though if you get special joy from working with your plants on very dim days or before or after work in the winter, you just might decide to put in an incandescent or fluorescent fixture over the potting bench, taking care to position it so shadows are not cast on plants. (Note: Poor wiring can be deadly in a damp, well-grounded place like a greenhouse, so be sure yours meets national and local electrical codes, that your cords, light fittings, and switches are waterproof, and that you don't overload circuits. You also should install a ground fault interrupter to guard against electric shock.)

But even if you do not plan to work in the greenhouse in the dark hours, if you plan

receive. You might also attach reflective panels made of aluminum or foil-covered plywood or Masonite to the outside of the greenhouse.

Even with such precautions, however, light intake will vary significantly from place to place and from house to house. For one thing, in coastal and industrial areas where smoke and extra water vapor exist in the air, the available light is often so reduced that little or no shading is ever needed. And in every location light is lost by being reflected off the surface of the glazing instead of passed through it to the plants inside. The extent of this loss depends on the slope of the roof and the angle at which sunlight strikes it, which depends in turn on the time of year, time of day, and the orientation of the greenhouse.

to grow chrysanthemums, poinsettias, kalanchoes, or other flowering plants whose bud initiation is controlled by photoperiod, you might need to use artificial light to extend daylength or interrupt night.

Some greenhouse gardeners use artificial lighting to boost the rate at which their plants make food, since this determines how fast they grow. Whether this is worth your while depends on the time of year, on your latitude, on the cloudiness of your climate, and on the kind of plants you grow. Such lighting can be used to special advantage in growing light-loving vegetables like cucumbers, peppers, and tomatoes, in growing plants under benches, and in rooting difficult cuttings such as those from azaleas, boxwood (*Buxus sempervirens*), broad-leaved evergreens, fruit trees, holly (*Ilex* spp.), and roses. By rigging light setups over high shelves along the back wall of an attached greenhouse, it is even possible to get dramatic tropicals like *Browallia* species to both grow and flower in a cool house.

But supplemental lighting can be used most economically to help along seedlings, for young plants make more efficient use of light than older ones, and you can fit more of them under a light source. (Take care, though, to provide sufficiently high temperatures and humidity when you germinate seeds or propagate cuttings under lights; night temperatures, for instance, should not drop below 60°F/16°C. In an unheated greenhouse, you can always start seeds late and make up for the delay by using lights after dark.)

For more information on choosing and using artificial lighting to best advantage, see chapter 25.

PEST AND DISEASE CONTROL

Sad to say, the warm, moist, cozy environment you so lovingly create to nurture your plants also can help disease organisms and insects to multiply. The best way to triumph over such spoilers is to keep them out, while taking anticipatory measures to destroy or discourage those which slip by your first line of defense. With this in mind, take the following general precautions, which will help you make your greenhouse and your plants unappealing to disease organisms and insects:

1. Keep the greenhouse and surrounding property scrupulously tidy, removing all weeds, plant debris, and rubbish where pathogens might linger or insects might hide and breed. This goes for the turf around your greenhouse, too, for viruses as well as insects may inhabit nearby weeds and are often carried into the greenhouse by bugs. One United States Department of Agriculture entomologist discovered he could reduce thrip damage by 90 percent just by mowing around the greenhouse.

2. Make sure all openings around foundations, doors, and so forth are sealed to keep out crawling insects, and screen all doors and ventilation openings in the summer to foil flying invaders. A man who runs five greenhouses in the southwest of England has developed a screening setup that reportedly protects against insect pests and even against spores of disease fungi while maximizing air flow. At each end of a plastic tunnel house he has installed screening about six feet (1.8 m) high and three feet (0.9 m) wide. This consists of three layers of metal mesh spaced two inches (5 cm) apart, with the center layer of coarse mesh and the two outer ones of fine mesh. When the temperature inside the greenhouse is higher than outside, the air naturally flows out of the house, carrying away airborne fungal spores. And insects can enter only by flying against the wind, which many serious pests (such as aphids) cannot do.

3. Make sure there is good air circulation around your plants, for still air helps many diseases and insects to thrive. For the same reason, don't crowd your plants.

4. Guard against humidity that is too low or too high. Actually, tests done in

Puerto Penasco, Mexico, by University of Arizona researchers suggest that high humidity will not contribute to the spread of disease *if* it is accompanied by high-intensity light and plenty of air movement; but in the absence of these factors, beware of very high humidity.

5. Keep your greenhouse cool. A constant temperature of 45° to 50°F (7° to 10°C) is much less encouraging to insect growth than a temperature of 70°F (21°C) or higher.

6. Use soilless growing media for starting seeds and rooting cuttings, or at least put a sterile layer of peat moss or scratchy coarse sand on top of your soil mix.

7. Pasteurize any soil you use.

8. Make sure any homemade compost you use (whether it's been made outdoors or right in the greenhouse) has been heated to 160°F (72°C)—the temperature required to kill off most pathogenic bacteria, fungi, viruses, and insects.

9. Destroy seriously infected or infested plants promptly, taking their remains far from the greenhouse so spores or scales cannot be blown or tracked back inside.

10. Make sure your plants are well nourished but not overnourished. It is known, for example, that a phosphorus deficiency encourages whiteflies, and that mites thrive where there is too little available magnesium relative to potassium. On the other hand, too much nitrogen produces oversucculent stem and foliage growth that attracts aphids. (To prevent the kind of nitrogen overkill linked to chemical fertilizers, use organic fertilizers, which release nutrients slowly and also help guard against the buildup of plant-sickening salt residues. See chapter 7 for more information on plant foods.)

11. Keep gardening tools and equipment—especially the end of the hose—off the floor, and don't use greenhouse tools in the outdoor garden.

12. Always wash your hands and cutting tools carefully on entering the greenhouse after working outside.

13. Do not smoke in the greenhouse or touch plants after smoking without washing your hands, for a virus called tobacco mosaic is spread by touch to plants like tomatoes.

14. Look over all new plants and cuttings carefully to be sure that there are no visible signs of disease or insect infestation. Then, and only then, take the plant into the greenhouse.

15. Do not reuse soil in which a plant has died, and be sure to sterilize any container linked to a plant death before you use it again.

16. Choose disease-resistant varieties.

17. Include some insect-repelling plants in your collection. Why not, for example, grow pyrethrum—an attractive daisylike perennial whose dried flowers have been used for well over a hundred years as a potent pesticide that does no harm to the environment? Or as a border plant try feverfew, another daisylike bug-chaser you can cultivate from seeds, root divisions, or cuttings. French or African marigolds (*Tagetes patula* or *T. erecta*) are especially effective against nematodes, and the shoofly plant (*Nicandra physalodes*)—more widely known as Peruvian ground cherry—repels whiteflies, which never come near it and are said to avoid plants in its vicinity. Petunias are reportedly anathema to ants and black aphids.

18. As a kind of preventive biological control, you can introduce chameleons into your greenhouse at the rate of one 3-inch (8 cm) lizard per 12 to 15 square feet (1 to 1.3 sq m) of floor area. Though they do best at about 80°F (27°C), even at much lower temperatures chameleons will continue to eat insects so small you cannot see them. They are also particularly appreciative of flies, mosquitoes, grasshoppers, spiders, and cockroaches. It is a good idea to supplement this fare with mealworms or crick-

ets for the first few weeks. Remember also to mist your plants daily since chameleons get their liquid from condensation on foliage. Needless to say, make sure vents are screened and doors kept closed when these fellows are in residence.

Even if you work hard at keeping disease and insects outside your green kingdom, you should inspect your plants weekly (and preferably with a 10x magnifying glass), for insects or signs of stunted, distorted growth; brown, dry, yellowing, spotted, ringed, holey, curled, or dwarfed foliage; winding white trails or powder on leaf surfaces; wilting, or unnatural growths; and blackened or rotting stems. In short, be on the lookout for any abnormal condition that appears unlinked to light, temperature, and humidity level or to watering practices.

At the first sign of trouble, look for evidence of infestation by any of the common indoor pests described in chapter 9, and take appropriate action.

But suppose your problem isn't visible pests on the plants or in the soil? In that case, it may be even harder to identify and more stubborn to treat, for there is a huge diversity of pathogens that can make plants sick. These can be environmental factors such as ozone, soot, chlorine, sulfur dioxide, and gases escaping from an improperly sealed or vented heating system. There are also a host of viruses, some causing mottling and spotting of leaves, others responsible for yellowing, leaf curling, dwarfing, or excessive branching, but all tending to result in stunted growth and small yields of lowered quality. And then there are bacteria, which cause rots that attack leaves, stems, branches, and tubers, or wilts resulting from the blockage of a plant's vascular system, or galls created by excessive cell growth. A third group of disease organisms is the fungi, which create various mildews, rust, leaf spot, gray mold, damping-off, and root rots. See chapter 9 for information on diagnosing and treating common plant ailments.

USING THE GREENHOUSE TO BEST ADVANTAGE
WAYS TO SAVE SPACE

Home greenhouses tend to shrink as gardening dreams expand, so it is a wise idea to arrange your interior for maximum capacity from the very start. In choosing your plan or prefabricated house, keep in mind that greenhouses with little overhead space at eaves and ridge not only make temperature control difficult, but rob you of the chance to increase the growing potential of your house by suspending additional plants above those growing on raised benches. To compensate for an English-style greenhouse or any other model with a low ridge, you can always mount the house atop 24 or 36 inch (61 or 91 cm) high side walls or create a semipit by excavating—an especially good option if you must build under a house eave.

To save horizontal as well as vertical space, put your potting bench, tools, and supplies in a foyer off the greenhouse, which will also act as an airlock in the winter. Or you might locate your workplace in an attached garage or cellarway or put up an adjoining shed which you also can use to store lawn and garden tools.

If you must have a work area in the greenhouse, you might put together a small portable potting bench which you can suspend between benches, or perhaps hinge a collapsible bench to a plant bench so it opens over an aisle. Or install the potting bench in the extreme northwest corner of the greenhouse, where you can hang your tools and equipment on the adjacent end wall. If you prefer to have a permanent workplace, one option is to use a waist-level bench and suspend lighting units underneath it over a heating cable in the floor, on which you can start seeds. Or put bins or containers below for potting components. Compost bins, by the way, can be built into the side of the greenhouse or even under a removable wooden walkway.

Most growers find that raised benches make for more efficient use of space than ground beds do, but if you do plant at ground level in soil borders or containers, you can squeeze more from the space by using the high-yielding block planting technique to grow cool-temperature vegetables like chard, kale, lettuce, and turnips. By planting such crops from one to three inches (2.5 to 8 cm) apart in checkerboard fashion, though individual plants will yield less, you will get more from the unit area. You also can make better use of ground beds by succession planting between maturing plants so their replacements will be needing more space just when it is time to harvest the first crop. You also might stand temporary tables over ground beds holding seedlings to get an extra deck of growing room.

As a space-saving alternative to growing vegetables from seeds in the greenhouse, consider building a nonfreezing cold frame nearby where you can start lots of plants at a very low cost, then transplant the healthiest inside, replacing them when they have peaked with more backup troops from the frame.

If you have two aisles and three benches running the length of your house, you can garner more vertical space by erecting an upper deck over part of the width and length of the bench and use the shaded space at waist level for begonias, coleus, impatiens, and other shade-lovers. (See Raised Staging, earlier in this chapter.)

And don't neglect to grow moisture- and shade-tolerant plants like asparagus fern (*Asparagus setaceus*), maidenhair fern (*Adiantum pedatum*), baby's tears (*Soleirolia soleirolii*), grape ivy and other ivies, and wandering Jews under your waist-high benches. Episcias also will thrive there if it is warm enough. So will garden cress (*Lepidium sativum*) or watercress (*Nasturtium officinale*). To

fill unusually shady nooks in a cool greenhouse, you can always bury chicory roots (*Cichorium intybus*) or dandelion (*Taraxacum officinale*) lifted from an autumn garden in a container filled with barely moist sand, cover, and harvest the new leaves for winter salads as they emerge in four to six weeks. You also can store root vegetables like carrots or celeriac, or even stem vegetables like cardoon (*Cynara cardunculus*), provided you pack them roots and all. Or winter-over bulb plants under the benches, keeping them barely moist.

To actually garden in greenhouse dark places, you can sow the spawn of champignon mushrooms (*Agaricus bisporus*) in compost-filled flats. Watering twice a week through coarse fabric used as covers, keep the spawn at about 70°F (21°C) until white threads show, then add more compost and grow the mushrooms under side benches near an attached wall or anywhere else you can maintain a temperature of about 55° to 60°F (13° to 16°C).

For optimum space for pot plants, use stair-step benches that climb from floor to shoulder level and make the step widths on the narrow side—say eight inches (20 cm) wide for the three lower levels and six inches (15 cm) for the two top steps. By leaving just six inches (15 cm) between steps instead of a more generous ten inches (25 cm), you can pack several extra steps into the same vertical space. To grab more horizontal space for growing, arrange your step or flat benches in the peninsular pattern instead of running them longitudinally (see Raised Staging, earlier in this chapter).

Another way to enlarge a shrinking greenhouse is to put up shelves. To cast a minimum of shade, these can be made 5 inches (13 cm) wide of acrylic or of glass at least 7/32 inch (6 mm) thick with polished edges. Or you can use lumber (preferably painted white) up to 10 inches (25 cm) wide, which will allow you to tack a 4 inch (10 cm) wide strip of hardware cloth to the front edge

Multi-Level Benches: In this greenhouse, the benches are installed at staggered levels to make optimum use of the space. This arrangement allows some low-light plants to be grown in the shade of the upper level benches.

to gain additional hanging space for smaller plants. Put your shelves along the eaves in a curved-eave house, between posts or below sash bars or at gable ends, perhaps using screw eyes and suspending slot shelves from them with ropes or chains. (Make sure that shelves hung this way are no more than 36 inches/91 cm long.) Using L-brackets or adjustable Garcy brackets you also can attach shelving above bench level to an opaque wall. With light fixtures attached above and under each, a series of such shelves along the north wall can be one of the most attractive and

productive parts of the greenhouse, housing such beauties as *Browallia* species or *Phalaenopsis* orchids.

You also can use walls to great advantage by sending cucumbers, morning glories, nasturtiums, squash, and other climbers up trellises made from redwood lath. Just remember that plants climbing on nonopaque greenhouse walls will decrease the amount of light available to plants in the interior of the house.

To save more space, consider narrowing

Use Ingenuity to Increase Space: Once all the available room on the ground level has been allotted and put to use, you can make the move upward. In this greenhouse, two metal shelves holding plants run lengthwise, and additional shelf space is created by suspending boards between these trays, on which potted plants can sit.

your greenhouse walks to 18 inches (46 cm) or even 16 inches (41 cm)—that is, if you don't need to accommodate a wheelbarrow or a second gardener.

For high-volume overhead gardening, hanging plants can be suspended from heavy-duty screw hooks placed 12 inches (30 cm) apart on roof bars and ridge poles, or they can be dangled on chains from upright supports. If your greenhouse is high enough to give clearance above bench plants, you can hang a row of plants from ½ inch (13 mm) wide electrical conduit run the length of the house just above or below where the roof and sides meet. Actually, if the house has a high ridge and gradually sloping sides, you may be able to hang 10-inch (25 cm) baskets from conduit at the side of the ridge and attach a second pipe lower down and close to the glazing for 6- to 8-inch (15 to 20 cm) hanging baskets. Another idea is to use chains to link together a vertical series of lightweight, shallow, plastic-bowl-like containers. Spaced 12 to 24 inches (30 to 61 cm) apart, such setups can give you a vertical column of growing space that stretches from near the ridge to the floor.

Solar houses that attempt to store heat face special challenges in the efficient use of space, since huge quantities of rock or water are needed in cold climates to maintain the greenhouse temperature. It is easy to lose an entire back wall to stacked water bottles or drums, or half your floor space to a fish pond. For less interference with growing space, it is possible to use fans to store heat in crushed rock beneath the floor or in thick masonry walls. Or you might keep water drums in dark areas under benches, perhaps using some drums to support benches. The hot ridge air can be sent toward the floor and into storage quite effectively by a circulating fan (see Year-Round Air Circulation, earlier in this chapter).

DECIDING WHAT TO GROW

It is easier to select plants that are adaptable to the environment you are able and willing to provide than to try to adjust the environment in ways that prove inconvenient or costly. With this in mind, you should assess the growing conditions you can offer in regard to duration and intensity of light, humidity, and minimum temperature, and choose plants reasonably compatible in their needs.

Actually, light will not be too limiting a factor since the structure and orientation of the greenhouse itself will create conditions ranging from intense light to heavy shade, and light scarcity related to season or climate can be remedied at relatively low expense by using supplemental lighting for some of your plants. Likewise, to some extent you can vary the humidity in parts of the greenhouse by such techniques as hand misting and the use of a mist chamber. It is important, though, to take into account extreme differences in humidity needs in choosing greenhouse companions; do not, for instance, try to accommodate both tropical foliage plants and cacti and other succulents.

Unless you partition your greenhouse with a polyethylene-covered wooden framework or something more lasting, the single factor most limiting the kinds of plants you can grow will be the minimum (nighttime) temperature you are prepared to maintain. Cool-season crops can be grown only when your greenhouse is in the 40° to 60°F (4° to 16°C) range, though most can tolerate an occasional dip to 35°F (2°C) or a rise to 75° to 90°F (24° to 32°C). Intermediate- or moderate-temperature plants need a minimum of 55° to 65°F (13° to 18°C), a range suitable to year-round growing of many plants—including almost all annuals, vegetables, house plants, and subtropical exotics—and to many propagation activities, when intense light can be provided. Warm-temperature plants need constant temperatures in the 65° to 80° or 85°F (18° to 27° or 29°C) range and often have little tolerance for lower or higher temperatures—obviously the orchids and tropicals in this group are not too practical for home gardeners without money to spend on fuel and automated equipment.

Greenhouses have come to be classified in terms of the lowest temperatures they maintain in the winter (obviously all of them are moderate-to-warm in the summer and can be used then to grow subtropicals and tropicals if you can provide enough light, air, and humidity). So-called cold or Alpine greenhouses are those in which no artificial heat is used and the "bottom line" expectation is to keep the temperature just above freezing for the culture of hardy, low-growing rock plants including shrubs, and to carry over chrysanthemums, geraniums, and even exotic vines. In mild winter climates, it is possible to grow cool-season crops in such houses—particularly if they are direct-planted in raised benches. Examples of some of the plants that can be grown successfully are hardy vegetable greens like collards and kales; root crops like turnips, rutabagas, and parsnips; alyssum; strawberry begonias; camellias; cyclamens; *Fatsia japonica;* forget-me-nots (*Myosotis* spp.); freesias; gentians; primulas; violets; wallflowers (*Cheiranthus cheiri*); all the Dutch bulbs; and tender woody plants like acacias, azaleas, daphne, Chinese evergreen (*Aglaonema modestum*), heather (*Erica* spp.), hydrangeas, jasmine, rhododendron, and rosemary. In the North, unless you live in a coastal area exposed to warm ocean currents, a cold house may be best suited to wintering-over dwarf fruit trees (peaches and persimmons, for example) and tender garden perennials such as *Salvia patens* and lemon verbena. Or it can be boarded over and sealed tight, and used to store root crops.

Cool greenhouses are variously defined as maintaining a minimum temperature of from 40° or 45°F (4° or 7°C) to 50° or 55°F (10° or 13°C) and may or may not need back-up heating to do so, depending on the severity of the climate and on how well the house conserves heat. (The average detached pit is said to hold a bottom temperature of 35° to 45°F/2° to 7°C, while the average attached pit maintains from 40° to 45°F/4 to 7°C.) Quite a few root and leaf vegetables and flowering plants are best suited to cool greenhouse conditions and many others—lettuce and petunias, for example—can adapt to the lower temperatures and diminished light although the time to maturity will be extended accordingly. (See How Seasonal Changes in Light and Temperature Affect Growth Rates in the Greenhouse.) For this reason, space- and heat-wise people gardening in a cool house tend to choose miniature or at least compact short-season species and varieties so that they can plant early in fall or later in the spring. They also look for crops that can handle fairly wide temperature swings between day and night and tolerate short days and low light levels. Examples of suitable crops include broad-leaved endive, 'Ruby' and 'Bibb' lettuce, parsley, and New Zealand spinach. Where it is impossible to turn up the heat in winter to counter humidity, it is also a good idea to choose plants resistant to *Botrytis* blight and downy mildew, such as the new Dutch lettuce developed by the Rijk Zwaan company.

In addition to the hardy plants mentioned above under cold greenhouses, the cool greenhouse does well by vegetables such as beets, carrots, Swiss chard, endive, leaf and looseleaf lettuce, radishes, and spinach, and by ornamental citrus fruits like the calamondin, kumquat, and Ponderosa lemon. If you prefer flowers and foliage to food, you can glory in asters (*Callistephus chinensis*), calceolarias, calendulas, carnations, Christmas rose (*Helleborus niger*), chrysanthemums, cinerarias, daisies (*Chrysanthemum* × *superbum*), fuchsias, gladiolas, *Iris* species, nasturtiums, *Plumbago* species, ranunculus, snapdragons, stock (*Matthiola* spp.), sweet pea (*Lathyrus odoratus*), and a host of bedding plants. A wide array of orchid genera native to heights of 5,000 to 8,000 feet (1,500 to 2,400 m) also will thrive in a cool house. These include *Coe-*

Cool Greenhouse: An assortment of root and leaf vegetables and flowering plants grows well under cool conditions, allowing you to harvest food for your table as well as blooms for your enjoyment.

logyne, Cymbidium species and hybrids, *Dendrobium, Odontoglossum, Oncidium,* and *Miltonia.* The cooler ferns—including many varieties of the bird's nest fern (*Asplenium nidus*), Boston fern (*Nephrolepis exaltata* cvs.), holly fern (*Cyrtomium falcatum*), and rabbit's foot fern (*Davallia fejeensis*)—are also tempting choices. Large-leaved *Philodendron* species and English ivy (*Hedera helix*) are other low-light possibilities for shady parts of a cool house. So are tender bulbs like angel lilies (*Crinum* spp.), blood lilies (*Haemanthus* spp.), pineapple lilies (*Eucomis* spp.), and florists' gloxinias (*Sinningia speciosa*), which can grow (or take a rest period inside paper bags) under benches during the winter. There are also many robust and dramatic begonias that like it cool. These include the highly decorative eyelash begonia (*Begonia boweri*), the angel-wing types (*B. cocci-*

nea and others), and the spectacular foliage plant *B.* 'Cleopatra'.

A cool greenhouse also makes a fine environment for specializing in a varied assortment of colorful gesneriads such as *Kohleria* and *Nematanthus* species. The dozens of sun-loving, easy-to-care-for bromeliads with their brilliant foliage and striking flower bracts are also a rewarding special interest in a cool house.

Offering a minimum night temperature of from 55° to 65°F (13° to 18°C), the intermediate or moderate greenhouse (sometimes called moderate-to-warm) is congenial to many of the flowering plants that can get by

How Seasonal Changes in Light and Temperature Affect Growth Rates in the Greenhouse

When the recommended minimum night temperature for a crop is . . .

65°F/18°C	55°F/13°C	45°F/7°C

but the actual average night temperature is . . .

45°F/7°C	55°F/13°C	65°F/18°C

the added time from sowing to maturity in poor light (midwinter) will be . . .

100%	50%*	25%
50%*	25%	0**
25%	0**	0**

the added time from sowing to maturity in good light (spring or fall) will be . . .

50%*	25%	0
25%	0	0**
0	0**	0**

*If a crop matures in 25 days at the recommended light and temperature, 50% added time means the time to maturity will be about 37 days.
**Cropping time may not be lost when higher than normal temperatures are used, but quality may be reduced or the crop may not mature properly.

Intermediate Greenhouse: This beautiful display of greenery gives an indication of the wide range of plants that thrive at this temperature. Found in this house are bromeliads, sedum, and several gesneriads: *Columnea, Nematanthus, Aeschynanthus,* and *Codonanthe.*

under cooler conditions but prefer it warmer—for instance, African violets, amaryllis, asters, azaleas, carnations, chrysanthemums, cinerarias, citrus trees, cyclamens, fuchsias, gardenias, geraniums, gloxinias, hyacinths, kalanchoes, primulas, and tulips. Others that will bask in the warmth of an intermediate house include *Cattleya, Phalaenopsis,* and *Epidendrum* orchids; achimenes, wax and tuberous begonias; bougainvillea; bouvardia; browallia; caladium; calla lilies (*Zantedeschia* spp.); Christmas cactus (*Schlumbergera bridgesii*); coleus; delphiniums; flowering maple (*Abutilon megapotamicum*); gardenias; impatiens; lantana; marigolds; roses; salpiglossis; strawberries; and zinnias.

The warm or tropical greenhouse, which is kept at a minimum of 65° to 75°F (18° to 24°C) is ideal for most foliage plants of tropical origin (most of these demand correspondingly high humidity). Indeed, the popular Swiss cheese plant (*Monstera deliciosa*), which is barren as a house plant, will produce delicious, edible fruit if pampered so appropriately. A host of heat-loving vegetables and fruits also will perform well in the warm greenhouse if the light is strong enough. However, you may have to help pollination along by shaking some fruiting plants or perhaps using a cotton-tipped swab or a fine brush. Plants that need to be pollinated include cucumbers, the edible dwarf banana (*Musa acuminata* 'Dwarf Cavendish'), eggplant, mangoes (*Mangifera indica*), melons, oranges, papayas (*Carica papaya*), peanuts (*Arachis hypogaea*), peppers, squash, and tomatoes. The tropical greenhouse in winter or summer is also ideal for luxuriant vines such as gloriosa lily, hoya, passionflower (*Passiflora* spp.), and *Stephanotis floribunda*; for tropical shrubs like the dwarf poinciana (*Caesalpinia pulcherrima*) and Surinam cherry (*Eugenia uniflora*); for many species of palms; and of course for warm-climate orchids of many genera. Heat-loving bulb plants like the amaryllis, Amazon lily (*Eucharis grandiflora*), butterfly lily (*Hedychium coronarium*), fancy-leaved caladium, and calla lily will also thrive if given full or partial shade in a warm house.

Considerations of temperature and humidity aside, another factor in selecting plants for your greenhouse is the amount of space you have to fill and how you can best utilize it. Accordingly, you might want to complement plants of upright, compact habit best suited to growth in benches or containers with procumbent types like campanulas, episcias, or thunbergias that will take up some vertical space in hanging baskets, and with vining, climbing, or trailing species such as clematis or star jasmine (*Trachelospermum jasminoides*) that can brighten corners and rafters.

Warm Greenhouse: The warmth, high humidity, and ample light in this house are ideal for the cultivation of tropical plants such as palms and orchids, which respond with lush foliage and breathtaking blooms.

You also will want to consider the potential size of plants that are not to be transplanted out. Will a fuchsia or petunia in a hanging basket cast too much shade where you plan to suspend it, and would a daintier ivy geranium (*Pelargonium peltatum*) or a petite basket of ivy be a better choice? Do you really want a single, mammoth, show-stopping staghorn fern (*Platycerium bifurcatum*), or would you get more pleasure out of the sizable cactus collection that could fit into the same amount of growing space? The same point applies on a smaller scale. One well-developed plant in a 6-inch (15 cm) pot may take up twice as much room on a bench as nine compact specimens in 3-inch (8 cm) pots. For example, in a modest 64 square feet

(5.8 sq m) of bench space, you can grow nine containers each of 21 vegetable crops, provided you choose compact, container-congenial vegetables and varieties and grow them in 6-inch (15 cm) pots at a 6- by 8-inch (15 by 20 cm) spacing—a quite feasible idea. In growing food, you also can get a better return on time and space by not selecting vegetables which are relatively inexpensive to buy at the market, such as carrots and onions—especially since such root crops can take up to five months to mature in a cool greenhouse, more than twice as much time as leaf crops. (For a list of some fruits and vegetables recommended for greenhouse conditions and container planting, see Some Food Plant Cultivars for Greenhouse Growing.)

Some Food Plant Cultivars for Greenhouse Growing

The following cultivars have been found to grow and bear well under greenhouse conditions. Information given in parentheses for some varieties indicates approximate days to maturity from sowing (S), or transplanting in (T) when variety is grown outdoors in season. Look for S or T after vegetable names.

Vegetable Cultivars
Broccoli
  (*Brassica oleracea*,
  Botrytis Group) **T**
  Green Comet (40)
  Southern Comet (55)
  Premium Crop F₁ (60)
  White Sprouting
  (continuous)
  Calabrese
  Italian
Brussels sprouts
  (*Brassica oleracea*,
  Gemmifera Group) **T**
  Lindo (80)
  Jade Cross (90)
  Focus F₁ (95)
Cabbage
  (*Brassica oleracea*,
  Capitata Group) **T**
  Dwarf Morden (60)
  Express Cross (60)
  Green Express F₁ (60)
  Hispi (60)
  Starlet (63)
  Ruby Ball F₁ (65)
  Savory Ace (78)
  Emerald Cross
  Golden Acre
  K-K Cross
Chinese cabbage
  (*Brassica rapa*,
  Pekinensis Group) **T**
  Burpee Hybrid (75)
  Michihli (80)
  Tropicana
  WR-55
Collards
  (*Brassica oleracea*,
  Acephala Group) **S**
  Vates (85)
Cucumbers
  (*Cucumis sativus*) **S**
  Burpless (25)
  Burgess Green Ice (48)
  Pot Luck (53)
  Burpless Green King
  (58)

Patio Pik (60)
Femfrance
Eggplant
  (*Solanum melongena*
  var. *esculentum*) **T**
  Morden Midget (65)
  Burpee Hybrid (70)
  Black Beauty (73)
  Beauty Hybrid
  Black Prince
  Dusky
  Early Beauty
  Money Maker
Endive
  (*Cichorium endiva*)
  Salad King
Green Beans
  (*Phaseolus vulgaris*) **S**
  bush-type:
    Limelight (38)
    Tenderpod (50)
  pole-type:
    Blue Lake (60)
    Violet-Padded
    Stringless (63)
Kale (*Brassica oleracea*,
  Acephala Group) **S**
  Dwarf Blue Curled (55)
  Dwarf Blue Scotch (55)
Lettuce
  (*Lactuca sativa*) **S**
  Oak Leaf (42)
  Black-Seeded Simpson
  (45)
  Salad Bowl (45)
  Slobolt (45)
  Ruby (47)
  Buttercrunch (60)
  Summer Bibb (65)
Peas (*Pisum sativum*) **S**
  Dwarf DeGrace (60)
  Dwarf White Sugar (60)
  Mighty Midget (60)
  Wando
Peppers
  (*Capsicum* spp.) **T**
  Sweet Canape (60)
  Burpee's Fordhook (65)

Park Wonder F₁ (65)
Slim Pin (65)
Christmas Pepper
Bell Boy
New Ace
Parsley
  (*Petroselinum crispum*)
  S
  Extra Triple Curled
  (75)
  Perfection (75)
Radishes
  (*Raphanus satuvus*) **S**
  for spring and summer:
    Champion (24)
    Cherry Bell (24)
    Half Long (24)
    Icicle (27)
    Red Prince
  for fall and winter:
    Summer Cross (45)
    White Chinese (50)
    China Rose (52)
Spinach
  (*Spinacia oleracea*) **S**
  Longstanding
    Bloomsdale (42)
  Monnopa (45)
  Melody
Malabar Spinach
  (*Basella alba*) (70)
New Zealand Spinach
  (*Tetragonia
  tetragonioides*) (70)
Swiss Chard
  (*Beta vulgaris*,
  Cicla Group) **S**
  Fordhook Giant (60)
  Lucullus (60)
  Rhubarb (60)
  Ruby (60)
  Vintage Green (60)
Tomatoes (*Lycopersicon
  lycopersicum*) **T**
  miniature:
    Sub-Arctic Cherry (43)
    Tiny Tim (55)
    Small Fry (65)

Patio (70)
regular size:
  Early Girl (45)
  Outdoor Girl (58)
  Better Boy (70)
  Superfantastic (70)
  Rutgers (85)

Fruit Cultivars
Edible Dwarf Banana
  (*Musa acuminata*
  'Dwarf Cavendish')
Citrus
  Calamondin
    (×*Citrofortunella
    mitis*)
  Nagami kumquat
    (*Fortunella
    margarita* 'Nagami')
  Mexican lime (*Citrus
    aurantiifolia* 'Bears')
  Meyer or dwarf lemon
    (*Citrus limon*
    'Meyer')
  Wonder lime (*Citrus
    limon* 'Ponderosa')
  Otaheite orange (*Citrus
    ×limonia*)
Strawberries
  Fragaria spp.
  seasonal:
    Earlibelle (early)
    Earli-dawn (early)
    Sequoia (early)
    Apollo (midseason)
    Surecrop
    (midseason)
    Tioga (midseason)
    Sparkle (late)
  everbearing:
    Fort Laramie
    Ogallala
    Ozark Beauty
    Quinault
  from seeds:
    Alexandria (75)
    Alpine Yellow (80)
    Tutti Frutti

When you choose your plants, it is also important to take into account how much time you want to invest in running your greenhouse. To get the most satisfaction for the least effort, concentrate on perennials, since annuals that require sowing and transplanting take up much more time. If you would like to enjoy the greater color and productivity of flowering annuals, grow just a few, such as the unusually colorful cineraria. To save yourself the fuss and bother of starting annuals from seeds in late summer for winter flowers or food, you can arrange to buy seedlings from a local nursery. In considering how involved you want to get, don't make the error of thinking that common vegetables and flowers are easy to grow,

whereas exotic or tropical plants are difficult. Given the proper temperature, orchids, for instance, are simpler to grow than carnations of decent quality, and fruits like oranges and lemons are easier to nurture indoors than top-flight tomatoes.

Actually, there is much to be said for deciding to work with plants of one type, since it becomes much easier to give individual specimens the culture best suited to optimum growth, and to avoid problems with pests. Besides, it can be fun to learn more and more about a particular plant family. If the idea of specializing intrigues you, seek out books on the plant group of your choice and consider joining one of the myriad special interest societies organized around individual plant

Cactus House: This greenhouse contains only cacti, and the conditions inside it have been adjusted to meet the growing needs of these particular plants, allowing for bright light, low humidity, and warm temperatures. Since the Cactus family alone contains up to 220 genera and 2,000 species, concentrating on this group imposes no limitation on the variety of plants which may be grown.

families or groups. (See the Appendix for names and addresses of plant societies.)

THE GREENHOUSE TOMORROW

Over the past decade radical changes in the cost of energy and food coupled with breakthroughs in plant science and greenhouse technology have caused us to see the home greenhouse in a new way. With each year that passes, it has become less of a resource-consuming hobby and more of a contributing part of our lives, offering uniquely restorative living space, fresh foods to nourish us around the year, and free heat. Responding to the economic and cultural factors that suggest the greenhouse will be an ever more important dimension of home life in the years ahead, agricultural engineers, architects, and interior designers are designing prototype greenhouse/residences in which "green rooms" are being integrated more and more completely with living areas and heating and cooling systems.

Some of these progenitors of the "green home" of tomorrow are strictly practical structures put together tentatively piece-by-piece by owner-builders who are groping toward their dream of a self-reliant life-style. Others are aesthetic conceptions made real, such as the central Connecticut home designed by New York architect John Johansen to be a kind of tall greenhouse in which plants and people live in environmental interdependence on five levels framed in actual greenhouse sections. There are also some experimental prototypes in various parts of the United States being carefully monitored to determine the greenhouse's contribution to food and heating needs. Two such formal projects are now being tested and refined by multidisciplinary teams at Clemson University in Clemson, South Carolina, and at Colorado State University.

The Clemson greenhouse/residence was planned to provide 75 percent of the energy and food costs for a family of four with a modest income—and a 10 percent annual return on the greenhouse-solar system investment. Built at a wooded site near Greenville, South Carolina, this rural residence consists of a manufactured aluminum-and-glass lean-to with a 134-square-foot (12 sq m) growing area attached to a two-story frame house with a rooftop solar collector. Preheated air from the greenhouse passes through this collector, then goes into 85 tons (77 metric tons) of rock storage under the floor or directly into the house. Backup auxiliary heating coils contribute when necessary. In summer the hot air collected is vented outside, and cooler outside air is drawn into storage and further chilled by an evaporative cooler.

The Colorado State greenhome at Fort Collins also sends preheated greenhouse air through air collectors and into rock storage. In this design, the greenhouse and residence are equal in square footage, and for both house and greenhouse, heat-conserving construction methods such as double glazing, caulking, and perimeter insulation were used to cut heating needs by half. As a result, 79 percent of the total space heating requirements were met by the solar system over the 1976–1977 heating season.

However different their looks and their functions, the innovative greenhouse of today and those that will take their place tomorrow may be seen as the ongoing expression of a need that becomes more compelling as the earth becomes more crowded—the longing to create a green and innocent place where we can once again live in mutuality and love with the natural world.

A GREENHOUSE GARDENING CALENDAR

Many greenhouse activities can be carried on at your convenience—you can, for example, propagate many foliage pot plants by seeds or stem or leaf cuttings at any time of the year and by division anytime you repot them.

You also can start African violets (*Saintpaulia* spp.) from seeds at any time and increase strawberry begonias (*Saxifraga stolonifera*) by runners, zonal geraniums (*Pelargonium ×hortorum*) by cuttings, and Christmas cactus (*Schlumbergera bridgesii*) from stems at any time. But where some foliage plants and shrubs and most flowering and fruiting plants are concerned, you will find that some seasonal planning is necessary to get optimum results from your efforts. The following calendar will give you just a sampling of the almost infinite variety of ways you can keep busy in the greenhouse year-round. In adapting these activities to your unique situation, take your climate and the minimum night temperature of your greenhouse into consideration in choosing which perennials and annuals to work with and in gauging when to propagate and transplant and the probable time to maturity.

JANUARY

Vegetables

Harvesting: Cucumbers (*Cucumis sativus*), lettuce (*Lactuca sativa*), onions (*Allium cepa*), radishes (*Raphanus sativus*), tomatoes (*Lycopersicon lycopersicum*), and other crops planted in fall.

Seeding: Sow radishes biweekly.

Flowering Plants

Seeding: From January to February, sow seeds of miniature pansy (*Viola tricolor*), Iceland poppy (*Papaver nudicaule*), and *Viola cornuta* cvs. From January to March, sow seeds of *Begonia ×semperflorens-cultorum* and *Streptocarpus* spp.; give bottom heat. Plant seeds of cineraria (*Senecio ×hybridus*) and gesneriads. Also, sow seeds of *Cyclamen* spp. in 4- to 4½-inch (10 to 11 cm) pots, to flower from December through February.

Cuttings: For summer flowering, take cuttings of geraniums (*Pelargonium*

spp.), *Fuchsia* spp., and *Lantana* spp. From January to April, take leaf and stem cuttings from *Begonia ×cheimantha* and *B. ×hiemalis*. Also, take cuttings from heather (*Erica* spp.). Root carnations (*Dianthus caryophyllus*) for flowering in April and May.

FEBRUARY

Vegetables

Harvesting: Cucumbers, lettuce, onions, radishes, and tomatoes.

Seeding: Sow radishes biweekly. Sow these seeds for spring harvest or to transplant outdoors: beets (*Beta vulgaris*); broccoli; (*Brassica oleracea,* Botrytis Group); cauliflower (*Brassica oleracea,* Botrytis Group); chard (*Beta vulgaris,* Cicla Group); onions; peas (*Pisum sativum*); peppers (*Capsicum frutescens*); spinach (*Spinacia oleracea*); and tomatoes.

Flowering Plants

Seeding: From February to April, sow slow-growing annuals: *Ageratum* spp.; carnations; *Chrysanthemum* spp.; marigolds (*Tagetes* spp.); *Petunia* hybrids; pin-cushion flowers (*Scabiosa* spp.); *Phlox* spp.; *Portulaca* spp.; *Salpiglossis sinuata; Salvia* spp.; *Statice* spp.; and *Stock* spp. Sow seeds of these perennials: chrysanthemums; *Dahlia* spp. (or plant tubers); *Gazania ringens;* and *Verbena* hybrids (sow from February to March). Also, sow seeds of tuberous begonias (or start tubers), pepper plants (*Capsicum annuum*), woolflowers (*Celosia argentea*), and marguerites (*Chrysanthemum frutescens* and *C. leucanthemum*).

Cuttings: From February to April, take cuttings from salvia. From February to June, take cuttings from fuchsia stock plants to bloom from next January through September. Take cuttings from star-of-Bethlehem (*Campanula* *isophylla*) and internodal stem cuttings from *Hydrangea* spp.

Division: Divide *Anthurium* spp.

Potting: Pot gesneriad tubers.

Foliage Plants

Seeding: Sow seeds for castor oil plant (*Ricinus communis*).

Division: Divide tubers of prayer plant (*Maranta leuconeura*). Divide roots of pothos (*Epipremnum aureum*).

MARCH

Vegetables

Harvesting: Cucumbers, lettuce, onions, and radishes.

Seeding: Sow radishes biweekly. From March to May, sow seeds of summer crops: cucumbers; eggplant (*Solanum melongena* var. *esculentum*); melons (*Cucumis melo* vars.); pole beans (*Phaseolus vulgaris*); and squash (*Cucurbita* spp.).

Transplanting: Move peppers and tomatoes into beds or pots.

Flowering Plants

Seeding: Sow seeds of faster-growing annuals to be set outdoors at a later date: flowering tobacco (*Nicotiana alata*); *Heliotrope* spp.; *Kochia scoparia;* morning glory (*Ipomoea* spp.); patience plant (*Impatiens wallerana*); *Zinnia* spp.; and others. From March to April, sow monkey-faced pansy (*Achimenes grandiflora*) seeds for June through October blooming (also can be started from rhizome). For summer flowering, sow *Browallia speciosa* 'Major'. For December blooms, sow cyclamen seeds in 3½- to 4-inch (9 to 10 cm) pots.

Cuttings: Take cuttings from *Camellia* spp. (leaf-bud cuttings), *Kalanchoe* spp. (or, seeds can be sown at this time), and patience plant.

Division: Tuberous begonias started from tubers in February can be divided and potted.

Bulbs: Plant tubers of glory lily (*Gloriosa* spp.), and florists' gloxinia (*Sinningia speciosa*). Plant bulbs or offsets of pineapple lily (*Eucomis* spp.).

Foliage Plants

Seeding: Sow presoaked seeds of parlor palm (*Chamaedorea elegans*). Plant seeds of false aralia (*Dizygotheca elegantissima*). From March to June, ferns can be propagated from spores.

Cuttings: Start cuttings of painted nettle (*Coleus blumei*) in propagation case. Take root cuttings of false aralia.

Division: Divide roots of Chinese evergreen (*Aglaonema commutatum*).

Shrubs

Seeding: Sow seeds of glorybower vine (*Clerodendrum thomsoniae*).

Cuttings: Give bottom heat to 3-inch (8 cm) cuttings of cape jasmine (*Gardenia jasminoides*) and *Hibiscus* spp.

APRIL

Vegetables

Harvesting: Cucumbers, onions, radishes, spinach, and others.

Transplanting: Start vegetables to be moved outdoors in mid-May to June.

Flowering Plants

Seeding: Sow seeds of the following plants: citrus trees; columbines (*Aquilegia* spp.); shasta daisies (*Chrysanthemum* × *superbum*); *Freesia* spp.; and poppies (*Papaver nudicaule* or *P. orientale*).

Cuttings: Take cuttings from perennials: *Calceolaria* spp.; feverfew (*Chrysanthemum parthenium*); heliotrope; geranium hybrids; *Lobelia* spp.; and *Penstemon* hybrids. Also, take cuttings from *Abutilon* hybrids, fibrous-rooted begonias (*B. coccinea, B. foliosa* var. *miniata, B. metallica, B. minor, B. scharffii*), bloodflower (*Asclepias curassavica*), and gesneriads (from young shoots). From April to June, take side-shoot cuttings from hen and chicks (*Echeveria* spp.). Root carnation cuttings to bloom from August through September.

Division: Divide bird-of-paradise (*Strelitzia reginae*) and cacti.

Potting: Grafted roses (*Rosa* spp.) can be planted now.

Foliage Plants

Cuttings: Take cuttings of ivies (*Hedera helix* cultivars). Plant 1-inch (2.5 cm) stem cuttings of ti plant (*Cordyline terminalis*) horizontally in sandy soil.

Division: Divide umbrella sedge (*Cyperus alternifolius*).

Shrubs

Seeding: From April through August, sow seeds of passionflower (*Passiflora* spp.).

Cuttings: Take cuttings from angel's trumpet (*Datura inoxia*). From April to June, take leadwort (*Plumbago* spp.) cuttings. From April to August, take heel cuttings of passionflower and supply bottom heat.

MAY

Vegetables

Harvesting: Broccoli, cauliflower, cucumbers, and onions.

Transplanting: Until mid-May, harden-off transplants for garden by setting in cold frame for two weeks.

Flowering Plants

Seeding: From May to June, sow *Primula* spp. Put ripened bulbs aside to rest. Repot and cut back most other

flowering plants. Move tender perennials intended for outdoor garden from greenhouse. Start tall or climbing annuals outside greenhouse for summer shading: hollyhocks (*Alcea rosea*); morning glories; and sunflowers (*Helianthus annuus*).

Foliage Plants

Cuttings: From May to July, take 3 to 6 inch (8 to 15 cm) long, 1-year-old shoots of pitcher plant (*Nepenthes* or *Sarracenia* spp.). From May to August, take leaf cuttings of silver-leaf peperomia (*Peperomia griseoargentea*) and snake plant (all *Sansevieria* spp. except *S. trifasciata* 'Laurentii').

JUNE

Vegetables

Harvesting: Continue to harvest early-planted vegetables.

Seeding: From mid-June to mid-July, sow tomatoes to be harvested throughout winter, beginning in October.

Flowering Plants

Seeding: Sow seeds of chimney bellflower (*Campanula pyramidalis*).

Cuttings: Take 4-inch (10 cm) cuttings from *Bouvardia* hybrids. Take cuttings from joints of bunny ear cactus (*Opuntia microdasys*).

Maintenance: Greenhouse can be closed down from end of June to early September for necessary cleaning, repairing, and painting. Move plants outdoors under a tree or arbor, or into a lath house.

JULY

Vegetables

Harvesting: Beans, peppers, squash, and others.

Flowering Plants

Seeding: For winter and spring bloom-ing, sow seeds of *Browallia speciosa* 'Major'. From July to October, sow seeds of snapdragons (*Antirrhinum majus*) for winter flowering. For flow-ering in autumn of next year, sow cy-clamen seeds. For flowering in March and April, sow *Calceolaria crenati-flora*. Also, sow anthurium seeds.

Cuttings: Take cuttings from some be-gonias (see April listing), hen and chicks, Japanese azaleas (*Rhododen-dron japonicum*), and florists' gloxinia (leaf cuttings). Take cuttings from *Justicia* spp. every second year. Propa-gate rose cuttings in mist chamber.

Division: After flowering, divide calla lily (*Zantedeschia aethiopica*).

Potting: Pot up bulbs and offsets of *Ne-rine* spp.

Foliage Plants

Division: Divide suckers of *Aloe barba-densis*.

Shrubs

Cuttings: Take cuttings from jasmine (*Jasminum* spp.) and perennial morn-ing glory. In mist chamber propagate cuttings of semiwoody side-shoots of *Acacia* spp., *Camellia japonica*, *Cle-matis* spp., and glorybower vine.

AUGUST

Vegetables

Seeding: From mid-August to beginning of November, sow lettuce weekly to be harvested from October through March. From mid-August to mid-Sep-tember, sow cucumbers to be har-vested from October or November through May or June. For fall and winter harvest, sow these crops: beans; broccoli; kale (*Brassica oleracea*, Acephala Group); kohlrabi (*Brassica*

oleracea, Gongylodes Group); parsley (*Petroselinum crispum*); peas; and spinach. Sow cabbage seeds (*Brassica oleracea*, Capitata Group) for continu-ous harvest.

Flowering Plants

Seeding: Sow winter-blooming annuals such as cinerarias and primulas in pit or cool greenhouse. From August to September, sow seeds of butterfly flower (*Schizanthus* spp.), *Lachenalia* spp., stock, and sweet pea (*Lathyrus odoratus*) for winter to spring flower-ing. From August to November, sow seeds of *Calendula* spp. and *Zante-deschia aethiopica* for December to May blooming.

Cuttings: Take root cuttings of outdoor herbs, rock-garden plants and lan-tanas. Start unrooted cuttings or cal-loused cuttings of poinsettias (*Euphorbia pulcherrima*) for Christ-mas bloom the following year. Take cuttings from carnations (can also be layered), marguerites, and star-of-Bethlehem. From August to April, take cuttings from geraniums (cuttings can be taken at any time from zonal geraniums).

Resting: Pots of cyclamens, freesias, *Oxalis* spp., and *Tritonia* spp. that have been resting can be started into growth again.

Shrubs

Cuttings: In mist chamber root cuttings of Norfolk Island pine (*Araucaria het-erophylla*). Also, root 4 inch (10 cm) long, half-ripe cuttings of *Bougainvil-lea glabra, B. spectabilis,* and bottle-brush tree (*Callistemon* spp.).

SEPTEMBER

Vegetables

Seeding: For late winter harvest, sow

seeds of celery (*Apium graveolens* var. *dulce*) and chinese cabbage (*Brassica rapa*, Pekinensis Group).

Cuttings: Plant runner cuttings from everbearing strawberries (*Fragaria* spp.) under benches.

Transplanting: Move healthy eggplants, melons, peppers, and tomatoes from garden to greenhouse.

Flowering Plants

Seeding: Sow seeds of *Saintpaulia ionantha* (now or at any time to flower six months later). Also, seeds of perennials can be sown at this time.

Cuttings: Take cuttings from calceolarias (herbaceous, rather than shrublike types), lobelias, and *Penstemon* hybrids.

Division: Divide *Astilbe* hybrids for indoor planting.

Bulbs: Plant bulbs of *Ixia* spp.

Transplanting: Bring in pot plants set outdoors for the summer, after careful inspection. Transplant in from the garden for winter blooming: marigolds; *Nasturtium* spp.; pansies (*Viola* ×*wittrockiana*); and petunias.

OCTOBER

Vegetables

Seeding: Sow seeds of dandelion (*Taraxacum officinale*), leeks (*Allium ampeloprasum*), and onions. Also, sow herb seeds for summer transplanting.

Flowering Plants

Seeding: For May blooming, sow seeds of *Calceolaria crenatiflora*. For flowering the following autumn, plant cyclamen seeds in 5- to 6-inch (13 to 15 cm) pots.

Bulbs: From October to November, plant hyacinth bulbs (*Hyacinthus orientalis*) for March flowering. From end of October to mid-February, plant 'Wedgwood' iris bulbs and sports to flower from January to April. From October to November, plant tulips (*Tulipa* spp.) and daffodils (*Narcissus* spp.) for January to April blooms. From October to January, plant amaryllis bulbs (*Hippeastrum* spp.) for November to May flowering.

Grooming: Bring tender perennials in from outdoors. Repot fast-growing annuals.

NOVEMBER

Vegetables

Harvesting: Broccoli, cucumbers, dandelions, lettuce, peas, tomatoes, and others.

Seeding: From November to March, sow seeds of onions and radishes (biweekly).

Flowering Plants

Seeding: From November to December, sow seeds of tuberous begonias.

Cuttings: From November to December, take cuttings from heather.

Potting: From November to December, plant cut-back, budded roses.

DECEMBER

Vegetables

Harvesting: Cucumbers, lettuce, onions, radishes, and tomatoes. Also, harvest last of broccoli and peas.

Option: Greenhouse can be closed down from mid-December to end of February, coinciding with the coldest time of the year, the shortest days, and in many places the dimmest light.

A Growing Guide for Some Popular Bedding and Pot Plants*

Plant Name	Best Temperature for Germination	Light or Darkness for Germination**	Approximate Days in Germinating Environment	Temperature for Seedlings after Germination	Weeks from Sowing to Transplanting	Minimum Night Temperature after Trans-planting***	Weeks from Transplanting to Blooming	Total Weeks from Sowing to Cropping
Alyssum spp. (annuals)	70°F/21°C	DL	3	50°-55°F/ 10°-13°C	4	40°F/4°C	7	11
Begonia spp. (fibrous-rooted)	70°F/21°C	L	14-21	70°F/21°C for 2 weeks, then 60°F/16°C	8	60°F/16°C	7	15
Brassica oleracea, Capitata Group (cabbage)	68°-86°F/ 20°-30°C	DL	3	55°F/13°C	2½	45°F/7°C	12	6½
Browallia speciosa 'Major' (bush violets)	70°F/21°C	L	7	60°F/16°C	4-5	55°F/13°C	12	16-17
Calendula spp. (pot or field marigolds)	70°F/21°C	D	7	50°-55°F/ 10°-13°C	4	40°F/4°C	5	9
Callistephus chinensis (asters)	70°F/21°C	DL	5	60°F/16°C	3	50°F/10°C	6	9
Capsicum spp. (peppers)	68°-86°F/ 20°-30°C	DL	7	65°F/18°C	3	55°F/13°C	5	8
Centaurea cineraria, C. gymnocarpa, C. maritima (dusty miller)	65°F/18°C	D	10	60°F/16°C	5	55°F/13°C	8	13
Coleus spp.	65°F/18°C	L	7	60°F/16°C	3	60°F/16°C	5	8
Dahlia cvs.	70°F/21°C	DL	3	55°F/13°C	3	55°F/13°C	6	9
Dianthus caryophyllus (carnations)	70°F/21°C	DL	7	55°- 60°F/ 13°- 16°C	6	45°F/7°C	8	14
Dianthus spp. (pinks)	70°F/21°C	DL	5	50°F/10°C	4	50°F/10°C	7	11
Impatiens spp.	70°F/21°C	L	7	70°F/21°C	4	55°F/13°C	6	10
Lobelia spp.	70°F/21°C	DL	5	50°F/10°C	4	40°F/4°C	7	11
Lycopersicon lycopersicum (tomatoes)	68°-86°F/ 20°-30°C	DL	5	60°F/16°C	3	55°F/13°C	4	7
Matthiola spp. (stock)	70°F/21°C	DL	7	50°F/10°C	4	40°F/4°C	7	11
Pelargonium spp. (geraniums)	70°-75°F/ 21°-24°C	DL	5	60°F/16°C	2-3	50°F/10°C	15	17-18

Plant Name	Best Temperature for Germination	Light or Darkness for Germination**	Approximate Days in Germinating Environment	Temperature for Seedlings after Germination	Weeks from Sowing to Transplanting	Minimum Night Temperature after Trans- planting***	Weeks from Transplanting to Blooming	Total Weeks from Sowing to Cropping
Petunia × hybrida (double petunias)	70°F/21°C	L	7	60°F/16°C	4	50°F/10°C	8	12
Petunia × hybrida (single petunias)	70°F/21°C	L	5	60°F/16°C	4	50°F/10°C	6	10
Phlox spp.	65°F/18°C	D	8-10	55°F/13°C	3	50°F/10°C	7	10
Portulaca spp.	70°F/21°C	D	3	60°F/16°C	6	50°F/10°C	8	14
Salvia spp. (sage)	70°F/21°C	L	5	60°F/16°C	3	55°F/13°C	7	10
Solanum melongena var. *esculentum* (eggplants)	68°-86°F/ 20°-30°C	DL	7	60°F/16°C	4	55°F/13°C	5	9
Tagetes erecta (tall marigolds)	70°F/21°C	DL	3	60°F/16°C	3	55°F/13°C	4	7
Tagetes tenuifolia 'Pumila' (dwarf marigolds)	70°F/21°C	DL	3	60°F/16°C	3	55°F/13°C	9	12
Verbena spp.	65°F/18°C	D	5	60°F/16°C	4	55°F/13°C	7	11
Viola × wittrockiana (pansies)	65°F/18°C	D	7	50°F/10°C	4	40°F/4°C	12	16
Zinnia elegans cvs. (dwarf zinnias)	70°F/21°C	DL	3	60°F/16°C	3	65°F/18°C	5	8
Zinnia elegans cvs. (tall zinnias)	70°F/21°C	DL	3	60°F/16°C	3	65°F/18°C	2	5

*For a more complete listing, see *Bedding Plants: A Manual on the Culture of Bedding Plants as a Greenhouse Crop* (University Park, Pennsylvania: Pennsylvania Flower Growers, 1976), from which this material has been compiled.

**D means that seeds must have total darkness to germinate. L signifies that seeds need light to germinate, either regular day-length or continuous light from an artificial source. Those receiving light around the clock will germinate more quickly. DL indicates that seeds germinate regardless of amount of darkness or light.

***These are the lowest temperatures recommended for quality plants. By providing night temperatures 10°F (6°C) higher, you can shorten the total time to cropping by about 2 weeks, though this is not recommended for *Zinnia*. Keep in mind, however, that plant growth and bloom dates are affected not just by temperature but by light intensities, length of photoperiod, and looseness of growing media, and may be delayed by less than ideal conditions.

CHAPTER 30

Using Plants

The use of plants can be viewed in psychological, aesthetic, and functional terms. We've shown throughout this book that plants seem to be a part of mankind's basic environment. We need to have them around us, both in work and in play. We enjoy plants for the aesthetic features they possess — the various colors, tones, forms, and textures of their leaves and flowers. Indoor plants can also be very functional. They can aid in directing traffic through a room, or serve as visual screens and sound diffusers, particularly in open-plan areas. Plants can also be used to soften hard architectural surfaces and lines, and they can provide textural patterns when used in front of nondescript surfaces.

Also, certain plants are excellent for brightening dull areas of the interior design. Flowering plants can add interest to a room with their bright splashes of color. Flowering plants, especially seasonal potted flowers, are useful in changing moods, too. Some plants, such as vegetables and herbs, have an added utility — you may use them for culinary purposes as well as visual enjoyment.

In making the best use of plants — to most successfully incorporate them into your home — it is necessary to consider the qualities of the plants themselves, and the qualities of the space you have to offer them.

DESIGN QUALITIES OF PLANTS

Effectively using plants indoors is much the same as landscaping with plants outdoors. The goal is to create a total composition which achieves unity of all the parts, and which is visually and aesthetically pleasing. Using plants can be fun. There is such a wide variety of colors, textures, and forms in the plant world that there is usually a number of plants available to complement any decorating scheme.

COLOR

The first design quality to consider when using plants is color. Color is probably the easiest design element to use because it is the most readily perceived and creates the most immediate response. Every homeowner knows how far a coat of paint can go in changing the character of a room. Plants offer a sort of living color, something which is hard to obtain with most functional materials.

The addition of plants can give you a vast array of colors and subtle shadings to work with in a room. Cut flowers or potted flowering plants provide concentrated spots of color to complement the basic color of the room, or to repeat a color that has already been used elsewhere in the room. The bright colors of flowering plants enliven a room and provide a focal point, while the subtler colors of foliage plants have a softening, harmonizing effect on the bold, sharp lines of architecture or furniture. All kinds of plants can be used to good advantage in decorating as long as they are chosen carefully to meet the needs of the particular room they occupy.

A good decorating scheme has one basic color that predominates. Flowers and plants can be used effectively if they match this color or pick up one of the accent colors also in the room. If the room is monochromatic, plants or flowers should be of the same color. Introducing a new color not already present in the room can confuse the design. Rooms that are basically neutral, with walls and furnishings in tones of gray, brown, or white, benefit most from a dash of color that adds variety and response.

Colors are also useful to create moods in

Opposite, palms create a tropical forest and soften the effect of a natural brick wall in a living area.   709 an indoor environment. Bright, warm colors (yellow, red, and orange) denote action, while neutral or cool colors (green, blue, and violet) exert a calming influence on the decor. Red or yellow flowers in a room with pale green walls, for example, will convey a sense of excitement and gaiety, and would be well suited to a festive party. On the other hand, blue or violet flowers in the same room would denote a more subdued mood, and would perhaps be more appropriate for a formal dinner.

In rooms which are decorated with green foliage plants, the gaiety or action response can be produced by careful attention to the textures and overall forms of the plants. Striking effects can also be obtained by making use of differently variegated foliage plants. A wide range of patterns and colors is often available within a single genus, such as coleus, foliage begonias, or wandering Jews, and the similar structure and shape of the plants used will help tie the room together.

Although we have offered here some very general guidelines for using plant colors to best effect in a room, it is impossible to lay down any hard-and-fast rules for the use of color. Your best guide is to trust your own instincts, and choose the color combinations that are most pleasing to you. Colors of some popular plants are noted in Design Qualities of Some Popular Indoor Plants, at the end of this chapter.

TEXTURE

Designers seldom overlook the quality of texture when dealing with the structural elements of a room. Texture is most often apparent in the use of differing fabrics in the furniture, draperies, and carpeting, but texture is also an important part of using plants correctly.

Texture can be defined as the relationship between the foliage and branch size, and the remainder of the plant. A small-leaved plant such as the weeping fig *(Ficus benjamina)* appears much more delicate than a

Adding Color to the Decor: The varying shades of green foliage along with the dabs of blooming color go a long way in creating a setting congenial to sharing food and conversation with friends and family. As a delightful touch, the pink flowers echo the floral pattern in the tablecloth.

bold-leaved fiddleleaf fig *(F. lyrata)* of the same size. This definition must in turn be qualified by the distance from which the plant is viewed. At close proximity, texture deals with the size, surface quality, and spacing of leaves and branches. From a distance, it deals with the entire mass of the plant, including the interplay of light and shadow among its leaves and branches.

Texture can also be defined as the coarseness or fineness, roughness or smoothness, heaviness or lightness, or thinness or density of leaves and of plants as a whole.

Leaf texture depends upon the quality of the leaf surface (glossy or hairy), and also the spacing and size of the leaves (see Design Qualities of Some Popular Indoor Plants). For example, leaves set on long petioles tend to move more in slight breezes and air currents than those on short petioles. This motion affects the shifting pattern of light and contrasting shadows in the room. Plants with long petioles look more delicate, and cast lacy, undulating shadows on walls and other surfaces. On the other hand, coarse-textured plants with leaves bunched closely together will cast large, solid shadows which appear to be strong and aggressive. Younger plants also tend to have larger leaves in proportion to their total size, so they, too, appear more coarse. The use of indoor lighting can enhance the textural differences created by shadows.

When grouping plants, try not to use too many textural contrasts. Always try to change texture in a graduated pattern; never put the coarsest plant next to the finest-textured one. Also, as the texture of the plants or structural element changes from coarse to fine, you can use a larger number or size of the finer element. For example, one coarse-textured plant may balance three medium-textured ones.

Evoking Sensations with Texture

There are two basic types of texture — visual, the part that is seen, and tactile, the part that is felt or experienced. Visual textures evoke a sensation which arises from how the plant and its leaves look: shiny leaf surfaces evoke happiness and spirit, whereas dull or hairy surfaces evoke a more subdued feeling. The smooth, glossy leaves of a peperomia may look almost good enough to eat, whereas the dull leaves of most African violets are hardly noticed. The tactile experience of textures is how plants feel, or how we imagine they would feel if we touched them. Words

like smooth, puckered, spiny, and velvety all denote tactile textures.

It is possible to use the textures of plants to provoke visual sensations, as well. For example, the coarse, massive leaves of a corn plant (*Dracaena fragrans* 'Massangeana') are usually sparse enough to make individual leaves noticeable. The coarse texture of the plant can accentuate the lines of the furniture in a room. Coarse plants can also lend a rugged, masculine appearance to a den or study, when that is desired. Delicately textured plants, on the other hand, can add contrast as well as soften. A fern, for example, can noticeably soften hard architectural lines in a room.

Flower texture can also be used effectively in indoor decor. In fact, the texture of the flower itself will influence the way in which its color is perceived. A velvety, hairy flower such as an achimenes will appear duller of hue than the smooth flower of a hibiscus, when in reality the color may be the same.

FORM

The third design quality to consider is the form or shape of the plant. Form is more than a simple outline of the plant. It is three dimensional and is determined by the line, direction, and arrangement of the leaves and branches. Plants that are weeping, pendulous, or vining in form (such as Swedish ivy) lead the eye back toward the floor, whereas ascending upright forms (like that of a columnar *Cereus* cactus) direct the eye upward.

The shape of the plant is most important in relation to the space into which you will place it. For example, a short, rounded plant such as a peperomia will not work visually in a tall, narrow space. A tall, rectangular plant such as a sansevieria would be more appropriate. Always match the shape of the plant to the available space.

The major directional emphasis of a plant is another aspect of its form, and must

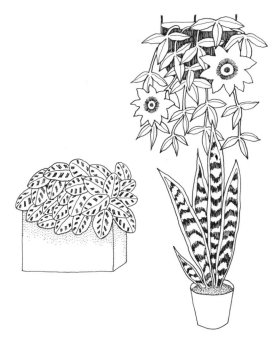

Basic Plant Forms: Three basic forms exist, based on the combination of shape and line exhibited by each plant. The trailing form, seen at top, directs the eye downward in a curved line created by varying stem lengths and flower positions. The spreading plant at left shows a more horizontal line with its squat, compact growth. The plant at lower right is an upright grower, with its leaves thrusting upward and creating a vertical line.

also be considered in an assessment of the plant's shape. The three basic types of line are horizontal, vertical, and curved. By considering plant shape and line together, all plants can be placed into three basic formal categories: upright, spreading, and weeping.

Upright-growing plants are those which are taller than they are wide and which have an overall rectangular appearance. We could call them vertical shaped. They can be used to add contrast to horizontal lines in a room, but more often to add unity to the already existing vertical features of the interior.

Plants which spread usually are relatively square in shape, since they are about as wide as they are tall. The vertical and horizontal lines are of equal importance, giving the plant a static quality. The use of square, spreading plants is most often successful

when associated with low, horizontal lines in a room.

Weeping, climbing, or trailing plants evoke active emotion. Climbing plants stimulate the observer's eye to move from level to level, upward along the stem, often softening the visual effect of strong horizontal features in the room. The weeping form can similarly be used to guide the viewer's eye in a specific direction.

In considering a plant's form and shape, it is necessary to consider also the individuality of its leaves, which in turn helps define the texture of the plant. The leaves of yuccas, for example, have a strong vertical line, whereas the leaves of spathiphyllums have a more drooping, static effect. Upon close examination, however, you'll find the basic leaf shape of the two plants to be similar.

One additional basic guide to keep in mind when working with plant forms is that the simpler a plant's overall form, the more it will attract attention. Using many bold plants in a room will cause them to compete for the viewer's attention and thus create an unsettling design. If you wish to use several plants in a room, they should generally be more delicate in form. On the other hand, if a single large plant is used to highlight a room (a specimen plant), it can be of a more severe, dramatic form, provided it complements the other furnishings in the room.

SOME BASIC CONSIDERATIONS OF SIZE

Plants vary in size from very small to very large, depending upon their identity and their age. Obviously, a plant's size determines to a great extent how it can be used — you wouldn't choose an African violet to fill an alcove, or place a five-foot (1.5 m) dieffenbachia on the dining room table for a centerpiece. For listings of some popular plants generally considered to be small, medium, or tall in size, see Plants for Living Areas.

Some plants will grow to six feet (1.8 m)

or higher, and are particularly useful where the ceiling height permits openings of over one story. Tall plants may be used one to a pot (a single stem or trunk), or they may be planted several to a container to give a group effect. Plants of this size rest on the floor and are useful to create dramatic, bold effects, especially in modern living and dining areas.

Larger plants can easily be used to counter architectural lines in the room. For example, a large rubber plant can create a strong vertical line where the horizontal lines of furnishings predominate. If a single-stemmed plant is too stark a contrast, then use a multi-stemmed plant, or group several plants together. An unusually shaped specimen may even be considered as a piece of living sculpture. But be sure to select a type of plant that will complement the total decor of the room. For example, the stark, sculpturesque form of a large dragon tree would not work well in a colonial living room — it would be much more attractive in an oriental atmosphere.

Plants between 1½ and 6 feet (0.5 and 1.5 m) tall are considered medium in size. They can sit on the floor or on shelves, or can be suspended in hanging containers, and may be used either as specimen plants, or as accessories to the room decor. They usually can be grouped together to form patterns of varying textures and heights. Such groupings are useful in filling corners or spaces, and in providing visual screens.

Small plants less than 12 inches (30 cm) high are most easily placed on tabletops, desks, windowsills, or pedestals, to be viewed at nearly eye level. Many of these plants can be used alone, particularly those with vining characteristics, showy foliage, or colorful flowers. Some types of plants can be used as tabletop plants early in their development before they get too large. Also don't forget the utility of smaller plants in terraria, dish gardens, hanging baskets, and window boxes. Small plants are easily moved around to change decor, and are far less expensive than larger plants. The vast array of individual plant textures, colors, and forms offers you the use of a multitude of plant combinations.

Some plants, particularly smaller ones, are much better displayed at close range where their specific leaf texture can be admired. African violets and the dwarf cyclamens, for example, are rich in contrast, so place them on a coffee table or desk. Sometimes a grouping of plants of the same type offers an interesting visual contrast. Try a cluster of differently variegated peperomias, or an assortment of ferns or begonias.

JUDGING THE QUALITIES OF THE ROOM

The qualities of the room environment need to be considered as carefully as plant attributes when choosing plants for various sites in the home. Other chapters of this book have described the various environmental conditions that are necessary before you can be successful with indoor plants — amounts and kinds of light, temperature ranges, growing media, humidity, and water. It is extremely important to understand these environmental conditions at the exact location of each plant (really its mini-environment, or microclimate) in the room. You will be at standing or sitting level, but the plant may be sitting on the floor, or next to a window, or near a door.

Probably the most important environmental condition is light. There are basically two approaches to dealing with the light levels available to plants at a given spot in a room.

First, you can actually grow a plant in that particular location, in which case you must be sure that ample natural or artificial light is available. Or, you can simply use and enjoy the plant for as long as it looks good and then move it. In other words, you can display the plant until it begins to suffer from lack of light, then rotate it to an "intensive

Plants for Living Areas

Plant	Light Requirement
Tall or Treelike Plants	
Araucaria heterophylla (Norfolk Island pine)	Moderate to low
Aucuba japonica (Japanese aucuba)	Moderate
Beaucarnea recurvata (elephant-foot tree)	Bright to moderate
Brassaia actinophylla (schefflera, umbrella tree)	Bright
Buxus sempervirens (boxwood)	Bright to moderate
Chamaedorea elegans (parlor palm neanthe bella), *C. erumpens*	Low
Cissus antarctica (kangaroo vine)	Bright
Cordyline terminalis (Hawaiian ti plant)	Bright
Dieffenbachia amoena, D. exotica, D. maculata 'Rudolph Roehrs' (dumb cane)	Bright to low
Dizygotheca elegantissima (false aralia)	Bright
Dracaena cincta, D. fragrans 'Massangeana' (corn plant), *D. marginata* (dragon tree), *D. sanderana* (Belgian evergreen)	Bright to moderate
Euonymus japonica (spindle tree)	Bright to moderate
Ficus benjamina (weeping fig), *F. elastica* 'Decora' (broad-leaved Indian rubber plant), *F. lyrata* (fiddle-leaf fig)	Bright to moderate
Howea belmoreana (Belmore sentry palm, curly palm)	Bright to low
Monstera deliciosa (Swiss cheese plant)	Moderate to low
Pandanus veitchii (veitch screw pine)	Moderate
Philodendron bipennifolium (fiddle-leaf philodendron)	Moderate
Phoenix roebelenii (pygmy date palm)	Bright
Pittosporum tobira (Australian laurel, mock orange)	Bright
Podocarpus macrophyllus var. *maki* (southern yew)	Bright
Rhapis excelsa (lady palm)	Bright
Tradescantia fluminensis 'Variegata' (variegated wandering Jew)	Bright
Zebrina pendula (wandering Jew)	Bright to moderate

Plant	Light Requirement
Medium Plants	
Acalypha wilkesiana, A. wilkesiana 'Godseffiana' (copperleaf)	Bright
Asparagus densiflorus 'Sprengeri' (emerald fern)	Bright
Aspidistra elatior (barroom plant, cast-iron plant)	Moderate to low
Begonia coccinea (angel-wing begonia), *B.* × *rex-cultorum* (rex begonia), *B. scharffii, B.* × *semperflorens-cultorum* (wax begonia)	Bright
Billbergia nutans (friendship plant, queen's tears)	Bright
Brassavola nodosa (lady of the night)	Bright
Buxus sempervirens (boxwood)	Bright to moderate
Calathea makoyana (peacock plant)	Bright to moderate
Callisia elegans (striped inch plant)	Bright
Cattleya skinneri (cattleya)	Bright
× *Citrofortunella mitis* (calamondin)	Bright
Codiaeum variegatum var. *pictum* (croton)	Bright
Crassula argentea (jade plant)	Bright
Dendrobium phalaenopsis	Bright
Episcia cupreata (flame violet)	Bright
Ficus deltoidea (mistletoe fig)	Bright to moderate
Guzmania lingulata	Moderate
Hoya carnosa (honey or wax plant)	Bright to moderate
Neoregelia marmorata (marble plant)	Bright
Nephrolepis exaltata 'Bostoniensis' (Boston fern)	Bright
Philodendron selloum (saddle-leaf philodendron), *P. wendlandii*	Low
Polyscias balfouriana (balfour aralia)	Bright
Syngonium angustatum 'Albolineatum' (arrowhead vine)	Moderate
Tolmiea menziesii (piggyback plant)	Bright to moderate

Plant	Light Requirement
Short or Tabletop Plants	
Adiantum capillus-veneris (southern maidenhair fern, Venus's hair)	Low
Begonia bogneri (grass-leaf begonia), *B. boweri*, *B. prismatocarpa* (miniature begonia)	Bright
Cissus rhombifolia (grape ivy)	Bright
Coleus blumei (coleus)	Bright
Cryptanthus zonatus 'Zebrinus' (earth star)	Bright
Epipremnum aureum (devil's ivy, golden pathos)	Bright to low
Fittonia verschaffeltii (mosaic plant, nerve plant), *F. verschaffeltii* var. *argyroneura* (silver-nerved fittonia)	Low
Hedera helix (English ivy)	Bright
Impatiens wallerana (patience plant)	Bright to moderate
Maranta leuconeura var. *kerchoviana* (prayer plant, rabbit's foot)	Moderate
Neoregelia carolinae (blushing bromeliad)	Bright
Pelargonium × *hortorum* vars. (miniature zonal geraniums), *P. peltatum* vars. (miniature ivy geraniums)	Bright
Peperomia argyreia (watermelon peperomia), *P. caperata* (emerald ripple peperomia), *P. griseoargentea* (ivy peperomia), *P. obtusifolia* (blunt-leaf peperomia)	Moderate to low
Philodendron scandens subsp. *oxycardium* (heart-leaf philodendron)	Moderate
Pilea cadierei (aluminum plant), *P. involucrata* (friendship plant, panamiga)	Bright to moderate
Saintpaulia spp. and cvs. (African violets)	Bright to moderate
Sinningia speciosa (florists' gloxinia)	Bright
Tradescantia albiflora 'Albovittata' (giant white inch plant)	Bright

care" area such as a greenhouse or light garden to recuperate, and replace it with a fresh, healthy plant. (Certain seasonal blooming plants, like kalanchoes and calceolarias, are often used and then discarded because they are very difficult to force into bloom a second time. These plants can be featured for a few weeks at a time to add a dash of color.) Setting up a rotation system for more permanent plants of course gives you a wider choice of which plants you can use where. It is a challenge to select a plant that not only will complement your decorative scheme but also will thrive in the location where you wish to use it.

Another important consideration in the room environment is air circulation. Drafts can be a problem in many rooms; modern heating systems often create virtual "wind tunnels" that can harm delicate foliage.

Location of heat sources can cause prob-

Plant-Proofing a Radiator: To offset the harmful effects of heat rising from a radiator, cover the top with a piece of heavy insulating material, then set a pebble-filled tray over this. The heat will evaporate drainage water from the tray and your plants will receive a greatly appreciated boost of humidity.

A Living Centerpiece

An arrangement of freshly cut flowers is a classic table decoration. A discussion of the principles of flower arrangement is beyond the scope of this book, but can be found in a host of others.

When planning a centerpiece for a dinner table or sideboard, don't overlook attractively potted flowering and foliage plants — they can be just as delightful as a bowl of cut flowers, and give you a chance to show off favorite specimens. The chief criterion to bear in mind is to keep the centerpiece low — dinner conversation inevitably falters when guests have to peer through a mass of leaves or blossoms to see one another.

lems, too. Radiators in older homes are often located directly under windows — an ideal place for plants. In winter, the heat from radiators can have ill effects on plants growing on the windowsills directly above. But this can be circumvented by placing a pad of heavy insulating material or other flameproof material on the radiator top and constructing a pebble tray for plants over this.

Specific rooms in the home tend to offer different kinds of challenges (and rewards) to indoor gardeners. Following is a brief review of some characteristics to keep in mind in relation to various rooms.

LIVING AND DINING AREAS

The living area of your home, or more specifically, the living room, is usually the showplace of your home, and the room where you most often entertain guests. This makes it an ideal place to display a large specimen plant, much the same as you might display a piece of sculpture or a large painting. The living room may also be the place where you want to house a collection of show plants or other favorites. You may wish to construct special stands and display cases to show off your favorite plants. In dining areas, the table is the focus of the decor, and plants can generally be used to best advantage as centerpieces and accessories around the perimeter of the room.

STAIRWAYS AND HALLWAYS

The stairways of most modern homes are open and airy, and receive a moderate amount of light. However, the stairways and halls of older homes are usually closed or partitioned off, often with doors at both ends. The selection of plants which can be safely used in such areas is determined by the amount of light available at the height at which the plants are growing. If the stairway or hall is too dim, no living plant will be able to survive there. But if you can provide 50 to 100 footcandles, a number of low-light plants can be maintained.

Plants as Accessories: The living room often becomes the showcase of the home where a great deal of attention is lavished on furnishings and pieces of art. For a change of pace, consider adding a living work of art. There are many bold, dramatic palms and other trees which can impart a sculptural quality through their very form, and which will do well indoors.

Greening Up the Stairway: What better way to brighten up a normally empty stairway corner than to tuck in a lovely foliage plant? Although the *Aspidistra* shown here can tolerate low light levels and would be suitable in a dim stairwell, the extra light provided by the window in this stairway will encourage more vigorous growth.

Curtain of Greenery for the Kitchen: This window full of plants can act as an eye-pleasing diversion for the person on kitchen duty. The sun-loving plants in this western exposure hang from hooks in the ceiling or rest on a glass shelf jutting out from the window frame. They stay in place year-round and benefit from the boosted humidity levels resulting from frequent use of the sink.

It is important that the plants are acclimated to this kind of dim environment before being placed there permanently. Never move a plant directly from a greenhouse to a dim

Plants for Stairways and Hallways

Aglaonema commutatum, A. modestum, A. pictum
(Chinese evergreen)
Araucaria heterophylla (Norfolk Island pine)
Aspidistra elatior, A. elatior 'Variegata' (barroom
plant, cast-iron plant)
Asplenium nidus (bird's nest fern)
Chamaedorea elegans (parlor palm, neanthe bella),
C. erumpens (bamboo palm)
Dieffenbachia amoena (dumb cane)
Epipremnum aureum (devil's ivy, golden pothos)
Ficus pumila (creeping fig)
Fittonia verschaffeltii (mosaic plant, nerve plant),
F. verschaffeltii var. *argyroneura* (silver-nerved
fittonia)
Howea belmoreana (Belmore sentry palm, curly
palm)
Monstera deliciosa (Swiss cheese plant)
Pellaea rotundifolia (button fern), *P. viridis* (green
cliff brake)
Philodendron erubescens, P. selloum (red-leaf
philodendron)
Sansevieria trifasciata 'Hahnii' (bird's nest
sansevieria), *S. trifasciata* 'Laurentii' (snake
plant)
Spathiphyllum spp. (peace lily, spathe flower)
Vriesea spp. (flaming sword)

hall or stairway. Whether you purchase a plant from a commercial greenhouse or grow it yourself, it is wise to gradually expose it to lowering light conditions before placing it in the darker location. A plant rotation system is often the best solution to the problem of maintaining plants in interior halls and stairways. For a list of some durable plants to use in such locations, see Plants for Stairways and Hallways.

Some additional considerations are in order for plants placed next to doorways or entranceways. When the door is opened, cold air rushes in and can chill the plants. Sudden or even gradual leaf dropping is a sure sign of this type of injury. It would be better to try to keep plants away from such areas, or to install a small enclosed entranceway that will act as a barrier to the first charge of cold air.

Despite the stresses of such an environ-ment, entrance halls and foyers offer a special opportunity to welcome guests to your home with a cheerful, attractive display of plants. Provided your entrance hall is not too drafty, try a group of low-light plants, or a vase of cut flowers. You can rotate plants, or install a couple of lights to help maintain them.

THE KITCHEN

Having aesthetically pleasing plants around where we work is most enjoyable. And the kitchen is one of the best rooms in which to enjoy plants, since we spend a great portion of our time working and sometimes dining there.

It is true that kitchens often are warmer and thus sometimes drier than other rooms of the house. But it is also true that they are sometimes filled with higher levels of humidity due to the amount of water vaporizing from cooking foods. Kitchens are also usually much brighter than other rooms since they may have one or two windows as well as a set of overhead lights for working purposes.

The kitchen, then, probably offers as versatile an environment for growing plants as any room in the home. Bear in mind, however, that light and temperature levels will vary widely from spot to spot within the kitchen. And it is never a good idea to place plants next to the stove, where escaping hot vapors would certainly scorch them.

Indoor gardening can take many turns in the kitchen. The lines of kitchen cabinetry and appliances are usually very harsh, and can be softened by the addition of ferns and other delicately textured plants. Of course, herbs and other edible plants are also natural candidates for the kitchen garden. If you have a large south-facing window, you might fill it with a combination of hanging baskets containing cucumbers, parsley, rosemary, strawberries, tomatoes, and other herbs and edibles. (See chapters 16 and 17 for information on growing these plants.) If you have a large window box or planter in the kitchen,

Plants for Kitchens

Acalypha wilkesiana (copperleaf)
Aphelandra squarrosa (zebra plant)
Beaucarnea recurvata (elephant-foot tree)
Codiaeum variegatum var. *pictum* (croton)
Coffea arabica (coffee plant)
Coleus blumei (coleus)
Cordyline terminalis (Hawaiian ti plant)
Crassula arborescens (silver jade plant)
×*Fatshedera lizei* (tree ivy)
Gynura aurantiaca (velvet plant)
Hedera canariensis 'Variegata' (variegated Canary
   Islands ivy)
Herbs (many varieties)
Impatiens wallerana (patience plant)
Justicia brandegeana (shrimp plant)
Kalanchoe blossfeldiana (Christmas kalanchoe),
   K. tomentosa (panda plant)
Osmanthus heterophyllus (false holly)
Pelargonium ×*hortatum* (fish or zonal geranium)
Pittosporum tobira 'Variegata' (mock orange,
   variegated Australian laurel)
Saintpaulia spp. and cvs. (African violet)
Vegetables (many varieties)

you may want to give it a neat border or edging. Try soaking whole or chopped corncobs in water and then sprinkling grass seed on them. Keep moist until the seeds sprout. Thereafter trim the grass to keep it low and attractive. Plants for Kitchens contains a general listing of plants that do well in the warm, bright conditions of a kitchen.

THE BATHROOM

In terms of humidity and temperature, the bathroom offers an excellent environment for a variety of plants. Since most people take showers or run steaming baths, the relative humidity usually reaches 80 to 100 percent at various times of the day. Most of us keep our

Bathing in a Tropical Setting: There are very few things as soothing as lying back in a tub of warm water and gazing upward into a canopy of lush green leaves. Tropical plants are a natural in the bathroom, where they thrive on the abundance of warmth and moisture.

Grass Border for a Window Box: For a neat edging, sprinkle prepared corncobs with grass seed, watch them sprout, then set the grass-laden cobs in your window box. Once in place, keep them trimmed for a well-groomed appearance.

Plants for Bathrooms

Achimenes spp. and hybrids (magic flower)

Adiantum raddianum (maidenhair fern)

Aechmea fasciata (living vase)

Aeschynanthus pulcher (lipstick plant)

Asplenium bulbiferum (mother spleenwort),
    A. nidus (bird's nest fern)

Billbergia nutans (friendship plant, queen's tears)

Columnea hybrids (goldfish plant)

Cryptanthus zonatus (earth star)

Cyrtomium falcatum (holly fern)

Davallia canariensis (deer's foot fern), *D. fejeensis*
    (rabbit's foot fern)

Gardenia jasminoides (gardenia)

Mimosa pudica (sensitive plant)

Nephrolepis exaltata 'Bostoniensis' (Boston fern)

Platycerium bifurcatum (staghorn fern)

Polypodium aureum (golden polypody fern or
    hare's-foot fern)

Pteris cretica (ribbon fern), *P. cretica* 'Cristata'
    (table fern), *P. ensiformis* (sword fern),
    P. ensiformis 'Victoriae' (silver leaf fern)

Saxifraga stolonifera, S. stolonifera 'Tricolor'
    (strawberry begonia)

Sinningia speciosa (florists' gloxinia)

Soleirolia soleirolii (baby's tears)

Streptocarpus ×*hybridus* (cape primrose)

Tillandsia ionantha

Vriesea spp. (flaming sword)

bathrooms fairly warm, too, and the humidity and warmth are a luxury that tropical house plants seldom experience in our homes.

The drawback to the bathroom environment is a tendency toward low levels of light. These rooms are often devoid of windows, making it necessary for gardeners to provide 12 to 16 hours of supplemental light a day for the plants.

Bathrooms, then, are ideal places to grow plants which insist upon high humidity, as long as sufficient light can be provided. Most of these types of plants also thrive on the moisture which accumulates on their leaves when showers are taken, much like the rains of a tropical rain forest. You might consider using various ferns, mosses, bromeliads, or even certain orchids for bathroom plants. See Plants for Bathrooms for a list of some plants that do well in these conditions.

USING PLANTS TO FILL SPACES

There are a number of ways to work with plants within a given room to fill the available space, to complement the decor, or to accent architectural features.

A single large specimen plant can serve as a focal point for the room. It can behave as a freestanding object of art.

Sometimes plants are an inexpensive way to remodel an existing room. One or more large plants can be used to "fill in" when newer furniture seems to be out of place in the existing decor. Don't be afraid to use a specimen plant as a piece of furniture. A weeping fig is a lot less expensive than a new chair or table, and can be a more versatile way of filling an empty corner. Rooms full of accessories like corner cupboards, decorative tables, and highboys are not necessary for the way many of us live today. Instead, groupings of furniture are massed away from walls for social ease, to encourage conversation and permit an easy flow of traffic through the room. The walls are then used to display works of art, and freestanding spaces can accommodate plants.

Plants can be used to hide heating pipes or unused doorways. They can be grouped at all levels in windows to take the place of blinds or curtains. Massed plants can also be used to shorten long, narrow rooms, to make them look and feel more comfortable.

Groupings of large plants on the floor or smaller plants on shelves and etageres can also serve as screens or room dividers. Perhaps the most obvious use for these living screens is in open-plan offices or loft dwellings, but even in the home, plants can be employed to create special areas for dining or relaxing with a good book or the stereo. In-

Plants as Room Divider: A grouping of plants can screen off a portion of a large room while still maintaining an open, airy feel. If you arrange plants in graduated heights, a graceful, sweeping line is created which is more pleasing to the eye than a block of plants identical in size.

stead of structural dividers, use a series of plants to cut down direct sunlight, and create special shadow patterns in various social areas. One excellent spot for plants is on top of the half-wall storage area found between many kitchens and dining rooms. The exact choice of plants will be governed by the ceiling height, size and type of furniture, and window and door patterns. The idea is not to divide the space completely — the goal is to encourage privacy while still maintaining the open, airy feel of a large room. Do not allow the plants to reach more than three-fourths of the way to the ceiling.

Plants can effectively offset hard architectural lines and surfaces in a number of ways to create a softening effect. One way is to place leafy hanging or upright plants in the corner of a room where they will mask the vertical lines of the converging walls. The plants visually become a part of the walls by joining them with an inward or outward curve instead of a sharp angle. Thus, a larger number of softer angles and curves are

formed in the room, which serve to soften its boundaries.

Another area where lines need to be softened is along the entranceway between two rooms, such as between a living room and a foyer. The harshness often associated with a foyer can be softened by a well-placed plant to blend into the more comfortable living room atmosphere.

MORE IDEAS FOR USING PLANTS

BRIDGING THE GAP BETWEEN INDOORS AND OUT

If you have a large window area, like a bay window or sliding glass doors, you can use the area to bring the outside indoors by visually associating your indoor plants with the plants outside the window. This technique also tends to make the room seem larger.

Softening Architectural Lines: The starkness and repetition caused by sharp vertical and horizontal lines in this room are softened by the full, round shape of a large Boston fern. The hard edges where walls meet ceiling are camouflaged by the presence of the fern, which is strategically hung to create an outward curve and to cover a harsh 90-degree angle.

If possible, use related species both indoors and out. Gardeners in the southwestern United States can focus on an assortment of cacti and other succulents. In the north, you might use a Norfolk Island pine to blend with the pines or other conifers outside, or indoor ferns to blend with a garden of native ferns outside the window. For homes in wooded areas, mass an array of plant textures along the inside of the window to simulate the large number of trees, shrubs, and herbaceous plants growing in the woods. In warmer climates, palms and lush tropicals can be planted both inside and out. In warmer climates all year and during summers elsewhere, a colorful planter of annual flowers can lead the eye outward to the private outdoor garden on a terrace or patio or lawn. Also, an aquarium or tub garden can be designed to echo an outdoor pool. Even though separated by glass, the effect can be that of a single continuous water garden.

Where the outdoor scenery is not so inviting, plants can be massed in a window to conceal the view. The drab vista of a neighboring high-rise can be transformed into a tranquil oasis of greenery. Angling plants inward from the windows to reflect more light creates a pleasant, diffused illumination in the room. They seem to bring the green from outdoors right into your home.

SPECIAL EFFECTS

Other special effects can be created by using plants under a glass-topped table or desk. It's as though the entire piece of furniture is alive. But be sure that either supplemental lighting or low-light-intensity plants are used. It also may be a good idea to select plants such as philodendron or cast-iron plant which will grow in shallow containers or even in water to make the best use of such limited space.

Another trick is to use plants in front of or beside large mirrors to turn one or two plants into a whole group, and also make the room look larger. Adding lighting from beneath or beside the plant will cast attention-getting shadows all around. The lighting adds drama to the room and also is necessary for the plant's growth.

In fact, the use of lights, both for plant growth and for aesthetic purposes, helps to create dramatic effects with any plant arrangement. There seems to be no end to the various types of lighting fixtures and methods by which plants can be lighted. Downlighting from ceiling or wall-mounted fixtures creates interesting shadow patterns on the walls and floors. Uplighting, from lights set on the floor, can be used to emphasize the foliage pattern on walls and ceilings. The effect usually enlarges the characteristics of the leaves, and is particularly striking with large, coarse plants such as dieffenbachias, dracaenas, monsteras, and palms. And by using light bulbs suitable for plant growth, your plants will also benefit from the added light.

DESIGNING PLANT GROUPINGS

Plants are valuable for the three-dimensional effect they create in a room, so don't line them all up like tin soldiers ready for a parade. Use different sizes and shapes when you group plants, and vary the depth and height to create an interesting grouping. If the plants are naturally of different sizes, then place a coarse-textured one or one with brightly colored foliage in front or to the side. Even a windowsill or kitchen cupboard arrangement can be staged; the technique can be as simple as setting some pots farther forward than others.

Another technique is to vary plant heights by the use of plant stands, carts, or pedestals. Or combine groupings of floor or pedestal plants with a hanging basket or two.

Small plants are usually grouped together for a better effect. One small, six-inch (15 cm) Norfolk Island pine is hardly noticeable on a large coffee table, unless you are practically sitting on top of it. Only when

Arranging for Maximum Impact: Randomly filling an empty window with a hodgepodge of plants isn't the best use of available space or the best means to show off specimen plants. It's a better idea to have a plan in mind before you begin hanging pots and setting them in place. The window arrangement here is a lovely example of how a dramatic effect can be created by varying the plant heights and by interspersing spots of color among green foliage.

grouped with other plants does it become a part of the total decor when viewed from a distance.

One of the most overlooked considerations when using plants is the selection of a complementary container for each plant. There are countless styles of pots, certainly you'll find one which will match your decor. For example, ordinary clay pots with their earthy tones and texture work well in a countryish room with wooden furniture and lots of natural materials. Be sure also that the color or form of the pot does not overwhelm the plant; you want to call attention to the plant, not the container.

Movable planters offer the opportunity to readily rearrange space within living and working areas. Choose a large rectangular planter on wheels to hold a variety of plants, or simply place heavy casters under a very large single potted plant. Move the planters

around to adjust for the number of people or special traffic patterns to be accommodated.

DISPLAYING PLANTS

Every indoor gardener has at least one favorite plant. It may have been a gift from a relative or friend, or it may be one which was grown from seeds or nurtured from a cutting. It is likely that you'll enjoy showing off this plant to everyone who visits your office or home. It may even become a central part of your decorating scheme with a prominent place of honor.

How you show off your favorite plant will depend upon the size and type of plant as well as the decorative mood of your room. Small plants should be placed on tables, desks, or other pieces of furniture so they can be viewed at eye level. Large plants can become the focal point of the entire room.

DISPLAYING A COLLECTION

There are any number of ways to display a collection of plants, but keep a few basic considerations in mind. First of all, are you displaying a collection of many kinds of plants, or are you a collector of one particular kind of plant such as ferns or orchids? Whatever your preference, plants to be displayed together must all thrive in the same environmental conditions. Choose the site for your display accordingly — site selection can be complicated when you are working with plants from a number of different families. A collection of related genera is much simpler to display.

Cacti and other succulents, for example, usually desire bright, sunny areas and of course they all look better (and grow better, too) when displayed in sand-filled containers. They could easily be placed in a series of dish gardens, or even a large "sandbox" where you can create a miniature desert scene. Add pieces of rock, weathered wood, or other desertlike materials. As the collection enlarges

(continued on page 725)

Build Your Own Multiple Hanging Plant Shelf

This hanging plant shelf is made up of three shelf units which are adjustable in height. The number of shelves used may be varied to accommodate the location and the type of plants being displayed.

Materials:

Item	Quantity	Description
Large shelves:		
A, G. Side rails	2	$3/4 \times 1\,1/2 \times 48$-inch select pine
B, H. End rails	2	$3/4 \times 1\,1/2 \times 9\,1/4$-inch select pine
C, I. Bottom	1	$1/4 \times 9\,1/4 \times 47\,1/4$-inch mahogany plywood
Nails	—	4d finish nails
Glue	—	White vinyl glue
Finish	—	Waterproof varnish
Small shelf:		
D. Side rails	2	$3/4 \times 1\,1/2 \times 30$-inch select pine
E. End rails	2	$3/4 \times 1\,1/2 \times 9\,1/4$-inch select pine
F. Bottom	1	$1/4 \times 9\,1/4 \times 29\,1/4$-inch mahogany plywood
Nails	—	4d finish nails
Glue	—	White vinyl glue
Finish	—	Waterproof varnish
Assembly:		
Chain	20 feet	Twist-link brass machine chain
Screw eyes	6	#108 ($3/4$-inch eye) screw eyes
Sash chain clips	8	$5/8$-inch diameter helix clips (copper-clad)

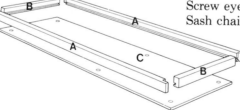

5. Rout a $1/4$-inch radius on all exposed edges, or break these edges with a sanding block.
6. Sand and finish each shelf.

Procedure for Shelf Construction:

1. Cut all pieces A through I to size, according to the dimensions in the materials list.
2. Cut a $3/8$-inch-deep $\times$ $3/4$-inch-wide rabbet on each end of all six side rails (A, D, and G).
3. Machine a $3/8$-inch-deep $\times$ $1/4$-inch-wide groove, $1/4$ inch from the bottom edge of all four rails (A, B, D, E, G, and H) of each shelf.
4. Glue and nail the shelf members together by nailing through the side rails with 4d finish nails. Remember to insert the bottoms (C, F, and I) into the grooves made for them before nailing on the fourth side.

Procedure for Shelf Assembly:

1. Insert screw eyes into the side rails (G) of the bottom shelf, 1 inch from the inside of each end rail (H).
2. Drill $1/2$-inch holes (clearance for the size of the chain) through the shelf bottom of the top and middle shelves, $1\,1/4$ inches from the outside edge of the side and end rails.
3. On the top shelf drill two $1/2$-inch holes $27\,1/2$ inches from one end. The holes should be spaced $1\,1/4$ inches from the outside edge of the side rails.
4. Insert a screw eye above each of these two middle holes.

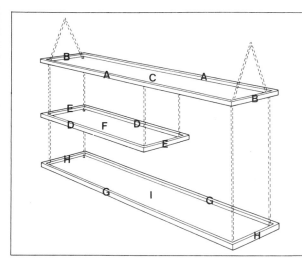

5. Cut two 22-inch and four 55-inch lengths of chain.
6. Attach the shorter chains to the screw eyes in the top shelf and allow them to hang through the holes. You will need to pry open the screw eyes and reclose them again.
7. Attach the longer chains to the screw eyes on the bottom shelf.
8. Thread the shelves onto the chains in the desired order.
9. Hang the assembly at the desired location.
10. Adjust the heights of the shelves. Secure them in position with sash chain clips.

and your plants grow, you may want to place larger plants in clay or decorative Mexican ceramic pots for further accent.

PEDESTALS, SHELVES, AND CASES

Plants can be displayed attractively on pedestals, stands, poles, and pieces of furniture, or hung from a variety of hangers. A quick look around in any flower shop which sells accessories will soon convince you of the large available array of plant display units.

Plant stands designed to hold varying numbers of plants are available in a wide range of styles and colors. They are suitable for use in areas of the home or office where growing conditions are less than ideal. Plants on lightweight stands can be moved periodically, stand and all, from poorly lighted areas to more ideal locations for revitalization.

If you are handy, you might try making your own pedestals from wood. You can purchase or construct wooden cubes of various sizes and shapes, and paint them according to your decorative scheme. By using different sizes of cubes and grouping them, you can create a changing effect as you vary the positions of the cubes and plants.

For a charming rustic look, try using an unusual section of log for a pedestal. Be sure to disinfect for termites, ants, and other creatures before bringing the log indoors. Saw the ends to make them flat, and if you wish, seal the cut ends with a nontoxic wood preservative.

Using decorator tension poles is also a popular way of displaying a number of different plants, usually of small sizes. Plant poles are available in a large number of styles; you can also construct one yourself, as described in Build Your Own Adjustable Plant Pole. They all stretch from floor to ceiling and can be set at appropriate places in the room. Some have extendable or movable arms, so you can position individual plants. Some will hold only hanging plants, whereas others have built-in saucers for pots. Be sure to balance the plants as you position them around the pole.

Plants can also be displayed on a wide variety of shelving ranging from wood through glass and plastic. Also, there are now available a large number of display cases, often made from wood, equipped with light fixtures for easy growth and maintenance of plants. Many are available ready-made or others can be easily constructed. For directions for building a simple case, see Build Your Own Plant Display Case.

Build Your Own Adjustable Plant Pole

This adjustable plant pole was designed to provide a vertical column of flowers and greenery by facilitating the use of both hanging and free-standing plant pots. It is adjustable for a friction fit between floor and ceiling by turning a carriage bolt at the bottom of the planter. This unit is designed for an 8-foot ceiling with an adjustment plus or minus 1 inch.

Materials:

Item	Quantity	Description
A. Pole columns	4	$1\frac{1}{8} \times 1\frac{1}{8} \times 94$-inch #2 pine
B. Column spacers	2	$\frac{3}{4} \times 3 \times 4$-inch #2 pine
C. Column spacers	4	$\frac{3}{4} \times 1\frac{1}{8} \times 4$-inch #2 pine
D. Support arms	4	$\frac{3}{4} \times 2\frac{1}{2} \times 27$-inch #2 pine
E. Pot supports	6	$\frac{3}{4} \times 6$-inch round #2 pine
Glue	—	White vinyl glue
Nails	—	6d finish nails
Screws	12	$1\frac{1}{4}$-inch #6 flat-head wood screws
Dowels	36 inches	$\frac{1}{4}$-inch maple dowel rod
Screw eyes	6	$\frac{5}{8}$-inch screw eyes
Varnish	1 pint	Polyurethane varnish
Adjustment bolt	1	$\frac{3}{8} \times 4$-inch carriage bolt
T-nut	1	$\frac{3}{8}$-inch T-nut

Special Tools: Router

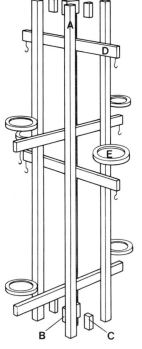

Procedure:

1. Cut pieces A through E according to the dimensions in the materials list.
2. Rout a $\frac{1}{4}$-inch radius on all edges of pieces A through E, or break the edges with a sanding block.
3. To assemble the frame, glue and nail through pole columns (A) into column spacers (C) with 6d finish nails at both the top and bottom.
4. Glue and nail these two sections together by nailing through pole columns (A) into column spacers (B).
5. Position the top and bottom support arms (D) 7 inches from the ends of the pole columns and center them. Position other two arms as desired.
6. Drill through the pole columns (A) and the support arms (D) with a $\frac{1}{4}$-inch drill and insert a glued $\frac{1}{4}$-inch dowel through the hole to secure the support arm.
7. Insert four dowels for each support arm. If adjustable arms are desired, the top and bottom arms may be held in place with dowels and no glue.
8. Rout out the 6-inch round pot supports (E) $\frac{1}{4}$ inch deep to form saucers.
9. Lay out, glue, and screw the saucers (E) to the support arms (D).
10. Install six screw eyes in the bottom of the support arms (D) to provide hanging hooks for the hanging plants.
11. Drill a $\frac{1}{2}$-inch hole $3\frac{1}{2}$ inches deep in the center of the bottom column spacer (B).
12. Install a $\frac{3}{8}$-inch T-nut in the hole for the $\frac{3}{8} \times 4$-inch carriage bolt.
13. Finish-sand all members and apply two coats of varnish.
14. To adjust the planter to fit your 8-foot ceiling securely, turn the carriage bolt.

Build Your Own Plant Display Case

This compact case was designed to provide a covered display area for small house plants. The clear polystyrene cover is removable to permit air circulation and easy access to plants. By making the cover from one piece of curved plastic, maximum light and visual exposure are provided.

Materials:

Item	Quantity	Description
A. End panels	2	$\frac{3}{4} \times 11\frac{1}{4} \times 18\frac{1}{2}$-inch #2 pine
B. Bottom rails	2	$\frac{3}{4} \times 1 \times 34\frac{1}{2}$-inch #2 pine
C. Handle	1	$\frac{3}{4} \times 36$-inch hardwood dowel
D. Cover	1	$35\frac{1}{8} \times 37\frac{1}{4}$-inch polystyrene sheet
E. Bottom tray	1	$\frac{3}{4} \times 9\frac{3}{8} \times 34\frac{3}{8}$-inch #2 pine
Screws	4	$1\frac{1}{4}$-inch #8 flat-head wood screws
Plugs	4	$\frac{3}{8}$-inch-diameter $\times \frac{1}{4}$-inch-long round wood plugs
Finish	—	Clear varnish
Glue	—	White vinyl glue

Special Tools:

Router
Saber saw or band saw
Mat knife

Procedure:

1. Lay out and cut two end panels (A), according to the dimensions in the materials list.
2. Lay out and rout a $\frac{1}{16}$-inch-wide $\times \frac{5}{16}$-inch-deep groove in each end panel (A) for the polystyrene cover (D).
3. Lay out and drill screw holes in each end panel (A) for the handle, and for fastening the bottom rails (B) to the end panels. Countersink $\frac{3}{8}$-inch-diameter $\times \frac{1}{4}$-inch-deep holes for plugs.
4. Cut two pieces of pine for the bottom rails (B), according to the dimensions in the materials list.
5. Rout a $\frac{1}{16}$-inch-wide $\times \frac{5}{16}$-inch-deep groove for the polystyrene sheet in one edge of the bottom rails (B) to match the groove in the end panels (A).
6. Rout a $\frac{1}{4}$-inch radius on the outside edges of the end panels (A), and on the top edges of the bottom rails (B).
7. Cut a piece of polystyrene sheet (D) to fit into the groove.
8. Assemble the unit, using a $\frac{3}{4} \times 34\frac{1}{2}$-inch dowel for the handle (C). Glue the

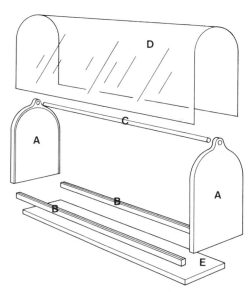

wood elements together with vinyl glue and use $1\frac{1}{4}$-inch #8 flat-head wood screws to fasten the end panels to the bottom rails.

9. Cut four $\frac{3}{8}$-inch-diameter pine plugs for the screw holes and glue in place.
10. Cut a piece of pine for the bottom tray (E).
11. Sand all surfaces of all wood pieces. Apply two coats of clear varnish for the finish.

Design Qualities of Some Popular Indoor Plants

PLANT NAME	COLOR				TEXTURE			FORM		
	Flowering	Brightly colored foliage	White or yellow markings	All-green foliage	Lacy, fine-leaved plants	Medium-leaved plants	Bold, large-leaved plants	Upright	Spreading	Weeping, trailing
Aglaonema commutatum 'Treubii' (Chinese evergreen)			X			X			X	
Aglaonema modestum (Chinese evergreen)				X		X			X	
Aphelandra squarrosa 'Dania' (zebra plant)			X			X			X	
Araucaria heterophylla (Norfolk Island pine)				X	X			X		
Asparagus densiflorus 'Sprengeri' (asparagus fern)				X	X					X
Beaucarnea recurvata var. *intermedia* (ponytail palm)				X		X		X		
Brassaia actinophylla (schefflera, umbrella tree)				X		X		X		
Caladium × *hortulanum* (caladium)		X					X	X		
Carissa grandiflora (natal plum)	X			X			X	X		
Caryota mitis (clustered fishtail palm)				X	X			X		
Chamaedorea elegans (neanthe bella or parlor palm)				X	X			X		
Chamaedorea erumpens (bamboo palm)				X	X			X		
Chamaedorea seifrizii (reed palm)				X	X			X		
Chamaerops humilis (European fan palm)				X			X	X		
Chlorophytum comosum 'Variegatum' (variegated spider plant)			X			X				X
Chlorophytum comosum 'Vittatum' (spider plant)			X			X				X
Chrysalidocarpus lutescens (butterfly palm)				X	X			X		
Cibotium chamissoi (Hawaiian free fern)				X		X		X		
Cissus rhombifolia (grape ivy)				X		X				X
Codiaeum variegatum var. *pictum* (croton)		X					X	X		
Coffea arabica (coffee plant)				X		X		X		
Coleus blumei (coleus)		X				X		X		
Cordyline terminalis (Hawaiian ti plant)		X				X		X		
Crassula argentea (jade plant)				X		X			X	
Cycas circinalis (fern palm, sago palm)				X	X			X		
Cycas revoluta (Japanese sago palm)				X	X			X		
Cyrtomium falcatum (holly fern)				X		X			X	
Dieffenbachia amoena (dumb cane)			X				X	X		
Dieffenbachia maculata (spotted dumb cane)			X				X	X		
Dizygotheca elegantissima (false aralia)				X	X			X		
Dracaena deremensis 'Warneckii' (dracaena)			X			X		X		
Dracaena fragrans 'Massangeana' (corn plant)			X				X	X		
Dracaena marginata (dragon tree)				X		X		X		
Dracaena sanderana (Belgian evergreen)			X			X		X		
Dracaena surculosa (gold-dust dracaena)			X			X			X	
Epipremnum aureum (devil's ivy, golden pothos)			X			X				X
Fatsia japonica (Japanese aralia)				X			X		X	
Ficus benjamina (weeping fig)				X		X		X		

Design Qualities of Some Popular Indoor Plants

PLANT NAME	Flowering	Brightly colored foliage	White or yellow markings	All-green foliage	Lacy, fine-leaved plants	Medium-leaved plants	Bold, large-leaved plants	Upright	Spreading	Weeping, trailing
	COLOR				TEXTURE			FORM		
Ficus elastica (rubber plant)				X			X	X		
Ficus lyrata (fiddle-leaf fig)				X			X	X		
Ficus retusa (Indian laurel)				X		X		X		
Gardenia jasminoides (gardenia)	X			X		X			X	
Grevillea robusta (silk oak)				X	X			X		
Hedera helix (English ivy)				X		X				X
Howea forsterana (kentia palm)				X			X	X		
Impatiens wallerana (patience plant)	X			X		X			X	
Livistona australis (cabbage palm)				X			X	X		
Livistona chinensis (Chinese fan palm)				X			X	X		
Maranta leuconeura var. *erythroneura* (red prayer plant)		X				X			X	
Maranta leuconeura var. *kerchoviana* (prayer plant, rabbit's foot)				X		X			X	
Monstera deliciosa (Swiss cheese plant)				X			X	X		
Nephrolepis exaltata 'Bostoniensis' (Boston fern)				X	X					X
Nephrolepis exaltata 'Fluffy Ruffles' (fluffy ruffles fern)				X	X					X
Pandanus veitchii (veitch screw pine)			X			X		X		
Pelargonium ×*hortorum* (geranium)	X	X				X			X	
Peperomia obtusifolia (baby rubber plant, blunt-leaf peperomia)				X		X			X	
Persea americana (avocado)				X			X	X		
Philodendron scandens subsp. *oxycardium* (heart-leaf philodendron)				X		X				X
Philodendron scandens subsp. *scandens* forma *micans* (velvet-leaf philodendron)				X		X				X
Philodendron selloum (saddle-leaf philodendron)				X			X	X	X	
Phoenix roebelenii (pygmy date palm)				X	X			X		
Pittosporum tobira (Australian laurel, mock orange)				X			X	X		
Plectranthus australis (Swedish ivy)				X		X				X
Podocarpus macrophyllus var. *maki* (southern yew)				X	X			X		
Polyscias balfouriana (balfour aralia)				X		X		X		
Polyscias balfouriana 'Marginata' (variegated balfour aralia)		X				X		X		
Polyscias filicifolia (fern-leaf aralia)				X		X		X		
Rhapis excelsa (lady palm)				X	X			X		
Senecio mikanioides (German ivy)				X		X				X
Spathiphyllum 'Clevelandii' (white anthurium)	X			X		X		X		
Spathiphyllum 'Mauna Loa' (white flag)				X		X			X	
Tradescantia albiflora 'Albovittata' (giant white inch plant)			X			X				X
Yucca elephantipes (spineless yucca)				X			X	X		

A House Plant Encyclopedia

This section contains concise, specific cultural information on 252 plants. The entries are organized alphabetically by genus name for quick reference.

Each entry begins with a brief paragraph describing the physical characteristics of the species that are most commonly grown or that are known to be reliable performers in the indoor garden.

Recipes for all-purpose potting soils and soil mixtures suitable for humus-lovers, succulents, and epiphytic plants can be found in chapter 6. For the more specific potting media called for in this section, consult the appropriate chapter (for example, the terrestrial and epiphytic bromeliad mixes can be found in chapter 14).

You will find in this section that many plants can be fed with all-purpose fertilizers or mild liquid fertilizers. For our purposes here, all-purpose fertilizers include various compost mixtures, compost tea, manure tea, and fish emulsion products. Mild liquid fertilizers include compost tea, manure tea, or fish emulsion diluted to ½ or ¼ of the usual strength. For information on organic plant foods, see chapter 7. The bone meal/clay pellets recommended for aquatic plants are discussed in chapter 24.

Temperature ranges and amounts of fertilizer and moisture recommended in this section are for periods of active growth unless otherwise noted. Special needs of plants during dormancy are mentioned under the Seasonal Care heading.

Propagation techniques and control measures for the pests and diseases that may attack these plants are detailed in chapters 8 and 9 respectively.

Opposite, blossom of a Camellia *hybrid.*

Ab–Ac

ABUTILON
Chinese lantern, flowering maple

150 species of shrublike plants make up this genus, with several species suited to indoor culture. Bell-shaped flowers hang gracefully from slender stalks in shades of white, yellow, orange, or purple, and appear in spring through autumn. Large plants, *Abutilon* require ample space and cutting back in spring to retain a nice bushy form. Flowers and slender branches are best displayed in hanging baskets or trained along a pole.

A. hybridum, Chinese lantern, features blooms patterned in red, yellow, or orange and speckled leaves.

A. megapotamicum 'Variegata' has green and yellow, arrow-shaped leaves; flowers are red and yellow.

A. pictum, also known as *A. striatum,* is a spreading shrub with leaves resembling those of the maple tree; yellow or orange flowers are marked with bright red veins.

Soil: All-purpose mix.
Temperature: Day, 68° to 72°F (20° to 22°C); night, 55° to 60°F (13° to 16°C).
Light: Winter, full sun from southern exposure; summer, partial shade with minimum of 4 hours full morning sun from eastern to southern exposure.
Moisture: Keep soil evenly moist. Mist daily. Humidity, 40% to 50%.
Feeding: Only when needed, to boost an undernourished plant, with low-nitrogen fertilizer.
Grooming: Remove yellow leaves. Pinch new shoots to promote bushy growth.
Propagation: By stem cuttings or seeds.
Pests and Diseases: Check for mealybugs, spider mites, scale, whiteflies.
Seasonal Care: No dormant period. In early spring, cut main stems back by half and trim lateral stems back to 3 or 4 inches (8 or 10 cm).

ACALYPHA
Chenille plant, copperleaf, three-seeded mercury

Containing about 430 species of flowering shrubs and trees, this genus graces both indoor and outdoor gardens with its distinctive flowers and brightly colored foliage. *Acalypha* are rapid growers, and require severe pruning to keep an attractive, bushy shape.

A. godseffiana grows to 20 inches (51 cm) tall; has bright green, yellow-edged leaves and greenish white flowers.

A. hispida, chenille plant, grows to 30 inches (76 cm) tall, sporting hairy green leaves and fuzzy, drooping spikes of tiny red blossoms.

A. wilkesiana grows to 30 inches (76 cm) tall; has coppery leaves with red and purple markings; blooms are red.

Abutilon hybridum

Acalypha hispida

Soil: All-purpose mix.
Temperature: Day, 70°F (21°C); night, 60° to 65°F (16° to 18°C).
Light: Winter, full sun from southern exposure; summer, partial shade from eastern to southern exposure for direct morning sun.
Moisture: Keep soil evenly moist. Mist twice daily. Spray only on leaves when plant is in bloom. Humidity, 45% to 50%.
Feeding: Monthly, with mild liquid fertilizer.
Grooming: Can be potbound. Pinch stems back for better bloom. To perk up old plant, prune back to 8 or 12 inches (20 or 30 cm) in early spring.
Propagation: By cuttings.
Pests and Diseases: Check for mealybugs, scale.
Seasonal Care: No dormant period, can be cultivated throughout the year.

ACHIMENES
Magic flower, monkey-faced pansy

26 species of flowering plants comprise this genus, which is a fibrous-rooted member of the Gesneriad family. Upright or trailing stems measure from 3 to 30 inches (8 to 76 cm) long, bearing deep green, heart-shaped leaves which may be covered with soft hairs or veined in red. The flowers, which appear throughout summer, are tubular, widening to 5 lobes, and are available in white, pink, red, yellow, orange, blue, lavender, and purple. After the blooming period is completed, the foliage dies back, and the plant enters a dormant period, with growth resuming in the spring. The attractive foliage and masses of blooms combine to make *Achimenes* a lovely choice for hanging baskets. Besides the species listed here, there are many cultivars available.

A. ehrenbergii produces lavender blooms resembling orchids, with white throats lined and spotted in orange and yellow.

A. erecta is covered with red- to rose-colored blooms; greenish red stems trail, bearing red-veined leaves.

A. grandiflora grows upright, bearing large purple flowers with purple-speckled white throats.

A. longiflora features trailing stems with hairy leaves; flowers range from pale to deep purple, with white throats.

Soil: All-purpose gesneriad mix.
Temperature: Day, 80° to 85°F (27° to 29°C); night, 62° to 65°F (17° to 18°C). Buds which turn brown and do not open indicate too much warmth.
Light: Bright light, with direct morning or winter sun, from eastern or southern exposure. Does well under artificial light, needing 14 to 16 light-hours daily.
Moisture: Once new growth appears in spring, and throughout flowering, keep soil evenly moist. If allowed to dry out completely after new growth appears, plant will enter dormancy. Mist daily. Humidity, 40% to 50%.
Feeding: Proportioned feeding of fish emulsion with each watering.
Grooming: Plant prefers to be potbound. Pinch back straggly stems to promote blooming and to maintain a nice, tidy shape.
Propagation: By rhizome division or tip cuttings.
Pests and Diseases: Check for aphids, *Botrytis* blight, cyclamen mites, mealybugs, powdery mildew,

***Achimenes* hybrid**

Adiantum raddianum

root or crown rot, scale, viruses, whiteflies.

Seasonal Care: After blooming is complete, decrease water and withhold fertilizer. Once leaves and floers have faded and dried, cut stems back to just above soil surface. Remove rhizomes from pot, store in bags of dry sand or peat moss in cool site, 60°F (16°C). Plant in early spring and resume regular schedule when new growth appears.

ADIANTUM
Maidenhair fern

Among the 200 species in this genus, several make good candidates for hanging baskets, where the fronds of a mature plant can arch attractively over the edges.

A. capillus-veneris has slender, erect fronds reaching 8 to 18 inches (20 to 46 cm) long.

A. caudatum grows to 36 inches (91 cm) tall; has dull, gray-green leaflets, with short brown hair on stalks.

A. hispidulum features stiff, hairy stalks with fronds 8 to 15 inches (20 to 38 cm) long.

A. pedatum has 12 inch (30 cm) tall, wiry, black, shiny stalks with leathery fronds measuring 18 inches (46 cm) wide.

A. raddianum sports dark stalks with light green leaflets; the feathery fronds measure 12 inches (30 cm) wide, 18 inches (46 cm) long.

A. tenerum grows to 4 feet (1.2 m) tall, has deeply notched, glossy green fronds.

Soil: Fern mix.
Temperature: Day, 80° to 85°F (27° to 29°C); night, 62° to 65°F (17° to 18°C).
Light: Provide subdued light from northern exposure, year-round. Does well under artificial light.

Moisture: Keep soil constantly moist, not soggy. Mist twice daily. Humidity, 50% to 80%.
Feeding: Every third or fourth watering, during growing season, with very mild all-purpose fertilizer.
Grooming: Repot when roots occupy ⅔ of pot space. Trim yellowed fronds close to soil level. Wipe fronds with a solution of 1 tablespoon (15 ml) white vinegar per 1 cup (236 ml) warm water. If spores are to be collected for propagation, do not wash underside of fronds when spores are maturing.
Propagation: By rhizome division. Plantlets on fronds may be set in rooting medium.
Pests and Diseases: Check for aphids, fungus gnats, mealybugs, scale, slugs, snails.
Seasonal Care: Plant may rest from fall through winter. Water sparingly; withhold fertilizer.

ADROMISCHUS
Calico hearts, leopard spots

A native of South Africa, this genus of succulents is well suited to artificial light situations. The flowers are insignificant, and they generally do not appear indoors.

A. clavifolius, called pretty pebbles, has gray-green, club-shaped leaves, flecked with red.

A. cooperii grows to 12 inches (30 cm) tall, with egg-shaped, light green leaves, speckled with dark green and tipped with purple.

A. cristatus, sea shells, has wedge-shaped, wavy-edged, light green leaves covered with fine hairs; grows to 10 inches (25 cm) tall. Greenish flowers appear on tiny red stems, measuring ½ inch (13 mm) long.

A. festivus, plover eggs, features egg-shaped, blue-green leaves spotted with reddish brown.

A. hemisphaericus has green frosted leaves and tubular green flowers.

A. maculatus sports clumps of thick, short-stemmed leaves that are gray-green hearts speckled with reddish brown.

Soil: Cactus/succulent mix.
Temperature: Day, 68° to 80°F (20° to 27°C); night, 50° to 70°F (10° to 21°C).
Light: Bright light from southern exposure, to enhance foliage color. Does well under artificial light, needing 16 light-hours daily. Fresh air circulation is important.
Moisture: Let soil become very dry between thorough waterings. Mist daily, not directly on plant. Humidity, 20% to 25%.
Feeding: Every 6 weeks, through spring and summer, with low-nitrogen, high-potassium fertilizer.
Grooming: Repot in early spring when roots occupy ½ of pot space.
Propagation: By offsets, leaf or tip cuttings. Avoid potting offsets in damp soil; don't water for 5 days after potting.
Pests and Diseases: Check for aphids, mealybugs, spider mites, scale. Also be alert for fungus disease.

Adromischus maculatus

Seasonal Care: Plant rests from fall to early spring. Place in cool, bright location where plant receives 5 hours of sunlight daily. Water only enough to keep soil barely moist; withhold fertilizer.

AECHMEA
Living-vase plant

150 species of epiphytic evergreen plants make up this genus of bromeliads. Vase-shaped, they feature a rosette of stiff, attractively colored leaves with spines. The striking flowers appear in fall or winter, rising on a spike from the rosette's center.

A. chantinii grows to 36 inches (91 cm), with dark green leaves edged in silver; flowers range from yellow to red with deep orange bracts.

A. fasciata has green or gray leaves with black spines and silver scales; light blue flowers change to rose as they mature. Plant grows to 24 inches (61 cm). Also called silver king.

A. fulgens var. *discolor* sports broad green leaves with tiny spines; blue flowers are followed by long-lasting, deep red berries.

Soil: Epiphyte mix.
Temperature: Day, 70°F (21°C); night, 60° to 65°F (16° to 18°C).
Light: Bright light, no direct sun, from southern exposure. Air circulation is important.
Moisture: For soft-leaved species, keep growing medium moist, not soggy. Keep stiff-leaved species moderately dry between waterings. Keep fresh water in cup during growing season. Mist several times a week. Humidity, 45% to 60%.
Feeding: Monthly, with mild all-purpose fertilizer diluted to ½ or ¼ strength. Avoid oil-based products such as fish emulsion. Spray on leaves, add to water in cup or apply to growing medium after watering; never fertilize a dry plant.
Grooming: Remove old, yellowed leaves and dried flowers and stalks. Change water in cup.
Propagation: By offsets or seeds.
Pests and Diseases: Check for scale.
Seasonal Care: Plant rests in late fall and winter. Place in cool site, 50° to 55°F (10° to 13°C). Keep growing medium barely moist and don't fill cup with water. Plant dies within 2 years after flowering.

AEONIUM
Pinwheel

This genus contains 38 species of succulents featuring a rosette structure. A spring bloomer, with pink, red, or yellow flowers, *Aeonium* is suitable as a windowsill or table plant.

A. arboreum grows to 36 inches (91 cm) tall; has a thick stem, green leaves, and yellow flowers.

A. decorum sports coppery red leaves and white flowers with dark pink markings; grows to 30 inches (76 cm) tall.

A. haworthii reaches 18 inches (46 cm) tall, with red-edged, blue-green leaves; blooms are pale yellow.

A. nobile has scarlet blooms and olive green leaves; grows to 24 inches (61 cm) tall.

A. tabuliforme reaches 20 inches (51 cm) tall, has yellow blooms and a rosette of small green leaves.

Soil: Cactus/succulent mix.

Aechmea fasciata

Aeonium arboreum

Temperature: Day, 45° to 60°F (7° to 16°C); night, 10° to 15° cooler.
Light: Bright light, no direct sun, from southern, southeastern or eastern exposure. Fresh air circulation is important.
Moisture: In spring and summer, let soil dry between thorough waterings. Overwatering causes plant to rot. Humidity, 10% to 20%.
Feeding: Every 6 weeks, during spring and summer growing period, with low-nitrogen, high-potassium fertilizer.
Grooming: Snug pot promotes top growth and reduces chance of root rot.
Propagation: Plant dies after blooming, so new plant must be grown each year. Use leaf cuttings or seeds. Allow cuttings to dry for 24 hours, place in peat and sand mixture, set in warm location.
Pests and Diseases: Check for aphids, mealybugs, spider mites, scale. Be alert for fungus disease.
Seasonal Care: Plant rests from fall to early spring. Place in cool, bright location where plant receives 5 hours of sunlight daily. Decrease water and withhold fertilizer.

AESCHYNANTHUS
Basket plant, lipstick plant

Numbering over 100 species, these epiphytic gesneriads are best dis-

played in hanging containers, to show off their 24 to 36 inch (61 to 91 cm) long trailing stems and tubular blooms.

A. longiflorus produces robust masses of deep red flowers.

A. marmoratus has green flowers with brown markings; waxy green leaves have deep purple undersides.

A. pulcher sports scarlet flowers with yellow throats; waxy leaves are light green.

A. radicans features clusters of bright red flowers, each with a purple-brown tubular calyx.

A. speciosus has rust-tipped orange blooms.

Soil: Mix 3 parts peat, 2 parts vermiculite, 1 part perlite.
Temperature: Day, at least 75°F (24°C); night, 60°F (16°C).
Light: Winter, full sun from southern exposure; summer, provide morning sun from southern to eastern exposure.
Moisture: Keep soil continuously moist. Mist daily. Humidity, 70%.
Feeding: Monthly, with mild liquid fertilizer.
Grooming: Repot only when roots occupy ¾ of pot space. After blooming, cut stems back to 6 inches (15 cm) to promote new growth. If new growth does not appear, reduce water and omit fertilizer.

Aeschynanthus pulcher

Propagation: By layering, stem cuttings in spring, or seeds.
Pests and Diseases: Check for leaf spot. Lower leaves that drop indicate drafts, too much or too little water, or root damage.
Seasonal Care: Plant has no dormant period, and given generous amounts of light and brief alternating periods of moisture and dryness, can bloom year-round. Most species, however, tend to flower sometime between spring and fall.

AGAPANTHUS
African lily, lily of the Nile

The 9 species of perennial plants in this genus have strap-shaped leaves and blooms similar to lilies. Commonly grown as tub or pot plants, they may be cultivated outdoors in warmer climates.

A. africanus grows to 36 inches (91 cm), with large umbels of light blue flowers.

A. campanulatus has crowded umbels of pale blue flowers; reaches 24 to 30 inches (61 to 76 cm) in height.

A. inapertus measures 18 inches (46 cm) tall; has compact heads of deep blue flowers.

A. orientalis features blue flowers; grows to 4 feet (1.2 m) tall.

Soil: All-purpose mix.
Temperature: Day, 68° to 72°F (20° to 22°C); night, 50° to 55°F (10° to 13°C).
Light: Winter, full sun from southern exposure; summer, morning sun and partial shade from eastern to southern exposure.
Moisture: Keep moist, never allowing soil to dry out. Mist twice daily. Humidity, 40% to 50%.
Feeding: Every 2 weeks during growing season, with mild liquid fertilizer.
Grooming: A potbound plant blooms more profusely; repot every 3 to 4 years. Remove dead stems and flower heads after blooming.

Propagation: By division of fleshy roots, or seeds.
Pests and Diseases: Check for mealybugs, scale.
Seasonal Care: Dormant period begins in late fall, when foliage dies. Store in cool location, 40° to 55°F (4° to 13°C). Water monthly, just enough to keep leaves from drying; withhold fertilizer.

AGAVE
Century plant

This genus contains over 300 species of succulents, featuring compact rosettes of pointed leaves and blooms borne on tall stems. Generally considered large tub plants, several smaller species are suitable for windowsill or tabletop. The common name refers to the time needed for

flowering—up to 50 years—although blooms may appear after 10 years. Plant dies after flowering.

A. americana grows to 5 feet (1.5 m), has yellow-edged green leaves; after 15 to 20 years the stalk bears yellow flowers.

A. filifera reaches 10 feet (3 m) tall; its shiny green leaves are etched with white.

A. parviflora is 4 inches (10 cm) tall, featuring leaves similar to *A. filifera*.

A. stricta has closely packed, slender, dark green leaves; grows to 14 inches (36 cm).

A. victoriae-reginae, 6 inches (15 cm) tall, has dark green leaves striped with white.

Soil: Cactus/succulent mix.
Temperature: Day, 68° to 80°F (20° to 27°C); night, 50° to 70°F (10° to 21°C).
Light: Bright, filtered sun from southern, southeastern, or eastern exposure. Fresh air circulation is important.

Moisture: In spring and summer, let soil dry between thorough waterings. Overwatering causes plant to rot. Mist daily around plant, not directly on it. Humidity, 20% to 25%.
Feeding: Every 6 weeks during growing season, with low-nitrogen, high-potassium fertilizer.
Grooming: Pot-on when roots occupy ½ of pot space or when foliage is crowded. Best done in spring.
Propagation: By suckers or seeds.
Pests and Diseases: Check for aphids, mealybugs, spider mites, scale. Also be alert for fungus disease.
Seasonal Care: Plant rests from fall to early spring. Place in cool, bright location where plant receives 5 hours of sunlight daily. Gradually reduce water, giving just enough to keep plant from shriveling; withhold fertilizer.

AGLAONEMA
Chinese evergreen

This genus contains 50 species of hardy foliage plants which can be grown in water, and adapt well to dimly lit areas.

A. commutatum has dark green leaves with silver markings and produces yellow or red berries; grows to 24 inches (61 cm).

A. costatum reaches 10 inches (25 cm) in height, with shiny green,

Agapanthus africanus

Agave victoriae-reginae

heart-shaped leaves bisected by a white vein and flecked with white.

A. crispum grows to 36 inches (91 cm) tall with a 36-inch (91 cm) spread, featuring gray leaves with light green edging and ribs.

A. modestum sports waxy, dark green foliage; reaches 24 to 36 inches (61 to 91 cm).

A. pictum, a dwarf variety, measures 12 inches (30 cm) tall; has silver-spotted, dark green, velvety leaves.

Soil: All-purpose mix, with good drainage.
Temperature: Day, 70° to 80°F (21° to 27°C); night, 62° to 69°F (17° to 21°C).
Light: Moderate to low light from northern to eastern exposure.
Moisture: Keep soil evenly moist. Mist twice daily. Humidity, 45% to 55%.
Feeding: Every 2 weeks during growing season, with mild all-purpose fertilizer.
Grooming: Repot when roots occupy ¾ of pot space. Remove withered or dried leaves. A tall plant can be trimmed by cutting growing ends.
Propagation: By cane cuttings or division of suckers.
Pests and Diseases: Check for aphids, mealybugs, spider mites, scale.
Seasonal Care: Growth slows during winter. Slowly reduce water, giving just enough to keep soil from drying out; withhold fertilizer.

ALLIUM
Garlic, chives

GARLIC

A. sativum is a hardy perennial usually grown as an annual. The bulb, made up of approximately 10 segments called cloves, is the part of the plant which lends its distinctive flavor and medicinal qualities to a wide variety of uses.

Soil: All-purpose mix, with good drainage.
Temperature: Tolerates wide range of household temperatures.
Light: Full sun from southern exposure.
Moisture: Keep soil evenly moist.
Feeding: A month after planting, work aged compost into topsoil. Every 2 weeks thereafter, feed with mild liquid fertilizer.
Grooming: Remove flowering stems. Cut a few shoots to use in cooking, for mild onion flavor.

Propagation: By seedlings or dried bulbs available in grocery stores. Separate bulbs into cloves; plant in late fall or early winter, with pointed end facing up.
Seasonal Care: Ready to harvest in about 8 months, when the leaves topple over and die. Store bulbs in mesh bags in dark, dry place at 60°F (16°C).

CHIVES

A. schoenoprasum is one of the easiest herbs to grow indoors. Kept on a sunny windowsill, it can be trimmed as needed for cooking. The plant is a perennial, with purple flowers.

Soil: Mix equal parts loam, sand, and well-rotted manure, with good drainage.
Temperature: Day, 68° to 72°F (20° to 22°C): night, 55° to 65°F (13° to 18°C).
Light: Full sun from southern exposure.
Moisture: Keep soil evenly moist. Humidity, 30%.
Feeding: Every 2 weeks, with mild liquid fertilizer.
Grooming: Trim plant to keep within pot.
Propagation: By division or seeds.

Aglaonema species

Allium sativum

Pests and Diseases: Generally healthy and free from infestation.
Seasonal Care: Set outdoors or in refrigerator for several weeks in winter to freeze roots and force new growth.

ALOE
Medicine plant

200 to 250 species of succulents comprise this genus, ranging in size from dwarf to 15-foot (4.5 m) treelike specimens. *Aloe* is a reluctant indoor bloomer, but when flowers appear, they range from pale pink to red to yellow.

A. arborescens, candelabra plant, features rosettes of blue-green, spiny leaves arranged along a woody stem.

A. aristata, lace aloe, grows to 6 inches (15 cm) tall, with a closely packed rosette of narrow gray-green leaves, 4 inches (10 cm) long; leaf edges bear white teeth, tips are bristled, undersides carry bands of white dots; flowers appear in summer.

A. barbadensis, medicine plant, often called *A. vera,* features fleshy green leaves in stemless clumps up to 24 inches (61 cm) tall, with white to red teeth on the edges; when cut, leaves ooze a sap which heals cuts and burns.

A. humilis, spider or crocodile jaws, sports stemless clumps of blue-green leaves with white teeth on the edges and white dots on the undersides; leaves curve upwards around 12 inch (30 cm) tall flower spike.

A. nobilis, golden-toothed aloe, features prickly-edged, pale to pea green leaves on a 24- to 36-inch (61 to 91 cm) stem.

A. variegata, partridge-breasted aloe, appears as 9 inch (23 cm) tall, stemless clumps; triangular leaves are blue-green, becoming coppery in strong light, with rough white edges and irregular pattern of white dots; flowers emerge on 12-inch (30 cm) spikes.

Soil: Cactus/succulent mix.
Temperature: Day, 68° to 75°F (20° to 24°C); night, 50° to 55°F (10° to 13°C).

Light: Bright, filtered light from southern, southeastern, or eastern exposure. Does well under artificial light, needing 12 to 16 light-hours daily. Air circulation is important.
Moisture: Let soil dry between thorough waterings. Avoid overwatering. Humidity, 20% to 25%.
Feeding: Monthly during growing season, with low-nitrogen, high-potassium fertilizer.
Grooming: Repot when roots occupy ½ of pot space. Mature plants may become top-heavy and topple over.
Propagation: By stem cuttings, suckers, or seeds.
Pests and Diseases: Check for aphids, mealybugs, spider mites, scale. Also be alert for fungus disease.
Seasonal Care: Plant rests during winter, except for *A. arborescens,* which rests in fall and grows in winter. Decrease exposure to light to 5 hours, site in cool location, 50°F (10°C). Give just enough water to keep leaves from withering; withhold fertilizer.

Allium schoenoprasum

Aloe barbadensis

ALTERNANTHERA
Copperleaf, Joseph's coat, parrotleaf

These attractive foliage plants, numbering 100 species, are most often used outdoors as border plants, but indoors with full sunlight they respond with luscious foliage colors.

A. ficoidea 'Amoena', parrotleaf, produces dense branches with reddish brown leaves covered with patterns of light red and orange.

A. ficoidea 'Bettzickiana', calico plant, features twisted, spoon-shaped, yellow to orange leaves.

A. ficoidea 'Versicolor', copperleaf, has coppery red foliage in plentiful sun, becoming green and bronze in low light; wavy edges are pink or white.

Soil: All-purpose mix.
Temperature: Day, 80° to 85°F (27° to 29°C); night, 62° to 65°F (17° to 18°C).
Light: Bright light, full sun from southern exposure.
Moisture: Keep soil evenly moist, not soggy. Humidity, 50%.
Feeding: Monthly, with mild liquid fertilizer.
Grooming: Repot yearly. Trim plant to avoid legginess. Pinch off flowers to promote lush foliage growth.

Propagation: By division or stem cuttings.
Pests and Diseases: Check for aphids, spider mites, whiteflies.
Seasonal Care: Plant rests slightly after blooming. Keep in cool location, 60°F (16°C). Gradually decrease water, keeping soil barely moist; feed half as frequently.

ANACHARIS, see *Elodea*

ANANAS
Pineapple

This bromeliad genus includes among its 9 species the edible pineapple. These terrestrial evergreen plants feature spiny leaves and produce pink, red, or white bracts on tall spikes in summer.

A. comosus has a 30- to 36-inch (76 to 91 cm) rosette of dark green leaves; blooms are red to light purple; mature plant produces edible fruit after flowering.

A. comosus 'Variegatus' features a rosette of ivory, green, and pink foliage; ornamental fruit is red, flowers are blue.

A. nanus, a dwarf, grows to 15 inches (38 cm), with green leaves and green fruit.

Soil: Terrestrial bromeliad mix.
Temperature: Day, 68° to 85°F (20° to 29°C); night, will tolerate drops to 60°F (16°C) or less.
Light: Full sun from southern exposure. Air circulation is important.
Moisture: Let soil dry slightly between thorough waterings. Mist daily. Humidity, 45% to 60%.
Feeding: Once a month, with mild liquid fertilizer. Avoid oil-based products such as fish emulsion. Apply to soil after watering.
Grooming: Remove dead and yellowing leaves.

Alternanthera ficoidea **'Bettzickiana'**

Ananas comosus

Propagation: By offsets, from leafy top of pineapple fruit (see chapter 14), or seeds.
Pests and Diseases: Check for scale.
Seasonal Care: Growth may slow in winter; reduce water. Plant dies within 2 years after flowering.

ANEMONE
Florists' anemone, lily of the field

120 species of flowering bulbs comprise this genus, which may be planted in early fall and forced, providing lovely cut flowers in early spring.

A. coronaria, florists' anemone, grows to 18 inches (46 cm) tall with lacy green foliage; flowers may be white, pink, red, purple, or blue.

A. × *hybrida,* Japanese anemone, measures up to 36 inches (91 cm) tall, and comes in a range of colors, from white to pink to rose.

Soil: All-purpose mix, with added lime.
Temperature: For 6 weeks, before growth appears, keep cool, 40° to

50°F (4° to 10°C). Once growth appears: day, 55° to 65°F (13° to 18°C); night, 40° to 50°F (4° to 10°C).
Light: Before growth appears, set in dark location. When active growth begins, gradually provide full sun from southern exposure.
Moisture: Water lightly until growth appears, then gradually increase amount, keeping soil evenly moist. Too much water causes rot.
Feeding: Weekly, when foliage has appeared, with mild liquid fertilizer.
Propagation: By division, offsets, or seeds.
Pests and Diseases: Check for aphids, slugs.
Seasonal Care: After blooming, allow foliage to die back. Plant is dormant during summer. Store pot in dark, cool location; keep soil barely moist. Resume watering and provide light when new growth appears.

ANETHUM
Dill

A. graveolens is an annual herb. Indoors it will rarely grow large enough to produce seed heads, but the feathery leaves are useful for flavoring a wide variety of dishes.

Soil: All-purpose mix, with good drainage.
Temperature: Day, 68° to 72°F (20° to 22°C); night, 55° to 65°F (13° to 18°C).
Light: Full sun from southern exposure.
Moisture: Keep soil evenly moist. Humidity, 30% or more.
Feeding: Every 2 weeks, with mild liquid fertilizer.
Grooming: Clip and use leaves as desired.
Propagation: By seeds.
Pests and Diseases: Generally healthy and free from infestation.
Seasonal Care: Discard plant after 1 season.

ANTHURIUM
Flamingo flower, painter's palette, tailflower

This genus consists of over 600 perennial species native to Central and South American tropical jungles. These plants are grown for their foliage and for their long-lasting flowers. The flower is made up of a bract with a spike growing from the center. This spike, the spadix, is densely packed with tiny flowers, and may be straight, curved, or spiral. *Anthurium* generally grows to 18 inches (46 cm) tall.

Anemone × hybrida

Anethum graveolens

An—Ap

A. andraeanum has heart-shaped green foliage with red, pink, coral, or white bracts and a yellow-tipped spadix.

A. bakeri produces dark green bracts with a yellow-green spadix.

A. crystallinum features heart-shaped, silver-veined, velvety green leaves.

A. scandens, a climber with dark green foliage, grows to 36 inches (91 cm).

A. scherzeranum bears brilliant red bracts with a yellow spadix.

A. warocqueanum, a climber, features long, oval, velvety leaves with pale green veins.

Soil: Mix equal parts potting soil and fir bark.
Temperature: Day, 72° to 85°F (22° to 29°C); night, 65° to 70°F (18° to 21°C).
Light: Bright to moderate light, with direct sun in winter, from eastern exposure.
Moisture: Keep soil evenly moist. Mist twice daily. Humidity, 80%.
Feeding: Every 2 weeks, with mild liquid fertilizer. Roots are easily burned by strong fertilizer.
Grooming: Repot when roots occupy ¾ of pot space. If new roots appear on surface of soil, cover with sphagnum moss.
Propagation: By division of suckers, or seeds.

Pests and Diseases: Check for mealybugs, spider mites, scale, whiteflies. Protect from drafts.

APHELANDRA
Zebra plant

The 80 species in this genus are admired for their distinctive, white-veined leaves and showy flower spikes with large bracts. These appear in spring through fall, lasting up to 6 weeks.

A. chamissoniana bears yellow flowers; leaves are 5 inches (13 cm) long.

A. squarrosa is adorned with pale yellow to orange blooms; leaves measure up to 12 inches (30 cm) long.

Soil: Humusy mix.
Temperature: Day, 70° to 75°F (21° to 24°C); night, 65° to 70°F (18° to 21°C).
Light: Bright light from eastern or western exposure.
Moisture: Keep soil evenly moist. Mist twice daily. Humidity, 65% to 75%.
Feeding: Every 2 weeks during growing season, with mild all-purpose fertilizer.
Grooming: In spring, prior to blooming, cut back previous season's growth, leaving one pair of leaves,

then repot. Do not remove roots appearing on stems and branches.
Propagation: By cuttings or seeds.
Pests and Diseases: Check for scale, whiteflies.
Seasonal Care: Plant rests following blooming. Keep soil barely moist; withhold fertilizer.

APONOGETON
Lace plant

This rooted aquatic plant is suitable for large aquaria or tub culture, where the feathery flowers and foliage lend a distinctive touch to aquascapes.

A. crispus bears white flowers on a 4- to 6-inch (10 to 15 cm) emersed spike; long, notched leaves are pale green.

A. madagascariensis, Madagascar lace plant, is noted for the lacy, open-vein pattern of the leaves, which grow to 12 inches (30 cm) long. Allow plenty of room.

Soil: Pot with rich mix of garden loam, sand, and bone meal. Top-dress with gravel, then submerge.
Temperature: 68° to 77°F (20° to 25°C).
Light: Indirect, filtered sunlight.

Anthurium scherzeranum

Aphelandra squarrosa

Does well under artificial light, needing 14 to 16 light-hours daily.
Water: Soft, slightly acid.
Feeding: Occasionally, with bone meal/clay pellets.
Grooming: Twice a month, replace ⅓ of water in tank; especially important for *A. madagascariensis*. Scrape algae from tank sides. Remove dead or discolored leaves.
Propagation: By rhizome division or runners.
Pests and Diseases: Check for snails. Rhizome rots easily.
Seasonal Care: Plant enters dormant period in midwinter. After foliage dies, remove bulb from water and store in moist soil or sphagnum moss at 60°F (16°C) to promote growth and blooming the following season.

APOROCACTUS
Rattail cactus

This genus contains 5 species of creeping, slender cacti, native to Mexico. These spiny plants with aerial roots must be kept some distance from other plants, since they tend to creep into other containers. The 1 inch (2.5 cm) thick stems may grow to 6 feet (1.8 m) and feature daytime blooms.

A. conzattii produces red flowers.

A. flagelliformis features bright pink to red flowers.

A. martianus sports deep rose blooms.

Soil: Cactus/succulent mix.
Temperature: Day, 70°F (21°C); night, 50° to 55°F (10° to 13°C).
Light: Bright, filtered sun from southern, southeastern, or eastern exposure. Fresh air circulation is important.
Moisture: Let soil dry between thorough waterings. Overwatering causes plant to rot. Humidity, 30% to 45%.
Feeding: Every 6 weeks during growing season, with low-nitrogen, high-potassium fertilizer.
Grooming: Repot after flowering.
Propagation: By stem cuttings or seeds.

Pests and Diseases: Check for aphids, mealybugs, spider mites, scale. Also be alert for fungus disease.
Seasonal Care: Plant rests from fall to early spring. Place in cool, bright location where plant receives 5 hours of sunlight daily. Decrease water; withhold fertilizer.

ARALIA, see *Dizygotheca* and *Fatsia*

ARAUCARIA
Norfolk Island pine

15 species of tall, evergreen, coniferous trees make up this genus. *A. heterophylla,* sometimes called *A. excelsa,* is the species commonly found indoors. An attractive pot plant, with a pyramidal shape composed of tiers of branches, it is a slow grower, eventually reaching 6 feet (1.8 m) in height with a 36-inch (91 cm) spread.

Soil: Mix 3 parts standard potting soil, 2 parts peat moss, and 1 part perlite.
Temperature: Prefers 50° to 60°F (10° to 16°C) range.

Aponogeton crispus

Aporocactus flagelliformis

Light: Moderate to low light from northern, eastern, or western exposure. Turn plant often to keep growth symmetrical. Air circulation is important.

Moisture: Keep soil moderately moist. Mist twice daily around plant, not directly on it. Humidity, 45% to 60%.

Feeding: Monthly, during growing season, with mild liquid fertilizer.

Grooming: Pot-on yearly, until 8- to 10-inch (20 to 25 cm) container is reached. Thereafter, repot every other year. Remove brown tips by pinching off.

Propagation: By air layering, cuttings from top shoots or from seeds.

Pests and Diseases: Check for aphids, mealybugs, spider mites, scale. Brown tips indicate improper watering or inadequate air circulation. Honey fungus can kill plant.

Seasonal Care: Plant rests during winter. Let soil dry slightly between thorough waterings; withhold fertilizer.

ARDISIA
Coralberry, spiceberry

250 species comprise this genus, of which *A. crenata* is the only one suitable for the indoors. Often mistakenly called *A. crispa*, this plant grows to 36 inches (91 cm) tall, producing clusters of star-shaped pink or white flowers in early summer. These flowers are replaced by clusters of long-lasting red berries, which along with the plant's topiary tree appearance make it a holiday favorite.

Soil: All-purpose mix.
Temperature: Day, 70°F (21°C); night, 50° to 55°F (10° to 13°C).
Light: Bright light from eastern or western exposure, with full sun in winter.

Moisture: Keep soil evenly moist. While flowering, mist around plant, not directly on blooms. Humidity, 50%.

Feeding: Weekly during growing season, with mild liquid fertilizer.

Grooming: Pot-on when roots occupy ½ of pot space. Pinch stems to prevent legginess. After berries have dried or fallen off, prune lightly.

Propagation: By air layering, cuttings, or seeds. Cuttings result in a fuller parent plant; air layering helps shape a leggy plant.

Pests and Diseases: Generally healthy and free from infestation.

Seasonal Care: Dormant period occurs in early spring. Cut plant back to 2 inches (5 cm); withhold water. When new shoots appear, remove all but 3 or 4 of the strongest ones. Repot in new soil or pot-on. Resume watering; 1 month after repotting, resume feeding.

ARECA, see *Chrysalidocarpus*

Araucaria heterophylla

Ardisia crenata

ARTEMISIA
Tarragon

A. dracunculus has gray-green, shiny leaves and panicles of tiny white flowers that appear in late summer. Tarragon is not the easiest of herbs to grow, but its mellow sweet flavor with just a hint of bitterness makes the effort worthwhile. Once the plant is established, it will thrive for several years, but after 2 or 3 seasons, the flavor fades. Leaves are at their best from summer to early fall.

Soil: All-purpose mix, with good drainage.
Temperature: Day, 68° to 72°F (20° to 22°C); night, 55° to 65°F (13° to 18°C).
Light: Moderate sun from southern exposure.
Moisture: Keep soil evenly moist. Humidity, 45% to 60%.
Feeding: Every 2 weeks with mild liquid fertilizer.
Grooming: Divide and repot every 2 years. To promote leaf growth, pinch off flower stems as soon as they appear.
Propagation: By division or tip cuttings.
Pests and Diseases: Generally healthy and free from infestation.

Seasonal Care: In early winter, must be chilled outdoors for several weeks, or set in refrigerator for a month. After chilling, cut back ⅔ of growth and repot in fresh soil.

ARUNDINARIA
Pygmy bamboo

This genus contains more than 30 species of clump-forming grasses. The commonly grown house plant, *A. pygmaea,* measures up to 12 inches (30 cm) in height, featuring slender, bright green stems with a slight purple cast and bright green leaves with toothed edges. With adequate water and fresh air, the pygmy bamboo can remain in the same pot for years, lending an oriental accent to room decor.

Soil: All-purpose mix, with good drainage.
Temperature: Day, 70°F (21°C); night , never below 50°F (10°C).
Light: Direct sun, from western or southern exposure. Air circulation is important.
Moisture: Keep soil evenly moist. 2 daily waterings may be necessary during growing season. Humidity, 45% to 60%.

Feeding: Monthly, during spring and summer, with a mild, high-nitrogen fertilizer.
Grooming: Stake tall plants. Clean foliage regularly.
Propagation: By division, in spring. First cut canes back to half the original height, leaving at least 2 internodes intact. Split clumps in halves or thirds.
Pests and Diseases: Check for slugs, snails. Leaf drop indicates too little water.

× ASCOCENDA

This orchid is a bigeneric hybrid, resulting from the crossing of *Asconcentrum* with the genus *Vanda.* There are now hundreds of ×*Ascocenda* hybrids available, all of which are epiphytic and monopodial. ×*Ascocenda* measures 4 to 20 inches (10 to 51 cm) tall, and is covered with medium to large flowers, resembling those of *Vanda.* A rapid grower, this orchid can flower several times a year if given excellent growing conditions. Its small size and profuse flowering habit make it an ideal selection for a home orchid collection. The following cultivars are among those that can be grown in-

Artemisia dracunculus

Arundinaria pygmaea

doors or in an intermediate to warm greenhouse:

A. 'Meda Arnold' bears flowers ranging from orange to red to lilac.

A. 'Tai Chai Beng' features clusters of blue to mauve blooms.

A. 'Yip Sum Wah' produces red, orange, or pink flowers, which may be mottled.

Soil: Osmunda fiber or orchid bark mix.
Temperature: Day, 70° to 85°F (21° to 29°C); night, 65°F (18°C).
Light: Bright light from southern exposure; shade during hottest part of the day. Does well under artificial light, needing 14 to 16 light-hours daily. Good circulation of fresh air.
Moisture: Keep growing medium evenly moist, never soggy. Mist frequently. Humidity, 40% to 65%.
Feeding: Every 3 weeks with all-purpose fertilizer, year-round.
Grooming: Repot when plant completely overcrowds pot or when growing medium has deteriorated. Best done in spring just prior to outset of active growth, when new roots are first visible.
Propagation: By detaching and potting plantlets.
Pests and Diseases: Check for bacterial, fungal, and viral infections, mealybugs, scale, slugs, snails, whiteflies.

Seasonal Care: Plant requires no rest period. Maintain regular feeding and watering schedule year-round, but decrease amounts slightly during cool, dark winter days when growth slows.

ASPARAGUS
Asparagus fern, emerald ripple

This genus comprises 100 to 300 species of perennial shrubs, woody vines, and herbaceous plants, including the popular spring vegetable. Many of these hardy species are adorned with graceful fernlike foliage and have fragrant flowers followed by berries.

A. asparagoides, used in florists' arrangements, has feathery, dark green foliage, orange flowers, and red berries.

A. densiflorus 'Myers' has 24 inch (61 cm) long, upright stems.

A. densiflorus 'Sprengeri' features light green, billowing needles and pink flowers.

A. setaceus has triangular branches bearing needles, pale pink blooms, and red or purple berries; older plants tend to climb.

Soil: All-purpose mix.
Temperature: Day, 70°F (21°C); night, 50° to 55°F (10° to 13°C).
Light: Bright to low light from any exposure, both indoors and out. Does well under artificial light, needing 14 to 16 light-hours daily.
Moisture: Keep soil evenly moist. Mist twice daily. Humidity, 30% to 35%.
Feeding: Weekly during growing season, with mild liquid fertilizer.
Grooming: Vigorous root growth may eventually displace soil and lift plant out of pot; pot-on when this occurs. For fuller effect, pinch centers of shoots. Pinch stems to prevent legginess.
Propagation: By division or seeds. After potting divisions, cut off stems at soil level.
Pests and Diseases: Check for aphids, fungus gnats, mealybugs, scale, slugs, snails.
Seasonal Care: Plant rests during winter. Keep soil barely moist; withhold fertilizer.

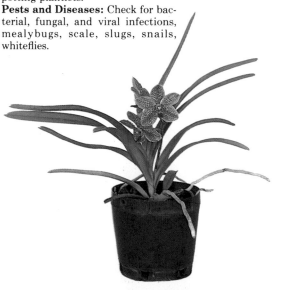

× *Ascocenda* **hybrid**

Asparagus densiflorus **'Sprengeri'**

ASPIDISTRA
Cast-iron plant

8 species of hardy foliage plants make up this genus. While it is known for its ability to tolerate some degree of neglect, *Aspidistra* responds well to a little attention.

A. elatior has shiny, dark green leaves measuring up to 36 inches (91 cm) long.

A. elatior 'Variegata' sports creamy white stripes running along the length of leaves.

Soil: All-purpose mix.
Temperature: Day, 70°F (21°C); night, 50° to 65°F (10° to 18°C).
Light: Moderate to low light from northern, eastern, or western exposure. Does well under artificial light, needing 14 light-hours daily.
Moisture: Keep soil barely moist, allowing top layer to dry slightly between waterings. Mist twice daily. Humidity, 30% to 35%.
Feeding: Every 2 weeks during growing season, with mild all-purpose fertilizer.
Grooming: Repot when roots occupy slightly more than ½ of pot space.
Propagation: By division.

Pests and Diseases: Check for scale.
Seasonal Care: Plant rests during winter. Gradually reduce water, never allowing soil to dry out completely; withhold fertilizer.

ASPLENIUM
Bird's nest fern, spleenwort

Several ferns among the 700 species in this genus are suitable for rock garden cultivation; the following do well indoors:

A. bulbiferum has 24-inch (61 cm), feathery, divided fronds harboring small plantlets, hence the common name hen and chickens fern, or mother fern.

A. nidus, bird's nest fern, has glossy, bright green, sheathlike fronds rising from a black, hairlike center, resembling a bird's nest.

Soil: Fern mix, with good drainage.
Temperature: Day, 68° to 75°F (20° to 24°C); night, 50° to 60°F (10° to 16°C).
Light: Subdued light from northern exposure, year-round. Does well under artificial light, needing 14 to 16 light-hours daily.
Moisture: Keep soil constantly moist, not soggy. Avoid overwatering. Mist twice daily. Humidity, 50% to 80%.
Feeding: Every third or fourth watering during growing season, with mild liquid fertilizer.
Grooming: Repot when roots occupy over ¾ of pot space. Yellowed fronds should be trimmed close to soil level. Sponge fronds with a solution of 1 tablespoon (15 ml) white vinegar per 1 cup (236 ml) warm water. If spores are to be collected for propagation, do not wash undersides of fronds when spores are maturing.
Propagation: By spores or rooting plantlets found on base of older plant.
Pests and Diseases: Check for aphids, fungus gnats, mealybugs, scale, slugs, snails.
Seasonal Care: Plant may rest during fall and winter. Water sparingly; withhold fertilizer.

Aspidistra elatior

Asplenium nidus

ASTROPHYTUM
Bishop's cap, star cactus

This genus consists of 6 cacti species native to Mexico. These smooth, globular cacti have white-scaled bodies. Blooms appear singly or in numbers, and last up to 5 days.

A. asterias, silver dollar, measures 2 inches (5 cm) tall, 3 inches (8 cm) wide; has tufts of white on its body and produces yellow flowers, 2 inches (5 cm) wide.

A. myriostigma, bishop's cap, is spineless, growing to 32 inches (81 cm) wide; produces yellow flowers that measure 2 inches (5 cm) across.

A. ornatum, star cactus, grows 14 inches (36 cm) tall and 6 inches (15 cm) thick; slightly curved spines are yellow to brown; blooms are large and yellow.

Soil: Cactus/succulent mix.
Temperature: Day, 80° to 85°F (27° to 29°C); night, 62° to 65°F (17° to 18°C).
Light: Bright, filtered sun from southern, southeastern, or eastern exposure. *A. myriostigma* prefers a semishady locale. Fresh air circulation is important.
Moisture: Let soil dry between thorough waterings. Overwatering causes plant to rot. Humidity, 30% to 35%.
Feeding: Every 6 weeks during

growing season, with low-nitrogen, high-potassium fertilizer.
Grooming: Pot-on when plant overcrowds container.
Propagation: By offsets or seeds.
Pests and Diseases: Check for aphids, mealybugs, spider mites, scale. Also be alert for fungus disease.
Seasonal Care: Plant rests from fall to early spring. Place in cool, bright location where plant receives 5 hours of sunlight daily. Decrease water; withhold fertilizer.

AUCUBA
Gold dust tree

7 species of easy-to-grow, hardy shrubs comprise this genus. Suitable for cultivation in tubs, under ideal conditions these plants may reach 15 feet (4.5 m), although indoors a height of 5 feet (1.5 m) is common.

A. japonica has 7 inch (18 cm) long, dark green, glossy leaves; berries may be red, yellow, or white.

A. japonica 'Aureo-maculata' features dark green leaves with a central yellow spot.

A. japonica 'Variegata', gold dust tree, has yellow-spotted green leaves.

Soil: Mix 3 parts standard potting soil with 1 part perlite or sharp sand.
Temperature: Day, at least 70°F (21°C); night, 40° to 64°F (4° to 18°C).
Light: Provide bright indirect or curtain-filtered sun from eastern or western exposure.
Moisture: Keep barely moist, allowing soil to dry between waterings. Humidity, 30% to 35%.
Feeding: Every 2 weeks during growing season, with mild liquid fertilizer.
Grooming: To shape plant, prune hard before new growth appears.
Propagation: By cuttings or seeds.
Pests and Diseases: Check for aphids, mealybugs, mites, scale. Black spots on leaves indicate improper soil condition.
Seasonal Care: Plant rests during winter. Gradually decrease water,

Astrophytum ornatum

Aucuba japonica 'Variegata'

never allowing soil to dry out completely; withhold fertilizer.

BACOPA
Water hyssop

This rooted aquatic plant is commonly found in aquaria, where its branching stems tend to emerge from the water unless trimmed back regularly.

B. caroliniana, also known as *B. amplexicaulis,* has thick, bright green leaves on a sturdy, hair-covered stem; measures to 24 inches (61 cm) tall.

B. monnieri features fleshy, bright green, oval leaves on a hairy stem.

Soil: Layer of medium size aquarium gravel or coarse sand.
Temperature: 59° to 72°F (15° to 22°C).
Light: Indirect, filtered sunlight. Does well under artificial light, needing 14 to 16 light-hours daily.
Water: Slightly acid.
Feeding: Occasionally, with bone meal/clay pellets.
Grooming: Once a month, replace 1/3 of water in tank. Scrape algae

from tank sides. Remove dead or discolored leaves. Trim tall plant to keep within tank.
Propagation: By division or stem cuttings.
Pests and Diseases: Check for snails. Leaves of *B. monnieri* rot if temperature is too high.

BEAUCARNEA
Bottle palm, elephant foot tree, ponytail palm

Containing 6 species of hardy tree-like plants, this genus is related to the yucca. The swollen trunk at soil level gives rise to the nickname elephant foot. In its natural habitat, this plant may eventually attain a height of 30 feet (9 m), but 2 to 5 feet (0.6 to 1.5 m) is the usual range for house plants.

B. recurvata produces leaves up to 6 feet (1.8 m) long, 3/4 inch (19 mm) wide.

B. recurvata var. *intermedia,* the most common house plant, has leaves less than 36 inches (91 cm) long.

Soil: All-purpose mix, with good drainage.
Temperature: Day, 68° to 75°F (20° to 24°C); night, 50° to 60°F (10° to 16°C).
Light: Bright to moderate light, with direct sun, from eastern, western, or southern exposure.
Moisture: Let soil dry slightly between thorough waterings. Humidity, 40% to 45%.
Feeding: Every spring, with mild liquid fertilizer, for established plants only.
Grooming: Plant may thrive for years in a small container. Pot-on in spring when roots occupy 1/2 of pot space.
Propagation: By offsets or seeds.
Pests and Diseases: Check for mealybugs, spider mites, scale, slugs, whiteflies.
Seasonal Care: Plant rests from fall through early spring. Reduce water, keeping soil slightly moist.

BEGONIA

There are over 1,000 species of *Begonia,* and new hybrids appear daily. Most house plants are fibrous-rooted or rhizomatous, but tuberous varieties are also available. There are va-

Bacopa monnieri

Beaucarnea recurvata var. intermedia

rieties that flower year-round, shrubby varieties that bloom seasonally, and others that are grown primarily for their foliage.

FIBROUS-ROOTED OR RHIZOMATOUS BEGONIAS

B. masoniana, iron cross begonia, is a rhizomatous plant, difficult to raise, but a distinctive addition to any collection; green leaves bear striking brown markings; waxy white flowers appear in spring.

B. metallica, a fibrous-rooted variety, has broadly ovate, olive green leaves with silver hairs and red veins; pale pink blossoms appear in fall.

B. ×rex-cultorum, rex begonia, belonging to the rhizomatous group, is the most common foliage plant; leaves are patterned in green, red, purple, silver, and white, reaching to 18 inches (46 cm) in length.

B. scharffii, a fibrous-rooted plant, has large brown-green leaves with red veins and red undersides; pink flowers, opening from late summer to early fall, have noticeable red hairs.

B. ×semperflorens-cultorum, wax begonia, has many popular, everblooming hybrids. These are small, fibrous-rooted, bushy plants with lustrous green or bronze-tinted leaves, and flowers ranging from white to red.

Soil: All-purpose mix, with good drainage.
Temperature: Day, 65° to 72°F (18° to 22°C); night, 55° to 60°F (13° to 16°C).
Light: Flowering varieties need up to 4 hours direct sun daily; foliage varieties need bright, indirect light. All do well under artificial light, needing 14 light-hours daily.
Moisture: Let *B. ×semperflorens-cultorum* dry slightly between waterings; others should be kept evenly moist. Mist daily, not directly on blooms. *B. ×rex-cultorum* needs 50% to 60% humidity; others need 30% to 35% humidity.
Feeding: Weekly during growing season, with mild liquid fertilizer.
Grooming: Repot when roots occupy ½ of pot space. Pinch stems to encourage bushier plant. Remove faded blossoms and withered foliage immediately.
Propagation: By division, leaf cuttings, or seeds.
Pests and Diseases: Check for mealybugs, scale, slugs, whiteflies. Powdery mildew is a common problem if air is too damp and warm.
Seasonal Care: Plant may rest during winter. Keep cool, 50° to 60°F (10° to 16°C). Reduce water, letting soil dry slightly between waterings; withhold fertilizer.

TUBEROUS-ROOTED BEGONIAS

Although seen most often in the outdoor garden, tuberous begonias can be cultivated indoors as well. Artificial light is often needed to induce blooming. There are many hybrid cultivars available, and new ones appear every year.

B. ×tuberhybrida is a group of cultivars with erect or trailing growth; clusters of 2 or 3 flowers appear in summer, in shades of white, pink, red, yellow, or orange.

Soil: Mix 1 part standard potting soil and 2 parts peat moss, with added bone meal.
Temperature: Day, 65° to 72°F (18° to 22°C); night, 55° to 60°F (13° to 16°C).
Light: At least 4 hours of direct sun daily. Does well under artificial light, needing 16 to 18 light-hours daily.
Moisture: Keep soil evenly moist. Avoid wetting foliage to prevent mildew.
Feeding: Weekly during growing season, with mild liquid fertilizer.
Grooming: Repot in fresh soil every spring. Stake heavy plants.
Propagation: By division or leaf cuttings.
Pests and Diseases: Check for mealybugs, scale, slugs, whiteflies.

Begonia × semperflorens-cultorum

Begonia × tuberhybrida

Powdery mildew is a common problem in stale, damp, warm air.
Seasonal Care: Dormant period extends over the winter. Keep cool, 55°F (13°C). Reduce water gradually, withholding completely once leaves have yellowed; do not fertilize.

BELOPERONE, see *Justicia*

BILLBERGIA
Queen's tears, vase plant

This bromeliad genus includes 52 species of epiphytic evergreen plants. Stiff leaves are multicolored and form rosettes. The unusual tubular blooms, which last for several weeks, appear erect on a spike or droop gracefully.

B. amoena has glossy, green leaves; blooms are pale green or rose.

B. morelii features lilac petals with red sepals.

B. nutans, queen's tears, sports red bracts and green flowers with blue edges.

B. pyramidalis produces bright orange bracts and red blooms with violet tips.

B. saundersii, rainbow plant, features a low-growing rosette; leaves have red undersides, red spines, and white spots; blooms are green with blue tips.

Soil: Epiphytic bromeliad mix.
Temperature: Tolerates wide range of household temperatures.
Light: Filtered bright light, with 4 hours of direct sun in winter, from eastern or western exposure. Air circulation is important.
Moisture: Let soil dry moderately between thorough waterings. Keep fresh water in cup. Mist several times a week. Humidity, 45% to 60%.
Feeding: Monthly, with mild liquid fertilizer. Avoid oil-based products such as fish emulsion. Spray on leaves, add to water in cup or apply to growing medium after watering; never fertilize a dry plant.

Grooming: Remove old, yellowed leaves and dried flowers and stalks. Change water in cup.
Propagation: By offsets or seeds.
Pests and Diseases: Check for scale.
Seasonal Care: To lengthen life of flowers, do not fill cup with water while in bloom. Plant dies within 2 years after flowering.

BOUGAINVILLEA
Paper flower

14 species of shrubs and vinelike plants comprise this genus. The flowers, appearing from spring through fall, are overshadowed by the brilliant-colored, petallike bracts that surround them. Under proper conditions, these papery bracts are long lasting. Many cultivars are available.

B. glabra features bracts in shades of

Billbergia saundersii

Bougainvillea hybrid

purple to magenta or orange to yellow.

B. spectabilis has purple to brick red bracts.

Soil: Mix 2 parts standard potting soil, 2 parts vermiculite, 1 part sand, and 1 part peat moss.
Temperature: Day, 70° to 80°F (21° to 27°C); night, 60° to 65°F (16° to 18°C).
Light: Winter and summer, place in southern exposure to ensure plenty of sun.
Moisture: Keep soil evenly moist. Mist twice daily during growing season. Humidity, 45% to 50%.
Feeding: Once a week during growing season, with mild liquid fertilizer.
Grooming: Pot-on in early spring. Pinch off dead blooms to prolong blooming period. Trim back plant after flowering. Tips may be pinched to promote branching.
Propagation: By stem cuttings taken in spring.
Pests and Diseases: Check for mealybugs, scale.
Seasonal Care: Plant rests following blooming. Reduce water, giving just enough to keep soil from drying out; withhold fertilizer.

BRASSAIA
Schefflera, umbrella tree

This popular tub plant, *B. actinophylla,* can grow to 15 feet (4.5 m), but is usually kept smaller. The common name comes from shiny green leaflets which project like ribs of an umbrella from the ends of narrow stems. Commonly called schefflera because of an early misclassification, it is sometimes incorrectly referred to as *Schefflera actinophylla.* A large specimen may have small red flowers, but these are rarely seen in cultivation. Easy to care for, it can stand some degree of neglect.

Soil: All-purpose mix.
Temperature: Day, 60° to 70°F (16° to 21°C); night, 50° to 55°F (10° to 13°C).
Light: Bright light, no direct sun, from southern, eastern, or western exposure.
Moisture: Let soil dry slightly between thorough waterings. Mist twice daily. Humidity, 45% to 60%.
Feeding: Monthly during growing season, with mild liquid fertilizer.
Grooming: Repot when roots occupy ¾ of pot space. Remove withered leaves. Clean leaves regularly to remove dust.
Propagation: By air layering.
Pests and Diseases: Check for aphids, mealybugs, spider mites, scale. Blackened leaf tips are caused by soggy soil and cool temperature. Leaf drop indicates too cool a temperature.
Seasonal Care: Plant rests from fall through early spring. Keep at 55° to 60°F (13° to 16°C). Reduce water, giving just enough to keep soil from drying out; withhold fertilizer.

BRASSAVOLA

Suitable for the beginner because it is easily grown, this orchid blooms throughout the year, producing an abundance of long-lasting flowers which release a pleasant fragrance in the evening. This plant closely resembles the orchid genus *Laelia*, and requires the same basic culture as the genus *Cattleya. Brassavola* is a pseudobulbous epiphyte exhibiting sympodial growth habit. Most of the 15 species do well in an intermediate greenhouse and the following species are recommended for home culture:

Brassaia actinophylla   **Brassavola glauca**

B. glauca is a dwarf, stocky plant measuring 4 to 7 inches (10 to 18 cm) tall; 3 to 4 heavy-textured flowers are produced, ranging from olive green to white to pale lavender; large, heart-shaped lip is white or yellow with purple spot in the throat; blooms in spring.

B. nodosa, lady of the night, bears 1 to 5 small, greenish white flowers; heart-shaped lip is white; plant measures from 6 to 9 inches (15 to 23 cm) tall, and can grow erect or hang; blooms throughout the year, with peak period in fall.

Soil: Osmunda fiber or orchid bark mix. In a greenhouse, it can be grown on section of tree limb, barn board, cork bark, or slab of tree fern fiber, but in the home should be grown in pots.
Temperature: Day, 70° to 85°F (21° to 29°C); night 55°F (13°C).
Light: Bright light from southern exposure, year-round; shade from strong summer sun at midday. *B. nodosa* does well under artificial light, needing 12 to 16 light-hours daily. Good circulation of fresh air.
Moisture: Let growing medium approach dryness between thorough waterings. Mist frequently. Humidity, 50%.
Feeding: Proportioned feedings of all-purpose fertilizer with each watering while in active growth.
Grooming: Repot when plant completely overcrowds pot space or when growing medium has deteriorated. Best done prior to outset of active growth, when new roots are first visible.
Propagation: By division of pseudobulbs.
Pests and Diseases: Check for bacterial, fungal, and viral infections, mealybugs, scale, slugs, snails, whiteflies.
Seasonal Care: To promote formation of flower buds, plant requires rest prior to flowering. For 2 weeks after new growth has matured, give just enough water to prevent pseudobulbs from shriveling; withhold fertilizer.

BROWALLIA
Bush violet, sapphire flower

This bushy perennial is well suited to hanging baskets, where trailing branches can display their blue-green leaves and flowers resembling violets. Best treated as an annual, *Browallia* naturally flowers in spring and summer, but depending when seed is sown, may be made to bloom at any time. Of the 8 species in the genus, the following do well indoors:

B. americana grows to 24 inches (61 cm) tall; small violet flowers have a yellow eye.

B. speciosa 'Major', sapphire flower, features 2 inch (5 cm) wide, violet flowers with white throats; measures 24 inches (61 cm) tall.

B. viscosa resembles *B. americana,* grows to 12 inches (30 cm) tall.

Soil: All-purpose mix.
Temperature: Day, 65° to 70°F (18° to 21°C); night, 50° to 55°F (10° to 13°C).
Light: Direct sun from eastern, western, or southern exposure.
Moisture: Keep evenly moist, never allowing soil to dry completely. Mist daily. Humidity, 45% to 50%.
Feeding: Every 2 weeks while in bloom, with mild liquid fertilizer.
Grooming: Pot-on when roots occupy at least ¾ of pot space. Pinch new stem growth to keep bushy shape. Remove faded flowers to promote new blooms.
Propagation: By stem cuttings or seeds.
Pests and Diseases: Check for aphids, whiteflies.

BUXUS
Boxwood

This genus, containing 30 species of slow-growing trees, lends itself to use in terraria and dish gardens. *Buxus* may be readily trained to grow as foot-tall (30 cm) bonsai trees.

B. microphylla is a hardy shrub with glossy green leaves.

B. sempervirens sports dark green leaves with yellow margins.

Soil: All-purpose mix.
Temperature: Day, 68° to 75°F (20° to 24°C); night, 50° to 65°F (10° to 18°C).

Browallia speciosa 'Major'

Light: Bright to moderate light from eastern or western exposure.
Moisture: Let soil dry out between thorough waterings. Mist twice daily. Humidity, 50%.
Feeding: Monthly, with mild liquid fertilizer.
Grooming: Remove dead stems and leaves. To promote full shape, pinch centers of new growth.
Propagation: By stem cuttings.
Pests and Diseases: Check for aphids, mealybugs, spider mites, scale.

CABOMBA
Fanwort, water shield

This bunch-type aquatic plant has both floating and submersed leaves and may produce small flowers. An easy specimen to grow in the aquarium, it reproduces readily.

C. aquatica has ¾ inch (19 mm), floating leaves and finely feathered submersed leaves arranged in rosette fashion along a waving stem.

C. caroliniana, water shield, features fanlike, feathery, submersed leaves and yellow-white flowers which bloom above water level.

Soil: Layer of medium size aquarium gravel or coarse sand.
Temperature: 50° to 76°F (10° to 24°C).
Light: Bright to filtered sunlight. Does well under artificial light, needing 14 to 16 light-hours daily.
Water: Slightly acid; can adapt to hard water.
Feeding: Occasionally, with bone meal/clay pellets.
Grooming: Once a month, replace ⅓ of water in tank. Scrape algae from tank sides. Remove dead or discolored leaves. Pinch back to control legginess.
Propagation: By cuttings or division.
Pests and Diseases: Check for bacterial rot, snails.

CALADIUM
Mother-in-law plant

15 species of colorful foliage plants belong to this genus, with leaf colors ranging between white, silver, pink, red, and green.

C. bicolor has 14 inch (36 cm) long, 6½ inch (16 cm) wide red leaves, bordered in green.

C. ×*hortulanum* features leaves in various shades of red, white, and green.

C. humboldtii is a miniature plant; its light green leaves are splotched with white.

Soil: Humusy mix.
Temperature: Day, 72° to 80°F (22° to 27°C); night, 65° to 70°F (18° to 21°C).
Light: Bright to moderate light from eastern, southeastern, or western exposure. Give plant a quarter turn after each watering.
Moisture: Keep soil evenly moist. Mist twice daily. Humidity, 45% to 50%.
Feeding: Every 2 weeks during growing season, with mild liquid fertilizer.
Grooming: Cut off yellowing leaves at soil level.

Buxus sempervirens

Cabomba caroliniana

Propagation: By division of tuber clumps in spring. Place in warm site, 75° to 80°F (24° to 27°C).

Pests and Diseases: Generally healthy and free from infestation.

Seasonal Care: Withhold fertilizer in early fall; foliage will yellow and fall off within a month. Then remove soil and roots from tubers, cut off withered foliage tops and store tubers in shallow box of peat or sphagnum moss at 55° to 60°F (13° to 16°C). Water sparingly, keeping soil barely moist.

CALANTHE

Most of the 120 species of orchids comprising this genus are terrestrial, with several considered to be epiphytic. Similarly, some members of the genus have pseudobulbs, while others do not — but all are sympodial. These orchids grow from 12 to 24 inches (30 to 61 cm) tall and are suitable for light gardens. *Calanthe* may exhibit one of two different growth habits: the plant can be deciduous, losing its leaves in fall before the flowers appear in winter; or it can be evergreen, meaning it keeps its

leaves year-round and blooms in spring or summer. All species mentioned here are terrestrial pseudobulbous plants, and do well under intermediate greenhouse conditions. These are rather temperamental orchids and are not recommended for the beginner.

C. masuca is an evergreen plant, bearing 10 to 15 flowers on a stem; blooms appear in late summer, and are violet to lilac in color.

C. rosea bears large rose- to pink-colored flowers with oblong, flat lips; a spur extends horizontally from each flower; a deciduous plant that blooms in early summer.

C. sanderiana produces numerous lilac flowers with purple edges, arranged in racemes; lip is dark purple with a brown spur; an evergreen plant that blooms in early summer.

C. vestita, a deciduous plant, bears 6 to 12 flowers in each raceme throughout the winter; blooms are white with an orange-yellow lip and slender spur.

Soil: Orchid bark mix or 2 parts bark-based potting mix, 1 part coarse compost, and 1 part decayed, aged cow manure.

Temperature: Day, 65° to 70°F (18° to 21°C); night, 55° to 60°F (13° to 16°C). A 10°F (6°C) drop at night is necessary to initiate buds.

Light: Bright, filtered light from southern or eastern exposure, with direct sun in winter. Does well under artificial light, needing 14 light-hours daily. Good circulation of fresh air.

Moisture: Let growing medium dry out moderately between thorough waterings. Mist daily. Humidity, 40% to 60%.

Feeding: Twice a month during growing season, with mild, all-purpose fertilizer.

Grooming: Repot when plant completely overcrowds pot space, or when growing medium has deteriorated.

Propagation: By division of bulbs just as new growth is visible.

Pests and Diseases: Check for bacterial, fungal, and viral infections, mealybugs, scale, slugs, snails, whiteflies.

Seasonal Care: For deciduous species, when growth stops in fall, stop watering altogether, keeping plant dry and cool (50° to 60°F/ 10° to 16°C). Flower spike will appear at this time. Resume regular watering and feeding when new growth appears in late winter or spring. For evergreen species, growth slows following blooming. Reduce water, withhold fertilizer, keep at 60°F (16°C).

Caladium × hortulanum

Calanthe rosea

Ca—Ca

CALATHEA
Peacock plant

Several of the 150 species in this genus are confused at times with the prayer plant. Their multicolored leaves make *Calathea* an attractive house plant.

C. bachemiana has gray-green leaves with dark green spots and borders.

C. lancifolia sports two-tone leaves, light green on the topsides, spotted with dark green, and purple-red on the undersides.

C. makoyana has cream-colored or olive green leaves, edged and speckled with dark green; undersides are purple.

C. ornata 'Roseo-lineata' features dark green, ovate leaves with rosy red stripes curving between the main veins.

C. picturata 'Argentea', a dwarf, has silver leaves bordered in dark green with deep red undersides.

C. roseopicta sports dark green leaves with red midribs, red margins fading to silver, and purple undersides.

Soil: All-purpose mix.
Temperature: Day, 75° to 85°F (24° to 29°C); night, 60° to 70°F (16° to 21°C).
Light: Bright to moderate light from northern, eastern, or western exposure.
Moisture: Keep evenly moist, never allowing soil to become soggy or dry out. Mist twice daily. Humidity, 45% to 60%.
Feeding: Every 2 weeks during growing season, with mild liquid fertilizer.
Grooming: Repot each year in midsummer. Cut growing ends of tall plant.
Propagation: By division or leaf cuttings.
Pests and Diseases: Generally healthy and free from infestation.
Seasonal Care: Plant enters dormant period from fall through late winter. Reduce water, letting soil dry slightly between waterings; withhold fertilizer.

CALCEOLARIA
Pocketbook plant, slipperwort

500 species of annuals and perennials comprise this genus. The first common name is derived from the unusual pouch-shaped blooms, which appear in late winter or early spring.

C. crenatiflora grows to 30 inches (76 cm) tall, has 1 inch (2.5 cm) wide, yellow or red blooms with orange-brown spots.

C. multiflora features yellow, orange, bronze, and yellow-brown flowers spotted with purple or brown.

Soil: All-purpose mix.
Temperature: Day, 65° to 70°F (18° to 21°C); night, 50° to 55°F (10° to 13°C).
Light: Moderate to low light from northern or eastern exposure.
Moisture: Keep evenly moist, never allowing soil to dry out completely.

Calathea ornata 'Roseo-lineata'

Calceolaria crenatiflora

Mist twice daily, not directly on flowers. Humidity, 45%.

Feeding: Weekly when not in bloom, with mild liquid fertilizer.

Grooming: Pinch back stems to promote blooming.

Propagation: By cuttings or seeds.

Pests and Diseases: Check for aphids, spider mites, slugs, whiteflies.

Seasonal Care: Plant is kept for 1 season, then discarded after flowering.

CALENDULA
Field marigold, pot marigold

This genus, commonly used for borders and cut flowers, includes among its 15 species several that are suitable as pot plants and are easily cultivated in a cool greenhouse. The petals are used to flavor and color butter, and can be used in cooking as a substitute for saffron. *C. officinalis,* an annual, bears yellow to orange flowers and grows to 24 inches (61 cm) tall.

Soil: All-purpose mix, with good drainage.

Temperature: Day, 55° to 65°F

(13° to 18°C); night, 40° to 50°F (4° to 10°C).

Light: Full sun from southern or western exposure. Air circulation is necessary.

Moisture: Keep soil evenly moist, not soggy. Mist twice daily.

Feeding: Every 2 weeks, with mild liquid fertilizer.

Grooming: For larger blooms, pinch off all but one bud per branch. For many small blooms, allow buds to develop naturally.

Propagation: For summer blooms, sow seeds in early spring. For late spring blooms, sow seeds in fall.

Pests and Diseases: Check for mildew, spider mites, whiteflies.

Seasonal Care: Plant is kept for one season, then discarded after flowering.

CALLISIA
Striped inch plant

8 species of foliage plants native to tropical America make up this genus. The brilliant leaf coloring makes *Callisia* an attractive choice for hanging baskets.

C. elegans measures 24 inches (61

cm) tall; has 3 inch (8 cm) long, dark green leaves striped with white or silver, with dark purple undersides.

C. fragrans grows to 36 inches (91 cm); has 10 inch (25 cm) long, glossy green leaves with white or pale yellow stripes and fragrant blooms.

Soil: All-purpose mix.

Temperature: Day, 68° to 80°F (20° to 27°C); night, 55° to 68°F (13° to 20°C).

Light: Bright light, with 4 hours direct sun, from eastern or western exposure.

Moisture: Keep soil evenly moist. Mist twice daily. Humidity, 40% to 45%.

Feeding: Every 2 weeks during growing season, with mild liquid fertilizer.

Grooming: Each spring, prune back hard to reestablish plants.

Propagation: By division or stem cuttings.

Pests and Diseases: Check for mealybugs, mites, scale, slugs, whiteflies.

Seasonal Care: Plant rests from fall to spring. Keep soil barely moist; withhold fertilizer.

CAMELLIA

Containing 80 species of flowering shrubs and trees, this genus produces and maintains the best blooms in cool temperatures. The large, waxy, fragrant flowers appear singly

Calendula officinalis

Callisia elegans

or in a cluster, and may be white, pink, red, or variegated. *C. japonica* is the common indoor species, with 2,000 known cultivars. These may feature single or double flowers, with many variations of form and color.

Soil: All-purpose mix.
Temperature: Day, 64° to 68°F (18° to 20°C); night, 40° to 45°F (4° to 7°C).
Light: Bright, filtered light from eastern, western, or southern exposure.
Moisture: Keep soil moist. Mist twice daily. Humidity, 60% to 65%.
Feeding: Every 2 weeks during growing season, with mild liquid fertilizer.
Grooming: Repot in spring when roots occupy ¾ of pot space. For larger flowers, remove all but one

bud from cluster. Prune after flowering, before new leaf growth. To grow along a trellis, stake and loosely tie the main trunk.
Propagation: By layering or stem cuttings.
Pests and Diseases: Check for aphids, mealybugs, mites, scale. Dropping buds indicate improper temperature or watering.
Seasonal Care: Plant rests for 6 weeks after flowering. Give just enough water to keep soil from drying out; fertilize monthly.

CAMPANULA
Bellflower, star of Bethlehem

This genus comprises 300 species of prolific blooming plants, which are

especially attractive when trained along a trellis or displayed in hanging baskets. The following perennials are suited for indoor cultivation:

C. elatines sports 1½-inch (4 cm), pale bluish lavender to purple, star-shaped flowers.

C. fragilis bears purple flowers with white centers; leaves are shiny green.

C. isophylla features 1½-inch (4 cm) violet-blue or white flowers and small oval leaves.

C. poscharskyana bears lilac-blue flowers on 18-inch (46 cm) stems.

Soil: Humusy mix.
Temperature: Day and night, 50° to 65°F (10° to 18°C).
Light: Bright light from eastern, western, or southern exposure.
Moisture: Keep soil evenly moist. Mist lightly. Humidity, 30% to 40%.
Feeding: Every 2 weeks during growing season, with mild liquid fertilizer.
Grooming: Repot each spring. To encourage a full plant, pinch centers of young shoots. Remove fading flowers.
Propagation: By cuttings taken in spring or fall, or seeds.
Pests and Diseases: Check for mealybugs, scale, slugs, whiteflies.
Seasonal Care: After flowering,

Camellia hybrid

Campanula isophylla

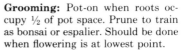

plant enters dormant stage, when it should be kept cool, 40° to 50°F (4° to 10°C). Trim stems back severely, even with top of pot. Keep soil barely moist; withhold fertilizer.

CAPSICUM
Red pepper plant

This genus contains 20 species of shrubby plants, grown for culinary or ornamental purposes. *C. annuum,* the common house plant, produces small, white flowers in summer, followed in winter by red fruits which last up to 12 weeks. This short-lived perennial is best treated as an annual, discarded after fruit shrivels.

Soil: All-purpose mix.
Temperature: Day, 70°F (21°C); night, 60° to 70°F (16° to 21°C).
Light: Full sun from southern exposure.
Moisture: Keep soil evenly moist. Mist daily. Humidity, 45% to 60%.
Feeding: Not necessary with plant grown for ornamental purposes.
Grooming: No pruning necessary.
Propagation: By seeds.
Pests and Diseases: Check for

whiteflies. Dropping fruit indicates too much warmth; dropping leaves indicate inadequate light. Clean foliage to prevent pest infestation.

CARISSA
Natal plum

Containing 35 species of evergreen vining shrubs, this genus includes specimens well suited for bonsai. Bearing thick, leathery leaves and glossy, fragrant flowers, edible fruit is a pleasant bonus.

C. bispinosa produces white flowers and ½ inch (12 mm) long red fruit.

C. grandiflora features 2 inch (5 cm) wide white flowers and red fruit, resembling cranberries, which make an excellent jelly.

Soil: All-purpose mix.
Temperature: Day, 70°F (21°C); night, 50° to 65°F (10° to 18°C).
Light: Bright light, with direct morning or winter sun, from eastern to southern exposure.
Moisture: Keep soil evenly moist. Mist twice daily. Humidity, 50%.
Feeding: Monthly, with mild liquid fertilizer.

Grooming: Pot-on when roots occupy ½ of pot space. Prune to train as bonsai or espalier. Should be done when flowering is at lowest point.
Propagation: By budding, layering, or stem cuttings.
Pests and Diseases: Check for aphids, mealybugs, scale, whiteflies.

CARYOTA
Dwarf fishtail palm

The resemblance between the divisions of the broad, deep green leaves of *Caryota* and the tail of a fish earned this palm its common name. Once the plant matures, it will bear green or purple flowers. *C. mitis* is the most common species.

Soil: All-purpose mix.
Temperature: Day, 68° to 75°F (20° to 24°C); night, 58° to 65°F (14° to 18°C).
Light: Bright light, no direct sun, from eastern or southern exposure. Does well under artificial light, needing 16 light-hours daily.

Capsicum annuum

Carissa grandiflora

Moisture: Keep soil constantly wet. Mist at least once daily, more often in warm weather. Humidity, 45% to 60%.

Feeding: Every 2 weeks during growing season, with mild liquid fertilizer.

Grooming: Prefers to be potbound; repot when roots occupy ¾ of pot space, in late winter or early spring.

Propagation: By division, suckers, or seeds.

Pests and Diseases: Check for mealybugs, spider mites, scale. Avoid drafts.

Seasonal Care: Plant rests in winter. Keep soil barely moist; withhold fertilizer.

CATTLEYA

The delicately scented flowers of this orchid are familiar sights in corsages.

The plant itself is relatively easy to grow and is suitable for beginners since it can tolerate a wide range of conditions. *Cattleya* is an epiphyte with a sympodial growth habit and pseudobulbs. The genus includes around 60 species, and there are thousands of hybrids. Once flower buds have formed, it takes from 1 to 2 months for them to open. The flowers appear pale and limp at first, but within 2 or 3 days the color deepens and the flower firms up. These blooms, with a trumpet-shaped, often ruffled lip, last from 10 to 14 days. *Cattleya* may be grown in an intermediate greenhouse, and any of the following species, as well as a wide range of hybrids, are suitable candidates for home orchid collections.

C. bowringiana features clusters of 10 to 25 glistening flowers on erect or arching stalks; petals and sepals are

pink or purple; lip is light pink on outside with golden yellow throat; blooms in late fall and winter.

C. gaskelliana is a small, compact plant measuring to 14 inches (36 cm), bearing 3 to 6 flowers; ruffled petals are medium to dark mauve; mauve lip is ruffled, with light yellow to orange throat; blooms in summer.

C. intermedia bears 4 to 10 flowers on a 10- to 15-inch (25 to 38 cm) plant; petals and sepals are pale pink; lip is white with dark purple markings and pale yellow throat; flowers in summer.

C. labiata measures 12 to 18 inches (30 to 46 cm) tall, bearing 2 to 5 flowers with ruffled petals; flower is rosy pink with dark purple lip, featuring deeply ruffled edge and yellow throat; blooms in fall.

C. mossiae, Easter orchid, bears 3 to 7 blooms on 12- to 18-inch (30 to 46 cm) plant; mauve petals are ruffled; showy, ruffled lip has orange throat with dark purple veining and mottling; flowers in spring.

C. percivaliana, Christmas cattleya, bears rosy lilac flowers with a dis-

Caryota mitis

Cattleya percivaliana

tinct scent; fringed purple lip has deep purple streaks and dark orange throat; blooms in winter.

Soil: Osmunda fiber or orchid bark mix. Can be grown in pots or hanging baskets or on slabs of tree fern fiber.
Temperature: Day, 70° to 85°F (21° to 29°C); night, 55°F (13°C).
Light: Bright light from southern exposure, year-round; shade from strong summer sun at midday. Does well under artificial light (especially hybrids), needing 12 to 16 light-hours daily. Good circulation of fresh air.
Moisture: Let growing medium approach dryness between thorough waterings. Mist frequently. Humidity, 50%.
Feeding: Proportioned feedings of all-purpose fertilizer with each watering while in active growth.
Grooming: Repot when plant completely overcrowds pot, or when growing medium has deteriorated. Best done just prior to outset of active growth, when new roots are first visible.
Propagation: Division of pseudobulbs when roots on newest growth are just starting, leaving at least 3 bulbs in each division.
Pests and Diseases: Check for bacterial, fungal, and viral infections, mealybugs, scale, slugs, snails, whiteflies.
Seasonal Care: Plant needs short to long rest period after flowers have opened. Once buds have swelled, reduce water and withhold fertilizer.

CEPHALOCEREUS
Old man cactus

This cactus, *C. senilis,* is barrel-shaped, with long white hair. It grows very slowly, but may eventually reach 30 inches (76 cm). Older plants will sometimes bear rose flowers.

Soil: Cactus/succulent mix.
Temperature: Day, 68° to 72°F (20° to 22°C); night, 55° to 65°F (13° to 18°C).
Light: Bright, filtered sun from southern, southeastern, or eastern exposure. Fresh air circulation is important.
Moisture: Let soil dry between thorough waterings. Overwatering causes plant to rot. Humidity, 30% to 45%.
Feeding: Once a year, in spring, with bone meal; for plants at least 1 year old.
Grooming: Pot-on every spring into slightly larger pot. Support for several days after repotting.
Pests and Diseases: Check for aphids, mealybugs, spider mites, scale. Also be alert for fungus disease.
Seasonal Care: Plant rests from

fall to early spring. Place in cool, bright location where plant receives 5 hours of sunlight daily. Decrease water.

CERATOPHYLLUM
Foxtail, hornwort

These hardy aquatic plants resist fish nibbling and prove to be long-lasting additions to an aquarium, where they may float just beneath the surface, or root on the bottom.

C. demersum, hornwort, features dense clusters of dark green, 1½ inch (4 cm) long leaves along the stem.

C. submersum, foxtail, has whorls of light green leaves fanning out along the stem.

Soil: Layer of medium size aquarium gravel or coarse sand.
Temperature: 50° to 80°F (10° to 27°C).
Light: Indirect, filtered sunlight. Does well under artificial light, needing 14 to 16 light-hours daily.
Water: Slightly acid; can adapt to hard water.
Feeding: When rooted, occasionally with bone meal/clay pellets.

Cephalocereus senilis

Ceratophyllum demersum

Ce—Ce

Grooming: Once a month, replace ⅓ of water in tank. Scrape algae from tank sides. Remove dead or discolored leaves.
Propagation: By cuttings.
Pests and Diseases: Check for bacterial rot, snails.

CEREUS
Peruvian apple cactus

These cylindrical cacti feature from 6 to 9 ribs, and branch into a shrubby or treelike form. A rapid grower, *Cereus* can reach 36 inches (91 cm) tall and 6 inches (15 cm) wide within 5 years. A large, mature plant can bear funnel-shaped summer blooms. These fragrant flowers open at night and fade by morning.

The following species are recommended:

C. jamacaru is blue-green with notched ribs, bearing white hairs and yellow spines; white flowers measure to 12 inches (30 cm).

C. peruvianus, Peruvian apple cactus, carries brown or black spines; white flowers have a trace of brownish green.

Soil: Cactus/succulent mix.
Temperature: Day, 70°F (21°C); night, 60° to 70°F (16° to 21°C).
Light: Bright, filtered light from southern, southeastern, or eastern exposure. Fresh air circulation is important.
Moisture: Let soil dry between thorough waterings. Overwatering causes plant to rot. Humidity, 30% to 35%.
Feeding: Once a year, in spring, with bone meal.
Grooming: Pot-on into slightly larger pot, when plant crowds container.

Propagation: By stem cuttings or seeds.
Pests and Diseases: Check for aphids, mealybugs, spider mites, scale. Also be alert for fungus disease.
Seasonal Care: Plant rests from fall to early spring. Place in cool, bright location where plant receives 5 hours of sunlight daily. Water just enough to keep plant from shriveling.

CEROPEGIA
Rosary vine, string of hearts

This vine has small, heart-shaped, succulent leaves, often mottled green with purple undersides. The thin stems, growing from a tuberous base, may reach 36 inches (91 cm), and bear small, light purple or pink flowers. The common name rosary vine comes from the fleshy, round bublets that appear at intervals, like beads on a rosary. Of the 150 species in this genus, the following are found indoors:

C. debilis, needle vine, has very narrow green leaves with purple markings, and red flowers.

Cereus peruvianus

Ceropegia woodii

C. haygarthii, the wine-glass vine, is noted for its cream-colored flowers with maroon spots.

C. sandersonii, parachute plant, has mottled green leaves and green flowers.

C. woodii, the most commonly grown species, has dark green leaves marked with silver; flowers are pink outside and purple-brown inside.

Soil: Cactus/succulent mix.
Temperature: Day, 68° to 72°F (20° to 22°C); night, 50° to 55°F (10° to 13°C).
Light: Bright light, direct sun from eastern, western, or southern exposure.
Moisture: Let soil dry moderately between thorough waterings. Never allow soil to become soggy or dry out. Mist lightly. Humidity, 30%.
Feeding: Every 2 weeks during growing season, with mild liquid fertilizer.
Grooming: Repot in late winter, keeping in small pots. To avoid stringy appearance, cut back or pinch stems near soil line.
Propagation: By stem cuttings.
Pests and Diseases: Check for mealybugs, spider mites.
Seasonal Care: Plant rests during winter. Reduce water, never allowing soil to dry out completely; withhold fertilizer.

CHAMAEDOREA
Bamboo palm, parlor palm

These palms often have slender, canelike stems and showy, lacy fronds which tend to grow upward rather than out. Some varieties may reach 8 to 10 feet (2.4 to 3 m), but this takes a while since they grow very slowly.

C. cataractarum, a dwarf clustering species, has black fruits.

C. elegans, parlor palm, sometimes listed as collinia elegans or neanthe bella, has erect stems with dark green fronds and grows to 36 inches (91 cm). Small pale yellow flowers appear occasionally, followed by black fruit.

C. erumpens, bamboo palm, has clusters of slender stems and arching dark green fronds with broad, drooping leaflets. Grows to 10 feet (3 m) tall.

C. glaucifolia is a decorative palm with narrow, blue-green fronds.

C. seifrizii has clusters of erect stems and narrow, grasslike leaflets. It bears fragrant male flowers, and tolerates more sun than other *Chamaedorea* species.

Soil: All-purpose mix, with good drainage.
Temperature: Day, 70° to 75°F (21° to 24°C); night, 65° to 70°F (18° to 21°C).
Light: Low light from eastern exposure; keep out of direct sun.
Moisture: Keep soil evenly moist. Drying causes brown leaf tips. Mist frequently. Humidity, 40% to 50%.
Feeding: Every 2 weeks during growing season, with mild liquid fertilizer or fish emulsion diluted to ½ strength.
Grooming: Keep potbound; repot when roots occupy ¾ of pot space.
Propagation: By division or seeds.
Pests and Diseases: Check for spider mites. Plant suffers in cool, drafty location.
Seasonal Care: Plant rests during winter. Keep soil barely moist; withhold fertilizer.

CHLOROPHYTUM
Spider plant

Although there are over 100 species in this genus, only 1, *C. comosum,* is grown as a house plant. Varieties may have solid green or green and white, grasslike leaves. An attractive basket plant, white flowers on the cascading stems precede the formation of plantlets. Plants will tolerate a great deal of abuse and will adapt to almost any growing situation.

Soil: All-purpose mix.
Temperature: Day, 68° to 75°F (20° to 24°C); night, 60° to 68°F (16° to 20°C).

Chamaedorea elegans

Light: Bright to moderate light from any exposure. Does not need direct sun, and will adapt to an unshaded northern exposure. Does well under artificial light, needing 14 to 16 light-hours daily.
Moisture: Let soil dry slightly between thorough waterings. Mist frequently. Humidity, 45% to 60%.
Feeding: Weekly, with mild liquid fertilizer.
Grooming: Keep somewhat potbound; pot-on when roots occupy ½ of pot space. Trim brown tips with sharp scissors.
Propagation: By division or plantlets.
Pests and Diseases: Check for scale.

CHRYSALIDOCARPUS
Areca palm, butterfly palm

C. lutescens is the only species of palm in this genus grown indoors. Sometimes referred to as *Areca lutescens,* it has a cluster of yellow, canelike stems with arching fronds, and stiff, shiny, yellow-green leaflets. A slow grower, it generally reaches 5 feet (1.5 m) in height.

Soil: All-purpose mix, with good drainage.
Temperature: Day, 70° to 80°F (21° to 27°C); night, 58° to 65°F (14° to 18°C).
Light: Bright light, no direct sun, from eastern or western exposure.
Moisture: Keep soil evenly moist, not soggy. Mist daily, twice in warm weather. Humidity, 45% to 60%.
Feeding: Every 2 weeks during growing season, with mild liquid fertilizer.
Grooming: Older plant prefers to be potbound; repot when roots occupy ¾ of pot space. Wipe leaves with damp cloth to keep pores unclogged. Cut off any brown leaf tips.
Propagation: By division or seeds.
Pests and Diseases: Check for mealybugs, spider mites, scale. Avoid drafts.
Seasonal Care: Plant rests during winter. Keep soil barely moist; withhold fertilizer.

CHRYSANTHEMUM
Chrysanthemum, mum

This delightful garden flower is now being brought into the house to pro-vide winter blooms. Plant needs 12 to 14 hours of darkness over a period of 8 to 10 weeks to induce flowering. There are 100 to 200 species and many hybrids of the florists' chrysanthemum, *C.* ×*morifolium.*

Soil: All-purpose mix, with good drainage.
Temperature: Day, 60° to 65°F (16° to 18°C); night, 45° to 50°F (7° to 10°C).
Light: Full sun from southern exposure.
Moisture: Keep soil evenly moist. Mist daily. Humidity, 35% to 40%.
Feeding: Every 2 weeks during blooming and after repotting in spring, with mild liquid fertilizer.
Grooming: Repot every spring. Pinch plant to keep it bushy. Some tall varieties may need staking.
Propagation: By tip cuttings of new shoots in spring.
Pests and Diseases: Check for aphids, whiteflies. Cold, wet soil causes yellow leaves.
Seasonal Care: After blooming, cut stems back to 3 inches (7 cm). Reduce water slightly until new growth starts.

Chlorophytum comosum

Chrysalidocarpus lutescens

CISSUS
Grape ivy, kangaroo ivy

This genus includes 350 species of vines and shrubs. The following do well in hanging baskets or on trellises:

C. antarctica, kangaroo ivy, may reach 6 feet (1.8 m) tall, with large, shiny green leaves.

C. discolor, begonia treebine, is a tropical plant with velvety leaves resembling those of the Rex begonia.

C. incisa, marine ivy, features heavily toothed, fleshy leaves.

C. quadrangula is a climbing succulent with shiny green leaves.

C. rhombifolia, grape ivy, is the best known species, with oval, leathery, dark green leaves.

C. striata, miniature grape ivy, bears small, bronze-green leaves.

Soil: All-purpose mix.
Temperature: Day, 68° to 75°F (20° to 24°C); night, 60° to 65°F (16° to 18°C).
Light: Bright light from southern exposure in winter; eastern or western exposure the rest of the year. Does well under artificial light, needing 14 to 16 light-hours daily.
Moisture: Keep soil evenly moist. Mist frequently. Humidity, 40% to 45%.
Feeding: Every 2 weeks during growing season, with mild liquid fertilizer.
Grooming: Repot every few years or when roots occupy ½ of pot space. Pruning may be done in early spring.
Propagation: By stem cuttings.
Pests and Diseases: Check for spider mites. Overwatering or too much light may cause spotting on leaves.
Seasonal Care: Plant rests from fall to early spring. Reduce water, never allowing soil to dry out completely; withhold fertilizer.

× CITROFORTUNELLA
Calamondin

Citrus trees are becoming increasingly popular as house plants. They grow from 2 to 15 feet (0.6 to 4.5 m) tall, depending on the variety, with shiny, oval, evergreen leaves. The calamondin, a cross between *Citrus* species and *Fortunella* species, is probably the best house plant, but several species in the closely related genus *Citrus* are also grown, such as *C. aurantiifolia* (lime), *C. aurantium* (sour orange), *C. limon* (lemon), *C. sinensis* (sweet orange), and *C. ×limonia* (otaheite orange).

Soil: Slightly acid all-purpose mix.
Temperature: Day, 69° to 72°F (21° to 22°C); night, 50° to 55°F (10° to 13°C).
Light: Full sun from southern exposure.
Moisture: Keep soil evenly moist. Mist daily. Humidity, 45% to 60%.
Feeding: Monthly, with mild liquid fertilizer.
Grooming: Repot when roots occupy ½ of pot space. Pinch back to keep plant from becoming straggly. Flowers must be pollinated with paintbrush to set fruit.
Propagation: By stem cuttings or seeds.
Pests and Diseases: Check for spider mites. Lack of soil acidity may cause yellow mottling of leaves.
Seasonal Care: Keep cool when growth slows, 50° to 60°F (10° to 16°C). Water only when soil is dry to the touch. Continue with light feedings.

Chrysanthemum × morifolium

Cissus rhombifolia

CI–CI

CLERODENDRUM
Bleeding heart, glory bower

400 species of shrubs, vines, and trees are found within this genus, but only a few are cultivated and used as house plants. These are fast growers which do best in hanging baskets or trained upright on supports, and should be pinched back frequently for attractive shape.

C. fragrans, Kashmir bouquet, has large, round, hairy leaves and dense clusters of rosy blooms which appear throughout the year.

C. thomsoniae features deep green, heart-shaped leaves with a pale vein pattern; clusters of 10 to 30 scarlet and white flowers appear in the spring.

Soil: All-purpose mix.
Temperature: Day, 70° to 75°F (21° to 24°C); night, 60° to 65°F (16° to 18°C).
Light: Bright light, filtered sun from eastern, western, or southern exposure.
Moisture: Keep soil evenly moist. Mist daily. Humidity, 50%. High hu-

midity is necessary during growing season for full flowering.
Feeding: Every 2 weeks during growing season, with mild liquid fertilizer.
Grooming: Repot when roots occupy ⅔ of pot space. Prune back old growth severely when growth appears, following dormant period. Flowers develop on new growth only.
Propagation: By stem cuttings in spring.
Pests and Diseases: Check for mealybugs, spider mites.
Seasonal Care: Plant is dormant throughout winter, when leaves may fall. Keep in cool site, 50° to 55°F (10° to 13°C). Water just enough to keep from drying out; withhold fertilizer.

CLIVIA
Kafir lily

Fragrant clusters of 10 to 15 blooms are eye catching as they rise on thick stems among spreading clumps of broad, waxy green leaves. The flowers resemble lilies, with red or yellow throats. They appear in the spring and are followed by red berries.

C. ×crytanthiflora, a hybrid cross of the following species, bears pale red flowers.

C. miniata features scarlet flowers with yellow interiors; leaves grow to 18 inches (46 cm) long.

C. nobilis sports red and yellow flowers with green tips; leaves are 12 inches (30 cm) long.

Soil: All-purpose mix.
Temperature: Day, 65° to 70°F (18° to 21°C); night, 60°F (16°C).
Light: Keep newly potted bulb in partial shade. Once growth appears, introduce bright, filtered light from eastern exposure.
Moisture: Water newly potted bulb moderately. When active growth begins, keep soil evenly moist. Mist daily when not in bloom. Humidity, 30% to 40%.
Feeding: Every 2 weeks during growing season, with mild liquid fertilizer.
Grooming: Blooms better when potbound; repot only when fleshy roots appear on surface, every 3 to 5 years. Remove red berries to promote blooming. Trim flower stalks after blooming.
Propagation: By division, offsets, or seeds.
Pests and Diseases: Check for spi-

×Citrofortunella mitis

Clerodendrum thomsoniae

der mites, root rot, scale.
Seasonal Care: Plant rests in early winter. Set in cool, dark location, 45° to 55°F (7° to 13°C). Keep soil nearly dry; withhold fertilizer until new flower stalks appear.

CODIAEUM
Croton

This genus has 6 species which have been crossed so often that it is very difficult to differentiate between them. The house plant, *C. variegatum* var. *pictum,* may eventually reach 5 feet (1.5 m). Leaves may be long, flat, wide, lobed, twisted, or crinkled. Foliage colors of the many cultivars include yellow, green, copper, red, pink, orange, brown, and white.

Soil: All-purpose mix.
Temperature: Day, 68° to 78°F (20° to 26°C); night, 60° to 68°F (16° to 20°C).
Light: Strong light, no direct midday sun, from eastern exposure to maintain bright foliage colors.
Moisture: Keep soil evenly moist. Mist daily. Humidity, 45% to 55%.
Feeding: Every 2 weeks during growing season, with mild liquid fertilizer.
Grooming: Prefers to be slightly potbound; repot when roots occupy

¾ of pot space. Wash foliage every few weeks.
Propagation: By air layering or cuttings.
Pests and Diseases: Check for mealybugs, spider mites, scale. Sudden temperature change causes rapid leaf fall.
Seasonal Care: Plant rests during winter. Reduce water, do not let soil dry out completely; withhold fertilizer.

COFFEA
Coffee plant

Although there are 40 species in this genus, only 1, *C. arabica,* is grown as a house plant. In outside cultivation, it may reach 15 feet (4.5 m), but indoors a maximum of 4 to 6 feet (1.2 to 1.8 m) is more common. Older plant will bear small white flowers in summer, followed by red berries containing the coffee beans. Leaves are a glossy, dark green.

Soil: All-purpose mix, with perlite or vermiculite in place of sand.
Temperature: Day, 70° to 75°F (21° to 24°C); night, 65° to 70°F (18° to 21°C).
Light: Bright, indirect light from

eastern or protected southern exposure.
Moisture: Keep soil evenly and thoroughly wet, not soggy. Mist frequently. Humidity, 60% to 70%.
Feeding: Monthly during growing season, with mild liquid fertilizer.
Grooming: Does not like to be potbound; repot in late winter with fresh soil. Pinch stems to keep plant from becoming straggly and to encourage better bloom. Wash leaves regularly to discourage pests; handle fragile leaves gently.
Propagation: By stem cuttings or seeds.
Pests and Diseases: Check for mealybugs, spider mites, scale. Direct sun will cause leaf burn.
Seasonal Care: Plant rests during winter. Reduce water, never allowing soil to dry out; feed monthly.

COLEUS
Flame nettle, painted leaf plant

This genus numbers 150 species of showy foliage plants, with *C. blumei*

Clivia miniata

Codiaeum hybrid

the common house plant. The soft leaves vary in size and shape, and appear in shades of red, yellow, orange, brown, and green. Spikes of tiny blue flowers may appear from time to time. A wide assortment of hybrids is available.

Soil: All-purpose mix, with good drainage.
Temperature: Day, 70°F (21°C); night, 55°F (13°C).
Light: Full sun from southern exposure to maintain bright colors, but will adapt to eastern or western exposure. Does well under artificial light, needing 14 light-hours daily.
Moisture: Keep soil moderately and evenly moist. Check daily, as plant may use a lot of water. Mist daily. Humidity, 40% to 45%.
Feeding: Every 2 weeks during growing season, with mild liquid fertilizer.
Grooming: Repot when roots occupy ½ of pot space. Pinch back frequently to prevent unsightly plant. Older plant with sparse, spindly foliage may be used for tip cuttings, then discarded. For fuller foliage, pinch off flower buds, which drain plant's energy.

Propagation: By herbaceous cuttings taken in spring or summer, or seeds.
Pests and Diseases: Check for mealybugs, spider mites, whiteflies. Older plant may develop root disease; discard plant. Overwatering causes rot.
Seasonal Care: Plant rests slightly during winter. Set in cool location, 55°F (13°C). Reduce water slightly; withhold fertilizer.

COLUMNEA

This gesneriad genus contains over 150 species which may be shrubby or vining in form. Considered at one time suited only to greenhouses, newer, hardier cultivars will thrive in the home environment with a little care, and do best in hanging baskets. Leaves are often hairy and range in size from ¾ inch (19 mm) to 6 inches (15 cm), on stems measuring up to 4 feet (1.2 m). Tubular flowers appear in yellow, red, orange, and pink. Besides the species listed below, many hybrids and cultivars are available.

C. arguta features trailing stems with large waxy leaves and salmon-red flowers.

C. gloriosa has brownish hairs covering small leaves and trailing stems; red flowers have yellow throats.

C. hirta sports scarlet-orange flowers and soft, hairy green leaves.

C. linearis grows upright and branches, bearing slender, shiny leaves and pink flowers with white hairs.

C. microphylla has copper-colored leaves covered with hairs; orange flowers bear yellow stripes; stems trail to 8 feet (2.4 m).

Soil: All-purpose gesneriad mix.
Temperature: Day, 65° to 85°F (18° to 29°C); night, 57° to 77°F (14° to 25°C).
Light: Bright light from eastern, western, or lightly shaded southern exposure with several hours of direct sun in winter. Does well under artificial light, needing 14 to 16 light-hours daily.
Moisture: Keep soil barely moist. Mist around plant but not directly

Coffea arabica

Coleus hybrid

on it, to avoid spotting leaves. Humidity, 70%.

Feeding: Every 2 weeks while blooming, with mild liquid fertilizer.
Grooming: Prefers to be potbound; repot only when roots occupy ¾ of pot space. Prune after flowering to encourage branching. Start a new plant every few years, as old growth tends to become woody and leafless.
Propagation: By tip cuttings taken immediately after flowering, or seeds.
Pests and Diseases: Check for mealybugs, spider mites. Soggy soil may cause root or crown rot.
Seasonal Care: To promote flowering, reduce water in fall, then withhold completely for a month before resuming normal schedule.

CORDYLINE
Hawaiian ti plant

This genus is related to, and closely resembles, *Dracaena*. They can be differentiated by their roots: *Cordyline* has white roots, while *Dracaena* has yellow. Mature plants may have white flowers, but blooming rarely occurs in house plants.

C. australis features narrow, leathery, bronze-green leaves.

C. banksii sports dark green leaves with yellow midribs.

C. stricta has narrow, red-green leaves.

C. terminalis, the most common species, has long, broad, tricolor leaves.

Soil: All-purpose mix, with good drainage.
Temperature: Day, 65° to 72°F (18° to 22°C); night, 62° to 68°F (17° to 20°C).
Light: Bright light from eastern or western exposure. Does well under artificial light, needing 14 to 16 light-hours daily.
Moisture: Let soil surface dry between thorough waterings. Mist daily. Humidity, 45% to 55%.
Feeding: Every 2 weeks during growing season, with mild liquid fertilizer. Top-dress with compost each spring.

Grooming: Prefers to be potbound; repot only when roots occupy ¾ of pot space. Remove withered leaves immediately. Wash foliage frequently to remove dust and prevent pest problems.
Propagation: By air layering or cane cuttings.
Pests and Diseases: Check for aphids, mealybugs, spider mites. Plant is very sensitive to drafts.
Seasonal Care: Plant rests in winter. Reduce water, never allowing soil to dry out completely; withhold fertilizer.

CORYPHANTHA
Pincushion cactus

These globular or cylindrical cacti grow to 12 inches (30 cm) tall and 4 inches (10 cm) thick. The genus, containing 60 species, resembles *Mammillaria,* but differs by producing blooms on the new growth instead of

Columnea 'Canary'

Cordyline terminalis

the old. Flowers appear in summer or fall.

C. bumamma is globelike, bearing brown spines and large yellow flowers.

C. clava has a cylindrical form; cone-shaped tubercles carry red, brown, or yellow spines; pale yellow flowers are tinged with red.

C. elephantidens is globular in shape, with a blue-green cast; features brown spines and white wool; produces large, rosy pink flowers.

Soil: Cactus/succulent mix.
Temperature: Day, 80° to 90°F (27° to 32°C); night, 60° to 70°F (16° to 21°C).
Light: Bright, filtered light from southern, southeastern, or eastern exposure. Fresh air circulation is important.
Moisture: Let soil dry between thorough waterings.
Feeding: Every 6 weeks while in bloom, with low-nitrogen, high-potassium fertilizer.
Grooming: Rarely needs repotting, as growth is very slow.
Propagation: By division or seeds.
Pests and Diseases: Check for aphids, mealybugs, spider mites, scale. Also be alert for fungus disease and rot.
Seasonal Care: Plant rests from fall to early spring. Place in cool,

bright location where plant receives 5 hours of sun daily. Give just enough water to keep plant from shriveling; withhold fertilizer.

COTYLEDON
Bear's toes, silver crown

35 species of succulent shrubs comprise this genus, growing from 12 to 36 inches (30 to 91 cm) tall. A mature plant can produce a cluster of 10 to 20 long-lasting flowers on a tall stalk in summer.

C. ladysmithiensis, bear's toes, grows erect and branching with triangular leaves covered with soft white hairs; flowers are brownish red.

C. orbiculata features gray-green, spoon-shaped leaves covered with a white powder and edged faintly in red.

C. undulata, silver crown, has a fan-like arrangement of leaves along a stiff stem; silvery leaves have white, ruffled top edges; pendent flowers are orange.

Soil: Cactus/succulent mix.
Temperature: Day, 68° to 72°F

(20° to 22°C); cooler at night.
Light: Bright, filtered light from southern, southeastern, or eastern exposure. Fresh air circulation is important.
Moisture: Let soil dry moderately between thorough waterings. Do not mist. Humidity, 30% to 35%.
Feeding: Once a year, in spring, with low-nitrogen, high-potassium fertilizer.
Grooming: Repot overcrowded plant in spring. Remove dried foliage and flowers.
Propagation: By tip cuttings or seeds.
Pests and Diseases: Check for mealybugs, spider mites. Moisture on leaves causes rot.
Seasonal Care: Plant rests from fall to early spring. Place in cool, bright location. Give just enough water to keep soil from drying out.

CRASSULA
Jade plant, silver dollar, string of buttons

The 300 species of succulents in this genus exhibit a wide range of ap-

Coryphantha elephantidens

Cotyledon ladysmithiensis

pearance from low growing to shrublike. Easy to care for, they grow from 18 to 30 inches (46 to 76 cm) tall.

C. arborescens, silver jade, has silvery leaves with red edges and a trunklike stem.

C. argentea, jade plant, produces thick, round, shiny leaves and has a treelike form; white flower heads may appear in winter.

C. falcata, propeller plant or scarlet paint brush, features densely arranged, sickle-shaped, gray-green leaves; clusters of orange-red flowers appear in summer.

C. lactea, tailor's patch, is a shrubby plant with spreading branches; oval leaves bear white dots along the edges; star-shaped white flowers appear in large clusters in winter.

C. lycopodioides, toy cypress, is noted for its 24 inch (61 cm) long, creeping stems, with densely overlapping scalelike leaves; small white flowers may appear.

C. perforata, string of buttons, grows to a shrubby 24 inches (61 cm); pairs

of pointed, oval leaves range along erect stems.

Soil: Mix equal parts garden loam and sand.
Temperature: Day, 68° to 72°F (20° to 22°C); night, 50° to 55°F (10° to 13°C).
Light: Bright light from eastern to western exposure. Does well under artificial light, needing 14 to 16 light-hours daily.
Moisture: Keep soil evenly moist, not soggy. Humidity, 30% to 35%.
Feeding: Every 3 weeks during growing season, with low-nitrogen, high-potassium fertilizer or bone meal.
Grooming: Prefers to be potbound; pot-on when roots occupy over ¾ of pot space. Clean foliage monthly.
Propagation: By stem or leaf cuttings or seeds.
Pests and Diseases: Check for aphids, mealybugs, spider mites, scale.
Seasonal Care: Plant rests during winter. Keep cool, 40°F (4°C). Reduce water; withhold fertilizer.

CROCUS

These harbingers of spring may be forced indoors and enjoyed during the winter months. The cup-shaped flowers come in shades of pink, purple, orange, and white, and are surrounded by grasslike leaves with a white stripe. Most plants available are cultivars of *C. chrysanthus* and *C. vernus.*

Soil: All-purpose mix.
Temperature: Before roots form, keep cool, 35° to 48°F (2° to 9°C). In 3 months, once roots have formed and plant is 2 inches (5 cm) tall, keep warm: day, 55° to 65°F (13° to 18°C); night, 40° to 50°F (4° to 10°C). When in bloom, keep cool for longer lasting flowers.
Light: Before roots form, site in dark location. Once roots have formed, gradually increase amount of light, eventually providing bright light, without direct sun, from eastern or southern exposure.
Moisture: Keep soil barely moist while roots are forming. Once foliage appears, keep evenly moist at all times. Mist daily around mature plant, not directly on blooms. Humidity, 35% to 40%.
Seasonal Care: After blooming, may be replanted outdoors. Or, once

Crassula argentea

***Crocus* hybrid**

foliage has yellowed, withhold water and store in cool, dark site; plant bulbs outdoors in fall. Blooms may appear in 1 to 2 years.

CROSSANDRA
Firecracker flower

This attractive shrubby plant has glossy, dark green leaves and tubular, orange to salmon-pink flowers. Blooms may be produced when plant is a mere 2 or 3 inches (5 to 8 cm) high, and appear on spikes from spring through fall. Although there are 50 species, only *C. infundibuliformis* is grown as a house plant, generally reaching 12 to 24 inches (30 to 61 cm) in height.

Soil: All-purpose mix, with good drainage.
Temperature: Day, 72° to 78°F (22° to 26°C); night, 60° to 68°F (16° to 20°C).
Light: Winter, direct sun from southern exposure; summer, direct morning sun from eastern exposure.
Moisture: Keep soil evenly moist. Mist daily. Humidity, 45% to 55%.
Feeding: Weekly during blooming, with mild liquid fertilizer.
Grooming: Repot in fresh soil every spring; pot-on only when roots completely crowd pot space. Prune in spring to maintain shape.
Propagation: By cuttings or seeds.
Pests and Diseases: Check for mealybugs, spider mites.
Seasonal Care: Plant rests slightly during winter. Reduce water, giving just enough to prevent soil from drying out; withhold fertilizer.

CRYPTANTHUS
Earth star

These beautiful terrestrial bromeliads have rippled, variegated leaves in a flat rosette. Leaves are often prickly, in shades of green, pink, copper, and bronze. Waxy white flowers appear on mature plant and signal the appearance of offsets. There are 20 species, with numerous hybrids available.

C. bivittatus sports variegations of salmon-pink and olive green; leaves measure up to 6 inches (15 cm).

C. bivittatus 'Minor' has green and cream to pink stripes; leaves are narrower and shorter.

C. bromelioides grows to 18 inches (46 cm) tall, bears white, rose, and green leaves.

C. 'It', a popular hybrid cultivar, has green leaves striped and edged with cream; blushes pink in good light.

C. 'Pink Starlite' is elegant and dainty, striped in cream, green, and pink.

C. zonatus has light green leaves crossbanded with light brown, grows 10 to 12 inches (25 to 30 cm) tall.

Soil: Terrestrial bromeliad mix.
Temperature: Day, 68° to 75°F (20° to 24°C); slightly cooler at night.
Light: Bright light, no direct sun, from eastern or western exposure for best color. Air circulation is important.
Moisture: Let soil dry moderately between thorough waterings. Humidity, 50% to 60%.
Feeding: Monthly, with mild liquid fertilizer. Avoid oil-based products such as fish emulsion. Spray on leaves or apply to soil after watering; never fertilize a dry plant.
Propagation: By offsets or seeds.
Pests and Diseases: Check for scale.
Seasonal Care: Growth may slow in winter. Set in cool site, 60°F (16°C), with full light. Reduce water.

CTENANTHE
Never-never plant

There are 9 species in this genus, with *C. oppenheimiana* grown as a

Crossandra infundibuliformis

Cryptanthus 'Pink Starlite'

house plant. Measuring up to 36 inches (91 cm) tall, it is prized for its decorative, oblong leaves which are carried on slender stalks. These leaves are green with regular silver-white markings between the veins and burgundy-red undersides.

Soil: All-purpose mix.
Temperature: Day, 70° to 75°F (21° to 24°C); slightly cooler at night.
Light: Bright light, no direct sun.
Moisture: Keep soil evenly moist. Mist frequently. Humidity, 50%.
Feeding: Every 2 weeks during growing season, with mild liquid fertilizer.
Grooming: Keep slightly potbound; repot every 3 or 4 years.
Propagation: By division in spring.
Pests and Diseases: Check for mealybugs, spider mites.
Seasonal Care: Plant rests during winter. Reduce water, never allowing soil to dry out completely; withhold fertilizer.

CUPHEA
Cigar plant, elfin herb

This genus has over 250 species, but only several are grown as house

plants. Blooming increases as plant matures, until it is literally covered with flowers.

C. hyssopifolia, elfin herb, is 6 to 8 inches (15 to 20 cm) tall with lavender bell-shaped flowers and needle-like leaves.

C. ignea, cigar plant, sometimes listed as *C. platycentra,* has fiery red, tubular flowers with black edges.

Soil: All-purpose mix.
Temperature: Day, 68° to 72°F (20° to 22°C); night, 60° to 65°F (16° to 18°C).
Light: Full sun from southern exposure.
Moisture: Keep soil evenly moist. Mist daily. Humidity, 35%.
Feeding: Every 2 weeks during growing season, with mild liquid fertilizer.
Grooming: Repot when roots take up ⅔ of pot space. Pinch stems to keep plant from becoming straggly.
Propagation: By cuttings or seeds.
Pests and Diseases: Check for mealybugs, spider mites, scale.
Seasonal Care: Reduce water while plant rests, never allowing soil to dry out completely; withhold fertilizer.

CYANOTIS
Pussy ears, teddy bear plant

40 to 50 species of foliage plants with climbing or creeping stems make up this genus, which resembles the wandering Jew. Generally low growing, the leaves and stems are covered with fine hairs, and appear somewhat fleshy.

C. kewensis, teddy bear plant, has deep green leaves and stems covered with short, reddish brown hairs; undersides of leaves are purple.

C. somaliensis, pussy ears, features shiny green foliage covered with long white hairs.

Soil: All-purpose mix.
Temperature: Day, 65° to 70°F (18° to 21°C); cooler at night.
Light: Full sun from eastern or western exposure.
Moisture: Keep soil evenly moist. Humidity, 35%.
Feeding: Monthly, with mild liquid fertilizer, year-round.
Grooming: Repot when roots occupy ⅔ of pot space. Pinch stems to encourage branching. Moisture on foliage causes spotting.

Ctenanthe oppenheimiana

Cuphea ignea

Cy—Cy

Propagation: By cuttings or seeds.
Pests and Diseases: Check for aphids, mealybugs.

CYCAS
Fern palm, sago palm

These palmlike foliage plants (not true palms) have rigid fronds growing from a thick trunk resembling a pine cone. A slow grower, *Cycas* may eventually reach 10 feet (3 m). Leaves are leathery, dark green and bruise very easily. Of the 20 species within the genus, *C. circinalis* and *C. revoluta* are most commonly available.

Soil: Mix 2 parts standard potting soil, 2 parts peat moss, and 1 part vermiculite.
Temperature: Day, 68° to 75°F (20° to 24°C); night, 60°F (16°C).
Light: Bright light, no direct sun, from northern, eastern, or western exposure.
Moisture: Let soil dry slightly between thorough waterings. Mist daily. Humidity, 65% to 70%.
Feeding: Monthly, with mild liquid fertilizer.
Grooming: Prefers to be potbound; do not repot until roots take up over ¾ of pot space. Work gently with roots that adhere to pot walls. Wash foliage regularly to remove dust.
Propagation: By offsets or seeds.
Pests and Diseases: Check for aphids, mealybugs, spider mites.

CYCLAMEN
Shooting star

Sometimes called the poor man's orchid or Persian violet, this tuberous plant has heart-shaped, dark green leaves and upright stems bearing waxy flowers with deeper shading around the eye. Of the 15 species in the genus, *C. persicum* is the common house plant, and new hybrids are continually introduced. Flowers appear midfall through winter, in shades of pink, red, white, purple, and salmon. *Cyclamen* prefers to be cool and will usually not survive average winter household conditions without special care.

Soil: Mix 2 parts standard potting soil and 1 part vermiculite.
Temperature: Keep cool, especially during flowering, 55° to 60°F (13° to 16°C) maximum.
Light: Bright light, no direct sun, from eastern exposure.
Moisture: Keep soil evenly moist during flowering. Mist daily, not directly on flowers. Humidity, 60% to 65%.
Feeding: Every 2 weeks during flowering, with mild liquid fertilizer.
Grooming: Repot each year after dormancy. Remove faded blossoms immediately.
Propagation: By separation of tubers, or seeds.
Pests and Diseases: Check for cyclamen mites, mealybugs, whiteflies.
Seasonal Care: When flowering stops in spring, move to cool, dark location. Allow leaves to die back, then remove all dead leaves and flowers. Keep barely moist, never allowing soil to dry out completely. Repot in late summer when corm begins to send up new shoots.

CYMBIDIUM

This well-known, popular orchid produces handsome, waxy flowers which are often featured in arrangements and corsages. The blooms are

Cyanotis kewensis

Cycas circinalis

long lasting even when cut, and remain attractive for 2 to 3 months on the plant. *Cymbidium* may be terrestrial or epiphytic, exhibiting sympodial growth and having pseudobulbs. There are thousands of hybrids derived from the 40 species within this genus, with the emphasis in breeding placed on miniature plants which are easy to grow as well as being prolific bloomers. These miniatures are sweetly scented and can bear up to 30 flowers in a single season; names of reliable, sturdy hybrids can be obtained from a commercial orchid grower. The following species are recommended for the home-grown collection, or they may be raised in an intermediate greenhouse.

C. finlaysonianum features hanging spikes laden with many flowers; petals and sepals are narrow, colored deep red with yellow edging; burgundy-colored lip has creamy yellow stripe down the center; blooms in summer.

C. lowianum bears 10 to 30 star-shaped flowers on an arching flower spike; petals and sepals are yellow-green, diffused with brown; lip is creamy white with red margin; flowers appear in spring.

Soil: Osmunda fiber or orchid bark mix. *C. finlaysonianum* should be grown in a hanging pot or in a slatted basket.

Temperature: Day, 75° to 80°F (24° to 27°C); night, 45° to 50°F (7° to 10°C).

Light: Bright light from northern, eastern, or full southern exposure indoors in winter. Needs lots of light to flower but should be protected from the heat of intense summer sun. Once buds begin to swell, gradually decrease amount of light to prevent bud drop; once flowering is finished, increase amount of light. Good circulation of fresh air.

Moisture: Let growing medium dry slightly between thorough waterings. Mist frequently, never allowing direct sun to strike moistened leaves. Humidity, 40% to 50%.

Feeding: For species plants, proportioned feedings of all-purpose fertilizer with each watering during active growth. Feed miniature hybrids only every 3 weeks during active growth to avoid burning leaf tips.

Grooming: Potbound plant blooms more vigorously. Repot only when plant completely overcrowds pot, or when growing medium has deteriorated. Best done at outset of active growth, when new roots are first visible. Stake and loosely tie arching flower spikes from time they measure 3 inches (8 cm) long until they lengthen enough to form a natural arch. Remove faded blooms immediately to avoid weakening plant.

Propagation: Division of pseudobulbs; single pseudobulb in each division is adequate.

Pests and Diseases: Check for bacterial, fungal, and viral infections, mealybugs, scale, slugs, snails, spider mites, whiteflies. "Honey" on flower spikes may attract ants.

Seasonal Care: As growth matures in late summer and fall, many plants require 2 to 3 weeks of low nighttime temperatures (40° to 50°F/4° to 10°C) in order to initiate spikes. Plant requires 2 periods of reduced watering; when new pseudobulb has matured and flower spikes are developing, and again when flowering is completed. Give only enough water to keep pseudobulb from shriveling. Rest period following flowering lasts 2 to 3 weeks; withhold fertilizer at this time. Because of light and temperature requirements, these plants do especially well summered outdoors in the partial shade of large trees. They can be left outdoors until just before the first frost.

Cyclamen persicum   **Cymbidium hybrid**

Cy–Cy

CYPERUS
Umbrella plant

This foliage plant can be grown in water culture or in a soil-filled tub, where it reaches from 3 to 4 feet (0.9 to 1.2 m) tall. Each slender stalk bears up to 20 narrow, grasslike leaves, and brown or green grasslike flower heads may appear in the crowns.

C. alternifolius, umbrella plant, features arching green leaves which radiate from the ends of stems like umbrella ribs.

C. papyrus, Egyptian paper plant, may eventually reach 8 feet (2.4 m) tall; dark green, triangular stems bear a few leaves on top with tufts of threadlike growths on which small flowers may appear.

Soil: All-purpose mix.
Temperature: Day, 68° to 72°F (20° to 22°C); night, 55° to 68°F (13° to 20°C).
Light: Bright light from eastern or western exposure, with direct sun in winter. Does well under artificial light, needing 14 light-hours daily.
Moisture: Keep thoroughly wet, not soggy. Mist frequently. Humidity, 45% to 60%.
Feeding: Every 2 weeks during growing season, with mild liquid fertilizer.
Grooming: Repot when roots occupy ½ of pot space. Needs frequent repotting due to rapid growth.
Propagation: By division or stem cuttings. Float cuttings in water; when plantlets sprout, plant each in moist sand for rooting.
Pests and Diseases: Check for mealybugs, scale, slugs, whiteflies.
Seasonal Care: Plant rests from fall through early spring. Keep soil barely moist; withhold fertilizer.

CYRTOMIUM
Holly fern

The stiff, dark green leaves on this fern resemble holly leaves. *C. falcatum* is the house plant species, which is extremely sturdy and will do well in less-than-ideal conditions.

Soil: Fern mix, with good drainage.
Temperature: Day, 68° to 72°F (20° to 22°C); night, 60° to 65°F (16° to 18°C).
Light: Does best in eastern exposure, but will adapt to poor light from northern exposure. Does well under artificial light.
Moisture: Let soil dry slightly between thorough waterings. Mist frequently. Humidity, 60% to 70%.
Feeding: Every third or fourth watering during growing season, with mild liquid fertilizer.
Grooming: Prefers to be potbound; repot when roots occupy over ¾ of pot space. Work gently with roots that adhere to pot walls. Cut off any aerial roots. Yellowed fronds should be trimmed close to soil level. To clean fronds, gently sponge with a solution of 1 tablespoon (15 ml) white vinegar per 1 cup (236 ml) warm water. If spores are to be collected for propagation, do not wash undersides of fronds when spores are maturing.
Propagation: By crown division or spores.
Pests and Diseases: Check for aphids, fungus gnats, mealybugs, scale, slugs, snails.
Seasonal Care: Plant may rest during fall and winter. Water sparingly; withhold fertilizer.

Cyperus alternifolius

Cyrtomium falcatum

DAVALLIA
Rabbit's foot fern

Davallia is noted for its hairy brown rhizome which resembles an animal's foot. The plant is suitable for hanging moss baskets and the rhizome will eventually cover the entire basket. An epiphyte, it sends down roots only to anchor the rhizome. The airy fronds appear at regular intervals along the rhizome. The most commonly grown species are *D. mariesii* and *D. fejeensis,* although others are sometimes available.

Soil: Fern mix, with good drainage.
Temperature: Day, 68° to 72°F (20° to 22°C); night, 60° to 65°F (16° to 18°C).
Light: Summer and winter, provide subdued light from northern or eastern exposure. Does well under artificial light, needing 14 to 16 light-hours daily.
Moisture: Let soil dry slightly between thorough waterings. Mist frequently. Humidity, 70%.
Feeding: Every third or fourth watering during growing season, with mild liquid fertilizer.
Grooming: Repot when rhizome becomes overcrowded. Yellowed fronds should be trimmed close to soil level. To clean fronds, gently sponge with a solution of 1 tablespoon (15 ml) white vinegar per 1 cup (236 ml) warm water.
Propagation: By sections of rhizome laid on top of rooting medium.
Pests and Diseases: Check for aphids, fungus gnats, mealybugs, scale, slugs, snails. Wilted foliage from over-dry soil cannot be revived.
Seasonal Care: Bring indoors before first frost. Plant may rest during fall and winter. Water sparingly; withhold fertilizer.

DENDROBIUM

Certain species in this genus are among the easiest orchids to grow and bring to flower. The blooms appear in a loose raceme or dense cluster. Some last only a week, but others remain in good shape on the plant for several months. This genus, numbering some 900 species, is mostly epiphytic with some semiterrestrial plants included, and also exhibits a sympodial growth habit with pseudobulbs. *Dendrobium* may be divided into 4 types: the deciduous plants which lose all their leaves prior to flowering; the deciduous plants which flower on leafless growths made the previous season; the warm-growing evergreen plants which retain their leaves year-round; and the evergreen types which require a cool, dry rest period. Each type requires different seasonal treatment. Not all *Dendrobium* are satisfactory for home growing, but the following species are those that are recommended for a home collection, and may also be grown in an intermediate or warm greenhouse:

D. crepidatum, a deciduous plant which sheds its leaves before blooming; bears racemes of 2 to 3 white flowers with lavender and yellow markings; blooms in late winter or early spring.

D densiflorum, evergreen, produces pendent spikes of many flowers; blooms are pale to golden yellow; lip is yellow to orange, with slightly hairy texture; blooms in spring.

D. farmeri, evergreen, has many flowers borne on a drooping spike, colored soft pink or white; lip is golden yellow, slightly hairy and tipped with pink; flowers appear in spring or early summer.

D. nobile, a deciduous plant which blooms on year-old, leafless canes; flowers are white with rosy tips in clusters of 2 or 3; white lip has pink rim and dark purple throat; flowers from spring to summer.

D. phalaenopsis, evergreen, grows to 36 inches (91 cm) and bears 5 to 15 flowers on long, arching sprays; blooms range from pink to white to red; lip is deep red with purple throat; flowers appear from spring to summer.

Soil: Osmunda fiber or orchid bark mix.
Temperature: Day, 70° to 80°F (21° to 27°C). Night: evergreen, 60°F (16°C); deciduous, 55° to 60°F (13° to 16°C).
Light: Bright light from southern exposure. Shade from direct summer sun at midday; can withstand several hours of direct sun in fall and winter. Smaller plants do well under artificial light, needing 12 to 16 light-hours daily. Good circulation of fresh air.
Moisture: Let growing medium be-

Davallia fejeensis

De—Di

come almost dry between thorough waterings, except for *D. phalaenopsis,* which should be kept evenly moist. Mist frequently, especially on aerial roots. Humidity, 50% to 70%; evergreen plants require higher humidity than deciduous plants.

Feeding: Deciduous plants, monthly during active growth with all-purpose fertilizer. Evergreen plants, twice a month during active growth with all-purpose fertilizer.

Grooming: Plant blooms more profusely when potbound. Repot only when plant crowds pot spare or when growing medium has deteriorated. Best done at outset of active growth, when new roots are first visible. *D. phalaenopsis* will need to be repotted more frequently than other plants, since its growing medium deteriorates more rapidly. It also may flower from the same pseudobulb for several years in a row; do not remove old pseudobulb without making certain that flowering is completed.

Propagation: By division of pseudobulbs. Deciduous plants produce plantlets which may be removed and potted, or cuttings of canelike stems may be taken.

Pests and Diseases: Check for bacterial, fungal, and viral infections, mealybugs, scale, slugs, snails, whiteflies.

Seasonal Care: Both deciduous and evergreen plants follow the same cycle of maturation of growth, rest, and flowering, but require different culture. Evergreen types that require a rest period will not flower if watered during this time; deciduous types will rot if watered when leafless and dormant. As growth of *D. crepidatum* matures, withhold fertilizer and water, misting just enough to keep canelike stems from shriveling. When blooms and new growth appear at same time in late spring, resume watering and feeding. *D. densiflorum* and *D. farmeri* require completely dry dormant period in order to bloom. When growth matures, withhold fertilizer and water, provide as much light as possible, and give cool (50°F/10°C) nights. When buds appear, resume watering, but then gradually reduce amount after flowering. Once active growth starts again, resume watering and feeding. *D. nobile* needs cold, dry dormancy to bloom; as growth matures, withhold water and fertilizer and provide cold (40° to 50°F/4° to 10°C) nights to initiate buds. Once buds appear, resume watering until flowering is finished, then gradually reduce amount until active growth has resumed. *D. phalaenopsis* is in active growth year-round under favorable conditions, and should be kept warm and evenly moist.

DIANTHUS
Carnation, pinks

There are some 300 species in this genus, which includes the carnation *(D. caryophyllus),* sweet William *(D. barbatus),* and common garden pinks, which are available in colors ranging from pink to red, purple, white, and yellow. Although best known in the outdoor garden, these plants can be grown indoors if given bright light and cool temperatures.

Soil: All-purpose mix.

Temperature: Day, 60° to 65°F (16° to 18°C); night, 55° to 60°F (13° to 16°C).

Light: Direct sun from southern exposure.

Moisture: Let soil dry slightly between thorough waterings. Humidity, 35%.

Feeding: Every 2 weeks, with mild liquid fertilizer.

Grooming: Does not like to be potbound; repot frequently. Pinch growing stems of *D. caryophyllus* to

Dendrobium phalaenopsis

Dianthus 'Magic Charms'

encourage branching. Remove all but crown buds to produce large single blooms.

Propagation: By cuttings.

Pests and Diseases: Check for spider mites. Plants are susceptible to blight and rust.

DIEFFENBACHIA
Dumb cane

This common house plant may reach 6 feet (1.9 m) tall, bearing broad, oblong leaves. Small flowers appear only rarely on mature plants. *Dieffenbachia* is poisonous and the sap in the leaves and stem will cause painful swelling of the mouth. Of the 30 species comprising the genus, the following are widely available:

D. amoena features blue-green leaves with white bands and blotches; grows to 5 feet (1.5 m).

D. ×bausei has pointed, yellow-green leaves with green edges and green and white spots; measures up to 18 inches (46 cm) tall.

D. bowmannii bears dark green leaves with bright yellow blotches; grows to 36 inches (91 cm).

D. maculata 'Baraquiniana' produces shiny green leaves with yellow or white markings; measures up to 4 feet (1.2 m).

D. seguine has dark green leaves with white bands and spots.

Soil: All-purpose mix.

Temperature: Day, 68° to 72°F (20° to 22°C); night, 60° to 65°F (16° to 18°C).

Light: Bright to low light from northern or eastern exposure.

Moisture: Let soil dry slightly between thorough waterings. Mist daily. Humidity, 45% to 50%.

Feeding: Monthly during growing season, with mild liquid fertilizer. Top-dress with compost in spring.

Grooming: Prefers to be potbound; repot when roots crowd pot. Remove withered bottom leaves as they appear. Wash foliage regularly to remove dust.

Propagation: By air layering or cane cuttings.

Pests and Diseases: Check for mealybugs, spider mites.

Seasonal Care: Plant rests during winter. Reduce water; withhold fertilizer.

DIONAEA
Venus' flytrap

This carnivorous plant is native to the eastern United States. It is best suited to the high humidity of a terrarium. There is only 1 species, *D. muscipula,* which bears small white flowers in late spring. Each half of the red- or green-lined trap has a row of hairlike extensions which hold insects captive when the trap snaps shut.

Soil: Live sphagnum moss or recommended carnivorous mix.

Temperature: Day, 60°F (16°C); night, 42° to 51°F (6° to 11°C).

Light: Large amount of bright light, no direct sun. Does well under artificial light. Air circulation is important.

Moisture: Keep growing medium constantly wet, not soggy. Mist daily. Humidity, 60% to 65%.

Feeding: When trap of fully mature plant appears pink, can be given small insects; light foliar spray of seaweed emulsion, diluted to $\frac{1}{10}$

Dieffenbachia amoena

Dionaea muscipula

Di—Dr

strength; or 1 drop gelatin-water solution. Avoid overfeeding.

Grooming: Every 1 to 2 months, add moistened tea leaves to live sphagnum moss to prevent fungus growth.

Propagation: By cuttings, division, or seeds.

Pests and Diseases: Check for aphids, fungus, mealybugs, scale.

Seasonal Care: Plant enters dormant period in winter when foliage dies back. Remove dried leaves. Reduce water; keep rhizomes in refrigerator for 2 to 3 months.

DIZYGOTHECA
False aralia

This genus comprises 15 species of shrubs and small trees, which can grow to 6 feet (1.8 m) indoors. Slender leafstalks radiate from the stem, and leaflets are arranged in a circular fashion at the tips. Often sold as *Aralia,* this plant is a slow grower and dislikes being moved.

D. elegantissima has a distinctive dark stem with creamy mottling; leaflets have toothed edges and are coppery colored on a young plant, changing to deep green-black as plant matures.

D. veitchii features green leaflets with waxy, toothed edges, copper-colored undersides and white mid-ribs.

Soil: All-purpose mix.

Temperature: Day, 70° to 75°F (21° to 24°C); night, 62° to 68°F (17° to 20°C).

Light: Bright filtered light, from northern or eastern exposure. Older plants will adapt to less light. Does well under artificial light, needing 14 to 16 light-hours daily.

Moisture: Keep soil constantly moist, year-round. Mist twice daily. Humidity, 45% to 60%.

Feeding: Monthly during growing season, with mild liquid fertilizer. Top-dress with compost in spring.

Grooming: Prefers to be potbound; repot when roots occupy more than ¾ of pot space, in early spring. Clean foliage monthly.

Propagation: By stem cuttings.

Pests and Diseases: Check for mealybugs, spider mites, scale. Lower leaves drop when plant is exposed to drafts.

Seasonal Care: Plant rests from fall through early spring. Keep in cool site, 55° to 60°F (13° to 16°C). Withhold fertilizer.

DRACAENA
Dragon tree

The 40 species of evergreen foliage plants within this genus vary widely in form and size. Most have green leaves with yellow or white vertical stripes. *Dracaena* often reach over 5 feet (1.5 m), but are slow growers. They will adapt to less-than-ideal conditions and are undemanding.

D. deremensis sports leathery green leaves, 2 inches (5 cm) wide and up to 24 inches (61 cm) long, which may be white striped.

D. fragrans 'Massangeana', corn plant, has 2 to 4 inch (5 to 10 cm) wide green leaves with broad, golden yellow stripes; sometimes bears clusters of fragrant yellow flowers.

D. hookerana bears 2 inch (5 cm) wide, thick, glossy, dark green leaves with translucent white edges.

D. marginata, dragon tree, has narrow green leaves edged in red.

Dizygotheca elegantissima

Dracaena marginata

D. reflexa 'Variegata', song of India, formerly listed as *Pleomele reflexa,* is a branching shrub with dense clusters of lance-shaped leaves; leaf margins are light green to yellow; growing tip angles off to right or left.

D. sanderana features narrow, dark green leaves, bordered in creamy white.

D. surculosa, gold dust dracaena, rises to a bushy 30 inches (76 cm); glossy oval leaves have random gold spots, and pale yellow flowers precede red berries.

Soil: All-purpose mix.
Temperature: Day, 68° to 72°F (20° to 22°C); cooler at night.
Light: Bright to moderate light, no direct sun, from eastern or western exposure. Will also adapt to strong northern light. Direct sun will cause leaves of *D. fragrans* 'Massangeana' to droop. Does well under artificial light, needing 14 to 16 light-hours daily.
Moisture: Keep soil evenly moist, not soggy. Let *D. reflexa* 'Variegata' dry slightly between waterings. Mist daily. Humidity, 45% to 50%.
Feeding: Monthly during growing season, with mild liquid fertilizer. Top-dress with compost in spring.
Grooming: Prefers to be potbound; pot-on when roots occupy over ¾ of pot space. Wash foliage regularly.
Propagation: By air layering, cuttings, or division.

Pests and Diseases: Check for mealybugs, scale, and spider mites.
Seasonal Care: Plant rests from early fall to early spring. Reduce water; withhold fertilizer.

DYCKIA
Miniature agave

This terrestrial bromeliad is a summer bloomer, bearing 15 to 20 waxy flowers on 12- to 24-inch (30 to 61 cm) stalks. Thick, spiny leaves form rosettes up to 16 inches (41 cm) across. Of the 103 species in this genus, the following are commonly cultivated indoors:

D. brevifolia has glossy, dark green leaves and bright orange flowers.

D. fosterana sports silver-gray leaves and golden flowers.

Soil: Terrestrial bromeliad mix.
Temperature: Day, 68°F (20°C) and up in summer, somewhat cooler in winter; night, 60° to 65°F (16° to 18°C).

Light: Full sun from southern exposure. Air circulation is important.
Moisture: Keep barely moist, allowing soil to dry moderately between waterings. Humidity, 35% or less.
Feeding: Monthly, with mild liquid fertilizer. Avoid oil-based products such as fish emulsion. Apply to soil after watering; never fertilize a dry plant.
Grooming: Remove dead or yellowed leaves and dried flowers and stalks.
Propagation: By offsets or seeds.
Pests and Diseases: Check for scale.
Seasonal Care: Growth slows in winter. Reduce water and frequency of feeding. Keep in cool site.

ECHEVERIA
Painted lady, plushplant

These succulents form compact rosettes of fleshy, almost stemless, leaves, measuring up to 9 inches (23 cm) across. They are often so symmetrical that they appear to be

Dyckia brevifolia

Echeveria 'Pulv-Oliver'

green flowers. Among the 100 species comprising the genus, dozens are available as house plants.

E. affinis has waxy, dark green leaves; red flowers appear in winter.

E. agavoides features very thick, pale green leaves with brown tips; spring blooms are red with yellow tips.

E. derenbergii sports smooth, pale green leaves with red edges; yellow or orange flowers appear in late winter.

E. elegans, Mexican snowball, has spoon-shaped, bluish leaves with pink tips; pale pink flowers bloom in summer.

E. gibbiflora features large, blue-green leaves with a bronze sheen, edged in red; scarlet flowers with yellow insides appear in late winter.

E. peacockii sports silver-blue leaves with red edges; red flowers appear in clusters.

E. pulvinata, chenille plant, produces silver-green leaves with white hairs; red flowers appear in winter.

E. 'Pulv-Oliver' features 2 inch (5 cm) long leaves arranged in a ro-sette with a dense covering of hair; flowers are deep red.

E. setosa, Mexican firecracker, has stemless, hairy green leaves with red tips; red flowers have yellow tips.

Soil: Cactus/succulent mix.
Temperature: Day, 70° to 85°F (21° to 29°C); night, 65° to 70°F (18° to 21°C).
Light: Full sun from southern exposure. Does well under artificial light, needing 16 light-hours daily.
Moisture: Let soil dry between thorough waterings. Overwatering causes plant to rot. Humidity, 20% to 25%.
Feeding: Every 6 weeks during growing season, with low-nitrogen, high-potassium fertilizer.
Grooming: Repot when plant crowds pot or roots occupy ⅔ of pot space.
Propagation: By offsets, or stem or leaf cuttings.
Pests and Diseases: Check for aphids, mealybugs, spider mites, scale. Also be alert for fungus disease.
Seasonal Care: Plant rests from fall to early spring. Place in cool, bright location where plant receives 5 hours of sunlight daily. Decrease water; withhold fertilizer.

ECHINOCACTUS
Golden barrel cactus

These barrel-shaped cacti usually are covered with golden spines, almost obscuring the green color of the plant itself. They are rapid growers and will reach 24 to 36 inches (61 to 91 cm) if given room. Yellow flowers appear only on large plants. The common house plant species is *E. grusonii.*

Soil: Cactus/succulent mix.
Temperature: Day, 68° to 72°F (20° to 22°C); night, 55° to 65°F (13° to 18°C).
Light: Bright, filtered sun from southern, southeastern, or eastern exposure. Fresh air circulation is important.
Moisture: Let soil dry completely between thorough waterings. Overwatering causes plant to rot. Humidity, 20% to 25%.
Feeding: Every 6 weeks during growing season, with low-nitrogen, high-potassium fertilizer.
Grooming: Repot when plant crowds pot. Roots are very fragile, so work gently.
Propagation: By offsets or seeds.
Pests and Diseases: Check for aphids, mealybugs, spider mites, scale. Also be alert for fungus disease.
Seasonal Care: Plant rests from fall to early spring. Place in cool, bright location where plant receives 5 hours of sunlight daily. Decrease water; withhold fertilizer.

ECHINOCEREUS
Hedgehog cactus, lace cactus, rainbow cactus

These spiny, globular cacti are natives of the western United States and Mexico. Plant blooms while still small, in spring or summer. The showy blooms measure up to 4 inches (10 cm) across and are long lasting. The following species are

Echinocactus grusonii

recommended out of the 35 making up this genus:

E. engelmannii grows to 10 inches (25 cm) tall; ribs are densely covered with white, yellow, or brown spines; flowers are red-purple.

E. pectinatus var. *rigidissimus* features symmetrical rows of pink, white, red, and brown spines; flowers are pink.

E. reichenbachii is covered with rosettes of yellow or white spines, and bears red and yellow flowers.

Soil: Cactus/succulent mix.
Temperature: Day, 68° to 72°F (20° to 22°C); night, 55° to 65°F (13° to 18°C).
Light: Bright, filtered sun from southern, southeastern, or eastern exposure. Fresh air circulation is important.
Moisture: Spring and summer, let soil dry slightly between thorough waterings. Overwatering causes plant to rot. Humidity, 30% to 45%.
Feeding: Every 6 weeks during growing season, with low-nitrogen, high-potassium fertilizer.
Grooming: Repot when plant crowds container.
Propagation: By offsets or seeds.
Pests and Diseases: Check for aphids, mealybugs, spider mites, scale. Also be alert for fungus disease.

Seasonal Care: Plant rests from fall to early spring. Place in cool, bright location where plant receives 5 hours of sunlight daily. Decrease water; withhold fertilizer.

ECHINODORUS
Cellophane plant, sword plant

This rooted aquatic plant makes a handsome addition to an aquarium and is a good oxygenator. Care must be taken to prevent the rampant growth from crowding out other plants.

E. berteroi, cellophane plant, has translucent oval leaves, 6 inches (15 cm) long.

E. intermedius, ruffled sword, has long, narrow, wavy leaves up to 4 inches (10 cm) long; inflorescence projects out of water, producing blue and white flowers along with new plants.

E. longistylis, melon sword, features broad, 10 inch (25 cm) long, dark green leaves with crinkled edges and prominent veins.

E. tenellus, Amazon sword plant, features dark green, slender leaves up to 4 inches (10 cm) long.

Soil: Pot larger specimens in garden loam mixed with bone meal. Top-dress with gravel, then submerge. Otherwise, set in layer of medium size aquarium gravel or coarse sand.
Temperature: 75° to 80°F (24° to 27°C).
Light: Moderate to bright sunlight. Does well under artificial light, needing 14 to 16 light-hours daily.
Water: Neutral to slightly alkaline.
Feeding: Occasionally, with bone meal/clay pellets.
Grooming: Once a month, replace 1/3 of water in tank. Scrape algae from tank sides. Thin plants regularly. Once leaves emerge from water, transfer to larger tank.
Propagation: By plantlets produced on old flower spikes, rhizome division, or runners.
Pests and Diseases: Check for bacterial rot, snails.

ECHINOPSIS
Easter lily cactus, sea urchin cactus

These globular cacti grow from 4 to 16 inches (10 to 41 cm) high and

Echinocereus pectinatus var. *rigidissimus*

Echinodorus species

Ec—Ep

have trumpet-shaped flowers in spring. They have been cultivated for over 100 years and most available today are hybrids.

E. calochlora has yellow spines, and bears showy white flowers.

E. eyriesii has a gray-green body with radial brown spines; its white flowers are sometimes flushed with purple.

E. multiplex, Easter lily cactus, has a dark green body with brown spines; bears fragrant rose flowers.

Soil: Cactus/succulent mix.
Temperature: Day, 75° to 85°F (24° to 29°C); night, 65° to 70°F (18° to 21°C).
Light: Full sun, with 4 hours direct sun daily, from southern exposure. Fresh air circulation is important.
Moisture: Let soil dry between waterings. Humidity, 30% to 35%.
Feeding: Every 6 weeks while in bloom, with low-nitrogen, high potassium fertilizer.
Grooming: Repot when plant crowds container.
Propagation: By offsets or seeds.
Pests and Diseases: Check for aphids, mealybugs, spider mites, scale. Also be alert for fungus disease.
Seasonal Care: Plant rests from fall to early spring. Place in cool, bright location where plant receives 5 hours of sun daily. Decrease water; withhold fertilizer.

ELODEA
Goldfish weed, water thyme, waterweed

Goldfish love to nibble on these bunch-type aquatic plants. Good oxygenators for aquaria, their rapid growth must be contained so they don't overcrowd their allotted space. Size ranges from 4 inches (10 cm) up to 36 inches (91 cm) tall. Also known as *Anacharis.*

E. callitrichoides features branching stems with whorls of ³⁄₄-inch (19 mm) leaves with finely toothed edges.

E. canadensis bears small, curling, dark green leaves on long, slender, branched stems.

E. densa, goldfish weed, can root or float on the surface; 1½ inch (4 cm) long, tapered leaves are densely arranged on a stem.

E. nuttallii has light green, finely toothed, narrow leaves.

Soil: Layer of medium size aquarium gravel or coarse sand.
Temperature: 50° to 68°F (10° to 20°C).

Light: Bright to filtered sunlight. Does well under artificial light, needing 14 to 16 light-hours daily.
Water: Slightly acid.
Feeding: Occasionally, with bone meal/clay pellets.
Grooming: Once a month, replace ⅓ of water in tank. Scrape algae from tank sides. Remove dead or discolored leaves. Thin to prevent overcrowding.
Propagation: By cuttings.
Pests and Diseases: Check for bacterial rot, snails. Goldfish may defoliate plants.

EPIDENDRUM
Buttonhole orchid

Over 1,000 species make up this orchid genus, exhibiting various growth habits. All are sympodial, some featuring pseudobulbs, others having canelike stems. They also may be terrestrial or epiphytic. *Epidendrum* is easily grown, and produces compact clusters of small, sweetly scented flowers which last up to several months on the plant. The following species may be grown in an intermediate greenhouse, and are especially suited to growing in the home:

E. atropurpureum, spice orchid, a pseudobulbous plant, produces an

Echinopsis multiplex

Elodea densa

erect or arching flower stalk bearing 4 to 20 flowers, colored brown with apple green edging; lip is white with rosy spot; flowers in spring.

E. difforme has canelike stems measuring to 20 inches (51 cm) tall; flowers are waxy and pale green; blooms in midwinter.

E. fragrans, a small pseudobulbous plant, features 2 to 5 richly fragrant flowers on a short stem; blooms are cream colored; lip is shaped like a shell and striped with purple; blooms from summer to fall.

E. tampense, butterfly orchid, is a pseudobulbous plant bearing long sprays of delicate flowers; blooms are yellow-green tinged with brown; lip is white with purple spot.

Soil: Osmunda fiber or orchid bark mix.
Temperature: Day, 70° to 85°F (21° to 29°C); night, 60° to 65°F (16° to 18°C).
Light: Plants with pseudobulbs re-quire bright light from southrn expo-sure; shade from summer sun at midday. Plants with canelike stems lacking pseudobulbs require slightly more shade. Smaller plants do well under artificial light, needing 12 to 16 light-hours daily. Good circula-tion of fresh air.
Moisture: Allow plants with pseudobulbs to become nearly dry between waterings. Plants with canelike stems should be kept moist, not wet, year-round. Mist foliage of-ten. Humidity, 50%.
Feeding: Twice a month during ac-tive growth with all-purpose fertil-izer.
Grooming: Repot when plant com-pletely overcrowds pot or when growing medium has deteriorated. Best done at outset of active growth, when new roots are first visible.
Propagation: Pseudobulbous plants by division. Remove plantlets from plants with canelike stems, or take stem cuttings.

Pests and Diseases: Check for bac-terial, fungal, and viral infections, mealybugs, scale, slugs, snails, whiteflies.
Seasonal Care: Pseudobulbous plants require a 2- to 3-month rest before flowering to promote buds. During this period keep cool, 50° to 55°F (10° to 13°C), and give little water, never allowing pseudobulbs to shrivel. Plants with canelike stems have no clearly defined rest period; never allow these plants to dry out.

EPIPREMNUM
Devil's ivy, golden pothos

This climbing or trailing vine was formerly classified as *Scindapsus au-reus,* but is now called *E. aureum.* Its 4 inch (10 cm) long, shiny, oval leaves are bright green with yellow marbling. Older leaves take on a heart shape. *Epipremnum* grows to 6 feet (1.8 m) long, and aerial roots along the stems attach readily to a moist moss stick or slab of tree bark. Several cultivars with attractive leaf

Epidendrum species

Epipremnum aureum

markings, including a white-marbled plant, are available.

Soil: All-purpose mix.
Temperature: Day, 70°F (21°C); night, 62° to 68°F (17° to 20°C).
Light: Bright to very low light, with no direct sun, from northern or eastern exposure. Does well under artificial light, needing 14 to 16 light-hours daily.
Moisture: Keep soil evenly moist. Mist twice daily. Humidity, 45% to 60%.
Feeding: Every 2 weeks during growing season, with mild liquid fertilizer.
Grooming: Repot every 2 years. To promote branching or to restrain a large plant, prune stem tips.
Propagation: By tip cuttings.
Pests and Diseases: Generally healthy and free from infestation.
Seasonal Care: Plant rests during winter. Set in cool site, 60°F (16°C). Keep soil barely moist; withhold fertilizer.

EPISCIA
Flame violet, peacock plant

This gesneriad is grown mainly for its foliage, but if given warm, humid air, it will produce an abundance of flowers in shades of white, yellow, red, or blue. The veined and varie-gated foliage often has a metallic sheen. The genus contains 10 species, and many of the available plants are hybrids.

E. cupreata bears copper foliage with white hairs and faint silver markings; scarlet flowers have yellow spots inside.

E. cupreata 'Tropical Topaz' produces yellow flowers.

E. dianthiflora has downy green leaves with purple midribs and fringed white flowers.

E. dianthiflora 'Cygnet' features scalloped, light green leaves; white flowers have purple throats.

E. lilacina sports coppery leaves and lavender flowers.

E. lilacina 'Lilacina' blooms in shades of lavender-blue.

E. lilacina 'Viridis' features emerald green leaves with faint silver markings; flowers are light blue.

E. reptans has green and white leaves; fringed red flowers are pink inside.

Soil: All-purpose gesneriad mix.
Temperature: Day, 70° to 75°F (21° to 24°C); night, 65° to 70°F (18° to 21°C).
Light: Bright light, no direct sun, from eastern, western, or southern exposure. Does well under artificial light, needing 14 to 16 light-hours daily.
Moisture: Keep soil evenly moist. Mist daily, not directly on plant. Humidity, 65% to 70%.
Feeding: Every 2 weeks during growing season, with mild liquid fertilizer.
Grooming: Repot when roots take up ⅔ of pot space or when runners crowd pot. Pinch stems to encourage growth.
Propagation: By leaf or stem cuttings or seeds.
Pests and Diseases: Check for aphids, *Botrytis* blight, cyclamen mites, mealybugs, powdery mildew, root or crown rot, scale, viruses, whiteflies. Cool temperatures will cause leaves to turn black.
Seasonal Care: Plant rests from late fall through winter. Let soil dry slightly between waterings; withhold fertilizer.

ERANTHEMUM
Blue sage

There are 30 species in this genus, but *E. pulchellum,* sometimes listed as *E. nervosum,* is best suited for indoors. The blue, rose, or purple tubular flowers appear in winter and early spring. Leaves are green with a silvery gloss.

Soil: All-purpose mix.
Temperature: Day, 70° to 75°F (21° to 24°C); night, 60° to 65°F (16° to 18°C).
Light: Moderate light, with full sun in winter, from eastern or southern exposure.
Moisture: Keep soil evenly moist. Mist frequently. Humidity, 60% to 70%.
Feeding: Monthly during growing season, with mild liquid fertilizer.
Grooming: Repot when roots occupy ⅔ of pot space. Prune back to 6 inches (15 cm) after flowering. Pinch stems to encourage branching.
Propagation: By root cuttings, or stem cuttings of new spring growth.

Episcia cupreata

Pests and Diseases: Overwatering will cause leaf drop.
Seasonal Care: Plant rests during spring. Let soil dry slightly between waterings; withhold fertilizer.

EUCHARIS
Amazon lily

This bulbous plant sends up fragrant, star-shaped, glistening white flowers 2 to 3 times a year on tall flower stalks. Each cluster contains 3 to 6 flowers, which resemble white daffodils. *E. grandiflora* is the common species grown indoors.

Soil: Humusy mix.
Temperature: For newly potted bulb and mature plant: day, 70° to 75°F (21° to 24°C); night, 55° to 60°F (13° to 16°C).
Light: Before growth appears, provide partial shade. As active growth begins, gradually provide bright light, with no direct sun, from eastern, western, or southern exposure.
Moisture: Water newly potted bulb moderately. As plant matures, gradually increase water. Keep soil evenly moist, almost wet, during flowering. Mist foliage, but not flowers. Humidity, 70%.
Feeding: Weekly during flowering, with mild liquid fertilizer.
Grooming: Prefers to be potbound; repot in fresh soil every 2 years.
Propagation: By offsets.
Pests and Diseases: Check for mealybugs, spider mites.
Seasonal Care: After blooming set in dark site; keep soil barely moist for 1 month and withhold fertilizer. Then, top-dress with compost and resume watering to induce bloom.

EUONYMUS
Spindle tree

Most of the 170 species of trees and shrubs making up this genus are recommended for outside hedging and ground cover, but *E. japonica* is found indoors as well. Trained as bonsai or grown in a terrarium, it requires both bright light and coolness, which may be difficult to provide. *E. japonica* 'Albomarginata' is a good grower featuring small, dark green leaves bordered in white.

Soil: All-purpose mix.
Temperature: Day, 55° to 60°F (13° to 16°C); night, 40° to 45°F (4° to 7°C).
Light: Bright to moderate light from eastern or western exposure.
Moisture: Let soil dry out between moderate waterings. Mist twice daily. Humidity, 40% to 50%.
Feeding: Every 2 weeks during growing season, with mild liquid fertilizer.
Grooming: Pot-on each spring until convenient pot size is reached. Growth becomes straggly if plant is kept too warm; prune back to retain nice shape.
Propagation: By tip cuttings taken in spring or late summer.
Pests and Diseases: Check for aphids, mealybugs, mildew, mites.
Seasonal Care: Plant rests from fall to early spring. Gradually reduce water, giving just enough to keep soil from drying out; withhold fertilizer.

Eranthemum pulchellum

Eucharis grandiflora

Eu–Eu

EUPHORBIA
Crown of thorns, poinsettia, and others

This genus of over 1500 species offers a wide diversity of appearance, from cactuslike succulents to flowering shrubs to tropical trees. Slicing the stem of any *Euphorbia* uncovers one common characteristic: the milky sap which oozes out and is an irritant to skin and eyes, even poisonous in some species.

FLOWERING SHRUBS
E. fulgens, scarlet plume, a winter bloomer, grows from 2 to 4 feet (0.6 to 1.2 m) tall; features scarlet bracts on graceful, drooping branches.

E. pulcherrima, poinsettia, is a common sight in winter with its bright red bracts surrounding small green and yellow flowers; varieties with white and pink bracts are also available.

Soil: Mix 2 parts potting soil, 1 part vermiculite, and 1 part sphagnum moss.

Temperature: Day, 65° to 70°F (18° to 21°C); night, 50° to 60°F (10° to 16°C).
Light: Bright, filtered light from southern exposure.
Moisture: Keep soil evenly moist, not soggy. Avoid overwatering. Humidity, 40% to 50%.
Feeding: Weekly, summer through fall, with mild liquid fertilizer.
Grooming: Trim back stalks and repot in spring.
Propagation: By cuttings. To stop flow of sap, dip end of cutting in water, dab plant ends with water.
Pests and Diseases: Check for aphids, mealybugs, spider mites, scale. Keep out of drafts.
Seasonal Care: Plant becomes dormant after blooming. Set in cool site with filtered light. Water just enough to keep soil from completely drying out; withhold fertilizer. Resume watering and repot in early spring, when new growth appears. To induce blooming, alternate 14 hours of darkness with 10 hours of light for 8 weeks.

SUCCULENTS
E. caput-medusae, Medusa's head, a dwarf spineless species, grows to 12 inches (30 cm) tall with green, ribbed branches snaking out from a sturdy stem; branch ends are tufted with small leaves and turn upwards.

E. milii var. *splendens,* crown of thorns, is a shrub growing to 36 inches (91 cm) tall, with spiny stem and branches. Leaves appear near branch tip, and fall off as plant matures. Blooms are also borne at tip, appearing spring through summer in shades of red, pink, or yellow. Excellent conditions may result in flowering throughout the year.

E. obesa, baseball plant, a dwarf spineless species, is a grayish green globe with horizontal bands of purple, measuring up to 8 inches (20 cm).

Soil: Mix equal parts potting soil and sharp sand.
Temperature: Day, 70° to 80°F (21° to 27°C); night, 55° to 65°F (13° to 18°C).
Light: Bright, filtered sun from eastern, western, or southern exposure.
Moisture: Keep soil barely moist, watering when soil is dry to touch. *E. milii* var. *splendens* needs slightly more water. Humidity, 30% to 45%.

Euonymus japonica **cultivars**

Euphorbia pulcherrima

Feeding: Every 2 weeks during growing season, with mild liquid fertilizer.
Grooming: Repot when roots occupy a little more than ½ of pot space.
Propagation: By stem cuttings or seeds.
Pests and Diseases: Check for aphids, mealybugs, spider mites, scale.
Seasonal Care: After flowering, reduce water slightly for *E. milii* var. *splendens,* withhold fertilizer, keep in normal room temperature. Other succulents, keep barely moist, let soil dry between waterings during winter rest period. Set in cool site, 55°F (13°C), with bright light. Withhold fertilizer.

EXACUM
Arabian violet, German violet

Only 1 of the 20 to 30 species in this genus is in general cultivation and can be grown as a flowering house plant. *E. affine* produces fragrant blue flowers in late summer through fall. This perennial is most attractive when young and no taller than 8 inches (20 cm), and is best treated as an annual and discarded in winter.

Soil: All-purpose mix.
Temperature: Day, 72° to 75°F (22° to 24°C); night, 60° to 65°F (16° to 18°C).
Light: Bright light, with direct sun in winter, from eastern exposure.
Moisture: Keep soil evenly moist. Humidity, 50%.
Feeding: Every 2 weeks, with mild liquid fertilizer, year-round.
Grooming: Remove faded flowers to prolong blooming period.
Propagation: By cuttings.
Pests and Diseases: Generally healthy and free from infestation.

×FATSHEDERA
Aralia ivy, botanical wonder, tree ivy

The result of a cross of 2 genera (*Fatsia* and *Hedera*), ×*Fatshedera* has foliage which resembles the leaves of an ivy, only thicker and wider. It can be trained to grow upright on a support or to trail as a vine.

F. lizei, aralia ivy, has leathery, waxy, green leaves and stems reaching from 4 to 8 feet (1.2 to 2.4 m).

F. lizei 'Variegata' features creamy white-margined leaves.

Soil: All-purpose mix.
Temperature: Day, 55° to 70°F (13° to 21°C); night, 40° to 55°F (4° to 13°C).
Light: Filtered bright to moderate light, with some direct sun, from eastern, western, or southern exposure.
Moisture: Keep soil evenly moist. Let *F. lizei* 'Variegata' dry slightly between waterings. Mist twice daily. Humidity, 45% to 55%.
Feeding: Monthly during growing season, with mild liquid fertilizer.

Euphorbia milii var. splendens

Exacum affine

Grooming: If plant grows too tall, pinch growing ends.
Propagation: By air layering or stem cuttings.
Pests and Diseases: Check for aphids, mealybugs, spider mites, scale.
Seasonal Care: Plant rests from late fall to late winter. Gradually reduce water, giving just enough to keep soil from drying out; withhold fertilizer.

FATSIA
Japanese aralia

This genus includes only 1 species of shrub with 2 cultivars, and is grown indoors as a decorative pot plant. Long lasting and quick growing, it routinely loses lower leaves as it matures.

F. japonica, formerly listed as *Aralia japonica,* grows to 5 feet (1.5 m) tall with woody stems and leafstalks bearing light green, shiny, many-lobed leaves.

F. japonica 'Moseri' is more compact, with yellow veining in the leaves.

F. japonica 'Variegata' features creamy white margins on leaves.

Soil: All-purpose mix.
Temperature: Day, 55° to 60°F (13° to 16°C); night, 40° to 45°F (4° to 7°C).
Light: Bright to moderate light, with direct sun in winter, from eastern, western, or southern exposure. Does well under artificial light, needing 14 to 16 light-hours daily.
Moisture: Keep soil evenly moist. Mist twice daily. Humidity, 40% to 50%.
Feeding: Monthly during growing season, with mild liquid fertilizer.
Grooming: Prefers to be potbound; pot-on when roots occupy ¾ of pot space. Prune back severely in spring to keep from growing too tall. Gently clean foliage once a month; tender leaves bruise easily.
Propagation: By stem cuttings, tip cuttings, suckers, or seeds.

Pests and Diseases: Check for aphids, mealybugs, spider mites, scale.
Seasonal Care: Plant rests from fall through late winter. Set in cool location, 40° to 45°F (4° to 7°C). Reduce water, letting soil surface dry between moderate waterings; withhold fertilizer.

FAUCARIA
Tiger's jaws

33 species of dwarf succulents comprise this genus. Triangular leaves are edged with white teeth which point inwards on young plants. As leaves mature, teeth expand outwards, resembling jaws. The daisy-like yellow or white flowers appear in spring and last several days.

F. tigrina has 2 inch (5 cm) long leaves in a rosette; flowers are 2 inches (5 cm) across.

F. tuberculosa features a rosette of 1 inch (2.5 cm) long leaves with white dots running along the edges.

Soil: Cactus/succulent mix.
Temperature: Day, 65° to 80°F (18° to 27°C); night, 50° to 70°F (10° to 21°C).

× *Fatshedera lizei*

Fatsia japonica

Light: Bright light, 4 to 6 hours direct sun, from southern or western exposure. Air circulation is important.

Moisture: Let soil dry between thorough waterings. Avoid overwatering. Humidity, 20% to 30%.

Feeding: Monthly during growing season, with mild, high-phosphorus fertilizer.

Grooming: Never requires repotting.

Propagation: By suckers or seeds.

Pests and Diseases: Check for mealybugs, scale.

Seasonal Care: Plant rests during winter. Provide 3 hours direct sun in cool site, 50°F (10°C). Water just enough to keep plant from shriveling; withhold fertilizer.

FEROCACTUS
Barrel cactus, fishhook cactus

25 species of barrel-shaped cacti make up this genus, noted for its colored spines which may be hooked or straight. Orange or yellow flowers appear on mature plants, at least 12 inches (30 cm) tall, in summer.

F. acanthodes may grow to 36 inches (91 cm) tall; bright green stems feature pink to bright red, hooked spines.

F. latispinus features gray-green stems with clusters of red and white spines; grows to 12 inches (30 cm) tall, bearing violet flowers.

F. wislizenii, fishhook cactus, bears white, needlelike radial spines with red, brown, or gray, hooked, central spines.

Soil: Cactus/succulent mix.

Temperature: Prefers 65° to 90°F (18° to 32°C) range.

Light: Bright light from southern exposure to enhance colored spines. Air circulation is important.

Moisture: Let soil dry between moderate waterings. Avoid overwatering. Humidity, 20% to 25%.

Feeding: Monthly during growing season, with high-potassium fertilizer.

Propagation: By seeds.

Pests and Diseases: Check for aphids, mealybugs, spider mites, scale. Also be alert for fungus disease.

Seasonal Care: Plant rests during winter. Place in cool site, 50°F (10°C). Water just enough to keep soil from drying out; withhold fertilizer.

FICUS
Fiddle-leaf fig, rubber plant, weeping fig

800 species of trees and shrubs in this popular genus offer a diversity of foliage shapes and colors, as well as varying growth habits, ranging from erect and treelike to trailing vines.

F. benghalensis, banyan tree, has dark green, oval leaves up to 8 inches (20 cm) long, covered with fine, reddish hairs.

F. benjamina, weeping fig, grows to 6 feet (1.8 m) tall, with slender, arching branches resembling those of poplar trees; immature leaves appear light green then darken with age.

F. deltoidea, mistletoe fig, has randomly spotted dark green leaves and may bear inedible fruit; grows to 36 inches (91 cm) tall, with many branches; formerly listed as *F. diversifolia.*

F. elastica, rubber plant, is single stemmed and grows to 6 feet (1.8 m) or more; thick, glossy leaves feature prominent midribs; cultivars with various leaf shapes and variegations are available.

F. lyrata, fiddle-leaf fig, also called *F. pandurata,* grows from 2 to 4 feet (0.6 to 1.2 m), producing fiddle-shaped leaves along a single stem.

F. pumila, creeping fig, also listed as *F. repens,* produces many branches bearing thin, heart-shaped leaves, which trail or cling to supports by aerial roots.

Faucaria tuberculosa

Ferocactus latispinus

F. religiosa, bo tree, has distinctive oval leaves with long, slender tips.

F. retusa, Indian laurel, has a shrubby form, measuring from 4 to 6 feet (1.2 to 1.8 m) tall, and deep green, shiny foliage.

Soil: All-purpose mix. *F. pumila* prefers humusy mix.
Temperature: Day, 80° to 85°F (27° to 29°C); night, 60°F (16°C). *F. pumila* prefers a cooler location.
Light: Bright to moderate light from eastern or western exposure. *F. pumila* prefers shade. Does well under artificial light, needing 14 to 16 light-hours daily.
Moisture: Let soil dry moderately between thorough waterings. Keep *F. pumila* evenly moist. Overwatering results in leaf drop. Mist twice daily. Humidity, 40% to 50%.
Feeding: Monthly during growing season, with mild liquid fertilizer.
Grooming: Prefers to be potbound; repot when roots occupy over ¾ of pot space, in spring. Gently clean shiny-leaved species; young leaves bruise easily. Clean *F. benghalensis* by misting leaves.
Propagation: By air layering, or stem cuttings of *F. pumila.*
Pests and Diseases: Check for aphids, mealybugs, spider mites, scale. Be alert for fungus disease.
Seasonal Care: Most species except *F. benjamina* rest from late fall through late winter. Keep in cool location, 50° to 60°F (10° to 16°C). Water only when soil is nearly dry; withhold fertilizer.

FITTONIA
Mosaic plant, nerve plant

This genus of low-growing foliage plants contains 2 species which best display their distinctive leaves in hanging baskets. *Fittonia* is also a delightful addition to terraria, featuring pointed, oval leaves covered with white or colored veining.

F. verschaffeltii, mosaic plant, has dark green leaves with pinkish red veins.

F. verschaffeltii var. *argyroneura* displays a silver or white pattern of veins on light green leaves.

F. verschaffeltii var. *pearcei* bears olive green leaves with pinkish veins.

Soil: Humusy mix.
Temperature: Day, 70° to 80°F (21° to 27°C); night, 62° to 68°F (17° to 20°C).
Light: Low light from northern or eastern exposure. Does well under artificial light, needing 14 to 16 light-hours daily.
Moisture: Let soil dry out between moderate waterings. Mist twice daily. Humidity, 45% to 55%.
Feeding: Monthly during growing season, with mild all-purpose fertilizer.
Grooming: Repot when roots occupy ½ of pot space, in early spring. Pinch or prune regularly to retain fullness.
Propagation: By stem cuttings in spring.
Pests and Diseases: Check for aphids, mealybugs, mites, slugs.
Seasonal Care: Plant rests during winter. Keep in cool location, 60°F (16°C). Water sparingly, never allowing soil to dry out completely; withhold fertilizer.

Ficus benjamina

Fittonia verschaffeltii

FORTUNELLA
Kumquat

Related to the citrus tree, this genus contains 4 or 5 species of easy-to-care-for trees with shiny, dark green foliage. Fragrant white flowers appear mainly in the spring, followed in fall by edible fruit which can be made into preserves.

F. japonica, Marum kumquat, can flower almost year-round; produces deep orange fruit, 1¼ inches (3 cm) in diameter.

F. margarita, Nagami kumquat, bears small, orange-yellow fruit.

Soil: All-purpose mix.

Temperature: Day, 68° to 72°F (20° to 22°C); night, 50° to 55°F (10° to 13°C).
Light: Direct sun from western or southern exposure.
Moisture: Keep soil evenly moist. Humidity, 20% to 30%.
Feeding: Monthly, with mild liquid fertilizer, year-round.
Grooming: Repot when roots occupy ¾ of pot space. Prune for bushier growth.
Propagation: By grafting, stem cuttings taken in late spring, or seeds.
Pests and Diseases: Check for aphids, mealybugs, mites, whiteflies.
Seasonal Care: Plant rests for several months, starting in late fall. Set in cool site, 55° to 60°F (13° to 16°C). Reduce water, never allowing soil to dry out completely. Continue with light feedings.

FUCHSIA
Lady's eardrops

100 species of blooming shrubs make up this genus, which may appear upright or with trailing stems, making them a natural for hanging baskets. Clusters of pendulous, bell-shaped flowers are featured against a backdrop of dark green, light green, or maroon-tinged foliage.

F. fulgens bears bright red flowers tipped with yellow.

F. × hybrida has single or double flowers that may be solid colors or combinations of red, pink, purple, and white.

F. triphylla grows to 24 inches (61 cm) tall, with deep red flowers.

Soil: All-purpose mix.
Temperature: Day, 60° to 65°F (16° to 18°C); night, 50° to 65°F (10° to 18°C).
Light: Bright light, with direct morning sun, from eastern or western exposure.
Moisture: Keep evenly moist, never allowing soil to dry out. Mist twice daily. Humidity, 60%.
Feeding: Weekly during growing season, with mild liquid fertilizer.
Grooming: Prefers to be potbound. Pinch back stems to retain attractive shape. Stake tall plants.

Fortunella margarita

Fuchsia × hybrida

Fu–Ga

Propagation: By cuttings of non-flowering shoots, taken in summer.
Pests and Diseases: Check for aphids, mealybugs, spider mites, scale.
Seasonal Care: Plant enters dormant period after flowering. Cut back half of growth and set in cool location, 45° to 50°F (7° to 10°C). Keep soil barely moist; withhold fertilizer. In spring, trim back slightly, give normal temperature and resume watering. Repot when new growth appears.

GARDENIA
Cape jasmine

Containing 200 species of low, bushy shrubs, this genus is famous for its snowy white, delicately scented, single or double flowers and waxy, dark green foliage. *Gardenia* proves to be a sensitive, demanding plant that does not tolerate drafts and changes in temperature, which result in bud drop. *G. jasminoides,* the most popular species, blooms throughout the summer and grows from 2 to 4 feet (0.6 to 2.1 m) tall.

Soil: Humusy mix.
Temperature: 62°F (17°C) when buds are forming. Otherwise: day, 60° to 75°F (16° to 24°C); night, 60° to 65°F (16° to 18°C).
Light: Bright light, no direct sun.
Moisture: Keep soil evenly moist. Mist twice daily. Humidity, 60%. Humidity must be high for bud formation.
Feeding: Every 2 weeks from early spring to late summer, with all-purpose fertilizer.
Grooming: Blooms better when potbound. Remove faded, brown flowers. Prune severely after flowering.
Propagation: By stem cuttings, with 3 or 4 buds, taken in early spring or fall.
Pests and Diseases: Check for aphids, mealybugs, scale, whiteflies. Low humidity causes black leaf tips; cold water results in yellow leaves.
Seasonal Care: Plant rests following blooming, lasting from early winter to early spring. Gradually reduce water, letting soil surface dry between waterings; withhold fertilizer.

GASTERIA
Ox-tongue

The 50 species of succulents in this genus present a variety of leaf shapes and patterns. Easy to grow, they produce rich red flowers borne on a stalk, from spring through summer.

G. ×hybrida, bowtie plant, is a name given to the numerous hybrids of unknown parentage; all plants under this name have long, tongue-like leaves, which may be speckled with white.

G. maculata features 8-inch (20 cm) leaves with tips curving upwards; white dots form an irregular pattern.

G. verrucosa, ox-tongue, sports 6-inch (15 cm) tapered leaves rising upwards, covered with white dots.

Soil: Recommended cactus/succulent mix.
Temperature: Day, 68° to 85°F (20° to 29°C); night, 50° to 70°F (10° to 21°C).
Light: Bright, indirect, or filtered light from southern exposure. Does well under artificial light, needing 14 to 16 light-hours daily.
Moisture: Let soil dry between thorough waterings. Avoid overwatering. Humidity, 20% to 25%.

Gardenia jasminoides

Gasteria × hybrida

Feeding: Monthly during growing season, with mild liquid fertilizer.
Grooming: Repot when roots occupy ½ of pot space, in spring.
Propagation: By division, leaf cuttings, or seeds.
Pests and Diseases: Check for aphids, mealybugs, spider mites, root rot, scale. Also be alert for fungus disease.
Seasonal Care: Plant rests during winter. Set in cool site, 50°F (10°C). Water just enough to keep leaves from shriveling; withhold fertilizer.

GERBERA
African daisy, transvaal daisy

This genus of blooming perennial plants includes 70 species which bear a single, daisylike flower per stalk. *G. jamesonii* is the species commonly grown, featuring leaves with woolly undersides, and 4 inch (10 cm) wide, orange-red flowers. The many hybrids which are available make attractive house plants, sporting single or double flowers in various shades of white, pink, red, yellow, and orange. The main blooming period extends from early spring to fall, but with the proper conditions, blooms can appear throughout the winter.

Soil: All-purpose mix.
Temperature: Day, 65° to 70°F (18° to 21°C); night, 55° to 60°F (13° to 16°C).
Light: Bright light, filtered sun, from eastern or western exposure.
Moisture: Let soil dry slightly between waterings. Humidity, 45% to 60%.
Feeding: Every 2 weeks with mild manure tea.
Grooming: Pot-on in spring when plant completely overcrowds pot space.
Propagation: By division or seeds.
Pests and Diseases: Check for aphids, mites.

GLORIOSA
Glory lily

5 or 6 species of climbing lilies comprise this genus, growing to 4 feet (1.2 m) tall indoors along a trellis. Leaves attach to supports by coiled tendrils on their tips. Late summer flowers resemble lily blooms, but with petals bent at the base and curving backwards.

G. rothschildiana bears bright red flowers with yellow and white along the margins and bases.

G. simplex features green flowers

Gloriosa rothschildiana

Gerbera jamesonii

changing to yellow and red as they mature.

G. superba has yellow blooms with crisped edges, changing to red as they mature.

Soil: All-purpose mix.
Temperature: Day, 72° to 75°F (22° to 24°C); night, 60° to 65°F (16° to 18°C).
Light: Bright light, with direct sun, from eastern, western, or southern exposure.
Moisture: Keep soil evenly moist. Mist twice daily. Humidity, 45% to 60%.
Feeding: Every 2 weeks while in bloom, with mild liquid fertilizer.
Grooming: Repot in early spring. Loosely tie stems laden with blooms to support.
Propagation: By division of tubers after dormancy, offsets, or seeds.
Pests and Diseases: Check for mealybugs.
Seasonal Care: Plant is dormant from late fall through winter. After flowering, let foliage die back. Store in pot at 50°F (10°C). Withhold water and fertilizer.

GREVILLEA
Silk oak

Several of the 250 species of evergreen trees and shrubs within this genus do well indoors in pots or tubs. A rapid grower, in 3 to 4 years *Grevillea* can reach 6 feet (1.8 m). The dark green leaves have a soft and silky feel, becoming slightly bronze colored with full sun.

G. robusta, the common indoor species, features finely divided leaves, resembling fern fronds, arching from a single stem.

G. rosmarinifolia has a bushy form, with pointed leaves resembling those of the herb, rosemary.

Soil: Mix 3 parts standard potting soil and 1 part coarse sand or perlite.
Temperature: Prefers 50° to 60°F (10° to 16°C) range.
Light: Bright light, with direct sun, from eastern, western, or southern exposure. Air circulation is important.
Moisture: Let soil dry slightly between thorough waterings. Mist daily around plant, not directly on foliage. Humidity, 45% to 60%.
Feeding: Monthly during growing season, with mild liquid fertilizer.
Grooming: Repot when roots occupy ¾ of pot space, before new growth appears in spring. Prune back severely in early spring. Remove old blooms.
Propagation: By seeds.
Pests and Diseases: Check for mealybugs, spider mites. Leaf drop indicates improper temperature.
Seasonal Care: Plant rests during winter. Set in cool location, at least 45°F (7°C). Water sparingly, allowing soil to dry moderately between waterings; withhold fertilizer.

GUZMANIA

These terrestrial or epiphytic bromeliads are valued for both their foliage and flowers. Basal leaf rosettes bear distinctive patterning or inner leaves change color as plant prepares to bloom. Flowers appear on stalk from center of rosette in late winter.

G. lingulata, an epiphyte, has 18 inch (46 cm) long, solid green leaves; small white flowers appear encased

Grevillea robusta

Guzmania sanguinea

within red or pink bracts. There are several popular hybrid cultivars of this species.

G. monostachia grows to 16 inches (41 cm) tall; has light green leaves and white flowers surrounded by orange-tipped white bracts borne on a long stalk.

G. musaica, a terrestrial, produces 30 inch (76 cm) long leaves, with dark green lines on tops and purple lines on undersides; flowers are yellow, golden bracts have pink markings.

G. sanguinea, a stemless species, grows to 8 inches (20 cm) tall; inner leaves in rosette turn red before green and white flowers emerge.

G. zahnii reaches 20 inches (51 cm) tall; leaves form a spreading rosette, flowers are bright yellow.

G. zahnii var. *variegata* has leaves striped with pink, white, and green.

Soil: Epiphytic or terrestrial bromeliad mix, according to species.
Temperature: 60° to 80°F (16° to 27°C).
Light: Moderate light from eastern exposure. In winter, tolerates direct sun. Does well under artificial light, needing 16 light-hours daily. Air circulation is important.
Moisture: Keep soil moist, not soggy. Keep fresh water in cup except while blooming. Mist daily. Humidity, 45% to 60%.

Feeding: Monthly, with mild all-purpose fertilizer. Avoid oil-based products such as fish emulsion. Spray on leaves, add to water in cup, or apply to growing medium after watering; never feed a dry plant.
Grooming: Remove old, yellowed leaves and dried flowers and stalks. Change water in cup.
Propagation: By offsets or seeds.
Pests and Diseases: Check for scale.

GYMNOCALYCIUM
Chin cactus, spider cactus

40 species of small, globe-shaped cacti comprise this genus. Ready bloomers, their daisylike flowers appear in spring or fall. Clefts beneath the areoles on plant's ribs give rise to the common name.

G. baldianum measures 3 inches (8 cm) across; dark green stem has gray spines; burgundy flowers measure up to 2 inches (5 cm) across.

G. denudatum, spider cactus, grows to 6 inches (15 cm) in diameter, with yellow-brown, thick, curving spines displayed along prominent ribs; 3 inch (8 cm) wide flowers are white to light pink.

G. mihanovichii, chin cactus, has angular ribs, red markings, thin yellow spines, and yellow to pink flowers; mutant forms, lacking chlorophyll,

appear red, yellow, pink, orange, or black; when grafted to *Hylocereus,* resultant plant is known as moon cactus.

G. quehlianum has a 6 inch (15 cm) wide, blue-green flattened globe with cream-colored curving spines; white flowers have red-tinged centers.

G. saglione, a larger species, features brick red, thick, curving spines; flowers are green-white to pink.

Soil: Cactus/succulent mix.
Temperature: Day, 68° to 72°F (20° to 22°C); night, 50° to 55°F (10° to 13°C).
Light: Bright light, at least 4 hours direct sun daily, from southern or western exposure. Air circulation is important.
Moisture: Let soil dry slightly between thorough waterings. Avoid overwatering. Humidity, 30% to 45%.
Feeding: Once a year, in spring, with high-potassium fertilizer.
Grooming: Pot-on when pot space is overcrowded.
Propagation: By offsets or seeds.
Pests and Diseases: Check for aphids, mealybugs, spider mites, scale. Also be alert for fungus disease.
Seasonal Care: Plant rests during winter. Site in cool location with 5 hours of light. Water just enough to keep plant from shriveling.

GYNURA
Purple passion plant, velvet plant

This branching foliage plant features a soft, hairy, purple leaf surface, creating a velvety texture. Although there are 100 species of *Gynura,* only *G. aurantiaca* is grown indoors, measuring up to 36 inches (91 cm) in height. Younger specimens have a deeper color than mature plants. Orange flowers with a sharp odor may appear in spring and summer, and can be plucked off before they open.

Gymnocalycium saglione

Gy–Ha

Soil: All-purpose mix.
Temperature: Day, 68° to 80°F (20° to 27°C); night, 55° to 68°F (13° to 20°C).
Light: Bright to moderate light, with some direct sun, from eastern or western exposure. Does well under artificial light, needing 14 light-hours daily.
Moisture: Keep soil evenly moist. Avoid getting water on leaves. Humidity, 45% to 60%.
Feeding: Monthly during growing season, with mild liquid fertilizer.
Grooming: Repot when roots occupy ½ of pot space. Prune often to avoid legginess; remove dead foliage.
Propagation: By stem cuttings taken in summer.
Pests and Diseases: Check for aphids, mealybugs, mites, scale, slugs, whiteflies.
Seasonal Care: Plant rests slightly from late fall through winter. Keep in cool, well-lit location, 55°F (13°C). Reduce water, keeping barely moist; feed half as frequently.

HAEMARIA
Jewel orchid

A single species, *H. discolor,* comprises this genus of terrestrial sym-podial orchids. It is prized for attractively colored foliage, which is a velvety dark green with a striking network of red and white veins. A raceme of small, fragrant white to pink flowers appears anytime from fall to early spring.

Soil: Mix equal parts screened tree fern fiber and orchid bark mix.
Temperature: Day, to 80°F (27°C); night, 62° to 65°F (17° to 18°C).
Light: Filtered light from northern or eastern exposure. Does well under artificial light, needing 14 to 16 light-hours daily. Tall flower spikes make it necessary to remove flower to windowsill while in bloom. Fresh air circulation is critical.
Moisture: Keep growing medium slightly moist at all times. Humidity, 50%.
Feeding: Every 3 weeks during active growth, with all-purpose fertilizer.
Grooming: Top-dress with fresh growing medium rather than repot.
Propagation: By rhizome cuttings or crown division.
Pests and Diseases: Check for bacterial, fungal, and viral infections, mealybugs, scale, slugs, snails, whiteflies.

Seasonal Care: Plant rests following blooming. Reduce water, never allowing growing medium to dry out.

HAWORTHIA
Pearl plant, wart plant

160 species of small, easy-care succulents comprise this genus. Their distinctive foliage shapes and patterning make them delightful additions to a window garden.

H. attenuata sports compact, erect rosettes of dark green leaves with bands of white dots.

H. fasciata, zebra haworthia, features a low rosette of dark green leaves, 2 inches (5 cm) long, marked with even bands of white dots.

H. limifolia, fairy washboard, has stiff, triangular, dark green leaves in a flattened rosette; white bands are less distinct than in *H. fasciata.*

H. margaritifera, pearl plant, features erect clusters of 3 inch (8 cm) long, pointed leaves, with scattered white dots.

H. reinwardtii, wart plant, has closely packed, small, wedge-shaped leaves on a 6-inch (15 cm) stem; undersides bear irregular patterns of white dots.

Gynura aurantiaca

Haemaria discolor

H. subfasciata has triangular leaves to 5 inches (13 cm) long, with rows of translucent spots on the lower leaf surface.

Soil: Cactus/succulent mix.
Temperature: Day, 68° to 80°F (20° to 27°C); night, 50° to 70°F (10° to 21°C).
Light: Bright, indirect, or filtered light from eastern or western exposure.
Moisture: Let soil dry moderately between thorough waterings. Avoid overwatering. Humidity, 20% to 25%.
Feeding: Once a year, in spring, with phosphorus-rich fertilizer; for plants at least 1 year old.
Grooming: Pot-on when roots occupy ½ of pot space, in spring. Remove dead leaves.
Propagation: By division, offsets, or seeds.
Pests and Diseases: Check for aphids, mealybugs, spider mites, root rot, scale.
Seasonal Care: Plant rests from winter to early spring. Keep in cool site, 60°F (16°C). Water only enough to keep leaves from shriveling.

HEDERA
Canary Island ivy, English ivy

2 of the 5 species of evergreen, woody vines in this genus are commonly found in hanging baskets or climbing along a trellis. Leaves may be ovate or lobed, with ruffled or crisped edges. *Hedera* is prized for its dense and bushy growth, with a wide range of foliage colors and variegations. Aerial roots often appear on stems and will attach to moist surfaces.

H. canariensis, Canary Island ivy, is a slow grower with glossy, deep green, ovate leaves, 6 inches (15 cm) across; stems are burgundy colored. Several variegated varieties are available.

H. helix, English ivy, features dark green leaves with white veins, 3 inches (8 cm) long, with 3 to 5 lobes. Many cultivars with lovely leaf variations are available.

Soil: All-purpose mix.
Temperature: Day, 60° to 68°F (16° to 20°C); night, 50° to 55°F (10° to 13°C).
Light: Bright light from southern, eastern, or western exposure. Variegated foliage needs 3 hours of sun daily to retain color. Does well under artificial light, needing 14 light-hours daily.
Moisture: Keep soil evenly moist. Mist twice daily. Humidity, 30% to 50%.
Feeding: Every 2 weeks during growing season, with mild liquid fertilizer.

Grooming: Repot when roots occupy ½ of pot space. For bushy plant, prune in spring before new growth appears. Rinse foliage often.
Propagation: By division, layering, or stem cuttings.
Pests and Diseases: Check for mealybugs, spider mites, scale.
Seasonal Care: Plant rests in fall and winter. Set in cool location, 50°F (10°C). Keep soil barely moist; withhold fertilizer.

HELXINE, see *Soleirolia*

HEMIGRAPHIS
Purple waffle plant, red ivy

More than 60 species of tropical plants with trailing branches comprise this genus. *H. alternata* is the common species, best grown in hanging baskets in a warm, shady greenhouse. Shimmering gray leaves are puckered, with burgundy-colored undersides. A head of small white flowers, enclosed by large bracts, appears in summer.

Soil: Mix equal parts peat moss and leaf mold.

Haworthia subfasciata

Hedera helix 'Glacier'

Temperature: 65° to 80°F (18° to 27°C), year-round.
Light: Filtered light, semishade.
Moisture: Keep soil evenly moist, not soggy. Mist daily. Humidity, 45% to 60%.
Feeding: Every 2 weeks during growing season, with mild liquid fertilizer.
Grooming: Repot every spring. Cut back leggy stems in late winter.
Propagation: By cuttings.
Seasonal Care: Plant rests for short period in winter. Reduce water, keeping soil barely moist; withhold fertilizer.

HIBISCUS
Rose mallow, rose of China

This genus includes 250 species of shrubs with dark green, toothed leaves and large, showy flowers. Grown in pots or tubs indoors, frequent pruning can keep them at a manageable height. Each bloom lasts for a single day, but new ones are continually being produced throughout the spring and summer.

H. rosa-sinensis, rose of China, features blooms in varying shades of red, darkening towards the base, with a white, yellow, red, or orange corolla. 2- or 3-colored cultivars with ruffled petals are available.

H. schizopetalus, Japanese lantern, has slender, arching branches; orange-red flowers with fringed edges hang from stalks, and long, dangling staminal columns emerge from the center.

Soil: All-purpose mix.
Temperature: Day, 65° to 70°F (18° to 21°C); night, 50° to 55°F (10° to 13°C).
Light: Direct sun, bright light from eastern or western exposure.
Moisture: Keep soil evenly moist. Mist frequently. Humidity, 45% to 60%.
Feeding: Weekly during growing season, with potassium-rich fertilizer.
Grooming: In early spring, cut back to 6 inches (15 cm), then repot. Pinch stems to retain good shape.
Propagation: By tip cuttings.
Pests and Diseases: Check for aphids, mealybugs, spider mites, scale, whiteflies.

Seasonal Care: Plant rests for 2 to 3 months in winter. Set in cool site, 55°F (13°C). Reduce water, never allowing soil to dry out completely; withhold fertilizer.

HIPPEASTRUM
Amaryllis, Barbados lily

This genus contains 75 species of perennial bulbs and belongs to the Amaryllis family. Confusion often arises over *Hippeastrum* because its common name, amaryllis, is the genus name of another closely related plant in the same family, *Amaryllis belladonna,* the belladonna lily. Most often, though, the name amaryllis refers to *Hippeastrum.* The large trumpet-shaped blooms come in a wide range of colors, with accenting streaks and veining. A single bulb produces 1 or 2 flower stems, each bearing a cluster of 2 to 6 blooms which may last up to 6 weeks. Many hybrids are available.

Hemigraphis alternata

Hibiscus rosa-sinensis

H. puniceum, Barbados lily, grows to 24 inches (61 cm) tall, with bright green, strap-shaped leaves developing after the flowers; clusters of red flowers with green or white stripes may appear continuously.

H. reticulatum var. *striatifolium* features dark green leaves with creamy white midribs; fragrant blooms are bright red, appearing mainly in fall.

H. striatum 'Fulgidum', a continuous bloomer, produces crimson flowers with yellow centers and bases.

Soil: All-purpose mix.
Temperature: For 1 to 2 months before growth appears, keep cool, 55° to 60°F (13° to 16°C). Once growth begins, keep at 65° to 70°F (18° to 21°C).
Light: Before growth appears, set in dark location. Once active growth begins, gradually introduce bright light, with some direct sun, from eastern, western, or southern exposure.
Moisture: Water newly potted bulb sparingly. As growth appears, increase water, keeping soil evenly moist. Mist daily. Humidity, 45% to 60%.
Feeding: Every 2 weeks during active growth, with compost or bone meal.
Grooming: Pot bulb, with top half exposed, 4 to 6 months before desired flowering. Blooms best when potbound; repot every 2 to 3 years. After flowering, cut off stalks.
Propagation: By offsets when repotting, or seeds.
Seasonal Care: After flowering, set outdoors. Bring indoors before first frost. Reduce water until foliage dies back, then withhold. Remove dead leaves. Store pot in dark, cool site, 50°F (10°C), until new growth appears. Then resume watering and provide light.

HOFFMANNIA
Taffeta plant

100 species of ornamental plants, grown for their foliage, make up this genus. *Hoffmannia* thrives in a warm greenhouse.

H. ghiesbreghtii, an erect plant growing to 4 feet (1.2 m), has velvety, bronze to deep green leaves with a glossy surface and deep veins, undersides are red; tubular yellow flowers have a red spot.

H. roezlii has pale green, glossy leaves with deep veining; flowers are dark red.

Soil: All-purpose mix.
Temperature: Day, up to 80°F (27°C); night, 62° to 65°F (17° to 18°C).
Light: Moderate filtered light, no direct sun, from northern or eastern exposure.
Moisture: Keep soil evenly moist, not soggy. Mist daily. Humidity, 45% to 60%.
Feeding: Every 2 weeks, with mild liquid fertilizer.
Grooming: Pinch tips to promote bushy growth.
Propagation: By cuttings taken in spring.

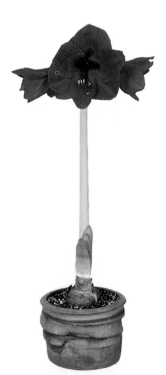

Hippeastrum **hybrid**

Hoffmannia roezlii

Ho—Ho

HOWEA
Kentia palm, paradise palm, sentry palm

2 species of palms with single-stemmed, arching fronds make up this genus. A common sight in nineteenth century hotel lobbies and parlors, *Howea* is still in demand because of its tolerance for air conditioned and poorly lit environments. A slow grower, it is easy to maintain indoors, where its waxy, deep green foliage enhances any decor.

H. belmoreana grows slowly to 8 feet (2.4 m) tall; leaflets are rigid near midrib, then arch downwards; fronds spread while plant is young.

H. forsterana has erect, flat leaflets; fronds spread only on mature plant; measures to 8 feet (2.4 m) in height.

Soil: All-purpose mix, with good drainage.
Temperature: Day, 70°F (21°C); night, 50° to 55°F (10° to 13°C).
Light: Bright to low light, no direct sun, from any exposure. Does well under artificial light. Air circulation is important.
Moisture: Keep soil evenly moist, not soggy. Can stand occasional dryness. Mist twice daily. Humidity, 45% to 60%.
Feeding: Every 2 weeks, with mild liquid fertilizer.
Grooming: Repot only when roots crowd pot space. Remove dead leaves and brown leaf tips. Rinse foliage monthly.
Propagation: By seeds.
Pests and Diseases: Check for mealybugs, spider mites, scale. Avoid drafts.
Seasonal Care: Plant rests in winter. Set in cool site, 55°F (13°C). Keep soil barely moist; withhold fertilizer.

HOYA
Porcelain flower, wax plant

This genus comprises 200 species of woody vines which climb on trellises or along wire, or trail from hanging baskets. Equally prized for its attractive foliage and flowers, *Hoya* features fleshy, glossy leaves and waxy, star-shaped, fragrant flowers that hang in clusters from woody spikes. A mature plant 2 to 3 years old will bloom profusely each year, from spring through fall, with long-lasting flowers.

H. australis sports greenish white flowers with red bases and white crowns.

H. bella, miniature wax plant, is a dwarf shrubby plant, best grown in a basket; white flowers have crimson centers.

Howea forsterana

Hoya carnosa

H. carnosa, honey plant or wax plant, produces pinkish white flowers with red crowns; many cultivars with various leaf shapes and colorings are available. The leaves of one popular cultivar, the Hindu rope plant, twist and curl into unusual, sculptural shapes.

H. imperialis features purple blooms with ivory-colored crowns.

Soil: All-purpose mix.
Temperature: Day, 70°F (21°C); night, 55° to 60°F (13° to 16°C).
Light: Bright to moderate light, with 3 to 4 hours of direct sun daily, from eastern or western exposure.
Moisture: Let soil dry slightly between moderate waterings. Mist daily. Humidity, 30% to 35%.
Feeding: Every 2 weeks, with potassium-rich fertilizer. Overfeeding causes buds to drop.
Grooming: Repot young plants each year, after rest period. Mature plants prefer to be potbound. Carefully remove faded blooms, leaving woody spur extending from leaf axil intact; from these spurs new blooms will emerge.

Propagation: By layering or stem cuttings.
Pests and Diseases: Check for aphids, mealybugs, mites, root rot, scale.
Seasonal Care: Plant rests from fall through winter. Set in cool site, 50°F (10°C). Give just enough water to keep soil from drying out; withhold fertilizer.

HYACINTHUS
Hyacinth

These spring-blooming bulbous plants with their dense flower spikes are easy to force indoors. The waxy, fragrant, bell-shaped flowers of the most common species, *H. orientalis,* and the many available cultivars may be red, pink, blue, yellow, or white, and appear on 1 to 3 stalks, surrounded by long, narrow, light green leaves. *Hyacinthus* also may be forced in special bulb glasses filled with water.

Soil: All-purpose mix.
Temperature: Before roots form, keep cool, 35° to 48°F (2° to 9°C). In 13 weeks, when roots have formed and plant is 3 inches (8 cm) tall, keep

Hyacinthus orientalis

warm: day, 55° to 65°F (13° to 18°C); night, 40° to 50°F (4° to 10°C). When in bloom, keep cool for longer-lasting flowers.
Light: Before roots form, site in dark location. Once roots have formed, gradually increase amount of light, eventually providing bright light, without direct sun, from eastern, western, or southern exposure.
Moisture: Keep soil evenly moist at all times while growing. Mist daily around mature plant, not directly on blooms. Humidity, 30% to 35%.
Grooming: Heavy flower heads may need to be staked.
Seasonal Care: After blooming, plant may be replanted outdoors. Or, once foliage has yellowed, withhold water and store in cool, dark site; plant bulbs outdoors in spring. Blooms may appear in 1 to 2 years.

HYDRANGEA

23 species of evergreen shrubs are found in this genus, with *H. macrophylla* the ornamental grown indoors. Formerly known as *H. hortensis,* this plant grows to 36 inches (91 cm) tall with shiny, dark green, toothed leaves, and round flower heads. Flowers, appearing in summer, may be white, pink, red,

Hydrangea macrophylla

purple, or blue, and last up to 6 weeks. Because *Hydrangea* is reluctant to rebloom indoors, after flowering it is often planted outdoors.

Soil: Mix 2 parts standard potting soil, 2 parts peat, and 1 part perlite.
Temperature: Day, 55° to 60°F (13° to 16°C); night, 45° to 55°F (7° to 13°C).
Light: Bright light, no direct sun, from eastern exposure.
Moisture: Keep thoroughly moist, never letting soil dry out. Mist twice daily. Humidity, 45% to 50%.
Feeding: Monthly during growing season, with mild liquid fertilizer.
Grooming: Cut back stems after flowering and plant outdoors.
Propagation: By stem cuttings, taken in spring and set in moist rooting medium. New plant will not bloom indoors unless given a cold period.
Pests and Diseases: Check for aphids, mites, scale, whiteflies.

HYPOESTES
Freckle face, polka dot plant

40 species of shrubby foliage plants comprise this genus. Moderate grow-

ers, they reach from 24 to 36 inches (61 to 91 cm) in height, and require frequent pruning to keep a nice compact shape.

H. aristata, ribbon bush, features hairy, light green leaves; rosy purple tubular flowers are spotted with purple and white.

H. phyllostachya, freckle face, incorrectly called *H. sanguinolenta,* has round, downy, dark green leaves with pink spots; insignificant lilac flowers appear in spring, and can be removed.

Soil: Humusy mix.
Temperature: Day, 70°F (21°C); night, 50° to 55°F (10° to 13°C).
Light: Bright, filtered sun from eastern or southern exposure for best foliage color. Does well under artificial light, needing 14 light-hours daily.
Moisture: Keep soil evenly moist. Mist daily. Humidity, 40% to 45%.
Feeding: Weekly during growing season, with mild liquid fertilizer.
Grooming: Repot when roots occupy ½ of pot space. Prune back before new growth appears; trim leggy stems. Rinse foliage frequently.
Propagation: By tip cuttings or seeds.

Pests and Diseases: Check for mealybugs, mites, scale, slugs, whiteflies.
Seasonal Care: Plant rests briefly during winter. Set in cool site, 55°F (13°C). Keep soil barely moist; withhold fertilizer.

IMPATIENS
Balsam, busy lizzie, patience plant

These bushy flowering plants are noteworthy because of their prolific blooms, which appear throughout the year in clusters at the tips of shoots. 500 species with succulent stems comprise this genus, with indoor specimens growing from 6 to 24 inches (15 to 61 cm) tall. Merely touching the seed pods can cause them to pop open and spill their seeds.

I. platypetala 'Tangerine' bears salmon-orange flowers with a bright red eye, on reddish purple stems.

I. repens has creeping red stems that may root where they touch soil; yellow flowers have long spurs.

Hypoestes phyllostachya

Impatiens wallerana

I. wallerana features green leaves with a reddish tinge; flowers range from white, pink, red, and orange to purple; many compact cultivars are available in a wide variety of colors.

Soil: All-purpose mix.
Temperature: Day, 70°F (21°C); night, 60° to 65°F (16° to 18°C).
Light: Bright to moderate light from eastern or western exposure. Does well under artificial light, needing 14 light-hours daily.
Moisture: Let soil surface dry slightly between moderate waterings. Mist twice daily. Humidity, 50% to 60%.
Feeding: Weekly while in active growth, with mild liquid fertilizer.
Grooming: Pot-on when roots overcrowd pot space, in spring. Pinch growing tips to prevent straggly appearance and to enhance blooming.
Propagation: By herbaceous tip cuttings, or seeds.
Pests and Diseases: Check for aphids, spider mites, whiteflies. Dropping buds indicate insufficient light or too low humidity.
Seasonal Care: Rest period may be induced by lowering amount of light. Reduce water, never allowing soil to dry out completely; withhold fertilizer. Generally treated as annuals, discarded when blooming is completed.

IPOMOEA
Morning glory, sweet potato vine

500 species of annual and perennial vines comprise this genus, suitable for training along supports or trailing from baskets. *Ipomoea* may grow from 5 to 10 feet (1.5 to 3 m) long, bearing large, trumpet-shaped blooms that open and fade in the same day, to be replaced by more the following day.

I. batatas, sweet potato vine, is a summer-blooming annual; flowers are rosy to pale pink.

I. horsfalliae is a common perennial in the greenhouse with thick, bright green leaves; bears rose to lilac flowers in late winter.

I. purpurea, morning glory, is an annual bearing pink, lilac, or blue flowers in summer.

Soil: All-purpose mix.
Temperature: Day, 70°F (21°C); night, 50° to 55°F (10° to 13°C).
Light: Moderate light, with some direct sun daily, from eastern, western, or southern exposure.
Moisture: Keep soil thoroughly moist, not soggy. Mist twice daily. Humidity, 45% to 50%.
Feeding: Every 2 weeks during growing season, with mild liquid fertilizer; for mature plants only.
Grooming: Prefers to be potbound; divide and repot when roots overcrowd pot space. Remove faded flowers for longer blooming.
Propagation: By cuttings or seeds.
Pests and Diseases: Check for aphids, spider mites. Avoid drafts.
Seasonal Care: Plant is dormant when no new buds appear. Water half as frequently; withhold fertilizer. *I. batatas* should be kept cool, 55°F (13°C). Water lightly, withhold fertilizer, and repot in spring.

IRESINE
Beefsteak plant, blood leaf

These easy-care ornamental foliage plants have a bushy form when young, but tend to trail as they mature. *Iresine* grows to 18 inches (46 cm) tall, and the leaf surface features noticeable veining. Of the 70 species, the following are commonly cultivated indoors:

Ipomoea species

Iresine lindenii

I. herbstii, beefsteak plant, has dark red stems and heart-shaped leaves with pale red veins.

I. herbstii 'Aureo-reticulata' produces greenish red leaves with yellow veins.

I. lindenii features narrow, pointed leaves, deep red with pale center veins.

Soil: All-purpose mix.
Temperature: Day, 68° to 80°F (20° to 27°C); night, 55° to 60°F (13° to 16°C).
Light: Bright light, with 3 hours direct sun daily for best foliage color, from eastern or southern exposure. Does well under artificial light, needing 14 light-hours daily.
Moisture: Keep soil evenly moist, not soggy. Mist twice daily. Humidity, 40% to 45%.
Feeding: Every 2 weeks during growing season, with mild liquid fertilizer.
Grooming: Pot-on when roots occupy ½ of pot space, in early spring. Prune frequently to retain nice shape. Small, insignificant flowers may appear; pinch off to promote fuller foliage. Clean leaves often.

Propagation: By division or tip cuttings.
Pests and Diseases: Check for mealybugs, mites, scale, slugs, whiteflies.
Seasonal Care: Plant rests slightly from fall through winter. Can be kept at normal room temperature. Gradually reduce water, keeping soil barely moist; withhold fertilizer.

IXORA
Flame of the woods, jungle geranium, starflower

This shrubby plant is prized for its foliage and flowers. Young leaves are bronze colored, deepening as they age to a dark, glossy green with red veining. Dense, flat-topped clusters of flowers appear in summer and fall, but *Ixora* may also bloom throughout the year. It is a temperamental plant, and flower clusters will drop if it is disturbed or moved about. Of the 400 species, the following are grown indoors:

I. coccinea grows to 4 feet (1.2 m), with bright salmon-red flowers.

I. javanica bears reddish orange blooms; grows from 3 to 4 feet (0.9 to 1.2 m).

Soil: Humusy mix.
Temperature: Day, 70° to 80°F (21° to 27°C); night, 65° to 68°F (18° to 20°C).
Light: Partial shade, with 4 hours of direct sun in winter, from eastern or southern exposure.
Moisture: Let soil dry slightly between thorough waterings. Mist twice daily. Humidity, 60% to 70%.
Feeding: Weekly during growing season, with mild all-purpose fertilizer.
Grooming: Pot-on when roots overcrowd pot space. Every 2 years, cut back and repot when new growth appears. Otherwise, before active growth begins, pinch growing tips for a fuller plant and profuse blooms. Remove flowers as they fade.
Propagation: By stem cuttings taken in spring.
Pests and Diseases: Check for aphids, mealybugs, scale. Yellowing leaves indicate too low a temperature; rolled leaf edges indicate too much light.
Seasonal Care: When blooming slows, in late summer or winter, set in cool site, 55°F (13°C). Reduce water, keeping soil barely moist; withhold fertilizer.

JASMINUM
Jasmine, jessamine

200 species of climbing or upright shrubs comprise this genus, with indoor specimens requiring support for their growth. *Jasminum* is prized for its sweetly scented flowers, which are used in perfume, and appear as long tubes broadening out to 4 to 9 petals.

J. mesnyi, primrose jasmine, bears nonscented yellow flowers with darker centers, which can be double; blooms appear in spring.

Ixora coccinea

J. officinale, poet's jasmine, features clusters of fragrant, double white blooms from late summer to fall.

J. polyanthum, a winter to spring bloomer, produces fragrant clusters of rosy pink flowers with white insides.

Soil: All-purpose mix, with good drainage.
Temperature: Prefers 50° to 60°F (10° to 16°C) range.
Light: Bright light, with direct morning sun, from eastern to southern exposure.
Moisture: Keep soil thoroughly moist. Mist twice daily. Humidity, 50% to 60%.
Feeding: Monthly during growing season, with mild liquid fertilizer.
Grooming: Pot-on when roots occupy ½ of pot space. Prune often to contain rapid growth by cutting back flowering shoots to 2 to 3 inches (5 to 8 cm) once flowers have faded. Thin out shoots of *J. officinale* rather than shortening them.
Propagation: By layering, tip cuttings taken in late summer or fall, or seeds.
Pests and Diseases: Check for aphids, mealybugs, scale, whiteflies.

Seasonal Care: After flowering, set outdoors and bring in before first frost. Plant rests following blooming. Set in cool, well-lit room. Keep soil barely moist; withhold fertilizer.

JUSTICIA
Shrimp plant

Commonly sold as *Beloperone guttata*, this plant is now classified as *J. brandegeana*. A bushy shrub with softly hairy leaves, it can grow to 36 inches (91 cm). The 4 to 6 inch (10 to 15 cm) long, drooping flower spikes appear continuously during the growing season, which may last for 10 months. The spikes consist of overlapping heart-shaped bronze, pink, or yellow-green bracts; between these bracts emerge white flowers with red spots on the lower lips.

Soil: All-purpose mix.
Temperature: Day, 70°F (21°C); night, 50° to 55°F (10° to 13°C).
Light: Bright light, with some direct sun daily for full-colored bracts, from eastern, western, or southern

exposure. Air circulation is important.
Moisture: Keep barely moist, letting soil dry between waterings. Mist daily. Humidity, 45% to 60%.
Feeding: Every 2 weeks during growing season, with mild liquid fertilizer.
Grooming: Pot-on each spring until largest convenient pot size is reached; top-dress thereafter. Pinch growing tips for bushy form and better blooms. Cut growth back by ½ each spring to retain nice shape.
Propagation: By tip cuttings taken in spring or summer.
Pests and Diseases: Check for aphids, whiteflies. Dropping leaves indicate too little water.
Seasonal Care: Plant rests in winter. Keep in cool site, 55° to 60°F (13° to 16°C). Water sparingly; withhold fertilizer.

KALANCHOE
Panda plant, velvet leaf

These succulents are prized for their foliage and spring and winter blooms. Generally growing to 12

Jasminum polyanthum

Justicia brandegeana

Ka–Ko

inches (30 cm) tall, they are good specimens for window gardens. The following species are recommended among the 125 in the genus:

K. blossfeldiana, a common sight in bloom in winter, has round, waxy, green leaves edged in red; brilliant red or orange flowers are borne on erect spikes.

K. daigremontiana features pale lilac flowers; leaves bear light green and red markings.

K. fedtschenkoi, rainbow kalanchoe, suited for hanging baskets, has bluish gray leaves with red-tinged, notched edges; flowers are peach colored.

K. tomentosa, panda plant, has thick, stubby leaves covered with short white hairs; teeth on edges are brown.

Soil: Cactus/succulent mix.
Temperature: Day, 68° to 70°F (20° to 21°C); night, 50° to 65°F (10° to 18°C).
Light: Bright light, with 4 hours direct sun daily, from southern exposure.
Moisture: Keep soil barely moist. Humidity, 20% to 25%.
Feeding: Every 2 weeks in spring before flowering, with mild high-phosphorus fertilizer. Feed *K. blossfeldiana* every 2 weeks while in flower.

Grooming: Pot-on when pot space is overcrowded. Trim stems to promote blooming and to retain bushy shape. Remove old flower stalks.
Propagation: By cuttings, small plantlets on leaf edges, or seeds.
Pests and Diseases: Check for aphids, mealybugs, spider mites, scale.
Seasonal Care: Plant enters dormant period in fall. Provide normal light in cool site, 50° to 55°F (10° to 13°C). Let soil dry between light waterings; withhold fertilizer. To make *K. blossfeldiana* bloom another season, trim stems below flowers, above first set of mature leaves, once flowering is completed. For 4 months alternate 14 hours of total darkness with 10 hours of light. Does not rebloom readily.

KOHLERIA
Tree gloxinia

50 species of flowering plants with attractive velvety foliage comprise this gesneriad genus. Both stems

and leaves are covered with soft hairs, and the notched or scalloped leaves may bear various colored markings. Tubular or bell-shaped flowers appear mainly from summer through fall, but blooming can be year-round under proper conditions.

K. amabilis has dark green leaves with brown veins and silver markings; rosy flowers are spotted and banded with purple-red.

K. bogotensis grows to 24 inches (61 cm) tall; dark green leaves have light green or white markings; flowers are yellow with red spots.

K. digitaliflora bears white flowers flushed with rose.

K. eriantha features leaves edged with red or white hairs; orange-red flowers have yellow spots; measures up to 4 feet (1.2 m).

K. hirsuta grows to 36 inches (91 cm), bearing soft-haired leaves with red undersides; orange-red flowers have yellow lobes.

K. lindeniana bears white flowers

Kalanchoe blossfeldiana

Kohleria hirsuta

with purple markings and flushed with yellow; grows to 12 inches (30 cm), with dark green leaves veined in silver.

Soil: Fibrous-rooted gesneriad mix.
Temperature: Day, 80°F (27°C); night, 70° to 75°F (21° to 24°C).
Light: Bright light, with direct early morning sun, from eastern or western exposure. Does well under artificial light, needing 14 to 16 light-hours daily.
Moisture: Keep soil evenly moist. Mist twice daily. Humidity, 50% to 60%.
Feeding: Every 3 weeks with mild all-purpose fertilizer, during active growth.
Grooming: Each spring, separate rhizome clusters and repot. Prune if necessary following blooming.
Propagation: By rhizome division, tip cuttings taken in spring, or seeds.
Pests and Diseases: Check for aphids, *Botrytis* blight, cyclamen mites, mealybugs, powdery mildew, root or crown rot, scale, viruses, whiteflies.
Seasonal Care: Plants grown under artificial lights with tip cuttings taken regularly will not go dormant unless allowed to dry out. Plants that do go dormant should be kept cool, 50° to 60°F (10° to 16°C). Water just enough to keep rhizome barely moist; withhold fertilizer until new growth appears.

LACHENALIA
Cape cowslip

This genus contains 50 species of small bulbous plants, and many hybrids. Terminal flower spikes consist of waxy, tubular, long-lasting flowers. These perennials are attractive displayed in hanging baskets, and when planted in late summer will yield early spring blooms.

L. aloides grows to 12 inches (30 cm) in height; dark green, strap-shaped leaves are spotted with purple; flowers are yellow with red tips.

L. bulbiferum bears yellow flowers with reddish purple insides; grows to 12 inches (30 cm).

L. glaucina measures 6 inches (15 cm) tall; white flowers may be tinged with blue, red, yellow, or green.

Soil: All-purpose mix.
Temperature: Newly potted bulb and mature plant, 50° to 55° (10° to 13°C).
Light: Bright light from any exposure, for newly potted bulb and mature plant.
Moisture: Water newly potted bulb thoroughly. Don't water again until growth appears, then water moderately, keeping mature plant evenly moist.
Feeding: Every 2 weeks during growing season, with mild liquid fertilizer; for mature plant.
Propagation: By offsets when repotting, or seeds.
Pests and Diseases: Generally healthy and free from infestation.
Seasonal Care: 1 month after flowering stops, gradually reduce water until leaves yellow, then withhold completely. Stop fertilizing. Store in dark location until late summer, then repot.

LACTUCA
Lettuce

L. sativa is the familiar green vegetable which turns up in salad bowls. Both leaf and head lettuce are suitable for greenhouse cultivation, with the leafy type quicker to develop and easier to grow. See chapter 16 for recommended varieties.

Soil: All-purpose mix.
Temperature: Keep newly planted seeds cool, 65°F (18°C). Maturing plants: day, 50° to 68°F (10° to 20°C); night, 45° to 50°F (7° to 10°C).
Light: 4 to 6 hours bright light daily from eastern or western exposure. Air circulation is important.
Moisture: Keep soil slightly moist. Avoid getting water on leaves.

Lachenalia **hybrid**

Feeding: Weekly, with mild liquid fertilizer.

Grooming: Pick outer leaves of maturing leaf lettuce to promote continuing inner leaf growth.

Propagation: By seeds.

Pests and Diseases: Check for aphids, mildew, rot, slugs, snails.

Seasonal Care: Sow seeds in late fall or winter so that plant's growing season corresponds with short day-length.

LAELIA

This orchid makes a delightful addition to any collection, bearing racemes of long-lasting, star-shaped flowers. The blooms, featuring a prominent tubular lip, last 1 month or longer on the plant, but fade quickly when cut. *Laelia* has been hybridized with the orchid genera *Cattleya, Brassavola,* and *Sophronitis.* Mainly epiphytic, this genus is sympodial in growth habit, having pseudobulbs. Most of the 30 species can be grown in an intermediate greenhouse, and the following species are recommended especially for the home:

L. anceps grows from 6 to 12 inches (15 to 30 cm), with slender, erect, or arching flower stalks; dark pink flowers with crimson lips are fragrant, appearing 2 to 6 in a cluster; blooms in winter.

L. autumnalis features clusters of 3 to 9 fragrant, waxy flowers; sepals and petals are rosy purple; lip is white or purple; blooms in late fall or early winter.

L. pumila produces drooping, 4 inch (10 cm) wide flowers; petals and sepals are rosy purple; lip is dark mauve with yellow throat; blooms appear in fall.

L. purpurata measures from 18 to 30 inches (46 to 76 cm) tall, bearing 3 to 5 flowers; wavy-edged petals and sepals are light pink; lip is mauve with purple veining and yellow throat; flowers in spring and summer.

Soil: Osmunda fiber or orchid bark mix. *L. anceps* tends to climb and does better mounted on section of tree limb, barn board, cork bark, or slab of tree fern fiber when grown in a greenhouse.

Temperature: Day, 70°F to 85°F (21° to 29°C); night, 55°F (13°C).

Light: Lots of bright light from southern exposure; shade from strong summer sun at midday. Good circulation of fresh air.

Moisture: Let growing medium approach dryness between thorough waterings. Mist frequently. Humidity, 50%.

Feeding: Proportioned feedings of all-purpose fertilizer with each watering during active growth.

Grooming: Repot when plant overcrowds pot, or when growing medium has deteriorated. Best done at outset of active growth, when new roots are first visible.

Propagation: By division of pseudobulbs.

Pests and Diseases: Check for bacterial, fungal, and viral infections, mealybugs, scale, slugs, snails, whiteflies.

Seasonal Care: Once flower buds have swelled, cut back on amount of food and water. Plant requires short to long rest period after flowers open; decrease watering; withhold fertilizer.

LANTANA
Red sage, yellow sage

155 species of perennial shrubs and herbs comprise this genus, featuring wrinkled leaves with a rough surface and sharp odor. Flowers appear mainly in spring and summer, in fragrant, flat-topped clusters. As these tubular flowers mature, they deepen in color. *Lantana* may grow to 4 feet (1.2 m) tall, but can be pruned to achieve a bushier, 10- to 15-inch (25 to 38 cm) form.

L. camara, yellow sage, has bright green, oval leaves; 2 inch (5 cm) wide

Lactuca sativa **'Buttercrunch'**

Laelia **hybrid**

flower clusters are orange-yellow, changing to red or white; a number of cultivars are available in shades of white, yellow, red, lilac, and blue.

L. montevidensis, weeping lantana, features 36 inch (91 cm) long, trailing branches with down-covered, dark green leaves; flowers are rosy pink with yellow centers.

Soil: All-purpose mix.
Temperature: Day, 68° to 75°F (20° to 24°C); night, 55° to 60°F (13° to 16°C).
Light: Bright light, with 3 hours direct sun daily for best flowering, from eastern, western, or southern exposure.
Moisture: Let soil dry slightly between thorough waterings. Mist daily. Humidity, 25% to 30%.
Feeding: Every 2 weeks during growing season, with mild liquid fertilizer.
Grooming: Blooms best when potbound; pot-on when roots occupy ½ of pot space. Repot each year in spring, after cutting growth back to 5 inches (13 cm). Pinch straggly stems, and pinch growing tips for bushy shape.
Propagation: By stem cuttings or seeds.

Pests and Diseases: Check for mealybugs, spider mites, scale, whiteflies.
Seasonal Care: Plant rests from late fall to late winter. Keep cool, 50°F (10°C). Reduce water, keeping soil barely moist; withhold fertilizer.

LAURUS
Bay tree, sweet bay, laurel

L. nobilis is the stately evergreen tree which offers up its bounty of deep green leaves to flavor foods. In addition, these leaves yield an essential oil which is used in perfume and medicine. *Laurus* is a slow grower which responds well to pruning, and generally measures 3 to 6 feet (0.9 to 1.8 m) indoors. Small greenish white flowers may appear.

Soil: Mix 3 parts standard potting soil and 1 part sand, with good drainage.
Temperature: Day, 65° to 75°F (18° to 24°C); night, 50° to 60°F (10° to 16°C).
Light: Indirect light from eastern exposure. Air circulation is important.

Moisture: Keep soil evenly moist. Mist twice daily. Humidity, 30% to 35%.
Feeding: Weekly during growing season, with mild liquid fertilizer.
Grooming: Pot-on when roots completely overcrowd pot space. Prune often to contain growth. Wash foliage frequently.
Propagation: By cuttings.
Pests and Diseases: Check for aphids, mealybugs, mites, scale.
Seasonal Care: Plant is dormant during winter. Set in cool site, 45° to 60°F (7° to 16°C). Reduce water, keeping soil barely moist; withhold fertilizer.

LAVANDULA
English lavender, French lavender

20 species of aromatic herbs in this genus produce lovely flower spikes which may be dried and used in sachets or potpourris. These perennials bloom in early summer when they are 2 years old, and may become leggy with age.

Lantana camara

Laurus nobilis

La–Li

L. angustifolia, English lavender, grows from 24 to 36 inches (61 to 91 cm) tall; young leaves are white changing to green; flower spikes are purple.

L. dentata, French lavender, features toothed, gray-green leaves; flower spikes are deep purple; measures 12 to 36 inches (30 to 91 cm) high.

Soil: Humusy mix, with good drainage.
Temperature: Tolerates 40° to 70°F (4° to 21°C) range.
Light: Bright light, with 4 hours direct sun daily, from southern or western exposure. Does well under artificial light, needing 12 to 14 light-hours daily.
Moisture: Keep soil slightly moist. Mist daily.
Feeding: Monthly during growing season, with mild liquid fertilizer.
Grooming: Remove faded flowers and stems. Prune in early spring to prevent straggly appearance. To dry flowers, pick before they open fully, when color has just appeared. Cut entire stalk; hang to dry in cool site with air circulation.
Propagation: By cuttings taken in spring or fall, division, or seeds.
Seasonal Care: After flowering stops, plant may rest through winter. Cut back growth by ⅓, reduce water slightly, and withhold fertilizer.

LEDEBOURIA
Squill

Planted in early spring, these bulbs will produce flowers in the same season. They will bloom indoors for several years, provided they are given a winter rest. A popular species, formerly known as *Scilla violacea,* it is now classified as *Ledebouria socialis.* This plant grows to 6 inches (15 cm) tall featuring olive green spotted, silvery leaves with pink or dark purple undersides; green flowers have white margins and purple filaments.

Soil: All-purpose mix.
Temperature: Keep at 60°F (16°C) at all times.
Light: Set newly potted bulb in partial shade. In 4 to 6 weeks when growth appears, introduce bright light, with 3 to 4 hours direct sun daily.
Moisture: Water newly potted bulb sparingly, allowing soil to dry between waterings. Once growth appears, let surface dry slightly between moderate waterings.
Feeding: Every 3 weeks once buds have appeared, with mild all-purpose fertilizer.
Propagation: By offsets.
Seasonal Care: Plant rests during winter. Set in cool site, 50° to 60°F (10° to 16°C). Water just enough to prevent foliage from drying out; withhold fertilizer.

LILIUM
Easter lily, Japanese lily

80 to 90 species of bulbous plants comprise this genus, producing fragrant, trumpet-shaped blooms in late summer. Each of the species listed here can be forced for earlier bloom, and requires 13 weeks from time of planting to produce flowers. Blooms are borne on 3- to 5-foot (0.9 to 1.5 m) stems.

L. auratum, gold banded lily, produces many 12 inch (30 cm) wide flowers in a raceme; blooms are white with brilliant red spots and yellow center stripes.

L. longiflorum var. *eximium,* Easter lily, features a single 4 to 5 inch (10

Lavandula dentata

Ledebouria socialis

to 13 cm) wide white bloom per stalk, lasting for 1 week.

L. speciosum, Japanese lily, bears 4 inch (10 cm) long white flowers with rosy red markings, singly or in a cluster.

Soil: All-purpose mix, with good drainage.
Temperature: Newly potted bulb: 40° to 45°F (4° to 7°C). Mature, blooming plant: day, 62° to 68°F (17° to 20°C); night, 40° to 55°F (4° to 13°C).
Light: Keep newly potted bulb in dark location. When growth appears, gradually introduce bright light from southern or eastern exposure. Air circulation is important.
Moisture: Keep soil evenly moist. Mist twice daily. Humidity, 30% to 45%.
Feeding: Every 2 weeks during growing season, with mild liquid fertilizer.

Grooming: Repot each year, in fall. Remove blooms as they fade.
Propagation: By offsets when repotting, or seeds.
Pests and Diseases: Check for rot.
Seasonal Care: After flowering, leaves will yellow. Keep soil barely moist. When leaves die back completely, plant is entering dormant period. Remove bulb from pot and store in damp sand in cool site, 45°F (7°C). Bulb can be forced next season or planted outdoors in spring.

LITHOPS
Living stones

The leaves of the 50 species comprising this succulent genus are colored and shaped to blend into the rocky terrain of their native Africa. Two semicircular leaves are fused along most of their surface, except for a slit across the top, and white and yellow flowers appear from this opening in late summer or fall. New leaves emerge from the slit following blooming, to replace old leaves.

L. marmorata features gray-green leaves with creamy green mottling; grows to 1½ inches (4 cm) tall; flowers are white and up to 1¼ inches (3 cm) wide.

L. olivacea grows to ¾ inch (19 mm) tall; olive green to brown, fleshy leaves have raised white dots; flowers are bright yellow.

L. salicola measures to 1 inch (2.5 cm) tall; leaf sides are gray to olive green; dark green rounded tops highlight white flowers.

L. turbiniformis sports rough, red-brown leaf tops with irregular tracings of dark brown lines; yellow flowers have white undersides.

Soil: Cactus/succulent mix.
Temperature: Day, 65° to 80°F (18° to 27°C); night, 50° to 70°F (10° to 21°C).
Light: Bright light from southern or western exposure. Does well under artificial light, needing 16 light-hours daily. Air circulation is important.
Moisture: Let soil dry between light waterings. Avoid overwatering. Humidity, 20% to 25%.
Grooming: Slow grower, no need to pot-on.
Propagation: By division or seeds.
Pests and Diseases: Check for mealybugs, root rot, scale.
Seasonal Care: Plant rests during winter. Set in cool location, 60°F (16°C). Withhold water until growth resumes in spring.

Lilium longiflorum var. eximium

Lithops turbiniformis, front left, and *L. marmorata*

Lo—Ly

LOBIVIA
Cob cactus

70 species of globe-shaped or cylindrical cacti make up this genus, which does well in window gardens or on tabletops. *Lobivia* is a summer bloomer with oversized, showy flowers in shades of red, pink, orange, yellow, or purple. Many hybrids are available.

L. allegraiana grows to 6 inches (15 cm); green stem bears yellow-brown spines along ribs; flowers are pink to red.

L. hertrichiana measures 4 inches (10 cm) across; glossy green stem has a pattern of yellow-brown radial spines surrounding a curved, yellow central spine; flowers are brilliant red.

L. jajoiana has 2 inch (5 cm) diameter; green stem features needlelike, red radial spines and black, hooked central spines; flowers are deep red.

Soil: Cactus/succulent mix.
Temperature: Day, 70°F (21°C); cooler at night.
Light: Bright light from southern or western exposure. Air circulation is important.
Moisture: Let soil dry between thorough waterings. Avoid overwatering. Humidity, 30% to 45%.

Feeding: Every 2 weeks during growing season, with high-potassium fertilizer.
Grooming: Repot when pot space is overcrowded, in spring.
Propagation: By offsets or seeds.
Pests and Diseases: Check for aphids, mealybugs, spider mites, scale. Also be alert for fungus disease.
Seasonal Care: Plant rests during winter. Site in cool location, 60°F (16°C), with maximum light. Water just enough to prevent plant from shriveling; withhold fertilizer.

LUDWIGIA
False loosestrife, swamp spoon

This bunch-type aquatic plant is a useful addition to aquaria plagued by algae. *Ludwigia* uses most of the available light, eventually starving the algae. *L. natans* has glossy, tapered leaves with deep burgundy undersides and grows to 8 inches (20 cm) tall. Yellow flowers appear in summer.

Soil: Pot in rich mix of garden loam and bone meal. Top-dress with gravel, then submerge.
Temperature: 50° to 75°F (10° to 24°C).

Light: Large amount of bright light. Does well under artificial light, needing 14 to 16 light-hours daily.
Water: Slightly acid.
Feeding: Occasionally, with bone meal/clay pellets.
Grooming: Once a month, replace ⅓ of water in tank. Scrape algae from tank sides. Remove dead or discolored leaves.
Propagation: By cuttings or division.
Pests and Diseases: Check for bacterial rot, snails.

LYCOPERSICON
Tomato

This familiar garden plant, *L. lycopersicum*, can produce edible fruit year-round when grown in the greenhouse. The fruit, usually seen as round and red, may also be pear- or plum-shaped in varying shades of red and yellow. There are many miniature and compact varieties suitable for greenhouse and indoor culture.

Soil: All-purpose mix.
Temperature: Day, 80°F (27°C); night, 60°F (16°C).
Light: 6 hours of full sun daily from southern exposure. Supplement with 2 hours of artificial light for every hour of natural light plant is lacking.

Lobivia hybrid

Ludwigia natans

Moisture: Keep soil evenly moist. Mist daily.
Feeding: Monthly, with fish emulsion or 1 tablespoon (15 ml) bone meal worked into soil.
Grooming: Stake large plants. Prune to control rapid growth. Pollinate blooming plants by gently shaking dry plant to distribute pollen.
Propagation: By seeds.
Pests and Diseases: Check for aphids, slugs, whiteflies. End rot and fruit rot indicate improper watering. Yellow foliage results from soil deficiency; add nitrogen, increase level of acidity.

MALPIGHIA
Miniature holly

30 species of evergreen shrubs and trees make up this genus, with *M. coccigera* commonly found indoors. Eventually reaching 36 inches (91 cm) in height, it can be pruned to retain a compact form and is often used as bonsai. The glossy green, holly-shaped leaves bear spines along the edges. Tiny, pinkish red flowers appear in spring through summer, and precede the small red fruit.

Soil: All-purpose mix.
Temperature: Day, 68° to 72°F (20° to 22°C); night, 60° to 65°F (16° to 18°C).
Light: Full sun from southern exposure.
Moisture: Let soil dry slightly between thorough waterings. Mist daily. Humidity, 30% to 35%.
Feeding: Once, in late winter, with potassium- and phosphate-rich fertilizer.
Grooming: Pot-on in late winter or early spring, when roots overcrowd pot space. Pinch straggly stems; pinch growing tips to retain attractive shape.
Propagation: By stem cuttings or seeds.
Pests and Diseases: Check for mealybugs, scale.
Seasonal Care: Plant is active year-round.

MAMMILLARIA
Pincushion cactus, powder puff cactus

The largest genus of cacti, numbering 150 species, *Mammillaria* includes low-growing clusters or single-stemmed plants, with an assortment of spines. Well suited to window gardens, even young plants produce a crown of flowers on top of the previous year's growth, in spring and summer. After flowering, red berries may replace blooms.

M. bocasana, powder puff cactus, rises to 1½ inches (4 cm) tall; 2-inch (5 cm) blue-green stems form a cluster, covered by soft white hairs interspersed with curving yellow spines; flowers are yellow.

M. candida, snowball pincushion, features cylindrical, blue-green stems measuring 3 inches (8 cm) thick, covered by needlelike white spines; bears pink flowers less than 1 inch (2.5 cm) long.

M. celsiana appears as a single stem, branching into clusters as it matures, up to 5 inches (13 cm) tall; blue-green leaves bear regular pattern of white and pale yellow spines; flowers are red.

M. microhelia forms small clusters, to 6 inches (15 cm) tall; radial yellow spines are curved, with white tips, while central spines are red-brown and needle shaped; flowers are white to yellow.

M. plumosa, feather cactus, appears to be a 3 inch (8 cm) thick, white, woolly mound, but individual stems

Lycopersicon lycopersicum 'Tiny Tim'

Malpighia coccigera

are hidden by dense cover of soft white spines; flowers are greenish white.

Soil: Cactus/succulent mix.
Temperature: Day, 70° to 85°F (21° to 29°C); night, 60°F (16°C).
Light: Bright light from western or southern exposure. Does well under artificial light, needing 12 light-hours daily. Air circulation is important.
Moisture: Let soil dry between thorough waterings. Avoid overwatering. Humidity, 30% to 45%.
Feeding: Once a year, in spring, with high-phosphorus fertilizer.
Grooming: Repot when pot space is overcrowded.
Propagation: By offsets or seeds.
Pests and Diseases: Check for aphids, mealybugs, spider mites, scale. Also be alert for fungus disease.
Seasonal Care: Plant rests during winter. Set in cool site, 65°F (18°C), with 5 hours of sun daily. Water just enough to keep foliage from shriveling.

MANETTIA
Firecracker plant

Twining stems which trail or climb characterize this genus of herbs and shrubs. Of the 100 species, *M. inflata* is the one commonly grown indoors. The thin stems with fleshy green leaves can be kept at a manageable length by frequent pinching. The small, tubular flowers, which appear mainly in spring and fall, are red with yellow tips, and have fine hair on the petals.

Soil: All-purpose mix, with good drainage.
Temperature: Day, 68° to 80°F (20° to 27°C); night, 68° to 70°F (20° to 21°C).
Light: Partial shade, with some morning sun or full winter sun, from eastern exposure. Does well under artificial light, needing 12 to 14 light-hours daily.
Moisture: Keep soil evenly moist. Mist twice daily. Humidity, 45% to 60%.
Feeding: Weekly during growing season, with mild liquid fertilizer.
Grooming: Pot-on young plant when roots occupy ¾ of pot space, in spring. Older plant does not like to be disturbed. Prune back ½ of growth after flowering. Provide support for twining stems.
Propagation: By tip cuttings taken in spring and summer.
Pests and Diseases: Check for aphids, whiteflies. Yellow leaves result from too low a temperature.
Seasonal Care: Plant rests after flowering, lasting from early fall to late winter. Keep in cool site, 55° to 60°F (13° to 16°C). Keep soil barely moist; withhold fertilizer.

MARANTA
Arrowroot, prayer plant

This genus contains 20 species of foliage plants, valued for their striking leaf patterns. At night the leaves fold up, resembling clasped hands. A low grower and easy to care for, *Maranta* usually measures from 8 to 15 inches (20 to 38 cm) tall.

M. leuconeura, prayer plant, the most common species, features light or dark green leaves with a satiny sheen; veins are red or gray and undersides are burgundy colored.

M. leuconeura var. *erythroneura* sports olive green leaves with light green markings; veins are bright red and leaf undersides are burgundy.

M. leuconeura var. *kerchoviana*, rabbit's tracks, features gray-green

Mammillaria candida

Manettia inflata

leaves with deep green markings along midribs; undersides are slate gray.

M. leuconeura var. *leuconeura* has dark green leaves with silver along the midribs and silver veins; undersides are burgundy-red.

Soil: Humusy mix.
Temperature: Day, 70° to 80°F (21° to 27°C); night, 62° to 68°F (17° to 20°C).
Light: Moderate light from northern or eastern exposure. Does well under artificial light, needing 14 to 16 light-hours daily.
Moisture: Keep soil evenly moist. Mist twice daily. Humidity, 45% to 60%.
Feeding: Every 2 weeks during growing season, with mild liquid fertilizer.
Grooming: Plant prefers to be potbound; pot-on when roots occupy ¾ of pot space, in spring. Remove dried leaves. Rinse foliage once a month.
Propagation: By layering, division, or stem cuttings.
Pests and Diseases: Check for aphids, mealybugs, spider mites, scale.
Seasonal Care: Plant rests from fall through early spring. Keep cool, 55°F (13°C). Reduce water, letting soil dry slightly between waterings; withhold fertilizer.

MELOCACTUS
Turk's cap cactus

These ribbed cacti bear a distinctive cap resembling white wool on their top, from which flowers emerge on a mature plant. The small pink blooms appear in spring and summer, and close at night. Containing 36 species, this genus features globe- or column-shaped cacti with various colored spines.

M. bahiensis is globular, measuring 4 inches (10 cm) high and 6 inches (15 cm) wide; brown radial spines emerge from areoles.

M. intortus features straight and curving spines, colored yellow, brown, or pink; measures 36 inches (91 cm) tall and 16 inches (41 cm) wide.

M. matanzanus, miniature Turk's cap, grows to a scant 3½ inches (9 cm) tall and 4 inches (10 cm) wide; curving spines are red, changing to yellow.

Soil: Cactus/succulent mix.

Temperature: Tolerates 65° to 90°F (18° to 32°C) range.
Light: Bright, filtered light from southern, southeastern, or eastern exposure. Does well under artificial light, needing 12 to 16 light-hours daily. Fresh air circulation is important.
Moisture: Let soil dry between moderate waterings. Avoid overwatering, which causes rot.
Feeding: For plants without caps: low-nitrogen, high-potassium fertilizer once in spring. Feed plants with caps every 2 months. Feed established plants only, and only during growing season.
Grooming: Repot when roots completely overcrowd pot space.
Propagation: By seeds.
Pests and Diseases: Check for aphids, mealybugs, spider mites, scale. Also be alert for fungus disease.
Seasonal Care: Plant may become dormant in winter. Keep in cool site; water just enough to keep plant from shriveling.

Maranta leuconeura **var.** *kerchoviana*

Melocactus **species**

MENTHA
Mint, peppermint, spearmint

25 species of aromatic perennial herbs comprise this genus. A fast grower suited to hanging baskets, the more cuttings of *Mentha* that are taken, the bushier the growth. Spikes of lilac, pink, or white flowers may appear in summer, and can be pinched out for better foliage growth.

M. ×*piperita*, peppermint, grows to 36 inches (91 cm) tall with dark green, purple-tinged leaves.

M. spicata, spearmint, grows to 24 inches (61 cm) tall with green, ovate leaves.

M. suaveolens, apple mint, measures 24 to 36 inches (61 to 91 cm) tall; leaves and stems are covered with white hairs.

M. suaveolens 'Variegata', pineapple mint, sports white variegated foliage.

Soil: All-purpose mix.
Temperature: 65° to 68°F (18° to 20°C).
Light: Indirect light from eastern exposure. Does well under artificial light, needing 12 to 14 light-hours daily.
Moisture: Keep evenly moist, never allowing soil to dry out. Mist daily. Humidity, 45% to 60%.
Feeding: Every 2 to 3 weeks during growing season, with mild liquid fertilizer.
Grooming: Repot and divide as plant becomes potbound. Pinch often to keep nice shape. Leaves may be plucked when stems are 3 inches (8 cm) tall.
Propagation: By cuttings or division.
Pests and Diseases: Generally healthy and free from infestation.
Seasonal Care: Plant rests in winter; cut back and keep cool, 55°F (13°C). Water sparingly; withhold fertilizer.

MONSTERA
Hurricane plant, split-leaf philodendron, Swiss cheese plant

M. deliciosa is the common ornamental among the 25 species comprising this genus of tropical foliage plants. It tends to climb, and sends out aerial roots that attach to bark slabs or moss-covered poles for support. *Monstera* may grow up to 8 or 10 feet (2.4 or 3 m) tall. Young leaves are heart-shaped and solid, but develop serrated edges and become riddled with holes as they age. Mature leaves are leathery and measure up to 18 inches (46 cm) wide. Flowers may appear, consisting of off-white spathes with a 10-inch (25 cm) spike projecting from the center. The edible fruit (called ceriman) ripens in a year and tastes somewhat like a combination of pineapple and strawberry.

Soil: All-purpose mix.
Temperature: Day, 70° to 80°F (21° to 27°C); night, 62° to 68°F (17° to 20°C).
Light: Moderate to low light from any exposure, with some direct winter sun. Does well under artificial light, needing 14 to 16 light-hours daily.

Mentha spicata

Monstera deliciosa

Moisture: Let soil dry between thorough waterings. Mist twice daily. Humidity, 30% to 55%.
Feeding: Every 2 weeks during growing season, with mild liquid fertilizer.
Grooming: Prefers to be potbound; pot-on when roots occupy ¾ of pot space, in spring. Cut ends of tall plant to limit growth. Rinse foliage frequently. Guide aerial roots onto support or into soil.
Propagation: By air layering, or stem cuttings taken in early summer.
Pests and Diseases: Check for aphids, mealybugs, spider mites, scale.
Seasonal Care: Plant rests during winter. Keep cool, 55°F (13°C). Reduce water, keeping soil barely moist; withhold fertilizer.

MUSA
Banana

These large plants with trunklike stems are interesting additions to a greenhouse. Growing from 4 to 7 feet (1.2 to 2.1 m) tall, they feature clumps of various colored foliage and produce fruit which may be edible, depending on the species.

M. acuminata 'Dwarf Cavendish' produces 36 inch (91 cm) long, bright green leaves; in summer, flower clusters appear surrounded by purple bracts, to be followed by edible fruits.

M. velutina features 36 inch (91 cm) long leaves, solid green or speckled with purple, borne on pink stems; 2 to 4 flower clusters appear in late summer, composed of pale pink to red bracts and yellow flowers; nonedible fruits are red with a velvety texture.

Soil: Humusy mix.
Temperature: Day, 80° to 85°F (27° to 29°C); night, 62° to 65°F (17° to 18°C).
Light: Lots of bright light, with direct winter sun, from eastern, western, or southern exposure.
Moisture: Keep wet at all times. Mist daily. Humidity, 45% to 60%.
Feeding: Every 2 weeks during growing season, with mild liquid fertilizer.
Grooming: Repot every 2 years, in spring. Remove dead flower stems.
Propagation: By division or suckers.
Pests and Diseases: Check for scale, mealybugs.
Seasonal Care: Plant is dormant in winter. Keep in cool site: *M. acuminata* 'Dwarf Cavendish' at 50°F (10°C); *M. velutina* at 60°F (16°C). Keep soil barely moist; withhold fertilizer.

MYRIOPHYLLUM
Milfoil, parrot's feather

This is an aquatic bunch-type plant which is easily grown in aquaria and makes an attractive addition to aquascapes.

M. elatinoides has whorls of feathery leaves both above and below water; grows to 15 inches (38 cm) tall.

M. hippuroides has featherlike submersed leaves, 1½ inches (4 cm) long; emersed leaves are ½ inch (13 cm) long.

M. verticillatum appears bushy, with leaves up to 1¼ inch (3 cm) long; flowers are borne on a spike.

Soil: Layer of medium size aquarium gravel or coarse sand.
Temperature: 65° to 75°F (18° to 24°C).
Light: Indirect, bright sunlight. Does well under artificial light, needing 14 to 16 light-hours daily.
Water: Slightly acid.
Feeding: Occasionally, with bone meal/clay pellets.
Grooming: Once a month, replace

Musa acuminata 'Dwarf Cavendish'

Myriophyllum verticillatum

My—Na

⅓ of water in tank. Scrape algae from tank sides. Remove dead or discolored leaves. Prune to promote bushiness.
Pests and Diseases: Check for bacterial rot, snails.

MYRTUS
Myrtle

This genus contains 16 species of evergreen shrubs and trees, with aromatic foliage which emits a fragrance when crushed. The small flowers are also delicately scented, and consist of white or pink petals surrounding many yellow stamens. These blooms appear in late summer through fall, and are later replaced by fruit. Generally growing under 4 feet (1.2 m) indoors, *Myrtus* can be trained as a bonsai specimen, and benefits by spending some time outdoors.

M. communis, Greek myrtle, features many branches with dense, shiny green leaves.

M. communis 'Microphylla', dwarf myrtle, has 1 inch (2.5 cm) long leaves and grows to 24 inches (61 cm) tall.

M. communis 'Variegata' features white-bordered leaves.

Soil: Mix 3 parts standard potting soil with 1 part coarse sand.
Temperature: Day, 68° to 78°F (20° to 26°C); night, 40° to 64°F (4° to 18°C).
Light: Bright light, no direct sun, from southeastern or southwestern exposure. Turn often to promote symmetrical growth. Air circulation is important.
Moisture: Let soil dry between thorough waterings. Mist twice daily. Humidity, 30% to 35%.
Feeding: Every 2 weeks during growing season, with mild all-purpose fertilizer.
Grooming: Pot-on when roots occupy a little over ½ of pot space. Prune occasionally to retain bushy shape; too much pruning results in fewer flowers.
Propagation: By heel cuttings taken in summer, or seeds.

Pests and Diseases: Check for aphids, mealybugs, mites, scale.
Seasonal Care: Plant is dormant from early fall to spring. Keep in cool site, 40° to 45°F (4° to 7°C). Reduce water, letting soil dry slightly between moderate waterings; withhold fertilizer.

NARCISSUS
Daffodil, narcissus

26 species of flowering bulbs comprise this genus, a member of the Amaryllis family. Flowers may appear singly on the stalk or several to a cluster, and consist of a large trumpet or small cup with a circle of petals. These parts may be yellow or white. Both hardy and fragile types may be forced indoors for winter or spring blooms. See chapter 18 for a list of some recommended hardy bulbs. The following are fragile bulbs which can be grown in water:

Myrtus communis 'Variegata'

Narcissus tazetta 'Paper-white'

N. tazetta var. *orientalis,* Chinese sacred lily, has a deep yellow trumpet.

N. tazetta 'Paper-white', paper-white narcissus, features pure white cups and petals.

Soil: Mix 2 parts garden loam and 1 part sand. Fragile bulbs may be grown in 3- to 4-inch (8 to 10 cm) deep glass containers filled with pebbles to ½ inch (13 mm) of top, and water.
Temperature: Keep newly potted hardy bulbs at 35° to 48°F (2° to 9°C). In 8 to 9 weeks, when roots have formed and growth is 1 inch (2.5 cm) tall, keep at 63°F (17°C). Keep fragile bulbs at 63°F (17°C) at all times.
Light: Keep fragile and hardy bulbs in dark location until growth appears. Gradually introduce bright light from eastern, western, or southern exposure.
Moisture: Keep hardy bulbs evenly moist. Humidity, 30% to 45%.
Feeding: Not necessary.
Seasonal Care: Fragile and hardy bulbs cannot be forced a second time indoors. Discard after flowering or plant permanently outdoors once foliage has died back.

NEMATANTHUS
Candy corn plant, guppy flower

These perennial plants in the Gesneriad family are grown for their attractive foliage and distinctively shaped flowers. Growth is generally trailing or spreading, with glossy, dark green leaves. The puffy, tubular, 1 inch (2.5 cm) long flowers are inflated, resembling a pouch, narrowing to a tiny opening with 5 petals. Several *Nematanthus* species were formerly classified in the genus *Hypocyrta.*

N. fritschii features speckled, lavender flowers; inside of tube is covered with rosy spots.

N. nervosus has spreading growth; flowers are orange and red.

N. perianthomegus produces yellow-orange flowers with maroon stripes which are long lasting and appear throughout the year; woody branches grow outward.

N. wettsteinii, clog plant, has thin, pendulous stems with polished, jade green leaves; profuse blooms are yellow and red and appear throughout the year.

Soil: Fibrous-rooted gesneriad mix.
Temperature: Day, 72° to 78°F (22° to 26°C); night, 65° to 70°F (18° to 21°C).
Light: Bright light, with direct winter sun, from southern or eastern exposure. Does well under artificial light, needing 14 light-hours daily.
Moisture: Let soil dry slightly between thorough waterings. Mist twice daily. Humidity, 50% to 60%.
Feeding: Every 2 weeks during growing season, with mild all-purpose fertilizer.
Grooming: Prefers to be potbound; pot-on when roots occupy ¾ of pot space. Prune straggly branches to retain nice shape.
Propagation: By division, stem cuttings, or seeds.
Pests and Diseases: Check for aphids, *Botrytis* blight, cyclamen

mites, mealybugs, powdery mildew, root or crown rot, scale, viruses, whiteflies.
Seasonal Care: Plant rests after main blooming period. Keep cool, 55°F (13°C). Reduce water; withhold fertilizer.

NEOREGELIA
Fingernail plant

These epiphytic bromeliads may bloom at any time during the year, when the changing color of the inner rosette or leaf tips signals the appearance of a flower. The compact heads of violet or blue flowers are not long lasting, but the foliage color remains for several months.

N. carolinae produces 16 inch (40 cm) long, spiny green leaves, with inner rosette changing to red-purple.

N. carolinae 'Meyendorffii' features 5 inch (13 cm) long, olive green leaves with brown bands on the undersides; center rosette deepens to burgundy.

N. carolinae 'Tricolor' sports variegated leaves of white, pink, and green; center leaves change to red.

Nematanthus fritschii

N. marmorata ×*spectabilis,* marble plant or fingernail plant, bears 16 inch (41 cm) long, mottled leaves with red tips.

N. spectabilis, fingernail plant, has two-tone leaves, green with red tips on the top and gray-striped on the underside; center rosette changes to purple before blue flowers appear.

Soil: Epiphytic bromeliad mix.
Temperature: Tolerates 50° to 85°F (10° to 29°C) range.
Light: Bright light, with direct winter sun, from eastern or western exposure. Foliage color is enhanced by full light. Air circulation is important.
Moisture: Keep growing medium slightly moist. Keep fresh water in cup. Mist occasionally. Humidity, 45% to 60%.
Feeding: Monthly, with mild liquid fertilizer. Avoid oil-based products such as fish emulsion. Spray on leaves, add to water in cup, or apply to growing medium after watering; never feed a dry plant.
Grooming: Remove old, yellowed leaves, dried flowers and stalks. Change water in cup.
Propagation: By offsets or seeds.
Pests and Diseases: Check for scale.
Seasonal Care: No specific rest period; growth continues slowly throughout the year. Plant dies within 2 years after flowering.

NEPHROLEPIS
Boston fern, sword fern

These popular, easy-care ferns are a common sight indoors and are noted for their longevity. The slender, arching fronds come in various sizes and shapes, and may carry spores on the leaf undersides. Furry runners emerge from rhizomes, and may root where they touch soil.

N. cordifolia, sword fern, grows erect to 36 inches (91 cm); bright green fronds appear in a close spiral; many cultivars are available.

N. exaltata 'Bostoniensis', Boston fern, features medium green, slender, arching fronds.

N. exaltata 'Compacta' or 'Dwarf Boston' grows from 15 to 18 inches (38 to 46 cm).

N. exaltata 'Fluffy Ruffles' is distinguished by the ruffled fronds.

N. exaltata 'Whitmanii', lace fern, is graced with feathery, delicate fronds.

Soil: Fern mix, with good drainage.

Temperature: Day, 68° to 75°F (20° to 24°C); night, 50° to 60°F (10° to 16°C).
Light: Bright, filtered light from eastern exposure. Does well under artificial light, needing 14 to 16 light-hours daily.
Moisture: Let soil dry slightly between thorough waterings. Mist twice daily. Humidity, 50% to 80%.
Feeding: Every third or fourth watering during growing season, with mild liquid fertilizer.
Grooming: Prefers to be potbound; pot-on when roots occupy over ¾ of pot space. Yellowed fronds should be trimmed close to soil level. To clean fronds, gently sponge with a solution of 1 tablespoon (15 ml) white vinegar per 1 cup (236 ml) warm water. If spores are to be collected for propagation, do not wash undersides of fronds when spores are maturing.
Propagation: By division, spores (for *N. cordifolia*), or stolons.
Pests and Diseases: Check for aphids, fungus gnats, mealybugs, scale, slugs, snails. Avoid drafts. Do not allow water to collect on dense mat of foliage.
Seasonal Care: Plant rests slightly from fall to winter. Keep at 50°F (10°C). Reduce water, keeping soil barely moist; withhold fertilizer.

Neoregelia carolinae 'Tricolor'

Nephrolepis exaltata

NEPHTHYTIS, see *Syngonium*

NIDULARIUM
Bird's nest bromeliad

These epiphytic bromeliads are noted for the long-lasting color change in the center of the leaf rosette prior to blooming. The soft, spiny leaves redden before a cluster of egglike flowers appears on a short, upright stem, at any time of the year.

N. billbergioides has 12 inch (30 cm) long, pale green leaves, often paler in center and marked with brown spots; bracts are pale pink to yellow, with white flowers.

N. fulgens, also sold as *N. regelioides,* blushing bromeliad, sports 12 inch (30 cm) long, light green leaves with dark green spots; scarlet bracts encircle white flowers.

N. innocentii var. *innocentii* has 12 inch (30 cm) long, two-tone leaves with dark red undersides and green tops; flower bracts are red with green tips, flowers are white.

N. innocentii var. *lineatum* has lengthwise white markings on leaves; green bracts have red tips.

Soil: Epiphytic bromeliad mix.
Temperature: 55° to 85°F (13° to 29°C).
Light: Bright, filtered sun from eastern or western exposure. Will tolerate low light. Air circulation is important.
Moisture: Keep growing medium moist, not soggy. Keep fresh water in cup. Mist often. Humidity, 45% to 60%.
Feeding: Monthly, with mild liquid fertilizer. Avoid oil-based products such as fish emulsion. Spray on leaves, add to water in cup, or apply to growing medium; never feed a dry plant.
Grooming: Remove old, yellowed leaves, dried flowers and stalks. Change water in cup.
Propagation: By offsets or seeds.
Pests and Diseases: Check for scale.
Seasonal Care: Growth slows in winter; reduce water.

NOTOCACTUS
Ball cactus

25 species make up this genus of small cacti. A flowering season from spring through summer produces bright yellow blooms, tinged with red on the outer petals. Most plants are round when young, but become columnar with age. Best suited as a windowsill or table plant.

N. apricus has a light green, globular stem with 15 to 20 nearly flat ribs that will eventually form a clump; grows to 3 inches (8 cm) with a 2-inch (5 cm) spread.

N. concinnus grows to 3 inches (8 cm) with a 4-inch (10 cm) spread; has a light green stem, slightly depressed at the top, with 18 notched ribs.

N. haselbergii, scarlet ball, is a slow grower with a height and width of 5 inches (13 cm); yellow spines fade to white as plant matures; bright red blooms are slow to fade.

Soil: Cactus/succulent mix.
Temperature: Day, 70°F (21°C); night, 50° to 55°F (10° to 13°C).
Light: Bright, filtered light, with 4 hours direct sun daily, from southern, southeastern, or eastern exposure. Does well under artificial light, needing 12 light-hours daily. Air circulation is important.
Moisture: Let soil surface dry between thorough waterings.
Feeding: Every 6 weeks during growing season, with full strength low-nitrogen, high-potassium fertilizer.
Grooming: Pot-on when roots completely overcrowd pot space.

Nidularium species

Notocactus species

No—Od

Propagation: By offsets or seeds.
Pests and Diseases: Check for aphids, mealybugs, spider mites, scale. Also be alert for fungus disease.
Seasonal Care: Plant rests during winter. Keep cool, 50°F (10°C). Water only enough to keep plant from drying out completely; withhold fertilizer.

OCIMUM
Basil, sweet basil

150 species make up this genus of annual herbs that produce a strong fragrance when the leaves are rubbed or crushed. Used primarily as a flavoring or for medicinal purposes, *Ocimum* can reach a height of 24 inches (61 cm), but can be kept smaller by regularly pinching the top shoots. Insignificant white flowers may appear in summer and should be pinched out. *O. basilicum,* the common species, has ovate, yellow-green to dark green leaves. *O. basilicum* 'Minimum' rarely exceeds 6 inches (15 cm).

Soil: All-purpose mix, with good drainage.
Temperature: Prefers 65° to 68°F (18° to 20°C) range.

Light: Requires 3 to 4 hours direct sun daily from southern or western exposure. Does well under artificial light, needing 14 light-hours daily.
Moisture: Keep soil evenly moist. Mist frequently. Humidity, 60%.
Feeding: Every 2 or 3 weeks, with mild liquid fertilizer.
Grooming: Pinch growing tips to keep bushy shape. Leaves are best when picked in summer.
Propagation: By seeds.
Seasonal Care: Treat as annual; discard after 1 season.

ODONTOGLOSSUM

These epiphytic orchids are prolific bloomers, bearing clusters of long-lasting flowers on erect or arching stalks, and a vigorous plant may even produce 2 flower stalks per pseudobulb. About 6 weeks elapse between the appearance of buds and the opening of the first bloom. There are 250 species of *Odontoglossum* and numerous hybrids, which may bloom twice a year. A pseudobulbous plant with sympodial growth habit, this orchid is suited for culture in a cool intermediate greenhouse. The following species are recommended for the home collections of experienced growers.

O. bictonienese produces an abundance of pale green or yellow flowers flecked with brown; lip is violet or white; blooms from late fall to spring.

O. grande, clown or tiger orchid, features stems which tilt at an angle; sepals carry alternating yellow and brown bands; petals are brown at base, tipped with yellow; wavy-edged lip is white with brown flecks; blooms in fall and winter.

O. pulchellum, lily-of-the-valley orchid, bears 8 to 10 fragrant white flowers; lip has yellow base with red speckles; blooms appear in fall and winter.

O. rossii, a compact plant, carries clusters of 1 to 5 flowers; sepals are yellow with rich brown flecks; petals

Ocimum basilicum

Odontoglossum rossii

are white with brown flecks at the base; ruffled lip is white or light pink; blooms in spring.

Soil: Osmunda fiber or orchid bark mix.
Temperature: Day, to 80°F (27°C); night, 50° to 55°F (10° to 13°C).
Light: Bright light from southern exposure; shade from direct summer sun at midday. Thin-leaved species always require some shade. *O. grande* requires more light than other species. Small plants, and especially hybrids, do well under artificial light, needing 12 to 16 light-hours daily. Good circulation of fresh air.
Moisture: Keep growing medium evenly moist in the home; allow to dry slightly between waterings in the greenhouse. Mist frequently. Humidity, 50% to 70%.
Feeding: With all-purpose fertilizer while in active growth. Plants in osmunda fiber require monthly feedings; plants in orchid bark mix need feeding every 3 weeks.
Grooming: Repot when plant overcrowds pot or when growing medium has deteriorated. Best done at outset of active growth, when new roots are first visible. Remove faded blooms before they weaken plant.
Propagation: By division of pseudobulbs.
Pests and Diseases: Check for bacterial, fungal, and viral infections, mealybugs, scale, slugs, snails, whiteflies.
Seasonal Care: In general, plants with hard pseudobulbs require longer rest period after flowering than those with soft pseudobulbs. Reduce water, never allowing pseudobulb to shrivel; provide bright light.

ONCIDIUM
Butterfly orchid, dancing lady orchid

This lovely, free-flowering orchid is especially recommended for beginners since it is easy to grow and tol-

erates a wide range of growing conditions. The long-lasting flowers appear in long sprays and appear to dance along the stem. The lip of *Oncidium* blooms is 3 lobed and often fiddle shaped, bearing a characteristic warty crest. An epiphyte exhibiting sympodial growth with pseudobulbs, it is suited to the conditions in an intermediate greenhouse. Among the 400 species, the following do especially well in home orchid collections:

O. flexuosum bears many small yellow flowers flecked with brownish red at the base; lip is golden yellow with brown flecks at the base; blooms from spring through summer.

O. ornithorhynchum bears many small, fragrant, rosy lilac flowers on a pendulous stem; blooms appear in fall.

O. sphacelatum features yellow blooms with slightly ruffled edges, flecked with reddish brown; yellow lip has brown flecks; flowers in spring.

O. varicosum 'Rogersii', dancing lady, grows to 8 inches (20 cm), bearing 100 to 250 bright yellow flowers on a 3- to 5-foot (0.9 to 1.5 m) spray; wide, round lip is golden yellow with cleft in front; blooms in fall.

Soil: Osmunda fiber or orchid bark mix. *O. sphacelatum* does well in slatted baskets.
Temperature: Day, 65° to 75°F (18° to 24°C); night, 55° to 60°F (13° to 16°C).
Light: Bright light from southern exposure; shade from direct summer sun at midday. Plants with thin leaves need more diffused light. Does well under artificial light, needing 12 to 16 light-hours daily. Good circulation of fresh air.
Moisture: Let growing medium dry slightly between thorough waterings. Mist frequently. Humidity, 50% to 70%.
Feeding: Plants in osmunda need no fertilizing. Plants in orchid bark mix need monthly feeding during ac-

tive growth with all-purpose fertilizer.
Grooming: Blooms vigorously when potbound. Repot when plant overcrowds pot space, or when growing medium has deteriorated. Best done at outset of active growth, when new roots are first visible.
Propagation: By division, with 3 to 4 pseudobulbs in each new pot.
Pests and Diseases: Check for bacterial, fungal, or viral infection, mealybugs, scale, slugs, snails, whiteflies.
Seasonal Care: Plant rests after new pseudobulb and leaves mature, prior to flowering. Reduce water, giving only enough to keep pseudobulb from shriveling. *O. flexuosum* requires little or no rest period; do not reduce watering at any point in growth cycle.

OPUNTIA
Beavertail, bunny ears, prickly pear

300 species make up this genus of cacti which may be cylindrical, globular, or flattened into rounded

***Oncidium varicosum* cultivar**

Op–Or

pads. The number of spines varies, but all species have tufts of barbed bristles in each areole. Care should be taken when handling *Opuntia* because these barbs easily pierce the skin and are difficult to remove.

O. basilaris, beavertail, is a slow grower which reaches 8 to 12 inches (20 to 30 cm) when fully grown; pink blooms appear on 4- to 5-year-old specimens.

O. cylindrica has a columnar, bright green stem growing to several feet with a diameter of 2 inches (5 cm); entire stem is covered with flat, diamond-shaped tubercles with a woolly white areole in the center.

O. microdasys, bunny ears, has oval pads that are 3 to 6 inches (8 to 15 cm) long; the pale green surface is dotted with clusters of deep yellow bristles; yellow flowers may appear in summer.

O. ovata grows to 6 inches (15 cm) with pale green, thick, oval pads which spread out to form a clump; bristles are pale yellow.

O. robusta is a large plant composed of flattened, gray-green, jointed segments with a bluish coating; circular in form, they vary from 2 inches (5 cm) to more than 12 inches (30 cm) across.

Soil: Cactus/succulent mix.
Temperature: Day, 75° to 85°F (24° to 29°C); night, 65° to 70°F (18° to 21°C).
Light: Bright light, with 4 hours direct sun daily, from southern to eastern exposure. Air circulation is important.
Moisture: Let soil dry between thorough waterings. Avoid overwatering.
Feeding: Every 6 weeks during growing season, with low-nitrogen, high-potassium fertilizer; for plants at least 1 year old.
Grooming: Repot each year.
Propagation: By stem cuttings or seeds.
Pests and Diseases: Check for aphids, mealybugs, spider mites, scale. Also be alert for fungus disease.
Seasonal Care: Plant rests during winter. Set in cool, bright location. Give just enough water to keep plant from shriveling; withhold fertilizer.

ORIGANUM
Oregano, sweet marjoram

These herbs, with their sweet, pungent taste, are familiar and popular flavorings, particularly in meat, egg, tomato, and vegetable dishes. The ovate leaves tend to spread, and small summer blooms appear on an erect stalk. This genus includes both oregano and sweet marjoram. Of the 15 to 20 species it contains, the following are pleasant additions to an outdoor herb garden:

O. heracleoticum, pot marjoram, is a slow-growing perennial with hair-covered leaves; 12-inch (30 cm) flower stalks bear white or purple flowers.

O. majorana, sweet marjoram, is an annual growing to 12 inches (30 cm); leaves are gray-green and woolly; flowers are pink or white.

Opuntia microdasys

Origanum vulgare

O. vulgare, oregano, is a perennial featuring dull, gray-green leaves with purple or white blooms.

Soil: All-purpose mix.
Temperature: Prefers 65° to 68°F (18° to 20°C) range.
Light: 4 to 5 hours direct sun daily from southern or western exposure. Does well under artificial light, needing 14 light-hours daily.
Moisture: Keep soil evenly moist. Mist daily. Humidity, 35% to 45%.
Feeding: Every 2 weeks during growing season, with mild liquid fertilizer.
Grooming: Leaves taste best when picked just before flowering.
Propagation: By cuttings, division, or seeds.
Seasonal Care: Plant rests during

winter. Reduce water; withhold fertilizer. *O. majorana* is an annual, best discarded after flowering.

OSMANTHUS
False holly, sweet olive

30 to 40 species of evergreen shrubs make up this genus, generally remaining under 5 feet (1.5 m) indoors. Leaves are glossy with spiny edges, resembling holly. Small white flowers have a pleasant fragrance, but are rare on indoor specimens.

O. fragrans, sweet olive, grows to 24 inches (61 cm) tall.

O. heterophyllus, also *O. aquifolium* or *O. ilicifolius,* false holly, measures

36 inches (91 cm) tall and 24 inches (61 cm) wide.

O. heterophyllus 'Variegatus' is distinguished by its white leaf margins.

Soil: Mix 3 parts garden loam and 2 parts sharp sand.
Temperature: Day, 68° to 78°F (20° to 26°C); night, 40° to 64°F (4° to 18°C).
Light: Bright light, with 3 to 4 hours direct sun daily, from southern exposure.
Moisture: Let soil dry slightly between moderate waterings. Mist twice daily. Humidity, 30% to 35%.
Feeding: Every 2 weeks during growing season, with mild liquid fertilizer.
Grooming: Repot yearly; pot-on when roots completely overcrowd pot space.
Propagation: By tip cuttings.
Pests and Diseases: Check for aphids, mealybugs, mites, scale.
Seasonal Care: Plant rests during winter. Keep soil barely moist; withhold fertilizer.

OXALIS
Lucky clover, shamrock plant

This genus contains 850 species of easy-care flowering plants with clo-

Osmanthus fragrans

Oxalis bowiei

verlike leaves. Clusters of delicate flowers appear throughout the year, with the heaviest blooming in summer and fall.

O. bowiei has leaves composed of 3 large leaflets; pink to purple blooms measure up to 1½ inches (4 cm) across.

O. deppei, lucky clover, bears 4 leaflets on each stalk, with a brown bar across the lower quarter; flowers are red with yellow centers; grows to 12 inches (30 cm).

O. herrarae grows to a bushy 4 inches (10 cm); 3 rounded leaflets comprise each leaf; flowers are red.

O. hirta grows to 12 inches (30 cm) with branched and trailing stems; blooms are large and rose to lilac colored.

O. ortgiesii, tree oxalis, sports hairy purple stems; longest of the 3 leaflets is notched at the tip; flowers are yellow; grows to 18 inches (46 cm).

Soil: Mix 2 parts garden loam and 1 part vermiculite.
Temperature: Day, 68° to 72°F (20° to 22°C); night, 50° to 60°F (10° to 16°C).
Light: Bright light, with direct morning or winter sun, from eastern or southern exposure. Does well under artificial light, needing 14 light-hours daily.
Moisture: Keep soil evenly moist.

Pachyphytum glutinicaule
'Cornelius Hybrid'

Mist daily. Humidity, 30% to 35%.
Feeding: Every 2 weeks during growing season, with mild liquid fertilizer.
Grooming: Repot each year, following dormant period. Dried foliage and flowers should be removed.
Propagation: By bulblets, root division, or seeds.
Pests and Diseases: Check for aphids, mites.
Seasonal Care: Plant becomes dormant over the winter, when foliage dies back. Keep cool, 50°F (10°C). Keep soil barely moist; withhold fertilizer.

PACHYPHYTUM
Moonstones, silver bract

These succulent shrubs are related to and resemble the genus *Echeveria.* Featuring rosettes of fleshy, rounded leaves, the plant also produces flower clusters borne on 2- to 6-inch (5 to 15 cm) stalks. Of the 12 species, the following are attractive additions to indoor displays:

P. bracteosum, silver bract, blooms in late fall and winter with red tubular flowers; grows to 12 inches (30 cm) tall, with light gray leaves that curve upwards.

P. glutinicaule 'Cornelius Hybrid' has fat, bluish gray leaves sometimes tipped with red or pink.

P. oviferum, moonstones, has egg-shaped leaves which are pearly white in winter, changing to pink in summer sun; late winter and spring blooms are bright red.

Soil: Cactus/succulent mix.
Temperature: Day, 75° (24°C); night, 50° to 55°F (10° to 13°C).
Light: Bright light, with 4 hours direct sun daily for best foliage color, from eastern, western, or southern exposure. Does well under artificial light, needing 12 to 16 light-hours daily. Fresh air circulation is important.
Moisture: Let soil dry between moderate waterings.

Propagation: By offsets, or stem and leaf cuttings.
Seasonal Care: Induce winter rest by setting in cool site, 50° to 60°F (10° to 16°C), with 5 hours of light daily. Water just enough to keep plant from shriveling; resume regular care in spring.

PACHYSTACHYS
Lollipop plant

P. lutea is the only species among the 6 in this genus which is grown indoors. A low-growing flowering shrub, it produces many stems, each bearing a 4-inch (10 cm) terminal flower spike. These flower heads consist of overlapping yellow bracts with green tips, and tubular white flowers, each lasting only a few days, emerge from the bracts throughout the summer. *Pachystachys* generally grows to 18 inches (46 cm) tall, featuring dark green leaves with a puckered surface and wavy margins.

Soil: All-purpose mix, with good drainage.
Temperature: Tolerates 55° to 65°F (13° to 18°C) range.
Light: Bright, filtered light from southern or western exposure, for best blooming.
Moisture: Let soil surface dry between moderate waterings.
Feeding: Weekly during growing season, with potassium-rich fertilizer to promote blooming.
Grooming: Repot and prune back in spring.
Propagation: By tip cuttings taken in spring.
Seasonal Care: Plant rests during winter. Keep cool, 55°F (13°C). Water sparingly; withhold fertilizer.

PANDANUS
Screw pine

This genus comprises 650 species of shrubs and trees, with several suitable for indoor culture. The glossy, leathery leaves are arranged in a spiral, and bear lengthwise stripes. *Pandanus* is long lasting and tolerates neglect.

P. baptistii, blue screw pine, features 1 inch (2.5 cm) wide, blue-green leaves with white stripes.

P. veitchii, veitch screw pine, grows from 24 to 36 inches (61 to 91 cm) tall; leaves have spiny margins with cream or yellow bands.

P. veitchii 'Compacta' has rigid leaves, measuring 15 inches (38 cm) long, with white stripes.

Soil: All-purpose mix.
Temperature: Day, 70° to 75°F (21° to 24°C); night, 62° to 68°F (17° to 20°C).
Light: Bright light, with 3 hours direct sun daily, from eastern or western exposure. Does well under artificial light, needing 14 to 16 light-hours daily.
Moisture: Keep soil evenly moist. Mist twice daily. Humidity, 45% to 55%.
Feeding: Every 2 weeks during growing season, with mild liquid fertilizer.
Grooming: Prefers to be potbound; pot-on when roots occupy ¾ of pot space. Trim growing ends of tall plant. Clean foliage monthly; remove dried leaves.
Propagation: By division of offsets.
Pests and Diseases: Check for aphids, mealybugs, spider mites, scale.
Seasonal Care: Plant rests during winter. Keep at 65°F (18°C). Reduce water, giving just enough to keep soil from drying out; withhold fertilizer.

PAPHIOPEDILUM
Lady's slipper

This popular orchid is among the easiest to grow in the home. The waxy blooms, shaped like a woman's slipper, all share a cuplike lip, called a pouch. These flowers can last up to 2 months on the plant. Hybrids can bloom twice a year, bearing rounder,

smoother, and waxier flowers than species plants. *Paphiopedilum* with mottled leaves do well in an intermediate greenhouse, while those plants with solid green leaves are suited to a cool greenhouse. This orchid is terrestrial and sympodial, with pseudobulbs. Formerly listed as *Cypripedium*, this genus contains about 60 species. The following are recommended for home collections:

P. callosum has mottled leaves; sepals are white with green and purple stripes; petals turn downward, are green at the base tipped with purple, and carry black warts on the upper edge; pouch is large, brownish purple; blooms in spring and summer.

P. concolor has mottled leaves; flowers are white to pale yellow, sprinkled with tiny purple spots; blooms appear in spring and summer.

P. fairieanum is a dwarf, green-leaved plant; flowers are white or light green with purple or brown stripes; pouch is green and red with purple veining; summer to fall bloomer.

P. insigne features green leaves; glossy flowers measure 5 inches (13 cm) across; sepals are bright green with brown spots and green veins; ruffled petals are pale yellow

Pachystachys lutea

Pandanus veitchii

with brown veins; pouch is yellow-green; flowers appear from fall to spring.

P. niveum has mottled leaves; white flowers are dotted with purple; pouch is pure white; blooms in spring.

P. villosum bears green leaves and a single flower; sepals are brown with narrow white margins; petals are ruffled and yellow-brown; yellow-brown pouch has light veining; blooms in winter.

Soil: Soft osmunda or finely chopped fir bark mixed with dried oak leaves; or orchid bark mix.
Temperature: For green-leaved plants: day, 60° to 75°F (16° to 24°C); night, 50° to 55°F (10° to 13°C). For mottled-leaved plants: day, 70° to 80°F (21° to 27°C); night, 60° to 65°F (16° to 18°C).
Light: Bright, diffused light from northern or eastern exposure. Does well under artificial light, needing 12 light-hours daily. Good circulation of fresh air.

Moisture: Keep growing medium evenly moist, not constantly wet. Humidity, 40% to 50%.
Feeding: Once or twice a month during active growth, with all-purpose fertilizer, mild manure tea, or fish emulsion.
Grooming: Repot when plant overcrowds pot space or when growing medium has deteriorated. Can be done at outset of active growth, when new roots are first visible, or, if plant is well established, before new growth begins.
Propagation: By crown division, including at least 3 growths in each group.
Pests and Diseases: Check for bacterial, fungal, and viral infections, mealybugs, scale, slugs, snails, whiteflies.
Seasonal Care: Plant requires brief rest period after new growth has matured. Withhold fertilizer and give less water. Also requires slightly less water after flowering is completed.

PASSIFLORA
Passion flower

The thin, wiry stems of these rapidly growing vines require some means of support. These stems, which have been known to reach 20 feet (6 m) in length, attach themselves by tendrils. The showy flowers may appear even on young plants, from late summer to early fall. Lasting only 1 day, they release a delightful fragrance before fading, but are replaced by many other blooms. The following species are grown for ornamental purposes, but among the 400 species in this genus several are grown for their edible fruit, the passion fruit.

P. ×alatocaerulea bears many large, showy blooms with white sepals, pinkish purple petals, and fringed coronas with variegations of blue, purple, and white.

P. caerulea, blue passion flower, has shiny, dark green leaves with 5 to 9 lobes; flowers measure 2 to 4 inches (5 to 10 cm) across, with white or pinkish petals and sepals surrounding a circle of filaments, colored pur-

Paphiopedilum callosum

Passiflora ×alatocaerulea

ple at the base, shading to white and then blue at the tip.

Soil: All-purpose mix.
Temperature: Day, 68°F (20°C); night, 55° to 65°F (13° to 18°C).
Light: Bright light, with 4 hours direct sun daily, from eastern or western exposure.
Moisture: Keep soil evenly moist. Mist twice daily. Humidity, 40% to 50%.
Feeding: Every 2 weeks during growing season, with mild liquid fertilizer.
Grooming: Repot each spring. Prune back shoots that have flowered the previous season to 6 inches (15 cm), in early spring. Older plants need only be trimmed back 2 to 3 inches (5 to 8 cm). Guide tendrils along support.
Propagation: By layering, stem cuttings, or seeds.
Pests and Diseases: Check for mealybugs, spider mites, scale.
Seasonal Care: Plant rests from fall through early winter. Keep at 50°F (10°C) and site in full sun. Water just enough to keep soil from drying out; withhold fertilizer.

PEDILANTHUS
Devil's backbone, Jacob's ladder, redbird cactus

Although this plant may be commonly referred to as a cactus, it is actually a succulent shrub. Out of the 30 species, *P. tithymaloides* is the species grown indoors, and measures 3 to 6 feet (0.9 to 1.8 m) tall with branching, spineless stems. These stems angle left, then right, in a zigzag pattern, with leathery leaves growing at the crook where the stem shifts direction. The stems contain a milky liquid which is poisonous and may irritate the skin. Red flowers appear at stem tips from time to time. *P. tithymaloides* 'Variegatus' features green leaves with red and white variegations.

Soil: Mix equal parts garden loam and coarse sand.
Temperature: Day, 65° to 80°F (18° to 27°C); night, 50° to 70°F (10° to 21°C).
Light: Bright, filtered light from southern exposure. Does well under artificial light, needing 14 light-hours daily.
Moisture: Let soil dry between moderate waterings. Humidity, 30% to 35%.
Feeding: Monthly during growing season, with mild all-purpose fertilizer.
Grooming: Prefers to be potbound; pot-on when roots overcrowd pot space. Prune to prevent legginess; stop flow of juice from cut ends by dabbing with water.
Propagation: By division or stem cuttings. Let cuttings dry several days before setting in rooting medium.
Pests and Diseases: Check for mealybugs, mites. Mildew and rot result from overwatering. Leaves drop if soil is allowed to dry completely.
Seasonal Care: Plant rests slightly from fall to late winter, when leaves may drop. Keep at 50°F (10°C). Water sparingly; withhold fertilizer. New leaves are formed when growth resumes.

PELARGONIUM
Geranium

These bushy plants, numbering around 280 species, can be grown for their bright flower clusters or for their foliage, in the case of those with scented leaves. The flowers consist of 1 or more layers of petals, and

Pedilanthus tithymaloides

Pelargonium peltatum 'Little Pinky'

Pe—Pe

are generally long lasting. The leaves come in varying shapes with accenting veins and accenting zones of color on a green background.

P. ×domesticum, show geranium, grows to 24 inches (61 cm) tall; solid green leaves have wavy edges; flowers appear from spring through mid-summer in clusters of 10, and in shades of white, pink, red, or purple with darker veins on the petals.

P. graveolens, rose geranium, has hairy, fragrant leaves; flowers are rosy with red veining; measures to 36 inches (91 cm).

P. ×hortorum, fish or zonal geranium, features scallop-edged leaves with bands of purple-brown; large clusters of red, pink, salmon, or white blooms appear throughout the year; grows to 4 feet (1.2 m).

P. odoratissimum, apple geranium, is a dwarf form with apple green and apple-scented leaves; white flowers with red veining appear in summer; branches sprawl to 18 inches (46 cm) long.

P. peltatum, ivy-leaved geranium, grows to 36 inches (91 cm) with stems that may trail or climb; shiny leaves with red zones resemble ivy leaves; small clusters of rosy pink to white blooms appear in spring.

P. tomentosum, peppermint geranium, measures 36 inches (91 cm) tall with peppermint-scented, velvety, bright green leaves.

Soil: All-purpose mix.
Temperature: Day, 68° to 75°F (20° to 24°C); night, 60° to 68°F (16° to 20°C).
Light: Bright light, with 4 hours of direct sun daily for full flowering, from eastern, western, or southern exposure. Does well under artificial light, needing 16 light-hours daily.
Moisture: Let soil dry between moderate waterings. Humidity, 30% to 40%.
Feeding: Monthly during growing season, with potassium-rich fertilizer.

Grooming: Prefers to be potbound; pot-on when roots occupy ¾ of pot space. Pinch straggly stems to promote blooming and to retain full shape. Remove faded blooms and yellowed leaves.
Propagation: By stem cuttings or seeds.
Pests and Diseases: Check for aphids, mealybugs, mites, whiteflies. Rot and mildew result from overwatering.
Seasonal Care: Plant may rest after heavy blooming period. Keep at 50°F (10°C). Give just enough water to keep soil from drying out; withhold fertilizer.

PELLAEA
Button fern, cliff brake fern

The 80 species of ferns making up this genus are considered xerophytic, meaning that in their natural habitat they adapted to a dry climate. Care must be taken when watering indoor plants, to see that they don't receive too much moisture.

P. rotundifolia, button fern, features 12-inch (30 cm) fronds which arch, then trail; pairs of round, dark green pinnae appear along a black midrib.

P. viridis, cliff brake fern, has bushy, upright fronds measuring 30 inches (76 cm) long; midrib becomes black as frond ages.

Soil: Fern mix, with good drainage.
Temperature: Day, 68° to 75°F (20° to 24°C); night, 50° to 60°F (10° to 16°C).
Light: Moderate, filtered light, with direct sun in winter, from eastern or western exposure. Does well under artificial light, needing 12 light-hours daily.
Moisture: Let soil dry, but not completely, between thorough waterings. Mist twice daily. Humidity, 30% to 35%.
Feeding: Every third or fourth watering during growing season, with mild liquid fertilizer.
Grooming: Repot when roots occupy ¾ of pot space. Yellowed fronds should be trimmed close to soil level. To clean fronds, gently sponge with a solution of 1 tablespoon (15 ml) white vinegar per 1 cup (236 ml) warm water. If spores are to be collected for propagation, do not wash undersides of fronds when spores are maturing.
Propagation: By rhizome division or spores.
Pests and Diseases: Check for aphids, fungus gnats, mealybugs, scale, slugs, snails.

Pellaea rotundifolia

Seasonal Care: Plant rests slightly during fall and winter. Keep at 50°F (10°C). Water sparingly; withhold fertilizer.

PELLIONIA
Trailing watermelon begonia

These perennial foliage plants feature creeping growth, and wherever a stem node touches soil, roots can form. Leaves are borne on pink or purple stems, and have striking patterns in many colors. *Pellionia* is very attractive in hanging baskets. Of the 50 species making up this genus, the following do well in the home:

P. daveauana has 24 inch (61 cm) long stems bearing leaves whose shape varies; uppersides are bronze and olive green with purple edges and a pale green center stripe; undersides are pale pink.

P. pulchra, rainbow vine, features green leaves with dull black midribs and veins and pale purple undersides; stems grow to 18 inches (46 cm).

Soil: Humusy mix.
Temperature: Day, 70°F (21°C); night, 50° to 55°F (10° to 13°C).
Light: Bright light, no direct sun, from eastern or western exposure. Does well under artificial light, needing 14 light-hours daily.

Moisture: Keep soil thoroughly moist. Mist twice daily. Humidity, 40% to 45%.
Feeding: Every 2 weeks during growing season, with mild liquid fertilizer.
Grooming: Pot-on in spring when roots occupy ½ of pot space. Prune back in early spring to prevent legginess. Rinse foliage often.
Propagation: By tip cuttings taken in spring or summer.
Pests and Diseases: Check for mealybugs, mites, rot, scale, slugs, whiteflies. Avoid drafts.
Seasonal Care: Plant rests slightly during winter. Reduce water, keeping soil barely moist; withhold fertilizer.

PENTAS
Egyptian star cluster

34 species of flowering plants comprise this genus, with *P. lanceolata* suitable for the indoors. Its growth is bushy, with woody, upright stems measuring from 12 to 24 inches (30 to 61 cm) tall. Bright green leaves are hairy with deep veining. Flat-topped clusters of star-shaped flowers appear mainly in fall and late winter, and may be white, pink, lilac, or deep purple.

Soil: All-purpose mix.
Temperature: Day, 68° to 80°F (20° to 27°C); night, 60° to 65°F (16° to 18°C).
Light: Bright light, with 4 hours direct sun daily, from southern exposure. Does well under artificial light, needing 14 light-hours daily.
Moisture: Let soil dry slightly between thorough waterings. Mist twice daily. Humidity, 50% to 60%.
Feeding: Every 2 weeks during growing season, with mild liquid fertilizer.
Grooming: Repot each spring; pot-on when roots occupy ½ of pot space. Prune to retain a bushy form; plant looks best when kept under 24 inches (61 cm).
Propagation: By tip cuttings of nonflowering shoots, or seeds.
Pests and Diseases: Check for scale.
Seasonal Care: Plant rests for 6 to 8 weeks following major blooming period. Keep cool, 55°F (13°C). Keep soil barely moist; withhold fertilizer.

PEPEROMIA

1,000 species of creeping or erect foliage plants within this genus offer a wide variety of attractive leaf colorations and textures. Generally grow-

Pellionia daveauana

Pentas lanceolata

ing to 12 inches (30 cm) in height, the leaves are borne on pink or red stems.

P. argyreia, watermelon peperomia, features slightly heart-shaped, dark green leaves with curved silver-gray bands running lengthwise.

P. caperata, emerald ripple, has clumps of dark green leaves with a silvery sheen and distinctive puckered surface; 6-inch (15 cm) slender, white flower spikes appear in winter and spring.

P. obtusifolia, blunt-leaved peperomia, produces waxy, rounded leaves which are deep green; various cultivars have yellow and white markings.

P. velutina, velvet peperomia, features red, hairy stems bearing thick, dark green, hair-covered leaves with silver midribs and silver veins.

Soil: Mix equal parts loam, peat moss, and perlite.
Temperature: Day, 68° to 80°F (20° to 27°C); night, 55° to 68°F (13° to 20°C).
Light: Filtered light, no direct sun, from northern, eastern, or western exposure. Does well under artificial light, needing 14 light-hours daily.
Moisture: Let soil dry between moderate waterings. Mist twice daily. Humidity, 40% to 45%.

Feeding: Monthly during growing season, with mild liquid fertilizer.
Grooming: Repot yearly in early spring; pot-on when roots occupy ¾ of pot space. Prune frequently to control leggy plant. Rinse foliage often.
Propagation: By stem or leaf cuttings.
Pests and Diseases: Check for mealybugs, mites, rot, slugs, whiteflies.
Seasonal Care: Plant rests slightly throughout the winter. Keep cool, 50° to 55°F (10° to 13°C). Keep soil barely moist; withhold fertilizer.

PETROSELINUM
Parsley

This genus contains 3 species of herbs commonly used for flavoring and garnishing. A hardy perennial, *Petroselinum* is usually grown as an annual for the best-tasting leaves. High in iron and rich in vitamins A and C, this popular herb is a healthy addition to any windowsill garden. 1 variety is grown as a root vegetable, resembling parsnips, and may be prepared and used in the same manner.

P. crispum var. *crispum* features curly leaf segments.

P. crispum var. *neapolitanum,* Italian parsley, has flat leaf segments.

P. crispum var. *tuberosum,* Hamburg parsley or parsley root, is a root vegetable with flat leaves; flavor is similar to celeriac.

Soil: All-purpose mix, with good drainage.
Temperature: Prefers cool range, 55° to 65°F (13° to 18°C).
Light: Lots of sun from southern exposure.
Moisture: Keep soil evenly moist. Mist frequently.
Feeding: Add well-aged compost or fish emulsion occasionally.
Propagation: By seeds.
Seasonal Care: Discard after 1 season.

PHALAENOPSIS
Moth orchid

This freely blooming, handsome orchid is especially recommended for

***Peperomia obtusifolia,* left, and *P. obtusifolia* 'Variegata'**

Petroselinum crispum* var. *crispum

beginning orchid growers. The waxy flowers, resembling butterflies or moths, open in succession along arching flower stalks which can then remain in bloom up to 5 months or more. This genus is epiphytic, monopodial, and lacks pseudobulbs. There are about 55 species and a vast number of hybrids; these may be white, pink, or yellow-green, with stripes, spots, or bars. The following species are good orchids for home collections:

P. amabilis bears 6 to 20 snowy white flowers on a slender stalk; white and yellow lip has red markings; blooms from fall through winter.

P. lueddemanniana features 3 to 4 white flowers with pink markings; purple lip has yellow base and light-colored markings; blooms appear at different times throughout the year.

Soil: Fir bark mixed with chopped tree fern fiber. Best when grown in pots in the greenhouse. In the home, does well in baskets, on section of tree limb or on slab of tree fern fiber.
Temperature: Day, 70° to 85°F (21° to 29°C); night, 60° to 65°F (16° to 18°C).
Light: Bright light from northern or eastern exposure; shade from direct sun at midday. Does well under artificial light, needing 12 to 16 light-hours daily. Good circulation of fresh air.
Moisture: Keep growing medium evenly moist; never allow plant to dry out. Mist aerial roots frequently. Humidity, 50% to 70%.
Feeding: Proportioned feedings of all-purpose fertilizer with each watering, year-round.
Grooming: Repot when plant overcrowds pot space, or when growing medium deteriorates. Best done at outset of active growth, when new roots are first visible. Remove faded blooms before they weaken plant. The flower stem that remains often will send out new side-shoots for a second blooming.
Propagation: By plantlets appearing along stem.
Pests and Diseases: Check for bacterial, fungal, and viral infections, mealybugs, scale, slugs, snails, whiteflies.
Seasonal Care: Plant rests briefly after vegetative growth stops; this is not easily recognized. At cooler times of the year continue watering, but give slightly less and lower humidity.

PHILODENDRON

200 species of foliage plants with glossy, leathery, deep green leaves comprise this genus. Appearing in a variety of forms, leaves may be lance-, arrow-, or heart-shaped. Some species grow upright, developing trunklike stems as they mature, while others are climbers, requiring moss-covered supports.

P. bipinnatifidum, tree philodendron, is a pot plant growing erect to 4 feet (1.2 m); young leaves are heart-shaped, becoming lobed and wavy as they mature, measuring 12 inches (30 cm) long.

P. erubescens, blushing philodendron, is a climber reaching to 6 feet (1.8 m); leaves are arrow-shaped, shiny dark green with burgundy-red undersides, borne on purple stalks.

P. melanochrysum, also listed as *P. andreanum,* black gold philodendron, climbs to 6 feet (1.8 m); young, heart-shaped leaves change to lance-

Phalaenopsis **hybrid**

Philodendron scandens

shaped; velvety foliage is metallic green, nearly black, with pale green veining.

P. scandens, heartleaf philodendron, may climb or trail; heart-shaped leaves are bronzy, changing to deep green as they age.

P. selloum, lacy tree philodendron, features a rosette of glossy green leaves with lobed segments; grows upright to 5 feet (1.5 m).

Soil: All-purpose mix.
Temperature: Tolerates 65° to 75°F (18° to 24°C) range.
Light: Filtered light from eastern or western exposure. Does well under artificial light, needing 14 to 16 light-hours daily.
Moisture: Let soil dry between thorough waterings. Mist twice daily. Humidity, 45% to 55%.
Feeding: Every 2 weeks during growing season, with mild liquid fertilizer.
Grooming: Prefers to be potbound; pot-on when roots occupy over ¾ of pot space. Cut growing tips on a tall plant to keep it at a manageable size. Pinch leggy plant to keep it shapely. Pick off dead leaves; rinse foliage monthly.
Propagation: By layering, tip or leaf cuttings, or seeds.
Pests and Diseases: Check for

aphids, mealybugs, spider mites, scale.
Seasonal Care: Plant rests during winter. Set in cool site, 55°F (13°C). Keep soil barely moist; withhold fertilizer.

PHYLLITIS
Hart's tongue fern

Among the 8 ferns within this genus, only 1 species, *P. scolopendrium,* is grown indoors. The tufts of fronds emerging from the rhizome are first erect, later arching as they grow longer, reaching from 12 to 36 inches (30 to 91 cm) in length. The straplike leaves may be straight, wavy, or frilled along the edges, bearing spores on the undersides. Many cultivars are available, with interesting crisped or divided leaf edges.

Soil: Fern mix, with good drainage, and additional ground limestone or crushed eggshells or crushed oyster shells.
Temperature: Day, 55° to 60°F (13° to 16°C); night, 40° to 45°F (4° to 7°C).
Light: Moderate light, no direct sun, from northern exposure. Does well under artificial light.
Moisture: Keep soil evenly moist,

not soggy. Humidity, 50% to 80%.
Feeding: Every third or fourth watering during growing season, with mild liquid fertilizer.
Grooming: Repot when roots occupy ¾ of pot space. Yellowed fronds should be trimmed close to soil level. To clean fronds, gently sponge with a solution of 1 tablespoon (15 ml) white vinegar per 1 cup (236 ml) warm water. If spores are to be collected for propagation, do not wash undersides of fronds when spores are maturing.
Propagation: By crown or rhizome division, or spores.
Pests and Diseases: Check for aphids, fungus gnats, mealybugs, scale, slugs, snails.
Seasonal Care: Plant may rest during fall and winter. Keep in cool location, 40°F (4°C). Water sparingly; withhold fertilizer.

PILEA
Aluminum plant, artillery plant

These small foliage plants are distinguished by their textured and patterned leaves. Leaf surfaces may be quilted, veined, or puckered, and the dark green coloration may be tinged with red, silver, or copper. *Pilea* is a slow grower, with upright or creeping stems growing to 12 inches (30 cm). Insignificant flowers may appear throughout the year. Of the more than 200 species, the following are handsome additions to indoor gardens:

P. cadierei, aluminum plant, features dark green leaves with raised silver bands along the center and edges.

P. cadierei 'Minima' is a dwarf growing to 6 inches (15 cm).

P. involucrata, friendship plant, bears rosettes of dark green leaves with a bronzy sheen, indented veins and scalloped edges; pink flowers may appear in summer.

Phyllitis scolopendrium

P. microphylla, also called *P. muscosa,* artillery plant, has dense leaves, ¼ inch (6 mm) long, creating a fernlike appearance; mature, yellow-green flowers send out a puff of pollen when touched.

P. 'Moon Valley', a popular compact form, bears leaves bordered in light green with sunken brown veins.

P. nummariifolia, creeping Charlie, produces creeping, reddish branches bearing tiny, round, pale green leaves with a quilted surface; flowers are green and pink.

Soil: Mix equal parts garden loam and peat moss.
Temperature: Day, 70°F (21°C); night, 55° to 65°F (13° to 18°C).
Light: Bright to moderate light, no direct sun, from eastern or western exposure. Does well under artificial light, needing 14 light-hours daily.
Moisture: Keep soil evenly moist. Mist twice daily. Humidity, 45% to 60%.
Feeding: Every 2 weeks during growing season, with mild liquid fertilizer.

Grooming: Pot-on when roots occupy ½ of pot space. Prune back stems in spring before new growth appears to prevent legginess. Rinse foliage often.
Propagation: By stem cuttings.
Pests and Diseases: Check for mealybugs, scale, slugs.
Seasonal Care: Plant rests from late fall to early winter. Set in cool site, 50° to 55°F (10° to 13°C). Keep soil barely moist; withhold fertilizer.

PITTOSPORUM
Australian laurel, mock orange

Among the 100 species of trees and shrubs in this genus, several are suitable for the indoors, growing from 4 to 5 feet (1.2 to 1.5 m) in a tub. The branch tips bear clusters of shiny, dark green leaves with rounded tips. Flat-topped clusters of white to yellow flowers appear in early summer, with a fragrance of orange blossoms.

P. tobira, Australian laurel, is the most common indoor species and is suitable for bonsai.

P. tobira 'Variegata' features off-white leaf margins and greenish white flowers.

P. undulatum, mock orange, has wavy-edged leaves; 4 to 15 fragrant yellow-white flowers appear in each cluster.

Soil: Mix 3 parts garden loam and 1 part sand.
Temperature: Day, 55° to 65°F (13° to 18°C); night, 40° to 50°F (4° to 10°C).
Light: Bright light, with 3 hours direct sun daily, from southern, eastern, or western exposure. Air circulation is important.
Moisture: Keep soil evenly moist. Mist twice daily. Humidity, 40% to 65%.
Feeding: Monthly during growing season, with mild liquid fertilizer.
Grooming: Pot-on when roots occupy over ¾ of pot space. Prune in spring to keep at a manageable size. Remove dead leaves; wash foliage every 2 weeks.

Pilea cadierei

Pittosporum tobira

Pi–Pl

Propagation: By tip cuttings taken in spring, or seeds.
Pests and Diseases: Check for aphids, mealybugs, mites, scale.
Seasonal Care: Plant rests after flowering. Keep at 50°F (10°C). Reduce water, giving just enough to keep soil from drying out; withhold fertilizer.

PLATYCERIUM
Staghorn fern

17 species of large, eye-catching epiphytic ferns comprise this genus. *P. bifurcatum* is commonly found indoors, growing on a piece of bark or tree fern, or hanging in a wooden basket. Each plant has 2 types of fronds, sterile and fertile. The single sterile frond is round and flat, changing from bright green to papery brown, when it is then replaced by new growth. Located at the base, this frond helps anchor the plant to its support. The fertile fronds are fleshy and grayish green. Measuring as much as 36 inches (91 cm) long, they spread and droop, resembling antlers with their many lobes. Brown spores are found on the tips of these fronds when plant reaches sufficient size.

Soil: Anchor to bark or tree fern

with a pad of long fiber sphagnum moss behind the sterile frond, or set in hanging wooden basket filled with equal parts peat moss and sphagnum moss.
Temperature: Day, 70° to 75°F (21° to 24°C); night, 55° to 65°F (13° to 18°C).
Light: Bright light, with no direct sun, from eastern or western exposure. Does well under artificial light, needing 14 to 16 light-hours daily. Air circulation is important.
Moisture: Let plant dry almost completely between thorough waterings. If sterile supporting frond covers surface of growing medium, submerge plant in water. Mist twice daily. Humidity, 50% to 80%.
Feeding: Every 3 weeks during growing season, with mild liquid fertilizer; for mature plants only.
Grooming: Mist gently with tepid water to remove dust or stray soil particles. The thin covering of gray scales is natural and need not be rubbed off.
Propagation: By detaching plantlets at least 4 inches (10 cm) wide, or spores.
Pests and Diseases: Check for aphids, fungus gnats, mealybugs, scale, slugs, snails.
Seasonal Care: Plant rests during fall and winter. Keep at 55° to 65°F (13° to 18°C). Reduce water, keeping barely moist; withhold fertilizer.

PLECTRANTHUS
Swedish ivy

250 species of foliage plants with trailing stems and a wide variety of leaf forms make this genus a natural for display in hanging baskets. Leaves are slightly fleshy and may have a velvety texture. Scalloped edges, veining, and a bronzy or purple cast are other leaf variations. Small flowers, which can be removed, may appear throughout the year.

P. australis, Swedish ivy, tends to grow erect, to a bushy 24 to 36 inches (61 to 91 cm); dark green leaves are waxy with scalloped edges; white flowers may appear.

P. coleoides 'Marginata', candle plant, grows upright, then trails as stems bear hairy, dark green leaves with white borders; flowers are purple and white.

P. oertendahlii, prostrate coleus, features round, velvety, bronze-green leaves edged in purple, with silver veins; trailing stems grow to 24 inches (61 cm); flowers are lilac.

Soil: All-purpose mix.
Temperature: Day, 60° to 70°F (16° to 21°C); night, 55° to 60°F (13° to 16°C).

Platycerium bifurcatum   *Plectranthus australis*

Light: Partial shade, with morning sun or direct winter sun, from eastern or southern exposure. Does well under artificial light, needing 14 to 16 light-hours daily.
Moisture: Let soil dry between thorough waterings. Mist twice daily. Humidity, 45% to 60%.
Feeding: Every 2 weeks during growing season, with mild liquid fertilizer.
Grooming: Pot-on when roots occupy ½ of pot space. Pinch growing tips for bushy shape and further branching.
Propagation: By tip cuttings.
Pests and Diseases: Check for aphids, mealybugs, whiteflies.
Seasonal Care: Plant rests from fall through early spring. Set in cool site, 55°F (13°C). Keep soil barely moist; withhold fertilizer.

PODOCARPUS
Buddhist pine, Japanese yew

This genus contains 75 species of trees and shrubs, with *P. macrophyl-lus* var. *maki* most suitable for indoor cultivation. Branches on a young specimen grow upright, then droop as they lengthen. Flat, yellow-green leaves curl at the tips and are spiraled along the dense branches. *Podocarpus* generally grows to 6 feet (1.8 m).

Soil: Mix 3 parts garden loam and 1 part sand.
Temperature: Prefers 50° to 60°F (10° to 16°C) range.
Light: Bright, filtered light from eastern or western exposure.
Moisture: Let soil surface dry between thorough waterings. Humidity, 30% to 35%.
Feeding: Monthly during growing season, with mild liquid fertilizer.
Grooming: Pot-on only when roots occupy over ¾ of pot space. Pot size is critical, since plant does not do well in a container too large for its size. For fuller growth, prune lateral branches back to ½ their length in spring or summer. Prune to keep at a manageable size. Rinse foliage often.
Propagation: By tip cuttings taken in spring, or seeds.
Pests and Diseases: Check for aphids, mealybugs, mites, scale.

Seasonal Care: Induce dormant period by setting in cool site, 55°F (13°C), in early fall. Give only enough water to keep soil from drying out and withhold fertilizer; resume regular schedule in spring.

POLYPODIUM
Hare's foot fern, polypody fern

This genus contains mostly epiphytic ferns with rhizomes that branch or creep along the soil. Relatively easy to care for, *Polypodium* is an attractive indoor plant with its deeply cut, arching fronds which may have a blue or gray cast and measure from 12 to 36 inches (30 to 91 cm).

P. aureum, golden polypody or hare's foot fern, features furry rhizomes covered with brown or rust-colored scales; wide, spreading fronds have deep lobes and change from green to brown as they mature.

P. punctatum, also listed as *P. polycarpon,* has light green, leathery leaves which may be ruffled, fringed, or forked at the tips.

P. scolopendria has creeping, fleshy rhizomes; leathery leaves are lobed.

Soil: Fern mix, with good drainage.

Podocarpus macrophyllus var. maki

Polypodium aureum

Po—Po

Temperature: Day, 60° to 75°F (16° to 24°C); night, 50° to 60°F (10° to 16°C).
Light: Moderate to bright light, with direct winter sun, from northern or eastern exposure. Does well under artificial light, needing 12 light-hours daily.
Moisture: Let soil dry slightly between thorough waterings. Mist twice daily. Humidity, 50% to 80%.
Feeding: Every third or fourth watering during growing season, with mild liquid fertilizer.
Grooming: Prefers to be potbound; repot when rhizome overcrowds pot surface. Yellowed fronds should be trimmed close to soil level. To clean fronds, gently sponge with a solution of 1 tablespoon (15 ml) white vinegar per 1 cup (236 ml) warm water. If spores are to be collected for propagation, do not wash undersides of fronds when spores are maturing.
Propagation: By rhizome sections or spores.

Polyscias balfouriana

Pests and Diseases: Check for aphids, fungus gnats, mealybugs, scale, slugs, snails.
Seasonal Care: Plant may rest during fall and winter, when it can be kept at 40°F (4°C). Water sparingly; withhold fertilizer.

POLYSCIAS
Ming aralia

80 species of trees and shrubs comprise this genus. Several are suited to tub culture, growing to 4 feet (1.2 m), and add interest indoors with their variegated and deeply dissected foliage. This genus was formerly classified as *Aralia*.

P. balfouriana, Balfour aralia, has many green branches which are speckled with gray; young, rounded leaves appear singly on a stalk, while older leaves develop into 3 leaflets.

P. balfouriana 'Marginata' features muted gray leaves with off-white borders.

P. fruticosa, ming aralia, features bright green, deeply divided leaves resembling ferns, borne on purple leafstalks.

P. guilfoylei 'Victoriae', lace aralia, has gray-green leaves divided into 7 leaflets with white margins.

Soil: Humusy mix.
Temperature: Day, 70° to 80°F (21° to 27°C); night, 62° to 68°F (17° to 20°C).
Light: Bright light, no direct sun, from eastern or western exposure. Does well under artificial light, needing 14 to 16 light-hours daily.
Moisture: Let soil surface dry between moderate waterings. Mist twice daily. Humidity, 50% to 60%.
Feeding: Monthly during growing season, with mild liquid fertilizer.
Grooming: Pot-on when roots occupy over ¾ of pot space. Cut growing ends of tall plant to keep at manageable size. Remove dead leaves; rinse foliage frequently.

Propagation: By air layering, root division, or tip cuttings taken in spring.
Pests and Diseases: Check for aphids, mealybugs, spider mites, scale.
Seasonal Care: Plant may rest slightly in winter. Keep cool, 55°F (13°C). Keep soil barely moist; withhold fertilizer.

POLYSTICHUM
Shield fern

Several species of ferns formerly classified under *Aspidium* have been transferred to this genus. Numbering 120 terrestrial species, *Polystichum* features erect rhizomes which partially emerge from the soil and are covered with black scales. Dense clusters of fronds grow from 12 to 36 inches (30 to 91 cm) tall, with many narrow divisions, pointed at the ends. *P. tsus-simense,* the most commonly grown species, features deep green pinnules with deeply notched edges; young fronds, not yet uncoiled, are covered with white scales.

Soil: Fern mix, with good drainage.
Temperature: Day, 68° to 75°F (20° to 24°C); night, 50° to 60°F (10° to 16°C).
Light: Bright, filtered light, no direct sun, from eastern exposure. Does well under artificial light, needing 12 light-hours daily.
Moisture: Keep soil evenly moist, not soggy. Mist twice daily. Humidity, 60% to 70%.
Feeding: Every third or fourth watering during growing season, with mild liquid fertilizer.
Grooming: Prefers to be potbound; pot-on when roots occupy ¾ of pot space. Yellowed fronds should be trimmed close to soil level. To clean fronds, gently sponge with a solution of 1 tablespoon (15 ml) white vinegar per 1 cup (236 ml) warm water. If spores are to be collected for propagation, do not wash undersides of fronds when spores are maturing.

Propagation: By crown division or spores.
Pests and Diseases: Check for aphids, fungus gnats, mealybugs, scale, slugs, snails.
Seasonal Care: Plant rests from fall through winter. Keep at 40°F (4°C). Water sparingly; withhold fertilizer.

PRIMULA
Indoor primrose

These flowering plants brighten up the indoors with winter and spring blooms. Flowers appear in a wide array of colors, either singly or clustered on a stem. *Primula* usually measures from 12 to 24 inches (30 to 61 cm) tall, and features rosettes of ovate, slightly hairy leaves. These perennials are usually treated as annuals, although several species may be kept for more than 1 season. Of the 400 species, the following are suitable indoors:

P. malacoides, fairy or baby primrose, features scented, star-shaped flowers in shades of white, red, pink, or lilac; pale green leaves have scalloped edges; discard after flowering.

P. obconica, poison primrose, bears short hairs on leaves which may irritate the skin; flower stalk bears white, pink, red, salmon, or mauve flowers, each with a central, light green eye.

P. sinensis, Chinese primrose, has toothed, lobed leaves; large flowers may be single or double with fringed petals; colors range from pink, red, and purple to white, with a central yellow eye.

P. veris, cowslip, grows to 12 inches (30 cm) tall; produces umbels of bright yellow, fragrant flowers.

Soil: Humusy mix.
Temperature: Day, 55° to 60°F (13° to 16°C); night, 40° to 50°F (4° to 10°C).
Light: Bright light from northern or eastern exposure. Does well under artificial light, needing 12 to 14 light-hours daily.
Moisture: Keep soil constantly moist. Mist daily, not directly on flowers. Humidity, 50% to 60%.
Feeding: Every 2 weeks while in bloom, with mild liquid fertilizer.
Grooming: Never allow plant to become potbound. Repot after flowering. Remove dead flower stems.
Propagation: By plantlets.
Pests and Diseases: Check for aphids, mealybugs, mites, slugs, whiteflies.
Seasonal Care: *P. obconica* and

P. sinensis can be made to bloom a second year. Plant rests in late spring, following blooming. Set in cool, partially shaded site, with plenty of air circulation. Keep soil barely moist; withhold fertilizer. In fall, remove dried leaves, top-dress, and resume regular watering schedule.

PTERIS
Brake fern, table fern

This sizable genus of terrestrial ferns contains 280 species, several of which are good specimens to be grown indoors and may be used in terraria. Long lasting and easy to care for, *Pteris* features clumps of erect, feathery fronds from 12 to 36 inches (30 to 91 cm) tall.

P. cretica, ribbon fern, has distinctive fronds with deep divisions, creating a ribbonlike appearance; many cultivars are available.

P. ensiformis 'Victoriae', silver leaf fern, bears fronds up to 20 inches (52 cm) long, with white bands on pinnae.

P. tremula, Australian brake fern, is a rapid grower, producing broad,

Polystichum tsus-simense

Primula veris

feathery fronds 36 inches (91 cm) in length.

Soil: Fern mix, with good drainage.
Temperature: Day, 68° to 75°F (20° to 24°C); night, 55° to 60°F (13° to 16°C).
Light: Filtered bright light, no direct sun, from northern or eastern exposure. Does well under artificial light, needing 12 light-hours daily.
Moisture: Keep soil evenly moist, not soggy. Mist twice daily. Humidity, 50% to 80%.
Feeding: Every third or fourth watering during growing season, with mild liquid fertilizer.
Grooming: Prefers to be potbound; pot-on when roots occupy ¾ of pot space. Unattractive older fronds on the outside of clump can be removed. To clean fronds, gently sponge with a solution of 1 tablespoon (15 ml) white vinegar per 1 cup (236 ml) warm water. If spores are to be collected for propagation, do not wash undersides of fronds when spores are maturing.
Propagation: By division or spores.
Pests and Diseases: Check for aphids, fungus gnats, mealybugs, scale, slugs, snails.
Seasonal Care: Plant may rest during fall and winter. Keep at 40°F (4°C). Water moderately; withhold fertilizer.

PUNICA
Pomegranate

Species of this genus grown in the tropics produce edible fruit, and although a plant grown indoors will produce fruit, it is not very palatable. *P. granatum* 'Nana' is the miniature form suited to tub culture, growing from 2 to 4 feet (0.6 to 1.2 m). Flowers, appearing in late spring and summer, are orange-red and bell shaped. These precede the fruit, which is round and 2 inches (5 cm) across, with a golden yellow color.

Soil: All-purpose mix.
Temperature: Day, 70°F (21°C); night, 45° to 55°F (7° to 13°C).
Light: Bright light, with 4 hours direct sun daily, from western or southern exposure.
Moisture: Keep soil thoroughly moist. Mist twice daily. Humidity, 45% to 60%.
Feeding: Every 2 weeks during growing season, with mild all-purpose fertilizer.
Grooming: Prefers to be potbound for better blooming. Pot-on every 2 years in spring. Prune back any straggly stems in late winter.
Propagation: By cuttings.

Seasonal Care: Plant rests during winter. In late fall after most of the leaves have dropped, set in cool site, 45° to 55°F (7° to 13°C). Water sparingly, never allowing soil to dry out completely; withhold fertilizer.

RANUNCULUS
Buttercup, florists' ranunculus

250 species of fibrous-rooted or tuberous flowering plants are included in this genus. *R. asiaticus* is a half-hardy, tuberous-rooted plant which is suitable for forcing indoors. The resultant blooms, measuring from 1 to 4 inches (2.5 to 10 cm) wide, can be single or double in form in shades of white, pink, red, yellow, and orange. Care must be taken when planting, so that the clawlike end of the tuber faces downward.

Soil: All-purpose mix.
Temperature: For 6 weeks before growth appears, keep cool, 40° to 50°F (4° to 10°C). Once growth appears: day, 55° to 65°F (13° to 18°C); night, 40° to 50°F (4° to 10°C).
Light: Before growth appears, set in dark location. When active growth

Pteris cretica

Punica granatum 'Nana'

begins, gradually provide full sun from southern exposure.

Moisture: Water lightly until growth appears, then gradually increase amount, keeping soil evenly moist. Too much water causes rot.

Feeding: Weekly, when foliage has appeared, with mild, all-purpose fertilizer.

Propagation: By division or seeds.

Pests and Diseases: Generally healthy and free from infestation.

Seasonal Care: Once flowering is over, allow the leaves to yellow, then remove tubers from pot and allow to dry. Store in cool, dark location until the following spring, when they can be planted outdoors.

REBUTIA
Crown cactus

27 species of small cacti comprise this genus, featuring cylindrical or spherical spine-laden stems. Their most outstanding feature is the funnel-shaped flowers, which are large in proportion to the plant. These appear profusely in spring and summer, opening in the morning, closing at night, and each lasting for several days. *Rebutia* only lives 3 to 4 years, seemingly exhausted by its flowering

effort, but produces numerous offsets before it dies.

R. kupperana, scarlet crown, has spherical, 1½ inch (4 cm) wide, red-green stems; blooms are orange-red and spines are brown.

R. minuscula, red crown cactus, features 2-inch (5 cm) globes with white spines; flowers are crimson.

R. senilis, fire crown cactus, grows 3 inches (8 cm) tall and 2¾ inches (7 cm) thick; brilliant red flowers are featured against dense white spines.

Soil: Cactus/succulent mix.

Temperature: Day, 65° to 85°F (18° to 29°C); night, 50° to 65°F (10° to 18°C).

Light: Filtered sun, with 4 hours direct winter sun daily, from southern or western exposure. Does well under artificial light, needing 12 light-hours daily. Air circulation is important.

Moisture: Let soil dry slightly between moderate waterings. Avoid overwatering. Humidity, 30% to 35%.

Feeding: Every 6 weeks during growing season, with low-nitrogen, high-potassium fertilizer; for plants at least 1 year old.

Grooming: Pot-on when offsets crowd against sides of pot or roots overcrowd pot space. Use broad pot to accomodate shallow roots.

Propagation: By offsets in summer, or seeds.

Seasonal Care: To encourage blooming, induce winter rest. Site in cool location, 40° to 50°F (4° to 10°C). Water just enough to keep plant from shriveling; withhold fertilizer. When buds appear, give slightly more water and warmer temperature. Resume regular care when buds show red.

RHIPSALIDOPSIS
Easter cactus

This genus is comprised of 2 species of epiphytic cacti, which are related to *Schlumbergera,* the Christmas and Thanksgiving cactus. The jointed stems are made up of flat, oval segments. Freely branching, they grow upright, then droop as stems lengthen. Soft, yellow-brown bristles are visible, growing from areoles. Blooms appear in spring, even on small plants, and will last for several days each, with the entire blooming period extending over several weeks. Many hybrids are available with a wide range of flower colors.

R. gaertneri, formerly *Schlumbergera gaertneri,* Easter cactus, produces bright red blooms; stems grow to 12 inches (30 cm) long.

Ranunculus asiaticus

***Rebutia* species**

R. rosea, dwarf Easter cactus, is a compact plant featuring rosy pink blooms.

Soil: Humusy mix.
Temperature: Day, 70°F (21°C); night, 60° to 70°F (16° to 21°C).
Light: Moderate light, filtered sun, from eastern or western exposure.
Moisture: Keep soil thoroughly moist. Mist daily. Humidity, 45% to 60%.
Feeding: Every 2 weeks once flower buds have formed, with high-potassium fertilizer. Give monthly dosage following rest period and before flower buds appear.
Grooming: Repot each year, after rest period.
Propagation: By cuttings or seeds.
Pests and Diseases: Buds may drop due to drafts, sudden change in temperature, or if soil is allowed to dry out.
Seasonal Care: Plant rests for 2 to 3 weeks after flowering. Water just enough to keep plant from shriveling; withhold fertilizer.

RHIPSALIS
Chain cactus, mistletoe cactus

A hanging basket will best simulate the tree perches these epiphytic cacti enjoy in their native jungles. Masses of slender, branching stems may be trailing or erect, bearing hair and bristles but no spines. The flowers are small, blooming in early spring and lasting up to 8 days. Fruit, resembling berries, appears after flowers have faded. Of the 60 species comprising this genus, the following may be grown indoors:

R. cereuscula, coral cactus, grows upright to 24 inches (61 cm) with slender, rounded stems branching at the tips and off to the sides; flowers are white, pink, or yellow; fruit is white.

R. cribrata has erect stems when young, which droop as they lengthen; bell-shaped white flowers have red centers; fruit is red.

Soil: Humusy mix.
Temperature: Day, 70° to 85°F (21° to 29°C); night, 50° to 65°F (10° to 18°C).
Light: Moderate sun from northern or eastern exposure. Does well under artificial light, needing 10 to 12 light-hours daily.
Moisture: Keep soil evenly moist. Mist daily. Humidity, 45% to 60%.
Feeding: Every 2 weeks while in bloom, with mild low-nitrogen fertilizer.
Grooming: Repot each spring.

Propagation: By cuttings taken in spring or summer, or division.
Pests and Diseases: Red, shriveled stems indicate too much sun.
Seasonal Care: In fall, set in cool site, 50° to 65°F (10° to 18°C), to encourage flower buds. Let soil dry between moderate waterings; feed monthly.

RHODODENDRON
Azalea

800 species of shrubs and small trees comprise this genus, and when grown indoors they measure anywhere from 6 inches to 4 feet (15 cm to 1.2 m). Clusters of flowers appear in spring, each lasting 2 to 4 weeks. These blooms are funnel shaped, may be single or double, and appear in shades of red, white, pink, yellow, and purple. *Rhododendron* will bloom indoors for several seasons. Many hybrids are available.

Soil: Humusy mix.

Rhipsalidopsis gaertneri

Rhipsalis cereuscula

Temperature: Prefers cool range, 45° to 60°F (7° to 16°C).
Light: When in bloom, bright light with no direct sun, from eastern or western exposure. When not flowering, moderate light.
Moisture: Use soft water only. Keep soil constantly moist. Mist twice daily. Humidity, 50% to 60%.
Feeding: Weekly when not in bloom and no buds are present, with all-purpose fertilizer.
Grooming: Pot-on every 2 to 3 years, after flowers fade and before setting outdoors. Remove blooms as they fade.
Propagation: By tip cuttings taken in spring.
Pests and Diseases: Check for aphids, mealybugs, scale, whiteflies.
Seasonal Care: To promote blooming the following season, when flowers have faded keep plant cool and allow soil to dry between moderate waterings. When danger of frost is past, set outdoors in shaded site. Keep soil moist; feed regularly. Bring indoors before first frost and keep at 45° to 55°F (7° to 13°C). *R. obtusum* can be planted permanently outdoors.

RHOEO
Boat lily, Moses in the cradle

Prized for both its foliage and flowers, *R. spathacea,* also listed as *R. discolor,* is the only known species in this genus. A good candidate for hanging baskets, it measures up to 15 inches (38 cm) tall, with rosettes of lance-shaped leaves. These leaves have a dark green upperside and purple underside. Small white flowers appear in late spring, nestled within purple, boat-shaped bracts. The flowers fade quickly but the colored bracts last for several months. *R. spathacea* 'Variegata' features bright yellow stripes running the length of its leaves.

Soil: All-purpose mix.
Temperature: Day, 65° to 70°F (18° to 21°C); night, 55° to 65°F (13° to 18°C).
Light: Bright light, no direct sun, from eastern or western exposure. Does well under artificial light, needing 14 light-hours daily.

Moisture: Keep soil evenly moist. Mist daily. Humidity, 45% to 60%.
Feeding: Every 2 weeks during growing season, with mild liquid fertilizer.
Grooming: Repot each spring; pot-on when roots occupy ½ of pot space. Rinse foliage often.
Propagation: By offsets or seeds.
Pests and Diseases: Check for mealybugs, mites.
Seasonal Care: Plant rests slightly after flowering. Keep cool, 50°F (10°C). Keep soil barely moist; withhold fertilizer.

RIVINA
Rouge plant

There is a single species in this genus, *R. humilis,* which is valued for its ornamental fruit. Growing to a bushy 24 inches (61 cm), it features thin, tapered, oval leaves. From summer through fall, pinkish white flowers appear on a spike, followed by a drooping cluster of tiny red berries. This fruit yields a red dye. *R. humilis* 'Aurantiaca' bears yellow-orange berries. Although *Rivina* is not commonly found, it is an undemanding plant to care for.

Soil: All-purpose mix.

Rhododendron hybrid

Rhoeo spathacea 'Variegata'

Temperature: Tolerates 65° to 80°F (18° to 27°C) range.
Light: Bright light, direct sun, from southern or western exposure. Air circulation is important.
Moisture: Keep soil evenly moist. Humidity, 30%.
Feeding: Monthly, with mild liquid fertilizer.
Propagation: By cuttings or seeds.
Pests and Diseases: If soil is allowed to dry out, berries will drop.
Seasonal Care: Plant grows actively year-round.

ROSMARINUS
Rosemary

Fresh or dried, the pungent leaves of this evergreen shrub lend themselves to a wide range of culinary uses. Of the 3 species comprising this genus, *R. officinalis* is the commonly grown plant. Leaves are shiny and narrow, dark green on top and fuzzy white underneath. Blue flowers appear from winter to early spring, in short spikes. Generally growing from 8 inches to 4 feet (20 cm to 1.2 m) tall, *Rosmarinus* can be kept in line by frequent pruning.

Soil: All-purpose mix.
Temperature: Day, 65° to 68°F (18° to 20°C); night, 50° to 55°F (10° to 13°C).
Light: Bright light, with 4 hours direct sun daily, from eastern, western, or southern exposure. Does well under artificial light, needing 14 light-hours daily.
Moisture: Keep soil evenly moist. Mist daily. Humidity, 30% to 35%.
Feeding: Every 2 to 3 weeks, with mild liquid fertilizer.
Grooming: Pinch growing tips to retain compact form.
Propagation: By tip cuttings or seeds.
Pests and Diseases: Check for spider mites.
Seasonal Care: Best treated as an annual, and discarded after 1 season.

RUELLIA
Monkey plant, trailing velvet plant

Good specimens for terraria, these plants are prized for their foliage and flowers. 250 species of shrubs comprise this genus, and remain under 36 inches (91 cm) when grown indoors. The ovate leaves are variegated and velvety. Large tubular flowers open to 5 lobes on the ends, and may be white, pink, or purple.

R. devosiana, Christmas pride, sports dark green leaves with white veining and purple undersides; white flowers tinged with lavender appear in spring.

R. graecizans, red spray, produces brilliant red, 2 inch (5 cm) long flowers in winter.

R. makoyana, trailing velvet plant, has trailing stems measuring to 24 inches (61 cm); gray-green leaves are tinted with purple, veined with white, and have purple undersides; rosy flowers appear in fall and winter.

Soil: Humusy mix.
Temperature: Day, 68° to 75°F (20° to 24°C); night, 55° to 65°F (13° to 18°C).
Light: Bright light, with no direct sun, from southern or eastern exposure.
Moisture: Keep soil evenly moist. Mist twice daily. Humidity, 60% to 70%.
Feeding: Every 2 weeks during growing season, with mild manure tea.
Grooming: Repot after flowering is completed. Pinch growing tips for compact shape and better blooming.
Propagation: By stem cuttings or seeds.

Rivina humilis

Rosmarinus officinalis

Pests and Diseases: Check for aphids, spider mites. Rolled leaf edges indicate insufficient humidity or too bright light.

Seasonal Care: After flowering, plant rests for about 2 months. Keep soil barely moist; withhold fertilizer.

SAGITTARIA
Arrowhead

These rooted aquatic plants are commonly found in aquaria, often used as focal points because of their graceful foliage. White flowers may appear above the water, although this is rare in aquarium specimens.

S. graminea var. *platyphylla* features a fountain-type arrangement of broad, thick leaves.

S. subulata var. *subulata* features narrow, densely arranged leaves, up to 12 inches (30 cm) long.

Soil: Layer of medium size aquarium gravel or coarse sand.

Temperature: 59° to 72°F (15° to 22°C).

Light: Moderate to bright sunlight.

Does well under artificial light, needing 14 to 16 light-hours daily.

Water: Slightly acid.

Feeding: Occasionally, with bone meal/clay pellets.

Grooming: Once a month, replace ⅓ of water in tank. Scrape algae from tank sides. Remove dead or discolored leaves. No need to prune, since plant generally grows according to water level, never exceeding it.

Propagation: By division.

Pests and Diseases: Check for bacterial rot, snails.

SAINTPAULIA
African violet

These well-known flowering plants are easy to propagate and bring to bloom throughout the year. Plants are divided into 2 groups according to their growth habit: they may be either rosette forming, or trailing or creeping. The 5-petaled flowers appear in clusters year-round, with summer and fall the peak blooming

seasons. They may be single or double in form, a single shade or bicolored, and have ruffled, fringed, or smooth edges. Available in many colors, the flowers can be white, pink, red, blue, or purple with yellow stamens. Most of the 21 species are available, as are a large number of cultivars and hybrids in which the simplicity and sublety of the species have been exchanged for larger, more vivid flowers and showier foliage. The following species merit consideration, in addition to the wide assortment of hybrids and cultivars. See chapter 13 for a list of durable, popular cultivars. Names of popular miniatures are given in chapter 22.

S. confusa features a rosette of scalloped, hairy, ovate leaves, colored a medium green with pale undersides; violet-blue flowers appear in clusters of 4.

S. grotei produces trailing, branching stems measuring to 8 inches (20 cm); round, thin leaves are covered with long and short hairs and fea-

Ruellia makoyana

Sagittaria species

ture prominent veining and notched edges; flowers are pale mauve with violet-blue centers, appearing in clusters of 2 to 4 blooms.

S. ionantha, the parent of a wide variety of cultivars, appears as a rosette of glossy, round leaves with a hair-covered, quilted surface; bears clusters of 8 to 10 light blue and violet flowers.

S. shumensis, a compact rosette, produces many small, hairy, toothed leaves, colored pale to dark olive green; flowers are pale violet-blue with a dark violet spot and appear in clusters of 5.

Soil: All-purpose gesneriad mix.
Temperature: 65° to 75°F (18° to 24°C) range, year-round.
Light: Filtered moderate to bright light, no direct sun, from eastern, western, southeastern or southwestern exposure. Does well under artificial light, needing 12 to 18 light-hours daily.
Moisture: Let soil surface dry between waterings. Use tepid water. Avoid overwatering. Leaves can be misted with lukewarm water with no danger of spotting if plant is out of direct sun. Humidity, 60% to 70%.
Feeding: Weekly, with mild all-purpose fertilizer.
Grooming: Blooms best when pot-bound; pot-on only when roots com-

pletely overcrowd pot space. Turn plants often to promote symmetry. Offsets creating a bunchy look on a rosette-forming plant may be removed and potted up.
Propagation: By crown division, leaf cuttings, offsets, or seeds.
Pests and Diseases: Check for aphids, crown rot, mealybugs, spider mites. Cold water droplets will spot foliage.
Seasonal Care: Plant will flower year-round if light intensity is high enough.

SANSEVIERIA
Mother-in-law plant, snake plant

A slow grower, this foliage plant will tolerate a great deal of abuse and neglect, and can do well in almost any location. Leaves are generally thick, stiff, and sword shaped, with interesting variegation and mottling on a dark green background. Growth

may be either erect, measuring up to 30 inches (76 cm) tall, or in low-lying rosettes, measuring to 3 inches (8 cm) across. Flowers are rare, appearing as whitish yellow clusters. Of the 60 species making up this genus, the following are commonly available:

S. ehrenbergii grows upright to 6 feet (1.8 m), with flat-margined leaves fanning out from a basal center stem; leaves are blue-green with white edges.

S. trifasciata 'Hahnii' is a dwarf form with a 6 inch (15 cm) tall leaf rosette featuring light and dark green patterning.

S. trifasciata 'Laurentii', snake plant, has rigid, erect leaves with golden yellow leaf margins and green patterning.

S. zeylanica, bowstring hemp, appears as a loose rosette of 30-inch (76

Saintpaulia ionantha

Sansevieria trifasciata 'Laurentii'

cm) leaves, which arch away from the base; leaves are gray-green with darker vertical bands.

Soil: All-purpose mix.
Temperature: Day, 65° to 80°F (18° to 27°C); night, 60° to 65°F (16° to 18°C).
Light: Bright light, with direct sun daily, from eastern or western exposure. Does well under artificial light, needing 14 to 16 light-hours daily.
Moisture: Let soil dry between thorough waterings. Avoid overwatering. Mist daily. Humidity, 25% to 30%.
Feeding: Monthly, with mild liquid fertilizer.
Grooming: Prefers to be potbound; pot-on when roots occupy over ¾ of pot space. Be careful when handling plant; if pointed tip is broken off, leaf will stop growing. Remove dead leaves; clean foliage monthly.
Propagation: By leaf cuttings, offsets, or rhizome division.
Pests and Diseases: Rot develops when water is allowed to collect in rosettes.
Seasonal Care: Plant rests slightly

during winter. Let soil dry almost completely between waterings; withhold fertilizer.

SAXIFRAGA
Mother of thousands, strawberry begonia

This dwarf perennial grows to 6 inches (15 cm) tall, producing 24 inch (61 cm) long, threadlike stolons which resemble strawberry runners. The olive green leaves are hairy, with white veining and burgundy undersides. Flower spikes appear in late summer, bearing clusters of small, star-shaped flowers. *Saxifraga* produces numerous offspring, which are the dangling plantlets found on the trailing stolons. Of the 300 species, *S. stolonifera,* also known as *S. sarmentosa,* is the common indoor plant. *S. stolonifera* 'Tricolor', magic carpet, is a smaller version, featuring pink-tinted leaves with green, gray-green, or creamy white variegations.

Soil: All-purpose mix.

Saxifraga stolonifera

Temperature: Day, 60° to 68°F (16° to 20°C); night, 50° to 60°F (10° to 16°C).
Light: Bright to moderate light from northern or eastern exposure. *S. stolonifera* 'Tricolor' requires 2 hours of direct sun to retain leaf coloration.
Moisture: Let soil dry slightly between thorough waterings. Humidity, 20% to 30%.
Feeding: Monthly during growing season, with mild liquid fertilizer.
Grooming: Pot-on in spring. When older plant begins to look leggy, replace with numerous plantlets. Remove blooms as they fade.
Propagation: By natural layering or offsets.
Pests and Diseases: Check for mealybugs, scale, whiteflies. Avoid drafts.
Seasonal Care: Plant rests during winter. Keep cool, 40°F (4°C). Gradually reduce water, keeping soil barely moist; withhold fertilizer. Resume regular schedule when flower buds appear.

SCHEFFLERA, see *Brassaia*

SCHLUMBERGERA
Christmas cactus, crab cactus, Thanksgiving cactus

These epiphytic cacti have blooming periods corresponding to holidays, hence their common names. The hanging branches measure from 12 to 36 inches (30 to 91 cm) long, composed of glossy green, flat segments. Flowers appear from stem tips, and measure from 1 to 3 inches (2 to 8 cm) long with several tiers of petals. Each bloom lasts for several days, and the entire blooming period spans several weeks. The Easter cactus, *Rhipsalidopsis gaertneri,* was formerly classified under this genus as *S. gaertneri.*

S. bridgesii, Christmas cactus, features arching, 12-inch (30 cm) branches made of scalloped segments with rounded tips; late winter, early spring blooms are bright red to purple.

S. truncata, also referred to as *Zygocactus truncatus,* crab cactus or Thanksgiving cactus, features notched stem tips; fall blooms are rosy pink.

Soil: Humusy mix.
Temperature: Day, 65° to 75°F (18° to 24°C); night, 55° to 65°F (13° to 18°C).
Light: Moderate light, partial shade and some direct sun in winter, from eastern exposure.
Moisture: Keep soil evenly moist. Mist frequently. Humidity, 45% to 60%.
Feeding: Once flower buds form, every 2 weeks with high-potassium fertilizer.
Grooming: Repot each year after flowering; prefers to be potbound.
Propagation: By cuttings taken in summer, or seeds.
Pests and Diseases: Dropping buds result from drafts, sudden change in temperature, or when soil is allowed to dry out.
Seasonal Care: Plant rests in summer, following blooming period.

Keep cool, 50° to 55°F (10° to 13°C). Keep soil barely moist; withhold fertilizer. When new growth appears, to encourage blooming follow this schedule for 4 to 6 weeks: Keep at 55° to 65°F (13° to 18°C), alternating 10 hours of light and 14 hours of total darkness. When buds appear, introduce to warmer temperature and begin regular culture. Blooming should occur in 6 weeks.

SCILLA, see *Ledebouria*

SCINDAPSUS,
see *Epipremnum*

SEDUM
Burro's tail, stonecrop

The 600 species of succulents comprising this genus are found worldwide. The fleshy leaves may be either cylindrical or flat, and are found on erect, creeping, or trailing stems. *Sedum* may occasionally bloom, producing 2- to 3-inch (5 to 8 cm) flower heads in spring and summer. Found at the stem tip, they can

be white, pink, red, or yellow. These plants are suitable for hanging baskets:

S. adolphi, golden sedum, has 12-inch (30 cm) upright stems covered with yellow-green leaves edged in red; white flowers may appear in early spring.

S. hirsutum features runners bearing dense rosettes of spicy-scented leaves; summer blooms are white with red veining.

S. morganianum, burro's tail, produces 12 to 36 inch (30 to 91 cm) long trailing stems, with densely overlapping tear-shaped leaves; yellow-green leaves are waxy with light blue powder; rose-colored flowers appear in spring.

S. ×rubrotinctum, Christmas cheer or jelly beans, is a 6- to 9-inch (15 to 23 cm) shrub; branches bear clusters of thick green leaves at the tips; leaf tips may turn red in full sun; yellow flowers appear in winter and spring.

Soil: Mix equal parts garden loam and sand.
Temperature: Day, 68° to 80°F (20° to 27°C); night, 50° to 65°F (10° to 18°C).
Light: Full sun from southern exposure, year-round. Does well under artificial light, needing 12 to 16 light-hours daily.

Schlumbergera truncata

Sedum morganianum

Moisture: Let soil surface dry moderately between thorough waterings. Humidity, 20% to 25%.
Grooming: Pot-on in spring when roots occupy ½ of pot space. As plant ages, it becomes less attractive; replace with cuttings. Remove dried leaves.
Propagation: By division, stem cuttings taken in spring, or seeds. Allow cuttings to dry for several days before placing in rooting medium.
Pests and Diseases: Check for mealybugs, root rot, scale.
Seasonal Care: Plant rests from fall through spring. Keep at 40° to 50°F (4° to 10°C). Give just enough water to keep plant from shriveling; withhold fertilizer.

SELAGINELLA
Club moss, moss fern

These fernlike foliage plants add a delicate, airy effect to terraria, and thrive under the moist, shady conditions found there. *Selaginella* may either appear as a low-growing clump or with upright branches. Stem tips contain spores which may be used for propagation. The following species are recommended out of the 700 within this genus for use indoors:

S. kraussiana, creeping club moss, features 12-inch (30 cm) creeping stems bearing bright green leaves which create a thick mat; a vigorous

grower, stems root when in contact with soil.

S. martensii has shiny, fleshy green leaves borne on 12-inch (30 cm) stems which grow erect, then arch in the lower half.

S. pallescens, also listed as *S. emmeliana,* moss fern or sweat plant, produces dense tufts of lacy fronds growing upright or horizontal; pale green leaves have white margins; stems measure to 12 inches (30 cm).

S. uncinata, rainbow fern, features 24 inch (61 cm) long creeping stems with metallic, blue-green leaves.

Soil: All-purpose mix.
Temperature: Day, 70°F (21°C); night, 50° to 55°F (10° to 13°C).
Light: Low light, partial shade from northern or eastern exposure. Does well under artificial light, needing 14 to 16 light-hours daily.
Moisture: Keep soil thoroughly moist. Mist twice daily. Humidity, 50% to 60%.
Feeding: Every 2 weeks during growing season, with mild liquid fertilizer.
Grooming: Repot each year; pot-on in spring when roots overcrowd pot space. Vigorous growth can be controlled by trimming.
Propagation: By cuttings taken in spring, layering, or spores.

Seasonal Care: Plant rests slightly during winter. Reduce water; withhold fertilizer.

SENECIO
Cineraria, parlor ivy, string of beads

A total of 2,000 to 3,000 species makes this one of the largest flowering plant genera, encompassing a wide range of plants with different growth habits. There are the nonsucculent climbers with ivylike foliage, the succulents with creeping stems, and the bushy flowering plants. Although grouped within the same genus, all require different culture.

SUCCULENTS
1 of these plants was formerly classified under the genus *Kleinia* and is often sold under this name. With trailing stems growing from 12 to 36 inches (30 to 91 cm) long, both of these species are attractive in hanging baskets.

S. herreianus, also known as *Kleinia gomphophylla,* gooseberry kleinia,

Selaginella kraussiana

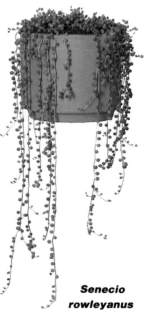

Senecio rowleyanus

has slender stems covered with globular, fleshy leaves marked with translucent bands.

S. rowleyanus, string of beads, features light green, globular leaves with a single translucent band and a pointed end; white flowers with red stigmas appear in winter.

Soil: Mix equal parts garden loam and sand.
Temperature: Day, 68° to 72°F (20° to 22°C); night, 50° to 55°F (10° to 13°C).
Light: Bright light, with 4 hours direct sun daily, from eastern or southern exposure. Does well under artificial light, needing 14 to 16 light-hours daily.
Moisture: Let soil surface dry between thorough waterings. Humidity, 45% to 60%.
Feeding: Monthly during growing season, with potassium-rich fertilizer; for plants at least 1 year old.
Grooming: Repot when necessary.
Propagation: By division or stem cuttings.
Pests and Diseases: Check for aphids, mealybugs, spider mites, scale.

Seasonal Care: Plant rests during winter. Place in cool, bright location, 50°F (10°C). Reduce water, keeping soil barely moist; withhold fertilizer.

NONSUCCULENT CLIMBER

S. mikanioides, parlor ivy or German ivy, has 4 foot (1.2 m) long, slender, stiff stems bearing dense, overlapping leaves resembling ivy; yellow, daisylike flowers appear in clusters at the ends of shoots.

Soil: Mix 3 parts garden loam and 1 part perlite, with good drainage.
Temperature: Day, 65° to 75°F (18° to 24°C); night, 55° to 62°F (13° to 17°C).
Light: Low light, with morning sun, from eastern exposure, or winter sun from southern exposure.
Moisture: Let soil dry between thorough waterings. Humidity, 30% to 35%.
Feeding: Every 2 weeks during growing season, with mild liquid fertilizer.
Grooming: Repot each spring; pot-on when roots occupy ½ of pot space.
Propagation: By tip cuttings.

Pests and Diseases: Check for aphids.
Seasonal Care: Plant rests during winter. Keep cool, 50° to 55°F (10° to 13°C). Keep soil barely moist; withhold fertilizer.

FLOWERING PLANT

Senecio ×hybridus, cineraria, grows to 36 inches (91 cm) with heart-shaped, softly hairy leaves. Velvety flowers resembling daisies appear in late winter or spring and last for several weeks. Blooms may be white, red, pink, purple, or blue. This plant is not long lasting indoors and is usually discarded after flowers fade.

Soil: All-purpose mix.
Temperature: Day, 55° to 60°F (13° to 16°C); night, 40° to 50°F (4° to 10°C).
Light: Bright light, no direct sun, from eastern or western exposure.
Moisture: Keep soil evenly moist. Humidity, 45% to 60%.
Pests and Diseases: Check for aphids, whiteflies. If soil dries out, plant will collapse and is hard to revive.

Senecio mikanioides

Senecio ×hybridus

SETCREASEA
Purple heart

The deep purple stems and leaves of this foliage plant create a striking effect when displayed in a hanging basket. Deep pink flowers appear on stem tips, each lasting 1 day with the entire blooming season extending over the summer. Of the 6 species of perennials, *S. pallida* 'Purple Heart', also listed as *S. purpurea,* is the plant grown indoors. The erect or sprawling stems grow to 24 inches (61 cm) long. *Setcreasea* is suitable for soil or water culture.

Soil: All-purpose mix.
Temperature: Day, 68° to 80°F (20° to 27°C); night, 55° to 68°F (13° to 20°C).
Light: Bright light, with 3 to 4 hours direct sun daily, from eastern, western, or southern exposure. Bright light enhances coloration, while shade causes foliage to turn green. Does well under artificial light, needing 14 light-hours daily.
Moisture: Let soil dry slightly between moderate waterings. Avoid overwatering. Mist twice daily. Humidity, 40% to 45%.
Feeding: Monthly during growing season, with mild liquid fertilizer.
Grooming: Pot-on when roots occupy ½ of pot space. Pinch growing tips to retain full shape. Handle gently to avoid rubbing off purple, dustlike substance on stems. Plant becomes less attractive as it ages; replace by cuttings.
Propagation: By division or stem cuttings.
Pests and Diseases: Check for mealybugs, mites, scale, slugs, whiteflies.
Seasonal Care: Plant rests slightly during winter. Keep soil barely moist; withhold fertilizer.

SINNINGIA
Florists' gloxinia

These plants, members of the Gesneriad family, are commonly sold under the name gloxinia. Grown from fibrous-rooted tubers, these plants are generally long lasting, producing brightly colored flowers from summer through fall. Among the 75 species comprising this genus, the following are commonly grown indoors:

S. cardinalis, cardinal flower, formerly listed as *Rechsteineria cardinalis,* produces 12-inch (30 cm) stems with white hairs; scalloped leaves have dark green veins and pale green undersides; scarlet blooms appear in fall.

S. pusilla, miniature slipper plant, is a tiny, ever-blooming, 1- to 2-inch (3 to 5 cm) plant; trumpet-shaped flowers are purple with darker lines and white throats; a good specimen for terraria.

S. regina, Cinderella slippers, is a dwarf measuring from 6 to 10 inches (15 to 25 cm) in height; velvety, dark green leaves have silver veins and purple undersides and serrated edges; erect stalks bear violet flowers resembling slippers in late summer.

S. speciosa, florists' gloxinia, features hairy, purple, 12-inch (30 cm) stems; velvety leaves have scalloped edges, pale green veins, and are flushed with red; flower stalks bear 1 to 3 bell-shaped white, red, or violet blooms in summer.

Soil: All-purpose gesneriad mix.
Temperature: Day, 68° to 75°F (20° to 24°C); night, 65° to 70°F (18° to 21°C).
Light: Bright, filtered light from southern exposure. Does well under artificial light, needing 12 to 14 light-hours daily.
Moisture: Keep soil evenly moist. Let *S. cardinalis* dry moderately between waterings. Mist twice daily. Humidity, 60% to 70%.
Feeding: Every 2 weeks after flowering until foliage dies back, with mild all-purpose fertilizer. *S. pusilla*

Setcreasea pallida

Sinningia speciosa

Si—So

can be fed every 2 weeks, year-round.

Grooming: Repot when new growth appears following dormant period.

Propagation: By stem or leaf cuttings taken in early spring, tubers, or seeds.

Pests and Diseases: Check for aphids, *Botrytis* blight, cyclamen mites, mealybugs, powdery mildew, root or crown rot, scale, viruses, whiteflies.

Seasonal Care: Except for *S. pusilla* and many hybrids of smaller species, most plants enter dormant period after flowering. Reduce water until foliage dies back, then remove foliage. Store tuber in pot in cool, dark site, 60° to 65°F (16° to 18°C). Withhold fertilizer and barely moisten soil every few weeks. When new growth appears, repot and increase water gradually, then resume regular schedule.

SOLANUM
Christmas cherry, Jerusalem cherry

This sizable genus, containing 1,700 species, includes both vegetable and ornamental plants. The ornamentals produce summer blooms, followed by berrylike fruits which last through the winter and are poisonous if eaten. These plants may be kept for 2 blooming and fruiting seasons, but are generally discarded after that.

S. pseudocapsicum, Christmas cherry or false Jerusalem cherry, a popular holiday plant with white flowers preceding scarlet berries, grows to a shrubby 4 feet (1.2 m).

S. pseudocapsicum 'Nanum' is a dwarf form, growing from 10 to 12 inches (25 to 30 cm).

Soil: All-purpose mix, with good drainage.

Temperature: Day, 68° to 72°F (20° to 22°C); night, 50° to 55°F (10° to 13°C).

Light: Low light, with direct morning or winter sun, from eastern or southern exposure.

Moisture: Keep soil evenly moist. Mist twice daily. Humidity, 40% to 50%.

Feeding: Every 2 weeks during growing season, with mild liquid fertilizer.

Grooming: Pot-on before setting outdoors. Pinch tips for bushy shape and to control straggly stems. Stake tall plant.

Propagation: By cuttings or seeds.

Pests and Diseases: Check for aphids, scale, whiteflies. If kept too warm or given insufficient light, fruit and leaves will fall.

Seasonal Care: To keep for a second season, let plant rest for 4 to 5 weeks in late winter. Keep at 60°F (16°C), or less. Water just enough to keep soil from drying out; withhold fertilizer. Let plant spend late spring and summer outdoors, and bring indoors before first frost.

SOLEIROLIA
Baby's tears, Irish moss, mind your own business

Commonly sold as *Helxine soleirolii,* the single species within this genus is correctly listed as *S. soleirolii.* A perennial creeping foliage plant, it is a rapid grower and easy to care for. Delicate, rounded leaves measure $\frac{1}{4}$ inch (6 mm) wide, appearing on threadlike, rooting stems. With its mounds of soft green foliage, it makes an attractive carpet for terraria.

Soil: Humusy mix.

Temperature: Day, 70°F (21°C); night, 50° to 55°F (10° to 13°C).

Light: Moderate to low light from northern or eastern exposure.

Moisture: Keep soil moderately moist. Humidity, 45% to 65%.

Propagation: By division.

Solanum pseudocapsicum

Soleirolia soleirolii

Seasonal Care: Growth slows in winter. Keep at 39° to 45°F (4° to 7°C), and reduce water.

SOPHRONITIS

This orchid genus contains 6 species, all dwarf in size, never growing beyond 4 inches (10 cm) in height. These epiphytic plants are sympodial and feature pseudobulbs, from each of which emerges a single, flat, leathery leaf. Flowers appear singly or up to 3 in a cluster and are noted for their vivid red and orange colors. *Sophronitis* is rather demanding to grow, but has been crossed with the orchid genera *Cattleya* and *Laelia* to unite the bright colors with plants of easier culture. *S. coccinea* is a widely available species, producing 3 inch (8 cm) wide, scarlet to orange flowers with yellow-streaked lips. These plants prefer a cool to intermediate greenhouse, but can be grown in the home as long as the temperature remains cool.

Soil: Osmunda fiber or orchid bark mix.
Temperature Day, 60° to 65°F (16° to 18°C); night, 55°F (13°C).
Light: Filtered light from northeastern or northwestern exposure. Does well under artificial light, needing 14 to 16 light-hours daily. Good circulation of fresh air.

Moisture: Keep evenly moist, year-round. Humidity, 60% to 70%.
Feeding: Every 3 weeks with all-purpose fertilizer, year-round.
Grooming: Repot when plant completely overcrowds pot space, or when growing medium has deteriorated. Best done before outset of active growth, when new roots are first visible.
Propagation: By division of pseudobulbs when active growth begins; divide so there are 3 to 4 pseudobulbs per plant.
Pests and Diseases: Check for bacterial, fungal, and viral infections, mealybugs, scale, slugs, snails, whiteflies.
Seasonal Care: Grows year-round; does not require rest period.

SPATHIPHYLLUM
Peace lily, spathe flower

This genus comprises 35 species of plants grown for their foliage and flowers, which resemble the calla lily. Clusters of oblong, dark green, shiny leaves grow from a rhizome.

Flower heads appear on erect stalks in spring and summer and last up to 5 weeks. These heads consist of a spathe and protruding spadix.

S. 'Mauna Loa' grows to 24 inches (61 cm) tall, with large leaves; 20-inch (51 cm) stalk bears creamy spathe and spadix.

S. wallisii measures 9 inches (23 cm) tall; pure white spathe shields yellow spadix.

Soil: All-purpose mix, with good drainage.
Temperature: Day, 80° to 85°F (27° to 29°C); night, 62° to 65°F (17° to 18°C).
Light: Moderate to low light, no direct sun, from northern or eastern exposure.
Moisture: Keep soil evenly moist. Mist twice daily. Humidity, 80%.
Feeding: Every 2 weeks during growing season, with mild liquid fertilizer.
Grooming: Repot each spring; pot-on when roots occupy over ¾ of pot space.

Sophronitis coccinea

Spathiphyllum 'Mauna Loa'

Propagation: By division or seeds.
Pests and Diseases: Check for mealybugs, spider mites, scale, whiteflies.
Seasonal Care: Growth may slow during winter. Reduce water; withhold fertilizer. *S. wallisii* should be kept cool, 50°F (10°C), in moderate light. Keep soil moist; give monthly dose of mild manure tea.

STAPELIA
Carrion flower, starfish flower

This genus, containing 90 species of succulents, merits its common name by producing star-shaped flowers which have a slight odor of decaying meat. 4 fleshy, leafless stems branch out from the base, from which a flower stalk emerges anytime from spring to fall.

S. hirsuta features 8-inch (20 cm) erect stems; purple flowers have cream and yellow markings, and measure 5 inches (13 cm) across.

S. variegata, starfish flower, produces 6-inch (15 cm) stems with brown markings; yellow-green flowers have purple bands or random spots; blooms measure 3 inches (8 cm) across.

Soil: Cactus/succulent mix.
Temperature: 60° to 65°F (16° to 18°C).
Light: Filtered sun from southern exposure, year-round.
Moisture: Let soil dry between thorough waterings. Humidity, 30% to 35%.
Feeding: Every 6 weeks during growing season, with low-nitrogen, high-potassium fertilizer.
Grooming: Repot each spring.
Propagation: By division, stem cuttings, or seeds. Let cuttings dry for several days before setting in rooting medium.
Pests and Diseases: Check for fungus, mealybugs. Overwatering causes rot.
Seasonal Care: Plant rests during winter. Keep cool, 50°F (10°C). Reduce water, never allowing soil to dry out completely.

STRELITZIA
Bird of paradise

4 species of perennial plants comprise this genus, and are noted for their distinctive blooms, which appear only on 7- or 8-year-old specimens. After that, flowers appear every year, in spring and summer. The flower heads appear on long stalks, each featuring a long, horizontal green bract from which a series of orange flowers emerges over a span of several weeks. Each flower has a purple, arrowlike projection from its center. Large, blue-gray leaves on long stalks appear in a clump. *S. reginae,* the familiar species, is relatively easy to grow.

Soil: Humusy mix, with good drainage.
Temperature: Day, 68° to 75°F (20° to 24°C); night, 60° to 65°F (16° to 18°C).

Stapelia hirsuta

Strelitzia reginae

Light: Bright light, with direct morning or winter sun, from southern or eastern exposure.
Moisture: Let soil dry slightly between moderate waterings. Mist daily. Humidity, 30% to 35%.
Feeding: Every 2 weeks during growing season, with mild liquid fertilizer.
Grooming: Must be potbound to bloom; pot-on only when roots occupy more than ¾ of pot space. Roots are easily damaged.
Propagation: By division. New plant will flower in half the time required by its parent.
Pests and Diseases: Check for mealybugs, scale.
Seasonal Care: Plant rests during winter. Set in cool spot, 55°F (13°C). Reduce water; withhold fertilizer.

STREPTOCARPUS
Cape primrose

132 species of flowering plants comprise this gesneriad genus. Most common house plants are stemless with a basal rosette of leaves or sometimes even a single leaf, but other plants may feature long, branching stems. The showy flowers are tubular with a wide end flaring into 5 petals. Under optimal condi-

tions, these plants may bloom continuously, and larger, longer-lasting blooms can be expected the second season.

S. dunnii produces a single gray-green leaf, 12 inches (30 cm) long, and pink to red flowers.

S. ×hybridus, cape primrose, a compact version of *S. rexii,* produces large flowers in shades of white, pink, red, blue, and purple.

S. rexii features a basal rosette of hairy, scalloped leaves, 12 inches (30 cm) long; 4 stalks appear, each bearing a cluster of 3 white, blue, or lilac flowers.

S. saxorum has 12 inch (30 cm) long, hair-covered, branching stems with whorls of velvety leaves; flower stalks bear a single white flower, tinged with purple.

Soil: For branching type, recommended all-purpose gesneriad mix. For rosette type, recommended fibrous-rooted gesneriad mix with crushed eggshells added.
Temperature: Rosette type prefers 65° to 80°F (18° to 27°C) range. Branching type shares that preference during the day, but needs cooler night temperature, 60° to 65°F (16° to 18°C).
Light: Bright light, without direct

sun, from eastern, western, or southern exposure. Except for *S. saxorum,* does well under artificial light, needing 12 to 14 light-hours daily.
Moisture: Let soil dry slightly between thorough waterings. Mist daily. Humidity, 60% to 70%.
Feeding: Give mild liquid fertilizer with each watering during active growth.
Grooming: Remove dead flower heads. Stake bushy plant. Repot when offsets crowd pot, following blooming.
Propagation: By crown division, leaf cuttings, suckers, or seeds.
Pests and Diseases: Check for aphids, *Botrytis* blight, cyclamen mites, mealybugs, powdery mildew, root or crown rot, scale, viruses, whiteflies.
Seasonal Care: Dormant period can be induced following blooming, by keeping in cool site: day, 65°F (18°C); night, 50°F (10°C). Provide moderate light, reduce water slightly, and withhold fertilizer.

SYNGONIUM
Arrowhead vine

Often mistaken for philodendron, the 20 species of tropical vines in this

Streptocarpus × hybridus

Syngonium podophyllum

genus are easily grown in soil or water. Stems, growing to 6 feet (1.8 m) long, can be trained to climb or trail from a hanging basket. As *Syngonium* ages, the leaf shape changes; leaves on a young plant are arrow shaped and undivided, while leaves on a mature plant are divided into distinct leaflets. Plants in this genus may also be sold under the name *Nephthytis*.

S. angustatum 'Albolineatum' features young leaves with white variegations and green margins; mature leaves have 3 to 5 leaflets and no variegations.

S. podophyllum, arrowhead vine, produces young leaves with white or yellow variegations; mature glossy green leaves have 9 leaflets.

S. wendlandii bears both young and mature leaves with 3 leaflets in a T-formation, which are a velvety dark green with light gray midribs.

Soil: Mix equal parts garden loam and peat moss.
Temperature: Day, 70°F (21°C); night, 55°F (13°C).
Light: Bright light, no direct sun, from northern or eastern exposure. Will adapt to moderate or low light. Does well under artificial light, needing 14 to 16 light-hours daily.
Moisture: Let soil dry moderately between thorough waterings. Mist daily. Humidity, 30% to 45%.
Feeding: Every 2 weeks during growing season, with mild liquid fertilizer. Top-dress with compost in spring.
Grooming: Prefers to be potbound; pot-on only when roots occupy more than ¾ of pot space. Rinse foliage and remove dead leaves.
Propagation: By 3-inch (8 cm) stem cuttings with node, taken in spring or summer.
Pests and Diseases: Check for aphids, mealybugs, spider mites.
Seasonal Care: Plant rests for

short time during winter. Water just enough to keep soil from drying out completely; withhold fertilizer.

THUNBERGIA
Black-eyed Susan vine

This popular ornamental may either grow erect or climb along a support. Depending on when seeds are sown, blooms may appear in summer or winter. These flowers feature black or deep purple centers with white, yellow, or orange petals. *Thunbergia* grows from 2 to 4 feet (0.6 to 1.2 m), and is best treated as an annual.

T. alata has serrated, triangular leaves; tubular flowers open to 5 bright orange petals and have a dark brown eye.

T. alata 'Alba' features white petals.

T. alata 'Aurantiaca', the most common plant, has orange-yellow petals.

T. alata 'Lutea' bears bright yellow petals.

T. mysorensis has long, pointed leaves; flowers appear in hanging clusters, purple-centered with yellow petals.

Soil: All-purpose mix, with good drainage.
Temperature: Day, 70° to 80°F (21° to 27°C); night, 60° to 65°F (16° to 18°C).
Light: Bright light, with 3 hours direct sun daily, from eastern or southern exposure.
Moisture: Keep soil evenly moist. Humidity, 30% to 35%.
Feeding: Every 2 weeks, with all-purpose fertilizer.
Grooming: Pot-on when roots overcrowd pot space. Remove flowers as they fade, to prolong flowering.
Propagation: By cuttings, layering, or seeds.
Pests and Diseases: Check for mealybugs, spider mites, scale.
Seasonal Care: Discard after flowering is completed.

Thunbergia alata

THYMUS
Thyme

300 to 400 species of perennial, aromatic shrubs comprise this genus, growing to 10 inches (25 cm) tall indoors. Fresh or dried leaves enhance many foods with their strong clove-like flavor.

T. ×citriodorus, lemon thyme, features large, lemon-scented leaves; pale lilac flowers appear in summer.

T. vulgaris, common thyme, features woody stems, narrow gray leaves, and white to lilac flowers.

Soil: Mix equal parts sphagnum moss, sand, and compost.
Temperature: Prefers 65° to 68°F (18° to 20°C) range.
Light: Full sun from southern or western exposure. Does well under artificial light, needing 14 light-hours daily.
Moisture: Let soil dry between thorough waterings. Mist frequently. Humidity, 45% to 60%.
Feeding: Every 2 weeks, with mild liquid fertilizer.
Grooming: Repot each spring. Leaves may be cut when plant is at least 3 inches (8 cm) tall.
Propagation: By cuttings taken in summer or fall, or division when repotting.

TIBOUCHINA
Glory bush, princess flower

This genus contains 350 species of shrubs, with *T. urvilleana* most suitable for indoor culture. Also listed as *T. semidecandra,* it will seldom grow more than 4 feet (1.2 m) tall. A young plant has soft, green branches which become woody as it matures, and are covered with red hairs. Velvety, bright green leaves are toothed and may be tinged with red. Flowers appear in summer and fall, clustered at branch tips. These rosy purple blooms measure 4 inches (10 cm) across, with prominent purple stamens.

Soil: All-purpose mix.
Temperature: Day, 70°F (21°C); night, 50° to 55°F (10° to 13°C).
Light: Bright, filtered light, with 4 hours of direct winter sun daily, from northern or eastern exposure.
Moisture: Keep soil thoroughly moist. Humidity, 45% to 60%.
Feeding: Every 2 weeks during growing season, with all-purpose fertilizer.
Grooming: Pot-on in spring until suitable container size is reached, then top-dress each year. Prune back shoots each spring. Large plants may need support.
Propagation: By stem or tip cuttings of nonflowering shoots.
Pests and Diseases: Generally healthy and free from infestation.
Seasonal Care: Plant rests during winter. Keep at 50°F (10°C). Keep soil barely moist; withhold fertilizer.

TILLANDSIA
Blue torch, Spanish moss

Comprising 375 species of epiphytic bromeliads, this genus includes many different forms. Given the proper setting, the plant remains attractive with relatively little care. Generally, *Tillandsia* prefers to be mounted on cork or a slab of tree fern bark, rather than being potted. Smaller species are suitable for use on a bromeliad tree.

T. bulbosa, dancing bulb, grows to 9 inches (23 cm) from a bulbous base;

Thymus vulgaris

Tibouchina urvilleana

contorted branches extend outward and may have red or purple margins; blooms consist of red or green bracts with blue-purple flowers, appearing in fall.

T. cyanea features a stemless rosette of arching, dark green leaves with sharp edges; 8-inch (20 cm) spike bears blue flowers and pink bracts; measures from 10 to 30 inches (25 to 76 cm) tall.

T. ionantha, sky plant, is a dwarf with pointed, silvery leaves arranged in a rosette; this rosette center turns pink or red as violet flowers develop.

T. lindenii, also listed as *T. lindeniana,* features a 24 inch (61 cm) tall, arching rosette of green leaves; deep blue flowers emerge from pink bracts in summer.

T. setacea bears many thin, filamentlike leaves.

T. usneoides, Spanish moss, is a rootless plant, with several feet of slender, silvery stems resembling lichen; in summer, pale green or blue flowers may appear.

Soil: Mount on cork or slab of tree fern. Pot *T. ionantha* and larger species in epiphytic bromeliad mix.

Temperature: Tolerates 50° to 90°F (10° to 32°C) range, year-round.
Light: Bright light, direct sun from southern exposure. Air circulation is important.
Moisture: Potted plants require only light watering. Mist plants that are not potted frequently. Humidity, 50% to 60%.
Feeding: Monthly, with mild liquid fertilizer. Avoid oil-based products such as fish emulsion.
Grooming: Remove old, yellowed leaves, dried flowers and stalks.
Propagation: By offsets.
Pests and Diseases: Check for scale.
Seasonal Care: Growth slows in winter.

TOLMIEA
Piggyback plant

This genus contains a single species of foliage plant, *T. menziesii.* The heart-shaped leaves are lobed and toothed and covered with soft hairs. The common name is derived from the plantlets which appear on the upper side of leaves at the point where each leaf joins a leaf stem. These plantlets cause the leaves to droop, which makes *Tolmiea* an attractive specimen for hanging bas-

kets. This perennial grows 12 inches (30 cm) tall and 15 inches (38 cm) wide.

Soil: All-purpose mix, with good drainage.
Temperature: Day, 65° to 75°F (18° to 24°C); night, 50° to 65°F (10° to 18°C).
Light: Bright to moderate light, no direct sun, from eastern or western exposure. Will tolerate some shade, but foliage becomes pale and spindly. Does well under artificial light, needing 14 light-hours daily.
Moisture: Keep soil evenly moist, not soggy. Humidity, 40% to 45%.
Feeding: Weekly during growing season, with mild all-purpose fertilizer.
Grooming: Pot-on only when roots overcrowd pot space. Lower leaves, as they age, shrivel and eventually die.
Propagation: By division or plantlets. Remove leaf with plantlets and set so that leaf rests flat on surface of rooting medium. Or, while still attached to parent plant, anchor plantlet-bearing leaf onto rooting medium; once roots have formed, cut leaf from parent plant.
Pests and Diseases: Check for mealybugs, spider mites, whiteflies. Brown leaf tips indicate overwatering.
Seasonal Care: Plant rests briefly during winter. Keep soil barely moist; fertilize once a month.

Tillandsia setacea

Tolmiea menziesii

TRADESCANTIA
Inch plant, spiderwort,
wandering Jew

This genus contains 20 species of foliage plants, which can be attractively displayed in hanging baskets and which also do well in water culture. Plants are easy to care for and rapid growers; their trailing stems measure up to 12 inches (30 cm) and bear flowers in spring and summer.

T. albiflora 'Albovittata', giant white inch plant, features ovate, blue-green leaves striped with white; flowers are white.

T. albiflora 'Laekenensis' has pale green leaves with white and purple stripes.

T. blossfeldiana, flowering inch plant, has dark green, oval leaves with hairy, reddish purple undersides; pink to purple flowers have white centers.

T. blossfeldiana 'Variegata' produces solid green, solid white, and green and white striped leaves on the same plant.

T. fluminensis 'Variegata', variegated wandering Jew, has green and purple stems bearing pointed leaves with white and yellow stripes.

T. sillamontana, white velvet, produces wavy-edged, green leaves covered with white hairs; stems and leaf undersides are purple; rosy purple flowers appear from summer through fall.

Soil: All-purpose mix.
Temperature: Day, 70°F (21°C); night, 50° to 55°F (10° to 13°C).
Light: Bright light, with direct sun to retain foliage color, from eastern or western exposure. Does well under artificial light, needing 14 light-hours daily.
Moisture: Let soil dry moderately between thorough waterings. *T. sillamontana* should be kept slightly drier. Mist twice daily. Humidity, 40% to 45%.
Feeding: Every 2 weeks during growing season, with mild liquid fertilizer.
Grooming: Repot each spring; pot-on when roots occupy ½ of pot space. Variegated species, except for *T. blossfeldiana* 'Variegata', should have solid green or white stems removed, otherwise the variegation will be lost. Pinch for bushy growth; remove dried leaves.
Propagation: By cuttings or division.
Pests and Diseases: Check for mealybugs, spider mites, scale, slugs, whiteflies. Overwatering causes rot.

Seasonal Care: *T. sillamontana* should be allowed to die back in the fall, then kept dry over winter. Resume watering in early spring, when new growth will appear. All other species rest during winter. Keep at 50°F (10°C). Keep soil barely moist; fertilize monthly.

TRIPOGANDRA
Fern leaf inch plant,
Tahitian bridal veil

T. multiflora, formerly classified as *Tradescantia multiflora,* is an attractive foliage plant with slender stems bearing tiny, olive green leaves and small, delicate white flowers.

Soil: All-purpose mix.
Temperature: Day, 70°F (21°C); night, 50° to 55°F (10° to 13°C).
Light: Bright light, with some direct sun daily, from eastern or western exposure. Does well under artificial light, needing 14 light-hours daily.
Moisture: Let soil dry moderately between thorough waterings. Mist twice daily. Humidity, 40% to 45%.
Feeding: Every 2 weeks during growing season, with mild liquid fertilizer.

Tradescantia albiflora 'Laekenensis'

Tripogandra multiflora

Grooming: Repot each spring; pot-on when roots occupy ½ of pot space. Pinch back tips for bushy growth; remove dried leaves.
Propagation: By cuttings or division.
Pests and Diseases: Check for mealybugs, spider mites, scale, slugs, whiteflies. Overwatering causes rot.
Seasonal Care: Plant rests during winter. Keep at 50°F (10°C). Keep soil barely moist; fertilize once a month.

TROPAEOLUM
Nasturtium

These flowering plants produce 2 inch (5 cm) wide, fragrant flowers in winter and spring. These appear in shades of white, yellow, orange, pink, red, or dark brown. The circular leaves, which have a peppery taste similar to watercress, can be used in salads, and the unripe seeds may be pickled to be used as a substitute for capers. Growing from 6 to 24 inches (15 to 61 cm), *Tropaeolum* requires support. There are 50 species comprising this genus; *T. minus* is a dwarf form, while *T. majus* is a climbing plant.

Soil: Mix 3 parts garden loam, 2 parts perlite, and 1 part peat, with good drainage.
Temperature: Day, 65° to 75°F (18° to 24°C); night, 45° to 55°F (7° to 13°C).
Light: Bright light, direct sun from southern exposure.
Moisture: Keep soil evenly moist. Humidity, 30% to 35%.
Feeding: Every 2 weeks, with mild low-nitrogen fertilizer.
Grooming: Pinch growing tips to promote blooms and to retain bushy shape. Climbing growth requires support.
Propagation: By cuttings or seeds.
Pests and Diseases: Check for aphids, mites.
Seasonal Care: Treat as an annual; discard after blooming.

TULIPA
Tulip

50 to 150 species of flowering bulbs comprise this genus. Growing from 3 to 36 inches (8 to 91 cm) tall, sturdy stalks bear cup-shaped flowers, available in a wide range of colors: white, red, pink, yellow, orange, blue, purple, brown, and green. Potted up in the fall, *Tulipa* may be forced indoors in the spring for a single blooming season, with flowers lasting from 3 to 4 weeks if kept cool. Following this, it may be planted outdoors. Cultivars rather than spe-

Tropaeolum majus

Tulipa **hybrid**

cies are commonly available, due to the amount of crossbreeding that has been done. See recommended list of cultivars in chapter 18.

Soil: Humusy mix.
Temperature: Keep newly potted bulb cold, 35° to 48°F (2° to 9°C), for 13 weeks, until growth measures 2 to 3 inches (5 to 8 cm) tall. Gradually introduce to warmer temperature, 55° to 65°F (13° to 18°C).
Light: Keep newly potted bulb in completely dark location for 13 weeks. Gradually introduce to moderate light, with no direct sun, from eastern or western exposure.
Moisture: Keep soil evenly moist during growing and blooming periods.
Feeding: Not necessary.
Grooming: Remove blooms as they fade.
Propagation: By offshoots.
Pests and Diseases: Check for aphids, mealybugs, mites, slugs.
Seasonal Care: After flowering, withhold water when foliage begins to yellow and die. Store bulb in pot in cool, dry site until fall, when it

may be planted outdoors for spring bloom.

VALLISNERIA
Eelgrass, tapegrass

These perennial, rooted aquatic plants resemble miniature shrubs. They are easy to grow and thrive in aquaria.

V. americana has tapered, ¾ inch (19 mm) wide leaves; becomes dormant in winter.

V. spiralis 'Torta', corkscrew val, has more closely spiraled leaves, and measures 8 to 10 inches (20 to 25 cm) tall.

Soil: Layer of medium size aquarium gravel or coarse sand.
Temperature: 50° to 80°F (10° to 27°C).
Light: Filtered, indirect sunlight. Does well under artificial light, needing 14 to 16 light-hours daily.
Water: Slightly alkaline.

Feeding: Occasionally, with bone meal/clay pellets.
Grooming: Once a month, replace ⅓ of water in tank. Scrape algae from tank sides.
Propagation: By division or runners.
Pests and Diseases: Check for bacterial rot, snails.

VANDA

These large and showy orchids are easy to grow and bring to flower. Epiphytes by nature, they are also monopodial, lacking pseudobulbs. The heavy-textured flowers can last anywhere from several days to 2 months, and *Vanda* has been known to bloom twice in a single year. The flowers open along the spike in succession, which means there are fresh flowers appearing over an extended period of time. The genus includes around 60 species, and there are many miniature hybrids which are very popular and widely available. The following plants are recommended for growing in the home; *Vanda* also may be cultivated in an intermediate to warm greenhouse.

Vallisneria americana

Vanda species

V. tricolor produces 6 to 12 blooms on an erect flower stalk; flowers have an odor reminiscent of grape juice and are pale yellow with brown spots; petals are twisted toward the back of the flower; fiddle-shaped lip is white with pink shading and purple stripes; blooms from spring to summer.

V. tricolor var. *suavis* bears 6 to 12 flowers on long and curving flower stalk; white blooms with purple stripes have twisted edges; white lip has pale yellow throat with purple stripes at base; flowers anytime throughout the year.

Soil: Osmunda fiber or orchid bark mix. Does well in baskets or slotted pots in the home; also can be grown on section of tree limb, barn board, cork bark, or slab of tree fern fiber in the greenhouse.
Temperature: Day, 65° (18°C) or higher; night, 58° to 65°F (14° to 18°C).
Light: Bright light from southern exposure; shade only during hottest part of the day. Good circulation of fresh air.
Moisture: Keep evenly moist; never allow growing medium to dry out. Mist aerial roots frequently. Humidity, 50%.

Feeding: Proportioned feedings of all-purpose fertilizer with each watering, year-round.
Grooming: Repot when plant overcrowds pot space, or when growing medium has deteriorated. Best done at outset of active growth, when new roots are first visible.
Propagation: By air layering, plantlets removed from stem, or stem cuttings.
Pests and Diseases: Check for bacterial, fungal, and viral infections, mealybugs, scale, slugs, snails, whiteflies.
Seasonal Care: Plant requires no rest period. Prefers slightly cooler and drier conditions prior to flowering.

VELTHEIMIA
Forest lily

5 species of bulbous plants comprise this genus, which blooms readily indoors. The bulbs are planted in late summer, with flowers appearing in late fall and lasting a month. There is a dormancy period of several months before the new, attractive foliage appears.

V. capensis features bright green, oblong leaves with wavy edges and purple mottling; green-tipped, pink flowers appear on dense, drooping spikes on an 18-inch (46 cm) stem that emerges from the leaf rosette.

V. viridifolia has glossy green, strap-shaped leaves with wavy edges; flowers are pink or purple with yellow spots.

Soil: 3 parts garden loam and 1 part coarse sand or perlite.
Temperature: 50° to 55°F (10° to 13°C).
Light: Partial shade, with 3 to 4 hours of direct morning sun daily.
Moisture: Keep newly potted bulb or one without foliage barely moist. Once leaves develop, water moderately, letting soil dry slightly between waterings.
Feeding: Once a month with potassium-rich fertilizer, once leaves have developed until they begin to yellow.
Grooming: Bulb should be planted so that one-half emerges from soil. Repot every 2 to 3 years.
Propagation: By offsets, when these begin to crowd base of plant.
Seasonal Care: In summer, reduce watering when leaves begin to yellow. Leave bulb in pot and withhold water during dormancy until new foliage appears. Provide 3 to 4 hours direct sun during dormant period.

VRIESEA
Flaming sword

This genus, containing 246 species of epiphytic bromeliads, does well indoors with a little extra care and the proper environment. The rosette consists of stiff, sword-shaped leaves with smooth edges and various markings. A flower spike may appear at any time of the year on a specimen that is several years old.

V. fenestralis grows to 36 inches (91 cm) with arching, light green leaves bearing irregular lines and purple undersides; 18-inch (46 cm) spike carries purple-spotted green bracts and yellow to orange flowers.

Veltheimia viridifolia

V. hieroglyphica, king of bromeliads, features glossy green leaves with purple bands and undersides; 24-inch (61 cm) stalk divides into many branches, each bearing light green bracts and yellow flowers; measures 24 inches (61 cm) tall.

V. saundersii, also listed as *V. botafogensis,* has stiff, dull, olive green leaves with purple-spotted undersides and tips that curve down; 12-inch (30 cm) stalk bears a loose, arching cluster of yellow bracts and flowers.

V. splendens 'Major', also listed as *V. speciosa,* flaming sword, features a loose rosette of 15 inch (38 cm) long leaves which are green with dark bands across their width; 24-inch (61 cm) spike bears orange-red bracts and yellow flowers.

Soil: Recommended epiphytic bromeliad mix.
Temperature: Tolerates 65° to 80°F (18° to 27°C) range, year-round.
Light: Moderate to low light from eastern or western exposure. Air circulation is important.
Moisture: Keep growing medium evenly moist. Keep fresh water in cup. Mist daily. Humidity, 45% to 60%.
Feeding: Monthly, with mild liquid fertilizer. Avoid oil-based products such as fish emulsion. Spray on leaves, add to water in cup, or apply to growing medium after watering; never fertilize a dry plant.
Grooming: Remove old, yellowed leaves, dried flowers and stalks. Change water in cup.
Propagation: By offsets or seeds.
Pests and Diseases: Check for scale.

Seasonal Care: Growth slows in winter. Plant dies within 2 years after flowering.

YUCCA
False agave

In its native habitat, this genus is capable of growing to 40 feet. Indoors, it is a slow grower and won't go beyond 6 feet (1.8 m) tall and 2 inches (5 cm) thick. Of the 40 species, those grown indoors may be stemless or have a single, woody, trunklike stem. Flowers are rare on indoor specimens.

Y. aloifolia, Spanish bayonet, has a slender trunk bearing clusters of stiff, pointed, blue-green leaves with toothed edges; a number of cultivars with yellow and white leaf margins are available.

Y. elephantipes, spineless yucca, has rosettes of arching, soft and shiny leaves borne on a trunklike stem.

Vriesea splendens

Yucca elephantipes

Yu–Za

Y. filamentosa, sometimes called *Y. smalliana,* Adam's needle, features a stemless basal rosette of succulent, narrow leaves, tapering at the ends and bearing curly threads on the margins.

Soil: All-purpose mix, with good drainage.
Temperature: Day, 70°F (21°C); night, 50° to 55°F (10° to 13°C).
Light: Bright light, with 3 hours direct sun daily, from eastern, western, or southern exposure.
Moisture: Let soil dry moderately between thorough waterings. *Y. filamentosa* should be kept somewhat drier. Humidity, 30% to 40%.
Feeding: Every 2 weeks during growing season, with mild liquid fertilizer. Feed *Y. filamentosa* once in spring.
Grooming: Pot-on when roots completely overcrowd pot space.
Propagation: By stem cuttings, offsets, or seeds.
Seasonal Care: Plant rests during winter. Keep at 50°F (10°C). Give just enough water to keep soil from drying out; withhold fertilizer.

ZAMIA
Sago cycas, Seminole tree

40 species of ornamental foliage plants comprise this genus, and although they closely resemble palms, they are not actual members of the Palm family. Generally a low grower, *Zamia* has a woody, non-branching trunk which remains underground or grows to only a few feet (approximately 1 m) high. Both specimens listed here are good specimens for the indoors.

Z. floridana is a compact grower with 24-inch (61 cm) fronds, divided into many shiny, dark green, stiff segments.

Z. pumila features a crown of fronds, each frond measuring to 4 feet (1.2 m) and divided into broad sections, tapered at the ends; clusters of cylindrical cones also may appear.

Soil: All-purpose mix.
Temperature: Day, 70°F (21°C); night, 50° to 55°F (10° to 13°C).
Light: Filtered light from northern, eastern, or western exposure.

Zamia floridana

Moisture: Keep soil evenly moist. Mist twice daily. Humidity, 45% to 60%.
Feeding: Monthly during growing season, with mild liquid fertilizer.
Grooming: Pot-on when roots occupy ⅔ of pot space. Rinse foliage once a month.
Propagation: By division, offsets, or seeds.
Pests and Diseases: Check for aphids, mealybugs, spider mites.
Seasonal Care: Plant rests during winter. Reduce water, letting soil dry moderately between waterings; withhold fertilizer.

ZANTEDESCHIA
Calla lily

These flowering perennial plants grow from tubers, and thrive indoors with the proper care. Foliage is broad or narrow, shaped like an arrowhead with white spots. The waxy flowers are made up of a spathe which curves around a slender spadix, in a trumpet form. *Zantedeschia* generally grows to 36 inches (91 cm). Of the 6 species, the following do well indoors:

Z. aethiopica 'Childsiana' is a compact plant bearing many flowers, winter through spring; white spathe surrounds a gold spadix.

Z. albomaculata, spotted calla lily, has a white spathe with a purple base, curved around a white spadix; flowers appear in summer.

Z. elliottiana, golden calla, features a spathe which is gold on the inside, tinged with green on the outside, and a yellow spadix; blooms in summer.

Z. rehmannii, pink calla, produces light to dark pink spathes and off-white spadix in summer.

Soil: All-purpose mix.
Temperature: Day, 70°F (21°C); night, 50° to 55°F (10° to 13°C).
Light: Filtered light, with direct

morning or winter sun, from eastern or southern exposure.

Moisture: Keep soil evenly moist. Mist frequently. Humidity, 50% to 60%.

Feeding: Weekly during growing season, with mild liquid fertilizer.

Propagation: By division of tubers.

Pests and Diseases: Check for aphids, mealybugs, mites, scale.

Seasonal Care: Plant rests during summer, following blooming. Let leaves yellow and die, then cut back and repot. Keep soil barely moist; withhold fertilizer.

ZEBRINA
Purple wandering Jew

Best suited for a hanging container, this genus contains 2 species with trailing stems and attractively marked leaves. Small clusters of flowers appear in spring. A rapid grower, *Zebrina* can reach 36 inches (91 cm) indoors.

Z. pendula has ovate leaves bearing 2 lengthwise silvery bands; undersides are purple; flowers are rose colored.

Z. pendula 'Discolor' features slender silver stripes on a coppery green background; flowers are purple.

Z. pendula 'Purpusii' bears dark red or reddish green leaves and lilac flowers.

Z. pendula 'Quadricolor' features coppery green leaves with green, red, and white stripes.

Soil: All-purpose mix.

Temperature: Day, 70° to 80°F (21° to 27°C); night, 55° to 60°F (13° to 16°C).

Light: Bright to moderate light from northern or eastern exposure.

Moisture: Keep soil evenly moist. Mist daily. Humidity, 40% to 45%.

Feeding: Every 2 weeks during growing season, with mild liquid fertilizer.

Grooming: Repot when roots occupy ½ of pot space. Pinch growing tips for bushy form.

Propagation: By stem cuttings.

Pests and Diseases: Check for mealybugs, mites, scale, slugs, whiteflies.

Seasonal Care: Plant rests slightly from late fall through winter. Slowly reduce water, keeping soil barely moist; feed once a month.

ZYGOCACTUS,
see *Schlumbergera*

Zantedeschia aethiopica

Zebrina pendula

Appendixes

PLANT SOCIETIES AND PUBLICATIONS

UNITED STATES

African Violet Society of America, Inc.
P.O. Box 1326
Knoxville, TN 37901
African Violet Magazine, 5/year.

American Begonia Society
10079 West Lilac Road
Escondido, CA 92026
The Begonia, monthly.

American Bonsai Society
1363 West Sixth Street
Erie, PA 16505
ABStracts, bimonthly; *Bonsai Journal,* quarterly.

American Gloxinia/Gesneriad Society
P.O. Box 174
New Milford, CT 06776
The Gloxinian, bimonthly.

American Horticultural Society
Mt. Vernon, VA 22121
American Horticulturist, bimonthly; *News and Views,* bimonthly.

American Orchid Society, Inc.
84 Sherman Street
Cambridge, MA 02140
American Orchid Society Bulletin, monthly.

American Plant Life Society/American Amaryllis Society
P.O. Box 150
La Jolla, CA 92038
Plantlife, annually.

Bonsai Clubs International
4943 Clydebank Avenue
Covina, CA 91722
Bonsai Source List, annually; *Bonsai Magazine,* 10/year.

The Bromeliad Club
13328 Lake George Lane
Tampa, FL 33618

Bromeliad Society, Inc.
P.O. Box 41261
Los Angeles, CA 90041
Journal of Bromeliad Society, bimonthly.

Cactus and Succulent Society of America, Inc.
P.O. Box 3010
Santa Barbara, CA 93105
Cactus and Succulent Journal, bimonthly.

Chicago Horticultural Society and Botanic Garden
Box 400
Glencoe, IL 60022
Garden Talk, bimonthly.

The Cycad Society
5988 South Pollard Parkway
Baton Rouge, LA 70808
Newsletter, quarterly.

Cymbidium Society of America
c/o Polly Eilau
469 West Norman Avenue
Arcadia, CA 91006
Orchid Advocate, bimonthly.

Epiphyllum Society of America
P.O. Box 1395
Monrovia, CA 91016
Epiphyllum Bulletin, biennially.

Gesneriad Hybridizers Association
c/o Meg Stephenson
1415 Goldsmith
Plymouth, MI 48170
Crossroads, quarterly.

Gesneriad Society International
628 North Cory Street
Findlay, OH 45840
Gesneria-Saintpaulia News, bimonthly.

The Herb Society of America
300 Massachusetts Avenue
Boston, MA 02115
The Herbarist: Primer for Herb Growing. Enclose a self-addressed, stamped envelope with all inquiries. You must be sponsored to become a member.

Hobby Greenhouse Association
P.O. Box 951
Wallingford, CT 06492
The Planter, bimonthly.

Horticultural Society of New York
128 West 58th Street
New York, NY 10019
Garden, bimonthly; newsletter, bimonthly.

Indoor Light Gardening Society of America, Inc.
c/o New York Horticulture Society
128 West 58th Street
New York, NY 10019
Light Garden, bimonthly.

International Cactus and Succulent Society
P.O. Box 5001
San Angelo, TX 76901

International Carnivorous Plant Society
Fullerton Arboretum
California State University
Fullerton, CA 92634
Magazine, quarterly.

International Fern Society
14895-J Gardenhill Drive
LaMirada, CA 90638

International Geranium Society
1413 Shoreline Drive
Santa Barbara, CA 93109
Geraniums Around the World, quarterly.

International Tropical Fern Society
8720 Southwest 34th Street
Miami, FL 33165
Rhizome Reporter, monthly.

The Marantaceae Newsletter
c/o Lyon Arboretum
3860 Manoa Road
Honolulu, HI 96822
Newsletter, quarterly.

Massachusetts Horticultural Society
300 Massachusetts Avenue
Boston, MA 02115
Horticulture, monthly; *The Leaflet,* monthly.

Pennsylvania Horticultural Society, Inc.
Independence National Historical Park
325 Walnut Street
Philadelphia, PA 19106

> *Gardeners Guide,* annually; *PHS News,* monthly; *The Green Scene,* monthly.

Peperomia Society
2013 Road 44
Pasco, WA 99301

> *Peperomia Gazette,* quarterly.

The Palm Society, Inc.
1320 South Venetian Way
Miami, FL 33139

> *Principes,* quarterly.

Terrarium Association
57 Wolfpit Avenue
Norwalk, CT 06851

> *Terrarium Topics;* terrarium plant lists.

CANADA

African Violet Society of Canada
c/o Mrs. Laura McLellan, President
119 Wesley Street
Moncton, New Brunswick E1C 4V9

> *Chatter,* 4/year.

Bonsai Society
c/o Mrs. E. Kenzie
495 Deloraine Avenue
Toronto, Ontario M5M 2C1

Canadian Geranium and Pelargonium Society
c/o Mrs. B. Van Assum
254 West Kings Road
North Vancouver, British Columbia V7N 2L9

Canadian Hobby Greenhouse Association
R.R. 3
Stouffville, Ontario L0H 1L0

> Bimonthly publication.

Indoor Light Garden Society
c/o L. Marsh
14 Bernadotte Drive
R.R. 2
Gormley, Ontario L0H 1G0

UNITED KINGDOM

British Bonsai Association
c/o Bill Horan
23 Nimrod Road
London SW16

> *The Quarterly Bulletin of the British Bonsai Association.*

British Bromeliad Society
c/o R. Lucibell
Plant Biology Department
Queen Mary College
London, E1 4NS

> *Bromeliads.*

British Pelargonium and Geranium Society
c/o H. J. Wood
129 Aylesford Avenue
Beckenham, Kent BR 3 3RX

> *The Pelargonium and Geranium News; The Year Book of the British Pelargonium and Geranium Society.*

British Pteridological (Fern) Society
c/o A. R. Busby
42 Lewisham Road
Smethwick
Warley, West Midlands B56 B2S

> *The Bulletin of the British Pteridological (Fern) Society; The Fern Gazette.*

Herb Society
c/o The General Secretary
34 Boscobel Place
London SW1

> *The Herbal Review;* several others.

National Begonia Society
c/o Dr. E. Catterall
3 Gladstone Road
Dorridge
Solihull, West Midlands

> *The National Begonia Society Bulletin.*

National Cactus and Succulent Society
c/o J. W. P. Mullard
19 Crabtree Road
Botley, Oxford

> *The National Cactus and Succulent Journal.*

Orchid Society of Great Britain
c/o L. E. Bowen
28 Felday Road
Lewisham
London SE13 7HJ

> *The Bulletin of the Orchid Society of Great Britain.*

The Royal Horticultural Society
c/o The Secretary
P.O. Box 313
Vincent Square
London SWIP 2PE

> *The Garden.*

Saintpaulia and Houseplant Society
c/o Miss N. Tanburn
82 Rossmore Court
Park Road
London NW1 6XY

> *The Saintpaulia and Houseplant Society Bulletin.*

SOME SOURCES OF GREENHOUSE PLANS

In addition to requesting greenhouse plans and information from your county extension agent or from the agricultural engineering department of your state college or university, you can write to the following places. Unless otherwise indicated, there is a fee for the plans offered and you probably should write ahead for a current price list.

Agricultural Engineering Extension
3022 Bainer Hall
University of California
Davis, CA 95616

> James F. Thompson, "Small Plastic Greenhouses," Leaflet 2387, reprinted August, 1978.

Northeast Regional Agricultural Engineering Service
Riley-Robb Hall
Cornell University
Ithaca, NY 14853

> Booklet, *Hobby Greenhouses and Other Gardening Structures.* Includes seven USDA or land grant university-developed greenhouse plans for a lean-to, a portable plastic greenhouse, an A-frame, a bar-

rel vault, a fiberglass/wood even-span, a tri-penta-shaped wood/polyester house, and an air-inflated double plastic-over-wood greenhouse. Also *Energy Conservation and Solar Heating for Greenhouses.*

Pennsylvania State University
Agricultural Engineering Extension
Room 204
Agricultural Engineering Building
University Park, PA 16802

"Greenhouse Packet," several fact sheets relating to greenhouses (heating, cooling, plans, materials). Free to Pennsylvania residents only.

Plans Service
Agricultural Engineering
Department
University of Kentucky
Lexington, KY 40546

Plans for a 10 by 16-ft. (or longer) hobby greenhouse, a "Kentucky specialty" field greenhouse (10 ft. wide by any length), a "Quonset field" greenhouse (10 ft. wide by any length), and an 8 by 12-ft. Gothic Arch greenhouse. Also plans for five larger greenhouses and many publications on greenhouse construction, operation, and management. Plans, publications, and prices listed on Leaflet AEN-4.

Public Service Cooperative
Extension
387 University Hall
University of California
Berkeley, CA 94720

Leaflet 2387, *Small Plastic Greenhouses,* free.

Superintendent of Documents
U.S. Government Printing Office
Washington, DC 20402

Bulletin #357, *Building Hobby Greenhouses,* Order #001-000-03692-1.

Vegetable Crops Department
Dr. Raymond Sheldrake, Jr.
Cornell University
Ithaca, NY 14853

Plastic Greenhouse Manual: Planning, Construction and Operation.

Western Regional Agricultural
Engineering Service (WRAES)
Agricultural Engineering
Department
Oregon State University
Corvallis, OR 97331

List of plans available, write for *Hobby Greenhouse Design Notes.*

INSTITUTIONS

BOTANIC GARDENS AND CONSERVATORIES

California:
County of Los Angeles
Department of Arboreta and
Botanic Gardens
301 North Baldwin Avenue
Arcadia, CA 91006

Huntington Botanical Gardens
1151 Oxford Road
San Marino, CA 91108

The Conservatory of Flowers
Golden Gate Park
San Francisco, CA 94117

University of California Botanic
Garden
Centennial Drive
Berkeley, CA 94720

Colorado:
Denver Botanic Garden
909 York Street
Denver, CO 80206

Florida:
Fairchild Tropical Gardens
10901 Old Cutler Road
Miami, FL 33156

Marie Selby Botanical Gardens
800 South Palm Avenue
Sarasota, FL 33577

Hawaii:
Pacific Tropical Botanical Garden
Apprentice Gardeners Program
P.O. Box 340
Lawai, Kauai, HI 96765

Wahiawa Botanical Gardens
Oahu, HI

Illinois:
Chicago Horticultural Society
Botanical Garden Library
P.O. Box 400
Glencoe, IL 60022

Garfield Park Conservatory
300 North Central Park
Chicago, IL 60624

Michigan:
University of Michigan
Matthaei Botanical Gardens
1800 Dixboro Road
Ann Arbor, MI 48105

Missouri:
Missouri Botanical Garden
2101 Tower Grove Avenue
St. Louis, MO 63110

New York:
Brooklyn Botanic Garden
1000 Washington Avenue
Brooklyn, NY 11225

New York Botanical Garden
Bronx Park
Bronx, NY 10458

North Carolina:
North Carolina Botanical Garden
University of North Carolina
Chapel Hill, NC 27514

Pennsylvania:
Longwood Gardens
Kennett Square, PA 19348

Phipps Conservatory
Schenley Park
Pittsburgh, PA 15213

South Carolina:
Riverbank Zoological Park
500 Wildlife Parkway
Columbia, SC 29210

Tennessee:
The Tennessee Botanical Gardens
and Fine Arts Center
Cheekwood
Nashville, TN 37205

Virginia:
Norfolk Botanical Gardens
Airport Road
Norfolk, VA 23518

Washington, DC:
United States National Arboretum
Washington, DC 20002

Canada:
Montreal Botanic Garden
4101 Rue Sherbrooke
Montreal, Quebec H2Y 1P5,
Canada

DEPARTMENTS OF AGRICULTURE

Agricultural Research Service
U.S. Department of Agriculture
Beltsville Agricultural Research
  Center
Room 251, Building 003
Beltsville, MD 20705

For USDA bulletins write: Superintendent of Documents, Government Printing Office, Washington, DC 20402

U.S. Department of Agriculture
Permit Unit
Room 635
Federal Building
Hyattsville, MD 20782

This is the office to contact when bringing plants into the United States from any foreign country — they cover the entire U.S. for permits.

Canadian Department of
  Agriculture
Plant Quarantine Division
1435 St. Alexander, Room 1275
Montreal, Quebec H3A 2G4,
  Canada

Credits and Acknowledgments

Contributing Writers:
Chapters 1-7: Jerry Minnich
Chapter 8: Susan A. Roth
Chapter 9: Anne Halpin
Chapter 10: Walter G. Neuhauser, Cooperative Extension Agent, N.Y.S. Cooperative Extension Service
Chapter 11: Frances M. Finkbeiner
Chapters 12, 14: Dr. Raymond P. Poincelot, Department of Biology, Fairfield University, Fairfield, CT
Chapter 13: Enola Jane N. Teeter
Chapter 15: Thomas W. Pew, Jr.
Chapter 16: Marjorie B. Hunt
Chapter 17: Gaea Laughingbird
Chapter 18: Hamilton Mason, former garden editor, *Better Homes and Gardens*
Chapter 19: John Philip Baumgardt, botany and greenhouse culture; Dr. Joseph Levine and Brenda Bortz, indoor culture
Chapter 20: Christopher J. Teasdale
Chapter 21: Allen Lowe
Chapter 22: William G. Scheller
Chapter 23: Dr. Roger B. Swain
Chapter 24: Suzanne L. Nelson
Chapter 25: Anna Carr
Chapter 26: Nancy E. Lee
Chapters 27, 29: Brenda Bortz
Chapter 28: Phyllis Wolff Banucci
Chapter 30: Dr. John A. Wott, Professor of Horticulture, Purdue University

Boxes, Features, and Additional Material: Doc and Katy Abraham, pp. 159-167; Iris August, 260-263; Michael Balick, 7-9, 12-13; Diana Branch, 64, 66, 72, 544-545, 610-611, 656-657, 659, 672-675, 682, 725, 726, 727; Bonnie Fisher, 351; William Hupping, 560-563; Rich Kline, 46-47, 380-381; Gaea Laughingbird, 2-3; Penny McConnell, 252-253, 580-581; Ray Wolf, 108, 109, 127, 154-155; Gayle Wood, 18-19, 373.

Horticultural Consultants and Reviewers: Lynn Perry Alstadt, American Bonsai Society; Iris August; Phyllis W. Banucci, Editor, *Light Garden*; Robert C. Baur, The Terrarium Association; Dr. William E. Ferguson, Professor of Entomology, San Jose State University; Frances M. Finkbeiner; Bonnie Fisher; Dr. Joseph S. Levine; Dr. Bruce W. McAlpin, Horticultural Specialist, New York Botanical Garden; Helga and William Olkowski, Co-Directors, Center for Integration of Applied Science, John Muir Institute; William A. Pierson; Dr. Henry A. Robitaille, Associate Professor of Horticulture, Purdue University; Michael A. Rothenberg, Shelldance Bromeliads; Dr. Gerald A. Wilcox, Professor of Horticulture, Purdue University; Dr. John A. Wott.

Photographs by the Rodale Press Photography Department, except for the following: Gary F. Leatham, pp. vi; viii; 25; 168; 170; 171, top left, and bottom right and left; 172, top;

173; 176; 208; 211, bottom; 213, left; 214; 215, right; 217; 219; 228; 236; 242, right; 248; 249; 264; 284; 294; 296; 304; 305; 308; 336; 360; 375, left; 378; 390; 395; 396: 413, top right and bottom left; 436; 476; 477; 486; 489; 490; 491, right; 492; 494; 509; 541; 697. Charles Marden Fitch, 115; 143; 149; 151; 152; 157; 158; 177; 216; 221; 235; 238; 320; 326; 374; 380; 384, bottom left and right; 385, top left and bottom; 391; 402; 409; 413, top left and bottom right; 416, right; 433; 460; 465; 469; 471; 472, left; 576; 588; 660. Michael J. Balick, 12; 13; 39; 211, top; 298; 300; 419; 621. Corliss Knapp Engle, 612. Ray R. Kriner, 142; 147; 150. Charles E. Lemieux, 384, top; 385, top right. Joseph S. Levine, 496; 499; 504; 506. Courtesy of the National Arboretum, 448, top; 453, right. Jerald Stowell, 448, bottom left and right; 449, right. Ray Wolf, 154.

Illustrations: Jacquelyn Diotte, pp. 31; 34; 36; 40; 42; 43; 49; 54; 60; 62; 69; 71; 78; 88; 131; 132; 134; 136; 137; 139; 145; 146; 178; 186; 194; 197, right; 257; 258; 274; 276; 279; 307; 309; 315; 317; 327; 333; 339; 356; 365; 366; 383; 386; 403; 404; 421; 427; 429; 438; 439; 440; 450, right; 451; 452; 460; 463; 466; 474; 485; 501; 502; 505; 510; 511; 559; 581; 597; 608; 609, left; 619; 641; 655; 668; 669; 712; 715; 719. Joan M. Frain, 13; 14; 15; 17; 91; 114; 121; 140; 174; 175; 190; 192; 204; 205; 210; 229; 231; 241; 266; 267; 278; 283; 286; 295; 297; 299; 302; 340; 341; 362; 373; 422; 426; 430; 447; 450, left; 480; 497; 558. Joseph Horvath, 63; 64; 66; 72; 108; 109; 127; 545; 607; 610; 623; 656; 659; 673, top; 674; 682; 725; 726; 727. Brian Swisher, 23; 97; 153; 179; 196; 197, left; 364; 367; 368; 424; 428; 446; 483; 533; 534; 535; 539; 542; 560; 561; 562; 563; 570; 592; 593; 594; 602; 609, right; 614; 615; 626; 627; 629; 634; 638; 662; 684. Ed Courrier, 673, bottom. Jerry O'Brien, 313; 337; 519; 522.
Reprinted by permission from a copy of *Flora Brasiliensis*, Vol. I, Pars. I, by C. F. PH. DeMartius, belonging to the library of the Massachusetts Horticultural Society, p. 265. Also reproduced by permission of the Library of the Massachusetts Horticultural Society, pp. 169, 281, 495, 557, 599

Special thanks to the following for their assistance in the preparation of this book: Jim Eldon; Rudy C. Keller; Suzanne Wymelenberg; Tom Cooper; Phyllis Banucci; Iris August; Marilyn Cox; Elvin Faust; Chris Hopka; William Saylor; Mitch Proffitt; Jerald Stowell; Corliss Engle; The Netherlands Bulb Institute; Anne Tinari, Tinari Greenhouses; Michael Kartuz, Kartuz Greenhouses; Bud Gahs, Fantom and Gahs Greenhouses; Lauray of Salisbury; Martin's Aquarium; Longwood Gardens; Meadowbrook Farm Greenhouses; J. Liddon Pennock; The Orchid Loft; My Indoor Garden; The Chestnut Greenery; Madeline Gonzales; Milan Fiske; Irwin Dibble; Gloria Ericson; Velta Hughes; Herbert and Ann Speanburg; John Jordan; Tomoko Yui; Joanne Fribush; Linda Weiner; Ceeb Leech; Berta White; Marg Whittlesey; Elinor Leen; Ruth Bois; Lucille Schwartz; Dick Wagner; Bob and Nancy Arobone; Penny McConnell; Pat Olver.

Glossary

Adventitious roots: Roots that arise from plant stems.

Annual: An herbaceous plant with a life cycle of one growing season.

Antheridium: The male sex organ of ferns and other lower vascular plants.

Anthers: Pollen sacs at the top of a stamen.

Archegonium: The female sex organ of ferns and other lower vascular plants.

Areole: An open area on the surface of a plant that is often ringed with hairs, spines, or glochids.

Auxins: A group of plant growth regulators that is responsible for cell elongation. Auxins occur naturally in the growth tips of plants.

Axil: The point at which a leaf stalk joins a stem, or a smaller stem joins a larger one.

Berry: A fleshy fruit with one or more seeds.

Bifoliate plant: A plant with two leaves supported by the main stem.

Blade: The wide, expanded part of a leaf or fern frond.

Bract: A leaflike organ that is often green, but in some plants quite colorful.

Bulb: A swollen underground stem with fleshy leaf scales which acts as a storage organ.

Calyx: A green or colored whorl of floral organs outside of the corolla; the floral envelope.

Cambium: A ring of meristematic cells around the stem which causes it to expand.

Cane: A thick stem with a pithy or hollow center.

Capsule: A dry fruit that opens to let the seeds escape; the spore case of some lower vascular plants.

Cellulose: The complex carbohydrate that forms cell walls, providing structure for the plant body.

Chlorophyll: The green pigment within the chloroplasts that aids in photosynthesis.

Chloroplasts: Chlorophyll-containing bodies within cells that give plants their green color.

Clones: Genetically identical plants that have been propagated vegetatively from a selected individual.

Corm: The enlarged base of a stem that acts as a storage organ.

Corolla: The inner whorl of floral organs.

Cotyledons: The first leaves to appear on a seedling; fleshy seed-leaves.

Crenate: Having scalloped leaf margins.

Crispate: Having curled leaf margins.

Crown: The portion of a plant just at soil level.

Crozier: See Fiddlehead.

Cultivar: A cultivated variety, not found in the wild. Written following the abbreviation cv. or in single quotation marks.

Cuticle: The shiny outer covering of the epidermis.

Cyme: A broad, flat-topped inflorescence with the central flowers opening first.

Dentate: Having toothed leaf margins.

Dicotyledons (dicots): Flowering plants with two cotyledons, or seed-leaves.

Dormancy: The state of arrested growth that is part of the life cycle of temperate perennials.

Epidermis: The waterproof outer layer of plant cells.

Epiphyte, epiphytic plant: A plant that physically grows upon another plant but does not parasitize it.

Family: A major unit of classification that is comprised of one or more closely related genera. Family names usually end in "aceae."

Fertilization: The union of the male gamete (pollen grain) with the female gamete (ovule or egg).

Fiddlehead (or crozier): The young, tightly curled fern frond.

Frond: The entire fern leaf, including the stipe and blade.

Genus (pl. genera): The unit of classification directly below family that is comprised of one or more closely related species. The genus

name is the first word of the scientific name of a plant (*Genus species*).

Germination: The time at which a seed sprouts a root and shoot.

Glochid: A tiny spine.

Hardwood: Wood of broad-leaved trees.

Head: A dense, often rounded spike of flowers.

Herb: An herbaceous, flowering plant; a plant which is valued for either its culinary, aromatic, cosmetic, or healing qualities.

Herbaceous: Nonwoody.

Hermaphroditic: Bisexual; containing both male and female parts.

Hibernaculum: A winter bud from which new growth emerges when dormancy is over.

Hybrid: The offspring of a cross between two species or less commonly, between two or more genera.

Imperfect flowers: Flowers of only one sex.

Indusium: The tissuelike covering over the sori of ferns.

Inflorescence: The arrangement of flowers on a flower stalk.

Keikis: Side-shoots growing from the latent lateral buds of orchids.

Labellum: The lip of an orchid.

LD$_{50}$: A measurement of the amount of an insecticide that kills 50 percent of a population of test animals; lethal dosage.

Leaflet: One unit of a compound leaf.

Lignin: The woody material of plants.

Meristems: Areas of a plant, especially the extremities, where cell division continues on through the life of the plant.

Monocarpic plant: A plant that flowers once during its life cycle.

Monocotyledons (monocots): Flowering plants with one cotyledon, or seed-leaf.

Monopodial orchids: Single-footed orchids that grow from the tip of the vertical stem with leaves arranged in two ranks on either side of the stem.

Offset: A new plant growing from the dormant bud at the crown of the original plant.

Ovary: The expanded, bottom portion of the pistil that contains the ovules or eggs.

Ovule: An individual egg.

Palisade layer: Vertically layered cells beneath the epidermal layer.

Palmately compound: Having leaflets arranged similar to a fan, radiating from a single point.

Panicle: An open, branched flower arrangement.

Pedicel: The stemlike stalk supporting an individual flower.

Perennial: A woody or herbaceous plant that lives from year to year.

Perfect flowers: Flowers having both sexes.

Petal: A single unit of the corolla.

Petiole: The stalk supporting the leaf; stemlike structure.

pH: The level of acidity or alkalinity expressed in units from 0 to 14, with 7 being the neutral point. The units below 7 become increasingly acid toward 0, and the units above 7 become increasingly alkaline toward 14.

Phloem: Conductive tissue that carries food from the leaves to all parts of the plant.

Photoperiod: Duration of light within a 24-hour day.

Photosynthesis: The production of carbohydrates within green leaves, using carbon dioxide and water, and releasing oxygen.

Phototropism: Plant movement in response to a one-sided source of light.

Pinna (pl. pinnae): An individual leaflet of a fern blade.

Pinnately compound: Having leaflets arranged on both sides of the rachis.

Pistil: The female reproductive organ, consisting of a stigma, style, and ovary.

Pollination: The transfer of pollen from an anther to a stigma of the same or a different flower; the first stage of fertilization.

Pollinium: A mass of orchid pollen fused by a clear, sticky fluid.

Prothallus: The heart-shaped, primary plant body of the fern that contains both male and female organs.

Pseudobulb: An enlarged orchid stem modified to store food and water.

Raceme: An elongated axis with pedicelled flowers spaced at intervals.

Rachis: A petiolelike organ bearing flowers or leaflets.

Rhizome: A horizontally growing stem that is partially or entirely underground.

Rosette: Leaves arranged in a circle around the stem, often at the base of a plant.

Rostellum: A sticky stigma lobe in orchids, modified to hang in front of the anther.

Saxicolous plants: Plants which grow among rocks.

Scarify: To create a break in the seed coat to speed germination.

Sepal: A single unit of the calyx.

Serrate: Having notched leaf margins.

Shrub: A woody plant, up to approximately 15 feet (4.5 m) in height, that has no central stem.

Sinuate: Having strongly waved leaf margins.

Softwood: Young, pliable wood; wood of coniferous trees.

Sorus (pl. sori): Clusters of sporangia arranged in patterns on the undersides of fern fronds.

Spadix: A fleshy, compact inflorescence that occurs mainly in plants of the Arum family.

Spathe: A large bract that encloses the spadix in plants of the Arum family.

Species: The basic unit of classification. The species name is the second word of the scientific name of a plant (*Genus species*).

Spike: An elongated or compact inflorescence with nonpedicelled flowers.

Sporangium (pl. sporangia): A spore case bearing masses of spores.

Spore: The tiny, seedlike reproductive body of most lower plants.

Sporophyte: A spore-bearing leaf or frond.

Stamen: The male reproductive organ, consisting of a stalk, or filament, and a pollen-bearing anther.

Stigma: The top portion of the pistil that receives the pollen on its sticky surface.

Stipe: The stalk supporting a fern blade.

Stolon (runner): A stem growing along the surface of the ground, rooting at the nodes of the stem.

Stomata: Small openings on the leaf surfaces, mostly on the lower sides, allowing for the exchange of gases and water vapor.

Stratify: To expose a seed to periods of cold temperatures to mimic winter weather. Often necessary for seeds of perennial plants native to the temperate zones.

Style: Necklike portion of the pistil.

Succulent: A plant with fleshy stems having the ability to store water.

Sucker: An offshoot that develops spontaneously from the roots.

Sympodial orchids: Many-footed orchids that produce a number of stems from a rhizome with the leaves growing vertically.

Tendril: A stem or leaf modified into a threadlike structure that coils around a support.

Trifoliate plant: A plant with three leaves supported by the main stem.

Tuber: An enlarged, fleshy, underground rhizome that acts as a storage organ.

Tuberous root: An enlarged, fleshy root that serves as a storage organ.

Undulate: Wavelike along the leaf margins and across the leaf.

Unifoliate plant: A plant with one leaf on the main stem.

Variegation: White or yellow coloring due to a genetic lack of the pigment chlorophyll.

Variety: The category of classification below the rank of species, thought of as a variant of the species. Written following the abbreviation var.

Xerophyte: A plant that has genetically adapted to dry or desert environments.

Xylem: Conductive tissue that carries water and dissolved minerals from the roots to all parts of the plant.

Selected Bibliography

Abraham, George and Katy. *Organic Gardening Under Glass.* Emmaus, Pa.: Rodale Press, 1975.

Bailey, Liberty Hyde Hortorium, Staff of. *Hortus Third: A Concise Dictionary of Plants Cultivated in the United States and Canada.* New York: Macmillan Co., 1976.

Baker, Kenneth F., and Cook, R. James. *Biological Control of Plant Pathogens.* San Francisco: W. H. Freeman & Co., 1974.

Ball, Vic, ed. *The Ball Red Book.* 13th ed. West Chicago: George J. Ball, 1975.

Baur, Robert C. *Gardens in Glass Containers.* Great Neck, N.Y.: Hearthside Press, 1970.

Behme, Robert L. *Bonsai, Saikei and Bonkei: Japanese Dwarf Trees and Tray Landscapes.* New York: William H. Morrow & Co., 1969.

Bickford, Elwood D., and Dunn, Stuart. *Lighting for Plant Growth.* Kent, Ohio: Kent State University Press, 1972.

Britton, Nathaniel L., and Rose, J. N. *Cactaceae: Descriptions and Illustrations of Plants in the Cactus Family.* 2 vols. 1937. Reprint. New York: Dover Publications, 1963.

Brooklyn Botanic Garden. *Handbook on African-Violets and Their Relatives.* New York: Brooklyn Botanic Garden, 1967.

————. *Handbook on Bonsai: Special Techniques.* New York: Brooklyn Botanic Garden, 1966.

————. *Handbook on Orchids.* New York: Brooklyn Botanic Garden, 1974.

————. *Handbook on Succulent Plants.* New York: Brooklyn Botanic Garden, 1963.

Burlingame, Alice. *Hoe for Health.* Birmingham, Mich.: Garden Consultant, 1974.

Carleton, R. Milton, ed. *Gardening under Artificial Light: A Handbook.* New York: Brooklyn Botanic Garden, 1970.

Cruso, Thalassa. *Making Things Grow Indoors.* New York: Alfred A. Knopf, 1971.

DeHertogh, August. *Holland Bulb Forcer's Guide.* Michigan Agricultural Experiment Station, Michigan State University.

Doerflinger, Frederic. *The Bulb Book.* North Pomfret, Vt.: David and Charles, 1973.

Downs, R. V. et al. *Light and Plants.* Beltsville, Md.: Agricultural Research Service, 1966.

Elbert, Virginie F. and George A. *Miracle Houseplants.* New York: Crown Publishers, 1976.

Emboden, William A. *Bizarre Plants: Magical, Monstrous, Mythical.* New York: Macmillan Co., 1974.

Fennell, F. A., Jr. *Orchids for Home and Garden.* New York: Holt, Rinehart & Winston, 1959.

Fisher, Rick, and Yanda, Bill. *The Food and Heat Producing Solar Greenhouse.* Santa Fe, N.M.: John Muir Publications, 1979.

Fitch, Charles Marden. *The Complete Book of Houseplants under Lights,* New York: Hawthorn Books, 1975.

————. *The Complete Book of Miniature Roses.* New York: Hawthorn Books, 1977.

Foster, F. Gordon. *Ferns to Know and Grow.* New York: Hawthorn Books, 1976.

Foster, Mulford B. *Bromeliads: A Cultural Handbook.* Orlando, Fla.: The Bromeliad Society, Inc., 1953.

Fuller, H. J. et al. *Plant World.* New York: Holt, Rinehart & Winston, 1972.

Glass, Charles, and Foster, Robert. *Cacti and Succulents for the Amateur.* New York: Van Nostrand Reinhold, 1976.

Gould, Deenagh Adams. *The Cool Greenhouse Today.* Levittown, N.Y.: Transatlantic Arts, 1970.

Graf, Alfred Byrd. *Exotic Plant Manual.* East Rutherford, N.J.: Julius Roehrs Co., 1978.

————. *Exotica Series Three: Pictorial Cyclopedia of Exotic Plants.* East Rutherford, N.J.: Julius Roehrs Co., 1978.

Grieve, M. *A Modern Herbal.* 2 vols. New York: Dover Publications, 1971.

Hawkes, Alex D. *Orchids: Their Botany and Culture.* New York: Harper & Row, 1960.

Hix, John. *The Glass House.* Cambridge, Mass.: The MIT Press, 1974.

Hoshizaki, Barbara J. *Fern Growers Manual.* New York: Alfred A. Knopf, 1975.

Hunter, Margaret K. and Edward H. *The Indoor Garden: Design, Construction and Furnishing.* New York: John Wiley & Sons, 1978.

Hutchinson, J., and Melville, R. *The Story of Plants.* London: P. R. Gawthorn, 1948.

Hylton, William H., ed. *The Rodale Herb Book: How to Use, Grow and Buy Nature's Plants.* Emmaus, Pa.: Rodale Press, 1974.

James, John. *Flowers When You Want Them: A Grower's Guide to Out-of-Season Bloom.* New York: Hawthorn Books, 1977.

Jordan, William H., Jr. *Windowsill Ecology.* Emmaus, Pa.: Rodale Press, 1977.

Kramer, Jack. *Plants under Lights.* New York: Simon & Schuster, 1974.

Kranz, Frederick H. and Jacqueline L. *Gardening Indoors under Lights.* New York: Viking Press, 1971.

Laurie, Alex et al. *Commercial Flower Forcing.* New York: McGraw-Hill, 1968.

McCullagh, James C., ed. *The Solar Greenhouse Book.* Emmaus, Pa.: Rodale Press, 1978.

McDonald, Elvin. *The Complete Book of Gardening under Lights.* New York: Popular Library, 1974.

McDonald, Elvin. *Plants As Therapy.* New York: Praeger Publishers, a division of Holt, Rinehart and Winston, 1976.

Mickel, John. *The Home Gardener's Book of Ferns.* New York: Holt, Rinehart & Winston, 1979.

Moment, Barbara C. *The Salad-Green Gardener.* Boston: Houghton Mifflin Co., 1977.

Mossman, Keith. *Indoor Light Gardening.* Newton, Mass.: Charles T. Branford Co., 1976.

Murata, Kenji. *Practical Bonsai for Beginners.* San Francisco: Japan Publications, 1977.

Nelson, Judith. *Money-Saving Garden Magic.* Englewood Cliffs, N.J.: Prentice-Hall, 1978.

Northern, Rebecca Tyson. *Home Orchid Growing.* New York: Van Nostrand Reinhold Co., 1970.

Olkowski, Helga and William. *The City People's Book of Raising Food.* Emmaus, Pa.: Rodale Press, 1975.

Orchidata. vol. 7, no. 2, New York: Greater New York Orchid Society, 1967.

Padilla, Victoria. *The Bromeliads.* New York: Crown Publishers, 1973.

Perry, Frances, ed. *Simon and Schuster's Complete Guide to Plants and Flowers.* New York: Simon & Schuster, 1976.

Perry, L. R. *Bonsai: Trees and Shrubs: A Guide to the Methods of Kyuzo Murata.* New York: Ronald Press Co., 1964.

Pietropaolo, J. and P. *The World of Carnivorous Plants.* Canandaigua, N.Y.: Peter Paul's Nurseries, 1974.

Plant Growth Lighting. Cleveland, Ohio: General Electric Co. Lighting Business Group.

Reynolds, Marc, and Meacham, William A. *The Complete Book of Garden Bulbs.* New York: Funk & Wagnalls, 1971.

Sander, David. *Orchids and Their Cultivation.* New York: Sterling Press, 1979.

Schnell, Donald E. *Carnivorous Plants of the United States and Canada.* Winston-Salem, N.C.: John F. Blair, 1976.

Sessler, Gloria Jean. *Orchids and How to Grow Them.* Englewood Cliffs, N.J.: Prentice-Hall, 1978.

Shuttleworth, Floyd S. et al. *Orchids — A Golden Nature Guide.* New York: Western Publishing Co., 1969.

Storms, Ed. *Growing the Mesembs.* Fort Worth, Tex.: the author, 1976.

Swenson, Allan A. *Cultivating Carnivorous Plants.* New York: Doubleday, 1977.

Taylor, Kathryn S., and Gregg, Edith W. *Winter Flowers in Greenhouse and Sun-Heated Pit.* New York: Charles Scribner's Sons, 1969.

Thompson, Mildred L. and Edward J. *Begonias: A Complete Reference Book.* New York: Times Books, 1979.

Tinari, Anne. *Our African Violet Heritage.* Huntingdon Valley, Pa.: Tinari Greenhouses.

Tompkins, Peter, and Bird, Christopher. *The Secret Life of Plants.* New York: Avon, 1974.

VanDersal, William R. *Why Does Your Garden Grow? The Facts of Plant Life.* New York: Times Books, 1977.

Whitman, John. *The Psychic Power of Plants.* New York: New American Library, 1974.

Wilson, Charles L. and James. *The World of Terrariums.* Middle Village, N.Y.: Jonathan David Publishers, 1975.

Wilson, Helen Van Pelt. *Helen Van Pelt Wilson's African-Violet Book.* New York: Hawthorn Books, 1970.

——. *The Joy of Geraniums.* New York: William Morrow & Co., 1965.

Wilson, Robert Gardener and Catherine. *Bromeliads in Cultivation.* Coconut Grove, Fla.: Hurricane House Publishers, 1963.

Withner, Carl L., ed. *The Orchids: A Scientific Study.* New York: John Wiley & Sons, 1959.

Index of Common Plant Names

Common Name	Botanical Name
Adam's needle	*Yucca filamentosa*
African milk tree	*Euphorbia trigona*
African violet	*Saintpaulia* spp.
Agave, miniature	*Dyckia* spp.
Air plant	*Kalanchoe pinnata*
Airplane plant	*Chlorophytum* spp.
Aloe	*Aloe* spp.
Aloe vera	*A. barbadensis*
Climbing	*A. ciliaris*
Golden-toothed	*A. nobilis*
Lace	*A. aristata*
Partridge-breasted	*A. variegata*
Short-leaved	*A. brevifolia*
Warty	*Gasteria verrucosa*
Alpine strawberry	*Fragaria vesca* 'Alpine'
Aluminum plant	*Pilea cadierei*
Amaryllis	*Hippeastrum* spp.
Andromeda	*Pieris japonica*
Anemone	*Anemone* spp.
Florists'	*A. coronaria*
Poppy	*A. coronaria*
Angel's trumpet	*Datura inoxia*
Angora plant	*Kalanchoe eriophylla*
Anise	*Pimpinella anisum*
Apostle plant	*Neomarica northiana*
Arabian coffee plant	*Coffea arabica*
Aralia	
Balfour	*Polyscias balfouriana*
False	*Dizygotheca elegantissima*
Japanese	*Fatsia japonica*
Ming	*Polyscias fruticosa*
Arrowhead	*Sagittaria* spp.
Arrowhead vine	*Syngonium podophyllum*
Arrowroot	*Maranta* spp.
Artillery plant	*Pilea microphylla*
Aster	*Callistephus chinensis*
Australian laurel	*Pittosporum tobira*
Avocado	*Persea americana*
Azalea	*Rhododendron* spp.
Kirishima mountain	*R. kiusianum*
Japanese	*R. japonicum*
Baby's tears	*Soleirolia soleirolii*
Baby's toes	*Fenestraria* spp.
Bald cypress	*Taxodium distichum*
Balsam	*Impatiens* spp.
Bamboo	*Arundinaria* spp., *Bambusa* spp., *Phyllostachys* spp., *Sasa* spp.
Black	*Phyllostachys nigra*
Dwarf fern-leaf	*Arundinaria disticha*
Golden	*Phyllostachys aurea*
Pygmy	*Arundinaria pygmaea*
Yellow running	*Phyllostachys bambusoides* 'Allgold'
Banana, dwarf	*Musa acuminata* 'Dwarf Cavendish'
Banana plant	*Nymphoides aquatica*
Banyan tree	*Ficus benghalensis*
Baseball plant	*Euphorbia obesa*

Common Name	Botanical Name
Basil	*Ocimum basilicum*
Bay	*Laurus nobilis*
Beans	*Phaseolus* spp.
Lima	*P. limensis*
Pole	*P. vulgaris*
Snap	*P. vulgaris*
Bear's toes	*Cotyledon* spp.
Beefsteak plant	*Iresine herbstii*
Beet	*Beta vulgaris*
Begonia	*Begonia* spp.
Angel-wing	*B. coccinea*
Beefsteak	*B.* ×*erythrophylla*
Black	*B.* 'Joe Hayden'
Bronze-leaf	*B.* ×*ricinifolia*
Christmas	*B.* ×*cheimantha*
Eyelash	*B. boweri*
Fairy carpet	*B. versicolor*
Fan	*B.* ×*rex-cultorum*
Fern-leaf	*B. foliosa*
Finger-leaf	*B.* ×*sunderbruchii*
Grape-leaf	*B. dregei*
Grass-leaved	*B. bogneri*
Iron cross	*B. masoniana*
Maple-leaf	*B. dregei*
Miniature	*B. mazae*
Painted-leaf	*B.* ×*rex-cultorum*
Pennywort	*B. hydrocotylifolia*
Pink spot angel-wing	*B. serratipetala*
Prism-fruited	*B. prismatocarpa*
Rex	*B.* ×*rex-cultorum*
Round-leaved	*B. rotundifolia*
Strawberry	*Saxifraga stolonifera*
Trailing watermelon	*Pellionia* spp.
Tuberous	*Begonia* ×*tuberhybrida*
Wax	*B.* ×*semperflorens-cultorum*
Belgian endive	*Cichorium intybus*
Bellflower	
Central American	*Codonanthe* spp.
Dwarf	*Koellikeria erinoides*
Italian	*Campanula isophylla*
Bird of paradise	*Strelitzia reginae*
Bird's-nest bromeliad	*Nidularium* spp.
Bishop's cap	*Astrophytum myriostigma*
Black alloplectus	*Nautilocalyx lynchii*
Black-eyed Susan vine	*Thunbergia alata*
Bladderwort	*Polypompholyx* spp., *Utricularia* spp.
Bleeding-heart	*Clerodendrum thomsoniae*
Bloodflower	*Asclepias curassavica*
Bloodleaf	*Iresine* spp.
Blue angel tears	*Ilysanthes grandiflora*
Blue torch	*Tillandsia* spp.
Blue-eyed grass	*Sisyrinchium* spp.
Blushing bromeliad	*Neoregelia carolinae* 'Tricolor'
Bo tree	*Ficus religiosa*
Bog rush	*Juncus effusus*
Botanical wonder	×*Fatshedera lizei*
Bottle-brush tree	*Callistemon* spp.

Common Name	Botanical Name
Bowtie plant	*Gasteria hybrida*
Boxwood	*Buxus* spp.
Common	*B. sempervirens*
Japanese	*B. microphylla* var. *japonica*
Kingsville dwarf	*B. microphylla* 'Compacta'
Broccoli	*Brassica oleracea*, Botrytis Group
Bugleweed	*Ajuga reptans*
Bunchberry	*Cornus canadensis*
Bunya-bunya	*Araucaria bidwillii*
Burnet	*Poterium sanguisorba*
Burro's tail	*Sedum morganianum*
Busy Lizzy	*Impatiens* spp.
Butterfly flower	*Schizanthus* spp.
Butterwort	*Pinguicula* spp.
Orchid-flowered	*P. moranensis*
Cabbage	*Brassica oleracea*, Capitata Group
Cactus	
Ball	*Notocactus* spp., *Parodia* spp.
Barrel	*Echinocactus* spp., *Ferocactus* spp.
Beaver-tail	*Opuntia microdasys*, *O. basilaris*
Bishop's-cap	*Astrophytum myriostigma*
Boxing glove	*Opuntia mamillata*
Brazilian	*Rhipsalidopsis rosea*
Bunny-ears	*Opuntia microdasys*
Button	*Epithelantha micromeris*
Candelabra	*Cereus peruviana*
Chain	*Rhipsalis* spp.
Chin	*Gymnocalycium* spp.
Christmas	*Schlumbergera bridgesii*
Cinnamon	*Opuntia microdasys* var. *rufida*
Cob	*Lobivia* spp.
Conehead	*Conophytum* spp.
Coral	*Rhipsalis cereuscula*
Crab	*Schlumbergera truncata*
Crown	*Rebutia* spp.
Cylinder	*Cephalocereus nobilis*
Devil's-head	*Echinocactus horizonthalonius*
Easter	*Rhipsalidopsis* spp.
Easter lily	*Echinopsis multiplex*
Feather	*Mammillaria plumosa*
Fishhook	*Coryphantha* spp., *Ferocactus wislizenii*, *Mammillaria* spp.
Giant chin	*Gymnocalycium saglione*
Goat's-horn	*Astrophytum capricorne*
Golden barrel	*Echinocactus grusonii*
Golden star	*Mammillaria elongata*
Green donkey ears	*Opuntia schickendantzii*
Hedgehog	*Echinocereus* spp., *Lobivia* spp.
Lace	*Echinocereus reichenbachii*
Lawyer's-tongue	*Gasteria* spp.
Mexican old man	*Cephalocereus senilis*
Mistletoe	*Rhipsalis* spp.
Old lady	*Mammillaria hahniana*
Orchid	*Epiphyllum* spp.
Organ-pipe	*Trichocereus spachianus*, *Lemaireocereus* spp.
Owl's eyes	*Mammillaria parkinsonii*
Ox-tongue	*Gasteria* spp.
Peanut	*Chamaecereus sylvestri*
Peruvian apple	*Cereus peruvianus*
Pincushion	*Coryphantha* spp., *Mammillaria* spp., *Opuntia erectoclada*
Powder-puff	*Mammillaria bocasana*
Prickly pear	*Opuntia* spp.
Rainbow	*Echinocereus pectinatus* var. *neomexicanus*, *E. engelmanii*

Common Name	Botanical Name
Rattail	*Aporocactus flagelliformis*
Redbird	*Pedilanthus tithymaloides*
Red crown	*Rebutia minuscula*
Redheaded Irishman	*Mammillaria spinosissima*
Rose	*Pereskia grandifolia*
Sand dollar	*Astrophytum asterias*
Scarlet ball	*Notocactus haselbergii*
Scarlet crown	*Rebutia kupperana*
Sea urchin	*Astrophytum asterias*, *Echinopsis* spp.
Silk pincushion	*Mammillaria bombycina*
Silver dollar	*Astrophytum asterias*
Snowball pincushion	*Mammillaria candida*
South American old man	*Espostoa lanata*
Spider	*Gymnocalycium denudatum*
Star	*Astrophytum ornatum*
Thanksgiving	*Schlumbergera truncata*
Thimble	*Mammillaria fragilis*
Turk's-head	*Melocactus* spp.
Watch-chain	*Crassula lycopodioides*
Calendula	*Calendula officinalis*
Calico hearts	*Adromischus maculatus* and *A.* spp.
Calico plant	*Alternanthera ficoides* 'Bettzickiana'
California live-oak	*Quercus agrifolia*
Camellia	*Camellia japonica*
Canadian hemlock	*Tsuga canadensis*
Canary Island broom	*Cytisus canariensis*
Candelabra plant	*Aloe arborescens*
Candle plant	*Senecio articulatus*
Candy corn plant	*Nematanthus* spp., *Hypocyrta wettsteinii*
Candy stick	*Senecio stapeliiformis*
Candytuft	*Iberis* spp.
Cape cowslip	*Lachenalia* spp.
Cape jasmine	*Gardenia jasminoides*
Cape primrose	*Streptocarpus* spp.
Caraway	*Carum carvi*
Cardinal flower	*Sinningia cardinalis*
Cardoon	*Cynara cardunculus*
Carnation	*Dianthus caryophyllus*
Carolina yellow jessamine	*Gelsemium sempervirens*
Carpet sedum	*Sedum lineare* 'Variegatum'
Carrion flower	*Stapelia* spp.
Carrot	*Daucus carota* var. *sativus*
Cast-iron plant	*Aspidistra elatior*
Castor oil plant	*Ricinus communis*
Catnip	*Nepeta cataria*
Cauliflower	*Brassica oleracea*, Botrytis Group
Celery	*Apium graveolens* var. *dulce*
Cellophane plant	*Echinodorus* spp.
Celtuce	*Lactuca sativa* var. *asparagina*
Century plant	*Agave* spp.
Champignon mushroom	*Agaricus bisporus*
Chard	*Beta vulgaris*, Cicla Group
Chenille plant	*Acalypha hispida*, *Echeveria pulvinata*
Cherry	
Acerola	*Malpighia glabra*
Barbados	*M. glabra*
Christmas	*Solanum capsicastrum*
Jerusalem	*S. pseudocapsicum*
Peruvian ground	*Nicandra physalodes*
Chervil	*Anthriscus cerefolium*
Chicory	*Cichorium intybus*
Chinese cabbage	*Brassica rapa*, Pekinensis Group

Common Name	Botanical Name
Fern (continued)	
Water	*Ceratopteris* spp.
Water clover	*Marsilea* spp.
Fern-leaf inch plant	*Tripogandra* spp.
Feverfew	*Chrysanthemum parthenium*
Fig	*Ficus* spp.
Celeste	*F. carica* 'Celeste'
Creeping	*F. pumila*
Fiddle-leaf	*F. lyrata*
Mistletoe	*F. deltoidea, F. diversifolia*
Weeping	*F. benjamina*
Fingernail plant	*Neoregelia* spp.
Firecracker flower	*Crossandra infundibuliformis*
Flame nettle	*Coleus blumei*
Flame of the woods	*Ixora* spp.
Flaming sword	*Vriesea splendens*
Flamingo flower	*Anthurium* spp.
Florists' gloxinia	*Sinningia speciosa*
Flower-of-an-hour	*Hibiscus trionum*
Flowering maple	*Abutilon megapotamicum*
Flowering stones	*Mesembryanthemum*
Flowering tobacco	*Nicotiana alata, N.* ×*sanderae*
Forget-me-not	*Myosotis* spp.
Foster's favorite	*Aechmea fasciata*
Foxglove	*Digitalis purpurea*
Foxtail	*Ceratophyllum submersum*
Freckle-face	*Hypoestes phyllostachya*
Friendship plant	*Pilea involucrata*
Frilled fan	*Euphorbia lactea* 'Cristata'
Frog'sbit	*Hydrocharis morsus-ranae*
Garden cress	*Lepidium sativum*
Gardenia	*Gardenia jasminoides*
Garlic	*Allium sativum*
Gasteria, miniature	*Gasteria liliputana*
Gazania	*Gazania ringens*
Genista	*Cytisus canariensis*
Gentian	*Gentiana farreri*
Geranium	*Pelargonium* spp.
Alpine	*Erodium chamaedryoides*
Apple	*Pelargonium odoratissimum*
Cactus	*P. echinatum, P. fulgidum*
Common miniature	*P.* 'Black Vesuvius'
Fish	*P.* ×*hortorum*
Garden	*P.* ×*hortorum*
Gouty	*P. gibbosum*
Ivy-leaved	*P. peltatum*
Jungle	*Ixora* spp.
Lady Washington	*Pelargonium* ×*domesticum*
Martha Washington	*P.* ×*domesticum*
Peppermint	*P. tomentosum*
Regal	*P.* ×*domesticum*
Rose	*P. capitatum, P. graveolens*
Show	*P.* ×*domesticum*
Zonal	*P.* ×*hortorum*
Ginger	*Asarum* spp., *Zingiber* spp.
Common	*Zingiber officinale*
European	*Asarum europaeum*
Wild	*A. shuttleworthii*
Glorybower vine	*Clerodendrum thomsoniae*
Glorybush	*Tibouchina urvilleana*
Gloxinia	*Sinningia speciosa*
Miniature	*S. pusilla*
Tree	*Kohleria* spp.
Gold-dust tree	*Aucuba japonica*
Golden carpet	*Sedum acre*
Golden glow	*Sedum dasyphyllum*
Goldfish plant	*Columnea* spp.
Goldfish weed	*Elodea densa*
Goodnight-at-noon	*Hibiscus trionum*
Gooseberry plant	*Senecio herreianus*

Common Name	Botanical Name
Guppy flower	*Nematanthus* spp.
Heather	*Erica* spp.
Heliotrope	*Heliotropium* spp.
Hen-and-chickens	*Echeveria secunda* var. *glauca,* *Sempervivum* spp.
Hindu rope	*Hoya* sp.
Hinoki cypress, dwarf	*Chamaecyparis obtusa* 'Nana'
Holly	
Dwarf Chinese	*Ilex cornuta* 'Rotunda'
False	*Osmanthus* spp.
Japanese	*Ilex crenata*
Miniature	*Malpighia coccigera*
Singapore	*M. coccigera*
Hollyhock	*Alcea rosea*
Honey bells	*Hermannia verticillata*
Honey plant	*Hoya carnosa*
Hornwort	*Ceratophyllum* spp.
Hound's tongue	*Cynoglossum amabile*
Houseleek	*Sempervivum calcareum*
Cobweb	*S. arachnoideum*
Huntsman horn	*Sarracenia flava*
Hurricane plant	*Monstera deliciosa*
Hyacinth	*Hyacinthus orientalis*
Grape	*Muscari* spp.
Water	*Eichhornia crassipes*
Hydrangea	*Hydrangea macrophylla*
Iceland poppy	*Papaver nudicaule*
Inch plant	*Callisia* spp., *Tradescantia* spp.
Indian hawthorn	*Raphiolepis indica*
Indian laurel	*Ficus retusa*
Indoor oak	*Nicodemia diversifolia*
Ivy	
Aralia	×*Fatshedera lizei*
Bird's-foot	*Hedera helix* 'Pedata'
Boston	*Parthenocissus tricuspidata*
Canary Islands	*Hedera canariensis*
Devil's	*Epipremnum aureum*
English	*Hedera helix*
German	*Senecio mikanioides*
Grape	*Cissus rhombifolia*
Kangaroo	*C. antarctica*
Marine	*C. incisa*
Miniature grape	*C. striata*
Parlor	*Senecio mikanioides*
Swedish	*Plectranthus australis*
Tree	×*Fatshedera lizei*
Wax	*Senecio macroglossus* 'Variegatum'
Jack-in-the-pulpit	*Arisaema triphyllum*
Jacob's ladder	*Pedilanthus tithymaloides*
Jade plant	*Crassula argenta*
Silver	*C. arborescens*
Jade vine, variegated	*Senecio macroglossus* 'Variegatum'
Japanese lantern	*Hibiscus schizopetalus*
Japanese yew	*Podocarpus macrophyllus*
Jasmine	*Jasminum* spp.
Arabian	*J. sambac*
Cape	*Gardenia jasminoides*
Confederate	*Trachelospermum jasminoides*
Madagascar	*Stephanotis floribunda*
Night	*Cestrum nocturnum*
Pink	*Jasminum polyanthum*
Poet's	*J. officinale*
Primrose	*J. mesnyi*
Star	*Trachelospermum jasminoides*
Jelly beans	*Sedum pachyphyllum*
Jessamin, night	*Cestrum nocturnum*
Joseph's coat	*Alternanthera* spp.
Joshua tree, miniature	*Sedum multiceps*

Common Name	Botanical Name
Needle vine	*Ceropegia debilis*
Nephthytis	*Syngonium podophyllum*
Nerve plant	*Fittonia verschaffeltii*
Never-never plant	*Ctenanthe oppenheimiana*
Night-blooming cereus	*Hylocereus undatus*
Norfolk Island pine	*Araucaria heterophylla*
Old-fashioned shamrock oxalis	*Oxalis rosea*
Oleander	*Nerium oleander*
Olive	
European	*Olea europaea*
Sweet	*Osmanthus fragrans*
Orchid	
Butterfly	*Oncidium* spp.
Clamshell	*Epidendrum cochleatum*
Cockleshell	*E. cochleatum*
Dancing lady	*Oncidium* spp.
Jewel	*Haemaria* spp.
Lady's slipper	*Paphiopedilum* spp.
Moon	*Vanda* spp.
Moth	*Phalaenopsis* spp.
Necklace	*Coelogyne dayana*
Nun's	*Phaius* spp.
Poor man's	*Schizanthus* spp., *Cyclamen persicum*
Swan	*Cycnoches*
Oregano	*Origanum heracleoticum, O. vulgare*
Oriental streptocarpus	*Boea hygroscopica*
Ox-tongue	*Gasteria* spp.
Painted lady	*Echeveria* spp.
Painted nettle	*Coleus blumei*
Painted tongue	*Salpiglossis sinuata*
Painter's palette	*Anthurium* spp.
Palm	
Areca	*Chrysalidocarpus lutescens*
Bamboo	*Chamaedorea erumpens*
Bottle	*Beaucarnea* spp.
Butterfly	*Chrysalidocarpus lutescens*
Chinese fan	*Livistona chinensis*
Clustered	*Caryota mitis*
Costa Rican	*Chamaedorea costaricana*
Curly sentry	*Howea belmoreana*
Dwarf fishtail	*Caryota mitis*
Elephant foot	*Beaucarnea* spp.
Fan	*Chamaerops humilis, Licuala* spp.
Fern	*Cycas* spp.
Fishtail	*Caryota urens*
Kentia	*Howea forsterana*
Lady	*Rhapis humilis*
Neanthe bella	*Chamaedorea elegans*
Paradise	*Howea forsterana*
Parlor	*Chamaedorea elegans*
Petticoat	*Washingtonia filifera*
Pony tail	*Beaucarnea recurvata*
Pygmy date	*Phoenix roebelenii*
Reed	*Chamaedorea seifrizii*
Sago	*Cycas* spp.
Showy	*Chamaedorea costaricana*
Thread	*Washingtonia robusta*
Palm trees	*Kalanchoe ×houghtonii*
Panda plant	*Kalanchoe tomentosa*
Pansy	*Viola ×wittrockiana*
Miniature	*V. tricolor*
Monkey-faced	*Achimenes* spp.
Papaya	*Carica papaya*
Paper flower	*Bougainvillea* spp.
Papyrus plant	*Cyperus papyrus* 'Nanus'
Parachute plant	*Ceropegia sandersonii*
Parrot leaf	*Alternanthera ficoidea*

Common Name	Botanical Name
Parrot's feather	*Myriophyllum*
Parsley	*Petroselinum* spp.
Common	*P. crispum* var. *crispum*
Curly-leaved	*P. crispum* var. *crispum*
Hamburg	*P. crispum* var. *tuberosum*
Italian	*P. crispum* var. *neapolitanum*
Turnip-rooted	*P. crispum* var. *tuberosum*
Partridgeberry	*Mitchella repens*
Passionflower	*Passiflora* spp.
Patience plant	*Impatiens wallerana*
Pea	
Chinese	*Pisum sativum* var. *macrocarpon*
Edible-podded	*P. sativum* var. *macrocarpon*
Snow	*P. sativum* var. *macrocarpon*
Sugar	*P. sativum* var. *macrocarpon*
Sweet	*Lathyrus odoratus*
Winged	*Lotus berthelotii*
Peacock plant	*Calathea makoyana, Episcia* spp.
Peanut	*Arachis hypogaea*
Pearl plant	*Haworthia margaritifera*
Pen wiper plant	*Kalanchoe marmorata*
Peperomia	*Peperomia* spp.
Blunt-leaved	*P. obtusifolia*
Emerald ripple	*P. caperata*
Ivy	*P. griseoargentea*
Silver-leaf	*P. griseoargentea*
Velvet	*P. velutina*
Watermelon	*P. argyreia*
Pepper plant	*Capsicum annuum*
Black	*Piper nigrum*
Celebes	*P. ornatum*
Ornamental	*Capsicum annuum*
Red	*C. annuum*
Saffron	*Piper crocatum*
Sweet	*Capsicum annuum*
Peppermint stick	*Senecio stapeliiformis, S. gregorii*
Persian squill	*Scilla tubergeniana*
Persian violet	*Cyclamen persicum*
Pewter plant	*Aglaonema* spp.
Philodendron	*Philodendron* spp.
Bird's-nest	*P. wendlandii*
Black-gold	*P. melanochrysum*
Blushing	*P. erubescens*
Fiddle-leaf	*P. bipennifolium*
Heart-leaf	*P. scandens* subsp. *oxycardium*
Lacy-tree	*P. selloum*
Silver-leaf	*P. ornatum*
Spade-leaf	*P. domesticum*
Split-leaf	*Monstera deliciosa*
Tree	*Philodendron bipinnatifidum*
Velvet-leaf	*P. scandens* subsp. *scandens* forma *micans*
Phlox, dwarf	*Phlox drummondii*
Piggyback plant	*Tolmiea menziesii*
Pilea	*Pilea* spp.
Creeping	*P. depressa*
Miniature	*P. depressa*
Pincushion flower	*Scabiosa* spp.
Pine	*Pinus* spp.
Balkan	*P. peuce*
Buddhist	*Podocarpus macrophyllus*
Dwarf Swiss mountain	*Pinus mugo*
Japanese black	*P. thunbergiana*
Japanese five-needle	*P. parviflora*
Japanese red	*P. densiflora*
Mugho	*P. mugo*
Screw	*Pandanus* spp.
Yew	*Podocarpus* spp.
Pineapple plant	*Ananas comosus*
Pink	*Dianthus* spp.
Pink agapanthus	*Tulbaghia fragrans*

Common Name	Botanical Name
Pinwheel plant	*Aeonium haworthii*
Pitcher plant	*Darlingtonia* spp., *Nepenthes* spp., *Sarracenia* spp.
Australian	*Cephalotus* spp.
Common	*Sarracenia purpurea*
Marsh	*Heliamphora* spp.
Parrot	*Sarracenia psittacina*
Tropical	*Nepenthes* spp.
White-topped	*Sarracenia leucophylla*
Plover eggs	*Adromischus festivus*
Plush plant	*Echeveria* spp.
Pocketbook plant	*Calceolaria* spp.
Poinciana, dwarf	*Caesalpinia pulcherrima*
Poinsettia	*Euphorbia pulcherrima*
Polka-dot plant	*Hypoestes phyllostachya*
Pomegranate	*Punica granatum*
Poppy	*Papaver orientale*
Iceland	*P. nudicaule*
Porcelain flower	*Hoya* spp.
Pothos	*Epipremnum aureum*
Powder puff, dwarf	*Calliandra surinamensis*
Prayer plant	*Maranta leuconeura*
Red-veined	*M. leuconeura* var. *erythroneura*
Primrose	*Primula* spp.
Baby	*P. malacoides*
Cape	*Streptocarpus rexii*
Chinese	*Primula sinensis*
English	*P. vulgaris*
Fairy	*P. malacoides*
Poison	*P. obconica*
Princess flower	*Tibouchina urvilleana*
Propeller plant	*Crassula falcata*
Prostrate coleus	*Plectranthus oertendahlii*
Purple heart	*Setcreasea pallida* 'Purple Heart'
Purple passion vine	*Gynura aurantiaca* 'Purple Passion'
Purple waffle plant	*Hemigraphis alternata*
Pussy ears	*Cyanotis somaliensis*
Pyrethrum	*Chrysanthemum cinerariifolium*
Queen's tears	*Billbergia nutans*
Rabbit's foot	*Maranta leuconeura* var. *kerchoviana*
Rabbit tracks	*Maranta leuconeura* var. *kerchoviana*
Radish	*Raphanus sativus*
Rainbow bush	*Portulacaria afra* 'Variegata'
Rainbow plant	*Billbergia saundersii*
Rainbow vine	*Crassula argentea* 'Variegata', *Pellionia pulchra*
Rattlesnake plantain	*Goodyera pubescens*
Red flame	*Oxalis hedysaroides*
Red herring bone	*Maranta leuconeura* var. *erythrophylla*
Rhubarb	*Rheum rhaponticum*
Ribbon bush	*Hypoestes aristata*
Rocket	*Eruca vesicaria* subsp. *sativa*
Rosary plant	*Crassula rupestris*
Rosary vine	*Ceropegia woodii*
Rose	*Rosa* spp.
China	*R. chinensis* 'Minima'
Rose grape	*Medinilla magnifica*
Rose mallow	*Hibiscus* spp.
Rose of China	*Hibiscus rosa-sinensis*
Rosemary	*Rosmarinus* spp.
Common	*R. officinalis*
Prostrate	*R. officinalis* 'Prostratus'
Rouge plant	*Rivina humilis*
Rubber plant	*Ficus elastica*
Sacred lotus	*Nelumbo nucifera*

Common Name	Botanical Name
Sage	*Salvia officinalis*
Blue	*Eranthemum pulchellum, E. nervosum*
Yellow	*Lantana camara*
Sapphire flower	*Browallia speciosa* 'Major'
Savory	*Satureja* spp.
Summer	*S. hortensis*
Winter	*S. montana*
Scarlet paint brush	*Crassula falcata*
Scarlet plume	*Euphorbia fulgens*
Schefflera	*Brassaia actinophylla*
Sea kale	*Crambe maritima*
Seersucker plant	*Geogenanthus undatus*
Sensitive plant	*Mimosa pudica*
Shallot	*Allium ascalonicum*
Shamrock plant	*Oxalis* spp.
Irish	*O. acetosella*
Tree	*O. ortgiesii*
Shepard's purse	*Capsella bursa-pastoris*
Shinleaf	*Pyrola elliptica*
Shoofly plant	*Nicandra physalodes*
Shooting star	*Cyclamen persicum*
Shrimp plant	*Justicia brandegeana, Beloperone guttata*
Shrub verbena	*Lantana camara*
Silk-oak	*Grevillea robusta*
Silver bract	*Pachyphytum bracteosum*
Silver crown	*Cotyledon undulata*
Silver dollar	*Crassula* spp.
Silver king	*Aechmea fasciata, Aglaonema* spp.
Silver lace vine	*Polygonum aubertii*
Silver panamiga	*Pilea pubescens*
Silver queen	*Aglaonema* spp.
Sky plant	*Tillandsia ionantha*
Slipper plant	*Sinningia* spp.
Cinderella	*S. regina*
Miniature	*S. pusilla*
Slipperwort	*Calceolaria* spp.
Snake plant	*Sansevieria* spp.
Snapdragon	*Antirrhinum majus*
Song of India	*Dracaena reflexa* 'Variegata'
Spiceberry	*Ardisia crenata*
Spider plant	*Chlorophytum* spp.
Spiderwort	*Tradescantia* spp.
Spinach	*Spinacia oleracea*
Malabar	*Basella alba*
New Zealand	*Tetragonia tetragonioides*
Spindle tree	*Euonymus* spp.
Spineless yucca	*Yucca elephantipes*
Spleenwort	*Asplenium* spp.
Ebony	*A. resiliens*
Split rocks	*Pleiospilos* spp.
Spoon flower	*Xanthosoma lindenii*
Spotted toad	*Stapelia variegata*
Spotted wintergreen	*Chimaphila maculata*
Spruce	*Picea* spp.
Alberta	*P. glauca* var. *albertiana*
Colorado	*P. pungens*
Oriental	*P. orientalis*
Squash	*Cucurbita* spp.
Star of Bethlehem	*Campanula isophylla, Ornithogalum umbellatum*
Starfish flower	*Stapelia* spp.
Giant	*S. gigantea*
Hairy	*S. hirsuta*
Stock	*Matthiola* spp.
Stonecrop	*Sedum* spp., *Sempervivum* spp.
Strawberry	*Fragaria* spp.

General Index

Page numbers in **boldface** indicate photographs or illustrations.

A

Abutilon spp., 215, 226, 732
  light needs of, 552
  temperature needs of, 22
A. hybridum, 732
A. megapotamicum 'Variegata', 221, 732
A. pictum, 732
Acacia armata, 220
Acalypha spp., 732-33
A. godseffiana, 732
A. hispida, 219, 732
  temperature needs of, 22
A. wilkesiana, 732
Acanthostachys spp., 269
Acer buergeranum, **448**
A. ginnala, for bonsai, 444, **448**
A. palmatum, for bonsai, 444
A. rubrum, for bonsai, 444
Achimenes spp., 241-42, 733-34
  light needs of, 254, 552
  temperature needs of, 22
A. andrieuxii, 242
A. antirrhina cvs., 242
A. ehrenbergii, 242, 733
A. erecta, 241, 733
A. grandiflora, 241, 733
A. longiflora, 241, 733
Acidity/alkalinity, of potting
  mixture, 87
Acorus calamus, 177
  temperature needs of, 22
Adaptation, of plant to
  environment, 11
Adiantum spp., **188**, 734
  grown from spores, 120
  potting mixture for, 193

propagation of, 203, **205**
structure of, 191
watering needs of, 199
A. capillus-veneris, 734
A. caudatum, 196, 734
  propagation of, 206
A. concinnum, spores on, **202**
A. hispidulum, 734
A. pedatum, 734
A. raddianum, 197, 734
  cultural needs of, 194-95
A. tenerum, 734
Adromischus spp., 734-35
A. clavifolius, 734
A. cooperii, 734
A. cristatus, 734
A. festivus, 734
A. hemisphaericus, 734
A. maculatus, 734
Aechmea spp., 269-70, 735
  division of, 277
  flower stalks of, 267
  temperature needs of, 22
A. chantinii, 735
A. fasciata, 269-70, 735
  light needs of, 27
A. 'Foster's Favorite', 271
  light needs of, 275
A. fulgens var. *discolor*, 735
Aeonium spp., 298-99, 735-36
A. arboreum, 299, 735
A. decorum, 735
A. haworthii, 298, 735
A. lindleyi, 295, 298
A. nobile, 735
A. tabuliforme, 735
Aeration
  of compost heap, 96
  of soil, 16

Aerides spp.
  structure of, 382
  temperature needs of, 388
Aeschynanthus spp., 248, 736
A. ellipticus, 248
A. evrardii, 248
A. longiflorus, 736
A. marmoratus, 248, 736
A. micranthus, 248
A. pulcher, 248, 736
A. radicans, 248, 736
A. speciosus, **245**, 248, 736
Agapanthus spp., **211**, 736-37
A. africanus, 736
A. campanulatus, 736
A. inapertus, 736
A. orientalis, 736
Agave spp., 302, 737
A. americana, 737
  'Marginata', 302
A. filifera, 737
A. parviflora, 302, 737
A. stricta, 737
A. victoriae-reginae, 302, 737
Aglaonema spp., 170, 737-38
  cane cuttings from, 133
  division of, 138
  grooming of, 185
  grown in water, 128
  light needs of, 27, 182, 552
  purchase of, 45
  temperature needs of, 21, 22, 181
A. commutatum, 737
A. costatum, 737
A. crispum, 738
A. modestum, 738
  seed-setting by, 113
A. pictum, 738